Cities of the United States

EIGHTH EDITION

Cities of the United States

EIGHTH EDITION

VOLUME 2

THE WEST

GALE
CENGAGE Learning·

Farmington Hills, Mich • San Francisco • New York • Waterville, Maine
Meriden, Conn • Mason, Ohio • Chicago

GALE
CENGAGE Learning®

Cities of the United States, 8th edition

Project Editor: Jeffrey Muhr

Editorial: Kristin Key

Product Management: Leigh Ann Cusack

Intellectual Property Project Manager: Lynn Vagg

Composition and Electronic Prepress: Evi Seoud

Manufacturing: Rita Wimberley

Imaging: John Watkins

For product information and technology assistance, contact us at
Gale Customer Support, 1-800-877-4253.

For permission to use material from this text or product,
submit all requests online at **www.cengage.com/permissions.**
Further permissions questions can be emailed to
permissionrequest@cengage.com

Cover photographs reproduced by permission of Shutterstock, except for Denver, CO, Des Moines, IA and New Orleans, LA permission of Getty Images; Chicago, IL and New York, NY permission of Laurie Fundukian; and Denver, CO, and Anchorage, AK permission of Alamy. Banner art within text reproduced by permission of photos.com/Jupiterimages.

While every effort has been made to ensure the reliability of the information presented in this publication, Gale, Cengage Learning, does not guarantee the accuracy of the data contained herein. Gale accepts no payment for listing; and inclusion in the publication of any organization, agency, institution, publication, service, or individual does not imply endorsement of the editors or publisher. Errors brought to the attention of the publisher and verified to the satisfaction of the publisher will be corrected in future editions.

Gale
27500 Drake Rd.
Farmington Hills, MI 48331-3535

ISBN-13: 978-1-5730-2337-5 (4-vol. set)   ISBN-10: 1-5730-2337-X (4-vol. set)
ISBN-13: 978-1-5730-2339-9 (vol. 1)   ISBN-10: 1-5730-2339-6 (vol. 1)
ISBN-13: 978-1-5730-2340-5 (vol. 2)   ISBN-10: 1-5730-2340-X (vol. 2)
ISBN-13: 978-1-5730-2341-2 (vol. 3)   ISBN-10: 1-5730-2341-8 (vol. 3)
ISBN-13: 978-1-5730-2342-9 (vol. 4)   ISBN-10: 1-5730-2342-6 (vol. 4)

ISSN 0899-6075

This title is also available as an e-book.
ISBN-13: 978-1-5730-2343-6
ISBN-10: 1-5730-2343-4
Contact your Gale, Cengage Learning sales representative for ordering information.

Printed in Mexico
1 2 3 4 5 6 7 18 17 16 15 14

Contents

VOLUME 2—THE WEST

VOLUME 3—THE MIDWEST

VOLUME 4—THE NORTHEAST

Introduction

Cities of the United States (CUS) provides a one-stop source for all the vital information you need on 219 of America's top cities—those fastest-growing, as well as those with a particular historical, political, industrial, and/or commercial significance. Spanning the entire country, from Anaheim to Virginia Beach, each geographically-arranged volume of CUS brings together a wide range of comprehensive data. The volumes include: The South; The West; The Midwest; and The Northeast.

Within each volume, the city-specific profiles organize pertinent facts, data, and figures related to demographic, economic, cultural, geographic, social, and recreational conditions. Assembling myriad sources, CUS offers researchers, travelers, students, and media professionals a convenient resource for discovering each city's past, present, and future.

For this completely updated eighth edition, ten new cities have been added, providing even greater access to the country's growing urban centers. The new city profiles include:

- Bellevue, NE
- Dover, NH
- Essex, VT
- Idaho Falls, ID
- Joliet, IL
- Key West, FL
- Rogers, AR
- Taos, NM
- Telluride, CO
- Wellesley, MA

Key Features Unlock Vital Information

Cities of the United States offers a range of key features, allowing easy access to targeted information. Features include:

- Section headings—Comprehensive categories, which include **History, Geography and Climate, Population Profile, Municipal Government, Economy, Education, Research, Health Care, Recreation, Convention Facilities, Transportation,** and **Communications** (including city Web sites), make it easy to locate answers to specific questions.

- Combined facts and analysis—Fact-packed charts and detailed descriptions provide statistics and the rest of the story.

- "In Brief" fact sheets—One-page "at a glance" overviews provide the essential facts for each state and each city profiled.

- Economic information—Detailed updates about such topics as incentive programs, development projects, and largest employers help rate the business climate using criteria that matters to people.

- Directory information—Contact information at the end of many entry sections provides addresses, phone numbers, and email addresses for organizations, agencies, and institutions.

- Selected bibliography listings—Historical accounts, biographical works, and other print resources suggest titles to read if one wishes to learn more about a particular city.

- Web sites for vital city resources—Access points to URLs for information-rich sources, such as city government, visitors and convention bureaus, economic development agencies, libraries, schools, and newspapers provide researchers an opportunity to explore cities in more detail.

- Enlightening illustrations—Numerous photographs highlight points of interest.

- Handy indexing—A referencing guide not only to main city entries, but also to the hundreds of people and place names that fall within those main entries, leading a reader directly to the information they seek.

Designed For a Variety of Users

Whether you are a researcher, traveler, or executive on the move, *CUS* serves your needs. This is the reference long sought by a variety of users:

- Business people, market researchers, and other decision-makers will find the current data that helps them stay informed.

- People vacationing, conventioneering, or relocating will consult this source for questions they have about what's new, unique, or significant about where they are going.

- Students, media professionals, and researchers will discover their background work already completed.

Definitions of Key Statistical Resources

Following are explanations of key resources used for statistical data:

ACCRA (The Council for Community Economic Research; formerly the American Chamber of Commerce Researchers Association): The Cost of Living Index, produced quarterly, provides a useful and reasonably accurate measure of living cost differences among urban areas. Items on which the Index is based have been carefully chosen to reflect the different categories of consumer expenditures, such as groceries, housing, utilities, transportation, health care, and miscellaneous goods and services; taxes are excluded. Weights assigned to relative costs are based on government survey data on expenditure patterns for midmanagement households (typically the average professional worker's home, new construction with 2,400 square feet of living space). All items are priced in each place at a specified time and according to standardized specifications. Information regarding ACCRA and the Cost of Living Index can be found at www.accra.org. Please note that the ACCRA Cost of Living Index and ACCRA housing price information are reprinted by permission of ACCRA.

Metropolitan Statistical Area (MSA): The U.S. Office of Management and Budget (OMB) provides that each Metropolitan Statistical Area must include (a) at least one city with 50,000 or more inhabitants, or (b) a U.S. Census Bureau-defined urbanized area (of at least 50,000 inhabitants) and a total metropolitan population of at least 100,000 (75,000 in New England). The term was adopted in 1983. The term "metropolitan area" (MA) became effective in 1990. During the 2000 Census, the MSA standards were revised, establishing Core Based Statistical Areas (CBSAs). CBSAs may be either Metropolitan Statistical Areas or Micropolitan Statistical Areas. It is important to note that standards, and therefore content of 1990 Census MSAs, are not identical to 2000 Census MSA standards. Additional information regarding MSAs can be found at http://census.state.nc. us/glossary/msa.html.

FBI Crime Index Total: The total number of index offenses reported to the FBI during the year through its Uniform Crime Reporting Program. The FBI receives monthly and annual reports from law enforcement agencies throughout the country. City police, sheriffs, and state police file reports on the number of index offenses that become known to them. The FBI Crime Index offenses are: murder and non-negligent manslaughter; forcible rape; robbery; aggravated assault; burglary; larceny; motor vehicle theft; and arson.

Estimates of population: Between decennial censuses, the U.S. Bureau of the Census publishes estimates of the population using the decennial census data as benchmarks and data available from various agencies, both state and federal, including births and deaths, and school statistics, among other data.

Method of Compilation

The editors of *Cities of the United States* consulted numerous sources to secure the kinds of data most valuable. Each entry gathers together economic information culled in part from the U.S. Department of Labor/Bureau of Labor Statistics and state departments of labor and commerce, population figures derived from the U.S. Department of Commerce/ Bureau of the Census and from city and state agencies, educational and municipal government data supplied by local authorities, historical narrative based on a variety of accounts, and geographical and climatic profiles from the National Oceanic and Atmospheric Administration. Along with material supplied by chambers of commerce, convention and visitors bureaus, and other local sources, background information was drawn from periodicals and books chosen for their timeliness and accuracy. Through print resources, web sites, email contact, and/or phone calls with agency representatives, the information contained reflects current conditions.

Acknowledgments

The editors are grateful for the assistance provided by dozens of helpful chambers of commerce and convention and visitors bureau professionals, as well as municipal, library, and school employees for their invaluable generosity and expertise.

Comments and Suggestions Welcome

If you have questions, concerns, or comments about *Cities of the United States*, please contact the Project Editor:

Cities of the United States

Gale

27500 Drake Road

Farmington Hills, MI 48331

Phone: (248)699-4253

Toll-free: (800)347-GALE

Fax: (248)699-8075

URL: www.gale.cengage.com

Alaska

The State in Brief

Nickname: Last Frontier; Land of the Midnight Sun

Motto: North to the future

Flower: Forget-me-not

Bird: Willow ptarmigan

Area: 665,384 square miles (2010; U.S. rank 1st)

Elevation: Ranges from sea level to 20,320 feet above sea level

Climate: Summers are short and hot, winters long and intensely cold

Admitted to Union: January 3, 1959

Capital: Juneau

Head Official: Sean Parnell (R) (until 2014)

Population

1990: 570,000
2000: 626,932
2010: 710,231
2012 estimate: 711,139
Percent change, 2000–2010: 13.3%
U.S. rank in 2012: 47th
Percent of residents born in state: 39.7% (2012)
Density: 1.2 people per square mile (2010)
2012 FBI Crime Index Total: 24,449

Racial and Ethnic Characteristics (2012)

White: 477,985
Black or African American: 24,219
American Indian and Alaska Native: 98,976
Asian: 37,968
Native Hawaiian and Pacific Islander: 7,363
Hispanic or Latino (may be of any race): 40,371
Other: 64,628

Age Characteristics (2012)

Population under 5 years old: 53,591
Population 5 to 19 years old: 153,503
Percent of population 65 years and over: 7.8%
Median age: 33.8

Vital Statistics

Total number of births (2012–13): 11,610
Total number of deaths (2012–13): 4,113
AIDS cases reported through 2011: 793

Economy

Major industries: Oil, government, commercial fishing, food processing, lumber, mining
Unemployment rate (2012): 5.8%
Per capita income (2012): $32,537
Median household income (2012): $69,917
Percentage of persons below poverty level (2012): 9.6%
Income tax rate: None
Sales tax rate: None

Anchorage

■ The City in Brief

Founded: 1915 (incorporated, 1920)

Head Official: Mayor Dan Sullivan (since July 2009; current term expires June 30, 2015)

City Population
- 1990: 226,338
- 2000: 260,283
- 2010: 291,826
- 2012 estimate: 298,610
- Percent change, 2000–2010: 12.1%
- U.S. rank in 1990: 69th (State rank: 1st)
- U.S. rank in 2000: 75th (State rank: 1st)
- U.S. rank in 2010: 64th (State rank: 1st)

Metropolitan Statistical Area Population
- 2000: 319,605
- 2010: 380,821
- 2012 estimate: 392,535
- Percent change, 2000–2010: 19.2%
- U.S. rank in 2000: 143rd
- U.S. rank in 2010: 133rd

Area: 1,955 square miles

Elevation: 132 feet above sea level

Average Annual Temperatures: 35.8° F

Average Annual Precipitation: 15.71 inches of rain; 70.6 inches of snow

Major Economic Sectors: government, trade, services, transportation (air)

Unemployment Rate: 5.1% (2012)

Per Capita Income: $34,565

2012 FBI Crime Index Property: 10,543

Major Colleges and Universities: University of Alaska Anchorage, Alaska Pacific University

Daily Newspaper: *Anchorage Daily News*

■ Introduction

Anchorage is the largest city in Alaska, and acts as the center of the state's communication, transportation, commercial, and finance industries. Nearly half of the state's residents call Anchorage home. Anchorage was founded in 1915 as a railroad construction headquarters, so the fact that the city has become a sophisticated metropolis in the midst of rugged wilderness can be appreciated as a phenomenon. In addition to being a great place to get ready to fish, hunt, climb and camp, the city has first-class hotels, four-star restaurants, and an outstanding Museum of History and Art. It is no surprise that in 2011, Anchorage was ranked by Businessweek.com as the 10th-best city in which to live in the United States. A visit to the city will dispel myths about its long, dark winters. Anchorage's climate is relatively mild with distinct seasons, winters similar to Denver's, and short daylight periods confined to late December. A relatively high per capita income, low taxes, and a low crime rate are among the positive qualities that have earned Anchorage a place among the country's most livable cities.

■ Geography and Climate

Anchorage is located in south-central Alaska in a wide valley surrounded by several mountain ranges, including the Chugach, Kenai, Talkeetna, Tordillo, Aleutian, and Alaska ranges. This port city is bordered on the west, north, and south by the Knik Arm and Turnagain Arm of Cook Inlet on the Gulf of Alaska. The city is conterminous with the borough of Anchorage. The Chugach Mountains to the east have a general elevation of 4,000 to 5,000 feet, with peaks from 8,000 to 10,000 feet.

Anchorage, Alaska skyline with Chugach mountains in background. © *Terri Chick/Alamy*

These mountains block warm air from the Gulf of Mexico, keeping precipitation relatively low. The Alaska Range to the north protects the city from cold air from the state's interior; thus temperatures in Anchorage are usually 25 to 30 degrees warmer than temperatures in the rest of the state. While the area has four seasons, their length and characteristics differ from those of the middle latitudes; snows generally arrive in October and leave in mid-April, while annual average snowfall is more than 70 inches. The average number of daylight hours in the summer is 19.3 hours; the winter average is 5.8 hours.

Area: 1,955 square miles

Elevation: 132 feet above sea level

Average Temperatures: 35.8° F

Average Annual Precipitation: 15.71 inches of rain; 70.6 inches of snow

■ History

Native American Trade Center Transformed by Discovery of Gold

The Anchorage area was settled more than 6,000 years ago as a summer fishing camp for the Tanaina tribe. The

Pacific Eskimos were a dominant presence in the area until the seventeenth century. In 1650 the Eskimos were defeated in battle by the Tanaina where Point Woronzof is now located on the shore of Knik Arm. By 1700 the area had become a major trade center for Native Americans, Eskimos, and Aleuts.

The first Russian sailors, led by Vitus Bering, may have arrived in about 1743 to establish trading posts. The first European to explore the territory around the inlet was the British explorer Captain James Cook, who claimed the land for England in 1778 and after whom Cook Inlet was named. Russian settlers moved onto Upper Cook Inlet in the late 1890s, establishing settlements inhabited by traders and missionaries. When Alaska was sold to the United States in 1867, Russia turned over its holdings on Cook Inlet to the Alaska Commercial Company of San Francisco. In 1882 gold was discovered in streams along Turnagain Arm, causing a population explosion as steamships from Seattle brought prospectors who settled in the Matanuska and Sustina Valleys to pan for gold. Alaska became an official U.S. territory in 1912.

City Becomes Major Railroad, Aviation, Military Center

Another growth spurt occurred in 1915 when the area known as Ship Creek valley was chosen as the mid-point construction headquarters for the government-owned Alaska Railroad that was to be built from Seward to Fairbanks. The town site of Anchorage was soon established at Ship Creek. By 1920, the year of its incorporation, Anchorage had become a major city. The Alaska Railroad was completed in 1923; that same year Anchorage's first airfield was built, initiating the aviation industry that within a decade became a vital part of the city's economy. Anchorage established its own airline in 1926 and Merrill Field opened in 1935. That same year the city also experienced another population boom with the migration of dust bowl farmers from the Midwest into the Matanuska Valley.

The foundation of another important element of Anchorage's economy, the military defense complex was formed with the military buildup in Alaska during the late 1930s and early 1940s. Fort Richardson and Elmendorf Field Air Force Base were established near the city. The Alaska Highway, the American military supply line to northern defense headquarters and a link between Anchorage and other parts of the country, was completed in 1942. The city expanded through World War II and into the early 1950s. The population increased to 43,314 in 1950 at a rate of more than 600 percent in a decade. The first terminal of the Anchorage International Airport opened in 1953, making Anchorage a primary connection for transpolar air traffic between Europe and Asia.

City Devastated by Earthquake; Oil Discovered

Anchorage suffered a severe setback in 1964 when it was struck by a devastating earthquake, one of the most serious ever recorded in North American history. Damage was extensive, but within the next few years the city had recovered and was moving into another phase of prosperity resulting from the discovery of oil on Cook Inlet. The city and borough governments merged in 1975 to form the municipality of Anchorage and, in 1978, Project 80s was initiated. A development plan of major proportions, Project 80s involved the construction of the George M. Sullivan Arena, the William A. Egan Convention and Civic Center, and the Anchorage Center for the Performing Arts; the final stage of the project, the Center for the Performing Arts, was completed in 1988. A collapse in world crude oil prices brought statewide recession in 1986, causing high unemployment rates and a population decrease in Anchorage.

Oil Spilled in Prince William Sound

Anchorage made international headlines on Good Friday, March 24, 1989, when the grounded oil tanker *Exxon Valdez* spilled nearly 11 million gallons of crude oil into nearby Prince William Sound, forming a slick that eventually reached into the Gulf of Alaska and beyond. Anchorage served as the command post for cleanup efforts costing more than $2.5 billion. Only a small amount of oil remained by the mid-1990s and seals, whales, and bald eagles had returned to the region. U.S. government biologists and scientists for the Exxon Corporation continued to disagree over the issue of damage to animals, with Exxon contending that the damage was less than what government scientists claimed. In 1994 an Anchorage jury ordered Exxon Corp. to pay more than $5 billion to fishermen and others who could demonstrate that they had been financially hurt by the oil spill.

A Time of Growth

In the 1990s Anchorage began to experience record economic growth that continued through the early 2000s. In 2002 Anchorage was one of 10 cities to receive the 2002 All-American City Award, an award designated by the National Civic League. In 2009 job growth in Anchorage came to a halt for the first time in 20 years. However, officials predicted that efforts to grow the local health-care industry would spur job increases in the 2010s.

Historical Information: Anchorage Museum at Rasmuson Center, 625 C Street, Anchorage, AK 99501; telephone (907) 929-9201. Municipality of Anchorage, 632 West Sixth Avenue, Anchorage, AK 99501; telephone (907) 343-7100.

■ Population Profile

Metropolitan Statistical Area Population
  2000: 319,605
  2010: 380,821
  2012 estimate: 392,535
  Percent change, 2000–2010: 19.2%
  U.S. rank in 2000: 143rd
  U.S. rank in 2010: 133rd

City Residents
  1990: 226,338
  2000: 260,283
  2010: 291,826
  2012 estimate: 298,610
  Percent change, 2000–2010: 12.1%
  U.S. rank in 1990: 69th (State rank: 1st)
  U.S. rank in 2000: 75th (State rank: 1st)
  U.S. rank in 2010: 64th (State rank: 1st)

Density: 171.2 people per square mile

Racial and ethnic characteristics
  White: 196,090
  Black or African American: 18,866
  American Indian and Alaskan Native: 19,165
  Asian: 27,691
  Native Hawaiian and Other Pacific Islander: 5,977

Hispanic or Latino (may be of any race): 24,593
Other: 30,821

Percent of residents born in state: 35.2%

Age characteristics

Population under 5 years old: 22,059
Population 5 to 9 years old: 21,049
Population 10 to 14 years old: 19,593
Population 15 to 19 years old: 20,242
Population 20 to 24 years old: 25,862
Population 25 to 34 years old: 48,250
Population 35 to 44 years old: 41,089
Population 45 to 54 years old: 40,501
Population 55 to 59 years old: 19,702
Population 60 to 64 years old: 16,319
Population 65 to 74 years old: 14,871
Population 75 to 84 years old: 7,006
Population 85 years and over: 2,067
Median age: 33.0

Births (2010–11 Metropolitan Area)

Total number: 5,875

Deaths (2010–11 Metropolitan Area)

Total number: 1,752

Money income (2012)

Per capita income: $34,565
Median household income: $74,648
Total households: 105,688

Number of households with income of ...

less than $10,000: 3,015
$10,000 to $14,999: 3,624
$15,000 to $24,999: 7,053
$25,000 to $34,999: 7,822
$35,000 to $49,999: 12,834
$50,000 to $74,999: 18,729
$75,000 to $99,999: 15,401
$100,000 to $149,999: 19,609
$150,000 to $199,999: 9,775
$200,000 or more: 7,826

Percent of families below poverty level: 8.5%

FBI Crime Index Property: 10,543

FBI Crime Index Violent: 2,479

■ Municipal Government

The municipality of Anchorage is administered by a mayor-assembly form of government, with the mayor and 11 assembly members elected to three-year terms.

Head Official: Mayor Dan Sullivan (since July 2009; current term expires June 30, 2015)

Total Number of City Employees: 4,100 (2013)

City Information: City of Anchorage, 632 West 6th Avenue, Anchorage, AK 99501; telephone (907) 343-7100.

■ Economy

Major Industries and Commercial Activity

Anchorage's prime location globally, stable economy, and low taxation help attract businesses to the area. Due to the nature of its economy, the city has weathered the recent economic downturn better than most. The United States government and the oil industry have been integral to the Anchorage economy. The federally funded Alaska Railroad gave Anchorage its start; later the military defense system supported an essentially undiversified economic base. This base expanded in the 1970s when the Trans-Alaska Pipeline, one of the largest construction projects in history, brought thousands of workers and increased service industries. Anchorage is the state's primary transportation, communications, trade, service, and finance center. The major growth sectors in the local economy are oil, health care, professional and business services, and leisure and hospitality.

While Anchorage is not a major center of oil production, the city acts as the administrative center for the industry. In 2008 BP and ConocoPhillips announced a plan named the Denali project, a 1,750-mile natural gas pipeline that would run from Alaska into Canada. The project was expected to result in the addition of more than 150 jobs by year's end. In 2010 Denali was still receiving bids for the $35 million venture, and was competing with other projects, such as TransCanada/ ExxonMobil's Alaska Pipeline Project, to secure shipping commitments. While the number of jobs in the sector is relative low, the importance to Anchorage's economy is great, accounting for a significant percentage of local salaries and wages each year.

Since Anchorage is a primary center for health care services for most Alaskans, health care has become a major economic driver in the city. The growth is attributed in part to increased federal spending and the increased need for health care in Alaska's growing population. Job growth in the professional and business services sector is seen primarily in engineering, architectural, and related services that meet the growing demand of construction, mining, and oil developments.

The leisure and hospitality industry, along with the service businesses that sprout up around the industry, are a major driving force in Anchorage economy. Mainly due to its central location, Anchorage acts as the gateway to the state of Alaska, thereby funneling tourists, conventioneers and other visitors through the area.

The military in Anchorage has been a constant presence. Elmendorf Air Force Base, Fort Richardson

Army Post, and Kulis Air National Guard base have all been located near Ted Stevens Anchorage International Airport. The three military posts have employed more than 10,000 military personnel. The family members of military personnel contribute to the local economy through employment and consumer spending. Because of the large number of military personnel based in the city, many businesses have experienced temporary slowdowns due to military deployments. In 2010, Elmendorf Air Force Base, and Fort Richardson Army Post were consolidated to become Joint Base Elmendorf-Richardson.

The transportation industry in Anchorage is the busiest in the state. Ted Stevens Anchorage International Airport officials have estimated that air transportation accounted for one in nine city jobs. The airport's economic impact is felt as far away as the North Pole, where jet fuel is refined and loaded onto the more than 100 rail cars that then travel by Alaska Railroad to service the airport daily. The Alaska Railroad transports freight and passengers; in summer months the Railroad transports passengers to popular destinations throughout the state. The Port of Anchorage accounts for delivery of more than 90 percent of the consumer goods arriving in Alaska.

Items and goods produced: fisheries' products, wood and wood products, petroleum products, coal, minerals

Incentive Programs—New and Existing Companies

Local programs: The most widely used local incentives include customized job training programs, low interest loans, municipal revenue bonds, and property tax abatement. Anchorage Economic Development Corporation, a public-private partnership, assists new and existing businesses with information on taxes and utilities and on available sites and buildings, which are said to be plentiful.

The Municipality of Anchorage offers a program that exempts some types of economic development properties from taxation. Inventory that is held for shipment outside of Alaska may also be exempt from local inventory taxes. Anchorage municipal code also provides for tax exemptions for property and inventory for economic development. New or expanding businesses may also be granted property tax abatement.

State programs: The Governor's Office of International Trade provides assistance and information to firms interested in foreign trade and investment, organizes trade missions and promotions, and sponsors trade shows and seminars. Several areas in the city are located in Anchorage's Foreign Trade Zone, the two most notable being the Ted Stevens Anchorage International Airport and the Port of Anchorage. The World Trade Center assists businesses seeking to enter or expand their role in international trade. The Alaska Export Assistance Center helps local businesses expand into foreign markets.

The Alaska Exploration Incentives Act allows mining and exploration credits of up to $20 million of qualified costs including personnel, transportation, fuel, camp, communications, geochemical, geophysical and contractual expenses for new mines. Oil & Gas Exploration Incentive Credits are available for exploratory wells on state-owned land. By 2013, 22 wells had qualified for this credit. A film incentive program provides transferable tax credits as an incentive to attract large-scale film production in Alaska. Bonus credits are available for shooting in rural areas. The New Business Incentive Program is an economic development grant program targeted at companies locating or expanding into new manufacturing or value-added businesses in Alaska. Deteriorated property and qualified inventory is exempt from taxation for up to 10 years. This exemption may be transferred to another owner. Targeted Jobs Tax Credits is a federal tax credit program that encourages employers to hire new employees.

Job training programs: The University of Alaska Anchorage offers classes and degree programs to businesses and individuals on logistics and on doing business in Pacific Asia and the former Soviet Union. The university also partners with the Alaska Economic Development Corporation to provide a Mentor Program that connects students with business leaders. Lunchtime forums highlight a different business industry each time.

Development Projects

In 2013 builders applied for approval of more than $223 million in construction projects. The Fred Meyer department store and grocery chain announced a $20 million overhaul of its oldest Anchorage store. The improvements, including high-rise glass panels at the entryways and a second floor mezzanine, involve a complete rebuild. Other retail projects include the Natural Pantry in Midtown, the first phase of the Bass Pro Shops at Glenn Square, a new Sam's Club, and a new Wal-Mart. The opening of the Dimond Center, Alaska' first factory outlet center, was planned for 2014. A Cabela's store is also expected to open in 2014 in South Anchorage.

The Anchorage Neighborhood Health Center opened a new 42,000-square-foot medical and dental facility in 2012. The Center is one of the largest medical and dental providers in the state. The expanded clinic will increase the health center's annual capacity to 25,000 patients, nearly doubling the volume of patients who can receive care. The new facility includes an on-site pharmacy, and lab and radiology services. Construction on the Blood Bank of Alaska's new $36.8 million facility remains in the planning stage. Scheduled for completion in the fall of 2014, the organization continues to seek funding.

The University of Alaska Anchorage's new 196,000-square-foot sports arena is projected to cost $109 million. Construction began in 2012 and is expected to be completed by 2014. The facility will house a 5,000-seat performance gymnasium for basketball and volleyball; a practice and performance gym for the gymnastics program; support space consisting of a fitness and training room, administration/coaching offices, laundry, A/V production, and locker and team rooms for basketball, volleyball, gymnastics, skiing, track and cross country programs. In 2013 the university also broke ground on a new Engineering and Industry Building scheduled to open in the fall of 2015. The new 81,500-square-foot facility will house labs for communications, electrical engineering, fluids, heat and mass transfer, foundation engineering, transportation and highway engineering and land surveying, in addition to machine and wood shops, a service yard and conferencing/collaborative learning areas.

New military construction included 12 planned projects costing a total of $355 million. In addition, 200,000 square feet of Class A office space construction went online in 2012, including the Class A Dankor building in midtown.

As of early 2014, the H2H (highway-to-highway) project to build an interchange that would link the Glenn and Seward highways was still under environmental review, with alternative routes being explored. The project, originally expected to be completed in 2008, is currently on hold.

To add an additional boost to the growing convention and tourism industry, in 2008 the city completed construction of a $103 million, 215,000 square-foot convention facility. Begun in 2006, the Dena'ina Center is located about one block away from the Egan Civic and Convention Center and the Alaska Center for the Performing Arts. All three buildings, marketed under the umbrella Anchorage Convention Centers, are linked by covered walkways.

Economic Development Information: Anchorage Economic Development Corporation, 510 L Street, Ste 603, Anchorage, AK 99501; telephone (907) 258-3700; fax (907) 258-6646. Municipality of Anchorage, 632 West Sixth Avenue, Anchorage, AK 99501; telephone (907) 343-7100 (public information).

Commercial Shipping

Anchorage's seaports and airports combine with its railroad to make the area the primary cargo distributor in the state.

The Port of Anchorage, the largest seaport in Alaska, is a year-round shipping point with five terminals served by three major carriers, which bring four to five ships from the Pacific Northwest and Asia each week. The port provides an estimated 90 percent of the merchandise goods for 80 percent of Alaska's populated area. In addition, more than 18,000 pieces of military cargo have passed through the port since 2005. More than four million tons of iron and steel products, 240,000 containers, cement, wood products, and various other commodities crossed the port's docks in 2013. The port is also an important fuel transport areas providing 100 percent of

the jet fuel used at Joint Base Elmendorf Richardson, 65 percent of the jet fuel used at Ted Stevens International Airport, and 1.4 million gallons of fuel to western Alaska for heating oil, gasoline, and diesel.

The Ted Stevens Anchorage International Airport (TSAIA) was among the top five in the world for cargo throughput in 2012. It is second in the United States for landed weight of cargo aircraft. (Memphis, Tennessee, is number one). The airport is less than 9.5 hours from 90 percent of the industrial world. It is also the world's largest and busiest floatplane base. More than 50 air carriers and 9 freight forwarders connect Anchorage to the rest of the country and the world beyond. Municipal Merrill Field airport serves the intrastate needs of business, banking, and commerce. The Airport is responsible for approximately 15,577 airport and community jobs, earning $1 billion.

The Alaska Railroad provides rail freight service including building products to construct Alaska homes and businesses, and support for critical resource industries such as coal, petroleum products and gas. In 2013 the railroad moved more than six million tons of freight across 651 miles of track. More than 30 motor freight carriers link Anchorage with major market areas.

Labor Force and Employment Outlook

Anchorage boasts an abundant and well-educated labor pool with a relatively low median age. In 2013 unemployment in Anchorage was 4.7 percent, well below the national rate of 7 percent. In 2013 the private sector grew by 1.5 percent, or 1,840 jobs. Seven of the 10 major job sectors were above the year-to-date monthly average, indicating that the increase in jobs is likely to remain strong into 2014. However, government employment declined by 840 jobs due to job losses in both the federal and local governments. The goods-producing category, which includes oil and gas, manufacturing and construction, showed the most growth. An increase of jobs was also seen in the construction industry.

Expansion and diversification have given Anchorage's economy the ability to absorb fluctuations in the business cycle or unexpected economic events. Anchorage now has a steady year-round employment base, with a summer boost from tourism and construction activities. The international cargo business in Anchorage continues to grow; Anchorage is equidistant to both Asia and Europe, and is nine hours flying time to nearly the entire industrialized world, making it a good location for warehousing and distribution.

The following is a summary of data regarding the 2012 Anchorage labor force:

Size of civilian labor force: 161,344

Number of workers employed in . . .

agriculture and mining: 4,813

construction: 9,642

manufacturing: 2,813

wholesale trade: 3,700

retail trade: 17,110

transportation: 10,431

information systems: 3,084

finance: 7,623

professional administration: 15,886

education and social services: 35,636

arts and leisure: 14,966

other: 6,332

public administration: 17,186

Average hourly earnings of production workers: $20.99

Unemployment rate: 5.1% (2012)

Employers

Largest employers (2012)	*Number of employees*
Providence Health & Services	more than 4,000
Wal-Mart/Sam's Club	3,000–3,249
Carrs/Safeway	2,750–2,999
Fred Meyer	2,500–2,749
ASRC Energy Services	2,250–2,499
BP Exploration Alaska	1,750–1,999
NANA Management Services	1,750–1,999
CH2MHill	1,750–1,999
Alaska Airlines	1,500–1,749
Alaska Native Tribal Health Consortium (ANTHC)	1,500–1,749
GCI Communications	1,250–1,499
Southcentral Foundation	1,250–1,499
FedEx	1,000–1,249
ConocoPhillips	1,000–1,249
Alaska USA Federal Credit Union	1,000–1,249

Cost of Living

The personal tax burden in Alaska is extremely low, while the cost of living is significantly higher than much of the rest of the nation. Residents benefit from distributions from the Permanent Fund, a savings account established in 1976 by voters allowing residents to receive 25 percent of the state's royalty oil revenue. Senior citizens enjoy a $150,000 property tax exemption or a renter's rebate.

The following is a summary of data regarding several key cost of living factors in the area.

2013 ACCRA Average House Price: $479,900

2013 ACCRA Cost of Living Index: 126

State income tax rate: None

State sales tax rate: None

Local income tax rate: None

Local sales tax rate: None

Property tax rate: 6.92 to 15.56 mills (2013)

Economic Information: Alaska Department of Labor and Workforce Development, Research and Analysis Section, P.O. Box 111149, Juneau, AK 99811-1149; telephone (907) 465-4500. Anchorage Economic Development Corporation, 510 L Street, Ste 603, Anchorage, AK 99501; telephone (907) 258-3700; fax (907) 258-6646.

■ Education and Research

Elementary and Secondary Schools

The Anchorage School District has schools in Anchorage, Eagle River, Chugiak, and Girdwood. The district prides itself on test scores that are better than state and national averages, and a diverse student body of 48,837 pupils. The district contains four schools that received gold, silver or bronze medals in U.S. News's Best High Schools rankings. In the 1990s Anchorage voters approved more than $500 million in school construction. Two middle schools and nine elementary schools were built and the new South Anchorage High School, serving 1,600 students, opened for the 2004–05 school year. The new Eagle River High School opened in fall 2005 with 740 students, relieving crowding at Chugiak High School. The Alaska Native Cultural Charter School opened in fall 2007 to kindergarten through sixth grade students. A preschool opened in fall 2009, followed by the addition of seventh grade in 2010.

The school system is administered by a nonpartisan, eight-member school board that appoints a superintendent on the recommendation of a selection task force. Stimulus money from the federal government became available in 2010; these funds were used to solidify a home-visit initiative within some schools. The program included teachers visiting childrens' homes to encourage higher academic performance and overall responsibility.

A small percentage of students attend private schools including four schools run by the Archdiocese of Anchorage and one independent Catholic school.

The following is a summary of data regarding the Anchorage School District.

Total enrollment: 49,206

Number of facilities

total: 99

elementary schools: 58

junior high schools: 10

high schools: 8

other: 23

Student/teacher ratio: 16.6:1

Teacher salaries

average (statewide): $61,093

Funding per pupil: $14,466

Public Schools Information: Anchorage School District, 5530 E. Northern Lights Blvd., Anchorage, AK 99504-3135; telephone (907) 742-4000.

Colleges and Universities

Two fully accredited universities are located in Anchorage: the University of Alaska Anchorage (UAA), and Alaska Pacific University, a private institution affiliated with the United Methodist church. Both institutions offer undergraduate degrees in a wide range of disciplines.

The University of Alaska Anchorage was founded in 1954. Its 362-acre urban campus served 17,129 students in 2013. The university ranked 71st among regional universities in the West in the 2013 *U.S. News & World Report* "Best Colleges" report. In 2013 in-state tuition and fees were $6,806, compared to $19,766 for out-of-state students. In addition to undergraduate degrees, the university offers master's degrees in such fields as biological sciences, business and management, logistics, and engineering.

Alaska Pacific University is a four-year liberal arts school on a 170-acre wooded main campus near the foothills of the Chugach Mountains. About 40 percent of APU's 436 students are from outside the state. Also located in the Anchorage area are several vocational, specialty, and technical schools.

Libraries and Research Centers

In addition to its main branch downtown, the Anchorage Municipal Libraries system operates five branches throughout the city. Holdings consist of more than 515,255 books, nearly 1,780 periodical subscriptions, and films, records, tapes, art reproductions, and sheet music. Special collections at the system's main Z. J. Loussac Library include the Alaska Collection, featuring more than 25,000 books and documents on Alaska and the North, and the Loussac Children's Collection, with materials for parents and people who work with children. Nearly 50 special libraries and research centers are located in Anchorage, most of them affiliated with the University of Alaska Anchorage and specializing in the fields of

environment, natural resources, art, history, law, and education. ARLIS, or Alaska Resources Library and Information Services, features a collection of more than 200,000 books, 700 journals, and a variety of other sources of information about Alaska. Housed on the University of Alaska campus, ARLIS contains the collection of The Oil Spill Public Information Center, featuring scientific data from the *Exxon Valdez* oil spill damage. The National Center for Infectious Diseases Arctic Investigations Program seeks to improve the quality of life of arctic and subarctic people.

Public Library Information: Anchorage Municipal Libraries, 3600 Denali St., Anchorage, AK 99503 (main branch); telephone (907) 343-2975.

■ Health Care

Anchorage is a primary medical treatment center for the state of Alaska and is home to the two largest hospitals in the state-Providence Alaska Medical Center and Alaska Regional Hospital. The $157 million 100-bed hospital on Elmendorf Air Force Base opened in 2001. The new Elmendorf Hospital replaced the existing 50-bed hospital, which suffered structural damage during the 1964 earthquake, and serves the state's military population. The hospital remained after Elmendorf merged with Fort Richardson in 2010.

Providence Alaska Medical Center, with 341 beds and more than 600 staff physicians, is the main medical referral center in the state, offering such specialized treatment as open heart surgery and neonatal care.

Alaska Regional Hospital provides neurosurgery and spinal and orthopedic surgery; a maternity center, critical care units, and emergency services, including an air ambulance, are maintained. A $7 million renovation at Alaska Regional Hospital included a new trauma and open-heart surgery room. The hospital was recognized for orthopedics in *U.S. News & World Report's* Best Hospitals 2010–11.

In 1974 Anchorage Neighborhood Health Center (ANHC) began service to Anchorage with a handful of clinicians in a trailer. Since that time, it has grown to become one of Alaska's largest and most comprehensive primary care medical and dental practices, serving over 12,000 individual patients through over 40,000 visits per year. Its new health center facility in Midtown contains 45 exam, procedure, and medical consultation rooms and a full-service state-of-the-art dental clinic.

Alaska Native Medical Center provides service to Alaskan and American Natives throughout the state free of charge. With 150 beds and a staff of about 250 physicians and 700 nurses, it is one of the largest facilities of its kind in the United States. Anchorage Neighborhood Health Center offers three family practice clinics featuring medical, dental, pharmaceutical, and mental health services. The North Star Behavioral Health System provides mental health and substance abuse treatment programs through several facilities.

■ Recreation

Sightseeing

An ideal way to see the points of interest in downtown Anchorage is to take a walking tour. A circular route-beginning at Old City Hall, original seat of the municipal government, and ending two blocks away at the Pioneer Schoolhouse, the first school in Anchorage-provides a leisurely stroll through the city's history. Principal attractions along the way include the Ship Creek Viewpoint with a view of the site of Tanaina summer fish camps. Nearby are the Leopold David House, built in 1917 for the city's first mayor and Boney Memorial Courthouse, housing fine examples of nineteenth-century art motifs of Alaskan natives and animals. The Oscar Anderson House Museum in Elderberry Park is Anchorage's only historic house museum, offering visitors a glimpse into the life of the family that occupied the home as well as Anchorage history. The Anchorage Light Speed Planet Walk, beginning at 5th and G streets in downtown Anchorage, is designed to offer an interactive tour of the solar system. The walk through town, in which one step is equal to the distance that light travels in one second, includes information kiosks at each planet location.

Resolution Park, featuring the Captain Cook Monument, commemorates the 200th anniversary of Cook's exploration of the area. Adjacent to the park are historic Anchorage homes, including the first permanent frame residence in the city. Located on the southern edge of downtown is Delaney Park, known as "The Park Strip," once a firebreak for the original town site and later the city's first airfield. Delaney Park is the oldest park in Anchorage.

The Alaska Zoo features hundreds of animals; special attractions are the natural land habitat for brown bears and an aquarium for seals and otters. Points of interest in north Anchorage include St. Nicholas Russian Church. The oldest building in the municipality, the church is located at Eklutna Historical Park, the site of the first Tanaina settlement east of Knik Arm; the cemetery's "spirit" houses are reminders of the blend of native tradition and missionary influence.

In south Anchorage are the Potter Section House and Crow Creek Mine, the first non-native settlement. An example of a nineteenth-century placer mine, Crow Creek is still in operation, and rental equipment is available for those wishing to pan for any gold that remains. Local fur factories provide regularly scheduled tours of their facilities. Sightseeing and "flightseeing" tours of the Anchorage area and day trips to attractions such as Mt. McKinley and Portage Glacier can be arranged through bus and air services. In 2010 Anchorage was named one of TripAdvisor's Top 25 Travelers' Choice Destinations.

Arts and Culture

Dating back to territory days when opera was staged regularly and when the city had an orchestra before it had paved streets, the performing arts have been an integral part of life in Anchorage. The city's arts community, with more than 75 organizations offering cultural experiences ranging from classical music to native dance, provides a striking contrast to the surrounding wilderness. The Anchorage Concert Association, founded in 1950 to bring international performers to local audiences, is still active, sponsoring about 22 music, dance, and theatre productions each year. The Alaska State Council on the Arts is based in Anchorage.

Many of these performances are presented in the downtown Alaska Center for the Performing Arts, a modern complex housing four theaters, including the Elvera Voth Hall, a 1,800-square-foot performance and rehearsal space opened in 2003. A significant contribution to the Anchorage arts community, the center offers a year-round schedule of more than 600 events and furnishes a showcase for local performers. The facility was built as part of Project 80's, along with the Anchorage Museum of History and Art, Egan Civic and Convention Center, Sullivan Arena and Z.J. Loussac Library. The 2013–14 performance season marked the Center's 25th Anniversary.

The center's resident companies include Alaska Dance Theatre, Alaska Junior Theater, Alaska Theatre of Youth, Anchorage Concert Association, Anchorage Concert Chorus, the Anchorage Symphony Orchestra, Anchorage Youth Symphony, Anchorage Opera, and Whistling Swan Productions. Anchorage Ballet, established in 1997, performs over seven performances per season. In 2010 the ballet was the recipient of the Mayor's Arts Award for Outstanding Arts Organization. Perseverance Theatre became a resident company in the 2011–12 season. It offers professional theatre by and for Alaskans.

The Anchorage Symphony Orchestra, formed in 1946, features about 80 musicians. The ASO performs between October and April in the Atwood Concert Hall. Performances include a six-event Classic Concerts Series, four Young People's Concerts, annual Halloween Family Concert, and projects that stimulate Alaskan musicians and composers. Randall Craig Fleischer has been the symphony's music director since 1999.

The Anchorage Opera, Alaska's only professional opera company, offers three full-scale opera productions per season in the Discovery Theatre. Anchorage Opera regularly partners with artists from Alaska Dance Theatre, Anchorage Concert Chorus, the Alaska Children's Choir, and the Anchorage Festival of Music. The Alaska Chamber Singers, a choral ensemble of approximately 40 voices, offer performances at various venues throughout the city.

Museums and galleries in Anchorage specialize in science, history, and arts and crafts. The Alaska Aviation Heritage Museum traces the history of state aviation and prominent aviators, with a theater, observation deck, and historic planes. The Alaska Museum of Natural History is located in Anchorage. The Alaska Museum of Science and Nature educates exclusively on Alaska's unique geological, cultural, and ecological history.

The Anchorage Museum at Rasmuson Center features a permanent collection of more than 25,000 objects and 2,000 artifacts; the museum is also responsible for a $5.8 million collection of 276 works of art viewable in public buildings around the city. An expansion project that started in 2006 included a 70,000 feet addition of galleries for the first regional office of the Smithsonian Institution's National Museum of Natural History Arctic Studies Center. The Arctic Studies Center houses more than 1,000 Alaska Native artifacts relocated from the Smithsonian. The museum includes a new 9,000-square-foot home for the city's Imaginarium, a science discovery center with a variety of hands-on experience exhibits, a planetarium, and a preschool learning area. The expansion project was scheduled for completion in 2009, but opened to the public in 2010. The 15,000-square-foot Alaska Gallery in the museum displays a collection of more than 1,000 objects of traditional and modern native art with demonstration exhibits.

At the Alaska Native Heritage Center (opened in 1999) the visitor can explore five distinct Alaska Native cultures through interpretive displays, films, and daily performances by traditional storytellers. A trail from the Welcome House leads to Native Tradition Bearers-artists and performers at five traditional village exhibits surrounding a lake on the 26-acre grounds.

Festivals and Holidays

The year kicks off in Anchorage with the Annual Anchorage Folk Festival, offering more than 120 musical performances by local and guest acts, and the Great Alaska Beer and Barleywine Festival. February offers the Fur Rendezvous, known as the "Fur Rondy" (Alaska's largest and oldest winter festival dating back to 1936), a popular 10-day celebration of the annual fur-auctioning and social gathering of trappers and miners. The event started as a three-day sporting event timed to coincide with the return of miners and trappers. The Crystal Gallery of Ice is an annual event in the heart of downtown Anchorage. Ice carvers come from all over the world to compete in ice carving competition.

The world-famous cross country Iditarod Trail Sled Dog Race starts in downtown Anchorage the first Saturday in March. Also in March, and coinciding with the Iditarod is the Tour of Anchorage, a cross-country ski event with varying race lengths.

April follows up with the Alyeska Spring Carnival and Slush Cup and May brings the Alaska Native Youth

Olympics. June events include the Three Barons Renaissance Faire and the Mayor's Midnight Sun Marathon.

Live music can be heard all summer long on Wednesday and Friday afternoons from the park at Fourth Avenue and E Street. An annual folk music festival and a monthly concert series spotlighting national up-and-coming artists enlivens the summer months.

Other summer fare includes the annual July 4th Celebration and the Bear Paw Festival at Eagle River in July; August offerings include the Alyeska Blueberry & Mountain Arts Festival and the Arctic Thunder Elmendorf Air Force Base Open House and Air Show.

Among the fall highlights are the Alaska State Fair in late August and early September, followed in October by the Kendall Hockey Classic. Thanksgiving weekend events include an annual production of *The Nutcracker* by the Cincinnati Ballet and the Town Square Tree Lighting Ceremony. The Anchorage International Film Festival takes place in December.

Sports for the Spectator

The Wells Fargo Sports Complex at the University of Alaska Anchorage hosts Seawolves National Collegiate Athletic Association (NCAA) hockey, basketball, and volleyball competition. The Alaska Aces of the East Coast Hockey League are based in Anchorage and play at Sullivan Arena. The Carrs/Safeway Great Alaska Shootout collegiate basketball tournament is a major event that draws fans from throughout the state and nation. The Anchorage Bucs are part of the Alaska Baseball League (summer collegiate league).

Sled dog racing is the official state sport and Anchorage hosts several main sledding events. The world famous Iditarod Trail Sled Dog Race originates in Anchorage and runs more than 1,000 miles to Nome, the course taking from 10 days to a month to complete. The Open World Championship Sled Dog Race, the most famous sprint race, is held during the Fur Rendezvous and draws racers from all over the world. The Native Youth Olympics, sponsored in part by the University of Alaska Anchorage, attracts students from across the state. Competition focuses on games and contests that were once played by Alaska Natives to hone their hunting and survival skills.

Sports for the Participant

With more than 223 parks, 82 playgrounds, and 250 miles of trails covering 10, 946 acres of municipal parkland, residents have a multitude of choices for year-round and seasonal outdoor activities. Park facilities include shelters, camping, more than 110 athletic fields, 5 pools, tennis courts, winter ice skating, and programming for recreational events. Mountain climbing can be pursued at the 500,000-acre Chugach State Park, situated within the city limits; hiking and horseback riding trails are located in several other municipal parks.

Salmon and trout fishing facilities are maintained on rivers, creeks, and lakes, and licensed hunting is regulated by the Alaska Department of Fish and Game.

During summer the midnight sun provides additional time for recreation. Popular activities include boating, kayaking, and river rafting on the flowing waters within the municipality limits. Free loaner bicycles are available for use on downtown bike trails; among other public facilities are golf courses, 5 pools, several lakes, and tennis courts. With 135 miles of paved trails and some 300 miles of unpaved and wilderness trail, Anchorage's extensive trail system attracts both residents and visitors. One of the most popular routes is the Tony Knowles Coastal Trail, an 11-mile asphalt trail that runs from downtown to Kincaid Park (which has its own system of 43 miles of wooded trail). Flattop Mountain is a popular hike; both beginner and expert hikers can summit the 3,510 foot mountain (3 miles roundtrip) as a day hike. Cyclists and runners enjoy the multitude of trails in and around Anchorage. Runners have been traveling to Anchorage to participate in the Mayor's Marathon & Half-Marathon since its inception in 1974. *Bicycling* magazine called Anchorage's trail system one of the best in the United States.

Winter sports enthusiasts can find a wide range of choices, including dog sledding, ice skating, skiing, sledding, snowshoeing, snowmobiling, and skating on several rinks, including two Olympic-sized hockey rinks. Dogsled rides and tours are available through local vendors. The municipality maintains more than 200 miles of cross-country ski trails, including 40 kilometers lit for night skiing, plus sledding hills and snowmobile trails. Alaska's largest ski resort is 40 minutes from downtown Anchorage. Alyeska Resort boasts an annual average of 742 inches of snowfall and a lift capacity of more than 10,000 skiers per hour on its nine lifts.

Shopping and Dining

More than a dozen shopping centers, including five major malls, are located in Anchorage. Downtown's Fifth Avenue Mall houses major national retail chains such as Nordstrom, The Gap, and J. C. Penney, but products native to Alaska are the major shopping attractions, with foods, ivory, jewelry, gold, furs, seal oil candles, and Eskimo and Aleut basketry among the most popular items. Shoppers can visit workshops to see fur styling, jewelry crafting, and wool making demonstrations. Dimond Center has more than 200 stores, a cinema, and an athletic club. The Anchorage Market & Festival operates both Saturday and Sunday throughout the summer at West Third Avenue and E Street. Shoppers will find fresh baked goods and vegetables, handmade jewelry and crafts, and unique Native art.

More than 350 restaurants in Anchorage offer a variety of ethnic cuisines. The local specialty is fresh seafood, particularly salmon, served at most restaurants in settings that offer views of mountain ranges and oceangoing vessels departing the Port of Anchorage.

Visitor Information: Anchorage Convention and Visitors Bureau, 524 West Fourth Avenue, Anchorage, AK 99501-2212; telephone (907) 276-4118; fax (907) 278-5559.

■ Convention Facilities

Anchorage is rapidly gaining distinction as a convention and meeting site. The city's downtown convention center is within walking distance of fine restaurants, unique shops, and world-class cultural events. The extraordinary experience of enjoying first-class amenities in close proximity to untouched wilderness attracts an increasing number of groups to Anchorage yearly.

The principal meeting venue in Anchorage is the Anchorage Convention Center, located in the heart of Anchorage in the middle of a pedestrian-friendly downtown convention district filled with hotels, high-end eateries, great shopping and art galleries featuring local artists. The complex includes the $103 million, 215,000-square-foot Dena'ina Center, completed in 2008, and the William A. Egan Civic and Convention Center, which adds an additional 85,000 square feet of meeting and exhibit space accommodating groups of 20 to 2,776 people and features 189 custom exhibit areas, simultaneous interpreting facilities, and complete catering service. The Egan Center completed a $3 million upgrade during 2009. Across the street from Egan Center and adjoined by a skybridge is the Alaska Center for the Performing Arts, which provides theater-style meeting halls seating 350 to 2,100 people. Covered walkways connect all three convention locations.

Located two miles from downtown is the George M. Sullivan Arena, which accommodates sporting events, and trade shows with 32,000 square feet of usable space and parking for more than 1, 000 vehicles. The Anchorage Museum at Rasmuson Center is available to host special events in its atrium. Other meeting facilities are available at the University of Alaska Anchorage, Alaska Pacific University, and major hotels in the metropolitan area. Anchorage features more than 8,000 hotel and motel rooms and more than 850 beds in bed and breakfast and hostel accommodations.

Convention Information: Anchorage Convention and Visitors Bureau, 524 West Fourth Avenue, Anchorage, AK 99501-2212; telephone (907) 276-4118; fax (907) 278-5559.

■ Transportation

Approaching the City

The majority of travelers come to Anchorage by plane, arriving at Anchorage International Airport located ten minutes west of downtown. A major stop for transpolar flights, the airport is one of the busiest in the country and is served by more than 50 freight and passenger air carriers. Nearly five million passengers were served in 2012.

For those heading to Anchorage by car, the major route into the city is Alaska 1, which is Glenn Highway as it enters from the northeast and Seward Highway (scenic S.R. 1/9) as it enters from the south. The Alaska Railroad, headquartered in Anchorage, provides passenger rail service within Alaska to more than 400,000 passengers annually.

Traveling in the City

Downtown Anchorage is laid out in a series of square blocks, a pattern typical of early western railroad towns. All lettered streets run north-south and numbered streets run east-west, with Northern Lights Boulevard dividing north from south and A Street dividing east from west.

Anchorage's bus-based public transit system is the People Mover, which provides a convenient way to see the city, as buses stop at major points of interest and extend to all suburbs. Bus Tracker is an online tool that tracks People Mover bus arrivals, and departures in real time. The Share-A-Ride service connects people living in the same area for car or vanpooling, and in some cases municipally-owned vans are provided. AnchorRIDES offers paratransit services to residents with disabilities. Taxi companies and several private shuttle companies offer transportations services throughout Anchorage.

■ Communications

Newspapers and Magazines

The major daily newspaper in Anchorage is the morning *Anchorage Daily News. The Anchorage Press* is an alternative weekly. Several other newspapers are published in Anchorage, including *Petroleum News,* a paper covering the petroleum industry in Alaska and Canada. The *Sourdough Sentinel,* a weekly covering happenings at Elmendorf Air Force Base, ceased operations in 2009 when Elmendorf was to become Joint Base Elmendorf-Richardson in 2010. The news publication for the joint base is *The Arctic Warrior.* Also published in Anchorage is *Alaska Business Monthly,* which focuses on state business developments. *Northern Pilot Magazine* was published in Anchorage until it was acquired by *Pilot Getaways,* which is published in Glendale, California.

Television and Radio

Anchorage has many affiliate and local cable television stations. NBC has an affiliate station, as well as FOX,

PBS, CBS, and ABC. The city is also served by AM and FM radio stations broadcasting a variety of formats such as adult contemporary, country, and broadcasts from National Public Radio and American Public Radio. KRUA is an FM station run by the University of Alaska Anchorage. KNBA is a station serving Native Americans. The Anchorage Media Group operates many of the radio stations. Telecommunication service companies include Alaska Communication Systems, General Communication, Inc., and AT&T Alascom.

Media Information: *Anchorage Daily News,* P.O. Box 149001, Anchorage, AK 99514-9001; telephone (907) 257-4200.

Anchorage Online

Anchorage Convention and Visitors Bureau. Available www.anchorage.net

Anchorage Daily News. Available www.adn.com

Alaska Department of Education and Early Development. Available www.eed.state.ak.us

Anchorage Economic Development Corporation. Available www.aedcweb.com

Anchorage Municipal Libraries. Available www.anchoragelibrary.org

Anchorage School District. Available www.asdk12.org

Municipality of Anchorage Home Page. Available www.muni.org

State of Alaska. Available www.state.ak.us

BIBLIOGRAPHY

Barnett, James K., *Alaska History—in Brief* (Anchorage, AK: Todd Communications, 2010)

Fanning, Kay, *Kay Fanning's Alaska Story: Memoir of a Pulitzer Prize-Winning Newspaper Publisher on America's Northern Frontier* (Kenmore, WA: Epicenter Press, 2006)

Muir, John, *Travels in Alaska* (Boston: Houghton Mifflin, 1915)

Rich, Kim, *Johnny's Girl: A Daughter's Memoir of Growing Up in Alaska's Underworld* (New York: Morrow, 1993)

Senkowsky, Sonya, and Amanda Coyne, *Alaska Then and Now: Anchorage, Juneau, and Fairbanks* (San Diego, CA: Thunder Bay Press, 2008)

Williams, Maria, ed., *The Alaska Native Reader: History, Culture, Politics* (Durham: Duke University Press, 2009)

Fairbanks

■ The City in Brief

Founded: 1901 (incorporated 1903)

Head Official: Mayor John Eberhart (since 2013; term expires 2016)

City Population
    1990: 30,843
    2000: 30,224
    2010: 31,535
    2012 estimate: 32,021
    Percent change, 2000–2010: 4.3%

Micropolitan Statistical Area Population
    2000: 82,840
    2010: 97,581
    2012 estimate: 100,272
    Percent change, 2000–2010: 17.8%
    U.S. rank in 2010: 399th

Area: 32.67 square miles

Elevation: 432 feet above sea level

Average Annual Temperatures: 30.4° F

Average Annual Precipitation: 11.5 inches with 67.8 inches of snowfall

Major Economic Sectors: government, services

Unemployment Rate: 5% (2012)

Per Capita Income: $26,563

2012 FBI Crime Index Property: 1,379

Major Colleges and Universities: University of Alaska Fairbanks

Daily Newspaper: *Fairbanks Daily News-Miner*

■ Introduction

Fairbanks is Alaska's second largest city. It is located in the heart of the state in east-central Alaska on the banks of the Chena River. It originated as a mining town where people flocked to discover gold. More recently, its character has been shaped by a large military presence, construction of the Trans-Alaska Pipeline, and the continuing oil economy. The city has become a cultural, trade, and transportation center of the Alaskan Interior since its beginnings in the early 1900s, but still retains its frontier character. Fairbanks, sometimes called the "Golden Heart of Alaska," boasts mining camps, swinging-door saloons, and unpaved roads that coincide with modern amenities such as hotels, and restaurants. The city is also home to an internationally renowned research university that is continually growing. The most distinctive feature of Fairbanks, however, is its weather. The city sees about 20 hours of sunlight during June and July, which contrasts greatly with only about 4 hours of sun daily during December and January. Long winter nights and snowy terrain during most of the year makes Fairbanks the epitome of Alaska.

■ Geography and Climate

Fairbanks is located in the Tanana Valley in east-central Alaska, about 358 miles north of Anchorage and 125 miles south of the Arctic Circle. The Alaska Range, including Mt. McKinley, lies to the south and the White Mountains are off to the north. The city is located near the confluence of the Chena and Tanana rivers. It is the largest city in the interior and the second-largest in the state (after Anchorage). It is part of Fairbanks North Star Borough. Significant changes in solar heat during the year produce a wide variation of temperatures from winter to summer. During the summer months (June and July) the sun is above the horizon an average of 20 hours per day and temperatures often reach 90° F. From November to March, daylight ranges from 10 to 4 hours daily and

© P.A. Lawrence, LLC./Alamy

temperatures can drop to −60° F. During the winter, ice fog can occur if the temperature drops below −20° F. The average annual precipitation is 11.5 inches. Fairbanks rarely experiences windy conditions.

Area: 32.67 square miles

Elevation: 432 feet above sea level

Average Temperatures: 30.4° F

Average Annual Precipitation: 11.5 inches with 67.8 inches of snowfall

■ History

Discovery of Gold Brings Prospectors, Settlers

Fairbanks was founded accidentally in 1901 by Captain E. T. Barnette. On his way to set up a trading post on the Tanana River, Barnette became stranded on the Chena River when the riverboat in which he was traveling was forced to turn back. As he was making plans to move his supplies to a more profitable location, gold was

discovered about 12 miles away, near Fox. Felix Pedro, an Italian prospector, is credited with having made the discovery on July 22, 1902. Every year on that date, Fairbanks commemorates the gold discovery with the Golden Days celebration.

During the resulting gold rush, Barnette's trading post became the center of activity for prospectors who swarmed into the area. A settlement developed and was named for Senator Charles Fairbanks of Indiana who served as vice president under Theodore Roosevelt from 1905–09; the town was incorporated in 1903. Barnette was elected the first mayor of Fairbanks. He is credited with establishing telephone service, fire protection, sanitation ordinances, electricity and steam heat, but he soon fell into disfavor as a result of his involvement in a bank failure that caused many citizens to lose their savings.

Oil and Military Buildup Replace Gold as Economic Pillars

By 1910 the population of Fairbanks grew to 3,541 people, although more than 6,000 miners lived and worked their claims north of town. During World War I, however, gold activity declined and the population of the town decreased. The start of the construction of the Alaska Railroad brought another boom period, so that by 1930 the population was restored to about half of its previous level.

In 1922 the Alaska Territorial legislature accepted lands granted by the United States Congress, creating the Alaska Agricultural College and School of Mines, which grew into the University of Alaska Fairbanks. During World War II the Alaska Highway was constructed as part of the military buildup and Fairbanks experienced yet another thriving period when thousands of military personnel were located at nearby Eielson Air Force Base and Ladd Field (now Fort Wainwright). Military personnel in the area grew from 10 in 1940 to 5,419 in 1950. Following the war, the Fairbanks population again declined, but during the following decade the community experienced gradual growth. Alaska became an official member of the United States in 1959.

The Fairbanks North Star Borough was established on January 1, 1964, by an act of the Alaska State Legislature. The borough includes the cities of Fairbanks and North Pole and several unincorporated communities. The borough encompasses about 7,361 square miles (4.7 million acres).

In August 1967, just weeks before the expected winter freeze-up, the city was swept by a flood that inundated 95 percent of its residences and left the city under eight feet of water. Fairbanks recovered from the extensive damage, and with the discovery in 1968 of oil on the north slope of the Brooks Mountain Range, the city entered a new era of expansion.

Construction of the Trans-Alaska oil pipeline triggered one of the city's largest booms. With the completion of the pipeline construction, the community's economy went into a serious decline, but it soon recovered with the injection of state revenues in the early 1980s. By the mid-1980s, however, crude oil prices had dropped and Alaska slipped into a severe recession, with Fairbanks experiencing the most abrupt decline in the state. However, the local economy recovered, and the per capita income has steadily risen since then, a trend that is expected to continue as Fairbanks expands its participation in new economic projects within the natural resources, U.S. security, and technology fields. As a regional center, the economy benefits from trade linkages with northern rural communities and villages. It is estimated that this trade contributes $250 million and hundreds of jobs to the Fairbanks economy annually.

Historical Information: City of Fairbanks, 800 Cushman Street, Fairbanks, AK 99701; telephone (907) 459-6774 (city clerk's office).

■ Population Profile

Micropolitan Statistical Area Population

2000: 82,840
2010: 97,581
2012 estimate: 100,272
Percent change, 2000–2010: 17.8%
U.S. rank in 2010: 399th

City Residents

1990: 30,843
2000: 30,224
2010: 31,535
2012 estimate: 32,021
Percent change, 2000–2010: 4.3%

Density: 1,063.1 people per square mile

Racial and ethnic characteristics

White: 21,498
Black or African American: 3,031
American Indian and Alaskan Native: 2,799
Asian: 1,278
Native Hawaiian and Other Pacific Islander: 381
Hispanic or Latino (may be of any race): 2,714
Other: 3,034

Percent of residents born in state: 28.4%

Age characteristics

Population under 5 years old: 3,023
Population 5 to 9 years old: 2,583
Population 10 to 14 years old: 1,910
Population 15 to 19 years old: 2,041
Population 20 to 24 years old: 4,202
Population 25 to 34 years old: 6,159
Population 35 to 44 years old: 3,723
Population 45 to 54 years old: 3,267
Population 55 to 59 years old: 1,913
Population 60 to 64 years old: 865
Population 65 to 74 years old: 1,171
Population 75 to 84 years old: 829
Population 85 years and over: 335
Median age: 28.1

Births (2010–11 Metropolitan Area)

Total number: 1,639

Deaths (2010–11 Metropolitan Area)

Total number: 383

Money income (2012)

Per capita income: $26,563
Median household income: $53,140
Total households: 11,811

Number of households with income of ...

less than $10,000: 799
$10,000 to $14,999: 478
$15,000 to $24,999: 1,284
$25,000 to $34,999: 1,366
$35,000 to $49,999: 1,714
$50,000 to $74,999: 2,377

$75,000 to $99,999: 1,746
$100,000 to $149,999: 1,413
$150,000 to $199,999: 466
$200,000 or more: 168

Percent of families below poverty level: 12.8%

FBI Crime Index Property: 1,379

FBI Crime Index Violent: 169

■ Municipal Government

The City of Fairbanks had no city council until 1960, when Alaska became a state and voters approved a home-rule charter adopting the council-manager form of government. In 1995 the voters amended the charter to adopt a council-mayor government with a full-time executive mayor. The city mayor is elected to a three-year term as the executive and administrative officer of the city; six elected council members serve for staggered three-year terms. The Fairbanks North Star Borough (similar to a county) is governed by a mayor who serves a term of three years and an assembly of nine members, who are elected at-large to three-year terms on a staggered schedule. Administration for the public school system is the responsibility of Fairbanks North Star Borough.

Head Official: Mayor John Eberhart (since 2013; term expires 2016)

Total Number of City Employees: 196 (2012)

City Information: City of Fairbanks, 800 Cushman Street, Fairbanks, AK 99701; telephone (907) 459-6774 (city clerk's office).

■ Economy

Major Industries and Commercial Activity

The city economy is closely related to that of the borough as well, and is primarily based on tourism, government services, and the military. Employment in the government services sector, including the military, was 12.2 percent as of September 2010, making it the largest employer behind education and health services. The city's international airport serves villages in the region, and is a supply point for North Slope oil fields, as well as a center for the transport of cargo by international carriers. The North Pole Refinery, southeast of Fairbanks, employed about 150 people from Fairbanks and contributed over $2.8 million in property taxes to the borough. In 2010, a lawsuit was filed against the refinery owners when contaminated water was discovered on a North Pole property.

The military presence at nearby Eielson Air Force Base and Fort Wainwright has a significant impact on the city and borough economy. According to the Fairbanks Economic Development Corporation, the total economic impact of the two military bases to the Greater Fairbanks community is about $800 million annually. Active-duty military personnel and their families make up a significant portion of consumer activity in Fairbanks.

Tourism comprises a large percentage of the commercial activity in the region.. Mining is an important industry as well. To the north of Fairbanks, the Fort Knox gold mine is the largest producing gold mine in the state. It produces about 330,000 ounces of gold annually, and employs between 400 and 425 year-round workers. More than $200 million in gold has been extracted from the mining district. The mine was expected to remain in operation through 2016.

Fairbanks is also beginning to see an emergence of wood products as a force of industry. Superior Pellet Fuels, a manufacturer of wood pellets, brought a 12,000-square-foot factory to the area in 2010. The company was the first large-scale wood pellet producer in the area. The pellets, which can be used in wood stoves, are a cleaner source of fuel and cause less air pollution. The addition of the factory to Fairbanks' business climate was expected to create 12 to 15 full-time jobs.

Items and goods produced: oil, ice, gold, wood, wood products

Incentive Programs—New and Existing Companies

Local programs: The Small Business Development Center (SBDC) offers seminars, counseling, and work-shops for new and established businesses to support their existence and help them grow. The Procurement Technical Assistance Center (PTAC) assists businesses who contract with local, state, or federal government. Services such as consultations, bid matching assistance, workshops, and general assistance are offered.

State programs: The Governor's Office of International Trade provides assistance and information to firms interested in foreign trade and investment, organizes trade missions and promotions, and sponsors trade shows and seminars. Several areas in the city are located in Anchorage's Foreign Trade Zone, the two most notable being the Ted Stevens Anchorage International Airport and the Port of Anchorage. The World Trade Center assists businesses seeking to enter or expand their role in international trade. The Alaska Export Assistance Center helps local businesses expand into foreign markets.

The Alaska Exploration Incentives Act allows mining and exploration credits of up to $20 million of qualified costs including personnel, transportation, fuel, camp, communications, geochemical, geophysical and contractual expenses for new mines. Oil & Gas Exploration Incentive Credits are available for exploratory wells on state-owned land. By 2013, 22 wells had qualified for this credit. A film incentive program provides transferable tax credits as an incentive to attract large-scale film production in Alaska. Bonus credits are available for shooting in rural areas. The New Business Incentive Program is an economic development grant program targeted at companies locating or expanding into new manufacturing or value-added businesses in Alaska. Deteriorated property and qualified inventory is exempt from taxation for up to 10 years. This exemption may be transferred to another owner. Targeted Jobs Tax Credits is a federal tax credit program that encourages employers to hire new employees.

Job training programs: A variety of training programs exist to help meet the business needs of Fairbanks employers; many are organized through the local educational institutions, training providers, or the state through the Alaska Job Center Network. Tanana Chiefs' Conference offers a wide array of programs for tribal populations through its Employment and Training Department. The Chamber of Commerce offers the School Business Partnership, which allows businesses and schools to work together.

Development Projects

In 2013 BP announced $1 billion in new investment in its Alaska North Slope fields over the next five years. The announcement came on the heels of changes to the state's oil tax policy. BP also continued to evaluate an additional $3 billion worth of new development projects scheduled for the next 10 years.

The proposed $9 billion Alaska Gasline Project involves a pipeline from Prudhoe Bay to Valdez, liquefaction and liquids extraction facilities in Valdez, and a gas conditioning plant in Prudhoe Bay. The project is expected to generate 75,000 construction and post-construction jobs and billions of dollars in royalties to the state and all Alaska municipalities. The first LNG tanker was projected to leave the terminal at Valdez sometime in 2011, but the project has so far failed to secure the federal approvals needed to start construction.

In 2010 a multi-million dollar construction project to build the Ruth Burnett Sport Fish Hatchery, funded in part by the state, was completed. The primary developmental goal was to boost tourism. Located near downtown Fairbanks, the hatchery sits just across the street from the Chena River near Pioneer Park and the Carlson Center. The hatchery will meet the sport fish stocking needs for Fairbanks region by providing fishing opportunities for 137 regional landlocked lakes.

Economic Development Information: Fairbanks Economic Development Corporation, 301 Cushman St., Ste 301, Fairbanks, AK 99701; telephone (907) 452-2185; toll-free (888) 476-FEDC; fax (907) 451-9534. Fairbanks North Star Borough, Economic Development Division, P.O. Box 71267, Fairbanks, AK 99707; telephone (907) 459-1000.

Commercial Shipping

Fairbanks is a major transportation hub both for the state and the world. Fairbanks International Airport functions as the air freight distribution and supply center for the region. With low fuel costs and a location that is within 9.5 hours away from major commercial centers in the northern hemisphere, the airport is also used as a major global flight refueling site. Cargo airlines serving the airport include Everts Air Cargo, FedEx, and Northern Air Cargo. Several motor freight carriers transport goods through facilities in the city. Goods are shipped via truck, air, and the Alaska Railroad.

Labor Force and Employment Outlook

The Fairbanks North Star Borough has seen its population steadily increase over the past four decades. The senior population was projected to nearly triple by 2020, while the school-age population was predicted to remain steady. Fairbanks-area businesses that cater to the needs of seniors were expected to prosper, but there will be more competition by employers to find workers. The construction industry was predicted to be the primary source of new jobs. The construction of the All-Alaska Pipeline was expected to bring more than 6,000 new jobs to the state. The city's Economic Opportunities Development Taskforce meets with University of Alaska scientists monthly to develop new opportunities for creating jobs.

The following is a summary of data regarding the 2012 Fairbanks AK Metro Area labor force:

Size of civilian labor force: 13,998

Number of workers employed in . . .

    agriculture and mining: 422
    construction: 680
    manufacturing: 217
    wholesale trade: 436
    retail trade: 1,816
    transportation: 825
    information systems: 226
    finance: 378
    professional administration: 820
    education and social services: 2,930
    arts and leisure: 1,393
    other: 513
    public administration: 1,679

Average hourly earnings of production workers: $26.07

Unemployment rate: 5% (2012)

Employers

Largest employers (2013)	*Employees*
Federal government	3,376
ASRC Energy Services (Houston/ NANA)	3,376
University of Alaska Fairbanks	1,968
Principal Employers	1,968
Fairbanks North Star Borough School District	1,918
State government	1,658
Banner Health	1,049
Tanana Chiefs Conference	750
Fairbanks Gold Mining, Inc. (Ft. Knox)	594
Sam's Club/ Wal-Mart	568
Carrs/Safeway	468
Fred Meyer .Stores Inc	418
Fairbanks North Star Borough (FNSB)	291

Cost of Living

Despite Alaska's reputation for its high cost of living, prices in Fairbanks compare favorably with those in some other North American cities. The personal tax burden for Fairbanks residents is extremely low. Residents benefit from distributions from the Permanent Fund, a savings account established in 1976 by voters allowing residents to receive 25 percent of the state's royalty oil revenue. Senior citizens enjoy a $150,000 property tax exemption or a renter's rebate.

The following is a summary of data regarding several key cost of living factors in the area.

2013 ACCRA Average House Price: $389,200

2013 ACCRA Cost of Living Index: 136

State income tax rate: None

State sales tax rate: None

Local income tax rate: None

Local sales tax rate: None

Property tax rate: 5.843 mills (2011)

Economic Information: Fairbanks Economic Development Corporation, 301 Cushman St., Ste 301, Fairbanks, AK 99701; telephone (907) 452-2185; toll-free (888) 476-FEDC; fax (907) 451-9534. Fairbanks North Star Borough, Economic Development Division, P.O. Box 71267, Fairbanks, AK 99707; telephone (907) 459-1000.

■ Education and Research

Elementary and Secondary Schools

Public elementary and secondary schools in Fairbanks are part of the Fairbanks North Star Borough School District (FNSBSD). The district is administered by a nonpartisan, seven-member school board with three non-voting advisory members, which appoints a superintendent. In 2013 there were 30 schools in the district, serving about 14,300 students. Schools range in size from a small rural elementary school of fewer than 100 students to comprehensive high schools with 1200 students. In addition to various charter, magnet, and specialized schools, two schools are on military bases. The school district also offers a native education program that provides special attention to Eskimo, Aleut, or Alaskan Native students.

The district maintains 21 elementary schools, many of which offer before and after school programs, breakfast programs, and tutoring. The average primary class has 23.5 students, while intermediate classes average 25.5 students per class. There are 3 middle schools for 7–8th grade and one junior high. There are 4 high schools, of which Lathrop and West Valley are the largest with 1,131 and 1,073 students, respectively. North Pole High has almost 900 students; Ben Eielson Junior/Senior High has over 340 high school students.

The Yukon-Koyukuk School District, headquartered in Fairbanks, covers the western interior of Alaska. Serving an area of 65,000 square miles, the district is larger than the state of Washington. More than 98 percent of the 1,400 students in the district are Athabaskan (Alaskan Native). The district sponsors nine village schools located along the Yukon, Koyukuk and Tanana river systems. These river schools serve about 300 students. The villages are remote with all but two accessible only by small aircraft. Local travel within the communities is by boats during the summer months, and snow machine or dog sleds in the winter. The district also sponsors a statewide correspondence program called Raven Correspondence School that enrolls about 1,000 students.

Private schools, including religious schools, provide alternative forms of education in the Fairbanks area. The Catholic Schools of Fairbanks, started in 1946, enrolled about 480 students in its K–12 program in 2013. The schools operate with a staff of 41 teachers and 10 administrative and support staff. They are a mixture of Catholic and non-Catholic professionals.

The following is a summary of data regarding the Fairbanks North Star Borough School District.

Total enrollment: 14,285

Number of facilities

  total: 30
  elementary schools: 21
  junior high schools: 4
  high schools: 4
  other: 1

Student/teacher ratio: 16.9:1

Teacher salaries

  average (statewide): $61,093

Funding per pupil: $16,147

Public Schools Information: Fairbanks North Star Borough School District, 520 Fifth Avenue, Fairbanks, AK 99701; telephone (907) 452-2000.

Colleges and Universities

Fairbanks is home to the University of Alaska Fairbanks (UAF), which enrolls 10,446 students and offers 168 degrees in 126 disciplines. The main campus has two lakes and miles of trails, as well as a major student recreation complex for indoor sports. Programs of study include developmental programs and certificate, associate, baccalaureate, and graduate/professional programs in the arts, sciences, career fields, and professions. It is Alaska's only doctoral-granting institution and the statewide university system's principal research center. It is also one of few Land, Sea, and Space Grant universities in the United States. UAF possesses unique strengths in both the physical and natural sciences and offers a broad array of engineering programs with particular emphasis on the northern environment. UAF is the state's center for the study of Alaska native cultures and languages, and also offers a northern studies program.

Libraries and Research Centers

The Noel Wien Public Library in Fairbanks is the central branch of the Fairbanks North Star Public Libraries. There is one branch located in the city of North Pole, 11 miles from Fairbanks. Mail library service is available. The library housed 428,534 books, audio, e-books, video, and periodicals in its collection in 2013. Registered borrowers numbered 56,352. Annual circulation is almost 670,000 items. The system also includes the North Pole Branch Library and the bookmobile, which brings library services to outlying areas, assistive living facilities, and to the homebound.

The Elmer E. Rasmuson Library at the University of Alaska Fairbanks houses more than 1.75 million items, making it the largest library in the state. Its holdings include books, periodicals, photography, manuscripts, films, oral histories, rare books, maps, microfiches, tapes, records, and prints. Its Alaska and Polar Regions collection is one of the world's finest. An array of computer databases provides access to hundreds of academic journals. Internet connections allow students at remote rural sites to use library resources

The University of Alaska Fairbanks (UAF) ranks among the top 100 universities in the nation for its research and development activities. Among UAF's many outstanding research schools and institutes are the School of Fisheries and Ocean Science, the Geophysical Institute, the Institute of Arctic Biology, the Polar Ice Coring Office, the Institute of Northern Engineering, and the Agriculture and Forestry Experiment Station. The Arctic Region Supercomputing Center, a collaboration between the UAF and the Department of Defense, supports computational research in science and engineering with emphasis on high latitudes and the arctic. A $32 million, 100,000-square-foot International Arctic Research Center provides office and research space for scientists from around the world. Research at the Center focuses on four major spheres: Arctic Ocean circulation, arctic atmosphere, permafrost/frozen soil, and arctic vegetation. The Office of Electronics Miniaturization (OEM) boasts a Class 10,000 Clean Room, equipped with Chip-Scale Packaging and related technologies. UAF is engaged in prototyping design development and production through a cooperative agreement with the Department of Defense's Defense MicroElectronics Activity (DMEA). The Poker Flats Research Range, located 33 miles north of Fairbanks, is a scientific rocket launching facility owned by the University of Alaska under contract to NASA's Wallops Flight Facility. Poker Flat houses many scientific instruments for the study of the arctic atmosphere and ionosphere. The Cold Climate Housing Research Center in Fairbanks researches and develops the latest building technologies and products for cold climate regions. Alaska's full range of climatic conditions and a cold season which lasts for six months or longer provides researchers ample time to conduct experiments and evaluations of housing performance. The Agricultural Research Service projects in the area focus on aquaculture, crop protection, plant diseases, and plant, microbial and insect genetics.

Public Library Information: Noel Wien Public Libraries, 1215 Cowles Street, Fairbanks, AK 99701; telephone (907) 459-1020. University of Alaska Fairbanks, P.O. Box 757500, Fairbanks, AK 99775; telephone (907) 474-7211.

■ Health Care

Fairbanks Memorial Hospital is the local community-owned hospital that serves an area covering about 250,000 square miles. It is the only major civilian hospital in the area. Operated by the Banner Health System, Fairbanks Memorial is a modern 152-bed facility that has been expanded and remodeled several times since its opening in 1972. The hospital occupies a five-building campus including a cancer treatment center, an imaging center, the Fairbanks Clinic (primary care) and a 24-room emergency department. The hospital logged 5,288 inpatient and 150,367 outpatient visits in 2012, The hospital's Denali Center, located on the same campus as the hospital, is a 90-bed short- and long-term care facility that is also managed by Banner Health System.

The Tanana Valley Clinic and a branch of the Interior Community Health Center also provide basic care in Fairbanks. Other facilities include the Fairbanks Regional Public Health Center and Fairbanks Community Behavioral Health Center. Bassett Army Hospital at Fort Wainwright serves military personnel and retirees.

■ Recreation

Sightseeing

Fairbanks is rich in frontier history. One of the main attractions is Pioneer Park, a 44-acre historic theme park on the banks of the Chena River. The Park features a Gold Rush Town with authentic historic buildings, a Native Village with Indian and Eskimo architecture and artifacts, the Pioneer Air Museum, and the stern-wheeler Nenana in drydock. The Kitty Hensley House, home of one of Fairbanks's early citizens, has been restored and is open to the public in Gold Rush Town. A narrow gauge railroad train meanders through the park, and a mini golf course, a mining operation, three museums, and an art gallery are also part of the fun.

There are several National Historic Register buildings within the Fairbanks area, including Creamer's Dairy at Creamer's Field Migratory Waterfowl Refuge; these sites are a living testament to the area's rich cultural history. Several churches and buildings in the city are of architectural interest. Muskoxen, caribou and reindeer can be seen at the Large Animal Research Station at the University of Alaska Fairbanks which offers tours of its facility from June through September.

Hot springs, gold dredges, gold camps, and engineering projects such as the first water system in permafrost ground and the Trans-Alaska Oil Pipeline are attractions in the outlying areas. The pipeline can be viewed at Milepost 8 on the Steese Highway north of Fairbanks in Fox.

The art of extracting gold from the frozen Alaskan ground is on display at Gold Dredge No. 8, which also has a dining hall and offers an opportunity to pan for gold. The Ester Gold Camp, a popular family attraction, features a 1900s gold camp site and town, a dining hall buffet dinner, a Saloon Show and a view of the Northern Lights set to music. The Ester Gold Camp is featured in the National Register of Historic Places. The El Dorado Gold Mine offers two-hour guided tours through a permafrost tunnel, a walking tour of a mining camp, and a chance to pan for gold.

A recommended day trip is a visit to Denali National Park and Preserve, 120 miles south of Fairbanks. Within its six million acres of pristine wilderness is North America's tallest mountain, Mt. McKinley (also known locally as Denali). Wildlife such as moose, grizzly bear, mountain sheep, and caribou can be seen in their natural habitat. During the summer months colorful carpets of wildflowers add to the beauty of the park.

The Georgeson Botanical Garden, on the University of Alaska Fairbanks campus, offers tours in the summer months. The sternwheeler Discovery paddles the Chena River for a three-and-a-half hour cruise and makes stops to visit Iditarod kennels, a traditional Athabaskan fish camp and an Old Chena Indian Village.

Fairbanks visitors can take advantage of one or more tour packages to explore the area's beauty, wildlife, and opportunities for outdoor fun. Choices for guided tours are plentiful and varied and can include tours by horseback, canoe, raft, boat, car, snowmobile, dogsled, or jet boat. Flightseeing in the form of balloon or helicopter rides is a unique way to enjoy the landscape. Day-long and multi-day trips are available to a number of destinations for individuals and groups.

The Aurora Borealis is one natural wonder that visitors shouldn't miss when visiting the area. While intensity varies, the most common yellow-green glow occurs heavily between late August and April (the midnight sun makes viewing difficult in the summer months). There are a variety of options for viewing the Northern Lights, with special guided tours of the Aurora Circle and lodges catering to Aurora viewers.

Arts and Culture

Fairbanks serves as a cultural center for the interior. The Fairbanks Arts Association was incorporated in 1966 and is the oldest community arts council in the state. The Davis Concert Hall of the University of Alaska Fairbanks Fine Arts Complex is home to the Fairbanks Symphony Orchestra and the Arctic Chamber Orchestra. There is also a city youth orchestra. Fairbanks is home to the Fairbanks Shakespeare Theatre and the Fairbanks Children's Theatre. Musical comedy revues and light opera productions are staged by the Fairbanks Light Opera Theatre, and the Palace Saloon. The Fairbanks Choral Society features an annual "Sing-it-Yourself-Messiah." In addition, the University of Alaska has some of the best performance facilities in the state. Performances are scheduled almost every weekend during the academic year at the Davis Concert Hall or Salisbury Theatre.

The city has several museums relating to the natural and cultural history of the area. The University of Alaska Museum of the North is one of the most frequently visited tourist attractions in the state as well as a resource for students. The 83,000-square-foot museum houses

Blue Babe, the Ice Age's only restored steppe bison mummy. Alaska's largest public display of gold and Alaskan native artifacts are on exhibit.

Fairbanks Community Museum chronicles the history of Fairbanks from its founding in 1901 to the present with a focus on the Gold Rush era and mining, including exhibits on the Flood of 1967 and the Klondike Gold Rush. The same building displays dog mushing memorabilia including sleds, clothing, harnesses, trophies, and cold weather expedition gear.

Life-size ice sculptures are on view at the Fairbanks Ice Museum which preserves year-round some of the sculptures carved during the World Ice Art Championships held annually in March. Museums located in Pioneer Park include the Alaska Native Museum, Kitty Hensley House, Pioneer Air Museum, Pioneer Museum, Riverboat Nenana, Tanana Valley Railroad Museum, and Wickersham House.

The Alaska Public Lands Information Center provides both exhibits and recreation information on state and federal land in Alaska for those planning a trip to the "back country." Information on camping grounds, hiking trails, scenic drives, and fishing spots is available. Several art galleries are also located in Fairbanks, including the Alaska House Art Gallery.

Festivals and Holidays

The North American Championship Preliminary Sled Dog Races are held in December and January. In February the Yukon Quest International Dog Sled Race is a 1,000-mile run on gold rush trails. The Tesoro Iron Dog Gold Rush Classic, also in February, is the world's longest snowmobile race.

In February or early March the Ice Alaska carnival showcases the World Ice Art Championships, an international ice carving competition. Ice Alaska has also become an exporter of ice with locally grown ice exported to the Bahamas and as far as Israel.

Folk, Celtic, bluegrass, orchestral, and gospel music are all on stage at the Fairbanks Folk Festivals held in February and June. March is the month for the Open North American Sled Dog Championships, which attracts top sprint mushers from the U.S., Canada, Europe, and Japan, as well as the Junior North American Sled Dog Championships. Native people from all over the state gather to share their dancing, singing, storytelling, and traditional arts and crafts at the Annual Festival of Native Arts, which is also held in March.

June is a busy month with a variety of events surrounding the summer solstice, such as the Midnight Sun Festival and Midnight Sun Dances. The Yukon 800 Marathon Riverboat Race also takes place in June. Fairbanks Summer Arts Festival takes place on the campus of the University of Alaska Fairbanks during the last two weeks in July. It is a unique, two-week study and performance festival with mini-workshops and full

weeklong classes in multiple music genres: dance, theatre arts, healing arts, visual arts, culinary arts, and creative writing. Also in July, Golden Days celebrates the rich gold-mining history of Fairbanks; a hairy chest, legs, and beard contest is one highlight of the five-day festival. In the World Eskimo-Indian Olympics, another July event, Native people from all over the Arctic compete in games of strength and endurance; among other highlights are storytelling and Native dances.

The Tanana Valley State Fair is held in August, followed by Oktoberfest. The Athabaskan Old-Time Fiddling Festival in November celebrates a musical format that is a composite of French Canadian and Scottish-Arcadian styles fused with Native tunes. Fairbanks celebrates the Alyeska Winter Solstice each weekend in December with Santa, live music, and family activities downtown.

Sports for the Spectator

Fairbanks is home to the Alaska Goldpanners of the Alaska Baseball League (a summer collegiate league). The University of Alaska Fairbanks Nanooks basketball and ice hockey teams host games on the University of Alaska campus and in the Carlson Center in town.

Dogsledding (mushing) is the official sport of the state of Alaska, and Fairbanks is the site of mushing competitions throughout the winter. Mushing demonstrations can be seen in summer, but serious racing requires cool temperatures and snow. Yukon Quest (in February) is a 1000-mile international sled dog race between Whitehorse, Yukon Territory, Canada, and Fairbanks, Alaska. The Fairbanks Curling Club hosts competitions with teams from throughout Alaska, Canada, and the United States. The Sundawgs Rugby Football Club plays rugby during the Golden Days festival in July. Fairbank's junior ice hockey team is the Ice Dogs, a North American Hockey League team.

Sports for the Participant

Running is a popular activity in Fairbanks. The Equinox Marathon, said to be one of the most challenging marathons in the U.S., is a 26-mile race to the top of Ester Dome. The Midnight Sun Run is held in conjunction with the celebration of the summer solstice, and the Chena River 5K Run is held in May.

Many city and area parks offer facilities for a variety of year-round indoor and outdoor recreational activities. Among the most popular pursuits are downhill and cross-country skiing, fishing, canoeing, goldpanning, hiking, hockey, hunting, ice skating, jogging, nature walks, tennis, swimming, volleyball, and racquetball. Smooth paved trails along the Chena River are ideal for biking and rollerblading. Fairbanks boasts three golf courses including one at Fort Wainwright. Winter is a favorite time for swimming in nearby hot springs. Volleyball courts are located at Growden Park. Birch Hill Recreation Area, a few minutes north of Fairbanks, has hiking and running trails, mountain biking, and bird watching in the summer.

Shopping and Dining

Fairbanks has a number of shopping malls and neighborhood stores. Specialty shops feature Alaska native arts and crafts and jewelry fashioned from ivory, jade, and hematite, as well as handmade fur garments. Visitors can watch the manufacture of Alaskan birch bowls at the Great Alaskan Bowl Company where they are also for sale. Santa Claus House, located 13 miles from Fairbanks in the city of North Pole, has become a landmark, drawing visitors from throughout the world to shop for Alaskan gifts, jewelry, and clothing. Local farmers and craft makers display their wares at the Farmers' Market, open Wednesdays and Saturdays from May through mid-September next to the Tanana Valley Fair Grounds. The city's main commercial district extends along Airport Way, between University Ave. and Cushman St. where most of the fast-food chains and malls can be found. Many bars, restaurants and businesses that cater to the university crowd are located along University Ave. and College Rd.

Dozens of restaurants in Fairbanks provide a wide range of cuisine in casual and elegant settings. Area restaurants specialize in fish from inland waters to more casual fare including miners's stew served in the dining halls of the local gold mines. Visitors can also enjoy Japanese, Korean, Mongolian, and Mexican specialties. Salmon, halibut and cod are the specialties at the Alaska Salmon Bake, one of the more popular venues with its Palace Theater and Saloon in Gold Rush Town. Located in Pioneer Park, it features evening entertainment in the summer with its "Golden Heart Revue."

Visitor Information: Fairbanks Convention and Visitors Bureau, 101 Dunkel Street, Ste 111, Fairbanks, AK 99701-4806; telephone (907) 457-3282; toll-free (877) 551-1728; fax (907) 459-3787.

■ Convention Facilities

Fairbanks offers a wide variety of meeting space. The largest meeting and exhibition facility is the Carlson Center, located on the banks of the Chena River in the heart of Fairbanks. The center features a 35,000-square-foot arena and 10,000 square feet of meeting rooms, for a combined total of 45,000 square feet of space that can accommodate more than 1,200 meeting participants, 200 trade show exhibits, or more than 6,000 people for a concert event.

The Alaska Centennial Center for the Arts at Pioneer Park houses a 384-seat theater, art gallery, exhibit areas, meeting rooms and all-purpose hall. Also at Pioneer Park is the Birch Hill Cross Country Ski Center which has a 2,500 square foot assembly room. The Chief Peter John

Tribal Hall and Mushers Hall are downtown banquet and meeting facilities. The University of Alaska Museum of the North and the Tanana Valley State Fair also provide many options for meeting spaces for any type of function.

Westmark Fairbanks Hotel and Conference Center has 400 guest rooms, an 800-square-foot fitness center, and more than 17,000 square feet of meeting space. It is located downtown near the Chena River and Morris Thompson Cultural and Visitor Center. Additional hotel properties with meeting and conference facilities include the Fairbanks Princess Riverside Lodge, River's Edge Resort, Pike's Waterfront Lodge, Regency Fairbanks Hotel, and Fountainhead Hotels.

Chena Hot Springs Resort, located 56 miles outside of Fairbanks, offers meeting space that can accommodate more than 100 people. The resort is world famous for its legendary healing mineral waters, beautiful Aurora Borealis displays in the winter, and Ice Museum.

Convention Information: Fairbanks Convention and Visitors Bureau, 101 Dunkel Street, Ste 111, Fairbanks, AK 99701-4806; telephone (907) 457-3282; toll-free (877) 551-1728; fax (907) 459-3787.

■ Transportation

Approaching the City

The Fairbanks International Airport is served by Alaska Airlines, Arctic Circle Air Service, Inc., Bettles Air, Delta Airlines, Era Aviation, 40-Mile Air, Ltd., Frontier Airlines, Northwest Airlines, and other smaller carriers that have daily flights to regional locales, as well as Anchorage and Seattle. Direct connections to major cities and international connections are made through Anchorage International Airport. Airport shuttle service into Fairbanks is available. The airport is located four miles southwest of the city.

Principal routes into Fairbanks are the Alaska Highway, running southeast to northwest, which connects the city with the lower 48 states through Canada, and the George Parks Highway, leading south to Anchorage. Fairbanks is also connected with Anchorage via the Richardson Highway. The Dalton Highway connects Fairbanks to Prudhoe Bay near the Arctic Ocean.

The Alaska Railroad, which links Fairbanks to Anchorage, Denali Park, and Seward on the Kenai Peninsula, has Fairbanks for its northern terminus.

Traveling in the City

Chartered bus tours operate throughout the tourist season in Fairbanks. The Metropolitan Area Commuter System (MACS) operates six bus routes. There are about 10 taxi services in Fairbanks.

■ Communications

Newspapers and Magazines

The major daily newspaper in Fairbanks is the *Fairbanks Daily News-Miner,* published in the morning. The award-winning *Sun Star Newspaper* is the student newspaper of the University of Alaska Fairbanks,.

Television and Radio

Fairbanks residents have access to many television stations, including ABC, FOX, PBS, NBC, and CBS affiliate stations; cable is also available. Various AM and FM radio stations, including stations from University of Alaska Fairbanks, provide a variety of music, news, and information programming.

Media Information: *Fairbanks Daily News-Miner,* P.O. Box 70710, Fairbanks, AK 99707-0710; telephone (907) 456-6661.

Fairbanks Online

City of Fairbanks website. Available www.ci. fairbanks.ak.us

Fairbanks Convention and Visitors Bureau. Available www.explorefairbanks.com

Fairbanks Daily News-Miner. Available www. newsminer.com

Fairbanks Economic Development Corporation. Available www.investfairbanks.com

Fairbanks North Star Borough Home Page. Available www.co.fairbanks.ak.us

Noel Wien Public Libraries. Available www.library. fnsb.lib.ak.us

Fairbanks North Star Borough School District. Available www.k12northstar.org

Greater Fairbanks Chamber of Commerce. Available www.fairbankschamber.org

State of Alaska. Available www.state.ak.us

University of Alaska Fairbanks. Available www.uaf. edu

BIBLIOGRAPHY

Anders, Joyce J., *Anders of Two Rivers* (Fairbanks, AK: Jenny M. Publishers, 1997)

Barnett, James K., *Alaska History—in Brief* (Anchorage, AK: Todd Communications, 2010)

Blunk, R. Glendon, *Yearning Wild: Exploring the Last Frontier and the Landscape of the Heart* (Montpelier, VT: Invisible Cities Press, 2002)

Cole, Dermot, *Fairbank:s A Gold Rush Town that Beat the Odds* (Fairbanks, AK: Epicenter Press, 1999)

Fejes, Claire, *Cold Starry Night: An Alaskan Memoir* (Fairbanks, AK: Epicenter Press, 1996)

Senkowsky, Sonya, and Amanda Coyne, *Alaska Then and Now: Anchorage, Juneau, and Fairbanks* (San Diego, CA: Thunder Bay Press, 2008)

Williams, Maria, ed., *The Alaska Native Reader:History, Culture, Politics* (Durham: Duke University Press, 2009)

Juneau

■ The City in Brief

Founded: 1880, incorporated, 1970

Head Official: Mayor Merrill Sanford (since 2010; current term expires 2015)

City Population
1990: 26,751
2000: 30,711
2010: 31,275
2012 estimate: 32,071
Percent change, 2000–2010: 1.8%

Micropolitan Statistical Area Population
2000: 30,711
2010: 31,275
2012 estimate: 32,071
Percent change, 2000–2010: 1.8%

Area: 3,255 square miles

Elevation: Ranges from sea level to 3,800 feet above sea level

Average Annual Temperatures: 41.9° F

Average Annual Precipitation: 91.32 inches

Major Economic Sectors: government, services

Unemployment Rate: 3.7% (2012)

Per Capita Income: $36,559

2012 FBI Crime Index Property: 1,099

Major Colleges and Universities: University of Alaska Southeast

Daily Newspaper: *Juneau Empire*

■ Introduction

The city and borough of Juneau is home to one of Alaska's most significant ports, and is also one of the state's most popular tourist areas. Unlike other cities, Juneau is only accessible by air and sea. It welcomes an influx of visitors, many of whom arrive via cruise ship, every year between May and September. Nearby Glacier Bay, Admiralty Island, and the Juneau Icefield offer spectacular scenery, and sightseeing flights are available year-round. While tourism is an important industry for Juneau, the city's economy relies heavily on the government workers who make up the majority of the work force, along with fishermen, loggers, and miners. The climate, with mild rain and moderate temperatures throughout the year, provides an ideal setting for participating in outdoor activities in the area. Residents and tourists alike can climb any of three challenging mountains, or ride the tramway that overlooks the Gastineau Channel.

■ Geography and Climate

The city of Juneau is located on the mainland of southeastern Alaska's Panhandle on the narrow southeastern strip bordering the Canadian province of British Columbia, approximately 1,000 miles northwest of Seattle, Washington. Most of the city lies on the mainland of Alaska, although Douglas Island, which is connected by a bridge, is also part of Juneau. The Gastineau Channel separates the island from the main part of the city, which is surrounded by the Tongass National Forest. The city climbs the tree-lined slopes of Mount Roberts and Mount Juneau, which rise from the water's edge to more than 3,500 feet.

The city has a mild, rainy climate with a year-round ice-free harbor. The Pacific Ocean currents temper the weather, and average summer temperatures are in the 60s with many days reaching into the high 70s or low 80s. Juneau's winters are comparable to those of Minneapolis or Chicago.

David Job/Getty Images

Area: 3,255 square miles

Elevation: Ranges from sea level to 3,800 feet above sea level

Average Temperatures: 41.9° F

Average Annual Precipitation: 91.32 inches

■ History

In the late 1800s when gold prospecting began in the Gastineau Channel region, the area was a fishing ground for local Tlingit Native Americans. A mining engineer from Sitka, George Pilz, offered a reward to any local native chief who could show him the site of gold-bearing ore. After Chief Kowee of the Auk Tlingit arrived in Sitka with ore samples from the Gastineau Channel, Pilz outfitted Joseph Juneau and Richard Harris for a trip to investigate the lode.

The prospectors reached the area in 1880, and although they found gold samples, they did not follow the gold to its source. After their return to Sitka, Pilz sent

them out again. On the second trip Harris and Juneau climbed Snow Slide Gulch at the head of Gold Creek and observed the mother lode of Quartz Gulch, and Silver Bow Basin. They staked a 160-acre town site on the beach. By the next year more than 100 prospectors had arrived in the settlement, which was later named in honor of Joseph Juneau.

Within a few years, Juneau grew to a center for large-scale hard-rock mining, and tunnels and shafts wound through the surrounding hills. Two great mills were developed, the Alaska-Juneau at the south end of the city and the Alaska-Gastineau at Thane.

In May 1882 John Treadwell established the Alaska Mill and Mining Company with the construction of a five-stamp mill. The Treadwell Gold Mining Company produced more than $70 million of gold before it closed. Treadwell's production peaked in 1915, but a 1917 flooding of three of its mines after a cave-in spelled its demise. The Alaska-Gastineau closed in 1921 when operations became too expensive. The final big mill, Alaska-Juneau, folded in 1944 as a result of high prices and labor shortages due to World War II.

By the beginning of the twentieth century, Juneau had become a transportation and regional trading center.

It assumed the title of Alaska's capital in 1906 following its transfer from Sitka. In 1931 the Federal and Territorial Building, now the State Capitol Building, was constructed. Juneau has remained the state capital despite attempts to move the capital elsewhere. In 2005 the city announced its desire to build a modern, $100 million facility to replace the aging Capitol Building. Today, government-local, state or federal-employs one out of every two workers and tourism is the largest private-sector employer in Juneau. A federally recognized Native American tribe lives within the Juneau community.

With its vast natural wonders, temperate climate, and position as the capital city, Juneau has the foundation for a long-term prosperous community as can be seen in its population growth since 1980. The Juneau Economic Development Council has programs in place to create positive business conditions for new and existing companies.

Historical Information: Juneau-Douglas City Museum, 155 S. Seward St., Juneau, AK 99801; telephone (907) 586-3572; fax (907) 586-4512;

■ Population Profile

Micropolitan Statistical Area Population
2000: 30,711
2010: 31,275
2012 estimate: 32,071
Percent change, 2000–2010: 1.8%

City Residents
1990: 26,751
2000: 30,711
2010: 31,275
2012 estimate: 32,071
Percent change, 2000–2010: 1.8%

Density: 11.6 people per square mile

Racial and ethnic characteristics
White: 22,256
Black or African American: 335
American Indian and Alaskan Native: 3,883
Asian: 1,773
Native Hawaiian and Other Pacific Islander: 264
Hispanic or Latino (may be of any race): 1,744
Other: 3,560

Percent of residents born in state: 40.8%

Age characteristics
Population under 5 years old: 1,980
Population 5 to 9 years old: 2,082
Population 10 to 14 years old: 1,949
Population 15 to 19 years old: 2,290
Population 20 to 24 years old: 1,890
Population 25 to 34 years old: 4,592
Population 35 to 44 years old: 4,404
Population 45 to 54 years old: 5,472
Population 55 to 59 years old: 2,692
Population 60 to 64 years old: 2,003
Population 65 to 74 years old: 1,789
Population 75 to 84 years old: 534
Population 85 years and over: 394
Median age: 37.8

Births (2010–11 Micropolitan Area)
Total number: 391

Deaths (2010–11 Micropolitan Area)
Total number: 121

Money income (2012)
Per capita income: $36,559
Median household income: $78,547
Total households: 12,314

Number of households with income of ...
less than $10,000: 360
$10,000 to $14,999: 252
$15,000 to $24,999: 613
$25,000 to $34,999: 884
$35,000 to $49,999: 1,188
$50,000 to $74,999: 2,538
$75,000 to $99,999: 2,302
$100,000 to $149,999: 2,477
$150,000 to $199,999: 956
$200,000 or more: 744

Percent of families below poverty level: 6.4%

FBI Crime Index Property: 1,099

FBI Crime Index Violent: 115

■ Municipal Government

Juneau, a home-rule municipality, has a council-manager type of government. In 1970 the city merged with the city of Douglas and other areas of the Juneau Borough to become the city and borough of Juneau. The Borough Assembly is comprised of the mayor and eight assembly members. Assembly members and the mayor are elected on rotating three-year terms at the regular municipal election held each first Tuesday in October. The Assembly's work is to set policy for the city manager to enact.

Head Official: Mayor Merrill Sanford (since 2010; current term expires 2015)

Total Number of City Employees: 1,641 (2012)

City Information: City and Borough of Juneau, 155 S. Seward St., Juneau, AK 99801; telephone (907) 586-5240.

■ Economy

Major Industries and Commercial Activity

Nearly half of Juneau's working population is employed by the federal, state, or local government. All state departments have offices in Juneau, including the Superior and District Courts. A large federal building houses the regional headquarters of several federal agencies. Those with the largest number of workers include the U.S. Forest Service, National Park Service, National Marine Fisheries Service, Bureau of Indian Affairs, U.S. Fish and Wildlife Service, U.S. Postal Service, and the U.S. Coast Guard. Having 41 percent of its workforce employed by the public sector greatly helped Juneau's economy weather a national economic recession during the late 2000s.

Tourism remains the largest private-sector employer. Most tourists arrive by cruise ship from Vancouver and Seattle. After a downturn in the cruise ship industry beginning in 2010, curies ships brought one million visitors to the city in 2013, which matched the number of passengers arriving in the city during the peak years of 2007–09. During the travel season (May 1–October 1) Juneau's harbor is filled with cruise ships from the "Lower 48" and around the world. The tourism industry has benefited from a new type of traveler who is younger, more independent, and interested in family, adventure, and environment-related activities.

Large-scale mining also helps support the local economy. There are two large operating mines in the area, the Hecla Greens Creek Mine and the smaller Coeur Kensington Mine. The Hecla Greens Creek Mine, located on Admiralty Island 18 miles west of downtown, employs 364 people and supports an annual payroll in excess of $35 million. In 2012 the mine produced 56,818 ounces of gold, 6,498,000 ounces of silver, and significant quantities of zinc and lead. The mine is expected to keep producing for the next 10 years. The Coeur Kensington mine is located 45 miles northwest of Juneau. The mine began production in 2010 and is expected to continue operations for the next 10 years. The mine employs 300 people and in 2012 produced approximately 83,000 ounces of gold, with reserves estimated at 1.3 million ounces.

Commercial fishing and fish processing are another important sector of the local economy. Salmon hatcheries and a cold storage facility operate in town, the latter processing salmon, halibut, black cod, and crab. In 2011 there were eight shore-based seafood processing facilities in Juneau that collectively processed 15.9 million pounds of product, with a wholesale value of $50.3 million.

Transportation and trading are the other important sectors of the economy. Manufacturing jobs had been almost nonexistent but that area has become a focal point for government programs resulting in a growth spurt.

The $900 million Regional Corporation Alaska Native Land Claims Settlement Act (ANCSA) was enacted in 1971 to help compensate the native Alaskans for the lands taken from them when the United States purchased the Alaskan Territory from Russia in 1867. Two of Alaska's many regional native Alaskan corporations are located near Juneau. Sealaska, the ANCSA regional corporation for Southeast Alaska that serves 17,600 Tlingit, Haida, and Tsimshian shareholders, has its headquarters in Juneau. Goldbelt Inc., the urban native village corporation, is also located near Juneau and handles about 3,200 shareholders of primarily Alaska Native heritage. The two corporations are in the business of money management, producing timber, and studying diversification into the area of mineral rights.

Items and goods produced: Processed fish, ore, forest products

Incentive Programs—New and Existing Companies

Local programs: The Southeast Alaska Revolving Loan Fund (RLF), since its formation in 1997, has developed a capital pool of about $4 billion to assist area businesses in retaining and creating jobs; only half of that number is allocated for Juneau. Entrepreneurs can go to the Business Assistance Center (BAC) for information, business counseling, workshops, and a variety of other services.

State programs: The Governor's Office of International Trade provides assistance and information to firms interested in foreign trade and investment, organizes trade missions and promotions, and sponsors trade shows and seminars. Several areas in the city are located in Anchorage's Foreign Trade Zone, the two most notable being the Ted Stevens Anchorage International Airport and the Port of Anchorage. The World Trade Center assists businesses seeking to enter or expand their role in international trade. The Alaska Export Assistance Center helps local businesses expand into foreign markets.

The Alaska Exploration Incentives Act allows mining and exploration credits of up to $20 million of qualified costs including personnel, transportation, fuel, camp, communications, geochemical, geophysical and contractual expenses for new mines. Oil & Gas Exploration Incentive Credits are available for exploratory wells on state-owned land. By 2013, 22 wells had qualified for this credit. A film incentive program provides transferable tax credits as an incentive to attract large-scale film production in Alaska. Bonus credits are available for shooting in rural areas. The New Business Incentive Program is an economic development grant program targeted at companies locating or expanding into new manufacturing or value-added businesses in Alaska. Deteriorated property and qualified inventory is exempt from taxation for up to 10 years. This exemption may be transferred to another owner. Targeted Jobs Tax Credits is a federal tax credit program that encourages employers to hire new employees.

Job training programs: Business start up services are offered by the state of Alaska on a case-by-case basis. The Alaska Department of Community and Economic Development and the Juneau Economic Development Council also offer support.

Development Projects

Bartlett Memorial Hospital underwent a multi-phase construction project in the 2000s that would included a new wing, and orthopedic center. In 2010, a Veterans Affairs Outreach Clinic opened downtown to serve the needs of local veterans. That same year, the U.S. Health Resources and Services Administration awarded a $1.3 million grant to expand the SouthEast Alaska Regional Health Consortium Haines Health Center. The addition added an extra 700 square feet, which allows for better patient accessibility and overall care.

In 2012 voters approved a five-year sales tax to partially fund a number of development projects including Dimond Park Library, a child and adolescent mental health facility, airport snow removal equipment facility, boat haul out and kayak launch ramp at Statter Harbor, water filtration, building maintenance, parks and trails maintenance, Lemon Creek neighborhood park, off-highway vehicle park, and expansions to the Performing Arts Center and Walter Soboleff Center.

In 2013 Juneau's Planning Commission approved the development of a 75-unit housing project. It is one of the largest developments the city has seen in at least a decade.

Economic Development Information: Alaska Department of Labor and Workforce Development, Research and Analysis Section; telephone (907) 465-4508; fax (907) 465-4506; email raweb@labor.state.ak.us. Juneau Economic Development Council, 612 W. Willoughby Ave., Ste. A, Juneau, AK 99801-1732; telephone (907) 523-2300; fax (907) 463-3929.

Commercial Shipping

The Juneau airport includes a paved 8,456-foot runway and a seaplane landing area. Marine facilities include a seaplane landing area at Juneau Harbor, two deep draft docks, launch ramps, and many small boat harbors. The Alaska Marine Highway System and cargo barges provide year-round services. Juneau's docks are used primarily for the cruise ships bringing tourists to Juneau.

Labor Force and Employment Outlook

As of 2012, the State of Alaska remains the most important source of Juneau jobs and income, accounting for a quarter of all direct local employment and 27 percent of total payroll. Retail trade, health care, and leisure and hospitality were the top three private employers with 29 percent of jobs. However, workers in these

three industries combined took home $144 million in wages, only 18 percent of total wages.

Because so many are employed in federal, state, tribal, and local government, Juneau's workforce is better educated than is the statewide workforce and per capita income is higher. However, dependence on one industry leaves Juneau vulnerable to severe economic distress when government falters. Ongoing efforts are being made to diversify Juneau's economy. The overall labor force demonstrated significant increases in all major categories. Education and health services have shown successes, as well as manufacturing, financial industries, construction and mining. Tourism is still a large industry, especially after rebounding from the down years between 2008 to 2011. The seafood industry constitutes another important sector of the local economy. About 760 Juneau residents fish commercially, landing 22.7 million pounds of fish with a value of $26.4 million in 2011.

The following is a summary of data regarding the 2012 Juneau labor force:

Size of civilian labor force: 18,256

Number of workers employed in . . .

agriculture and mining: 775
construction: 983
manufacturing: 193
wholesale trade: 106
retail trade: 1,106
transportation: 1,280
information systems: 384
finance: 525
professional administration: 1,269
education and social services: 3,700
arts and leisure: 1,583
other: 720
public administration: 4,660

Average hourly earnings of production workers: $17.76

Unemployment rate: 3.7% (2012)

Employers

Largest employers (2012)	*Number of employees*
State of Alaska	4,276
City & Borough of Juneau	910
Federal Government	840
Coeur Alaska Inc.	767
Hecla Greens Creek Mine	364
Alaska Travel Adventures Inc.	300
Coeur Kensington Mine	300

Bartlett Regional
    Hospital   Not available
University of Alaska
    Southeast   Not available
Reach Inc   Not available
Fred Meyers Stores
    Inc   Not available

Cost of Living

The personal tax burden in Alaska is extremely low, but the cost of living remains high in Juneau as among some other national cities. Senior citizens enjoy a $150,000 property tax exemption or a renter's rebate. However, in Juneau, the overall costs are significantly higher than the U.S. average. Housing costs are primarily what makes the cost of living so high.

The following is a summary of data regarding several key cost of living factors in the area.

2013 ACCRA Average House Price: $472,833

2013 ACCRA Cost of Living Index: 131

State income tax rate: None

State sales tax rate: None

Local income tax rate: None

Local sales tax rate: 5.0%

Property tax rate: 10.66 mills (2014)

Economic Information: Alaska Department of Labor and Workforce Development, Research and Analysis Section, P.O. Box 25501, Juneau, AK 99802-5501; telephone (907) 465-4500; fax (907) 465-2101; email raweb@labor.state.ak.us.

■ Education and Research

Elementary and Secondary Schools

The Juneau School District is the fifth largest district in the State of Alaska with 745 employees, including 387 teachers, and an annual budget of approximately $90 million. It serves about 5,000 students in six elementary schools; two mid-sized middle schools, two medium sized high schools, an alternative high school and a K-8 Charter School. Other district programs include Montessori Borealis, HOMEBridge home school, and a Tlingit Culture, Language, and Literacy program. Due to Juneau's geographic location, the schools also offer programs focusing on the sea. Almost 25 percent of the student body has Alaskan Native heritage.

The following is a summary of data regarding the Juneau Borough School District.

Total enrollment: 5,094

Number of facilities

    total: 12
    elementary schools: 6
    junior high schools: 2
    high schools: 2
    other: 2

Student/teacher ratio: 15.16:1

Teacher salaries

    average (statewide): $61,093

Funding per pupil: $16,406

Public Schools Information: Juneau School District, 10014 Crazy Horse Dr., Juneau, AK 99801; telephone (907) 523-1821; fax (907) 523-1829.

Colleges and Universities

The University of Alaska Southeast's (UAS) Juneau location on the shores of the Inside Passage serves as the main campus, with two other administrative units of the University of Alaska statewide system (in Ketchikan and Sitka), and focuses on general liberal arts education. In 2011, 3,977 students were enrolled region-wide, with 800 full-time and 1,600 part-time students at its Juneau campus. The university proper offers certificate, associate of arts, associate of applied science, baccalaureate, professional, and master's degree programs in the applied areas of business, fisheries, liberal arts, science, public administration, and teacher education. The university's two-year and certificate program in vocational and technical education supplies employees for local business and industry.

Libraries and Research Centers

The Juneau Public Library has a unique design built upon a parking garage in a beautiful waterfront location, with holdings of about 124,000 items throughout its branches. The collection includes books, e-books, books on tape/CD, audiobook downloads, videos and DVDs, music on compact disc and for download, periodicals, microfiche, microfilm and online electronic databases. In March 2005 it began offering the Alaska Library Network Catalog (ALNCAT) which provides access to all state libraries' collections. The Juneau Public Library and its two branches are part of the Capital City Libraries consortium, a cooperative catalog and circulation system shared with the Alaska State Library since 1989, the University of Alaska Southeast Egan Library, the Juneau-Douglas High School Library, and the Alyeska Central School Library. Holders of library cards at one of these libraries may borrow from any of the others and have access to library resources from home.

Other libraries in the city include the Alaska State Libraries, Archives and Museums, which encompass legislative information, policy issues and Alaskan history; and other governmental libraries.

Public Library Information: Juneau Public Libraries, 292 Marine Way, Juneau, AK 99801; telephone (907) 586-5249.

■ Health Care

Juneau is served by Bartlett Regional Hospital, a city-owned facility that began an extensive $40 million expansion project in 2005. The expansion included building a new wing, improving the original hospital, and adding a new admissions lobby and an orthopedic center. The project was completed in 2009. Bartlett Regional also operates the Rainforest Recovery Center, a medical model facility for the detoxification and rehabilitation of persons with alcohol or other drug dependencies. In 2013 Bartlett was licensed for a total of 57 inpatient beds and 16 residential substance abuse treatment facility beds in the Rainforest Recovery Center. Bartlett serves a 15,000 square-mile region in the northern part of southeast Alaska. Other Juneau health facilities are the Juneau Alliance for Mental Health, Inc. (JAMHI), and a Veterans Affairs Outreach Clinic that opened in 2010.

■ Recreation

Sightseeing

Juneau's Downtown Historic District contains many buildings dating back to 1880 and has wider sidewalks reminiscent of the old boardwalks. The Governor's Mansion, built in 1912, is not open to the public on a regular basis but tours can be arranged by contacting the governor's office. Alaska's State Capitol Building, with columns fashioned from a quarry on Prince of Wales Island, houses both the governor's office and state legislative offices and is open for tours. From January through May visitors may watch floor sessions from the galleries. The House of Wickersham, built in 1898 and the former home of famous local judge, James Wickersham, contains historic memorabilia as well as a genuine Chickering grand piano circa late 1800s, and is listed on the National Register of Historic Places.

The Juneau-Douglas City Museum includes various exhibits related to the area's rich history and provides educational and public programs while concentrating on the city's mining history. Tours are available of the St. Nicholas Orthodox Church, the oldest original Russian Orthodox church in the state, which was constructed in 1893. The Shrine of St. Therese, a chapel located on an island north of Juneau that is connected to the city by a narrow path, has stations of the cross on a trail circumnavigating the chapel in the surrounding woods and can be visited year-round.

The Last Chance Basin Historic District, usually referred to as the Jualpa Mining Camp, features many old mine buildings and attractions for visitors such as gold panning and, in summer, an outdoor salmon bake. A 5,000-gallon aquarium full of local sea life is the highlight of the Macaulay Salmon Hatchery, which is located three miles from downtown. Green Angel Gardens is a botanical facility featuring a variety of local plants and a salmon stream located near a low, active volcano.

Nature is the star at Juneau, and the walk-up Mendenhall Glacier, located 12 miles from downtown, is a must-see experience. It features a visitor center, built in 1962, which describes the progression of the glacier and the icecap from which it descends; the visitor center also features a movie and self-guided walking tour map. The 1,500-square-mile Juneau Icefield, the birthplace of the Mendenhall Glacier and 38 others, is located just over the mountains behind the city and is the fifth largest in North America. Light plane charters and helicopters offer an up-close tour.

Many visitors enjoy taking walking tours of Juneau's four local harbors, where fishing boat captains are usually amenable to discussing the day's catch. Whalewatching and wildlife viewing charter boat tours are a popular visitor attraction; a variety of companies offer tours from in or around Juneau, and many guarantee sightings.

Arts and Culture

The Alaska State Museum, established in 1900 when the state was a territory, offers more than 27,000 fine historical, cultural, and artistic collections under one roof. Juneau's gold rush history is captured at the Juneau-Douglas City Museum, which also contains a hands-on exhibit room for children, and a large relief map of Juneau's topography. Juneau has a very active artists' community, and there are many works of art located in public areas throughout downtown, including sculptures and totem poles.

Alaska's leading professional theater company, Perseverance Theatre of Juneau, presents a variety of classic, comedic, and dramatic plays during its fall-winter-spring season that typically draws thousands annually. The Naa Kahidi Theater, supported by the Sealaska Heritage Foundation, performs ancient Tlingit legends via storytelling for special events.

Festivals and Holidays

April is the time for the annual Alaska Folk Festival, which has been running since the mid-1970s. Music lovers assemble for the 10-day Juneau Jazz and Classics Music Festival in May. August's Golden North Salmon Derby, a tradition since 1947, offers big prizes, including scholarships, for catching big fish.

The Annual Juneau Maritime Festival offers live entertainment, free fish and activities, over 50 exhibits, and multiple maritime-themed contests. The festival features the popular Wild Alaskan Marinade Contest, where signature fish marinades are prepared with sockeye salmon then grilled by festival grill masters and tasted by a panel of judges.

Sports for the Spectator

Juneau-Douglas High School sports receive plenty of media coverage from the daily newspaper, *The Juneau Empire*. Spectators have the chance to cheer on the 2005 State Champion football team, the Crimson Bears, as well as a variety of other athletics programs, such as those centered around baseball, basketball, soccer, track and field, hockey, and volleyball. Spectators should also try to catch one of the men's, women's or co-ed softball games organized by the Juneau Sports Association.

Sports for the Participant

Juneau has five mountain peaks within reasonable day-trip distances, affording many hiking and climbing opportunities. Hiking trails lead from downtown to overlooks on 3,576-foot Mt. Juneau, 3,819-foot Mt. Roberts, and 3,337-foot Mt. Bradley (also known as Mt. Jumbo). The Mt. Roberts tramway travels from Juneau's waterfront to an elevation of nearly 2,000 feet. Guided tours, a restaurant, and theater are available at the upper terminal. The Juneau visitor's center offers free guides to more than two dozen trails to glaciers and historic gold mining ruins.

Fishing, sailing, kayaking, and river rafting are available on the protected waters of the Inside Passage. In summers, operators offer gentle river rafting, salmon watching, and gold panning. Picnics, camping, fishing, and beachcombing are popular on the area's beaches.

Mendenhall is the only golf course in Southeast Alaska, a par-three, nine-hole course built on private land behind the airport and only 10 miles from downtown. Winter downhill skiing and snowboarding are offered at Eaglecrest, 12 miles from the city's downtown, with 34 alpine runs, 2 loops of Nordic trails, and a vertical drop of 1,400 feet. Helicopter ski packages are available.

Juneau also has a racquet club, indoor rock-climbing, several aerobic studios, yoga classes, and local Parks and Recreation Department seasonal sports programs that welcome visitors. The Alaska Club, which has locations in Fairbanks, Mat-Su Valley, plus numerous sites in Anchorage, offers racquetball, spa facilities, tennis, fitness, and other athletic activities.

Shopping and Dining

Visitors will find galleries, shops, and restaurants throughout the downtown Juneau area. Specialty shops and gift shops offer hand-crafted work by local artists. Nugget Mall, the largest shopping destination, is within walking distance of the airport; its stores feature Alaskan gifts and clothing, and the mall has a visitor information center. Senate Shopping Mall houses eight eclectic shops from Native art to flyfishing supplies. Merchant's Wharf, an office and shop complex, is located at harborside. Gift shops and taverns line South Franklin Street. The Emporium Mall contains specialty shops and stores, as well as the Heritage Coffee Co., a sandwich and coffee shop on the main floor. Fantastic mountain views and a traditional steak and seafood menu are signatures of the historic Hangar on the Wharf restaurant.

The state's most famous bar, the lively Red Dog Saloon, provides local pictorial history, music, and excitement, especially when cruise ships are in port.

Visitor Information: Juneau Convention and Visitors Bureau, 101 Egan Drive, Juneau, AK 99801; toll-free (888) 581-2201; fax (907) 586-6304; email info@traveljuneau.com.

■ Convention Facilities

Centennial Hall Convention Center, just across the street from the waterfront, is three blocks away from the heart of Juneau's downtown with its shops and restaurants. Built in 1983, Centennial Hall has many meeting rooms ranging from 288 square feet to a 12,389-square-foot, column-free ballroom. The ballroom can be divided into three separate rooms, each with state-of-the-art light and sound systems. Centennial Hall also has two lobbies that provide additional space for receptions, displays, and relaxation. Juneau also offers meeting spaces in majestic settings atop Mt. Roberts, on the banks of the Gastineau Channel, or overlooking Auke Lake.

Convention Information: Juneau Convention and Visitors Bureau, 101 Egan Drive, Juneau, AK 99801; toll-free (888) 581-2201; fax (907) 586-6304; email info@traveljuneau.com.

■ Transportation

Approaching the City

Juneau International Airport is serviced daily by Alaska Airlines, and many smaller planes, and helicopter lines. The city is about a two-hour flight north from Seattle, or approximately a 90-minute flight southeast from Anchorage.

The Alaska Marine Highway ferry system provides car and passenger connections into Juneau from other southeast communities, as well as Bellingham, Washington (a two and one-half day trip) and Prince Rupert, British Columbia (a 24-hour trip). In 2011, the Highway announced it would begin weekly ferry service to Gustavus . The ferries have staterooms, observation decks, cocktail lounges, and heated solariums. After increasing port stops in Juneau by 55 in 2011, the highway reduced stops by 80 in 2012. Despite this decrease, the number of disembarking passengers in Juneau increased 2.8 percent to a new high of 262,798.

A variety of regional air taxi services and chartered flights are available to nearby attractions and smaller towns. Barge lines serve Juneau from Seattle several times per week. Power boats, sailboats, and kayaks are also available to rent for trips to the Inside Passage.

Traveling in the City

Egan Drive is one of the major streets in Juneau, running from one end of town to the other and following the shoreline of the Gastineau Channel. The downtown area is divided into a grid with Main Street crossing the numbered streets and passing the Capitol building and other major sites. Bus service is provided by the Capitol Transit line with 18 buses, and 10 paratransit vans in its fleet. Buses and vans meet every ferry from mid-April to the end of September, providing inexpensive service to downtown and the airport. Local air taxi operators fly both wheel and float planes.

■ Communications

Newspapers and Magazines

Juneau Empire is the city's daily newspaper and *Inside Passage,* the official newspaper of the Catholic Diocese of Juneau, is produced biweekly and monthly from January until September.

Television and Radio

ABC and PBS television stations are based in Juneau. Cable television is available, and there are various AM and FM radio stations broadcasting news, adult contemporary music, public radio, and album-oriented rock.

Media Information: Juneau Empire, Morris Communications Corp., 3100 Channel Dr., Juneau, AK 99801; telephone (907) 586-3740; fax (907) 586-9097.

Juneau Online

Alaska Communications Systems. Available www.acsalaska.com

Alaska Department of Labor & Workforce Development, Research & Analysis Section. Available almis.labor.state.ak.us

Alaska State Library. Available www.library.state.ak.us

Alaska State Museum. Available www.museums.state.ak.us/asmhome.html

City of Juneau Home Page. Available www.juneau.org

Juneau Borough Schools. Available www.juneauschools.org

Juneau Chamber of Commerce. Available www.juneauchamber.com

Juneau Convention and Visitors Bureau. Available www.traveljuneau.com; www.juneau.com

Juneau Economic Development Council. Available www.jedc.org

Juneau Empire. Available www.juneauempire.com

Juneau Public Library. Available www.juneau.org/library/index.php

State of Alaska. Available www.state.ak.us

BIBLIOGRAPHY

Raban, Jonathan, *Passage to Juneau: A Sea and Its Meanings* (New York: Pantheon Books, 1999)

Senkowsky, Sonya, and Amanda Coyne, *Alaska Then and Now: Anchorage, Juneau, and Fairbanks* (San Diego, CA: Thunder Bay Press, 2008)

Williams, Maria, ed., *The Alaska Native Reader: History, Culture, Politics* (Durham: Duke University Press, 2009)

Arizona

The State in Brief

Nickname: Grand Canyon State

Motto: Ditat Deus (God enriches)

Flower: Blossom of the saguaro cactus

Bird: Cactus wren

Area: 113,990 square miles (2010; U.S. rank 6th)

Elevation: Ranges from 100 feet to 12,670 feet above sea level

Climate: Dry and sunny, but heavy snows in the high central area

Admitted to Union: February 14, 1912

Capital: Phoenix

Head Official: Jan Brewer (R) (until 2015)

Population

    1990: 3,750,000
    2000: 5,130,632
    2010: 6,392,017
    2012 estimate: 6,410,979
    Percent change, 2000–2010: 24.6%
    U.S. rank in 2012: 16th
    Percent of residents born in state: 37.6% (2012)
    Density: 56.3 people per square mile (2010)
    2012 FBI Crime Index Total: 260,038

Racial and Ethnic Characteristics (2012)

    White: 5,085,954
    Black or African American: 262,284
    American Indian and Alaska Native: 283,805
    Asian: 177,598
    Native Hawaiian and Pacific Islander: 12,506
    Hispanic or Latino (may be of any race): 1,902,946
    Other: 588,832

Age Characteristics (2012)

    Population under 5 years old: 455,375
    Population 5 to 19 years old: 1,354,773
    Percent of population 65 years and over: 14%
    Median age: 36.0

Vital Statistics

    Total number of births (2012–13): 85,994
    Total number of deaths (2012–13): 50,274
    AIDS cases reported through 2011: 13,073

Economy

    Major industries: Services, trade, manufacturing, agriculture, aerospace and aviation
    Unemployment rate (2012): 6.0%
    Per capita income (2012): $25,571
    Median household income (2012): $50,256
    Percentage of persons below poverty level (2012): 17.2%
    Income tax rate: 2.59% to 4.54%
    Sales tax rate: 5.6%

Flagstaff

■ The City in Brief

Founded: 1881

Head Official: Mayor Jerry Nabours (since 2012; current term expires 2014)

City Population
1990: 45,857
2000: 52,894
2010: 65,870
2012 estimate: 67,472
Percent change, 2000–2010: 24.5%
U.S. rank in 1990: 543rd (State rank: 10th)
U.S. rank in 2000: 673rd (State rank: 13th)
U.S. rank in 2010: 501st (State rank: 15th)

Metropolitan Statistical Area Population
2000: 122,366
2010: 134,421
2012 estimate: 136,011
Percent change, 2000–2010: 9.9%
U.S. rank in 2000: 293rd
U.S. rank in 2010: 309th

Area: 63.58 square miles

Elevation: 6,899 feet above sea level

Average Annual Temperatures: 45.8° F

Average Annual Precipitation: 21.3 inches of rain

Major Economic Sectors: government, trade, manufacturing, research and development, tourism, retail

Unemployment Rate: 5.3% (2012)

Per Capita Income: $23,678

2012 FBI Crime Index Property: 2,834

Major Colleges and Universities: Northern Arizona University, Coconino County Community College

Daily Newspaper: *Arizona Daily Sun*

■ Introduction

Flagstaff, sometimes referred to as "the Gateway to the Grand Canyon," is the largest city in northern Arizona; it is also the county seat for Coconino County, which is the second largest in the nation by area. There are many tales surrounding how the city got its name: a popular one holds that a group from Boston stripped a pine tree on the Fourth of July and raised a flag to the top of it. At nearly 7,000 feet, Flagstaff is one of the highest cities in the United States. The city has become a regional center for northern Arizona, and boasts a refurbished downtown and a lively college student atmosphere. The city also is the site of many monuments and museums that pay tribute to the land and native tribes. But Flagstaff has more to offer than cultural merits from the past; it has taken big steps to become a center of bioscience research, as demonstrated by construction of a major telescope in 2012 and expansion of the city's technology incubator in 2013.

■ Geography and Climate

Flagstaff is located 145 miles due north of Phoenix, 323 miles west of Albuquerque, and 467 miles east of Los Angeles.

Flagstaff enjoys a four-season climate. Because of its high elevation, the city has cool summers in which air conditioners are mostly unnecessary, not the desert conditions one might expect. The altitude and low humidity result in clean air and relatively mild weather year round. Occasional late-afternoon thundershowers are common from July through September, and snow

© Tim Roberts Photography/Shutterstock.com

usually occurs first in mid-October, and is heaviest December through March. The snow, which averages more than 100 inches per year, generally melts off rather quickly. The city experiences nearly 300 days of sunshine annually.

Area: 63.58 square miles

Elevation: 6,899 feet above sea level

Average Temperatures: 45.8° F

Average Annual Precipitation: 21.3 inches of rain

■ History

Local Springs and Railroad Draw Settlers

It is said that the springs first drew people to the Flagstaff area of otherwise dry northern Arizona. The Sinagua, Anasazi, and Cohonino tribes were the first to settle there. Ruins of the pueblos and cliff dwellings belonging to the Navaho nation and Hopi tribes can still be found in the forests and lands surrounding present-day Flagstaff. A mountain man named Antoine Leroux knew the location of a source of water at the base of the San Francisco Peaks, and in 1876 a group of New Englanders left from Boston in search of the excellent farm land that they had heard about in highly exaggerated stories. They started a settlement in present-day Leroux Springs later in the year. According to legend, it was this group who placed a flag on top of a barren pine tree, celebrating the Centennial of the Declaration of Independence, and thus gave the city the name by which it has been known ever since.

In 1882, the arrival in Flagstaff of the Atlantic and Pacific Railroad started a building boom. The site of what is today downtown Flagstaff was selected because the railroad wanted to build its new depot on flat land. Shortly after the arrival of the railroad, a sawmill began operations to accommodate the railroad's need for wooden ties. The new sawmill provided jobs for more than 250 people. Wood was easily attainable, as the city is near the world's largest forest of ponderosa pines.

For more than half a century, beginning in the 1880s, miles of spur rail line extended in all directions from the city. The men who engaged in the sawmill industry developed their own culture. Author Rose Houk describes "logger lingo" in which "coffee was referred to by its brand name, Arbuckle; pancakes were 'blankets;' [and] biscuits were 'doorknobs.'"

Sheep ranching got started in the mid-1880s and became big business in Flagstaff. Many of the sheep ranchers were of Basque or Spanish heritage. At the same time, a group of Mormons began to raise cattle at Leroux Spring.

City Becomes Observatory Site

In 1894, Andrew E. Douglass of Boston chose Flagstaff as the site for an astronomical observatory. Douglass placed the Lowell Observatory there in part because of the clear skies that good telescope viewing requires. During that same year a reform school was built, which was later to serve as the first building of what is now Northern Arizona University. In 1930 astronomer V.M. Slipher discovered the planet Pluto at the observatory. Lowell Observatory has stayed in the forefront of science, notably with its research in the area of bodies within the solar system, such as satellites (moons), near-Earth asteroids, and comets.

Wildland-Urban Interface

In June and July 2002 the catastrophic Rodeo-Chediski fire grabbed national attention as the worst fire in Arizona history. Affecting Coconino County and its contiguous neighbors Navajo, Apache, and Gila counties, the fire burned approximately 468,000 acres, the bulk of which was Ft. Apache Indian Reservation and national forest land, destroyed almost 500 homes, and cost $43 million to quell. More than $34 million in federal disaster aid was directed to the area. Flagstaff itself was not directly affected because of city leaders' and civic groups' proactive work in land use planning and response training.

Into the 2000s and 2010s, some of Flagstaff's citizens became concerned about increasing development, mostly due to tourism, and preserving the natural environment that makes the area special. Master development plans have focused on sustainability and the retention and expansion of green space. The growing bioscience industry, furthered by the expansion of the city's entrepreneurial and technology business incubator in 2013, promised to add more high-wage jobs to the local economy.

Historical Information: Arizona Historical Society, Northern Arizona University, Cline Library, Building 28, Knoles Drive, P.O. Box 6022, Flagstaff, AZ 86011-6022; telephone (928) 523-5551; fax (928) 523-3770.

■ Population Profile

Metropolitan Statistical Area Population

2000: 122,366
2010: 134,421
2012 estimate: 136,011
Percent change, 2000–2010: 9.9%
U.S. rank in 2000: 293rd
U.S. rank in 2010: 309th

City Residents

1990: 45,857
2000: 52,894
2010: 65,870
2012 estimate: 67,472
Percent change, 2000–2010: 24.5%
U.S. rank in 1990: 543rd (State rank: 10th)
U.S. rank in 2000: 673rd (State rank: 13th)
U.S. rank in 2010: 501st (State rank: 15th)

Density: 1,031.3 people per square mile

Racial and ethnic characteristics

White: 50,596
Black or African American: 1,906
American Indian and Alaskan Native: 7,870
Asian: 1,348
Native Hawaiian and Other Pacific Islander: 82
Hispanic or Latino (may be of any race): 12,759
Other: 5,670

Percent of residents born in state: 43.3%

Age characteristics

Population under 5 years old: 4,518
Population 5 to 9 years old: 3,519
Population 10 to 14 years old: 3,927
Population 15 to 19 years old: 9,218
Population 20 to 24 years old: 12,473
Population 25 to 34 years old: 9,043
Population 35 to 44 years old: 8,601
Population 45 to 54 years old: 6,077
Population 55 to 59 years old: 3,478
Population 60 to 64 years old: 2,558
Population 65 to 74 years old: 2,582
Population 75 to 84 years old: 1,085
Population 85 years and over: 393
Median age: 25.1

Births (2010–11 Metropolitan Area)

Total number: 1,802

Deaths (2010–11 Metropolitan Area)

Total number: 703

Money income (2012)

Per capita income: $23,678
Median household income: $46,033
Total households: 22,385

Number of households with income of …

less than $10,000: 2,359
$10,000 to $14,999: 1,618
$15,000 to $24,999: 2,035
$25,000 to $34,999: 2,432
$35,000 to $49,999: 3,412
$50,000 to $74,999: 3,833

$75,000 to $99,999: 2,543
$100,000 to $149,999: 2,698
$150,000 to $199,999: 789
$200,000 or more: 666

Percent of families below poverty level: 24.7%

FBI Crime Index Property: 2,834

FBI Crime Index Violent: 262

■ Municipal Government

Flagstaff has a council/manager form of government with a mayor and six council members elected at large. Mayoral elections are held every two years; council members serve four years, and elections are staggered every two years.

Head Official: Mayor Jerry Nabours (since 2012; current term expires 2014)

Total Number of City Employees: 657 (2012)

City Information: Flagstaff City Hall, 211 West Aspen Ave, Flagstaff, AZ 86001; telephone (928) 744-5281.

■ Economy

Major Industries and Commercial Activity

New scientific and high-tech research and development industries have located to Flagstaff, broadening the economic base of tourism, government, education, and transportation, which replaced the lumber, railroad, and ranching eras.

W.L. Gore & Associates, Inc., makers of GORE-TEX, anchor the city's bioscience industry. Translational Genomics Research Institute in Flagstaff, known as TGen North, conducts epidemiologic research for public health and biodefense. Also contributing to the local bioscience industry is SenesTech, Inc., which specializes in reproductive physiology to work toward non-surgical sterilization methods for controlling pest populations. Research at the University of North Arizona, as well as the college's graduates, have contributed to the growth of the industry.

Research activities are important to the city's economy. The most well-known facility, Lowell Observatory, was responsible for the discovery of Pluto and has done pioneering work in observations of near-Earth phenomena such as asteroids, comets, and belt systems; and in the field of interferometric studies, in which a distributed network of small telescopes together create images of celestial bodies with much higher resolutions than any other single telescope can produce.

Other important industries included advanced manufacturing; emerging technology, buoyed by the local Northern Arizona Center for Entrepreneurship and Technology (NACET) incubator; and clean energy, a gift of the city's natural environment and its average 288 days of sunshine annually.

Items and goods produced: dog and cat food, specialty fabrics, wind turbines, medical devices, ice cream cones, packaging materials

Incentive Programs—New and Existing Companies

Local programs: Most programs in Arizona are offered at the state level. Local programs, such as the Business Retention and Expansion Program, connect local companies and provide access to important resources like job training and tax incentive programs.

The city offers tax exemptions for buying, constructing, or improving buildings. The city also offers Community Development Block Grant funds for infrastructure improvements.

State programs: State incentives are offered through the Arizona Commerce Authority, which organizes its programs through an "Incentive Tool Box." Among the cash assistance or loan programs are the Arizona Competes Fund, which provides cash assistance to attract business with stable, high-wage jobs; Arizona FAST Grant, offering up to $7,500 for technology commercialization; Arizona Innovation Accelerator Fund Program, with loans from $50,000 to $2 million for business expansion or job creation; Arizona Innovation Challenge, another cash assistance program providing up to $250,000 to technology ventures; and Arizona STEP grant targeting international export opportunities with cash assistance up to $10,000. Private Activity Bonds and Qualified Energy Conservation Bonds give companies access to low-interest financing.

Tax incentives provided include the Commercial and Industrial Solar Energy Program, offering a tax credit of up to 10 percent of the installed cost of solar energy devices; Healthy Forest Tax Incentives, which supplies several tax incentives to forestry and forest-product companies related to equipment purchases, transportation, and training; Military Reuse Zone tax credits that reduce property taxes by up to 75 percent for five years and also offer $10,000 in tax credits per new employee hired; Quality Jobs Program with $9,000 tax credits for new hires that meet certain criteria; Qualified Facilities Tax Credit that refunds up to 10 percent or $20,000 of a company's investment in new job creation; Renewable Energy Tax Incentives and Research and Development Program tax credits; and a Small Business Capital Investment Tax Credit amounting to as much as 35 percent of investment over a three-year period.

Job training programs: The state of Arizona offers matching funds of up to 75 percent to businesses for the training of workers for new jobs in the state. This cash assistance may total as much as $1.5 million per business. Training of incumbent workers is still eligible for cash assistance covering up to 50 percent of training expenses. The State of Arizona also operates the Arizona Job Training Program to tailor training plans to the evolving industry landscape. The Arizona Apprenticeship System maintains more than 100 registered apprenticeship opportunities that pair education with on-the-job training.

The Small Business Development Center is jointly sponsored by the U.S. Small Business Administration and Coconino County Community College. This one-stop center offers free one-on-one counseling, training, and technical assistance in all aspects of small business management.

Development Projects

Flagstaff 2020 Vision Project, unveiled in the 1990s, represented a comprehensive development plan for the city. However, some citizens questioned whether increasing development was compatible with preservation of what made the area special. In 2002 it was replaced by the Flagstaff Area Regional Land Use and Transportation Plan, which governs land use, transportation, open space, and trail systems. Sustainable development was a critical aspect of the plan.

Flagstaff has continued to work on its non-motorized urban trail network (FUTS), part of the aforementioned master plan. FUTS was to interconnect virtually all areas of the city when completed and promised to be important for both transportation and recreation. Flagstaff had completed approximately 50 miles of FUTS as of 2013. When the system was finished, it was to consist of 130 total miles. A 2009 survey showed that some 78 of city residents utilized the trail system.

In 2003, the Lowell Observatory and Discovery Communications announced a cooperative effort on a $53 million telescope to bring unprecedented wide-range views and deep-imaging surveys of the night skies. The Discovery Channel telescope's unique design allow it to switch from extremely wide-field focus to much more detailed spectroscopy, infrared imaging, and other applications. In addition to significantly advancing capacity for research, the telescope was capable of real-time worldwide broadcasting and science education programs for the public. The 4.3-meter (14.1-foot) telescope was completed in 2012 and began observations in 2013. The University of Arizona negotiated 80 nights of use of the telescope over a period of five years for $1 million, or about $12,500 per night.

Flagstaff is investing in bioscience. The city constructed the Northern Arizona Center for Emerging Technologies (NACET), which is a technology incubator that provides space for up to two dozen companies and many researchers. Construction of the incubator, funded by a $2.5 million federal economic development grant and $1 million from Flagstaff, was completed in 2008. The construction of the technology incubator was followed by the construction of a 200,000-square-foot Science and Technology Park. A 25,000-square-foot expansion to the original 10,000-square-foot incubator facility was underway in 2013, with the intention of offering a "soft landing" space to companies that graduated from the incubator. NACET won the 2012 Governor's Award for economic development. At that time, it reported creation of more than 200 high-wage jobs and client companies with estimated revenues of $6 million.

In 2012 the city completed repairs to its Inner Basin water pipeline. The pipeline, which provides as much as 20 percent of the city's water supply, was damaged after a forest fire in 2010 cleared lands that then flooded in a subsequent monsoon and severed the pipeline in two locations. The arduous construction, at high altitude and over rugged terrain, protected the city's most economical source of water, as drawing water from other sources, such as wells, cost as much as $6,000 per day.

Economic Development Information: City of Flagstaff Economic Development Department, 211 W. Aspen Avenue, Flagstaff, AZ 86001; telephone (928) 213-2906.

Commercial Shipping

US Airways serves Flagstaff Pulliam Airport, while multiple carriers are available in Phoenix. The city has a number of motor freight carriers. Flagstaff can reach some 34 million consumers within six hours of driving time. In particular, the city boasts its proximity to California, offering a low-cost alternative to operating within that state. Flagstaff is served by Burlington Northern Santa Fe Railway.

Labor Force and Employment Outlook

Northern Arizona, which includes Flagstaff, Sedona, and Payson, has experienced a massive influx of tourists and retirees. After concerns were voiced by residents about the continued development and its impact on the environment, developers and environmentalists worked together to achieve a balance between economy and landscape preservation. The bioscience industry, nurtured by the city's technology incubator, NACET, has been a primary driver of economic growth and new jobs. Some 40 percent of Flagstaff residents hold at least a bachelor's degree, significantly higher than both state and national rates. Northern Arizona University and Coconino Community College graduate thousands of highly qualified job-seekers each year.

The following is a summary of data regarding the 2012 Flagstaff labor force:

Size of civilian labor force: 38,846

Number of workers employed in . . .
  agriculture and mining: 485
  construction: 1,589

manufacturing: 1,880
wholesale trade: 546
retail trade: 5,473
transportation: 1,301
information systems: 371
finance: 1,456
professional administration: 2,335
education and social services: 10,384
arts and leisure: 6,108
other: 1,294
public administration: 2,087

Average hourly earnings of production workers: $15.37

Unemployment rate: 5.3% (2012)

Employers

Largest employers (2012)	*Number of employees*
Northern Arizona University	2,571
Flagstaff Medical Center	2,200
W.L. Gore & Associates	1,950
Flagstaff Unified School District	1,375
Coconino County	1,200
City of Flagstaff	657
Wal-Mart	630
Walgreens & Distribution Center	407
SCA Tissue	255
Nestle Purina	240

Cost of Living

The cost of living in Flagstaff is about 2.2 percent above the national average. Still, the city is considerably less expensive than neighboring California, a fact it uses to market itself to relocating businesses.

The following is a summary of data regarding several key cost of living factors in the area.

2013 ACCRA Average House Price: $472,600

2013 ACCRA Cost of Living Index: 114

State income tax rate: 2.59% to 4.54%

State sales tax rate: 5.6%

Local income tax rate: None

Local sales tax rate: 2.846%

Property tax rate: 6.3553 mills (2013)

Economic Information: Flagstaff Chamber of Commerce, 101 W. Route 66, Flagstaff, AZ 86001; telephone (928) 774-4505; fax (928) 779-1209.

■ Education and Research

Elementary and Secondary Schools

The Flagstaff Unified School District is widely recognized as one of the finest in the Southwest. It offers a wide range of programs to meet the needs of students with diverse backgrounds, interests, and abilities. Through use of non-traditional approaches, Project New Start helps students who have difficulty learning in the traditional setting. The district also offers services for students and families who might find themselves homeless. Flagstaff was the first school system in the United States to implement drug-and-alcohol prevention programs in both its elementary and secondary schools. Other programs include artists-in-residence, after-school classes for high school credit, the Suzuki violin program, parenting programs, bilingual education, and magnet and alternative programs, among others.

The following is a summary of data regarding the Flagstaff Unified School District.

Total enrollment: 10,130

Number of facilities
total: 16
elementary schools: 10
junior high schools: 2
high schools: 2
other: 2

Student/teacher ratio: 16.24:1

Teacher salaries
average (statewide): $47,553

Funding per pupil: $8,793

Public Schools Information: Flagstaff Unified School District, 3285 East Sparrow Avenue, Flagstaff, AZ 86004; telephone (928) 527-600.

Colleges and Universities

Northern Arizona University (NAU) had 21,774 undergraduates and more than 5,000 graduate students during the 2013–14 school year. It offers small classes, respected and accessible faculty and advisers, comprehensive libraries, computer labs, research opportunities, career placement, cultural programs and events, recreational facilities, and intramural and NCAA athletics. NAU students can choose from more than 300 minors, majors, certificates, master's and doctoral degrees. Unique programs range from Colorado Plateau-based forestry to global-ranging bioterrorism. Fields such as physical therapy and hotel/restaurant management are also available. The university's Center for Excellence in Education promotes a competency-based approach to teacher education.

Coconino County Community College, a two-year college educating nearly 10,000 students throughout its four campus locations, offers programs for students to continue their higher education or to enter the business world.

Libraries and Research Centers

The Flagstaff City-Coconino County Public Library consists of a main library, as well as the East Flagstaff Community Library, a bookmobile, and eight branch and county-affiliate libraries. (One is located within the Coconino County Correctional Facility.) The main library, built in an attractive ski-lodge style, features four fireplaces and local Native American art. The library contains an extensive collection of Arizona and Southwest publications. Other special collections include a U.S. genealogy collection, the Economic Development Information Center, a large print collection, and the City of Flagstaff Archives.

Considering its small population, the city is home to a large number of research collections and special libraries, including Lowell Observatory Library, the Museum of Northern Arizona Library, the U.S. Geological Survey Library, the Arboretum at Flagstaff (Transition Zone Horticultural Institute), the Cross Cultural Dance Resources, and Northern Arizona University's Cline Library Special Collections and Archives Division.

The many research centers and institutes at Northern Arizona University include the Colorado Plateau Research Station, the Quaternary Sciences Program, and the Native American Cultural Center. The U.S. Geological Survey Flagstaff Field Center supports such research as space mission support, water locating, earth geology, and image processing.

Public Library Information: Flagstaff City-Coconino County Public Library, 300 West Aspen Avenue, Flagstaff, AZ 86001; telephone (928) 213-2331.

■ Health Care

Flagstaff Medical Center (FMC) is Northern Arizona's regional referral medical facility and has the only Level I trauma center in the area. Prominent departments of Flagstaff Medical Center are the Heart and Vascular Center of Northern Arizona, Cancer Center of Northern Arizona, Imaging/Radiology, Sports Medicine, Women and Infants' Center, and a Bariatric Surgical Weight Loss Center. FMC had 267 inpatient beds and handled about 13,500 admissions annually as of 2013. The center's parent corporation, Northern Arizona Healthcare, also has facilities in nearby Sedona and Verde Valley. In 2013

U.S. News & World Report ranked FMC the eighth-best hospital in Arizona, with high-performing marks in five adult specialties.

■ Recreation

Sightseeing

Flagstaff, originally a railroad town, now houses its visitors center in the Tudor revival-style Santa Fe Station, where one can pick up maps for walking tours of the city. The Lowell Observatory, possibly the city's most famous structure, presents visitors with hands-on exhibits, historic displays, and a scenic campus located near downtown. Tours, sky shows, demonstrations, and lectures are offered throughout the year. The observatory's oldest telescope is housed in an historic wooden dome, and night-sky viewing is offered in evening hours during most of the year. Construction of the Discovery Channel Telescope was completed in 2012, with operations beginning in 2013.

The Arboretum at Flagstaff, with the highest elevation of a botanical research garden in the nation, displays a fascinating variety of plant life native to the region, and features an Endangered Species Refugia. The Arboretum is home to 2,500 species of plants. Its gardens include an herb garden, a constructed wetland wherein native plants purify water, a butterfly garden, organic vegetable garden, and other gardens spread over 200 acres with scenic trails. Visitors to Coconino National Forest may spot American bald eagles and black bear in the world's largest ponderosa pine forest, which ranges in elevation from 2,600 to 12,633 feet. The Elden Pueblo Archaeological Project at the National Forest informs visitors about archaeological concepts, values, laws, and practices through personal experience including hands-on mapping, and excavation. Programs for children are also available.

Guides escort tourists through the Riordan Mansion State Historic Park, a mansion with 40 rooms and more than 13,000 square feet of living area. This 1904 duplex contains original artifacts, handcrafted furniture, and personal mementos of the Riordan family, who lived there early in the twentieth century. The park also offers a visitor center, a self-guided tour of the grounds, and picnic tables. Reservations are recommended for tours.

Three national monuments in the area draw visitors for their history and breathtaking beauty. The pristine, stream-cut gorge at Walnut Canyon National Monument offers walking trails that reveal the ancient cliff dwellings built into the steep canyon walls where the Sinagua people lived nearly a thousand years ago. The on-site museum displays artifacts that paint a picture of what life was like for these early inhabitants of the area. Located in the shadow of the San Francisco Peaks, the Wupatki National Monument was once home to the farmers and traders of the Anasazi and Sinagua tribes. Four pueblos offering a glimpse into the past can be seen at this monument. (Wupatki is Hopi for "big house.")

Fifty thousand years ago an enormous iron-nickel meteorite, falling through space at about 30,000–40,000 miles per hour, struck a rocky plain of northern Arizona with an explosive force greater than 20 million tons of TNT. It left behind a crater, called the Meteor Crater, which today is 570 feet deep and 2.4 miles in circumference. The adjacent Museum of Astrogeology offers exhibits, movies and lectures that vividly describe the impact and the awesome results.

The Grand Canyon is about 80 miles northwest of Flagstaff. There one can view one of the most spectacular examples of arid land erosion in the world. The park covers 1,900 square miles, including 277 miles of the Colorado River. South Rim facilities are open year-round, and North Rim facilities are open mid-May through mid-October. The Grand Canyon Railway lets one travel in grand style on a vintage train from Williams, Arizona, to the South Rim, across 65 miles of beautiful Arizona countryside.

Arts and Culture

The Coconino Center for the Arts, a modern glass-front building, is the site of many cultural activities in Flagstaff, including symphonic, orchestral, and choral performances. Visual arts and literary and educational programs edify both locals and visitors. The center's 4,000-square-foot gallery presents the work of a variety of artists throughout the year. Annual exhibits of note held at the center include the Youth Celebrate Art and Culture exhibit held in March, which features the works of students throughout Coconino County; and the Flagstaff Folk Music Festival exhibit in June, which features folk, and acoustic musical performances.

The Flagstaff Symphony Orchestra has been bringing enjoyment to local audiences since its founding in 1950. The orchestra performs in the 1,500-seat Ardrey Memorial Auditorium, giving seven concerts during its September through April season, as well as youth concerts, a Lollipop concert in December for very young children, and Summer Chamber Music Series that began in 2008. Theatrikos, a popular local theatre company, performs six main stage productions per year; is involved in project P.E.A.C.E (Prevention, Education, and Creative Expression), which helps to prevent teen violence through theatre and peer interaction; and offers classes on acting, scene building, lighting design, voice, and the like. Theatrikos's home, the Flagstaff Playhouse, was renamed the Doris Harper-White Community Playhouse after one of its founders. It is an intimate black box theatre that can seat 100 people.

Flagstaff's premier museum is the Museum of Northern Arizona, which introduces museum-goers to the native peoples and natural sciences of the Colorado Plateau region. Permanent galleries and changing exhibits explore anthropology, biology, geology, and fine art. Native American art is for sale at the museum shop and there is a nature trail on the grounds. The Museum of Northern Arizona also hosts many entertainment events throughout the year.

The history of Flagstaff from the time of cowboys and lumberjacks to the railroaders and astronomers is presented at the Arizona Historical Society Pioneer Museum. Exhibits include early medical equipment, saddles, household and livestock items, and a 1929 Baldwin locomotive.

Festivals and Holidays

Summer events in Flagstaff center on ethnic culture and cuisine. Every June, the annual Flagstaff Chili Festival features live music and contests for both adults and children, in addition to the food. The Arizona Highland Celtic Festival offers music, Irish dancing, and whiskey tastings.

Several Native American festivals dot the cultural calendar, including the Zuni Festival of Arts and Culture in May, the Hopi Festival of Arts and Culture in July, and the Navajo Festival of Arts and Culture in August. Mexican influence is honored with the Celebraciones de la Gente festival in October.

Every Labor Day Weekend the Coconino County Fair takes place at the fairgrounds in Fort Tuthill Park. Highlights of the fair include exhibits, livestock, entertainment, a demolition derby, and a carnival. Pickin' in the Pines Bluegrass and Acoustic Music Festival takes place mid-September, and features music, and dance performances by various groups. The Flagstaff Festival of Science, a 10-day event held annually at the end of September, promotes science awareness through hands-on exhibits, interactive displays, field trips, and world-class scientist participants.

During December, Riordan Mansion offers holiday tours of its festively decorated turn-of-the-century rooms. February's Flagstaff Winterfest features nearly 100 events: sled dog races, skiing competitions, and other snow events; The Arizona Special Olympics is a competition for mentally and physically challenged athletes that holds some events in Flagstaff.

Sports for the Spectator

Until 2013, the Arizona Cardinals of the National Football League held preseason training camps in Flagstaff at the Northern Arizona University. The Phoenix Suns of the National Basketball Association still held camp in Flagstaff as of that year. A variety of NCAA-sanctioned sports are hosted at Northern Arizona University, including football, men's and women's basketball, volleyball, track, and swimming, among others. NAU's J. Lawrence Walkup Skydome, where many athletic events are held, is one of the largest wood-domed structures in the world; the university's Douglas J. Wall Aquatic Center is a high-altitude training site for U.S. and international Olympic swimmers and divers.

The Coconino County Horse Races—a tradition for more than 50 years—featured thoroughbreds and quarter horses and was held annually over the Fourth of July weekend at Fort Tuthill Downs until budget woes forced its cancellation in 2011.

Sports for the Participant

Flagstaff has 24 parks, including a swimming pool, ice-skating rink, tennis courts, basketball courts, ball fields, disc-golf courses, skate parks, a BMX park, and three recreation centers. FUTS, the Flagstaff Urban Trails System, runs through the city and provides 50 miles of multi-use trails varying in length from one to five miles. Long-term expansion plans are scheduled to extend FUTS to 130 total miles. Northern Arizona University's Douglas J. Wall Aquatic Center has an Olympic-size pool that is open to the public. The city's transportation network of interstate highways makes it easy to explore the national forests surrounding the city. Popular forest-based activities include hiking, mountain biking, and horseback riding. Coconino National Forest offers more than 320 miles of hiking trails. In town, trailheads access Mount Elden from the east and west. The Arizona Snowbowl atop the San Francisco Peaks, with a base elevation of 9,200 feet, is higher in elevation than most resorts in Utah, Colorado, and California. It offers skiers a vertical drop of 2,300 feet, 6 chairlifts and more than 30 slopes, the longest of which stretches more than a mile. Its chairlift becomes a 6,450-foot-long "Scenic Skyride" during the summer. Flagstaff Nordic Center, about 15 miles north of the city, offers 25 miles of groomed trails for every level of skier.

Shopping and Dining

Flagstaff is the primary commercial center in northern Arizona. The city boasts many fine art galleries, antique shops and specialty shops, as well as a number of major shopping centers. Flagstaff's proximity to a number of Native American reservations provides shoppers with a variety of Native American arts and crafts. The historic downtown shopping area has some 200 gift shops, boutiques, and clothing stores. Import stores downtown specialize in South American and Mexican goods. The Flagstaff Mall and Marketplace is an enclosed shopping center with more than 80 stores. The Gallery Shop at Coconino Center for the Arts specializes in hand-made arts and crafts by area artists.

Flagstaff's restaurants range from casual southwestern to European-style, with food served in the historic atmosphere of turn-of-the-century buildings. Ethnic cuisine ranges from Italian, Mexican, and Asian to Middle Eastern and Bohemian. Music fans enjoy visiting

the Museum Club, a Depression-era Route 66 road house and the Southwest's largest log cabin, which continues to present popular country musicians.

Visitor Information: The Flagstaff Visitor Center, 1 East Route 66, Flagstaff, AZ, 86001; telephone (928) 774-9541.

■ Convention Facilities

Flagstaff's largest conference hotel, with 247 guest rooms, is the Little America Hotel. With more than 10,000 square feet of conference space, the facility can accommodate hundreds of people classroom-style, the-ater-style, and for banquets. The Radisson Woodlands Hotel, with more than 180 guest rooms, has 6,400 square feet of conference space for classroom-style, theater-style, and banquet-style meetings. Some 70 area hotels offer 5,000 rooms.

■ Transportation

Approaching the City

Interstate 40, providing east–west coast access, runs through the center of Flagstaff. Access to the south is via Interstate 17. U.S. routes 89 and 180 run between Flagstaff and the Grand Canyon. At Flagstaff Pulliam Airport, located just six miles south of downtown Flagstaff, US Airways provides daily service to Phoenix. Amtrak offers trains from Flagstaff that connect with trains to Chicago and Los Angeles, and Greyhound-Trailways has interstate and intrastate bus service.

Traveling in the City

Over the years, Flagstaff has developed many of the traffic congestion problems that come with rapid growth. Some estimates say that traffic has more than tripled since 1974. Heavy snowfall brings additional congestion as skiers flock to the area. Major traffic improvements have been underway on Interstate 40, and other streets in the city continue to see improvements as well. Shuttle and tour bus service is provided by Nava-Hopi Tours (Gray Line) and Mountain Line.

■ Communications

Newspapers and Magazines

The city's daily newspaper, the *Arizona Daily Sun*, is published six days a week, Tuesday through Sunday. The *Navajo-Hopi Observer* serves the Native American peoples of northern Arizona. *Flagstaff Live* is an alternative weekly publication that is distributed at locations throughout Flagstaff, Sedona, and northern Arizona.

Television and Radio

Flagstaff has 14 local television stations. Cable is available throughout the city. Two AM and 14 FM radio stations broadcast out of the city, offering a wide range of formats including news, public radio, contemporary, country, and religious programming.

Media Information: The *Arizona Daily Sun*, 1751 S Thompson St., Flagstaff, AZ 86001; telephone (928) 774-4545.

Flagstaff Online

Arizona Daily Sun. Available azdailysun.com
City of Flagstaff Economic Development Department. Available www.chooseflagstaff.com
City of Flagstaff home page. Available www.flagstaff.az.gov
Flagstaff Chamber of Commerce. Available www.flagstaffchamber.com
Flagstaff Unified School District. Available www.fusd1.org

BIBLIOGRAPHY

Aitchison, Stewart, *Red Rocks, Sacred Mountains: The Canyons and Peaks from Sedona to Flagstaff* (Stillwater, MN: Voyager Press, 1992)

DeGraff, John G., *Flagstaff* (Charleston, SC: Arcadia Publishing, 2011)

Cline, Platt, *Mountain Town: Flagstaff's First Century* (Flagstaff, AZ: Northland Press, 1994)

Hait, Pam, *Shifra Stein's Day Trips from Phoenix, Tucson, and Flagstaff* (Guilford, CT: GPP Travel, 2009)

Houk, Rose, *The Peaks* (Phoenix, AZ: Arizona Highways, 1994)

Kupel, Douglas E., *Fuel for Growth: Water and Arizona's Urban Environment* (Tucson, AZ: University of Arizona Press, 2003)

Mangum, Richard K., *Flagstaff: Past and Present* (Flagstaff, AZ: Northland Pub., 2003)

Mesa

■ The City in Brief

Founded: 1878 (incorporated in 1883)

Head Official: Mayor Scott Smith (since 2008; current term expires 2016)

City Population
- 1990: 288,091
- 2000: 396,375
- 2010: 439,041
- 2012 estimate: 452,068
- Percent change, 2000–2010: 10.8%
- U.S. rank in 1990: 53rd (State rank: 3rd)
- U.S. rank in 2000: 51st (State rank: 3rd)
- U.S. rank in 2010: 38th (State rank: 3rd)

Metropolitan Statistical Area Population
- 2000: 3,251,876
- 2010: 4,192,887
- 2012 estimate: 4,329,534
- Percent change, 2000–2010: 28.9%
- U.S. rank in 2000: 14th
- U.S. rank in 2010: 14th

Area: 125.18 square miles

Elevation: 1,241 feet above sea level

Average Annual Temperatures: 84.5° F

Average Annual Precipitation: 8.5 inches

Major Economic Sectors: aerospace/aviation, health care, education, tourism, transportation, advanced manufacturing

Unemployment Rate: 5.7% (2012)

Per Capita Income: $23,731

2012 FBI Crime Index Property: 14,140

Major Colleges and Universities: Arizona State University Polytechnic, Mesa Community College, East Valley Institute of Technology

Daily Newspaper: *East Valley Tribune*

■ Introduction

Founded by Mormon agricultural pioneers, Mesa today is growing like the crops of its ancestors. Located in Maricopa County, one of the largest counties in the nation, Mesa began as a suburb of Phoenix but has risen to become the third largest city in the state and among the top-40 cities in the nation. The city's economy has been sustained primarily by the robust aerospace industry, and local education has worked to form a workforce capable of meeting its growing needs. Additionally, Mesa is far enough from Phoenix to retain its small town feel, yet near enough to the big city to encourage the growth of technological and manufacturing industries. Layers of native, frontier, and Mexican history have combined to form a city of eclectic tastes and offerings, from the prehistoric farming canals deep in the ground to the aviation businesses that take to the skies.

■ Geography and Climate

Desert, mountains, water—Mesa has it all. Located along a spit of the Sonoran Desert, called the Valley of the Sun, Mesa is warm and arid every month of the year and enjoys the flora and fauna of the desert biome. Saguaro and prickly pear cacti are abundant, along with varieties of cholla. The dry soil outside the city is wandered by rattlesnakes, jack rabbits, bobcats, hawks, and owls. While Mesa gets 320 days of sunshine annually and temperatures in the 100s during the summer, the evenings are marked by cool breezes. The city receives less than 10 inches of annual precipitation a year. Mesa has easy access

View of downtown Mesa, AZ. © *Ivan Martinez Photography*

to six local lakes and two nearby rivers. The Superstition Mountain range just to the east of the city provides some altitude to the mesas and valleys of the area, specifically the Salt River Valley, adjoining Tempe and the Salt River Indian reservation.

Area: 125.18 square miles

Elevation: 1,241 feet above sea level

Average Temperatures: 84.5° F

Average Annual Precipitation: 8.5 inches

■ History

The First Farmers

More than 2,000 years ago, Mesa's agricultural destiny was carved out by the Hohokam Indians who settled the area. The Hohokam were peaceful farmers who developed a sophisticated and effective network of irrigation canals that turned the arid land around Mesa into arable soil. Eventually, the Hohokam people seemed to disappear from the area; it is theorized that the tribe may have morphed into the Tohono O'dham tribe or that the Hohokam were driven out of the future Mesa area by

Apache Indians. Regardless, the tribe left an indelible mark on the desert that served farmers of all nationalities well for centuries.

Spanish explorers and conquistadores followed—both Francisco Vasquez de Coronado and Father Eusebio Kino passed near Mesa as they searched for treasure and sought to convert Native Americans. The Mesa-Phoenix area also lay along the route to the legendary seven cities of Cibola sought by Estevanico (or Esteban), a former Muslim slave who became an explorer after hurricanes and battles with Native Americans decimated his former crew in Florida. As quickly as the Spanish attempted to put down roots in southwestern Arizona, the Apache tribe drove them out again in a tradition that lasted through the 1700s.

The Mexican War and the U.S. Civil War largely occupied the time and resources of the United States military during the early and mid-1800s, and its forces were operating at less than full power when the government decided to intervene in the clashes between native peoples and European settlers in the Southwest after a portion of Arizona was ceded to the U.S. The Western Indian Wars in the later 1800s were spotted with massacres and relocations; in the Mesa area, the U.S. Army did battle with the Apaches until the tribe agreed to resettlement. Unfortunately, several competing Apache tribes were co-located, resulting in a resumption of hostilities until the military was able to negotiate a surrender by Apache Chief Geronimo in 1886. It was in relative peace that a group of Mormon farmers, dealing with relocation and persecution themselves, established the settlement of Fort Utah in Lehi, just north of Mesa.

Mesa Takes Root

A decade before Chief Geronimo's surrender, the 85 intrepid members of the First Mesa Company left Utah and Idaho. The group was composed of Latter-day Saints, some of whom practiced polygamy and who had been intrigued by the descriptions of Arizona brought back to church elders by the Mormon Battalion that fought during the Mexican War and traveled through Arizona on its way back to Utah. Stopping briefly in Lehi, the First Mesa Company moved on to the mesa, where they discovered and began clearing the irrigation canals left by the Hohokam people. The Second Mesa Company set out from Idaho about a year later; with the best land in Mesa already claimed, these pioneers established a nearby community called Stringtown, which was eventually absorbed into modern Mesa.

In the late 1800s, a flood in Lehi washed away Fort Utah; it had become evident over time that the lower desert lands were prone to sudden and unexpected flooding, allowing table-top Mesa to flourish. It began to look like a city, complete with an adobe pesthouse to control smallpox outbreaks, a city hall, saloons, and *The Mesa Free Press*, which has existed continuously under a variety of names since 1892 and is currently known as *The East Valley Tribune*.

Dr. A.J. Chandler played a significant role in the foundation of Mesa. Using heavy machinery, he enlarged the Hohokam canals and made them more effective in agricultural enterprises. Dr. Chandler was the force behind the construction of the first office complex in Mesa, and he started the first electric power plant. When the municipal government purchased the utility in 1917, it became one of a handful of Arizona cities to own such a service. Earnings from utilities solely funded capital expenditures until the 1960s and also provided the financial underpinning for Works Progress Administration (WPA) projects during the Great Depression. WPA projects included the first dedicated hospital facility, a new city hall and library, sidewalks, paved streets, parks, and a recreation department for the city.

Layers of Culture

By 1940, Mesa had achieved its standing as the third largest city in Arizona, boasting 7,000 inhabitants. Joining the Tohono O'dham Indians, the Hispanics, and the Mormons living in Mesa in the early 1900s were African American families (including a veterinarian) and families of Chinese and Japanese heritage who farmed and owned a variety of local businesses. This eclectic populace provided an interesting backdrop for events during the second World War, particularly considering the proximity of the internment camp at the Gila River Indian Reservation nearby.

World War II had another lasting cultural and industrial impact with the development of Falcon Field Airport and Williams Air Force Base as training sites for pilots. British pilots trained at Falcon Field, while U.S. pilots trained at Williams; many of those military families stayed in the Mesa area after the war ended. The aeronautical training and supply facilities at Falcon Field and Williams Air Force Base attracted aviation and aerospace companies to Mesa, propelling a switch from citrus and cotton farming to high-tech employment in the mid-1960s.

Twenty-First Century Mesa

Williams Air Force Base was closed in September of 1993 and was quickly reborn as Williams Gateway Airport, later renamed Phoenix-Mesa Gateway Airport. The aviation industry gives Mesa its wings today, with weather conditions that are near-perfect for training and testing every month of the year. Mesa accounts for around 20 percent of aerospace related jobs within the Phoenix-Mesa metropolitan area. Both Gateway and Falcon Field are home to national and international aeronautical companies that develop aircraft and aviation systems both for the commercial aviation industry as well as for the military. Development related to unmanned aerial vehicles (UAVs) has provided the next aerospace revolution for Mesa-area industries. The climate and geography have also made Mesa a golf destination, to the extent that local universities have developed golf-related research programs and academic concentrations.

Mesa offers a low cost of doing business, reasonable tax structure, well-educated workforce, low crime rate, high performing schools, affordable housing, and a good regional transportation system. These benefits are some of the reasons why Mesa was one of the fastest-growing cities in the country. With the exception of the 1920s, Mesa's population increased by at least 79 percent every decennial census through 1990, when Mesa had the highest growth rate of any city over 100,000 people in the country. As a result of the high growth, Mesa's planning revolved around it, mostly related to housing. By 2010, growth had declined to just under 11 percent, slipping Mesa into its spot as the 38th largest city in the country. With growth at least temporarily slowed, city planners have solicited feedback from the community to plot out the next 30 years with the "This is My Mesa" development plan, slated for adoption in 2014.

Historical Information: Mesa Historical Museum, 51 East Main Street, Mesa, AZ 85211; telephone (480) 835-2286; email info@mesamuseum.org.

■ Population Profile

Metropolitan Statistical Area Population

2000: 3,251,876
2010: 4,192,887
2012 estimate: 4,329,534
Percent change, 2000–2010: 28.9%
U.S. rank in 2000: 14th
U.S. rank in 2010: 14th

City Residents

1990: 288,091
2000: 396,375
2010: 439,041
2012 estimate: 452,068
Percent change, 2000–2010: 10.8%
U.S. rank in 1990: 53rd (State rank: 3rd)
U.S. rank in 2000: 51st (State rank: 3rd)
U.S. rank in 2010: 38th (State rank: 3rd)

Density: 3,217.5 people per square mile

Racial and ethnic characteristics

White: 375,765
Black or African American: 14,982
American Indian and Alaskan Native: 9,780
Asian: 8,021
Native Hawaiian and Other Pacific Islander: 1,138
Hispanic or Latino (may be of any race): 125,469
Other: 42,382

Percent of residents born in state: 39.1%

Age characteristics

Population under 5 years old: 31,020
Population 5 to 9 years old: 34,658
Population 10 to 14 years old: 30,472
Population 15 to 19 years old: 28,661
Population 20 to 24 years old: 32,939
Population 25 to 34 years old: 64,904
Population 35 to 44 years old: 51,775
Population 45 to 54 years old: 56,708
Population 55 to 59 years old: 24,545
Population 60 to 64 years old: 24,874
Population 65 to 74 years old: 36,481
Population 75 to 84 years old: 25,375
Population 85 years and over: 9,656
Median age: 35.6

Births (2010–11 Metropolitan Area)

Total number: 59,738

Deaths (2010–11 Metropolitan Area)

Total number: 26,891

Money income (2012)

Per capita income: $23,731

Median household income: $46,496
Total households: 165,344

Number of households with income of . . .

less than $10,000: 11,224
$10,000 to $14,999: 8,918
$15,000 to $24,999: 20,704
$25,000 to $34,999: 20,130
$35,000 to $49,999: 27,112
$50,000 to $74,999: 31,201
$75,000 to $99,999: 18,830
$100,000 to $149,999: 18,236
$150,000 to $199,999: 5,419
$200,000 or more: 3,570

Percent of families below poverty level: 16.7%

FBI Crime Index Property: 14,140

FBI Crime Index Violent: 1,804

■ Municipal Government

The city of Mesa has established a charter government under which it operates, with citizens of the municipality electing a mayor and six district council members. Council members serve four-year terms. Every two years, there is an election for three seats on the council. The mayor serves a four-year term in office. A vice mayor, chosen by the council, assists the mayor and council in administration of the city government.

Head Official: Mayor Scott Smith (since 2008; current term expires 2016)

Total Number of City Employees: approximately 3,491 (2012)

City Information: City of Mesa, P.O. Box 1466, Mesa, AZ 85211-1466; telephone 480-644-2011; email citymgt.info@Mesaaz.gov.

■ Economy

Major Industries and Commercial Activity

Economic growth in Mesa was sparked by its proximity to Phoenix, its sunny climate, the low cost of doing business, and quality of life. The arid, warm climate of Mesa has made it a top-flight locale for aeronautical industries that range from manufacturing to educational. Boeing maintains a facility at Falcon Field Airport where flight control panels are created, tested, and installed in freighters. The Mesa plant was the site of the development of the Apache Longbow helicopter during the 1990s and continues to research and develop military aeronautical equipment. Boeing Training Services and Systems not only equips pilots with the latest knowledge in flight but puts together training packages that can be administered to prospective pilots in other locations. More than a dozen other aerospace, defense, and aviation companies operate in Mesa. Their presence, combined with that of more than 100 companies surrounding the airport in support of the aerospace industry, employs more than 10,000 citizens in jobs ranging from advanced manufacturing to software development.

Unmanned aerial technology is one of the newest aerospace industries in Mesa. Boeing, as well as other companies, are involved in development of both planes and guidance systems for unmanned aerial vehicles (UAVs), commonly referred to as drones. While most current applications are relevant to the defense industry, potential use by commercial organizations was considered in research and testing as well. The city of Mesa and supporting development agencies sought designation as one of six national test sites for UAVs; the decision from the Federal Aviation Administration was expected in 2015.

Health care is a $19.2 billion industry in Maricopa County, supporting more than 160,000 jobs with an average wage above $56,000 as of 2013. Health-care development in the Phoenix metropolitan area has been a response to the region's rapid population growth. Mesa alone has more than 1,300 hospital beds, as well as major training centers and higher education institutions focused on health care delivery. Bioscience industries have followed on the heels of the core health-care industry, growing by 23 percent between 2002 and 2007, more than double the national average.

The growth of high-technology industries such as aerospace and health care has also fueled growth in higher education in and around Mesa, as universities have developed curriculum specifically to prepare graduates to enter the local workforce.

Tourism is also an important component of the local economy.

Items and goods produced: aeronautical equipment, military equipment, vehicle safety systems

Incentive Programs—New and Existing Companies

Local programs: Local business development assistance is available through the Neighborhood Economic Development Corporation (NEDCO), a partnership between the public and private sectors in support of community development and community reinvestment. NEDCO oversees loans for new and start-up businesses, upgrades and expansions for existing businesses, non-profit organizations, and homeowner associations. It offers development assistance in the form of entrepreneur education, loan readiness assessment, business credit repair, and loan application assistance. Loans from NEDCO are available for amounts between $5,000 and $50,000, with larger amounts available through NEDCO's partnerships with

local banks. The local chamber of commerce provides assistance to its members. Mesa's Enterprise Zone reduces property taxes by 80 percent for five years and also provides tax benefits worth $3,000 for the hiring of new employees in designated areas.

State programs: State incentives are offered through the Arizona Commerce Authority, which organizes its programs through an "Incentive Tool Box." Among the cash assistance or loan programs are the Arizona Competes Fund, which provides cash assistance to attract business with stable, high-wage jobs; Arizona FAST Grant, offering up to $7,500 for technology commercialization; Arizona Innovation Accelerator Fund Program, with loans from $50,000 to $2 million for business expansion or job creation; Arizona Innovation Challenge, another cash assistance program providing up to $250,000 to technology ventures; and Arizona STEP grant targeting international export opportunities with cash assistance up to $10,000. Private Activity Bonds and Qualified Energy Conservation Bonds give companies access to low-interest financing.

Tax incentives provided include the Commercial and Industrial Solar Energy Program, offering a tax credit of up to 10 percent of the installed cost of solar energy devices; Healthy Forest Tax Incentives, which supplies several tax incentives to forestry and forest-product companies related to equipment purchases, transportation, and training; Military Reuse Zone tax credits that reduce property taxes by up to 75 percent for five years and also offer $10,000 in tax credits per new employee hired; Quality Jobs Program with $9,000 tax credits for new hires that meet certain criteria; Qualified Facilities Tax Credit that refunds up to 10 percent or $20,000 of a company's investment in new job creation; Renewable Energy Tax Incentives and Research and Development Program tax credits; and a Small Business Capital Investment Tax Credit amounting to as much as 35 percent of investment over a three-year period.

Job training programs: The state of Arizona offers matching funds of up to 75 percent to businesses for the training of workers for new jobs in the state. This cash assistance may total as much as $1.5 million per business. Training of incumbent workers is still eligible for cash assistance covering up to 50 percent of training expenses. The State of Arizona also operates the Arizona Job Training Program to tailor training plans to the evolving industry landscape. The Arizona Apprenticeship System maintains more than 100 registered apprenticeship opportunities that pair education with on-the-job training.

Employment and staffing assistance is provided by the Mesa Chamber of Commerce. Maricopa Workforce Connections is a county branch of the state workforce development office, serving Maricopa County businesses and job seekers. Employers can access recruitment, screening, job matching, corporate restructuring, and job training services, while county residents in search of employment can tap into education and job training opportunities, career planning services, vocational counseling, specialized support services, job placement, and a national job database.

Development Projects

Despite its renown for intense growth at the end of the twentieth century, the city still has vast tracts of undeveloped land, especially in its southeastern corner. This region is the home of the Phoenix-Mesa Gateway Airport, also known as the Williams Gateway Area, and prospective urban development that the city hopes will create 100,000 jobs over the next few decades.

The "Mesa 2025" strategic plan, adopted in 2002, identified areas of focus for economic development, including the 4,560 acres that comprise the Falcon Field Airport corridor (business park and industrial usage), the Town Center/Main Street corridor (light rail, other rapid transit, business development, historical, and cultural development), and the Santan Freeway corridor (a combination of residential, commercial, industrial and mixed use). The city's "This is My Mesa" development plan sought to expand the existing plan by covering city development to 2040. The plan was scheduled for finalization and adoption in 2014, although a 2012 review panel found that the core of the Mesa 2025 plan was still very applicable.

In 2010 the voters approved a complete overhaul of the city's facility that serves the Chicago Cubs of Major League Baseball during Spring Training, as well as the accompanying Riverview Park. Construction finished in late 2013 and added a brand stadium six practice fields, and additional team facilities. Total cost for the development was $84 million, with an additional $15 million for surrounding infrastructure. Hohokam Stadium, home of the Oakland Athletics' Spring Training facilities, won approval for enhancements to their facilities, slated for completion in 2015, after signing a 20-year agreement with the city. The city invested $17.5 million in improvements, while the team was expected to cover the remaining $2.5 million. Spring Training contributed $632 million annually to the state's economy, according to a 2013 study.

In 2013 Grand Canyon University announced that it had chosen Mesa for a new East Valley campus. The satellite campus development was expected to include a total investment of $150 million. The university was given the right to purchase 100 acres at Eastmark in Mesa, with the option to add another 60 acres. Construction, set to begin in 2014, had a target completion date of 2015. If the university purchases the remaining 60 acres, construction was expected to continue into 2017.

Banner Health, already the city's largest employer, announced $45.2 million expansion in 2013 via the construction of four new Banner Health Centers in Maricopa County, one of which was located in East Mesa.

In 2012 the city announced that the Barry and Peggy Goldwater Library and Archives would be located in downtown Arizona. The $30 million research facility was to include documents from the Arizona politician, as well as other prominent public servants of the state. Construction was to begin in 2014 with an opening scheduled for 2016.

Major streetscape improvements to the city's Fiesta District began in 2013, with an anticipated completion in 2014. Improvements included lane adjustments, sidewalk widening, landscaping, benches, streetlights, and decorative pavements. The streetscape improvements were made to lure more businesses to the area, and encourage existing businesses to renovate their properties.

A 3.1-mile extension of the city's light rail system was under preliminary construction in 2013 after completion of the design phase in 2010. All construction was expected to finish by early 2016. Funding derived from a half-cent sales tax passed by voters in 2004, which was paired with matching federal funds.

Economic Development Information: City of Mesa Office of Economic Development, P.O. Box 1466, 20 East Main Street, Suite 200, Mesa, AZ 85211; telephone (480) 644-2398; fax (480) 644-3458.

Commercial Shipping

Mesa is served by two local airports, a major international airport 12 miles to the west, and a network of freeways, highways, and rail. The Phoenix-Mesa Gateway Airport can accommodate corporate, cargo, military, and general aviation craft. A 21,500-square-foot storage hangar and a 25,000-square-foot air cargo facility are available for shipping concerns, and the airport resides in Foreign Trade Zone #221, allowing for landing and storing import merchandise without full customs formalities.

Falcon Field Airport doubles as an industrial park, offering a variety of charter, general aviation, and cargo flights daily. Phoenix Sky Harbor International Airport, located between Mesa and Phoenix, is a major aeronautical enterprise that handles more than 800 tons of cargo daily. Phoenix Sky Harbor joins Phoenix-Mesa Gateway Airport in Foreign Trade Zone #221, easing customs requirements for imported goods and providing some tax relief for those businesses.

Several freeways, U.S. highways, and state highways pass through Mesa, including U.S. Highway 60 (known as Superstition Freeway) and state highways 87 and 89. The Santan Freeway 202 creates a bypass around the more congested downtown area, and Interstates 10 and 17 are quickly accessible from the city. Mesa is the headquarters for several trucking companies of national scope and is located conveniently near many more in Phoenix. Driving conditions are good year-round, and Mesa is within an eight-hour drive of Albuquerque, El Paso, Las Vegas, Los Angeles, San Diego, Tucson, and several major cities in Mexico. Mesa is also served by Union Pacific Railroad.

Labor Force and Employment Outlook

More than 30 percent of Mesa's labor force holds at least an associate's degree or higher, qualifying it as a well-educated workforce prepared to staff positions in the health-care and aerospace industries that buoy the local economy. The labor force has also grown rapidly, increasing by more than 25 percent since 2000. (This was slightly below the 28 percent increase in nearby Phoenix.) Arizona is a right-to-work state with a low rate of unionization.

The following is a summary of data regarding the 2012 Mesa labor force:

Size of civilian labor force: 214,836

Number of workers employed in ...

> agriculture and mining: 1,163
> construction: 15,803
> manufacturing: 16,187
> wholesale trade: 4,245
> retail trade: 24,635
> transportation: 8,156
> information systems: 3,669
> finance: 15,896
> professional administration: 23,768
> education and social services: 42,984
> arts and leisure: 19,795
> other: 9,598
> public administration: 7,083

Average hourly earnings of production workers: $16.03

Unemployment rate: 5.7% (2012)

Employers

Largest employers (2012)	*Number of employees*
Banner Health System	8,287
Mesa Public Schools	8,042
Boeing	4,700
City of Mesa	3,491
Maricopa County Government	2,644
Wal-Mart	2,537
Maricopa Community College	1,951
Gilbert Unified School District	1,230
The Kroger Company (Fry's)	1,059
West Direct II Inc.	800

Cost of Living

The cost of living in the Phoenix-Mesa-Scottsdale metropolitan area is about equal to the national average. Housing prices in Mesa are among the most affordable in the metropolitan area.

The following is a summary of data regarding several key cost of living factors in the area.

2013 ACCRA Average House Price: $297,175

2013 ACCRA Cost of Living Index: 96

State income tax rate: 2.59% to 4.54%

State sales tax rate: 5.6%

Local income tax rate: None

Local sales tax rate: 2.45%

Property tax rate: $8.41 per $100 for 10% of total value (2013)

Economic Information: City of Mesa Office of Economic Development, P.O. Box 1466, 20 East Main Street, Suite 200, Mesa, AZ 85211; telephone (480) 644-2398; fax (480) 644-3458.

■ Education and Research

Elementary and Secondary Schools

The Mesa Public Schools have come a long way from its pioneer farmer roots, when classes were taught in a shack made of cottonwood. These days, the emphasis is on preparing students to function in the new technology of the information age. Classes are geared toward the development of students who can use the latest technology and can think critically in the course of their learning experiences. The school district plans for every student to graduate with a skill or trade that will lead to future employment; to that end, the district has created and implemented a Career and Technical Education (CTE) curriculum. The program is comprised of six "pathways," including agricultural sciences, business and technology, industrial technology, family and consumer sciences, biotechnology, and graphics and video production. Hands-on learning is stressed, with some high school students enrolled in a Cooperative Office Education program that allows them to attend classes in the morning and work at local businesses in the afternoon.

Mesa Public Schools offers alternative education programs spanning kindergarten to 12th grade and running the gamut from early education centers, to support for home-schooled students, to institutions created for drop-out prevention and retrieval.

Mesa Public Schools also coordinates with technical schools, Maricopa Community Colleges, and Arizona's three state universities so that students can continue their studies at the post-secondary level. Adult education courses are also available through Parent University, Family Literacy, and General Education Development programs, among others.

Mesa is also home to approximately 45 charter schools and dozens of private schools.

The following is a summary of data regarding the Mesa Unified School District.

Total enrollment: 65,123

Number of facilities

    total: 82
    elementary schools: 55
    junior high schools: 11
    high schools: 6
    other: 10

Student/teacher ratio: 19.27:1

Teacher salaries

    average (statewide): $47,553

Funding per pupil: $7,530

Public Schools Information: Mesa Public Schools, 63 E. Main Street, Mesa, AZ 85201-7422; telephone (480) 472-0000; email info@mpsaz.org.

Colleges and Universities

Arizona State University Polytechnic, Arizona School of Health Sciences, Chandler-Gilbert Community College, East Valley Institute of Technology, Embry-Riddle Aeronautical University, Keller Graduate School of Management, Mesa Community College, Ottawa University, AT Still University, Arizona School of Dentistry and Oral Health, and the University of Phoenix all have locations in the Mesa area.

Arizona State University in Mesa functions as a polytechnic institute, or vocational college, offering its more than 9,700 students degrees in some 75 educational concentrations including business, agribusiness, engineering technology, professional pilot training, health and wellness, and education. Baccalaureate, master's, and doctoral degrees are all available through the Mesa campus. In June 1999, the university received accreditation by the Professional Golfers Association and was one of the first state universities west of the Mississippi to offer a Golf and Facilities Management major. It decided to drop the major in 2011, relisting it as a concentration within a bachelor's of science in agribusiness.

Master's and doctoral degrees are available through the Arizona School of Health Sciences, which offers programs such as medical informatics, advanced physician assistant studies, sports medicine, occupational therapy, and audiology. Fieldwork experiences occur in a variety of urban and rural placements, allowing for practical application of academic concepts.

The largest of the 10 Maricopa Community Colleges, Mesa Community College (MCC) offers its student body of more than 40,000 degrees in more than 40 departments. Well-respected Fire Science and Nursing academic programs are underscored by a service learning program that has become a blueprint for community colleges across the country. Courses within a variety of disciplines send their students out into the local community to do meaningful volunteer work that employs the theoretical concepts learned in class. Additionally, MCC provides AmeriCorps service scholarships to students who are performing volunteer work or completing unpaid internships.

East Valley Institute of Technology (EVIT) is billed as Arizona's first regional technological education district, serving high school students from 10 East Valley school districts (including Mesa Public Schools). The programs at EVIT are the result of partnerships with local industry and business in an effort to prepare students with the skills needed for future employment. High school students can attend half-days at EVIT and the rest of the school day at their own school. EVIT additionally offers adult education classes under the banner of Evenings at EVIT.

Highly specialized training is available to would-be pilots and transitioning former members of the military at Phoenix-Mesa Gateway Airport Educational Campus, which includes tenants such as Advanced Training Systems International, Inc., and Airline Transport Professionals. Keller Graduate School of Management, part of DeVry University, also maintains a Mesa branch with a range of business-related master's degrees. Adult learners can also enroll at the Mesa campus of Ottawa University and the University of Phoenix.

Grand Canyon University announced in 2013 that it was locating a satellite campus in Mesa, expected to enroll students by 2015.

Libraries and Research Centers

The Mesa Public Library system is comprised of one centrally located main library facility, with two branch libraries covering the southwest and northeast portions of the city—Dobson Ranch and Red Mountain branches—as well as an express library in Power Square Mall. The main library is home to the Mesa Room, an archive of local history items and special collections regarding Mesa. Besides offering general library services, the City of Mesa Library coordinates reading programs for children, book discussion groups, special exhibits and lectures.

The Research Library at the Arizona Museum of Natural History contains non-circulating materials dedicated to the natural and cultural history of the Southwest. There are approximately 58,000 objects in the collections of the museum.

The Arizona State University Polytechnic campus library offers access to hundreds of databases and thousands of online journals and periodicals, which can be searched remotely. The library provides a call center for help, along with live tech support. The library features the Naxos Music Library, an online compendium of classical music with a sprinkling of other musical genres.

Arizona State University Polytechnic also houses several high-tech facilities for specialized research, including the Golf Driving Range and PING Swing Analysis Lab, which refine the work of students in golf facilities management concentrations. ASU's Agribusiness Center incorporates a Consumer Behavior Research Lab with a Market/Trading Room, along with a testing theater for students in the pre-veterinary medicine program. An altitude chamber and a simulator lab provide the latest facilities for pilot training, while the College of Technology and Applied Sciences benefits from the Microelectronics laboratory, a 15,000-square-foot manufacturing facility available to both students and local industry partners. The university constructed a 34,600-square-foot research facility to house Applied Biological Sciences Laboratories, the Applied Cognitive Sciences Center, the Health Lifestyles Research Center, and the Laboratory for Plant Biotechnology and Pharmaceutical Research.

Public Library Information: City of Mesa Main Library, 64 East First Street, Mesa, AZ 85201; telephone (480) 644-3100.

■ Health Care

Mesa is home to eight medical centers, three of which are part of the Phoenix-based Banner Health company. Banner Desert Medical Center offers the community 583 licensed beds for adult acute care, emergency services, intensive care, oncology and cardiology specialties, orthopedics, and neurology. Banner Desert also operates a Children's Hospital staffed by medical specialists in pediatric emergency, and surgical, intensive, and rehabilitative care. The second Banner facility is Banner Baywood Medical Center, with 340 beds, admitted more than 21,000 patients in 2013. The third is Banner Heart Hospital, which offers 111 beds that provide specialized cardiology services to the East Valley community, including advanced cardiac diagnostics and treatment.

Other health facilities include Mountain Vista Medical Center, with 172 beds; Restora Hospital of Mesa, a 120-bed acute long-term care hospital; the 23-bed Arizona Spine and Joint Hospital; and the HealthSouth East Valley Rehabilitation Hospital, which has 40 beds. Mesa General Hospital, also known as the Arizona Regional Medical Center, had served the community since 1965 until it closed in 2013 due to financial insolvency.

Mesa's proximity to Phoenix allows access to hundreds of medical professionals in family practice, specialty practices, outpatient psychiatric services and alternative medicine practices.

■ Recreation

Sightseeing

The only skyscraper in Mesa is the 16-story Financial Plaza building. Part of the sprawling Southwest, the modern Mesa prefers visitors to see the city's history rather than a jungle of steel. A tour of Mesa might best be started at the very beginning, at the Park of the Canals near the intersection of McKellips Road and Horne Street north of the downtown area. In addition to the Mesa Grande Ruins, the Park of the Canals is a major archaeological site. Visitors can see the innovative irrigation systems established by the original Hohokam Indian residents of Mesa, with the effectiveness of the canals demonstrated by the Brinton Desert Botanical Garden at the same location. The Botanical Garden hosts special events in season, along with desert gardening workshops and concerts in what can be a surreal setting. The Salt River is just northwest from the Park of the Canals, making for a water-themed day in the desert.

On the way back to Mesa's town center, it's an easy stop at the former Lehi School, circa 1913, which housed the Mesa Historical Museum until 2013, when the museum moved downtown, and has served as an annex for alternative museum programming thereafter. The historic downtown section of Mesa features attractions ranging from the Wild West era to modern arcades. The Ellis-Johnson home, the Alhambra Hotel, the Vance Auditorium, and the former Southside Hospital all echo back to the beginnings of Mesa. The Sirrine House, built in 1895, is an attractive brick structure restored by the Mesa Historical Society and the City of Mesa.

Immediately east of the original Mesa town site is the Temple Historic District, encompassing two residential divisions. Homes from the early 1920s line streets that were named for the Mormon pioneers who helped shape present-day Mesa and who laid the foundations for the Arizona Temple of the Church of Jesus Christ of Latter-Day Saints built in 1927. The large temple is the location of the denomination's Easter Pageant, held every spring. The temple is open for tours.

From Mesa, visitors and history buffs can embark on sightseeing adventures such as the Apache Trail Jeep Tour, which follows the stagecoach and freight wagon route from Mesa to Globe through the Superstition Mountains. Somewhere in those mountains, the Lost Dutchman's Mine waits to be found again. The Goldfield Ghost Town resurrects its history as a thriving mining community that bit the dust when the mine petered out. At its height, there were three saloons, a boarding house, a general store, blacksmith shop, brewery, schoolhouse, and bordello. Along the finger of the Sonoran Desert that points across the East Valley, a smorgasbord of desert succulents can be encountered: saguaro, prickly pear, varieties of cholla, hedgehog cactus, and ocotillos. When the mountains and desert become too dry, visitors can head northeast to Saguaro Lake for a paddleboat excursion on the *Desert Belle* past canyon walls and Arizona wildlife.

Arts and Culture

The Mesa Arts Center is the largest arts center in Arizona at 212,775 square feet of space for performing arts facilities, visual arts galleries and studios, and art education classrooms. The outside of the complex is as inviting as the inside, with a design reflective of the surrounding Sonoran Desert in hue, shape and landscaping. A 700-foot Shadow Walk serves as a cool outdoor plaza for events or relaxing during a tour. Located in the heart of downtown Mesa, the Arts Center campus contains three buildings, including a four-theater complex. The theater spaces are: the 1,588-seat Tom and Janet Ikeda Theater; the 550-seat Virginia G. Piper Repertory Theater; the 200-seat Nesbitt/Elliott Playhouse; and the 99-seat Anita Cox Farnsworth Studio Theater. The other facilities on the Arts Center campus are the Mesa Contemporary Arts Building and the Art Studios' classrooms and work areas.

The Mesa Arts Center is home to Ballet Etudes, offering serious ballet performers an experience akin to a professional dance company. Ballet Etudes stages *The Nutcracker* annually, along with a Spring Repertory performance. The dancers have performed with the Symphony of the Southwest, also located under the Arts Center roof. Besides its four scheduled orchestral performances each season, the orchestra does outreach in the public schools and provides vouchers that allow students and their families to attend future performances at a reduced rate. The Youth Symphony of the Southwest, established in 2006, involves excellent young musicians in a minimum of three concerts each season, providing a professional-level experience for aspiring performers. The Sonoran Desert Chorale's 60 vocalists present concerts throughout the year, with selections ranging from classical to the Broadway stage.

Billed as "theatre for children by children," the East Valley Children's Theatre encourages creativity, self-confidence, and expression through community theatrical performances. The company puts on four productions each season, along with a host of workshops and classes for youth between the ages of 8 and 18. Offering seven plays per season is the Southwest Shakespeare Company, which strives to bring classical theater to the masses through dynamic live performances. The actors are able to share their appreciation for the Bard via student matinees, post-show seminars, and play introductions.

For theater along with edible fare, the Broadway Palm West Dinner Theatre is recommended.

At the Arizona Museum for Youth, exhibits are tailored for young children up to 12 years of age, although adults will also enjoy the explanatory and interactive displays. Tours, opportunities to contribute to masterpieces, art classes, and workshops all happen at this fun and stimulating site located at Robson and Pepper streets.

Until 2013, the Mesa Historical Museum was housed in the original 1913 Lehi Schoolhouse; it has since moved to downtown, maintaining the schoolhouse as an annex for other museum initiatives. The Mesa Historical Museum contains a wealth of artifacts donated by Mesa's pioneer families and linked to the city's colorful past.

The natural and cultural histories of Mesa and its environs are the focus of the Arizona Museum of Natural History. With 80,000 square feet, the museum hosts various collections, including Spanish Colonial relics, artifacts of mining, reflections of Arizona's role in World War II (including Japanese relocation camps), Hohokam ceramics and jewelry, and evidence of Arizona's former function as ocean floor. The museum's Archaeology Team has several active excavations that are open to the public.

The Arizona Wing of the Commemorative Air Force Aviation Museum is also located in the city.

Festivals and Holidays

The Mesa Arizona Easter Pageant is the annual production of the Church of Jesus Christ Latter-day Saints set on the grounds of the Mesa Arizona Temple annually. It is renowned as the largest annual outdoor Easter pageant in the world, with a 450-member cast depicting a 65-minute version of the life of Jesus Christ in song and dance. The free, 10-night pageant happens in April. Two of the performances are done completely in Spanish.

The desert heat in summer dictates that festivals and outdoor events in Mesa are concentrated in winter, spring, and fall months, with a bit of a summer siesta in between. The year kicks off in January with the Mesa Martin Luther King Jr. Celebration, where the civil rights pioneer is feted with music, food, and carnival rides. For many years each February, Mesa joined forces with Phoenix and other East Valley communities to put on the Blues Blast at the Mesa Amphitheatre; the festival moved to M. T. Hance Park in Phoenix in 2012. At the festival, national and local blues artists perform a day-long concert that gets central Arizona in the groove.

Cinco de Mayo festivities start May off, with cultural fiestas at locations throughout the city. For half a century, Mesa has sponsored a Fourth of July party; the Southwest Symphony Orchestra typically provides a rousing rendition of "The Star Spangled Banner." Ushering in cooler weather in September, Mesa honors its history during the

Annual Constitution Celebration, featuring a parade, picnics and music.

Native American art, culture, music, dancing, and food are the focus of the Mesa Pow Wow in late October. Elaborate native dress and dance competitions attract visitors from many tribes and states. Also in late October is the Mesa Storytelling Festival, which presents the art of the spoken word. National, regional, and youth talent gather to share a wide range of stories: folk tales, tall tales, myths, humor, American legends, and tales from all over the world. In December, Main Street is again the destination for holiday celebrations in the downtown area. Mesa's Merry Main Street decks the halls with lights, gingerbread houses, tempting wrapped packages and a visit by Santa.

Sports for the Spectator

While Mesa does not have its own professional sports teams, it has become a place where sports lovers gather. The Chicago Cubs and Oakland Athletics both get ready for the Major League Baseball season in Mesa as part of the Cactus League, which gets started in early March and wraps up the Spring Training season the following month. Both teams received major ballpark and facilities upgrades, at Riverview Park and Hohokam Stadium, respectively, in the 2010s after signing long-term lease agreements with the city. Locals and visitors get the opportunity to preview not just the Cubs but also their impressive roster of opponents.

Baseball doesn't end in March, though—both facilities host Fall League baseball. In October and November, Fall League baseball features the Mesa Solar Sox, providing a preview of the next generation of Major League Baseball players for the Anaheim Angels of Los Angeles, Oakland Athletics, Chicago Cubs, Washington Nationals, and Detroit Tigers.

Mesa Community College's Thunderbirds compete in a more than a dozen men and women's sports at the National Junior College Athletic Association level. Phoenix offers more professional and collegiate sports options, from the Arizona Cardinals of the National Football League to the Phoenix Suns of the National Basketball Association, as well as the National Hockey League's Phoenix Coyotes and Arizona Diamondbacks of Major League Baseball.

Sports for the Participant

The name of the game in Mesa is golf—local courses abound, and a short drive provides access to even more holes stunningly situated in desert and mountain terrain. Local courses in Mesa include Fiesta Lakes Golf Club, Royal Palms Golf Course, Augusta Ranch Golf Club, Las Sendas Golf Club, and Superstition Springs Golf Club, just to name a few. Toka Sticks Golf Course on the grounds of the Phoenix-Mesa Gateway Airport offers the unique opportunity to fly in, play 18 holes, and fly out

again. Mountain Brook Golf Club is located outside of Mesa, but is set in the desert just below the Superstition Mountains, making it a dramatic experience for the golfer.

The Gene Autry Sports Complex contains tennis courts, indoor volleyball courts and beach volleyball pits. Lessons are offered, and players can join leagues or drop in on specified days.

Mesa may be in the desert, but watersports are still available. Rafting and tubing on the Salt River are popular summertime thrills, while local lakes like Saguaro are typically good spots for anglers to try for walleye, largemouth and brown trout, bluegills, channel catfish, and crappie.

The Superstition Mountains east of Mesa offer hikes of all levels of difficulty and duration, including the 1.5-mile Massacre Grounds trail, the Peralta Trail to the Fremont Saddle, and the steep Siphon Draw trail. The Tonto National Forest to the north of Phoenix and Mesa is the fifth largest forest in the United States, providing opportunities for a range of outdoor activities such as hiking, rock climbing, and camping. For a classic hiking adventure, trekkers can head north to the Grand Canyon.

Shopping and Dining

The Mesa Market Place Swap Meet covers 55 acres with more than 1,600 booths under a canopy to give an outdoor shopping experience with shade and water misters to keep customers cool. The Swap Meet is open year-round with great bargains and unusual merchandise. Antiques and collectibles are often found among the shops in the historic downtown area of Mesa, while more recognizable stores can be encountered at the newly expanded Fiesta Mall in West Mesa, Superstition Springs Center in East Mesa, the Village at Las Sendas, and The Village Square at Dana Park. Mesa holds a Community Farmers Market downtown all year, with vendors providing fresh produce and other goods in a street fair atmosphere. The Mesa Riverview, the latest shopping addition, is an outdoor shopping mall in the northwestern part of the city.

As might be expected, Mesa's culinary specialty is Mexican-Southwestern food, with burgers and pizza coming in second and third. There's something for every taste, though, in Mesa's menu of Chinese, Japanese, Italian, Greek, and home-style eateries. Local and chain coffee shops abound as well.

Visitor Information: Visit Mesa, 120 N. Center Street, Mesa, AZ 85201; telephone (480) 827-4700 or (800) 283-6372; email info@visitmesa.com.

■ Convention Facilities

Mesa has several convention centers (not including the nearby Phoenix-area convention centers). The Mesa

Convention Center features 19,000 square feet of exhibit space, along with an additional 19,000 square feet of flexible meeting space that can be used for trade show exhibits, banquets, dances, concerts and other events. The Conference Center features a 100-seat conference theatre that possesses multimedia capabilities for presentations and teleconferences. Breakout rooms and an executive conference room are also available. The Mesa Amphitheatre hosts more than 70 events per year; festival-style seating can accommodate 4,200 for commercial shows and outdoor festivals.

The Arizona Golf Resort and Conference Center has a 12,000-square-foot space for meetings and exhibitions, bolstered by an additional 5,000 square feet of general session rooms, training rooms, board rooms, outdoor courtyards, and onsite championship golf. The Phoenix Marriott Mesa Hotel and Convention Center offers 52,000 square feet of meeting and function space. The 18,000-square-foot Exhibit Hall is accompanied by the 9,000-square-foot Arizona Ballroom and an outdoor amphitheatre that can accommodate up to 5,200 people.

■ Transportation

Approaching the City

Phoenix Sky Harbor Airport is located approximately 12 miles to the west of Mesa and is served by 17 airlines that connect the East Valley–area to more than 80 cities in the United States and another 20 around the world. Sky Harbor is a major hub for Southwest Airlines. Non-stop international flights are available to the United Kingdom, Mexico, Costa Rica, and Canada. The local airfields Phoenix-Mesa Gateway and Falcon Field offer charter flights in the Southwest.

Several interstates and U.S. and state highways pass through or near Mesa, including U.S. Highway 60 (known as Superstition Freeway) and state highways 87 and 89. The Santan Freeway 202 creates a bypass around the more congested downtown area, and Interstates 10 and 17 are quickly accessible from the city. Greyhound Bus service maintains a branch in Mesa, with daily departures and arrivals. West Mesa is connected to the METRO Light Rail line.

Traveling in the City

From east to west, Mesa is 18 miles long; as a result, the city's residents are bisected between East Mesa and West Mesa. Mesa is laid out on a straightforward north–south, east–west grid pattern for its major streets. Center Street and Main Street are perpendicular to each other and, as their names suggest, intersect in the city center, providing a handy reference point and making city navigation relatively easy. Mesa has styled itself as a bicycle-friendly city, with 70 miles of bicycle routes and 40 miles of bicycle lanes. The city plans for more bicycle route and lane construction in the future, along with facilities at bike destinations.

Bus service within Mesa is provided by Valley Metro, which runs buses seven days a week for about 16 hours per day. Mesa operates a Dial-A-Ride program for people with mobility or vehicle operation issues, plus the city offers RideChoice options to elderly and disabled patrons who either use the bus, cabs, or are driven to their destinations by friends or family members.

■ Communications

Newspapers and Magazines

The Mesa area is served by *The East Valley Tribune,* which is delivered daily and is available online. *Get Out,* an affiliate of the daily paper, supplies dining and entertainment information for Mesa residents and tourists alike. Mesa Community College publishes its campus paper, *The Mesa Legend.* Spanish-language speakers can check out *La Voz* and *Prensa Hispana,* while other local publications write to the interests of the Catholic, Jewish, and senior populations in Mesa.

Television and Radio

Phoenix is Mesa's source for network television broadcast stations, being home to affiliates of CBS, ABC, NBC, and Fox. Mesa is within hearing distance of a wide variety of AM and FM radio stations with signals originating in Phoenix; formats run the gamut from talk radio to National Public Radio to classical music to rock and roll.

Media Information: East Valley Tribune, 1620 W. Fountainhead Parkway, Ste. 219, Tempe, AZ 85282; telephone (480) 874-2863.

Mesa Online

City of Mesa home page. Available www.cityofmesa. org

Mesa Public Library. Available www.mesalibrary.org

Downtown Mesa Association. Available www. downtownmesa.com

Mesa Chamber of Commerce. Available www. mesachamberofcommerce.org

Mesa Convention and Visitors Bureau. Available www.visitmesa.com

Mesa Historical Museum. Available www. mesamuseum.org

BIBLIOGRAPHY

Our Town: The Story of Mesa, Arizona, 1878–1991 (Mesa, AZ: Mesa Public Schools, 1991)

Samson, Karl, *Frommer's Arizona and the Grand Canyon 2011* (Hoboken, NJ: Wiley, 2011)

Phoenix

■ The City in Brief

Founded: 1864 (incorporated, 1881)

Head Official: Mayor Greg Stanton (since 2012; current term expires 2015)

City Population
  1990: 983,015
  2000: 1,321,045
  2010: 1,445,632
  2012 estimate: 1,488,759
  Percent change, 2000–2010: 9.4%
  U.S. rank in 1990: 9th (State rank: 1st)
  U.S. rank in 2000: 10th (State rank: 1st)
  U.S. rank in 2010: 6th (State rank: 1st)

Metropolitan Statistical Area Population
  2000: 3,251,876
  2010: 4,192,887
  2012 estimate: 4,329,534
  Percent change, 2000–2010: 28.9%
  U.S. rank in 2000: 14th
  U.S. rank in 2010: 14th

Area: 475.09 square miles

Elevation: 1,058 feet above sea level

Average Annual Temperatures: 72.6° F

Average Annual Precipitation: 8.3 inches

Major Economic Sectors: services, government, manufacturing, health care, aviation/aerospace

Unemployment Rate: 6.5% (2012)

Per Capita Income: $22,594

2012 FBI Crime Index Property: 60,777

Major Colleges and Universities: University of Phoenix, Arizona State University, Maricopa Community Colleges

Daily Newspaper: *The Arizona Republic*

■ Introduction

Phoenix, the capital of Arizona, originated as a legendary frontier town teeming with stagecoaches, saloons, and bandits. The city has since evolved into a resort area for tourists, as well as a haven for retirees. While it retains much of its Old West heritage, Phoenix has also become known as one of the "newest" cities in the nation. It is among the fastest growing metropolitan areas in the country. Phoenix has attracted younger residents to the area and shed its image as a traditional retirement area. Not only has it been ranked among the best places for business, but it has also been recognized as an ideal area for young professionals. Private companies and public-private partnerships continue to grow Phoenix into a national leader in several technology fields, including solar power, bioscience, and aerospace and aviation.

■ Geography and Climate

Located in the Salt River Valley in the south central part of the state, Phoenix is situated on flat desert terrain, bordered by lakes and the Superstition Mountains to the east, and surrounded by the Phoenix Mountain Preserve. The climate is warm, with low humidity. The most remarkable weather feature is sunshine more than 300 days per year, making Phoenix one of the sunniest cities in the country.

Area: 475.09 square miles

Elevation: 1,058 feet above sea level

Average Temperatures: 72.6° F

Average Annual Precipitation: 8.3 inches

© *Andrew Zarivny/Shutterstock.com*

■ History

Native Americans Removed to Make Way for White Settlers

The city of Phoenix stands on the site of a prehistoric settlement built by the Hohokam tribe, a group of Native Americans who had established a thriving culture but then vanished without a trace around 1450 A.D. Thought to be the ancestors of the Pima—"Hohokam" means "those who have gone" in Pima—the Hohokam had constructed a sophisticated system of irrigation canals, many of which are still in use today, that remain as evidence of their existence.

Permanent resettlement of the Hohokam site did not come until the late 1860s; in the interim the area shared the history of the rest of the state. Hispanic conquistadors invaded Arizona in the 1500s in search of the Seven Cities of Cibola, bringing with them cattle, horses, and new agricultural methods. They were followed by miners, traders, and farmers whose presence was tolerated by the Native Americans until the 1850s, when it became apparent that the white settlers were encroaching on their land. Battles between the settlers and the tribes brought intervention by the U.S. military, and the tribes were eventually confined to reservations.

City Thrives as Trade Center; Irrigation Aids Farms, Industry

In 1864 a U.S. Army post, a supply camp for nearby Camp McDowell, was set up on the ruins of the Hohokam settlement. Then in 1867 the Hohokam's irrigation canals were rebuilt by two settlers, one of whom called the place "Phoenix." He predicted that, like the mythical phoenix bird rising from its own ashes, a great city would emerge from the ruins. Incorporated in 1881, Phoenix rapidly developed into a major trading center with the building of the railroad in 1887 and became the capital of the Arizona territory in 1889; it was named the capital of the state of Arizona in 1912.

Phoenix gained a reputation as a rowdy frontier town because of its saloons, gambling places, and general outlaw atmosphere. Law and order were restored by the turn of the century, however, and Phoenix entered a new phase. The railroad, bringing settlers from throughout the country, established an immigration pattern that continued steadily without interruption; during the three decades that followed World War II, for instance, the population of Phoenix increased from roughly 107,000 to nearly 790,000 people.

Major technological advances during the first half of the twentieth century—the Roosevelt Dam on the Salt River, the Southern Pacific Railroad, the advent of air conditioning, and the Central Arizona Project aqueduct system—brought about agricultural and industrial development that also spurred tremendous growth. In the 1990s Phoenix went through its third major growth boom in four decades, partly a result of a large influx of people from California. The city has experienced the effects of urban sprawl, including serious air pollution.

The Next Hundred Years

Entering the twenty-first century, Phoenix has introduced light rail to help alleviate traffic congestion and the associated pollution, and a steady stream of mixed-use downtown development projects have lured residents back to the city center. The contemporary city landscape consists of Hispanic colonial and Indian pueblo architecture interspersed with gleaming high-rise office buildings. And while general population growth has fueled economic development in the health-care industry, Phoenix's young and well-educated workforce has encouraged growth in high-technology businesses and made the city one of the nation's entrepreneurial capitals.

Historical Information: Arizona Science Center, 600 E. Washington Street, Phoenix, AZ, 85004; telephone (602) 716-2000; fax (602) 716-2000.

■ Population Profile

Metropolitan Statistical Area Population

2000: 3,251,876
2010: 4,192,887
2012 estimate: 4,329,534
Percent change, 2000–2010: 28.9%
U.S. rank in 2000: 14th
U.S. rank in 2010: 14th

City Residents

1990: 983,015
2000: 1,321,045
2010: 1,445,632
2012 estimate: 1,488,759
Percent change, 2000–2010: 9.4%
U.S. rank in 1990: 9th (State rank: 1st)
U.S. rank in 2000: 10th (State rank: 1st)
U.S. rank in 2010: 6th (State rank: 1st)

Density: 2,797.8 people per square mile

Racial and ethnic characteristics

White: 1,141,686
Black or African American: 105,152
American Indian and Alaskan Native: 29,472
Asian: 51,432
Native Hawaiian and Other Pacific Islander: 2,772
Hispanic or Latino (may be of any race): 600,451
Other: 158,245

Percent of residents born in state: 40.3%

Age characteristics

Population under 5 years old: 117,486
Population 5 to 9 years old: 114,608
Population 10 to 14 years old: 108,774
Population 15 to 19 years old: 104,932
Population 20 to 24 years old: 115,603
Population 25 to 34 years old: 228,885
Population 35 to 44 years old: 216,220
Population 45 to 54 years old: 196,303
Population 55 to 59 years old: 82,968
Population 60 to 64 years old: 66,402
Population 65 to 74 years old: 80,239
Population 75 to 84 years old: 39,845
Population 85 years and over: 16,494
Median age: 32.9

Births (2010–11 Metropolitan Area)

Total number: 59,738

Deaths (2010–11 Metropolitan Area)

Total number: 26,891

Money income (2012)

Per capita income: $22,594
Median household income: $44,649
Total households: 516,383

Number of households with income of ...

less than $10,000: 49,174
$10,000 to $14,999: 30,640
$15,000 to $24,999: 60,480
$25,000 to $34,999: 62,473
$35,000 to $49,999: 77,784
$50,000 to $74,999: 88,605
$75,000 to $99,999: 55,029
$100,000 to $149,999: 55,968
$150,000 to $199,999: 19,068
$200,000 or more: 17,162

Percent of families below poverty level: 23.1%

FBI Crime Index Property: 60,777

FBI Crime Index Violent: 9,458

■ Municipal Government

The capital of Arizona and the Maricopa County seat, Phoenix has a council-manager form of government. The eight council members serve staggered four-year terms, representing districts of the city, while the mayor is elected at large to a four-year term and also serves as the ninth member of the council. Phoenix has won international recognition and many awards for the quality of management of the city.

Head Official: Mayor Greg Stanton (since 2012; current term expires 2015)

Total Number of City Employees: 15,100 (2012)

City Information: City of Phoenix, 200 W. Washington St, Phoenix, AZ 85003; telephone (602) 262-6011.

■ Economy

Major Industries and Commercial Activity

Manufacturing and tourism, traditionally the base of the city's economy, continue to be important to Phoenix. Major manufacturing or distribution companies with a significant presence in the Phoenix area include Amazon, Boeing, Bose, Daisy Brand, Dick's Sporting Goods, eBay/PayPal, Freescale Semiconductor, Frito Lay, Gap, Inc., Intel Corporation, ON Semiconductor, PetSmart, PING, and Target. Distribution companies benefit from the city's access to transportation infrastructure as well as its proximity to California, which hosts millions of consumers but requires comparatively expensive operating costs for companies or distribution centers based in the state.

Tourism is an especially vital part of the economy. Some 16 million visitors from throughout the United States and Canada visit annually to enjoy the warm weather and sunshine in the Valley of the Sun. Visitor spending, which averaged $30 million per day in 2013, generated $730 million annually in city, county, and state tax revenue.

Sunshine has also attracted solar energy companies to the Phoenix area, both for manufacturing, installing solar capacity, and conducting solar research. Solar-power companies in the Phoenix area include Abengoa Solar, Centrosolar, First Solar, Gestamp, Kyocera, Maxwell Technologies, Power-One, and Rioglass Solar. Also a player in high-technology research is the city's bioscience industry, which utilizes its area institutions of higher education in addition to private companies. The Mayo Clinic, Dignity Health, and Banner Healthcare all have offices in and around Phoenix. Research institutions such as the Alzheimer's Institute and International Genomics Consortium are located in Phoenix as well.

Corporate or regional headquarters located in Phoenix include Avnet, Dial Corporation/Henkel, Fender, Freeport McMoRan, Go Daddy, Hensley & Co., Microchip Technology, PetSmart, Poore Brothers, Shamrock Farms, U-Haul, and Viad Corporation. Several aerospace and aviation companies have a major presence in the Phoenix area.

Items and goods produced: aircraft and aircraft parts, electronic equipment, steel castings and fabrications, flour, boxes, agricultural chemicals, aluminum products, radios, creamery products, saddles and leather goods, apparel

Incentive Programs—New and Existing Companies

Local programs: Employers locating facilities in the 200-square-mile City of Phoenix Enterprise Zone (COPEZ), as designated by the Arizona Department of Commerce, can earn state corporate income tax credit for each net new job created in the zone. Tax credits can total up to $3,000 per hire (with a maximum of 200 annually) over a three-year period. The city of Phoenix is the administrator of Foreign Trade Zone #75, which allows companies to reduce or defer payment of customs duties on imported products; companies operating in the zone can benefit from an 80 percent reduction in real and personal property tax. EXPAND (Expansion Assistance and Development Program) was formed to facilitate a growing company's need for funds to acquire capital. EXPAND reserve deposits are pledged in amounts up to 25 percent of a loan with a ceiling of $150,000. Phoenix Industrial Development Authority (PIDA) bonds provide tax-exempt financing utilizing industrial revenue bonds up to $20 million for most aspects of manufacturing projects, including construction, equipment, and improvement expenses. The Phoenix Community Development Investment Corporation encourages businesses to operate or expand in underserved areas of the community, targeting job creation for low-income residents.

State programs: State incentives are offered through the Arizona Commerce Authority, which organizes its programs through an "Incentive Tool Box." Among the cash assistance or loan programs are the Arizona Competes Fund, which provides cash assistance to attract business with stable, high-wage jobs; Arizona FAST Grant, offering up to $7,500 for technology commercialization; Arizona Innovation Accelerator Fund Program, with loans from $50,000 to $2 million for business expansion or job creation; Arizona Innovation Challenge, another cash assistance program providing up to $250,000 to technology ventures; and Arizona STEP grant targeting international export opportunities with cash assistance up to $10,000. Private Activity Bonds and Qualified Energy Conservation Bonds give companies access to low-interest financing.

Tax incentives provided include the Commercial and Industrial Solar Energy Program, offering a tax credit of up to 10 percent of the installed cost of solar energy devices; Healthy Forest Tax Incentives, which supplies several tax incentives to forestry and forest-product companies related to equipment purchases, transportation, and training; Military Reuse Zone tax credits that reduce property taxes by up to 75 percent for five years and also offer $10,000 in tax credits per new employee hired; Quality Jobs Program with $9,000 tax credits for new hires that meet certain criteria; Qualified Facilities Tax Credit that refunds up to 10 percent or $20,000 of a company's investment in new job creation; Renewable Energy Tax Incentives and Research and Development

Program tax credits; and a Small Business Capital Investment Tax Credit amounting to as much as 35 percent of investment over a three-year period.

Job training programs: The state of Arizona offers matching funds of up to 75 percent to businesses for the training of workers for new jobs in the state. This cash assistance may total as much as $1.5 million per business. Training of incumbent workers is still eligible for cash assistance covering up to 50 percent of training expenses. The State of Arizona also operates the Arizona Job Training Program to tailor training plans to the evolving industry landscape. The Arizona Apprenticeship System maintains more than 100 registered apprenticeship opportunities that pair education with on-the-job training. Phoenix development organizations partner with nearly 20 local technical and four-year colleges to support job training and workforce development for area businesses.

Development Projects

A rapidly growing young city, Phoenix has required more recent construction activities than more mature cities. Between 2006 and 2011, some $4 billion in public and private investment went to the 1.5-square-mile downtown area alone. Among the major projects was a $600-million Phoenix Civic Plaza and Convention Center, completed in 2009 and tripling the existing facility's size. A light rail system that effectively transports nearly one million riders throughout the city per month launched the year before. The Phoenix Sky Harbor International Airport, which continues to see improvements, has constructed and continues to expand the PHX Sky Train, a light rail extension that transports passengers between the city's METRO Light Rail and the airport grounds. The initial stage of the project opened in 2013, and subsequent phases were to be completed by 2020. The total project had an estimated cost of $1.58 billion, funded entirely through airport revenues and passenger fees.

In private developments, WinCo Foods announced in 2013 its plans to open an 800,000-square-foot distribution facility in west Phoenix, expected to open in 2014 and create at least 200 jobs. The distribution center was to help the company reach markets in Arizona and southern California and Nevada. CityScape, a 600,000-square-foot mixed-use facility, opened in 2010 at a cost of $600 million. Included within the facility was the Hotel Palomar, 224 apartments, and a number of office, restaurant, and retail venues. A 500,000-square-foot mixed-use facility with office, hotel, and retail space opened in 2011 and housed the headquarters of Freeport-McMoRan Copper & Gold, Inc., in addition to a 242-room Westin Hotel.

Private investment from the health-care industry was led by developments in the Phoenix Biomedical Campus. The Arizona Cancer Center, expected to open in 2015 after construction began in 2013, was intended to treat some 60,000 patients annually on the campus. The Phoenix Biomedical Campus was anchored by the IGC/TGen headquarters and the Arizona Biomedical Collaborative. The master plan for the campus included 6.5 million square feet of medical development; annual estimated impact for the completed campus registered $2.1 billion and was to support 14,000 jobs.

Maricopa County completed a 16-story courthouse tower in 2012, with 32 new courtrooms and a cafeteria. The county also broke ground on a new $92.5 million Maricopa County Sheriff's Headquarters that year, expected to open in 2013. The headquarters, capable of housing 300 employees, had five stories and a total of 128,000 square feet.

Economic Development Information: City of Phoenix Community and Economic Development Department, 200 W. Washington St., 20th Floor, Phoenix, AZ 85003; telephone (602) 262-5040; fax (602) 495-5097; email phx.business@phoenix.gov.

Commercial Shipping

Phoenix is located at the center of market areas stretching along interstate highways from southern California to western Texas, Colorado, Utah, and Mexico. Importantly, Phoenix offers distributors focused on the California market a low-cost alternative for warehousing and shipping. More than 50 companies provide motor freight service. Rail service is available from two transcontinental rail lines, Union Pacific and Burlington Northern Santa Fe. The Phoenix metropolitan area economy benefits from air cargo service through Phoenix Sky Harbor International Airport. The airport handled more than more than 800 tons of cargo daily as of 2013.

Labor Force and Employment Outlook

The local labor force is described as young, plentiful, and well-educated. Arizona consistently ranks among the top-five growth states, and workers are attracted by the quality of life to be enjoyed. A right-to-work state, Arizona has union membership of around 5 percent.

In 2012 professional and business services employed the largest number of Phoenix residents, followed by government, retail trade, health care and social assistance, leisure and hospitality, and manufacturing. Labor-force projections to 2020 anticipated the greatest growth in construction, education and health services, professional and business services, and leisure and hospitality.

The following is a summary of data regarding the 2012 Phoenix labor force:

Size of civilian labor force: 730,359

Number of workers employed in . . .

    agriculture and mining: 2,669
    construction: 48,712
    manufacturing: 49,547

wholesale trade: 17,423
retail trade: 77,079
transportation: 33,240
information systems: 12,356
finance: 64,488
professional administration: 90,558
education and social services: 128,024
arts and leisure: 67,292
other: 35,258
public administration: 25,609

Average hourly earnings of production workers: $16.03

Unemployment rate: 6.5% (2012)

Employers

Largest employers (2012)	Number of employees
State of Arizona	49,800
Wal-Mart	30,634
Banner Health Systems	24,825
City of Phoenix	15,100
Wells Fargo	13,308
Bank of America	13,300
Maricopa County	12,792
Arizona State University	11,185
Apollo Group	11,000
JPMorgan/Chase	10,600

Cost of Living

The cost of living in the Phoenix-Mesa-Scottsdale metropolitan area is about equal to the national average and below that of several other major cities in the West, such as Las Vegas or Denver, as well as most locations in California.

The following is a summary of data regarding several key cost of living factors in the area.

2013 ACCRA Average House Price: $297,175

2013 ACCRA Cost of Living Index: 96

State income tax rate: 2.59% to 4.54%

State sales tax rate: 5.6%

Local income tax rate: None

Local sales tax rate: 2.7%

Property tax rate: 6.6755 to 12.6878 mills (2013)

Economic Information: Greater Phoenix Economic Council, Two North Central Ave., Ste. 2500, Phoenix, AZ 85004; telephone (602) 256-7700; fax (602) 256-7744.

■ Education and Research

Elementary and Secondary Schools

The city of Phoenix is home to 325 public schools in 30 school districts along with more than 200 charter and private schools. The Greater Phoenix area has an extensive magnet school program with an emphasis on specialized course work in career fields such as aeronautics and aerospace, agri-business, and computer studies, among others.

The following is a summary of data regarding Arizona and Maricopa County Schools.

Teacher salaries
average (statewide): $47,553

Funding per pupil: $7,898

Public Schools Information: Maricopa County Superintendent of Schools, 4041 N. Central Avenue, Suite 1100, Phoenix, AZ 85012; telephone (602) 506-3866; fax (602) 506-3753.

Colleges and Universities

Phoenix has some 80 private technical and business colleges, including the University of Phoenix and Maricopa Community Colleges, the latter being one of the largest higher education systems in the world. The University of Phoenix has garnered recognition via its innovative online degree program and more than 100 campuses throughout North America. Both offer undergraduate degrees in a wide range of disciplines and graduate degrees in such fields as business and management and education. Other colleges in Phoenix include Grand Canyon University and two campuses of Arizona State University (ASU), the largest university in the Rocky Mountain area with an enrollment of more than 73,000 students and more than 2,000 full-time faculty, based in nearby Tempe. ASU boasts a strong science orientation; the 9,000-student Phoenix West Campus focuses on upper division and graduate courses.

Libraries and Research Centers

The Phoenix Public Library system consists of the main branch downtown, Burton Barr Central Library, and 16 branches throughout the city. Located across 280,000 square feet, the central library's collection numbers nearly one million volumes as well as magazines, newspapers, tapes, films, slides, and art reproductions. Special collections include the Arizona Room, which features a variety of resources related to Arizona's rich history. The Arizona State Library, Archives, and Public Records also focuses on the state's history and includes law, government, and genealogy holdings. More than 50 special libraries and research centers are located in Phoenix; most are affiliated with colleges, medical centers, and government agencies and specialize in such fields as medicine, business, and technology. Arizona State University's Engineering Center focuses on microelectronics, CAD/CAM, telecommunications, and computer science.

The Translational Genomics Research Institute (TGen) held its grand opening in March 2005 with a 170,000-square-foot facility. It is the centerpiece of a massive downtown medical complex with various tenants, some involved in research, expected to total 2.5 million square feet after all development finished; construction projects were ongoing through at least 2015. The Biodesign Institute at Arizona State University contributes to Phoenix's growth by beckoning scientists and biotechnological companies to the area. Other medical research institutes included the Alzheimer's Institute and the International Genomics Consortium.

Public Library Information: Phoenix Public Library, 1221 N. Central Ave., Phoenix, AZ 85004; telephone (602) 262-4636.

■ Health Care

Along with population growth in Phoenix has come an increased demand for health-care services; meeting this need, the Phoenix medical community has become a major industry in the metropolitan area. More than 33,000 medical personnel are employed in the region. One of the largest health-care providers in Phoenix, the Maricopa Integrated Health System oversees the Maricopa Medical Center, Arizona Burn Center, Comprehensive Healthcare Center, McDowell Healthcare Clinic, 11 community-oriented family health centers, and an attendant care program. The Maricopa Medical Center has 578-beds and is also a teaching hospital.

Banner Health operates several facilities in and around Phoenix and is one of the area's largest employers. In Phoenix proper Banner Estrella Medical Center and Banner Good Samaritan Medical Center. St. Joseph's Hospital and Medical Center, housing 697 beds, was ranked nationally for its neurology and neurosurgery care in 2013–14 by *U.S. News & World Report*. The Barrow Neurological Institute also serves the Phoenix community with specialized care.

In 2008, Cancer Treatment Centers of America (CTCA) opened its fourth hospital near Phoenix. It was the first CTCA hospital to be located in the West. Numerous other research and hospital facilities were under construction in Phoenix during 2013, including the Arizona Cancer Center, expected to open in 2015.

■ Recreation

Sightseeing

A visitor to the Phoenix metropolitan area will find many sights and attractions, some of them related to frontier history and the natural beauty of Salt River Valley. A principal attraction in Phoenix since 1939 is the Desert Botanical Garden on 65 cultivated acres of Papago Park, containing thousands of desert plants. Also located in Papago Park is the Phoenix Zoo, a privately funded, non-profit zoo, where 1,400 animals are exhibited.

Historic Heritage Square near downtown is a city block of restored Victorian houses preserved as replicas of homes in the late 1800s and converted into museums, shops, and restaurants; a highlight is the elegant Rosson House. In neighboring Scottsdale is Taliesin West, a national historic landmark built as the desert home of architect Frank Lloyd Wright. Scottsdale is also the site of Rawhide, a replica of a 1880s western town that offers a variety of activities, including stagecoach and burro rides, a petting zoo, and stunt shows. Located in nearby Tempe is Big Surf Water Park, sometimes referred to as "Arizona's ocean."

Old West-style entertainment, such as stagecoach rides, covered wagon campfire circles, and simulated gunfighter shoot-outs, is available to groups by reservation through various commercial enterprises in the area. Scenic day trips to the Grand Canyon and other sites near metropolitan Phoenix are provided by several bus and airplane charter services. Encanto Park is the home of the Enchanted Island Amusement Park with a variety of rides geared for the younger set.

Arts and Culture

Phoenix has a vital performing arts community, which was enriched with the 1989 opening of the Herberger Theater Center. Located downtown next to the Phoenix Convention Center and Symphony Hall, the complex is designed to augment existing cultural facilities. The Herberger Theater is used primarily for music, dance, and dramatic performances and includes an art gallery.

The Phoenix Center for the Arts was run by the city until 2011, when restricting threatened its closure. The organization reshuffled to become a privately run non-profit. The center is home to City Jazz and a number of youth and adult classes and outreach activities, as well as performances in its 210-seat theater. Founded in 1920, the Phoenix Theatre is one of the oldest continuously running companies in the country. The Arizona Theatre Company, based in Phoenix, is in residence at the Herberger Theater Center and offers about 25 weeks of performances. Other local troupes include Childsplay, Actors Theatre of Phoenix, and Center Dance Ensemble.

Housed in Symphony Hall, the Phoenix Symphony Orchestra performs an extensive classical repertoire and presents pops concerts with well-known guest artists. Phoenix hosts the state's professional ballet company and other international dance companies. The Arizona Opera also gives regular performances for Phoenix-area audiences. Touring artists perform at the US Airways Center, Celebrity Theatre, Gammage Auditorium on the campus of Arizona State University, and the Ak-Chin Pavilion.

Many museums and art galleries in the Phoenix area offer a range of educational and cultural experiences. The Arizona Hall of Fame Museum, opened in 1902, honors people who have contributed to Arizona heritage. Featuring the history of central Arizona, the Arizona Historical Society Museum includes replications of old-time shops and stores. The family-oriented Shemer Art Center and Museum presents primarily local and state artists. The Arizona Science Center provides interactive exhibits for children and adults in such areas as energy, life science, and health. The Hall of Flame Fire Museum houses the world's most extensive collection of fire-fighting apparatus, equipment, and memorabilia. Anthropological exhibits, fine arts, and historic arts of Native American cultures of the Southwest are specialties at the Heard Museum, which boasts 18,000 works of art and artifacts. The Phoenix Art Museum contains a permanent collection of more than 18,000 pieces focusing on European, American, Western American, Latin American, and Asian arts and costume design.

Festivals and Holidays

Since 2006, the Tostitos Fiesta Bowl has been held at the University of Phoenix Stadium in Glendale, Arizona; it was previously held in Sun Devil Stadium. The contest features two of the nation's top collegiate football teams and is held in early January. Also held in January, since 1948, is the Arizona National Livestock Show.

The Heard Museum Guild Annual Indian Fair and Market takes place in March, featuring Native American culture. Also in March is the St. Patrick's Day Parade and Faire. In May the Cinco de Mayo festival celebrates an 1862 Mexican military victory over the French with various activities throughout the Phoenix area. The Arizona State Fair, billed as one of the most successful in the nation, takes place in October and November. The fair attracts more than one million people annually. The fall also brings the Oktoberfest at Tempe Town Lake. The year ends with the Electric Light Parade, a holiday celebration in downtown Phoenix.

Sports for the Spectator

Phoenix fields teams in all major league sports. The city is home to two professional basketball teams—the Phoenix Suns of the National Basketball Association and the Phoenix Mercury of the Women's National Basketball Association, both of which play their games at US Airways Center. Professional football is represented by the National Football League's Arizona Cardinals and the Arena Football League's Rattlers, while professional hockey is represented by the National Hockey League's Phoenix Coyotes. In 1998 the city's Major League Baseball team, the Arizona Diamondbacks, were formed and began play at Bank One Ball Park, later renamed Chase Field, built especially for the expansion team. In 2001 the Diamondbacks defeated the powerhouse New York Yankees to capture their first World Series.

From March through early April, exhibition baseball games are held nearly every day by the 15 major league baseball teams that hold spring training in Phoenix at as part of the Cactus League. Other popular sporting events are polo matches and greyhound, horse, and auto racing. The Phoenix Greyhound Park features greyhound races year round, and Turf Paradise schedules thoroughbred racing from October through May. The Phoenix International Raceway, built in 1964, boasts one of the world's fastest one-mile oval paved tracks for auto racing.

Annual sporting events in the Phoenix area include professional golf tournaments, such as the Waste Management Phoenix Open, with about 500,000 attendees, and the LPGA Founders Cup at the JW Marriott Phoenix Desert Ridge Resort & Spa.

Sports for the Participant

Phoenix's consistently warm climate permits such year-round outdoor activities as camping, backpacking, hiking, horseback riding, mountain climbing, swimming, boating, fishing, water skiing, skating, tennis, and golf. In metropolitan Phoenix and the surrounding valley area, there are more than 1,100 tennis and racquetball courts, more than 190 championship golf courses—many designed by golfing legends Arnold Palmer and Jack Nicklaus—and many natural and man-made lakes and waterways with facilities for a variety of water sports. Contained within the city limits is South Mountain Park, said to be the largest municipal park in the world, with horseback riding, hiking trails, and a view of the city across its more than 16,000 acres. Several snow-skiing resorts are within traveling distance of the city.

Shopping and Dining

Retail establishments in Phoenix range from large malls and shopping centers—including several downtown—that feature nationally known department stores to small specialty shops offering products made by local artists and craftsmen. Located downtown, the Arizona Center is a uniquely landscaped mall on three acres of land. Close to the center city is Biltmore Fashion Park, a collection of exclusive stores anchored by Macy's and Saks Fifth Avenue. Nearby is Town & Country Shopping Center, considered Arizona's original open-air mall. The Shops at Norterra, a 350,000-square-foot shopping and lifestyle center, opened in 2007 in north Phoenix. It offers a variety of specialty retail stores, restaurants, a movie theatre, and a fitness center. A variety of shops in metropolitan Phoenix specialize in such items as native American arts and crafts, products made from Arizona copper, leather crafts, and Western apparel. Phoenix Premium Outlets in Chandler, Arizona, opened in 2013.

Restaurants in Phoenix have become more sophisticated with the city's growth and prosperity. They offer a variety of cuisines, including traditional American, Italian, Continental, Oriental, and French fare. Specialties are

Southwestern and Mexican dishes with an emphasis on regional foods such as chilies, jicama, local game, and citrus. A popular attraction is Rustler's Rooste Steakhouse, a landmark and one of the busiest dining establishments west of the Mississippi. With a scenic mountaintop view of the surrounding area, the restaurant features a mineshaft entrance and walls decorated with the brands of local cattle ranches. Restaurants such as Different Pointe of View and Vincent's on Camelback have been recognized among "Distinguished Restaurants of North America."

Visitor Information: Greater Phoenix Convention & Visitors Bureau, 400 E. Van Buren St., Ste. 600, Phoenix, AZ 85004; telephone (602) 254-6500 or (877) 225-5749; email visitors@visitphoenix.com.

■ Convention Facilities

Phoenix is a popular gathering place for large and small groups that wish to conduct business in a pleasurable environment. Known for its resorts, Phoenix offers more than 200 hotel properties and additional resort space, a year-round warm climate, and a variety of leisure activities. These factors have contributed to an increase in group business in metropolitan Phoenix since 1980.

The Phoenix Convention Center, formerly the Phoenix Civic Plaza and Convention Center, has nearly 900,000 square feet of meeting and exhibit space providing a total seating capacity for more than 29,000 people. It has been the city's primary convention facility since 1972 and underwent a $600 million expansion in 2007 that increased the space by 600,000 square feet. Completed in three phases, the final phase of the project opened in 2009. The convention center hosts more than one million visitors annually for trade shows, conventions, meetings, and other events. Meeting space is also available at the Arizona Exposition and State Fair grounds, Arizona State University, and area hotels.

Convention Information: Phoenix Convention Center, 100 North Third St., Phoenix, AZ 85004; telephone (602) 262-6225; (800) 282-4842.

■ Transportation

Approaching the City

Located near downtown, Phoenix Sky Harbor International Airport is serviced by 17 airlines with direct flights from most cities in the United States and several locations abroad. More than 100,000 passengers are served on a daily basis, comparable to airports in Miami and San Francisco. Its importance to the area is highlighted by an estimated $79 million daily economic impact.

Interstate routes into the city are Interstate 10 (the Papago Freeway), entering from the west, and Interstate

17 (the Black Canyon Freeway), entering from the north. These highways join at Van Buren Street and 27th Avenue, becoming the Maricopa Freeway and then forming the Pima Freeway southeast of the city. State Route 89 (Grand Avenue Expressway) enters diagonally from the northwest, joins State Route 60 at Van Buren Street downtown, then intersects the city laterally to the east, becoming the Superstition Freeway. A 20-year "Regional Transportation Plan" was passed by voters in November 2004 to alleviate excessive traffic congestion by building new or renovating existing freeways; since that time, the METRO Light Rail system has been created to effectively transport commuters.

Traveling in the City

Travel in the city is facilitated by the simple grid layout. The Valley Metro Transit System provides daily bus service in the metropolitan area. The METRO Light Rail, part of Valley Metro Transit System, began providing rail service to residents in 2008.

■ Communications

Newspapers and Magazines

Phoenix's major daily newspaper is the morning daily *The Arizona Republic*. Among the many other daily and weekly periodicals published in Phoenix are the *Arizona Business Gazette, Arizona Informant, Jewish News of Greater Phoenix*, and *Phoenix New Times*, which features arts, entertainment, and restaurants. Magazines published in Phoenix include *Phoenix Magazine, Phoenix Home & Garden, Desert Living Today, Arizona Foothills Magazine*, and *Arizona Highways*.

Television and Radio

Phoenix is served by 24 television stations, including affiliate stations of major networks and public broadcasting. Cable and satellite television service is readily available. Eleven AM and 14 FM radio stations, including Hispanic-language radio, are broadcast in Phoenix, with additional stations broadcast nearby accessible to Phoenix-area listeners.

Media Information: The Arizona Republic, 200 E. Van Buren St., Phoenix, AZ 85004; telephone (602) 444-8000; toll-free (800) 331-9303.

Phoenix Online

The Arizona Republic. Available www.azcentral. com/arizonarepublic

Arizona School Report Cards. Available http:// www10.ade.az.gov/reportcard

City of Phoenix Home Page. Available phoenix.gov

Greater Phoenix Convention & Visitors Bureau. Available www.visitphoenix.com

Greater Phoenix Economic Council. Available www. gpec.org

Phoenix Public Library. Available www. phoenixpubliclibrary.org

BIBLIOGRAPHY

Bartlett, Michael H., and Thomas M. Kolaz, *Archaeology in the City: A Hohokam Village in Phoenix, Arizona* (Tucson, AZ: University of Arizona Press, 1986)

DeBarbieri, Lili, *Location Filming in Arizona: The Screen Legacy of the Grand Canyon State* (Charleston, SC: The History Press, 2014)

Booth-Clibborn, Edward, ed., *PHX: Phoenix 21st Century City* (London: Booth Clibborn Editions, 2006)

Hait, Pam, *Shifra Stein's Day Trips from Phoenix, Tucson, and Flagstaff* (Guilford, CT: GPP Travel, 2009)

Scottsdale

■ The City in Brief

Founded: 1888 (incorporated, 1951)

Head Official: Mayor W. J. "Jim" Lane (R) (since 2009; current term expires 2016)

City Population

1990: 130,099
2000: 202,705
2010: 217,385
2012 estimate: 223,517
Percent change, 2000–2010: 7.2%
U.S. rank in 1990: 139th
U.S. rank in 2000: 99th (State rank: 5th)
U.S. rank in 2010: 92nd (State rank: 6th)

Metropolitan Statistical Area Population

2000: 3,251,876
2010: 4,192,887
2012 estimate: 4,329,534
Percent change, 2000–2010: 28.9%
U.S. rank in 2000: 14th
U.S. rank in 2010: 14th

Area: 184.5 square miles

Elevation: 1,250 feet above sea level

Average Annual Temperatures: 70.3° F

Average Annual Precipitation: 7.05 inches

Major Economic Sectors: services; trade; finance, insurance and real estate; manufacturing

Unemployment Rate: 3.9% (2012)

Per Capita Income: $50,419

2012 FBI Crime Index Property: 6,047

Major Colleges and Universities: Scottsdale Community College

Daily Newspaper: *The Arizona Republic*

■ Introduction

Scottsdale is a popular winter vacation destination that is known for its consistently sunny climate. The city began as a small farming community of merely 2,000 residents in 1981; since then, it has evolved into a vibrant city with more than 220,000 people living in its nearly 200 square miles. The area boasts golf courses, resorts, restaurants, and nightclubs, all situated among looming palm trees. However, reminders of the west in the form of ranches, ruins, and the occasional rodeo are also nearby. Besides the tourism industry, Scottsdale has also found strength as a technology center, and has begun to garner a reputation for being a leader in health care and research. A branch of the Mayo Clinic is located in Scottsdale, as well as SkySong, an innovative office, research, and retail space project. Scottsdale also offers a variety of activities that can be done in the sun, such as hiking, biking, and horseback riding. Scottsdale's cultural assets are anchored by the national reputation of its more than 100 art galleries.

■ Geography and Climate

Scottsdale is located in central Arizona, just northeast of Phoenix. With an area of more than 184 square miles, the distance between the most extreme northern and southern points in Scottsdale is about 30 miles; the distance between the farthest east and west points is more than 10 miles. Scottsdale enjoys more sunshine than any other area in the United States. Low humidity year-round makes even high temperatures comfortable. Most of the yearly rainfall occurs July through September and December through March.

Area: 184.5 square miles

Elevation: 1,250 feet above sea level

Average Temperatures: 70.3° F

Photo courtesy of City of Scottsdale Downtown Group.

Average Annual Precipitation: 7.05 inches

■ History

Irrigation Leads to Thriving Agriculture Industry

Prior to its founding, the Scottsdale area was made up of barren desert lands, distinguished only by the intricate canals of the Hohokam Indians.

Scottsdale was founded in 1888 by U.S. Army Chaplain Winfield Scott, a Baptist minister from New York. That same year the construction of the Arizona Canal, which provided irrigation to a wide geographic area, was completed by Frank Murphy. Winfield Scott and his brother, George Washington Scott, who shared a dream of developing a thriving town in the desert, first grew citrus and other fruits, peanuts, and sweet potatoes on their land.

Air Quality Attracts Settlers, Manufacturers, Artists

Early settlers included people searching for better health and others who were attracted by the fresh desert air.

History shows that many of these people were culturally-minded and nurtured the arts from the beginning. The city was first called Orangedale because of the orange orchards along Camelback Mountain, but the name was changed to Scottsdale in 1894 in honor of its founder.

From 1894 through the 1940s Paradise Valley ranchers drove their cattle through the city each spring and fall on their way to the stockyards or the train depot at Tempe, where the cattle were shipped to market.

Modern development began after World War II when Motorola opened a plant in Scottsdale, the first of many electronics manufacturing plants to locate in the area. Artists and crafts persons also became attracted to the city, and the population grew from 2,000 people in 1950 to 10,000 people by 1960. By 1965 the city had grown to 55,000 residents. The city was incorporated in 1951 and received its city charter in 1961.

Through the 1960s the city preserved an Old West look of wood buildings and quaintly lettered signs, calling itself "the West's most Western town." As the "Old West" theme became less prominent, the city began billing itself as the "Arts Capital of the Southwest." Galleries shared the avenues with western-wear stores, and the magnificent Scottsdale Center for the Arts was built, permitting year-round exhibits and concerts for residents and visitors.

Scottsdale's area was greatly increased by the annexation of territory north of the city in the 1980s. A great part of this area is made up of uninhabited desert and hilly land, much of which is maintained in its natural state. Into the twenty-first century, Scottsdale has spent millions on the renovation of the downtown area with new landscaping, entrances, signage and public art, making it a most appealing desert oasis for tourists. Complementing the city's vibrant tourist industry is the growth of high-technology and research facilities, best exemplified by SkySong, a partnership between the city and Arizona State University.

Historical Information: Scottsdale Historical Museum, 7333 E. Scottsdale Mall, Scottsdale, AZ 85251; telephone (480) 945-4499; email info@scottsdalemuseum.com.

■ Population Profile

Metropolitan Statistical Area Population

2000: 3,251,876
2010: 4,192,887
2012 estimate: 4,329,534
Percent change, 2000–2010: 28.9%
U.S. rank in 2000: 14th
U.S. rank in 2010: 14th

City Residents

1990: 130,099
2000: 202,705
2010: 217,385
2012 estimate: 223,517
Percent change, 2000–2010: 7.2%
U.S. rank in 1990: 139th
U.S. rank in 2000: 99th (State rank: 5th)
U.S. rank in 2010: 92nd (State rank: 6th)

Density: 1,182.0 people per square mile

Racial and ethnic characteristics

White: 201,917
Black or African American: 5,342
American Indian and Alaskan Native: 1,320
Asian: 9,901
Native Hawaiian and Other Pacific Islander: 399
Hispanic or Latino (may be of any race): 20,488
Other: 4,638

Percent of residents born in state: 24.3%

Age characteristics

Population under 5 years old: 8,295
Population 5 to 9 years old: 9,723
Population 10 to 14 years old: 11,956
Population 15 to 19 years old: 13,034
Population 20 to 24 years old: 12,501
Population 25 to 34 years old: 29,261
Population 35 to 44 years old: 28,975
Population 45 to 54 years old: 33,913
Population 55 to 59 years old: 15,833
Population 60 to 64 years old: 14,226
Population 65 to 74 years old: 27,369
Population 75 to 84 years old: 12,664
Population 85 years and over: 5,767
Median age: 44.4

Births (2010–11 Metropolitan Area)
Total number: 59,738

Deaths (2010–11 Metropolitan Area)
Total number: 26,891

Money income (2012)
Per capita income: $50,419
Median household income: $69,876
Total households: 99,734

Number of households with income of . . .
less than $10,000: 4,974
$10,000 to $14,999: 3,004
$15,000 to $24,999: 9,283
$25,000 to $34,999: 8,058
$35,000 to $49,999: 11,909
$50,000 to $74,999: 15,889
$75,000 to $99,999: 11,943
$100,000 to $149,999: 14,824
$150,000 to $199,999: 8,142
$200,000 or more: 11,708

Percent of families below poverty level: 8.8%

FBI Crime Index Property: 6,047

FBI Crime Index Violent: 329

■ Municipal Government

Scottsdale's government consists of a mayor and six city council members elected at large who serve staggered four-year terms. The council appoints a city manager, city clerk, city treasurer, city attorney, and city judge.

Head Official: Mayor W. J. "Jim" Lane (R) (since 2009; current term expires 2016)

Total Number of City Employees: 2,465 (2013)

City Information: City of Scottsdale, 3939 N. Drinkwater Blvd., Scottsdale, AZ 85251; telephone (480) 312-3111; fax (480) 312-2888.

■ Economy

Major Industries and Commercial Activity

Hospitality is Scottsdale's major industry and largest employer. In addition to tourism facilities located within Scottsdale, the city hosts regional or corporate headquarters of many companies involved in the industry, including Barrett-Jackson Auction Company, Troon Golf, AirSprint, International Cruise & Excursion, Inc., and Starwood Hotels and Resorts Worldwide, Inc., among others.

The city is also home to numerous high-technology firms such as a JDA Software Group, which has headquarters in Scottsdale. It is also the site of Microsoft's first retail store. Data storage facilities have located to Scottsdale in part because of the area's low risk of natural disasters. SkySong is a technology incubator launched by a partnership between the city and Arizona State University. Like several surrounding cities, Scottsdale is also home to a number of solar power firms. The Bioscience industry is represented by Scottsdale's "Cure Corridor" on Shea Boulevard, which supports several premier cancer research and treatment facilities.

Aviation is one of the fastest growing sectors of the Arizona economy. The Scottsdale Airport/Airpark was begun in the 1960s as a fully planned facility specifically designed to meet the needs of employers with air transportation requirements. By the 2000s, the Airport/Airpark had become one of Scottsdale's top employment centers, with some 52,000 employees and 2,800 businesses by 2013. Aerospace and defense companies in Scottsdale included Dillon Precision, Fire-Trace, General Dynamics C4 Systems, Guardian 8, G&H Aerospace, and Taser.

Items and goods produced: electronics, radiology solutions, military equipment

Incentive Programs—New and Existing Companies

Local programs: Scottsdale rarely offers financial assistance but considers requests from new or existing companies on a case-by-case basis. The city does invest in public infrastructure improvements to support area businesses. Review of proposed business projects are delegated to a project manager and team to expedite the review and permitting process. The Scottsdale Area Chamber of Commerce partners with various organizations to connect businesses with resources, and offers events throughout the year.

State programs: State incentives are offered through the Arizona Commerce Authority, which organizes its programs through an "Incentive Tool Box." Among the cash assistance or loan programs are the Arizona Competes Fund, which provides cash assistance to attract

business with stable, high-wage jobs; Arizona FAST Grant, offering up to $7,500 for technology commercialization; Arizona Innovation Accelerator Fund Program, with loans from $50,000 to $2 million for business expansion or job creation; Arizona Innovation Challenge, another cash assistance program providing up to $250,000 to technology ventures; and Arizona STEP grant targeting international export opportunities with cash assistance up to $10,000. Private Activity Bonds and Qualified Energy Conservation Bonds give companies access to low-interest financing.

Tax incentives provided include the Commercial and Industrial Solar Energy Program, offering a tax credit of up to 10 percent of the installed cost of solar energy devices; Healthy Forest Tax Incentives, which supplies several tax incentives to forestry and forest-product companies related to equipment purchases, transportation, and training; Military Reuse Zone tax credits that reduce property taxes by up to 75 percent for five years and also offer $10,000 in tax credits per new employee hired; Quality Jobs Program with $9,000 tax credits for new hires that meet certain criteria; Qualified Facilities Tax Credit that refunds up to 10 percent or $20,000 of a company's investment in new job creation; Renewable Energy Tax Incentives and Research and Development Program tax credits; and a Small Business Capital Investment Tax Credit amounting to as much as 35 percent of investment over a three-year period.

Job training programs: The state of Arizona offers matching funds of up to 75 percent to businesses for the training of workers for new jobs in the state. This cash assistance may total as much as $1.5 million per business. Training of incumbent workers is still eligible for cash assistance covering up to 50 percent of training expenses. The State of Arizona also operates the Arizona Job Training Program to tailor training plans to the evolving industry landscape. The Arizona Apprenticeship System maintains more than 100 registered apprenticeship opportunities that pair education with on-the-job training.

Scottsdale Community College offers training classes for local businesses ranging from nursing to the hospitality industry, to computer operations and other skills.

Development Projects

Groundbreaking began in 2000 on the $250 million Scottsdale Waterfront development, a retail, dining, entertainment, office, and residential complex planned on 12 acres southwest of Scottsdale and Camelback roads on the north side of the Arizona Canal. The development is also home to the Fiesta Bowl headquarters and museum. Phase One of the project (retail, office, and restaurants) was completed and opened in 2005; approval of the final phase occurred in 2012 and was expected to add 259 apartments and 10,000 square feet of retail and restaurant space.

In 2004, the City of Scottsdale, Arizona State University, and the ASU Foundation entered into a partnership to develop the ASU Scottsdale Center for New Technology and Innovation on 42 acres of land that was the former site of the Los Arcos Mall. The city agreed to purchase the site, called "SkySong," from the ASU Foundation for $41.5 million with the provision that the site would be available to the ASU Foundation to develop the ASU Scottsdale Center. The Center is designed to focus on technology commercialization, entrepreneurship, and business development SkySong, which was expanding existing facilities in 2013.

Scottsdale Quarter, a $270 million shopping and entertainment district, opened its first phase in 2009. William-Sonoma Home and West Elm stores were the first to open and were followed by other major retailers and a movie theater. More stores, restaurants, and nightclubs followed in the later phases, with work on a third phase that included 275 apartments beginning in 2013 with a target completion date of 2015.

City projects were led by development of Scottsdale's Museum of the West, a $13.6 million museum with 40,000 square feet of space to feature six art galleries, retail space, a theater, and a central courtyard. The museum was expected to earn a gold LEED certification for its environmentally responsible design and was scheduled to open as early as 2014. A $42.8 million expansion of the Tony Nelsen Equidome at WestWorld completed in late 2013 and allowed the facility to host events year-round with 40,000 additional square feet of space.

Economic Development Information: Scottsdale Area Chamber of Commerce, 7501 E. McCormick Parkway, Suite 202-N, Scottsdale, AZ 85258; telephone (480) 355-2700; fax (480) 355-2710; email info@scottsdalechamber.com.

Commercial Shipping

Air freight is handled at Phoenix Sky Harbor International Airport, a 20-minute drive from downtown Scottsdale. Arizona is crisscrossed by five U.S. interstate highways and by a growing system of state roadways. The interstates permit rapid motor freight delivery because of their by-pass features, no slowdown in the metro areas, and no toll roads or toll bridges. Numerous general interstate and transcontinental truck lines serve the city and state. Although there are no railroads in Scottsdale's city limits, several railways serve the surrounding suburbs. Arizona's proximity to California—but substantially lower costs of doing business—has made the state attractive to distribution companies.

Labor Force and Employment Outlook

Scottsdale's labor force offers a complex blend of skills, abilities, and experience levels. The city's unemployment rate is consistently below that of the metropolitan area. More broadly, the Phoenix metropolitan area has been recognized nationally for its young, growing, and well-educated workforce.

The following is a summary of data regarding the 2012 Scottsdale labor force:

Size of civilian labor force: 118,951

Number of workers employed in . . .

agriculture and mining: 366
construction: 3,689
manufacturing: 7,003
wholesale trade: 4,388
retail trade: 12,024
transportation: 3,784
information systems: 2,822
finance: 15,744
professional administration: 16,699
education and social services: 24,295
arts and leisure: 12,848
other: 3,449
public administration: 3,253

Average hourly earnings of production workers: $16.03

Unemployment rate: 3.9% (2012)

Employers

Largest private employers (2013)	*Number of employees*
Scottsdale Healthcare Corporation	6,600
General Dynamics C4 Systems	2,764
City of Scottsdale	2,465
CVS–CareMark	2,400
Vanguard Insurance	2,186
Mayo Clinic	1,972
Scottsdale Unified School District	1,828
Scottsdale Insurance Company	1,525
Veri Fone Inc.	1,431
International Cruise and Excursion	1,130

Cost of Living

The cost of living in the Phoenix metropolitan area, of which Scottsdale is a part, is about equal to the national average. It is below that of Las Vegas or Denver, and almost all of California.

The following is a summary of data regarding several key cost of living factors in the area.

2013 ACCRA Average House Price: $297,175

2013 ACCRA Cost of Living Index: 96

State income tax rate: 2.59% to 4.54%

State sales tax rate: 5.6%

Local income tax rate: None

Local sales tax rate: 2.35%

Property tax rate: 5.7433 to 8.9142 mills (2013)

Economic Information: Scottsdale Area Chamber of Commerce, 7501 E. McCormick Parkway, Suite 202-N, Scottsdale, AZ 85258; telephone (480) 355-2700; fax (480) 355-2710; email info@scottsdalechamber.com.

■ Education and Research

Elementary and Secondary Schools

The Scottsdale Unified School District (SUSD) consistently receives outstanding support from city voters. For the 2012–13 school year, the district received an "A" rating from the state, with 15 schools receiving the top "A" rating and another 10 graded as "B." In a scale that goes down to "F," no SUSD school received below a "C."

The district offers special education services for handicapped children, including programs for those that are moderately and severely handicapped, which are strategically located throughout the district. An English-as-a-Second Language program is available to help children who are limited in their ability to speak English. Elementary and middle school students with high academic ability are tested for participation in the district's gifted program. Desert Mountain High School offers the International Baccalaureate (IB) program to qualified students. The accelerated courses across all content areas allow students to complete pre-university work for college credit. Scottsdale Online Learning offers an Internet-based high school program to students.

BASIS Scottsdale, a charter school, has been ranked nationally by *Newsweek* and the *Washington Post*. The Scottsdale/Paradise Valley area also has a number of private academies, college prep, charter day, and child-care schools.

The following is a summary of data regarding the Scottsdale Unified School District.

Total enrollment: 26,235

Number of facilities
    total: 31
    elementary schools: 16
    junior high schools: 9
    high schools: 5
    other: 1

Student/teacher ratio: 18.51:1

Teacher salaries
    average (statewide): $47,553

Funding per pupil: $8,038

Public Schools Information: Scottsdale Unified School District, 3811 North 44th Street, Phoenix, AZ 85018; telephone (480) 484-6100; fax (480) 484-6287.

Colleges and Universities

Scottsdale Community College is part of the Maricopa Community College system, one of the largest such systems in the country. It offers an extensive selection of educational programs including associate's degrees and technical degrees. The college provides training classes for local businesses, continuing education courses, and community service programs. Also located in or near Scottsdale are Phoenix Seminary, Le Cordon Bleu College of Culinary Arts, Scottsdale Artists' School, and Taliesin, the Frank Lloyd Wright School of Architecture.

Students in Scottsdale also have access to several major institutions nearby, most notably Arizona State University, with some 73,000 students in adjacent Tempe, and the University of Phoenix.

Libraries and Research Centers

The Scottsdale Public Library System, established in 1960, includes one main library and four branch libraries. The libraries within the system are the Civic Center Library, Mustang Library, Palomino Library, Arabian Library, and Appaloosa Library. Two of the branches are relatively recent expansions: The Arabian Library was completed in 2007, and the Appaloosa Library opened in 2009.

At the Samuel C. Johnson Medical Research Building on the grounds of Mayo Clinic Scottsdale, scientists study molecular genetics, molecular immunology and chemistry, and molecular and cell biology. The Mayo Clinic Collaborative Research Building, a 110,000-square-foot biomedical research facility, was completed in 2005.

Public Library Information: Civic Center Library (Main Library), 3839 N. Drinkwater Blvd., Scottsdale, AZ 85251-4452; telephone (480) 312-7323.

■ Health Care

Scottsdale offers the services of more than 1,000 doctors and has a full range of medical services available. The largest health-care providers are Scottsdale Healthcare and Mayo Clinic Scottsdale. Since its inception in 1962 as the City Hospital of Scottsdale, Scottsdale Healthcare has grown to include three hospitals, and outpatient centers. Scottsdale Healthcare offers one of the busiest Level 1 trauma centers in the state, as well as outpatient surgery, cardiology and oncology services, a diabetes center, and weight reduction surgery.

Mayo Clinic Scottsdale, with 240 beds, offers outpatient surgery, laboratory and diagnostic testing, imaging, and pharmacy services. The Mayo Clinic

Hospital in nearby Phoenix provides inpatient care as well as emergency rooms and urgent care services.

■ Recreation

Sightseeing

Scottsdale celebrates the life of the West through a variety of attractions. Old Town Scottsdale hearkens back to pioneer days with its wooden sidewalks, blacksmith shop, mission, church, and the 1909 Little Red School House, which used to be home to the Scottsdale Historical Society Museum. Rawhide Wild West Town is the state's largest western theme attraction, with a replica of a frontier town, stagecoach and burro rides, gunfights, petting ranch, museum, gold panning, and country music and food. Rawhide closed at the Scottsdale location in 2005 and reopened 35 miles from North Scottsdale in Chandler. WestWorld of Scottsdale is an equestrian center and special events facility that the city paid more than $40 million to expand in 2013, allowing it to host events year-round. Many local companies offer trips via jeep, covered wagon, helicopter, and air balloon to the mountains, desert, and canyons surrounding Scottsdale. Day trips can be arranged to the Kinishba Ruins, and Tuzigoot National Monument or Canyon de Chelly, which are prehistoric pueblo villages. In Verde Valley, the 20-room Montezuma Castle National Monument is a twelfth-century cliff dwelling carved into solid rock by the Sinagua Indians.

Arts and Culture

Scottsdale is a nationally recognized art mecca with more than 100 art galleries, the Scottsdale Center for the Performing Arts, the Scottsdale Artists' School, and a variety of public artworks, primarily downtown. Scottsdale has an "ArtWalk" every Thursday night that offers an opportunity to meet artists and observe their work. Cosanti, an Arizona Historic Site, is a unique complex of concrete structures designed and constructed by Paolo Soleri. Tours of where Soleri Windbells are made and sold are offered. Frank Lloyd Wright's Taliesin West is an architectural masterpiece and Wright's former home and studio. The Scottsdale Museum of Contemporary Art, located in the city's Old Town district, houses modern and contemporary works from around the world. The House of Broadcasting, Inc., celebrates Arizona's radio and television history.

Other museums of interest in Scottsdale include the Heard Museum North, focusing on Native American artists, and the Fiesta Bowl museum, which traces the history of the college football game since 1971.

Scottsdale's showcase for the performing arts is the Scottsdale Center for the Performing Arts, where symphonies and Broadway plays are performed. Scottsdale Desert Stages Theatre presents children's, main stage, and professional productions. Theatre 4301 presents live theatre in an intimate setting.

Festivals and Holidays

Scottsdale's annual Barrett-Jackson Collector Car Event in January is one of the largest in the world. In February and March, the Parada del Sol includes a rodeo and ends with the world's largest "horse-drawn parade." Also in February, the Scottsdale Arabian Horse Show—one of the world's largest all-Arabian horse shows—attracts Arabian horse breeders and buyers from around the world.

The Festival of the West, a four-day celebration of cowboy life each March, features western film and television stars, western antiques, western art and music, cowboy poetry, and other events. While held in 2013, the event's future remained uncertain. Also in March, the Scottsdale Arts Festival showcases the work of nearly 200 nationally acclaimed artists.

The Scottsdale Culinary Festival in April showcases local and nationally known chefs. Scottsdale celebrates the holiday season with the Tree Lighting and Concert at the Scottsdale Mall in December, and with displays featuring holiday lights at McCormick-Stillman Railroad Park.

Sports for the Spectator

Although Scottsdale fields no major league sports teams, sports fans have easy access to events in Phoenix. Scottsdale is the spring training home of the San Francisco Giants of Major League Baseball. Scottsdale Stadium is also one of the playing sites for the Arizona Fall League, where the stars of the future, including those on the Scottsdale Scorpions, vie for a shot at the big leagues. Salt River Fields at Talking Stick, which opened in 2011, is the spring training complex for the Arizona Diamondbacks and Colorado Rockies.

Professional golf has an enthusiastic following in Scottsdale. TPC Scottsdale hosts the Waste Management Phoenix Open in January. Boys & Girls Clubs of Greater Scottsdale Celebrity Invitational is held each February, with all proceeds benefiting the local Boys & Girls Clubs.

Sports for the Participant

Scottsdale has more than 500 acres of developed park land, more than 35 acres of lakes, some 40 miles of bike trails, and about 200 miles of non-paved multi-use recreational trails. Many of Scottsdale's 41 parks are located within the Indian Bend Wash Greenbelt, a 7.5-mile-long flood control project that uses a system of parks, lakes, and golf courses as an alternative to a conventional concrete channel. Pools and recreation centers also meet the needs of Scottsdale residents year-round. Residents may participate in youth and adult sports and recreation programs.

There are nearly 200 golf courses in the Scottsdale area, including more than 25 public golf courses. The course for P.F. Chang's Rock 'n' Roll Marathon runs through Scottsdale and nearby cities, beginning in downtown Phoenix and ending in Tempe. Held in January, the marathon attracts thousands of distance runners due to its flat, fast course and live musical entertainment. Tennis, horseback riding, swimming, rollerblading, and fishing are among the other year-round recreational opportunities available in Scottsdale.

Shopping and Dining

Scottsdale has more than 2,500 retail shops with everything from hand-stitched leather boots to designer fashions. Upscale shopping centers such as Scottsdale Fashion Square and Biltmore Fashion Park (in Phoenix) feature retailers such as Burberry, Gucci, Louis Vuitton, and Tiffany & Company. The Microsoft store is also located at Scottsdale Fashion Square. Old Town Merchants Association, with more than 150 shops and restaurants, captures the flair of the Old West with traditional and southwestern merchandise. Scottsdale Pavilions is a shopping center that offers mass retailers such as Target, Home Depot, and Toys R Us. El Pedregal at the Boulders has courtyard amphitheater facilities surrounded by boutiques, galleries and restaurants. Native American arts and crafts are available at Chief Dodge Indian Jewelry & Fine Arts, and other stores in the area. Scottsdale Quarter, with some phases of construction still ongoing in 2013, includes an array of upscale shopping options.

Scottsdale has an excellent selection of first-class dining establishments among its more than 500 restaurants. Ethnic offerings include Southwestern specialties, Italian, French, Japanese, Chinese, Polynesian, Greek, Thai, Indian, and Continental cuisine. Mesquite grills abound, and Western fare served in cookout or ranch settings is popular.

Visitor Information: Scottsdale Convention and Visitors Bureau, 4343 N. Scottsdale Rd., Ste 170, Scottsdale, AZ 85251; telephone (800) 782-1117; email visitorcenter@scottsdalecvb.com.

■ Convention Facilities

El Zaribah Shrine Auditorium is a multiuse facility with a 12,000-square-foot ballroom, break-out rooms, and a stage that can be used for banquets, seminars, and trade shows. Many hotels and resorts provide meeting space within the city. The Phoenician Resort's Camelback Ballroom Complex has 99,000 square feet of meeting space. Among others resorts are the Hyatt Regency Scottsdale Resort and Spa at Gainey Ranch, offering 70,000 square feet of indoor and outdoor space; JW Marriott Scottsdale Camelback Inn Resort; and the

Scottsdale Marriott at McDowell Mountains. The Hilton Scottsdale Resort & Villas offers versatile meeting and conference space. WestWorld is one of the most sought-after equestrian show facilities in the country.

Convention Information: Scottsdale Convention and Visitors Bureau, 4343 N. Scottsdale Rd., Ste 170, Scottsdale, AZ 85251; telephone (800) 782-1117; email visitorcenter@scottsdalecvb.com.

■ Transportation

Approaching the City

Phoenix Sky Harbor International Airport, located about 15 miles west of downtown Scottsdale, is served by 17 airlines with direct flights from most cities in the United States and several locations abroad. Scottsdale is served by Greyhound Bus Lines and Valley Metro—the regional public transportation authority responsible for public transit in Phoenix and Maricopa County. Interstates 10 and 17, U.S. highways 60 and 89, and Arizona Highway 87 are near the city.

Traveling in the City

Scottsdale Road is the major north–south thoroughfare through the city. Scottsdale Trolley operates a free downtown shuttle and neighborhood trolley for tourists and shoppers. Valley Metro operates public transit bus routes throughout Paradise Valley and also operates paratransit service through "Dial-a-Ride" for disabled commuters.

■ Communications

Newspapers and Magazines

The *Scottsdale Tribune* was the city's daily newspaper until it ceased operations in 2009; the newspaper continued to be published for nearby cities under the name *East Valley Tribune*. *The Arizona Republic*, published from Phoenix, covers Scottsdale news. The *Scottsdale Airpark News* is published in Scottsdale. Magazines published locally are *American Indian Art Magazine* and *Frank Lloyd Wright Quarterly*.

Television and Radio

Although Scottsdale does not have any television stations within its borders, stations do broadcast in Paradise Valley, and cable service is available. Scottsdale is home to one AM station and three FM stations, with many more stations accessible to Scottsdale listeners but broadcast from surrounding cities.

Media Information: *The Arizona Republic,* 200 E. Van Buren St., Phoenix, AZ 85004; telephone (602) 444-8000; toll-free (800) 331-9303.

Scottsdale Online

Arizona School Report Cards. Available www10.ade. az.gov/reportcard

Choose Scottsdale. Available www.choosescottsdale. com

City of Scottsdale Home Page. Available www. scottsdaleaz.gov

Scottsdale Area Chamber of Commerce. Available www.scottsdalechamber.com

Scottsdale Convention and Visitors Bureau. Available www.experiencescottsdale.com

Scottsdale Public Library. Available library. scottsdaleaz.gov

BIBLIOGRAPHY

Pfeiffer, Bruce Brooks, *Under Arizona Skies: The Apprentice Desert Shelters at Frank Lloyd Wright's Taliesin West* (San Francisco: Pomegranate, 2011)

Samson, Karl, *Frommer's Arizona and the Grand Canyon 2011* (Hoboken, NJ: Wiley, 2011)

Sedona

◼ The City in Brief

Founded: 1902 (incorporated, 1987)

Head Official: Mayor Rob Adams (since 2008; current term expires 2014)

City Population
 1990: 7,720
 2000: 10,192
 2010: 10,031
 2012 estimate: 10,037
 Percent change, 2000–2010: −1.6%

County Population
 2000: 167,517
 2010: 205,098
 2012 estimate: 211,280
 Percent change, 2000–2010: 22.4%

Area: 19 square miles

Elevation: 4,350 feet above sea level

Average Annual Temperatures: Not available

Average Annual Precipitation: Not available

Major Economic Sectors: tourism, film, and television

Unemployment Rate: 3.3% (2012)

Per Capita Income: $53,842

2012 FBI Crime Index Property: 219

Major Colleges and Universities: University of Sedona, Yavapai College's Sedona Center for Arts & Technology

Daily Newspaper: *Sedona Red Rock News*

◼ Introduction

In the northern Verde Valley region of Arizona, 30 miles southwest of Flagstaff, lies a small city packing a big punch. There, visitors will find Sedona, Arizona, known for its stunning red sandstone formations, the Red Rocks of Sedona. Named after the city's first postmaster, celebrated for her hospitality, it is fitting that the picturesque Sedona is now one of Arizona's top tourist destinations, the city's core industry and economic generator. Incorporated in 1988, Sedona is a young city of nearly 12,000 year-round residents—and 3.5 million annual tourists. While it is a newer city, Sedona has a rich history in the Oak Creek Canyon. *USA Today* has previously ranked Red Rock Country the most beautiful places in America, and *U.S. News and World Report* has listed Sedona as one of the best places to retire. From a rural, ranching society, the city has risen to become a premier tourism, recreation, resort, retirement, and art center.

◼ Geography and Climate

Sedona is a 19-mile square city located in the Upper Sonoran Desert of northern Arizona. The city is approximately an average of 4,300 feet above sea level (though red rock formations in the region soar to more than one mile in elevation). The highest point is about 5,600 feet at Coffee Pot Rock, and the lowest point is about 4,000 feet at Oak Creek. Only 51 percent of the city's land is privately owned; the rest is part of the Coconino National Forest. The city straddles the county line between Coconino and Yavapai counties in the Verde Valley region of Arizona. Sedona is known for its geographic beauty, located at the mouth of the Oak Creek Canyon and characterized by large red rock formations distinct to the region. The red rocks provide a red-orange sandstone that appear to glow when illuminated by the rising and setting sun. The various

Nick Martucci/Shutterstock.com

monoliths surrounding the city are named Coffeepot, Cathedral, and Thunder mountains.

While Sedona is located in a temperate high desert climate, the city is marked by four distinct, but mild, seasons abundant in sunshine and clean air. The annual average temperature is topped around 75 degrees Fahrenheit and bottoms around 46 degrees, a comfortable range. Annual precipitation is about 20 inches.

While beautiful, the geographic conditions could also be a danger, as it was in 2006, when a wildfire one mile north of the city caused major damage on the Brins Mesa at a cost of $6.4 million, destroying over 4,000 acres of land.

Area: 19 square miles

Elevation: 4,350 feet above sea level

Average Temperatures: Not available

Average Annual Precipitation: Not available

■ History

Prehistoric Red Rock Country

Archaeologists continue to debate how long this region had been inhabited. Millions of years ago, the area now

known as Sedona, the Red Rock Country, was covered with sea. As the waters receded, the natural formations unique to the region were created, sculpted by wind and erosion, creating large, crimson colored mesas. Though the history is muddy, historians and researchers somewhat disagree on the timeline of Sedona's ancient dwellers. Artifacts, prehistoric dwellings, and other archaeological evidence indicate that various civilizations inhabited the area beginning in about 8,000 B.C.; those civilizations have become known as Paleo Indians.

Evidence suggested the Anasazi Indians and the Hohokam inhabited the area from 500 A.D. to 700 A.D. It is unknown why the Anasazi left the area. The Hohokam began irrigation farming in the region, indicated by ancient canals viewable in the rocks. The Sinaqua Tribe, also known as Sinagua, then moved into the area, but scientists believe a large volcanic eruption around 1060 A.D., which created the Sunset Crater, forced the Sinaquans to flee. During these traders' reign, there were reportedly up to 5,000 residents in the area.

Colonialists Search for Resources

Hunters and gatherers roamed the area looking for sustenance in the red rock canyons, but most left; archaeologists have speculated that people left due to invasions, resource depletions, and drought, though the evidence is not telling. Various native American tribes inhabited the region before the late 1500s, when a quest or gold and silver invited Spanish explorers to the Sedona area in 1583. The area was in the hands of Spain until Mexico gained its independence in 1821; the region would transfer to the United States in 1848 when Arizona became a U.S. territory. While the Spanish did find copper, when gold and silver were not discovered, the Spanish left the region as well, leaving behind a variety of colonial architecture.

In the 1870s, the Apache and Yavapai Indians were forced to leave the area and sent to the San Carlos Reservation by American soldiers to make way for American settlers seeking to farm, mine, and explore the land. The region was marked by a natural resources along the creeks, where plants, berries, and fish were abundant; in addition, a unique climate allowed for forests where deer, bears, and other game were available. Nonetheless, the land was still harsh, and settlers continued to be few throughout the nineteenth century. By the beginning of the twentieth century, the region ultimately became a place for Anglo-American squatters on their way to the West.

A Settlement Begins

In 1876, the first Anglo-American settler, John J. Thompson, moved into the Oak Creek Canyon. After he began raising his family in present-day Uptown Sedona, other families arrived, settling in Crimson Cliffs, and other rock niches, allowing the general area to become known as Red Rock. The homes were far apart, and socializing as a community was difficult as a result. In 1891, a school was built to educate the few families' children, and the area started to become a town. Settlers sold produce and livestock in the nearby mining town of Jerome and in Flagstaff further north.

The main trade route was Munds Trail, the main route from Red Rock to Flagstaff. When a Theodore Carl Schnebly and his wife, Sedona, moved to the area from Missouri, the few families living there convinced them to establish a post office on the trail, since their home was located at the end of the trail and had already become the community's hotel. When the federal government authorized the post office in 1902, the post office was named "Sedona." Munds Trail would later become known as Schnebly Hill Road.

The Region Grows

With the advent of the post office, the settlement now known as Sedona began to slowly gain a population. Apples and peaches were the city's first main industry, using water from the Oak Creek to irrigate the orchards. The areas farms and ranches suffered heavily during the Great Depression of the 1930s. In 1948, the establishment of the Verde Valley School invited many new potential residents.

Starting in the 1930s, and expanding greatly in the 1950s, Hollywood discovered the Sedona region and began to use the geographically unique area as a backdrop to western films, attracting movie producers and the entertainment industry. In 1951, a groundwater aquifer under West Sedona was discovered, opening the way for more residents. Sedona began to develop as a tourist destination, vacation home, and retirement center, first as a second-home region to Hollywood types. Other new residents came for the spiritual and serene atmosphere created by the outdoor beauty of the region and in order to form an artist community. The opening of the Tlaquepaque shopping center in 1971 invited even more tourists and residents. However, it was not until 1988 that the city of Sedona was incorporated. Most development seen today is a result of construction in the 1980s and 1990s stemming from second-home owners.

The Modern Spirit of Sedona

In the latter half of the twentieth century, Sedona began to invite less traditional practitioners of religion and artists who believe the area holds a spiritual presence. As early as 1958, alternative personal development and self-help religions called Sedona home. Other examples include the "Ruby Focus" movement to find "vortex" energy centers, the Sedona Institute for improving self-awareness, and the Sri Aurobindo Center for "Indian religious thought." In the 1980s, Sedona had become known as a center for "New Age" consciousness. The "New Age" movement reached a peak in Sedona in 1987 when thousands of believers came to town to witness the "harmonic convergence" of the planets.

While the spiritual element has waned, the effect is still present in Sedona, inviting religious and artistic individuals. Moreover, the climate and natural beauty of the city's landscape are the most attractive qualities of the area. Today, Sedona continues to amaze visitor with its panoramic views of unique prehistoric geological creations. Sedona is a very young city, attracting artist communities and retirees, creating an eclectic blend of history, archeology, geology, and art. Tourism is Sedona's primary industry, attracting more than 3.5 million visitors a year. It is said that the city is second only to the Grand Canyon as Arizona's most visited destination.

Historical Information: Sedona Heritage Museum, 735 Jordan Road, Uptown Sedona, AZ 86339; telephone (928) 282-7038; email sedonamuseum@esedona.net.

■ Population Profile

County Population

2000: 167,517
2010: 205,098
2012 estimate: 211,280
Percent change, 2000–2010: 22.4%

City Residents

> 1990: 7,720
> 2000: 10,192
> 2010: 10,031
> 2012 estimate: 10,037
> Percent change, 2000–2010: −1.6%

Density: 524.1 people per square mile

Racial and ethnic characteristics

> White: 9,716
> Black or African American: 51
> American Indian and Alaskan Native: 157
> Asian: 85
> Native Hawaiian and Other Pacific Islander: 0
> Hispanic or Latino (may be of any race): 968
> Other: 64

Percent of residents born in state: 19.8%

Age characteristics

> Population under 5 years old: 488
> Population 5 to 9 years old: 181
> Population 10 to 14 years old: 392
> Population 15 to 19 years old: 343
> Population 20 to 24 years old: 411
> Population 25 to 34 years old: 372
> Population 35 to 44 years old: 1,292
> Population 45 to 54 years old: 1,339
> Population 55 to 59 years old: 1,354
> Population 60 to 64 years old: 1,206
> Population 65 to 74 years old: 1,581
> Population 75 to 84 years old: 830
> Population 85 years and over: 342
> Median age: 56.3

Births (2010–11 Metropolitan Area)

> Total number: Not Available

Deaths (2010–11 Metropolitan Area)

> Total number: Not Available

Money income (2012)

> Per capita income: $53,842
> Median household income: $41,165
> Total households: 5,293

Number of households with income of ...

> less than $10,000: 333
> $10,000 to $14,999: 328
> $15,000 to $24,999: 613
> $25,000 to $34,999: 652
> $35,000 to $49,999: 637
> $50,000 to $74,999: 983
> $75,000 to $99,999: 508
> $100,000 to $149,999: 536
> $150,000 to $199,999: 237
> $200,000 or more: 466

Percent of families below poverty level: 10.9%

FBI Crime Index Property: 219

FBI Crime Index Violent: 20

■ Municipal Government

A mayor, a vice mayor, and five council members make up the Sedona city council. Three of the council seats are served in four year terms, while two seats are held for two year terms. The mayor, elected every two years, runs the city council meetings and votes as a member of the council.

Head Official: Mayor Rob Adams (since 2008; current term expires 2014)

Total Number of City Employees: 108 (2013)

City Information: City of Sedona, 102 Roadrunner Drive, Sedona, AZ 86336; telephone (982) 282-3113.

■ Economy

Major Industries and Commercial Activity

While fruit growing and cattle trading were the most significant part of Sedona's early economy, agriculture and ranching play minimal roles in the modern Sedona. Today, Sedona's economy revolves around tourism, entertainment, and the arts. Of these, there is no question that tourism is the largest sector of Sedona's economy: The visitors center served more than 346,000 walk-in visitors in 2012 alone, and an estimated 3.5 million people visit annually. Overall, the tourism industry supported 8,900 jobs and sparked $439 million of economic activity in 2012.

Tourism started in the region as cabins along trade routes for overnight stays. Starting in the 1960s, visitors came to enjoy the seclusion and beauty of the Sedona area, kept as natural as possible by residents. The local chamber even removed all billboards from the area during this time so as not to obstruct the views of the surrounding rocks. Also during this time, local ranchers and homesteaders sold their property to developers, converting former agricultural property to new residential developments. In addition, shopping centers and resorts were also built to capture tourists who came to enjoy the outdoor scenery and activities in the area. With high tourism rates, employment in accommodation and food services, real estate, and rental and leasing sectors are highest in the city, and higher than average in the country. As an extension of tourism, art and religion also play a role in the city. Sedona serves as a location for all kinds of artistic and spiritual interpretations. Many artists have called the red rocks home. In addition, seasonal residents and in-migrating retirees contribute to the economic base.

During the 1940s, government buildings were transformed into a lodge and sound stage as Hollywood found Sedona the picturesque setting for new movies. Sedona became the film capital during the "golden age" of Western films. Other new businesses cropped up to cater to the needs of movie crews. Over 100 films and television productions have been shot either partially or entirely on location in Sedona. Today, development of the city is limited to ensure certain scenes and backdrops are available to current and future film crews.

Items and goods produced: fruits, cattle, films, commercials

Incentive Programs—New and Existing Companies

Local programs: The city's economic planning department is one of the local information sources for new and existing businesses, providing resources on taxation requirements and other economic information. A Small Business Development Center is offered to cultivate new businesses. The local chamber offers the Sedona Film Office, providing assistance for site locations, talent and crew provisions, permitting, and as a general resource between production companies and the necessary government agencies. The Sedona Main Street Program seeks to cultivate a vibrant pedestrian-friendly destination by providing business enhancement and promotion services. Free one-on-one business counseling is offered by Yavapai College's Small Business Development Center and Northern Arizona's SCORE program.

State programs: State incentives are offered through the Arizona Commerce Authority, which organizes its programs through an "Incentive Tool Box." Among the cash assistance or loan programs are the Arizona Competes Fund, which provides cash assistance to attract business with stable, high-wage jobs; Arizona FAST Grant, offering up to $7,500 for technology commercialization; Arizona Innovation Accelerator Fund Program, with loans from $50,000 to $2 million for business expansion or job creation; Arizona Innovation Challenge, another cash assistance program providing up to $250,000 to technology ventures; and Arizona STEP grant targeting international export opportunities with cash assistance up to $10,000. Private Activity Bonds and Qualified Energy Conservation Bonds give companies access to low-interest financing.

Tax incentives provided include the Commercial and Industrial Solar Energy Program, offering a tax credit of up to 10 percent of the installed cost of solar energy devices; Healthy Forest Tax Incentives, which supplies several tax incentives to forestry and forest-product companies related to equipment purchases, transportation, and training; Military Reuse Zone tax credits that reduce property taxes by up to 75 percent for five years and also offer $10,000 in tax credits per new employee hired; Quality Jobs Program with $9,000 tax credits for new hires that meet certain criteria; Qualified Facilities Tax Credit that refunds up to 10 percent or $20,000 of a company's investment in new job creation; Renewable Energy Tax Incentives and Research and Development Program tax credits; and a Small Business Capital Investment Tax Credit amounting to as much as 35 percent of investment over a three-year period.

Job training programs: The state of Arizona offers matching funds of up to 75 percent to businesses for the training of workers for new jobs in the state. This cash assistance may total as much as $1.5 million per business. Training of incumbent workers is still eligible for cash assistance covering up to 50 percent of training expenses. The State of Arizona also operates the Arizona Job Training Program to tailor training plans to the evolving industry landscape. The Arizona Apprenticeship System maintains more than 100 registered apprenticeship opportunities that pair education with on-the-job training.

Several community colleges in the area offer technical training. The University of Sedona is a non-traditional institute providing ministerial training. Yavapai College's Sedona Center for Arts & Technology provides training in independent filmmaking. The Center also provides a Community Education facility for the Verde Valley and a local branch of the Yavapai College Foundation.

Development Projects

Development in Sedona centers on tourism, which, ironically, often limits development to preserve the environment that attracts millions of visitors and limit obstructions of the natural landscape. Nearly 50 percent of Sedona's land area is part of the Coconino National Forest. Much development is infill development of single family residences, condominiums, and other residential development.

Projects planned or underway in 2013 included the restaurant Mariposa; the conversion of an existing two-story office space into a six-unit condominium building known as Kayenta Plaza; a 12-suite addition to Sedona Rouge Hotel & Spa; and a 40-unit expansion of Sky Ranch Lodge.

Economic Development Information: City of Sedona, Community and Economic Development Department, 102 Roadrunner Drive, Sedona, AZ 86336; telephone (928) 282-1154.

Commercial Shipping

Trade and transportation, while once important to the development of the city, is not highly relevant in the city's modern economy. Nationwide Pack and Ship provides packing and shipping services locally.

Labor Force and Employment Outlook

As a result of high tourism rates, and relatively low year-round residency rate, the labor force and employment in the region is geared toward the maintenance of tourist industries. Retail, services, and real estate are the highest labor markets. Many residents of the area are part-time or seasonal and do not actually live and work in the area. Resort companies are the area's largest employers.

The following is a summary of data regarding the 2012 Sedona labor force:

Size of civilian labor force: 5,061

Number of workers employed in…

agriculture and mining: 0
construction: 323
manufacturing: 172
wholesale trade: 52
retail trade: 412
transportation: 74
information systems: 336
finance: 254
professional administration: 448
education and social services: 1,121
arts and leisure: 1,196
other: 257
public administration: 114

Average hourly earnings of production workers: $15.37

Unemployment rate: 3.3% (2012)

Employers

Largest regional employers (2013)	*Number of employees*
Enchantment Resorts	500
Diamond Resorts International	450
L'Auberge de Sedona Resort	270
Hilton Resort & Spa	200
Sedona/Oak Creek School District	160
Pink Jeep Tours	160
Sedona Rouge	115
City of Sedona	108
Poco Diablo Resort	89

Cost of Living

The following is a summary of data regarding several key cost of living factors in the area.

State income tax rate: 2.59% to 4.54%

State sales tax rate: 5.6%

Local income tax rate: None

Local sales tax rate: 3.75%

Property tax rate: $0.9359 to $2.9134 per $100 of assessed value for Yavapai County; the city of Sedona does not assess property taxes (2010)

Economic Information: Sedona Chamber of Commerce, 331 Forest Road, Sedona, AZ, 86336; telephone (800) 288-7336 or (928) 282-7722.

■ Education and Research

Elementary and Secondary Schools

The Sedona-Oak Creek Joint Unified School District includes Sedona Red Rock High School, West Sedona School, and Big Park Community School. The high school's campus is a series of single-story buildings, located opposite the Sedona campus of Yavapai College. Red Rock Academy is the school system's online offering for distance learning.

Founded in 1995, Sedona Charter School is the oldest charter school in Arizona. Serving about 160 students, the school provides a small-school atmosphere employing the Montessori method in its curriculum. In addition, numerous private elementary and college prep schools serve students in this area. Valley School, a boarding International Baccalaureate high school, serves many international and Native American students. The school, serving about 110 students per year, is located between the Village of Oak Creek and Red Rock Crossing. It hosts numerous performances open to the community.

The following is a summary of data regarding the Sedona-Oak Creek Unified School District.

Total enrollment: 1,250

Number of facilities
total: 3
elementary schools: 1
junior high schools: 1
high schools: 1
other: 0

Student/teacher ratio: 18.73:1

Teacher salaries
average (statewide): $47,553

Funding per pupil: $8,450

Public Schools Information: Sedona-Oak Creek Unified School District, 221 Brewer Road, Sedona, AZ 86336; telephone (928) 204-6800; fax (928) 282-0232.

Colleges and Universities

Several small post-secondary institutes and campuses serve Sedona. The University of Sedona is a non-traditional institute providing ministerial training and education in metaphysics. Yavapai College serves about 4,000 students and offers a variety of certificate, degree, and transfer options to students in over 60 programs. Yavapai College, based in Prescott, Arizona, offers classes in a variety of fields in its Sedona Center, from the arts to computer systems to foreign languages to mathematics. The college's Sedona Center for Arts & Technology includes the Zaki Gordon Institute for Independent Filmmaking and the Osher Lifelong Learning Institute. The center also provides a Small Business Development Center, Community Education for the Verde Valley, and a local branch of the Yavapai College Foundation. Coconino Community College is located in nearby Flagstaff, as is Northern Arizona University. Arizona State University in Tempe is approximately 100 miles away.

Libraries and Research Centers

The Sedona Public Library has a main library in Sedona and a branch library in the Village of Oak Creek of Sedona, opened in 2005. The public library, originally opened in 1958 with only three shelves of donated books and magazines, provides over 600,000 resources to Sedona residents, along with the Yavapai Library Network. The Sedona Public Library also offers a children's library. The building is marked by the Sedona Schnebly statue, the first of its Art in Public Places project. Volunteers provide roughly 50 percent of staff hours annually for the system.

Public Library Information: Sedona Public Library, 3250 White Bear Road, Sedona, AZ 86336; telephone (928) 282-7714.

■ Health Care

The Verde Valley Medical Center provides an outpatient facility, specializing in primary healthcare, emergency services, and cancer treatment. The center is a part of Northern Arizona Healthcare, the parent corporation of Flagstaff Medical Center and Northern Arizona Homecare. Northern Arizona Healthcare also provides additional services, including emergency search and rescue complemented by a medical evacuation helicopter, available to Sedona residents. Residents of Sedona also are served by numerous skilled practitioners who operate in private offices and clinics throughout this immediate area, as well as Sedona's NextCare Urgent Care.

■ Recreation

Sightseeing

The hallmark of Sedona is its natural beauty, intentionally preserved by the local residents. The list of unique geographic formations can seemingly be endless, but all belong to Red Rock country, marked by the red orange glow of the unique sedimentary makeup of the region. Visitors can obtain a Red Rock pass for recreational passage in the area. Specific rock formations include: the Devil's Kitchen in Soldier's Pass, in which the giant rock in the center is called The Grand Piano; Cathedral Rock; and Courthouse Butte. The Coconino National Forest is also one of the most diverse national forests in the country, ranging from the red rocks to pine forests to alpine tundra. Sedona is also about 120 miles from the Grand Canyon.

There are a variety of modes tourists can use to see the city. At Sedona Airport, scenic sightseeing biplane and helicopter tours are available at one of the most unique airports in the nation, sitting atop a red rock mesa. For those who need to touch the ground, jeep tours or hiking and bicycling the Red Rock region provide for spectacular views. Hikers must see the West Fork Oak Canyon Trail, providing a lush, green contrast to the surrounding rocky region. In addition, a scenic train ride, the Verde Canyon Railroad, is available through the Verde Valley. In the city, the Sedona Trolley offers daily 55-minute rides throughout the city's historic and scenic tourist sites.

Distinct areas of Sedona include the Village of Oakcreek, a quaint census-designated area located in Sedona. In Uptown Sedona, charming southwestern architecture is evidenced throughout the area, such as the Sinagua fountain in Sinagua Plaza. Also in Uptown, a stagecoach tour explores back roads and hidden historic corners of town off the scenic Route 89A. Visitors should also see Tlaquepaque, what some call the "heart and soul" of Sedona. The historic building features Mexican style architecture, fine Sedona dining indoor and outdoor, and a private non-denominational chapel.

Historic archaeological finds are also scattered throughout the region, such as the Sinagua Indian ruins among and cut into the canyons and plateaus of the red rocks. The Palatki ruins and rock art provide visitors insight into the ancient Native American ruins of the Sinaqua Cliff Dwelling, in addition to over 1,000 petroglyphs and pictographs carved and painted into the rocks and formations by prehistoric natives that occupied the area during various times in ancient history. Similarly, Montezuma Castle, a national monument, and Montezuma Well are popular tourist locations. Montezuma Castle is a five-story cliff dwelling carved into limestone cliffs near Sedona.

Spiritual visitors often frequent the area due to energy "vortexes" popularized in the 1980s. However, for more literal religious visitors, more than 30 churches, many in beautiful buildings specifically oriented to capture inspirational views of this spectacular area, are located in Sedona. One example is the Chapel of the Holy Cross, considered a remarkable work of art and architecture from the 1940s and one of Sedona's most visible artistic and historic artifacts. The chapel and its surroundings inspired others to construct religious monuments in Sedona, such as the Shrine of the Red Rocks on Airport Mesa, which was built as a monument to cooperation and religious beliefs.

The Jordan Historical Park was developed in collaboration with the Sedona Historical Society and Heritage Museum. There, the society opened the Sedona Heritage Museum in the Jordan farmstead historic landmark structures, and now operates the museum seven days a week.

Arts and Culture

Sedona is a mecca for alternative artists and spiritual-healing seekers. Sedona touts itself as home to a diverse art community, from cutting-edge contemporary to visionary, Native American to modern realism. Where there is art, there are galleries. Over 40 Sedona galleries showcase contemporary and traditional artists who are known nationally and internationally. This creates a full calendar of openings, artist receptions, demonstrations and workshops to keep the art aficionado entertained all year long. The Sedona Arts Center, founded in 1958, is the oldest arts center in northern Arizona.

In addition to art and religion, Sedona also offers music. For over 25 years, Chamber Music Sedona has sponsored a chamber music program annually from October to May. Musical events, like GumptionFest, are held in the city throughout the year.

Festivals and Holidays

The Sedona International Film Festival was established in 1995. The week-long annual festival takes place in late February and early March at Harkins Theatres while supplemental events take place at area resorts. Since 1970, the city has hosted an annual St. Patrick's Parade and Festival in March. The Sedona Photofest occurs in June, as does the Sedona Bluegrass Festival. The Red Rocks Music Festival in August features classical and jazz music as well as modern dance. GumptionFest, established in 2006, is an annual grassroots, local-art street festival held over a weekend in early September. It is one of the largest free music and arts festivals in Northern Arizona. Other events hosted annually include the Sedona Marathon and the Sedona Miracle Annual Charity Fundraiser.

Sports for the Spectator

The Sedona FC Strikers, a W-League women's professional soccer team, were slated to have their inaugural season in 2014. Yavapai College in Prescott, Arizona, features junior college athletics.

Sports for the Participant

The Red Rocks form a breathtaking backdrop for everything from spiritual pursuits to the hundreds of hiking and mountain biking trails. Hiking and mountain biking through Red Rock Country are popular sport activities to explore the breadth of natural beauty the Red Rock Country has to offer.

Shopping and Dining

In the 1970s, as population grew in Sedona, retail shops and businesses began to cater to the new tourist population with unique arts-and-crafts offerings. Sedona has dozens of art galleries, food emporiums, New Age metaphysical shops, specialty stores, antiques, and even more traditional shopping areas with both national stores and local businesses. With many local artists, Sedona offers shoppers the opportunity to purchase very unique gifts. Sedona's world-class galleries feature original paintings and multi-media works, jewelry, photography, sculpture, pottery, rugs, art glass, woven textiles, hand-crafted furniture, and collectibles. Sedona's shopping districts are nestled among the city's world-famous red rocks, making shopping a sightseeing trip as well. Two popular stops for unique Sedona gifts include the Sedona Arts Center gift store, which represents dozens of local artists, and the Sedona Heritage Museum shop, which offers items with a historic flair. Another unique place to shop is the Tlaquepaque Arts & Crafts Village, a replica of Guadalajara, Mexico.

Multiple Sedona restaurants can be found in Hillside, Tlaquepaque, Oak Creek Canyon, Uptown, the Village of Oak Creek, and West Sedona. Several Sedona restaurants have earned national acclaim for their exceptional food and atmosphere. Restaurants cover the food gamut, from bakeries and bistros to many styles of fine dining, southwestern cuisine, and catering. Sedona restaurants offer a variety of menu choices, including American and Mexican cuisine, and international specialties, including Italian, French, Indian, Chinese, Korean, Thai, and Japanese food. Many restaurants change their menus seasonally and, due to the mild climate, offer outdoor dining three seasons a year.

Sedona is also known for unique wines and wineries. Verde Valley is home to several vineyards and wineries, specifically creating handcrafted, limited production wines in both white and red varietals in addition to library wines and multi-grape bottling.

Visitor Information: Sedona Visitor Information Center, 331 Forest Road, Sedona, AZ 86336; telephone (800) 288-7336 or (928) 282-7722.

■ Convention Facilities

Sedona does not offer an official convention center. Sedona's visitors tend to be more recreational than business-oriented. However, the Sedona Chamber of Commerce Tourism Bureau offers a free one-stop service for meeting planners to assist in providing facilities and services for meetings, retreats, and workshops. Sedona offers more than 100 lodging facilities, including large-scale resorts and hotels as well as smaller, unique bed and breakfast establishments. The largest meeting facilities can hold up to 400 people.

■ Transportation

Approaching the City

About 30 miles southwest of the larger city of Flagstaff, those going to Sedona can make their way via Route 89A after flying into Flagstaff Pulliam Airport. *USA Today* has rated Route 89A from Flagstaff to Prescott—through Sedona and the Verde Valley—the most scenic drive in America. Some visitors fly into Phoenix Sky Harbor International Airport and drive 119 miles to Sedona. The Sedona Phoenix Shuttle provides daily scheduled stops in the city from the Phoenix airport. State Route 179, a federally designated All American Road, is the main highway moving south from the city, connecting to Interstate 17 toward Phoenix and Route 89A toward Flagstaff. The Sedona Airport, located atop a mesa at an elevation of more than 4,800 feet, is itself an attraction known as the USS Sedona (SEZ). The non-towered airport provides one runway and one helipad. While not able to accommodate commercial jets larger than a Boeing 727, it attracts a number of smaller business jets and aircraft. Nearest Amtrak and Greyhound rail and bus lines are in Flagstaff.

Traveling in the City

State highway 89A is the major throughway to and through the city. The intersection of state routes 179 and 89A is known as the "Y," often used as a point of reference for Sedona attractions and businesses. The Sedona Trolley provides daily city and scenic tours in Sedona.

■ Communications

Newspapers and Magazines

Sedona Red Rock News is the city's only local newspaper, published twice weekly. The *Sedona Observer* is an online newspaper, founded in 2007, focused on investigative journalism. The *Gateway to Sedona* online magazine is a visitor's guide covering local events and entertainment. *Four Corners Magazine* focuses on nontraditional medicine science.

Television and Radio

Sedona benefits from the Flagstaff listening and viewing area. Sedona broadcastse three FM stations and one AM station—KAZM radio (780 AM), the main radio station for Sedona with one of the largest listening audience in Northern Arizona.

Media Information: *Sedona Red Rock News;* telephone (928) 282-7795; fax (928) 282-6011.

Sedona Online

City of Sedona. Available www.sedonaaz.gov
Sedona Chamber of Commerce. Available
  sedonachamber.com
Sedona Red Rock News. Available www.redrocknews.
  com.
Visit Sedona. Available www.visitsedona.com.

BIBLIOGRAPHY

Bailey, Christine, *Phoenix, Scottsdale, Sedona and Central Arizona: A Complete Guide* (Woodstock, VT: Countryman Press, 2008)

McNeill, Joe, *Arizona's Little Hollywood: Sedona and Northern Arizona's forgotten film history 1923–1973* (Sedona, AZ: Northedge & Sons, 2010)

Samson, Karl, *Frommer's Arizona and the Grand Canyon 2011* (Hoboken, NJ: Wiley, 2011)

Tucson

■ The City in Brief

Founded: 1775 (incorporated, 1853)

Head Official: Mayor Jonathan Rothschild (since 2011; current term expires 2015)

City Population
> 1990: 415,444
> 2000: 486,699
> 2010: 520,116
> 2012 estimate: 524,278
> Percent change, 2000–2010: 6.9%
> U.S. rank in 1990: 34th
> U.S. rank in 2000: 37th (State rank: 2nd)
> U.S. rank in 2010: 33rd (State rank: 2nd)

Metropolitan Statistical Area Population
> 2000: 843,746
> 2010: 980,263
> 2012 estimate: 992,394
> Percent change, 2000–2010: 16.2%
> U.S. rank in 2000: 55th
> U.S. rank in 2010: 52nd

Area: 194.7 square miles

Elevation: 2,390 feet above sea level

Average Annual Temperatures: 68° F

Average Annual Precipitation: 11 inches

Major Economic Sectors: government, military, high-technology industry, education, tourism

Unemployment Rate: 6.8% (2012)

Per Capita Income: $19,796

2012 FBI Crime Index Property: 3,851

Major Colleges and Universities: University of Arizona, Pima Community College, University of Phoenix

Daily Newspaper: *Arizona Daily Star*

■ Introduction

Tucson is the second largest city in Arizona, and has a reputation for having a sunny and dry climate. With more than 300 sunny days per year, Tucson has become a popular tourist area because of its warm weather and beautiful surroundings. Its population has an array of ethnic backgrounds, including Native American, Spanish, and Mexican. Tucson has been referred to as "Old Pueblo" because of the area's numerous tributes to its past, and residents' dedication to their respective heritages. While the city is known for its frontier past, it has also developed a technologically advanced future, with the local military presence supporting defense companies and the University of Arizona leading the way in bioscience and environmental research.

■ Geography and Climate

Tucson is located in southeastern Arizona, 60 miles north of the Mexican border. Established in the valley of the Sonoran Desert, the city is surrounded by the Sierrita and Santa Rita mountain ranges to the south and the Rincon Mountains rising to 7,000 feet above sea level to the east. With more than 300 days of sunshine a year, and minimal rain, Tucson's climate lends itself to a variety of outdoor activities and enjoyment.

Area: 194.7 square miles

Elevation: 2,390 feet above sea level

Average Temperatures: 68° F

Average Annual Precipitation: 11 inches

Todd Taulman/Shutterstock.com

■ History

Four Governments Claim Tucson Territory

Tucson is an extremely old settlement with a rich layering of history and pre-history. Archaeological excavations have revealed adobe huts, pit houses, and irrigation systems built by the Hohokam tribe who inhabited and farmed the area nearly 2,000 years ago. The Hohokam have since vanished; in fact, their name, meaning "those who have vanished," was given to them by the Pimas, the Native Americans who occupied the site of present-day Tucson when the first white settlers arrived, and after whom Pima County is named. "Tucson" is also derived from a Pima word, "Stjukshon" or "Chuk-son," meaning "spring at the foot of a black mountain."

Since its founding Tucson has operated under four governments: Spain, Mexico, the United States, and the Confederacy. One of the first Spanish visitors was Father Eusebio Francisco Kino, a Jesuit missionary who arrived in 1687. Tucson was officially founded as a Spanish colony less than one hundred years later, in 1775, and the Spanish settlers built the Presidio of San Augistin del Tucson as protection from the Apache. Part of this walled presidio still exists today, and its nickname, "Old Pueblo," is now extended to the city as a whole.

When Mexico won independence from Spain in 1821, Tucson became a Mexican town. In 1853 the United States acquired from Mexico the Gadsden Purchase, a strip of land that included Tucson. Before 1863, when Arizona gained territorial status, Tucson briefly belonged to the Confederacy, then became the capital of the Arizona Territory in 1867.

Tucson played an integral role in the romance of the Old West. The city was the scene of gunfights, brawls, and attacks by Native Americans; neighboring Tombstone was the site of the legendary gunfight at the O.K. Corral. Tucson also participated in the great gold rush when prospectors moved east from California into Arizona. The effects of this migration were lasting, since Tucson became the center of a mining industry that continued unabated into the 1970s.

Healthy Climate Attracts Settlers, Tourists

By the time it became the 48th state in 1912, Arizona was famous for the sunny climate and dry air that made it ideal as a healthful spot where people could visit and settle. In 1920 Tucson became the first city in the nation to have a municipal airport. At the same time, major highways were being built. Tourism became one of Tucson's strongest industries and remains so today. During World War II the city contributed to the war effort when the government established the Davis-Monthan Air Force Base nearby. Tucson has since emerged as a major cultural center and one of the most sophisticated cities in the Southwest.

Tucson is the second largest city in Arizona with nearly one million people living in its metropolitan area as of 2012. Public and private sectors continue to join forces to improve Tucson's standard of living and business environment. With an expanding economy based on high-technology industries, modern Tucson aggressively preserves its multicultural heritage and pioneer spirit.

Historical Information: Arizona History Museum, 949 East Second Street, Tucson, AZ 85719; telephone (520) 628-5774; email AHSTucson@azhs.gov.

■ Population Profile

Metropolitan Statistical Area Population

2000: 843,746
2010: 980,263
2012 estimate: 992,394
Percent change, 2000–2010: 16.2%
U.S. rank in 2000: 55th
U.S. rank in 2010: 52nd

City Residents

1990: 415,444
2000: 486,699
2010: 520,116
2012 estimate: 524,278
Percent change, 2000–2010: 6.9%
U.S. rank in 1990: 34th
U.S. rank in 2000: 37th (State rank: 2nd)
U.S. rank in 2010: 33rd (State rank: 2nd)

Density: 2,294.2 people per square mile

Racial and ethnic characteristics

White: 384,306
Black or African American: 27,562
American Indian and Alaskan Native: 11,165
Asian: 13,327
Native Hawaiian and Other Pacific Islander: 755
Hispanic or Latino (may be of any race): 228,510
Other: 87,163

Percent of residents born in state: 43.9%

Age characteristics

Population under 5 years old: 32,485
Population 5 to 9 years old: 34,037
Population 10 to 14 years old: 31,988
Population 15 to 19 years old: 38,704
Population 20 to 24 years old: 57,053
Population 25 to 34 years old: 79,190
Population 35 to 44 years old: 64,469
Population 45 to 54 years old: 61,339
Population 55 to 59 years old: 31,460
Population 60 to 64 years old: 28,609
Population 65 to 74 years old: 34,930
Population 75 to 84 years old: 20,321
Population 85 years and over: 9,693
Median age: 33.3

Births (2010–11 Metropolitan Area)

Total number: 12,223

Deaths (2010–11 Metropolitan Area)

Total number: 8,255

Money income (2012)

Per capita income: $19,796
Median household income: $36,050
Total households: 200,627

Number of households with income of . . .

less than $10,000: 24,500
$10,000 to $14,999: 17,864
$15,000 to $24,999: 28,662
$25,000 to $34,999: 26,596
$35,000 to $49,999: 30,313
$50,000 to $74,999: 32,858
$75,000 to $99,999: 18,242
$100,000 to $149,999: 15,653
$150,000 to $199,999: 3,522
$200,000 or more: 2,417

Percent of families below poverty level: 25.9%

FBI Crime Index Property: 3,851

FBI Crime Index Violent: Not available

■ Municipal Government

Tucson, the seat of Pima County, has a council-manager form of government. City Council has six members represented wards; the mayor is elected at-large. All serve four-year terms and are elected on a staggered schedule in odd-numbered years.

Head Official: Mayor Jonathan Rothschild (since 2011; current term expires 2015)

Total Number of City Employees: 4,944 (2012)

City Information: City of Tucson, City Hall, 255 W. Alameda St., Tucson, AZ 85701; telephone (520) 791-4201 (Mayor's office).

■ Economy

Major Industries and Commercial Activity

Copper mining has traditionally been a vital part of the city's economy; in 1976, for instance, one of every 20

Tucson residents was a copper miner. Seven years later, a combination of foreign competition and depressed copper prices forced a dramatic downturn in mining industries nationwide, with the result that only 0.4 percent of the working population was employed in mining by the mid-1980s. The early 1990s saw an upturn in the mining industry again. Throughout Arizona, the mining industry continues to contribute to the economy—Freeport-McMoRan Copper & Gold employed nearly 5,000 Tucson residents in 2012—but locally and globally the industry has experienced a slowdown.

At the time of the mining crisis, Tucson and southern Arizona looked to diversify economically. In the 1980s the area experienced economic growth from Davis-Monthan Air Force Base, with more than 8,200 employees in 2012, and the University of Arizona, with more than 11,600 employees, as well as growth in the high-tech and service industries.

Tucson's residential and tourist economy benefits from Tucson ballet, symphony, live theater, and opera performances—a remarkable array for a city its size. Tucson's dependably dry and sunny climate assures continuing growth in tourism, an industry that brings in more than $2.67 billion in direct travel spending annually to Pima County as of 2012. The industry supports some 22,340 tourism jobs.

Manufacturing activity doubled from the 1990s to the 2000s, and included such companies as AlliedSignal, Weiser Lock, 3M, Environmental Air Products, Inc., and Krueger Industries, Inc., all of which have either since ceased operations or moved to another city. Raytheon Missile Systems remains the city's most important manufacturer, employing 11,500 citizens in 2012. The manufacturer's dependence on government defense contracts was a potential vulnerability to the company and the city. Also vulnerable to federal government cutbacks were the U.S. Army Intelligence Center at Fort Huachuca and Davis-Monthan Air Force Base, which combined provided jobs to more than 17,000 area residents.

Tucson has actively promoted expansion in the high-technology industry. The military presence has supported development in aerospace and defense industries, including Raytheon, and the University of Arizona continues to churn out highly qualified graduates and conduct cutting-edge research. The Optical Sciences Center at the university is considered a national asset for technological advances in optics related to data storage, medicine, manufacturing, telecommunications, and military guidance systems.

Tucson has become more involved in international trade and has developed close partnerships with Mexico. The state of Sonora, Mexico, the southern neighbor to Arizona, is the leader of Mexico's aerospace industry, furthering opportunities for partnerships. Tucson also actively encourages the growth of twin-plant or "maquiladora" industries locating part of their operations in Tucson. Increased expansion is predicted in the manufacture of electronics, aerospace, and computer component products. Proximity to Mexico also has supported a sustained presence of the transportation industry.

Items and goods produced: electronic equipment, missiles and related components, aircraft and aircraft parts, ceramics, concrete

Incentive Programs—New and Existing Companies

Local programs: The Tucson Regional Economic Opportunities (TREO) serves as the lead economic development agency for the greater Tucson area. TREO focuses on promoting and developing the region's industry strengths. As of 2013, TREO promoted aerospace; bioscience, solar, and transportation industries. The Tucson Metropolitan Chamber of Commerce works to promote a favorable business atmosphere conducive to attracting, sustaining, and expanding industrial and service sector employers. The University of Arizona, one of the top research universities in the country, plays an active role in attracting businesses and encouraging the entrepreneurial spirit in Tucson.

The city of Tucson offers a number of financial incentives, such as the Government Property Lease Excise Tax, which provides up to eight years of tax abatement for projects in the Central Business District that increase property value by at least 100 percent. During the abatement period, the city takes ownership of the property. Tucson's Primary Jobs Incentive provides up to 100 percent credit on construction sales tax for job-training expenses or public infrastructure improvements. The credit requires a minimum $5 million investment and the creation of at least 25 jobs with an average wage of no less than $60,000, with at least 75 percent of employee health insurance premiums covered by the employer. Additional benefits may be available on a case-by-case basis, or for business relocations to specific inventive areas.

State programs: State incentives are offered through the Arizona Commerce Authority, which organizes its programs through an "Incentive Tool Box." Among the cash assistance or loan programs are the Arizona Competes Fund, which provides cash assistance to attract business with stable, high-wage jobs; Arizona FAST Grant, offering up to $7,500 for technology commercialization; Arizona Innovation Accelerator Fund Program, with loans from $50,000 to $2 million for business expansion or job creation; Arizona Innovation Challenge, another cash assistance program providing up to $250,000 to technology ventures; and Arizona STEP grant targeting international export opportunities with cash assistance up to $10,000. Private Activity Bonds and Qualified Energy Conservation Bonds give companies access to low-interest financing.

Tax incentives provided include the Commercial and Industrial Solar Energy Program, offering a tax credit of up to 10 percent of the installed cost of solar energy devices; Healthy Forest Tax Incentives, which supplies several tax incentives to forestry and forest-product companies related to equipment purchases, transportation, and training; Military Reuse Zone tax credits that reduce property taxes by up to 75 percent for five years and also offer $10,000 in tax credits per new employee hired; Quality Jobs Program with $9,000 tax credits for new hires that meet certain criteria; Qualified Facilities Tax Credit that refunds up to 10 percent or $20,000 of a company's investment in new job creation; Renewable Energy Tax Incentives and Research and Development Program tax credits; and a Small Business Capital Investment Tax Credit amounting to as much as 35 percent of investment over a three-year period.

Job training programs: The state of Arizona offers matching funds of up to 75 percent to businesses for the training of workers for new jobs in the state. This cash assistance may total as much as $1.5 million per business. Training of incumbent workers is still eligible for cash assistance covering up to 50 percent of training expenses. The State of Arizona also operates the Arizona Job Training Program to tailor training plans to the evolving industry landscape. The Arizona Apprenticeship System maintains more than 100 registered apprenticeship opportunities that pair education with on-the-job training.

Pima County assists employers in recruiting, screening, and training processes at its OneStop Employment Centers. County training is funded in part by the federal Workforce Investment Act.

Development Projects

The Rio Nuevo project received voter support for millions in taxpayer funding in 1999 for a variety of mixed-use developments that were to add new attractions, shopping, restaurants, infrastructure, office space and residential housing to downtown Tucson. However, gross mismanagement by the Rio Nuevo board resulted in essentially no progress—despite the expenditure of as much as $250 million. A state investigation into the mismanagement began in 2011 but found, in 2013, that mismanagement did not reach criminal levels, and no charges were filed. Funds were lost on design, mitigation, and infrastructure projects, as well as contractor over-billing and other more dubious costs. As of 2013 the city planned to use remaining funds to complete smaller projects, such as $7.8 million for repairs to the Tucson Convention Center Arena.

The University of Arizona's Science Park was a center of development in the 2010s. In 2012 a 6.1-megawatt solar system was installed on the grounds, with the power to be sold to the Tucson Electric Power Company under a 20-year agreement. The solar power generated was sufficient to provide electricity for some 1,000 homes and was installed at a cost of $13 million.

American Tire Distributors, Inc., constructed a 125,000-square-foot distribution center in Tucson in 2012 at a cost of $19.5, with a project annual economic impact of $5.5 million on the city. Iowa-based Involta constructed a 40,000-square-foot, multi-tenant data center in 2012 at a cost of $15 million.

OptumRx announced the creation of 400 jobs in 2012 through the creation of a customer service facility in Tucson. The jobs, added through the end of 2013. LivingSocial hired 180 residents for a Tucson-based call center in 2012. In 2013 Sorenson Communications opened a Tucson support center that employed 270 residents in a 24,000-square-foot facility; Sorenson Communications specializes in products and services for the deaf and hard-of-hearing.

Economic Development Information: Tucson Metropolitan Chamber of Commerce, 465 West St. Mary's Road, Tucson, AZ 85702; telephone (520) 792-2250. Tucson Regional Economic Opportunities (TREO), 120 N. Stone Ave., Suite 200, Tucson, AZ 85701; telephone (520) 243-1900 or (866) 600-0331.

Commercial Shipping

Tucson is linked to national and worldwide markets via Tucson International Airport, which receives service from major air cargo carriers. The Union Pacific railroad provides freight service; some 40 motor freight carriers ship goods through facilities in Tucson.

Labor Force and Employment Outlook

Tucson attracts 18,000 to 20,000 new residents each year and offers a work force from which employers can draw relatively young and productive workers. Tucson has committed itself, through its educational institutions, to train and retrain potential employees. The city's proximity to the Mexican border has enhanced its importance in transportation and logistics.

The following is a summary of data regarding the 2012 Tucson labor force:

Size of civilian labor force: 252,734

Number of workers employed in . . .

    agriculture and mining: 1,304
    construction: 14,060
    manufacturing: 13,334
    wholesale trade: 3,647
    retail trade: 27,418
    transportation: 7,514
    information systems: 4,182
    finance: 10,855
    professional administration: 26,288
    education and social services: 58,112
    arts and leisure: 27,144
    other: 12,919
    public administration: 13,408

Average hourly earnings of production workers: $16.06

Unemployment rate: 6.8% (2012)

Employers

Largest employers (2012)	*Number of employees*
University of Arizona	11,604
Raytheon	11,500
U.S. Army Intelligence Center and Fort Huachuca	9,039
Davis-Monthan Air Force Base	8,215
Pima County	8,132
Wal-Mart Stores, Inc.	7,900
Tucson Unified School District	6,739
Freeport-McMoRan Copper & Gold, Inc.	4,800
Tohono O'Odham Nation	4,679
Carondelet Health Services	4,566

Cost of Living

The cost of living in the Tucson metropolitan area is slightly below the national average overall. Only transportation costs rate above the national average.

The following is a summary of data regarding several key cost of living factors in the area.

2013 ACCRA Average House Price: $228,617

2013 ACCRA Cost of Living Index: 94

State income tax rate: 2.59% to 4.54%

State sales tax rate: 5.6%

Local income tax rate: None

Local sales tax rate: 2.5%

Property tax rate: $0.4213 per $100 of assessed value (2014)

Economic Information: Tucson Metropolitan Chamber of Commerce, 465 West St. Mary's Road, Tucson, AZ 85702; telephone (520) 792-2250. Tucson Regional Economic Opportunities (TREO), 120 N. Stone Ave., Suite 200, Tucson, AZ 85701; telephone (520) 243-1900 or (866) 600-0331.

■ Education and Research

Elementary and Secondary Schools

Pima County has 18 school districts, the largest being Tucson Unified School District with an enrollment in excess of 50,000 students. All districts focus on building basic skills. Gifted, honors, advanced placement, English-as-a-Second-Language, computer literacy, special education, extended school year, sports, music, theater, arts, and homebound programs are among the special offerings. Vocational and business programs prepare students for entry into jobs or further occupational education. All elementary schools offer full-day kindergarten.

About 35 self-regulating and parochial schools operate in Pima County. These range from boarding schools offering a college preparatory curriculum to schools that provide basic education with religious instruction. Tucson is also home to the Arizona School for the Deaf and Blind.

The following is a summary of data regarding the Tucson Unified School District.

Total enrollment: 53,275

Number of facilities
total: 101
elementary schools: 63
junior high schools: 21
high schools: 12
other: 5

Student/teacher ratio: 18.8:1

Teacher salaries
average (statewide): $47,553

Funding per pupil: $8,202

Public Schools Information: Tucson Unified School District, 1010 E. Tenth Street, Tucson, AZ 85719; telephone (520) 225-6000; email webmaster@tusd1.org.

Colleges and Universities

Institutions of higher learning located in Tucson include the University of Arizona, Pima Community College, Tucson College, and the University of Phoenix–Tucson. The University of Arizona enrolled more than 40,000 students in 2013–14. That year, *U.S. News & World Report* ranked it 119th among national universities. The university is highly regarded for its extensive research programs, earning the number-one ranking for environmental research in the United States in 2013—and second internationally—according to the journal *Science of the Total Environment*. Management Information Systems and Geology programs were also rated among the best of any university.

Pima Community College consists of six campuses in southern Arizona offering on-campus, alternative-style and online courses. It also provides learning and education centers throughout Tucson.

Libraries and Research Centers

The Pima County Public Library has a main library located in Tucson, and 26 additional branch locations throughout the area. The library also has a bookmobile and bookbike program to reach homebound patrons. The system manages 5.7 million annual visitors and circulates nearly 7.4 million items annually. A special collection focuses on Southwestern literature for children.

The University of Arizona main library holds about 5 million volumes and more than 25,000 serials and collections that include East Asian studies, government documents, maps, and the Middle East. Also located in the city are a number of specialized libraries associated with the university, including its Science-Engineering Library, Fine Arts Library, and Arizona Health Sciences Library..

Biosphere 2, located 30 miles northeast of Tucson, was formerly the site of research into global climate change by Columbia University's Lamont-Doherty Earth Observatory. Tours of the inside and outside of the glass-and-steel geodesic structure are available. Research activities in such fields as architecture, engineering, astronomy, geology, geochemistry, minerals and mining, agriculture, fish and wildlife, arid lands and water, biotechnology, immunology, gerontology, sleep disorders, anthropology, Southwestern culture, and international studies are conducted at centers in the Tucson area, with the University of Arizona a primary driver of research activity.

Public Library Information: Pima County Public Library System, Joel D. Valdez Main Library, 101 N. Stone Avenue, Tucson, AZ 85701; telephone (520) 594-5500.

■ Health Care

Tucson has long had a reputation for its healthful climate. For the past century its warm, dry air has attracted people suffering from such respiratory illnesses as asthma and tuberculosis. The city continues to attract wealthy residents who travel to Tucson across the Mexican border for health care.

The 365-bed University Medical Center, the teaching hospital of the University of Arizona, specializes in the research of respiratory illness, cancer, and heart disease. The hospital was ranked second in the state in 2013 by *U.S. News & World Report*, achieving a national ranking in ear, nose, and throat and geriatric care. Providing health care to residents throughout southern Arizona, Tucson Medical Center, with 553 beds, houses southern Arizona's only child-focused emergency department. The 58-bed Carondelet Heart and Vascular Institute offers inpatient and outpatient cardiovascular and cardiology services. Tucson also has internationally known health and spa retreats and alternative health-care centers. A total of 16 hospitals serve the Tucson area.

■ Recreation

Sightseeing

The variety of things to do and see in Tucson extends from the heart of the city to the surrounding area. Three historic districts—El Presidio, Armory Park, and Barrio Historico—provide convenient focal points for a walking tour of downtown Tucson. Around El Presidio, the old adobe wall that was part of the original town, are clustered other historic structures, among them restored homes of the city's early settlers and political leaders, as well as an artisans' marketplace housed in an adobe.

Located in the Barrio Historico district, El Tiradito—the "Wishing Shrine"—is one of the nation's genuine folk shrines. A few blocks away, at the edge of the Armory Park district, is the site of the printing office of a Spanish-language newspaper founded in 1878. Other popular attractions in the city include the Reid Park Zoo, situated in Gene C. Reid Park, and the Tucson Botanical Gardens.

The ideal way to view the landscape surrounding Tucson is to take a leisurely driving tour that winds through miles of scenic Sonora desert, the only place where Saguaro cactus grows, ending at Mount Lemmon. Covered with stands of aspen, Ponderosa pine, and Douglas fir, Mount Lemmon offers vistas of the desert.

Other interesting excursions include Colossal Cave, one of the largest caves in the world, and Sabino Canyon, in nearby Coronado National Forest. Kartchner Caverns State Park, home of the world's largest living cave, offers guided cave tours, hikes, and group use areas. Popular visitor attractions are Old Tucson Studios, a western theme park and the site of a television and movie set, and Mission San Xavier del Bac, called the "White Dove of the Desert" because of its striking appearance from a distance.

Arts and Culture

Tucson is the "arts mecca" of the American Southwest, offering a wealth of cultural activities: theater, opera, ballet, and symphony, as well as galleries and museums. Tucson's Arizona Theater Company, the leading professional theater company in the state, has received national recognition, including grants and citations from the Ford Foundation, the National Endowment of the Arts, and the White House Committee on the Arts. Its productions range from the classics to recent Broadway hits during a September-to-April season at the Temple of Music and Art; the company also performs at the Herberger Theater in downtown Phoenix. Off-Broadway shows and musicals are the forte of the Invisible Theatre. The award-winning Tucson Symphony Orchestra performs classical music at the Tucson Music Hall. The Arizona Opera makes Tucson and Phoenix its home, performing a standard repertoire along with less-frequently performed works. Dance lovers can see performances of Ballet Tucson. The Gaslight Theatre presents old-fashioned melodrama. The "UApresents" series at the University of Arizona Centennial Hall brings performances and groups like the Martha Graham Dance Company, the St. Petersburg Ballet Theatre, I Musici, Herbie Hancock, Forever Tango, David Sedaris, and Itzhak Perlman to delight audiences.

Tucson is home to several museums and galleries. The Arizona State Museum, specializing in the archaeology and ethnology of Arizona, is noted for having one of the most comprehensive southwestern archaeology collections in existence. The Arizona Historical Society houses a museum, research library, and Arizona mining exhibit; the society also administers Fort Lowell Museum and Sosa-Carrillo-Frèmont House. Featuring military equipment, the Fort Lowell Museum is an 1865 reconstruction of the home of the fort's commanding officer. The Sosa-Carillo-Frèmont House, built around 1858, is one of the oldest adobe houses in Tucson and is furnished in original period pieces. Exhibits such as the enchanted rain forest, whistle stop gallery, and bodyology can be found at the Tucson Children's Museum. The Pima Air and Space Museum features more than 300 different kinds of military and civilian aircraft from around the world.

Arizona-Sonora Desert Museum, 14 miles west of downtown, is one of southern Arizona's most popular attractions. It exhibits hundreds of native plants and animals in their natural habitats. The Flandrau Science Center and Planetarium, on the campus of the University of Arizona, presented exhibits pertaining to optical science, astronomy, and space exploration, many of them encouraging visitor experimentation. The center closed in 2009 because of financial difficulties, but the planetarium and exhibits were reopened in 2010 after Biosphere 2 took over operations. For those interested in astronomy, the 56-mile trip to Kitt Peak National Observatory to gaze through one of the telescopes in the world's largest collection of optical solar telescopes is well worth the drive.

The Tucson Museum of Art specializes in crafts, textiles, furnishings, and fine arts, including pre-Columbian and western American pieces. The University of Arizona Center for Creative Photography offers permanent and changing exhibitions of photographs and is home to more than 80,000 works by 2,000 photographers such as Ansel Adams, Richard Avedon, and Edward Weston. Tucson boasts an active community of artists and artisans. Local commercial galleries show their work, which includes paintings, jewelry, and pottery.

Festivals and Holidays

Tucson celebrates its history and multicultural heritage with a variety of activities throughout the year. February's La Fiesta de los Vaqueros Tucson Rodeo features riding and roping events. The Tucson Winter Chamber Music Festival takes place in March. The month of April offers the Tucson International Mariachi Conference featuring a full week of culture, music and dancing. In May, Tucson's Mexican-American community commemorates Mexico's victory against France with a four-day Cinco de Mayo Festival. Tucson's patron saint is honored in the Fiesta de San Augustin in August, and in September the Latin community celebrates Mexico's independence from Spain. El Nacimiento, on the grounds of the Tucson Museum of Art, ushers in the Christmas holiday season with displays of folk art. It is followed by Fiesta Navidad, a Mexican mariachi Christmas celebration.

Tucson is the site of other events of interest to both residents and visitors. For several weeks in the winter colored stones, gems and beads are on show at various locations in the city. The Fourth Avenue Street Fair is held twice each year, usually in March and December.

Sports for the Spectator

Although Tucson does not field any top-level professional sports teams, there is plenty of action for sports fans. Tucson is home to the University of Arizona Wildcats, which compete in the Pacific Athletic Conference (PAC-12). The University of Arizona's hockey team, known as the Icecats, plays hockey at the Tucson Convention Center.

The city of Tucson has often been home to minor league baseball. The Tucson Padres were a Triple-A affiliate playing in Tucson until 2014, when the team relocated to El Paso. Greyhound races are held year-round at Tucson Greyhound Park. Stock car races are on view at Tucson Raceway Park, the only asphalt short track in Arizona.

Golf is very popular in Tucson, and major annual events include the Accenture Match Play Championship at the Ritz-Carlton Golf Club at Dove Mountain. Tucson hosts the prestigious El Tour de Tucson cycling event each fall, as well as many tennis tournaments.

Sports for the Participant

Tucson's warm, sunny climate offers the outdoor sports enthusiast weather that rarely disrupts planned activities. The city of Tucson maintains more than 100 parks with jogging tracks, bike paths, riding trails, swimming pools, five municipal golf courses and several tennis centers. Swimming, boating, and fishing can be enjoyed in public and private pools and lakes. More than 4,500 participants run or walk in the Tucson Marathon each December, which also includes a half-marathon, 10-K, 5-K, and 1-mile races. Surrounding mountain ranges offer a variety of recreational opportunities. Mount Lemmon ski area receives an average of 175 inches of snow and offers three months of skiing each year. In keeping with Tucson's western traditions, local ranches offer horseback riding; and for those who want to step back into the past, there are even opportunities to pan for gold or participate in a cattle drive.

Shopping and Dining

Shopping for necessities or for pleasure can be equally rewarding in Tucson at neighborhood retail centers, regional malls, shopping plazas, and numerous shops and boutiques conveniently located throughout the area. Downtown's Fourth Avenue historic shopping and arts district is a popular destination, with its more than 100 galleries and unusual shops. Many shops specialize in indigenous goods and crafts such as Mexican handicrafts and decorative items, Indian kachina dolls, baskets, pottery, and moccasins. Traditional western clothing, boots, and other leather goods are also available in Tucson.

The city's restaurants are famous for Southwestern cuisine. Local specialties include carne seca, beef that has been marinated in lime and cilantro and then sun-dried; cinnamon chicken; black bean hummus; and prickly pear cactus. Diners can find a wide diversity of other ethnic fare, ranging from Greek to Thai, as well as traditional American food.

Visitor Information: Metropolitan Tucson Convention and Visitors Bureau, 100 S. Church Ave., Tucson, AZ 85701; telephone (520) 624-1817; fax (520) 884-7804.

■ Convention Facilities

With an expanded convention center and with additional meeting facilities available in many of the more than 200 hotels and 16 resorts, Tucson is emerging as a primary convention and meeting destination in the Southwest. A consistently warm climate and a wealth of leisure activities have drawn planners to the Tucson area.

To keep pace with hotel and resort developments that have gained for Tucson a reputation as an ideal setting for large and small group functions, the Tucson Convention Center offers flexible facilities for all types of meeting and convention needs. The center offers 205,000 square feet of meeting space and 3 exhibition halls as well as a music hall, arena, small auditorium, and eight meeting rooms for groups of 50 to 1,000 people. A spacious foyer and galleria are designed to accommodate pre-function activities. About $8 million in repairs and improvements to the convention center were funded by the city in 2013.

Convention Information: Metropolitan Tucson Convention and Visitors Bureau, 100 S. Church Ave., Tucson, AZ 85701; telephone (520) 624-1817; fax (520) 884-7804.

■ Transportation

Approaching the City

Visitors arriving in Tucson by plane are greeted by the expanded Tucson International Airport, located a few miles south of the city. Since a terminal expansion in 2005, the airport has been capable of handling seven million passengers in ticketing and baggage claim. A comprehensive master plan for even more development to accommodate the area's rapidly growing needs was underway in 2013. The Federal Aviation Administration was funding construction of a new $40 million control tower, while the local airport was working to develop large amounts of surrounding land for both aviation and non-aviation purposes. A 2012 study by the University of Arizona determined that the airport generated $3.3 billion in annual economic activity, which supported 35,000 direct or indirect jobs. Tucson International Airport is served by Alaska Airlines, American, Delta, Southwest, United, and US Airways.

Principal highway routes into the city are Interstate 10, which runs between Los Angeles and El Paso and passes through downtown on a northwest–southeast axis, and Interstate 19, which originates at the Mexican border and merges with Interstate 10 in Tucson. Amtrak provides train service and Greyhound provides bus service.

Traveling in the City

Tucson, located in a narrow, elliptical valley, is laid out in a grid pattern. The city is essentially serviced by surface roads, which can be congested during rush hours. Some major cross-town roads may suddenly dead end, necessitating a switch to a roundabout route. Numbered streets south of Speedway Boulevard run east–west, and numbered avenues west of Euclid Avenue run north–south. Residential and commercial pockets are scattered throughout the city, which can cause confusion. Drivers should be aware that during rush hours, the center or left-turn lane on major east–west thoroughfares becomes a one-way traffic lane.

Tucson's public mass transit system, operated by the regional Sun Tran Transit, provides service to major points within the city and the surrounding area, including the airport. The system provides more than 20 million passengers trips annually. Arizona has deregulated the ground transportation industry so that cab fare in Tucson is negotiable. Sun Link, Tucson's streetcar service, is part of a $2.1 billion regional transportation plan implemented by Pima County in 2006. The plan utilizes funding from federal and local sources. As of 2013, Sun Link operated one main route that wound its way from the Mercado district through downtown, the Fourth Avenue Business District, and the University of Arizona campus, ending at the Arizona Health Sciences Center.

■ Communications

Newspapers and Magazines

Tucson's primary newspaper is the *Arizona Daily Star* (every morning), with business information provided by the publication *Inside Tucson Business*. The *Tucson Citizen* is an online publication about life in the region. *Desert Airman* is a weekly newspaper for military personnel at Davis-Monthan U.S. Air Force Base. Magazines published in Tucson include *Tucson Weekly*, which contains information about the arts and area news, and *Tucson Guide*, which publishes *Tucson Official Visitors Guide* and *Tucson Lifestyle*. Several scholarly journals are also published in Tucson.

Television and Radio

Tucson's 15 television stations include network affiliates such as PBS, NBC, ABC, FOX, and CBS; independent stations and cable or satellite service are also available. Ten AM and 22 FM radio stations broadcast from Tucson, which also receives programming from neighboring communities.

Media Information: *Arizona Daily Star*, 4850 S. Park Avenue, Tucson, AZ, 85714; telephone (800) 695-4492.

Tucson Online

Arizona Daily Star. Available azstarnet.com

Arizona School Report Cards. Available www10.ade.az.gov/reportcard

City of Tucson home page. Available cms3.tucsonaz.gov

Metropolitan Tucson Convention & Visitors Bureau home page. Available www.visittucson.org

TucsonCitizen.com. Available www.tucsoncitizen.com

Tucson Metropolitan Chamber of Commerce home page. Available www.tucsonchamber.org

Tucson-Pima Public Library home page. Available www.library.pima.gov

BIBLIOGRAPHY

Griffith, James S., *Hecho a Mano: The Traditional Arts of Tucson's Mexican American Community* (Tucson, AZ: University of Arizona Press, 2000)

Hait, Pam, *Shifra Stein's Day Trips from Phoenix, Tucson, and Flagstaff* (Guilford, CT: GPP Travel, 2009)

Van Ham, Lane Vernon, *A Common Humanity: Ritual, Religion, and Immigrant Advocacy in Tucson, Arizona* (Tucson, AZ: University of Arizona Press, 2011)

California

The State in Brief

Nickname: Golden State

Motto: Eureka (I have found it)

Flower: Golden poppy

Bird: California valley quail

Area: 163,695 square miles (2010; U.S. rank 3rd)

Elevation: Ranges from 282 feet below sea level to 14,494 feet above sea level

Climate: Extremely varied, with zones ranging from subtropical to subarctic, but in the main two seasons—wet from October to April, dry from May to September

Admitted to Union: September 9, 1850

Capital: Sacramento

Head Official: Jerry Brown (D) (until 2015)

Population

1990: 30,380,000
2000: 33,871,653
2010: 37,253,956
2012 estimate: 37,325,068
Percent change, 2000–2010: 10.0%
U.S. rank in 2012: 1st
Percent of residents born in state: 53.8% (2012)
Density: 239.1 people per square mile (2010)
2012 FBI Crime Index Total: 1,210,409

Racial and Ethnic Characteristics (2012)

White: 23,252,553
Black or African American: 2,254,160
American Indian and Alaska Native: 291,505
Asian: 4,921,543
Native Hawaiian and Pacific Islander: 144,236
Hispanic or Latino (may be of any race): 14,024,109
Other: 6,461,071

Age Characteristics (2012)

Population under 5 years old: 2,543,777
Population 5 to 19 years old: 7,869,786
Percent of population 65 years and over: 11.5%
Median age: 35.2

Vital Statistics

Total number of births (2012–13): 503,634
Total number of deaths (2012–13): 250,567
AIDS cases reported through 2011: 168,692

Economy

Major industries: Agriculture, manufacturing (transportation equipment, electronics, machinery), biotechnology, information technology, aerospace, tourism
Unemployment rate (2012): 7.1%
Per capita income (2012): $29,551
Median household income (2012): $61,400
Percentage of persons below poverty level (2012): 15.3%
Income tax rate: 1.00% to 13.3%
Sales tax rate: 7.5%

Anaheim

■ The City in Brief

Founded: 1857 (incorporated, 1876)

Head Official: Mayor Tom Tait (since 2010; term expires 2014)

City Population
>1990: 266,406
>2000: 328,014
>2010: 336,265
>2012 estimate: 343,241
>Percent change, 2000–2010: 2.5%
>U.S. rank in 1990: 59th (State rank: 10th)
>U.S. rank in 2000: 64th (State rank: 10th)
>U.S. rank in 2010: 54th (State rank: 10th)

Metropolitan Statistical Area Population
>2000: 2,846,289
>2010: 3,018,181
>2012 estimate: 3,090,132
>Percent change, 2000–2010: 6.0%

Area: 48.9 square miles

Elevation: 137 feet above sea level

Average Annual Temperatures: 70.0° F

Average Annual Precipitation: 11.0 inches

Major Economic Sectors: services, trade, manufacturing

Unemployment Rate: 7.9% (2012)

Per Capita Income: $22,309

2012 FBI Crime Index Property: 10,070

Major Colleges and Universities: None

Daily Newspaper: *Orange County Register*

■ Introduction

The tourism industry is synonymous with Anaheim, one of the top vacation destinations in the United States. The city is home to the world famous theme park, Disneyland, which attracts flocks of tourists each year. The cornerstone attraction is supplemented by other tourist attractions such as Knott's Berry Farm and the San Juan Capistrano Mission. Millions of dollars invested in the city's convention center during the 2000s has allowed it to welcome one million event attendees annually and generate almost $1 billion in annual revenue. Both pleasure and business tourists have sustained a robust hospitality industry and allowed the city to work to diversify its economy toward advanced manufacturing.

■ Geography and Climate

Anaheim is located approximately 21 miles south of downtown Los Angeles and 13 miles from the Pacific coast. Anaheim is the second-largest city in Orange County, which consists of 34 cities. The Santa Ana Mountains lie to Anaheim's east. The Santa Ana River, which rises in the San Bernardino Mountains, flows past the southeast of Anaheim to the Pacific. Industrial and commercial areas along with a majority of the residential sections are relatively flat. The newer residential areas are in rolling terrain in the foothills of the Santa Ana Mountains. Summers are moderate to hot with cool evenings and winters are mild with very little rain. There are only about 38 days each year with even a one one-hundredth inch sprinkle. The region of Southern California, with several fault lines, is susceptible to earthquakes, though most are of a relatively low magnitude. The Santana Winds (or Santa Ana Winds) that typically occur from late summer to spring, bring warm and dry air down from the high deserts to the San Bernardino Mountains and through the Los Angeles-Orange County Basin. These winds are sometimes accompanied by brush and wildfires.

Courtesy of the Anaheim/Orange County Convention and Visitors Bureau.

Area: 48.9 square miles

Elevation: 137 feet above sea level

Average Temperatures: 70.0° F

Average Annual Precipitation: 11.0 inches

■ History

City Settled By German Winemakers

Anaheim was founded in 1857 by a group of German settlers who gave it the German name meaning "home by the river." The settlers were part of a group who first came to the United States during the German Revolution of 1848 and settled in San Francisco. Fifty members of that German community decided to move south when they learned about an abundance of cheap land that was once part of a Spanish land grant. The German colonists purchased the 1,165 acres of coastal plains for $2 an acre. Two of the Germans had a wine-making business. Attracted by the area's moderate climate, the settlers decided to make wine production the region's economic foundation. A civil engineer named George Hansen was hired to plan a carefully thought-out community with fences to protect the planned vineyards from roaming cattle. To allow future growth, specific parcels were set aside for construction of a school and other public buildings.

With the introduction of irrigation, Anaheim remained a prosperous wine producing region until the 1880s. During the period of 1860 to 1885, Anaheim wineries produced more than 1.25 million gallons of wine annually. In the 1880s, a blight completely wiped out the vineyards, destroying a thriving business. The orange and citrus industry was then developed and prospered, as did the city of Anaheim. The Southern California Fruit Growers Exchange, which was later renamed Sunkist, was organized in 1893.

The railroad had a positive effect on the city's development. Railroad service was provided by the Southern Pacific Railway, which established itself in the city in 1875. The Santa Fe Railroad followed soon after. The coming of the railroads permitted the city to expand to include other markets. Businesses prospered and the population grew.

Despite earlier failed attempts to become independent of the city of Los Angeles, Orange County was formed in 1889. Beginning in the late 1920s the city underwent rapid industrial development. A huge flood in 1938 caused the creation of a program to control the Santa Ana River, and the Prado Dam was built upstream to regulate the flow of the sometimes violent waterway.

Disneyland Displaces Agriculture as Major Industry

Agriculture remained the principal industry of the city until the mid 1950s, when the legendary Walt Disney chose Anaheim as the site for construction of his world-famous Disneyland amusement park. Millions of people each year are drawn to the area to enjoy this wonderful fantasy world.

The growth of Anaheim as a recreational attraction increased in the 1960s with the opening of Anaheim Stadium, home to Major League Baseball's Los Angeles Angels of Anaheim, and since renamed Angel Stadium of Anaheim. In 1967 the Anaheim Convention Center was opened. In 2000 the center was expanded by 40 percent, adding 815,000 square feet of exhibit space to become the largest exhibit facility on the West Coast. An additional 100,000 square feet of functional outdoor space was added in 2013.

Disney's California Adventure, an additional 55-acre park that pays homage to California's past, opened in 2001 and was renovated during 2007–12 at a cost of $1 billion. The addition of Cars Land, based on the Disney/Pixar animated films, was the central and final feature of the upgrade. An adjacent Downtown Disney District was also added during the 2000s, offering restaurants, shopping, and entertainment and firmly establishing Anaheim as the center of the Orange County tourism industry.

While mixed-use developments continued to appear throughout the city, a long-awaited economic development project finally broke ground in 2013: the Anaheim Regional Transportation Intermodal Center The $188 million, 67,000-square-foot transportation hub, located between the Honda Center and Angel Stadium, was set to provide residents and visitors with a landmark structure that provided easy access to and from some of the city's most popular attractions.

■ Population Profile

Metropolitan Statistical Area Population

2000: 2,846,289
2010: 3,018,181
2012 estimate: 3,090,132
Percent change, 2000–2010: 6.0%

City Residents

1990: 266,406
2000: 328,014
2010: 336,265
2012 estimate: 343,241
Percent change, 2000–2010: 2.5%
U.S. rank in 1990: 59th (State rank: 10th)
U.S. rank in 2000: 64th (State rank: 10th)
U.S. rank in 2010: 54th (State rank: 10th)

Density: 6,747.5 people per square mile

Racial and ethnic characteristics

White: 233,546
Black or African American: 7,450
American Indian and Alaskan Native: 1,057
Asian: 52,130
Native Hawaiian and Other Pacific Islander: 2,313
Hispanic or Latino (may be of any race): 182,446
Other: 46,745

Percent of residents born in state: 51%

Age characteristics

Population under 5 years old: 27,800
Population 5 to 9 years old: 25,063
Population 10 to 14 years old: 25,706
Population 15 to 19 years old: 23,625
Population 20 to 24 years old: 26,161
Population 25 to 34 years old: 52,244
Population 35 to 44 years old: 51,888
Population 45 to 54 years old: 43,640
Population 55 to 59 years old: 18,439
Population 60 to 64 years old: 14,529
Population 65 to 74 years old: 18,654
Population 75 to 84 years old: 10,446
Population 85 years and over: 5,046
Median age: 33.2

Births (2010–11 Metropolitan Area)

Total number: 38,498

Deaths (2010–11 Metropolitan Area)

Total number: 17,161

Money income (2012)

Per capita income: $22,309
Median household income: $57,345
Total households: 98,137

Number of households with income of ...

less than $10,000: 4,738
$10,000 to $14,999: 5,169
$15,000 to $24,999: 9,348
$25,000 to $34,999: 9,662
$35,000 to $49,999: 13,913
$50,000 to $74,999: 18,051
$75,000 to $99,999: 13,407
$100,000 to $149,999: 14,163
$150,000 to $199,999: 5,478
$200,000 or more: 4,208

Percent of families below poverty level: 16.4%

FBI Crime Index Property: 10,070

FBI Crime Index Violent: 1,279

■ Municipal Government

Anaheim has a council-manager form of government. The four members of the city council are elected to four-year, staggered terms. Council elections are held every two years. A mayoral election is held every four years. The city council appoints a manager who serves as the head of the government.

Head Official: Mayor Tom Tait (since 2010; term expires 2014)

Total Number of City Employees: 1,847 (2013)

City Information: City of Anaheim, City Hall 7th Floor, 200 S. Anaheim Blvd., Anaheim, CA 92805; telephone (714) 765-5247.

■ Economy

Major Industries and Commercial Activity

Tourism is the major industry in Anaheim. An ever-growing number of visitors has caused hotels, motels, restaurants, and retail centers to be built to meet their demands. At the time of Disneyland's opening in 1955, Anaheim had only 87 hotel rooms; presently, those numbers had grown to some 20,000 by 2013. The rise in tourism has encouraged the city to update and add to its facilities. Since being dedicated in 1967, the Anaheim Convention Center has undergone major expansions; an expansion completed in 2000 enlarged the center by 40 percent, to 1.6 million square feet. Tremendous infrastructure changes in the 1,100-acre Anaheim Resort district (surrounding Disneyland and Anaheim Convention Center area) during the 2000s included 15,000 new trees, shrubs, and flowers, as well as improved signage, with a total price tag of some $5 billion. As of 2013, the convention center was the largest on the West Coast. It drew nearly 1 million meeting attendees and generated $834 million in revenue in 2012.

More than 43 million tourists come to Anaheim and Orange County annually. Tourism supports an estimated 150,000 jobs county-wide, with tourist expenditures reaching nearly $8.7 billion in 2012.

Tourism and business have built a healthy interdependence over the years. The city has become more economically diverse with the development of business and manufacturing firms; Anaheim is currently home to thousands of businesses. It is a center of enterprise for multinational firms, as well as regional and local companies. The city of Anaheim has been successful in retaining some businesses that had considered leaving by offering loans, tax and utility rebates, subsidies, and job-training incentives.

In addition to the Walt Disney Resort, by far the largest employer in Anaheim, top employers in 2013 included Kaiser Permanente, Hilton Anaheim, CashCall Inc., Anaheim Regional Medical Center, and Republic Services.

Items and goods produced: aerospace devices, kitchen products and accessories, shelving and cabinets, countertops, fixtures

Incentive Programs—New and Existing Companies

Local programs: Anaheim offers qualifying firms economic development rates, new construction incentives, and energy efficiency incentives. Anaheim has programs to help businesses relocate into designated redevelopment areas, and offers consultations, workshops, and seminars. The Anaheim Redevelopment Agency considers financial support of business projects on a case-by-case basis if located within a Merged Redevelopment Project Area. The Orange County Small Business Development Center also offers assistance to new and expanding businesses.

State programs: California business incentives include the state's Alternative Energy and Advanced Transportation Authority Sales and Use Tax Exemptions for Zero Emission Vehicle Manufacturing. Initially targeting vehicle manufacturing only when it was passed in 2010, the sales and use tax exemption has since been expanded to all renewable energy technologies. In 2012 it was expanded again to include advanced manufacturing. More than one dozen additional incentives encourage green development or pollution-reducing business decisions.

Research and development tax credits offers companies a 15 percent credit against their bank and corporation tax liability for qualifying in-house research expenses; a 24 percent tax credit for basic research payments to outside organizations is also available. Industrial development bonds finance investment in land, buildings, and new equipment related to domestic manufacturing operations in the state. California Capital Access Program and Collateral Support Program also offer alternative methods of financing for businesses. Enterprise Zones and Local Agency Military Base Recovery Area regions provide incentives for development in targeted geographic regions. A New Jobs Tax Credit offers $3,000 per hire of qualifying new employees, and the state's Film and Television Tax Credit Program supports productions with a 20 percent tax credit against qualified expenses.

In 2011 California began offering companies the option to calculate their corporate income tax through the single sales factor method, rather than the existing triple apportionment derived from calculations of a company's payroll, property, and sales.

California's Innovation Hub Program, with 12 locations throughout the state, supports the commercialization of innovation and technology businesses through public-private partnerships, knowledge sharing, venture capital sources, and business incubators. The state also undertakes trade missions to form partnerships for trade and export promotion.

Job training programs: The state of California offers an Employment Training Panel to assist companies with post-hire training and reimbursement. The Employment Development Department also partners with Local Workforce Investment Areas to recruit, screen, test, evaluate, and hire qualified workers.

Anaheim's Career Employment Center (CEC), created by the Job Training Program Division, offers subsidies of up to 50 percent of an employee's wages for up to six months in order to assist with customized on-the-job training programs that can help new and expanding businesses. Industry-specific customized training programs are also offered, as are retraining and new-hire training assistance. Anaheim supports school-to-career training programs to increase the employability of its secondary school graduates.

Development Projects

In 2001 a massive $5 billion renovation of the Anaheim Resort District (the greater Anaheim Convention Center/ Disneyland area, comprised of 1,100 acres) was completed. The project began in 1994 when the city of Anaheim approved a $174 million Anaheim Resort Capital Improvement Program designed to transform the district into a more attractive, pedestrian-friendly destination.

Among the results was the 55-acre theme park called Disney's California Adventure, brought about by a $1.4 billion investment in all Disney properties. California Adventure, which opened in 2001 adjacent to Disneyland, received a $1 billion transformation that concluded in 2012 and added Cars Land, based on the Disney/Pixar animated films, as a centerpiece of the renovation. Other additions between 2007 and 2012 centered on popular Disney films and characters, such as *Toy Story, The Little Mermaid,* Mickey, and Goofy.

The Anaheim Convention Center underwent a $177 million expansion that completed in 2000. The expansion increased the size of the center by 40 percent, making it the largest exhibit facility on the West Coast. Also completed was a $396 million "freshening" of the entire Resort District with landscaping and infrastructure improvements, including the addition of 15,000 new trees, shrubs, and flowers, and improved signage. In 2013 the city completed work on the Anaheim Convention Center Grand Plaza, 100,000 square feet of outdoor space between the Hilton and Marriot hotels leading up to the convention center. The Grand Plaza is capable of hosting outdoor concerts, cocktail receptions, dinners, and automobile shows.

In 2007 John Wayne Airport began an Airport Improvement Program to meet the needs of its passengers.

Among other changes, the program included an update to existing facilities, the addition of a third terminal, Terminal C, which completed in 2011, additional parking, and installation of wireless Internet in all terminals.

The city's biggest project was the Anaheim Regional Transportation Intermodal Center (ARTIC), which broke ground in 2013. The $188 million transportation hub included a 67,000-square-foot, three-story terminal building located between the Honda Center and Angel Stadium. The project was set to be completed in 2014 and serve more than 10,000 passengers daily via Amtrak and Metrolink rail, and local bus service, in addition to charter buses, taxis, and bicycles. Plans for ARTIC dated to the mid-1980s but had been long delayed. Funding came from federal and state sources, in addition to a half-cent sales tax in Orange County.

Economic Development Information: City of Anaheim Economic Development, 200 S. Anaheim Blvd., Suite 162, Anaheim, CA 92805; telephone (714) 765-4323.

Commercial Shipping

The city's transportation access is excellent and is in proximity to several airports, two major ports of call, interstate access, and an extensive public transit system. The Port of Los Angeles, about 28 miles from the city, is the busiest container port in the United States. It is designated as a Foreign Trade Zone. The Port of Long Beach, about 25 miles from the city, is a major gateway to Asian markets.

The Los Angeles International Airport (LAX) has 1,000 cargo flights each day. Handling facilities include the 98-acre Century Cargo Complex, the 57.4-acre Imperial Complex, the Imperial Cargo Center, and several terminals on the south side of the airport. As of 2013, LAX ranked 14th in the world and 5th in the United States for most air cargo tonnage handled. In 2012, the airport handled 1.96 million tons of freight worth a total of $87 billion. The John Wayne Airport added a new cargo facility in 2009 as part of a larger airport improvement program. Freight service is provided by Southern Pacific, Santa Fe, and Union Pacific railroads, which maintain about 30 miles of railroad track in the city. Many major interstate trucking companies are located within the area.

Labor Force and Employment Outlook

As of 2012, 16 percent of people employed in Anaheim worked in wholesale or retail trade; 11 percent in professional, scientific, and business services; 15 percent in manufacturing; 7 percent in construction, agriculture, mining, and fishing; 7 percent in finance, real estate, and insurance; 17 percent in education, health care, and social assistance; 13 percent in arts, entertainment, recreation, hospitality, and food services services; and 14 percent in a variety of other fields.

The following is a summary of data regarding the 2012 Anaheim labor force:

Size of civilian labor force: 175,535

Number of workers employed in . . .

agriculture and mining: 628
construction: 10,460
manufacturing: 23,227
wholesale trade: 5,453
retail trade: 19,363
transportation: 5,622
information systems: 2,499
finance: 9,823
professional administration: 16,829
education and social services: 27,052
arts and leisure: 19,634
other: 8,669
public administration: 4,310

Average hourly earnings of production workers: $15.78

Unemployment rate: 7.9% (2012)

Employers

Largest employers (2013)	Number of employees
Walt Disney Resort	23,512
Kaiser Foundation Hospital	6,040
Hilton Anaheim	1,572
CashCall Inc. Mortgage Division	1,400
AHMC Anaheim Regional Medical Center	1,300
Republic Services	1,300
Angels Baseball LP	1,051
Anaheim Marriot Hotel	1,030
L-3 Interstate Electronic Corporation	940
Northgate Gonzalez Markets	850

Cost of Living

The cost of living in Anaheim is significantly above the national average, as are home prices.

The following is a summary of data regarding several key cost of living factors in the area.

2013 ACCRA Average House Price: $729,578

2013 ACCRA Cost of Living Index: 144

State income tax rate: 1.00% to 13.3%

State sales tax rate: 7.5%

Local income tax rate: None

Local sales tax rate: 0.5%

Property tax rate: Limited to 1% of assessed value by state law. In some cases the local taxing body can add additional taxes.

Economic Information: Anaheim Chamber of Commerce, 201 East Center Street, Anaheim, CA 92805; telephone (714) 758-0222; fax (714) 758-0468.

■ Education and Research

Elementary and Secondary Schools

Anaheim is served by the Anaheim City School District, which operates the elementary schools, and the Anaheim Union High School District, which oversees the junior high and high schools. The city is noted for excellent schools offering a full array of learning programs from basic curriculum instruction to college preparation, athletics, and special education. A Spanish-English Dual Language program is available in some schools. The Gifted and Talented Education Program (GATE) is available to students in grades three to six.

Lexington Junior High School, Cypress High School, Western High School, and Oxford Academy all have been recognize by the state as Distinguished Schools. Oxford Academy has been ranked nationally by *U.S. News & World Report,* with another six schools receiving other recognition from the publication. The district's Career Technical Education pathway program includes 28 pathways across 12 industries that seek to prepare future graduates for immediate employment. Some 900 students are enrolled in 19 courses conducted online.

The following is a summary of data regarding the Anaheim City and Anaheim Union High School Districts.

Total enrollment: 52,251

Number of facilities

total: 48
elementary schools: 24
junior high schools: 11
high schools: 13
other: 0

Student/teacher ratio: 25.56:1

Teacher salaries

average (statewide): $69,434

Funding per pupil: $9,023

Public Schools Information: Anaheim City School District, 1001 South East Street, Anaheim, CA 92805; telephone (714) 517-7500. Anaheim Union High School District, 501 N. Crescent Way, Anaheim, CA, 92801; telephone (714) 999-3511; fax (714) 520-9754.

Colleges and Universities

Although there are no major universities in the city of Anaheim proper, there are several smaller institutions offering post-secondary education. Anaheim University, based in the city, serves students around the globe with online courses in English teacher education, business administration, and sustainable management.

The Southern California Institute of Technology offers four bachelor's degree programs in biomedical engineering, electrical engineering, electronic engineering, and information systems. The North Orange County Community College District Anaheim Campus houses a Schools of Continuing Education. The school offers a variety of basic adult education and vocational programs. Associate degrees are offered through Cypress College and Fullerton College, both of which are operated by the Orange County Community College District. Everest College has an area location that offers career training programs in dental assisting, medical assisting, massage therapy, nursing, and medical billing and coding. The national ITT Technical Institute maintains a campus in Anaheim.

South Baylo University offers master's and doctoral degree in acupuncture and oriental medicine. It is considered one of the best schools of its kind in the nation and offers instruction in Chinese and Korean as well as English. The school operates a clinic in Anaheim.

In the greater Orange County area, California State University–Fullerton offers both undergraduate and graduate programs through eight colleges. Chapman University in Orange offers programs in eight colleges, with one of the most popular being studies in film and television through the Lawrence and Kristina Dodge College of Film and Media Arts. The University of California–Irvine is a research university with 16 colleges and schools.

Libraries and Research Centers

The Anaheim Public Library holds more than 500,000 volumes and more than 40,000 audio and video materials. The library's special collections include the Anaheim History Collection. The library is comprised of a central library and five main branches—Haskett, Euclid, Sunkist, East Anaheim, and Canyon Hills—in addition to a joint-use center at Ponderosa School and the Heritage Center at Carnegie Plaza. Bookmobile services were suspended in 2010 due to budget cuts but resumed operations in 2011. The Sunkist Branch holds foreign language books in Chinese, Spanish, and Vietnamese. Card holders of the Anaheim Public Library system may also borrow books through the Fullerton Public Library, Placentia Public Library, and Yorba Public Library.

Other Anaheim libraries consist of those of local hospitals and companies, including Anaheim Regional Medical Center and Western Medical Center. The Richard Nixon Presidential Library & Museum is in Yorba Linda, a 15-minute drive from Anaheim.

The South Baylo University Research Center was established 2000. It conducts research in acupuncture treatments for high-risk populations, such as those with cancer or AIDS, in part by providing free services to patients seeking such care. Research training takes place at the Well Healthcare One Clinic, part of the South Baylo University Integrative Medical Center.

Public Library Information: Anaheim Public Library, 500 West Broadway, Anaheim, CA 92805; telephone (714) 765-1880.

■ Health Care

Area hospitals boast state-of-the-art facilities and top-quality care. Several hospitals are located within the city. Anaheim Regional Medical Center offers general medical, critical care, and surgical services, as well as centers for specialized care. As of 2013, the hospital had 223 beds and more than 600 physicians. Its emergency department served some 44,000 patients annually..

The 219-bed West Anaheim Medical Center is another general medical and surgical hospital. Western Medical Center–Anaheim has 188 beds and offers general medical and surgical service, and features the Cardiac Institute of Anaheim, offering both diagnostic and interventional treatments that include access to a Cardiac Cath Lab. Kaiser Permanente also has a facility in Orange County.

South Baylo University Integrative Medical Center offers Western medicine practice as well as treatments including acupuncture, herbal medicine, and massage in a holistic approach to health care.

The Karlton Residential Care Center in Anaheim is a 70-bed faculty for those with Alzheimer's or related disorders.

■ Recreation

Sightseeing

Anaheim's crown jewel attraction is Disneyland, America's most popular theme park. Visitors can stroll through the park's eight "lands," which together offer more than 60 major rides, shops, and restaurants: futuristic Tomorrowland provides an out-of-this-world atmosphere; Adventureland reproduces the exotic surroundings of

Asia, the Middle East, and the South Seas; Frontierland is based on the Wild West; Fantasyland, with Sleeping Beauty's Castle and the It's a Small World ride, is the heart of Disneyland; Critter Country is home to cute woodland creatures; Main Street U.S.A. is based on small-town America of a century ago; New Orleans Square reproduces the atmosphere of turn-of-the-century New Orleans; and Mickey's Toontown is a cartoon playland. Special entertainment, shopping, and dining are featured at Disneyland year-round. Special attractions include Indiana Jones Adventure; Space Mountain and Star Tours, exciting flight-simulation journeys; Splash Mountain, an 87-foot-high log flume ride based on Disney's "Song of the South" characters; Big Thunder Mountain Railroad; and the Haunted Mansion.

One of Disneyland's newest areas is California Adventure. Requiring a separate admission ticket, it was originally based on the fun adventures offered by California and divided into four themed districts: Paradise Pier with classic "Golden Age" amusement park attractions along the beach; Hollywood Land celebrating the movie business; The Golden State, a tribute to California's natural beauty; and "a bug's land," inspired by the film *A Bug's Life* and designed from a bug's perspective. Between 2007 and 2012, the park spent $1 billion to add more Disney- and Pixar-themed lands, including those based on the films *Toy Story*, *The Little Mermaid*, and *Cars*.

Knott's Berry Farm in nearby Buena Park, once a small berry farm business, has grown into one of the most popular theme parks in the country. The park, a 150-acre complex with more than 100 rides and dozens of shops and restaurants, is especially known for its thrill rides. Distinct theme areas are Ghost Town, an Old West mining town reproduction; Camp Snoopy, which features special rides and activities for small children; The Boardwalk, a colorful tribute to the Southern California beach culture that features ocean-related rides and attractions, three of which were added in 2013; Indian trails, which showcases the traditions and cultures of Native Americans; Fiesta Village, a celebration of Spanish California; and Soak City water park. Special attractions include MonteZOOMa's Revenge, a roller coaster that goes from 0 to 60 miles per hour in just three seconds; Supreme Scream ascends 214 feet and then plunges straight down at about 50 miles per hour; XCELERA-TOR blasts riders to 82 miles per hour in 2.3 seconds, travels up to 205 feet, then descends at 90 degrees; and Bigfoot Rapids is a whitewater river raft ride.

The Discovery Science Center, in Santa Ana, houses hands-on exhibits in themed areas: Eco Challenge, Boeing Rocket Lab, Science of Hockey, and Dino Quest. Adventure City is a two-acre theme park for children ages 2 to 12. The Mission San Juan Capistrano, 30 miles south of Anaheim, was founded in 1776 and is the birthplace of Orange County. Beautiful and romantic, it is considered the "jewel of the missions." Its Serra Chapel is believed to be California's oldest standing building.

Arts and Culture

The 3,000-seat Segerstrom Hall at the Orange County Performing Arts Center in nearby Costa Mesa hosts world-class performances of symphony, ballet, and opera, as well as Broadway shows; the 250-seat Founders Hall in the Center offers innovative jazz and cabaret programming as well as the best in chamber music. The Center also includes a 2,000-seat Renée and Henry Segerstrom Concert Hall and the multi-functional Samueli Theater. The Center is home to the Philharmonic Society of Orange County, Pacific Symphony Orchestra, and Pacific Chorale.

Numerous other theaters dot Orange County. Fullerton Civic Light Opera Company, based in nearby Fullerton, is one of the largest musical theater companies in Southern California; it presents four productions annually at Plummer Auditorium. The auditorium, built in 1930, seats more than 1,300 and hosts a variety of theatrical productions and community-oriented cultural programs. South Coast Repertory Theatre, in Costa Mesa, is a Tony award–winning theater that presents professional productions of contemporary and classical plays on its three stages. Garden Grove is home to the 158-seat Gem Theater and 550-seat Festival Amphitheater.

The Honda Center is a 650,000-square-foot arena that hosts concerts and family shows as well as being home to the Anaheim Ducks of the National Hockey League. Pearson Park Amphitheater is an open-air facility that features family entertainment all summer long and the Grove of Anaheim presents comedy and music artists in an intimate setting.

The Anaheim Museum highlights the history of the city's original German settlers, its establishment as a wine and citrus colony, and the early Disneyland days depicted in changing exhibits. Mother Colony House, one of the city's first buildings, showcases antiques and other historical items of Anaheim's earliest periods. Bowers Museum of Cultural Art, in nearby Santa Ana, occupies a landmark mission-style building; its exhibits reflect cultural arts from California and around the world. Bowers features a hands-on children's section known as the Kidseum.

The Muzeo, opened in 2007 as part of the city's downtown revitalization projects, offers an exhibit hall, a cultural and art museum, and a history center.

Festivals and Holidays

The St. Patrick's Day Festival at the Anaheim Farmer's Market features Irish dancers, music, and food. St. Boniface Parish Fiesta in April features international foods, rides, and games. The first weekend in May brings the Cinco de Mayo Fiesta and Carnival, featuring a soccer tournament, the crowning of a fiesta queen, and a Sunday bilingual Mass, as well as rides, food, and entertainment; the fiesta draws more than 100,000 people throughout the weekend. The OC Greek Fest, also in May, features Greek foods, pastries, music, and folk dancers, and a marketplace with vendors selling a variety of items. The

Anaheim Children's Art Festival in late May features art-and-craft projects in staffed booths. Taste of Anaheim offers ethnic food, fun, and displays in May, as well. Anaheim Hills 4th of July Festival & Parade includes a pancake breakfast, dog show, 5K and 10K run/walk, parade, food and game booths, and fireworks. At nearby Laguna Beach's Pageant of the Masters, famous paintings and statuary come to life through the use of live models and an orchestra each night during the months of July and August. The Anaheim Fall Festival & Halloween Parade in late October features a parade, pancake breakfast, rides, games, and live entertainment. Knott's Berry Farm transforms into Knott's Camp Spooky and then Knott's Merry Farm to celebrate Halloween and Christmas. The Christmas Parade at Disneyland features many popular Disney characters as well as Santa Claus. Nutcracker Holiday, held the first Saturday in December, features musicians, carolers, and a tree-lighting ceremony.

Sports for the Spectator

Major League Baseball's Los Angeles Angels of Anaheim, World Series Champions in 2002 and American League West Champions in 2007, 2008, and 2009, play home games at Angel Stadium of Anaheim, a baseball-only facility with seating for 45,050. The Anaheim Ducks, a National Hockey League team formerly owned by the Walt Disney Company, won the Stanley Cup in 2007. They play at the four-level, 17,174-seat Honda Center. The Honda Center also hosts the Wooden Legacy tournament, formerly the J.R. Wooden Classic, which features some of the nation's top basketball teams. The Anaheim Bolts area professional indoor soccer team, and Anaheim serves as the training home for both the men and women's USA Volleyball teams.

Los Alamitos Race Course, 15 minutes west of Disneyland, features the world's fastest horses in quarter horse, Arabian, thoroughbred, paint, and Appaloosa racing. Costa Mesa Speedway at Orange County Fairgrounds holds speedway races on Saturday nights, April through September.

Sports for the Participant

Anaheim has 51 parks totaling more than 600 acres. Among them is Oak Canyon Nature Center, a 58-acre natural park in the Anaheim Hills providing excellent opportunities for short hikes. A year-round stream meanders through the park, which consists of three adjoining canyons with four miles of hiking trails. Tennis is available at several Anaheim hotels and the city maintains more than 50 public courts. Anaheim Hills, a public country club, offers a challenging 18-hole golf course in the natural terrain of the Santa Ana Canyons. Dad Miller Golf Course is a well-kept course surrounded by lovely old trees and a natural lake; it was Tiger Woods's home course during high school. Anaheim Ice, the official training facility of the Anaheim Ducks, offers public skating and pick-up hockey.

Orange County has a 42-mile coastline filled with public and state beaches. Sailing cruises, whale watching, surfing, and swimming are available at sites along the coastline. The county has a regional trail system consisting of 220 miles of built trails. The 30-mile Santa Ana River Trail is a running/bike path that follows the Santa Ana River in the San Bernardino Mountains. Snow skiing is available at nearby Bear Mountain ski resort. Orange County is home to 38 public golf courses.

Shopping and Dining

Downtown Disney, a 120-acre shopping, restaurant, and entertainment complex adjacent to Disneyland, features one-of-a-kind Disney-themed shops and trend-setting restaurants. It is open to the public, with no admission charge. Anaheim Indoor Marketplace is an outlet mall with more than 200 variety stores. South Coast Plaza in Costa Mesa offers an immense collection of international stores clustered around a Village Green in an open-air environment. Fashion Island in Newport Beach is an upscale shopping area with open-air courtyards and covered patios overlooking the ocean; it features more than 200 shops, about 40 restaurants, and a movie theater. Westfield MainPlace Mall in Santa Ana is another large upscale center, with more than 180 specialty shops and restaurants. The Anaheim Hills Festival Shopping Center offers a variety of stores similar to those found in typical shopping malls. The Shops at Anaheim Garden-Walk along Katella Avenue opened in 2007 and feature more than 40 stores and restaurants.

Dining experiences in Anaheim run the gamut from ethnic specialties such as Armenian, Cajun, Chinese, Cuban, German, Indian, Italian, Japanese, Mexican, Middle Eastern, Peruvian, and Thai to places with unique ambiance such as canneries, gold mines, and Victorian houses. There are more than 60 restaurants and cocktail lounges in the immediate area of the Anaheim Convention Center. In nearby Orange, Watson Drugs and Soda Fountain, established in 1899, has been the set for several movies; it offers burgers and sweets.

Visitor Information: Anaheim/Orange County Visitor and Convention Bureau, 800 W. Katella Avenue, Anaheim, CA 92802; telephone (855) 405-5020.

■ Convention Facilities

The Anaheim Convention Center, a sparkling, glass-walled facility, completed a $177 million expansion and redesign in December 2000. The expansion enlarged the center by 40 percent to 1.6 million square feet. The center houses 815,000 square feet of exhibit space, making it the largest exhibit facility on the West Coast. Pre-function lobby space totals 200,000 square feet; an additional 100,000 square feet of outdoor space was added in 2013. There are also 130,000 square feet of meeting space and a 38,000 square-foot main ballroom. The center hosts more than one million attendees annually at events such as national conventions, conferences, corporate meetings, trade shows, concerts, and home and garden shows. Situated in the 1,100-acre Anaheim Resort district, the center is within walking distance of more than 12,000 hotel rooms.

The Disneyland Hotel at Disneyland Resort offers dozens of meeting spaces, the largest one being the 50,000-square-foot Disneyland Exhibit Hall in Magic Tower. There is a banquet hall to accommodate up to 2,000 people and three restaurants. The Marriott Anaheim offers 82,000 square feet of meeting space that includes exhibit space, flexible ballrooms and 44 total meeting rooms. Several other area hotels and restaurants offer meeting and banquet spaces.

Convention Information: Anaheim/Orange County Visitor and Convention Bureau, 800 W. Katella Avenue, Anaheim, CA 92802; telephone (855) 405-5020.

■ Transportation

Approaching the City

The main artery running through Anaheim is Interstate 5 (the Santa Ana Freeway), which also connects Los Angeles and San Diego. Interstate 5 links Anaheim with the Riverside Freeway, the Garden Grove Freeway, the Orange Freeway, and the Costa Mesa Freeway.

There are four airports serving the area. Los Angeles International Airport, located about 31 miles northwest of Anaheim, is the sixth busiest airport in the world for passengers handled and third busiest in the United States. The airport is served by more than 25 major airlines with thousands of flights each year. Long Beach Airport to the west is served by four airlines, and LA/Ontario International Airport to the northeast supports seven airlines. The John Wayne Airport in Santa Ana, owned and operated by Orange County, is about 16 miles southwest of Anaheim. It is served by 11 airlines.

Metrolink, a regional commuter rail system, links travelers to activity centers in Orange and surrounding counties. Amtrak provides railway transportation, and Greyhound offers daily bus service into the city. The city broke ground in 2013 on a $188 million transportation hub located between the Honda Center and Angel Stadium. The project was set to be completed in 2014 and serve more than 10,000 passengers daily via Amtrak and Metrolink rail, in addition to local and regional bus service and local bus service.

Traveling in the City

The Santa Ana Freeway traverses Anaheim's downtown running northwest to southeast. The Garden Grove Freeway runs east and west through the city, and the Orange Freeway runs north and south through the city.

The Orange County Transportation Authority operates buses daily with 77 routes and nearly 6,200 stops throughout Orange County. Anaheim Resort Transportation (ART) buses, trams, and trolleys provide connections between hotels, Anaheim attractions, the convention center, shopping, dining, and evening entertainment locations, along 20 interchangeable routes.

■ Communications

Newspapers and Magazines

The primary daily newspapers serving Anaheim and surrounding Orange County are the *Orange County Register,* published in Santa Ana, the *Daily Pilot,* published in Costa Mesa, and the *Los Angeles Times.* The *Press-Telegram* is published in Long Beach.

The *OC Weekly* is an alternative weekly press that is published in Orange County.

Television and Radio

Only one television station broadcasts directly from Anaheim. Most local programming and news is provided through Los Angeles–based stations. Cable television and satellite service is also available. And although just one AM radio station broadcasts from within the city, a multitude of AM and FM stations are broadcast from the surrounding Orange County area and Los Angeles.

Media Information: Orange County Register, 625 N. Grand Ave., Santa Ana, CA 92701; telephone (877) 469-7344.

Anaheim Online

> Anaheim City School District. Available www.acsd. k12.ca.us
> Anaheim Orange County Visitor & Convention Bureau. Available anaheimoc.org
> Anaheim Public Library. Available library.anaheim. net/Library
> City of Anaheim home page. Available www. anaheim.net
> Greater Anaheim Chamber of Commerce. Available www.anaheimchamber.org
> Orange County Department of Education. Available www.ocde.us
> *Orange County Register.* Available www.ocregister. com

BIBLIOGRAPHY

Faessel, Stephen J., *Early Anaheim* (Mount Pleasant, SC: Arcadia Publishing, 2006)

Newhan, Ross, *The Anaheim Angels: A Complete History* (New York: Hyperion, 2000)

Telotte, J. P., *The Mouse Machine: Disney and Technology* (Urbana: University of Illinois Press, 2008)

Fresno

■ The City in Brief

Founded: 1872 (incorporated 1885)

Head Official: Mayor Ashley Swearengin (since 2009; term expires 2017)

City Population
1990: 354,091
2000: 427,652
2010: 494,665
2012 estimate: 505,870
Percent change, 2000–2010: 15.7%
U.S. rank in 1990: 47th
U.S. rank in 2000: 40th
U.S. rank in 2010: 34th (State rank: 5th)

Metropolitan Statistical Area Population
2000: 799,407
2010: 930,450
2012 estimate: 947,895
Percent change, 2000–2010: 16.4%
U.S. rank in 2000: 58th
U.S. rank in 2010: 55th

Area: 99.1 square miles

Elevation: 328 feet above sea level

Average Annual Temperatures: January, 46.0° F; July, 81.4° F; annual average, 63.2° F

Average Annual Precipitation: 11.23 inches of rain; 0.1 inches of snow

Major Economic Sectors: agriculture, trade, manufacturing, government, technology

Unemployment Rate: 9.5% (2012)

Per Capita Income: $18,360

2012 FBI Crime Index Property: 25,737

Major Colleges and Universities: California State University, Fresno; Fresno City College; Fresno Pacific University

Daily Newspaper: *The Fresno Bee*

■ Introduction

Fresno is the commercial, financial, and cultural center of the San Joaquin Valley and the central California region; it is also the seat of Fresno County. The city is the business and transportation hub for four separate agricultural regions in what has been called the agribusiness center of the world. The economy, though largely based in farming, has also expressed strength in technology as software companies have moved into the area. Fresno is also known as the gateway to three national parks: Yosemite, Kings Canyon, and Sequoia. Rapid publication growth during the last decades of the twentieth century—and a roughly 16 percent growth rate in the first decade of the twenty-first—led to considerable suburban sprawl and inspired city efforts to refocus energy on the downtown area. Growth also created an ethnically diverse city, as many immigrants flocked to Fresno seeking work in local agriculture.

■ Geography and Climate

Fresno is located in the fertile San Joaquin Valley in the central part of California, about halfway between San Francisco and Los Angeles. It is the sixth largest city in the state and is the seat of Fresno County. The terrain in Fresno is relatively flat, with a sharp rise to the foothills of the Sierra Nevada Mountains about 15 miles eastward. A network of irrigation canals runs through and round the

© Gary Crabbe/Enlightened Images/Alamy

city. The weather is usually sunny, with more than 200 clear days each year. Summers are typically hot and dry, while winters are mild and rainy. Spring and fall are the most pleasant seasons. The area is occasionally subject to severe droughts or winter storms that can cause damage to croplands and homes.

Area: 99.1 square miles

Elevation: 328 feet above sea level

Average Temperatures: January, 46.0° F; July, 81.4° F; annual average, 63.2° F

Average Annual Precipitation: 11.23 inches of rain; 0.1 inches of snow

■ History

Settlement of Fresno Delayed Until Arrival of Railroad

Fresno means "ash tree" in Spanish and was the name given by early Spanish explorers to a stretch of white ash trees along the banks of the San Joaquin River. These explorers did not settle in the region where Fresno is now located, however, because they considered it uninhabitable. The site was in fact to remain undeveloped until the late nineteenth century. In the early part of the century, potential settlers were discouraged from staying permanently by the presence of the native population. Unlike other California cities Fresno did not get its start during the gold rush. Prospectors simply passed through the area on the way to the Sierras. After the gold rush the land was used for cattle grazing.

The first permanent settlement is said to have been established in the 1860s by an immigrant from Holland who was joined by a few other people; the cluster of dwellings was not actually considered a town. In 1872 the Central Pacific Railroad was constructed through the San Joaquin Valley; the railroad builders laid out a town, calling it Fresno Station for the name of the county. A station was built on the present site of downtown Fresno.

The county seat at that time was Millerton, a town 25 miles to the south. In order to gain access to rail transportation, Millerton residents voted to transfer the seat to Fresno Station and the entire population moved. The town was rough and desolate, and the countryside barren. The introduction of irrigation and grape-growing in the valley brought prosperity and Fresno was established as a city in 1885. Soon vineyards were being planted by local inhabitants as well as Italian, French, and Swiss immigrants who had bought 20-acre parcels of land.

Development of Raisin and Fig Industries

When the dry white wine produced from the area's vineyards proved less than satisfactory, the grapes were cultivated for raisins, which were naturally produced by the continuous sunlight in the valley. Following an unusually large yield of more than one million pounds of raisins that drove the price down to two cents a pound in 1894, the Raisin Growers Association was organized (in 1898) to protect the raisin industry. In 1886 Frank Roeding and his son began growing figs in the area; having experimented with caprification, the cross-fertilization of the Smyrna fig by the fig wasp, they started another successful industry.

By 1900 the population of Fresno had reached 12,470 people and the city drafted its first charter. During the following decade, agriculture continued to flourish, with cotton growing and sweet wine production emerging as new industries. Fresno became the residential and commercial center of an increasingly prosperous region. With the expansion of manufacturing along with agriculture, Fresno was a major metropolitan area by the end of World War II.

Rapid population growth began to strain the city's boundaries. In the late 1970s the city had about 190,000 people. In 1990 the population was 354,000. From 1990 to 2000 the population grew by 20.3 percent. Newcomers included a large number of immigrants, particularly those from Southeast Asia. To keep up with the surge of residents, farmlands were rezoned to allow for new housing developments and the city began to diversify its economy, particularly in retail, strip-mall type developments.

Scandal rocked the town in the early 1990s as the FBI discovered a web of political corruption known as Operation Rezone. It came to light that a number of city council members from Fresno and nearby Clovis were accepting bribes from developers in return for favorable votes on rezoning issues. Several officials were later convicted. At about the same time, downtown retail centers began to decline as suburban shopping centers became more popular. In the 2000s and 2010s, city officials have taken measures to strengthen the city through redevelopment. The city became a federal Empowerment Zone in 2002 and unveiled comprehensive revitalization and rezoning plans in the 2010s that were expected to guide sustainable downtown development for decades.

An increase of gang-related violence in Fresno plagued the city in the late 2000s, although Mayor Ashley Swearengin reported significant progress in the reduction of violent crime into the 2010s, with violent crime falling by 4 percent in 2011, 6 percent in 2012, and 9 percent in 2013. The city's "Operation Bulldog" has taken a five-pronged approach to gang stem violence—prevention, intervention, suppression, rehabilitation and economic development—and was viewed as a national model.

Historical Information: California History & Genealogy Room, Fresno County Public Library, 2420 Mariposa Street, Fresno, CA 93721; telephone (559) 600-7323.

■ Population Profile

Metropolitan Statistical Area Population
2000: 799,407
2010: 930,450
2012 estimate: 947,895
Percent change, 2000–2010: 16.4%
U.S. rank in 2000: 58th
U.S. rank in 2010: 55th

City Residents
1990: 354,091
2000: 427,652
2010: 494,665
2012 estimate: 505,870
Percent change, 2000–2010: 15.7%
U.S. rank in 1990: 47th
U.S. rank in 2000: 40th
U.S. rank in 2010: 34th (State rank: 5th)

Density: 4,418.4 people per square mile

Racial and ethnic characteristics
White: 245,070
Black or African American: 43,739
American Indian and Alaskan Native: 6,128
Asian: 68,813
Native Hawaiian and Other Pacific Islander: 935
Hispanic or Latino (may be of any race): 237,175
Other: 141,185

Percent of residents born in state: 65.6%

Age characteristics
Population under 5 years old: 45,090
Population 5 to 9 years old: 42,186
Population 10 to 14 years old: 38,871
Population 15 to 19 years old: 39,531
Population 20 to 24 years old: 41,860
Population 25 to 34 years old: 81,747
Population 35 to 44 years old: 60,952
Population 45 to 54 years old: 58,081
Population 55 to 59 years old: 26,444
Population 60 to 64 years old: 22,150
Population 65 to 74 years old: 27,195
Population 75 to 84 years old: 13,814
Population 85 years and over: 7,949
Median age: 30.2

Births (2010–11 Metropolitan Area)
Total number: 15,958

Deaths (2010–11 Metropolitan Area)

Total number: 6,161

Money income (2012)

Per capita income: $18,360
Median household income: $40,761
Total households: 157,154

Number of households with income of ...

less than $10,000: 14,601
$10,000 to $14,999: 12,878
$15,000 to $24,999: 23,617
$25,000 to $34,999: 18,149
$35,000 to $49,999: 22,569
$50,000 to $74,999: 26,733
$75,000 to $99,999: 15,452
$100,000 to $149,999: 14,223
$150,000 to $199,999: 4,867
$200,000 or more: 4,065

Percent of families below poverty level: 30.2%

FBI Crime Index Property: 25,737

FBI Crime Index Violent: 2,748

■ Municipal Government

Fresno has a strong-mayor form of government. There are seven council members elected by district to four-year, staggered terms. The mayor is elected at large for a four-year term, with a two-term limit. A city manager is appointed by the mayor. Fresno is also the Fresno County seat.

Head Official: Mayor Ashley Swearengin (since 2009; term expires 2017)

Total Number of City Employees: 3,244 (2012)

City Information: City of Fresno, 2600 Fresno Street, Fresno, CA 93721; telephone (559) 621-2489.

■ Economy

Major Industries and Commercial Activity

Agriculture has historically been the backbone of the Fresno area, employing upwards of 20 percent of all residents during peak seasons. Much of America's produce is grown in California's Central Valley, and Fresno County is the number-one agricultural county in the United States. Major crops are grapes, cotton, cattle, tomatoes, milk, plums, turkeys, oranges, peaches, and nectarines. A large food processing industry has developed around the agricultural activity; a number of canning, curing, drying, and freezing plants are located in the area.

However, Fresno's has seen other industries emerge, such as government, education and health services, and trade and transportation, each of which employed more people that farming as of 2013. The health-care industry contributes more than $2 billion annually to the county economy. Fresno is an ideal location for manufacturing and distribution due to its proximity within one day's drive of 35 million people. Manufacturing concerns in this Port of Entry region produce farm machinery, metal products, transportation equipment, stone, clay, and glass products, lumber and wood products, furniture and fixtures, and electrical equipment.

Fresno has also demonstrated strength in software and market research. The city is home to many company headquarters, such as ShoWare, Ticketmaster's largest competitor. Redcort Software, maker of employee time clocks, sheets, and cards, is headquartered in Fresno, as well as Decipher, an online market research company. The Python and Django software developers Bixly have been headquartered in Fresno since 2008.

Items and goods produced: agricultural products, machinery, metal and glass products, wood products, electrical equipment

Incentive Programs—New and Existing Companies

Local programs: The City of Fresno offers programs such as Fresno Startup and the Fresno Redevelopment Agency (RDA) and its finance authority that can be useful when considering Industrial Development Bonds. The City has also developed relationships with other agencies such as the Fresno Regional Workforce Investment Board and the Fresno Chamber of Commerce and Economic Development Corporation, which offer assistance to the developer and other companies considering a move to the City of Fresno.

The city of Fresno received a designation as an Enterprise Zone beginning in 1986, and in 2006 was granted an extension through October 14, 2021. Fresno is one of the largest Enterprise Zones in California. Benefits of operating in the Enterprise Zone include sales and use tax credits; hiring tax credits; business expense deductions; net operating loss carryover and net interest deduction for lenders programs. Fresno businesses may also receive tax incentives as part of a Foreign Trade Zone.

State programs: California business incentives include the state's Alternative Energy and Advanced Transportation Authority Sales and Use Tax Exemptions for Zero Emission Vehicle Manufacturing. Initially targeting vehicle manufacturing only when it was passed in 2010, the sales and use tax exemption has since been expanded to all renewable energy technologies. In 2012 it was expanded again to include advanced manufacturing. More than one dozen additional incentives encourage green development or pollution-reducing business decisions.

Research and development tax credits offers companies a 15 percent credit against their bank and corporation tax liability for qualifying in-house research expenses; a 24 percent tax credit for basic research payments to outside organizations is also available. Industrial development bonds finance investment in land, buildings, and new equipment related to domestic manufacturing operations in the state. California Capital Access Program and Collateral Support Program also offer alternative methods of financing for businesses. Enterprise Zones and Local Agency Military Base Recovery Area regions provide incentives for development in targeted geographic regions. A New Jobs Tax Credit offers $3,000 per hire of qualifying new employees, and the state's Film and Television Tax Credit Program supports productions with a 20 percent tax credit against qualified expenses.

In 2011 California began offering companies the option to calculate their corporate income tax through the single sales factor method, rather than the existing triple apportionment derived from calculations of a company's payroll, property, and sales.

California's Innovation Hub Program, with 12 locations throughout the state, supports the commercialization of innovation and technology businesses through public-private partnerships, knowledge sharing, venture capital sources, and business incubators. The state also undertakes trade missions to form partnerships for trade and export promotion.

Job training programs: The state of California offers an Employment Training Panel to assist companies with post-hire training and reimbursement. The Employment Development Department also partners with Local Workforce Investment Areas to recruit, screen, test, evaluate, and hire qualified workers.

The Fresno Regional Workforce Investment Board offers assistance in on-the-job skills training and training subsidies. Additional services are available through the Fresno Regional Occupational Program, Fresno City College–Career Advancement Academy, Heald College, San Joaquin Valley Junior College, and ITT Technical Institute.

Development Projects

Revitalization of Fresno's downtown area remained a development priority into the 2010s, even after a number of projects were completed during the 2000s. The city sought to establish its 7,200-acre urban core as a primary development site through a total revision of its building codes and planning—itself a $2.7 million investment. Existing zoning ordinances were established in the 1960s and did not prioritize preservation of historic buildings or environmentally conscious design. City officials hoped that efforts would create a number of "shovel-ready" lots downtown and expedite any remaining permitting processes.

A major component of downtown development was construction of a high-speed rail station. High-speed rail in California was anticipated to run from San Francisco to the Los Angeles basin by 2029 at speeds of more than 200 miles per hour—and a cost of $68.5 billion—with later development reaching Sacramento and San Diego. Fresno is the starting point for the first 30-mile segment of the rail network; a second, 60-mile segment was in the bidding process during 2013. High-speed rail development had a number of critics, including several local business and homeowners in Fresno, who were forced to move out of their properties to make way for the rail construction. Additionally, long-term funding remained uncertain, as agreed financing covered only the initial few stages of development.

Development proposals under consideration in 2013 included retail developments such as the 238-acre El Paseo in northwest Fresno and a mixed-use project known as Westlake, also in northwest Fresno, that was slated to cover 460 acres with 2,600 residential units and 295,000 square feet of community and neighborhood commercial buildings.

Economic Development Information: Fresno Economic Development Corporation, 906 North Street, Ste 120, Fresno, CA 93721; telephone (559) 476-2500.

Commercial Shipping

International freight shipments to and from the entire region flow through the Fresno Yosemite International Airport, a direct port of entry and part of a Federal Foreign Trade Zone. The nation's largest parcel carriers, FedEx, and UPS operate from there. Rail freight services are provided by both the Burlington Northern-Santa Fe (BNSF) and Union Pacific railroads. Nearly 200 truck firms are based within the Fresno County borders.

Labor Force and Employment Outlook

Fresno continues to diversify its economy toward non-agricultural industries. The city is home to headquarters such as ShoWare, Bixly, Decipher, and Redcort—all of which are either software, market research, or Web-related businesses. Fresno's labor force is productive, motivated, flexible, and relatively young. Steady population growth has occurred faster than local business expansion or new business development. Unemployment rates fluctuate seasonally, due mainly to the high demand for agricultural labor at certain times of the year. A large number of immigrants, both regional and international, provide a continuous supply of employable people with diverse skills. If high-speed rail projects in the area move forward, they were expected to add thousands of local jobs directly, and also benefit indirect job growth as businesses enjoyed an influx of workers to the city.

The following is a summary of data regarding the 2012 Fresno CA Metro Area labor force:

Size of civilian labor force: 230,125

Number of workers employed in . . .

agriculture and mining: 11,166
construction: 10,029
manufacturing: 13,005
wholesale trade: 7,078
retail trade: 22,840
transportation: 9,744
information systems: 2,849
finance: 11,675
professional administration: 17,274
education and social services: 45,530
arts and leisure: 19,168
other: 9,700
public administration: 10,584

Average hourly earnings of production workers: $14.82

Unemployment rate: 9.5% (2012)

Employers

Largest private employers (2012)	*Number of employees*
County of Fresno	6,178
Community Medical Centers	6,000
City of Fresno	3,244
Saint Agnes Medical Center	2,710
California State University, Fresno	1,564
State Center Community College	1,221
Kaiser Permanente Medical Center	981
AmeriGuard Security Systems	700
Zacky Farms, LLC	500
Guarantee Real Estate	442

Cost of Living

The cost of living in Fresno is slightly above the national average, with the average cost of a home in 2013 estimated at $322,143.

The following is a summary of data regarding several key cost of living factors in the area.

2013 ACCRA Average House Price: $322,143

2013 ACCRA Cost of Living Index: 106

State income tax rate: 1.00% to 13.3%

State sales tax rate: 7.5%

Local income tax rate: None

Local sales tax rate: 0.725%

Property tax rate: Limited to 1% of assessed value by state law. In some cases the local taxing body can add additional taxes.

Economic Information: Greater Fresno Area Chamber of Commerce, 2331 Fresno Street, Fresno, CA 93721; telephone (559) 495-4800; fax (559) 495-4811.

■ Education and Research

Elementary and Secondary Schools

The Fresno Unified School District, which serves more than 74,000 students, is the fourth largest district in the state. A seven-member, nonpartisan board of education hires a superintendent. Overall the district has underperformed due to a wide variety of problems including financial woes, mismanagement, and a highly diverse student population with large numbers of immigrant and non-English-speaking students, many of whom are impoverished. As of 2011–12, some 83 percent of students were eligible for free or reduced meals, and nearly one-quarter of all students were English learners. However, significant progress was reported between 2011 and 2013; Fresno was the only Trial Urban District in the Department of Education's National Assessment of Educational Progress to report a significant decrease in the eighth-grade achievement gap between 2009 and 2013 among students with significant income disparities.

The district supports 20 magnet programs, nine charter schools, and an adult education school. The Central Unified School District (CUSD) also serves students in the city and county. As of 2013, there were 21 CUSD sites. CUSD offers a full array of programs for all ages. Additionally, there are several private schools serving K–12 students in Fresno, including Catholic elementary and high schools, other Christian and religious schools, and secular private institutions.

The following is a summary of data regarding the Fresno Unified School District.

Total enrollment: 74,833

Number of facilities

total: 101
elementary schools: 65
junior high schools: 17
high schools: 8
other: 11

Student/teacher ratio: 24.2:1

Teacher salaries

average (statewide): $69,434

Funding per pupil: $9,263

Public Schools Information: Fresno Unified School District, 2309 Tulare Street, Fresno, CA 93721; telephone (559) 457-3700. Central Unified School District, 4605 N. Polk Avenue, Fresno, CA 93722; telephone (559) 274-4700; fax (559) 271-8200.

Colleges and Universities

California State University, Fresno (commonly known as Fresno State) is part of the 23-campus California State University system. It is a four-year accredited university offering doctoral, graduate, and undergraduate degrees in about 100 fields to its more than 22,500 students. Fresno State is the largest post-secondary institution in the city and sits on a 388-acre campus and adjacent to a 1,011-acre University Farm in the northeast section of Fresno. In 2013–14 *U.S. News & World Report* ranked the school 36th among regional universities in the West.

Fresno City College is a two-year community college with nearly 21,000 students. California's oldest community college, Fresno City College offers associate's degrees in more than 100 disciplines. Many are designed to transfer to four-year institutions. The University of California, San Francisco School of Medicine operates a campus in Fresno that hosts a medical education program, providing medical internship and residency training.

Fresno Pacific University is a Christian liberal arts school affiliated with the Mennonite Brethren. It offers associate's, bachelor's, and master's degrees through five schools: the School of Business; the School of Education; the School of Humanities, Religion, and Social Sciences; the School of Natural Sciences; and Fresno Pacific Biblical Seminary. Enrollment is about 3,500 students.

The Fresno campus of Alliant International University is one of six locations in the state. Programs at Alliant focus on careers in human relations, applied behavioral, cognitive and economic sciences, and the humanities. The Fresno campus offers graduate degrees to 400 students in applied criminology, clincial psychology, infant-preschooler mental health, organizational behavior, and organizational development..

Libraries and Research Centers

The Fresno County Public Library has a Central Resource Library and 34 branches throughout the Fresno area. The system further links to the San Joaquin Valley Library system, a cooperative network of 10 public library systems with shared information databases across seven counties in the Central Valley. The Fresno County Library circulates nearly four million materials annually and has greatly expanded wireless Internet access across

its branches, as well as adding to its e-book collection—5,000 new titles in 2012 alone. There are special services for the handicapped and visually impaired, as well as special collections on the Japanese and Hmong languages, Pulitzer Prize-winning author and Fresno native William Saroyan, oral history, and holdings of the Fresno Genealogical Society. The library has been a complete depository for California state documents and a partial depository for the U.S. Government since 1920.

The Henry Madden Library at Fresno State has a collection of more than 1 million books, 47,000 scores, and more than 60,000 online journal, magazine, and newspaper subscriptions. Special collections include the Arne Nixon Center for the Study of Children's Literature, Lewis Carroll Collection, Helen Monnette Amestoy Collection, and an LGBTQ Collection. The library also contains the University Archives, which contains various scholarly papers.

The Center for Mennonite Brethren Studies, formerly part of the Mennonite Brethren Biblical Seminary, is now part of Fresno Pacific University as the Mennonite Library and Archives. The library maintains records and personal papers relating to the Mennonite Brethren Church in North America.

Fresno State sponsors several research centers and institutes, including the California Water Institute, the Central Valley Cultural Heritage Institute, the Center for Food Science and Nutrition Research, and the Department of Viticulture and Enology. The Fresno campus of the University of California, San Francisco School of Medicine is home to the Center for Medical Education and Research.

Public Library Information: Fresno County Public Library, 2420 Mariposa Street, Fresno, CA 93721; telephone (559) 600-7323.

■ Health Care

Community Medical Centers operates the largest health system in the city. Community Regional Medical Center in Fresno, with 677 beds, is the only hospital in the region with a Level I Trauma Center and specialized burn center. The hospital finished a 340,000-square-foot critical care addition in 2007, which included a 52-bed Neuroscience Center of Excellence, 50-bed cardiovascular unit, and 65-bed Level III neonatal intensive care unit. It also serves as a teaching hospital for the University of California San Francisco School of Medicine's Center for Medical Education and Research in Fresno.

Other facilities operated by the network include the Fresno Heart and Surgical Hospital is a 60-bed facility primarily dedicated to the full range of cardiac care services. This hospital also offers bariatric and general surgery services. The Clovis Community Medical Center offers women's services, sports medicine, screenings, diagnostic procedures, and minimally invasive surgeries. The center began a $300 million expansion project to add a five-story tower, women's pavilion, nursery, and parking facility in 2010, with construction continuing into 2013. The renovation was set to increase the number of patient beds and transform the center into a private patient bed facility. The Community Subacute and Transitional Care Center has 33 beds. Outpatient care is offered through the California Cancer Center.

The St. Agnes Medical Center, a full-service regional hospital, is affiliated with Trinity Health. The Medical Center campus includes the California Eye Institute at Saint Agnes, a comprehensive outpatient facility offering services from routine eye exams to complex eye surgeries, and the Cancer Center at Saint Agnes, offering a holistic approach to cancer care.

Nearby Children's Hospital Central California has 356 beds on a 50-acre campus in Madera.

■ Recreation

Sightseeing

The 62-mile self-guided motor tour of Blossom Trail offers the best look at what makes the Fresno area unique, with a plunge into some of the most productive agricultural land in the world. The annual Blossom Trail kickoff comes each February, and motorists and hikers can come upon stunning displays of blossoming peach, nectarine, plum, orange, and almond trees. The family-run Simonian Farms at the end of the trail cultivate more than 100 varieties of fruits and vegetables and can be toured via a hay wagon.

The Forestiere Underground Gardens offers a unique experience of underground rooms, passageways, and gardens covering 10 acres. Baldassare Forestiere designed and excavated the complex—by hand—in the early 1900s. It includes his five-room underground home, a multilevel aquarium, and an auto tunnel. The gardens include a variety of fruit trees, such as date palm and olive. Guided tours are available at this state landmark.

Fresno is less than one hour from the Sierra Nevada Mountains and three of the nation's most popular national parks. Yosemite, King's Canyon, and Sequoia National Parks offer spectacular canyons, waterfalls, and forests of 4,000-year-old bristlecone pine trees and giant sequoias, the largest trees in the world.

Downtown Fresno offers the Fulton Mall, an area of stores, restaurants, landscaped grounds, fountains, and sculpture that covers a six-block area. It contains one of the finest collections of public art in the nation, arranged throughout the central business district. The mall, which suffered from high vacancy rates into the 2010s, was a principal target of downtown redevelopment by the city. Roeding Park, two miles northwest of the downtown area, contains the Fresno Chaffee Zoo, the third largest in

California; and Rotary Storyland and Playland, an amusement park for children.

Arts and Culture

The William Saroyan Theater is the cultural center of Fresno. Luxurious seating for 2,300 people and near-perfect acoustics highlight the theater, home to the Fresno Philharmonic Orchestra, Fresno Broadway Series, and Fresno Grand Opera. The Fresno Grand Opera offers two major productions each year at the Saroyan. Other venues for the performing arts are the Good Company Players' Second Space Theatre, presenting comedy and drama; Roger Rocka's Dinner Theater; historic Tower Theatre, presenting touring performers; and Warnor's Center for the Performing Arts. Children's Musical Theaterworks offers young actors a chance to perform at the Fresno Memorial Auditorium. Save Mart Center at Fresno State and the Selland Arena at the Fresno Convention and Entertainment Center offer a wide variety of programs and concerts.

The Fresno City and County Historical Society operates the Kearney Historical Site, extensive archives on the history of Fresno, and tours of the city's historic buildings. Meux Home Museum, a restored historical structure in downtown Fresno, features a number of exhibits relating to the region's history, displayed on a rotating basis. Architecture buffs might wish to contemplate the futuristic design of the City Hall, located near the historic district containing Meux Home and St. John's Cathedral.

The Discovery Center is a hands-on science museum and outdoor education center; it features Native American exhibits, a cactus garden, worm farms, ponds, and a greenhouse. Downing Planetarium at the California State University, Fresno offers public programs on weekends.

The Fresno Art Museum is the only modern art museum between San Francisco and Los Angeles and has three main galleries and an exhibition concourse. It also offers ArtSmart enrichment classes for adults and children. The Fresno Metropolitan Museum of Art and Science contained collections of European still lifes, tromp l'oeil oil paintings, and exhibits focused on the cultural heritage of Central California, including exhibits dedicated to author and Fresno native William Saroyan; the museum closed in January 2010 due to financial difficulties.

The Legion of Valor Museum in Veteran's Memorial Auditorium is the first museum in the country dedicated to the recipients of the Medal of Honor, Distinguished Service Cross, Navy Cross, and Air Force Cross.

Festivals and Holidays

Fresno schedules a number of special cultural and ethnic events throughout the year. A variety of activities are planned by communities along the Blossom Trail to coincide with the peak growing season, beginning in late February or early March. A Grand Mardi Gras Parade and festival takes place in the Tower District, usually in

February. An annual Mariachi Festival also takes place in March at the Selland Arena. The Rogue Festival in March is a non-juried art festival for theater, dance, music, film, puppetry, storytelling, visual arts, and more. Beginning each June there are bi-weekly free concerts in Woodward Park. The High Sierra Regatta at Huntington Lake is a prestigious yachting event held on two consecutive weekends in July. Fiestas Patrias, the Mexican Independence Day festival, features music, food, and folk dancing and takes place in September. The Big Fresno Fair happens at the Fairgrounds in October. Several special tree-lighting and musical events occur throughout the month of December.

Sports for the Spectator

The Fresno Grizzlies, a Triple-A affiliate of the San Francisco Giants, play baseball at the downtown ballpark, Chukchansi Park. The Fresno State University Bulldogs play basketball at Selland Arena and football at Bulldog Stadium. Men's and women's teams from the university compete in an array of other sports as well.

Sports for the Participant

A number of area lakes and reservoirs provide a full range of water recreation in the immediate Fresno area. With three of America's great national parks within a 90-minute drive, Fresno offers arguably the greatest range of recreational options of any large metropolitan area in the United States. Nearby Yosemite, Sequoia/Kings Canyon, and Death Valley National Parks offer flat, scorching desert vistas to high mountain streams and skiing, and everything in between. The numerous streams and rivers in the area offer some of California's finest trout and largemouth bass fishing, as well as rafting and canoeing. The hills and nearby mountains contain many campsites and hiking trails; snow skiing is less than 90 minutes away at Sierra Summit, while Lake Tahoe is just a bit farther in the Sierra Nevada range.

The city of Fresno operates three major regional parks, including the highly popular Chaffee Zoo, and nearly 80 total community parks, playgrounds, community centers, as well as standard and learner swimming pools, seven golf courses, and numerous tennis courts. Municipal golf courses include the Brighton Crest Golf Course and Country Club, designed by Johnny Miller.

Shopping and Dining

Fulton Mall, a popular sightseeing spot along the six-block stretch of historic Fulton Street, has historically been a major shopping complex in Fresno's downtown area, although increased vacancy in the 2000s and 2010s spurred the city to focus on the area's revitalization. Other important shopping centers are the Fashion Fair Mall and Manchester Center. Fig Garden Village and River Park offer both offer national chains as well as unique boutiques. The Tower District offers a variety of shops, restaurants, and nightclubs. The Sierra Vista Mall in Clovis contains several large retail outlets and a number of smaller specialty shops. Numerous smaller centers and antique shops are spread throughout the city. Of unique interest is the international gift shop in the Mennonite Quilt Center in downtown Reedley.

More than 500 restaurants in Fresno, many housed in historic buildings, offer a wide selection of dining experiences for every taste and price range, including hearty regional and western dishes, Mexican specialties, and European and international cuisines. Visitors might want to stop in at one of the area's local wineries, including Engelmann Cellars, Milla Vineyards, Nonini Winery, and Los Californios Winery.

Visitor Information: Fresno/Clovis Convention and Visitors Bureau, 1550 E. Shaw Avenue, Suite 101, Fresno, CA 93710; telephone (559) 981-5500; toll-free (800) 788-0836.

■ Convention Facilities

The Fresno Convention and Entertainment Center is an award-winning complex covering five city blocks in the downtown district. It contains a large exhibit hall, 20 breakout meeting rooms, a theater that seats about 2,300 people, an 11,000-seat arena, and a 32,000-square-foot multi-use hall that can seat up to 2,700 attendees. The William Saroyan Theatre in the convention center complex is home to the Fresno Philharmonic Orchestra and the Fresno Ballet, and is also available for meetings. California State University, Fresno offers several large facilities, and the major hotels in the area feature extensive meeting, banquet, and ballroom accommodations.

Convention Information: Fresno/Clovis Convention and Visitors Bureau, 1550 E. Shaw Avenue, Suite 101, Fresno, CA 93710; telephone (559) 981-5500; toll-free (800) 788-0836.

■ Transportation

Approaching the City

The Fresno Yosemite International Airport is served by 9 passenger air carriers and offers non-stop service to 12 major cities throughout the western United States, and Mexico. Fresno Chandler Executive Airport is a secondary general aviation airport serving the area.

State Routes 99, 41, and 180 are the primary entryways into the city. Interstate 5, which runs generally north–south to the west of the city, connects directly with State Route 99 at points north and south of the city. State Route 180 runs east and west to connect the city with the Sierra Nevada Mountains and western California.

Amtrak provides daily service to the downtown Fresno Amtrak Station through Fresno County with connections to northern and southern California. Fresno is poised to maintain its dominant rail position in California as the state continues with plans for high-speed rail service to connect the Central San Joaquin Valley with San Francisco and the Los Angeles basin. The proposed rail service would transport passengers at more than 200 miles per hour, with segments operational as early as 2022, although securing long-term funding remained a concern. Greyhound also makes a daily stop to a downtown Fresno station.

Traveling in the City

Most of Fresno is laid out in a grid of streets running east–west and north–south. West Avenue is the dividing line for east and west designations and Whites Bridge Avenue and Kings Canyon Road divide the city north and south. State routes 99, 180, and 41 circle the downtown area.

Fresno Area Express (FAX) has 16 fixed-route bus service lines and Handy Ride Para transit service, all with a fleet of more than 100 buses. Taxi service is plentiful.

■ Communications

Newspapers and Magazines

The Fresno Bee is the only daily paper published in the city. It had a daily circulation of more than 100,000 in 2013, with monthly Web traffic averaging about 750,000 unique visitors. *Vide en el Valle* is a bilingual weekly publication managed by the *Fresno Bee*. *The Business Journal*, which covers business news in Fresno, Kings, Madera, and Tulare, is published weekly. *Fresno Magazine* comes out monthly.

Television and Radio

Among the 18 television broadcasters in Fresno, viewers have access to CBS, ABC, NBC, and PBS affiliate stations. Spanish, religious, shopping, sports, and musical programming is also available. Cable television is available throughout Fresno. As expected of any mid-sized American city, a wide variety of radio programming is available from Fresno's 11 FM and 14 AM stations, including foreign language broadcasts.

Media Information: *The Fresno Bee*, 1626 E. Street, Fresno, CA 93786; telephone (559) 441-6111; toll free (800) 877-3400.

Fresno Online

City of Fresno Home Page. Available www.fresno.gov

The Fresno Bee. Available www.fresnobee.com

Fresno Chamber of Commerce. Available fresnochamber.com

Fresno/Clovis Convention & Visitors Bureau. Available www.playfresno.org

Fresno County Economic Development Corporation. Available www.fresnoedc.com

Fresno County Library. Available www.fresnolibrary.org

Fresno Unified School District. Available www.fresno.k12.ca.us

BIBLIOGRAPHY

Burnett, Brenda Preston, *Andrew Davidson Firebaugh and Susan Burgess Firebaugh: California Pioneers* (Rio Del Mar, CA: Rio Del Mar Press, 1995)

Hunter, Pat, *Fresno's Architectural Past* (Fresno, CA: Craven Street Books, 2006)

Putirka, Keith, ed., *Geologic Excursions from Fresno, California, and the Central Valley: A Tour of California's Iconic Geology* (Boulder, CO: Geological Society of America, 2013)

Los Angeles

■ The City in Brief

Founded: 1781 (incorporated 1850)

Head Official: Mayor Eric Garcetti (since 2013; current term expires 2017)

City Population
> 1990: 3,485,557
> 2000: 3,694,820
> 2010: 3,792,621
> 2012 estimate: 3,857,786
> Percent change, 2000–2010: 2.6%
> U.S. rank in 1990: 2nd (State rank: 1st)
> U.S. rank in 2000: 2nd (State rank: 1st)
> U.S. rank in 2010: 2nd (State rank: 1st)

Metropolitan Statistical Area Population
> 2000: 12,365,627
> 2010: 12,828,837
> 2012 estimate: 13,052,921
> Percent change, 2000–2010: 34.8%
> U.S. rank in 2000: 2nd
> U.S. rank in 2010: 2nd

Area: 469.1 square miles

Elevation: 340 feet above sea level

Average Annual Temperatures: January, 58.3° F; July, 74.2° F; annual average, 66.2° F

Average Annual Precipitation: 15.14 inches of rain

Major Economic Sectors: services; manufacturing; government; finance, insurance, and real estate

Unemployment Rate: 7.6% (2012)

Per Capita Income: $26,391

2012 FBI Crime Index Property: 87,478

Major Colleges and Universities: University of California, Los Angeles (UCLA), University of Southern California (USC), California Institute of Technology

Daily Newspaper: *Los Angeles Times*

■ Introduction

With more than 13 million people in the five-county metropolitan area, Los Angeles has one of the largest urban populations in the United States and is one of the largest cities in terms of area. Commonly known by its initials, Los Angeles is considered the prototype of the future metropolis—a city on the cutting edge with all the advantages and challenges of large urban areas. The city sprawls across 500 square miles of southwestern California, creating an opportunity for great geographic, cultural, and economic diversity. Los Angeles incorporates one of the largest Hispanic populations in the United States, a major Asian community, and sizable populations of nearly every ethnic background in the world. The glamour of Hollywood, Beverly Hills, the Sunset Strip, and the famous beaches added to Los Angeles's reputation as a California paradise and have contributed to the area's phenomenal growth. Los Angeles is also the "Entertainment Capital of the World," the lead creator of motion pictures, television shows, video games, and recorded music. Many celebrities call Los Angeles and its surrounding suburbs home. Los Angeles is a center of international trade and banking, entertainment, media, fashion, and tourism. The city offers something for everyone in its large conglomeration of separate and very distinct districts: a sleek, ultra-modern downtown, miles of beautiful beaches, opulent mansions and stunning canyon homes, and some of the world's most glamorous shopping and dining. Beneath the glitter, though, lingers the historic and present reality of a racially divided city in which disproportionately high unemployment rates still plague young African Americans and Latinos.

Jon Varsano/Shutterstock.com

■ Geography and Climate

Los Angeles lies on a hilly coastal plain with the Pacific Ocean as its southern and western boundaries. It is the seat of Los Angeles County. The greater Los Angeles Metropolitan Area is known for its sprawling nature, which covers the five counties of Los Angeles, Orange, Riverside, San Bernardino, and Ventura. The harbor at San Pedro Bay offers a port of entry. The communities of Hollywood, San Pedro, Bel Air, Central City, Sylmar, Watts, Westwood, and Boyle Heights are all part of the city of Los Angeles. The city of Los Angeles stretches north to the foothills of the Santa Monica Mountains and is bounded by the San Gabriel Mountains to the east. Numerous canyons and valleys also characterize the region, making it an area of diverse climatic conditions. The highest point in the city is Mount Lukens, also known as Sister Elsie Peak, which reaches a height of 5,080 feet above sea level.

Los Angeles is known to have a subtropical, Mediterranean climate. The predominant weather influence is the warm, moist Pacific air, keeping temperatures mild throughout the year. Summers are dry and sunny—the city averages 329 days of sun per year—with most of the precipitation occurring during the winter months. Smog and air pollution are major environmental problems, gathering in the coastal basin during periods of

little air movement. Attributed to the geography, heavy reliance on automobiles, industrial activities, and insufficient rainfall to clear the air, the Los Angeles Basin and the San Fernando Valley are often the victim of atmospheric inversion, which holds the exhaust and fumes, creating smog and prompting air quality alerts for residents. The American Lung Association consistently ranks the city as the most polluted in the country.

Other unusual weather phenomena include the Santa Ana winds, which bring hot, dusty winds of up to 50 miles per hour from the surrounding mountains, and the occasional flash floods in the canyon areas, causing mudslides and rockslides. Wildfires during the driest season can be very destructive. The San Andreas Fault runs to the north of the Los Angeles area, making the area susceptible to earthquakes, though most are of a low magnitude. The numerous faults in the area cause approximately 10,000 earthquakes annually. Parts of the city are also susceptible to tsunamis.

Area: 469.1 square miles

Elevation: 340 feet above sea level

Average Temperatures: January, 58.3° F; July, 74.2° F; annual average, 66.2° F

Average Annual Precipitation: 15.14 inches of rain

■ History

Spanish and Anglos Settle, Trade Industry Thrives

The area around present-day Los Angeles was first explored by Europeans in 1769 when Gaspar de Portola and a group of missionaries camped on what is now called the Los Angeles River. Franciscans built Mission San Gabriel about 9 miles to the north in 1771. In 1781 Felipe de Neve, governor of Alte California, founded a settlement called El Pueblo de Nuestra Senora la Reina de los Angeles, which means "the pueblo of our lady the queen of angels." In its early years, the town was a small, isolated cluster of adobe-brick houses and random streets carved out of the desert, and its main product was grain.

Although the Spanish government placed a ban on trading with foreign ships, American vessels began arriving in the early 1800s, and the first English-speaking inhabitant settled in the area in 1818. He was a carpenter named Joseph Chapman, who helped build the church facing the town's central plaza, a structure that still stands. After Mexico, including California, gained its independence from Spain in 1821, trade with the United States became more frequent. The ocean waters off the coast of California were important for whaling and seal hunting, and a number of trading ships docked at nearby San Pedro to buy cattle hides and tallow. By the 1840s, Los Angeles was the largest town in southern California.

City Becomes American Possession; Gold Discovered

During the war between the United States and Mexico in 1846, Los Angeles was occupied by an American garrison, but the citizens drove the fifty-man brigade out of town. The Treaty of Cahuenga, signed in 1847, ended the war in California, adding Los Angeles and the rest of California to American territory. The Sierra Nevada gold strike in 1848 in the mountains to the north of Los Angeles provided the town with a booming market for its beef, and many prospectors settled in the area after the gold rush. Los Angeles was incorporated in 1850 with a reputation as one of the toughest towns in the West. "A murder a day" only slightly exaggerated the town's crime problems, and suspected criminals were often hanged by vigilante groups. Lawlessness reached a peak in 1871, when, after a Chinese immigrant accidentally killed a white man, an angry mob stormed into the Chinatown district, murdering sixteen people. After that, civic leaders and concerned citizens began a successful campaign to bring law and order to the town.

The Southern Pacific Railroad reached Los Angeles in 1876, followed by the Santa Fe Railroad nine years later. The two rival companies conducted a rate war that eventually drove the price of a ticket from the eastern United States down to five dollars. This price slashing brought thousands of settlers to the area, sending real estate prices to unrealistically high levels. By 1887, lots around the central plaza sold for up to one thousand dollars a foot, but the market collapsed in that same year, making millionaires destitute overnight. People in vast numbers abandoned Los Angeles, sometimes as many as three thousand a day. This flight prompted the creation of the Chamber of Commerce, which began a worldwide advertising campaign to attract new citizens. By 1890, the population had climbed back up to fifty thousand residents.

Oil, Agriculture, Moving Pictures, Manufacturing Build City

In the 1890s, oil was discovered in the city, and soon another boom took hold. By the turn of the century almost fifteen hundred oil wells operated throughout Los Angeles. In the early 1900s, agriculture became an important part of the economy, and a massive aqueduct project was completed. The city's growth necessitated the annexation of the large San Fernando Valley, and the port at San Pedro was also added to give Los Angeles a position in the international trade market.

The motion picture industry thrived on the Los Angeles area's advantages after the first decade of the twentieth century, and by 1930 it had earned the city the nickname of "Tinseltown." Large manufacturing concerns also began opening factories during that time, and the need for housing created vast areas of suburban neighborhoods and the beginnings of the city's massive freeway system. The Depression and the Midwestern drought of the 1930s brought thousands of people to California looking for jobs.

To accommodate its growing population, the city instituted a number of large engineering projects, including the construction of the Hoover Dam, which channeled water to the city from the Colorado River and provided electricity from hydroelectric power. The area's excellent weather made it an ideal location for aircraft testing and construction, and World War II brought hundreds of new industries to the area, boosting the local economy. By the 1950s, Los Angeles was a sprawling metropolis. It was considered the epitome of everything new and modern in American culture—a combination of super highways, affordable housing, and opportunity for everyone.

City Grapples with Pollution, Racial Unrest

The Los Angeles dream began to fade in the 1960s. Despite the continued construction of new freeways, traffic congestion became a major problem; industry and auto emissions created smog and pollution. Frustration over living conditions came to a head in August 1965, when riots erupted in the African American ghetto of Watts, and more unrest developed in the Hispanic communities of East Los Angeles. Reacting to these new problems, the city adopted strict air pollution guidelines and took steps to bring minorities into the political process, culminating in the 1973 election of Mayor Tom Bradley, the city's first African American mayor. Over the next two decades, public transportation was improved, and a subway system was funded and began limited operations. The downtown area became a thriving district of impressive glass skyscrapers.

In 1984, the city hosted the Summer Olympics Games for the second time. Due to the international Cold War at the time, the games were boycotted by 14 countries. Nonetheless, the 1984 Olympics became the most successful in history, having been only the second Olympics to turn a profit (the first being the 1932 Summer Olympics also held in Los Angeles).

The city's reputation was severely tarnished by a rebellion that broke out in April 1992 following the acquittal of four white police officers accused of beating an African American motorist—a beating that was captured on videotape by a bystander and broadcast worldwide, now known as the Rodney King controversy. The ensuing melee left more than 50 people dead and resulted in an estimated $1 billion in damage.

The region's violence problems are not solely a racial issue; the problem of gang violence in the city has been a constant challenge. The Los Angeles Police Department reported in 2013 that there were more than 450 active gangs in the city, with many active for more than 50 years. Total gang membership was estimated at 45,000 individuals, with the narcotics trade driving an increase in gang activity during the 2010s, even as the overall crime rate decreased. Gangs were responsible for more than 150 homicides annually.

Los Angeles Enters Twenty-First Century

Los Angeles began to emerge from the recession of the mid-1990s, but like much of the country, the city was dealt another blow after the terrorist attacks of September 11, 2001. In response to the ensuing economic downturn, the Los Angeles Economic Impact Task Force was developed to bring together business leaders from across the city and to develop recommendations for strengthening the local economy. The result was an increase in tourism, retail sales, and other continuing signs of recovery.

Continuing into the early 2000s, the city also made progress toward improvement of the environment. City officials set a goal of recycling 70 percent of all waste by the year 2015, and a Million Trees LA program was launched to add 35 new parks to the city. The city also began investing in renewable energy resources and established water conservation programs. A nationwide recession in the late 2000s stalled economic development across the country. As economic growth returned during the 2010s, so too did progress on major development projects, but privately and publically funded. Urban renewal and mixed-use facilities—especially those that

might mitigate urban sprawl and commuter travel—were priorities.

Historical Information: The Historical Society of Southern California, Charles F. Lummis Home and Garden, 200 East Avenue 43, Los Angeles, CA 90031; telephone (323) 222-0546. Los Angeles City Historical Society, P.O. Box 862311, Los Angeles, CA 90086-2311; email info@lacityhistory.org.

■ Population Profile

Metropolitan Statistical Area Population

2000: 12,365,627
2010: 12,828,837
2012 estimate: 13,052,921
Percent change, 2000–2010: 34.8%
U.S. rank in 2000: 2nd
U.S. rank in 2010: 2nd

City Residents

1990: 3,485,557
2000: 3,694,820
2010: 3,792,621
2012 estimate: 3,857,786
Percent change, 2000–2010: 2.6%
U.S. rank in 1990: 2nd (State rank: 1st)
U.S. rank in 2000: 2nd (State rank: 1st)
U.S. rank in 2010: 2nd (State rank: 1st)

Density: 8,092.3 people per square mile

Racial and ethnic characteristics

White: 2,013,642
Black or African American: 360,124
American Indian and Alaskan Native: 16,392
Asian: 442,498
Native Hawaiian and Other Pacific Islander: 4,853
Hispanic or Latino (may be of any race): 1,868,759
Other: 1,020,277

Percent of residents born in state: 45.2%

Age characteristics

Population under 5 years old: 253,336
Population 5 to 9 years old: 234,783
Population 10 to 14 years old: 232,640
Population 15 to 19 years old: 258,854
Population 20 to 24 years old: 315,877
Population 25 to 34 years old: 651,837
Population 35 to 44 years old: 568,855
Population 45 to 54 years old: 510,777
Population 55 to 59 years old: 223,664
Population 60 to 64 years old: 181,864
Population 65 to 74 years old: 228,450
Population 75 to 84 years old: 135,211

Population 85 years and over: 61,638
Median age: 34.7

Births (2010–11 Metropolitan Area)

Total number: 171,737

Deaths (2010–11 Metropolitan Area)

Total number: 75,587

Money income (2012)

Per capita income: $26,391
Median household income: $47,742
Total households: 1,317,210

Number of households with income of . . .

less than $10,000: 110,913
$10,000 to $14,999: 97,377
$15,000 to $24,999: 159,699
$25,000 to $34,999: 137,920
$35,000 to $49,999: 174,511
$50,000 to $74,999: 212,991
$75,000 to $99,999: 135,274
$100,000 to $149,999: 148,199
$150,000 to $199,999: 61,377
$200,000 or more: 78,949

Percent of families below poverty level: 22.5%

FBI Crime Index Property: 87,478

FBI Crime Index Violent: 18,547

■ Municipal Government

The city has a mayor-council form of government. The city council is comprised of 15 council members. The council members, the mayor, the city attorney, and the city controller are elected to four-year terms. The council members are elected to single-member districts through staggered elections and a two-term limit. There are 43 departments, bureaus, commissions, and offices operating as part of city government. The Board of Harbor Commissioners assists in governance of the Port of Los Angeles. As the city is part of the greater Los Angeles area, the county also plays a major role in governance. The county of Los Angeles is governed by a five-member board of supervisors, although many districts are separate and self-governing. Neighborhood Councils serve to promote public participation in city government.

Head Official: Mayor Eric Garcetti (since 2013; current term expires 2017)

Total Number of City Employees: 44,947 (2012)

City Information: City Hall, 200 North Spring Street, Los Angeles, CA 90012; telephone (213) 485-2121.

■ Economy

Major Industries and Commercial Activity

California has always been known as an "incubator" of new ideas, new products and entrepreneurial spirit. Southern California has led the way in celebrating and nurturing that spirit. The people, institutions of knowledge, great climate and infrastructure have enabled the Los Angeles region to emerge as a leading business, trade and cultural center—a creative capital for the twenty-first century. The leading industries are direct international trade, tourism, motion picture and television production, technology, and business and professional services. The city is part of the largest manufacturing center in the West, one of the world's busiest ports, a major financial and banking center, and one of the largest retail markets in the United States. In addition to its reputation as the entertainment capital of the world, Los Angeles is highly diversified, making it a major player in the national and international economy.

International trade is an important segment of the economy. Los Angeles is considered the West Coast gateway to North America. The Port of Los Angeles is part of the nation's largest Customs District in terms of value of two-way trade. It is also the busiest container port in the United States. Top containerized exports include wastepaper, animal feeds, scrap metal, cotton, and resins; top imports are furniture, apparel, automobile parts, electronic products, and footwear. About $6 billion in state and local tax revenue is generated by the port for California, with $23 billion generated throughout the United States. The city's prominence in international trade is also evidenced by the 20 U.S. headquarters of foreign companies in the area that had annual revenues of more than $2 billion in 2012. The largest are automobile makers Toyota and Honda, grocer Fresh & Easy, and food manufacturer Nestle.

California had 53 *Fortune* 500 companies 2012—more than any other state—with Los Angeles County home to 14. The highest ranked from Los Angeles is the Walt Disney Company, with $42.3 billion in annual revenue in 2013. Other *Fortune* 500 companies include international and national names such as Dole Food Company, Health Net, AECOM Technologies, DirecTV, Avery Dennison, Occidental Petroleum, Reliance Steel & Aluminum, Molina Healthcare, Mattel, Edison International, CB Richard Ellis, Jacobs Engineering Group, and Live Nation. In addition, many companies, while not headquartered in the city, maintain a Los Angeles office.

Tourism is also a major factor in the Los Angeles economy; the city lures visitors with its celebrities and cosmopolitan lifestyle. Los Angeles County annually hosts about 21 million overnight visitors, whose spending pumps nearly $15 billion into the economy. Entertainment, in the form of film, television, and music production, is the best known industry in Los Angeles, focusing worldwide attention on the city and forming a critical part of the city's status as a major tourist destination. All six major studios—Paramount Pictures, 20th Century Fox, Columbia Pictures, Warner Bros., Universal Pictures, and Walt Disney Studios—are located within the county. Some 13,100 business operate in support of the entertainment industry, employing nearly 160,000 people. Including other aspects of the region's "creative economy," such as fashion, home furnishings, and visual and performing arts, the total economic impact exceeded $230 billion in 2011.

Technology is considered to lead the "new economy" of Los Angeles. This sector includes computer and electronics manufacturing, aerospace products manufacturing, software publishing, Internet services, computer system design, scientific and technical consulting, and wholesale electronic markets, agents, and brokers. The banking and finance industry in Los Angeles is one of the largest in the country. More than 8,400 businesses offering financial services operate in Los Angeles; local firms manage some $2 trillion worth of portfolio assets.

Los Angeles is the largest major manufacturing center in the United States. Within the manufacturing industry, the most important sectors for employment and production were apparel, fabricated metals, food products, and aerospace parts and products. The manufacture of heavy machinery for the agricultural, construction, mining, and oil industries contributes significantly to the local economy. Los Angeles is also a major producer of furniture and fixtures, as well as petroleum products and chemicals, print material, rubber goods, electronic equipment, and glass, pottery, ceramics, and cement products.

Items and goods produced: agricultural and seafood products, aircraft and aircraft parts, furniture, electrical and electronic equipment, jewelry, apparel, textiles, toys, fabricated metals, rubber, plastic, motion pictures, petroleum

Incentive Programs—New and Existing Companies

Local programs: Los Angeles's Business Source, part of the Mayor's Office of Economic Development, is a one-stop shop for business developers. The website provides interactive tools to find appropriate incentives for business attraction and retention. The site links businesses to a network of opportunities including financing, tax incentives, real estate, low-interest loans, job training programs, permits, and more.

Financial incentives include the Technology Advancement Program (TAP), related to the ports of Los Angeles and Long Beach. The program provides grants to companies investing in carbon reduction technologies with seaport applications. The South Coast Air Quality Management District Technology Advancement Program uses cooperative partnerships among private, academic, and government agencies to support development of clean

energy. Southern California Edison Programs offer investor-owned utilities to support lower electricity costs; the Southern California Gas Company has a variety of incentives available. The City of Los Angeles supports tax-free water usage, no signalization fees, 31 business improvement districts, and two state enterprise zones.

The Los Angeles Regional Technology Alliance (LARTA) supports small, technology-related businesses. The Southern California Bio-Medical Council offers similar support.

Business advocates for the city also state that, especially for businesses in the creative economy, claiming Los Angeles as headquarters provides an often undervalued advantage related to marketing and consumer appeal.

State programs: California business incentives include the state's Alternative Energy and Advanced Transportation Authority Sales and Use Tax Exemptions for Zero Emission Vehicle Manufacturing. Initially targeting vehicle manufacturing only when it was passed in 2010, the sales and use tax exemption has since been expanded to all renewable energy technologies. In 2012 it was expanded again to include advanced manufacturing. More than one dozen additional incentives encourage green development or pollution-reducing business decisions.

Research and development tax credits offers companies a 15 percent credit against their bank and corporation tax liability for qualifying in-house research expenses; a 24 percent tax credit for basic research payments to outside organizations is also available. Industrial development bonds finance investment in land, buildings, and new equipment related to domestic manufacturing operations in the state. California Capital Access Program and Collateral Support Program also offer alternative methods of financing for businesses. Enterprise Zones and Local Agency Military Base Recovery Area regions provide incentives for development in targeted geographic regions. A New Jobs Tax Credit offers $3,000 per hire of qualifying new employees, and the state's Film and Television Tax Credit Program supports productions with a 20 percent tax credit against qualified expenses.

In 2011 California began offering companies the option to calculate their corporate income tax through the single sales factor method, rather than the existing triple apportionment derived from calculations of a company's payroll, property, and sales.

California's Innovation Hub Program, with 12 locations throughout the state, supports the commercialization of innovation and technology businesses through public-private partnerships, knowledge sharing, venture capital sources, and business incubators. The state also undertakes trade missions to form partnerships for trade and export promotion.

Job training programs: The state of California offers an Employment Training Panel to assist companies with post-hire training and reimbursement. The Employment Development Department also partners with Local Workforce Investment Areas to recruit, screen, test, evaluate, and hire qualified workers.

The Los Angeles Workforce Investment Board (WIB) helps to provide educational facilities and mentoring programs for both youth and adult students. The WIB sponsors WorkSource Centers to assist both businesses and individuals. The Los Angeles Area Chamber of Commerce offers a variety of workforce development programs, such as the Pillar program, Cash for College, Hire LA's Youth, and LA Youth at Work. The chamber's programs facilitate interaction between businesses and future employees by supporting education initiatives.

Development Projects

Since the turn of the twenty-first century, greater Los Angeles has bustled with construction activity and continues to be a constantly changing city marked by constant development. In the new century, the Los Angeles downtown area has undergone a renaissance, with new museums, entertainment centers, sports venues, and more.

LA Live, a $2.5 billion development with more than 4 million square feet of residences, hotels, and entertainment venues, opened in 2008 and was completed in 2010. Also called Times Square West, the development is located south of downtown. A 54-story tower with a Marriott hotel and Ritz-Carlton condominium development is the centerpiece of the project. LA Live also maintains a 7,100-seat theatre; a 14-screen movie theatre; West Coast broadcast facilities for ESPN; and eight restaurants, including concepts by famous Los Angeles chef Wolfgang Puck.

The needs of the city's public institutions also constitute a major portion of development. Part of a major expansion plan, the Los Angeles Unified School District opened the $232 million Central Region High School No. 9, otherwise known as the High School for the Visual and Performing Arts, in 2008. In 2010 the Robert F. Kennedy Community Schools opened at a cost of $578 million, reportedly the most expensive school construction in the United States. The project was controversial as it was developed on the site where Senator Robert F. Kennedy was shot, and demolition of the site was strongly opposed by preservationists. At a cost of $440 million, a new headquarters for the Los Angeles Police Department opened in 2010.

In 2006 NBC/Universal unveiled a $3 billion, 25-year plan to expand Universal City from a movie studio and theme park into a major residential and office center, including two 500-room hotels. The proposal represents the single largest investment in the San Fernando Valley and is expected to double the number of jobs at the studio. City approval of a slightly scaled-back version was achieved in 2012. Universal officials have estimated it could take up to 20 years to complete and create 3,000 to 5,000 jobs.

Another development project in the works is Grand Avenue, with hopes of revitalizing downtown Los Angeles. It has been compared to the Champs-Élysées of Paris and the Central Park of New York City. The $3 billion Grand Avenue project includes up to 3.6 million square feet of development, designed primarily by the famous architect Frank Gehry. The project, initially proposed in 2003, had several projects under development in 2013, with a 271-unit mixed-use tower scheduled located next to ongoing construction for the Broad, a contemporary museum funded by billionaires Eli and Edythe Broad. Both were expected to open in 2014. Additional private investments included more than 40 major projects in various stages as of 2014, with four mixed-use developments investing more than $1 billion.

Renovation of Los Angeles International Airport's Tom Bradley International Terminal, completed in 2013, represented the first phase of a $1.9 billion upgrade scheduled to wrap up in 2015. The initial terminal renovation was intended to facility the airport's handling of big aircraft like that Airbus A380. Increasing energy efficiency was a central component of airport improvements. New taxiways, a utility plant, and infrastructure upgrades were also included in plans.

The Port of Los Angeles was also investing heavily in its infrastructure, with $1 billion in capital investments planned for 2010–15. Port improvement projects focused on creating new terminals for existing clients, adding additional cranes, and deepening water depth to 53 feet across the port's containership berths. Related to port developments was a planned $1.2 billion improvement project for the San Pedro Waterfront, which included creating new open spaces, harbors, public piers, and general revitalization to support the quality of life for local community members and ensure positive experiences for the thousands of visitors drawn to the area for cruise travel.

City investment in a regional connector for its underground light rail service tallied $1.37 billion, with construction for a 1.9-mile underground route and three underground stations expected to complete in 2019.

Economic Development Information: Los Angeles County Economic Development Corporation, 444 South Flower Street, 34th Floor, Los Angeles, CA 90071; telephone (213) 236-4800.

Commercial Shipping

International trade is a major component of the Los Angeles area economy. The Los Angeles Customs District (including the ports of Long Beach and Los Angeles, Port Hueneme, and Los Angeles International Airport) is the nation's largest customs area based on value of two-way trade. Also called Los Angeles Harbor and Worldport LA, the Port of Los Angeles's complex sits on 7,500 acres of land, adjoining the separate Port of Long Beach. The Port of Los Angeles is the busiest container port in the United States, with 43 miles of waterfront and 24 passenger and cargo terminals. It is designated as a Foreign Trade Zone; top trading countries include China, Japan, Taiwan, Vietnam, and South Korea. The Los Angeles International Airport (LAX) averages 1,000 cargo flights each day and handled nearly two million tons of cargo in 2012. Handling facilities include the 98-acre Century Cargo Complex, the 57.4-acre Imperial Complex, the Imperial Cargo Center, and several of terminals on the south side of the airport.

The Alameda Corridor, a 20-mile high-speed cargo rail system, connects the Port of Long Beach and the Port of Los Angeles to the transcontinental rail network links near the city of Los Angeles. An average of nearly 50 trains per day make the trip, generally carrying containers. Several transcontinental rail lines serve the area. All of the major interstate truck companies maintain large facilities in the metropolitan area.

Labor Force and Employment Outlook

Los Angeles offers a diverse employment pool, with a wide range of schooling and skills. A large number of immigrants—international, national, and regional—provide a steady source of labor with strong links to important trading partners like Mexico and Asia. With Los Angeles International Airport serving as the so-called new Ellis Island for foreign immigration into the United States, the metropolitan region has achieved a new ethnic and cultural diversity in its workforce.

Services, wholesale and retail trade, manufacturing, government, financial service industries, transportation, utilities, and construction contribute significantly to local employment. Employment growth in 2012 was paced by the construction sector, which was driven primarily by resurgence in the housing market.

The following is a summary of data regarding the 2012 Los Angeles labor force:

Size of civilian labor force: 2,027,681

Number of workers employed in . . .

agriculture and mining: 9,100
construction: 103,798
manufacturing: 157,206
wholesale trade: 50,906
retail trade: 184,118
transportation: 71,873
information systems: 102,770
finance: 112,847
professional administration: 244,071
education and social services: 351,825
arts and leisure: 210,411
other: 129,138
public administration: 42,995

Average hourly earnings of production workers: $15.29

Unemployment rate: 7.6% (2012)

Employers

Largest employers (2012)	*Number of employees*
City of Los Angeles	44,947
County of Los Angeles	40,691
Los Angeles Unified School District	36,881
University of California Los Angeles	32,300
Cedars-Sinai Medical Center	17,000
University of Southern California	16,623
Kaiser Foundation Hospitals	11,775
Veterans Health Administration	10,400
Farmers Insurance Group	9,167
Team-One Employment Specialists LLC	5,000
United States Postal Service	1,500
The Walt Disney Company	350

Cost of Living

Living costs in the metropolitan area are significantly higher than the national average. Los Angeles ranks as the most expensive U.S. city for "living well", with an estimated $350,000 of annual income necessary to maintain a high-end lifestyle.

The following is a summary of data regarding several key cost of living factors in the area.

2013 ACCRA Average House Price: $550,115

2013 ACCRA Cost of Living Index: 130

State income tax rate: 1.00% to 13.3%

State sales tax rate: 7.5%

Local income tax rate: None

Local sales tax rate: 1.5%

Property tax rate: Limited to 1% of assessed value by state law. In some cases the local taxing body can add additional taxes.

Economic Information: Los Angeles Area Chamber of Commerce, 350 South Bixel Street, Los Angeles, CA 90017; telephone (213) 580-7500; fax (213) 580-7511.

■ Education and Research

Elementary and Secondary Schools

The Los Angeles Unified School District (LAUSD) is the country's second largest district, serving more than 640,000 students. Geographically, it encompasses 720 square miles, an area that includes the City of Los Angeles and parts or all of 31 smaller municipalities, and some unincorporated areas of Los Angeles County. Over 70 percent of all students are Hispanic. Dual Language Programs, in which instruction is given in English and a second language, are sponsored district-wide for students who speak Spanish or Korean. Several classes are available for those learning English as a second language.

Most district schools are on a single-track schedule with a school year running September through June. Thirty-one schools operate on year-round schedules. The school district has historically had a reputation for having very crowded schools, high dropout rates, and general difficulty with insufficient funding. Throughout the 2000s and into the 2010s, the district tried to change those tides. New school building projects funded by a voter-approved $19.3 billion construction program added more than 115 schools to the district by 2013. One of these schools, the Robert F. Kennedy Community Schools, opened in 2010 as the most expensive school construction in the country at a cost of $579 million.

The district also has 187 public charter schools and centers, 58 elementary magnet centers and schools, 44 middle school magnet centers, and 53 high school magnet programs. There are 18 special education schools.

There are over 75 private schools in the city of Los Angeles and well over 100 including those in the LAUSD area. These include religious affiliated schools, independent schools, Montessori's, and special education facilities

The following is a summary of data regarding the Los Angeles Unified School District.

Total enrollment: 667,273

Number of facilities

> total: 848
> elementary schools: 519
> junior high schools: 120
> high schools: 121
> other: 88

Student/teacher ratio: 21.46:1

Teacher salaries

> average (statewide): $69,434

Funding per pupil: $10,816

Public Schools Information: Los Angeles Unified School District, Office of the Superintendent, 333 South Beaudry Avenue, 24th floor, Los Angeles, CA 90017; telephone (213) 241-7000.

Colleges and Universities

Los Angeles is home to a long list of colleges and universities, some among the best in the country and many receiving a broad variety of accolades for academic achievement. The two largest schools in Los Angeles are the University of California, Los Angeles (UCLA) and the University of Southern California (USC). UCLA consistently ranks among the top 30 best universities in the nation by *U.S News & World Report*. It was ranked 23rd for 2013–14. The university has 125 majors across nearly 150 departments and also offers doctoral degrees in 40 programs that all place among the top 10 nationally.

USC is also consistently ranked among the top 30 best universities by *U.S News & World Report*, and its programs are also highly distinguished in the academic community. It tied with UCLA for the 23rd spot among national universities in 2013–14. Serving about 40,000 students—more than half of whom are graduate or professional students— the university consists of the College of Letters, Arts, and Sciences; a Graduate School; and more than one dozen professional schools.

California Institute of Technology (Caltech) is consistently ranked in the top 10 universities by *U.S News & World Report* and was ranked 10th in 2013–14. Enrollment that year was 2,243. Caltech offers an array of undergraduate degrees as well as graduate degrees in engineering, biology, chemistry, computer science, earth sciences, mathematics, and physics. A major research university, it receives significant funding from institutions such as NASA, the National Science Foundation, and Department of Health and Human Services.

Loyola Marymount University, a private Jesuit-affiliated institution, has a total enrollment of about 9,500 students. They offer 60 undergraduate degree programs and 43 graduate programs through seven schools and colleges. Pepperdine University, an independent university affiliated with the Churches of Christ, ranks as the 57th best national university according to *U. S News & World Report* in 2013–14. There are about 7,300 students enrolled in five colleges and schools. The Graduate School of Education and Psychology has a campus location in Los Angeles. The main campus, however, is in Malibu. Mount St. Mary's College is an independent Catholic liberal arts college for women. The school offers associate's degrees in five fields, bachelor's degrees in 32 fields, as well as master's and doctoral degrees. Enrollment is about 3,100 women. The Claremont Colleges, a consortium of five undergraduate and two graduate institutions, are located to the east of the city.

Other major institutions include: California State University, Los Angeles; California State University, Northridge; Alliant International University; American InterContinental University; Charles R. Drew University of Medicine and Science; Los Angeles Film School; Marymount College; National University of California; Occidental College; Otis College of Art and Design; Southern California Institute of Architecture; and Southwestern Law School, among others. Los Angeles hosts branch campuses of Syracuse University, the American Musical and Dramatic Academy, Antioch University, the Fashion Institute of Design & Merchandising.

The Los Angeles Community College District has nine campuses in the Los Angeles area, three of which are in the city limits (Los Angeles City College, Los Angeles Southwest College, and Los Angeles Trade-Technical College). A wide variety of programs are offered throughout the system. The colleges had a combined enrollment of 132,601 in 2012.

The American Film Institute's Conservatory offers graduate programs for those entering the film industry. A Master of Fine Arts degree is available in six discipline specific programs: cinematography, directing, editing, producing, production design, and screenwriting.

There are many other specialized schools in the city that offer both general higher educational opportunities and career specific programs. These include such schools as the American Barber College, National Bartenders School, Samara University of Oriental Medicine, and American Jewish University.

Libraries and Research Centers

The Los Angeles Public Library system operates a central library and 72 branches throughout the metropolitan area with a total of more than 6.2 million volumes. Forty-four branches and the central library are located in Los Angeles. The Mexicana Collection, with information on Mexico and the impact of Mexican culture on California, is considered to be a core collection with items located at several branches in the system. Other core collections cover special topics such as bullfighting, pacific voyages, food and wine, costumes, the history of the book and printing, California history, and ornithology. Special collections include the George Smith Biblioteca Taurina (Bullfight Collection), photographs by Ansel Adams and Edward Weston, the Tom Owen Collection of Bookplate Art, and the Paul Fritzche Collection of Culinary Literature. The system also maintains holdings of maps, audio tapes, films and videos, art reproductions, mobile libraries, and special services for the visually impaired.

The County of Los Angeles Public Library, headquartered in Downey, operates 84 regional and community library branches and 3 bookmobiles. With over 7.5 million titles, the system was ranked as one of the largest public library systems in the nation by a report from the American Library Association. There are 10 library branches within the city of Los Angeles. The Anthony Quinn Library branch contains over 3,000 items of memorabilia related to the actor. Special homework centers are located at several branches.

The UCLA library collection ranks among the top 10 academic libraries in the nation with over 8 million volumes. The Clark Library holds special collections on Oscar Wilde and Western Americana. The East Asian Library includes numerous Chinese, Japanese, and Korean language materials. The USC libraries contain about 4.5 million volumes. Special collections include American Literature, the Boeckmann Center for Iberian and Latin American Studies, the California Social Welfare Archives, the Natural History Collection, and the Shoah Foundation Visual History Archive. There are several regional history collections as well.

The Los Angeles County Law Library is the second largest law library in the country—trailing only the Library of Congress—with a collection of more than 700,000 volumes in all areas of law and legal issues. More than 150 other specialized and private libraries serve the Los Angeles area.

The Louis B. Mayer Library of the American Film Institute holds over 10,000 books and 30 journal titles on industry related topics such as film, television, video, photography, theater, and costume design. The library also holds over 5,000 unpublished American film scripts. Special collections include the Martin Scorsese Collection, the Charles K. Feldman Collection, the Robert Aldrich Collection, and the Fritz Lang Collection. Most items are non-circulating, but are available for in-house use by visitors as well as students and film professionals.

Some of the most advanced research in the world is conducted at Los Angeles's three major institutions of higher learning: UCLA, USC, and the California Institute of Technology. There are dozens of research centers and institutes at UCLA with topics ranging from scientific to social and religious. Scientific and technological research facilities include Basic Plasma Science Facility, Center for High Frequency Electronics, Institute of Geophysics and Planetary Physics, Electronic Thin Film Lab, and Fusion Science and Technology Center. Health research centers include the Alzheimer's Disease Research Center, Cardiovascular Research Laboratory, Center for Collaborative Research on Drug Abuse, Center for Human Nutrition, Center for Molecular Medicine, and Gonda Neuroscience and Genetics Research Center. Cultural studies are supported by the Center for Buddhist Studies, Center for Chinese Studies, Center for East Asian Studies, Center for Jewish Studies, and Institute for America Cultures. Other research topics include business, communications, labor and industry, and environmental studies.

Research at USC is just as extensive. Centers for scientific research include Center of Excellence in Genomic Science, Center for Robotics and Embedded

Systems, Loker Hydrocarbon Research Institute, and Space Science Center. Cultural and social research is covered through the Center for Feminist Research, Center for Religion and Civic Culture, East Asian Studies Center, Institute of Modern Russian Culture, and Center for Research on Children, Youth and Families. Health research institutes include the Andrus Gerontology Center, Research Center for Alcoholic Liver and Pancreatic Diseases and Cirrhosis, Hepatitis Clinical Research Center, and the Research Center for Liver Diseases. The Southern California Earthquake Center is also located at USC. The USC Stevens Institute for Innovation helps students and faculty turn new inventions and discoveries into practical applications.

Research institutes at Caltech are known worldwide. They include the Beckman Institute, a multi-disciplinary center for research in the chemical and biological sciences; Infrared Processing and Analysis Center; NASA Jet Propulsion Laboratory; Laser Interferometer Gravitational Wave Observatory; and NASA Spitzer Space Telescope. There are nine observatories sponsored in part by Caltech. The Keck Observatory at Mauna Kea, Hawaii, is a joint program of Caltech and the University of California.

Public Library Information: Los Angeles Public Library System, Central Branch, 630 West Fifth Street, Los Angeles, CA 90071-2097; telephone (213) 228-7000. USC Office of Research, Credit Union Building, Suite 325, 3720 S. Flower Street, University of Southern California, Los Angeles, CA 90089; telephone (213) 740-6709. UCLA Office of the Vice Chancellor of Research, UCLA, 2147 Murphy Hall, Los Angeles, CA 90095; telephone (310) 825-7943.

■ Health Care

Los Angeles is the primary health-care and treatment center for the southern California region. It is one of the largest health-care markets in the country and is at the forefront of major changes taking place in the health-care industry. In the vast metropolitan area, there are over 800 hospitals and clinics.

With 466 beds, UCLA Medical Center is known worldwide as a health-care innovator. Its highly experienced staff consists of more than 1,000 physicians and 3,500 nurses, therapists, technologists, and support personnel. Offering comprehensive care from the routine to the highly specialized, its physicians are some of the best in the country. Other factors contributing to the Center's top rankings include specialized intensive care units, state-of-the-art inpatient and outpatient operating suites, a Level 1 trauma center, and the latest diagnostic technology. UCLA Medical Center includes the Mattell Children's Hospital; Jules Stein Eye Institute; Doris Stein Eye Research Center; Jonsson Comprehensive Cancer

Center, officially designated by the National Cancer Institute as one of the most comprehensive cancer centers in the country; and a network of health-care facilities that brings UCLA-quality care to a growing number of California communities. The UCLA Medical Center consistently receives high marks from the annual *U.S News & World Report* as one of the best hospitals in the nation. These include a third place ranking in geriatrics; fourth place in urology; fifth place in ophthalmology; eighth in rheumatology, nephrology, and gastroenterology and related surgery; ninth in neurology and neurosurgery, and psychiatry; and top-20 rankings for five other adult specialties in 2013–14. Pediatric care was ranked nationally in 10 specialties.

The private, non-profit Children's Hospital Los Angeles is affiliated with the Keck School of Medicine of the University of Southern California. The 317-bed hospital features Level I Pediatric Trauma Center, a Newborn and Infant Critical Care Unit, a Pediatric Intensive Care Unit, and a Cardiothoracic Intensive Care Unit. The hospital made headlines in 2006 when a team of doctors successfully separated conjoined twins who were joined at the mid-abdomen and pelvis. The hospital was ranked nationally in 10 pediatric specialties by *U.S News & World Report* in 2013–14, including six specialties among the top eight: cancer, cardiology and heart surgery, diabetes and endocrinology, gastroenterology and related surgery, neonatology, and orthopedics.

The Los Angeles County-University of Southern California (LAC-USC) Medical Center is among the largest teaching hospitals in the country. Specialized facilities and services include a state-of-the-art burn center, Level III neonatal intensive care unit, Level I trauma service, an NIH-funded clinical research center, and an HIV/AIDS outpatient center. Keck Hospital of USC is a private, 220-bed referral, teaching, and research hospital. Advanced services include neurointerventional radiology, cardiac catheterization, and interventional cardiology. The hospital is also known for its surgical care in organ transplantation, neurosurgery, and plastic and reconstructive surgeries. The Doheny Eye Institute, also affiliated with USC, was ranked ninth in the nation for ophthalmology by *U.S News & World Report* in 2013–14. The 408-bed Good Samaritan Hospital is also affiliated with USC.

Cedars-Sinai Medical Center (CSMC), with 892 beds, is one of the largest non-profit hospitals in the West. The CSMC Campus is located near the borders of Los Angeles, Beverly Hills, and West Hollywood. *U.S. News & World Report* consistently ranks Cedars-Sinai among the top hospitals in the country. In 2013–14 the hospital was ranked nationally in 12 specialties, including among the top 10 for cardiology and heart surgery, gastroenterology and related surgery, orthopedics, and urology. The CSMC Samuel Oschin Comprehensive Cancer Institute is one of the largest of its kind in Southern California. Other Specialty centers include the Cedars-Sinai Spine Center, Heart Institute, and Center for Chest Diseases. The hospital has a comprehensive transplant center.

The Los Angeles County Department of Health Services operates several community clinics in the area.

■ Recreation

Sightseeing

The immense size of Los Angeles and the innumerable activities offered by the city make its attractions seem limitless. Different sections of the city offer a wide range of sights and diversions, from the more than 40 miles of city-operated Pacific beaches in the west to the mountains in the east and the vast urban areas in between. The downtown district not only forms one of the nation's most modern skylines, but also preserves many historic buildings. Some of the original structures in the city can be found in El Pueblo de Los Angeles State Historic Park. To the east is Olvera Street, a Hispanic district that recreates the atmosphere of old Mexico's open-air markets. Chinatown is just north of the downtown area, and to the south Little Tokyo is the social, cultural, religious, and economic center for Southern California's more than 200,000 Japanese American residents, the largest concentration of Japanese people outside of Asia.

Hollywood and other districts devoted to the film and television industry are among the most popular attractions in Los Angeles. Universal Studios Hollywood features guided tours of some of the world's most famous imaginary places, and live tapings of television shows can be viewed at several studios. Nearby Beverly Hills, an independent community completely surrounded by the city, is home to many film stars, where opulent mansions enjoy proximity to some of the world's most exclusive stores and restaurants. A trip to Los Angeles is not complete without a visit to the newly refurbished TCL Chinese Theatre and the "Walk of Fame" sidewalk featuring the handprints and footprints of movie legends.

Griffith Park, the city's largest municipal park, features the Los Angeles Zoo, with more than 1,100 animals; Griffith Observatory, which contains refracting and solar telescopes; and the Greek Theatre, a natural outdoor amphitheater. Train rides are also available in the park. Hancock Park contains the Rancho La Brea Tar Pits, where prehistoric fossil remains are displayed alongside life-size renditions of the species common to the area in prehistory.

Three of the nation's most popular theme parks are located in the Los Angeles area. Six Flags Magic Mountain is 25 minutes north of Hollywood in Valencia and features 260 acres of rides and family-oriented fun. Knott's Berry Farm in Buena Park offers rides, attractions, live entertainment, shops, and restaurants. World-famous Disneyland, located in Anaheim, is home to eight imaginary lands, rides, adventures, and the famous Disney characters.

The Pacific oceanfront provides a variety of attractions, including carnival-like Venice Beach and Muscle Beach, home to hundreds of bodybuilders. Marina Del Ray, known as "LA's Riviera," is the world's largest man-made marina. Catalina Island features island tours and a casino.

Arts and Culture

The performing arts thrive in the city of Los Angeles. Many consider it the entertainment capital of the world, where major television and film projects develop daily. One of America's premier symphony orchestras, the Los Angeles Philharmonic, performs during the winter at the Walt Disney Concert Hall; the orchestra gives summer concerts at the Hollywood Bowl, an open-air amphitheater designed by Frank Lloyd Wright. The Los Angeles Opera and Master Chorale perform at the 3,200-seat Dorothy Chandler Pavilion.

Theater in Los Angeles benefits from the motion picture and television industry. Famous personalities can often be seen in area theaters, including the Fonda Theatre, Ahmanson Theatre, and Center Theatre Group. The internationally acclaimed Joffrey Ballet performs in Los Angeles but maintains headquarters in Chicago.

The Los Angeles area is filled with museums for every taste. The Natural History Museum of Los Angeles County features displays of paleontology and history, minerals, animal habitats, and pre-Columbian culture. The Page Museum located at the La Brea Tar Pits is one of the world's most famous fossil localities, recognized for having the largest and most diverse collection of extinct Ice Age plants and animals in the world. The Hollywood Wax Museum houses more than 350 wax figures depicting famous people. The California Science Center is one of the most visited museums in the West and includes an IMAX Theatre, extensive ecosystem exhibit, and air and space exhibit. The history of California comes alive at the Autry National Center in Griffith Park, the Southwest Museum, Hollywood Museum, and Wells Fargo History Museum. The early Spanish colonial history of the region can be experienced by visiting one of nine mission churches located in and around the city. The Museum of Tolerance is a high-tech, hands-on experiential museum that focuses on racism and prejudice in America and the history of the Holocaust through unique interactive exhibits.

The Museum of Contemporary Art houses a large permanent collection of approximately 5,000 objects in all visual media, ranging from masterpieces of abstract expressionism and pop art to recent works by young and emerging artists. Paintings, drawings, sculpture, illuminated manuscripts, decorative arts, and European and American photographs are on display at the J. Paul Getty Museum. The Los Angeles County Museum of Art features permanent installations of pre-Columbian, Far Eastern, European, and American artwork, as well as a number of traveling exhibits. Fundraising to build an Academy Museum of Motion Pictures next to the Los Angeles County Museum of Art was underway in 2014. The Broad, a contemporary art museum funded by billionaires Eli and Edythe Broad, was scheduled to open in 2014.

Other museums in the region include the California African American Museum, Chinese American Museum, Armand Hammer Museum of Art at UCLA, and the many museums to be found on "Museum Row" on the city's west side.

Festivals and Holidays

Los Angeles' events calendar begins with the Tournament of Roses Parade in Pasadena on New Year's Day, an event featuring floral floats decorated by hand. The Los Angeles Art Show, also in January, offers for-sale, museum-quality artworks from around the world. Chinese New Year is celebrated each February in Chinatown with the Golden Dragon Parade and other celebrations. The annual Academy Awards event sponsored by the Academy of Motion Picture Arts and Sciences is held in early March. In March or April Olvera Street is host to a Blessing of the Animals festival on the Saturday before Easter. April features the spectacular Easter Sunrise services at the Hollywood Bowl.

Cinco de Mayo, a Mexican festival in May, is celebrated in a number of places throughout the Southern California area. May also brings the Bluegrass in the Spring Festival at Calico Ghost Town in Yermo and the elegant Affaire in the Garden, a fine arts and crafts show in Beverly Hills. June features the Ojai Wine Festival in Ojai and the Playboy Jazz Festival at the Hollywood Bowl. The Fourth of July is celebrated in a variety of ways throughout the city, including fireworks on the oceanfront. July also features the Orange County Fair in Costa Mesa and the International Surf Festival on the South Bay. One of the oldest Japanese American festivals, the Nisei Week Japanese Festival occurs each August in Little Tokyo.

Los Angeles celebrates its birthday each September in the downtown Plaza, and Catalina Island hosts the Annual Art Festival, a September tradition since 1958. September also brings the LA County Fair in Pomona, a two-week celebration of agriculture and livestock featuring horse races and prize pies. Mexican Independence Day is also celebrated with a fiesta for three days in mid-September in El Pueblo de Los Angeles State Historic Park. The October Eagle Rock Music Festival is a street fair that is family-friendly, offering food from local restaurants and live entertainment. The Screamfest Horror Film Festival also takes place in October at the TCL Chinese Theatre. November features the Dia de Los Muertos, the "Day of the Dead," a traditional Mexican festival on the first of November. The AFI Film Fest, a week-long event in November, is the longest running

film festival in Los Angeles (established 1987) and is considered to be one of the most influential in North America. The holiday season begins in December with the Holiday Afloat Boat Parade. Las Posadas, a traditional Mexican festival recreating the New Testament story of Mary and Joseph's journey to Bethlehem, takes place each year during the week before Christmas.

Sports for the Spectator

Los Angeles is a coveted location for major international sports competitions. Los Angeles has hosted two Olympics and was the site of the final match of the 1994 FIFA World Cup.

Los Angeles is also home to a variety of well-known professional sports teams. The 21,000-seat Staples Center is home to the National Basketball Association's Los Angeles Clippers and Los Angeles Lakers, the Lakers' development team the D-Fenders, and the National Hockey League's Los Angeles Kings. Baseball's National League Los Angeles Dodgers play an April–October season at a refurbished Dodger Stadium. Los Angeles is also home to the Women's National Basketball Association team, the Sparks, and Major League Soccer's Galaxy and Chivas USA. The Los Angeles Angels of Anaheim of Major League Baseball and the Anaheim Ducks of the National Hockey League play in nearby Anaheim. The city is the largest in the United States without a National Football League team, though the city's Memorial Coliseum formerly hosted the Raiders, now in Oakland, and the Rams, now in St. Louis, Missouri. Locating an expansion franchise in Los Angeles continued to be a frequent source of speculation by commentators and sports fans through 2014.

Collegiate sports are represented by UCLA and USC, both Division I National Collegiate Athletic Association (NCAA) institutions. Both schools field championship caliber teams in many major sports. The annual Rose Bowl, one of the major traditional post-season college football games, is played on New Year's Day in Pasadena. Hollywood Park and Santa Anita Park are both nationally known thoroughbred racing facilities.

Sports for the Participant

The Los Angeles area offers a broad range of activities for the athletically inclined. The miles of city-operated beaches along the Pacific are popular for swimming, surfing, and all forms of boating. Winter skiing areas are less than an hour's drive away from the city. The Los Angeles Parks and Recreation Department operates several hundred parks and recreation centers. These include 21 year-round public swimming pools and 37 summer pools, 21 skate parks, and 9 dog parks. There are special Therapeutic Recreation Centers for children and adults with disabilities. The city also has universally accessible playgrounds, designed to accommodate children of all ability levels. The city also maintains several bike trails.

Shopping and Dining

Los Angeles is a shopper's paradise, with more than 1,500 department stores as well as countless smaller specialty shops, a number of fashionable shopping plazas, and many large urban malls. With high-powered celebrities with cash to burn at every turn, the fashion industry, in which Los Angeles is a major player, makes shopping in Los Angeles a unique ritual. An exclusive group of stores along Rodeo Drive is the most famous shopping district in the area, and the epicenter of the "Golden Triangle" shopping area of Beverly Hills. There is also Melrose Avenue, whose luxury goods start with the ivy-covered Fred Segal store to the infamous Sunset Strip. Westwood Village is a collection of interesting boutiques and restaurants that offers a thriving night life. Abbot Kinney Boulevard is one of Los Angeles's hippest areas for unique shopping, featuring home-grown artists and designers in a mix of modern chic and old school vintage goods. The Beverly Center in West Los Angeles is one of the nation's busiest malls. Celebrity sightings there are not uncommon, and tourists come by the thousands to shop as part of planned sightseeing tours. The Hollywood and Highland Center in Hollywood offers dining, shopping, and entertainment all at one stop. Other shopping districts include Larchmont Village, West Third Street, Pacific Palisades, Brentwood Country Mart, Third Street Promenade and Montana Avenue in Santa Monica, and boutique shopping on Ventura Boulevard in the San Fernando Valley. The Valley also has some of Los Angeles's largest shopping malls, including Westfield Fashion Square Mall in Sherman Oaks and the Sherman Oaks Galleria. Los Angeles is home to several large shopping malls. Among the latest is the $400 million Americana at Brand, featuring a two-acre park complemented by fountains, public art and generous open space. Promenades, meandering walkways and open-air plazas invite guests to shop, stroll, and dine in this outdoor mall.

Ethnic specialty shops can be found in Little Tokyo, Koreatown, Chinatown, East Los Angeles, and on Olvera Street. The Farmer's Market and Shopping Village in downtown Los Angeles offers fresh produce, import shops, and elegant cafes. Westwood Village and the neighboring UCLA campus are a cultural and entertainment hub filled with shops, bistros, and architectural landmarks.

The Los Angeles area, home to some of America's finest restaurants, enjoys some 20,000 dining establishments, from fast food chains to exclusive gourmet restaurants frequented by Hollywood stars. Ethnic specialties from nearly every country in the world can be found in Los Angeles. Fresh seafood and beef, as well as produce from the nearby agricultural regions, are served in most of the city's restaurants. While in the city, visitors might want to stop at a few of the Los Angeles "original" restaurants. Philippe the Original restaurant, for instance, is the home of the first French dip sandwich, created by accident by then-chef and owner Philippe Mathieu in 1918. Wood-fired pizzas were introduced to the nation by Wolfgang Puck, the famous chef and owner of Spago.

Visitor Information: Los Angeles Convention & Visitors Bureau, Visitor Center, 6801 Hollywood Blvd., Hollywood, CA 90028; telephone (323) 467-6412.

■ Convention Facilities

Los Angeles is a popular destination for meetings and boasts high attendance records, with more than 250 event venues listed with the visitor's bureau. The major convention and meeting facility in Los Angeles is the Los Angeles Convention Center. Situated on 63 landscaped acres, the complex is centrally located within easy access of hotels, restaurants, nightlife, shops, recreational activities, and sightseeing attractions. With 720,000 square feet of exhibition and 147,000 square feet of meeting room space, the center is one of the largest convention facilities on the West Coast. There are more than 14,000 hotel rooms and two major airports near the convention center. The California Market Center downtown offers 168,000 square feet of exhibit and banquet space. The Kodak Theatre and the Pantages Theatre are sometimes available for private events. L.A. Live boasts a four-million-square-foot entertainment complex. Nokia Theatre, part of the L.A. Live Complex, hosts more than 150 live annual performances and also features 235,000 square feet of flexible hospitality areas. Meeting spaces may also be available at local universities.

Convention Information: Los Angeles Convention & Visitors Bureau, Visitor Center, 6801 Hollywood Blvd., Hollywood, CA 90028; telephone (323) 467-6412.

■ Transportation

Approaching the City

Several airports service the Los Angeles region. Los Angeles International Airport (LAX), just west of the downtown area, is one of the top-six airports in the world in terms of passengers handled, with more than 63 million people passing through annually as of 2012. The airport is served by approximately 60 airlines, including all major airlines, taking passengers to 910 non-stop destinations in 30 countries. Special FlyAway buses take visitors from LAX to Union Station in downtown Los Angeles or to the Van Nuys Airport (a noncommercial regional airport). A free, frequent shuttle bus connects LAX with Metro Transit Authority's Green Line Light Rail. The LA/Ontario International Airport (ONT) is a medium-hub, full-service airport with commercial jet service to major U.S. cities and international destinations. Located in the Inland Empire, ONT is approximately 35 miles east of downtown Los Angeles. The airport has more than 114 daily flights on seven airlines. The closest airport to Hollywood is the Bob Hope Airport, served by seven airlines. Travelers may also choose to enter the area through Long Beach Airport to the south, which is served by four airlines and is a primary hub for JetBlue. Long Beach Airport is among the busiest general aviation airports in the world. Even busier is another general aviation airport, Van Nuys Airport (VNY). This 730-acre airport averages more than one-quarter million takeoffs and landings annually. More than 100 businesses are located on the airport grounds. VNY also is home to numerous companies that provide aviation support activities.

Greyhound carries passengers to a terminal in downtown Los Angeles. Amtrak carries passengers to Los Angeles from Seattle, Portland, Sacramento, Oakland, Santa Barbara, Chicago, and New Orleans. The local *Pacific Surfliner* carries passengers from San Diego through Los Angeles on multiple daily available trips, with routes to Santa Barbara and San Luis Obispo. Four other Amtrak routes pass through the city, with about 17 trains passing through Los Angeles's Union Station, which also services two Metro subway lines and one light rail line. Metrolink passenger trains also pass through the hub, servicing regional lines to various Southern California counties.

Three interstate highways converge in the Los Angeles area: Interstate 5 approaching from Canada in the north, Interstate 15 from Las Vegas to the west, and Interstate 10 connecting Los Angeles with Arizona and the Southwest. State Highway 1, the Pacific Coastal Highway, skirts the city along the ocean.

The World Cruise Center in San Pedro, located in the Port of Los Angeles, also offers visitors a way to Los Angeles by sea. About 18 miles south of the LAX airport, the cruise center is easily accessible. With more than a dozen of the world's largest cruise lines, passengers set sail every day on voyages to Mexico and Hawaii. Visitors can also take cruises to nearby locations, such as Catalina Island.

Traveling in the City

The sprawling Los Angeles is perhaps best navigated by automobile. However the city's massive, complex web of limited-access freeways, one of the most extensive in the nation, still struggles to accommodate heavy commuter traffic. The Los Angeles Department of Transportation has implemented a state-of-the-art computer system to manage the city's street traffic, but Los Angeles was still among the places with the worst traffic congestion in the nation according to numerous 2012 reports. Downtown Los Angeles is bounded by the Hollywood Freeway to the north, the Santa Monica Freeway to the south, and the Harbor Freeway to the west, with the east bounded by the Los Angeles River.

The Los Angeles County Metropolitan Transit operates one of the largest public transportation networks in the country, including subways, light rail, buses, and shuttles. Local and express bus service with 170 routes carry more than 1.5 million riders throughout the city each weekday. Color-coded subway and light-rail lines offer visitors another way of getting from one destination to the next, with 80 stations across 87 miles. The Metro Blue Line runs north and south between Long Beach and Los Angeles. The Metro Green Line runs between Norwalk and Redondo Beach. The Metro Red Line subway provides service through Downtown to North Hollywood, then connects to the Orange Line, which travels west into the San Fernando Valley. The Metro Purple Line subway runs through Downtown and continues to the Mid-Wilshire area. The Metro Gold Line connects with the Red Line at Union Station and runs northeast to Pasadena.

The City of Los Angeles Department of Transportation operates the DASH shuttle system. Six downtown DASH lines link major business, government, retail and entertainment centers within downtown. The Convention Center, the Garment and Jewelry districts, Olvera Street, the Metro Blue Line, and Union Station are easily accessible via DASH lines.

■ Communications

Newspapers and Magazines

The *Los Angeles Times* is the city's major daily newspaper. It is among the largest newspapers in the nation with a daily readership of 1.5 million across the Los Angeles metropolitan area. The paper also supports 22 million unique Web visitors each month. The *Daily News*, published out of Oxnard, focuses on the San Fernando Valley in general. The *Los Angeles Business Journal* is a weekly publication. The *Los Angeles Daily Journal* also serves the business community. *La Opinión*, published in the city, is the largest Spanish-language newspaper in the United States. Other Spanish-language papers published in Los Angeles include *La Prensa de Los Angeles* and *LA Voz Libre*.

Dozens of foreign language, special interest, business, alternative, and neighborhood papers are published weekly in the Los Angeles area. Those published within the city include the *Los Angeles Independent* and the *Los Angeles Downtown News*. *LA Weekly* is an alternative press publication distributed on Thursday. Weekly newspapers serving the African American community include the *Los Angeles Sentinel*. Numerous English and foreign language papers serve the ethnic communities, including the *Beirut Times* (Arabic), *Rafu Shimpo* (Japanese), and *Korea Times* (Korean). The *Jewish Journal of Greater Los Angeles* is published weekly.

Los Angeles magazine, a monthly covering events and topics of importance to the metropolitan area, and a number of nationally distributed magazines, such as *Motor Trend* and *Muscle & Body,* are also published in the city.

Television and Radio

Los Angeles is the second largest designated market area in the nation. Twenty-one television stations broadcast from Los Angeles. Twelve AM and 20 FM radio stations broadcasting there feature a wide assortment of music, news, and information programming; stations broadcasting in surrounding communities are also received in Los Angeles. Many television and radio stations are language specific, from Korean television broadcasting to Spanish radio.

Media Information: Los Angeles Times, 202 W. First Street, Los Angeles, CA 90012; telephone (213) 237-5000.

Los Angeles Online

City of Los Angeles Home Page. Available www.lacity.org

La Opinión. Available www.laopinion.com

Los Angeles Area Chamber of Commerce. Available www.lachamber.org

Los Angeles Convention and Visitors Bureau. Available discoverlosangeles.com

Los Angeles Economic Development Corporation. Available www.laedc.org

Los Angeles Public Library. Available www.lapl.org

Los Angeles Times. Available www.latimes.com

BIBLIOGRAPHY

Allende, Isabel, *The Infinite Plan* (New York: Harper-Collins, 1993)

Cameron, Robert W., *Above Los Angeles* (San Francisco, CA: Cameron and Co., 1990)

Cole, Carolyn Kozo, and Kathy Kobayashi, *Shades of Los Angeles: Pictures from Ethnic Family Albums* (New York: Norton, 1996)

Culver, Lawrence, *The Frontier of Leisure: Southern California and the Shaping of Modern America* (New York: Oxford University Press, 2010)

Widener, Daniel, *Black Arts West: Culture and Struggle in Postwar Los Angeles* (Durham, NC: Duke University Press, 2010)

Monterey

■ The City in Brief

Founded: 1770 (incorporated, 1850)

Head Official: Mayor Chuck Della Sala (since 2006; current term expires 2014)

City Population
  1990: 31,954
  2000: 29,674
  2010: 27,810
  2012 estimate: 28,492
  Percent change, 2000–2010: −6.3%

County Population
  2000: 401,762
  2010: 407,435
  2012 estimate: 416,199
  Percent change, 2000–2010: 1.4%

Area: 8.44 square miles

Elevation: 10 feet above sea level

Average Annual Temperatures: 57° F

Average Annual Precipitation: 19.29 inches

Major Economic Sectors: agriculture, tourism, government, education

Unemployment Rate: 3.7% (2012)

Per Capita Income: $33,130

2012 FBI Crime Index Property: 1,016

Major Colleges and Universities: Monterey Peninsula College, Monterey Institute of International Studies

Daily Newspaper: *The Monterey County Herald*

■ Introduction

Monterey, the largest city on the Monterey Peninsula, is a pristine seaside community that boasts a variety of recreational, cultural, and other activities. It is the site of the Monterey Bay Aquarium, which is home to a wide variety of marine animals. Monterey Bay itself has a diverse and interesting marine ecosystem. Another important offering is Cannery Row, the district made famous by novelist John Steinbeck that once marked Monterey as the "Sardine Capital of the World"; the area has become a bustling retail site with trendy restaurants, shops, and nightspots. Although Monterey offers entertainment opportunities for residents and tourists, it has preserved more of its history than any other California city. The area has become an important military research and educational center, as well as a popular tourist destination. The Salinas Valley in which the city is located is one of the prime agricultural areas of the United States.

■ Geography and Climate

Monterey is located on the Monterey Peninsula, which is 120 miles south of San Francisco, 60 miles south of San Jose, and 345 miles north of Los Angeles. The peninsula is bordered by Monterey Bay to the north, the Pacific Ocean to the west, and Carmel Bay to the south.

Although characterized by cool, dry summers and wet winters, the regions of Monterey County exhibit considerable climatic diversity. The warmest months are July through October, and the rainiest are November and April. Summer months often can be foggy, especially early and late in the day, due to the chilly and unchanging water temperatures of the Pacific Ocean. The city lies in an area surrounding by six active fault lines putting the city at risk for earthquakes.

Area: 8.44 square miles

Elevation: 10 feet above sea level

Old Fisherman's Wharf, Monterey, CA. © *Joseph S Giacalone/Alamy*

Average Temperatures: 57° F

Average Annual Precipitation: 19.29 inches

■ History

Early Settlements

Native Americans known as the Esalen lived in the area of present-day Monterey from 500 B.C. to 500 A.D. and probably much longer. The Esalen were displaced in 500 B.C. by the Ohlone Indians, who were drawn to the area by the abundance of fish and wildlife and other natural resources. The Indians hunted quail, geese, rabbit, bear, and other wildlife, gathered plants, and caught fish, mussels, abalone, and shellfish. Several of their village sites have been identified and preserved.

Monterey was first seen by Europeans when Portuguese explorer Juan Rodriquez Cabrillo spotted La Bahia de los Pinos (Bay of Pines) in 1542 on a journey in search of riches in the New World. But high winds prevented him and his crew from landing. In 1602 Spanish explorer Don Sebastian Viscaino officially named the port in honor of Spain's Count of Monte Rey under whose order he was sailing. Viscaino's 200 men gave thanks for their safe journey in a ceremony held under a large oak tree overlooking the bay.

In 1770 an expedition by land and sea brought Gaspar de Portol and Franciscan Father Junipero Serra to Monterey. There they established the Mission and Presidio (military post) of San Carlos de Borromeo de Monterey and the City of Monterey. Under the same oak tree where Viscaino's crew members had prayed, Father Serra said mass for his brave group. A year later Father Serra moved the mission to nearby Carmel, which offered a better agricultural and political environment; the Presidio Church in Monterey, however, continued in use.

Becomes Capital of Spanish California

In 1776 Spain named Monterey the capital of Baja (lower) and Alta (upper) California. This same year Captain Juan Bautista de Anza arrived with the first settlers for Spanish California, most of them bound for San Francisco. For decades Monterey's soldiers and their wives lived at the Presidio. In 1818 Argentinean revolutionary Hippolyte Bouchard sacked the town in an effort to destroy Spain's presence in California. Soon the residents began to expand outside the Presidio, creating homesteads throughout Monterey.

In April 1822, when Mexico gained its independence from Spain, Monterey became the Mexican capital. California soon pledged its loyalty to the Mexican government.

Spain had not allowed foreigners to trade with California, but Mexico opened up the area to international trade, and Monterey was made California's sole port of entry. Traffic with English and American vessels for the hide and tallow trade became an important part of the economy. A dried steer hide valued at about a dollar was termed a "California bank note." The hides were shipped to New England, where they were used to make saddles, harnesses, and shoes. Tallow was melted down in large rendering pots and poured into bags of hides or bladders to be delivered to the trading ships; in the end, most of the tallow was made into candles.

By 1827 foreign trade had become very important and a custom house was built in Monterey. The booming trade, especially with New England, attracted a number of Americans—called "Yanquis"—to Monterey. Many of them married into Mexican families and became Mexican citizens. In the mid-1830s, Mexican rulers redistributed much of the local land formerly run by the Catholic Church and huge cattle ranches were formed. An elite class of landed "Californios" grew up in the area. In 1842 the U.S. government sent Thomas Larkin to Monterey to head the first American consulate in California.

Statehood Attained

In July 1846 Commodore John Drake Sloat's flagship arrived in Monterey Bay and his troops raised the American flag, claiming the region for the United States, and gaining the territory without a fight from the Mexicans. American occupation continued until the Treaty of Guadalupe Hidalgo was signed in 1848, making all of Alta California part of the United States. This included the land now known as California, Utah, Nevada, and parts of Arizona, Colorado, New Mexico, and Wyoming.

In Monterey, U.S. Naval Chaplain Walter Colton was appointed to serve as Monterey's first American Alcalde, a position defined as mayor and judge. Colton, a well-educated and just man, was considered well qualified to hold this important position. In 1846 he and Robert Semple established California's first newspaper, *The Californian*. Colton also designed and supervised the construction of the first public structure built under the American flag, Colton Hall, which served as a public school and town meeting hall.

In 1849 delegates from throughout Alta California met in Colton Hall in Monterey to create a constitution for the people of the new U.S. territory. The new constitution was signed on October 13, 1849. In 1850 the U.S. Congress voted to adopt California as the thirty-first state of the Union. San Jose was chosen as the seat for the first legislature. (The official definition of a state capital is where the legislature sits; therefore Monterey never was the state capital.)

During the next decade Monterey lost much of its political influence. But at the same time it was becoming an important center for the whaling industry. Asian and European fishermen began arriving there, drawn by the developing fishing industry. Influences from these Japanese, Chinese, Portuguese, and Italian immigrants formed a basis for the city's culture that lives on to today.

Serves as County Seat; Sardine Trade Develops

After California gained its statehood, the legislature formed counties. Monterey served as the Monterey County seat of government until 1873, when Salinas was named to that role. Further transformation of Monterey took place in the 1870s when the first railroad was built, connecting the quiet fishing town with cosmopolitan San Francisco and cities beyond. In the 1880s the local whaling industry disappeared and civic leaders turned to tourism to revive the local economy. By the mid-1880s tourism flourished in the area, with thousands flocking to the seaside resort annually.

By the 1920s the sardine market had grown greatly and the section of Monterey known as Cannery Row was established. During the next two decades, a score of canneries and reduction plants grew up in the area. Workers processed an estimated 250,000 tons of sardines each year. Monterey became known as the "Sardine Capital of the World." The rough and rollicking vicinity of Cannery Row was made famous in the John Steinbeck novels *Cannery Row* and *Sweet Thursday*.

Abandoned Warehouses Revitalized; Tourism Grows

In the 1940s, for reasons still in dispute, the sardine population began a rapid decline. Theories explaining the sardines' disappearance range from water pollution to a change in currents to warmer climates or just being "fished out." The once-thriving Cannery Row soon became a ghost town of empty warehouses.

That changed in the second half of the twentieth century, as the old abandoned warehouses were converted into shops, restaurants, and galleries, and tourism began to take root. By the early 2000s, tourism had become a major industry in Monterey, growing out of the city's efforts to preserve its historic and natural resources. Into the 2010s, annual tourists numbered more than 8 million. Beyond tourism, the robust agricultural industry continued to buoy the area economically, with the remaining defense installations contributing a solid, if less certain, economic boost.

Historical Information: Monterey County Historical Society, PO Box 3576, Salinas, CA 93912; telephone (831) 757-8085.

■ Population Profile

County Population

2000: 401,762
2010: 407,435
2012 estimate: 416,199
Percent change, 2000–2010: 1.4%

City Residents

> 1990: 31,954
> 2000: 29,674
> 2010: 27,810
> 2012 estimate: 28,492
> Percent change, 2000–2010: −6.3%

Density: 3,284.9 people per square mile

Racial and ethnic characteristics

> White: 22,099
> Black or African American: 959
> American Indian and Alaskan Native: 126
> Asian: 2,659
> Native Hawaiian and Other Pacific Islander: 40
> Hispanic or Latino (may be of any race): 5,010
> Other: 2,609

Percent of residents born in state: 39.4%

Age characteristics

> Population under 5 years old: 1,547
> Population 5 to 9 years old: 1,298
> Population 10 to 14 years old: 1,119
> Population 15 to 19 years old: 1,575
> Population 20 to 24 years old: 3,347
> Population 25 to 34 years old: 5,076
> Population 35 to 44 years old: 3,373
> Population 45 to 54 years old: 2,979
> Population 55 to 59 years old: 1,703
> Population 60 to 64 years old: 1,844
> Population 65 to 74 years old: 2,122
> Population 75 to 84 years old: 1,488
> Population 85 years and over: 1,021
> Median age: 35.7

Births (2010–11 Metropolitan Area)

> Total number: Not Available

Deaths (2010–11 Metropolitan Area)

> Total number: Not Available

Money income (2012)

> Per capita income: $33,130
> Median household income: $61,374
> Total households: 11,812

Number of households with income of . . .

> less than $10,000: 928
> $10,000 to $14,999: 504
> $15,000 to $24,999: 1,034
> $25,000 to $34,999: 918
> $35,000 to $49,999: 1,374
> $50,000 to $74,999: 2,587
> $75,000 to $99,999: 1,823
> $100,000 to $149,999: 1,551
> $150,000 to $199,999: 554
> $200,000 or more: 539

Percent of families below poverty level: 8.8%

FBI Crime Index Property: 1,016

FBI Crime Index Violent: 153

■ Municipal Government

Monterey operates with a council-city manager form of government. The city council is the policymaking branch of the city government and consists of five members. The mayor is elected to a two-year term and four council members are elected to four-year terms. The city manager, appointed by the council, serves as the city's professional administrator.

Head Official: Mayor Chuck Della Sala (since 2006; current term expires 2014)

Total Number of City Employees: 463 (2012)

City Information: City of Monterey, 580 Pacific Street, Monterey, CA 93940; telephone (831) 646-3799.

■ Economy

Major Industries and Commercial Activity

Once a leading fishing and whaling port, Monterey County's economic mainstays now are tourism and the military. While tourism has always been a major component in the city's economy, it has become the dominant industry in the last 30 years. The prime tourist season runs April through Thanksgiving. The Monterey Bay Aquarium is the prime attraction, and numerous restaurants, art galleries, gift shops, and an Antiques Mall have created a wide variety of shopping opportunities. Tourists also come to observe special events tied to the historic Cannery Row Area, made famous by novelist John Steinbeck, local son of the nearby city of Salinas. Its reputation as a world class golfing destination brings golfers to the championship golf courses at Pebble Beach and other area courses. Monterey has also become an intriguing dive spot for scuba diving enthusiasts because of its unique aquatic environment: harbor seals, otters, sea lions, and a variety of kelp and other marine features sit beneath the bay's surface. Some eight million tourists descend on Monterey annually, sustaining a $2 billion industry.

Due to its strategic location, Monterey has historically been a key military outpost. Today, the city's military installations continue to provide tremendous support to the economy, particularly through its educational institutions. The Army's Defense Language Institute provides language instruction for agents of the FBI, Drug Enforcement Administration, and Border Patrol. The Naval Postgraduate School offers advance classroom training for Naval officers. The Fleet Numerical Meteorology and Oceanography Center, operated by the Navy, is one of the world's leading numerical weather prediction centers. While the military installations offer a significant economic benefit to the city and surrounding area, the city has attempted to avoid dependence on the defense industry due to the unpredictability of military base closures.

Agriculture is the largest industry in Monterey County. Salinas Valley agriculture generates $3.8 billion of economic valley. Monterey County is the top vegetable-producing region in the nation, producing 80 percent of all U.S. lettuce and a majority of the country's artichokes. Other important crops include broccoli, cauliflower, spinach, strawberries, peppers, squash, carrots, asparagus, celery, tomatoes, mushrooms, Brussels sprouts, garlic, onions, and flowers. The wine industry also has a major presence, with 40,000 acres under cultivation. Some 570 million pounds of Monterey County produce is exported annually, with most going to Canada, Mexico, Asia, or Europe.

Items and goods produced: vegetables, fruits, seafood, light manufactured products

Incentive Programs—New and Existing Companies

Local programs: The Central Coast Small Business Development Center (SBDC) provides no-cost, hands-on technical assistance and support to small businesses on California's Central Coast. Confidential counseling, classes, workshops, seminars, and loan programs are available through the SBDC.

State programs: California business incentives include the state's Alternative Energy and Advanced Transportation Authority Sales and Use Tax Exemptions for Zero Emission Vehicle Manufacturing. Initially targeting vehicle manufacturing only when it was passed in 2010, the sales and use tax exemption has since been expanded to all renewable energy technologies. In 2012 it was expanded again to include advanced manufacturing. More than one dozen additional incentives encourage green development or pollution-reducing business decisions.

Research and development tax credits offers companies a 15 percent credit against their bank and corporation tax liability for qualifying in-house research expenses; a 24 percent tax credit for basic research payments to outside organizations is also available. Industrial development bonds finance investment in land, buildings, and new equipment related to domestic manufacturing operations in the state. California Capital Access Program and Collateral Support Program also offer alternative methods of financing for businesses. Enterprise Zones and Local Agency Military Base Recovery Area regions provide incentives for development in targeted geographic regions. A New Jobs Tax Credit offers $3,000 per hire of qualifying new employees, and the state's Film and Television Tax Credit Program supports productions with a 20 percent tax credit against qualified expenses.

In 2011 California began offering companies the option to calculate their corporate income tax through the single sales factor method, rather than the existing triple apportionment derived from calculations of a company's payroll, property, and sales.

California's Innovation Hub Program, with 12 locations throughout the state, supports the commercialization of innovation and technology businesses through public-private partnerships, knowledge sharing, venture capital sources, and business incubators. The state also undertakes trade missions to form partnerships for trade and export promotion.

Job training programs: The state of California offers an Employment Training Panel to assist companies with post-hire training and reimbursement. The Employment Development Department also partners with Local Workforce Investment Areas to recruit, screen, test, evaluate, and hire qualified workers.

The Monterey County Workforce Investment Board offers many links to specialized job training services designed for potential workers. The city of Monterey can also provide information about agencies that assist international businesses with training employees. Monterey County Virtual OneStop provides links to employment and training opportunities and services to job seekers including veterans, youths, and seniors. Monterey Peninsula College, a two-year school, provides job training. The Rancho Cielo Youth Campus in Salinas provides vocational training and education to youths who are at risk of committing crimes.

Development Projects

When a change in military needs led to the downsizing of Fort Ord in 1993, the 13,000 soldiers and family members who lived there were relocated. A Base Reuse Plan was developed to guide the planning and implementation process through 2014. The Fort Ord Reuse Authority received approval from the California state legislature in 2012 to extend its management of the area through 2020. Development plans in 2012 included a 150,000-square-foot medical facility on 14.3 acres within the Dunes on Monterey Bay Specific Plan area. The proposed medical center was to fill a long-standing gap in Veterans Administration care for Central Coast residents. The closure of Fort Ord had removed the area's only clinic serving military personnel. Other projects on the land area included the California Central Coast Veterans Cemetery, the South County Housing University Villages Apartments, and the Mid-Peninsula Housing Coalition Manzanita Place. Demolishing unused buildings and repairing environmental contamination were also parts of the program. As of 2013, some 22 percent of the original reuse plan had completed.

Due to the natural beauty of Monterey that attracts millions of tourists, city-sponsored development projects were typically small and focused on maintaining or improving infrastructure. As of 2013, the largest projects, not including street resurfacing, were $2.33 million for sewer line replacement and repairs on State Highway 68, $1.46 million for repairs to Wharf No. 2, and a $931,500 investment in marina dredging. Encouragement of mixed-used and transit-oriented development were central features of the city's plans guiding future downtown development. Long-term planning was studying the addition of light-rail service near the city's waterfront.

Economic Development Information: Central Coast Small Business Development Center at Cabrillo College, 6500 Soquel Drive, Aptos, CA 95003; telephone (831) 479-6136; fax (831) 479-6166; email sbdc@cabrillo.edu.

Commercial Shipping

Monterey is not a major commercial transportation hub; however, there are a number of motor freight carriers that serve the surrounding area.

Labor Force and Employment Outlook

Monterey employs both temporary and year-round workers, as the seasonal tourism and agriculture industries support a flexible labor force. One challenge to attracting new employees to Monterey has been its lack of affordable housing, with median home prices in Monterey estimated at $600,000 by the local chamber of commerce. The lack of low-cost housing is a particular challenge given the number of persons employed in the comparatively low-paying hospitality sector. Redevelopment of Fort Ord included multiple projects to add affordable housing to the area.

The following is a summary of data regarding the 2012 Monterey labor force:

Size of civilian labor force: 13,001

Number of workers employed in . . .

agriculture and mining: 185
construction: 653
manufacturing: 402
wholesale trade: 167
retail trade: 1,289
transportation: 284
information systems: 424
finance: 591
professional administration: 1,492
education and social services: 2,317
arts and leisure: 2,570
other: 736
public administration: 942

Average hourly earnings of production workers: $17.51

Unemployment rate: 3.7% (2012)

Employers

Largest employers (2012)	Number of employees
Community Hospital of the Monterey Peninsula	1,000–4,999
Naval Postgraduate School	1,000–4,999
CTB McGraw-Hill LLC	500–999
Monterey Peninsula College	500–999
City of Monterey	250–499
Dole Fresh Vegetables Co	250–499
Hyatt Regency–Monterey	250–499
Macy's	250–499
McGraw-Hill Co	250–499
Monterey Institute–International Study	250–499
Monterey Peninsula College	250–499
Monterey Plaza Hotel & Spa	250–499
Monterey-Salinas Transit	250–499
Portola Hotel & Spa	250–499
Robert Talbott Inc	250–499
Trancredi Enterprises	250–499

Cost of Living

The following is a summary of data regarding several key cost of living factors in the area.

State income tax rate: 1.00% to 13.3%

State sales tax rate: 7.5%

Local income tax rate: None

Local sales tax rate: None

Property tax rate: Limited to 1% of assessed value by state law. In some cases the local taxing body can add additional taxes.

Economic Information: Monterey Peninsula Chamber of Commerce, 30 Ragsdale Dr., Ste 200 Monterey, CA 93940; telephone (831) 648-5360; fax (831) 649-3502; email info@montereychamber.com.

■ Education and Research

Elementary and Secondary Schools

The Monterey Peninsula Unified School District encompasses Monterey City schools as well as those of Marina, Sand City, Seaside, and Del Rey Oaks. In addition to a well-rounded curriculum, the schools offer a gifted and talented program (GATE) for accelerated students and an independent study program for motivated students who wish to study on their own. The district has adopted the Common Core State Standards and supports an Advancement Via Individual Determination (AVID) program, used throughout the country and designed to increase graduate enrollment in four-year colleges.

Monterey is also home to several religious schools, including the York School associated with the Episcopal Faith, and Santa Catalina School (Catholic school for boys and girls grades Pre-K–8, and girls grades 9–12). Auburn's House Montessori School, located in nearby Seaside, serves children ages three to six.

The following is a summary of data regarding the Monterey Peninsula Unified School District.

Total enrollment: 11,167

Number of facilities

    total: 19
    elementary schools: 12
    junior high schools: 3
    high schools: 4
    other: 0

Student/teacher ratio: 22.56:1

Teacher salaries

    average (statewide): $69,434

Funding per pupil: $9,014

Public Schools Information: Monterey Peninsula Unified School District, 700 Pacific St., Monterey CA 93940; telephone (831) 645-1200.

Colleges and Universities

Monterey's major institution of higher learning is Monterey Peninsula College. It is one of 112 schools in the California Community College system. The college offers associate's degrees and certificate programs in a wide variety of fields, with major departments in business and technology, creative arts, humanities, life science, physical education, physical science, social science, and cooperative work experience.

The Monterey Institute of International Studies, an affiliate of Vermont-based Middlebury College, offers graduate programs in development policy and practice, international business, international education management, international environmental policy, nonproliferation

and terrorism studies, teaching English and other languages, and translation and interpretation. The school also offers tailored courses for individuals requiring intensive language and cultural training for work outside their native country or with foreign nationals in the United States.

The Naval Postgraduate School is an academic institution whose emphasis is on study and research programs relevant to the U.S. Navy's interests, as well as to the interests of other arms of the Department of Defense. Its campus houses state-of-the-art laboratories, academic buildings, a library, government housing, and recreational facilities. The school enrolls nearly 1,500 students annually. The student body consists of officers from the five U.S. uniformed services and a small number of civilian employees. The school offers master of arts degrees in a wide variety of fields, including national security affairs, defense-focused master's of business administration, aeronautical engineering, and physical oceanography, among many others. Another educational institution associated with the military is the Defense Language Institute operated by the Army. Its 2,000 instructors teach some 3,500 serviceman annually.

Brandman University, a part of Orange County-based Chapman University, is located in Monterey and offers baccalaureate degrees in a variety of subjects. The school system has 26 campuses throughout California and Washington, and also offers online programs. California State University–Monterey Bay on the grounds of Fort Ord offers 23 undergraduate and 8 graduate programs to approximately 5,600 students.

Libraries and Research Centers

Monterey Public Library is the largest public library on the Monterey Peninsula. The library operates one bookmobile. In 2012–13 it circulated more than 507,000 items, welcomed 335,000 patrons, and sponsored 224 cultural and informational programs. The California History Room contains a unique collection of books, selected magazine and newspaper articles, maps, government documents, photographs, and archival material about the city of Monterey and the Monterey Peninsula. Additional library programs and collections include the Local History Partners, which provides access to local history materials through a partnership with the Colton Hall Museum, the Monterey History and Art Association, and the Teen Zone and Youth Services collections.

Other local libraries include the Colton Hall Museum Library, Museum of Monterey, Monterey Bay Aquarium Research Institute Library, Community Hospital of the Monterey Peninsula Health Resource Library, and U.S. Navy library facilities. College libraries are housed at the Monterey Institute of International Studies and Monterey Bay Peninsula College.

The Monterey Institute of International Studies is home to the Center for the Blue Economy, Center for

Conflict Studies, Center for East Asian Studies, James Martin Center for Nonproliferation Studies, Mixed-Methods Evaluation, Training and Analysis (META) Lab, Monterey Cyber Security Initiative (MCySec), and Monterey Terrorism Research and Education Program (MonTREP). The Naval Postgraduate School is home to dozens of research institutes and centers that support the Navy and Department of Defense, including the Turbo-Propulsion Laboratory, Center on Terrorism and Irregular Warfare, Spacecraft Research and Design Center, and the Center for Autonomous Underwater Vehicle Research.

The Monterey Bay Aquarium Research Institute's research program focuses on deep-sea exploration in Monterey Bay, one of the most biologically diverse bodies of water in the world. The Institute's three research vessels and remotely-operated vehicles provide access to the Monterey Canyon, an underwater canyon two miles deep. The Marine Meteorology Division (NRL-MRY) is the Navy and Marine Corps' corporate research lab. The lab conducts research on the atmosphere, develops weather interpretation systems for the Department of Defense, and studies the effects of the atmosphere on Naval weapons systems.

Public Library Information: Monterey Public Library, 625 Pacific St., Monterey, CA 93940; telephone (831) 646-3932; fax (831) 646-5618. Naval Postgraduate School, Office of the Dean of Research, Halligan Hall, Monterey, CA 93943.

■ Health Care

Community Hospital of the Monterey Peninsula is a nonprofit system serving the Monterey Peninsula and surrounding communities with seven main locations that include outpatient facilities, satellite laboratories, mental-health clinics, and hospice facilities. The main 235-bed hospital houses a comprehensive cancer-care center, an emergency department, a family birth center, and a health resource library. The system also includes the Breast Care Center, the Carmel Hill Professional Center, the Diabetes and Nutrition Therapy center, the Hartnell Professional Center, and Ryan Ranch Outpatient Campus. The 172-bed Natividad Medical Center, an acute-care hospital in nearby Salinas, is owned and operated by Monterey County and is affiliated with the University of California at San Francisco School of Medicine.

■ Recreation

Sightseeing

Monterey's Cannery Row, popularized by the books of Nobel and Pulitzer award winner John Steinbeck, is one of America's most famous streets. Cannery Row features

more than 200 shops, restaurants, galleries, and attractions, including American Tin Cannery retail center and A Taste of Monterey Wine Tasting Room. The Blue Fin Cafe & Billiards overlooks Steinbeck Plaza and offers a panoramic view of Monterey Bay and Cannery Row. Steinbeck's Spirit of Monterey Wax Museum recreates the history of Cannery Row through life-sized characters and narration. Other amusements in Cannery Row include a shop which rents reproductions of old roadster convertibles, an old-fashioned portrait studio, and a ceramic painting studio.

Fisherman's Wharf and Wharf No. 2 stretch side-by-side into the Monterey Harbor. Fisherman's Wharf is lined with seafood restaurants, fish markets, art galleries, shops, candy stores, a theater, and fish and diving companies. Municipal Wharf No. 2 is a working fish pier where commercial fishing boats can be seen unloading their daily catch. On holidays, the fisherman often decorate their crafts with colorful strings of lights.

Cannery Row's Monterey Bay Aquarium features marine life ranging from playful sea otters to drifting jellyfish, octopuses, giant ocean sunfish, green sea turtles, swirling yellow-fin tuna, and hundreds of other creatures. The aquarium showcases one of the tallest ocean sanctuaries in the United States in a three-story living kelp forest, the million-gallon Outer Bay exhibit, a jellyfish gallery, expanded touch pools, and dozens of other galleries and exhibits.

Monterey State Historic Park downtown marks the spot where the U.S. flag was first officially raised on July 7, 1846, heralding California's statehood. Ten buildings, including the Custom House, California's first theater, and several former 1830s residences, now museums, preserve the area's heritage.

Tours are available of Colton Hall, a local landmark from the time when Monterey was the capital of Alta California. The hall was built to serve as a public school and town meeting hall and now is a museum. California's first constitution was drafted there more than 150 years ago.

Visitors to the area enjoy whale watching (best in winter) and fishing trips. Other popular tours departing from Monterey can be guided or self-guided. Wine tasting, sightseeing, and agricultural education tours are available, as well as movie tours of scenes from popular movies filmed in the area. Point Pios Lighthouse at the northernmost tip of the Monterey Peninsula is open for guided tours. The 17-mile drive along the coast through Pebble Beach affords spectacular views of rugged coastline and animals in their natural habitats.

Arts and Culture

The Monterey Museum of Art has a fine collection of early Christian, Asian, American folk, ethnic, and tribal art. It also offers photographic exhibits and rotating exhibits of major American artists. The museum is housed in two facilities, Pacific Street and La Mirada. Pacific Street, located across from Colton Hall in the historic center of Monterey, includes eight galleries. The Monterey Museum of Art at La Mirada is situated in one of Monterey's oldest neighborhoods and is surrounded by magnificent gardens and picturesque stone walls. It began as a two-room adobe structure and later became an elegant home where international and regional celebrities were entertained. Visitors today experience the same exquisitely furnished home and spectacular rose and rhododendron gardens. Visitors view the museum's permanent collection and changing exhibitions in four contemporary galleries, including the Dart Wing designed by renowned architect Charles Moore, that complement the original estate.

The Monterey Conference Center features impressive permanent and rotating collections. Sculptures, paintings, and tapestries from contemporary local artists adorn its walls and public spaces. Visitors are greeted by *Two Dolphins*, a nine-foot-tall sculpture composed of thousands of pieces of inlaid wood. The work, created by Big Sur artist Emile Norman, depicts two dolphins in flight as they dance across the sea. On the center's second floor, the Alvarado Gallery presents an ever-changing array of art from Peninsula artists.

The Golden State Theatre features live shows and concerts by musical guests and comedians and also serves as a film theater for old movies. It is the site for the Monterey International Film Week. The Bruce Ariss Wharf Theater at Fisherman's Wharf offers live shows as well.

Festivals and Holidays

Colorful events fill Monterey's calendar throughout the year. In January the annual migration of the gray whales is saluted through a variety of events such as art projects, storytelling, whale watching, and exhibits. The sounds of Dixieland and Swing fill the March air during the three days of Monterey's Jazz Bash by the Bay, held in various venues with dance floors and special events.

The spotlight is on young, up-and-coming musicians during the three-day Next Generation Jazz Festival held annually in April. The Subaru Sea Otter Classic, the largest bicycle festival in the country, features road cycling, mountain biking, downhill, and BMX events. Original hand-made arts and crafts are for sale at the Spring Arts & Crafts Fair.

On May 15, Cannery Row celebrates the life and times of Ed "Doc" Ricketts, a revolutionary marine biologist and mentor of John Steinbeck. The Monterey Beer Festival is a lively celebration of great beers in June. Three days of blues music on three stages is the focus of the three-day Monterey Bay Blues Festival at the Monterey Fairgrounds in June. The Monterey Wine Festival, also held in June, features California wines exclusively, and consists of tastings, educational seminars, and cooking demonstrations.

July's big events include the Community Fourth of July Parade, picnic and fireworks, the commemoration of John Drake Sloat's landing in Monterey on July 8, and the Obon Festival at the Buddhist Temple. August is enlivened by the Turkish Festival and Monterey County Fair. The Rolex Monterey Motorsports Reunion takes place at the Mazda Raceway Laguna Seca. Crowds enjoy August's Monterey Bay ReggaeFest and September's Greek Festival, Festa Italia-Santa Rosalia Festival, and Cherry's Jubilee Motorsports Festival. The world-famous Monterey Jazz Festival offers non-stop jazz by top performers as well as food, art, and jazz clinics for a weekend each September. A re-enactment of California's first Constitutional Convention takes place each October on California Constitution Day. A week-long focus on the history of Monterey is History Fest Monterey.

November's annual Great Wine Escape Weekend showcases the products of local vintners. Runners participate in the Big Sur Half Marathon, also in November, and the Cannery Row Christmas Tree Lighting welcomes the arrival of Santa Claus to the city. Christmas in the Adobes showcases Monterey's historic buildings illuminated and decorated for the holidays. December also brings the Monterey Cowboy Poetry and Music Festival. First Night Monterey draws crowds throughout the city to music, dance, and poetry events to welcome in the New Year.

Sports for the Spectator

World-class automobile racing events are held at the Mazda Raceway Laguna Seca, east of downtown Monterey. The raceway hosts five major events each year: TUDOR United SportsCar Championship, Ferrari Racing Days, FIM Superbike World Championship, Rolex Monterey Motorsports Reunion, and SCCA National Championship Runoffs.

Sports for the Participant

The City of Monterey Sports Center is the largest family fitness facility on the Monterey Peninsula, offering a full range of fitness activities, as well as two pools and a water slide. The city has 14 neighborhood parks. The El Estero Park complex, a 45-acre city-wide multi-use recreation area in the center of the city, offers paddleboats, swimming, picnicking, and an exercise course. Located in the park complex are a number of recreational facilities including the Dennis The Menace Playground, designed by the popular cartoon character's creator Hal Ketcham. It features a steam engine, sway bridge, a sandy hills slide, a rollers-slide, sun bridge, garden maze, and a handicap play area. The Monterey Youth Center is a multi-use recreation facility for youth and adult activities. The Youth Center includes a professional dance studio with a wooden floor, wall mirrors, ballet bars, and a public address system. Located next to Lake El Estero is the Monterey Skate Park designed for skateboarders and inline skaters. The Monterey Tennis Center has six courts. The city has five ball fields.

Monterey Bay Waterfront Park offers 4.1 acres of turf and landscaped areas adjacent to the beach that feature five sand volleyball courts and picnic and grill facilities.

Private sea kayak outfitters help visitors discover Monterey by sea, by paddling through the kelp forest along Cannery Row and observing sea otters and the abundant marine life. Diving, skydiving, and sailing are all available to sports enthusiasts on Monterey Bay.

Shopping and Dining

Del Monte Center, Monterey's traditional regional shopping center, anchored by Macy's, has approximately 675,000 square feet of space occupied by businesses offering a wide variety of goods and services. The retail center includes a 13-screen Century Theatres. Monterey has a busy downtown shopping area. The Old Monterey Market Place is one of the largest in the United States, attracting thousands of tourists and residents downtown every Tuesday afternoon. New Monterey, an emerging commercial area with an eclectic mix of businesses, includes Lighthouse Avenue, and is located three blocks up the hill from Cannery Row. The former sardine canning factories of Cannery Row have become the center of more than 50 factory outlets. North Fremont, adjacent to the Monterey Fairgrounds, is a high-traffic area and serves the many tourists who attend activities at the Monterey Fairgrounds.

The Salinas Valley has been called the "Salad Bowl of the Nation" for the wide variety of vegetables and fruits produced there. These, plus Monterey's extensive marine life and the Native American, Spanish, Mediterranean Rim, and Asian heritages of its citizens from various eras, have influenced the local cuisine. Restaurant choices run the gamut from regional American to Asian, British, California, Continental, French, Indian, Island Grill, Italian, Mexican, and Swiss cuisines. Monterey restaurant chefs are inspired by the abundance of robustly flavored signature area crops such as lettuce, artichokes, garlic, strawberries, and a variety of mushrooms. Visitors may want to explore the local wineries, including A Taste of Monterey, Silver Mountain Vineyards, and Ventana Vineyards.

Visitor Information: Monterey County Convention & Visitors Bureau, P.O. Box 1770, Monterey, CA 93942; telephone (888) 221-1010; email info@seemonterey.com.

■ Convention Facilities

Convention activity in Monterey is heaviest from early April through Thanksgiving. The Monterey Conference Center, with 61,000 square feet of meeting and banquet space, a 19,600-square-foot exhibit hall, and a 500-seat amphitheater, hosts more than 220 events annually. The Monterey County Fairgrounds has eight buildings for exhibits or meeting spaces and two outdoor arenas seating 5,850 and 2,000 people.

The Monterey Meeting Connection, located in the heart of the city's historic district and adjoining Fisherman's Wharf, is an alliance of the Monterey Conference Center and its adjoining hotels—the Portola Hotel and Spa and Monterey Marriott—offering a total 700 guest rooms and suites. Other hotels that offer a variety of spaces for meetings are the Hyatt Regency Monterey, Hilton Garden Inn Monterey, Monterey Plaza Hotel and Spa, Casa Munras Hotel, and the Beach Resort Monterey. A variety of other facilities also feature spaces for large functions including Adventures by the Sea and the Monterey Bay Aquarium.

Convention Information: Monterey Conference Center, One Portola Plaza, Monterey, CA 93940; telephone (831) 646-3770; fax (831) 646-3777. Monterey County Convention & Visitors Bureau, P.O. Box 1770, Monterey, CA 93942; telephone (888) 221-1010; email info@seemonterey.com.

■ Transportation

Approaching the City

Direct access to Monterey is provided from San Jose and San Francisco via Highway 156 off State Route 101. Access from Los Angeles is achieved via State Route 101 and Highway 68. Monterey Peninsula Airport, 3.5 miles from downtown Monterey, provides passenger service on five airlines with non-stop flights from Monterey to Los Angeles, San Diego, San Francisco, Phoenix, Denver, and Las Vegas, and connections to domestic and foreign locations. Airlines serving Monterey include Alaska Airlines, American Eagle, Allegiant Air, United, and US Airways. Major car rental companies operate from the airport. Monterey Salinas Transit buses also service the airport.

The Monterey Airbus provides 11 trips daily to the San Jose and San Francisco international airports from downtown Monterey. Pick up service is available from hotels and private homes. Greyhound offers regular bus service in Salinas with connections to Monterey. Amtrak's Coast Starlight train also stops at Salinas, with free bus service into downtown Monterey.

Traveling in the City

Taxi companies operate in Monterey County. Monterey-Salinas Transit (MST) has a fleet of 111 buses on 60 routes and covers the Monterey Peninsula and Salinas Valley. MST provides rural transit service to Carmel Valley and seasonal service to Big Sur. MST served 4.33 million passengers in 2012. The Waterfront Area Visitors Express (WAVE) Shuttle Service provides free trolley transportation to the Monterey Bay Aquarium and other waterfront areas during summer months.

■ Communications

Newspapers and Magazines

Monterey's local daily newspaper is *The Monterey County Herald,* which also publishes a Salinas edition. *Monterey County Weekly* is an alternative press publication covering news, art, and entertainment.

Television and Radio

Monterey is home to seven local television stations. Commercial television stations are picked up from nearby cities, and cable and satellite service is available. There are two AM and three FM radio stations broadcasting from Monterey.

Media Information: The Monterey County Herald, 8 Upper Ragsdale Drive, Monterey, CA 93940; telephone (831) 372-3311.

Monterey Online

City of Monterey home page. Available www. monterey.org

Community Hospital of the Monterey Peninsula. Available www.chomp.org

Monterey Conference Center. Available www. montereyconferencecenter.com

Monterey County Convention & Visitors Bureau. Available www.seemonterey.com

The Monterey County Herald. Available www. montereyherald.com

Monterey County Historical Society. Available mchsmuseum.com

Monterey Jazz Festival. Available www. montereyjazzfestival.org

Monterey Peninsula Chamber of Commerce. Available www.mpcc.com

Monterey Peninsula Unified School District. Available www.mpusd.k12.ca.us

Monterey Public Library. Available www.monterey. org/library

BIBLIOGRAPHY

Benson, Jackson J., *True Adventures of John Steinbeck, Writer: A Biography* (New York: Penguin Books, 1990)

Fisher, Anne B., *No More a Stranger* (Stanford, CA: Stanford University Press, 1946)

Ford, Tirey Lafayette, *Dawn and the Dons: The Romance of Monterey, with Vignettes and Sketches by Jo Mora* (San Francisco, CA: A.M. Robertson, 1926)

Hobbs, Fredric, *The Spirit of the Monterey Coast* (Palo Alto, CA: Tioga Pub., 1995)

Jeffers, Robinson, *Selected Poems* (New York: Vintage, 1965)

McKibben, Carol Lynn, *Beyond Cannery Row: Sicilian Women, Immigration, and Community in Monterey, California, 1915–99* (Urbana: University of Illinois Press, 2006)

Shields, Scott A., *Artists at Continent's End: The Monterey Peninsula Art Colony, 1875–1907* (Berkeley: University of California Press, 2006)

Shillinglaw, Susan, *A Journey into Steinbeck's California* (Berkeley, CA: Roaring Forties Press, 2011)

Steinbeck, John, *Cannery Row* (New York: Viking, 1945)

Steinbeck, John, *Tortilla Flat* (New York: Grosset and Dunlap, 1935)

Oakland

■ The City in Brief

Founded: 1820 (incorporated, 1854)

Head Official: Mayor Jean Quan (elected 2010; current term expires 2014)

City Population
  1990: 372,242
  2000: 399,484
  2010: 390,724
  2012 estimate: 400,740
  Percent change, 2000–2010: −2.2%
  U.S. rank in 1990: 39th
  U.S. rank in 2000: 50th (State rank: 8th)
  U.S. rank in 2010: 47th (State rank: 8th)

Metropolitan Statistical Area Population
  2000: 4,123,740
  2010: 4,335,391
  2012 estimate: 4,455,560
  Percent change, 2000–2010: 5.1%
  U.S. rank in 2000: 12th
  U.S. rank in 2010: 11th

Area: 56 square miles

Elevation: 42 feet above sea level

Average Annual Temperatures: 56.7° F

Average Annual Precipitation: 23 inches

Major Economic Sectors: Government, health care, trade, services

Unemployment Rate: 7.6% (2012)

Per Capita Income: $31,130

2012 FBI Crime Index Property: 26,342

Major Colleges and Universities: Holy Names College, Mills College, Patten College, Merritt College, California College of Arts & Crafts

Daily Newspaper: *Oakland Tribune*

■ Introduction

The city of Oakland is the seat of Alameda County. An important seaport, Oakland has been a major business and manufacturing center for San Francisco and its East Bay section. Oakland was among the first ports globally to specialize in the intermodal container operations whose advantages have revolutionized international trade. With its strategic Pacific Rim location, a majority of Oakland's foreign trade is with Asia, and the city itself is one of the most ethnically and culturally diverse populations in the state. In the new millennium, the city has sought to build its reputation for green business. These efforts saw the arrival of many solar-centric companies at the front of major energy projects, some of which failed to survive the still-volatile alternative energy climate. Still, Oakland has continued to struggle to reduce crime and unemployment, and stabilize control over its school district. The pending fate of development projects connected to the Port of Oakland and the city's sports franchises—as well as the health of its green industries—were to serve as a primary indicator of the city's future.

■ Geography and Climate

Oakland lies near the center of the Pacific Coast between Canada and Mexico. It is located on the east side of the San Francisco Bay and is connected to the city of San Francisco by the San Francisco-Oakland Bay Bridge. Oakland boasts 19 miles of coastline to the west and magnificent rolling hills to the east. The flat plain of San

Lynn Watson/Shutterstock.com

Francisco Bay comprises about two-thirds of the city and the remainder of the city's terrain lies in the foothills and hills of the East Bay range. Residents and area visitors can take advantage of one of the most beautiful views in the world-the San Francisco Bay, the Golden Gate and Oakland Bay Bridges, and the sparkling Pacific Ocean. Cities adjacent to Oakland include Berkeley to the north; San Leandro to the south; Alameda across the estuary; Piedmont, a small city completely surrounded by Oakland; and Emeryville, a city that lies on the bay between Oakland and Berkeley. Oakland is the seat of Alameda County. Oakland is the only city in the United States with a natural saltwater lake wholly contained within its borders-the 115-acre Lake Merritt.

Oakland has earned the nickname "bright side of the Bay" because of its sunny skies and moderate year-round climate. Humidity remains high while precipitation is low. Almost all the city's rainfall occurs between October and January. The temperature usually reads about five degrees warmer than San Francisco, and the warmest months are September and October. The entire San Francisco Bay area lies between the Pacific and North American Tectonic Plates. The city of Oakland itself rests on the Hayward

Fault, which is one of seven fault lines (also including the San Andreas Fault) affecting the area. This zone of continual seismic activity marks the city as highly susceptible to damaging earthquakes and landslides.

Area: 56 square miles

Elevation: 42 feet above sea level

Average Temperatures: 56.7° F

Average Annual Precipitation: 23 inches

■ History

Spaniards Settle Area, Followed by Hunters, Loggers

The first inhabitants of present-day Oakland were the Ohlone (also known as Costanoans), peaceful tribes known for their basket making and the success of their hunting and gathering way of life.

In 1772 the first Europeans arrived through an expedition from Spain led by Lieutenant Pedro Fages and

Father Crespi, who camped along Lake Merritt. The area that is now Oakland came more directly under European control in 1820, when Don Luis Maria Peralta received the land as a grant from the Spanish crown in recognition of his soldiering career. Don Luis never lived on his ranch, but divided the land among four of his sons who settled and operated ranches in the area. At that time the territory was governed by the Republic of Mexico, which had become independent of Spain in 1821.

In the 1840s hunters and loggers came to the area, followed by adventurers traveling to the gold fields. Some stayed and built squatter shacks on the Peralta land, creating several small settlements which later became part of Oakland.

In 1848, the Treaty of Guadalupe-Hidalgo officially ceded California to the U.S. and, two years later, California became the 31st state in the Union. Regulation of land deeds became the responsibility of the new state government. The Peraltas presented their claim to the Federal Land Commission in 1852.

Railroad Spurs Growth

In 1850 Edson Adams, Horace Carpentier, and Andrew Moon had settled on land near the present foot of Broadway. They planned a town, sold lots, and secretly rushed "An Act to Incorporate the Town of Oakland" to the State Legislature. The city, which was named for the groves of lovely oaks that grew along the hills, was granted a charter on May 4, 1852, about the same time that ferry service to San Francisco was initiated. It became an incorporated city with an elected mayor and council two years later. During this period the Peralta land case continued through the American legal system. By the time the land claim was finally confirmed in 1877, the Peraltas had sold most of their property to pay legal fees and taxes.

The completion of the Southern Pacific railroad line in 1869 transformed Oakland, which had been chosen as the terminus of the transcontinental railroad, into an important part of the Metropolitan Bay Area, second only to San Francisco. For the next several decades the railroad controlled the city's political and economic life. The railroad also stimulated economic development and the creation of an electric street car system which spurred rapid population and territorial growth.

Originally, the area of the city was quite small, but annexations in 1872, 1891, 1897, and finally in 1910 brought the city to its present size. Along with the 1906 earthquake in San Francisco, which resulted in a sizable number of new residents in-migrating, Oakland experienced a rapid rise in population that reached over 150,000 people by 1910 and continued its growth through World War II. By the 1920s Oakland had become the core city of the East Bay, the Alameda County seat, and a rival to San Francisco for leadership in the Bay Area as a whole.

Oakland experienced great losses from the 1989 Loma Prieta earthquake, which caused the upper deck of the Nimitz freeway in West Oakland to collapse, killing 41 people. The earthquake also caused part of the San Francisco Bay Bridge to fall down on the Oakland side and a number of buildings in the business district and residential areas suffered severe damage. In 1991 Oakland was struck by a firestorm, which burned more than 3,000 homes to the ground, killed 25 people, and accrued $1.5 billion in damage. The fire remains one of the most damaging firestorms in the history of the state.

By the end of the 1980s, Oakland was the sixth largest city in the state with a highly diverse and integrated population of more than 350,000 residents. Population growth continued into the 1990s, when Oakland began to experience an increasing vitality. In 1998 former California governor and presidential candidate Jerry Brown was overwhelmingly elected mayor of Oakland. Brown brought sweeping change to the city, ranging from fixing potholes to increasing the size of the police force to forcing the resignations of entrenched managers and department heads, and encouraging business development in the city. In March 2004, Oakland voters approved a measure that affirmed the "strong mayor" system by altering the city charter to give the mayor chief executive power rather than the city manager, as had been the case.

As the city entered the new millennium, it was still faced mounting challenges of a high crime rate, a troubled school system, and a lack of affordable housing. In 2003 the state of California took over control of the financially strapped Oakland Unified School District and appointed a state administrator to oversee the district's operations. The state returned control to the city in 2009, but a 2013 audit of the district's 2010–11 finances, according to the state, suggested that the local school board had not resolved all issues.

Ron Dellums, mayor from 2007 to 2010, worked to make Oakland a "model city" in health, education, economy, environmental issues, and social and cultural strength and diversity. The city partnered with schools and the county hospital to offer new health prevention and education projects for both children and adults. His Green Initiative continued programs already in place that encouraged green business and sustainability in the city. In 2007 Oakland was ranked first in the nation for renewable energy by SustainLane Government and received a City Solar Award from the NorCal Solar Energy Association.

Jean Quan replaced Dellums as mayor in 2010, inheriting some of the city's lingering issues such as high crime, unemployment, and a struggling school system. Quan was both the first woman and Asian mayor of Oakland. Her mayoral legacy was believed to be tied to progress on the potential City Coliseum development, which would provide new stadiums for the city's sports franchises and add thousands of office, retail, and residential spaces to a blighted area of the city. Approval of plans was set to occur in 2014.

Historical Information: Oakland History Room, Oakland Public Library, 125 14th Street, Oakland, CA 94612; telephone (510) 238-3222.

■ Population Profile

Metropolitan Statistical Area Population

2000: 4,123,740
2010: 4,335,391
2012 estimate: 4,455,560
Percent change, 2000–2010: 5.1%
U.S. rank in 2000: 12th
U.S. rank in 2010: 11th

City Residents

1990: 372,242
2000: 399,484
2010: 390,724
2012 estimate: 400,740
Percent change, 2000–2010: −2.2%
U.S. rank in 1990: 39th
U.S. rank in 2000: 50th (State rank: 8th)
U.S. rank in 2010: 47th (State rank: 8th)

Density: 7,004.0 people per square mile

Racial and ethnic characteristics

White: 164,376
Black or African American: 102,456
American Indian and Alaskan Native: 2,536
Asian: 64,663
Native Hawaiian and Other Pacific Islander: 2,570
Hispanic or Latino (may be of any race): 107,279
Other: 64,139

Percent of residents born in state: 49.6%

Age characteristics

Population under 5 years old: 27,630
Population 5 to 9 years old: 23,766
Population 10 to 14 years old: 21,669
Population 15 to 19 years old: 22,100
Population 20 to 24 years old: 27,661
Population 25 to 34 years old: 69,414
Population 35 to 44 years old: 61,341
Population 45 to 54 years old: 53,564
Population 55 to 59 years old: 25,317
Population 60 to 64 years old: 23,086
Population 65 to 74 years old: 26,145
Population 75 to 84 years old: 12,521
Population 85 years and over: 6,526
Median age: 36.3

Births (2010–11 Metropolitan Area)

Total number: 51,720

Deaths (2010–11 Metropolitan Area)

Total number: 27,781

Money income (2012)

Per capita income: $31,130
Median household income: $50,326
Total households: 154,737

Number of households with income of …

less than $10,000: 12,725
$10,000 to $14,999: 12,452
$15,000 to $24,999: 19,112
$25,000 to $34,999: 14,240
$35,000 to $49,999: 18,402
$50,000 to $74,999: 24,240
$75,000 to $99,999: 16,097
$100,000 to $149,999: 18,021
$150,000 to $199,999: 8,841
$200,000 or more: 10,607

Percent of families below poverty level: 21.9%

FBI Crime Index Property: 26,342

FBI Crime Index Violent: 7,963

■ Municipal Government

In 2004 voters approved Measure P, which altered the city charter to create a strong-mayor form of government in place of the previous city-manager form. The city manager position was redefined as a city administrator, appointed by and reporting to the mayor. The mayor and eight council members are elected to four-year terms. Seven council members are elected as district representatives and one member serves at large.

Head Official: Mayor Jean Quan (elected 2010; current term expires 2014)

Total Number of City Employees: 5,082 (2013)

City Information: City of Oakland, One Frank H. Ogawa Plaza, Oakland, CA 94612; telephone (510) 444-2489.

■ Economy

Major Industries and Commercial Activity

Oakland's business community faced some major problems in the 1980s and 1990s. The Loma Prieta Earthquake in 1989 not only caused physical damage but caused many companies to consider relocation.

Although Alameda County had economic growth in the 1980s, Oakland did not participate in that growth, and the economy actually declined. Major plant closures in the late 1980s and 1990s included Gerber Products, General Electric, National Lead, American Can, and Oakland's largest manufacturing facility, Transamerican Delaval, which had employed 1,600 workers. The ripple effect of these closures led to the closing of many small businesses that had been suppliers to these firms. The city received a designated Urban Enterprise Zone to help alleviate the employment situation, particularly for inner-city residents. By the late 1990s Oakland's economy was showing some vitality.

As of 2013, nine of Oakland's 10 largest employers were in government or health-care sectors. The city's coastal location has made its port one of the most important drivers of economic activity. Key industries targeted by the city included the creative economy, food and beverage manufacturing, green and clean technology, health and wellness, international trade and logistics, industrial, office, and retail.

The Port of Oakland is one of the busiest ports in the world for container ships. Chief exports at the port include fruits and vegetables, waste paper, red meat and poultry, resins, chemicals, animal feed, raw cotton, wood and lumber, crude fertilizers/minerals, industrial machinery, and cereal. Oakland's principal imports include auto parts, computer equipment, apparel, toys, games and items made of plastic, processed fruits and vegetables, fasteners and household metal products, red meat, pottery, glassware and ceramics, iron and steel, beverages, and lumber products.

Rated among the 10 greenest cities in the United States, Oakland has done much to expand its work with sustainable energy in an effort to grow the economy and create jobs while improving environmental conditions. It has attracted many solar and green energy companies to the area including Sungevity and BrightSource Energy. However, renewable energy firms were volatile if lucrative additions to the local economy; Solar Millennium, which had relocated to Oakland in 2010, declared bankruptcy in 2012.

Items and goods produced: processed foods, transportation equipment, fabricated metal products, non-electrical machinery, electrical equipment, clay, and glass products

Incentive Programs—New and Existing Companies

Local programs: Oakland has been designated as an Enterprise Zone, a designation that allows businesses that hire from the zone to be eligible for tax incentives. Companies within the zone can also qualify for net operating loss carryover incentives, business expense deductions and other benefits, including the Work

Opportunity Tax Credit and Welfare to Work Credits. The Enterprise Zone was extended in 2009 to include companies in West Berkeley.

Incentives offered by the city include Oakland's Tenant Improvement Program and Façade Improvement Program, both of which offer architectural assistance and grants to supported aesthetic improvements to commercial properties on certain streets. The Tenant Improvement Program supports interior improvements, while the Façade Improvement Program works to increase building exteriors. Oakland also supports a Brownfields Revolving Loan Fund to encourage development in areas that have suffered environmental damage. Funding for the program comes from the federal Environmental Protection Agency. A similar city program is the Urban Land Redevelopment Program. The Oakland Business Development Corporation manages all loans to area businesses under $249,500 for companies that might not otherwise qualify for traditional bank financing.

Local tax incentives include the Jobs and Tax Base Stimulus Incentive, which offers up to two years of business and sales tax incentives to companies bringing at least 20 jobs to the area and thereby growing the city's tax base. Target industries for these medium and large employers were retail, health care and life sciences, international trade and logistics, green technology, creative arts and digital media, and specialty foods manufacturing.

State programs: California business incentives include the state's Alternative Energy and Advanced Transportation Authority Sales and Use Tax Exemptions for Zero Emission Vehicle Manufacturing. Initially targeting vehicle manufacturing only when it was passed in 2010, the sales and use tax exemption has since been expanded to all renewable energy technologies. In 2012 it was expanded again to include advanced manufacturing. More than one dozen additional incentives encourage green development or pollution-reducing business decisions.

Research and development tax credits offers companies a 15 percent credit against their bank and corporation tax liability for qualifying in-house research expenses; a 24 percent tax credit for basic research payments to outside organizations is also available. Industrial development bonds finance investment in land, buildings, and new equipment related to domestic manufacturing operations in the state. California Capital Access Program and Collateral Support Program also offer alternative methods of financing for businesses. Enterprise Zones and Local Agency Military Base Recovery Area regions provide incentives for development in targeted geographic regions. A New Jobs Tax Credit offers $3,000 per hire of qualifying new employees, and the state's Film and Television Tax Credit Program supports productions with a 20 percent tax credit against qualified expenses.

In 2011 California began offering companies the option to calculate their corporate income tax through the single sales factor method, rather than the existing triple apportionment derived from calculations of a company's payroll, property, and sales.

California's Innovation Hub Program, with 12 locations throughout the state, supports the commercialization of innovation and technology businesses through public-private partnerships, knowledge sharing, venture capital sources, and business incubators. The state also undertakes trade missions to form partnerships for trade and export promotion.

Job training programs: The state of California offers an Employment Training Panel to assist companies with post-hire training and reimbursement. The Employment Development Department also partners with Local Workforce Investment Areas to recruit, screen, test, evaluate, and hire qualified workers.

The city of Oakland serves as the liaison between new and existing companies and all of the educational and training organizations in the East Bay, including Eastbay Works One-Stop Career Center, Alameda County Workforce Investment Board, and the Oakland Private Industry Council. The Youth Employment Partnership coordinates the Mayor's Summer Jobs Program, which places teens and young adults in seasonal jobs based on their interests.

Development Projects

The "Oak to Ninth" project is a redevelopment of 65 acres of waterfront property owned by the Port of Oakland, first considered in the late 2000s. After several years of legal hurdles to ensure the project met environmental standards, a 2013 announcement unveiled an agreement with Signature Development Group of Oakland and Zarsion Holdings Group Co. Ltd of Beijing to develop the property, which was rebranded as the Brooklyn Basin. Plans for the $1.5 billion development call for the construction of 3,100 residences, 200,000 square feet of commercial and retail space, and a marina with 200 boat slips. Also included are 30 acres of waterfront parks and open space. Some aspects of project were not expected to complete until the mid-2020s.

In 2010 the city of Oakland signed a deal to redevelop the former Oakland Army Base, which closed in 1999. The base, which has since been owned by the city and the Port of Oakland, was to be developed into a logistics and warehousing center called Oakland Global Trade & Logistics Center. Construction on the $500 million project began in late 2013, with an expected completion date of 2018. Most funding was coming from state grants and private developers, with supplemental funding from two federal grants, the city, and the Port of Oakland.

The Oakland Airport Connector project broke ground in 2010. The $484 million project included building a 3.2-mile electric train-to-plane connector that would transport passengers to-and-from the airport

quickly and efficiently, thus eliminating the need to drive cars to the airport. The connector was expected to begin operations in 2014.

Still in the planning stages was Oakland's Coliseum City, a major development initiative tied to the city's sports franchises. In addition to new stadiums, potentially for all three sports teams, the 850-acre development would include 14 million square feet of office and light industrial space for biotechnology, science, and technology firms, as well as retail space and 6,000 housing units. New stadiums for the area's sports teams were considered critical to ensuring their continued presence in Oakland. A final plan was expected to be completed in 2014, at which point the city would decide whether to go forward with the project.

Economic Development Information: City of Oakland Economic Development, 250 Frank H. Ogawa Plaza, Ste 3315, Oakland, CA 94612; telephone (510) 238-3941. Oakland Metropolitan Chamber of Commerce, 475 Fourteenth Street, Suite 100, Oakland, CA 94612; telephone (510) 874-4800; fax (510) 839-8817.

Commercial Shipping

The Port of Oakland is one of the largest container ports in the United States and the world. The Port of Oakland occupies 19 miles on the mainland shore of San Francisco Bay, one of the finest natural harbors in the world. There are five container terminals, with 90 percent of berths dredged to a depth of 50 feet. The port's facilities are backed by a network of local roads and interstate freeways, warehouses, and intermodal rail yards. Rail service is provided through Burlington Northern Santa Fe and Union Pacific. All major motor freight carriers serve the port and many maintain terminals in the harbor area. The port is part of the Oakland Foreign Trade Zone No. 56. Cargo service is also provided at Oakland International Airport through major carriers, with an average of nearly 500,000 metric tons of cargo handled annually during 2009–12. On-site U.S. Customs personnel are available at the airport on a scheduled basis.

Cargo service is also available at San Francisco International Airport. The Port of San Francisco has five berths, on-dock rail, and more than 550,000 square feet of covered storage for weather-sensitive cargo. Many shipping service companies serve the port. The port is part of Foreign Trade Zone No. 3.

Labor Force and Employment Outlook

The Oakland labor force is described as skilled, educated, and available to employers who need managerial/executive, professional, sales, technical, and clerical staff. Following a nationwide recession in the late 2000s, the unemployment rate in Oakland failed to dip below 13 percent during 2009–13, though it had declined from its high of 17 percent in 2010. Employment growth rates through 2015 were projected to be highest in the area of manufacturing. An estimated 50,000 new jobs were expected to be added by 2040.

The following is a summary of data regarding the 2012 Oakland labor force:

Size of civilian labor force: 210,237

Number of workers employed in . . .

agriculture and mining: 652
construction: 10,029
manufacturing: 12,558
wholesale trade: 4,260
retail trade: 17,750
transportation: 8,844
information systems: 5,951
finance: 10,599
professional administration: 27,664
education and social services: 46,624
arts and leisure: 19,511
other: 11,955
public administration: 7,089

Average hourly earnings of production workers: $19.41

Unemployment rate: 7.6% (2012)

Employers

Largest employers (2013)	*Number of employees*
Kaiser Permanente Medical Group	10,914
Oakland Unified School District	7,664
State of California	7,480
County of Alameda	6,218
City of Oakland	5,082
Alta-Bates Summit Medical Center	3,623
Children's Hospital & Research Center	2,600
Internal Revenue Service	2,500
Southwest Airlines	2,100
Peralta Community College District	1,420

Cost of Living

The cost of living in the San Francisco-Oakland-Fremont is significantly above the national average, with the median cost of a home in 2013 averaging $648,714. Housing costs in Oakland tend to be lower than the median.

The following is a summary of data regarding several key cost of living factors in the area.

2013 ACCRA Average House Price: $648,714

2013 ACCRA Cost of Living Index: 134

State income tax rate: 1.00% to 13.3%

State sales tax rate: 7.5%

Local income tax rate: None

Local sales tax rate: 1.5%

Property tax rate: Limited to 1% of assessed value by state law. In some cases the local taxing body can add additional taxes.

Economic Information: Oakland Metropolitan Chamber of Commerce, 475 Fourteenth Street, Suite 100, Oakland, CA 94612; telephone (510) 874-4800; fax (510) 839-8817.

■ Education and Research

Elementary and Secondary Schools

The Oakland Unified School District (OUSD) is one of the largest school districts in the state. The district has a rich ethnic diversity with nearly 39 percent Hispanic and 31 percent African American students, and the rest a mixture of white, Asian, and other students. In 2010 the district created the Office of African American Male Achievement to accelerate development of African American boys in the school system, which followed on the heels of an Urban Strategies report that showed disproportionate suspension rates for black males. Gifted and Talented Education (GATE)/High Potential programs are available for students of all ages, as are special education programs. The district supports adult education programs. There were 32 charter schools as of 2013–14.

In 2003 the district's financial crisis led to a takeover by the State of California and the appointment of a state administrator. In 2009 the local school board regained control over all aspects of community relations, but the state continued to maintain primary control over decisions relating to financial management, facilities, student achievement, and personnel. An audit of the 2010–11 district finances, completed in 2013, rekindled state concerns as to whether sufficient improvements had been made to district operations. The school board disputed the findings.

Oakland has more than 50 private schools, including both independent and faith-based schools. Of particular note is the Mills College Children's School, a laboratory school that is operated through the Mills College School of Education.

The following is a summary of data regarding the Oakland Unified School District.

Total enrollment: 46,586

Number of facilities

   total: 100
   elementary schools: 56
   junior high schools: 19
   high schools: 15
   other: 10

Student/teacher ratio: 21.2:1

Teacher salaries

   average (statewide): $69,434

Funding per pupil: $9,141

Public Schools Information: Oakland Unified School District, 1000 Broadway, Oakland, CA 94607; telephone (510) 434-7790.

Colleges and Universities

Mills College is a private liberal arts school with an enrollment of more than 1,500 students that serves female undergraduates, but admits men to its graduate school. The college grants bachelor's and master's degrees and offers courses leading to California teaching credentials. Mills College was ranked fifth among regional universities of the West in 2013–14 by *U.S. News & World Report*.

Two of the four Peralta Community College District campuses are located in Oakland; they are Merritt College, a publicly supported coeducational junior college with an enrollment under 7,000 students and Laney College, which offers associate's degrees in arts and science, pre-apprenticeship programs, and job retraining to its more than 14,000 students. The school offers liberal arts, technical-vocational, and general education programs in both day and evening schools. Holy Names University is a Catholic, liberal arts college that enrolls more than 1,300 students. The college provides both bachelor's and master's programs, including a Master of Science in Nursing and a Master of Music.

More than 700 students are enrolled at Patten University, a private co-educational school affiliated with the Christian Evangelical Churches of America, Inc. Patten awards associate's and bachelor's degrees in about 15 majors. The school also offers a master's degree in education. Certificate and training programs are offered through the Division of Continuing and Extended Education.

California College of the Arts is a four-year independent college of art and design. Its Oakland campus houses undergraduate art students and hosts the Center for Art and Public Life. The San Francisco campus of the California College of the Arts houses the schools graduate program and hosts the CAA Watts Institute for Contemporary Arts. The Oakland campus of

Samuel Merritt University offers degrees at the undergraduate and graduate level in five disciplines: nursing, occupational therapy, physician assistant, physical therapy and podiatric medicine.

The San Francisco State University College of Extended Learning in Oakland offers a number of certificate and professional development programs, as well as degree credit courses through its Open University.

Libraries and Research Centers

The Oakland Public Library consists of a main library and 16 branches. The library has more than 1.2 million books and other materials system wide. The main library houses a special Business Collection and Oakland History Room, and is also a government documents repository. The system has a few unique collections. The Asian Library contains over 74,000 print and audio materials, with both reference and general subject titles, in eight Asian languages: Chinese, Japanese, Korean, Vietnamese, Thai, Cambodian, Tagalog and Laotian. The branch also features an in-depth English-language Asian Studies collection.

Also unique to the system is the Temescal Tool Lending Library, which offers over 2,700 tools available for loan, as well as books and how-to videos for home repairs. The Temescal branch offers workshops on tool safety and home repair topics.

The African American Museum and Library at Oakland is a non-circulating reference library system. The collection contains 12,000 volumes by or about African Americans, including materials about the military, Martin Luther King, Jr., Malcolm X, the Black Panther Party, Africa, genealogy, and California history. The museum houses exhibits on African American art, history, and culture.

Oakland has two research centers associated with the University of California: the California Agricultural Experiment Station and the Tobacco-Related Disease Research Program. Another major research center in the city is the Children's Hospital Oakland Research Institute (CHORI). It is one of the top-10 federally funded pediatric research facilities in the nation. CHORI contains eight specialized centers: the Center for Cancer Research; Center for Critical Care Medicine; Center for Genetics; Center for Immunobiology and Vaccine Development; Jordan Family Center for Blood and Marrow Transplantation and Cellular Therapies Research; Center for Nutrition and Metabolism; the Center for Prevention of Obesity, Cardiovascular Disease and Diabetes; and the Center for Sickle Cell Disease and Thalassemia. The Earthquake Engineering Research Institute, a non-profit technical professional society, is based in Oakland as well.

Public Library Information: Oakland Public Library, 125 Fourteenth Street, Oakland, CA 94612; telephone (510) 238-3134.

◾ Health Care

Oakland's largest private, not-for-profit medical center is the Alta Bates Summit Medical Center with three campuses and two acute-care hospitals in the Oakland region. The Medical Center was formed from the merger of Summit Medical Center, Alta Bates Medical Center, and Sutter Health in 2000. Its Summit campus specializes in cardiovascular care, orthopedics, women and infants, wellness and prevention, and seniors. The Alta Bates campus, based in Berkeley, is recognized for its care of women and infants, In Vitro Fertilization Program, and its high-risk obstetrics program. Alta Bates includes the Herrick Campus, once known as Herrick Hospital and Health Center. In 2010 ground was broken on an addition to Altat Bates Summit Medical Center, which included a 250,000-square-foot Patient Care Pavilion and structure for parking. A 30-bed emergency department was also to be built as part of the project. The $385 million project was expected to complete in 2014. The 190-bed Children's Hospital and Research Center Oakland has the most active pediatric trauma center in the region, and one of largest sickle cell treatment and research programs in the world.

The 236-bed Highland Hospital is part of the Alameda County Medical Center (ACMC) system. Highland is home to a Level II Emergency/Trauma Center and the Bright Beginnings Family Birthing Center. The hospital also serves as a teaching and training facility with accredited programs in emergency medicine, internal medicine, general surgery, and oral and maxillo-facial surgery. The ACMC Eastmont Wellness Center is home to more than 40 primary and medical specialty services, including an immigration clinic and refugee health screening clinic.

A new Kaiser Permanente Oakland Medical Center with 349-beds, considered to be Kaiser's flagship hospital for Northern California, was slated to open in 2014. Specialty offices that were part of the facility opened in 2013. Kaiser Permanente Oakland Medical Center offers a full range of acute care services. Urgent care and primary care services are located on the campus as well. The hospital supports a drop-in HIV testing clinic and a domestic violence support services program. The Friday Fresh Farmers' Market, located outside the Oakland hospital entrance each Friday, sells produce to the community to encourage healthy eating habits.

◾ Recreation

Sightseeing

Historic buildings in Oakland include the Camron-Stanford House, a beautifully restored Victorian house on Lake Merritt. The Pardee Home Museum is an historical treasure in the heart of the Preservation Park Historical District. Dunsmuir-Hellman Historic Estate features 50 acres of hills and gardens that are the site of public events. The Greek Orthodox Cathedral of the Ascension is a modern Byzantine architectural gem, with icons painted on the dome; the cathedral is nestled in the Oakland Hills. The Oakland Temple and Visitors' Center, of the Church of Jesus Christ of Latter-day Saints, is another notable architectural site. The visitors' center offers exhibits on the Mormon faith. The Morcom Rose Garden (formerly Morcom Amphitheater of Roses) provides a stunning horticultural display of rose bushes surrounded by Mediterranean architecture. The landmark Paramount Theatre is a restored 1930s movie palace that still hosts a variety of arts events.

Popular entertainment and amusement sites include Children's Fairyland, a three-dimensional theme park with more than 60 sets recreating nursery rhymes, fairy tales, and legends; and the Oakland Aviation Museum (formerly Western Aerospace Museum), displaying aeronautical artifacts and housing an aircraft library and gift shop. The Oakland Zoo in Knowland Park is home to more than 660 native and exotic animals and an African Savannah exhibit. The Wayne and Gladys Valley Children's Zoo is a four-acre site within the larger zoo that includes a Malaysian Fruit Bat exhibit, Wilds Discovery Area, and a playground area. Curious persons of all ages are welcome at the Chabot Space and Science Center, which features a planetarium, observatory, and exhibits.

Another popular spot is the Jack London Square, which was once the stomping grounds of the city's most colorful literary figures. It houses many quaint shops, restaurants, and a Farmer's Market along its scenic Boardwalk. The Presidential Yacht U.S.S. *Potomac*, Franklin Delano Roosevelt's "floating white house," hosts dockside tours and history cruises from its port at Jack London Square.

Arts and Culture

The Oakland East Bay Symphony presents symphonic music during its November through May subscription concert series, which is presented at the Paramount Theatre. The Malonga Casquelourd Arts Center (the former Alice Arts Center) is home to Axis Dance Company, Citicentre Dance Theater, Dimensions Dance Theater, Oakland Youth Orchestra, and Bay Area Blues Society. Woodminster Summer Musicals are performed July through September in the open-air Woodminster Amphitheater in the scenic Joaquin Miller Park in the Oakland hills.

Several museums are part of the Jack London Square complex, including the African American Museum and Library, Lightship Relief floating lighthouse, Museum of Children's Art, and the Oakland Museum of California. The Oakland Museum of California is lauded for its displays of California art, history and natural science. The Museum of African American Technology Science Village, opened in 2004, sponsors exhibits on the technical achievements of African Americans.

Festivals and Holidays

The African Cultural Festival features dance in its many African forms performed by various artists. Oakland celebrates its birthday on May 4th with its annual Celebration in the Plaza, featuring live music with guest performers, famous Oakland celebrities, living history exhibits, walking tours, food booths, and art exhibits. Oakland's rich Spanish heritage is saluted at the annual Cinco de Mayo celebration which includes a parade and many festival activities. The Annual Scottish Highland Games take place in June. August's Chinatown Streetfest with its arts, food and crafts of the cultures of China, Vietnam, Japan, Korea, the Philippines, and others, celebrates the city's Asian community.

Art & Soul Oakland, with more than 150 artisans displaying their music and crafts at multiple stages around the city, takes place in August. An annual fall occurrence is the Black Cowboy Parade downtown, always held the first Saturday in October. The holiday season is greeted by a Holiday Tree Lighting Celebration at Jack London Square.

Sports for the Spectator

The National Football League's Oakland Raiders play at the O.co Coliseum (formerly Oakland-Alameda County Coliseum,) also home to the Oakland Athletics of Major League Baseball's American League. The National Basketball Association's Golden State Warriors play at the ORACLE Arena. Both the arena and coliseum are part of the Oakland-Alameda County Coliseum Complex. Major development proposals to create Coliseum City, a massive redevelopment in the area to potentially include new stadiums for all three major franchises, were to be reviewed in 2014.

Nearby Sonoma Raceway offers a wide variety of motorsports events year-round. The excitement of thoroughbred racing is offered at Golden Gate Fields in Berkeley, only minutes from Oakland.

Sports for the Participant

Joaquin Miller Park offers trails across 500 acres that feature spectacular views of the entire Bay Area. Joggers enjoy the 3.18-mile jogging path that encircles the shoreline of Lake Merritt. Surrounded on three sides by Lake Merritt, 122-acre Lakeside Park offers picnic areas, putting greens, lawn bowling, boat rentals, and Japanese and herb gardens. The Redwood Regional Park and Roberts Regional Recreation Area covers more than 2,000 acres in the city of Oakland and Contra Costa County. They include an amphitheater fire circle, horse and hiking trails, picnic and play areas, volleyball court, exercise course, and heated outdoor swimming pool. The Temescal Regional Recreation Area's 48 acres, which include a 13-acre lake, provide swimming, fishing, picnicking, and a children's play area. Ice skating is available seven days a week at the Oakland Ice Center. Oakland's three municipal golf courses, Metropolitan Golf Links, Lake Chabot Golf Course, and Montclair Golf Course, accommodate avid and beginning golfers alike. Oakland also maintains 52 athletic fields, outdoor tennis courts, and public outdoor pools located throughout the city.

Shopping and Dining

Boutiques and specialty shops offering men's and women's apparel, household goods, toys and ethnic gift items are featured at Jack London Village. Other shopping areas include the City Center downtown, Rockridge, Piedmont Avenue, Lakeshore, and Grand Avenues. City Center is a popular pedestrian plaza with a mix of shops and restaurants. The Oakland Artisan Marketplace is open Fridays in Oakland's Frank Ogawa Plaza, and Saturdays and Sundays in Jack London Square. One of the oldest and most culturally diverse markets in the city is the Old Oakland Farmer's Market, open year-round on Fridays downtown, where shoppers find Asian produce, fresh flowers, potted plants, herbs, bakery items, fresh fish and seafood, and wild game and poultry. Visitors might want to enjoy the Asian restaurants, specialty shops, and bakeries of Chinatown, located along Broadway, Alice, 13th, and 7th Streets.

From upscale to modest, Oakland has offerings for traditionalists as well as adventurous gourmets. The Jack London Square is home to a variety of restaurants in a wonderful waterfront setting. Unusual fare and cuisine from around the world is offered at many eateries on the Square. Restaurants include specialties such as Mexican, Indonesian, Cajun, Northern Italian, Greek, Japanese, sushi, seafood, and classic American cuisine. Some favorite stops for both locals and visitor's include Yoshi's Jazz Club and Japanese Restaurant, and Ratto's Market and Deli.

Local wineries are well worth a stop for visiting wine connoisseurs. JC Cellars, founded by winemaker Jeff Cohn, offers winemaking demonstrations and a selection of Rhone varietals. Dashe Cellars feature wines made from grapes from Dry Creek, Alexander Valley, and Mendocino counties.

Visitor Information: Oakland Convention and Visitors Bureau, 481 Water Street, Oakland, CA; telephone (510) 839-9000.

■ Convention Facilities

The Oakland Convention Center/Oakland Marriott City Center complex is one of the first structures in California to house both a convention center and hotel. An atrium lobby joins the two-story convention center with the 483-room hotel. The largest convention center facilities can accommodate more than 6,000 people and more than 3,000 for banquets. There is a 48,000-square-foot exhibition hall that can be divided into smaller halls, 12 additional meeting rooms, and a parking garage. The

Marriott offers an additional 25,000 square feet of flexible function space. The rooftop ballroom can accommodate 200 guests for banquets.

The Henry J. Kaiser Convention Center was a multifunction facility consisting of the Kaiser Arena, Calvin Simmons Theatre and two banquet/ballrooms. Financial issues caused the center to close in 2006 and revert to city control; efforts to sell the complex to a private redeveloper were ongoing as of 2014.

Other large facilities include the ORACLE Arena and Oakland-Alameda County Coliseum Complex; the state-of-the-art County of Alameda Conference Center; and the California Ballroom. Several local museums and theaters offer meeting and event space for smaller groups.

Visitor Information: Oakland Convention and Visitors Bureau, 481 Water Street, Oakland, CA; telephone (510) 839-9000.

■ Transportation

Approaching the City

Oakland International Airport, located only 12 minutes from downtown, has 11 domestic and international airlines serving 10 million passengers each year as of 2012. Bay Area Rapid Transit (BART) offers a dedicated connection to and from the airport and high-speed rail service between East Bay cities and San Francisco with eight stations in Oakland. Shuttles also serve the airport. The Alameda-Contra Costa Transit District (AC Transit) provides bus service to and from the airport via the 73 and 805 lines. Amtrak schedules frequent arrivals through its terminal at Jack London Square. Greyhound bus service is also available.

Interstate 980 is the main north–south artery to the city. Interstates 880 and 580 connect to Interstate 980, as does State Route 24.

Some travelers may wish to fly in through the San Francisco International Airport. Oakland can be reached from San Francisco by traveling east across the Bay Bridge via Interstate 80 and continuing south to Oakland on Interstate 580 or 980.

Traveling in the City

The Alameda-Contra Costa Transit District (AC Transit) is the third-largest public bus system in the state, serving 13 cities in Alameda and Contra Costa counties. There are dozens of routes through the city, with some routes connecting to the Bay Area Transit System (BART), which provides wide-ranging subway service on four East Bay lines into San Francisco. The Broadway Shuttle service began in 2010 to transport locals to various destinations within Jack London Square, Chinatown, Old Oakland, City Center, Uptown, and the Lake Merritt Financial District. The Alameda/Oakland Ferry cruises into Jack London Square from San Francisco's Ferry terminal and Pier 41. Several taxi companies service the city. The city had about 100 miles of bicycle lanes and routes as of 2013.

■ Communications

Newspapers and Magazines

The *Oakland Tribune* is the city's daily newspaper. The *Berkeley Voice*, *The Montclarion*, and *Piedmonter* are popular weeklies published by the Bay Area News Group. The Post News Group maintains an online news site focusing on the African American Community; it controls the former print publication with a similar mission, the *Oakland Post*.

Among the magazines and journals published in Oakland are *Oakland Magazine* and *The Black Scholar*.

Television and Radio

Oakland has one commercial network television station (KTVU-Fox) and 3 AM radio stations offering talk radio and children's programming. Several television and radio stations are picked up from the surrounding area and cable programming is available.

Media Information: *Oakland Tribune,* 7677 Oakport Street, Ste 950, Oakland, CA 94621; telephone (510) 208-6300.

Oakland Online

City of Oakland Home Page. Available www2. oaklandnet.com

Oakland Convention & Visitors Bureau. Available www.oaklandcvb.com

Oakland Metropolitan Chamber of Commerce. Available www.oaklandchamber.com

Oakland Public Library. Available www. oaklandlibrary.org

Oakland Tribune. Available www.insidebayarea. com/oakland-tribune

BIBLIOGRAPHY

Bartlett, Serena, *GrassRoutes Oakland and Berkeley: Urban Eco Travel* (Seattle: Sasquatch Books, 2009)

Bradford, Amory, *Oakland's Not for Burning* (New York: McKay, 1968)

Murch, Donna Jean, *Living for the City: Migration, Education, and the Rise of the Black Panther Party in Oakland, California* (Chapel Hill, NC: University of North Carolina Press, 2010)

Rhomberg, Chris, *No There There: Race, Class, and Political Community in Oakland* (Berkeley, CA: University of Press, 2004)

Self, Robert O., *American Babylon: Race and the Struggle for Post-War Oakland* (Princeton, NJ: Princeton University Press, 2003)

Riverside

■ The City in Brief

Founded: 1870 (incorporated, 1883)

Head Official: Mayor Rusty Bailey (since 2013; current term expires 2017)

City Population
    1990: 226,546
    2000: 255,166
    2010: 303,871
    2012 estimate: 313,700
    Percent change, 2000–2010: 19.1%
    U.S. rank in 1990: 68th
    U.S. rank in 2000: 78th
    U.S. rank in 2010: 61st (State rank: 12th)

Metropolitan Statistical Area Population
    2000: 3,254,821
    2010: 4,224,851
    2012 estimate: 4,350,096
    Percent change, 2000–2010: 29.8%
    U.S. rank in 2000: 13th
    U.S. rank in 2010: 13th

Area: 85.6 square miles

Elevation: 847 feet above sea level

Average Annual Temperatures: 66.0° F

Average Annual Precipitation: 10.2 inches

Major Economic Sectors: government, health care, education, light and medium manufacturing, retail trade

Unemployment Rate: 8.6% (2012)

Per Capita Income: $21,417

2012 FBI Crime Index Property: 10,818

Major Colleges and Universities: University of California, Riverside; California Baptist University, La Sierra University, Riverside Community College

Daily Newspaper: *The Press-Enterprise*

■ Introduction

Riverside is located within one hour of the city of Los Angeles, and began as the center for the navel orange–growing industry in the United States. The city has since developed a diverse economy that includes a growing number of high-tech and research and development firms. The city's government hopes that the influx of these companies, paired with new developments and cultural renovations, will help reinvent the city as an artistic and innovative center. A more than $1 billion Riverside Renaissance program updated and expanded many city facilities during the late 2000s and early 2010s. Riverside is home to an array of recreational opportunities such as beaches, ski slopes, and desert resorts that are within an hour's drive. Cultural activities range from community theater to symphonic concerts to ballet. The Mission Revival style hotel built in the city's early days has become the world-famous Mission Inn favored by presidents, royalty, and movie stars. Through coordinated city planning, Riverside has combined the best of the past with the promise of unlimited future possibilities.

■ Geography and Climate

Riverside is located in Southern California at the center of the metropolitan area that encompasses Riverside County and San Bernardino County. This area is typically known as the Inland Empire. Riverside is 10 miles southwest of San Bernardino and 53 miles east of Los Angeles. The city is located on the Santa Ana River, near the San Bernardino Mountains.

The climate is characterized as mild and semi-arid. Summer highs frequently reach more than 90 degrees, but

David Liu/iStockPhoto.com

evening temperatures can drop as much as 30 to 49 degrees accompanied by cool breezes. Low humidity generally keeps even hot summer days from being oppressive. The Santana Winds (or Santa Ana Winds) that typically occur from late summer to spring bring warm and dry air down from the high deserts to the San Bernardino Mountains and through the counties of Los Angeles, Orange, San Bernardino, and Riverside. These often strong winds are sometimes accompanied by brush and wildfires. The San Andreas Fault line lies just to the northeast of Riverside. This area in Southern California is highly susceptible to earthquakes, some of which can be very severe.

Area: 85.6 square miles

Elevation: 847 feet above sea level

Average Temperatures: 66.0° F

Average Annual Precipitation: 10.2 inches

■ History

The Rancho Era

The first European visitors to the area of present-day Riverside were Captain Juan Bautista de Anza and his 34 seasoned soldiers, who arrived in the area from Arizona in 1774 in search of a land route to California. At that time the Valley of Paradise was inhabited by Native Americans who lived in the niches of rocky hills and foraged for food. The natives lived in the area relatively undisturbed until 1821, when the lands of California became the property of Mexico.

Shortly thereafter Juan Bandini, a prominent political figure in California, was given a piece of land called El Rancho Jurupa, which he later presented to his son-in-law, Abel Stearns. The Stearns sold the land to Louis Rubidoux, who ruled the land along with other ranchers. After Rubidoux's death part of the land was purchased by John North. He decided to build a community of ethical people devoted to establishing good schools, churches, and libraries. The new town was called Riverside and its original square, called "Mile Square," remains the heart of the city. Within a few years of its founding, railroad tracks were built connecting the city to far-off places.

In 1873 James Roe, a druggist and teacher, moved to the city and by the late 1870s had launched the *Riverside Press* weekly newspaper that later became the current daily publication, *The Press-Enterprise*.

Oranges and Irrigation

Around 1875 a mutant Brazilian orange tree that produced fruit with no seeds was brought to the city. In the rich soil by the Santa Ana River the fruit flourished under the abundant sunshine. By 1887 the navel orange had become the dominant crop in Riverside and other California cities.

About the same time, with the financial aid of people from England, Matthew Gage, an immigrant from Canada, began work on a canal to bring water to all of Riverside, parts of which had no water available. With the irrigation made possible by Gage's canal, Riverside's greatest growth period began. Three new subdivisions—White's Addition, Hall's Addition, and Arlington Heights—were developed.

Economic strides were made in the 1880s when a number of local fruit growers joined together to pick and sell fruit under one brand name and to grade their oranges for quality. The plan expanded and by 1893 a group of all California growers was formed under the name of the Southern California Fruit Exchange, now known as Sunkist. The development of refrigerated railroad cars and innovative irrigation systems established Riverside as the state's wealthiest city per capita by 1895.

World Wars Establish Military Presence

During World War I, March Field, now the March Air Reserve Base, was established for the training of aviators. In 1920, Ernest Louis Yeager began the E. L. Yeager Construction Company, Inc., which, with the assistance of his three sons, completed more than a half century of master construction projects. In the latter half of this century the Food Machinery Corporation was formed to produce machinery for packing citrus fruits efficiently and rapidly. During World War II March Field was expanded and another base, Camp Haan, was begun across from March Field. The site is now occupied by the new National Veteran's Cemetery. A third base was built, called Camp Anza, which later became a subdivision called Arlanza.

In 1997 a joint use agreement with the U.S. Air Force allowed for over 300-acres of March Field to be used as a civilian airport, which is now known as the March Inland Port.

A Promising Future

In the late 1990s and into the early 2000s, Riverside began to focus attention on diversifying its economy and creating a sustainable community. One major development was an agreement between the city, county, and the University of California, Riverside for the creation of University Research Park (URP), a 39-acre site designed to house high-tech research facilities as well as office spaces for technology-based companies. The first lot opened in 2000. As of 2014, 19 companies were tenants at the park. *Forbes* magazine named Riverside the number-two Hot Spot for Tech Growth in the United States in 2013.

An innovative Riverside Renaissance Initiative was set in place in the 2000s to redevelop and expand the general infrastructure of the city as well as allow for capital improvements. Through the initiative, more than $1 billion was invested in parks, libraries, museums, public safety facilities, office and retail developments, utilities upgrades, and general transportation improvements. More than 90 percent of projects had completed by 2011. In a move toward sustainable community, the city began to promote the use of alternative fuel vehicles for public and private use and opened a compressed natural gas fast-fill fueling station for the public.

Historical Information: Riverside Metropolitan Museum, 3580 Mission Inn Ave., Riverside, CA 92501; telephone (951) 826-5273.

■ Population Profile

Metropolitan Statistical Area Population

2000: 3,254,821
2010: 4,224,851
2012 estimate: 4,350,096
Percent change, 2000–2010: 29.8%
U.S. rank in 2000: 13th
U.S. rank in 2010: 13th

City Residents

1990: 226,546
2000: 255,166
2010: 303,871
2012 estimate: 313,700
Percent change, 2000–2010: 19.1%
U.S. rank in 1990: 68th
U.S. rank in 2000: 78th
U.S. rank in 2010: 61st (State rank: 12th)

Density: 3,745.0 people per square mile

Racial and ethnic characteristics

White: 201,768
Black or African American: 18,038
American Indian and Alaskan Native: 2,976
Asian: 20,773
Native Hawaiian and Other Pacific Islander: 648
Hispanic or Latino (may be of any race): 163,543
Other: 69,497

Percent of residents born in state: 61.5%

Age characteristics

Population under 5 years old: 22,172
Population 5 to 9 years old: 22,055
Population 10 to 14 years old: 23,473
Population 15 to 19 years old: 27,390
Population 20 to 24 years old: 34,768
Population 25 to 34 years old: 47,030
Population 35 to 44 years old: 36,777
Population 45 to 54 years old: 40,211

Population 55 to 59 years old: 16,677
Population 60 to 64 years old: 12,851
Population 65 to 74 years old: 16,570
Population 75 to 84 years old: 8,654
Population 85 years and over: 5,072
Median age: 30.7

Births (2010–11 Metropolitan Area)

Total number: 61,923

Deaths (2010–11 Metropolitan Area)

Total number: 26,097

Money income (2012)

Per capita income: $21,417
Median household income: $53,893
Total households: 89,588

Number of households with income of ...

less than $10,000: 5,414
$10,000 to $14,999: 4,941
$15,000 to $24,999: 9,943
$25,000 to $34,999: 9,178
$35,000 to $49,999: 12,137
$50,000 to $74,999: 17,364
$75,000 to $99,999: 10,962
$100,000 to $149,999: 11,555
$150,000 to $199,999: 4,562
$200,000 or more: 3,532

Percent of families below poverty level: 19.5%

FBI Crime Index Property: 10,818

FBI Crime Index Violent: 1,389

■ Municipal Government

Riverside has a council-manager form of government. The seven-member council is comprised of persons elected for four-year terms from geographically designated wards. A mayor is elected from the city at large for a four-year term and acts as the presiding officer of the council.

Head Official: Mayor Rusty Bailey (since 2013; current term expires 2017)

Total Number of City Employees: 2,687 (2013)

City Information: City of Riverside, 3900 Main St., Riverside, CA 92522; telephone (951) 826-5311.

■ Economy

Major Industries and Commercial Activity

Although Riverside's beginnings are steeped in agriculture, today the economy has become more diversified while still relying heavily on government, education, health care, professional and business services, and retailing.

Among the largest city employers are the University of California, Riverside and the Riverside Unified School District. The city is also home to many state and county government offices as well as county, state, and federal courts. In addition, the city has become an important center for financial and professional services. There are numerous legal and accounting firms, software firms, architectural and engineering offices, and banking institutions that call the city home.

In recent years Riverside has placed a major emphasis on expanding its technology areas by developing high-tech industrial business parks. The city, county, and University of California, Riverside have partnered together to create University Research Park within the 856-acre Riverside Regional Technology Park. The complex offers a high-speed fiber optic telecommunications system that supports voice, video, and data information. As of 2014, 19 companies were tenants at the park. Electronic component manufacturer Bourns Inc., Centrum Analytical Labs, and Luminex Software, Inc. have all chosen Riverside for new headquarters operations. Goodrich (aerospace) has a branch in Riverside. *Forbes* magazine named Riverside the number-two Hot Spot for Tech Growth in the United States in 2013.

Riverside has taken strides in developing its industrial and manufacturing sectors. Riverside has attracted more than 125 industrial employers since 2000. Riverside's diverse manufacturing base now includes such sectors as injection molding, food safety preparation, medical device manufacturing, and aerospace products.

Major health-care providers in Riverside include Kaiser Permanente, Riverside Community Hospital, and Loma Linda Medical Center. Riverside's retail industry continues to grow as population continues to rise.

Items and goods produced: injection molds, medical devices, electronics, aerospace products

Incentive Programs—New and Existing Companies

Local programs: The City of Riverside Office of Economic Development offers many programs and services to help businesses grow and succeed in the Southern California marketplace. Support programs and services include site selection assistance, business liaison services, pre-development meetings, fast-track permitting and review, expedited plan check and inspection, and technology ombudsman service. Riverside Public Utilities provides discounted rates for qualifying economic development projects; a sewer treatment rate is also available for businesses with large water and sewer consumption. The city offers micro loans of between $5,000 and $10,000 to small businesses, with up to a three-year term of repayment.

The Inland Empire Small Business Development Center and Inland Empire Economic Partnership, both located in the research park, offer additional assistance to small, emerging and technology-based businesses. The TriTech Regional Small Business Development Center Network promotes high-tech and high-growth business sectors, including bioscience, computer hardware and software, and communications.

State programs: California business incentives include the state's Alternative Energy and Advanced Transportation Authority Sales and Use Tax Exemptions for Zero Emission Vehicle Manufacturing. Initially targeting vehicle manufacturing only when it was passed in 2010, the sales and use tax exemption has since been expanded to all renewable energy technologies. In 2012 it was expanded again to include advanced manufacturing. More than one dozen additional incentives encourage green development or pollution-reducing business decisions.

Research and development tax credits offers companies a 15 percent credit against their bank and corporation tax liability for qualifying in-house research expenses; a 24 percent tax credit for basic research payments to outside organizations is also available. Industrial development bonds finance investment in land, buildings, and new equipment related to domestic manufacturing operations in the state. California Capital Access Program and Collateral Support Program also offer alternative methods of financing for businesses. Enterprise Zones and Local Agency Military Base Recovery Area regions provide incentives for development in targeted geographic regions. A New Jobs Tax Credit offers $3,000 per hire of qualifying new employees, and the state's Film and Television Tax Credit Program supports productions with a 20 percent tax credit against qualified expenses.

In 2011 California began offering companies the option to calculate their corporate income tax through the single sales factor method, rather than the existing triple apportionment derived from calculations of a company's payroll, property, and sales.

California's Innovation Hub Program, with 12 locations throughout the state, supports the commercialization of innovation and technology businesses through public-private partnerships, knowledge sharing, venture capital sources, and business incubators. The state also undertakes trade missions to form partnerships for trade and export promotion.

Job training programs: The state of California offers an Employment Training Panel to assist companies with post-hire training and reimbursement. The Employment Development Department also partners with Local Workforce Investment Areas to recruit, screen, test, evaluate, and hire qualified workers.

The city offers a Municipal Internship Program that provides college and university students the opportunity to work with city staff and learn about local government as part of their school training. The federal Workforce Investment Act (WIA) provides a cooperative effort between employers and the Riverside County Workforce Investment Board. An employer can receive assistance with employer-specific training and financial incentives, such as reimbursements, tax credits, and direct payments for the training of new employees. Employers can also receive reimbursement for a portion of the employee's wages during an on-the-job training period.

Development Projects

Riverside has seen its industrial sector grow with the addition of the 56-acre University Research Park, a collaborative project with the University of California, Riverside. The research park is housed within Hunter Park and is the core of the 856-acre Riverside Regional Technology Park.

The Riverside Renaissance Initiative was the city's plan, approved in 2006, for $785 million worth of projects from 2007 to 2012. Projects ranged from electric power plant and substation construction to railroad underpasses to parks, libraries, and cultural facilities. Renovating the historic Fox Theater was a centerpiece of cultural improvements and finished in 2010. Initial cost estimates fell short of actual costs, with the total price tag of the Riverside Renaissance settling at $1.57 billion by 2011, when 90 percent of projects were complete. A $45 million expansion of the Riverside Convention Center was expected to complete in 2014.

Construction of the new Fox Entertainment Plaza next door to the Fox Theater began in 2010. The $14.4 million project provided a 400-spot parking facility, museum exhibit space, restaurant, and retail space. A 4,000-seat Black Box Theater was also added, with performances beginning in 2013.

Capital improvement plans for the city allotted $832 million for the period 2011–16. Some $373.5 million were devoted to sewer improvements, while another $198 million were dedicated to the electrical system and $106.9 million to transportation projects. The remainder served needs for storm drains, local and regional parks, airport, refuse, and public parking projects.

Economic Development Information: City of Riverside Office of Economic Development, 3900 Main St., 7th Floor, Riverside, CA 92522; toll-free (877) 748-7433; email econdev@riversideca.gov.

Commercial Shipping

Riverside is adjacent to one of the major rail-freight centers in the state. Burlington Northern Santa Fe and Union Pacific railroads both link to the Ports of Los Angeles and Long Beach. The Port of Los Angeles is the busiest container port in the United States. It is designated as a Foreign Trade Zone. The LA/Ontario International Airport shipped 454,880 tons of cargo in

2012. John Wayne Airport, about 44 miles away in Santa Ana, also has air-cargo service. About 70 miles away, Los Angeles International Airport has 1,000 cargo flights each day. The March Inland Port/March Airfield, just outside of the city limits, is a joint use facility serving both military and commercial interests. It has been designated as a Foreign Trade Zone. The Riverside Municipal Airport, an excellent general aviation facility, accommodates private aircraft, charter services, and air-related businesses. More than sixty-five trucking companies are based in or have facilities in Riverside and provide a broad range of interstate, regional, and local freight services.

Labor Force and Employment Outlook

The Inland Empire used to be the bedroom community for the larger metropolitan area. A relatively high percentage of the labor force commuted to jobs outside the two counties. But from 1980 to 2000 about 1.3 million people migrated to the area because it offered large tracts of affordable residential land, more than in coastal areas. The California Employment Development Department notes that Inland Empire's affordable housing and advantageous location have helped it create more new jobs than any other area. The influx of skilled professionals has helped the Inland Empire's economy become more focused on high-tech, professional, and corporate jobs.

Projections to 2020 for jobs with the greatest growth potential in the metropolitan area were led by automotive and watercraft service attendants, mental health counselors, health-care social workers, database administrators, interpreters and translators, veterinarians, and industrial machinery mechanics, all of which were expected to see more than 33 percent growth between 2010 and 2020.

The following is a summary of data regarding the 2012 Riverside labor force:

Size of civilian labor force: 147,486

Number of workers employed in . . .

    agriculture and mining: 816
    construction: 9,059
    manufacturing: 13,194
    wholesale trade: 4,383
    retail trade: 18,314
    transportation: 7,464
    information systems: 1,599
    finance: 5,749
    professional administration: 11,802
    education and social services: 29,348
    arts and leisure: 10,504
    other: 7,087
    public administration: 6,183

Average hourly earnings of production workers: $15.36

Unemployment rate: 8.6% (2012)

Employers

Largest employers (2013)	*Number of employees*
County of Riverside	11,187
Riverside Unified School District	5,580
University of California	5,497
Kaiser	4,500
City of Riverside	2,687
Riverside Community College District	2,087
Riverside Community Hospital	1,880
Riverside County Office of Education	1,765
Alvord Unified School District	1,445
Parkview Community Hospital	1,350

Cost of Living

Residential housing costs within Riverside are among the lowest in Southern California, a fact that has caused numerous companies and individuals to relocate to the area in recent years.

The following is a summary of data regarding several key cost of living factors in the area.

2013 ACCRA Average House Price: $409,633

2013 ACCRA Cost of Living Index: 113

State income tax rate: 1.00% to 13.3%

State sales tax rate: 7.5%

Local income tax rate: None

Local sales tax rate: 0.5%

Property tax rate: Limited to 1% of assessed value by state law. In some cases the local taxing body can add additional taxes.

Economic Information: Greater Riverside Chambers of Commerce, 3985 University Ave., Riverside, CA 92501; telephone (951) 683-7100; fax (951) 683-2670.

■ Education and Research

Elementary and Secondary Schools

There are two school districts serving the city. Riverside Unified School District (RUSD serves an area that includes most of Riverside as well as the Highgrove and Woodcrest areas just outside of the city. The district enrolls more than 42,000 in its K–12 programs, and nearly 7,000 students in adult education. Some 93 percent of 2010 graduates were enrolled in college, with 83 percent of those enrolled full-time. The RUSD GATE Program offers special cluster classes or day classes for elementary students beginning in second grade. Advanced programs are offered for middle school and high school GATE students, including Advanced Placement classes, an International Baccalaureate, and college credit classes.

The Alvord Unified School District accommodates the southwestern part of the city and adjacent unincorporated areas. Alvord also offers a GATE program for students in elementary school through high school. Both districts offer magnet schools for science and the performing arts, regional occupational programs, a wide variety of special education programs (generally serving students through age 21), and adult education classes.

There are several independent and religiously affiliated private schools in and around the city. The California School for the Deaf, Riverside is part of the state Department of Education. The school has an enrollment of about 500 students from Southern California with day and residential programs. Students range in age from about 18 months to 22 years. Educational programs are also available for parents and community members.

The following is a summary of data regarding the Riverside Unified School District.

Total enrollment: 42,532

Number of facilities

    total: 48
    elementary schools: 29
    junior high schools: 7
    high schools: 7
    other: 5

Student/teacher ratio: 26.47:1

Teacher salaries

    average (statewide): $69,434

Funding per pupil: $7,869

Public Schools Information: Riverside Unified School District, 3380 14th Street, Riverside, CA 92501; telephone (951) 788-7135. Alvord Unified School District, 10365 Keller Ave., Riverside, CA 92505; telephone (951) 509-5000.

Colleges and Universities

The University of California, Riverside (UCR) is a major research university and national center for the humanities. UCR enrolls more than 21,000 students. The School of Education offers master's and doctoral programs in addition to teaching credentials in several other programs; UCR also offers a College of Engineering. The UCR California Center for the Native Nations, established in 2003, encourages research and educational programs for Native populations. The UCR/UCLA Thomas Haider Program in Biomedical Sciences offers a unique pathway into medical school for students; UCR received preliminary accreditation from the Liaison Committee on Medical Education in 2013 to open a comprehensive four-year medical school.

La Sierra University (LSA), with about 2,000 students, is a Seventh-Day Adventist institution that offers course work in undergraduate and graduate programs. LSA has four schools: the College of Arts and Sciences, the School of Business, the School of Education, and the School of Religion. It also has a Division of Continuing Studies.

California Baptist University, affiliated with the Southern Baptist Convention, is a liberal arts institution with more than 6,000 students that offers 150 undergraduate majors and concentrations and 35 graduate majors and credentials in such areas as behavioral sciences, business administration, liberal arts, and Christian studies. The school was ranked 42nd among Best Regional Universities in the West for 2013–14 by *U.S. News & World Report*.

California Southern Law School, which operates part-time evening classes, offers programs in the practice and theory of law as students prepare for the state bar exam. Riverside City College, part of the Riverside Community College District, is a two-year school serving more than 19,000 students each semester. Its main campus in downtown offers a number of associate degree programs in a variety of fields, including a School of Nursing. Moreno Valley and Norco also have campuses that are part of the Riverside Community College District.

Other institutions of higher learning within the greater Riverside area include California State University, San Bernardino; California State University, Fullerton; Chapman University; University of Redlands; and Cal Poly Ponoma.

Libraries and Research Centers

The Riverside Public Library has approximately 425,000 books and other library materials, as well as 400 public-access computers. The library has a circulation of 1.23 million materials per year. Casa Blanca Library and Family Center features a collection of more than 7,000 volumes in Spanish. The main library facility is located in historic downtown and seven other branches operate within the city. The Riverside Local History Resource Center is a partnership between Riverside Municipal Museum and Riverside Public Library. Special collections at the Riverside Public Library include genealogy, local history, historical photographs, and U.S. documents.

The Riverside County Library System has 33 libraries and 2 bookmobiles serving the county. The Riverside County Library, San Bernardino County Library, Moreno Valley Public Library, Murrieta Public Library, and College of the Desert libraries are part of the Inland Library System, a network of 103 service outlets serving 4 million people throughout the region.

The Riverside County Law Library is a state government document depository library. The University of California, Riverside (UCR) libraries contain more than 3.2 million volumes and more than 94,770 paid electronic journals, 2,908 print serial subscriptions, and 2.3 million micro formats. There are four facilities. The Tómas Rivera Library is home to the famed Eaton Collection, the world's largest cataloged collection of science fiction and fantasy. There is also the Orbach Science Library, the Music Library, and the Multimedia Library.

The University of California, Riverside sponsors many research projects and facilities. The Agricultural Experiment Station Citrus Research Center has developed more than 40 new citrus varieties and provided research to help growers fight pests and diseases for more than a century. The Institute for Integrative Genome Biology is another leading research facility. The Insectary and Quarantine Facility is an advanced laboratory for research in the study of non-native insects.

University Research Park is a cooperative development between the city, the county, and UCR. The development covers 39 acres in the Hunter Park Area and includes such companies as Alden Botanica, Ambryx Biotechnology, Microbac Laboratories, Surado Solutions, and Viresco Energy. The Inland Empire Small Business Development Center and Inland Empire Economic Partnership also operate within the research park.

Public Library Information: Riverside Public Library, 3581 Mission Inn Ave., Riverside, CA 92501; telephone (951) 826-5201.

■ Health Care

With 373 beds, Riverside Community Hospital is one of the largest acute-care community hospitals in the county. The facility includes a Level II Trauma Center, Heart-Care Institute, Cancer Center, Center for Surgical Weight Loss, CyberKnife Center, and Transplant Program. A full array of other medical services is provided. Kaiser Permanente Riverside Medical Center offers a wide variety of hospital and primary care services, with 215 beds and a high-performing rating in orthopedics from *U.S. News & World Report* in 2013–14. Other Kaiser facilities in Riverside include the Magnolia Village geriatric and long-term care facility, Canyon Crest Mental Health Offices, and Polk Street Medical Offices. Parkview

Community Hospital, with 193 beds, is a not-for-profit acute-care hospital.

The 362-bed Riverside County Regional Medical Center in Moreno Valley adds to the health-care service options, with specialty clinics and research facilities that are easily accessible to area residents. A separate psychiatric facility that is also part of the center has 77 additional beds.

■ Recreation

Sightseeing

One of Riverside's most attractive sites, Victoria Avenue, was constructed in 1891–92. The 8.3 miles of divided street are planted with hedgerow roses, eucalyptus, palm, and crepe myrtle trees with a multipurpose trail. Forty acres of hilly tree-lined paths with more than 3,500 blooming plant species from around the world are on view at the Botanic Gardens of the University of California, Riverside. The Gardens are also a wildlife sanctuary with almost 200 bird species officially observed. The Mission Inn, a completely renovated National Historic Landmark hotel, is a unique blend of architectural styles and houses priceless pieces of art. The Teen Challenge Program is headquartered in the Spanish-style Benedict Castle, built in 1931, which is also used for weddings and events. Overlooking the city of Riverside is the 1,337-foot Mt. Rubidoux, which is the site of the World Peace Tower and a large cross dedicated to Father Junipero Serra.

Heritage House, a restored two-story Victorian home completed in 1892 in the Queen Anne style, is open for tours. Visitors are also welcome at the Jensen-Alvarado Ranch, a historic ranch completely restored to portray rural life. The ranch features a variety of live animals, a duck pond, and citrus groves and fruit orchards.

Castle Park, a 25-acre family recreation park, features miniature golf, arcades, amusement rides, and a restored 1909 carousel. A model railroad at Hunter Park offers train rides when operating. Cuttings from the Parent Navel Orange Tree, planted in 1873, started the entire billion-dollar citrus industry in the United States. The tree, which can be seen at the Magnolia and Arlington area, still bears fruit.

Arts and Culture

Riverside is home to a variety of performing arts, theater, dance, and music organizations. The performing arts program of the University of California, Riverside offers quality plays, musicals, and other acts through its University Theatre and other campus venues. The historic Riverside Municipal Auditorium—located in downtown Riverside—showcases live performances ranging from popular music acts to comedy to dance throughout the year. It underwent a $10 million renovation in 2010. The Riverside County Philharmonic performs four subscription concerts each year October through May at the Fox Theater, which was renovated in 2007 and reopened in 2010. The Culver Center for the Arts opened in 2010 and consists of exhibit and gallery space, art collections, and offices. It is also used for film screenings, performing arts shows and other programs.

The Riverside Community Players, founded in 1926, is one of the oldest continuously active community theater groups in the United States and holds workshops in acting and staging techniques in addition to performing six productions annually. The Riverside Youth Theatre provides training for much younger thespians and showcases their talents with a few reasonably priced performances per year.

The free public concerts of the Riverside Concert Band provide an opportunity for young musicians to perform with more experienced players at official functions in the city. Riverside Community College offers its Performance Riverside season at the college's Landis Auditorium.

Dance enthusiasts will enjoy traditional Mexican dances performed by the Ballet Folklorico de Riverside, whose members range in age from 5 to 28 years old. Annual professional productions of the *Nutcracker* plus a spring performance are offered by the California Riverside Ballet, founded in 1969.

Riverside has an interesting variety of museums to be enjoyed by residents and visitors alike. The March Field Air Museum displays more than 70 aircraft and missiles, both inside and outside, on a 35-acre site adjacent to March Field. The Riverside Metropolitan Museum tells the story of the city's history, depicts the development of the citrus and other local manufacturing industries, and features touring exhibits. One of the largest collections of cameras and photos in the world is on display at the University of California, Riverside/California Museum of Photography. Rare Indian artifacts, basketry, pottery, and handicrafts are on view at the Sherman Indian Museum. The Mission Inn Museum, located at the historic Mission Inn, presents an eclectic display of historic artifacts, paintings of the California Missions painted in the 1800s, oriental *objects d'art*, arts and crafts furniture, marble sculptures, and many photographs. The Riverside Arts Museum, which offers many major exhibits a year, also is located downtown near the Mission Inn Museum. Built as a YMCA in 1909, the Life Arts Center is home to artists' studios.

Festivals and Holidays

January brings the annual Dickens Festival, a literary festival honoring the writer Charles Dickens that encourages reading and enjoyment of the dramatic and cultural arts by the general public. Riverside also hosts the Black History Parade and Expo on the third Saturday in February. The Riverside County Fair and Date Festival is also a February highlight.

In March the Riverside Arts Council presents Evening for the Arts to benefit the local arts community. March also brings the annual Riverside Airshow at the Riverside Municipal Airport. Apple Festival Weekend is typically in April. May's Cinco de Mayo is a celebration with music, entertainment, and food. The Vintage Home Tour, Restoration Faire and Vintage Mercantile featuring historically significant homes also take place in May. Riverside Wednesday Nights, which offered arts and crafts, food, and live entertainment during the summer, was replaced by a year-round Saturday farmers' market, and Thursday family activities nights in 2007.

In the summer months Fairmount Park offers a wide range of family programs and a peaceful setting. Independence Day features fireworks atop Mt. Rubidoux and two other city sites, which can be viewed from Riverside's Wheelock Field and surrounding streets. Riverside Ultimate Jazz Festival goes on for a weekend in August at Fairmount Park.

Fall ushers in a new lineup of programming in Riverside. September is the month of the annual Mayor's Ball for Arts and Innovation, with an evening of banquets, costumes, prizes, and awards. October features Festa Italiana, an Italian food festival. Halloween weekend brings spooky tales of ghouls with Ghostwalk Riverside.

November brings the Mission Inn Run through notable areas of downtown. It also kicks off the holiday season with the Christmas Tree Lighting and Mission Inn Festival of Lights. December's Christmas Open House brightens spirits with music and entertainment at the Riverside Metropolitan Museum, and the Riverside Ballet Theatre Company performs the annual *Nutcracker* ballet.

Sports for the Spectator

The University of California, Riverside is part of the NCAA Division I and participates in the Big West Conference. Men's and women's competitions include soccer, basketball, tennis, golf, cross country, and track and field. Men's baseball is played at the Riverside Sports Complex, which is jointly owned by the city and the university. Women's softball is played at the Amy S. Harrison Field; the university also fields a women's volleyball team.

Sports for the Participant

Riverside has 51 city parks and 2 state parks available to sports enthusiasts. Among the parks are seven swimming pools and many tennis courts in select city parks and community centers. The city parks have many soccer fields and more than 40 ballfields, which includes the lighted baseball stadium at Riverside Sports Complex that seats 2,500.

County parks offer natural environments for hiking, horseback riding, cycling, fishing, and camping. The 180-plus acre Fairmount Park offers fishing and sailing on

Lake Evans, paddleboats, wildlife and bird watching, lawn bowling, golfing, playgrounds, and evening concerts. Rancho Jurupa Park (a county park) has hiking and horseback riding trails, stocked lakes, campsites with utility hookups, and the Louis Rubidoux Nature Center. The park has added an 18-hole miniature golf course, driveway, and 61 new campsites.

The California Citrus State Historic Park has expanded for visitors. Lake Perris State Recreation Area has 8,800 lakeside acres waiting for water-skiing, boating, sailing, and windsurfing. Skiing in the nearby Big Bear area and hot-air ballooning near the Temecula wineries are two popular winter activities.

Golfers can choose from six public and three private courses. Bicyclists may learn about a wealth of trails and events through the Riverside Bicycle Club. Riverside bike trails connect with Crest to Coast trails along the Santa Ana River. Skaters have numerous options within Riverside's city limits.

Shopping and Dining

The Inland Empire's shopping outlet is Ontario Mills, home to more than 200 specialty stores and eight anchor and department stores. Riverside has two other major shopping malls: the 1.1-million-square-foot Galleria at Tyler and Riverside Plaza. The Riverside Plaza, housed within Riverside's Magnolia Center and historic craftsman-era "Wood Street" neighborhood, now sports a "Main Street" look and feel to its stores and shops. Downtown Riverside also offers a wide arrange of specialty stores. The Canyon Springs shopping center located on the eastern edge of Riverside has national retail stores, while Canyon Crest Towne Centre has specialty shops in a residential area five minutes from downtown.

From coffeehouse fare to Cantonese favorites, Riverside has restaurants for every taste. Sandwich shops and casual eateries abound along with purveyors of ethnic delights including Mexican, French, Italian, Greek, Japanese, Thai, and British fish 'n' chips. The Mission Inn restaurant, Citrus City Grille, Creola's Restaurant, and Café Sevilla are just a few of the local restaurants listed as the best in the city.

Visitor Information: Riverside Convention and Visitors Bureau, 3750 University Ave., Ste 175, Riverside, CA 92501; telephone (951) 222-4700.

■ Convention Facilities

Riverside Convention Center is located near downtown and enjoyed a $45 million renovation and expansion that completed in 2014. The enhanced convention center has more than 65,000 square feet of multiuse space and cutting-edge technology in its exhibit halls, ballrooms, and meeting facilities. The Convention Center also has a well-lit outdoor plaza available for open-air exhibits. Numerous hotels are within walking and easy driving distance from the Convention Center. Meeting spaces are available at Riverside Marriot and Mission Inn Hotel, as well as at several other hotels. The Riverside Municipal Auditorium, built in the Spanish Revival style with Moorish accents, has been home to the local symphony orchestra, opera, and ballet and is available for special events.

Convention Information: Riverside Convention and Visitors Bureau, 3750 University Ave., Ste 175, Riverside, CA 92501; telephone (951) 222-4700.

■ Transportation

Approaching the City

Most travelers take advantage of services at the LA/Ontario International Airport, which is located about 17 miles northwest of Riverside and is served by seven commercial airlines. Riverside Municipal Airport serves small corporate and business travelers. The John Wayne Airport is about 44 miles away in Santa Ana and is served by 10 commercial and commuter lines.

Several interstate highways passing through or near the city of Riverside include Interstate 215 and Interstate 15, which run north–south, and Interstate 10, which runs east–west just north of the city. Other major freeways in the area are State Route 60 and State Route 91. These routes provide direct access to metropolitan areas of Los Angeles and Orange County. Nearly 3,000 miles of county-maintained roads and nearly 700 miles of roads maintained by the state provide service to business, industry, and motorists in the region. A toll lane for commuters traveling between Riverside and Orange County on Highway 91 is the newest freeway addition.

Metrolink is a regional rail system that includes commuter and other passenger services and links Riverside to employment and activity centers in Los Angeles, Orange, Ventura, San Bernardino, and San Diego counties.

Greyhound Bus Lines offers both intrastate and interstate service. The Riverside Transit Agency provides service to Riverside County within a 2,500-square-mile area; it also maintains eight CommuterLink routes. Amtrak serves the city through its Southwest Chief route, with daily trips to Chicago through Albuquerque and Kansas City.

Traveling in the City

Within the city of Riverside, State Route 91 runs northwest and southeast through the city, and State Highway 60 runs northwest to southeast through the northern part of the city. Major thoroughfares include Magnolia Avenue, Allesandro Boulevard, University Avenue, and Arlington Avenue. The Riverside Transit Agency (RTA) has 36 routes in and around the city. Bike racks are available on all fixed-route busses. RTA has a Dial-A-Ride service for those with disabilities.

■ Communications

Newspapers and Magazines

The city's daily newspaper is *The Press-Enterprise*. Other newspapers are the University of California, Riverside's *Highlander*, California Baptist University's online publication *The Banner*, *Black Voice News* (weekly), and *La Prensa* (Spanish weekly). Magazines, newsletters, and journals published in Riverside include *Riverside Magazine*, *Inland Empire Magazine*, *Inland Empire Family Magazine*, and *Hispanic Lifestyle*. *Inland Empire Business Journal* serves the business community.

Television and Radio

Two local television stations are based in Riverside, and cable and satellite service is available. Riverside has two AM and four FM radio stations featuring contemporary hits, adult contemporary, and religious programming. One station is hosted by the University of California, Riverside.

Media Information: The Press-Enterprise, 3450 14th Street, Riverside, CA 92501; telephone (951) 684-1200.

Riverside Online

Alvord Unified School District. Available www. alvord.k12.ca.us

City of Riverside home page. Available www. riversideca.gov

Greater Riverside Chambers of Commerce. Available www.riverside-chamber.com

Press-Enterprise. Available www.pe.com

Smart Riverside. Available www.smartriverside.com

Riverside Convention and Visitors Bureau. Available www.riversidecvb.com

Riverside County. Available www.countyofriverside. us

Riverside County Library System. Available rivlib. info/riverside-county-library-system

Riverside Unified School District. Available www. rusdlink.org/site/default.aspx?PageID=1

BIBLIOGRAPHY

Dixon, Lloyd, ed., *Balancing Environment and Development: Costs, Revenues, and Benefits of the Western Riverside County Multiple Species Habitat Conservation Plan* (Santa Monica, CA: RAND Corp., 2008)

Lech, Steve, *Pioneers of Riverside County: The Spanish, Mexican, and Early American Periods* (Charleston, SC: The History Press, 2012)

Patterson, Tom, *A Colony for California: Riverside's First Hundred Years* (Riverside, CA: The Museum Press of the Riverside Museum Associates, 1996)

Traf, Clifford, *Native Americans of Riverside County* (San Francisco, CA: Arcadia Publishing, 2006)

Sacramento

■ The City in Brief

Founded: 1839 (incorporated, 1850)

Head Official: Mayor Kevin Johnson (since 2008, term expires 2016)

City Population

    1990: 369,365
    2000: 407,018
    2010: 466,488
    2012 estimate: 475,524
    Percent change, 2000–2010: 14.6%
    U.S. rank in 1990: 41st
    U.S. rank in 2000: 49th
    U.S. rank in 2010: 35th (State rank: 6th)

Metropolitan Statistical Area Population

    2000: 1,796,857
    2010: 2,149,127
    2012 estimate: 2,196,482
    Percent change, 2000–2010: 19.6%
    U.S. rank in 2000: 27th
    U.S. rank in 2010: 24th

Area: 97.2 square miles

Elevation: 30 feet above sea level

Average Annual Temperatures: January, 46.3° F; July, 75.4° F; annual average, 61.1° F

Average Annual Precipitation: 17.93 inches of rain

Major Economic Sectors: government, trade, education, energy, health care

Unemployment Rate: 9% (2012)

Per Capita Income: $24,882

2012 FBI Crime Index Property: 19,967

Major Colleges and Universities: California State University, Sacramento; University of California, Davis

Daily Newspaper: *The Sacramento Bee*

■ Introduction

Sacramento, the capital of California, started out as a Gold Rush city when thousands of prospectors descended upon Captain John Sutter's settlement, New Helvetia, in hopes of striking rich. Today Sacramento has become a city of gracious tree-lined streets, famous for flowers that bloom all year—the "Camellia Capital of the World." A significant percentage of the food that America consumes is produced in Sacramento, which is at the center of the fruitful Sacramento Valley. Since the nineteenth century the city has been a major transportation hub for the West Coast. More recently, it has evolved into a sophisticated center for many medical and other research facilities on the forefront of scientific breakthroughs. The city's development plans for the early decades of the twenty-first century focused on reviving underutilized areas and concentrating residents and businesses near the city center.

■ Geography and Climate

Sacramento lies in the center of California's broad and fruitful Sacramento Valley at the confluence of the Sacramento and American Rivers, 72 miles northeast of San Francisco. Shielded by the Sierra Nevada Mountains to the east, the California Coast ranges to the west, and the Siskiyou Mountains to the north, the city enjoys a mild climate for most of the year. In the summer, however, "northers" blow from the Siskiyou Mountains, bearing pollen and heat. This is mitigated by Sacramento's extremely low humidity and the cool ocean breezes. The winters are rainy. The city lies to

© Anthony Dunn/Alamy

the northeast of several major fault lines, making the area susceptible to earthquakes. However, most quakes experienced in the city are of lower, less damaging magnitudes than those that may occur in the coastal San Francisco Bay Area.

Area: 97.2 square miles

Elevation: 30 feet above sea level

Average Temperatures: January, 46.3° F; July, 75.4° F; annual average, 61.1° F

Average Annual Precipitation: 17.93 inches of rain

■ History

Gold Rush Begins in Sacramento

The Sacramento area was originally inhabited by the Nisenan, a branch of the Maidu, who lived in the valley for 10,000 years before white settlers arrived. Spanish soldiers from Mission San Jose under the command of Lieutenant Gabriel Morago discovered the Sacramento and American rivers in 1808. The area was not settled until 1839. That year, with the permission of Mexico,

Captain John Sutter, a Swiss immigrant who had fled his homeland to escape debtor's prison, built a settlement on 76 acres and called it New Helvetia after his homeland. He built a fort called Sutter's Fort (which has been restored and can still be seen today). Sutter also constructed a landing on the Sacramento River that he called the Embarcadero and contacted a millwright, James Marshall, to help build the settlement. It was Marshall who in 1848 discovered a gold nugget, thus precipitating the great California Gold Rush of 1849. Sutter's Embarcadero became the gateway to the mines, but Sutter was financially ruined by the influx of newcomers from all over the world who trampled his settlement; even his employees left him to make their fortune.

Sacramento, Spanish for "Holy Sacrament," was originally the name of a nearby river that is now called the Feather River; in 1849 the name was taken for the town, which was incorporated in 1850. Sacramento was a rowdy place, full of successful miners who spent their money on gambling and dance halls. In its early days the town encountered difficulties, with floods in 1849 and 1853 and a fire in 1852. But Sacramento survived to become the capital of California in 1854, paying the state $1 million for the honor.

Railroad Arrives; Agriculture Surpasses Gold Mining

In 1855 construction began on the Sacramento Valley Railroad with the financial backing of shopkeepers known as the Big Four: Collis P. Huntington, Mark Hopkins, Charles Crocker, and Leland Stanford (after whom Stanford University is named). In 1856 Sacramento became the terminus of California's first railroad. Then came the Pony Express and, in 1861, the transcontinental telegraph. The Central Pacific Railroad joined the east and west coasts in 1869, permitting Sacramento farmers to ship their produce to the east. The railroad also transformed what had been a six-month trip between the coasts to six days; in time it also superseded the river as a means of transportation. In another important change, agriculture eventually replaced the gold mines as the primary industry.

Mather Field was established to prepare planes to fly to Europe during World War I; McClellan Air Force Base was established in 1937 and was an important base of operations during World War II. These military installations drew a large influx of people into the area, many of whom stayed after World War II and spurred the development of the private sector. The first suburban shopping mall in the United States was established in North Sacramento in 1945. However, like many cities in the United States, downtown Sacramento had fallen into decay by the end of the 1950s, since most of the moneyed population had moved to the suburbs. The city eventually experienced a resurgence marked by the redevelopment of the downtown area, with the city's historical sections being preserved and restored. Sutter's Embarcadero, for instance, was redeveloped to house shops and restaurants.

The 1990s brought a decrease in the once major military presence. Mather Air Force Base officially ceased military operation in 1993. The Air Force transferred the base to the County of Sacramento, which opened the Mather Airport for civilian use in 1995. McClellan Air Force Base officially ceased operations in 2001, but the site continued to house federal employees from the Department of Defense and is the site of the Veteran's Administrations medical and dental clinics.

Into the early 2000s, federal, state, and local government services continued to be a major source of employment in the city; however, city officials also continued to work on development projects that encouraged the reemergence of retail, entertainment, culture, and arts as primary forces in the downtown economy. The prospect of infill development was highlighted by consideration of a multi-purpose development to be anchored by a new arena for the city's National Basketball Association franchise, the Sacramento Kings, which was under consideration in 2014.

Historical Information: Sacramento Room, Sacramento Public Library, 828 I Street, Sacramento, CA 95814; telephone (916) 264-2700.

■ Population Profile

Metropolitan Statistical Area Population

2000: 1,796,857
2010: 2,149,127
2012 estimate: 2,196,482
Percent change, 2000–2010: 19.6%
U.S. rank in 2000: 27th
U.S. rank in 2010: 24th

City Residents

1990: 369,365
2000: 407,018
2010: 466,488
2012 estimate: 475,524
Percent change, 2000–2010: 14.6%
U.S. rank in 1990: 41st
U.S. rank in 2000: 49th
U.S. rank in 2010: 35th (State rank: 6th)

Density: 4,764.2 people per square mile

Racial and ethnic characteristics

White: 232,757
Black or African American: 71,297
American Indian and Alaskan Native: 2,665
Asian: 87,977
Native Hawaiian and Other Pacific Islander: 6,729
Hispanic or Latino (may be of any race): 132,097
Other: 74,099

Percent of residents born in state: 60.3%

Age characteristics

Population under 5 years old: 34,120
Population 5 to 9 years old: 32,413
Population 10 to 14 years old: 27,955
Population 15 to 19 years old: 32,023
Population 20 to 24 years old: 41,235
Population 25 to 34 years old: 75,158
Population 35 to 44 years old: 64,087
Population 45 to 54 years old: 59,901
Population 55 to 59 years old: 28,875
Population 60 to 64 years old: 26,199
Population 65 to 74 years old: 29,306
Population 75 to 84 years old: 14,904
Population 85 years and over: 9,348
Median age: 34.2

Births (2010–11 Metropolitan Area)

Total number: 27,593

Deaths (2010–11 Metropolitan Area)

Total number: 14,934

Money income (2012)

Per capita income: $24,882

Median household income: $48,692

Total households: 175,723

Number of households with income of ...

less than $10,000: 13,604

$10,000 to $14,999: 14,037

$15,000 to $24,999: 20,530

$25,000 to $34,999: 17,453

$35,000 to $49,999: 23,826

$50,000 to $74,999: 33,175

$75,000 to $99,999: 20,031

$100,000 to $149,999: 20,058

$150,000 to $199,999: 7,567

$200,000 or more: 5,442

Percent of families below poverty level: 22.7%

FBI Crime Index Property: 19,967

FBI Crime Index Violent: 3,520

■ Municipal Government

Sacramento has a council-manager form of government. The council is comprised of a mayor elected at large and eight council members elected by district; all serve staggered four-year terms. A city manager is hired by the council.

Some urbanized areas within the county of Sacramento are not part of any incorporated city, therefore, they are still governed by a system designed for rural counties.

Head Official: Mayor Kevin Johnson (since 2008, term expires 2016)

Total Number of City Employees: 4,083 (2012)

City Information: Sacramento City Hall, 915 I Street, Sacramento, CA 95814; telephone (916) 264-5011.

■ Economy

Major Industries and Commercial Activity

Sacramento began as a city rich from gold and railroad money. Productive mines still operate in the area, and the city remains an important transportation center. Sacramento's deep-water port, connected to the San Francisco Bay via a 43-mile channel, is an important West Coast hub for the handling of cargo from ocean-going ships. As the junction of the state's major railroad, the Union Pacific, Sacramento maintains its position at the top of the rail transportation industry.

As state capitol of California, Sacramento's largest employment sector has historically been federal, state, and local government. As is true of California in general, the Sacramento area is rich in agriculture; products of the fertile Sacramento Valley region include fruits and

vegetables, rice and other grains, meat, beet sugar, and almonds. Agribusiness and food manufacturing employ about 6,400 residents and take part in a $3 billion regional industry. The University of California, Davis conducts extensive research on sustainable agricultural practices, representing an industry unto itself and also attracting food manufacturing firms. Higher education in general is an important area industry, with several major universities located in and around Sacramento.

Green energy industries have been encouraged by three regional initiatives—Green Capital Alliance, CleanStart, and Greenwise—that provide 3,000 jobs and $846 million in annual sales from some 200 area businesses. Another important industry related to science and technology is health care. The city hosts four major non-profit medical centers, which, in addition to other providers, support 279,000 jobs.

Other industries include advanced manufacturing, business and financial services, retail, and entertainment and tourism.

Items and goods produced: high-technology items, medical equipment and other health-related products, dairy products, feeds, meat, brick and clay products, mining equipment, lumber boxes

Incentive Programs—New and Existing Companies

Local programs: A number of organizations work to attract and assist businesses in the Sacramento area. Among them are the Sacramento Metro Chamber of Commerce, and the Sacramento Area Commerce and Trade Organization (SACTO). Sacramento's Economic Development Department and its partners offer loan programs to assist the development of small businesses. The city of Sacramento sponsors a Brownfields Program to redevelopment sites that may suffer from environmental contamination; assistance includes both financial and technical support. The Grow Sacramento Fund is a partnership among several government and development agencies to help small businesses obtain necessary financing. Most financing is for amounts above $100,000. A Sewer Credit Program reduces fees for connecting to the city's sanitary sewer system, and the Sacramento Streamline Program reduces requisite permitting and application hurdles for new and expanding businesses. The Local Business Enterprise Program gives preferential treatment to area businesses during bidding on city contracts.

State programs: California business incentives include the state's Alternative Energy and Advanced Transportation Authority Sales and Use Tax Exemptions for Zero Emission Vehicle Manufacturing. Initially targeting vehicle manufacturing only when it was passed in 2010, the sales and use tax exemption has since been expanded to all renewable energy technologies. In 2012 it was expanded again to include advanced manufacturing. More than one dozen additional incentives encourage green development or pollution-reducing business decisions.

Research and development tax credits offers companies a 15 percent credit against their bank and corporation tax liability for qualifying in-house research expenses; a 24 percent tax credit for basic research payments to outside organizations is also available. Industrial development bonds finance investment in land, buildings, and new equipment related to domestic manufacturing operations in the state. California Capital Access Program and Collateral Support Program also offer alternative methods of financing for businesses. Enterprise Zones and Local Agency Military Base Recovery Area regions provide incentives for development in targeted geographic regions. A New Jobs Tax Credit offers $3,000 per hire of qualifying new employees, and the state's Film and Television Tax Credit Program supports productions with a 20 percent tax credit against qualified expenses.

In 2011 California began offering companies the option to calculate their corporate income tax through the single sales factor method, rather than the existing triple apportionment derived from calculations of a company's payroll, property, and sales.

California's Innovation Hub Program, with 12 locations throughout the state, supports the commercialization of innovation and technology businesses through public-private partnerships, knowledge sharing, venture capital sources, and business incubators. The state also undertakes trade missions to form partnerships for trade and export promotion.

Job training programs: The state of California offers an Employment Training Panel to assist companies with post-hire training and reimbursement. The Employment Development Department also partners with Local Workforce Investment Areas to recruit, screen, test, evaluate, and hire qualified workers.

Sacramento Works provides an array of support to hiring businesses and job seekers. The Sacramento Training and Response Team (START), a partnership of 13 job assistance and training programs, helps companies recruit, train, and hire employees. Business Information Centers operated by Sacramento Works provide access to libraries of information as well as workshops and seminars relating to business management. Sacramento Works further sponsors recruitment events, career fairs, and skills assessments. Its Rapid Response Team aids businesses in worker retraining, layoffs, or closures.

Development Projects

The city's 2030 General Plan focused on infill development—taking advantage of existing, underutilized spaces rather than expanding outward—environmental sustainability, making the city more pedestrian and bicycle friendly, retaining the diversity and cultural milieu of its neighborhoods. The city had several "shovel-ready"

planned development areas in 2014, including 54 city blocks downtown, the 773-acre River District industrial area, and 244 acres at the Sacramento Railyards.

Two of Sacramento's medical centers—University of California at Davis Medical Center and Kaiser Permanente's South Sacramento Hospital—underwent major expansions in the early 2010s. The University of California at Davis's Medical Center completed a $424 million Surgery and Emergency Services Pavilion in 2010. Kaiser Permanente added a new $300 million tower to its facility in 2011, with 48 private medical-surgery beds, a 30-bed intensive care unit, outpatient pharmacy, meditation room, gift shop, and cardiac catheterization unit.

In 2010 the city unveiled plans for a new Powerhouse Science Center, a project costing $78 million that broke ground in 2013 to transform a rehabilitated Power Station into a science and technology museum. The 48,200-square-foot center was expected to open in 2015 and generate more than $10 million per year in revenue with an estimated 320,000 annual visitors.

Proposals to construct a new downtown arena for the Sacramento Kings, the city's National Basketball Association franchise, were under consideration in early 2014. If approved, the new arena would receive $258 million in city support, with team owners paying for the remainder of the $448 million project. In addition to the arena, development would include 1.5 million square feet of hotel, office, residential, and entertainment space. Relocation of the team to downtown was in line with the city's infill development efforts. Economic impact estimates conducted by proponents of the building plan were placed at $11.5 billion.

Sacramento International Airport completed its Big Build capital improvement project in 2011. The $1.04 billion project replaced the airport's Terminal B, giving it the ability to handle some 10 million passengers annually.

Economic Development Information: Sacramento Metro Chamber of Commerce, One Capitol Mall, Suite 300, Sacramento, CA 95814; telephone (916) 552-6800; fax (916) 443-2672.

Commercial Shipping

With an international airport, rail hub, seaport, and junction of three freeways within 10 miles of downtown, Sacramento is ideally situated for commercial shipping. Inland 79 miles from San Francisco, the Port of West Sacramento admits international ocean-going vessels through a deep-water channel connecting it with San Francisco Bay. The port's specialty is handling dry-bulk cargos and it utilizes the most modern equipment on the West Coast for that purpose. The port is served by more than 50 major trucking companies and three major rail lines: BNSF Railway, Union Pacific Railroad, and Sierra Northern Railway. The Sacramento International Airport is served by 9 cargo airline carriers, including the all-cargo Federal Express and U.S. Postal Service–Express Mail Services.

Labor Force and Employment Outlook

Employers have access to a large and well-educated labor pool. The labor force of Sacramento grew by more than 7.2 percent between 2002 and 2012, above the state average. After an increase in unemployment following a national recession in the late 2000s, Sacramento has enjoyed a decline in its unemployment rate that outpaced that of the state of California during 2011–12. According to a 2013 report from the Center for Strategic Economic Research, the strongest growth industries in the city from 2006 to 2011 were life, physical, and social science; health care practitioners and technical workers; and computer and mathematical science.

The following is a summary of data regarding the 2012 Sacramento labor force:

Size of civilian labor force: 236,209

Number of workers employed in . . .

agriculture and mining: 1,383
construction: 10,085
manufacturing: 9,865
wholesale trade: 5,487
retail trade: 21,983
transportation: 9,481
information systems: 4,693
finance: 11,819
professional administration: 25,186
education and social services: 45,530
arts and leisure: 19,625
other: 9,845
public administration: 24,902

Average hourly earnings of production workers: $17.77

Unemployment rate: 9% (2012)

Employers

Largest employers (2012)	*Number of employees*
State of California	69,763
Sacramento County	11,450
University of California, Davis Health System	7,725
Dignity Health	7,069
Intel Corporation	6,633
Kaiser Permanente	6,360
Sutter Health Sacramento Sierra Region	5,765
Elk Grove Unified School District	5,021
Sacramento City Unified School District	4,700
City of Sacramento	4,083

Cost of Living

Sacramento's housing prices relative to San Francisco and southern California have been kept low by an abundance of cheap land.

The following is a summary of data regarding several key cost of living factors in the area.

2013 ACCRA Average House Price: $399,184

2013 ACCRA Cost of Living Index: 114

State income tax rate: 1.00% to 13.3%

State sales tax rate: 7.5%

Local income tax rate: None

Local sales tax rate: 1.0%

Property tax rate: Limited to 1% of assessed value by state law. In some cases the local taxing body can add additional taxes.

Economic Information: Sacramento Area Commerce and Trade Organization, 400 Capitol Mall, Suite 2500, Sacramento, CA 95814; telephone (916) 441-2144; email locate@sacto.org.

■ Education and Research

Elementary and Secondary Schools

The Sacramento City Unified School District, among the largest in the state, is Sacramento's main school district. Students of all ages are served throughout the district, which offers a full range of programs that include 15 charter schools as well as alternative schools, independent study, preschool, and adult education. About 36 percent of students in the district are Hispanic, 18 percent Asian, 16 percent African American, and 19 percent white. Also reflecting the district's ethnic diversity are the more than 40 languages spoken by residents within the district; 38 percent of students do not speak English at home.

Other districts with schools in Sacramento include the Elk Grove Unified School District, Folsom Cordova Unified School District, San Juan Unified School District, Natomas Unified School District, Robla Elementary School District, and Two Rivers Unified School District, which resulted from a merger between Grant Joint Union High School District and three elementary school districts.

Sacramento also has about 80 private and parochial schools.

The following is a summary of data regarding the Sacramento City Unified School District.

Total enrollment: 47,897

Number of facilities

total: 81
elementary schools: 46

junior high schools: 14
high schools: 13
other: 8

Student/teacher ratio: 57.19:1

Teacher salaries
average (statewide): $69,434

Funding per pupil: $9,682

Public Schools Information: Sacramento City Unified School District, 5735 47th Avenue, Sacramento, CA 95824; telephone (916) 643-7400.

Colleges and Universities

Sacramento is home to a number of colleges and universities. Four-year institutions include California State University, Sacramento (CSUS), typically known as Sacramento State, with an enrollment of about 28,500 students. CSUS has academic divisions of Arts and Letters; Business Administration; Education; Engineering and Computer Science; Health and Human Services; Natural Sciences and Mathematics; Social Sciences and Interdisciplinary Studies; and Continuing Education. CSUS offers 58 undergraduate degree programs, 41 master's programs, and 2 doctoral programs.

Golden Gate University, which offers undergraduate and graduate programs in business and management, information technology, taxation, and law, has a Sacramento campus. (Its main campus is in San Francisco.) Nearby is the University of California at Davis, which boasts a highly regarded medical center—the primary teaching facility of the university's School of Medicine—located in Sacramento. UC Davis School of Medicine was ranked among the top 20 schools for primary care and 45 for research in 2014 by *U.S. News & World Report.*

The University of Southern California's Price School of Public Policy is located in Sacramento. There is a regional campus of the University of San Francisco in Sacramento as well, offering both bachelor's and master's degree programs. The University of the Pacific's McGeorge School of Law at Sacramento offers full-time and part-time study programs. Joint degrees are available with UC Davis and CSUS.

Two-year colleges in Sacramento are American River, Cosumnes River, and Sacramento City colleges.

Libraries and Research Centers

The Sacramento Public Library operates a 160,000-square-foot Central Library, and 28 branches and bookmobile services. Holdings include more than 2 million volumes and thousands of periodical subscriptions, plus audio and video tapes, recordings, maps, and art reproductions. Circulation averages in excess of 7.5 million items annually, and patrons log more than 600,000 hours on public computers located at library branches. Among the special collections are Californiana, the history of printing, and city planning and urban development. The Arden-Dimick Library branch houses more than 75,000 items and a special collection for the deaf including books, magazines, and sign language videos. The Schwab-Rosenhouse College Resource Center and the Sacramento Room (for local history) are located at the Central Library. A College and Career Center is based at the Colonial Heights branch. The Sacramento Public Library system is the fourth largest system in California and serves a population of more than 1.3 million people.

The University Library of California State University, Sacramento held more than 1.4 million volumes as of 2013, as well as thousands of e-books, periodical subscriptions, audio/visual materials, and maps and government documents.

Sacramento is also the headquarters of the California State Library with special collections of federal and state government documents; its holdings include more than 777,509 volumes. The Braille and Talking Book Library is one of the special collections at the State Library. It has more than 55,000 titles and 15 periodical subscriptions, including a limited number of materials in foreign languages. The Witkin State Law Library of California is also part of the State Library.

The Western Ecological Research Center (WERC), which has 13 field stations in California and one in Nevada, is headquartered in Sacramento. WERC offers its clients and partners the research and technology needed to support the management of Pacific Southwestern ecosystems. WERC's scientists are experts in such fields as herpetology, conservation biology, wetlands ecology, and ecological restoration.

The research centers and institutes of the nearby University of California at Davis (UC) perform research in a wide variety of areas such as food safety and cleaner fuel technologies. UC Davis Health System, which is based in Sacramento, conducts hundreds of research studies through its specialized clinics. The UC Davis Health System research centers include the Alzheimer's Disease Center, Mouse Biology Program, Genome Center, and the Center for Nursing Research. The university's MIND Institute has performed cutting-edge research in such areas as autism, cancer, and ADHD.

The California National Primate Research Center is a federally funded biomedical research facility affiliated with UC Davis. The center is part of a network of eight national primate research centers sponsored by the National Institutes of Health for studies of human and animal health.

California State University, Sacramento sponsors several research institutes and centers, including the Institute for Social Research, Center for Pacific Asian Studies, and the Archaeological Research Center.

Public Library Information: Sacramento Public Library, Central Library, 828 I Street, Sacramento, CA 95814; telephone (916) 264-2700.

■ Health Care

Sacramento is well served by medical facilities. The acclaimed University of California, Davis Medical Center is located in Sacramento. Its campus includes a 619-bed hospital that admits more than 32,000 patients annually. Originally founded in 1852 as Sacramento County Hospital, it was acquired by the university and renamed The University of California, Davis Medical Center in 1973. The campus's Shriner's Hospital for Children, providing pediatric care in three specialty programs—orthopaedics, spinal cord injury treatment and rehabilitation, and acute burn treatment and rehabilitation—was built in 1997. The medical center is the region's only Level I comprehensive adult and pediatric trauma center. Specialty services include a trauma service that utilizes Life Flight; a Burn Center; a Transplant Center for kidney, pancreas, and liver transplants; a regional poison control center; a corneal transplant service; a regional mental health program; an extensive family practice program; a neonatal intensive care unit; a comprehensive rehabilitation center; and seven specialized intensive care units including a neurological surgery intensive care unit. The UC Davis Cancer Center was the 41st comprehensive cancer center in the United States designated as such by the National Cancer Institute. Research at the Cancer Center engaged some 225 scientists with $99 million in annual funding for 377 projects in 2013.

Sutter Medical Center, Sacramento, includes Sutter General Hospital, Sutter Memorial Hospital, and Sutter Center for Psychiatry. In 2003 Sutter Memorial Hospital and Sutter General Hospital became the first hospitals on the West Coast to begin utilizing electronic ICU with advanced video and electronic monitoring as a remote high-tech surveillance system of their most critically ill patients. Sutter Medical Center includes a total of 659 beds that admits nearly 31,000 patients annually.

Mercy General Hospital, operated by Dignity Health, offers care through the Mercy Heart and Vascular Institute, Neurological Institute, Cancer Institute, and family birth centers, and also offers treatment in the fields of orthopedics and women's health. Mercy has 286 beds and admits about 19,000 patients annually. Mercy also sponsors the Mercy Clinic Norwood primary health-care facility and Mercy Clinic Loaves and Fishes, a medical clinic for homeless residents in Sacramento. Methodist Hospital of Sacramento, also operated by Dignity Health, has 325 beds. Inpatient services include a birthing room, heart catheterization, end-of-life services, heart surgery, and a neonatal intensive care unit, among others. Bruceville Terrance is a long-term skilled nursing facility licensed to Methodist Hospital.

Kaiser Permanente's South Sacramento Medical Center has one of the largest labor and delivery services in the area. Along with standard services such as 24-hour emergency care, surgery, nuclear medicine, and cardiology, the hospital provides HIV/AIDS programs, home health, hospice, a nutrition service, pain management, and a sleep lab. South Sacramento Medical Center is a teaching hospital for UC Davis School of Medicine. The center underwent a $300 million expansion that finished in 2011.

The Veteran's Administrations maintains a 60-bed inpatient medical center in Sacramento.

■ Recreation

Sightseeing

Sacramento is a river town, virtually created by the California Gold Rush. Along the bank of the Sacramento River is the Old Sacramento Historic Area, a 28-acre National Historic Landmark that attracts more than five million visitors annually. This atmospheric area, with wooden-slat sidewalks and horse-drawn carriages on its cobblestone streets, gives the visitor a sense of the vitality and bustle generated by the thousands of hopeful prospectors who streamed through Sacramento in the mid-nineteenth century. Old Sacramento's museums, shops, and restaurants preserve its historical character. The Old Sacramento Waterfront offers a variety of activities, including touring and riding on nineteenth-century boats, visiting the depots of the Central Pacific railroad, and exploring the bustling Public Market.

In midtown Sacramento, Sutter's Fort, the first Euro-American settlement in Sacramento, has been restored and preserved. The 1839 adobe fort contains relics of pioneer and Gold Rush days. Exhibits include living quarters, a blacksmith shop, a bakery, a prison, and livestock areas. The State Capitol building within 40-acre Capitol Park was built in 1869; it is similar in style to the U.S. Capitol building. Underneath its 120-foot-high rotunda are ornate chandeliers, imposing staircases, and marble floors. Visitors can tour the offices of the governor, attorney general, secretary of state, and treasurer, and view exhibits about the history of California's state government. In Sacramento's south side, the Sacramento City Cemetery, established in 1849, contains the graves of more than 25,000 pioneers, immigrants, their families, and descendants; among its first interments were more than 600 victims of the 1850 cholera epidemic.

The Sacramento Zoo displays more than 400 exotic animals in their natural settings, including red pandas, snow leopards, lemurs, zebras, chimpanzees, jaguars, and many others. The zoo emphasizes protection of endangered animals, and faithful recreation of natural habitats. Adjacent to the zoo is Fairytale Town for children, a park based on themes from fairy tales and nursery rhymes. Waterworld California in Concord has a wave pool, sprayground, and the highest water slides in the West, including the Honolulu Halfpipe and the Cliffhanger.

Sacramento is within easy driving distance of other atmospheric Gold Country towns: Coloma has Marshall

Gold Discovery State Historic Park, where James Marshall's discovery of gold in 1848 started the Gold Rush; Placerville features Hangtown's Gold Bug Park and Mine, a fully-lighted mine shaft; Sutter Creek has a charming array of Victorian homes and balconied buildings; Jackson retains a European character from its early Italian- and Serbian-American miners; Columbia has Columbia State Historic Park, where visitors can ride a stagecoach and pan for gold. Sacramento is conveniently located for day trips to Northern California's outdoor attractions. The city is only a few hours away from Yosemite National Park; from the Napa-Sonoma Valley, where most of California's finest wines are produced; and from Lake Tahoe.

Arts and Culture

Sacramento is rich in theater. California's largest nonprofit musical theatre—the California Musical Theatre—is based here. It provides Music Circus productions during the summer and Broadway Series productions during the rest of the year. Since its first performance in 1951, Music Circus has staged numerous productions of some 150 musicals; classics such as *The King and I, Oklahoma!,* and *Show Boat* are well represented. Music Circus presented its music theatre under a circus-style open-air tent until its move in 2003 to the 2,200-seat Wells Fargo Pavilion. Performances are in the round, with 360-degree seating. California Musical Theatre's Broadway Series, begun in 1989, offers Broadway shows with national stars. Productions are at the 2,452-seat Sacramento Community Center Theater, across from the Capitol building.

The Sacramento Community Center Theater is also home to the Sacramento Ballet, Sacramento Opera, Sacramento Philharmonic, Sacramento Community Concerts, and the Sacramento Speakers Series. The Sacramento Opera has performed more than 40 operas; the opera season runs from September to March and includes about three performances. The Sacramento Philharmonic Orchestra generally presents five concerts annually from November through May. Special chamber orchestra concerts are also offered throughout the season. Both the Opera and Philharmonic are joined together as the Sacramento Region Performing Arts Alliance, referred to as Two in Tune. The Sacramento Ballet performs both classical and contemporary ballet. They present about five performance series annually. Also for music lovers, the all-volunteer (by audition) Camellia Symphony Orchestra season runs from October through mid-May and includes about four concerts (one of which, at the Sunrise Mall on Mother's Day, is free) and several special fundraising concerts.

The 24th Street Theatre, a 296-seat auditorium at the Sierra 2 Center for the Arts and Community, is home to Runway Stage Productions, which performs six Broadway-style productions during its season. The company also performs theatricals geared toward younger crowds. The Sacramento Theatre Company maintains its own resident company offering classical and modern plays at its 300-seat Mainstage and 85-seat Pollock Stage. The B Street Theatre produces contemporary theatrical works. Sutter Street Theatre, in the Historic Folsom District, offers an off-Broadway series and productions for younger audiences. In all, more than 80 groups present live theatrical performances throughout the region.

Sacramento is home to the oldest art museum in the West. Purchased by the Crocker family, the Crocker Art Museum's permanent collection features European paintings by such masters as Rembrandt and Bruegel; a renowned collection of drawings; Indian and Persian miniature paintings; American (especially Californian) paintings; decorative arts and ceramics; photography; and contemporary art. The California State Railroad Museum displays the history of the railroads and makes special note of the fact that Sacramento was once the terminus of the transcontinental railroad. The 100,000 square-foot main museum displays 21 locomotives and railroad cars, half of which may be walked through, as well as many other exhibits. On weekends between April and September, visitors can ride the Museum's Sacramento Southern Railroad on a six-mile route along the Sacramento River. The Discovery Museum Science and Space Center features interactive history, science, and technology exhibits examining the evolution of everyday life in Sacramento, on such topics as the gold rush and other periods of local California history, the history of the Sacramento Valley's topomorphology, and food processing technology. The California Automobile Museum explores car culture and automotive history, and has more than 150 vintage automobiles on display. The State Indian Museum on the grounds of Sutter's Fort displays the jewelry, art, clothing, baskets, and other artifacts of Native Americans who lived in the area.

Festivals and Holidays

Sacramento Music Festival, once focused exclusively on jazz, takes place during Memorial Day weekend; it now features blues, rock, jazz, and dance bands and attracts more than 100,000 listeners. The California Grape and Gourmet event in July features more than 700 wines, represented by 200 wineries. There are numerous Fourth of July events throughout the area. July is also the month that Sacramento hosts the California State Fair, one of the largest agricultural fairs in the country, at the California Exposition; the fair's features include a concert series, rides, horse racing, numerous competitions, extreme sports demonstrations, indoor and outdoor exhibits and shows, and a kids park. During the four-day Gold Rush Days festival over Labor Day weekend, the Gold Rush era is recreated in Old Sacramento, with historic characters, covered wagons and horse-drawn carriages, street dramas, musicians, dancers, arts and crafts, and exhibits; the streets of Old Sacramento are covered with dirt and only horse-drawn vehicles are permitted.

Sports for the Spectator

The Sacramento Kings of the National Basketball Association bring professional basketball to the city; they play at Sleep Train Arena. A proposal to build a new, downtown arena for the team was under consideration by the city in 2014. Efforts by suitors to buy and relocate the team from Sacramento to Seattle nearly succeeded in 2013 but eventually were rebuffed. The Sacramento Monarchs, a WNBA team, that dispersed at the end of 2009 after 13 seasons.

In 2000 professional minor league baseball returned to Sacramento after a 27-year absence when the Sacramento River Cats, formerly the Vancouver Canadians, moved to 11,092-seat Raley Field. The River Cats are a Triple-A affiliate of the Oakland Athletics. Professional tennis is represented by the Sacramento Capitals, who play as part of the Mylan World TeamTennis league, which features coed team competitions.

The Sacramento State Hornets and University of California, Davis Aggies fill the local college sports calendar.

Sports for the Participant

Sacramento, the "River City," provides many forms of water recreation. The American River offers boating, swimming, and calm- and white-water rafting. Nearby Folsom Lake and Lake Natoma offer sailing and windsurfing. All the waters in the Sacramento area are stocked with fish; king salmon run in the American and Sacramento Rivers. The American River Bike Trail, stretching from Sacramento's Discovery Park to Folsom Lake, provides nearly 35 miles of scenic trail used by cyclists, walkers, joggers, and bird watchers. More than 210 city parks and recreation areas dot Sacramento encompassing more than 2,000 acres, including sites for skate parks, dog parks, a rifle and pistol range, bocce ball, disc golf, playgrounds, and community gardens. There are five municipal golf courses and four county courses.

Sacramento is roughly two hours from five national forests. Sacramento has several equestrian centers and many horseback riding trails. More than two dozen ski resorts, most within 120 miles, are located in the nearby Sierra-Nevada Mountains. The California International Marathon in December starts in Folsom and ends at the Sacramento State Capitol building.

Shopping and Dining

Sacramento is home to several shopping malls and hundreds of boutiques and specialty shops. Old Sacramento is a popular and atmospheric shopping area; its Public Market is a European-style, open-air market featuring bakeries, fish, poultry, meat, produce, flowers, and assorted ethnic shops. Other major shopping areas in Sacramento include: Westfield Downtown Plaza, with more than 75 shops, many restaurants, and a cinema; Town and Country Village, with some 55 shops, was built in 1946, making it Sacramento's oldest shopping center; Arden Fair has more than 165 shops, restaurants, a cinema, and food court; Pavilions offers cosmopolitan shopping and fine dining; Sunrise Mall has about 100 shops and restaurants; and Folsom Premium Outlets has more than 80 stores.

Restaurants are plentiful in Sacramento, featuring cuisine ranging from traditional American, to inventive Californian, to a wide variety of ethnic fare. Many eateries are concentrated in Old Sacramento, as well as along J Street and Capitol Avenue between 19th and 29th streets, and Fair Oaks Boulevard between Howe and Fulton streets. A few local favorites include Aioli Bodega Espanola (Spanish), Ambrosia Café (Californian), Bangkok Garden (Thai), and La Bonne Soupe Café (French), which reopened under new ownership in 2011.

Visitor Information: Sacramento Convention and Visitors Bureau, 1608 I Street, Sacramento, CA 95814; telephone (800) 292-2334.

■ Convention Facilities

The principal meeting place is the Sacramento Convention Center Complex, located downtown. The complex contains three buildings: the 134,000-square-foot Exhibit Hall can be divided into five areas and is equipped with risers to create arena seating for 6,500 people; the elegant 24,000-square-foot Ballroom, which can be divided into 10 meeting rooms, accommodates 1,500 people banquet-style or 2,600 theater-style; and another building that features 12 meeting rooms. Nearby Memorial Auditorium, opened in 1927 and registered as a historic landmark, provides seating for a maximum of 3,800 people; the building contains Memorial Hall, the Little Theater, and meeting rooms. The 2,452-seat Sacramento Community Center Theater is located near Capitol Park.

Located five miles from downtown is the California Exposition (Cal Expo), a large facility with more than 200,000 square feet of exhibit space on a 780-acre site. Designed for events such as agricultural shows and trade conventions, the center provides outdoor exhibit areas and unlimited parking. Sleep Train Arena also hosts trade shows and business events on its 442,000-square-foot main floor.

Hotels and motels in the metropolitan area, providing more than 10,000 rooms, offer meeting facilities for large and small groups.

Convention Information: Sacramento Convention and Visitors Bureau, 1608 I Street, Sacramento, CA 95814; telephone (800) 292-2334.

■ Transportation

Approaching the City

The Sacramento International Airport, 12 miles northwest of downtown, receives service from 11 major carriers. The airport served 3.7 million passengers annually as of 2013. There are non-stop and direct flights to 38 cities. Also in Sacramento, the Executive Airport serves private and business planes.

The primary north–south routes to Sacramento are Interstate 5 (the Pan American Highway) and U.S. Highway 99; the major east–west routes are Interstate 80 and U.S. Highway 50, connecting Sacramento to San Francisco to the southwest, and Lake Tahoe to the northeast.

Passenger train service is available through Amtrak on three lines. Greyhound also has a route to the city, and boat or bus excursions are offered between Sacramento and San Francisco.

Traveling in the City

Most of Sacramento's downtown streets are one-way, with a synchronized traffic light system. The major thoroughfares are the freeways: Interstate 80 and Business 80, which run from the west to the northeast, and Interstate 5, which runs north and south. Other important roads are the Garden Highway, running east and west, and State Highway 99, coming from the southern part of the city to join Business 80. In downtown Sacramento, the streets running east and west are named by letter; streets running north and south are designated by number.

Sacramento Regional Transit District (RT) operates 67 area bus routes. The RT also owns the electrically powered light rail system, which consists of 38.6 miles of light rail, connecting the suburbs with downtown. The bus and rail systems are accessible to the disabled community. The system had a combined ridership of 26.4 million passengers in 2012.

■ Communications

Newspapers and Magazines

Sacramento offers one major daily newspaper, *The Sacramento Bee*. The "Sacbee," as it is sometimes called by locals, is one of the top newspapers in the state and has consistently had a circulation among the 50 largest of all U.S. newspapers. The newspaper celebrated its 155th anniversary in 2012. The *Sacramento News & Review*, a weekly alternative paper, is distributed for free throughout the city. The *Sacramento Gazette* is a small weekly paper that began publication in 1996. *The Sacramento Observer* is considered one of the finest African American newspapers in the country. *El Hispano* is a weekly Spanish and English publication for the Hispanic community.

Nearly 30 magazines and journals are published in Sacramento. The *Sacramento Business Journal* reports on happenings in business and industry. *Sacramento Magazine* highlights local entertainment and lifestyles. *Sacramento Parent* is a family-oriented magazine. *Catholic Herald*, for the Diocese of Sacramento, is published twice a month.

Television and Radio

Sacramento broadcasts 18 television stations, including major network affiliates as well as independent and other stations. Cable and satellite service is also available. Sacramento broadcasts 6 AM and 13 FM radio stations with music, news, talk, Spanish, and Christian programming; additional stations broadcasting from the surrounding area are also audible.

Media Information: The Sacramento Bee, 2100 Q Street, Sacramento, CA 95852; telephone (916) 321-1000.

Sacramento Online

City of Sacramento Home Page. Available portal. cityofsacramento.org

The Sacramento Bee. Available www.sacbee.com

Sacramento City Unified School District. Available www.scusd.edu

Sacramento Commerce and Trade Organization. Available sacto.org

Sacramento Convention & Visitors Bureau. Available www.discovergold.org

Sacramento Metro Chamber. Available metrochamber.org

Sacramento Public Library. Available www.saclibrary.org

BIBLIOGRAPHY

Burg, William, *Sacramento Renaissance: Art, Music, and Activism in California's Capital City* (Charleston, SC: The History Press, 2013)

Mathews, Joe, *California Crackup: How Reform Broke the Golden State and How We Can Fix It* (Berkeley: University of California Press, 2010)

San Diego

■ The City in Brief

Founded: 1769 (incorporated, 1850)

Head Official: Interim Mayor Todd Gloria (since 2013)

City Population
- 1990: 1,110,623
- 2000: 1,223,400
- 2010: 1,307,402
- 2012 estimate: 1,338,354
- Percent change, 2000–2010: 6.9%
- U.S. rank in 1990: 6th
- U.S. rank in 2000: 11th
- U.S. rank in 2010: 8th (State rank: 2nd)

Metropolitan Statistical Area Population
- 2000: 2,813,833
- 2010: 3,095,313
- 2012 estimate: 3,177,063
- Percent change, 2000–2010: 10%
- U.S. rank in 2000: 17th
- U.S. rank in 2010: 17th

Area: 324.3 square miles

Elevation: Ranges from sea level to 1,591 feet above sea level

Average Annual Temperatures: January, 57.8° F; July, 70.9° F; annual average, 64.4° F

Average Annual Precipitation: 10.77 inches of rain

Major Economic Sectors: military, manufacturing, government, trade, services, agriculture

Unemployment Rate: 5.9% (2012)

Per Capita Income: $31,950

2012 FBI Crime Index Property: 31,700

Major Colleges and Universities: University of California, San Diego, University of San Diego, San Diego State University

Daily Newspaper: *San Diego Union-Tribune*

■ Introduction

San Diego, a favorite among travelers, is a city of many strengths. Not only is it a top tourist attraction and resort area, but it also home to many naval centers and a critical natural harbor. San Diego is a prominent high-technology, aerospace, and aviation production community, and a fertile agricultural area. The port and its proximity to Mexico give the city an international flavor and an advantage over other cities in two-way trade capabilities. An ongoing downtown revitalization has added to the exciting atmosphere. The mild climate attracts many new residents and industries. A nondescript town until the 1940s, San Diego now has more than three million residents in its metropolitan area and is California's second largest city. San Diego's phenomenal growth has brought it well-deserved national attention. Still, the city has balanced growth with careful preservation of history and a strong emphasis on art, culture, and recreation.

■ Geography and Climate

San Diego is just 20 miles north of Mexico, situated in the rolling hills and mesas that rise from the Pacific shore to join with the Laguna Mountains to the east. Its bay is one of the country's finest natural harbors. The city covers a large area of vastly different terrain: miles of ocean and bay shoreline, densely forested hills, fertile valleys, and mountains, canyons, and desert. The climate varies in a similar manner. On the coast, the temperatures are mild and constant, while in the desert areas, the temperature can fluctuate as much as 30 degrees in one day. San Diego is about 120 miles south of Los Angeles.

iofoto/Shutterstock.com

The climate in San Diego is tempered by the Pacific Ocean air, keeping the summers cool and the winters warm. Severe weather is rare in the area; snow is almost unknown, and the city averages only three thunderstorms a year. September and October often bring hot eastern winds from the desert, producing what are usually the hottest days of the year.

Area: 324.3 square miles

Elevation: Ranges from sea level to 1,591 feet above sea level

Average Temperatures: January, 57.8° F; July, 70.9° F; annual average, 64.4° F

Average Annual Precipitation: 10.77 inches of rain

■ History

Spanish, Mexicans, Americans Lay Claim to San Diego Region

Portuguese explorer Juan Rodriguez Cabrillo, the discoverer of California, sailed into what is now San Diego Bay and claimed the surrounding region for the King of Spain in 1542. The bay was named in 1602 by another Spanish explorer, Don Sebastian Viscaino. The first European settlement there was established in 1769, when the Franciscan fathers established a mission on a hill overlooking the bay, close to a large Native American village. The mission was the first in a chain of twenty-one that the sect built throughout California. The mission was burned down by the local tribes and later almost completely destroyed by an earthquake, but the determined Franciscans rebuilt each time. Today, the restored mission still conducts Mass every Sunday.

By the 1830s, a small but thriving trading village had developed on the bay, in the district now called "Old Town." The town was an important shipping point for cattle hide and quarried stone. The famous cobblestone streets of Boston are said to have been paved with San Diego stone. San Diego became the capital of Mexican California after Mexico achieved independence from Spain in 1822. It was a much fought-over prize during the Mexican War, changing hands numerous times before the U.S. Army established permanent American rule in late 1846. The town was incorporated as a city in 1850.

City Thrives, Declines, Thrives Again

Throughout the next twenty years the town was an important whaling port. Then in 1867, San Francisco land-developer Alonzo E. Horton bought a 1,000-acre plot of what was to become downtown San Diego. Horton laid out streets, built a wharf and a hotel, and donated land for churches. A gold strike in 1870 and numerous land booms in the area increased the population rapidly. In 1885, when the Santa Fe Railroad and a number of eastern investors arrived, 40,000 people lived in the city.

By the turn of the century, however, San Diego was plunged into a slump. Failed businesses and unwise real estate speculations caused the population to dwindle to 17,000 people. The city began a period of slow, steady growth, helped by the Panama-California Exposition in celebration of the completion of the Panama Canal in 1915. The fledgling aircraft industry, which found the desert climate and terrain an ideal testing environment, also aided San Diego's recovery. An aggressive policy of attracting new people and industry contributed to growth, but the city remained relatively obscure, over-shadowed by Los Angeles and San Francisco to the north.

City Becomes Naval Base; Rise of Agriculture and Industry

Japan's bombing of Honolulu's Pearl Harbor at the beginning of World War II forced the U.S. Navy to seek another suitable Pacific base. They chose San Diego, and almost overnight the city became a busy military center, home base for a large number of naval trainees, many of whom relocated to the city as civilians after the war. In the post-war era the city emerged as the headquarters of the Eleventh Naval District and the Naval Air Command; installations included major U.S. Navy and Marine training centers, the West Coast's main supply depot, a naval hospital and laboratories, and a large fleet stationed in the bay. Along with the military came related support industries and a large number of naval and aviation defense contractors.

Growth begun during World War II has continued unabated. San Diego spread to extend almost 20 miles in each direction, developing small, distinct communities in the nearby canyons and valleys; these areas retain a separate identity while being incorporated into San Diego. With this growth came diversity. To the south, San Diego connects with a rich agricultural area that produces much of California's famous fruit and vegetable produce, shipped worldwide from the easily accessible port. To the north the wealthy leisure class developed a resort community of hotels, spectacular cliff homes, and recreational amenities. Throughout the city commercial and industrial corridors began growing, and many corporations moved their headquarters to the region.

Downtown Declines, Revives

During the 1960s and early 1970s the San Diego downtown area declined when businesses and residents moved to the suburbs in large numbers. The city's growth continued despite these problems, and by the mid-1970s San Diego had surpassed San Francisco as California's second largest city. An efficient freeway system and a coordinated effort by the Centre City Development Corporation—a comprehensive group of developers, financial experts, and civic leaders—kept the downtown area alive.

Today, downtown San Diego is revitalized with new energy and is experiencing a renaissance as growth continues through ventures such as the North Embarcadero Visionary Plan, which seeks to redevelop 12 acres of waterfront area into attractive parks and open spaces. Thoughtful planning has produced an impressive skyline of mirrored office towers blended with innovative shopping and residential developments, parks, and historic districts, all designed to serve the people who use them.

Historical Information: San Diego History Center, 1649 El Prado, Ste 3, San Diego, CA 92101; telephone (619) 232-6203.

■ Population Profile

Metropolitan Statistical Area Population

2000: 2,813,833
2010: 3,095,313
2012 estimate: 3,177,063
Percent change, 2000–2010: 10%
U.S. rank in 2000: 17th
U.S. rank in 2010: 17th

City Residents

1990: 1,110,623
2000: 1,223,400
2010: 1,307,402
2012 estimate: 1,338,354
Percent change, 2000–2010: 6.9%
U.S. rank in 1990: 6th
U.S. rank in 2000: 11th
U.S. rank in 2010: 8th (State rank: 2nd)

Density: 4,020.4 people per square mile

Racial and ethnic characteristics

White: 852,307
Black or African American: 87,569
American Indian and Alaskan Native: 11,130
Asian: 230,434
Native Hawaiian and Other Pacific Islander: 5,814
Hispanic or Latino (may be of any race): 408,788
Other: 151,100

Percent of residents born in state: 45.9%

Age characteristics

Population under 5 years old: 83,310
Population 5 to 9 years old: 72,977
Population 10 to 14 years old: 73,083
Population 15 to 19 years old: 93,466
Population 20 to 24 years old: 128,619
Population 25 to 34 years old: 237,054
Population 35 to 44 years old: 184,189
Population 45 to 54 years old: 171,933
Population 55 to 59 years old: 81,869
Population 60 to 64 years old: 60,496
Population 65 to 74 years old: 82,647
Population 75 to 84 years old: 46,495
Population 85 years and over: 22,216
Median age: 33.9

Births (2010–11 Metropolitan Area)

Total number: 44,076

Deaths (2010–11 Metropolitan Area)

Total number: 19,373

Money income (2012)

Per capita income: $31,950
Median household income: $63,034
Total households: 469,700

Number of households with income of . . .

less than $10,000: 29,227
$10,000 to $14,999: 23,536
$15,000 to $24,999: 42,132
$25,000 to $34,999: 38,963
$35,000 to $49,999: 56,275
$50,000 to $74,999: 79,051
$75,000 to $99,999: 61,851
$100,000 to $149,999: 71,708
$150,000 to $199,999: 34,384
$200,000 or more: 32,573

Percent of families below poverty level: 16.1%

FBI Crime Index Property: 31,700

FBI Crime Index Violent: 5,529

■ Municipal Government

San Diego used a city-manager form of government until the city transitioned to a strong-mayor form of government on a trial basis in 2006; the change was made permanent through passage of Proposition D in 2010. The system calls for the mayor to be the primary executive with the most power; eight council members serve as the legislative branch. Like the mayor, they are elected every four years.

Bob Filner, elected in 2012, resigned in 2013 following a sexual harrassment scandal. An election in November 2013 to replace him required a secondary runoff election in February 2014.

Head Official: Interim Mayor Todd Gloria (since 2013)

Total Number of City Employees: 10,026 (2013)

City Information: City Hall, 202 C Street, San Diego, CA 92101; telephone (619) 236-5555.

■ Economy

Major Industries and Commercial Activity

San Diego's economy, once dominated by military and defense endeavors, has since broadened to other areas. Still, San Diego region has the largest military concentration in the nation, and military employment accounts for one of every four jobs in the city, or about 311,000 regional jobs. The Eleventh Naval District Headquarters, the base for the U.S. Navy Pacific fleet, is located in San Diego, as are Marine Corps Base Camp Joseph H. Pendleton, Marine Corps Recruit Depot, Marine Corps Air Station at Miramar, Naval Air Station North Island, Naval Station San Diego, and Naval Submarine Base Point Loma.

Defense-related spending contributes $20.6 billion to the regional economy, and the large military presence has attracted major companies that depend on the defense industry such as BAE Systems, Lockheed Martin, and Raytheon. Research and development of unmanned aerial vehicles is the largest single component of San Diego's military-dependent companies, representing some 12 percent of all defense contracts awarded to area businesses.

Manufacturing is an important component of the San Diego economy, particularly in the areas of shipbuilding and repair. Maritime industries employ some 46,000 residents and contribute $14 billion to the economy. As of 2013, industry growth projected an additional 6,000 jobs by 2020. Major maritime companies included Cubic Corporation, General Atomics, NASSCO/General Dynamics, Orca Maritime, Poseidon Resources, Sea Con, SeaBotix, and Seacoast Science.

Since the founding of San Diego, the city's economy has been tied to San Diego Bay, a natural harbor that is one of California's five major ports. It is an important link in the nation's international shipping trade; the port's two marine cargo facilities are the National City Marine Terminal, which is a primary port of entry for several vehicle manufacturers, and Tenth Avenue Marine Terminal, which handles a wide variety of commodities. The port also has robust cruise ship operations. Land trade is important as well: The border between the San Diego area and Tijuana is the busiest in the world.

With the San Diego Zoo and Sea World, a variety of historical and cultural attractions, and year-round good weather, San Diego is a top destination for tourists. *Travel and Leisure* magazine has ranked it America's second favorite city (behind Honolulu). San Diego's tourism industry is the third largest segment of its economy, employing 160,000 residents. San Diego attracted 31 million visitors in 2011, who spent a total of $7.5 billion. Events at the San Diego Convention Center generated nearly $600 million in direct spending.

San Diego has become a center for high technology and biotechnology. High-technology growth areas include the biomedical, software, telecommunications and security sectors. Software firms have an estimated $9.8 billion annual economic impact on the local economy. Quick growth in the wireless and telecommunications sectors has earned San Diego the nickname "Telecom Valley." An estimated 60 percent of venture capital invested in the region targets biomedical industries; traditional health-care services employ one of every 10 San Diego residents.

San Diego has the state's highest concentration of clean technology businesses, with more than 850 companies calling the area home in 2013. Industry growth between 1995 and 2010 registered 73 percent. Clean technology products ranged from algae biofuels to smart-grid development. Major companies were Enel Green Power, Iberdrola Renewables, Soitec, Kyocera Solar, Sapphire Energy, and Synthetic Genomics. San Diego generates some 37 megawatts of solar energy.

San Diego County is also a top producer of nursery products, flowers, foliage plants, and avocados.

Items and goods produced: airplane parts, biofuels, dairy products, electronics, flowers, plastics, rubber products, beverages, paper, clothing, computers, biofuels, telecommunications equimpment

Incentive Programs—New and Existing Companies

Local programs: The city of San Diego offers permit and regulatory assistance, problem solving, regulatory reform, and project troubleshooting for large companies interested in expanding in the San Diego area. San Diego claims the lowest business license fees among the nine largest cities in California and also charges no utility users' taxes. The city's Business Cooperation Program offers a tax rebate of up to 50 percent of the local 1 percent sales or use tax. A Guaranteed Water for Industry Program exempts industrial and research firms from mandatory water conservation measures in the event of a drought and also supplies discounted monthly rates for reclaimed water usage and one-time cost savings on water capacity

charges. The Cleantech Initiative, launched by the city in 2007, promotes expansion, attraction, and retention of businesses that develop environmentally sustainable products. San Diego has multiple business improvement districts, redevelopment project areas, one enterprise zone, a foreign trade zone, recycling market development zones, and a renewal community.

State programs: California business incentives include the state's Alternative Energy and Advanced Transportation Authority Sales and Use Tax Exemptions for Zero Emission Vehicle Manufacturing. Initially targeting vehicle manufacturing only when it was passed in 2010, the sales and use tax exemption has since been expanded to all renewable energy technologies. In 2012 it was expanded again to include advanced manufacturing. More than one dozen additional incentives encourage green development or pollution-reducing business decisions.

Research and development tax credits offers companies a 15 percent credit against their bank and corporation tax liability for qualifying in-house research expenses; a 24 percent tax credit for basic research payments to outside organizations is also available. Industrial development bonds finance investment in land, buildings, and new equipment related to domestic manufacturing operations in the state. California Capital Access Program and Collateral Support Program also offer alternative methods of financing for businesses. Enterprise Zones and Local Agency Military Base Recovery Area regions provide incentives for development in targeted geographic regions. A New Jobs Tax Credit offers $3,000 per hire of qualifying new employees, and the state's Film and Television Tax Credit Program supports productions with a 20 percent tax credit against qualified expenses.

In 2011 California began offering companies the option to calculate their corporate income tax through the single sales factor method, rather than the existing triple apportionment derived from calculations of a company's payroll, property, and sales.

California's Innovation Hub Program, with 12 locations throughout the state, supports the commercialization of innovation and technology businesses through public-private partnerships, knowledge sharing, venture capital sources, and business incubators. The state also undertakes trade missions to form partnerships for trade and export promotion.

Job training programs: The state of California offers an Employment Training Panel to assist companies with post-hire training and reimbursement. The Employment Development Department also partners with Local Workforce Investment Areas to recruit, screen, test, evaluate, and hire qualified workers.

The city of San Diego works closely with the San Diego Workforce Partnership, a nonprofit community corporation that supports the region's workforce and employers through education, training, and employment services.

Development Projects

In 2002, a $312.3 million program to build or improve 24 San Diego libraries was approved. Since then, several new branches were built, including a new central library, which opened to the public in 2013 at a cost of $185 million. The nine-story facilities covered almost 500,000 square feet and included a career center, cafe, and outdoor garden. A charter high school, e3 Civic High, occupied two floors of the building.

The San Ysidro Port of Entry that connects San Diego and Tijuana, the busiest border crossing in the world, was under consideration for $226 billion in federal funding to complete the second and third phases of a crossing overhaul. Mexico completed improvements on its side of the border in 2012. A study by the San Diego Association of Governments concluded that border delays cost the economy of Southern California some $7 billion annually. Plans for the overhaul had been under discussion since 2009, with Southern California lawmakers pushing for the U.S. Congress to appropriate funding.

Redevelopment of Horton Plaza was expected to take place during 2014–15. The plaza, which formerly served as a central meeting and event area for the city, had been filled mainly with vacant storefronts. With the vision of replicating Union Square in San Francisco or Bryant Park in New York City, planners anticipated a mixture of demolishing and restoring area buildings and monuments.

The North Embarcadero Visionary Plan was a redevelopment of 12 acres of waterfront area in San Diego—sometimes referred to locally as the city's "front porch"—to create park and open space along the downtown coastline. First conceived in 1997, Phase I of redevelopment was underway in 2014. The project was estimated to cost $228 million and add seven acres of gardens and 1,700 trees to the area.

Private developments in downtown San Diego included plans for a new corporate headquarters for Sempra, expected to complete in 2015 and add a 16-story, 320,000-square-foot building to the city skyline. Ballpark Village, a $250 million mixed-use facility located near the Petco Park, home of the San Diego Padres, received city approval in 2013 and was scheduled to finish construction in 2017. Also receiving city approval that year was Blue Sky, slated to become downtown San Diego's largest apartment complex with 939 units and two 21-to-25-story towers. The apartments were scheduled to be ready by 2015, with total construction costs estimated at $300 million.

Economic Development Information: City of San Diego Economic Development Division, 1200 Third Avenue, 14th Floor, San Diego, CA 92101; telephone (619) 236-6700.

Commercial Shipping

The Port of San Diego handles hundreds of merchant ships each year and some three million tons of cargo annually. The National City Marine Terminal handles vehicle imports for some 15 motor companies as well as exports for Chrysler, Ford, and General Motors. The port maintains a 140-acre terminal capable of handling 500,000 vehicles annually. Nearby Tijuana, Mexico, is also a duty-free port. The Burlington Northern Santa Fe (BNSF) railroad connects San Diego to major market areas. More than 80 trucking companies are established in metropolitan San Diego, providing freight, hauling, or equipment services. Air cargo services are maintained at San Diego International Airport, which handled 155,715 tons of cargo in 2012.

Labor Force and Employment Outlook

A large portion of the San Diego work force is derived from in-migration, creating a diverse population. The workforce is also young, since the median age of San Diego's population is 33.9. More than 42 percent of the city's workforce over age 25 has at least a bachelor's degree. The plethora of higher education and research institutions in and around San Diego are a major reason for the city's well-educated workforce and also support economic development in high-technology fields such as green energy and bioscience. Many of the military personnel stationed in San Diego stay in the area after leaving the military, adding to the workforce; their spouses also provide an influx of labor.

The following is a summary of data regarding the 2012 San Diego labor force:

Size of civilian labor force: 692,183

Number of workers employed in . . .

agriculture and mining: 2,367
construction: 25,178
manufacturing: 57,074
wholesale trade: 12,932
retail trade: 64,754
transportation: 21,578
information systems: 15,354
finance: 43,814
professional administration: 99,159
education and social services: 139,268
arts and leisure: 73,043
other: 32,821
public administration: 35,814

Average hourly earnings of production workers: $17.04

Unemployment rate: 5.9% (2012)

Employers

Largest employers (2013)	*Number of employees*
United States Navy	30,664
University of California, San Diego	28,071
Sharp Healthcare	15,906
County of San Diego	15,727
San Diego Unified School District	13,552
Qualcomm, Inc.	13,524
City of San Diego	10,026
Kaiser Permanente	8,800
University of California, San Diego Medical Center	6,235
San Diego Gas & Electric Compnay	4,753

Cost of Living

The cost of living in the San Diego-Carlsbad-San Marcos metropolitan area is about 32 percent higher than the national average. In 2013 the average cost of a home was $593,643; home prices are the primary driver of the high cost of living in San Diego.

The following is a summary of data regarding several key cost of living factors in the area.

2013 ACCRA Average House Price: $593,643

2013 ACCRA Cost of Living Index: 131

State income tax rate: 1.00% to 13.3%

State sales tax rate: 7.5%

Local income tax rate: None

Local sales tax rate: 0.5%

Property tax rate: Limited to 1% of assessed value by state law. In some cases the local taxing body can add additional taxes.

Economic Information: San Diego Regional Chamber of Commerce, 402 West Broadway, Suite 1000, San Diego, CA 92101; telephone (619) 544-1300.

■ Education and Research

Elementary and Secondary Schools

The San Diego Unified School District is the second largest school district in the state and one of the largest urban school districts in the country. There are nearly 132,000 students enrolled in the district. Its nonpartisan five-member board is elected every four years, and the superintendent is hired by the board. The student body is comprised of more than 15 ethnic groups speaking more than 60 languages. About 47 percent of all students are Hispanic, with 23 percent white and 10 percent African American. Filipino, Indo-Chinese, and other Asian students each comprise at least 3 percent of the student body. Ocean Air Elementary School was named a National Blue Ribbon School by the U.S. Department of Education in 2013. The district operates 49 charter schools.

The San Diego area is also served by a number of parochial and private schools.

The following is a summary of data regarding the San Diego Unified School District.

Total enrollment: 131,785

Number of facilities

total: 226
elementary schools: 117
junior high schools: 25
high schools: 24
other: 60

Student/teacher ratio: 22.58:1

Teacher salaries

average (statewide): $69,434

Funding per pupil: $9,505

Public Schools Information: San Diego Unified School District, Eugene Brucker Education Center, 4100 Normal Street, San Diego, CA 92103; telephone (619) 725-8000.

Colleges and Universities

Major universities in San Diego include the University of California, San Diego (UCSD), San Diego State University (SDSU), and the University of San Diego (USD), which is a Catholic university. UCSD, one of the University of California's 10 campuses, is regarded as a top institution for higher education and was rated 39th among national universities by *U.S. News & World Report* in 2013. Campus undergraduate enrollment is nearly 23,000. UCSD has six undergraduate colleges, all on one campus, with each maintaining its own set of requirements while sharing departmental majors: Thurgood Marshall College, John Muir College, Revelle College, Roosevelt College, Sixth College, and Warren College. UCSD's graduate and professional schools include: the acclaimed Scripps Institution of Oceanography, one of the oldest and largest centers for marine science research and graduate training in the world; School of Medicine, School of International Relations and Pacific Studies, Skaggs School of Pharmacy and Pharmaceutical Sciences, Jacobs School of Engineering (graduate and undergraduate), and Rady School of Management.

SDSU, the oldest and largest university in San Diego and third largest in California, had a total enrollment of about 32,000 students in 2013. SDSU offers bachelor's undergraduate majors and minors in nearly 160 fields, 16 preprofessional programs, and almost100 graduate degrees and credentials. In 1970 the university founded the first women's studies program in the country.

USD, a private, Roman Catholic university, has an enrollment of more than 7,500; the university offers more than 60 bachelor's, master's and doctoral degrees, and is particularly noted for its law and nursing schools.

Libraries and Research Centers

San Diego is served by two major library systems, the city and county. The San Diego Public Library operates 35 branches in addition to the central library. In 2002 the mayor and city council approved a $312.3 million program to build or improve 24 libraries. Since then several new branches have been built, including the $185 million new Central Library, which opened in 2013. The library's collection includes more than 3.8 million books, 3,313 periodical subscriptions, 1.6 million government documents, and more than one-quarter books in 25 languages other than English. READ/San Diego is the library's adult literacy program.

The San Diego County Library system consists of 33 branches, 2 bookmobiles, and a virtual branch. The collection is made up of more than 33 million books, films, and music materials. In 2010-11, 5.8 million people visited the library, checking out 12.4 million materials. Special collections include audio and video-tapes, films, art reproductions, extensive Filipino, Spanish, and Vietnamese collections, and special services for the deaf, including closed-captioned video tapes and talking books. A new branch at Lincoln Acres opened in 2013. More than 30 other public, private, and research libraries serve the metropolitan area.

A large number of specialized research centers functioning in such subject areas as oceanography, nuclear energy, astronomy, and biological sciences are scattered throughout San Diego. Among the most prominent research centers are the Salk Institute for Biological Studies, which focuses on molecular biology, genetics, neuroscience, and plant biology; and the Palomar Observatory, a center for astronomy research, located atop San Diego County's Mount Palomar.

Public Library Information: San Diego Public Library, 330 Park Blvd., San Diego, CA 92101; telephone (619) 236-5800.

■ Health Care

The San Diego county medical community includes many accredited hospitals, with a total of more than 6,600 beds. The largest networks are Scripps Health and Sharp Healthcare, which maintain hospitals and walk-in clinics throughout the county.

Scripps Health comprises of four acute care hospitals including Scripps Mercy Hospital, which is the city's longest-running hospital with 700 licensed beds, more than 3,000 employees and 1,300 physicians. Scripps is one of the largest hospitals in California. Scripps Mercy Hospital was rated as high-performing in 12 adult specialties by *U.S. News & World Report* in 2013. In 2010 Scripps Health announced a 25-year, $2 billion expansion plan to renovate most of its facilities.

Sharp Healthcare consists of four full-service hospitals and four specialty hospitals. Its largest hospital is Sharp Memorial, the designated trauma center for San Diego. Sharp Memorial's best-known programs include cardiac and vascular care, cancer treatment, pulmonary care services, rehabilitation, and multi-organ transplantation. The Stephen Birch Healthcare Center opened at Sharp Memorial in 2009.

San Diego's research and specialty institutions include the Salk Institute of Biology—established by Jonas Salk, developer of the polio vaccine—which conducts research in such areas as genetics and neuroscience; the 330-bed Rady Children's Hospital, which was ranked nationally in 10 specialties by *U.S. News & World Report* in 2013; the Naval Medical Center, which provides care to officers, personnel, and their dependents and is among the largest and most technologically advanced military health-care centers in the world; and the Scripps Research Institute, internationally recognized for its research in immunology, molecular, and cell biology.

■ Recreation

Sightseeing

San Diego and its surrounding communities offer a wide range of tourist attractions for every taste, from amusement parks to historic buildings and scenic wilderness.

The center of San Diego preserves two separate historic districts representing two different periods. Old Town evokes San Diego's Spanish and Mexican heritage. Many of its nineteenth-century adobe buildings have been restored and filled with museums, shops, and restaurants. Old Town was preceded, in 1769, by the Spanish establishment of California's first mission and military fortress, on nearby Presidio Hill. Gaslamp Quarter is a 16-block restored Victorian district downtown, featuring antiques, arts and crafts, offices, shops, and restaurants. Walking tours of the district depart from William Heath Davis House, one of the area's first residences, on Saturdays.

Several of the original missions in the area, including California's first—Mission Basilica San Diego de Alcalá, which moved from Presidio Hill to its present site in 1774—still hold Mass and are open to the public for tours. San Diego Bay harbors the *Star of India*, a 100-year-old sailing vessel, and several U.S. Navy ships that are open to the public. At Point Loma the Cabrillo National Monument commemorates the spot where California was discovered and includes a restored lighthouse, a whale overlook, and a visitor's center.

The nearby 600,000-acre Anza-Borrego Desert State Park, east of San Diego, is a unique collection of geological formations, plants, and animals that has been described by *Flower and Garden* magazine as "a perfect first desert encounter." The Cleveland National Forest north of the city, and other local cliffs, mesas, and canyons offer an abundance of natural scenic features on 460,000 acres, as do the many flower plantations in the hills outside of San Diego. Tijuana, Mexico, the most visited border town in the world, is an exciting and exotic adventure for shoppers, sightseers, and sports enthusiasts. The Mexican border is a 20 minute ride away, accessed by restored trackless trolleys that depart from the renovated Santa Fe Depot in downtown San Diego.

Animals play a major role in San Diego's tourist trade. The world-famous San Diego Zoo, 100 acres of lush, tropical landscape filled with more than 3,700 animals representing some 650 species and subspecies, contains some of the rarest species in captivity. Moving sidewalks, an aerial tramway, and open-air buses run through the exhibits. Highlights include giant pandas, Australian koalas, rare Chinese golden monkeys, a large reptile collection, and a beautiful free-flight walk-through aviary. Habitats have been crafted to replicate desert, tropical rain forest, savanna, scrubland, island, tundra, ocean and coastline, prairie and steppe, temperate forest and taiga, river, lake, and wetland ecosystems as closely as possible. Among the habitat zones are Panda Canyon, Urban Jungle, and the Elephant Odyssey. The Asian Passage features lion-tailed macaque and sun bears, while the Lost Forest is home to orangutans, siamangs, bonobos, tigers, and other exotic animals.

The San Diego Zoo Safari Park, formerly known as the Wild Animal Park, is an 1,800-acre preserve operated by the San Diego Zoo. Designed to protect endangered species, the park features more than 3,500 animals living in natural habitats modeled after African, Asian, and Australian terrain. The park is known for its successful breeding of such species as the southern white rhino and Arabian oryx. Visitors can walk the park or use the monorail system that traverses through the heart of the park. During summer months, the rail system also operates after dark, and lamps light the active animal areas. Nairobi Village provides special exhibits, refreshments, and other services.

Sea World San Diego, home of Shamu the killer whale (the original Shamu died long ago, but his successors bear his name), is a 150-acre marine park, located along Mission Bay, that offers a number of marine exhibits, live shows, aquariums, the world's largest shark exhibit, playgrounds, and rides. Sea World's Wild Arctic area is a massive, multimillion-dollar project combining motion simulation theater technology, live marine mammal viewing, and interactive educational exhibits. At Shark Encounter, visitors come face to face with sharks by walking through a 57-foot tube that passes through a 280,000-gallon habitat. Shipwreck Rapids transforms visitors into island castaways who journey on raft like inner tubes trying to find their way back to civilization.

LEGOLAND California, located in Carlsbad, stimulates creativity and imagination through hands-on recreation. Play areas feature attractions, rides, building opportunities, and more than 1,000 LEGO models. The Chima Water Park features a 45-foot tall tower, a lazy river that allows kids to make their own LEGO rafts, and tube slides among its many activity areas. The Water Park won the World Waterpark Association's Industry Innovation Award in 2011.

Arts and Culture

San Diego's citizens and business community are very supportive of the arts. Drama, music, and the visual arts are important elements of the city's personality. Theater, in all its varieties, is available year-round. Musical offerings range from formal affairs, symphonies, and operas, to oceanside picnic concerts under the stars and arena-sized rock concerts. More than 90 area museums as well as a number of small art galleries cater to the historic- and artistic-minded.

A large theater community is rising to national prominence in San Diego, and the area's proximity to Hollywood attracts many stars to the more than 40 innovative local theater companies. The centerpiece of San Diego culture is the Old Globe theatre complex. It consists of the Lowell Davies Festival Theatre, a large outdoor arena; Sheryl and Harvey White Theatre, a 225-seat theater-in-the-round; and the Tony Award–winning 580-seat Old Globe Theatre, a reproduction of Shakespeare's Globe Theater. The theatre complex stages classic and contemporary works throughout the year, with an emphasis on Shakespeare during the summer.

Numerous other theater groups are located in the area, including the La Jolla Playhouse at University of San Diego at La Jolla, which stages plays and musicals from April through December at the university's 492-seat Mandell Weiss Theatre and 400-seat Mandell Weiss Forum; the San Diego Repertory Theatre, which produces progressive, culturally diverse plays at the Lyceum Space Theatre and Gallery at the Lyceum; and the Lamb's Players Theater, which stages musicals, dramas, comedies, and adventurous world premieres, primarily at the company's 350-seat Resident Theatre in Coronado and the 250-seat Horton Grand Theatre. San Diego has a thriving dinner-theater population as well.

Music and dance are also well-represented in San Diego. The San Diego Symphony performs classical masterworks, interactive performances, outdoor summer pops, family festivals, and community concerts. The La Jolla Music Society presents visiting orchestras, soloists, and ensembles. The Orchestra Nova San Diego presented its classical repertoire and Nova Classics Concerts Series at venues across San Diego County until its bankruptcy in 2012. The acclaimed San Diego Opera attracts star international performers; its grand productions at the San Diego Civic Theatre run from January through May. The California Ballet provides year-round contemporary and classical professional ballet, while historical and cultural dance exhibitions are offered by organizations such as the Samahan Philippine Dance Company, the PASACAT Philippine Performing Arts Company, and Teye Sa Thiosanne, an African drum and dance company.

Balboa Park is the nation's largest urban cultural park. Covering 1,200 acres, it is home to the San Diego Zoo, most of San Diego's museums, performing arts venues, and restaurants, as well as cultivated and wild gardens and a number of historic buildings and exhibits. In all, more than 85 cultural and recreational organizations are located here. The park was originally the site of the Panama-California International Exhibition in 1915 and 1916 (which celebrated the opening of the Panama Canal), and most of the buildings are restored exhibit halls from that period, serving as examples of Spanish Revival architecture.

There are 15 museums located in Balboa Park. Among them is the San Diego Museum of Art, established in 1922; it is the oldest and largest art museum in the region. Highlights of the museum's permanent collections include its Spanish baroque, Renaissance, and contemporary California paintings; Indian miniatures; South Asian art; and numerous works by Toulouse-Lautrec. Traditional and modern sculpture is exhibited in an outdoor garden.

The Mingei International Museum emphasizes traditional and modern folkart, craft, and design from outside the United States and Europe. The Museum of Photographic Arts, devoted to collecting, conserving and exhibiting still photography and film, has a permanent collection of more than 7,000 works, as well as a state-of-the-art 226-seat movie theater and a 20,000-volume library. The San Diego Natural History Museum features exhibits on local plants, animals, and geological specimens. The San Diego Air & Space Museum features aeronautical exhibits, from the dawn of flight through the space age. The Reuben H. Fleet Science Center houses more than 100 scientific hands-on exhibits, the nation's first Omnimax theater, a virtual reality attraction, and a motion simulation ride. The San Diego Museum of Man, devoted to anthropology, is comprised of a group of buildings documenting the history of mankind, Indians of the three Americas, and human birth, plus various temporary exhibits. The San Diego Model Railroad Museum is the world's largest operating model railroad museum, at 28,000 square feet; highlights include four massive scale model layouts and a toy train gallery. The

San Diego Hall of Champions Sports Museum is the largest multi-sport museum in the country at nearly 70,000 square feet.

The Museum of Contemporary Art San Diego (MCASD), with downtown San Diego and La Jolla locations, presents more than 3,000 artworks, created after 1950, in its permanent collection; across the street from the San Diego location, the historic 1915 Santa Fe Depot baggage building was remodeled to become part of MCASD and opened in 2006.

Other attractions in the park include the House of Pacific Relations, a cluster of cottages representing 32 nationalities, and the Spreckels Organ Pavilion, containing the largest outdoor organ in the nation, played on Sundays by a civic organist. The Spanish Village Art Center presents artists and craftspeople at work in buildings resembling a charming town square in Spain, and the San Diego Art Institute features prominent local artists.

The Junípero Serra Museum is located on the site where Father Junípero Serra and Captain Gaspar de Portola established California's first mission and military fortress, in Presidio Park overlooking Old Town. It displays exhibits covering the history of the San Diego area from 1562 to the present. The Maritime Museum of San Diego, located on the waterfront, is comprised of three historic ships—the 1863 tall ship *Star of India,* the 1898 ferry *Berkeley,* and the 1904 steam yacht *Medea*—as well as numerous nautical exhibits.

Festivals and Holidays

San Diego's events calendar begins with the New Year's Day Race, a yacht regatta in San Diego Bay. In March, the San Diego Latino Film Festival, spanning 10 days, is the largest Latino film festival in the country. ArtWalk is a two-day April event showcasing visual and performing fine arts exhibits in San Diego's Little Italy neighborhood. May events include the Fiesta Old Town Cinco de Mayo celebration, which brings historical reenacts, folkloric music and dance, and Mexican food and fun; Gator by the Bay two-day Cajun zydeco, blues and crawfish festival; and the Ethnic Food Fair, featuring food from more than 25 nations.

A gala celebration on the Fourth of July features special events throughout the region, including several parades, outdoor concerts, a hot-air balloon race, and fireworks. Another July event, held at Imperial Beach, is the U.S. Open Sandcastle Competition, the world's longest-running and largest sand castle competition. America's Finest City Week is celebrated city-wide in August and features a large variety of events including concerts, sports events, carnivals, and more. In late September, the city celebrates the Cabrillo Festival to commemorate the discovery of California by Spanish explorer Juan Rodríguez Cabrillo.

The San Diego Film Festival in early October celebrates American and international cinematic arts.

The San Diego Bay Wine and Food Festival in November is a culinary celebration featuring more than 150 wineries and cuisine from many fine area restaurants. The San Diego Thanksgiving Dixieland Jazz Festival is a five-day classic jazz event held during Thanksgiving weekend, showcasing traditional, swing, and Dixieland jazz. The Christmas season inspires some of the major celebrations of the year, sparking festivals, parades, and light displays in many locations. Other Christmas events include the Parade of Lights, a display of decorated boats in San Diego Bay; the festive rituals of Las Posadas; and the Holiday Bowl, a postseason college football game. December also marks the beginning of the whale migration season off Point Loma.

Sports for the Spectator

Sports are varied in San Diego. Major League Baseball's San Diego Padres play April through September at Petco Park; located downtown, it has 42,000 seats, and its seating bowl sections are named after neighborhoods. The National Football League's San Diego Chargers play at 70,561-seat Qualcomm Stadium. Qualcomm is also home to San Diego State University's Aztecs. San Diego also hosts a major bicycle race, the Barrio Logan Grand Prix. Nearby Del Mar Thoroughbred Club, founded by entertainer Bing Crosby in 1937, offers horseracing from July through September, and Tijuana, Mexico features the excitement of jai alai, bullfighting, and greyhound racing.

Sports for the Participant

Sports Illustrated magazine has called San Diego "the sports and fitness capital of the U.S." The Pacific Ocean and numerous bays in the area provide a wide range of activities: swimming, sailing, water skiing, snorkeling, and deep sea sport fishing, among others. Mission Bay Park is the largest aquatic park in the nation; it consists of 4,235 acres. The park offers 44 miles of beachfront recreation area, as well as inland trails and jogging tracks. San Diego-La Jolla Underwater Park and Ecological Reserve at La Jolla Cove provides excellent snorkeling and scuba diving opportunities. San Diego's public park system maintains extensive recreation facilities, public pools, jogging paths, and playing fields. There are more than 1,300 public and private tennis courts in the county, as well as more than 90 golf courses, including three municipal golf courses. The most popular bike and running route in the area is Route S21, which extends 15 miles along the beach between La Jolla and Oceanside. Winter sports such as skiing are available in the nearby mountains.

Shopping and Dining

San Diego offers a wide variety of shopping experiences, from small shops in renovated historical districts such as Old Town, which resembles a Mexican marketplace, and the Gaslamp Quarter, where Victorian buildings house antique stores, art galleries, and boutiques, to the large suburban shopping malls, many located in the Mission Valley region. Downtown San Diego's massive Westfield Horton Plaza Mall, adjacent to the Gaslamp district, is a five-level, open-air plaza filled with department stores and more than 130 upscale specialty shops. Seaport Village is a 14-acre shopping, dining, and entertainment complex featuring more than 50 shops and restaurants in a harborside setting. Nearby Tijuana provides a colorful variety of bazaars, open-air markets, and handcrafted goods.

Seafood and authentic Mexican cuisine are dining specialties in the San Diego area. Many distinctive restaurants, ranging from formal luxury dining to sidewalk cafes, can be found in the historical districts, the modern plazas, and along the waterfront. A large number of international and ethnic restaurants add variety to the dining fare.

Visitor Information: San Diego Convention & Visitors Bureau, 750 B Street, Suite 1500, San Diego, CA 92101; telephone (619) 232-3101; email sdinfo@sandiego.org.

■ Convention Facilities

The San Diego Convention Center, which doubled in size following an expansion in 2001, is located downtown along San Diego Bay. The 2.6-million-square-foot facility features 615,701 square feet of exhibit space; 204,114 square feet of meeting space, including two 40,000-square-foot ballrooms; and 284,494 square feet of pre-function, lobby, and registration space. The center is within a mile of 7,500 first-class hotel rooms, and is only 10 minutes from the airport. Meeting space is also available at the 2,967-seat Civic Theatre, a multipurpose convention and performing arts center adjacent to City Hall.

A number of downtown hotels are designed to accommodate major conventions, providing extensive meeting and banquet facilities, as well as exhibit space. More than 50,000 rooms are available in the San Diego area.

Convention Information: San Diego Convention & Visitors Bureau, 750 B Street, Suite 1500, San Diego, CA 92101; telephone (619) 232-3101; email sdinfo@sandiego.org.

■ Transportation

Approaching the City

San Diego International Airport, also known as Lindbergh Field, is located three miles from downtown and provides major domestic and foreign air service from 22 passenger carriers. There were more than 500 takeoffs and landings daily in 2012, serving 17.3 million passengers. Amtrak's *Pacific Surfliner* route carries passengers from San Diego through Los Angeles,

Oxnard, and Santa Barbara, to San Luis Obispo. Amtrak's San Diego station is in the historic Santa Fe Depot, north of Seaport Village. A commuter rail service, The Coaster, runs between San Diego, Solana Beach, Encinitas, Carlsbad, and Oceanside.

San Diego is located at the junction of two major north–south routes that originate in Canada. Interstate 5 from Los Angeles and Interstate 15 from Las Vegas meet in San Diego and continue to the Mexican border. Interstate 8 enters San Diego from the east.

Traveling in the City

The San Diego Metropolitan Transit System serves 88 million riders annually and operates 93 bus routes covering San Diego, El Cajon, La Mesa, National City, as well as portions of San Diego County's unincorporated area. The San Diego Trolley travels in the downtown area, through Mission Valley and east county communities, and to the Mexican border. In 2010 construction began on new tracks, and station platforms that would help rejuvenate the blue and orange lines. New trolleys were also planned. The $660 million project was expected to finish in 2015. Carriage rides through the downtown area are available from Embarcadero Marina Park.

■ Communications

Newspapers and Magazines

San Diego is served by the *San Diego Union-Tribune,* the result of the 1992 merger of the city's two dailies. Readers can choose from among a number of weekly, ethnic, and community papers as well, such as *La Prensa San Diego,* a weekly English/Spanish newspaper. *San Diego Magazine* publishes articles of regional interest; several other technical and special interest magazines, such as *San Diego Home/Garden Lifestyles, Computor-Edge* (online), and *San Diego Metropolitan* (focusing on business news), are also published in the area.

Television and Radio

The San Diego area is represented by ABC, CBS, NBC, FOX, Univision, PBS, and other local and independent stations. The region is also serviced by cable and satellite television. Various radio stations serve the San Diego area, providing a wide variety of musical and information programming, some broadcasting in Spanish.

Media Information: *San Diego Union-Tribune,* 350 Camino de la Reina, San Diego, CA 92108; telephone (800) 533-8830.

San Diego Online

City of San Diego Home Page. Available www.sandiego.gov

San Diego Convention & Visitors Bureau. Available www.sandiego.org

San Diego County Library. Available www.sdcl.org

San Diego Daily Transcript. Available www.sddt.com

San Diego Public Library. Available www.sannet.gov/public-library

San Diego Regional Chamber of Commerce. Available www.sdchamber.org

San Diego Regional Economic Development Corporation. Available www.sandiegobusiness.org

San Diego Unified School District. Available www.sandi.net

San Diego Union-Tribune. Available www.utsandiego.com

BIBLIOGRAPHY

Cameron, Robert, *Above San Diego: A New Collection of Historical and Original Aerial Photographs of San Diego* (San Francisco, CA: Cameron and Co., 1990)

Ford, Larry, *Metropolitan San Diego: How Geography and Lifestyle Shape a New Urban Environment* (Philadelphia: University of Pennsylvania Press, 2005)

Lee, Murray K., *In Search of Gold Mountain: A History of the Chinese in San Diego, California* (Virginia Beach, VA: Donning Co. Publishers, 2010)

Nevins, Joseph, *Operation Gatekeeper and Beyond: The War on "Illegals" and the Remaking of the U.S.-Mexico Boundary* 2nd ed. (New York: Routledge, 2010)

San Francisco

■ The City in Brief

Founded: 1776 (incorporated, 1850)

Head Official: Mayor Edwin M. Lee (since 2011; current term expires 2016)

City Population
> 1990: 723,959
> 2000: 776,733
> 2010: 805,235
> 2012 estimate: 825,863
> Percent change, 2000–2010: 3.7%
> U.S. rank in 1990: 14th
> U.S. rank in 2000: 18th
> U.S. rank in 2010: 13th (State rank: 4th)

Metropolitan Statistical Area Population
> 2000: 4,123,740
> 2010: 4,335,391
> 2012 estimate: 4,455,560
> Percent change, 2000–2010: 5.1%
> U.S. rank in 2000: 12th
> U.S. rank in 2010: 11th

Area: 47 square miles

Elevation: 155 feet above sea level

Average Annual Temperatures: January, 52.3° F; July, 61.3° F; annual average, 58.3° F

Average Annual Precipitation: 22.28 inches of rain

Major Economic Sectors: services; trade; finance, insurance, real estate, government

Unemployment Rate: 5.5% (2012)

Per Capita Income: $47,274

2012 FBI Crime Index Property: 38,898

Major Colleges and Universities: San Francisco State University; University of California, San Francisco; University of San Francisco; Golden Gate University

Daily Newspaper: *San Francisco Chronicle; San Francisco Examiner*

■ Introduction

San Francisco is one of the truly international cities in the United States. The neighborhoods are different, yet each fits cohesively into the city. Rows of elegant houses, the famous cable cars, and the colorful waterfront also add to the distinctive international flavor of San Francisco. The city's well-known hills offer stunning views of the Pacific Ocean and San Francisco Bay and feature a wide array of shops, restaurants, and cosmopolitan nightlife. In addition to its diversity and charm, San Francisco is a major financial and insurance center, an international port, and the gateway to Silicon Valley, America's premier high-technology center. The consistently spring-like weather and unique atmosphere attract corporations as well as visitors, and the solid economic base keeps them there.

■ Geography and Climate

San Francisco occupies the tip of a peninsula halfway up the coast of northern California, surrounded by the Pacific Ocean to the west, the Golden Gate strait to the north, and the San Francisco Bay to the east. The city is laid out in a grid over some 40 hills, reaching heights of nearly 1,000 feet; this sometimes causes wide variations in temperature and sky conditions in different areas of town. The Pacific air keeps the temperatures generally moderate, rarely ranging above 75 degrees or below 45 degrees, leading San Francisco to be called "the air-conditioned city." The climate is very similar to coastal areas on the Mediterranean.

CAN BALCIOGLU/Shutterstock.com

Although temperatures remain relatively constant, there are two definite seasons—wet and dry—with more than 80 percent of annual precipitation taking place between November and March. Perhaps the most distinctive feature of the local climate is the banks of fog that can roll in off the ocean, quickly covering various areas of the city, and then disappear just as quickly. The fog is most common on summer mornings, coming off the cooler ocean and backing up against the hills, but it also comes from the colder inland areas during the winter. The fog affects different elevations in varying amounts, covering the city in complex patterns of fog and sunshine.

The San Francisco Bay area lies between the Pacific and North American Tectonic Plates. The city of San Francisco itself rests in the San Andreas Fault, which is one of seven fault lines affecting the area. This zone of continual seismic activity marks the city as highly susceptible to damaging earthquakes and at high-risk for tsunamis. Landslides are another natural hazard.

Area: 47 square miles

Elevation: 155 feet above sea level

Average Temperatures: January, 52.3° F; July, 61.3° F; annual average, 58.3° F

Average Annual Precipitation: 22.28 inches of rain

■ History

Spanish Discover City; Franciscan Friars Build Missions

Because thick fog banks usually obscure the narrow entrance to the bay, the area where San Francisco now stands and the adjacent natural harbor remained undiscovered by seafaring adventurers for more than 200 years after the original Spanish explorers found California. It was left to an overland expedition of Spanish soldiers from Mexico to stumble upon the bay by accident in 1769 while trying to reach Monterey. In 1776 Colonel Juan Bautista de Anza founded the first European settlement in the Bay Area by establishing a military garrison, or Presidio, on the southern shore of the Golden Gate. That same year the Franciscan Order built Mission Dolores, the sixth Roman Catholic mission in what eventually became a chain of 21 missions along the coast of California.

Until the 1830s almost all of the inhabitants were missionaries, trying—without much success—to convert the local Costanoan tribe to Christianity, but eventually a small village was built up around the Presidio and the mission. The village, called Yerba Buena, was mapped out in 1839 by Jean Jaques Vioget, a Swiss surveyor, but it continued to be small and remote throughout most of the 1840s. The quiet town of a few hundred inhabitants was visited infrequently by whaling ships, traders from the East Coast, and frontier hunters and trappers. Farming and a small but steady market in trading cattle hides and tallow were the main sources of commerce.

America Wins California; Gold Discovered

The American flag was raised in the town's central square in 1846, marking the annexation of California by the United States after the war with Mexico; one year later the name of the town was changed to San Francisco. Soon after the annexation, the town's population was nearly doubled by the arrival of a group of 238 Mormon settlers, led by Sam Brannan. It was Brannan who ran through the muddy streets of San Francisco less than two years later shouting "Gold!," thus altering the city's fate. Within a year, more than 40,000 people had journeyed through the area on their way to the gold fields around Sutter's Mill in the Sierra foothills, about 140 miles away. Some 35,000 of those people stayed on to live in San Francisco. The city was incorporated in 1850.

The gold prospectors came from all corners of the globe and tended to settle in areas according to their nationalities, one reason for the distinctive international flavor of modern San Francisco. Demand for food and shelter outstripped the supply, and many people lived in tents, cooking over campfires. Whole crews abandoned their ships in the harbor, leaving hundreds of empty hulls that were brought ashore and used as temporary warehouses, stores, and as the foundations of the town's new buildings. Gambling halls, saloons, hotels, and stores sprang up almost daily, only to be destroyed by frequent fires and then quickly rebuilt. It was a wild and reckless time; rampant lawlessness was common, so much so that in 1851 concerned citizens banded together into vigilante groups and rounded up the worst violators, eventually restoring order to the town.

Gold Boom Goes Bust; Industry, Shipping Thrive

The gold boom declined by the mid-1850s, but the town continued to grow with increases in industry and shipping. The 1859 silver boom in Nevada and the completion of the transcontinental railroad in 1869 also contributed their share to the city's prosperity. The downtown area grew full of large stone buildings and warehouses along the docks, and the surrounding hills were filled with impressive residential homes. By the turn of the century, San Francisco was home to a population of more than a third of a million people and was the ninth largest city in the country.

April 18, 1906, brought disaster to the city in the form of a major earthquake and fire that killed more than 500 people, devastated 3,000 acres in the heart of the city, and left almost 1,000 residents homeless. Among the heroes of the day were the U.S. Navy, who stretched a mile-long fire hose from Fisherman's Wharf over Telegraph Hill and down to Jackson Square, saving historic buildings. Before the ashes were cold, the townspeople set out to rebuild the city, and by 1915, when San Francisco hosted the Panama-Pacific International Exposition in honor of the opening of the Panama Canal, no traces of the fire and earthquake were visible.

Rise of Finance, Commerce, Culture

During the mid-twentieth century, San Francisco secured its position as the financial, commercial, and cultural center of northern California. The completion of the Golden Gate Bridge in 1937, after four years of exhausting work, was the major event of the period and a symbol of the city's new-found prominence. Designer Joseph Strauss tried for more than a decade to convince disbelievers that the plans for the construction of the bridge were feasible, and many people still doubted that it could stand for long even after its completion. The structure is more than three-quarters of a mile in length, supported by two 746-foot towers. It was one of the outstanding engineering achievements of all time and continues to draw hundreds of thousands of tourists each year.

World War II boosted the already strong economy of the city, which became a major supply and troop shipping port for the Pacific fronts and an important area for defense industries. It was also during this time that large numbers of the area's Asian citizens were interred in work camps in the region. After the war, the city pointed the way to peace when delegates representing almost all of the world's countries gathered in San Francisco to draw up the charter of the United Nations.

The post-war era brought continued growth and prosperity. San Francisco's downtown area began to develop a skyline of high-rise buildings while carefully preserving many of the historical structures and green spaces. A large stretch of high-technology industries eventually built up in the nearby area known as Silicon Valley. The city fought problems of urban blight encountered in the 1960s and 1970s with an extensive urban-renewal program, developing the downtown section and introducing a major Rapid Transit System in 1974 to provide access to the center city. The assassinations of Mayor George Moscone and City Supervisor Harvey Milk in November 1978 were a blow to the city's progressive image. The city elected its first woman mayor, Diane Feinstein, in 1979.

Another major earthquake occurred on October 17, 1989, ending decades of tranquility in the San Francisco Bay Area. But the region recovered strongly, showing a spirit of cooperation and determination. San Francisco was home to many dot-com operations in the 1990s. When the dot-com bubble began to burst in 2000, the city was quickly left with many vacant offices. The recession of the early 2000s brought more unemployment to the city.

In 2004 Gavin Newsom took office as mayor and began a number of ambitious, and sometimes controversial, programs. In February 2004 Newsom directed the city clerk to allow issuance of marriage licenses to same-sex couples, a direct violation of California state law that prohibited same-sex marriages. Within one month, thousands of same-sex couples from across the country came to San Francisco to be married. In March 2004 the Supreme Court of California, based in San Francisco, ordered the county to stop issuing the licenses pending future legal review. These events set off a national controversy and brought the issue of same-sex marriage into national court systems, where debate has persisted. As of 2014, 18 states, including California in 2013, had legalized same-sex marriage.

With somewhat less controversy, within the first three years in office Newsom initiated measures that decreased unemployment by about 26 percent and welcomed more than 50 new companies into the city. Newsom also initiated a Climate Action Plan to reduce local greenhouse gas emissions. Newsom left office in 2011 to become Lieutenant Governor of California, with Edwin Lee appointed in his place by the Board of Supervisors. Lee was elected to serve a full term later that year, which began in 2012.

During the 2010s, the city has continued to repair and expand its infrastructure, from subway service to Chinatown, to a cruise terminal at the Port of San Francisco, to a new domestic terminal at the San Francisco International Airport, to the new San Francisco-Oakland Bay Bridge. Central to these projects was the environmentally responsible design of the facilities, a fitting reflection on the city that has become a driving force for technology innovation in the United States.

Historical Information: California Historical Society, 678 Mission Street, San Francisco, CA 94105; telephone (415) 357-1848. Chinese Historical Society of America, 965 Clay Street, San Francisco, CA 94108; telephone (415) 391-1188. San Francisco African American Historical and Cultural Society, 762 Fulton St., San Francisco, CA 94102; telephone (415) 292-6172.

■ Population Profile

Metropolitan Statistical Area Population

2000: 4,123,740
2010: 4,335,391
2012 estimate: 4,455,560
Percent change, 2000–2010: 5.1%
U.S. rank in 2000: 12th
U.S. rank in 2010: 11th

City Residents

1990: 723,959
2000: 776,733
2010: 805,235

2012 estimate: 825,863
Percent change, 2000–2010: 3.7%
U.S. rank in 1990: 14th
U.S. rank in 2000: 18th
U.S. rank in 2010: 13th (State rank: 4th)

Density: 17,179.2 people per square mile

Racial and ethnic characteristics

White: 409,803
Black or African American: 46,406
American Indian and Alaskan Native: 2,640
Asian: 274,340
Native Hawaiian and Other Pacific Islander: 3,381
Hispanic or Latino (may be of any race): 126,876
Other: 89,293

Percent of residents born in state: 38%

Age characteristics

Population under 5 years old: 37,043
Population 5 to 9 years old: 30,225
Population 10 to 14 years old: 26,352
Population 15 to 19 years old: 33,365
Population 20 to 24 years old: 54,042
Population 25 to 34 years old: 180,603
Population 35 to 44 years old: 135,141
Population 45 to 54 years old: 112,252
Population 55 to 59 years old: 51,660
Population 60 to 64 years old: 49,650
Population 65 to 74 years old: 58,703
Population 75 to 84 years old: 38,288
Population 85 years and over: 18,539
Median age: 38.5

Births (2010–11 Metropolitan Area)

Total number: 51,720

Deaths (2010–11 Metropolitan Area)

Total number: 27,781

Money income (2012)

Per capita income: $47,274
Median household income: $72,888
Total households: 341,721

Number of households with income of . . .

less than $10,000: 23,378
$10,000 to $14,999: 21,910
$15,000 to $24,999: 28,937
$25,000 to $34,999: 23,572
$35,000 to $49,999: 29,865
$50,000 to $74,999: 46,512
$75,000 to $99,999: 36,583
$100,000 to $149,999: 55,168
$150,000 to $199,999: 31,103
$200,000 or more: 44,693

Percent of families below poverty level: 13.8%

FBI Crime Index Property: 38,898

FBI Crime Index Violent: 5,777

■ Municipal Government

The governments of the city and county of San Francisco are consolidated into one unit. San Francisco adopted a mayor-council form of government in 1932. The council, however, is known as the Board of Supervisors. There are eleven supervisors, who represent specific districts, elected to four-year terms. The mayor is directly elected to a four-year term. A city administrator is appointed by the mayor, with approval of the board, to serve a five-year term.

Head Official: Mayor Edwin M. Lee (since 2011; current term expires 2016)

Total Number of City Employees: 25,458 (2012)

City Information: City Hall, Mayor's Office, Room 200, 1. Dr. Carlton B. Goodlett Place, San Francisco, CA 94102; telephone (415) 554-6141; fax (415) 554-6160.

■ Economy

Major Industries and Commercial Activity

Since the days of the Gold Rush, San Francisco has been an important financial center. Located halfway between London and Tokyo as well as between Seattle and San Diego, San Francisco is at the center of global business. Because of its natural, landlocked harbor, San Francisco has thrived on trade and shipping since its early days. Today, through its main port in Oakland, eight smaller ports, and three key airports, the Bay area handles some 30 percent of West Coast trade. The port system is augmented by San Francisco International Airport.

San Francisco's economic activity attracts and supports a range of industries. As the base for some of the country's largest banks and scores of international financial institutions, San Francisco is a center for world commerce. Most recently San Francisco is being considered the birthplace of new media; its South Park neighborhood houses some of the most innovative new technology companies in the world. San Francisco's Mission Bay neighborhood is a model for collaborative innovation between the biotechnology industry and academic researchers.

World War II started a local boom in defense industries, resulting in subsequent high-technology development that hasn't ceased. Nearby Silicon Valley, along with Stanford University, are considered among the places where the worldwide technology boom began, and

they remain on the leading edge today. More than 6,700 Bay Area companies produce computers, semiconductors and related components, scientific instruments, and various other electronic systems and equipment. The IT industry employs more than 272,000 people in San Francisco. With more than 78 percent of households wired to the Internet, San Francisco is one of the top 10 cities for high-speed connection. San Francisco has become a center for digital entertainment companies with more than 50 companies in the city, including LucasArts, Pixar, Electronic Arts, Dolby, Sega of America, and PDI DreamWorks SKG. Aerospace industries such as the National Aeronautic and Space Administration (NASA) and Lockheed Martin also maintain major research facilities in the area.

Another important high-technology industry in the area is bioscience; several hundred companies in the Bay Area are setting the pace in research and development of pharmaceutical products, medical electronics, and genetic engineering. More bioscience companies are located in Northern California than any other place in the world, employing some 90,000 directly and 250,000 directly or indirectly. An estimated 30 new bioscience companies are started in the area each year. Companies operating in San Francisco include Pfizer, Bayer, FibroGen, Nektar, Medivation, Celgene, and the California Institute for Regenerative Medicine..

San Francisco and the Silicon Valley also boast the largest concentration of environmental technology investors in the United States. Some 225 such companies operate in San Francisco. Other prominent industries are tourism, which brought in $8.5 billion from 16.4 million visitors in 2012; fashion apparel, with the Bay Area home to the world's largest apparel maker, Levi Strauss & Co.; health care; and education. Regarding the tourism industry, the number of visitors to San Francisco in 2009 was 15.4 million, only a slight decrease from 15.8 in 2006. In 2009 visitors spent $7.8 billion.

San Francisco is also the headquarters of the non-profit Wikimedia Foundation, which relocated from St. Petersburg, Florida, to San Francisco in 2008.

Items and goods produced: paper boxes, confectionery, paints, chemicals, glass, leather, lumber, textiles, steel, clothing, bags, furniture, auto parts, electric machinery, matches, clay, rubber products, tools, beverages

Incentive Programs—New and Existing Companies

Local programs: The city offers several business incentives, with many targeted toward specific industries. The Biotechnology Payroll Tax Exclusion provides a local payroll tax exclusion for up to seven-and-a-half years to biotechnology research and development firms. The Clean Technology Payroll Tax Exclusion offers the same local payroll tax exclusion to clean technology companies with fewer than 100 employees for up to 10 years. San Francisco refunds up to $600,000 in payroll tax and city fees to film and television production crews operating in the city. A Central Market/Tenderloin Payroll Tax Exclusion provides businesses in defined exclusion areas with the ability to exclude any new jobs they create payroll taxes for six years. GreenFinanceSF, a collaboration between the city and the Clinton Climate Initiative, secures financing for buildings attempting to make environmentally conscious design improvements to their structures.

There are several local business associations assisting entrepreneurs, including the San Francisco Black Chamber of Commerce and the Bayview Merchants Association.

State programs: California business incentives include the state's Alternative Energy and Advanced Transportation Authority Sales and Use Tax Exemptions for Zero Emission Vehicle Manufacturing. Initially targeting vehicle manufacturing only when it was passed in 2010, the sales and use tax exemption has since been expanded to all renewable energy technologies. In 2012 it was expanded again to include advanced manufacturing. More than one dozen additional incentives encourage green development or pollution-reducing business decisions.

Research and development tax credits offers companies a 15 percent credit against their bank and corporation tax liability for qualifying in-house research expenses; a 24 percent tax credit for basic research payments to outside organizations is also available. Industrial development bonds finance investment in land, buildings, and new equipment related to domestic manufacturing operations in the state. California Capital Access Program and Collateral Support Program also offer alternative methods of financing for businesses. Enterprise Zones and Local Agency Military Base Recovery Area regions provide incentives for development in targeted geographic regions. A New Jobs Tax Credit offers $3,000 per hire of qualifying new employees, and the state's Film and Television Tax Credit Program supports productions with a 20 percent tax credit against qualified expenses.

In 2011 California began offering companies the option to calculate their corporate income tax through the single sales factor method, rather than the existing triple apportionment derived from calculations of a company's payroll, property, and sales.

California's Innovation Hub Program, with 12 locations throughout the state, supports the commercialization of innovation and technology businesses through public-private partnerships, knowledge sharing, venture capital sources, and business incubators. The state also undertakes trade missions to form partnerships for trade and export promotion.

Job training programs: The state of California offers an Employment Training Panel to assist companies with post-hire training and reimbursement. The Employment Development Department also partners with Local Workforce Investment Areas to recruit, screen, test, evaluate, and hire qualified workers.

SFWorks is a program that assists employers in hiring low-income individuals who are transitioning to work or trying to advance their careers. The Jobs Now! Program, an initiative of the San Francisco Human Services Agency, disperses federal funding to expand subsidized employment opportunities. Local employers are provided referrals for new hires and a wage subsidy of $5,000, paid over a five-month period in equal installments.

Development Projects

A multiyear, $2.4 billion program to bring San Francisco International Airport into the twenty-first century included new parking garages, a consolidated rental car center, and other amenities. A $383 million project to create a new domestic terminal, Terminal 2, remodeled the airport's old international terminal and was completed in 2011. The new Terminal 2 added 587,000 square feet to the airport's terminal space. In keeping with the city's green development priorities, the terminal was LEED Gold certified, making it one of the most modern and sustainable terminals in the country.

Additional improvements to the city's transportation infrastructure highlighted public investment. As of 2013, Phase 2 of the San Francisco Municipal Transportation Agency's efforts to provide transportation links to southeastern neighborhoods of the city was underway. Phase 1, completed in 2007, restored light rail service to residents along the Third Street corridor—for the first time in 50 years. Phase 2 planned to construct a central subway to Chinatown, which, despite being one of the city's most densely population neighborhoods, did not have modern rail service. The 1.7-mile line was targeted for completed by 2018.

Another transportation project, the Transbay Transit Center Project, was expected to complete in 2017 at a cost of $4.2 billion. The new Transbay Terminal at First and Mission Streets was to connect eight Bay Area counties by providing a hub for 11 regional transit systems, including the proposed high-speed rail that was to connect San Francisco to the Los Angeles basin in future decades. The terminal was to have a 5.4-acre public park on its roof as part of the one-million-square-foot, five-story facility. The city began construction in 2010.

In September 2013, the East Coast Span of the new San Francisco-Oakland Bay Bridge opened to traffic after six years of construction. The $6.4 billion project was managed by the California Department of Transportation and featured the world' largest self-anchored suspension span. The original Bay Bridge, constructed in 1936, handled about 280,000 vehicles each day. A new cruise terminal at Pier 27 on the Port of San Francisco was slated for completion in 2014 and was expected to be a LEED certified building and carbon-neutral facility.

Treasure Island, also formerly used by the Navy until 1997, was to be site of up to 8,000 housing units; almost a third of those units would be used to house the area's lower income residents. More development on the island would include space for offices, shops, and even hotels, leaving some 300 acres of green space. The project was expected to begin construction in 2014.

The San Francisco Museum of Modern Art was in the process of a major expansion to triple its gallery and public spaces by added a additional 120,000 square feet. Expected to complete in 2016, the $555 million project was to showcase many of the museum's recent acquisitions gained through a collections campaign that preceded the expansion.

The University of California San Francisco was building a new 289-bed medical center at Mission Bay. The planned 43-acre, $1.5 billion medical campus, expected to completed in 2015, was to focus on care for children, women, and cancer patients and also include a life sciences campus for teaching and research. The facility anchored the broader development of Mission Bay, which has been undergoing development since 2003.

Beginning in 2014, the city's National Football League franchise, the San Francisco 49ers, were to begin playing in a new $1.3 billion stadium in Santa Clara.

Economic Development Information: San Francisco Center for Economic Development, 235 Montgomery St., 12th Floor, San Francisco, CA 94104; telephone (415) 352-8855; email info@sfced.org.

Commercial Shipping

Cargo service at San Francisco International Airport is available from 48 airlines, including 8 cargo-only airlines. The airport supports 11 cargo facilities with a total of approximately 1,026,271 square feet of warehouse and office space. Cargo service is also provided at Oakland International Airport through major carriers, with an average of nearly 500,000 metric tons of cargo handled annually during 2009–12. The Port of San Francisco has five berths, on-dock rail, and more than 550,000 square feet of covered storage for weather-sensitive cargo. Many shipping service companies serve the port. The port is part of Foreign Trade Zone No. 3.

Labor Force and Employment Outlook

San Francisco has one of the highest concentration of new immigrants in the nation, providing a continuous supply of workers at all levels of expertise. The city also boasts some of the most well-trained professionals in the United States, with 85 percent of San Franciscans having educational training beyond high school, and more than 50 percent having at least a four-year degree. Nearly 20 percent of San Franciscan residents hold a graduate

degree. San Francisco tops all cities in educational attainment density.

The city's workforce is a magnet for business and employment. According to the U.S. Department of Labor, San Francisco's diverse and educated population results in one of the most productive workforces in the country and the world. Job growth was led by technology firms, which enjoyed a 12 percent jump in employment between 2011 and 2012. They were also responsible for 25 percent of all new jobs in the city during that period. Despite rapid growth, technology companies employed only six percent of all workers in the city—a nonetheless remarkable statistic considering it represented only 1 percent in 1990—while finance and insurance continued to form the backbone of high-paying employment. As the sixth largest metropolitan market in the United States, San Francisco offers continual opportunities in areas such as retail trade, service industries, and restaurants.

The following is a summary of data regarding the 2012 San Francisco labor force:

Size of civilian labor force: 490,876

Number of workers employed in . . .

agriculture and mining: 828
construction: 15,464
manufacturing: 27,043
wholesale trade: 8,394
retail trade: 46,036
transportation: 16,051
information systems: 20,539
finance: 39,287
professional administration: 94,274
education and social services: 86,231
arts and leisure: 57,080
other: 24,577
public administration: 15,769

Average hourly earnings of production workers: $19.14

Unemployment rate: 5.5% (2012)

Employers

Largest employers (2012)	*Number of employees*
City and County of San Francisco	25,458
University of California, San Francisco	22,664
California Pacific Medical Center	8,559
Wells Fargo & Co.	8,300
San Francisco Unified School District	8,189

Gap, Inc.	6,000
PG&E Corporation	4,415
State of California	4,184
Salesforce.com Inc.	4,000
Kaiser Permanente	3,581

Cost of Living

San Francisco's cost of living is one of the highest in the country, due in part to the tight labor market and the high cost of housing, food, and other consumer goods. The workforce is highly educated and jobs are concentrated in high-paying industries. Although the residential property tax is low, because property values are high, the absolute payment is relatively high.

The following is a summary of data regarding several key cost of living factors in the area.

2013 ACCRA Average House Price: $814,857

2013 ACCRA Cost of Living Index: 160

State income tax rate: 1.00% to 13.3%

State sales tax rate: 7.5%

Local income tax rate: 1.50% (This payroll tax is being phased out during 2014–18 in favor of a gross receipts tax.)

Local sales tax rate: 1.25%

Property tax rate: Limited to 1% of assessed value by state law. In some cases the local taxing body can add additional taxes.

Economic Information: San Francisco Center for Economic Development, 235 Montgomery St., 12th Floor, San Francisco, CA 94104; telephone (415) 352-8855; email info@sfced.org.

■ Education and Research

Elementary and Secondary Schools

Founded in 1851, the San Francisco Unified School District (SFUSD) was the first public school district established in California. The SFUSD is a multicultural, multilingual, major urban public school system in which ethnic and racial diversity are considered strengths. English is the second language of nearly one-third of SFUSD students. With this in mind, the district offers Language Immersion Programs in Spanish, Mandarin, Cantonese and Korean.

The school has also ranked as the top performing large urban school district in the state. Student achievement on both mathematics and language arts exams in 2012 outpaced state averages at all grade levels. Gifted and Talented Education (GATE) Programs and special education programs are offered for all grade levels. Special

programming for high school students is available at schools such as the International Studies Academy and the School of the Arts. Advanced Placement and honors classes are also available.

The SFUSD encompasses all of San Francisco County, making it one of the largest in the state of California. The school board consists of seven partisan members who appoint the superintendent. The district oversees 13 charter schools.

A number of private and parochial schools provide alternative forms of education in the San Francisco area.

The following is a summary of data regarding the San Francisco Unified School District.

Total enrollment: 55,571

Number of facilities

total: 102
elementary schools: 72
junior high schools: 12
high schools: 17
other: 1

Student/teacher ratio: 20.67:1

Teacher salaries

average (statewide): $69,434

Funding per pupil: $9,839

Public Schools Information: San Francisco Unified School District, 555 Franklin Street, San Francisco, CA 94102; telephone (415) 241-6000.

Colleges and Universities

The eight academic colleges of San Francisco State University offer bachelor's degree programs in 124 fields, along with 105 master's programs and a doctorate in educational leadership. The University of California, San Francisco (UCSF) is the only University of California campus dedicated exclusively to health sciences. The UCSF campus serves about 3,100 degree-seeking students, offering graduate degrees in several scientific fields, including its renowned school of medicine. The campus supports the UCSF Medical Center, the UCSF Children's Hospital, and Langley Porter Psychiatric Institute. UCSF also hosts more than 60 specialized research centers and institutes.

Golden Gate University offers certificate programs and undergraduate and graduate degree programs in accounting, business and management, finance, law, taxation, information technology, and related professions such as psychology and public administration. While San Francisco is the main campus site, there are three other campuses on the West Coast. Total enrollment is about 3,500 students.

The University of San Francisco is a private, Jesuit Catholic university that enrolls about 10,000 undergraduate and graduate students annually. The school offers graduate and undergraduate degrees in five schools: Arts and Sciences, Business and Professional Studies, Education, Law, and Nursing and Health Professions. Advanced study options are available through 18 specialized centers and institutes, including the Center for Latino Studies in the Americas, the Ricci Institute for Chinese-Western Cultural History, and the Center for Law and Global Justice.

City College of San Francisco offers associate's degrees and certificate programs across 50 academic programs and more than 100 occupational disciplines..

The University of California Hastings College of the Law, in downtown San Francisco, has a total enrollment of about 1,100. The school offers more than 20 advanced degrees. The Academy of Art University offers undergraduate and graduate programs in a wide spectrum of art-related fields, such as architecture, fashion, industrial design, motion pictures and television, digital arts, and advertising. The San Francisco campus of the California College of the Arts houses the school's graduate program and hosts the CAA Wattis Institute for Contemporary Arts, established in 1998 as a forum for the presentation and discussion of international contemporary art and curatorial practices. The undergraduate programs of the school are located at the Oakland campus.

Nearby Stanford University and the University of California, Berkeley, two schools with international reputations, provide still more opportunities for educational pursuits.

Libraries and Research Centers

The San Francisco Public Library consists of the main library and 28 branches throughout the city, providing a total of more than 3.5 million volumes, as well as films, videotapes, CDs, and other recordings. The collection of exclusively digital resources numbers more than 75,000. There are also three bookmobiles, and one wheelchair-accessible bookmobile for senior citizens. The main library houses several special collections and centers, including special collections on calligraphy, the history of printing, Panama Canal manuscripts, science fiction and fantasy, San Francisco history, gay and lesbian history, and a document department featuring United Nations, federal, state, and local documents. The library is one of six in the state to be designated as a U.S. Patent and Trademark Depository Library. The Deaf Services Center and the Library for the Blind and Print Disabled are also at the main branch.

The J. Paul Leonard Library at SFSU holds more than 1.1 million books and government documents and serves as a federal depository library of the 12th congressional district. Special collections include the Marguerite Archer Collection of Historic Children's Materials, the San Francisco State College Strike Collection, and San Francisco Bay Area Television Archives.

The Labor Archives and Research Center collection includes historic documents and materials from several surrounding counties. Many unions have made the Labor Archives the official repository for their historical records. This center also contains personal memorabilia, photographs, and oral histories that document the lives and stories of working men and women from the region. The library completed a major, $104 million expansion in 2012 to provide visitors with more space, seating, and computers and capacity for additional collections.

The city's proximity to Silicon Valley produces a large amount of research activity. The University of California, San Francisco hosts more than 60 specialized research centers and institutes. These include California Institute for Quantitative Biosciences, Center for Aging in Diverse Communities, Center for BioEntrepreneurship, Center for Consumer Self Care, Center of Regeneration Medicine and Stem Cell Research, and the Gladstone Institute of Virology and Immunology. There are centers conducting research on HIV/AIDS and cancer.

The Public Research Institute (PRI) at San Francisco State University offers a wide variety of research services to government agencies, non-profit organizations, community groups, and academic researchers.

Public Library Information: San Francisco Public Library, 100 Larkin Street, San Francisco, CA 94102; telephone (415) 557-4400.

■ Health Care

The major hospitals in San Francisco are affiliated with the University of California, San Francisco. UCSF Medical Center, part of the UCSF campus at Parnassus, features a 15-story, 660-bed main hospital occupying two buildings. Along with a full spectrum of medical care and services, the hospital has special departments for cancer care, fertility treatments, nanosurgery, cardiac care, ophthalmology, and orthopedics. There is also a transplant department for liver, kidney, pancreas, heart, and heart-lung transplants. The hospital was ranked nationally in 13 specialties in 2013–14 by *U.S. News & World Report,* including a top-eight ranking in seven specialties.

Within UCSF Medical Center is the UCSF Benioff Children's Hospital, a 180-bed center with a specialized pediatric surgical suite, pediatric and neonatal intensive care units, and a Birth Center. *U.S. News & World Report* ranked the hospital nationally in nine specialties for 2013–14.

Outpatient clinics of the UCSF Medical Center are part of the Ambulatory Care Center near the hospital. Specialized clinics include an AIDS treatment center, a cochlear implant center, epilepsy care, occupational medicine, and dermatology center, among others. The UCSF Medical Center at Mount Zion, only a few miles away from Parnassus, features specialized clinics and surgery services as well as a center for comprehensive cancer care. UCSF planned to open a $1.5 billion, 289-bed facility at Mission Bay in 2015, specializing in children's, women's, and cancer care.

The San Francisco General Hospital is a public general acute care hospital that serves as a regional teaching hospital through partnership with UCSF. The hospital complex contains an internationally-recognized emergency and Level I Trauma Center (the only one in the city), psychiatric services, the nation's first AIDS unit, an Alternative Birth Center, and the innovative Women's Health Center. In 2004 the Avon Comprehensive Breast Center opened within the hospital, seeking to increase the number of underserved women who received mammograms; the center had provided more than 45,000 screenings by 2013. The Psychiatric Care and Psychiatric Emergency Services department is a 24-hour, 7-day-a-week specialized emergency assessment, stabilization, and hospital placement program. Primary care services are also available through the San Francisco General Medical Center complex.

■ Recreation

Sightseeing

San Francisco contains so many interesting attractions in such a small area that visitors find something unique on almost any street. Most points of interest are within walking distance or a short ride away. The ride itself can be an attraction when taken on one of the city's famous cable cars, the nation's only moving historical landmarks, now restored and servicing an 8.8-mile route in the heart of the city.

Historic and scenic beauty is evident all over the city. The original mission and the Presidio, both built in 1776 out of simple adobe brick, can still be toured. Jackson Square, the former Barbary Coast, and Portsmouth Square, the original center of the early town, are both in renovated areas that highlight different periods of the city's history. Many of the residential sections that surround the downtown district were spared destruction in the earthquake and fire of 1906, and they offer examples of Victorian architecture. Displayed in hillside vistas, the colorful houses give the city a Mediterranean look. The downtown area also contains a number of striking modern structures like the pyramidal Transamerica Building, and the impressive Civic Center complex, including the domed City Hall.

Perhaps the most unique features of San Francisco are its clusters of distinct ethnic neighborhoods. The most famous is Chinatown, the largest Chinese district outside of Asia, a 24-block area of authentic bazaars, temples, restaurants, and distinctive Oriental architecture. The area includes a two-level gateway to the district,

ornately carved by Taiwanese craftsmen, and the Chinese Culture Center. Next to Chinatown is the North Beach area, once home to the "beatnik" culture. Filled with Italian influences—cafes, gelato parlors, delicatessens, cappuccino houses, and restaurants—the area also contains a number of jazz clubs, art galleries, and theaters. The Mission District, a business and residential area of colorful Victorian buildings, is home to a predominantly Spanish-speaking population and the original Levi Strauss clothing factory, still in operation. A five-tiered pagoda welcomes visitors to Nihonmachi, a section of sushi bars, theaters, shops, restaurants, and hotels that reflect the Japanese culture.

Golden Gate Park, just west of the downtown area, is more than 1,000 acres of landscaped greenery that was once a barren area of windswept sand dunes. The park was created in 1846 and houses flowered meadows, an arboretum and botanical garden containing more than 10,000 plants, and a five-acre Japanese tea garden. Also located in the park are the Conservatory of Flowers, a children's playground with an antique carousel, and a small herd of bison, a tradition since 1890.

The city's waterfront offers a variety of entertainments. Several islands in the bay provide scenic picnic areas. Alcatraz Island, home of "The Rock," the former escape-proof federal prison, is open for tours; advance reservations are suggested. Ocean Beach, on the Pacific side of the peninsula, provides a view of Seal Rocks, a small island occupied by a colony of sea lions. At the northern end of Ocean Beach is the San Francisco Zoo, one of the top zoos in the nation. More than 250 species inhabit the exhibits, including snow leopards, red kangaroos, and a colony of koala bears. The zoo also features the Insect Zoo, Jones Family Gorilla Preserve, one of the nation's foremost gorilla habitats, and a children's zoo.

Golden Gate National Recreation Area, one of the largest urban parks in the world and host to about 17 million visitors each year, is located on both sides of the Golden Gate, the entrance to San Francisco Bay. Its 75,500 acres contain stunning cliff-top views of the bay and the ocean, a network of hiking trails, valleys, and beaches, and the Fort Point National Historic Site, a brick fort built in 1861. The Golden Gate Bridge, with its pedestrian walkway, connects the two sides of the park.

The Randall Museum is a special hands-on facility for families sponsored by the San Francisco Recreation and Parks Department. Situated on a 16-acre hill overlooking San Francisco and the Bay, the museum features a live animal exhibit, a greenhouse and garden, an earthquake exhibit with a working seismograph, and a replica of a 1906 Earthquake Refugee Shack. The Randall Museum Theatre hosts concerts, movies, plays and lectures year-round. A hiking trail leads to the top of Corona Heights with stunning views of San Francisco and the Bay.

Arts and Culture

San Francisco enjoys a cultural scene as varied as its population. Theater, music, and dance can be found in a multitude of outlets. The heart of the city's cultural life is located in the area around the Civic Center Plaza, where the San Francisco War Memorial and Performing Arts Center blends in with the neighboring civic buildings. The Center's Louise M. Davies Symphony Hall is home of the San Francisco Symphony, a world-class orchestra that is one of the oldest in the United States. The War Memorial Opera House is home to the internationally acclaimed San Francisco Opera and the equally renowned San Francisco Ballet. The SFJAZZ Center, the nation's first stand-alone center dedicated to jazz performance, opened in 2013.

Visitors and residents enjoy Broadway shows, improvisational comedy, musical revues, and dramatic theater throughout the city. Situated on San Francisco's Union Square is TIX Bay Area, a half-price ticket booth that has day-of tickets to performances at many of the large and smaller houses. Within walking distance are American Conservatory Theater, Curran Theater, Golden Gate Theater, and Orpheum Theater.

Museums in San Francisco are varied and plentiful. Located on the waterfront is the San Francisco National Maritime National Historical Park, a collection of ship models, relics, photographs, and paintings, as well as several restored vessels docked at the adjacent pier. Other area museums include the San Francisco African American Historical and Cultural Society, the Museum of the California Historical Society, and the Wells Fargo History Museum.

The California Academy of Sciences, located in Golden Gate Park, consists of an aquarium, a planetarium, and a natural history museum. The Steinhart Aquarium houses more than 38,000 aquatic specimens including African penguins, stingrays, sharks, crocodiles, and rare Australian lungfish. The Kimball Natural History Museum houses many exhibits of natural science including the Gem and Mineral Hall.

The Exploratorium: The Museum of Science, Art and Human Perception, in the Palace of Fine Arts, was founded by the renowned physicist and educator Dr. Frank Oppenheimer in 1969. The museum offers hands-on exhibits on what might be considered an eclectic range of topics, including weather, the human body, space and astronomy, earth science, cooking, languages, the science of wine, and sports science. In 2013 the Exploratorium moved to Pier 15 on the Embarcadero, renovating an existing space and tripling its original indoor and outdoor exhibit space to 330,000 square feet.

The M. H. de Young Museum in Golden Gate Park houses a diverse collection, including galleries tracing the history of art, as well as displays of American art, pre-Columbian gold work, and works by masters such as El Greco and Rembrandt. The nearby Asian Art Museum houses the Avery Brundage Collection, which contains more than 500 examples of Chinese art in addition to art of the Middle East, the Indian subcontinent, and Southeast Asia.

At the heart of San Francisco's Yerba Buena Gardens, situated south of Market Street near the Financial District, is a bustling center for arts and culture that includes the San Francisco Museum of Modern Art, which is the first museum on the West Coast devoted solely to twentieth-century art. The museum was undergoing a $555 million expansion slated to finish in 2016. The Contemporary Jewish Museum and Mexican Museum are two of the many organizations that have built their new facilities nearby. Other area art museums include the Museum of Craft and Folk Art, Chinese Culture Center, Galería de la Raza, Cartoon Art Museum, and the Museo Italo Americano.

The Mint Plaza, opened in 2007, consists of an 290-foot-long portion of Jessie Street (between Fifth and Mint) that has been closed to vehicle traffic. The area is lined with cafes and art, with open spaces available for events including theater, live music, and street fairs.

Festivals and Holidays

San Francisco is known for its celebratory spirit, which is reflected in the calendar of festivals and special events. One of the biggest celebrations occurs in February with the week-long Chinese New Year Festival, an exotic blend of parades, outdoor festivals, and other cultural programs in America's largest Chinese community. March brings the seven-day St. Patrick's Day Celebration. The attention shifts to the Japanese district for the annual Cherry Blossom Festival in April, consisting of cultural programs, exhibitions, and a parade of dancers and costumed performers.

For almost a century, thousands of runners have flocked to San Francisco in May for the annual Bay to Breakers, which is part fundraiser for a variety of charities and part celebration of the city's diversity. June brings the two-day San Francisco Pride, a celebration and parade for the city's lesbian, gay, bisexual, and transgender community. The San Francisco Waterfront Festival is an Independence Day party that unfailingly delivers brilliant fireworks over the Bay. Also in July is the Fillmore Street Jazz Festival. In September, people can sample the sinful fruits of chocolatiers at the Ghirardelli Square Chocolate Festival. October is the month for the Hardly Strictly Bluegrass Festival at Golden Gate Park, as well as the Oktoberfest celebration. The San Francisco World Music Festival takes place in November. The Holiday Festival of Lights in December takes place at Fisherman's Wharf and launches the Bay Area holiday season in style.

Sports for the Spectator

The Bay Area is home to two Major League Baseball franchises, the American League Oakland Athletics and the National League San Francisco Giants, as well as to the National Basketball Association's Golden State Warriors (Oakland), the National Hockey League's San Jose Sharks, and Major League Soccer's San Jose Earthquakes. The National Football League's San Francisco 49ers were the first professional sports franchise on the West Coast; they have made several successful trips to the Super Bowl. The Oakland Raiders, also of the National Football League, are nearby.

Thoroughbred racing can be enjoyed at Golden Gate Fields, one of America's premier horse racing facilities. The Mazda Raceway Laguna Seca and the Sonoma Raceway provide a variety of motor sports nearby. The city annually sponsors one of the largest marathons in the country, the San Francisco Marathon, as well as several other running events throughout the year. Area colleges and universities also field teams in most sports and maintain extensive spectator facilities.

Sports for the Participant

San Francisco offers a wide array of choices for those who are sports minded. Aquatic sports are especially popular because of the city's proximity to water. Yachting, boating, swimming, water skiing, boardsailing, surfing, fishing, and hang gliding from cliffs are among the favorite activities. The 75,398-acre Golden Gate Recreation Area is filled with hiking and bicycling trails, campgrounds, and wildlife preserves. The San Francisco Recreation and Parks Department administers and maintains more than 200 parks, playgrounds, and open spaces throughout the city, including two outside the city limits: Sharp Park in Pacifica and Camp Mather in the High Sierras. The system also includes 25 large recreation centers; 9 swimming pools; 6 golf courses; and more than 100 tennis courts. Indoor and outdoor soccer facilities, ball diamonds, athletic fields, and basketball courts are readily available. The department is also responsible for the Marina BayYacht Harbor, Candlestick Park, San Francisco Zoo, and the Lake Merced Complex, which is operated for recreational purposes under the San Francisco Water Department.

Shopping and Dining

San Francisco offers some of the best shopping in the world, so it is no wonder that tourists and serious shopaholics alike want to spend some time and money in San Francisco's varied shopping centers, districts and malls. Union Square, Hayes Valley, upper Fillmore, the Mission, Sacramento Street, Chinatown and downtown's San Francisco Centre offer a unique style with one-of-a-kind shops; each mall and neighborhood offers a distinctive feel suited to any shopper's mood. Other major shopping districts include Ghirardelli Square, which is a group of stores built around the Ghirardelli chocolate factory, and the Cannery, a lavishly remodeled former produce processing plant. Other popular shopping destinations are the Anchorage Square at Fisherman's Wharf and downtown's Embarcadero Center. In addition, each ethnic neighborhood supports its own distinctive section of shops, open-air markets, and restaurants.

San Francisco has been called "the weight watcher's Waterloo" because of its tempting restaurants, many holding international reputations. San Francisco's 3,588 restaurants are geographically concentrated at the rate of about 95 per square mile. The prestigious Michelin star rating system, giving one, two, or three stars to elite restaurants, featured several San Francisco eateries. Atelier Crenn, Benu, Coi, Quince, and Saison all earned two stars in 2014, and another 14 restaurants in the city were honored with a single star. Dining styles and venues include supper clubs, American grills, California-Asian hybrids, haute vegetarian, modest bistros, and fine-dining destinations.

Seafood fresh off the boat can be obtained at restaurants along Fisherman's Wharf; farmland, vineyards, and cattle ranches in the surrounding area provide an abundance of other fresh ingredients. Sourdough bread is a San Francisco specialty. Many international restaurants, serving dishes from around the world and prepared with exact authenticity, are scattered throughout the city's numerous ethnic neighborhoods.

Visitor Information: San Francisco Convention and Visitors Bureau, Convention Plaza, 900 Market St., San Francisco, CA 94102; telephone (415) 391-2000.

■ Convention Facilities

The city of San Francisco hosts more than one million meeting, convention, and trade show delegates annually. Convention planners come to San Francisco not only because of the attractions in the Bay Area, but also for the excellent facilities. The city's Civic Center, called "the grandest Civic Center in the country" by architectural critics, houses extensive meeting facilities. The Bill Graham Civic Auditorium seats 7,000 people, with two adjoining halls that seat another 900 people. The Moscone Center offers more than 900,000 totalt square feet. The Concourse Exhibition Center can accommodate up to 6,800 for a reception and has a total of about 125,000 square feet of meeting and exhibit space.

The city has nearly 33,000 hotel rooms. All rooms are within easy traveling distance of the main convention sites. Most of the major hotels in the area provide ample meeting space, ballrooms, registration lobbies, and exhibit areas. Several local theaters, galleries, and museums also offer rental spaces for meetings, banquets, and other special events.

Convention Information: San Francisco Convention and Visitors Bureau, Convention Plaza, 900 Market St., San Francisco, CA 94102; telephone (415) 391-2000.

■ Transportation

Approaching the City

The San Francisco International Airport is one of the busiest in the nation, handling some 37.5 million passengers every year on more than 40 domestic and international airlines. An efficient customs clearance, modern facilities, and computerized ground transportation information make the airport easy to use. A 24-hour AirTrain people-mover system helps passengers navigate the airport grounds. Terminal 2, a fully renovated building that was the airport's old international terminal, opened in 2011.

SamTrans provide 24-hour service from the airport to parts of San Francisco, Palo Alto, and San Mateo County. Many downtown hotels offer free transportation to and from the airport. Travelers may choose to arrive at Oakland International Airport, which is served by 11 domestic and international airlines.

The city is at the intersection of several major highways. U.S. Highway 101 and S.R. 1, the Pacific Coastal Highway, converge on San Francisco from the north and south. From the east, Interstate 80 and U.S. Highway 50 serve the city. Interstate Loops 580 and 680 provide access to Interstate 5, the major north–south route from Canada to Mexico.

Amtrak rail service is available, as is Caltrain, a commuter service that operates from San Francisco to Gilroy. Bus service is offered via Greyhound Bus Lines.

Traveling in the City

Because of the city's compact size, walking is a favored means of transportation, but when the distance is too great, several public transportation options are available. The famous cable cars are not only a tourist attraction, but also a convenient way for commuters to travel in the downtown area. The city's Municipal Railway System (Muni) light-rail vehicles, descendants of the cable cars, travel underground in the inner city and above ground in the outlying areas. A Muni Visitor Passport allows unlimited access to Muni's entire fleet of buses, trolleys, light-rail vehicles, and cable cars. Passports are available for one, three, or seven days. There are about 80 Muni routes in the city.

The Bay Area Rapid Transit (BART) is an ultra-modern train system linking the city with 44 stations in the East Bay Area. Ferry services also connect the city with Oakland and Berkeley across the bay.

■ Communications

Newspapers and Magazines

San Francisco has a prominent publishing industry on both regional and national levels. The city is served by two major daily newspapers, the morning *San Francisco Chronicle* and, in the evening, *The Examiner*. Historically, the *San Francisco Chronicle* has been one of the largest newspapers in the country. While it remains a prominent newspaper, its circulation has slipped, as have those of many other major newspapers. Daily circulation in 2007 was estimated at about 398,246; print circulation had dropped to 165,000 by 2012, with total circulation—which included digital-only subscriptions—standing at 229,174.

The city's diversity is reflected in the community's special interest and ethnic publications. The *Sun-Reporter* (Thursdays), *Metro Reporter* (Tuesdays), and *California Voice* (Sundays) are weeklies serving the African American community; all three are published by Sun-Reporter Publishing Company, one of the oldest black presses in the nation. The *San Francisco Bay Guardian* and *SF Weekly* are alternative press publications. The *Bay Area Reporter* is a weekly serving the gay and lesbian community. Spanish weeklies include *El Bohemio News* and *El Latino*. The Japanese *Nichi Bei Times* was a weekly newspaper that ceased operations in 2009. *Vestkusten*, in both English and Swedish, came out twice a month, but was absorbed by long-established New York newspaper *Nordstjernan* in December 2007. The *Jewish News Weekly of Northern California* is distributed on Fridays, and also has an online edition available.

Several nationally distributed magazines are based in the city, as are many trade, industry, and technical journals. Among the many local and national publications are *San Francisco, Mother Jones*, and *Macworld*. A variety of scholarly, medical, and professional journals are published in San Francisco.

Television and Radio

Many television stations provide viewing choices from commercial network affiliates (CBS, ABC, PBS), public television, and foreign-language stations. Additional channels are available through cable service. AM and FM radio stations broadcast in San Francisco, offering a range of music, news, and informational programming.

Media Information: *San Francisco Chronicle*, 901 Mission Street, San Francisco, CA 94103-2988; telephone (415) 777-1111. *The Examiner*, 225 Bush, 17th Floor, San Francisco, CA 94104; telephone (415) 359-2661.

San Francisco Online

California Historical Society. Available www. californiahistoricalsociety.org

City of San Francisco Home Page. Available www. sfgov.org

San Francisco Chamber of Commerce. Available www.sfchamber.com

San Francisco Chronicle. Available www.sfchronicle. com

San Francisco Convention & Visitors Bureau.
Available www.sanfrancisco.travel
San Francisco Examiner. Available www.sfexaminer.
com
San Francisco Public Library. Available www.sfpl.org
San Francisco Unified School District. Available
www.sfusd.edu

BIBLIOGRAPHY

Birt, Rodger C., *History's Anteroom: Photography in San Francisco, 1906–1909* (Richmond, CA: William Stout Publishers, 2011)

Caen, Herb, *Baghdad by the Bay* (Garden City, NY: Doubleday, 1949)

Richards, Rand, *Historic San Francisco: A Concise History and Guide* (San Francisco, CA: Heritage House Publishers, 2007)

Solnit, Rebecca, *Infinite City: A San Francisco Atlas* (Berkeley: University of California Press, 2010

Twain, Mark, *Mark Twain's San Francisco* (New York: McGraw-Hill, 1963)

Twain, Mark, *Roughing it in California* (Kentfield, CA: L-D Allen Press, 1953)

Twain, Mark, *The Washoe Giant in San Francisco* (San Francisco, CA: G. Fields, 1938)

Wheeler, Richard S., *Aftershocks* (New York: Forge, 1999)

San Jose

■ The City in Brief

Founded: 1777 (incorporated, 1850)

Head Official: Mayor Chuck Reed (since 2006; current term expires 2014)

City Population
> 1990: 782,224
> 2000: 894,943
> 2010: 945,942
> 2012 estimate: 982,783
> Percent change, 2000–2010: 5.7%
> U.S. rank in 1990: 11th
> U.S. rank in 2000: 11th
> U.S. rank in 2010: 10th (State rank: 3rd)

Metropolitan Statistical Area Population
> 2000: 1,735,819
> 2010: 1,836,911
> 2012 estimate: 1,894,388
> Percent change, 2000–2010: 5.8%
> U.S. rank in 2010: 31st

Area: 175 square miles

Elevation: 67 feet above sea level

Average Annual Temperatures: 57.1° F

Average Annual Precipitation: 18.5 inches

Major Economic Sectors: manufacturing, technology, services, government

Unemployment Rate: 7% (2012)

Per Capita Income: $33,142

2012 FBI Crime Index Property: 28,463

Major Colleges and Universities: San Jose State University, San Jose/Evergreen Community College District

Daily Newspaper: *San Jose Mercury News*

■ Introduction

Once an average-sized town of agricultural strength, San Jose underwent a large transformation during a span of 30 years to become a technological stronghold. The area's "Silicon Valley" was the product of the computer revolution, and includes an array of electronic companies stretching throughout California's Santa Clara County. Along with the birth of Silicon Valley came a large increase in population. But growth and prosperity came with a price; traffic congestion, air pollution, housing shortages, and a strained infrastructure have all been problems due to swift development and the population's fourfold increase. While the type of technological growth has shifted over the years, most recently to social networking startups and bioscience firms, the central importance and economic power of San Jose, the capital of Silicon Valley, has not wavered.

■ Geography and Climate

San Jose is located in the Santa Clara Valley at the southern tip of San Francisco Bay, 48 miles south of San Francisco and 40 miles south of Oakland. The area is known as the Southern Peninsula. San Jose is the seat of Santa Clara County and the center of a large and expanding metropolitan area bordered by the Santa Cruz Mountains on the west and the Diablo Mountain range on the east. The Coyote and Guadalupe rivers run through the city. San Jose's climate is mild and semi-arid, with humidity varying from 67 percent in January to 51 percent in July. The city boasts of having about 300 sunny days per year.

The city of San Jose lies on the boundary zone between two of the major tectonic plates: the Pacific and North American plates. The city also lies between three

Albert Cheng/Shutterstock.com

active fault lines, including the San Andreas to the west. As such, the city is highly susceptible to earthquakes, which are sometimes quite damaging.

Area: 175 square miles

Elevation: 67 feet above sea level

Average Temperatures: 57.1° F

Average Annual Precipitation: 18.5 inches

■ History

San Jose Begins as Agricultural Center for State

San Jose was California's first civic settlement, founded in 1777 by Mexican colonists and named El Pueblo de San Jose de Guadalupe for St. Joseph and the Guadalupe River near the town site. The town was established in order to bring agricultural development to the Alta California territory; each settler was issued animals, farm implements, seeds, and a $10 monthly stipend. These farmers joined Spanish missionaries who were already in the area. The Native American inhabitants of the region were the Olhone. The disruption of their culture by the

missionaries and farmers and the spread of diseases eventually led to their virtual extermination.

As a supply station for prospectors during the gold rush, San Jose underwent a population explosion; upon incorporation in 1850 the city's inhabitants numbered 5,000 people. San Jose was the state capital from 1849 to 1851, and then became an important stage and boat link on the route to San Francisco until the advent of the railroad in 1864. Growth continued through the 1880s, reaching a culmination with the real estate boom and bust of 1887 when land sales totaled $2 million per day before the market collapsed. By the turn of the century San Jose was a major center for the cultivation of apricots, prunes, and grapes; with rail connections to other cities, it was also an important regional shipping hub.

High-Technology Revolution

Prior to World War II, San Jose, with its 18 canneries and 13 packing houses, was the world's largest canning and dried-fruit packing center. The city also pioneered the manufacture of specialized mechanical farm equipment in California; among the other products introduced by local inventors were the spray pump and the steam-powered stemmer-crusher for wine making. In the 1950s, however, San Jose was transformed from a farming community to a high-technology capital by another of its natural resources: silicon. This element is used in making semiconductors, a basic component in high-technology industries. Thus San Jose and Santa Clara County came to be known as "Silicon Valley." Originating at Stanford University, a vast military-industrial complex, which includes the Ames Research Facility of the National Aeronautics and Space Administration (NASA) at Moffett Field, ultimately spread throughout the Southern Peninsula.

San Jose's largest population boom was triggered by this high-technology revolution. This growth continued unabated from the 1950s through the early 1980s. It was in 1971 that a journalist first referred to the area as the "Silicon Valley," and the name has since stuck. Buoyed by the success of computer companies, a steady flow of venture capital poured into San Jose and Santa Clara County to finance new firms that sprang up almost overnight. Companies that got their start in the Silicon Valley area include Hewlett-Packard, Apple, Intel, Adobe, eBay, and Sun Microsystems. Expansion began to moderate only with the 1985 recession in the computer industry, followed by a new swell in the economy that developed with the growth of the dot-com industry in the 1990s.

When that bubble burst in 2000, so did many local businesses. The strength of other, more established businesses seemed to help the city avoid a major recession—more than 20 percent of the semiconductors and related devices made in the United States continue to be produced in the Silicon Valley—but the city has faced problems resulting from uncontrolled development. The city government faced regular budget shortfalls throughout the 2000s and into the 2010s. Since the city charter requires a balanced budget, the shortfalls resulted in the reduction of services.

In 2012 San Jose sought to control costs via a referendum that required public employees to accept lowr pay and pension cuts. The referendum passed but led to a court battle over whether public voters had the legal authority to mandate such cuts. A December 2013 state court ruling found that the city could not reduce pensions through the referendum but could cut worker salaries in order to fund higher retirement costs. A number of other cash-strapped cities, included several in California, looked to the ruling to guide their own efforts to reduce budget deficits.

Historical Information: History San Jose, 1650 Senter Road, San Jose, CA 95112; telephone (408) 287-2290; fax (408) 287-2291.

■ Population Profile

Metropolitan Statistical Area Population

2000: 1,735,819
2010: 1,836,911
2012 estimate: 1,894,388
Percent change, 2000–2010: 5.8%
U.S. rank in 2010: 31st

City Residents

1990: 782,224
2000: 894,943
2010: 945,942
2012 estimate: 982,783
Percent change, 2000–2010: 5.7%
U.S. rank in 1990: 11th
U.S. rank in 2000: 11th
U.S. rank in 2010: 10th (State rank: 3rd)

Density: 5,358.6 people per square mile

Racial and ethnic characteristics

White: 453,617
Black or African American: 30,619
American Indian and Alaskan Native: 6,287
Asian: 325,098
Native Hawaiian and Other Pacific Islander: 5,174
Hispanic or Latino (may be of any race): 325,828
Other: 161,988

Percent of residents born in state: 48.3%

Age characteristics

Population under 5 years old: 68,580
Population 5 to 9 years old: 71,342
Population 10 to 14 years old: 61,820
Population 15 to 19 years old: 62,138
Population 20 to 24 years old: 65,765
Population 25 to 34 years old: 152,284
Population 35 to 44 years old: 148,870
Population 45 to 54 years old: 141,239
Population 55 to 59 years old: 56,417
Population 60 to 64 years old: 47,432
Population 65 to 74 years old: 59,224
Population 75 to 84 years old: 34,430
Population 85 years and over: 13,242
Median age: 35.6

Births (2010–11 Metropolitan Area)

Total number: 24,727

Deaths (2010–11 Metropolitan Area)

Total number: 9,351

Money income (2012)

Per capita income: $33,142
Median household income: $80,155
Total households: 305,787

Number of households with income of ...

less than $10,000: 13,433
$10,000 to $14,999: 11,378
$15,000 to $24,999: 23,011

$25,000 to $34,999: 21,626
$35,000 to $49,999: 31,304
$50,000 to $74,999: 43,911
$75,000 to $99,999: 38,906
$100,000 to $149,999: 56,663
$150,000 to $199,999: 30,948
$200,000 or more: 34,607

Percent of families below poverty level: 12.5%

FBI Crime Index Property: 28,463

FBI Crime Index Violent: 3,547

■ Municipal Government

San Jose operates under a council-manager form of government. The council consists of ten council members elected by districts and the mayor, who is elected at-large. All council members serve four-year terms. The city manager is appointed by the mayor and the council to an open-ended term. San Jose is the seat of Santa Clara County.

Head Official: Mayor Chuck Reed (since 2006; current term expires 2014)

Total Number of City Employees: 5,651 (2013)

City Information: City of San Jose, 200 East Santa Clara St., San Jose, CA 95113; telephone (408) 535-3500; fax (408) 292-6731.

■ Economy

Major Industries and Commercial Activity

The rapid expansion of high-technology industries triggered uninterrupted growth in the Silicon Valley—San Jose and Santa Clara County—from the 1950s through the early 1980s. The 1985 recession, however, left a stagnant economy, pointing to a need to diversify the economic base of the area. Studies indicated that high-technology companies had to move toward decreased reliance on the defense industry. By the early 1990s, businesses in San Jose and Santa Clara County showed less than 20 percent of their budgets devoted to government contracts. The city was encouraged by a 1992 study that reported the nation's beleaguered semiconductor industry claimed 43.8 percent of the world market, up from a low of 36.9 percent in 1988.

By 1997 the nation was riding the wave of the booming new economy centered on the Internet and how to use it to change the way businesses, economies, and societies operated. High technology had become a major factor in the economic growth of U.S. cities, and

San Jose was at the center of it all. By 2000 San Jose was a mecca for hot startup companies and venture capital dollars. The bursting of the dot-com bubble in 2000 and subsequent economic recession stymied growth. However, once economic growth returned, San Jose still stood at the center of the information technology industries that continued to contribute significantly to general economic growth into the 2010s. In addition, a growing bioscience sector offered another pathway for economic growth.

The Silicon Valley region has received more patents than any other technology region in the United States. Technology businesses centered there continue to grow and expand, as does the growth of service and support businesses operating in conjunction with the industry. The San Jose Metropolitan Area is home to more than 6,600 high technology companies employing more than 254,000 people. Some 12 percent of all private-sector businesses in the city are high-technology companies, the greatest concentration of any city in the United States.

Companies in the Silicon Valley area include Hewlett-Packard, Apple, Intel, Intuit, Oracle, Yahoo!, Google, Adobe, and eBay. Recent additions include Netflix and social media marvels Facebook, Twitter, and LinkedIn.

Items and goods produced: missiles; rocket boosters; computers; atomic electrical equipment; fruit, vegetable, and fish cans; dairy products; chemicals; aluminum; paint; fiberglass; medical equipment

Incentive Programs—New and Existing Companies

Local programs: The city of San Jose adopted a Local Preference Policy in 2004. The policy works to encourage local companies to work with other local companies and the city to promote further job growth for residents and to keep local spending within the regional economy. The Local Preference Policy goes hand in hand with the Small Business Opportunity Program, which works to smooth the process for small businesses of selling their products and services to the city.

A variety of loans, bonds, and special funds are available to local businesses in San Jose. Among them are the North San Jose Traffic Impact Fee Reduction that offers reduced traffic impact fees for qualifying industrial developments of at least 100,000 square feet. The Downtown Parking Incentive Program offers businesses free parking when they lease office space in the downtown area and also provides existing firms with a 50 percent reduction for up to two years. A Downtown High Rise Incentive reduces fees and taxes for all projects of more than 12 stories. Construction taxes on tenant improvements are eligible for a reduction from 4.5 percent to 1 percent.

The San Jose Silicon Valley Chamber of Commerce works to develop and maintain the metropolitan area economy. Their particular focus is on aiding small and medium-sized companies involved in international business. The chamber's international trade program includes seminars, networking events, and exhibitions. The San Jose Downtown Association also works to stimulate and improve business conditions. The Silicon Valley Association of Startup Entrepreneurs and other local business organizations help members launch companies by providing access to resources and interactions with peers. Business incubators include the San Jose BioCube, U.S. Market Access Center, Silicon Valley Global Accelerator, and San Jose Entrepreneur Center.

State programs: California business incentives include the state's Alternative Energy and Advanced Transportation Authority Sales and Use Tax Exemptions for Zero Emission Vehicle Manufacturing. Initially targeting vehicle manufacturing only when it was passed in 2010, the sales and use tax exemption has since been expanded to all renewable energy technologies. In 2012 it was expanded again to include advanced manufacturing. More than one dozen additional incentives encourage green development or pollution-reducing business decisions.

Research and development tax credits offers companies a 15 percent credit against their bank and corporation tax liability for qualifying in-house research expenses; a 24 percent tax credit for basic research payments to outside organizations is also available. Industrial development bonds finance investment in land, buildings, and new equipment related to domestic manufacturing operations in the state. California Capital Access Program and Collateral Support Program also offer alternative methods of financing for businesses. Enterprise Zones and Local Agency Military Base Recovery Area regions provide incentives for development in targeted geographic regions. A New Jobs Tax Credit offers $3,000 per hire of qualifying new employees, and the state's Film and Television Tax Credit Program supports productions with a 20 percent tax credit against qualified expenses.

In 2011 California began offering companies the option to calculate their corporate income tax through the single sales factor method, rather than the existing triple apportionment derived from calculations of a company's payroll, property, and sales.

California's Innovation Hub Program, with 12 locations throughout the state, supports the commercialization of innovation and technology businesses through public-private partnerships, knowledge sharing, venture capital sources, and business incubators. The state also undertakes trade missions to form partnerships for trade and export promotion.

Job training programs: The state of California offers an Employment Training Panel to assist companies with post-hire training and reimbursement. The Employment Development Department also partners with Local Workforce Investment Areas to recruit, screen, test, evaluate, and hire qualified workers.

The Silicon Valley Workforce Investment Network works with local businesses and residents. The network's one-stop system offers resources for job seekers, as well as services to businesses that include pre-employment screening, access to qualified applicants, training programs, and assistance with employee transitions. Work2-future offers training and workforce assistance for local businesses and job-seekers.

Development Projects

A massive plan for the redevelopment of North San Jose, or the Innovation Triangle, was adopted by the city council in 2005. The North San Jose 2030 plan calls for a redevelopment of approximately 42 million square feet of industrial space in the Innovation Triangle, which is currently home to more than 1,200 multinational companies employing more than 55,000 people. The plan cites that the space is currently "functionally obsolete," and calls for renovations as well as an additional 26.7 million square feet of new research and development space and office space, 32,000 new housing units, and 1.4 million square feet of retail space. It was estimated that up to 83,000 new jobs would be brought to San Jose as a result of the North San Jose redevelopment.

A $2.8 billion expansion of the San Jose International Airport included expansions and improvements ranging from new concourses and parking garages, terminal and roadway improvements, and an Automated People Mover. The project was completed in 2010, with new terminals and car rental centers to serve the public. The improvements allowed the airport to handle 17 million passengers annually. In 2014 Bay Area Rapid Transit, an ultra-modern train system based in San Francisco, was constructing a $2.3 billion, 10-mile route extension to San Jose, expected to complete in 2017.

Plans were unveiled in 2013 for a two-million-square-foot office complex on the city's north side. Believed to be the largest office construction ever proposed in San Jose, the project was set to include 10 total buildings, each seven stories in height. The space could hold as many as 10,000 employees and was expected to cost at least $400 million to construct.

Other major private projects included Misora, a 424,825-square-foot residential complex expected to complete by 2014; Domain Apartments, 450,000 square feet of residential space that opened in 2013; Epic, a multi-family residential space slated for completion in 2014; Evergreen Place, a 636,000-square-foot complex of single-family homes completed in 2013; and the 1.6-

million-square-foot Crescent Village Apartment Homes, which also finished construction in 2013.

Economic Development Information: San Jose Silicon Valley Chamber of Commerce, 101 West Santa Clara St., San Jose, CA 95113; telephone (408) 291-5250; fax (408) 286-5019; email hals@sjchamber.com.

Commercial Shipping

Nearly half of the traffic at Mineta San Jose International Airport is business related, which makes the facility an important factor in the Silicon Valley economy. There are two cargo or freight airlines—Federal Express and United Parcel Service—and six freight-only airlines. Approximately 144.6 million pounds of cargo was handled during 2012. Two major rail freight lines and a number of motor freight carriers also operate in the metropolitan area. The city is part of Foreign Trade Zone 18, and the U.S. Customs services are available at the airport.

Labor Force and Employment Outlook

A well-educated and abundant work force coupled with the great quantity of high-level jobs created annually combine to create a shortage of qualified employees in the region. San Jose has ranked first among large metropolitan areas as a world class manufacturing community based on manufacturing strength and the high productivity of its workers. Calculations by the U.S. Department of Commerce estimated worker productivity at $130,000 per employee, more than double the national average. The workforce is highly educated, with 43 percent of workers having earned a college degree. World-class educational institutions nearby, such as Stanford University and the University of California, Berkeley provide an ample supply of highly qualified graduates each year.

The following is a summary of data regarding the 2012 San Jose labor force:

Size of civilian labor force: 513,208

Number of workers employed in . . .

agriculture and mining: 1,533
construction: 27,045
manufacturing: 86,729
wholesale trade: 10,422
retail trade: 51,130
transportation: 14,394
information systems: 13,093
finance: 22,213
professional administration: 73,989
education and social services: 83,020
arts and leisure: 38,675
other: 23,132
public administration: 11,122

Average hourly earnings of production workers: $18.84

Unemployment rate: 7% (2012)

Employers

Largest employers (2013)	*Number of employees*
County of Santa Clara	15,360
Cisco Systems	13,600
City of San Jose	5,651
eBay Inc.	4,700
IBM	4,200
U.S. Postal Service	3,920
San Jose State University	3,119
San Jose Unified School District	2,330
Hitachi	2,070
Adobe Systems, Inc.	2,000
Good Samaratin Hospital	1,950
Kaiser Permanente	1,940
Cadence Design Systems	1,800
Sanmina-SCI	1,770
Maxim Integrated	1,650

Cost of Living

San Jose suffers from a severe shortage of affordable housing and is among the most expensive cities in which to live.

The following is a summary of data regarding several key cost of living factors in the area.

2013 ACCRA Average House Price: $804,813

2013 ACCRA Cost of Living Index: 153

State income tax rate: 1.00% to 13.3%

State sales tax rate: 7.5%

Local income tax rate: None

Local sales tax rate: 1.25%

Property tax rate: Limited to 1% of assessed value by state law. In some cases the local taxing body can add additional taxes.

Economic Information: San Jose Silicon Valley Chamber of Commerce, 101 West Santa Clara St., San Jose, CA 95113; telephone (408) 291-5250; fax (408) 286-5019; email hals@sjchamber.com.

■ Education and Research

Elementary and Secondary Schools

The city of San Jose is served by many school districts, but not every district serves all ages of students. For instance, the Evergreen School District serves elementary and middle school students, while the East Side Union High School District serves only high school students. Charter schools are available in some districts. The largest district in the city is the San Jose Unified School District, which serves children of all ages with a variety of curriculums, including programs for advanced students as well as those for at-risk or special education students.

More than 60 private and parochial schools serve San Jose. The following is a summary of data regarding the San Jose Unified School District.

Total enrollment: 33,018

Number of facilities

total: 45
elementary schools: 27
junior high schools: 6
high schools: 8
other: 4

Student/teacher ratio: 23.59:1

Teacher salaries

average (statewide): $69,434

Funding per pupil: $9,016

Public Schools Information: San Jose Unified School District, 855 Lenzen Avenue, San Jose, CA 95126; telephone (408) 535-6000.

Colleges and Universities

San Jose State University is the oldest public institution of higher learning on the West Coast, as well as one of the largest universities in the 23-campus California State University system. San Jose State University educates more than 30,000 students and offers 69 bachelor's and 65 master's degrees in 110 concentrations; the university prides itself on being the top supplier of engineering, computer science, and business graduates to the Silicon Valley high-tech workforce. SJSU is one of the top 200 research universities in the United States.

The San Jose/Evergreen Community College District is comprised of San Jose City College and Evergreen Valley College; both award associate of arts and science degrees and offer occupational and technical training to 20,000 students every semester.

The National Hispanic University is a four-year institution offering associate's and bachelor's degrees in business administration, child development, computer information, criminal justice, education, mathematics and science, and psychology. Master's degrees are available in business administration, early childhood development, and education. The school offers special programs for middle and high school students to encourage their educational goals. The Lincoln Law School of San Jose offers part-time evening study programs for students seeking a legal education leading to the Bar Examination. Most students complete their course of studies in about four years.

The University of Phoenix has a facility in San Jose that awards bachelor's and master's degrees. Also located in the San Jose area are technical and vocational schools, adult learning centers, and extension facilities. Several colleges and universities—some of them considered among the best in the nation—are within driving distance of San Jose. They include Stanford University, Santa Clara University, and the University of California campuses at Berkeley and Santa Cruz.

Libraries and Research Centers

The San Jose Public Library system operates the Dr. Martin Luther King Jr. Main Library, 22 branches, and a bookmobile. Library holdings consist of more than two million items. The Dr. Martin Luther King, Jr. Main Library opened in 2003 as a joint development effort between the city, San Jose State University, and the now-defunct San Jose Redevelopment Agency. It is the first library of its kind in that the combined services and collections of the city system and the university library are made available to all. With eight floors and more than 475,000 square feet, the library is among the largest in the country and serves more than one million visitors annually. The Main Library also houses a special collection in the California Room, featuring state and local history from 1849 to the present; the Cultural Heritage Center; and the Ira F. Brilliant Center for Beethoven Studies. The Steinbeck Research Center contains the writings and memorabilia of novelist John Steinbeck, a San Jose area native, as well as the world's largest collection of the writer's first edition books.

San Jose State University has partnerships with more than 45 research institutes and facilities serving a wide variety of fields. These include the Bay Area Earth Science Institute, Carl W. Sharsmith Herbarium, Center for the Development of Recycling, and the Institute for Nursing Research and Practice. Other fields of interest include gerontology, the environment, and telecommunications. IBM's Almaden Research Center conducts industrial research in computer science, software, computer storage technology, and physical and materials science and technology.

Public Library Information: Dr. Martin Luther King, Jr. Main Library, 150 E. San Fernando Street, San Jose, CA 95112; telephone (408) 808-2000.

■ Health Care

HCA Healthcare owns two major hospitals in San Jose. The Regional Medical Center of San Jose admits some

10,680 patients annually to its 216 beds. The hospital features six Centers of Excellence: Emergency and Trauma, Cardiovascular, Women and Children's Health, Neurosciences, Cancer Care and Medical/Surgical Services. The trauma department is a Level II facility. Good Samaritan Hospital is a general acute-care hospital with 349 beds that has an accredited primary stroke center and offers one of the few behavioral health centers in the area. Other specialized departments include maternity care, the Cardiac and Vascular Institute, and the Arthritis and Joint Replacement Center.

Santa Clara Valley Medical Center, one of California's most high-tech public hospitals, is a 554-bed acute-care facility that houses a burn center, a rehabilitation center for patients with spinal and head injuries, a Level I trauma center, a high-risk maternity program, and a neonatal intensive-care unit. The 358-bed O'Connor Hospital, sponsored by the Daughters of Charity of St. Vincent de Paul, offers heart and cancer care, sports medicine, and a Wound Care Center. O'Connor Hospital also supports a satellite pediatric facility and a family health center.

Stanford Hospital in nearby Palo Alto is highly regarded for its work in a wide variety of specialties, notably cardiovascular treatment, and is the teaching facility for the Stanford University School of Medicine. Only 20 minutes from San Jose, the hospital's 477 beds and more than 2,000 medical staff personnel serve some one million area residents annually. Stanford Hospital was ranked nationally in 13 specialties in 2013–14 by *U.S. News & World Report*.

■ Recreation

Sightseeing

Most of the attractions in San Jose are related to the natural beauty of the area or to its historical past. Kelley Park is a popular site, offering a variety of diversions, including Happy Hollow Park and Zoo, where visitors can enjoy family-oriented amusements and view wildlife in a 12-acre natural setting. The 14-acre San Jose History Park Museum on the grounds features a recreated turn-of-the-century town with such exhibits as a working blacksmith shop, a Victorian home, and a doctor's office. Also located in Kelley Park is the Japanese Friendship Garden, featuring flowering trees and shrubs, waterfalls, and koi fish. Other botanical gardens in San Jose are Overfelt Botanical Gardens and the Municipal Rose Garden.

Alum Rock Park is a wildlife refuge containing mineral springs, trails, and picnic facilities; the Youth Science Institute based in the park offers educational programs and special events to acquaint children with nature. Ardenwood Historic Farm in neighboring Fremont is a working farm that demonstrates agrarian life

from 1880 through the 1920s; among the exhibits are soap and candle making and the planting and harvesting of crops with horse-drawn equipment.

Especially popular with tourists is the Winchester Mystery House; according to legend, this "haunted" Victorian mansion, containing 160 rooms, was built by the wealthy but eccentric widow of the maker of the Winchester rifle to appease the spirits of the rifle's victims.

Families with children will not want to miss a trip to several of the special areas in Guadalupe River Park Conservancy. The park's Discovery Meadow is home to the Children's Discovery Museum, featuring 28,000 square feet of interactive exhibits, and Monopoly in the Park, the world's largest Monopoly game board at 930 square feet. McEnery Park includes a playground and 12 sculptures that represent the wildlife of the river. Arena Green has a carousel, and large art work in honor of Olympic champion ice skaters of the area. The Guadalupe Gardens are a relaxing place for a stroll or a guided tour, for a small fee.

Nationally known for its table wines, the San Jose area boasts dozens of wineries; many offer wine-tasting and tours of their facilities. Several theme parks operate in Santa Clara County, including Raging Waters in San Jose's Lake Cunningham Regional Park and California's Great America in nearby Santa Clara.

Arts and Culture

San Jose is becoming a regional center for the arts as local performing groups and organizations consistently draw larger audiences from throughout the Bay Area. The San Jose Repertory Theatre produces classic and contemporary drama. Plays for children are staged by the Children's Musical Theater San Jose. The San Jose Wind Symphony holds concerts at many area venues. The California Theatre is home to the Symphony Silicon Valley and Opera San Jose. Ballet San Jose is considered one of the country's most innovative ballet companies, with a repertoire of more than 120 modern and traditional classical ballets. The San Jose Stage Company produces plays by contemporary playwrights. SAP Center at San Jose hosts varied performers such as U2 and the Mormon Tabernacle Choir.

San Jose's museums and galleries specialize in a variety of fields. Attractions include the Children's Discovery Museum, offering hands-on exhibits, and The Tech Museum of Innovation, offering an IMAX theater and interactive experiences in new technologies. The Rosicrucian Egyptian Museum features the city's only planetarium as well as astronomical and scientific displays, a full-scale Egyptian tomb exhibit, and a collection of Egyptian artifacts.

The San Jose Museum of Art holds 1,400 objects in its permanent collection, which includes a variety of media with a focus on twentieth- and twenty-first century artwork, particularly of artists from the West Coast. The San Jose Museum of Quilts and Textiles, one of the few museums of its kind in the country, provides a showcase for the history of quilts and textiles. The work of local and Bay Area artists is shown at the Institute of Contemporary Art and at Works San Jose gallery. Works San Jose is a mixed-use space for contemporary art, music, and other performances. Movimiento de Arte y Cultura Latino Americana (MACLA) offers a place for the contemporary art and performances of Latino artists.

Festivals and Holidays

Special events and celebrations take place in the San Jose area throughout the year, many focusing on the varied cultural heritage of the region's population. Winter events include January's Silicon Valley International Auto Show; in February, the Vietnamese Spring Festival and Parade offers food, entertainment, games, and other fun events highlighting Vietnamese culture in the city. March offerings include the Golden Circle Theatre Party, an annual black-tie benefit for Santa Clara University, and the annual Cinequest Film Festival. May brings cultural celebrations including the Nikkei Matsuri, and Cinco de Mayo Parade and Festival. The Juneteenth Festival occurs during its namesake month of June. In July, visitors and residents can enjoy the Tahiti Fete San Jose. August ushers in the San Jose Jazz Summer Fest, the Santa Clara County Fair, and the San Jose PRIDE, a festival and parade sponsored by the area's gay, lesbian, bisexual, and transgender community. The Tapestry Arts Festival falls on Labor Day weekend, although funding shortages left its future uncertain as of 2014. Autumn offers the International Mariachi and Mexican Heritage Festival. San Jose's year winds down at Gilroy Gardens, which hosts holiday lighting events during December.

Sports for the Spectator

San Jose is in an advantageous location for fans of professional sports. The National Hockey League's San Jose Sharks play at the SAP Center. The SAP Center also hosts the Arena Football League's SaberCats, who returned in 2011 after a two-year hiatus. Other sporting events held at the center include figure skating, boxing, among other events. Major League Soccer's San Jose Earthquakes play at Buck Shaw Stadium; they were scheduled to move to a new, soccer-specific stadium in 2015. The San Jose Giants, the Advanced Single-A farm club for the San Francisco Giants of Major League Baseball, play their home games at Municipal Stadium in San Jose. Horse racing can be watched at the San Jose Fair Downs at the Santa Clara County Fairgrounds.

Several professional teams compete within driving distance of San Jose; among them are baseball's San Francisco Giants and Oakland Athletics, Oakland's Golden State Warriors of the National Basketball Association, and the San Francisco 49ers and Oakland Raiders of the National Football League.

Sports for the Participant

A variety of neighborhood and regional parks in the San Jose area provide facilities for a variety of activities such as water sports, baseball, tennis, golf, hiking, horseback riding, and wildlife study. San Jose's has more than 100 large and small neighborhood and regional parks and gardens; especially popular are Almaden Quicksilver Park, Alum Rock Park, and Lake Cunningham Regional Park. There are 53 miles of trails and more than 200 miles of on-street bikeways throughout the city. Numerous reservoirs and lakes are located throughout the region for sailing, waterskiing, and windsurfing. More than 15 local and championship golf courses exist in the area, including two Jack Nicklaus-designed golf courses spanning Coyote Creek and the Los Lagos Golf Course. Runners have two major fall events to choose from: the Silicon Valley Marathon and the Rock 'n' Roll Half Marathon San Jose.

Shopping and Dining

With several major and outlet malls, regional shopping centers, and myriad neighborhood stores and specialty shops, San Jose can meet the needs of most consumers. San Jose's largest shopping center is Westfield Valley Fair, boasting more than 250 stores and various dining establishments. Santana Row, directly across the street from the mall, includes shops, restaurants, spas, and a full-service hotel in a complex set up like European streets. The Westfield Oakridge Mall has more than 200 shops as well as cafes and restaurants. The San Jose Flea Market is one of the nation's largest flea markets and attracts more than 2,000 sellers and more than 80,000 shoppers per week to its eight miles of corridors and alleys. Shoppers will find anything from antiques and collectibles to freshly made foods. The "Produce Row" section of the market is touted as California's largest farmer's market. San Jose Market Center downtown features about 50 retail and dining establishments.

Restaurants are plentiful in San Jose, offering American cuisine and ethnic specialties ranging from German and French to Mexican, Persian, Moroccan, and Thai dishes. Several authentic Japanese restaurants are clustered in historic Japantown. Santana Row offers ethnic restaurants such as Amber India and Left Bank. Local favorites include Paolo's, an Italian restaurant with a 6,500-bottle wine collection; Emile's, hosted by the Swiss Chef Emile; and Original Joe's, featuring Italian-American family-style dining. Santa Clara Valley wineries combine brunches, luncheons, and picnics with wine tastings; the area is noted for its Chardonnay, Zinfandel, and Johannisburg Riesling wines.

Visitor Information: Team San Jose, 408 Almaden Blvd., San Jose, CA 95110; telephone (408) 295-9600; toll-free (800) 726-5673.

■ Convention Facilities

The principal convention and meeting place is the San Jose Convention Center. It offers a total of 550,000 square feet of event space with 43 meeting rooms and ballrooms of 35,194 square feet and 22,000 square feet. South Hall, adjacent to the convention center, has 80,000 square feet of column-free exhibit space. Directly across the street from the convention center is the City National Civic, a Spanish Mission style dual-level auditorium seating 3,060. The 536-seat Montgomery Theater is in the same building as the City National Civic. Next door is Parkside Hall, featuring 30,000 square feet of unobstructed exhibit space. This space can be divided into two smaller sections. The 1,100-seat California Theatre downtown has conference and meeting rooms available.

There are more than 4,000 hotel and motel rooms in San Jose's downtown and another 4,400 citywide. Hotels and motels in the San Jose metropolitan area, many of them new or recently renovated, provide accommodations for a variety of group functions. Among the unique meeting facilities are the many museums and wineries in the area.

Convention Information: Team San Jose, 408 Almaden Blvd., San Jose, CA 95110; telephone (408) 295-9600; toll-free (800) 726-5673.

■ Transportation

Approaching the City

The Norman Y. Mineta San Jose International Airport, located 10 minutes from downtown, handles 3.7 million passengers annually; it is served by 11 airlines with more than 40 non-stop destinations as of 2014. Construction projects at the airport expanded and enhanced facilities and completed in 2010. Corporate and private aircraft are accommodated at the Reid-Hillview Airport.

Three interstate highways serve San Jose: Interstate 680 (north–south), which becomes Interstate 280 (east–west), and Interstate 880 (north–south). U.S. Route 101 runs northeast–southwest. State routes 87 and 17 also lead into the city.

Amtrak serves the San Jose Diridon Station; rail commuter service to San Francisco is provided by Caltrain. Other intercity rail connections are made via the county bus system that links with BART (Bay Area

Rapid Transit), an ultra-modern train system based in San Francisco; a $2.3 billion, 10-mile route to reach San Jose was under construction in 2014, with an anticipated opening in 2017.

Traveling in the City

The Santa Clara Valley Transportation Authority (VTA) operates a 42.2-mile-long light rail system out of the downtown Transit Mall, which also provides antique trolleys and county transit buses in and around the city and connecting the city with Bay Area Rapid Transit (BART) to East Bay and San Francisco. The light rail system runs from Mountain View through downtown San Jose and ends in south San Jose residential and shopping areas. DASH Shuttles provide service around downtown and connect the VTA Light Rail to the Diridon Caltrain Station, the convention center, and San Jose State University. The Altamont Commuter Express train runs between Stockton and San Jose.

■ Communications

Newspapers and Magazines

San Jose's daily newspaper is the *San Jose Mercury News.* Weekly community papers include the *Almaden Resident, Rose Garden Resident,* and *Willow Glen Resident,* all published by Silicon Valley Community Newspapers. The metropolitan area is also served by such publications as the weekly *Silicon Valley Business Journal. El Observador* and *Alianza Metropolitan News* are published weekly in Spanish and English.

Television and Radio

Because of the proximity of communities in the Bay Area, San Jose shares a number of television and radio stations with other cities. Eight television stations are based in San Jose. The area also broadcasts four AM and eight FM radio stations.

Media Information: *San Jose Mercury News,* 750 Ridder Park Drive, San Jose, CA 95190; telephone (800) 870-6357; fax (408) 288-8060.

San Jose Online

City of San Jose home page. Available www. sanjoseca.gov

History San Jose. Available www.historysanjose.org

Team San Jose. Available www.sanjose.org

San Jose Mercury News. Available www.mercurynews. com

San Jose Public Library. Available www.sjpl.org

San Jose Silicon Valley Chamber of Commerce. Available www.sjchamber.com

San Jose Unified School District. Available www. sjusd.org

BIBLIOGRAPHY

Beers, David, *Blue Sky Dream: A Memoir of America's Fall From Grace* (New York: Doubleday, 1996)

Branson, Po, *The First $20 Million is Always the Hardest: A Silicon Valley Novel* (New York: Random House, 1997)

Brookner, Jackie, *Urban Rain: Stormwater as Resource: A City of San Jose Public Art Project at Roosevelt Community Center* (Pt. Reyes Station, CA: ORO Editions, 2009)

Johnson, Bob, *San Jose* (Charleston, SC: Arcadia Publishing, 2010)

Lecuyer, Christopher, *Making Silicon Valley: Innovation and the Growth of High Tech, 1930–1970* (Cambridge, MA: MIT Press, 2006)

Santa Ana

The City in Brief

Founded: 1869 (incorporated, 1886)

Head Official: Mayor Miguel A. Pulido (since 1994; current term expires 2014)

City Population
> 1990: 293,827
> 2000: 337,977
> 2010: 324,528
> 2012 estimate: 330,913
> Percent change, 2000–2010: −4%
> U.S. rank in 1990: 52nd
> U.S. rank in 2000: 51st
> U.S. rank in 2010: 57th (State rank: 11th)

Metropolitan Statistical Area Population
> 2000: 12,365,627
> 2010: 12,828,837
> 2012 estimate: 13,052,921
> Percent change, 2000–2010: 3.7%
> U.S. rank in 2000: 2nd
> U.S. rank in 2010: 2nd

Area: 27.2 square miles

Elevation: 110 feet above sea level

Average Annual Temperatures: 65.0° F

Average Annual Precipitation: 13.17 inches

Major Economic Sectors: services, trade, manufacturing

Unemployment Rate: 7.1% (2012)

Per Capita Income: $16,012

2012 FBI Crime Index Property: 7,389

Major Colleges and Universities: Rancho Santiago Community College

Daily Newspaper: *Orange County Register*

Introduction

Santa Ana is the seat and largest city of California's Orange County. The city is surrounded by the rich farmland of the Santa Ana Valley and is included in a large area that encompasses nearby Anaheim, Buena Park, and Fullerton. Situated not far from the Pacific Coast, Santa Ana is also close to the Los Angeles metropolitan area to the northwest, as well as the San Diego metropolitan area to the southeast. The majority of the city's residents are Hispanic, and the community has retained much of its rich cultural heritage as seen through festivals and celebrations throughout the year. The city was once a farming town, but has since evolved into a financial and governmental center for Orange County. The city has placed much emphasis on reviving historical landmarks and its arts scene.

Geography and Climate

Santa Ana is located in the Santa Ana Valley in southwestern California. The seat and largest city of Orange County, it is located about 30 miles southeast of Los Angeles and 90 miles north of San Diego. Situated on the Santa Ana River, it is near the Santa Ana Mountains and about 12 miles from the coast of the Pacific Ocean. For statistical purposes, the city is sometimes linked in a metropolitan division with Anaheim and Irvine and sometimes listed as part of a Metropolitan Statistical Area (MSA) encompassing Los Angeles and Long Beach. The weather is typically warm and sunny, as in most of Southern California. The sun shines approximately 300 days out of the year. Year-round humidity at noon is usually around 53 percent. The Santana Winds (or Santa Ana Winds) that typically occur from late summer to spring bring warm and dry air

Santa Ana Courthouse in Orange County California. © *Nik Wheeler/Alamy*

down from the high deserts to the San Bernardino Mountains and through the Los Angeles-Orange County Basin. These winds are sometimes accompanied by brush and wildfires. The region of Southern California, with several fault lines, is susceptible to earthquakes, though most are of a relatively low magnitude.

Area: 27.2 square miles

Elevation: 110 feet above sea level

Average Temperatures: 65.0° F

Average Annual Precipitation: 13.17 inches

■ History

Franciscans Settle Santa Ana Valley

The valley in which Santa Ana is located was discovered in July 1769, during a Franciscan expedition led by Don Gaspar Portola. The explorers christened the valley Santa Ana in honor of Saint Anne, also giving the name Santa Ana to the river flowing through the valley. One of the members of the Portola party, Father Junipero Serra, later founded a chain of Franciscan missions that still can be seen

today. The El Camino Real, the King's Highway, which linked the missions, passes through the Santa Ana Valley.

Another member of the Portola group, a soldier named Antonio Yorba, and his nephew, Juan Peralta, received a Spanish grant for land extending from the foothills of the Santa Ana Canyon to the ocean. They used the land for grazing cattle and later developed irrigation systems fed by water from the Santa Ana River. The land was thus quite fertile, and the area soon became an agricultural center, with several ranches established in the valley.

City of Santa Ana Prospers

The 1849 California Gold Rush brought the region a population boom, which was followed by another major expansion during the Civil War. The valley's large ranches were subdivided and sold to the newcomers, many of whom later founded the cities of Santa Ana, Orange, and Tustin. Santa Ana's modern history began in 1869 when William H. Spurgeon purchased 70 acres from the Yorba heirs and drew up a town plan. Since the land had been part of the Santiago de Santa Ana ranch and since it was also near the Santa Ana River, the town was called Santa Ana.

Soon the new town became prosperous, boasting mail delivery twice a week and a number of stores and residences within its boundaries. Farms also were established throughout the valley; the rich soil and favorable climate permitted the cultivation of several crops. Santa Ana became a commercial center; its central location in the valley made it a natural marketplace for crops produced in the surrounding region that is now Orange County. When rail transport arrived in the area in 1877, the town developed and population increased; in 1886 Santa Ana was incorporated. Three years later Orange County was separated from Los Angeles County and Santa Ana was named the county seat.

World War II brought further development as industry moved into the area. The population of Santa Ana increased from around 49,000 people in 1900 to nearly 210,000 residents in 1950. A city charter, providing for a council-manager form of government, was adopted in 1952. Since World War II Santa Ana has become a financial and governmental center of Orange County.

Efforts began in the 1980s to restore and revitalize the city of Santa Ana, especially its downtown. As a result the city became known for its historic downtown and MainPlace shopping center (Westfield MainPlace Mall), which created thousands of jobs in the heart of the city. In 1993 the city gained designation as an Enterprise Zone by the State of California and in 1999 was recognized as a Federal Empowerment Zone. The tax credits allowed by these designations encouraged development of new and existing business. The development of Artists Village in the downtown area contributed significantly to the city's pride in its arts and culture, and the development of neighborhood associations also helped bring city residents together. Into the twenty-first century, the city continued to focus development on revitalization of existing buildings that preserved the city's history and culture.

Historical Information: Santa Ana Public Library, History Room, 26 Civic Center Plaza, Santa Ana, CA 92701; telephone (714) 647-5280. Santa Ana Historical Preservation Society, 120 W Civic Center Drive, Santa Ana, CA 92701; telephone (714) 547-9645.

■ Population Profile

Metropolitan Statistical Area Population

2000: 12,365,627
2010: 12,828,837
2012 estimate: 13,052,921
Percent change, 2000–2010: 3.7%
U.S. rank in 2000: 2nd
U.S. rank in 2010: 2nd

City Residents

1990: 293,827
2000: 337,977

2010: 324,528
2012 estimate: 330,913
Percent change, 2000–2010: −4%
U.S. rank in 1990: 52nd
U.S. rank in 2000: 51st
U.S. rank in 2010: 57th (State rank: 11th)

Density: 11,900.8 people per square mile

Racial and ethnic characteristics

White: 174,088
Black or African American: 3,887
American Indian and Alaskan Native: 1,843
Asian: 32,089
Native Hawaiian and Other Pacific Islander: 655
Hispanic or Latino (may be of any race): 260,734
Other: 118,351

Percent of residents born in state: 46.3%

Age characteristics

Population under 5 years old: 27,213
Population 5 to 9 years old: 24,558
Population 10 to 14 years old: 26,483
Population 15 to 19 years old: 28,974
Population 20 to 24 years old: 33,175
Population 25 to 34 years old: 52,774
Population 35 to 44 years old: 47,904
Population 45 to 54 years old: 42,454
Population 55 to 59 years old: 15,646
Population 60 to 64 years old: 9,519
Population 65 to 74 years old: 12,258
Population 75 to 84 years old: 7,081
Population 85 years and over: 2,874
Median age: 29.2

Births (2010–11 Metropolitan Area)

Total number: 171,737

Deaths (2010–11 Metropolitan Area)

Total number: 75,587

Money income (2012)

Per capita income: $16,012
Median household income: $52,961
Total households: 71,546

Number of households with income of ...

less than $10,000: 3,022
$10,000 to $14,999: 3,381
$15,000 to $24,999: 8,050
$25,000 to $34,999: 7,393
$35,000 to $49,999: 11,727
$50,000 to $74,999: 15,382
$75,000 to $99,999: 9,256
$100,000 to $149,999: 8,923
$150,000 to $199,999: 2,886
$200,000 or more: 1,526

Percent of families below poverty level: 22.0%

FBI Crime Index Property: 7,389

FBI Crime Index Violent: 1,334

■ Municipal Government

In accordance with a charter adopted in 1952, Santa Ana operates under a council-manager form of government. The city is governed by a council consisting of six council members and an elected mayor. Council members are nominated from wards but are elected by voters from the entire city. Council members are elected to four-year terms and are limited to three consecutive terms. The mayor is elected every two years. The council hires a city manager.

Head Official: Mayor Miguel A. Pulido (since 1994; current term expires 2014)

Total Number of City Employees: 1,500 (2013)

City Information: City of Santa Ana, 20 Civic Center Plaza, Santa Ana, CA 92701; telephone (714) 647-5400.

■ Economy

Major Industries and Commercial Activity

Santa Ana's major industries include a mix of retail trade, services, and manufacturing firms.

Government is a major employer in Santa Ana; as the county seat, the city has offices at the county, state, and federal levels. Santa Ana is also a financial center. The aerospace and electronics industries, among the area's largest employers, figure significantly in the city's economy. Among Santa Ana's major private employers in 2014 were TTM Technologies, Tenet Healthcare System Medical, Aluminum Products Inc., and Brasstech.

Ingram Micro ranked 76th on the 2013 *Fortune* 500 list. Headquartered in Santa Ana, the company is the world's largest wholesale technology distributer and distributes and markets products for major companies such as Apple, Cisco, IBM, Microsoft, and Samsung, among others.

Tourism is a major industry in Santa Ana and Orange County. Within a radius of 10 miles of the city are several of California's most popular tourist attractions, such as Disneyland, Knott's Berry Farm, and southern California beaches.

Items and goods produced: sugar; glass products; plumbing material; foam rubber products; dehydrating, electronic, and sporting equipment; concentrates; extracts; agricultural machinery; perfumes; feed; cement pipes; soft drinks; rivets; fasteners; canned and dried fruits and vegetables; packaged walnuts and oranges; poultry

Incentive Programs—New and Existing Companies

Local programs: The Orange County Business Council (OCBC) concentrates on attracting and retaining high-quality, high-paying and low-polluting jobs to Orange County. For business development, the OCBC is the single business point-of-contact for economic development and related business information in Orange County. As well, the OCBC leads the county in ensuring a quality workforce and advocating legislation to benefit businesses.

State programs: California business incentives include the state's Alternative Energy and Advanced Transportation Authority Sales and Use Tax Exemptions for Zero Emission Vehicle Manufacturing. Initially targeting vehicle manufacturing only when it was passed in 2010, the sales and use tax exemption has since been expanded to all renewable energy technologies. In 2012 it was expanded again to include advanced manufacturing. More than one dozen additional incentives encourage green development or pollution-reducing business decisions.

Research and development tax credits offers companies a 15 percent credit against their bank and corporation tax liability for qualifying in-house research expenses; a 24 percent tax credit for basic research payments to outside organizations is also available. Industrial development bonds finance investment in land, buildings, and new equipment related to domestic manufacturing operations in the state. California Capital Access Program and Collateral Support Program also offer alternative methods of financing for businesses. Enterprise Zones and Local Agency Military Base Recovery Area regions provide incentives for development in targeted geographic regions. A New Jobs Tax Credit offers $3,000 per hire of qualifying new employees, and the state's Film and Television Tax Credit Program supports productions with a 20 percent tax credit against qualified expenses.

In 2011 California began offering companies the option to calculate their corporate income tax through the single sales factor method, rather than the existing triple apportionment derived from calculations of a company's payroll, property, and sales.

California's Innovation Hub Program, with 12 locations throughout the state, supports the commercialization of innovation and technology businesses through public-private partnerships, knowledge sharing, venture capital sources, and business incubators. The state also undertakes trade missions to form partnerships for trade and export promotion.

Job training programs: The state of California offers an Employment Training Panel to assist companies with post-hire training and reimbursement. The Employment Development Department also partners with Local Workforce Investment Areas to recruit, screen, test, evaluate, and hire qualified workers.

The Santa Ana Work/Opportunities/Resources/Knowledge (W/O/R/K) Center is a non-profit organization comprised of a partnership between several agencies: the Santa Ana Workforce Investment Board, State Employment Development Department, Santa Ana College, and Orange County Social Services. The W/O/R/K Center is designed to meet the job training and placement needs of the community. The Workplace Learning Resource Center, available in Santa Ana through the Rancho Santiago Community College District, is part of a statewide network that offers assessments and low cost customized on-site training for some businesses.

Development Projects

In 2010 Santa Ana adopted a development plan for a centralized area encompassing 457 acres including the train depot, downtown, the Civic Center, the Santa Ana Boulevard Corridor, and the Logan and Lacy neighborhoods. The Renaissance Specific Plan created a land use plan that built upon the urban environment, while at the same time ensuring that future development continued to enhance the area's strengths. The plan was used, in part, to help the city compete for and win funding for mass transit projects, as the plan detailed how the city's broader development policies supported use of mass transit.

Improvements to Interstate 5 in Orange County, including in and around Santa Ana, were underway in 2013, with major construction expected to begin in 2016. The $45 million transportation project was slated to add carpool lanes and improve entrance and exit ramps for the freeway.

City Place, a multi-use urban village with residential and commercial space developed in the late 2000s and early 2010s, was seeing ongoing development into 2014, with additional proposals for new residential spaces under consideration by the city.

Economic Development Information: Orange County Business Council, 2 Park Plaza, Suite 100, Irvine, CA 92614; telephone (949) 476-2242; fax (949) 476-9240.

Commercial Shipping

The John Wayne Airport has two all-cargo airlines. Rail freight service is provided by the Southern Pacific and Union Pacific railroads. The Los Angeles International Airport (LAX), about 37 miles northwest of the city, has 1,000 cargo flights each day. Handling facilities include the 98-acre Century Cargo Complex, the 57.4-acre Imperial Complex, the Imperial Cargo Center, and several terminals on the south side of the airport. Motor

freight carriers link Santa Ana with markets throughout the country; overnight delivery service is available to several West Coast cities as well as to Tucson, Phoenix, Las Vegas, and Reno.

Labor Force and Employment Outlook

Santa Ana has a young, well-trained work force; the median age is the lowest of the county's seven largest cities. Projections to 2015 estimated that 5.6 percent of residents would hold an associate's degree, 12.3 percent a bachelor's degree, and 6.2 percent a graduate degree. Unionization is prevalent in manufacturing, trucking, retailing, the hotel industry, warehousing, and some grocery and drugstore chains.

The following is a summary of data regarding the 2012 Santa Ana labor force:

Size of civilian labor force: 162,634

Number of workers employed in . . .

    agriculture and mining: 1,663
    construction: 10,848
    manufacturing: 25,814
    wholesale trade: 4,092
    retail trade: 17,569
    transportation: 4,114
    information systems: 2,164
    finance: 7,370
    professional administration: 19,565
    education and social services: 18,358
    arts and leisure: 19,332
    other: 10,909
    public administration: 2,693

Average hourly earnings of production workers: $15.78

Unemployment rate: 7.1% (2012)

Employers

Largest employers (2013)	*Number of employees*
County of Orange	17,447
Santa Ana Unified School District	4,665
Santa Ana College	2,390
Integrated Healthcare Holdings	1,932
City of Santa Ana	1,500
Corinthian Colleges Inc	1,400
First American Financial	1,215
Orange County Register (Freedom Communications)	1,100

Ingram Micro	985
Abbott Medical	
Optics Inc	750

Cost of Living

The cost of living in the Los Angeles-Long Beach-Santa Ana metropolitan area is significantly higher than the national average, with the median cost of a home in 2013 estimated at nearly $730,000.

The following is a summary of data regarding several key cost of living factors in the area.

2013 ACCRA Average House Price: $729,578

2013 ACCRA Cost of Living Index: 144

State income tax rate: 1.00% to 13.3%

State sales tax rate: 7.5%

Local income tax rate: None

Local sales tax rate: 0.5%

Property tax rate: Limited to 1% of assessed value by state law. In some cases the local taxing body can add additional taxes.

Economic Information: Santa Ana Chamber of Commerce, 1631 W. Sunflower Ave. #C-35, Santa Ana, CA 92704; telephone (714) 541-5353; fax (714) 541-2238.

■ Education and Research

Elementary and Secondary Schools

The Santa Ana Unified School District (SAUSD), the largest in Orange County, is comprised of more than 57,000 students. It was the sixth largest school district in California as of 2014. The district is administered by a five-member, nonpartisan board of education that appoints a superintendent.

About 82 percent of students in the district are English learners, with Spanish, Vietnamese and Khmer the most common languages spoken at home. Additionally, some 91 percent of students are eligible for free or reduced lunches.

The Achievement Reinforcement Center opened in 2006 as an alternative school environment for at-risk students. A number of pre-K/early childhood programs are available. The system also has a Gifted and Talented Education (GATE) program. Occupational programs are available for high school students. There were five charter schools in the district in 2014.

A variety of private schools also operate in the city.

The following is a summary of data regarding the Santa Ana Unified School District.

Total enrollment: 57,319

Number of facilities

total: 61
elementary schools: 36
junior high schools: 9
high schools: 7
other: 9

Student/teacher ratio: 26.25:1

Teacher salaries

average (statewide): $69,434

Funding per pupil: $9,065

Public Schools Information: Santa Ana Unified School District, 1601 E. Chestnut Avenue, Santa Ana, CA 92701; telephone (714) 558-5501.

Colleges and Universities

Santa Ana College, the fourth oldest junior college in the state, offers numerous programs leading to an associate's degree in science or arts or a vocational certificate of competency. Enrollment for credit in 2012 was 18,764 students; an additional 10,554 students were enrolled in non-credit courses. The college offers a number of local off-site programs. The Centennial Education Center offers non-credit continuing education that includes English-as-a-Second-Language courses, citizenship preparation, high school completion, parent education, and vocational training. A Regional Fire Training Center offers classes for students enrolled in the Fire Academy program as well as for fire professionals seeking continuing education credits. Santa Ana College is part of the Rancho Santiago Community College District, which also sponsors Santiago Canyon College in Orange.

The Santa Ana campus of Newbridge College offers diploma programs for surgical technology, medical laboratory technicians, medical assistants, ultrasound technicians, and medical office administration. The Southern California Institute of Technology in nearby Anaheim offers engineering, computer science, and accounting degree programs.

Located within commuting distance of Santa Ana, other Orange County colleges include the University of California, Irvine; California State University, Fullerton; and Chapman College in Orange.

Libraries and Research Centers

The Santa Ana Public Library system operates a main library at Civic Center Plaza and the Newhope Library Learning Center. The main library houses the Santa Ana History Room, a computer lab, and a Passport Application Acceptance Service center. The Newhope Library Learning Center also contains computer labs for youth, high school students, and adults. Holdings consist of more than 240,000 books and more than 300 periodicals, plus CDs, tapes, videos, and maps. Special collections include California and Santa Ana history, foreign language books and cassettes, and federal and state documents.

The Orange County Public Library operates 33 branches throughout the county, and holds more than 2.5 million volumes and 5,000 periodicals and maintains a special collection of the Orange County Law Library documents. Other libraries and research centers are affiliated with government agencies, colleges, hospitals, and private corporations.

Research activities in botany are conducted at the Ranch Santa Ana Botanical Garden. The Apex Research Institute in Santa Ana conducts clinical trials for several major pharmaceutical companies.

Public Library Information: Santa Ana Public Library, 26 Civic Center Plaza, Santa Ana, CA 92701; telephone (714) 647-5250.

■ Health Care

Three general hospitals are located in Santa Ana. They offer a range of specialties such as cardiac rehabilitation and hospice care. The largest medical facility is Western Medical Center with 282 beds, a Level II Trauma Center, and 700 primary care physicians. Western also hosts the Grossman Burn Center, a seven-bed specialized care unit; a 16-bed Neonatal Intensive Care Unit; and a kidney transplant unit.

Coastal Communities Hospital is a 178-bed acute care hospital offering community health programs as well as basic health-care services, an emergency room, and outpatient surgical units. Kindred Hospital–Santa Ana is a long-term, acute-care facility.

Nearby is the teaching hospital of the medical school at the University of California, Irvine; other medical schools in the area are the University of California, Los Angeles; University of Southern California; and Loma Linda University.

■ Recreation

Sightseeing

A major tourist attraction in Orange County is the historical district in downtown Santa Ana. Placed on the National Register of Historic Places in 1984, the 21-block area is among the largest such districts in the state of California. It contains 100 buildings constructed between 1877 and 1934; among them are the Old Orange County Courthouse (now a museum featuring changing exhibits related to local and regional history), the Fox West Coast Theatre, and Old City Hall. The district also features homes of prominent Santa Ana

citizens. Tours of the Dr. Willella Howe-Waffle House, a restored Queen Anne Style home built in the 1880s, are available the first Saturday of each even month.

Fairhaven Memorial Park is situated on 73 acres and features an arboretum harboring nearly 1,000 trees and numerous plants from around the world. The park's historic mausoleum was built in 1916 of European marble and granite, with handcrafted stained-glass windows.

The Santa Ana Zoo at Prentice Park is home to many animals and species; among the rare and endangered species living at the zoo are the ring-tailed lemur, the black and white ruffled lemur, the cotton-top tamarin, and the golden lion tamarin; the zoo welcomes 270,000 visitors each year. There are several other points of interest in Orange County, including world-famous Disneyland amusement park in Anaheim, and Knott's Berry Farm. Within driving distance of Santa Ana are the Universal Studios tour, Six Flags Magic Mountain, Raging Waters amusement park, SeaWorld, and the San Diego Zoo.

Arts and Culture

More than 1,000 cultural organizations are active in Orange County; among them are symphony orchestras, ballet companies, theater groups, and modern and folk dance troupes. Santa Ana is the headquarters for the Pacific Symphony Orchestra, which presents its summer season at Verizon Wireless Amphitheater in Irvine and performs its regular season concerts at Segerstrom Hall, part of Segerstrom Center for the Arts in Costa Mesa.

Among the other orchestras in the metropolitan area are the Orange County Youth Symphony Orchestra and the American Youth Symphony. Theater groups include the South Coast Repertory. Tibbies Great American Cabaret dinner theater performs on board the Queen Mary, located in Long Beach; the group also performs at the Center Stage Theater in Fontana. A variety of special events and banquets are held in the region throughout the year.

Santa Ana boasts a thriving art scene, comprised of galleries and studios. The Cal State Fullerton Grand Central Art Center houses a student gallery and studios. The Orange County Center for Contemporary Art is also located in the Artists Village.

One of Orange County's most prominent museums is located in Santa Ana. The famous Bowers Museum, a Spanish mission–style building, houses cultural collections pertinent to Orange County and California history; Native American, Pacific Rim, and African cultures; and natural history. It also features a hands-on Kidseum, a five-star restaurant, and shops. The Discovery Science Center houses hands-on exhibits in themed areas that include Eco Challenge, Dino Quest Adventure, Science of Hockey, and Boeing Rocket Lab.

The Heritage Museum of Orange County has exhibits that chronicle the history of Orange County back to the nineteenth century. Special demonstrations and hands-on activities draw visitors to imagine what life was like in that earlier time in history. Art museums in the area include the Laguna Beach Art Museum, the Muckenthaler Cultural Center, and the Orange County Museum of Art, which holds nearly 2,500 works focusing on twentieth-century Californian art.

The Santa Ana Fire Museum opened in August 2013. Fire services were transferred by the city to Orange County in 2012, and the museum, established by the Santa Ana Historical Preservation Society, was established in an operational Orange County fire station to honor the more than 100 years of service by the Santa Ana Fire Department.

Festivals and Holidays

Santa Ana has an annual Memorial Day celebration in May. The annual Imagination Celebration (usually in April and May) features art and cultural programs at a variety of venues throughout Orange County, including some within Santa Ana. The annual Fiestas Patrias Santa Ana celebrates the independence day of Mexico (September 16). The Santa Ana Zoo hosts an annual Boo at the Zoo event for families in October. The same month, the Santa Ana Historic Preservation Society sponsors a Cemetery Tour. The Black History Parade and Festival occurs in early February.

Sports for the Spectator

While there are no professional sports teams in Santa Ana, residents are within an easy drive of sporting events in Anaheim. Major League Baseball's Los Angeles Angels of Anaheim play home games at Angel Stadium of Anaheim. The National Hockey League's Anaheim Ducks play at Honda Center.

The Santa Ana College Dons play in the Orange Empire Conference, part of the California Community College Athletic Association. Sports include football, soccer, water polo, volleyball, cross country, basketball, baseball, badminton, football, track and field, and wrestling. The California State University, Fullerton Titans and the Anteaters of the University of California, Irvine field National Collegiate Athletic Association (NCAA) Division I teams. Los Alamitos Race Course features parimutuel thoroughbred and harness racing.

Sports for the Participant

Santa Ana's mild climate invites year-round athletic enjoyment. Some of Southern California's finest beaches are minutes away, and the city is located only 12 miles from the Pacific Ocean. The city maintains a system of 39 parks, as well as bicycle trails. There are also 19 city recreation centers, five of which have swimming pools. Mountain ski resorts are within easy driving distance.

Shopping and Dining

With 25 incorporated cities in Orange County, each with its own central shopping district and community shopping centers, the shopper has endless opportunities. More than 20 major regional shopping malls feature national department stores, specialty shops, and boutiques. Santa Ana is also within easy driving distance of Beverly Hills' famous Rodeo Drive, which is lined with luxury and designer shops.

In the city itself, prime shopping locations include South Coast Plaza, which is a European-style marketplace, and Westfield MainPlace Mall.

Santa Ana has dozens of restaurants that offer a variety of cuisine, including traditional American, Continental, Italian, Asian, and Mexican dishes.

Visitor Information: Anaheim/Orange County Visitor and Convention Bureau, 800 W. Katella Avenue, Anaheim, CA 92802; telephone (855) 405-5020.

■ Convention Facilities

The largest convention facilities are located in nearby Anaheim. These include the Anaheim Convention Center, which houses 815,000 square feet of exhibit space, making it the largest exhibit facility on the West Coast. The Marriott Anaheim offers 82,000 square feet of meeting space that includes exhibit space, flexible ballrooms and 44 meeting rooms. The Disneyland Hotel at Disneyland Resort offers dozens of meeting spaces, the largest one being the 50,000-square-foot Disneyland Exhibit Hall in Magic Tower. There is a banquet hall to accommodate up to 2,000 people and three restaurants.

A number of Santa Ana's hotels and motels provide conference and convention facilities. Among the major hotels with meeting rooms are the Embassy Suites and Quality Inn Suites. The Doubletree Hotel Santa Ana offers 253 hotel rooms, two board rooms, a 7,680-square-foot ballroom, reception space for more than 1,000 participants, and private dining.

Convention Information: Anaheim/Orange County Visitor and Convention Bureau, 800 W. Katella Avenue, Anaheim, CA 92802; telephone (855) 405-5020.

■ Transportation

Approaching the City

Several airports are located in the Santa Ana metropolitan area. The John Wayne Airport in Santa Ana, owned and operated by Orange County, is about 5 miles from downtown. It is served by 10 commercial airlines that provide transportation for millions of passengers each year. Los Angeles International Airport (LAX), located about 37 miles northwest of the city, is one of the top-six airports in the world in terms of passengers handled. The airport is served by approximately 60 airlines with thousands of flights each year. Long Beach Airport and LA/Ontario International Airport provide additional travel alternatives. The Fullerton Municipal Airport is a general aviation airport accommodating about 600 planes.

Four major highways lead into Santa Ana: Interstate-5 (the Santa Ana Freeway), State Route 55 (Costa Mesa Freeway), State Route 57 (Orange Freeway), and State Route 22 (Garden Grove Freeway). Amtrak and Greyhound have stops at the Santa Ana Regional Transportation Center.

Traveling in the City

The Orange County Transportation Authority (OCTA) operates buses daily with about 77 routes throughout Orange County. OCTA Metrolink, a regional commuter rail system, links travelers to activity centers in Orange and surrounding counties. The Metrolink stops at the Santa Ana Regional Transportation Center. Special services are available for the handicapped and the hearing impaired. The Regional Transportation Center, often called "The Depot," is a hub for Amtrak, intercity buses, urban transit, a future rapid transit system, taxi cabs, an airport shuttle, and other transportation services.

■ Communications

Newspapers and Magazines

The *Orange County Register* is the morning daily published in Santa Ana with a circulation of about 280,000 as of 2012. Readers also find some local news in the *Los Angeles Times*. *OC Weekly* is an alternative press that is published in Orange County.

Television and Radio

The city sponsors its own local access television station, KTBN-TV, channel 33. While there are no major television stations in the city, there are many affiliate television stations serving the city from the surrounding area; cable is also available. One AM and four FM radio stations are based in Santa Ana. However, the city receives broadcasts from many AM and FM radio stations broadcast from other cities in the region.

Media Information: *Orange County Register*, 625 N. Grand Ave., Santa Ana, CA 92701; telephone (877) 469-7344.

Santa Ana Online

City of Santa Ana. Available www.ci.santa-ana.ca.us

Orange County Business Council. Available www.ocbc.org

Orange County Register. Available www.ocregister.com

Santa Ana Chamber of Commerce. Available www.santaanachamber.com

Santa Ana History (Historical Preservation Society). Available www.santaanahistory.com

Santa Ana Public Library. Available www.ci.santa-ana.ca.us/library

Santa Ana Unified School District. Available www.sausd.k12.ca.us

BIBLIOGRAPHY

Allen, Robert L., *Wildflowers of Orange County and the Santa Ana Mountains* (Laguna Beach, CA: Laguna Wilderness Press, 2013)

Haas, Lisbeth, *Conquests and Historical Identities in California, 1769–1936* (Berkeley, CA: University of California Press, 1995)

Colorado

The State in Brief

Nickname: Centennial State

Motto: Nil sine numine (Nothing without providence)

Flower: Rocky Mountain columbine

Bird: Lark bunting

Area: 104,094 square miles (2010; U.S. rank 8th)

Elevation: Ranges from 3,350 feet to 14,433 feet above sea level

Climate: Dry and sunny, with a wide daily and seasonal variation in temperature and with alpine conditions in the high mountains

Admitted to Union: August 1, 1876

Capital: Denver

Head Official: John Hickenlooper (D) (until 2015)

Population
> 1990: 3,377,000
> 2000: 4,302,015
> 2010: 5,029,196
> 2012 estimate: 5,042,853
> Percent change, 2000–2010: 16.9%
> U.S. rank in 2012: 22nd
> Percent of residents born in state: 42.2% (2012)
> Density: 48.5 people per square mile (2010)
> 2012 FBI Crime Index Total: 155,293

Racial and Ethnic Characteristics (2012)
> White: 4,243,753
> Black or African American: 201,424
> American Indian and Alaska Native: 49,099
> Asian: 136,882
> Native Hawaiian and Pacific Islander: 6,034
> Hispanic or Latino (may be of any race): 1,040,478
> Other: 405,661

Age Characteristics (2012)
> Population under 5 years old: 340,829
> Population 5 to 19 years old: 1,020,024
> Percent of population 65 years and over: 11.1%
> Median age: 36.1

Vital Statistics
> Total number of births (2012–13): 65,831
> Total number of deaths (2012–13): 33,159
> AIDS cases reported through 2011: 10,381

Economy
> Major industries: Services, manufacturing, communications, transportation, agriculture, aerospace, bioscience
> Unemployment rate (2012): 5.5%
> Per capita income (2012): $31,039
> Median household income (2012): $58,244
> Percentage of persons below poverty level (2012): 12.9%
> Income tax rate: 4.63%
> Sales tax rate: 2.9%

Aurora

■ The City in Brief

Founded: 1891 (incorporated, 1903)

Head Official: Mayor Steve Hogan (since 2011; current term expires 2015)

City Population
> 1990: 222,103
> 2000: 276,393
> 2010: 325,078
> 2012 estimate: 338,835
> Percent change, 2000–2010: 17.6%
> U.S. rank in 1990: 73rd
> U.S. rank in 2000: 61st
> U.S. rank in 2010: 56th (State rank: 3rd)

Metropolitan Statistical Area Population
> 2000: 2,179,240
> 2010: 2,543,482
> 2012 estimate: 2,645,209
> Percent change, 2000–2010: 16.7%
> U.S. rank in 2000: 22nd
> U.S. rank in 2010: 21st

Area: 142.7 square miles

Elevation: 5,435 feet above sea level

Average Annual Temperatures: 64° F

Average Annual Precipitation: 17.69 inches

Major Economic Sectors: Aerospace and defense, bioscience, transportation, renewable energy

Unemployment Rate: 7.1% (2012)

Per Capita Income: $24,008

2012 FBI Crime Index Property: 10,059

Major Colleges and Universities: Community College of Aurora, University of Colorado at Denver Anschutz Medical Campus, University of Denver

Daily Newspaper: *Aurora Sentinel*

■ Introduction

Aurora began as a small farmer's and rancher's town on the frontier. For much of the twentieth century, Aurora was seen as a suburb of its larger neighbor Denver, but its strong growth and easy livability soon distinguished Aurora as a city in its own right. Today, set on 144 square miles beneath the towering Rocky Mountains, Aurora is Colorado's third-largest city. It is known for its beautiful weather, proximity to a plethora of outdoor activities and cultural opportunities, and pro-business climate. In recent years it has also developed a reputation as an up-and-coming center for bioscience research, with $5.2 billion dedicated to bioscience development in the Fitzsimons Life Science District, which continued to attract new tenants and lucrative employment opportunities throughout the 2010s.

■ Geography and Climate

Aurora is located just east of Denver on high plains at the foot of the Rocky Mountains. These mountains, reaching higher than 14,000 feet, are the dominant feature of the area. Much of the area's precipitation tends to fall as snow on the Rockies rather than as storms on the plains, sparing Aurora itself, and the city thus enjoys abundant sunshine.

Aurora has four seasons and an annual average high temperature of 64 degrees. The region's climate is semi-arid and relatively mild. The city has the lowest average relative humidity of 25 major cities surveyed on a list that includes Los Angeles, San Francisco, Dallas, and Minneapolis.

Area: 142.7 square miles

Elevation: 5,435 feet above sea level

Average Temperatures: 64° F

Average Annual Precipitation: 17.69 inches

■ History

The City of Aurora got its start under a different name, in 1891, when westward-moving Chicagoan Donald Fletcher staked out a town named Fletcher on the high plains beneath the Rocky Mountains. In 1907 residents decided to rename their town Aurora, after the Latin word for dawn. The town remained a sleepy one until 1921, when the United States government selected Aurora to build a new army hospital, Fitzsimons Army Hospital. The new facility treated the wounded—especially those affected by mustard gas and tuberculosis—during World War I and provided an impetus to growth in the small town just outside of Denver.

By 1929, the town had reached 2,000 residents and was finally recognized by the state of Colorado. Sewers, roads and fire stations were built. During the Great Depression, Fitzsimons was considered for cost-cutting closure by the Army, but the congressional delegation from Aurora managed to save the facility from that fate; in fact, when President Roosevelt visited the facility, shortly afterwards, he decided instead to allocate more funds for its improvement.

The Second World War proved to be another boon for Aurora's infrastructure. In 1942 the Army Air Corps built Buckley Field (later renamed the Naval Air Station, then Buckley Air National Guard Base), followed by Lowry Field, further increasing the military presence in the city. By 1960, Aurora had accumulated 60,000 residents. Growth continued through the 1970s, helped along in part by the construction of a new highway system through the Denver area that connected Aurora to more of its Western neighbors. Though Aurora's economy was based strongly on the U.S. military presence, it remained closely tied in with that of nearby Denver.

In the 1980s Denver, along with most of Colorado and its close neighbor Aurora, experienced serious economic setbacks as energy prices fell and plans for oil shale development were curtailed. The 1990s represented an economic comeback of sorts for Aurora, as population grew to 292,393 residents by the end of the decade. The decade also saw the expansion of the aerospace engineering sector in Aurora, as well as the beginning of biotechnology as a major local industry. However, the city suffered during the mid-1990s when first Lowry Air

Force Base and then Fitzsimons were targeted for closure. In 1995 officials from the City of Aurora, University of Colorado Health Sciences Center, and the University of Colorado Hospital presented the U.S. Department of Defense with a plan to transform the decommissioned base into a world-class medical campus. The government agreed, and work continued for over a decade on Fitzsimons. The plan proved to be a defining moment in the history of the city.

By 2004, a number of facilities within the base had been completed, including the University of Colorado Hospital and Health Sciences Center, Rocky Mountain Lions Eye Institute, Nighthorse Campbell Native Health Building, Research Complex I and Colorado Bioscience Park Aurora. By the 2010s, some 6.4 million square feet of building space had been constructed or renovated, with more development on the way, including a new Veterans Administration hospital to open in 2015. Total investment in the renamed Fitzsimons Life Science District was estimate at $5.2 billion.

Historical Information: Boulder Public Library, Carnegie Branch Library for Local History, 1125 Pine St., Boulder, CO 80302; telephone (303) 441-3110; fax (720) 406-7452.

■ Population Profile

Metropolitan Statistical Area Population
> 2000: 2,179,240
> 2010: 2,543,482
> 2012 estimate: 2,645,209
> Percent change, 2000–2010: 16.7%
> U.S. rank in 2000: 22nd
> U.S. rank in 2010: 21st

City Residents
> 1990: 222,103
> 2000: 276,393
> 2010: 325,078
> 2012 estimate: 338,835
> Percent change, 2000–2010: 17.6%
> U.S. rank in 1990: 73rd
> U.S. rank in 2000: 61st
> U.S. rank in 2010: 56th (State rank: 3rd)

Density: 2,100.9 people per square mile

Racial and ethnic characteristics
> White: 223,122
> Black or African American: 56,817
> American Indian and Alaskan Native: 3,243
> Asian: 14,916
> Native Hawaiian and Other Pacific Islander: 808
> Hispanic or Latino (may be of any race): 94,916
> Other: 39,929

Percent of residents born in state: 38%

Age characteristics

Population under 5 years old: 25,379
Population 5 to 9 years old: 27,777
Population 10 to 14 years old: 23,957
Population 15 to 19 years old: 23,142
Population 20 to 24 years old: 22,975
Population 25 to 34 years old: 54,083
Population 35 to 44 years old: 47,613
Population 45 to 54 years old: 43,070
Population 55 to 59 years old: 20,166
Population 60 to 64 years old: 17,151
Population 65 to 74 years old: 19,873
Population 75 to 84 years old: 9,643
Population 85 years and over: 4,006
Median age: 33.5

Births (2010–11 Metropolitan Area)

Total number: 35,028

Deaths (2010–11 Metropolitan Area)

Total number: 15,031

Money income (2012)

Per capita income: $24,008
Median household income: $51,019
Total households: 121,540

Number of households with income of ...

less than $10,000: 7,507
$10,000 to $14,999: 5,531
$15,000 to $24,999: 12,428
$25,000 to $34,999: 14,119
$35,000 to $49,999: 19,880
$50,000 to $74,999: 25,914
$75,000 to $99,999: 14,374
$100,000 to $149,999: 14,702
$150,000 to $199,999: 4,284
$200,000 or more: 2,801

Percent of families below poverty level: 16.4%

FBI Crime Index Property: 10,059

FBI Crime Index Violent: 1,433

■ Municipal Government

Aurora operates under a council-manager form of government. Ten council members are elected by ward and four at-large; the mayor is also elected at large. The city manager is appointed by the council and is in charge of hiring city officials and preparing a recommended budget for the council, while the city council and mayor set long- and short-term goals and engage in strategic planning.

Head Official: Mayor Steve Hogan (since 2011; current term expires 2015)

Total Number of City Employees: 3,770 (2012)

City Information: City of Aurora, 15151 E. Alameda Parkway, First Floor, Aurora, CO 80012; telephone (303) 739-7000; email access@auroragov.org.

■ Economy

Major Industries and Commercial Activity

The bioscience and aerospace industries are the two most significant industries in Aurora.

Bioscience research is conducted at the University of Colorado Anschutz Medical Campus and its Children's Hospital Colorado. Part of the 578-acre Fitzsimons Life Science District, the facilities anchor the bioscience industry in Aurora's local economy. The $5.2 billion Fitzsimons Life Science District development project also includes plans for a Veterans Administration hospital, and spaces for private expansion.

The aerospace and defense industry of Colorado, which encompasses the development of products such as satellites and control software, boasts nearly 130 companies and more than 25,000 private-sector aerospace and defense workers. Aurora itself is home to major aerospace suppliers that include the Boeing Company, Lockheed Martin, Northrop Grumman, and Raytheon. Raytheon is one of the city's largest employers, and all of the aforementioned defense companies rank among the city's top-25 private employers. Aurora's Buckley Air Force Base contributes more than $1 billion to the region annually, hosting 3,100 active-duty members and 4,000 National Guard personnel and reservists, in addition to employing more than 5,000 civilians and contractors.

The city has also become a hub for transportation and logistics industries; between 1995 and 2007, the warehouse and distribution real estate inventory in Aurora's Interstate 70 corridor more than doubled. Growth in the industry has been attributed to the availability of business parks, warehouses, and developable land, proximity to Denver International Airport, and a favorable business climate.

Renewable energy has become a boon to Aurora's economy in recent years as well. The Solar Technology Acceleration Center in Aurora was the first shared solar technology center of its kind and is the largest test facility for solar technology in the United States. The research site comprises 74 acres of the 1,762-acre Aurora Campus for Renewable Energy (ACRE).

Items and goods produced: airplane parts, defense technology, solar energy components

Incentive Programs—New and Existing Companies

Local programs: Aurora's low tax rates are a draw for businesses looking to relocate to the city. City council also has the power, on a case-by-case basis, to offer new, expanding, and existing businesses financial incentives, usually in the form of Aurora local sales and use tax rebates. Additionally, portions of Aurora have been designated by the state as enterprise zones to encourage investment and job creation.

City incentive programs include Arts District and Brownfields loan funds, a Business Revolving Loan Fund, Commercial Renovation Program, Homebuyer Resources, Housing Rehabilitation, New Job Reward Program, and Water Conservation Rebates.

State programs: Colorado offers a variety of business assistance and incentive programs for expanding or relocated companies. Incentives include the Job Growth Tax Incentive, which provides a state income tax credit to job-creating projects in Colorado dependent on the incentive; Strategic Fund Initiative, for business development, expansion, or relocation that results in job creation; Enterprise Zone Tax Credits, which incentive development in economically distressed areas; Public Infrastructure Grants, to retain or add employment opportunities for low- or moderate-income residents; and sales and use tax refunds, exemptions, and credits for developments in biotechnology, manufacturing, and aviation sectors.

State financing support can be obtained through an array of general and industry-specific programs. Advanced Industries Accelerator Programs, created in 2013, offer access to capital for advanced manufacturing, aerospace, bioscience, electronic, energy and natural resource, infrastructure engineering, and technology and information industries. Private Activity Bonds offer tax-exempt bond financing to small manufacturing companies. Bioscience Discovery Evaluation Grants were available from 2007 to 2013 to support growth of companies in the bioscience industry. The Regional Tourism Act allows local governments to apply to the state for financial support for major tourism development initiatives likely to draw out-of-state visitors.

Venture capital funding is offered through the state's Certified Capital Companies Program, which makes available a statewide pool of $75 million for investment throughout the state, with an additional $25 million available for rural investment. The Colorado Venture Capital Authority manages venture capital investments for the state. Colorado Capital Access, Cash Collateral Support, and Colorado Credit Reserve support financing needs of small and medium businesses.

Job training programs: The Colorado Community College System has joined with the Colorado Office of Economic Development & International Trade to administer Colorado FIRST/Existing Industry Customized Training Programs. These programs are designed to fund employee training for transferable job skills to benefit a company's competitive strength as well as an employee's long-term employment opportunities.

Development Projects

Children's Hospital Colorado, located in Aurora, broke ground in 2010 on a 10-story, 350,000-square-foot expansion for a new tower to add 124 beds to the hospital. The tower opened in 2012 and included the Colorado Institute for Maternal and Fetal Health. Similarly, the University of Colorado Hospital added a second inpatient tower at a cost of about $400 million, which held an additional 144 beds—with space to add 132 more at a later date—across 734,000 square feet of space. The expansion project brought 1,400 full-time jobs to the medical campus along with around 650 construction jobs. The new building was completed in 2013.

The Fitzsimons Life Science District continued to add tenants and facilities to its campus throughout the 2010s. In 2013 alone, eight new companies took up residence at the park, and four expanded operations. A planned four-story Bioscience 2 facility, launched in 2013, was to house the University of Colorado's bioengineering program and space for commercial companies across its 112,000 square feet. The largest addition to the park, the Aurora Veterans Administration Hospital, was on track for completion in 2015, although concerns over budget overruns related to the $800 million project have threatened to delay progress. The facility was to have 182 beds, the majority in private rooms.

In 2013 BMC Investments and Kentro Group purchased four acres of land adjacent to the Fitzsimons Life Science District for $3.6 million, with plans to establish a 40,000-square-foot retail center. The steady growth of the district has made surrounding land a coveted asset for retail developers. Other private developments announced in 2013 included a 386,000-square-foot expansion by Steven Roberts Original Desserts and Ticklebelly Desserts, undertaken through the renovation of existing warehouse space; a 52,000-square-foot expansion by Advanced Circuits, a circuit board fabricator based in Aurora; and a new 81,000-square-foot facility to double the operations of Electronic Recyclers International in Aurora.

Economic Development Information: Aurora Economic Development Council, 14001 E. Iliff Avenue, Suite 211, Aurora, CO 80014; telephone (303) 755-2223; fax (303) 755-2224.

Commercial Shipping

Aurora's extensive warehouse industry means that it is also a shipping hub. Nearly 700 motor freight companies traverse the network of major interstates and highways that flow in and around Aurora. Nearby Denver International Airport handled more than 410 million pounds of cargo in 2013. Front Range Airport, just 6 miles from the Denver International Airport, also offers 24-hour air cargo operations and railway track access. Burlington Northern Santa Fe and Union Pacific Railroad provide freight service to the area. The Metro Denver area, which includes Aurora and is located strategically between Canada and Mexico, is an ever-expanding center for international trade.

Labor Force and Employment Outlook

Colorado has one of the nation's most highly educated workforces, with approximately 89 percent of the population having graduated high school and more than 37 percent with college degrees. The Aurora workforce is spread fairly evenly throughout a variety of industries. Efficient mass transit allows Aurora to draw employees from the surrounding metropolitan area anchored by Denver.

The following is a summary of data regarding the 2012 Aurora labor force:

Size of civilian labor force: 179,211

Number of workers employed in ...

agriculture and mining: 998
construction: 14,123
manufacturing: 8,656
wholesale trade: 5,067
retail trade: 20,216
transportation: 10,111
information systems: 5,599
finance: 11,678
professional administration: 18,828
education and social services: 29,346
arts and leisure: 18,468
other: 7,907
public administration: 7,565

Average hourly earnings of production workers: $17.32

Unemployment rate: 7.1% (2012)

Employers

Largest employers (2012)	*Number of employees*
Buckley Air Force Base	12,100
University of Colorado Anschutz Medical Campus	7,180
Aurora Public Schools	5,000
Children's Hospital Colorado	4,400
University of Colorado Hospital	4,400
Cherry Creek Public Schools	3,840
City of Aurora	3,770
Raytheon	2,230
Kaiser Permanente	1,730
ADT Security Systems	1,600

Cost of Living

Aurora's cost of living, while slightly above the national average, is lower than most major cities.

The following is a summary of data regarding several key cost of living factors in the area.

2013 ACCRA Average House Price: $349,217

2013 ACCRA Cost of Living Index: 105

State income tax rate: 4.63%

State sales tax rate: 2.9%

Local income tax rate: $2 per month on compensation over $250

Local sales tax rate: 5.1%

Property tax rate: $0.075541 for every $1 of assessed value; residential assessed value is 7.96% of total value (2013)

Economic Information: Aurora Chamber of Commerce, 14305 E. Alameda Ave., Suite 300, Aurora, CO 80012; telephone (303) 344-1500; fax (303) 344-1564; email info@aurorachamber.org.

■ Education and Research

Elementary and Secondary Schools

Aurora Public Schools had an operating budget of $302 million in 2012-2013. Some 37 percent of the students in the district speak English as a second language, with 86 percent of those native Spanish-speakers. Nearly 70 percent of students qualify for free or reduced lunch. In 2007 the district was taking the first steps toward creating a "Pilot Schools" program, wherein individual schools would have a greater level of control over budget and curriculum, in order to foster a culture of high expectations. In 2008 the district opened William Smith, the district's first autonomous Pilot School. Three other schools have since been approved for Pilot School status. The District operates six charter schools and several alternative and vocational high schools. The district developed VISTA 2015, an effort to get every graduating senior to the level of academic achievement needed to be admitted to college without remediation.

Part of the city of Aurora is also served by the Cherry Creek Public Schools District, known for consistently exceeding state and national achievement standards.

There are over 20 private and parochial schools located within the city of Aurora.

The following is a summary of data regarding the Aurora Joint District No. 28.

Total enrollment: 38,605

Number of facilities

    total: 59
    elementary schools: 31
    junior high schools: 10
    high schools: 6
    other: 12

Student/teacher ratio: 19.89:1

Teacher salaries

    average (statewide): $49,938

Funding per pupil: $6,933

Public Schools Information: Aurora Public Schools, Educational Services Center 1, 15701 E. 1st Avenue, Aurora, CO 80011; telephone 303-344-8060; email webmaster@aps.k12.co.us.

Colleges and Universities

In the Aurora-Denver metropolitan area, there are more than 20 institutions offering two-year, four-year and graduate degrees. The Community College of Aurora offers more than 40 degrees and certificates in vocational education and technical fields. Enrollment for 2011–12 was 7,842 students. The school has two campuses, located at Lowry and CentreTech, and offers classes at seven outreach locations throughout Aurora.

A branch of the University of Colorado at Denver is the Anschutz Medical Campus in Aurora is one of the newest and largest academic health centers between Chicago, Texas, and the West Coast. The campus is divided up threefold, providing an education zone for training future physicians and health professionals; a research zone offering world-renowned research; and a clinical care zone.

Nearby Denver offers a number of opportunities in higher education, including the University of Denver, which enrolled 17,729 students in 2013 and boasted more than 130 study programs in 13 schools and colleges. The University of Denver awards more graduate degrees than any other public Colorado institution, accounting for roughly one-third of all graduate degrees.

Other area private colleges are Johnson & Wales University, Regis University, and Colorado Heights University. Public schools include the Metropolitan State College of Denver, Community College of Denver, and the Colorado School of Mines. Non-traditional education is well represented by such institutions as the Colorado Free University, which has an open admissions policy and is known for its adult and continuing education programs.

Libraries and Research Centers

There are 10 libraries within 15 miles of Aurora, four of which are part of the Aurora Public Library system. The library offers some 300,000 books and also operates four computer centers and a book outlet, which sells former library books at deeply discounted prices. The Learning Resource Center at the Community College of Aurora features a lending library, career resources, and computer access to online resources.

The greater Denver area, which includes Aurora, boasts a number of other public, special interest, and research libraries. Among them are the Colorado Talking Book Library, Denver Medical Library, University of Colorado Law Library, and many high-technology and university-related libraries. The University of Denver libraries feature rare book and manuscript collections, the Beck Memorial Archives of Rocky Mountain Jewish History, and the Carson Brierly Griffin Dance Library.

Research activities in such fields as environmental sciences, allergy and immunology, biochemical genetics, health services, mass spectrometry, biochemical parasitology, alcohol, taste and smell, sports sciences, applied mechanics, public management, social science, mineral law, mass communications, family studies, the Holocaust, Islamic-Judaic studies, and international relations are conducted at centers in the Denver area.

The former Fitzsimons Medical Center, now home to the Anschutz Medical Center, among other facilities, is a major research site for biotechnology firms.

Public Library Information: Aurora Public Library Central Library, 14949 E. Alameda Parkway, Aurora, CO 80012; telephone (303) 739-6600.

■ Health Care

In 2011 *Men's Health* and *Women's Health* magazines ranked Aurora the ninth best city for men and women's health, an achievement attributed at least in part to the city's health-care system. The Medical Center of Aurora is Aurora's only full-service hospital and has a total of 303 licensed beds. The Center offers services in cardiac care, breast cancer care, and emergency response, in addition to a number of educational services and programs. In 2013 it was named the fourth-best hospital in the state by *U.S. News & World Report,* with high-performing marks in eight specialties.

The University of Colorado Hospital, part of the Anschutz Medical Campus, is a nationally ranked medical institution in five specialties according to *U.S. News & World Report* in 2013. It ranked second in the nation for care in pulmonology. The hospital has 467 beds and is a teaching hospital. Major facilities include the hospital's two inpatient towers, an outpatient pavilion, Rocky Mountain Lions Eye Institute, and the Center for Dependency, Addiction, and Rehabilitation (CeDAR). The Children's Hospital Colorado, part of the Anschutz Medical Campus, is also a nationally ranked facility.

Aurora is close to other facilities throughout the Denver metropolitan area.

■ Recreation

Sightseeing

There are a number of historical, natural, and cultural sites for tourists to see, both within Aurora proper or just a daytrip away. Nearby Manitou & Pikes Peak Cog Railway is the highest cog railroad in the world and offers tours to the summit of Pikes Peak at 14,110 feet. Near the peak of the mountain lies Garden of the Gods, the famous red rock sandstone formation that is a popular destination for hikers and walkers. Free tours are available. The Cave of the Winds, which also offers free guided tours, features 20 beautiful caverns. The Flying W Ranch, in nearby Colorado Springs, is a recreated Old West town from the late 1800s. Visitors love to experience its authentic chuck wagon supper and famous Flying W Wranglers stage show. Also in Colorado Springs is the U.S. Olympic Training Center, where 12,000 athletes train annually.

The Royal Gorge is the world's highest suspension bridge and spans the Arkansas River at a height of 1,050 feet. At the base of the Royal Gorge is offered a 24-mile scenic train ride around the gorge that has been called "the most arresting scenic site in all of American railroading"; another option includes an aerial tram ride though the gorge itself. Tours are available at the Stanley House, an historic hotel dating from 1909, which inspired Stephen King to write *The Shining*. Within driving distance of Aurora are over 30 casinos in Central City and Blackhawk, with over 10,000 slot machines, blackjack tables and poker tables. Central City, a historic mining town featuring Victorian homes and storefronts, is itself a tourist destination and was once called the "Richest square mile on Earth." The Gilpin County Historical Society features artifacts from Colorado's mining days, in addition to featuring the Teller House Museum, where President Grant once stayed. The Leanin' Tree Museum of Western Art displays over 200 paintings and 85 bronze statues. Tours are available at the nearby Anheuser-Busch Brewery for the beer aficionado. The Aurora History Museum features exhibits on the city's past, in addition to the environment, diversity, and contemporary life in Aurora.

Arts and Culture

Although Aurora's Arts District is small, in the early twenty-first century city leaders placed strong emphasis on maintaining and growing a cultural presence in the city's downtown area. Aurora's East End Arts District, a collaborative partnership of artists, businesses, neighborhood residents on East Colfax Avenue, is home to the Aurora Fox Arts Center, which holds a capacity crowd of 245 and is home to the Aurora Fox Theatre Company and the Aurora Fox Children's Theatre. The theater also co-sponsors with the Colorado Cultural Connections, *Aurora Sentinel, LaVoz,* and Colorado Folk Arts Council an annual multi-cultural performance series that highlights Aurora's various ethnic groups. In addition to staging several productions annually, the Children's Theatre Company hosts theater classes, workshops, and summer camps. The Aurora Dance Arts Office, established in 1973, offers 100 classes weekly in various dance disciplines. The Bicentennial Arts Center, originally a satellite building operated as part of the Lowry Air Force Base, is now a pottery center that also organizes music and fine arts programs throughout the city. The nearby Central City Opera House opened in 1878 and is home to an ensemble repertory each summer that performs opera classics in English.

Festivals and Holidays

Art Walks are held by the City of Aurora each June and November and lead participants through local studios, galleries, and shops in Aurora's East End Arts District. Banks in Harmony is a free concert series held on Thursday nights each summer at various parks throughout Aurora, featuring jazz, big band, Motown, and country performers. Another ongoing summer festival is Flicks on the 'FAX, held on seven summer Saturday nights in Fletcher Plaza, where popular, family-friendly films are shown on the big screen. Java Fest, held in May, is Colorado's only coffee-dedicated festival. June brings KidSpree @ YumFest, with music and a bevy of food trucks. The Fourth of July Spectacular is the largest fireworks display in the metro region. In October, the city hosts Punkin Chunkin Colorado, which features hay rides, scarecrow making, a pumpkin patch, music—and a pumpkin catapulting contest. The November Aurora Veterans Salute honors the area's military veterans and heritage.

Sports for the Spectator

Although Aurora has no professional sports teams of its own, fans can root for the Buffalos at nearby University of Colorado Boulder, who compete in a number of National Collegiate Athletic Association (NCAA) Division I sports.

They can also cheer for any of Denver's pro teams, which include the Nuggets of the National Basketball Association, Major League Baseball's Rockies, the National Hockey League's Colorado Avalanche, the National Football League's Broncos, and the Rapids of Major League Soccer.

Sports for the Participant

In 2004 Aurora was selected as the *Sports Illustrated* Colorado "Sportstown" for its 50th anniversary issue. The city was chosen for its involvement in facilitating and enhancing the athletic experiences of its residents. The same year, the metro region was chosen as the fourth fittest area in the nation by *Men's Fitness Magazine,* and the city has continued to win accolades in successive years for the promotion of active lifestyles.

Aurora maintains 1,800 acres of developed parkland, which includes a variety of athletic fields, playgrounds, picnic shelters, tennis courts, a skateboard bowl, basketball courts, a disc golf course, and a water sprayground. The city offers 8,000 recreation classes, more than 100 parks, and over 60 miles of trails. Major trail corridors for biking or walking include Cherry Creek Spillwood Trail, High Line Canal Trail, and Sand Creek Regional Greenway Trail. Popular parks in the region include Horsetooth Reservoir, a state park featuring a mountain lake, and Rocky Mountain National Park, with numerous opportunities for wildlife viewing and hiking. Aurora boasts six municipal golf courses: Saddle Rock, Murphy Creek, Meadow Hills, Aurora Hills, Fitzsimons, and Springhill. The 220-acre Aurora Sports Park, opened in 2003, is home to 23 full-sized soccer fields and 12 baseball/softball fields.

Shopping and Dining

Aurora is a mecca for mall shopping. Local complexes include Southlands Shopping Center, Tamarac Square Shopping Center, and Town Center at Aurora. Shoppers can also drive to nearby Denver, Boulder, or Littleton for more options.

Aurora boasts a variety of restaurants, with both national chains and local favorites, such as Helga's German Restaurant & Deli or Lupita's Restaurant. Cuisines include Italian, American, German, Mexican, Hawaiian, and more.

Visitor Information: Visitor Information Department, Aurora Chamber of Commerce, 14305 E. Alameda Ave., Suite 300, Aurora, CO 80012; telephone (303) 344-1500; fax (303) 344-1564; email info@aurorachamber.org.

■ Convention Facilities

The Summit Conference and Events Center in Aurora has 9,000 square feet of meeting space and can accommodate groups of up to 500 people. Nearby Denver offers a plethora of convention and meeting options; the Colorado Convention Center in downtown Denver is within walking distance of more than 7,000 hotel rooms and 300 restaurants. The convention center, located along the river in the heart of downtown, contains more than 600,000 square feet of exhibit space, 100,000 square feet of meeting rooms, two ballrooms (including a 35,000-square-foot ballroom and a 50,000-square-foot ballroom), theater-style seating for 7,000 people, 1,000 covered parking spaces, and state-of-the-art multimedia facilities. The center underwent a massive $268 million expansion that nearly doubled its space in 2003.

The National Western Complex, also in Denver, is located at the northern end of the downtown area and contains a 6,600-seat stadium arena, a two-story stadium hall with over 32,000 square feet of space on each floor, a 34,000-square-foot expo hall, a multi-use events center, and the Hall of Education, which can seat 450.

Other meeting and exhibition facilities include the Denver Coliseum, Red Rocks Amphitheatre, Denver Mart, and the Adams County Regional Park Complex.

Convention Information: Visit Denver, 1600 California St., Denver, CO 80202; telephone (303) 892-1505; email visitorinfo@visitdenver.com.

■ Transportation

Approaching the City

Aurora is served by the Denver International Airport, which is the fifth busiest airport in the United States and 13th busiest in the world. In 2012 its 17 commercial airlines served a total of 44.7 million passengers. Front Range Airport also provides services for commercial, corporate, and private aircraft, just six miles from the Denver International Airport. Aurora is also easily accessible through the Interstate 70, Interstate 225, and Express Toll 470 thoroughfares.

Traveling in the City

Aurora is served by Denver's Regional Transportation District (RTD), which offers 125 bus routes throughout the metropolitan area, Park-n-Ride facilities, six light-rail routes, and SkyRide transportation to and from Denver International Airport. The RTD has been named a top transit agency in the United States and is cited by the Aurora city government as an economic advantage, allowing highly skilled workers throughout the metropolitan area to commute to or from Aurora. FasTracks, an ambitious expansion of Denver's public transportation system, was scheduled to be completed by 2016 and include 122 miles of new rail service, among other enhancements.

■ Communications

Newspapers and Magazines

The only paid newspaper published in Aurora is the *Aurora Sentinel,* a weekly with a subscription of around 4,000. The company also distributes the *Aurora Sentinel Free Daily* four days a week. Residents can get their daily news from *The Denver Post* and the *Rocky Mountain News,* both published in nearby Denver. *Minority Golf Magazine* is published in Aurora, and other area magazines include *Colorado Country Life, Colorado Outdoors,* and *The Bloomsbury Review.*

Television and Radio

Aurora is largely served by nearby Denver's broadcast media. Six major television stations in the Denver area represent commercial networks, public television, independent stations, and special interest channels; a number of channels are offered by area cable systems as well. Two AM and one FM radio stations broadcast from Aurora, with many more area stations providing listeners with a variety of musical and special programming.

Media Information: *Aurora Sentinel,* 12100 East Iliff Avenue, Suite 102 Aurora, CO 80014; telephone (303) 750-7555; fax (303) 750-7699.

Aurora Online

Aurora Economic Development Council. Available www.auroraedc.com

Aurora Public Library. Available www.auroragov. org/ThingsToDo/AuroraPublicLibrary/index. htm

Aurora Public Schools. Available aurorak12.org

Aurora Sentinel. Available www.aurorasentinel.com

Chamber of Commerce. Available www. aurorachamber.org

City of Aurora Home Page. Available www. auroragov.org

The Medical Center of Aurora. Available www. auroramed.com

BIBLIOGRAPHY

Knopper, Steve, *Colorado* (Berkeley, CA: Avalon Travel, 2009)

Pettem, Silvia, *Behind the Badge: 125 Years of the Boulder, Colorado, Police Department* (Boulder, CO: The Book Lode LLC, 2003)

Whitney, Gleaves, *Colorado Front Range: A Landscape Divided* (Boulder, CO: Johnson Books, 1983)

Boulder

■ The City in Brief

Founded: 1859 (incorporated 1871)

Head Official: Mayor Matthew Appelbaum (since 2011; current term expires 2017)

City Population
1990: 85,127
2000: 94,673
2010: 97,385
2012 estimate: 101,812
Percent change, 2000–2010: 2.9%
U.S. rank in 1990: 257th
U.S. rank in 2000: 283th (State rank: 9th)
U.S. rank in 2010: 291st (State rank: 11th)

Metropolitan Statistical Area Population
2000: 291,288
2010: 294,567
2012 estimate: 305,318
Percent change, 2000–2010: 1.1%
U.S. rank in 2000: 159th
U.S. rank in 2010: 160th

Area: 25.37 square miles

Elevation: 5,340 feet above sea level

Average Annual Temperatures: 51.8° F

Average Annual Precipitation: 102.13 inches total (83.1 inches of snow)

Major Economic Sectors: services, trade, manufacturing, government

Unemployment Rate: 5% (2012)

Per Capita Income: $35,140

2012 FBI Crime Index Property: 2,937

Major Colleges and Universities: University of Colorado at Boulder, Naropa University, Front Range Community College

Daily Newspaper: *Daily Camera*

■ Introduction

Boulder is sometimes called the "Athens of the West" in tribute to its dedication to education and the arts. The University of Colorado at Boulder and a host of private industries make the city one of America's leading research towns, particularly in the fields of bioscience and aerospace. Boulder also maintains a commitment to the arts, presenting a number of renowned music, theater, and arts festivals each year. The city's attractive setting near the Rocky Mountains and its abundant cultural and entertainment offerings make it a popular stop for business or recreation. Outdoor life is prized in Boulder, and the city's residents are often noted as some of the most physical fit in the nation. These quality-of-life features consistently land Boulder on lists as one of the best places to live in America.

■ Geography and Climate

Boulder lies in a wide basin beneath Flagstaff Mountain just a few miles east of the continental divide and about 30 miles west of Denver. The large Arapahoe glacier provides water for a number of mountain streams that pass through Boulder, including Boulder Creek, which flows through the center of the city. The climate in Boulder is typically mild with dry, moderate summers and relatively comfortable winters. The city boasts around 300 sunny days each year. Nearby mountains shield Boulder from the most severe winter storms. Most precipitation occurs during the winter and spring months, with snowfall averaging about 83 inches.

© James Frank/Alamy

Area: 25.37 square miles

Elevation: 5,340 feet above sea level

Average Temperatures: 51.8° F

Average Annual Precipitation: 102.13 inches total (83.1 inches of snow)

■ History

A City Born of a Newspaper

For centuries before the coming of European explorers, the area surrounding what is now Boulder was a favorite winter campsite for a number of Native American groups, including the Arapaho, Ute, Kiowa, Comanche, Cheyenne, and Sioux. The area was rich in buffalo, elk, and antelope.

Economic depression in the East brought many pioneers and gold seekers to Colorado in the 1850s, and the first settlement in Boulder County was established at Red Rocks in 1858. An early settler, A. A. Brookfield, organized the Boulder City Town Company in 1859. The company laid out more than 4,000 lots, each with a price of $1,000. Few people could afford such a price, and by 1860 the population numbered only 364 residents.

Boulder City grew slowly through the 1860s, competing for prominence in the county with nearby Valmont, where the only newspaper in the area was printed. A group of Boulder citizens stole the printing press, and soon Boulder City was named the county seat, selected because it published the only newspaper in the area. In November 1871, Boulder was incorporated as a Colorado town, and "City" was dropped from the name.

A site for the University of Colorado was chosen in Boulder in 1872, and the Colorado state legislature appropriated funds for the institution in 1874, the same year that Boulder's first bank opened its doors. The city grew steadily through the turn of the century. In 1880 the population totaled 3,000 people, but modern conveniences like the installation of electricity in 1887 and a new railway depot in 1890 boosted the population to more than 6,000 people by 1900.

The twentieth century brought moderate growth for Boulder. In the late 1950s and early 1960s the development of high-technology industries had a great impact in the area. Companies like IBM and Rockwell and governmental agencies like the National Oceanic and

Atmospheric Administration and the National Bureau of Standards moved into the area, resulting in an economic surge due to the creation of many new jobs. The development of the Boulder-Denver Turnpike further bolstered the area, driving Boulder's population from 20,000 in 1950 to 72,000 in 1972.

Pushing Through a Rocky Period

The convergence of the university environment with research centers and science and technology companies fueled continued growth in the 1990s. At the turn of the century, however, a national and international recession contributed to a migration of residences and businesses from Boulder to neighboring communities, where real estate was often cheaper.

Yet the University of Colorado at Boulder has continued to anchor the city's economy, providing stability—and a strong allure to private industry—during economically difficult times. Research by both the university and private companies into the 2010s focused on three fields central to the economic future of the nation and the world: bioscience, aerospace, and green energy.

Historical Information: Boulder Public Library, Carnegie Branch Library for Local History, 1125 Pine St., Boulder, CO 80302; telephone (303) 441-3110; fax (720) 406-7452.

■ Population Profile

Metropolitan Statistical Area Population

2000: 291,288
2010: 294,567
2012 estimate: 305,318
Percent change, 2000–2010: 1.1%
U.S. rank in 2000: 159th
U.S. rank in 2010: 160th

City Residents

1990: 85,127
2000: 94,673
2010: 97,385
2012 estimate: 101,812
Percent change, 2000–2010: 2.9%
U.S. rank in 1990: 257th
U.S. rank in 2000: 283th (State rank: 9th)
U.S. rank in 2010: 291st (State rank: 11th)

Density: 3,948.4 people per square mile

Racial and ethnic characteristics

White: 91,562
Black or African American: 1,352
American Indian and Alaskan Native: 93
Asian: 3,726
Native Hawaiian and Other Pacific Islander: 19

Hispanic or Latino (may be of any race): 8,923
Other: 5,060

Percent of residents born in state: 25.4%

Age characteristics

Population under 5 years old: 3,942
Population 5 to 9 years old: 4,461
Population 10 to 14 years old: 4,059
Population 15 to 19 years old: 12,252
Population 20 to 24 years old: 21,248
Population 25 to 34 years old: 15,950
Population 35 to 44 years old: 10,468
Population 45 to 54 years old: 10,747
Population 55 to 59 years old: 4,802
Population 60 to 64 years old: 4,378
Population 65 to 74 years old: 5,249
Population 75 to 84 years old: 2,904
Population 85 years and over: 1,352
Median age: 27.7

Births (2010–11 Metropolitan Area)

Total number: 3,066

Deaths (2010–11 Metropolitan Area)

Total number: 1,510

Money income (2012)

Per capita income: $35,140
Median household income: $56,205
Total households: 40,913

Number of households with income of . . .

less than $10,000: 4,667
$10,000 to $14,999: 2,329
$15,000 to $24,999: 3,903
$25,000 to $34,999: 3,480
$35,000 to $49,999: 4,284
$50,000 to $74,999: 6,345
$75,000 to $99,999: 3,879
$100,000 to $149,999: 5,331
$150,000 to $199,999: 2,946
$200,000 or more: 3,749

Percent of families below poverty level: 23.4%

FBI Crime Index Property: 2,937

FBI Crime Index Violent: 249

■ Municipal Government

Boulder has a council-manager form of government with a nine-member council elected to two- or four-year terms. The council member receiving the least number of votes serves a two-year term; all others serve for four years. The council elects the mayor from among its number for a two-year term and appoints the city manager.

Head Official: Mayor Matthew Appelbaum (since 2011; current term expires 2017)

Total Number of City Employees: 1,243 (2012)

City Information: City of Boulder, 1777 Broadway, Boulder, CO 80302; telephone (303) 441-3388.

■ Economy

Major Industries and Commercial Activity

The predominant industries in the Boulder are science and technology related. Buoyed by research activity at the University of Colorado at Boulder, a large high-technology, electronic, and aerospace industry has developed in and around the city. The phenomenal growth of these industries attracted the establishment of defense contractors, applied and pure research centers, and satellite and communications companies, which bring millions of dollars into the local economy each year. Boulder is home to nearly 50 bioscience businesses, including such companies as Agilent Technologies, Array BioPharma, Dharmacon, Roche, and Somalogic. Total employment is in excess of 4,100.

The aerospace industry is also represented by many big-name businesses in or very near Boulder, including Lockheed Martin, Northrop Grumman, DigitalGlobe, and SpaceDev. Boulder's aerospace industry has been further secured by the presence of several federally funded aerospace research labs as well as a nationally recognized aerospace engineering sciences program at the University of Colorado at Boulder. Some 6,315 people are employed by aerospace companies in Boulder.

The technology boom has filtered down into other Boulder industries, increasing the city's manufacturing and retail base. Other key industries include the manufacture of natural and organic products, and sporting goods. Education, health care, and government are also important sectors of the Boulder economy.

The arts and culture sectors have also become important to Boulder's economy in recent years and contribute to its tourist industry. The city is currently home to some 30 art galleries, four museums, 32 movie and stage theaters, and dozens more cultural performances and events, all of which have contributed to the quality of life for the city's residents and drawn visitors to Boulder.

Items and goods produced: electronic devices, space hardware, recreational equipment, natural and organic food products

Incentive Programs—New and Existing Companies

Local programs: In an effort to reverse a downward economic trend early in the twenty-first century, the City of Boulder established an Economic Vitality Program in 2003. Guided by the Economic Vitality Advisory Board, the program's primary purpose is to attract new businesses and retain and expand existing businesses. Among the challenges it faces are Boulder's high facility costs, limited space for expansion, and poor condition of many older buildings. As a remedy, the program applies industry-cluster initiatives—partnerships between businesses, government agencies, and research institutions involved in similar industries—to foster innovation and efficiency. The city's clusters include aerospace, bioscience, creative services, natural and organic food, and sustainable technologies.

With the help of both public and private financial institutions, a Microloan Program was initiated to help small businesses and nonprofit organizations that may have difficulty finding funding through traditional sources. Loans of up to $50,000 are available to small businesses with annual gross revenue of less than $2 million. A Flexible Rebate Program targets existing businesses by allowing the city manager to structure custom incentive packages of tax and fee rebates. A Parks and Recreation Discount Program is available to all employees of Boulder companies, regardless of city of residence, and offers resident pricing for use of recreational facilities operated by the city.

Additionally, the Boulder Small Business Development Center provides valuable assistance to new and established small businesses. It offers three types of support: counseling, short- and long-term training, and access to such resources as market data, financing, and competitive information.

State programs: Colorado offers a variety of business assistance and incentive programs for expanding or relocated companies. Incentives include the Job Growth Tax Incentive, which provides a state income tax credit to job-creating projects in Colorado dependent on the incentive; Strategic Fund Initiative, for business development, expansion, or relocation that results in job creation; Enterprise Zone Tax Credits, which incentive development in economically distressed areas; Public Infrastructure Grants, to retain or add employment opportunities for low- or moderate-income residents; and sales and use tax refunds, exemptions, and credits for developments in biotechnology, manufacturing, and aviation sectors.

State financing support can be obtained through an array of general and industry-specific programs. Advanced Industries Accelerator Programs, created in 2013, offer access to capital for advanced manufacturing, aerospace, bioscience, electronic, energy and natural resource, infrastructure engineering, and technology and information industries. Private Activity Bonds offer tax-exempt bond financing to small manufacturing companies. Bioscience Discovery Evaluation Grants were available from 2007 to 2013 to support growth of companies in the bioscience industry. The Regional Tourism Act allows local governments to apply to the state for financial support for major tourism development initiatives likely to draw out-of-state visitors.

Venture capital funding is offered through the state's Certified Capital Companies Program, which makes available a statewide pool of $75 million for investment throughout the state, with an additional $25 million available for rural investment. The Colorado Venture Capital Authority manages venture capital investments for the state. Colorado Capital Access, Cash Collateral Support, and Colorado Credit Reserve support financing needs of small and medium businesses.

Job training programs: The Colorado Community College System has joined with the Colorado Office of Economic Development & International Trade to administer Colorado FIRST/Existing Industry Customized Training Programs. These programs are designed to fund employee training for transferable job skills to benefit a company's competitive strength as well as an employee's long-term employment opportunities.

The Small Business Development Center of Boulder provides both short- and long-term employee training to businesses seeking to expand or relocate to the area. Front Range Community College offers a variety of training programs for both employer and employee.

Development Projects

The Economic Vitality Program has several specific initiatives, in various stages of development. Among them is the development of Boulder Junction, formerly known as the Boulder Transit Village, a 160-acre site that combines transit service, including commuter rail, with residential and commercial space. The 25-year plan includes renovation and redevelopment of the area, including new neighborhoods, a new transit center and other transportation improvements, improved business and industrial districts, and development of other public spaces. The first phase of the project began in 2007, with rail service expected by 2017. Several projects received funding in 2011, while others awaited financial support.

Boulder's Capital Improvements Program is a six-year plan (2011–16) for public physical improvements within the city. The program will encompass some 138 projects and includes proposed funding of $139.5 million. These projects encompass renovations and redevelopment of open space, parks, and transportation infrastructure, among other initiatives.

In private developments, Ball Aerospace completed a 90,000-square-foot, $75 million expansion in 2013. The new facility, known as the Fisher Integration Facility, allowed the company to design, build, test, and ship satellites and instruments from the same plant.

Economic Development Information: Boulder Chamber of Commerce, 2440 Pearl St., Boulder, CO 80302; telephone (303) 442-1044; fax (303) 938-8837.

Economic Vitality Program, City of Boulder, 1300 Canyon Boulevard, Boulder, CO 80306; telephone (303) 441-3287.

Commercial Shipping

Commercial air shipping is available from a number of carriers at Denver International Airport (DIA). The airport handled 410 million pounds of cargo in 2012. Major cargo carriers are the U.S. Postal Service, DHL, UPS, FedEx, and United Airlines. The airport is the site of Foreign Trade Zone #123, as well as areas for U.S. Customs and Department of Agriculture clearance. Approximately 50 freight forwarders and customs brokers also serve in the area. More than one dozen motor freight carriers maintain facilities in Boulder.

Labor Force and Employment Outlook

Boulder business managers and owners cite a high quality of life and a talented work base among the advantages of doing business in Boulder. The workforce is educated well above the national average; 76 percent of adults 25 and older living in the city have a bachelor's degree or higher, compared to a national average of 29 percent. The university and the many technology- and research-oriented companies draw a large number of college graduates and professionals into the labor market.

Boulder is also a noteworthy region for up-and-coming young business professionals, offering such resources as Boulder 2140, an affiliate of the Boulder Chamber of Commerce, which annually hosts more than 40 different events for more than 1,000 young professionals in the city. The volunteer-driven group, which launched in 2009, focuses on bringing professional development opportunities, philanthropy, and social and cultural opportunities to the local community of young professionals.

The following is a summary of data regarding the 2012 Boulder labor force:

Size of civilian labor force: 58,881

Number of workers employed in . . .

    agriculture and mining: 367
    construction: 1,508
    manufacturing: 3,122
    wholesale trade: 921
    retail trade: 5,699
    transportation: 929
    information systems: 1,540
    finance: 2,624
    professional administration: 10,223
    education and social services: 15,453
    arts and leisure: 7,098
    other: 3,533
    public administration: 1,335

Average hourly earnings of production workers: $17.72

Unemployment rate: 5% (2012)

Employers

Largest county employers (2012)	*Number of employees*
University of Colorado at Boulder	7,312
Boulder Valley School District	4,000
St. Vrain Valley School District	3,238
Ball Corporation	2,982
IBM Corporation	2,800
Level 3 Communications Inc.	2,478
Boulder Community Hospital	2,300
Covidien	1,860
Boulder County	1,848
University Corporation for Research	1,394

Cost of Living

Boulder's cost of living is higher than in neighboring communities. Real estate in Boulder has held its value more than other parts of the nation.

The following is a summary of data regarding several key cost of living factors in the area.

State income tax rate: 4.63%

State sales tax rate: 2.9%

Local income tax rate: None

Local sales tax rate: 5.46%

Property tax rate: $0.01398 for every $1 of assessed value; residential assessed value is 7.96% of total value (county, 2013)

Economic Information: Boulder Chamber of Commerce, 2440 Pearl St., Boulder, CO 80302; telephone (303) 442-1044; fax (303) 938-8837.

■ Education and Research

Elementary and Secondary Schools

The Boulder Valley School District regulates the public schools in Boulder as well as the neighboring communities of Broomfield, Ward, Lafayette, Louisville, Gold Hill, Erie, Nederland, and Superior. The district's open enrollment policy enables students to enroll in a variety of schools, including focus or alternative schools. The board, comprised of seven members elected at-large to four-year terms, employs the superintendent.

The Boulder Valley District provides 56 schools to its nearly 30,000 students. The District boasts the distinction of consistently ranking among the top three large Front Range school districts in Colorado as measured by the Colorado Student Assessment Program. Ponderosa Elementary School was honored as a National Blue Ribbon School of Excellence in 2013 by the U.S. Department of Education, one of only five schools in the state to receive the honor.

A number of private and parochial schools also serve the Boulder area.

The following is a summary of data regarding the Boulder Valley School District .

Total enrollment: 29,526

Number of facilities

total: 56
elementary schools: 32
junior high schools: 12
high schools: 12
other: 1

Student/teacher ratio: 17.5:1

Teacher salaries

average (statewide): $49,938

Funding per pupil: $9,409

Public Schools Information: Boulder Valley School District, 6500 Arapahoe, Boulder, CO 80303; telephone (303) 447-1010.

Colleges and Universities

Boulder is the main campus of the University of Colorado (CU) system. Other campuses in the system include the University of Colorado at Colorado Springs, and the University of Colorado at Denver and Health Sciences Center. The Boulder campus is a major research and educational institution, with an enrollment of more than 30,000 students who choose from 3,600 courses in 150 fields of study. *U.S. News & World Report* ranked the university 86th among national universities for 2013–14. CU has strong ties to the astronautics and astrophysics disciplines. The university is a primary research center in space sciences, and at least 17 of its alumni have become astronauts in the National Aeronautics and Space Administration (NASA) program. The university received is estimated to have an annual economic impact of $5.3 billion on the state of Colorado.

Front Range Community College promotes academic and career advancement through associate degree and certificate programs in business, health, mathematics, advanced sciences, arts and humanities, world languages, computer information sciences, communication, and social sciences. Naropa University is a Buddhist-inspired institution offering four-year degrees in an academic program that blends intellectual, artistic, and meditative disciplines. Accredited by the North Central Association of Colleges and Schools, Naropa enrolls some 400 undergraduates and 600 graduate students; the school also features internship programs and a study-abroad program in Prague, Czech Republic, and is home to the Jack Kerouac School of Disembodied Poetics, founded by Allen Ginsberg and Anne Waldman. The Boulder College of Massage Therapy closed in 2013 following financial difficulties.

Libraries and Research Centers

The Boulder Public Library consists of a main building and four branches, the newest of which, NoBo Corner Library, opened in 2014. The library maintains special collections of children's literature, a Colorado Artists Registry, and municipal government. The Carnegie Branch Library for Local History contains a manuscript collection of more than 700,000 items, including some from before the area received the name Colorado, as well as historic photographs, newspapers, and oral histories. The University of Colorado library system consists of the central Norlin Library, which hosts the humanities and social science collections, and five discipline-specific branch libraries. The total system contains more than 12 million books, periodicals, and microforms, as well as special collections in juvenile literature, the history of silver, mountaineering, and Western history. The National Indian Law Library, which houses 4,000 items, is the only law library specializing in practice materials relating to federal and tribal Indian law. The Allen Ginsberg Library of the Naropa University houses books, journals, audio/visual media, and artwork, as well as special collections in university recordings, Tibetan volumes, and small press and chapbooks. A number of private and special interest libraries are also located in the city.

In fiscal year 2012 the University of Colorado at Boulder (CU) received more than $380 million in sponsored research awards. CU's nearly 100 research centers and institutes are involved in everything from music entrepreneurship to high energy physics. Some of the largest facilities are the Institute of Arctic and Alpine Research, Institute for Behavioral Genetics, Institute of Cognitive Science, Colorado Center for Information Storage, Joint Institute for Laboratory Astrophysics, and the Laboratory of Atmospheric and Space Physics. The Biofrontiers Institute, studying an array of human diseases, opened in 2012. Five CU professors and research faculty members have been recipients of a Nobel Prize, four in physics and one in chemistry; another four have won the National Medal of Science.

Boulder is home to several research institutions of the federal government. The Cooperative Institute for Research in Environmental Sciences is a joint venture of CU and the National Office of Oceanic and Atmospheric Research. The National Weather Service maintains a weather forecast office in the city, which provides weather forecasts and data for a large chunk of Colorado. The National Center for Atmospheric Research offers free, guided tours of such exhibits as lightning, a tornado, a solar eclipse telescope, and aircraft models. Visitors can view the atomic clock and other science displays at the National Institute of Standards and Technology Boulder Laboratories, which attracts 100 visiting researchers each year in addition to its 350 resident scientists, engineers, and other personnel.

Public Library Information: Boulder Public Library, 1001 Arapahoe Avenue, Boulder, CO 80302; telephone (303) 441-3100.

■ Health Care

Boulder Community Hospital is the largest health-care institution in the Boulder area, with 159 beds and a $250 million operating budget. It is a full-service hospital with a 24-hour emergency room, an intensive care unit, a cardiac care unit, and a network of facilities that includes the Boulder Center for Sports Medicine, Boulder Community Foothills Hospital, Community Medical Center (an urgent care facility), the Sleep Clinic, and the Miriam R. Hart Regional Radiation Therapy Center.

Top-rated hospitals in nearby Aurora included the University of Colorado Hospital, part of the Anschutz Medical Campus, a nationally ranked medical institution in five specialties according to *U.S. News & World Report* in 2013. The hospital has 467 beds and is a teaching hospital. Also part of the Anschutz Medical Campus in the Children's Hospital of Colorado, a nationally ranked facility.

■ Recreation

Sightseeing

A highlight of downtown Boulder is the 16-mile Boulder Creek Path, which runs along the creek through the center of the city. The banks of the creek have been restored to their natural state, parks and picnic areas have been formed—including the attractive Boulder Sculpture Park—and many small waterfalls along the way are perfect for kayaking and tubing. The Open Space & Mountain Parks division of the City of Boulder encompasses 43,000 square feet and a number of free public nature hikes of varying difficulty, each offering some of the most scenic views in the region. Among them is Sawhill Ponds, featuring 18 ponds; Flagstaff Mountain, a 6,850-foot peak that is home to the Flagstaff Nature Center; Royal Arch, a sandstone arch through which the city of Boulder can be viewed from above; and Boulder Falls, a five-acre site known as the "Yosemite of Boulder Canyon."

Boulder also caters to those who prefer less strenuous sightseeing excursions. Free tours are offered by the Celestial Seasonings Tea Co., including a tea sampling bar and a walk through the Mint Room, and by the Redstone Meadery, brewer of a honey wine known as mead. Gateway Park Fun Center features go-karts, batting cages, and miniature golf.

Arts and Culture

The Boulder Philharmonic Orchestra has been performing since 1958, and holds the majority of its performances at the Macky Auditorium Concert Hall on the campus of the University of Colorado at Boulder. Also performing at the Macky is Boulder Ballet, the major dance company of Boulder County. The Boulder Concert Band, comprised of 70 community members, offers a concert series and summer concerts in the area parks. Other musical institutions include the Boulder Chorale, Greater Boulder Youth Symphony, and the Boulder Chamber Orchestra, founded in 2004. The Nomad Theatre is Boulder's only professional resident theater. The Upstart Crow Theatre Company is an ensemble acting company whose season runs from early fall to mid-summer and offers four major works. Boulder's Dinner Theatre entertains thousands of attendees each year with food, drink, and major Broadway musicals.

The University of Colorado (CU) Museum of Natural History houses nearly four million specimens of biology, anthropology, and geology, including fossils, local animals, and Southwestern cultural artifacts. The CU Heritage Center contains exhibits that chronicle the university's past, such as the baseball bat and glove used by alumnus Robert Redford in *The Natural,* as well as space suits worn by former graduates who became astronauts. CU is also the site of the Sommers-Bausch Observatory and the Fiske Planetarium, which features the largest projection dome between Chicago and Los Angeles.

The city's many museums are not limited to the CU campus. The Boulder History Museum houses nearly 35,000 objects from Boulder's past, dating back to the 1800s. The Leanin' Tree Museum of Western Art houses one of the largest collections of contemporary Western art in America.

Boulder offers a variety of art galleries, as well as several art museums. The Boulder Museum of Contemporary Art features regional, national, and international exhibitions and performances. The CU Art Museum, which reopened in 2010 in the CU Visual Arts Complex, offers five galleries including both changing and permanent exhibitions, as well as a video gallery. The Charles A. Haertling Sculpture Park displays the work of such artists as Jerry Wingren, Dennis Yoshikawa Wright, Tom Miller, and Beth Juliar-Skodge.

Festivals and Holidays

Boulder's most famous festival is the Colorado Shakespeare Festival, regarded as one of the best in the nation. The festival is held each summer at the University of Colorado at Boulder's outdoor Mary Rippon Theatre and the indoor University Theatre. February brings the Boulder Bach Festival, a three-day event featuring an orchestra, chorus, and soloists performing the works of Johann Sebastian Bach. For more than a month during the summer, the Colorado Music Festival presents classical music performed by musicians from around the world. The Pearl Street Art Fair is held each July, and the Aerial Dance Festival, featuring demonstrations of dancing through the air, takes place the following month. Film festivals include the Boulder International Film Festival, held for four days in February, and the adventure-themed films of the Boulder Adventure Film Festival, shown each April.

The city hosts a number of unique festivals and events. The annual Polar Plunge attracts participants intrepid enough to jump into the Boulder Reservoir on New Year's Day. The International Mead Festival, held in February, features more than 80 meads from seven countries and is the world's largest competition for mead, a beverage made of wine fermented with honey. Another record-setting event is held the following month, as the world's shortest parade—Boulder's St. Patrick's Day Parade—takes place over a course covering less than one city block. The Kinetics Sculpture Challenge, preceded a week earlier by the Kinetics Parade, invites teams to race kinetically designed sculptures over both land and water. The Boulder Creek Festival, which draws approximately 130,000 people over Memorial Day Weekend, features a rubber duck race, a children's fishing derby, and dog-agility demonstrations along with typical festival activities and fare. The Shoot-Out Boulder, held since 2007, is a filmmaking festival in which contestants have 24 hours to produce a seven-minute video. Several holiday events take place in November and December, including Switch on the Holidays, the Holiday Festival, and the Lights of December Parade.

Sports for the Spectator

The University of Colorado at Boulder provides the major sporting attractions in the city. The university's football team, the Buffaloes, is a member of the Pac 12 conference. The university also offers 12 other sports, from soccer to golf to skiing to volleyball.

Professional sports fans can turn to any of nearby Denver's clubs: the Nuggets of the National Basketball Association, Major League Baseball's Colorado Rockies, National Hockey League's Colorado Avalanche, National Football League's Broncos, and the Colorado Rapids of Major League Soccer.

Sports for the Participant

Boulder consistently has been rated one of the top towns in the county for sports or other outdoor activities. Some of its more recent such accolades include the 2013 designation by *USA Today* as the city with the Best Urban Green Spaces in North America, *MSN Healthy Living* noting Boulder as the Fittest City in America, and a 2012 Gallup honor as the nation's Least-obese Metro Area. Boulder is more than great location for sports lovers in general; it is a haven specifically for bicyclists, with residents able to access 150-plus miles of bike paths and more than 200 miles of bike lanes. The city has even been known to plow snow off important bike paths before plowing certain roads. Each year, Boulder turns national Bike to Work Day in June into Bike to Work Week and offers free tune-ups and safety clinics.

Boulder offers a variety of outdoor activities the year round. Natural areas like the seven-mile-long Boulder Creek Path and the city's large mountain park feature hiking, camping, and boating. The city operates more than 60 parks—800 acres of maintained park land and an additional 200 acres of natural land—offering recreational facilities of all kinds. There are 54 tennis courts, three main sports complexes, 14 satellite athletic fields, and the public Flatirons Golf Course. Boulder is also a short distance away from several popular ski resorts and dozens of state and national parks.

Boulder hosts several athletic competitions. The BolderBOULDER 10K race brings 50,000 runners from around the world to the city on Memorial Day. Three weeks later is the 5430 Sprint Triathlon, the first of three races making up the Boulder Triathlon Series. The second race is the Boulder Peak Triathlon, held in July, followed in August by the Ironman 70.3 Boulder. Colorado's largest running event is the Boulder Marathon , which takes place each September at the Boulder Reservoir.

Shopping and Dining

A major attraction in the downtown area is the historic Pearl Street Mall district. Set up for pedestrian traffic, the mall is lined with shops, galleries, and restaurants. Along the way, street performers, gardens, and sculptures make the stroll enjoyable. Several large suburban malls add to countless smaller shops and specialty stores scattered throughout the area. Twenty Ninth Street is an 850,000-square-foot shopping center with an open-air environment anchored by Foley's and a 16-theater cinema.

More than 300 restaurants in Boulder offer a wide variety of foods, from traditional Western fare to exotic ethnic foods. The Flagstaff House and Frasca possess global bragging rights for having landed on Zagat's competitive "World's Top Restaurants" list, making it no wonder that *Bon Appetit* magazine declared Boulder the "Foodiest Town in America" in 2010.

Visitor Information: Boulder Convention & Visitors Bureau, 2440 Pearl St., Boulder, CO 80302; telephone (303) 442-2911; toll-free (800) 444-0447; fax (303) 938-2098; email visitor@bouldercvb.com.

■ Convention Facilities

Although lacking a full-fledged convention center, Boulder has 14 facilities offering meeting space. The Millennium Harvest House can accommodate small functions as well as up to 500 people on its outdoor pavilion and up to 600 in its Grand Ballroom. The historic Hotel Boulderado, a national registered landmark, accommodates meetings for up to 200 people and receptions up to 300. Several other hotels provide meeting space, as do facilities at the University of Colorado at Boulder, namely the 2,047-seat Macky Auditorium Concert Hall and the University Memorial Center, whose 9,418-square-foot Glenn Miller Ballroom can accommodate 700 attendants. The Boulder Theater can seat up to 860 conference delegates.

Convention Information: Boulder Convention & Visitors Bureau, 2440 Pearl St., Boulder, CO 80302; telephone (303) 442-2911; toll-free (800) 444-0447; fax (303) 938-2098; email visitor@bouldercvb.com.

■ Transportation

Approaching the City

The majority of air traffic comes through the Denver International Airport, which is the fifth busiest airport in the United States and 13th busiest in the world. In 2012 its 17 commercial airlines served a total of 44.7 million passengers. The Northwest Parkway toll road connects the airport with Boulder. Hourly shuttle service and limousine service from the airport to Boulder is also available. Rocky Mountain Metropolitan Airport is located 11 miles from Boulder, and provides commuter air service in addition to corporate air facilities. Boulder Municipal Airport, located three miles northeast of the central business district, also provides commuter air service.

Interstate 25, Colorado's major north–south highway, runs just to the east of Boulder. The Boulder-Denver Turnpike connects the two cities, and Interstate 70 at Denver provides links east and west. Other major highways include U.S. highways 36, 52, 93, and 287.

FasTracks, a metro-wide passenger train system to connect Boulder to Denver and Longmont, was under construction in 2013, with a segment reaching Westminster—located between Denver and Boulder—expected to open by 2016.

Traveling in the City

Boulder ranks second in the United States for non-auto transit, trailing only Manhattan, a feat made possible because of its numerous biking campaigns and comprehensive bus service. Major thoroughfares in the city include Broadway and Twenty-Eighth Street, running north and south, and Iris Avenue, Pearl Street, Canyon Boulevard, Arapahoe Road, and Baseline Road, all running east and west. The Regional Transportation District (RTD) operates a fleet of buses serving the metropolitan area. The HOP line makes 40 stops in a loop throughout central Boulder, while the SKIP lines runs north and south along Broadway; other RTD bus lines in Boulder are the BOLT, DASH, BOUND, HOP, SKIP, and STAMPEDE.

Bicycling is extremely important to travel in Boulder, as 10 percent of residents ride bikes on a regular basis. Bicycle paths parallel all major traffic arteries, and total more than 200 miles. The Annual Walk and Bike Week encourages commuters to get out of their cars and either pedal or walk to and from work. Local businesses, such as restaurants and bicycle mechanics, offer free incentives to participants.

■ Communications

Newspapers and Magazines

Boulder is served by two daily newspapers, the morning *Daily Camera* and the morning *Colorado Daily*. *Boulder Weekly* is a free, alternative newspaper, and the *Boulder County Business Report* focuses on economic, industrial, and business news every other week. The *Campus Press*, written by and for students of the University of Colorado at Boulder, is distributed each Thursday. Boulder's love of outdoor sports is reflected in some of the nationally distributed magazines published in the city, including *Inside Triathlon, Ski, Skiing,* and the competitive bicycling magazine *VeloNews*. Other publications include *Delicious Living* and *Soldier of Fortune,* as well as a number of several scholarly journals and trade publications.

Television and Radio

Numerous television stations broadcast to Boulder audiences, and cable service is available. Two AM and 10 FM radio stations broadcast music, talk radio, and University of Colorado programming.

Media Information: *Daily Camera,* 5450 Western Avenue, Boulder, CO 80301; telephone (303) 466-3636.

Boulder Online

Boulder Chamber of Commerce. Available www.boulderchamber.com

Boulder Community Hospital. Available www.bch.org

Boulder Convention & Visitors Bureau. Available www.bouldercoloradousa.com

Boulder Public Library System. Available www.boulder.lib.co.us

Boulder Valley School District. Available www.bvsd.org

City of Boulder Home Page. Available www.ci.boulder.co.us

Daily Camera. Available www.thedailycamera.com

Economic Vitality Program. Available www.ci.boulder.co.us/economic_vitality

University of Colorado at Boulder. Available www.colorado.edu

BIBLIOGRAPHY

Brosnan, Kathleen A. and Amy L. Scott, eds., *City dreams, Country Schemes: Community and Identity in the American West* (Reno, NV: University of Nevada Press, 2011)

Knopper, Steve, *Colorado* (Berkeley, CA: Avalon Travel, 2009)

Lipker, Kim, *Sixty hikes within 60 miles, Denver and Boulder: including Colorado Springs, Fort Collins, and Rocky Mountain National Park,* 2nd ed. (Birmingham, AL: Menasha Ridge Press, 2010)

Pettem, Silvia, *Behind the Badge: 125 Years of the Boulder, Colorado, Police Department* (Boulder, CO: The Book Lode LLC, 2003)

Pettem, Silvia, and Liston Leyendecker, *Boulder: Evolution of a City* (Niwot, CO: University Press of Colorado, 1994)

Colorado Springs

■ The City in Brief

Founded: 1871 (incorporated, 1872)

Head Official: Mayor Steve Bach (since 2011; current term expires 2015)

City Population
> 1990: 283,112
> 2000: 360,890
> 2010: 416,427
> 2012 estimate: 431,846
> Percent change, 2000–2010: 15.4%
> U.S. rank in 1990: 54th
> U.S. rank in 2000: 48th (State rank: 2nd)
> U.S. rank in 2010: 41st (State rank: 2nd)

Metropolitan Statistical Area Population
> 2000: 537,484
> 2010: 645,613
> 2012 estimate: 668,353
> Percent change, 2000–2010: 20.1%
> U.S. rank in 2000: 86th
> U.S. rank in 2010: 82nd

Area: 186 square miles

Elevation: 6,035 feet above sea level

Average Annual Temperatures: January, 28.1° F; July, 69.6° F; annual average, 47.8° F

Average Annual Precipitation: 17.40 inches of rain; 42.4 inches of snow

Major Economic Sectors: military, tourism, aerospace, computers and electronics, manufacturing, health care

Unemployment Rate: 6.1% (2012)

Per Capita Income: $28,035

2012 FBI Crime Index Property: 17,899

Major Colleges and Universities: University of Colorado at Colorado Springs, United States Air Force Academy, Colorado College

Daily Newspaper: *The Gazette*

■ Introduction

At the foot of Pikes Peak, the highest of the Rocky Mountains, Colorado Springs is a city surrounded by natural beauty that draws millions of visitors a year. Its municipal parks include the breathtaking Garden of the Gods, once sacred Native American tribal grounds. Upon ascending Pikes Peak in 1893, Katharine Lee Bates wrote the words to "America the Beautiful;" the lyrics "purple mountains' majesty" refer to the vistas around Colorado Springs. Now an important center of military installations, Colorado Springs is home to the United States Air Force Academy, the North American Aerospace Defense Command (NORAD), U.S. Air Force and U.S. Space Commands, Consolidated Space Operations Center, and Fort Carson. The military presence, in turn, has attracted private defense contractors that provide high-quality jobs in advanced fields such as aerospace.

■ Geography and Climate

Colorado Springs is located on a high, flat plain at the foot of the Rocky Mountains in eastern central Colorado. To the east of the city are rolling prairie lands and to the north is Monument Divide. The climate of Colorado Springs is relatively mild and dry, since the city is protected from harsh weather by the Rocky Mountains in the west. The city sees about 300 days of sunshine each year. In the winter, Colorado Springs is warmed by the Chinook, a wind whose name means "snow eater."

Area: 186 square miles

Colorado Springs Convention & Visitors Bureau. Reproduced by permission.

Elevation: 6,035 feet above sea level

Average Temperatures: January, 28.1° F; July, 69.6° F; annual average, 47.8° F

Average Annual Precipitation: 17.40 inches of rain; 42.4 inches of snow

■ History

Rowdiness and Refinement Coexist in City's Early Days

The history of Colorado Springs is the history of two very different communities, one wild and rowdy, the other a model of controlled growth. The area was first discovered by settlers of European descent in 1806 when Zebulon Montgomery Pike came upon a mountain he named Pikes Peak and attempted to climb it. Later, several tribes of Native Americans, namely the Ute, Arapaho, and Cheyenne, lived and battled in the region. They declared what is now called the Garden of the Gods to be sacred ground where the tribes could meet in peace and bathe in the mineral springs.

Mountains rich in silver and gold brought miners into the area. A settlement developed and was called El

Dorado City, because of its proximity to the gold mines. This became Colorado City, a rough town full of saloons where frequent brawls and gun fights raged. In 1871, the Denver & Rio Grande Western Railroad, the first narrow-gauge line in Colorado, came to the region. The railroad was directed by General William Jackson Palmer, who began to plan a community near Colorado City. Palmer envisioned the town as a playground for the rich, rivaling the elegant resorts on the East Coast. First called the Fountain Colony, the town was incorporated as Colorado Springs in 1872. According to what was called "The Palmer Pattern of Responsibility," Colorado Springs was planned with schools, libraries, churches, parks, and a college. Citizens of "good moral character and strict temperance habits" were purposely sought; intemperance and industry were relegated to Colorado City across the railroad tracks.

City Becomes Tourist and Military Center

Tourists from throughout the country flocked to Colorado Springs and to the spa at nearby Manitou Springs. By the turn of the century Colorado Springs was the wealthiest city per capita in the United States. At this time it earned the nickname Little London, reflecting the number of Tudor-style houses constructed in the area.

During this age of the elegant hotel, the rich and the titled were drawn to the Rocky Mountains—especially Colorado Springs—to play polo and hunt foxes. Colorado City, after suffering great economic vicissitudes tied to the mining industry, was absorbed by Colorado Springs in 1971.

Since World War II, Colorado Springs has become a focal point for the U.S. military. Fort Carson Army Base was established in the early 1940s; the United States Air Force Academy was completed in 1958. In 1966 the North American Air Defense Command (NORAD) was installed inside Cheyenne Mountain as the first warning system for North America against a nuclear missile strike.

The United States Olympic Committee created an Olympic Training Grounds in Colorado Springs in 1978. Athletes come from throughout the world to train there, surrounded by the beauty of the Rocky Mountains. In 2010 the United States Olympic Committee decided to establish its headquarters in the city, solidifying the Olympic presence.

Meanwhile, the extensive military presence in the city has attracted major defense contractors and supported growth of high-technology in Colorado Springs, especially aerospace.

Historical Information: Colorado College, Tutt Library, 1021 North Cascade Avenue, Colorado Springs, CO 80903; telephone (719) 389-6184.

■ Population Profile

Metropolitan Statistical Area Population

2000: 537,484
2010: 645,613
2012 estimate: 668,353
Percent change, 2000–2010: 20.1%
U.S. rank in 2000: 86th
U.S. rank in 2010: 82nd

City Residents

1990: 283,112
2000: 360,890
2010: 416,427
2012 estimate: 431,846
Percent change, 2000–2010: 15.4%
U.S. rank in 1990: 54th
U.S. rank in 2000: 48th (State rank: 2nd)
U.S. rank in 2010: 41st (State rank: 2nd)

Density: 2,140.6 people per square mile

Racial and ethnic characteristics

White: 348,013
Black or African American: 28,963
American Indian and Alaskan Native: 2,172
Asian: 13,552

Native Hawaiian and Other Pacific Islander: 636
Hispanic or Latino (may be of any race): 74,559
Other: 38,510

Percent of residents born in state: 32.3%

Age characteristics

Population under 5 years old: 29,214
Population 5 to 9 years old: 28,432
Population 10 to 14 years old: 28,174
Population 15 to 19 years old: 30,811
Population 20 to 24 years old: 37,439
Population 25 to 34 years old: 64,489
Population 35 to 44 years old: 53,305
Population 45 to 54 years old: 61,499
Population 55 to 59 years old: 27,151
Population 60 to 64 years old: 21,431
Population 65 to 74 years old: 28,995
Population 75 to 84 years old: 14,554
Population 85 years and over: 6,352
Median age: 34.5

Births (2010–11 Metropolitan Area)

Total number: 9,070

Deaths (2010–11 Metropolitan Area)

Total number: 3,749

Money income (2012)

Per capita income: $28,035
Median household income: $52,896
Total households: 167,862

Number of households with income of ...

less than $10,000: 11,028
$10,000 to $14,999: 8,882
$15,000 to $24,999: 18,128
$25,000 to $34,999: 17,109
$35,000 to $49,999: 23,494
$50,000 to $74,999: 32,873
$75,000 to $99,999: 19,723
$100,000 to $149,999: 22,913
$150,000 to $199,999: 7,683
$200,000 or more: 6,029

Percent of families below poverty level: 14.4%

FBI Crime Index Property: 17,899

FBI Crime Index Violent: 1,968

■ Municipal Government

Colorado Springs operates under a council-mayor form of government; it had operated under a manager-council form until 2010. The city council is composed of nine non-partisan officials elected by the citizens. Elections are held every four years for mayor, three at-large council members, and six district-based council members. Colorado Springs is the seat of El Paso County.

Head Official: Mayor Steve Bach (since 2011; current term expires 2015)

Total Number of City Employees: 4,116 (2012)

City Information: City Hall, 107 N. Nevada Ave, Colorado Springs, CO 80903; telephone (719) 385-2489.

■ Economy

Major Industries and Commercial Activity

The economy of Colorado Springs is based primarily on the military installations in the area, as well as the aerospace and electronics industries, and tourism. Colorado Springs is home to five major military installations: Fort Carson, Schriever Air Force Base, Peterson Air Force Base, Cheyenne Mountain Air Station, and the U.S. Air Force Academy. The military and supporting businesses account for roughly one-third of the region's economy, and Fort Carson is Colorado's largest non-state employer.

The state of Colorado has the nation's second-largest aerospace industry, and Colorado Springs is a center for space research and other aerospace endeavors, with both the U.S. Air Force Space Command and North American Aerospace Defense Command (NORAD) headquartered there. The U.S. Space Foundation and the Space Command at Peterson Air Force Base also provide an environment conducive for developing space-related projects. Resultantly, several high-technology firms have been attracted to Colorado Springs; the Colorado Springs Technology Incubator supports firms seeking to launch in the area. As of 2014, an estimated 10,000 workers employed by several hundred defense contractors were in Colorado Springs. Aerospace companies continued to relocate and expand into the area through the 2010s, with ARES Corporation, Cosmic Advanced Engineering Solutions, and National Aviation all coming to Colorado Springs in 2011 alone.

Since the turn of the century, when the city's grand hotels made it famous, Colorado Springs has been a major tourism center. Pikes Peak and the natural beauty of the surrounding area draw an average of nearly six million visitors per year. Total visitor spending approaches $1.2 billion annually and employs some 13,000 residents. The United States Olympic Committee established their headquarters in downtown Colorado Springs in 2010, bringing with it tourism and sports-related growth projected to amount to about $340 million in direct and indirect economic impact.

Items and goods produced: medical devices, semiconductors, aerospace parts, electronics, special plastics, granite, concrete, dairy products, chemicals

Incentive Programs—New and Existing Companies

Local programs: At the local level, El Paso County contains an Enterprise Zone offering state and local credits for new jobs, investment, and research and development expenditures. El Paso County also supports a revolving loan fund. The Colorado Springs Regional Business Alliance packages private and public incentives for relocating or expanding companies that are tailored to the specific needs of the company. Incentives available from the city government include sales and use tax rebates, alternative tax rates for machinery and equipment, and private activity bonds. Pikes Peak Regional Development Corporation offers a small business loan program.

State programs: Colorado offers a variety of business assistance and incentive programs for expanding or relocated companies. Incentives include the Job Growth Tax Incentive, which provides a state income tax credit to job-creating projects in Colorado dependent on the incentive; Strategic Fund Initiative, for business development, expansion, or relocation that results in job creation; Enterprise Zone Tax Credits, which incentive development in economically distressed areas; Public Infrastructure Grants, to retain or add employment opportunities for low- or moderate-income residents; and sales and use tax refunds, exemptions, and credits for developments in biotechnology, manufacturing, and aviation sectors.

State financing support can be obtained through an array of general and industry-specific programs. Advanced Industries Accelerator Programs, created in 2013, offer access to capital for advanced manufacturing, aerospace, bioscience, electronic, energy and natural resource, infrastructure engineering, and technology and information industries. Private Activity Bonds offer tax-exempt bond financing to small manufacturing companies. Bioscience Discovery Evaluation Grants were available from 2007 to 2013 to support growth of companies in the bioscience industry. The Regional Tourism Act allows local governments to apply to the state for financial support for major tourism development initiatives likely to draw out-of-state visitors.

Venture capital funding is offered through the state's Certified Capital Companies Program, which makes available a statewide pool of $75 million for investment throughout the state, with an additional $25 million available for rural investment. The Colorado Venture Capital Authority manages venture capital investments for the state. Colorado Capital Access, Cash Collateral Support, and Colorado Credit Reserve support financing needs of small and medium businesses.

Job training programs: The Colorado Community College System has joined with the Colorado Office of Economic Development & International Trade to administer Colorado FIRST/Existing Industry Customized Training Programs. These programs are designed to fund employee training for transferable job skills to benefit a company's competitive strength as well as an employee's long-term employment opportunities. The Pikes Peak Workforce Center helps with placement, job matching, and training workers, and also leads collaborative efforts with local community colleges and private institutions.

Development Projects

The Copper Ridge at Northgate retail development includes 2.4 million square feet of space and construction of a new Powers Boulevard extension. While development of the boulevard, intended to provide a more direct link to the Colorado Springs airport, was stalled due to lack of funding—possibly until 2035—the retail space developed rapidly. A 117,000-square-foot Bass Pro Shops was set to anchor the development and opened in late 2013. Additional projects were in various stages of development, with a 400-rooom hotel and 50,000-square-foot waterpark among the possibilities for major future projects.

Development projects led by the Colorado Springs government centered on its City for Champions proposal, a $120.5 million project with four major components intended to solidify the city's reputation as a tourist and sports haven, and build upon the 2010 relocation of the United States Olympic Committee. The four projects were a United States Olympic Museum, Colorado Sports and Event Center, Sports Medicine and Performance Center, and Air Force Academy Visitors Center. During late 2013 and early 2014, the project was under review to determine its eligibility for funding through the state's Regional Tourism Act.

Development projects at the University of Colorado at Colorado Springs included an $18.5 million Lane Center for Academic Health Sciences and a $17.5 million addition to student housing, both of which were scheduled to complete in 2014.

Location of customer service centers in the area provided some of the largest job growth during 2012 and 2013. A Comcast customer service center added 150 jobs in 2012, while centers operated by UnitedHealth Group and Sorenson Communications generated 500 new jobs during 2013.

Economic Development Information: Colorado Springs Regional Business Alliance, 102 S. Tejon Street, Suite 430, Colorado Springs, CO 80903; telephone (719) 471-8183; fax (719) 471-9733.

Commercial Shipping

Established as a Foreign Trade Zone, Colorado Springs is a link in the country's import-export shipping network.

Federal Express is the only exclusively air cargo carrier operating from Colorado Springs Airport. The metropolitan area is served by two major rail freight lines: Burlington Northern Santa Fe and Union Pacific. A number of motor freight carriers ship goods through terminals in the city.

Denver International Airport, a 75-minute drive from Colorado Springs, offers extensive commercial shipping opportunities.

Labor Force and Employment Outlook

Colorado Springs boasts a youthful, well educated labor force. Prime sources of labor include former military personnel, military dependents, retirees, college students, and commuters from other Colorado cities. An estimated 600 military personnel based in Colorado Springs finish their term of service each month. Labor/management relations are described as excellent; there is a low level of unionization throughout Colorado. More than 92 percent of adult residents have a high school diploma, and some 36 percent have at least a bachelor's degree.

The following is a summary of data regarding the 2012 Colorado Springs labor force:

Size of civilian labor force: 217,460

Number of workers employed in . . .
agriculture and mining: 1,385
construction: 12,128
manufacturing: 13,240
wholesale trade: 3,479
retail trade: 23,093
transportation: 7,438
information systems: 5,572
finance: 12,403
professional administration: 25,482
education and social services: 42,775
arts and leisure: 21,526
other: 12,564
public administration: 13,612

Average hourly earnings of production workers: $16.63

Unemployment rate: 6.1% (2012)

Employers

Largest employers (2012)	*Number of employees*
Fort Carson Army Post	52,063
Peterson Air Force Base	20,966
Schriever Air Force Base	14,578
United States Air Force Academy	11,705

Memorial Health Services	8,446
Colorado Springs School District #11	7,160
Academy School District #20	4,931
Penrose-St. Francis Health Services	4,716
City of Colorado Springs	4,116
El Paso County	3,773

Cost of Living

The average sale price of a house in Colorado Springs as of 2013 was $270,948. Prices for utilities and other basic items are highly competitive with other communities.

The following is a summary of data regarding several key cost of living factors in the area.

2013 ACCRA Average House Price: $270,948

2013 ACCRA Cost of Living Index: 96

State income tax rate: 4.63%

State sales tax rate: 2.9%

Local income tax rate: None

Local sales tax rate: 4.73%

Property tax rate: $0.058992 for every $1 of assessed value; residential assessed value is 7.96% of total value (2013)

Economic Information: Colorado Springs Regional Business Alliance, 102 S. Tejon Street, Suite 430, Colorado Springs, CO 80903; telephone (719) 471-8183; fax (719) 471-9733.

■ Education and Research

Elementary and Secondary Schools

In Colorado, school district boundaries are independent of city or other political boundaries. A 1993 state law allows parents to send their children to any public school, as long as there is room in the facility. There are 10 public school districts within El Paso County. Colorado Springs School District #11 is the primary school district for the city. The district offers a variety of alternative programs throughout its school system, including international baccalaureate programs at the primary, middle, and high school levels as well as Advanced Placement courses. The school system also provides a Career and Technology Education program and the only public Montessori program for elementary school students in the region. Columbia Elementary School was named a National Blue Ribbon School in

2013 by the U.S. Department of Education. As of 2013–14, the district had seven charter schools.

Colorado Springs is also home to dozens of parochial and private schools, spanning all grades.

The following is a summary of data regarding the Colorado Springs School District No. 11.

Total enrollment: 29,498

Number of facilities
  total: 59
  elementary schools: 33
  junior high schools: 9
  high schools: 4
  other: 13

Student/teacher ratio: 15.98:1

Teacher salaries
  average (statewide): $49,938

Funding per pupil: $8,880

Public Schools Information: Colorado Springs School District 11, 1115 North El Paso Street, Colorado Springs, CO 80903; telephone (719) 520-2000.

Colleges and Universities

Colorado Springs is home to the University of Colorado at Colorado Springs (UCCS), United States Air Force Academy, and Colorado College, as well as several other two- and four-year colleges located in the surrounding area. UCCS is a state school offering both undergraduate and master's degrees in interdisciplinary programs such as geography, earth sciences, and environmental studies. UCCS enrolls nearly 9,000 students annually. The highly selective United States Air Force Academy, ranked 25th among all liberal arts colleges by *U.S. News & World Report* in 2013, enrolls about 4,100 cadets annually. Colorado College, opened in 1874, has grown with the city, and offers an unusual learning environment: the Block Plan has students take only one intensive course at a time.

Other schools include Nazarene Bible College, DeVry University, and Everest College. Technical, professional, and business schools include Colorado Technical University, which has locations in Colorado Springs, Denver, Kansas City, Pueblo, and Sioux Falls.

Libraries and Research Centers

The Pikes Peak Library District (PPLD) serves the residents of El Paso County, except for Manitou Springs and Widefield School District #3. Residents in those two areas can check out PPLD materials through the Colorado Library Card program. Library facilities include two main facilities—Penrose Public Library and the East Library and Information Center—as well as 13 branches and bookmobile services. The library district maintains several diverse and specialized collections. The circulating collection includes books, vertical file materials, audio and video cassettes, record albums, CDs, and DVDs. The library subscribes to hundreds of periodicals and newspapers. The Local History and Genealogy collections, housed in the 1905 Carnegie Library, include books, photographs, manuscripts, maps, blueprints, newspapers, city directories, oral histories, and other items spanning more than 125 years of local and regional history.

A number of other libraries and research centers are housed in the city; most are affiliated with educational institutions, government agencies, hospitals, and churches. The United States Air Force Academy McDermott Library, with nearly 1.9 million volumes, maintains a collection on aeronautics history before 1910; special interests also include falcony and military history. The Charles Leaming Tutt Library at Colorado College houses periodicals, a government documents repository, the college's Special Collections & Archives, and the Crown-Tapper Teaching and Learning Center devoted to exploring ways to improve teaching in the electronic age.

Public Library Information: Pikes Peak Library District, PO Box 1579, Colorado Springs, CO 80901; telephone (719) 531-6333.

■ Health Care

The Colorado Springs metropolitan area is served by several major hospitals. Memorial Hospital is a regional center for high-risk pregnancies, with a Level III Neonatal Intensive Care Unit. It opened its North Hospital facility, with nearly 500 beds, in 2007. Memorial Hospital admitted about 25,600 patients annually as of 2013. The hospital is accredited by the Commission on Accreditation of Rehabilitation Facilities.

Penrose-St. Francis Health Services runs Penrose Hospital, St. Francis Medical Center, and an array of urgent-care and sports clinics, as well as a health learning center. It was named one of "America's 50 Best Hospitals" by HealthGrades from 2008 through 2013. The hospital system includes 522 licensed beds and employs nearly 800 physicians, admitting almost 22,000 patients annually and caring for some 88,000 in its emergency department.

There are a variety of rehabilitation centers, nursing homes and behavioral health centers in the city and surrounding county. In addition, there are a number of alternative centers of healing and medicine, including Health Quarters Ministries.

■ Recreation

Sightseeing

Colorado Springs is one of the premier vacation spots in the United States, the majestic natural beauty of Pikes Peak being a principal attraction. Visitors can venture up High Drive, a one-way road without guardrails, to see the spectacular vistas. North Cheyenne Canyon contains unusual rock formations and waterfalls that cascade down the mountains. In the Garden of the Gods, northwest of the city, visitors can hike or horseback ride through huge red sandstone rock formations; the Garden of the Gods is particularly lovely to visit at sunrise or sunset, when the sun's rays set off the natural splendor of the rocks. At High Point a camera obscura is provided for viewing the landscape that surrounds the point.

Cheyenne Mountain Zoo displays more than 800 animals from around the world in the United States' only mountain zoo. The African Rift Valley area features Colobus monkeys, giraffes, other African animals and birds, and an interactive African Play Village for kids. The price of admission includes a visit to the Will Rogers Shrine of the Sun, which exhibits mementos of this famous American humorist and an 80-foot-high observation tower. The May Natural History Museum of the Tropics houses more than 7,000 exotic insects from jungles around the globe.

The U.S. Air Force Academy is one of Colorado Springs's most popular tourist attractions. Visitors can tour the unusual multi-spired chapel, Honor Court, and visitor's center. The Pikes Peak Cog Railway takes visitors on a 3-hour round trip tour to the summit of the mountain, at 12,110 feet above sea level. At the U.S. ProRodeo Hall of Fame, rodeo memorabilia is on display.

Arts and Culture

The Colorado Springs Philharmonic presents classical, pops and jazz performances October through May at the Pikes Peak Center. The Chamber Orchestra of the Springs performs five programs a year of pieces meant for small orchestras. The Da Vinci Quartet plays concerts in various venues in Colorado Springs and Denver and offers community outreach to local schools. The Colorado Springs Chorale has been performing classical and modern pieces since 1956. Students from Colorado College perform during the school year and during the Summer Music Festival, Vocal Arts and New Music Symposia, and during Extraordinary Dance Festival. The famous Broadmoor Hotel resort complex features international performers and hosts concerts.

The Star Bar Players present four plays per season in the Lon Chaney Theater at the Civic Auditorium. Theatreworks at the University of Colorado presents Shakespeare and contemporary and classic plays. The Fine Arts Theatre Company presents musicals at the Fine Arts Center of Colorado Springs. Drama and dance students at Colorado College perform regular seasons at the college. Colorado Springs Dance Theatre sponsors national and international companies to perform at the Pikes Peak Center.

Colorado Springs is home to a number of major museums and galleries, including the Museum of the

American Numismatic Association, which houses one of the largest collections of coins and medals in the world. The Fine Arts Center of Colorado Springs is a regional center for all the arts, containing the Taylor Museum of Art, the Bemis School of Art, and a performing arts department presenting plays, dance, music, and films. Also located in Colorado Springs are the World Figure Skating Hall of Fame and Museum and the Pioneers Museum, which exhibits displays pertaining to the history of the region. Featuring demonstrations of gold-panning techniques, the Western Museum of Mining and Industry showcases machinery used in early gold and silver mining operations. The Peterson Air and Space Museum displays historic aircraft and a moon rock. The Taylor Collection, which includes collections of Native American and Hispanic Art, is maintained at the Fine Arts Center. The Rock Ledge Ranch Historic Site celebrates the history of Colorado Springs by recreating the settlements of Native Americans and the lives of the settlers of the frontier in the 1800s, with costumed interpreters and special programs.

Festivals and Holidays

Among the annual events in Colorado Springs is the impressive Easter Sunrise Service, celebrated at Gateway Rocks in the Garden of the Gods. Territory Days on Memorial Day weekend brings 100,000 visitors to Colorado Avenue for free entertainment, food, and crafts. In early July is the Firefighter Chili Cook-off, featuring a beer garden and car displays. Pikes Peak or Bust Rodeo in Penrose Stadium, one of the top outdoor rodeos in the country, takes place in July as well. The celebration includes a parade through downtown Colorado Springs and a street breakfast. August brings the national Little Britches Rodeo in which children from ages 8 to 18 compete for titles at Penrose Stadium. Labor Day weekend features the Colorado Balloon Classic, with the ascension of scores of colorful hot air balloons. December brings the Festival of Lights Christmas Parade.

Sports for the Spectator

Most notably, Colorado Springs has long been home to the United States Olympic Training Center. Approximately 130,000 visitors tour the facility each year, where they are able to watch Olympic training in fencing, gymnastics, judo, shooting, swimming, taekwondo, weightlifting and wrestling.

A number of other sports events are available for viewing in Colorado Springs. The Colorado Springs Sky Sox, a Triple-A affiliate of the Colorado Rockies, play baseball at Security Service Field. College sports fans enjoy watching U.S. Air Force Academy teams compete against top college teams. Basketball, hockey, and other college sports are also played at the University of Colorado at Colorado Springs and Colorado College.

Pikes Peak International Hill Climb and rodeo events also interest spectators in the Colorado Springs

area. Pikes Peak International Raceway has a 1.3-mile road course and 1-mile banked oval to serve several different racing organizations.

Sports for the Participant

Outdoor activities abound in Colorado Springs, including climbing, white-water rafting, fishing, hiking, horseback riding, cave exploring, and gliding. The city maintains over 14,000 acres of parks and open spaces, with 15 community and regional parks (including Garden of Gods and North Cheyenne Canon Parks), biking and hiking trails, 5 sports complexes, and 136 neighborhood parks. The El Pomar Youth Sports Complex includes 9 baseball fields of various sizes, 8 soccer/lacrosse fields, a seven-station batting cage, and a playground. Approximately 250,000 visitors come to the park annually. The Broadmoor Hotel resort complex offers skeet and trap shooting as well as skiing and ice skating in the winter and golfing on three challenging courses during the warmer months. Echo Canyon River Expeditions offers half- and multi-day rafting adventures on the Arkansas River. Summit Expeditions and Pikes Peak Alpine School offers instruction for all levels in rock and ice climbing, mountaineering, and back-country skiing.

Shopping and Dining

Colorado Springs is served by four major malls: The Citadel, Outlets at Castle Rock, Promenade Shops at Briargate, and Chapel Hills Mall. Stores specializing in Western gear and Native American art can be found in many areas. In addition, the Old Colorado City Historic District contains many small shops, and the Garden of the Gods Trading Post stocks fine Indian jewelry and Colorado giftware.

Because Colorado Springs is at the center of a popular resort area, it enjoys cuisine from around the world, as well as local Western-style establishments offering barbecue and chuck-wagon fare and Mexican foods. Rocky Mountain trout is a local delicacy. The Broadmoor Hotel maintains seven dining rooms with a range of prices and cuisines. Gourmet food is served at the historic Briarhurst Manor Inn. The Flying W Chuckwagon Supper and Western Show combines fine dining for the family with cowboy music.

Visitor Information: Colorado Springs Convention and Visitors Bureau, 515 South Cascade Avenue, Colorado Springs, CO 80903; telephone (719) 635-7506.

■ Convention Facilities

Since the turn of the century, Colorado Springs has drawn a steady flow of tourists; beginning in the 1970s the city made itself equally amenable to conventions and conferences, providing a number of meeting facilities. The Colorado Springs World Arena accommodates 8,000 people for general sessions and the exhibit floor offers 19,500 square feet of space or 180 booths. The Phil Long Expo Center, which had over 90,000 square feet of exhibition space, closed in 2010.

There are many hotels that offer convention and meeting facilities. The luxurious Broadmoor features the expanded Broadmoor Events Center Complex which is home to Broadmoor Hall, a 60,000-square-foot exhibit space which can accommodate as many as 6,500 people on top of the hotel's 46 already existent meeting rooms. The Broadmoor Connection, an alliance of surrounding properties, provides capacity for 1,700 guest rooms and 185,000 square feet of total meeting space. The 316-room Cheyenne Conference Mountain Resort offers 40,000 square feet. There is also the Marriott Colorado Springs and the DoubleTree by Hilton Colorado Springs World Arena, with 299 rooms and 21,135 square feet of meeting space. There are more than 14,000 hotel rooms in the city.

Convention Information: Colorado Springs Convention and Visitors Bureau, 515 South Cascade Avenue, Colorado Springs, CO 80903; telephone (719) 635-7506.

■ Transportation

Approaching the City

The Colorado Springs Airport, located east of the city, is served by five major airlines, with 90 arrivals and departures each day to 13 U.S. cities. More than two million people travel through the airport each year. The airport sits on more than 7,200 acres with two parallel runways and one crosswind runway. It has one of the lowest rates of delays of major airports in the country, and also boasts valet parking service and free wireless Internet access.

Four major highways lead into Colorado Springs: Interstate 25 (north–south), U.S. Highway 85/87 (north–south), Interstate 70 (east–west), and U.S. Highway 50 (north–south). Commercial bus transportation into the city is available through interstate bus lines, including Greyhound.

Traveling in the City

The main north–south thoroughfare in Colorado Springs is Interstate 25, called Monument Valley Freeway within the city. Midland Expressway (U.S. Highway 24) runs east and west, becoming Platte Avenue after it crosses Interstate 25. Other important arteries are Garden of the Gods Road, Uintah Street, and Fillmore Street, all running east and west. Some of the mountain roads are not furnished with guardrails and are not accessible to such vehicles as recreational vans.

Mountain Metropolitan Transit is the city's mass transportation system, which offers 18 bus routes Monday through Friday, as well as limited Saturday service.

■ Communications

Newspapers and Magazines

The major daily newspaper in Colorado Springs is the morning *The Gazette*. Weekly publications include the *Colorado Springs Independent* and the *Colorado Springs Business Journal*. The *Hispania News* and *Colorado Catholic Herald* are also published in Colorado Springs. Local concerns publish sports and hobby oriented magazines of interest to fans of hockey, whitewater kayaking, rafting, canoeing, cycling, hang gliding, rodeo, skating, coin collecting, and table tennis.

Television and Radio

Eleven television stations broadcast from Colorado Springs; cable service is available. The city also receives broadcasts from television stations located in nearby Grand Junction and Pueblo. Six AM and 15 FM radio stations in Colorado Springs schedule a range of music, news, and information programming.

Media Information: *The Gazette*, 30 E. Pikes Peak Avenue, Suite #100, Colorado Springs, CO 80903; telephone (716) 632-5511.

Colorado Springs Online

City of Colorado Springs Home Page. Available www.springsgov.com

Colorado Springs Convention & Visitors Bureau. Available www.visitcos.com

The Gazette. Available www.gazette.com

Colorado Springs Business Alliance. Available www. coloradospringsbusinessalliance.com

Colorado Springs School District 11. Available www. d11.org

Pikes Peak Library District. Available library. ppld.org

BIBLIOGRAPHY

Blevins, Tim, et al., eds., *Enterprise & Innovation in the Pikes Peak Region* (Colorado Springs, CO: Pikes Peak Library District with Dream City Vision 2020, 2011)

Finley, Judith Reid, *On the Wings of Modernism: The United States Air Force Academy* (Urbana, IL: University of Illinois Press, 2004)

Knopper, Steve, *Colorado* (Berkeley, CA: Avalon Travel, 2009)

Lipker, Kim, *Sixty hikes within 60 miles, Denver and Boulder: including Colorado Springs, Fort Collins, and Rocky Mountain National Park*, 2nd ed. (Birmingham, AL: Menasha Ridge Press, 2010)

Nauman, Robert Allen, *Time Capsule 1900: Colorado Springs a Century Ago* (Colorado Springs, CO: Pastword Publications, 1998)

Denver

■ The City in Brief

Founded: 1858 (incorporated, 1861)

Head Official: Mayor Michael B. Hancock (D) (since 2011; current term expires 2015)

City Population

    1990: 467,610
    2000: 554,636
    2010: 600,158
    2012 estimate: 634,265
    Percent change, 2000–2010: 8.2%
    U.S. rank in 1990: 26th
    U.S. rank in 2000: 31st (State rank: 1st)
    U.S. rank in 2010: 26th (State rank: 1st)

Metropolitan Statistical Area Population

    2000: 2,109,282
    2010: 2,543,482
    2012 estimate: 2,645,209
    Percent change, 2000–2010: 20.6%
    U.S. rank in 2000: 22nd
    U.S. rank in 2010: 21st

Area: 153 square miles

Elevation: 5,332 feet above sea level

Average Annual Temperatures: January, 29.2° F; July, 73.4° F; annual average, 50.1° F

Average Annual Precipitation: 15.81 inches of rain; 60.3inches of snow

Major Economic Sectors: aerospace/aviation, finance, transportation, bioscience, information technology, energy

Unemployment Rate: 6.1% (2012)

Per Capita Income: $32,818

2012 FBI Crime Index Property: 23,343

Major Colleges and Universities: University of Denver, University of Colorado at Denver

Daily Newspaper: *The Denver Post*

■ Introduction

Denver, dubbed the Mile High City, is the commercial, financial, and transportation capital of the Rocky Mountain region. A concentration of federal government offices also makes it an administrative center. Denver's history has included frequent boom periods, but redirection and economic diversification became necessary during the late 1960s through the early 1980s. The city has undergone a renaissance, with downtown development paving the way for Denver's ascendance in high-technology industries as the nation's population shifts southwestward. Set in a verdant plain at the foot of the Rocky Mountains, Denver is noted for its quality of life and the blending of modern innovation and western tradition. With the city's universities, hospitals, and convention centers receiving high marks in national rankings, it is no wonder that people continue to flock to the area at a rate that is expected to double the Denver metropolitan population by 2030.

■ Geography and Climate

Denver is situated in the high plains at the eastern edge of the Rocky Mountains, which protect the city from severe winter weather. These mountains, reaching higher than 14,000 feet, are the dominant feature of the area. The South Platte River bisects the city, and many creeks, small lakes, and reservoirs grace the metropolitan area. Denver's climate is semiarid and relatively mild, with more sunny days than either Miami, Florida or San Diego, California, and an average of less than 16 inches of

© *Jim Havey/Alamy*

precipitation each year. Although visitors must make some adjustment to the high altitude, they find that the area's low humidity makes even the highest and lowest temperatures seem less extreme.

Area: 153 square miles

Elevation: 5,332 feet above sea level

Average Temperatures: January, 29.2° F; July, 73.4° F; annual average, 50.1° F

Average Annual Precipitation: 15.81 inches of rain; 60.3inches of snow

■ History

Discovery of Gold Brings Settlers to Denver Area

For centuries, the mountains and plains of Colorado were used as hunting grounds by Native Americans, and eventually the more sophisticated, agricultural tribes like the Anasazi established villages. In the sixteenth century, the Spanish explored the region where Denver is now located, but no Europeans established permanent settlements until the mid-1800s, when gold was discovered at Pikes Peak. In 1858, a supply center for the mining towns was established on the site of a tribal village at the junction of the South Platte River and Cherry Creek. The town was called St. Charles; later it was renamed Denver City after James W. Denver, governor of the Kansas Territory, and was incorporated in 1861.

The gold boom soon ended, but some of the fortune hunters stayed on to settle in the new town. During the 1860s, much of the town was destroyed by fire; a ravaging flash flood killed 20 people; and the citizens repelled frequent attacks from the Plains tribes and even an assault by a Confederate Army. With the arrival of rail transportation in 1870 a steady influx of settlers insured the future of the thriving town, and when Colorado attained statehood in 1876, Denver was named the state capital. By 1879 it boasted a population of 35,000 people and the first telephone service in the West.

Silver Boom and Bust; Economy Diversifies

A silver boom in the 1880s ushered in another period of rapid growth, filling Denver with the Victorian mansions of silver barons and making it the most elegant city in the West. The collapse of the silver market in the panic of

1893 staggered the city's economy, so the city began to diversify. By the early 1900s, Denver had become the commercial and industrial center of the Rocky Mountain region, as well as a leader in livestock sales, agriculture, and tourism.

Denver sustained a period of relatively slow development until the 1930s. Prior to World War II, when such federal government agencies as the Geological Survey, the U.S. Mint, Lowry Air Force Base, the Bureau of Land Management, and the Air Force Accounting Center were established in the area, Denver experienced another population surge that continued through the 1950s. During the 1960s Denver lost population as residents moved to the suburbs to escape inner city deterioration. Growth slowed again in the mid-1970s as a result of the oil industry crisis. The effects of this downturn, however, were ultimately positive. As a result of efforts to diversify the economy, Denver became known as "the energy capital of the west," with a focus on alternative energy sources such as solar and wind power. By 1980, approximately 1,200 energy companies were located in Denver.

Growth slowed again in the mid-1980s when plans for oil shale development were curtailed; construction of high-rise office buildings downtown nevertheless continued unabated. A sleek, modern landscape has emerged in Denver where a western frontier town once stood. Following two national economic recessions during the 2000s, Denver stabilized and strengthened into the 2010s, remaining the principal commercial, financial, and industrial hub of the Rocky Mountain region, and growing in prominence in bioscience and information technology industries. New businesses and urban development attracted thousands to the downtown area, where population increased 142 percent between 2000 and 2013.

Historical Information: Colorado Historical Society, Stephen H. Hart Library, 1300 Broadway, Denver, CO 80203; telephone (303) 866-2305; email research@chs.state.co.us

■ Population Profile

Metropolitan Statistical Area Population

2000: 2,109,282
2010: 2,543,482
2012 estimate: 2,645,209
Percent change, 2000–2010: 20.6%
U.S. rank in 2000: 22nd
U.S. rank in 2010: 21st

City Residents

1990: 467,610
2000: 554,636
2010: 600,158

2012 estimate: 634,265
Percent change, 2000–2010: 8.2%
U.S. rank in 1990: 26th
U.S. rank in 2000: 31st (State rank: 1st)
U.S. rank in 2010: 26th (State rank: 1st)

Density: 3,922.6 people per square mile

Racial and ethnic characteristics

White: 479,745
Black or African American: 64,566
American Indian and Alaskan Native: 5,941
Asian: 21,689
Native Hawaiian and Other Pacific Islander: 464
Hispanic or Latino (may be of any race): 199,866
Other: 61,860

Percent of residents born in state: 41.9%

Age characteristics

Population under 5 years old: 46,794
Population 5 to 9 years old: 40,378
Population 10 to 14 years old: 33,202
Population 15 to 19 years old: 31,711
Population 20 to 24 years old: 44,195
Population 25 to 34 years old: 135,555
Population 35 to 44 years old: 95,341
Population 45 to 54 years old: 74,089
Population 55 to 59 years old: 34,697
Population 60 to 64 years old: 31,586
Population 65 to 74 years old: 36,489
Population 75 to 84 years old: 20,417
Population 85 years and over: 9,811
Median age: 33.7

Births (2010–11 Metropolitan Area)

Total number: 35,028

Deaths (2010–11 Metropolitan Area)

Total number: 15,031

Money income (2012)

Per capita income: $32,818
Median household income: $49,049
Total households: 266,248

Number of households with income of …

less than $10,000: 24,306
$10,000 to $14,999: 16,239
$15,000 to $24,999: 29,980
$25,000 to $34,999: 28,178
$35,000 to $49,999: 36,375
$50,000 to $74,999: 44,311
$75,000 to $99,999: 29,645
$100,000 to $149,999: 29,055
$150,000 to $199,999: 13,175
$200,000 or more: 14,984

Percent of families below poverty level: 19.7%

FBI Crime Index Property: 23,343

FBI Crime Index Violent: 3,871

■ Municipal Government

The city and county of Denver share the same boundaries and operate under a government that performs both municipal and county functions. Denver's mayor-council form of government invests its mayor, who is elected to a four-year term, with strong executive powers. The 13 council members also serve for four years.

Head Official: Mayor Michael B. Hancock (D) (since 2011; current term expires 2015)

Total Number of City Employees: 9,704 (2012)

City Information: City of Denver, Office of the Mayor, 1437 Bannock St., Room 350, Denver, CO 80202; telephone (720) 865-9000.

■ Economy

Major Industries and Commercial Activity

Following record economic and population growth in the 1950s, Denver weathered reversals tied to the fluctuating petroleum market in the 1970s and 1980s. By the late 1980s the city had taken measures toward establishing a diversified economic base. Major companies in the Denver metropolitan area employ workers in a range of fields such as air transportation, telecommunications, aerospace, and manufacturing, along with a growing high-tech sector.

A whopping 19,600 individuals are employed at aerospace companies in the Metro Denver area, and some of the top aerospace contractors in the country call the area home, including Boeing, Lockheed Martin, Northrop Grumman, Sierra Nevada Corporation, and the United Launch Alliance. Denver is first among the 50 largest cities for private aerospace employment and contributes mightily to the state of Colorado's standing as the second-largest aerospace economy.

With Denver International Airport, the fifth busiest airport in the nation and 13th busiest in the world, calling the city its home, it is not surprising that the aviation industry also provides many job opportunities for the Denver area. Aviation companies operating out of Denver International Airport, along with the area's three reliever airports, directly employ nearly 16,000 workers.

The financial and commercial capital of the Rocky Mountain region, Denver's downtown banking district—dubbed the "Wall Street of the Rockies"—is composed of major national and international institutions. The

financial services industry in Denver and its surrounding Metro area employs some 87,750 people at 13,020 companies.

The city is the transportation hub for a large portion of the western United States; consumer and industrial goods are transported by air, rail, and truck through Denver to more than 30 million people annually. Denver is a Foreign Trade Zone, providing advantages to companies involved in international trade. Denver's central location—it is 346 miles west of the exact geographic center of the country—places it in an advantageous position for future economic development and growth. Analysts predict that the U.S. population is shifting south and west, with future concentration expected in the area from California to Utah and to the Gulf Coast in Texas. Denver is at the center of this region.

Emerging industries in Denver include bioscience, with much of the activity centered in the suburb of Aurora; health and wellness, which grew 22 percent between 2006 and 2011 and employs more than 175,000; and information technology and software, with Denver boasting one of the 10-highest concentrations of technology workers among the top 50 metropolitan areas.

Items and goods produced: computer storage and peripherals, beverages, mining and farming machinery, rubber goods, fabricated metals, chemicals and allied stone and clay products, western clothing, transportation equipment, scientific instruments, feed, flour

Incentive Programs—New and Existing Companies

Local programs: The Denver Office of Economic Development works to retain and create quality jobs within the city, offering a variety of incentives to encourage relocation to the city and also expansion of existing businesses within the city. The office also will work with companies to figure out which of various economic development-financing programs are available and a good fit for their business. Also available to certain qualified businesses are tax rebates for specific business taxes paid to the city or county of Denver and gap financing under certain circumstances. Additionally, the Metro Denver WIRED initiative, administered by the Metro Denver EDC and the Denver Office of Economic Development, coordinates workforce development, economic development, and education on a regional level for the aerospace, bioscience, energy, and information technology sectors.

State programs: Colorado offers a variety of business assistance and incentive programs for expanding or relocated companies. Incentives include the Job Growth Tax Incentive, which provides a state income tax credit to job-creating projects in Colorado dependent on the incentive; Strategic Fund Initiative, for business development, expansion, or relocation that results in job creation; Enterprise Zone Tax Credits, which incentive development in economically distressed areas; Public Infrastructure Grants, to retain or add employment opportunities for low- or moderate-income residents; and sales and use tax refunds, exemptions, and credits for developments in biotechnology, manufacturing, and aviation sectors.

State financing support can be obtained through an array of general and industry-specific programs. Advanced Industries Accelerator Programs, created in 2013, offer access to capital for advanced manufacturing, aerospace, bioscience, electronic, energy and natural resource, infrastructure engineering, and technology and information industries. Private Activity Bonds offer tax-exempt bond financing to small manufacturing companies. Bioscience Discovery Evaluation Grants were available from 2007 to 2013 to support growth of companies in the bioscience industry. The Regional Tourism Act allows local governments to apply to the state for financial support for major tourism development initiatives likely to draw out-of-state visitors.

Venture capital funding is offered through the state's Certified Capital Companies Program, which makes available a statewide pool of $75 million for investment throughout the state, with an additional $25 million available for rural investment. The Colorado Venture Capital Authority manages venture capital investments for the state. Colorado Capital Access, Cash Collateral Support, and Colorado Credit Reserve support financing needs of small and medium businesses.

Job training programs: The Colorado Community College System has joined with the Colorado Office of Economic Development & International Trade to administer Colorado FIRST/Existing Industry Customized Training Programs. These programs are designed to fund employee training for transferable job skills to benefit a company's competitive strength as well as an employee's long-term employment opportunities.

Denver's Division of Workforce Development offers six workforce centers around the city, which help to recruit applicants for various job positions through activities such as company-specific recruiting events and/or big job fairs. The division also helps to develop customized training programs whose goal is to improve the skills of both new recruits and already-existent workers.

Development Projects

The FasTracks mass transit expansion, a 12-year, $7.4 billion project begun in 2004, plans to bring 122 miles of new light rail and commuter rail, 18 miles of bus rapid transit service, and 21,000 new parking spaces to Denver by 2017. Several aspects of the project were in various stages of development as of 2014. The East Rail Line, slated to connect Denver Union Station to Denver International Airport and passing through Aurora was under major construction, with an anticipated opening of 2016. Denver's Union Station was also in the midst of a complete renovation, estimated to cost $1 billion. Some phases of the project may not be completed until as a late as 2022.

Denver's popular cultural venues have recently been the recipients of expansions and redevelopments as well. From 2010 to 2012, the Denver Zoo constructed a $50 million, 10-acre Asian Tropics exhibit that included a habitat for Asian elephants and Indian rhinos along with many other Asian animals. The exhibit opened in June 2012 and received LEED Platinum certification for its environmentally conscious design.

A number of companies relocated headquarters or expanded in Denver during 2012 and 2013. Trimble, a GPS technology company, announced plans in 2012 to build a 125,000-square-foot building that would allow the company to add nearly 200 employees, for a total of 550. Frontier Airlines relocated its headquarters to Denver that year, and Southwest Airlines announced plans to open a new pilot crew base in Denver as well, expected to be home for some 250 pilots and 400 flight attendants. Dozens of other companies planned expansions throughout the metropolitan area.

During 2012, some $630 million was invested in downtown Denver, primarily in residential construction. Total available residential units downtown, estimated at 2,800 by 2014, was double the total available just seven years earlier. The city sought to match private investment with public money for downtown improvements, including $14.3 million for a downtown plaza at 14th and California, $30 million for improvements to 16th Street Mall, and a $5 million homeless facility. The downtown population increased 142 percent from 2000 to 2013, with an additional 18 percent increased expected by 2018.

Economic Development Information: Denver Office of Economic Development; 201 W. Colfax Ave., Dept. 208, Denver, CO 80202; telephone (720) 913-1999; fax (720) 913-1802; email oed@DenverGov.org.

Commercial Shipping

Denver is the commercial transportation center for an eight-state area, providing a hub for two major rail freight companies, more than 160 motor freight carriers, and a number of air cargo services. With negotiated motor freight rates and the city's designation as a Free Trade Zone, Denver has created a competitive marketplace for the import and export of goods. Denver International Airport handled 410 million pounds of cargo in 2012. Major cargo carriers are the U.S. Postal Service, DHL, UPS, FedEx, and United Airlines. Cargo and mail facilities cover some 375,000 square feet. The airport is the site of Foreign Trade Zone #123, as well as areas for U.S. Customs and Department of Agriculture clearance. WorldPort at DIA, adjacent to the freight operations site, provides an additional 100,000 feet of office space. The city, located strategically between Canada and Mexico, is an ever-expanding center for international trade.

Labor Force and Employment Outlook

Employers in Denver choose from a highly educated labor pool. As of 2014, more than 40 percent of adult residents had at least a college degree and nearly 86 percent held a high school diploma. With a diverse employment base across many sectors, Denver is in a prime position for growth well into the twenty-first century. Industries with strongest growth projections to 2022 included management, professional, scientific and technical services, construction, and health care and social assistance. Employment in downtown Denver is projected to grow to 145,000 individuals by 2030. It is also predicted that, by 2030, the population of Metro Denver will almost double to 3.9 million, with some 800,000 new jobs being created in the metro area.

The following is a summary of data regarding the 2012 Denver labor force:

Size of civilian labor force: 353,231

Number of workers employed in . . .

agriculture and mining: 3,373
construction: 21,568
manufacturing: 17,826
wholesale trade: 9,392
retail trade: 28,846
transportation: 13,546
information systems: 10,999
finance: 25,910
professional administration: 55,240
education and social services: 64,903
arts and leisure: 38,727
other: 16,185
public administration: 13,323

Average hourly earnings of production workers: $17.32

Unemployment rate: 6.1% (2012)

Employers

Largest employers (2012)	*Number of employees*
Denver Public School District #1	11,332
City and County of Denver	9,704
State of Colorado Central Payroll	9,606
U.S.D.A. National Finance Center	7,593
Denver Health & Hospital Authority	5,314
United Airlines, Inc.	4,209
CHC Payroll Agent, Inc.	4,180
University of Denver	3,713
University of Colorado	3,314
Accounting Service Center (U.S. Postal Service)	3,262

Cost of Living

Metro Denver's cost of living is slightly above the national average, and yet it is more affordable than California, Chicago, and most major East Coast cities.

The following is a summary of data regarding several key cost of living factors in the area.

2013 ACCRA Average House Price: $349,217

2013 ACCRA Cost of Living Index: 105

State income tax rate: 4.63%

State sales tax rate: 2.9%

Local income tax rate: $5.75 per month on compensation over $500

Local sales tax rate: 4.72%

Property tax rate: $0.084071 for every $1 of assessed value; residential assessed value is 7.96% of total value (2013)

Economic Information: Metro Denver Chamber of Commerce, 1445 Market Street, Denver, CO 80202; telephone (303) 534-8500; fax (303) 534-3200.

■ Education and Research

Elementary and Secondary Schools

The Denver Public Schools are regarded as one of the best urban school systems in the nation and are directed by a seven-member board of education that administers policy and establishes direction. The Denver public schools provide programs for slow and gifted learners, college preparation, and career training. It also features a Junior ROTC program. About 58 percent of students in the district are Hispanic, with another 20 percent white, and 15 percent African American. English language learners account for 35 percent of the student population. Seventy-two percent of students qualify for free or reduced lunch; nearly 13 percent qualify as gifted and talented according to district metrics. The four-year graduation rate is nearly 59 percent, and the dropout rate 5.7 percent.

The metropolitan area is served by 22 other public school districts, and Denver features an open enrollment policy and the opportunity for charter school formation.

There are numerous private and parochial institutions, including the Colorado Academy and St. Mary's Academy for Girls in Englewood.

The following is a summary of data regarding the School District No. 1 in the County of Denver.

Total enrollment: 78,339

Number of facilities

    total: 185
    elementary schools: 106
    junior high schools: 37
    high schools: 42
    other: 0

Student/teacher ratio: 16.73:1

Teacher salaries

    average (statewide): $49,938

Funding per pupil: $10,468

Public Schools Information: Denver Public Schools, 900 Grant Street, Denver, CO 80203; telephone (720) 423-3200; fax (720) 423-3318; email info@dpsk12.org

Colleges and Universities

The metropolitan Denver area supports 11 four-year public and private colleges and universities with enrollments totaling over 145,000; eight major colleges and universities can be found within a 45-mile radius of the city. A wide variety of undergraduate degrees and numerous graduate and professional degrees are offered along with the opportunity to study at several excellent research institutions. The University of Denver enrolled 17,729 students in 2013 and boasted more than 130 study programs in 13 schools and colleges. The University of Denver awards more graduate degrees than any other public Colorado institution, accounting for roughly one-third of all graduate degrees. The school's Daniels College of Business frequently is ranked among the top business schools of the region and the nation, especially for its part-time and online study options.

Other area private colleges are Johnson & Wales University, Regis University, and Colorado Heights University. Public schools include University of Colorado at Denver, Metropolitan State College of Denver, Community College of Denver, and the Colorado School of Mines. Non-traditional education is well represented by such institutions as the Colorado Free University, which has an open admissions policy and is known for its adult and continuing education programs. More than 60 vocational and technical schools serve the region.

Libraries and Research Centers

Denver's Central Library underwent expansion in the mid-1990s to expand its square footage to 540,000. The addition houses the Children's Library, the Burnham Hoyt Room popular adult library, and Marietta Baron Teen Space. The Denver Public Library maintains 24 additional branches, including an African-American research library, and two bookmobiles. Circulation in 2012 was 9.5 million items, loaned to the library's 3.8 million visitors. A Summer of Reading program serves some 36,000 area children.

The greater Denver area boasts a number of other public, special interest, and research libraries. Among them are the Colorado Talking Book Library, Denver Medical Library, University of Colorado Law Library, and many high-technology and university-related libraries. The University of Denver libraries feature rare book and manuscript collections, the Beck Memorial Archives of Rocky Mountain Jewish History, and the Carson Brierly Griffin Dance Library.

Research activities in such fields as environmental sciences, allergy and immunology, biochemical genetics, health services, mass spectrometry, biochemical parasitology, alcohol, taste and smell, sports sciences, applied mechanics, public management, social science, mineral law, mass communications, family studies, the Holocaust, Islamic-Judaic studies, and international relations are conducted at centers in the Denver area.

Public Library Information: Denver Public Library, 10 West Fourteenth Avenue Parkway, Denver, CO 80204; telephone (720) 865-1111.

■ Health Care

For years Denver has attracted those seeking to enjoy the respiratory benefits of the area's climate and mountain air. Today, Denver is the medical center of the Rocky Mountains, operating more than 25 major hospitals, many of which have earned national and international reputations as leading medical research and treatment facilities. The city has a large number of physicians practicing in every specialty. Additionally, since Colorado has the lowest obesity rate in the nation, annual health insurance rates in the Denver area are lower than the national average.

Several of Metro Denver's hospitals have expanded during the 2010s. The Rocky Mountain Hospital for Children opened a $128 million pediatric center in 2010. The expansion offers 53 inpatient beds, a pediatric intensive care unit and emergency department, two endoscopy suites, and six pediatric specialty operating rooms, among other additions. The Swedish Medical Center has completed new neonatal and pediatric intensive care units, a remodeled ER, and a new lobby.

Children's Hospital Colorado, located in Aurora, opened a new 10-story, 350,000-square-foot tower in 2012. In 2013 the University of Colorado Hospital, also in Aurora, added a second inpatient tower at a cost of about $400 million.

The aforementioned Children's Hospital Colorado is a state-of-the-art children's hospital serving a 10-state area. The Children's Hospital has more than 1,000 pediatric specialists and 3,000 full-time employees. It was ranked seventh nationally in pediatric care by *U.S. News & World Report* in 2013. The University of Colorado Hospital was ranked nationally in five specialties. National Jewish Health, part of the University of Colorado Hospital system, is a teaching and research center for respiratory, allergic, and immunological diseases; the center also houses the Environmental Lung Center. It has consistently been ranked as one of the best—often the best—hospitals in the country for the treatment of respiratory diseases.

The Rose Medical Center offers a wide range of services and specializes in diabetes treatment, obstetrics, and videoscopic surgery. Other major hospitals in the city include the Denver Health Medical Center and St. Anthony Hospital.

■ Recreation

Sightseeing

Denver offers attractions ranging from historic Western landmarks to modern amusement parks. Downtown, the Colorado State Capitol features a 24-carat gold-plated dome; the 13th step of its stairway is set at the altitude of exactly one mile above sea level. A few blocks away is the United States Mint, where nearly a third of the nation's gold supply is stored. Larimer Square, Denver's first main street and a restored Victorian historical district, is an especially popular tourist site. Also downtown is Elitch Gardens, a year-round amusement park offering thrill rides, formal gardens, restaurants, and shops. Across the river, the renovated Downtown Aquarium combines the qualities of aquariums and sea life parks in an exciting interactive experience that is both fun and educational. The 80-acre Denver Zoo is a modern facility, housing more than 4,000 animals in natural environments. The zoo's master plan seeks to transform itself into a major conservation center; the second of four phases of development, the addition of an Asian Tropics exhibit, opened in 2012.

The Denver area is filled with historic buildings, homes, and mansions that are open to the public. Many neighborhoods retain a large part of their historical and architectural integrity, offering excellent examples of Victorian, Georgian, and Italianate styles. Popular tour sites in the area include the Coors Brewery in nearby Golden; Denver Botanic Gardens; and Washington Park, a replica of President Washington's gardens at Mount Vernon. Another area landmark, located in City Ditch, is a statue of "Wynken, Blynken, and Nod," dedicated to Denver poet Eugene Field, author of the popular children's rhyme "Dutch Lullaby." Several bus and guided walking tours of Denver are also available.

Arts and Culture

The arts are well supported in Denver, both in modern facilities and elegantly preserved historic buildings. The Denver Center for the Performing Arts, covering a four-block area and 12 acres, is an architecturally stunning complex that offers almost every facet of the cultural world from Shakespearean drama to popular music, serving more than 750,000 visitors a year. It regularly hosts Colorado Ballet, Colorado Symphony Orchestra, Denver Center Theatre Company, and the National Theatre Conservatory. Many small theaters, galleries, and open-air exhibits can also be found throughout the city.

Denver enjoys a thriving performance community comprised of a number of theater and dance companies, as well as music and opera groups. Germinal Stage Denver, a non-profit avant-garde theater, stages five or six productions a year, and each summer the University of Colorado at Boulder sponsors a nationally recognized Shakespeare Festival. Dance in all its forms, from folk to ballet to modern, is performed frequently throughout the area. The Boettcher Concert Hall, considered one of the nation's great music halls, was the first symphony hall in the round in the United States, and is the home of the renowned Colorado Symphony Orchestra. Opera is presented by Opera Colorado in the restored Ellie Caulkins Opera House.

The History Colorado Center displays exhibitions highlighting the history of Colorado and the West with changing and permanent exhibits on Native Americans, miners, and other settlers. The Museum of Outdoor Arts is a unique museum without walls that showcases a blend of architecture, fine art, and landscaping. Offering a versatile collection of activities for children of all ages, the Children's Museum of Denver includes live theater, playscapes for children of all ages, a market, assembly plant, and a fire station.

The Denver Art Museum is an impressive seven-story structure containing more than 40,000 art objects; a highlight is the world's leading collection of Native American art. The addition of its Hamilton Building, a work of art in itself, was designed by world-renowned architect Daniel Libeskind and brings its own form of visually stunning artwork to the city streets with its astonishing and unique architecture. The Colorado Railroad Museum, housed in a replica of an 1880s depot, is considered one of the best privately supported rail museums in the United States. Also of interest are the

Denver Museum of Miniatures, Dolls and Toys and the Denver Firefighters Museum.

Festivals and Holidays

Denver schedules an abundance of festivals and special events throughout the year. The National Western Stock Show, Rodeo and Horse Show, which has been called the "Super Bowl of cattle shows," occurs each January. It features nearly a month of western music performances, prize-winning livestock exhibitions, and rodeo events with the country's top rodeo stars. The show culminates with the award for Livestock Person of the Year. From May through September, outdoor shows and musical events are held at Red Rocks and Cricket Wireless amphitheaters and in the LoDo District.

Another special event in Denver is the nation's largest St. Patrick's Day Parade west of the Mississippi in March. The Colorado Renaissance Festival, a recreation of medieval England, takes place each weekend during June and July. The Colorado Indian Market, featuring the art, dances, food, and culture of native Americans, is held in January. Larimer Square is the site of the annual Oktoberfest.

Sports for the Spectator

Denver fields a professional team in almost every major sport, and more than six million fans attend sporting events in the city each year. The Denver Broncos of the National Football League won back-to-back Super Bowls in 1998 and 1999. The team moved to Sports Authority Field at Mile High Stadium in 2001. Other major franchises include the National Basketball Association's Denver Nuggets and the Colorado Rockies of Major League Baseball. The Colorado Avalanche, Denver's National Hockey League team, won the Stanley Cup in 1996 and 2001. Dick's Sporting Goods Park is home to Denver's Major League Soccer (MLS) franchise, the Colorado Rapids, who won the MLS Cup in 2010. Denver area colleges and universities compete in a variety of sporting events.

Auto racing takes place at the Colorado National Speedway, and for those who enjoy parimutuel betting, the greyhound races at the Mile High Kennel Club in Commerce City provide plenty of excitement. Denver is also a major stop on the Professional Bull Riders circuit.

Sports for the Participant

The nearby Rocky Mountains provide abundant opportunities for sports-minded individuals year round. In the winter, skiers from the world over come to try their luck on the famous slopes. Rock and mountain climbing, fly fishing in the clear mountain streams, white-water canoeing and rafting, and hiking through the splendid mountain vistas are among the most popular recreations in spring, summer, and fall.

A $45 million, 24-year project to clean up the stretch of the South Platte River that runs through Denver has resulted in bike paths and a series of 11 beautiful parks; man-made boat chutes provide kayaking and rafting opportunities, and the banks of the river are lined with picnic areas and wetlands. Denver County maintains 250 urban parks, over 285 athletic fields, 11 dog parks, 14,000 acres of mountain park land, and an extensive urban trail system in addition to 27 recreation centers and 29 swimming pools. There are more than 75 public and private golf courses in the metropolitan area and several area lakes offering water skiing, sailing, swimming, and fishing. There are also 24 lakes to choose from for both fishing and boating.

Shopping and Dining

Denver is home to more than a dozen major shopping centers as well as a number of shopping districts. Denver's Colorado Mills, a Simon-operated mall, offers some 200 stores. Downtown, Denver Pavilions retail and entertainment center covers two square blocks in the heart of downtown Denver. Flatiron Crossing offers indoor/outdoor shopping in 200 stores and a 14-theater movie complex. The 16th Street Mall, a sculptured pedestrian walkway stretching for over a mile in the downtown district, is lined with shops and restaurants. The revitalized Cherry Creek Shopping Center, one of the area's top tourist destinations, features upscale department stores and more than 160 specialty shops in an enclosed mall. The adjacent Cherry Creek Shopping District is known for its aesthetically appealing shops and galleries.

With the success of Larimer Square, a renovated historical area of specialty stores, the entire lower downtown area is rapidly attracting unique shops, galleries, and restaurants. Denver's Tattered Cover Book Store has been hailed by *The New York Times* as "one of the truly great independent book stores in America." Several other popular shopping areas are found in metro Denver, with Belmar offering shopping a short distance away in Lakewood, and Southlands, a 1.5-million-square-foot shopping center nestled in nearby Aurora.

Other interesting areas include Sakura Square, a group of Asian markets and art galleries; and Tivoli, a converted brewery that houses many shops, movie theaters, and some of Denver's finest restaurants. Park Meadows Mall is a 1.5-million-square foot shopping center located 12 miles south of the city designed to resemble a mountain ski resort.

Denver is well known for its fine beef and traditional Western fare, but a much wider range of dining experiences is also available, from fast food to haute cuisine. Area specialties include spicy Mexican dishes, local fish and game delicacies such as buffalo, elk, venison, and Rocky Mountain trout, and native Southwestern food. A large number of international and ethnic restaurants complete the dining choices. A favorite nighttime gathering spot is LoDo, or Lower Downtown, which has been transformed since the opening of nearby Coors Field from an industrial warehouse district into a thriving area of elegant restaurants and sports bars that attracts Denver's young population.

Visitor Information: Visit Denver, 1600 California St., Denver, CO 80202; telephone (303) 892-1505; email visitorinfo@visitdenver.com.

■ Convention Facilities

The Colorado Convention Center in downtown Denver is within walking distance of more than 8,400 hotel rooms and 300 restaurants. The convention center, located along the river in the heart of downtown, contains more than 584,000 square feet of exhibit space on one level, 100,000 square feet of meeting rooms, two ballrooms (including a 35,000-square-foot ballroom and a 50,000-square-foot ballroom), theater-style seating for 5,000 people, 1,000 covered parking spaces and state of the art multimedia facilities. In 2013 the center underwent a massive $268 million expansion that nearly doubled its space.

The National Western Complex, located at the northern end of the downtown area near Interstate 70, contains a 6,600-seat stadium arena, a 40,000-square-foot exhibit hall, a multi-use events center, and the 120,000-square-foot Hall of Education.

Other meeting and exhibition facilities include the Denver Coliseum, Red Rocks Amphitheatre, Denver Mart, and the Adams County Regional Park Complex. Most of the major hotels in the city offer extensive meeting, banquet, and ballroom facilities, as do many of the larger mountain resorts.

Convention Information: Visit Denver, 1600 California St., Denver, CO 80202; telephone (303) 892-1505; email visitorinfo@visitdenver.com.

■ Transportation

Approaching the City

Denver International Airport is the fifth busiest airport in the United States and 13th busiest in the world. In 2012 its 17 commercial airlines served a total of 44.7 million passengers. The airport had 1,625 daily flights to 180 locations in 2012, with an annual economic impact of some $22.3 billion. Amtrak provides passenger rail service with westbound passengers treated to a scenic route through the Rocky Mountains.

Denver is at the crossroads of three major interstate highways. A beltway highway system encircles the metro area and provides easy access to the airport via C-470, E-470, and the Northwest Parkway.

Traveling in the City

Orienting oneself in Denver is made considerably easier by the natural landmark of the Rocky Mountains, readily visible to the west. Denver's street numbers are divided north and south by Ellsworth Avenue and east and west by Broadway. In general, east–west roads are called "avenues," with north–south roads designated as "streets." Above Ellsworth, the streets bear numbers; below Ellsworth the streets are named.

The Regional Transportation District (RTD) offers 125 bus routes, 47 miles of light rail, and SkyRide transportation to and from Denver International Airport. The RTD transported about 100 million passengers annually as of 2012. FasTracks, an ambitious expansion of Denver's public transportation system, was scheduled to be largely complete by 2017.

■ Communications

Newspapers and Magazines

Denver readers are served by one major daily newspaper, *The Denver Post.* Another daily, the *Rocky Mountain News,* was published until 2009. The city is also served by many smaller neighborhood weeklies and a business weekly—the *Denver Business Journal.* Local magazines include *Colorado Country Life, Colorado Outdoors,* and *The Bloomsbury Review.* Many trade and collegiate publications are based in the city as well.

Television and Radio

Numerous television stations in the Denver area represent commercial networks, public television, independent stations, and special interest channels. Eleven AM and 13 FM radio stations provide listeners with a variety of musical and special programming.

Media Information: *The Denver Post,* 101 W. Colfax Ave, Denver, CO 80202; telephone (303) 954-1010; toll-free (800) 336-7678.

Denver Online

City of Denver. Available www.denvergov.org

Colorado Historical Society. Available www.coloradohistory.org

Visit Denver. Available www.denver.org

The Denver Post. Available www.denverpost.com

Denver Public Library. Available www.denverlibrary.org

Denver Public Schools. Available www.denver.k12.co.us

Downtown Denver. Available www.downtowndenver.com

Metro Denver Chamber of Commerce. Available www.denverchamber.org

Metro Denver Economic Development
Corporation. Available www.metrodenver.org

BIBLIOGRAPHY

Everett, Derek R., *The Colorado State Capitol: History, Politics, and Preservation* (Boulder, CO: University Press of Colorado, 2005)

Lipker, Kim, *Sixty hikes within 60 miles, Denver and Boulder: including Colorado Springs, Fort Collins, and Rocky Mountain National Park,* 2nd ed. (Birmingham, AL: Menasha Ridge Press, 2010)

Madigan, Michael, *Historic Photos of Denver in the 50s, 60s, and 70s* (Nashville, TN: Turner Publishing Company, 2010)

Noel, Thomas J., *The City and the Saloon: Denver, 1858–1916* (Lincoln, NE: University of Nebraska Press, 1982)

Fort Collins

The City in Brief

Founded: 1862 (incorporated 1869)

Head Official: Mayor Karen Weitkunat (since 2011; current term expires 2015)

City Population
    1990: 87,491
    2000: 118,652
    2010: 143,986
    2012 estimate: 148,634
    Percent change, 2000–2010: 21.4%
    U.S. rank in 1990: 230th (State rank: 7th)
    U.S. rank in 2000: 206th (State rank: 5th)
    U.S. rank in 2010: 169th (State rank: 4th)

Metropolitan Statistical Area Population
    2000: 251,494
    2010: 299,630
    2012 estimate: 310,487
    Percent change, 2000–2010: 19.1%
    U.S. rank in 2000: 167th
    U.S. rank in 2010: 156th

Area: 47 square miles

Elevation: 5,003 feet above sea level

Average Annual Temperatures: 47.9° F

Average Annual Precipitation: 15 inches of rain; 55 inches of snow

Major Economic Sectors: technology, manufacturing, research, education, government

Unemployment Rate: 5.7% (2012)

Per Capita Income: $28,828

2012 FBI Crime Index Property: 4,119

Major Colleges and Universities: Colorado State University

Daily Newspaper: *Fort Collins Coloradoan*

Introduction

Fort Collins is located on the Cache la Poudre River at the foot of the Rocky Mountains. The city's clean water and clean air make for a healthy environment. Fort Collins boasts an active cultural scene, which is enhanced by events offered at Colorado State University. The surrounding countryside has breathtaking cliffs, clear skies, and beautiful lakes and waterfalls—nature at its best. Fort Collins is regularly honored as one of the best places to live, work, or retire, with its extensive outdoor life bringing frequent accolades for cycling and the general physical fitness of its residents. With high-technology industries flourishing during the 2010s, the city turned its attention to improving transportation infrastructure and growing its retail sector.

Geography and Climate

Located at the western base of the "Front Range" of the Rocky Mountains, Fort Collins is about 65 miles north of Denver, 45 miles south of Cheyenne, Wyoming, and almost 5,000 feet above sea-level. The city lies along the banks of the Cache La Poudre River, and the Great Plains lie to the east.

Fort Collins lies in a semi-arid region and experiences four seasons. The city has 300 days per year with sunshine, and the average summer high temperature is 85 degrees. Annual snowfall averages 55 inches, and the snow generally melts within a few days.

Area: 47 square miles

Elevation: 5,003 feet above sea level

Landscape Imagery Nature photography.

Average Temperatures: 47.9° F

Average Annual Precipitation: 15 inches of rain; 55 inches of snow

■ History

Travelers crossing the country on the Overland Trail often stopped at Camp Collins, which was established on the Cache La Poudre River in 1862. The camp was named for Colonel W. O. Collins, a commander of the eleventh Ohio Cavalry at Fort Laramie, Wyoming. The fort was built to protect the important trading post from attacks by Native Americans. In 1864 a community grew around the fort and became a center of trading, shipping, and manufacturing. Fort Collins was incorporated in 1869.

As farmers settled in the outlying areas, other settlers began moving to the new town, where they opened stores, livery stables, and other businesses. The first buildings of the state agricultural college, located in Fort Collins by vote of the state legislature, were erected in the 1870s. By that time the town boasted a post office, a general store, a rooming house, a mill, and its first school house.

During the first half of the 1870s the town population began to dwindle due to the failure of the town's first bank, a grasshopper infiltration, and business problems. The economy was given a boost by the arrival of the Colorado Central Railroad later in the decade. Soon after, the development of irrigation canals brought water to the area, greatly expanding farming options. Barley, wheat, and oat growing were especially successful, as were the cultivation of sugar beets and alfalfa.

The 1880s saw the construction of a number of elegant homes and commercial buildings. Beet tops proved to be excellent and abundant food for local sheep, and by the early 1900s the area was being referred to as "Lamb feeding capital of the world." In 1903 the Great Western sugar processing plant was built in the city.

Fort Collins gained a reputation as a very conservative city in the twentieth century, with prohibition of alcoholic beverages being retained from the late 1890s until 1969. Although the city was affected by the Great Depression, it nevertheless experienced slow and steady growth throughout the early part of the twentieth century. During the middle of the century, the population of the city doubled, and an era of economic prosperity occurred. Old buildings were razed to make way for new, modern structures. By the 1960s, though, citizens had formed a group to preserve and restore the older buildings that add such beauty and character to the city. The Fort Collins Historical Society was formed in 1974 to encourage the preservation of historic buildings and documents, and to provide educational opportunities for people to learn about the city's past.

Today's Fort Collins is known above all for its small-town familiarity, outdoor activities, cultural amenities, and active lifestyle. The city offers a rich mix of history with the cultural interest of a university town, whose extensive research apparatus has attracted new, high-tech businesses.

Historical Information: Poudre River Public Library District, 201 Peterson Street, Fort Collins, CO 80524; telephone (970) 221-6740.

■ Population Profile

Metropolitan Statistical Area Population

    2000: 251,494
    2010: 299,630
    2012 estimate: 310,487
    Percent change, 2000–2010: 19.1%
    U.S. rank in 2000: 167th
    U.S. rank in 2010: 156th

City Residents

    1990: 87,491
    2000: 118,652
    2010: 143,986
    2012 estimate: 148,634
    Percent change, 2000–2010: 21.4%
    U.S. rank in 1990: 230th (State rank: 7th)
    U.S. rank in 2000: 206th (State rank: 5th)
    U.S. rank in 2010: 169th (State rank: 4th)

Density: 2,652.8 people per square mile

Racial and ethnic characteristics

    White: 131,686
    Black or African American: 2,081
    American Indian and Alaskan Native: 751
    Asian: 4,415
    Native Hawaiian and Other Pacific Islander: 373
    Hispanic or Latino (may be of any race): 16,819
    Other: 9,328

Percent of residents born in state: 39.3%

Age characteristics

    Population under 5 years old: 8,912
    Population 5 to 9 years old: 8,772
    Population 10 to 14 years old: 6,634
    Population 15 to 19 years old: 12,225
    Population 20 to 24 years old: 24,602
    Population 25 to 34 years old: 25,701
    Population 35 to 44 years old: 16,528
    Population 45 to 54 years old: 18,624
    Population 55 to 59 years old: 7,700
    Population 60 to 64 years old: 6,478
    Population 65 to 74 years old: 7,136
    Population 75 to 84 years old: 3,587
    Population 85 years and over: 1,735
    Median age: 30.1

Births (2010–11 Metropolitan Area)

    Total number: 3,380

Deaths (2010–11 Metropolitan Area)

    Total number: 1,739

Money income (2012)

    Per capita income: $28,828
    Median household income: $51,830
    Total households: 56,319

Number of households with income of ...

    less than $10,000: 4,743
    $10,000 to $14,999: 3,145
    $15,000 to $24,999: 6,350
    $25,000 to $34,999: 4,942
    $35,000 to $49,999: 8,003
    $50,000 to $74,999: 10,414
    $75,000 to $99,999: 7,077
    $100,000 to $149,999: 7,014
    $150,000 to $199,999: 2,601
    $200,000 or more: 2,030

Percent of families below poverty level: 18.5%

FBI Crime Index Property: 4,119

FBI Crime Index Violent: 391

■ Municipal Government

The City of Fort Collins operates within a council-manager form of government. The City Manager is the chief executive officer of the city and is responsible for the overall management of city operations. The City Council is composed of six district council members who are elected for a term of four years, and a Mayor who is elected at-large for a two-year term. The Mayor Pro Tem is chosen from among the entire council and serves a term of two years.

Head Official: Mayor Karen Weitkunat (since 2011; current term expires 2015)

Total Number of City Employees: 2,000 (2012)

City Information: City of Fort Collins, 300 LaPorte Avenue, Fort Collins, CO 80521; telephone (970) 221-6878.

■ Economy

Major Industries and Commercial Activity

Fort Collins, which started out as a hub for agricultural production, specifically sugar beet manufacturing, has since shifted its focus to a high-technology economy. High-tech firms, including major information technology companies like Hewlett Packard, Intel, Advanced Microdevices, and I-cubed, have become an integral part of the Northern Colorado economy. Many of these high-tech companies have relocated to Fort Collins because of the resources of Colorado State University and its research facilities.

Clean energy is also an emerging field in the Fort Collins area, with local businesses focusing on aspects such as distributed power generation, biofuels, energy efficiency, power management and intelligent grid technologies. Fort Collins also has a strong manufacturing base and is home to such firms as WaterPik, Woodward, Advanced Energy, In-Situ, Otter Products, Tolmar, and Anheuser-Busch.

Colorado State University is the city's largest employer, providing nearly 7,000 jobs. The school's research efforts, attract some $300 million in annual funding in fields such as vector-borne infectious disease, veterinary medicine, atmospheric science, clean energy technologies, and environmental science. The Colorado State University Research Foundation and CSU Ventures partner with the university to commercialize its research findings.

The Federal government has several facilities in Fort Collins, including the National Seed Storage Laboratory, U.S. Forest Service Visitor Center for the Arapahoe and Roosevelt National Forest, Natural Resources Research Center, Agricultural Research Service, National Wildlife Research Center, National Institute of Standards and Technology, and the State Division of Wildlife.

Items and goods produced: pharmaceuticals, electronic components and accessories, scientific instruments, industrial chemicals, beer, protective cases, semiconductors

Incentive Programs—New and Existing Companies

Local programs: The city of Fort Collins is unique in that it doesn't offer a one-size-fits-all incentive package to local businesses. Instead, the city works collaboratively with businesses to develop an incentive package that best meets their needs. The advantage of such an approach is that a wider variety of incentives can be utilized by a business if the needs of a project demand it.

The city offers a variety of tax rebates, including a personal property tax rebate which will allow qualified employers a ten-year rebate for 50 percent of an expansion/relocation project's personal property. Also available to qualified businesses are rebates for associated infrastructure fees like fire and police protection, as well construction material use taxes and building permit fees.

A Larimer County Revolving Loan Fund and Private Activity Bond Financing provide local financing alternatives for businesses.

Additionally, the Northern Colorado Economic Development Corporation works with individual firms to locate resources or assist in the development of a financial package. In 1998, the community created the Fort Collins Technology Incubator, which in 2004, acquired 6,500 square feet of office space, transforming the seven-year-old Fort Collins's "Virtual Incubator" into an incubator with walls. The incubator was later renamed the Rocky Mountain Innovation Initiative. It is a cluster of programs designed to nurture startup businesses. Incubator companies receive discounted business services from top-notch community resources, advisory groups, Colorado State University resources, and strategic planning counseling as well as idea sharing amongst other entrepreneurs.

The Northern Colorado Economic Development Corporation supports existing employers and recruits new employers to the region. It assists local companies to grow and expand and, in partnership with Colorado State University, encourages technology transfer to nurture local start-up companies.

State programs: Colorado offers a variety of business assistance and incentive programs for expanding or relocated companies. Incentives include the Job Growth Tax Incentive, which provides a state income tax credit to job-creating projects in Colorado dependent on the incentive; Strategic Fund Initiative, for business development, expansion, or relocation that results in job creation; Enterprise Zone Tax Credits, which incentive development in economically distressed areas; Public Infrastructure Grants, to retain or add employment opportunities for low- or moderate-income residents; and sales and use tax refunds, exemptions, and credits for developments in biotechnology, manufacturing, and aviation sectors.

State financing support can be obtained through an array of general and industry-specific programs. Advanced Industries Accelerator Programs, created in 2013, offer access to capital for advanced manufacturing, aerospace, bioscience, electronic, energy and natural resource, infrastructure engineering, and technology and information industries. Private Activity Bonds offer tax-exempt bond financing to small manufacturing companies. Bioscience Discovery Evaluation Grants were available from 2007 to 2013 to support growth of companies in the bioscience industry. The Regional Tourism Act allows local governments to apply to the state for financial support for major tourism development initiatives likely to draw out-of-state visitors.

Venture capital funding is offered through the state's Certified Capital Companies Program, which makes available a statewide pool of $75 million for investment throughout the state, with an additional $25 million available for rural investment. The Colorado Venture

Capital Authority manages venture capital investments for the state. Colorado Capital Access, Cash Collateral Support, and Colorado Credit Reserve support financing needs of small and medium businesses.

Job training programs: The Colorado Community College System has joined with the Colorado Office of Economic Development & International Trade to administer Colorado FIRST/Existing Industry Customized Training Programs. These programs are designed to fund employee training for transferable job skills to benefit a company's competitive strength as well as an employee's long-term employment opportunities.

Front Range Community College and Colorado State University provide excellent employee training resources. Larimer County offers comprehensive, coordinated employment and training services at its WorkForce Center.

Development Projects

Development of the downtown Fort Collins area is largely spurred by the Downtown Development Authority (DDA), which uses tax increment financing to stimulate redevelopment in the central business district. Total expenditures by the DDA in 2012 approached $4 million. Major projects supported that year included the deconstruction of the 1907 Elks Building, formerly a YMCA, improvements to the library park landscape, façade projects for a 37,000-square-foot mixed-use development under construction by Encompass Technologies, and nearly $800,000—the DDA's largest single investment—for the Canyon place office and restaurant development, located across the street from Lincoln Center. During 2010–11, Lincoln Center underwent $7.2 million in renovations.

The Fort Collins Museum of Discovery opened in 2012 after a $24 million investment. The museum's exhibits span a massive time from, from million-year-old fossils to showcases of current digital technology. The museum has a total of 16,000 square feet of exhibit space, with 5,000 feet dedicated to temporary traveling exhibits. The new building received LEED certification for its environmentally conscious design.

The Mason Corridor Project includes bicycle and pedestrian trails and the MAX Bus Rapid Transit. The Mason Corridor was to connect Downtown, Colorado State University, and local businesses and neighborhoods. With nearly 60 percent of all Fort Collins jobs located within one mile of the Corridor, the project was expected to boost the local economy by providing efficient public transportation. Most aspects of the project completed in 2013, with operations expected to begin in 2014. Of the project's $87 million price tag, some 80 percent was federally funded.

In private developments, Avago Technologies Wireless Manufacturing announced a $20 million expansion of its 70-acre campus in Fort Collins, which would add a three-story building and 138,000 square feet of space. The addition was expected to add 100 employees to the company roster. The expansion follows an additional $9 million in upgrades to existing office space made by the company in 2012. In 2013 Woodward Inc. announced plans to redevelop the former Link-N-Greens golf course into its global headquarters.

Redevelopment of Foothills Mall received approval for a $53 million public assistance package in 2013. Mall redevelopment was seen as essential to restore much-needed local sales tax, and construction was expected to complete by 2015. The mix of private investment, public assistance, and surrounding infrastructure projects was estimated to total $312 million.

Economic Development Information: Northern Colorado Economic Development Corporation, 3553 Clydesdale Parkway, Suite 230, Loveland, CO 80538; telephone (970) 667-0905; fax (970) 669-4680.

Commercial Shipping

Parcel service for Fort Collins is provided by major companies that include Federal Express and United Parcel Service. Fort Collins has two-day rail freight access to the west coast or the east coast and has a number of motor freight carriers. Many local industrial sites have rail freight spur service. The city is served by the Union Pacific and Burlington Northern Santa Fe railroads.

Labor Force and Employment Outlook

Fort Collins's labor force has been described as young, well-educated, and energetic. Many graduates of Colorado State University stay in the city. Some 48 percent of Fort Collins residents hold some type of college degree, and 14 percent have a doctoral degree. About 11.5 patents are issued for every 10,000 people, a rate four times greater than average communities.

The following is a summary of data regarding the 2012 Fort Collins labor force:

Size of civilian labor force: 84,429

Number of workers employed in . . .

    agriculture and mining: 1,321
    construction: 3,534
    manufacturing: 6,366
    wholesale trade: 1,801
    retail trade: 9,177
    transportation: 1,965
    information systems: 1,712
    finance: 4,024
    professional administration: 9,848
    education and social services: 21,381
    arts and leisure: 9,415
    other: 3,671
    public administration: 2,577

Average hourly earnings of production workers: $17.58

Unemployment rate: 5.7% (2012)

Employers

Largest employers (2012)	*Number of employees*
Colorado State University	6,753
Poudre R-1 School District	3,957
Poudre Valley Health Care Inc.	3,100
City of Fort Collins	2,000
Larimer County	1,910
Woodward Inc.	1,302
Center Partners	1,112
Hewlett Packard Company	927
Employment Solutions Personnel Services	713
Other Productions LLC.	468

Cost of Living

In 2013 the median cost of purchasing a home was $166,400, and other cost-of-living measures were roughly 10 percent below the national average. Utility rates are among the lowest in Colorado.

The following is a summary of data regarding several key cost of living factors in the area.

State income tax rate: 4.63%

State sales tax rate: 2.9%

Local income tax rate: None

Local sales tax rate: 4.45%

Property tax rate: $0.09797 for every $1 of assessed value; residential assessed value is 7.96% of total value (2013)

Economic Information: Northern Colorado Economic Development Corporation, 3553 Clydesdale Parkway, Suite 230, Loveland, CO 80538; telephone (970) 667-0905; fax (970) 669-4680.

■ Education and Research

Elementary and Secondary Schools

The Poudre School District is led by a seven-member Board of Education committed to actively recruiting administrators and teachers displaying high standards of excellence. The school district is the second-largest employer in Fort Collins and covers some 1,856 square miles. About 31 percent of students qualify for free or reduced lunch. The dropout rate is only 1.33 percent, and the graduation rate is above 84 percent. Programs within the district include specialized non-neighborhood elementary schools that offer bilingual immersion and a multi-age, non-graded program; two charter schools; and multiple alternative secondary schools.

The metro area is also served by the Loveland-based Thompson School District.

The following is a summary of data regarding the Poudre School District.

Total enrollment: 27,510

Number of facilities

total: 50
elementary schools: 31
junior high schools: 10
high schools: 7
other: 2

Student/teacher ratio: 15.41:1

Teacher salaries

average (statewide): $49,938

Funding per pupil: $8,415

Public Schools Information: Poudre School District, 2407 La Porte Avenue, Fort Collins, CO 80521; telephone (970) 482-7420; fax (970) 490-3403.

Colleges and Universities

Three doctoral-level universities and two community colleges in the greater Fort Collins area turn out approximately 14,600 newly minted graduates each year. Colorado State University (CSU), with 30,700 total students, is a land-grant institution that consists of eight colleges and more than 150 programs of study. The colleges are agricultural sciences, business, engineering, health and human services, liberal arts, natural sciences, veterinary medicine and biomedical sciences, and natural resources. Founded in 1870, its campuses cover 5,612 acres in Larimer County, including the main campus, a foothills campus, an agricultural campus, and the Pingree Park mountain campus, which is the summer campus for natural resources education. Research is a major component of the university, and it received $252.3 million in federal funding in 2012, with total external funding above $300 million.

The University of Northern Colorado, located in nearby Greeley, offers more than 100 undergraduate programs and 100 graduate programs, with a total enrollment of more than 12,000 students. Focus areas include education, physics, business, and jazz.

Front Range Community College (FRCC), the largest community college in Colorado, grants associate's degrees in arts, science, general studies, and applied science at its four campuses. The college offers high school vocational programs and more than 100 degree and certificate programs, in addition to a growing online learning program. The Larimer Campus of FRCC offers partnerships with Colorado State University, Poudre Valley Hospital, McKee Medical Center, Columbine Health Systems, Village Homes' Observatory Village, Microsoft, and Oracle.

Libraries and Research Centers

The Poudre River Public Library District has three libraries, all in Fort Collins. The Old Town Library is the main facility, with Harmony Library and Council Tree Library serving as branch facilities. The system was established in 2006 via voter approval to serve 177,000 people across an 1,800-square-mile area in Larimer County. Annual circulation averages more than 2.3 million items.

Special collections of the Colorado State University Library include agriculture, agricultural economics, biomedical science, engineering, hydrology, and natural resources. The university has over two million books in its total library holdings. The University of Northern Colorado is home to two of its own libraries, the Michener Library and the Skinner Music Library. Michener Library houses more than 1.5 million items, and the Skinner Music Library is composed of more than 100,000 scores, recordings, books, and periodicals. The Colorado Division of Wildlife maintains a research library.

Fort Collins has a great range of research institutes covering a myriad of subjects. Facilities are maintained by the Centers for Disease Control Division of Vector-Borne Infectious Diseases, Colorado Cooperative Fish and Wildlife Research Unit, Colorado Water Institute, and the Cooperative Institute for Research in the Atmosphere. The Rocky Mountain Research Station of the U.S. Forest Service conducts research on experimental forests, ranges, and watersheds, and oversees research on more than 200 natural areas.

Colorado State University has a variety of research groups focusing on subjects such as animal reproduction, biotechnology, engineering, environmental toxicology, irrigation management, microscopy, nutrition, hydraulics, manufacturing, marrow transplantation, vehicle emissions, and solar energy. The University spent about $375 million on research in 2012, with about $300 million financed externally, most from the federal government.

Public Library Information: Poudre River Public Library District, 201 Peterson St., Fort Collins, CO 80524; telephone (970) 221-6740.

■ Health Care

By virtue of the broad scope of medical services available, Fort Collins has become a regional health center. The Poudre Valley Health System, part of University of Colorado Health, has several area facilities, including Poudre Valley Hospital, specializing in orthopedic surgery, neuroscience, cancer, bariatric weight-loss surgery, and women and family services. The hospital serves residents in northern Colorado, southern Wyoming, and western Nebraska. It is a Level II trauma center and was named a Top 100 Hospital by Thomson Reuters for five consecutive years during 2003–07. In 2013 *U.S. News & World Report* gave the hospital high-performing marks in eight adult specialties.

McKee Medical Center, owned by Banner Health System, is based in Loveland and has 121 beds. It offers heart, cancer, trauma and intensive care units, rehabilitation programs, home-health services, inpatient and outpatient surgical facilities and a birthing center. Banner Health System also operates North Colorado Medical Center in Greeley.

■ Recreation

Sightseeing

More than 40 historic sites can be visited in the Fort Collins Area, with over half of them listed in or eligible for the National Register of Historic Places. Tours of Avery House, a restored Victorian residence built by one of the city's prominent citizens, are offered year round. The two-story Strauss Cabin, which was built in 1864 by George Strauss and modeled after structures found in South Carolina, exists only as a brick shell following a 1999 fire. The Old Federal Building is a 1912 structure that housed the post office on its main floor for 60 years. The 1881 Spruce Hall on the campus of Colorado State University is the oldest complete building still standing on the campus. Ammons Hall, also on the campus, is a 1922 Italian Renaissance building that is still being used as a welcome center. Many other sites worth observing are on the Historic Buildings map available through the Fort Collins Convention and Visitors Bureau.

Fort Collins boasts of being the "Napa Valley of Beer." Beer enthusiasts and those merely curious will enjoy touring the Anheuser-Busch Brewery, which includes a visit with the famous Clydesdale horses and a trip to the sampling room. Several of its award-winning craft breweries—such as New Belgium, Odell,l and Equinox—also invite visitors to enjoy their variety of offerings. A metal menagerie of mythical and real creatures is on view at farmer/sculptor Bill Swets's dairy farm, known as the Swetsville Zoo. The zoo also has a miniature live steam railroad train and a display of antique farming equipment. Young and old enjoy hopping a ride aboard the Fort Collins Municipal Railway streetcar, which runs May to September, weather permitting.

Arts and Culture

The premier facility for the performing arts in Fort Collins is Lincoln Center, with its 1,180-seat performance hall, two theaters, and four exhibit galleries, all of which draw in over 225,000 visitors each year. The center hosts over 1,500 events each year, among them an annual season of Broadway shows, dance, and musical events. Renovations that completed in 2011 added 17,000 square feet of space.

OpenStage Theater Company, a regional professional theater group, stages its seasons in the Lincoln Center's 220-seat Mini-Theater. Based on the tradition of eighteenth-century salons, the 48-seat Bas Bleu Theater provides an intimate setting for poetry, plays, and musical performances. Bas Bleu has produced, performed, exhibited, or hosted over 600 events. Good food and theater can be combined at the Carousel Dinner Theater, which presents dramas, comedies, and popular musicals. Colorado State University presents several plays each year at the school's Johnson Hall. Other theater groups in the city include the Debut Theatre Company, Fort Collins Children's Theatre, and the Front Range Chamber Players. A variety of dance performances is offered by the Canyon Concert Ballet. Several performing halls are located on the campus of Colorado State University.

Musical experiences in the city come in many forms, featuring such groups as the Larimer Chorale, Opera Fort Collins, and the Fort Collins Symphony. The primary visual arts center of the city is the Fort Collins Museum of Art, located on the first floor of the city's old post office building.

In 2007 the Fort Collins Museum and the Discovery Science Center merged with a goal of fusing history, culture, and hand's on science exploration into a single location. The combined Fort Collins Museum of Discovery, which opened its new joint facility in 2012, continues to highlight the area's past, including a display of pre-Columbian Folsom points discovered at a major archaeological site in northern Larimer County, while also offering experiences with hands-on science to youngsters.

Festivals and Holidays

Fort Collins's festival season begins with its annual St. Patrick's Day Parade downtown. The city's Hispanic community is honored at the Cinco de Mayo celebration, which features dancing, entertainment, and food. Patrons are invited to tap kegs of beer at June's Colorado Brewers' Festival downtown. Fireworks light the sky at City Park's annual Fourth of July Celebration. On Skookum Day, also in July, Fort Collins's history is re-enacted with demonstrations of blacksmithing, milking, quilting, branding, and weaving. August is enlivened by the Larimer County Fair & Rodeo, and by the NewWestFest, featuring more than 300 booths, events, performances, evening concerts, and children's activities.

The city celebrates the harvest during Oktoberfest, and the holiday season is launched with Lincoln Center's Great Christmas Hall, with its juried art exhibit, homemade crafts, and decorated trees. In December, festivities include carolers and Christmas celebrations in Old Town, and the New Year is welcomed in with a community-wide celebration for the whole family called First Night.

Sports for the Spectator

Colorado State University students engage in a variety of sporting competitions throughout the year. The CSU Rams are represented by both male and female teams in a variety of sports, including football, basketball, cross country, golf, softball, swimming and diving, tennis, track and field, volleyball, and water polo.

Sports for the Participant

Fort Collins is home to a variety of walking, running, and bicycling events and tournaments. In 2012 *Bicycle Magazine* ranked Fort Collins as the 11th-most Bike Friendly City; the prior year, *Triathlete Magazine* named Fort Collins one of the 15 best places to live and train. The Cache La Poudre River provides some of the finest fishing in the state. The city is home to more than 30,000 acres of natural areas and 600 acres of parks, and it maintains some 200 miles of on-street and off-street trails for hikers and cyclists. Lory State Park offers 2,400 acres for horseback riding, boating, hiking, and picnicking. Duffers may choose from three public golf courses in Fort Collins, in addition to several area private courses. Of its three swimming pools, the Edora Pool and Ice Center and Mulberry Pool feature swimming and exercise programs, as well as youth and adult hockey and public ice skating. The young or young at heart will enjoy skateboarding at Northside Azatlan Community Center, Edora Skateboard Park, and Fossil Creek Skateboard. In winter, Lory State Park's trails and rolling hills attract cross country skiers; tubing and sledding are also popular. Several renowned Colorado mountain ski resorts are within a few hours of Fort Collins. Rocky Mountain National Park offers scenic drives and hikes and is only one hour's drive away.

Shopping and Dining

Shopping in Fort Collins can involve browsing antique stores and flea markets or seeing the latest fashions at major malls. An extensive redevelopment of Foothills Mall was planned scheduled to take place during 2014 and 2015. At Historic Old Town, restored buildings filled with specialty shops, galleries, boutiques, and outdoor cafes beckon the visitor. Fort Collins boasts over 300 restaurants, with American and ethnic cuisines.

Visitor Information: Fort Collins Convention and Visitors Bureau, 19 Old Town Square, Suite 137, Ft. Collins, CO 80524; telephone (970) 232-3840; fax (970) 232-3841; email information@ftcollins.com.

■ Convention Facilities

Fort Collins has nearly 2,000 hotel rooms, ranging from budget rooms to luxury suites. Colorado State University, in the heart of Fort Collins, has 50,000 square feet of convention facilities at its Lory Student Center, with 25 meeting rooms, five ballrooms, a 630 seat theater, and other miscellaneous meeting space. Its main ballroom can seat up to 1,200. An expansion of the building, scheduled for completion in 2014, was to add another 40,000 square feet of space. The school's Moby Arena seats 6,000 for a conference, and up to 100 classrooms are available depending on the conference date. Auditoriums with accommodations for up to 400 are available in the Clark Building, as are a total of 4,400 beds in the residence halls, and dining facilities in each residence hall.

The Pingree Park Conference Center, 53 miles west of Fort Collins and affiliated with Colorado State University, offers seven meeting rooms, two dorms, and seven cabins on its 1,200 acre campus. Campus lodging is available late May through mid-August. There are several facilities around the city that can handle small group meetings.

Convention Information: Fort Collins Convention and Visitors Bureau, 19 Old Town Square, Suite 137, Ft. Collins, CO 80524; telephone (970) 232-3840; fax (970) 232-3841; email information@ftcollins.com.

■ Transportation

Approaching the City

Fort Collins/Loveland Airport is a jointly-owned, general aviation facility. The airport offers charter flights and mainly serves the private and corporate needs of Northern Front Range. However, it was actively seeking a commercial carrier to provide scheduled air service. Denver International Airport, which is 25 miles to the south, is the closest major commercial airport. Fort Collins can be approached from Denver by car via Interstate 25. Greyhound offers bus service into the city.

Traveling in the City

Fort Collins's downtown streets form a grid with Interstate 25 running north and south on the east side of the city. U.S. Highway 287 runs east and west in the northwest sector of the city. Transfort, Fort Collins's local bus transportation system, operates daily, with 18 bus routes. MAX Bus Rapid Transit was scheduled to begin in 2014, providing a dedicated and efficient means of traveling along the city's main corridor. Alternative transportation is encouraged in the city; bicycle commuters benefit from city incentives and excellent bike paths through town.

■ Communications

Newspapers and Magazines

The *Fort Collins Coloradoan*, which appears Monday through Sunday mornings, is the city's daily paper.

The bimonthly *Northern Colorado Business Report*, reports on the growing business market in Northern Colorado with an increasing emphasis on high-tech and e-business. Other publications include *Scene Magazine*, focusing on entertainment and lifestyle.

Television and Radio

There are five television stations in the greater Fort Collins area, in addition to available cable television. One local AM and nine FM stations serve the city with a variety of programming including public radio, news/talk, adult contemporary, and alternative music formats.

Media Information: The *Fort Collins Coloradoan*, 1300 Riverside Ave., Fort Collins, CO 80524; telephone (970) 493-6397

Fort Collins Online

City of Fort Collins Home Page. Available www. fcgov.com
Coloradoan. Available www.coloradoan.com
Fort Collins Area Chamber of Commerce. Available www.fortcollinschamber.com
Fort Collins Convention & Visitors Bureau. Available www.visitftcollins.com
Larimer County. Available www.co.larimer.co.us
Northern Colorado Economic Development Corporation. Available www.ncedc.com
Poudre River Public Library. Available www. poudrelibraries.org

BIBLIOGRAPHY

Fleming, Barbara, and Malcolm McNeill, *Fort Collins* (Charleston, SC: Arcadia Publishing, 2010)

Fort Collins Friends of the Library, comp. *Talking About Fort Collins: Selections from Oral Histories* (Fort Collins, CO: City of Fort Collins, 1992)

Horan, Bob, *Colorado Front Range Bouldering: Fort Collins* (Evergreen, CO: Chockstone Press, 1995)

Lipker, Kim, *Sixty hikes within 60 miles, Denver and Boulder: including Colorado Springs, Fort Collins, and Rocky Mountain National Park*, 2nd ed. (Birmingham, AL: Menasha Ridge Press, 2010)

Swanson, Evadine Burris, *Fort Collins Yesterdays* (Fort Collins, CO: G & H Morgan, 1993)

Telluride

■ The City in Brief

Founded: 1878

Head Official: Mayor Stu Fraser (since 2007; current term expires November 2015)

City Population
    1990: 1,309
    2000: 2,221
    2010: 2,325
    2012 estimate: 2,120
    Percent change, 2000–2010: 4.7%

County Population
    2000: 6,594
    2010: 7,359
    2012 estimate: 7,406
    Percent change, 2000–2010: 11.6%

Area: 0.74 square miles

Elevation: 9,813 feet above sea level

Average Annual Temperatures: January, 21.2° F; July, 59.2° F

Average Annual Precipitation: 23.1 inches of rain; 167 inches of snow

Major Economic Sectors: tourism, hospitality, services

Unemployment Rate: 6.0% (2012)

Per Capita Income: $28,051

2012 FBI Crime Index Property: 115

Major Colleges and Universities: University Centers of San Miguel

Daily Newspaper: *Daily Planet*

■ Introduction

Surrounded by the spectacular San Juan Mountains of western Colorado, Telluride is a popular tourist destination year-round. In winter, skiing is the primary attraction, while in summer, hiking, golfing, mountain biking, and the town's many festivals draw visitors to Telluride's many resorts and charming downtown, designated a National Historic Landmark District in 1961. Citizens and visitors alike value Telluride's unique architecture, spectacular scenery, and mountain resort ambience. From its rugged remote location in southwest Colorado in the San Juan mountain range, Telluride functions as the San Miguel County seat.

■ Geography and Climate

Telluride is situated a diverse geographic region that includes both rugged mountain plateaus and arid ranch lands. The city is surrounded on three sides by 14,000-foot peaks. To the south and west is desert, which plays a role in the city's 300 days of annual sunshine, as well as its 10 percent humidity. Winters are mild compared to other ski resorts in the state and northward, with summers featuring comfortable days and cool nights.

Area: 0.74 square miles

Elevation: 9,813 feet above sea level

Average Temperatures: January, 21.2° F; July, 59.2° F

Average Annual Precipitation: 23.1 inches of rain; 167 inches of snow

■ History

For centuries, summers found Ute Indians camped in the area of modern-day Telluride, hunting elk, deer, and Rocky Mountain bighorn sheep. In winter, the Ute

© Blaine Harrington III/Alamy

would move to lower elevations. This cycle went unchanged until the 1700s.

In the late 1700s, Spanish explorers encountered and named the San Juan Mountains (and the San Juan River that runs through them). They established a 1,200-mile route, from Santa Fe, New Mexico, to Colorado. This route is now known as the Old Spanish Trail. The Spanish explorers did not establish permanent settlements. Eventually, the trappers and traders continued moving westward toward the California coast.

Gold and Silver Lures Miners

Gold was discovered in the mid-1800s, and miners following tales of gold and silver deposits soon established settlements in the area around Telluride. One such mining encampment, known as Columbia, was established in 1878 at the site of modern-day Telluride, elevation 8,750 feet. Local mining claims drew fortune-seekers to the San Juan Mountains of western Colorado. By 1887, Telluride was formally established as a town.

Most mining towns, including Telluride, were very isolated. To serve the booming mining towns in the San Juan Mountains, the 162-mile Rio Grande Southern Railroad was built in the late 1800s. Comprised of narrow-gauge track, the Rio Grande Southern carried

people and supplies across rugged mountain terrain to the young towns of Telluride, Durango, and Ouray. Miners did not find gold, but they did find ores rich in zinc, lead, copper, and silver, and the railroad helped connect the miners to supplies and to markets for their products.

Tales of riches also attracted a criminal element. On June 24, 1889, Robert Leroy Parker, later known as Butch Cassidy, made his first major heist. With two conspirators, Parker robbed the San Miguel Valley Bank of $24,580.

Fortune-seekers flocked to Telluride, and the town grew quickly. Rows of elegant Victorian homes and brick buildings lined the streets and helped earn today's Telluride a listing on the National Register of Historic Places. From 1905 to 1911 alone, more than $16 million in silver and other precious minerals were mined in the Telluride area.

In 1891, Telluride got another boost. Telluride citizen L. L. Nunn, with Nikola Tesla and George Westinghouse, built the Ames Hydroelectric Generating Plant, the first commercial-grade alternating current power plant near Telluride. The plant supplied power to a mine 3.5 miles away, which was the first time alternating current was transmitted over such a long distance. The Ames plant sparked a competition between the Westinghouse Electric Corporation and the General

Electric Company, which was headed by Thomas Edison and financed by J. P. Morgan.

Telluride's historic mines (the Tomboy, Pandora, Smuggler-Union, Nellie, and Sheridan) eventually were consolidated. From 1939 to 1953, the Idarado Mining Company acquired and consolidated mining operations and continued mining until 1978. Miners and their families left Telluride. Some questioned whether Telluride would become a ghost town.

Winter Sports Bring a New Rush

The Telluride Ski Resort installed a ski lift in 1972, and people with different interests were drawn to Telluride. Wealthy skiers began to discover all that the area had to offer. Folksingers and other musicians appreciated the scenery and saw Telluride as a perfect festival setting. Bu the 1990s, Telluride's image had transformed from rough mining town to laid-back resort. Population growth was dramatic. In 1970 Telluride's population was just 553; San Miguel County's total population was 1,949. By 2012, Telluride's population had grown to about 2,400, and that of the county reached more than 7,500.

As of 2014, management and control of the area's growth was one of the town's principal concerns.

■ Population Profile

County Population

> 2000: 6,594
> 2010: 7,359
> 2012 estimate: 7,406
> Percent change, 2000–2010: 11.6%

City Residents

> 1990: 1,309
> 2000: 2,221
> 2010: 2,325
> 2012 estimate: 2,120
> Percent change, 2000–2010: 4.7%

Density: 3,141 people per square mile

Racial and ethnic characteristics

> White: 2,103
> Black or African American: 9
> American Indian and Alaskan Native: 25
> Asian: 27
> Native Hawaiian and Other Pacific Islander: 0
> Hispanic or Latino (may be of any race): 219
> Other: 161

Percent of residents born in state: 29.3%

Age characteristics

> Population under 5 years old: 109
> Population 5 to 9 years old: 126
> Population 10 to 14 years old: 118
> Population 15 to 19 years old: 88
> Population 20 to 24 years old: 154
> Population 25 to 34 years old: 530
> Population 35 to 44 years old: 452
> Population 45 to 54 years old: 341
> Population 55 to 59 years old: 168
> Population 60 to 64 years old: 123
> Population 65 to 74 years old: 98
> Population 75 to 84 years old: 16
> Population 85 years and over: 2
> Median age: 35.9

Births (2010–11 Metropolitan Area)

> Total number: Not available

Deaths (2010–11 Metropolitan Area)

> Total number: Not available

Money income (2012)

> Per capita income: $28,051
> Median household income: $64,189
> Total households: 1,008

Number of households with income of ...

> less than $10,000: 11
> $10,000 to $14,999: 39
> $15,000 to $24,999: 104
> $25,000 to $34,999: 73
> $35,000 to $49,999: 142
> $50,000 to $74,999: 190
> $75,000 to $99,999: 147
> $100,000 to $149,999: 170
> $150,000 to $199,999: 36
> $200,000 or more: 96

Percent of families below poverty level: 5.0%

FBI Crime Index Property: 115

FBI Crime Index Violent: 6

■ Municipal Government

The Town of Telluride is a home-rule municipality. The mayor and six council members are elected for four-year terms. The mayor and town council members do not have offices at Town Hall. The town manager is Telluride's chief administrator. The town manager reports to the town council.

The town council meeting schedule is set at the end of the year for the next calendar year. Town council meetings are held approximately every third Tuesday at Rebekah Hall.

Head Officials: Town Manager Greg Clifton (since 2012); Mayor Stu Fraser (since 2007; current term expires November 2015)

Total Number of City Employees: 95 (2014)

City Information: Town of Telluride, P.O. Box 397, Telluride, CO 81435; telephone (970) 728-2170.

■ Economy

Major Industries and Commercial Activity

Tourism related to skiing and other mountain recreational activities (hiking and climbing) is an important segment of the economy. Summer activities attracting tourists include golf, hiking, climbing, fly fishing, and the many festivals staged at Telluride Town Park.

Telluride Ski Resort offers 1,700 acres of skiable terrain and a mountain experience for all levels of skiers. The resort operates 18 lifts, including two high-speed gondolas and seven high-speed quads, and offers one of North America's largest vertical drops at 4,425 feet, of which 3,845 vertical feet are served by ski lifts. The Telluride Golf Course is a par 70, 18-hole mountain resort course. It serves as a private club for members as well as a public course for locals and guests.

Providing services for tourists is a key economic activity in Telluride.

Incentive Programs—New and Existing Companies

Local programs: From 2009 to 2013, Telluride operated under a Major Recession Plan, which involved curtailing investment in economic development projects. In 2014, with the regional economy in recovery, the town council elected to ease its plan to the Moderate Recession Plan level. The 2014 budget included a small increase in support for arts and special events, including reallocating funding to support the expansion of the Telluride Creative District, which serves as an umbrella organization.

The city planned to expand support for small business with "Buy Local" programs. In addition, programs to minimize impact of development on the fragile environment, which is critical to Telluride's economy, were prioritized.

State programs: Colorado offers a variety of business assistance and incentive programs for expanding or relocated companies. Incentives include the Job Growth Tax Incentive, which provides a state income tax credit to job-creating projects in Colorado dependent on the incentive; Strategic Fund Initiative, for business development, expansion, or relocation that results in job creation; Enterprise Zone Tax Credits, which incentive development in economically distressed areas; Public Infrastructure Grants, to retain or add employment opportunities for low- or moderate-income residents; and sales and use tax refunds, exemptions, and credits

for developments in biotechnology, manufacturing, and aviation sectors.

State financing support can be obtained through an array of general and industry-specific programs. Advanced Industries Accelerator Programs, created in 2013, offer access to capital for advanced manufacturing, aerospace, bioscience, electronic, energy and natural resource, infrastructure engineering, and technology and information industries. Private Activity Bonds offer tax-exempt bond financing to small manufacturing companies. Bioscience Discovery Evaluation Grants were available from 2007 to 2013 to support growth of companies in the bioscience industry. The Regional Tourism Act allows local governments to apply to the state for financial support for major tourism development initiatives likely to draw out-of-state visitors.

Venture capital funding is offered through the state's Certified Capital Companies Program, which makes available a statewide pool of $75 million for investment throughout the state, with an additional $25 million available for rural investment. The Colorado Venture Capital Authority manages venture capital investments for the state. Colorado Capital Access, Cash Collateral Support, and Colorado Credit Reserve support financing needs of small and medium businesses.

Job training programs: The Colorado Community College System has joined with the Colorado Office of Economic Development & International Trade to administer Colorado FIRST/Existing Industry Customized Training Programs. These programs are designed to fund employee training for transferable job skills to benefit a company's competitive strength as well as an employee's long-term employment opportunities.

Development Projects

Providing for adequate water has been an ongoing priority for Telluride. By the 1990s, scarcity of water in Mill Creek, the primary source of municipal water, drove city leaders to find a solution. The resulting Pandora Project was envisioned to provide access to water in Blue Lake, located high within the Bridal Veil basin. The Idarado Mining Company owns most of the land and substantial water rights within the basin. After 20 years of complex negotiations and litigation over easement issues, water rights, and related topics, construction on the Pandora Project began in 2011. The construction of the Water Treatment Plant began in 2013. The entire Pandora Project was scheduled for completion in the late 2014. Telluride has had to implement restrictions on water use for irrigation and general consumption; in addition, in 2014 a 20 percent increase in water utility rates was enacted.

The Telluride Regional Airport undertook a multi-year $50 million runway project beginning around 2010. The project replaced the 6,770-foot runway and runway lighting, widened the remaining safety areas, and added an engineered material arresting system. These improvements allow the airport to serve larger aircraft.

In 2013 a partnership with the Telluride Film Festival allowed the city to prioritize enclosing the Town Park Pavilion. Similarly, with partnerships involving intergovernmental contributions and grants, Telluride prioritized the 2014 replacement and enlargement of its community swimming pool.

Federal funding to cover 80 percent of the costs enabled the city to schedule its Public Works Facility for completion in 2014.

Telluride Ski Resort, which experiences an average of 300 inches of snowfall each year, continued to expand. In 2008 the Resort expanded by nearly 400 acres and opened a new slope for advanced skiers, the Revelation Bowl, which is situated above the tree line. In 2010 the Resort installed a new bridge and staircase on Gold Hill. The Resort opened an outdoor restaurant, The Bon Vivant, located at the top of the Polar Queen Express (Chair 5) in 2012. The restaurant, which features a sun deck, serves a menu of "country French" items for up to 75 diners, seated under a 40-foot motorized umbrella.

Economic Development Information: Telluride Tourism Board/Chamber of Commerce, 630 W. Colorado Avenue, P.O. Box 1009, Telluride, CO 81435; telephone (888) 355-8743.

Commercial Shipping

There is little commercial shipping in Telluride. A unique shipping enterprise, High Country Shipping, serves vacation and other travelers who wish to ship equipment, such as skis, bicycles, and golf bags, to a resort destination. High Country Shipping is based in Mountain Village, Colorado, Telluride's neighboring town.

Labor Force and Employment Outlook

The Telluride area economy is rooted in the hospitality industry. The remote location and sparse population of western Colorado are factors that somewhat limit the growth of this industry in Telluride. In addition, infrastructure (such as water supply and sewage treatment) limits the rate of growth for tourism in the area.

The following is a summary of data regarding the 2012 Telluride labor force:

Size of civilian labor force: 1,668

Number of workers employed in . . .

    agriculture and mining: 60
    construction: 116
    manufacturing: 13
    wholesale trade: 0
    retail trade: 160
    transportation: 42
    information systems: 20

    finance: 213
    professional administration: 225
    education and social services: 135
    arts and leisure: 522
    other: 40
    public administration: 38

Average hourly earnings of production workers: $18.36

Unemployment rate: 6.0% (2012)

Employers

Largest employers (2014)	Number of employees (winter; summer)
TSG Ski & Golf LLC (ski resort)	1,000; 250
The Peaks Resort & Spa (resort)	181; 181
Town of Mountain Village (government)	123; 152
Hotel Madeline Telluride (hotel)	140; 120
San Miguel County (government)	117; 117
Telluride School District R-1	115; 115
Fairmont Heritage Pl., Franz Klammer Lodge	105; 90
Telluride Sports Ski (sports equipment)	100; 40
Town of Telluride (government)	95; 95
Telluride Medical Center (health care)	36; 36

Cost of Living

Telluride's status as a prime ski destination has driven up real estate prices and, consequently, the cost of living.

State income tax rate: 4.63%

State sales tax rate: 2.9%

Local income tax rate: None

Local sales tax rate: 5.5%

Property tax rate: 34.783 mills (2014)

Economic Information: Telluride Tourism Board/Chamber of Commerce, 630 W. Colorado Avenue, P.O. Box 1009, Telluride, CO 81435; telephone (888) 355-8743.

■ Education and Research

Elementary and Secondary Schools

The first school in the area, Telluride Elementary School, was built in 1895. The Board of Education purchased the present school site for $3,200 in May of that year. Using locally produced bricks, construction began on a school building, but the structure collapsed before it could open. Rebuilding began immediately, and by fall 1896, the school opened with six teachers and a principal. In 1902 a belfry and bell and four additional rooms were added. This building served the Telluride community until 1967.

In 1984 the school district again acquired the historic building and undertook a major renovation, seeking to preserve its historic character. Original materials were used, and when the renovation was completed in 1987, the results were award-winning. The school is now listed on the National Register of Historic Places. In 1998 voters passed a bond to build a two-story addition to house a gymnasium, stage, and three additional classrooms. This annex was completed in 2000.

Voters again supported a bond measure in 2003 to expand the school district's facilities with the addition of thirteen new classrooms, including a library, technology laboratory, and 600-seat auditorium. Upon its completion in 2004, this addition became the Telluride Intermediate School (grades 4 through 8) and Palm Theatre. Telluride Elementary School was reorganized to house kindergarten through third grade.

Telluride High School opened in November 1995. Located in Telluride, the high school is built on 10.8 acres. Telluride High School is a public, four-year college preparatory school with an enrollment of 184 students in grades 9 through 12. *U.S. News & World Report* ranked Telluride High School number one among public high schools and number four among all high schools (including charter and private schools) in Colorado. There are 482 high schools in Colorado.

Telluride also operates the Telluride Early Childhood Center. In 2013 the Early Childhood Center launched a dual-language English-Spanish program.

In addition to taxpayer support, public schools receive financial support from the nonprofit Telluride Education Foundation, known as We R-1. It is operated by an all-volunteer board of parents and administrators who raise funds for supplemental programs that fall outside the school system's budget. Examples of projects funded by We R-1 include experiential learning for students, grants for teachers, and college scholarships.

Telluride Academy offers summer programs. It was begun in 1980 as a summer daycare option for working families. Within 20 years of its founding, the Academy offered 100 programs for international summer study and hosted more than 700 students.

The following is a summary of data regarding the Telluride School District.

Total enrollment: 697

Number of facilities

    total: 3
    elementary schools: 1
    junior high schools: 1
    high schools: 1
    other: 0

Student/teacher ratio: 11.5:1

Funding per pupil: $12,000

Public Schools Information: Telluride School District R-1, 725 W. Colorado Avenue, Telluride CO 81435; telephone (970) 728-6617.

Colleges and Universities

Established in 2005, University Centers of San Miguel (UCSM) is a non-profit college access program. On its website, UCSM describes its educational functions as similar to those of a rural community college branch campus. UCSM brokers with regional colleges to provide accredited courses locally. UCSM provides access to lower-level core academic courses to prepare students to transfer to four-year programs. Among UCSM's partners are Colorado Mesa University and Colorado Northwestern Community College. In 2010 UCSM became the Regional Center for Colorado Northwestern Community College by supporting the College's Virtual Classroom and high school outreach efforts.

Libraries and Research Centers

The Wilkinson Public Library began as a bookmobile service in 1965. Larry and Betty Wilkinson, for whom the library is named, arranged for a small library to open in a building provided by the city's fire department. All books in the collection were donated. Donations were collected to cover the cost of heating the small building. In 1974 citizens voted to approve the creation of a community library, with Betty Wilkinson as the first director. As the library grew, an old jail building was identified as a possible location. The building was rehabilitated with support from the National Park Service and the Colorado State Historical Society, and by Betty and Larry Wilkinson, who personally hauled 20 tons of rock in their family van. The new library was dedicated in 1976. In 1984 voters passed a bond issue to add on to the building. In 1997 a referendum to build a new library passed by only two votes. The Wilkinson Public Library Building opened in August 2000. The library's collection includes books, audio and video media, and historic documents. Its meeting rooms are used for a wide variety of community events and lecture programs.

Public Library Information: Wilkinson Public Library, 100 West Pacific Avenue, Telluride, CO 81435; telephone (970) 728-4519.

■ Health Care

The Telluride Medical Center provides health-care services to the region. Founded in 1896 as the Telluride Community Hospital in a building that is now the Telluride Museum on Fir Street, the hospital later moved to the Idarado Mining Clinic, its current site. In 2013 the Medical Center employed approximately 40 people and handled 13,500 patient visits. Some 8,876 patients received primary-care services and 3,014 patients received emergency room services.

In 1978 the region that includes Telluride created a tax district, the Telluride Hospital District, to support health care. Because of this tax-based funding, the Emergency Department provides 24-hour emergency care, digital radiology, and CT services. The Medical Center also houses primary care services, the Institute for High Altitude Medicine, and welcomes about 12 visiting specialists in various disciplines each year. The Hospital District is operated by an elected board of community members serving four-year terms. As of 2014, the Hospital District has initiated a process to identify and obtain a new site to build a new medical center facility. The Medical Center was built on land that is leased from the Idarado Mining Company for $1 a year. The Hospital District predicts that the Medical Center will not be adequate to meet the needs of the growing Telluride population.

■ Recreation

Sightseeing

Telluride is located in San Miguel County, named for the 90-mile-long San Miguel River. Among the county's attractions is Bridal Veil Falls, the longest free-falling waterfall in Colorado. The Old Spanish Trail, a 1,200-mile historic route, starts in Santa Fe, touches the Telluride region, and continues on to Los Angeles.

Telluride is connected to neighboring Mountain Village by a gondola, which is free for all to ride. The gondola is the only transportation system of its kind in North America.

The Telluride Historic District consists of 80 acres of downtown Telluride and 7 acres of Lone Tree Cemetery. The streets of the Historic District are lined with late Victorian and Gothic Revival architecture; the District was declared a National Historic Landmark in 1961.

Arts and Culture

Telluride is dedicated to supporting the arts. The town has been recognized by the state of Colorado for its commitment to the arts, sharing the prestigious Governor's Arts Award with the town of Creede in 2010.

Major arts events include the Mountainfilm Festival, founded in 1979 and held each year in May, and the Telluride Film Festival, held over Labor Day Weekend. In 1999 the Mountainfilm Festival introduced Mountainfilm on Tour, a program through which festival films travel to selected cities across North America. Since 1977, Telluride has been site of the annual Telluride Jazz Festival, held each August and produced by the Telluride Society for Jazz.

Festivals and Holidays

The Telluride Town Park, an outdoor music venue, hosts a number of annual festivals. Major festivals include the Telluride Blues & Brews Festival (held in September, staged since 1994); the Telluride Jazz Festival (held in August, staged since 1977), and the Telluride Bluegrass Festival (held in June, staged since 1973). Other festivals include a Mushroom Festival, Ride Festival, and the Imogene Pass Run.

Sports for the Spectator

In December 2012, Telluride Ski Resort hosted the FIS (International Ski Federation) World Cup Snowboard-cross, the only U.S. site for this sport's competition that year. The event included—for the first time in the competition's history—the FIS World Cup Skiercross, a combined event. Competitive skiing events are regularly staged in Telluride and champion skiers compete on Telluride slopes. At the 2014 Olympic Winter Games in Sochi, Russia, Telluride's Gus Kenworthy won the silver medal in the first-ever Olympic slopestyle competition.

Sports for the Participant

Telluride offers opportunities for participation in recreational sports in winter and summer. Winter sports include skiing and related mountain sports; summer sports include biking, climbing, rafting, and golf. The readers of *Conde Nast Traveler* ranked Telluride Ski Resort as the number-one ski resort in North America in 2012.

Shopping and Dining

There are no chain stores or restaurants in Telluride. The towns of Telluride and Mountain Village offer plenty of shopping, however, in unique retail stores. Stores offer the latest styles in clothing, home décor, jewelry, and outdoor recreation equipment. In 2011 and 2012, Telluride Ski Resort opened three new retail stores (Mountain Standard Time Telluride, Alpenglow Beauty, and Heritage Apparel) in Mountain Village. These and other stylish boutiques have earned the shopping area the nickname "Mountain Village Fashion District."

Dining options vary from small independent coffee shops and casual restaurants to fine gourmet dining. A unique dining option is Allred's, a fine-dining restaurant with a casual atmosphere located at the midpoint of the gondola ride between Telluride and Mountain Village.

Visitor Information: Telluride Tourism Board, Telluride Information Center, 700 W. Colorado Avenue, Telluride, CO 81435; telephone (888) 605-2578.

■ Convention Facilities

The Telluride Conference Center is located in neighboring Mountain Village. Since 2012, it has been managed by the Telluride Ski & Golf Company. The Conference Center features more than 20,000 square feet of meeting space

Convention Information: Telluride Conference Center, 580 Mountain Village Blvd., Conference Center Plaza, Telluride, 81435; telephone (970) 369-5120.

■ Transportation

Approaching the City

Telluride Regional Airport, elevation 9,078 feet above sea level, is the highest commercial airport in North America. During normal operations, two commercial airlines provide daily flights from Denver and Phoenix. Airport administration reported 20,573 enplanements in 2012, 22,429 in 2011, and 20,251 in 2010. The nearest airport with major airline service is Montrose Regional Airport, approximately 70 miles north of Telluride. Montrose Regional has service to Denver year-round. Summer service extends to Houston and Dallas–Fort Worth, and winter service to those cities plus Newark, Chicago, Atlanta, Los Angeles, and Phoenix.

Traveling in the City

Telluride does not have any traffic lights; the nearest traffic signal is 45 miles away.

The city's bus system, the Galloping Goose Transit System, is jointly funded by the town of Telluride and San Miguel County. It operates 365 days a year, with buses following six routes. Galloping Goose also provides contract transportation services for nonprofit groups. The Galloping Goose's oldest bus, #101, runs on biodiesel fuel.

The Galloping Goose Transit System was established in 1931. The Galloping Goose operated throughout the region, carrying U.S. Mail, passengers, and freight until the 1950s. Since then, operations have been restricted to

Telluride, with historic buses preserved and on display. Galloping Goose #4 is on display at the San Miguel County Courthouse in Telluride. Goose #5, fully restored and rail worthy, may be seen at the historical museum in Dolores, Colorado. Several other Geese are exhibited at the Colorado Railroad Museum in Golden.

■ Communications

Newspapers and Magazines

The Telluride *Daily Planet,* founded in 1898 as the *Telluride Times,* is an independently owned newspaper serving Telluride and the greater region. The *Daily Planet* is published on Sunday, Tuesday, Wednesday, Thursday and Friday. The paper is distributed to the communities of Telluride, Mountain Village, Ridgway, Norwood, Rico, and other areas of San Miguel and Ouray counties. The *Daily Planet* reaches an estimated 30,000 readers each week in print and online. The *Daily Planet* has earned journalism awards from the Colorado Press Association, including awards for Best News Reporting and Best Layout and Design.

In 1982 the Telluride Times (now the Daily Planet) launched Telluride Magazine. The first issue was successful, and an independent publishing company, Telluride Publishing, was established to produce two issues (summer and winter) each year. In 2008 Telluride Publishing became a division of Big Earth Publishing. The winter issue of *Telluride Magazine* covers the ski season, and the summer issue covers summer activities and the many festivals staged in the Telluride area.

Television and Radio

Founded in 1986, Telluride TV, also known as Telluride Community Television (TCTV), is a non-commercial public access cable television station. The office is located in the Telluride High School. Telluride TV, with a slogan "The Rest of the World Doesn't Get Us," airs on cable channel 12 on Time Warner Cable in Telluride and on Mountain Village Cable in Mountain Village. Telluride TV archives 25 years of town and regional events in its library. A Telluride TV Community Media Center, planned to offer video education courses and to allow community members and students to produce programs, was scheduled to open in 2013; however, fundraising continued into 2014 to support completion of the project.

In 1975 a listener-supported radio station, KOTO, was established. KOTO's radio mission is "to entertain, educate, and inform while reflecting the needs, desires, and diversity of our community." KOTO is affiliated with Public Radio International and National Public Radio.

Media Information: Daily Planet, 307 East Colorado Avenue, P.O. Box 2315, Telluride, CO 81435; telephone (970) 728-9788; fax (970) 728-8061.

Telluride Online

Colorado Historical Society. Available www. coloradohistory.org

San Miguel County. Available www. sanmiguelcounty.org

San Miguel County Historic Preservation Commission. Available openspacerec. sanmiguelcounty.org/Historic.htm

Telluride Council for the Arts & Humanities. Available telluridearts.org

Telluride Foundation. Available http://telluride foundation.org

Telluride Historical Museum. Available www. telluridemuseum.org/

Telluride Visitor's Center. Available www. visittelluride.com/

Town of Telluride. Available www.telluride-co.gov

Wilkinson Public Library. Available www. telluridelibrary.org

BIBLIOGRAPHY

Hanna, Rod, *Colorado's Seasons of Gold* (Steamboat Springs, CO: Hanna Enterprises, LLC, 2010)

Turner, Carol, *Notorious Telluride: Tales from San Miguel County* (Charleston, SC: The History Press, 2010)

Hawaii

The State in Brief

Nickname: Aloha State

Motto: Ua mau ke ea o ka aina i ka pono (The life of the land is perpetuated in righteousness)

Flower: Hibiscus

Bird: Hawaiian goose

Area: 10,932 square miles (2010; U.S. rank 43rd)

Elevation: Ranges from sea level to 13,796 feet above sea level

Climate: Mild, tropical

Admitted to Union: August 21, 1959

Capital: Honolulu

Head Official: Neil Abercrombie (D) (until 2014)

Population
    1990: 1,135,000
    2000: 1,211,537
    2010: 1,360,301
    2012 estimate: 1,362,730
    Percent change, 2000–2010: 12.3%
    U.S. rank in 2012: 40th
    Percent of residents born in state: 54.5% (2012)
    Density: 211.8 people per square mile (2010)
    2012 FBI Crime Index Total: 46,147

Racial and Ethnic Characteristics (2012)
    White: 339,079
    Black or African American: 22,399
    American Indian and Alaska Native: 3,079
    Asian: 527,745
    Native Hawaiian and Pacific Islander: 133,873
    Hispanic or Latino (may be of any race): 122,882
    Other: 336,555

Age Characteristics (2012)
    Population under 5 years old: 88,203
    Population 5 to 19 years old: 248,714
    Percent of population 65 years and over: 14.5%
    Median age: 38.4

Vital Statistics
    Total number of births (2012–13): 19,016
    Total number of deaths (2012–13): 11,433
    AIDS cases reported through 2011: 3,408

Economy
    Major industries: Government, services, finance, agriculture, tourism
    Unemployment rate (2012): 4.2%
    Per capita income (2012): $29,227
    Median household income (2012): $67,492
    Percentage of persons below poverty level (2012): 10.8%
    Income tax rate: 1.4% to 11.00%
    Sales tax rate: 4.0%

Hilo

■ The City in Brief

Founded: 1822 (incorporated, 1911)

Head Official: Mayor William P. Kenoi, County of Hawaii (since 2008; current term expires 2016)

City Population
    1990: 37,808
    2000: 40,759
    2010: 43,263
    2012 estimate: 41,705
    Percent change, 2000–2010: 6.1%

Micropolitan Area Statistical Population
    2000: 148,677
    2010: 185,079
    2012 estimate: 189,191
    Percent change, 2000–2010: 24.5%
    U.S. rank in 2010: 227th

Area: 54 square miles

Elevation: 38 feet above sea level

Average Annual Temperatures: January, 71.4° F; July, 75.9° F; annual average, 73.9° F

Average Annual Precipitation: 126.27 inches of rain

Major Economic Sectors: agriculture, trade, tourism, government

Unemployment Rate: 5.3% (2012)

Per Capita Income: $24,259

Major Colleges and Universities: University of Hawaii at Hilo, Hawaii Community College

Daily Newspaper: *Hawaii Tribune-Herald*

■ Introduction

On the coast of a crescent bay, where the lower foothills of two shield volcanoes, Mauna Loa and Mauna Kea, emerge, one can find the city of Hilo. The second largest city in the state and home to over 40,000 residents, Hilo is the main port of the Island of Hawaii, the largest island in Hawaii. The island of Hawaii is known as the "Big Island" so as to avoid confusion between the name of the island and the state itself. Hilo, the county seat of the County of Hawaii, serves as the business and government center of the Big Island, as well as the shipping and service center of the various industries in the vicinity. With more than 100 inches of rain annually, the city is the rainiest in the United States. The rainfall not only provides for lush greenery, but also encourages the city's agricultural economy, based upon raising tropical flowers, fruits, and nuts. Tourism has also grown rapidly in the "City of Flowers," spurred in part by its proximity to Hawaii Volcanoes National Park, which is 30 miles away. Nonetheless, tourism has affected Hilo much less than many large cities in Hawaii, and Hilo has been able to maintain its laid back, traditional, old Hawaii "Aloha spirit." In recent years the city has attracted retirees and escapees from the faster-paced life on other islands. The city boasts a modern, convenient airport and a deep water harbor, and serves as the transportation hub for the island. The city, whose name means "new moon," is slowly transforming itself from a plantation town whose economy centered on sugar cane to a university town that is attracting a slew of new construction and research dollars. With the addition of the Imiloa Astronomy Center of Hawaii and the Hilo Art Museum in the 2000s, the city continues to create an even more enriching environment than the natural beauty that graces it.

■ Geography and Climate

Because the state of Hawaii does not incorporate its cities, Hilo is technically a census designated place (CDP) according to the U.S. Census Bureau. Hilo is located on

Aerial view of Hilo. *Daniel Stein/Used under license from iStockPhoto.com*

Hilo Bay on the eastern side of the island of Hawaii, 216 miles southeast of Honolulu (on the island of Oahu). Two rivers flow through the city and into the bay: the Wailuku and Wailoa Rivers. The area's topography is mostly sloping, from the tops of the scenic Mauna Kea and Mauna Loa volcano mountains to the sea. The city was partially built upon lava flows from the late nineteenth century. From top to oceanic bottom, Mauna Kea is over 33,000 feet tall and considered the largest mountain in the world, taller than Mauna Everest. While Mauna Kea is considered dormant, Mauna Loa is an active volcano, slowly erupting for at least 700,000 years. Hilo is located less than 30 miles from Kilauea, one of the most active volcanoes on earth, which has been slowly emitting lava since 1983. While the volcano was generally known for its non-explosive eruptions, a crater explosion in 2008, the first explosive event since 1924 and first eruption since 1983, changed the trend, and periodic eruptions continued through 2013. Considered one of the most active volcanoes in the world and the most dangerous in the country, lava flows from Kilauea have been responsible for the slow destruction of many homes since then, often one or a couple at a time. Much of the lava has reached the ocean, enlarging the island of Hawaii by at least 500 acres and growing, making the Big Island

the youngest of the Hawaii island chain. According to the Pacific Tsunami Museum, Hilo's location on the funnel-shaped bay also makes it particularly vulnerable to devastating tsunamis; some have even called Hilo the tsunami capital of the United States.

While the island has everything from lush rain forests to volcanic deserts and snow-capped mountaintops to black sand beaches, the Hilo region has a warm tropical rainforest climate and experiences abundant rainfall without droughts or shortages that can trouble other parts of the island. Hilo is one of the wettest cities in the world; Hilo receives rain for an average of 275 days a year. At some weather stations in Hilo, the annual rainfall is over 200 inches; at some points on the island, annual rainfall can reach 300 inches. The rain, which generally falls during the night, keeps the area fresh and green. It also results in many waterfalls. Hilo's rich soil is conducive to the growth of a variety of diversified agricultural products. Hilo's weather is generally static throughout the year, with little change in seasons. July and August are the warmest months, when temperatures reach daily highs above 80 degrees and lows in the low-60s. While January and February are the cooler months, daily highs and lows are also around 80 degrees and the low 60s, respectively. At the summit of Mauna Kea the temperature ranges from about 31 to 43 degrees. In winter there is frost above the 4,000-foot level and snow above the 10,000-foot level.

Area: 54 square miles

Elevation: 38 feet above sea level

Average Temperatures: January, 71.4° F; July, 75.9° F; annual average, 73.9° F

Average Annual Precipitation: 126.27 inches of rain

■ History

Ancient Hawaii to 1810

Oral history, in lieu of harder archaeological evidence, makes many references to the people of Hilo, living along the Wailuku and Wailoa rivers in the time of "ancient Hawaii"—the period before 1810, when Kamehameha the Great united the Hawaiian islands. The Hawaii islands have been inhabited for centuries, and the Big Island is no different, but Hilo is the oldest city in the Hawaiian archipelago. Polynesians arrived in the Hilo area in the 1100s, establishing farming and fishing communities. A rich island culture developed, diversified by the arrival of many Asian ancestors, in addition to English explorers. In 1796, Kamehameha the Great came to Hilo to build 800 war canoes to help him conquer the Hawaiian islands and include the city in the new constitutional monarchy.

Popular Trading Post Attracts Missionaries, Scientists

The city of Hilo has been a trading place from the time Hawaiian tribes came up the Wailuku River, which separated Hilo from Hamakua, and shouted out what goods they had to offer. In the 1800s, although Honolulu reigned supreme as the principal whaling base of the Pacific, Hilo came in third behind Koloa as alternative anchorages. Foreign ships found anchorages between the coral heads of Hilo's wide bay, and thereafter the dredging of a channel permitted steamships to enter the area.

Missionaries settled Hilo in 1822, teaching reading and writing to the locals. The region was first studied scientifically by Lord Byron and his men of the ship *Blonde* in 1825. Titus Cona, a missionary at Hilo, was the foremost volcanologist of his time and made frequent visits to the volcano.

Hilo Develops an Economy and a City

During the 1800s, trade in sandalwood was a major economic driver, but collapsed when the resources were exhausted. Instead, residents turned to the sugarcane. Metcalf Plantation, started on the outskirts of Hilo, was the first major sugar cane plantation in the area, and its first crop was harvested in 1859. The beginnings of Hilo's tourist industry also date back to the 1870s when Hilo was one of a number of sites on a standard sightseeing route. Particularly popular were visits to the volcano of Kilauea east of Mauna Loa.

By the late 1800s and early 1900s, Hilo's sugar industry was booming and the city became the commercial trading center of the island of Hawaii. This attracted many immigrants, as Chinese, Japanese, Filipinos, Koreans, and Portuguese workers in Hilo were recruited long before Hawaii was a State or even a territory of the United States as contractors on sugar cane and pineapple plantations. A railroad connected Hilo with other parts of the island. Hilo became the seat of Hawaii County in 1905 and was incorporated as a city in 1911.

Hilo Beset by Volcanic Eruptions and Tidal Waves

Hilo is known by some as the U.S. tsunami capital. In March 1868, a volcanic eruption resulted in formidable destruction. The city experienced close calls from the eruptions of Mauna Loa in 1942 and in 1984. Two tsunamis have also caused major damage. In 1946, a tsunami sent tidal waves sweeping through half the town inland and dragging the remains out to sea. Hilo rebuilt and constructed a stone breakwater across the bay to protect the harbor. Another tidal wave destroyed a major part of the waterfront business district and the city's beachfront in 1960, sweeping 61 Hiloites out to sea. Civic leaders, vowing that such destruction would never recur, drained the lowland crescent and raised a new hill 26 feet above sea level and mounted a new government and commercial center. Today, however, the beach is still gone. In 1984, Mauna Loa erupted and lava flows nearly reached Hilo.

Aloha Spirit in the Turn of a Modern Century

Hilo remained largely coastal until it began to expand inland in the 1960s. The city's downtown became popularized as a cultural center. Hilo's historic cultural diversity also contributed to the city's developing charm as a tourist destination. Japanese, Polynesian, Filipino, Chinese, Puerto Rican, Portuguese, and Russian residents make up the city's mixed-race culture of today. Since their arrival, Japanese people have had an important influence on the city, from serving on the city council to starting businesses.

In the latter half of the twentieth century, many sugar plantations began to downsize, with many shutting down in the 1990s. Hilo turned to the state's largest economic driver: tourism. Plantations were turned into resorts. While tourism is apparent, the city still strives to preserve its presence as one of the few surviving examples of a Hawaiian plantation town, and the Hilo Downtown Improvement Association serves to provide leadership in developing a safe and attractive community. Known for traditional Hawaiian festivals and dance, Hilo is a more easygoing alternative to other tourist sites in the state, maintaining the friendly "aloha" spirit of the Polynesian culture of its ancestors.

■ Population Profile

Micropolitan Area Statistical Population

2000: 148,677
2010: 185,079
2012 estimate: 189,191
Percent change, 2000–2010: 24.5%
U.S. rank in 2010: 227th

City Residents

1990: 37,808
2000: 40,759
2010: 43,263
2012 estimate: 41,705
Percent change, 2000–2010: 6.1%

Density: 810.3 people per square mile

Racial and ethnic characteristics

White: 6,646
Black or African American: 211
American Indian and Alaskan Native: 120
Asian: 15,180
Native Hawaiian and Other Pacific Islander: 5,057
Hispanic or Latino (may be of any race): 4,149
Other: 14,491

Percent of residents born in state: 78.7%

Age characteristics

Population under 5 years old: 2,104
Population 5 to 9 years old: 2,713
Population 10 to 14 years old: 1,973
Population 15 to 19 years old: 2,891
Population 20 to 24 years old: 3,255
Population 25 to 34 years old: 4,643
Population 35 to 44 years old: 4,303
Population 45 to 54 years old: 5,377
Population 55 to 59 years old: 3,217
Population 60 to 64 years old: 3,231
Population 65 to 74 years old: 3,647
Population 75 to 84 years old: 2,694
Population 85 years and over: 1,657
Median age: 42.3

Births (2010–11 Micropolitan Area)

Total number: 2,376

Deaths (2010–11 Micropolitan Area)

Total number: 1,397

Money income (2012)

Per capita income: $24,259
Median household income: $49,065
Total households: 14,352

Number of households with income of ...

less than $10,000: 1,443
$10,000 to $14,999: 896
$15,000 to $24,999: 1,385
$25,000 to $34,999: 1,571
$35,000 to $49,999: 1,997
$50,000 to $74,999: 2,236
$75,000 to $99,999: 1,780
$100,000 to $149,999: 1,973
$150,000 to $199,999: 699
$200,000 or more: 372

Percent of families below poverty level: 16.8%

■ Municipal Government

The Big Island has one governmental unit: the County of Hawaii. There is no formal government at the city or municipal level, although Hilo is the county seat, and serves as the headquarters for all government activities on the Island. Hilo is governed by the County of Hawaii, which has a mayor-council government. The mayor is elected for up to two four-year terms and nine council members representing each of the county's nine districts are elected to two-year terms. Hilo has two council members, serving the North Hilo and South Hilo districts. Mayor Harry Kim, first elected to office in 2000, is the first mayor of Korean descent in the United States.

Head Official: Mayor William P. Kenoi, County of Hawaii (since 2008; current term expires 2016)

Total Number of City Employees: 2,357 (2013)

City Information: Hawaii County, 25 Aupuni Street, Hilo, HI 96720; telephone (808) 961-8255.

■ Economy

Major Industries and Commercial Activity

While government is one of Hilo's major employers, the Hilo area has a diversified economy that includes agriculture, tourism, aquaculture, livestock, trade, education, and government.

The Big Island was a world center for the production of raw sugar from 1876 to 1994, when the last plantation closed. Today, the tremendous rainfall in the Hilo area produces a genuine paradise of flowers, from exotic anthuriums and orchids to tropical blooms of all sorts. As the "City of Flowers," Hilo, which is the center for the world's largest tropical flower industry, exports fresh cut flowers, spray, and potted plants from various farmer cooperatives and flower farms. The island's orchid agriculture is the largest in the state, and resulted in the unofficial nickname "The Orchid Isle." About 1 million acres of the island's total 2.4 million acres are devoted to agriculture, an over $500 million per-year industry.

Livestock is an economic mainstay, with sales of beef, hogs, dairy and poultry products, and honey totaling more than $25 million annually. Cattle ranches, including Parker Ranch, one of the largest in the country (150,000 acres), produce the majority of the state's beef supply About 440 cattle farms are run on the Big Island with a value of about $27 million; most are shipped to the U.S. mainland and Canada for processing. The Big Island is Hawaii's largest producer of honey, with its honey and queen bee industries producing about 900,000 pounds a year.

Aquaculture, another important industry on the island, has been a mainstay of economic life since the first Polynesian settlers came to the Big Island. Abalone, carp, catfish, clams, flounder, milkfish, moi, mullet, ornamental fish, oyster, prawns, sea cucumber, seaweed, shrimp, snails, sturgeon, tilapia, and rainbow trout are among the fish and seafood harvested. Several types of microalgae are also cultivated for pharmaceutical and nutritional products.

One of Hilo's more famous crop is the macadamia nut. The Hilo area is home to Mauna Loa Macadamia Nut Company, the world's largest processor of macadamia nuts. Despite serious agricultural problems ranging from drought to harmful bacteria, the Big Island produces almost the whole of the state's production of fruit (other than pineapples), including bananas, guavas, oranges, tangerines, and avocados; the bulk of the state's macadamia nuts and papaya; the vast majority of its coffee; crops such as ginger, Chinese cabbage, leaf lettuce, greenhouse tomatoes, and cucumbers; and orchids, anthuriums, and other nursery products for domestic and foreign markets. A recent problem for Hilo's agricultural industry has been the infestation of the coqui frog. The increasing population of this amphibian has threatened the island's ecosystem. It is a community effort to control and prevent further coqui infestations; coqui control classes are held in partnership with the State of Hawaii Department of Agriculture.

Until recently, the tourism industry had all but bypassed the town of Hilo due to its lack of a decent beach and the annual surplus of rainfall. Since Hilo had never been a tourist destination, the town retained its historic character and has not suffered from the infrastructure problems associated with high-rises and big-city development. However, it just may be that historic character that is attracting new visitors to the city. In 2013 the county experienced a 7 percent increase in the total number of visitors to the island from the prior

fiscal year. More significantly, spending for this sector has been increasing since the beginning of 2010.

Leisure and hospitality services grew in the new century and comprised the largest of the major industrial sectors in the area throughout the 2000s. The number of visitors to Hilo, both domestic and international, averages over 40,000 visitors per month, with over 700,000 per year, not including transient general tourists of the Big Island.

Hilo's Foreign Trade Zone (FTZ) is ideally situated adjacent to Hilo Harbor and the Hilo International Airport, less than a mile from downtown Hilo. This 31-acre site is the first such zone designated by the State of Hawaii to attract manufacturers to Hawaii. The FTZ allows companies locating there to import parts for assembly and export the finished product without paying import duties. It was given a boost when NIC Americas, Inc., became its first tenant. NIC Americas manufactures a device that uses electrical arcing to destroy used needles from health care facilities.

Hilo, like much of Hawaii, provides scenic backdrops sometimes used as a backdrop for television, film, and commercial productions. While much of the entertainment industry filming happens on other islands, Hilo and the Big Island are working toward increasing its entertainment industry. Hilo is also known for a unique astronomical research market, where telescopes and space research stations are operated on the summit of Mauna Kea, where atmospheric clarity is excellent and there is little light (and air) pollution.

The county's unique geographic characteristics have attracted scientists in the fields of astronomy, meteorology, volcanology, and agriculture/aquaculture. Significant investments have been made in scientific research. Eleven facilities with an annual budget of $75 million support 527 county-based staff.

Given its special connection to the purity of its natural surroundings, Hilo is also attempting to build a "green economy," in the 2000s and beyond. According to the county, on Hawaii Island, about $47 million have been awarded to preserve or create additional jobs in green sectors such as: restoration of watersheds and national park facilities, energy efficiency retrofits of federal buildings, solar energy installations, residential energy evaluations, and mass transit improvements. The local university also provides programs in sustainability, such as specializations in agroecology and sustainable livestock production.

Items and goods produced: flowers, fruit, cattle, fish, macadamia nuts, coffee

Incentive Programs—New and Existing Companies

Local programs: Local incentives and business assistance is offered through the Department of Research and Development of the County of Hawaii. The department annually solicits proposals for projects or activities that support sustainable economic development for the county in agriculture, tourism, film, and new businesses. Community-based nonprofit organizations in Hilo can receive free access to the County's eCivis Grants Network, a grant and grant training database. The county also has the Big Island Film Office, which helps market the Hawaii Island for film productions and to develop its workforce. The U.S. Department of Agriculture's Rural Development Hawaii State Office is located in Hilo, providing financial assistance to rural businesses.

State programs: Most business incentives are offered at the state level. These include direct financial incentives such as Industrial Development Bonds, a Capital Loan Program, customized industrial training, and investment of public funds in return for equity or ownership positions in private businesses. Tax incentives are also offered along with the Hawaii Urban Enterprise Zones Program. Other tax incentives for businesses on the Big Island include no personal property taxes; no taxes on inventory, equipment, furniture and machinery; no tax on goods manufactured for export; no unincorporated business tax; and only one business tax for banks and financial institutions. High technology businesses can also take advantage of unparalleled tax breaks through legislative initiatives and the State Foreign Trade Zone program and Enterprise Zone Partnership. Hawaii's economy relies heavily on small business entrepreneurs, as they account for over 96 percent of all businesses in the state. Hawaii's Small Business Development Center Network is a partnership of the University of Hawaii at Hilo and the U.S. Small Business Administration. With the aim of helping small business become established or expand, the Network offers one-on-one counseling, seminars, workshops and conferences. Three separate tax credits can be applied to film and television productions: the motion picture, digital media, and film production income tax credits, which range from 15 to 20 percent.

Job training programs: The Workforce Development Division of Hawaii's Department of Labor and Industrial Relations oversees One-Stop Workforce Assistance Centers, a job placement and training system to help people find work and employers find suitable workers, and the Employment & Training Fund (ETF), a job skills upgrade program for current workers. Employers can receive customized training grants for their workplace or they can nominate a current worker for an established training course. One-Stop Workforce Assistance Centers provide free services to job seekers and employers, including job search assistance, personal career planning services, training opportunities. Hire Net Hawaii provides support and a library resource center.

Development Projects

In 2013 the County of Hawaii acquired 217 acres in Kona, between Kohanaiki Shores and the Natural Energy Laboratory of Hawai'i pursuant to its Public Access, Open Space, and Natural Resource Preservation program. The purchase helps preserve ocean quality and contribute to a healthy reef. The County anticipates preserving 'O'oma in its current natural condition as a buffer between the mauka urban area and the ocean, while allowing access for passive recreation and subsistence fishing. Since 2008, the County has acquired 1,247 acres of open space.

Astronomy continues to be a major factor in the success of the County's economy, with an estimated nearly 500 new jobs opening up through 2023 to meet the needs of the current observatories and the creation of new jobs with the development of the Thirty Meter Telescope (TMT) by the TMT Observatory Corporation. Permits have been issued for the TMT, but a final appeal has been lodged with the courts. Once construction begins, it is anticipated that the construction and equipment costs will be $1.2 billion, and the TMT will have an annual operating budget of $27 million.

Since the fall of the Big Island's sugar plantations in the mid-1990s, "Hilo has transformed itself from a plantation town to a university town," according to Richard West, executive director of the Hawaii Island Economic Development Board, in *Hawaii Business Magazine.* Hilo has seen the addition of several new science and technology developments in the early 2000s. One of the largest projects was the Imiloa Astronomy Center of Hawaii (formerly the Mauna Kea Astronomy Education Center) in 2005, a $28 million facility that showcases exhibits that focus on the connection between Hawaiian culture and astronomy. The center opened in the University of Hawaii at Hilo's University Park of Science and Technology. Additional research dollars came to Hilo in the late 2000s with the opening of the U.S. Forest Service Institute of Pacific Islands Forestry, a $12 million forest research laboratory. The laboratory is one of few that studies invasive plants in native ecosystems-important to the region, as invasive exotic species of plants are a major threat to Pacific Island forests.

The U.S. Department of Agriculture's Agricultural Research Service broke ground on the second phase of a $60 million research lab in 2010; the second phase involves additional offices, screen houses, and head houses. In three additional phases, the Pacific Basin Agricultural Research Center (PBARC) will eventually encompass 120,000 square feet of laboratories, an administration building, greenhouse facilities, and insect rearing facilities. In 2010, the state contributed $5.7 in "green" economy dollars to the project. The first phase of the new PBARC facility-a $19 million, 35,000-square-foot office and laboratory building-officially opened in 2007.

Economic Development Information: County of Hawaii Department of Research and Development, 25 Aupuni Street, Hilo, HI 96720; telephone (808) 961-8366. Hawaii Department of Labor and Industrial Relations; telephone (808) 586-8842. Hilo Hamakua Community Development Corporation, County of Hawaii, 25 Aupuni Street, Hilo, HI 96720.

Commercial Shipping

Hilo is one of the Big Island's main ports of entry. Hilo Harbor is a deep-water port with an entrance depth of 35 feet. The harbor basin has a length of 2,300 feet and a width of 1,400 feet. There are 2,787 linear feet of piers, and storage area totals 122,000 square feet of shedded and 492,000 square feet of open space. Combined cargo handling and storage area totals over 595,000 square feet. An expansion plan scheduled to continue through 2020 recommends more passenger terminals at Hilo Harbor to accommodate the growing number of cruise passengers.

Hilo International Airport provides cargo services via Aloha Cargo and Hawaiian Airlines. It is capable of handling fully loaded wide-bodied aircraft. Despite being smaller than Kona, overall, Hilo's airport handles over 22,000 U.S. tons of cargo annually, only slightly less than the larger Kona airport. Kona International Airport cargo operators include Aloha Air, Big Island Parcel Service, Inc., Commodity Freight Forwarders, Delta Airlines, Inc., Direct Freight Service, FedEx, Hawaiian Airlines, Japan Airlines, United Airlines, and UPS.

Labor Force and Employment Outlook

The Big Island is the most diversified of the neighbor island economies. As a result, it is buffered to some extent when any one industry lags. Nevertheless, despite recent improvements, unemployment remains a concern. In 2013 the county's unemployment rate (8.3 percent) was almost a full percent lower than that of the prior year (9.2 percent). Construction jobs have recovered by one-third of the decline experienced in recent years, and private building permits are up 25 percent in the first part of 2013 compared to the same period the year before. Astronomy continues to be a major provider of jobs, with an estimated 500 new jobs opening up through 2023 to meet the needs of the current observatories and the creation of new jobs with the development of the Thirty Meter Telescope (TMT) by the TMT Observatory Corporation.

The following is a summary of data regarding the 2012 Hilo labor force:

Size of civilian labor force: 19,379

Number of workers employed in . . .

    agriculture and mining: 428
    construction: 918
    manufacturing: 657

    wholesale trade: 267
    retail trade: 2,330
    transportation: 1,152
    information systems: 326
    finance: 888
    professional administration: 1,480
    education and social services: 4,624
    arts and leisure: 1,680
    other: 972
    public administration: 1,954

Average hourly earnings of production workers: $17.91

Unemployment rate: 5.3% (2012)

Employers

Largest county employers (2013)

	Number of employees
State of Hawaii	7,962
County of Hawaii	2,630
United States Government	1,429
Hilton Waikoloa Village	935
KTA Super Stores	750
Walmart	741
Four Seasons Resort Hualalai	650
The Fairmont Orchid, Hawaii	616
Mauna Kea Beach Hotel	513
Mauna Lani Resort (Operations) Inc.	450

Cost of Living

While tourist costs are lower in Hilo than in other Hawaiian locales, the cost of living in Hilo is much higher than the national average. This effect may be attributed to the high value of island living for those interested in coastal living, particularly in the Pacific islands.

The following is a summary of data regarding several key cost of living factors in the area.

2013 ACCRA Average House Price: $485,920

2013 ACCRA Cost of Living Index: 149

State income tax rate: 1.4% to 11.00%

State sales tax rate: 4.0%

Local income tax rate: None

Local sales tax rate: None

Property tax rate: $6.15 per $1,000 assessed value (2013)

Economic Information: County of Hawaii, Department of Economic Development and Tourism, 25 Aupuni Street Room 219, Hilo, HI 96720; telephone (808) 961-8366; fax (808) 935-1205. Hawaii Island Chamber of Commerce, 106 Kamehameha Ave, Hilo, HI 96720; telephone (808) 935-7178; fax (808) 961-4435; email hicc@interpac.net.

■ Education and Research

Elementary and Secondary Schools

Hawaii is the only state with a single, unified statewide school system, comprised of seven districts, one of which is the Hawaii District, which covers the island of Hawaii. An elected board of education formulates educational policy and supervises the public school system. Ten members are elected from Oahu and a total of three from all other islands. One non-voting student member from grades 7–12 is appointed.

All Department schools are rolled into what is known as a complex: a high school, and the elementary and middle schools that feed into it. Anywhere from two to four complexes are grouped into a complex area, which has its own complex area superintendent and support staff. The complex area superintendent reports to the deputy superintendent in the state office.

The Hilo Bay area is served by the Hilo-Laupahoehoe-Waiakea complex area, with three even smaller districts within it. The Hilo complex maintains eight elementary and intermediate schools and one high school. Hilo has three charter schools. The Waiakea complex maintains three elementary, one intermediate, and one high school. The Laupahoehoe complex offers one joint intermediate and high school. The major complex also offers the Hilo Community School for alternative adult education. There are six major private schools in Hilo. They include: E Makaala School; Haili Christian School; Hale Aloha Nazarene School; Kamehamaha Schools; Mauna Loa School; and St. Joseph School of Hilo.

The following is a summary of data regarding the Hawaii Department of Education.

Total enrollment: 179,601

Number of facilities

 total: 204
 elementary schools: 101
 junior high schools: 55
 high schools: 41
 other: 7

Student/teacher ratio: 15.8:1

Teacher salaries

 average (statewide): $55,063

Funding per pupil: $12,004

Public Schools Information: Hawaii State Department of Education, 390 Miller St. Honolulu, HI 96813; telephone (808) 586-3230.

Colleges and Universities

The city of Hilo is the home to the University of Hawaii at Hilo, one of 10 branches of the state university system. The school serves over 4,000 students and offers two- and four-year programs in areas such as agriculture, arts and sciences, and vocational and technical training, with particular renown in its marine biology, volcanology, and astronomy programs. Their College of Hawaiian Language is the only school in the country to offer a graduate program in the study of indigenous languages. The university's College of Pharmacy is the only pharmacy school in the state accredited by the Accreditation Council for Pharmacy Education. *U.S. News & World Report* has ranked UH Hilo among the top 10 for both ethnic diversity and the low percentage of students with debt at graduation. Hawaii Community College is also part of the state system. Less than one mile from UH Hilo, the community college shares some of its facilities with the larger university and offers career and technical programs in addition to general academic courses. Akamai University is an alternative, private online graduate school designed for mid-career adult students.

Libraries and Research Centers

The Hilo Public Library, part of the Hawaii State Public Library System, contains books, periodicals, videotapes, sound recordings, and provides internet access to its patrons. It is the largest public library on the island and the second busiest in circulation statewide. They are open Tuesday through Saturday. Other libraries in the city include the Hilo Hospital Medical Library, which features consumer health materials; the State Supreme Court Third Circuit Court Law Library; and the University of Hawaii at Hilo Libraries, whose system holds more than 250,000 volumes, 1,650 periodical subscriptions, and 225,000 microfiche titles.

Because of its mid-Pacific location near the equator, the Big Island and the Hilo area is especially known for its clear skies and high visibility, making it an ideal location for astronomical observations. University Park of Science and Technology on the campus of the University of Hawaii at Hilo (UH-Hilo) is home to several U.S. and international observing facilities. They include the British-Canada-Netherlands Joint Astronomy Centre, Gemini North Telescope, Caltech Submillimeter Observatory, Subaru National Astronomical Observatory of Japan, University of Hawaii Institute for Astronomy, and Smithsonian Submillimeter Array. The Imiloa Astronomy Center of Hawaii (formerly the Mauna Kea Astronomy Education Center) is a state-of-the-art interpretive research center and planetarium, located in University Park. Over 10 nations have telescopes set up in the area, including the world's largest telescope. The U.S. Geological Survey's Hawaiian Volcano Observatory is located at the rim of Kilauea, 30 miles from Hilo; Kilauea is said to be the most studied volcano in the world.

Public Library Information: Hilo Public Library, 300 Waianuenue Avenue, P.O. Box 647, Hilo, HI 96720; telephone (808) 933-8888.

■ Health Care

Hilo Medical Center is the city's primary hospital with 264 beds offering general medical, surgical and obstetric care, as well as emergency services. Other east Hawaii medical facilities include the Hale Ho'ola Hamakua long-term care facility in Honokaa and the Ka'u Hospital in Pahala. Ka'u is a rural health clinic providing acute and long term care in a 21-bed critical access facility. The North Hawaii Community Hospital in Kameula serves the 30,000 residents in the northern region of the Big Island. These facilities have led to growth in the island's medical profession and to an expectation that the region will become the health and medical center of the Pacific Rim. The VA Hilo Community Based Outpatient Clinic offers services to U.S. veterans. With 95 beds, the hospital provides long-term care and adult day-care.

■ Recreation

Sightseeing

Rainbows often hover over the charming city of Hilo. The city blends its traditional Hawaii culture with the modern expectations of tourism, surrounded by a plethora of natural beauty, the main attraction in the area.

Hilo is known as the gateway to Hawaii Volcanoes National Park, a mere 30 miles away from the center of the city. A popular attraction, the park is the most visited site in the state, with almost 3.7 million visitors in fiscal year 2013 representing an almost 7 percent increase from the prior fiscal year. At Hawaii Volcanoes National Park, a powerful active volcano can be glimpsed firsthand by car or helicopter at the fire pit crater of Kilauea. Rangers can provide maps and directions for optimum viewing of the volcano and for walks or hikes along 150 miles of trail. Educational programs and seminars are available to the public and include talks on topics such as endangered and unique local animal species and technology used to monitor volcanoes.

The Imiloa Astronomy Center, a 12,000 foot gallery set up among three titanium cone domes representing the three largest mountains on Hawaii Island, houses interactive exhibits showcasing Hawaii's astrological connection. Exhibits include a "walk" through a koa (native hardwood) forest and an IMAX-style movie presentation that makes viewers feel like they're flying through space.

The natural grandeur of the volcanoes is supplemented by the tropical rainforest that surrounds it. Trails lead sightsee-ers to waterfalls, such as the 442 foot Akaka Falls and nearby 100 foot Kahuna Falls, about 8 miles from Hilo. From Wailuku River State Park, visitors can see Rainbow Falls, which provides a view of cascading water surrounded by flowers, fruits, and wild ginger. Nearby the Boiling Pots are turbulent rapids with deep, swirling pools and falls. Coconut Island, just offshore from Liliuokalani Park, contains picnic tables and shelters and is often used for local cultural events. Leleiwi Beach Park, one of few beaches of the Hilo area, provides another ideal picnic spot and a good place for swimming, snorkeling, surfing, and netfishing since its seawall offers easy access to the ocean. The park's Richardson Ocean Center is a free marine life interpretive center.

The Hawaii Tropical Botanical Garden, just a little over eight miles north of Hilo, provides views of hundreds of waterfalls and numerous varieties of flowers and native animals. The Nani Mau Gardens feature 20 acres of flowers, fruit trees, walking paths, pools and waterfalls. The World Botanical Gardens, north of Hilo, is home to some 5,000 species and the 300 foot Umauma Falls. The Pana 'Ewa Rainforest Zoo and Gardens claims to be the only natural tropical rainforest zoo in the United States. It is part of the Pana 'Ewa Recreational Complex, which also has an equestrian center. The Nani Mau Gardens claims to host every flowering plant in Hawaii.

The Hilo-Hamakua Heritage Coast Drive, organized by the Hawaii Island Economic Development Department, provides a free guide to historic sites and museums, as well as provide an introduction to the scenic and culture-rich region along the Hawaii Belt Road in the Hilo area. A drive down Banyan Drive offers views of tree-lined lanes with 50-year-old banyan trees planted by President Franklin D. Roosevelt and other celebrities of the times. Old Mamalahoa Highway Scenic Drive, five miles north of the city, follows the Hamakua Coast through beautiful rainforest jungles with scenic views of the coast.

After enjoying the natural sights, visitors can delight in the town itself. Downtown Hilo is a small, quaint neighborhood, with rows of wooden clapboard and stucco buildings and corrugated tin overhangs covering the sidewalks. A walk through town reveals flower and fruit stalls, fish markets, butcher shops, soda fountains, seed shops, and luncheonettes. Hilo has many magnificent gardens and parks within the city.

The center of the historic downtown is Kalakaua Park, a grassy square with a large banyan tree, a statue of the king, and a reflecting pool. On one side of the square is the 1919 Federal building, which combines

Neo-Classical and Spanish Mission characteristics. Opposite the Federal Building is the East Hawaii Cultural Center. Other buildings of interest are the Zen Buddhist Temple, Taishoji Soto Mission, and the Haili Church, built in 1857 by missionaries from New England. Lilioukalani Gardens is an elaborate 30 acre oriental park at the edge of the bay. It is designed and maintained in authentic Japanese style. This lovely landscape is the largest formal oriental park outside of Japan.

The Naha Stone, a gigantic stone sitting in front of the Hilo Public Library, is said to have been upended by King Kamehameha with his bare hands. Legend has it that only a chief of royal blood can budge it at all and anyone who can turn it over is a potential island king.

Visitors can watch fishermen pull in their daily weekday catch, then follow them to the Suisan Fish Market. The Suisan Fish Market Auction is a multilingual auction, held Monday through Saturday, of tuna and other tropical fish and seafood delicacies. On Wednesdays and Saturdays the Hilo Farmers' Market features breadfruit, papaya, avocados, stalks of ginger and other tropical flowers, as well as craft and gift items from more than 100 area farmers and crafters. Visitors can also tour the world famous Maunalao Macadamia Nut Company for an insider's look at the factory and processing plant-not to mention a few samples.

Arts and Culture

The East Hawaii Cultural Center features changing art exhibits and dance and musical performances. The University of Hawaii-Hilo Performing Arts Center is the primary center for performing arts in the area. The theater seats 600 and each season hosts over 150 performances including dance, mime, lectures, and children's programs. The Hawaii County Band provides music for special community functions throughout the county. The Culture and Arts Section of the County of Hawaii also offers courses in various traditional dances and art in Hilo, assisting in retaining the unique Hawaiian cultural traditions.

The Palace Theater in downtown Hilo has been entertaining residents since 1925. In addition to plays and musical productions, every Wednesday, the "Hawai'iana Live" program provides a 45 minute peak into the history and traditions of the Hawaiian culture through storytelling, film, music, oli and hula. The Lyman Mission House and Museum, built in 1839, is the oldest wooden structure in Hilo. The restored house is furnished with period antiques that reflect the time when early Christian missionaries lived on the island. Hilo is rich in Polynesian, Asian, and some western culture.

An attached museum features exhibits of Stone Age implements, feather leis, a large house made of grass, and various artifacts from Japan, Portugal, Korea, and the Philippines. The museum's Earth Heritage Gallery showcases the island's natural history including specimens of volcanic minerals and Hawaiian land shells, and the Island Heritage Gallery showcases native history and culture. Part of this cultural narrative can also be seen in the churches in Hilo. The Portuguese community is represented by the Victorian-era Central Christian Church. The Latin St. Joseph's Catholic Church is said to have been influenced by "cowboys" who immigrated as cattle herders from Spanish California. Hilo Hongwanji Temple is a Japanese Buddhist center. Several churches provide services in Hawaiian and English.

The Pacific Tsunami Museum in Downtown Hilo provides educational exhibits about tsunamis, which have caused more damage in Hilo than anywhere on all the Hawaiian Islands. The Hilo Art Museum, founded by resident Ted Coombs, opened in 2007 with a small permanent collection featuring original pieces by Picasso, Salvador Dali, and several local artists.

Festivals and Holidays

In historic Downtown Hilo, the town hosts the annual, world renowned Merrie Monarch Festival each spring. There, hula troupes from around the islands, the country, and sometimes from Asia come to compete in the feature event: an internationally acclaimed, prestigious hula competition. Started in 1971, the week-long festival also offers a crafts fair, an art show, hula shows, and a grand parade through Hilo town. Hilo welcomes the Chinese New Year in February with a festival in Kalakaua Park featuring food, crafts, art, exhibitions, demonstrations, fireworks, and traditional dancers. The Kona Brewers Festival, on the other side of the island, in March showcases 60 types of beer and chefs from 25 local restaurants preparing tropical culinary creations. Bluegrass, Hawaiian, and rock music, a "trash fashion show," hula and fire dancers are also part of the festivities. The Annual Parker Ranch Horseraces & Rodeo is a Fourth of July celebration. Festivities at the rodeo include children's activities, food, and paniolo (Hawaiian cowboys) competing in traditional rodeo events.

Sports for the Spectator

Hilo does not have any major professional sports teams. The University of Hawaii at Hilo Vulcans offer intercollegiate basketball, volleyball, baseball, and softball competitions.

Sports for the Participant

Water sports reign supreme in Hilo and include fishing, scuba diving, snorkeling, freediving, and sailing. Also popular are hunting, horseback riding, mountain biking, and other outdoor activities. The Big Island offers black, white, and green sand beaches; among them are Leleiwi Beach Park, a black sand beach that offers swimming, snorkeling and fishing, and Onekahakaha Beach Park, the city's only white sand beach with a safe inlet for swimming. The best surfing is found off Leleiwi and

Richardson beaches. Protected inlets in this area create shallow pools free from the characteristically large currents. Attracts sea turtles, making it a popular snorkeling location to see them. Southern swells. For experienced surfers only. One of the oldest surf contests on the Big Island is the Quiksilver-Kamaaina Nissan Big Island Pro AM Surfing Trials. Held on the bayfront in downtown Hilo, amateur surf athletes use this open tournament as a platform toward a professional surfing career.

Two golf courses are located in the town of Hilo-the Hilo Municipal Golf Course and the Naniloa Golf Club. Several more public and semi-private courses are a short drive away. Skiing is occasionally possible atop Mauna Kea. The County also offers the Ho'olulu Complex, where reservations can be made for the Afook-Chinen Civic Auditorium, Walter Victor Baseball Complex, Dr. Francis F.C. Wong Stadium, Aunty Sally Kaleohano's Lu`au Hale, Edith Kanakaole Multi-Purpose Stadium, and Hilo Drag Strip.

Shopping and Dining

Hilo offers a variety of shopping opportunities, ranging from national chain stores to bookstalls and specialty shops that carry such items as Hawaiian handicrafts, wooden bowls, jewelry, and native furniture. The major shopping centers in the city include the multimillion-dollar Prince Kuhio Plaza shopping center, Hilo Shopping Center, and Puainako Town Center, as well as the revitalized "Main Street" of downtown Hilo. Hilo's Bayfront area along Kamehameha Avenue is home to shops in historic buildings featuring native Hawaiian art and authentic Hawaiian wear. The East Hawaii Cultural Center is a good spot to find authentic, locally made Hawaiian gifts and souvenirs such as books, cards, jewelry, sculptures, and wood objects.

Downtown Hilo is overflowing with casual eateries; many are closed for a few hours in the middle of the afternoon. Trendy restaurants interject the many ethnic restaurants in the area, particularly many Japanese restaurants. In addition, Hilo's residents and visitors enjoy a variety of dining spots that feature Cajun, Mexican, Italian, Thai, Filipino, Chinese, Hawaiian, and traditional American fare. The fresh catch of the day is forever popular with visitors, especially the Aholehole, or Hawaiian flagtail, a reef fish raised in island ponds. Ahi (tuna), Mahi-Mahi and Opakapaka (pink snapper) are also served in area restaurants. Suman, a Filipino sticky-rice sweet wrapped in a banana leaf and cooked in coconut milk, is a favorite dish sold by street vendors in Hilo. Café Pesto is a popular local restaurant that features fresh local Hawaiian Regional foods. Other unique dining spots include an espresso bar featuring pure Kona coffee and various places with evening luaus.

Visitor Information: Big Island Visitors Bureau, 250 Keawe Street, Hilo, HI 96720; telephone (808) 961-5797; fax (808) 961-2126. Destination Hilo, 106 Kamehameha Ave, Hilo, HI 96720; telephone (808) 969-4999; fax (808) 969-4999.

■ Convention Facilities

The county of Hawaii's Hoolulu Park Complex provides the Afook-Chinen Civic Auditorium, with 11,342 square feet that can accommodate 3,550 people theater-style, 1,000 people classroom-style, and 500 people banquet-style. The Conference Center at the University of Hawaii at Hilo can host groups as small as 25 and as large as 600, with reception facilities for 1,000 people. The Edith Kanakaole Multipurpose Pavilion, with 18,720 square feet of space, can seat 4,500 people theater-style, 2,000 people for a reception, and 750 people banquet-style. The Seven Seas Luau House's 5,000 square feet can seat 700 people theater- or classroom-style, and 500 people for banquets. The Hilo Hawaiian Hotel offers a 5,040-square-foot banquet room that can accommodate small and large groups. The Hawaii Naniloa Resort offers seating for up to 400 people.

Convention Information: Big Island Visitors Bureau, 250 Keawe Street, Hilo, HI 96720; telephone (808) 961-5797; fax (808) 961-2126.

■ Transportation

Approaching the City

The county of Hawaii's airports are Hilo International and Kona International. Hilo Airport (ITO) serves about 4,500 passengers daily. Four hotels are located within a five mile radius of the Hilo airport. There are frequent inter-island flights by Aloha Airlines, Island Air, Pacific Wings, and Hawaiian Airlines, as well as flights to major U.S. cities; daily direct flights from Tokyo are available. Kailua-Kona and South Kohala, major tourist destination areas on the west side of the Big Island, are served by flights from the United States mainland and Canada through the Kona International Airport. Waimea-Kohala Airport, about one and a half hour away, is a general aviation airport also available to visitors of the Big Island; Pacific Wings offers one daily flight here.

Kona International Airport is the major airport on the Big Island. Kona serves an average over 8,000 daily passengers. Kona offers services by US Airways, United, Delta, Alaska Airlines, Air Canada, and several inter-island operators, such as GO! Mokulele, Hawaiian Airlines, and Island Air. A major highway system known as Hawaii Belt Road encircles the island of Hawaii, and driving time from Hilo to the Kona International Airport, on the opposite side of the island, is about two hours and 15 minutes. Route 19 approaches Hilo from the north and Route 11 approaches from the south. R 200 runs west into the interior of the island, and north toward Waimea.

Traveling in the City

The island of Hawaii has more than 1,450 miles of highways. Since the area surrounding the city of Hilo is large, a rental car may be preferable. Hilo itself is contained within the bounds of the scenic highways on the coast, state highway 11 bordering the eastern portion of the city, and state highway 200 bordering the western side. Downtown starts at Front Street (officially Kamehameha Avenue). Major streets in Hilo include Kinoole St. and Kilauea Avenue, which run northwest to southeast, and Waianuenue Avenue, which runs east and west. Bayfront Highway follows the coastline and scenic Banyan Drive curves around the major resort area. County bus service is provided by "Hele-On." The Hawaii County Mass Transit Agency offers a Shared Ride Taxi program, which provides inexpensive door to door transportation in the cities of Hilo and Kona.

■ Communications

Newspapers and Magazines

The *Hawaii Tribune-Herald* is Hilo's only daily newspaper. *Big Island Weekly* is a free publication published every Wednesday. Both are run by Stephens Media Group, who, with the demise of the *Hawaii Island Journal* in 2008, run all major commercial publications on the Big Island.

Television and Radio

No network television stations broadcast from Hilo, but all major networks are available for viewing from Hilo via programming from neighboring Oahu. Hawaiian Cablevision system offers a wide selection of programming. The county is served by about 20 AM and FM radio stations.

Media Information: *Hawaii Tribune-Herald*, 355 Kinoole Street, Box 767, Hilo, HI 96720; telephone (808) 935-6621; fax (808) 969-9100.

Hilo Online

Destination Hilo. Available www.destinationhilo.org

Downtown Improvement Association. Available www.downtownhilo.com

Hawaii County Home Page. Available www.hawaii-county.com

Hawaii Department of Education. Available doe.k12.hi.us

Hawaii Department of Labor and Industrial Relations. Available www.hawaii.gov/labor

Hawaii Island Chamber of Commerce. Available www.hicc.biz

Hawaii Tribune-Herald. Available www.hawaii tribune-herald.com

Hawaii Visitors and Convention Bureau. Available www.gohawaii.com/big_island

Hilo Public Library. Available www.librarieshawaii.org/locations/hawaii/hilo.htm

State of Hawaii. Available www.ehawaii.gov/dakine

BIBLIOGRAPHY

Ball, Pamela, *Lava: A Novel* (New York: Henry Holt, 1998)

Ingram, Scott, *Tsunami! The 1946 Hilo Wave of Terror* (New York: Bearport Pub., 2005)

Honolulu

■ The City in Brief

Founded: 1100 (by Hawaiians); 1795 (incorporated, 1907)

Head Official: Mayor Kirk Caldwell (D) (since 2013; current term expires 2017)

City Population
    1990: 377,059
    2000: 371,657
    2010: 337,256
    2012 estimate: 1,571,550
    Percent change, 2000–2010: −9.3%
    U.S. rank in 1990: 44th
    U.S. rank in 2000: 55th
    U.S. rank in 2010: 53rd (State rank: 1st)

Metropolitan Statistical Area Population
    2000: 876,156
    2010: 953,207
    2012 estimate: 976,372
    Percent change, 2000–2010: 8.8%
    U.S. rank in 2000: 52nd
    U.S. rank in 2010: 53rd

Area: 86 square miles

Elevation: 15 feet above sea level

Average Annual Temperatures: January, 73.0° F; July, 80.8° F; annual average, 77.5° F

Average Annual Precipitation: 18.29 inches of rain

Major Economic Sectors: services (especially tourism), military, agriculture, construction

Unemployment Rate: 3.2% (2012)

Per Capita Income: $29,314

Major Colleges and Universities: University of Hawaii at Manoa, Chaminade University of Honolulu, Hawaii Pacific University, Brigham Young University-Hawaii

Daily Newspaper: *The Honolulu Advertiser; Honolulu Star-Bulletin*

■ Introduction

Honolulu, the capital of Hawaii and the seat of Honolulu County, is a cosmopolitan city located in the scenic setting of the Hawaiian island of Oahu. Its name means "protected harbor," and it serves as the crossroads of the Pacific Ocean with ship and air connections to the U.S. mainland, Asia, Australia, and New Zealand. The city is the principal port for the Hawaiian Islands and an important center for military defense with several bases, including the infamous Pearl Harbor Naval Base, located in the area. Millions of visitors are drawn annually to Honolulu's mild, semitropical climate and to the beautiful beaches of Waikiki. Oahu is the third largest and most populated of the islands, and Honolulu is the state's most populous city. About 75 percent of the residential population of the entire state is located on Oahu, and about 75 percent of those individuals live in the Honolulu area.

■ Geography and Climate

Honolulu as a city is defined by the U.S. Census Bureau as the area from Makapuu south of the Koolau Mountain range summit to the western edge of Halawa Valley. Located along the southern coast of Oahu, Honolulu is the third largest of the Hawaiian Islands, just south of the Tropic of Cancer in the Pacific Ocean. The city is situated on a narrow plain between the ocean and the Koolau mountain range; it climbs the Punchbowl, an extinct volcano. Although the climate is semi-tropical, the trade winds usually keep the city comfortable, until the "kona,"

Andy Z./Shutterstock.com

or southerly winds, blow for a few weeks in the summer. Honolulu's weather exhibits the least seasonal change of any city in the United States, with only a few degrees difference between winter and summer. Average high temperatures range in the 80s, while the average lows are in the upper 60s. Rainfall generally occurs from October through March, with very little throughout the summer.

Area: 86 square miles

Elevation: 15 feet above sea level

Average Temperatures: January, 73.0° F; July, 80.8° F; annual average, 77.5° F

Average Annual Precipitation: 18.29 inches of rain

■ History

Native Hawaiians Meet Westerners, Begin Trading Goods

Historians estimate that the first settlers, Polynesians, came to the Hawaiian Islands fifteen hundred years ago, with the last migration occurring around 750 A.D. By the time Westerners came to the islands, the Hawaiian people had developed a highly structured society composed of chiefs, who claimed the right of divine rule, and commoners, who worked the land and the sea.

British Captain James Cook first sighted Oahu in 1778, when he named the islands the Sandwich Islands after the Earl of Sandwich. William Brown was the first to enter Honolulu's harbor, in 1794. In 1795, King Kamehameha I unified the Hawaiian Islands, conquering the king of Oahu. Kamehameha settled at Waikiki, turning the harbor at Honolulu into a center of trade with the West for such goods as fur, sandalwood, and whale products. While bringing the islands into the modern world, such trade also threatened the native Hawaiian culture.

Rise of Sugar Industry Erodes Traditional Way of Life

Honolulu was such a convenient center of trade between the Orient and the West that it became the seat of a series of European occupations: Russia in 1816, England in 1843, and France in 1849. New England missionaries began arriving in 1820; some of their buildings, preserved by the Mission Houses Museum, can be seen today. The missionaries established schools and also functioned as government advisors to the royal Hawaiians. During the mid-nineteenth century the whaling industry began to decline and the sugar industry grew. The cultivation of sugar cane brought in a great influx of immigrant labor from throughout the Pacific basin; the descendants of these peoples are partially responsible for modern Honolulu's cosmopolitanism. An 1876 treaty that admitted sugar duty-free into the United States strengthened the power of this industry.

King Kamehameha III proclaimed Honolulu as the capitol city in 1850. The territorial legislature created county level governments in 1905. Incorporated that year, the County of Oahu included that island plus all the small islands beyond Niihau to, but not including, Midway Island 2,000 miles away. In 1907 the county was renamed the City and County of Honolulu.

At the time, Honolulu was named the capitol city; traditional Hawaiian life was breaking down. The sugar interests consisting of an oligarchy of plantation owners ruled the islands. Native customs were declining through both the breakdown of taboos and the introduction of guns and liquor. Furthermore, the Hawaiian people were not immune to diseases brought to them by the Westerners; within a hundred years of the islands' discovery by the West, 80 percent of the native population was dead. The language and history of the Hawaiians is nevertheless preserved, partly through native dance and folklore.

In 1893 Queen Liliuokalani, the last Hawaiian monarch, was deposed by a group of American businessmen and U.S. Marines, and in 1898 the islands were annexed by the United States. In 1907, Honolulu was incorporated as a city and county. Through the efforts of Prince Jonah Kuhio Kalanianaole, a member of Congress from 1902 to 1922, Pearl Harbor was dredged, extending the sea power of the United States. On December 7, 1941, the Japanese bombed Pearl Harbor, but it survived to become the most important staging area for the United States in the Pacific during World War II. The area around Honolulu is still an important constellation of military bases.

A State Capital Emerges

Hawaii achieved statehood in 1959 and joined the Union as the 50th state with Honolulu as its capital. Today Honolulu is the Aloha state's center of business, culture, and politics. In recent years, Hawaiian sovereignty has become a contested political issue. In 1993 President Clinton signed an official apology acknowledging the U.S. role in the overthrow of the Hawaiian kingdom. A 2003 U.S. Supreme Court decision addressed the issue of sovereignty and the elections of government officials in Hawaii. In 2005 and 2009, the Native Hawaiian Government Reorganization Act was reintroduced in the House and Senate. The legislation calls for the U.S. government to recognize Native Hawaiians as it does American Indians and Native Alaskans. The legislation would also provide a process by which the United States recognizes the Native Hawaiian governing entity.

With about 8 million visitors a year, Honolulu retains a reputation as a tourist destination. As Honolulu continued to be a prime location for travelers and developers alike, in the 21st century officials turned their focus toward preservation of the lush land. Taking initiative towards maintaining a balance between the natural setting of Hawaii and the ongoing development as a center for business and tourism. Honolulu's economic development is most apparent in the rapid growth of tourism in the region, particularly in the Waikiki neighborhood adjacent the waterfront. There, numerous high rises and resorts line the shore.

Historical Information: Bernice P. Bishop Museum Library, 1525 Bernice Street, Honolulu, HI 96817; telephone (808) 847-3511; fax (808) 841-8968.

■ Population Profile

Metropolitan Statistical Area Population

2000: 876,156
2010: 953,207
2012 estimate: 976,372
Percent change, 2000–2010: 8.8%
U.S. rank in 2000: 52nd
U.S. rank in 2010: 53rd

City Residents

1990: 377,059
2000: 371,657
2010: 337,256
2012 estimate: 1,571,550
Percent change, 2000–2010: −9.3%
U.S. rank in 1990: 44th
U.S. rank in 2000: 55th
U.S. rank in 2010: 53rd (State rank: 1st)

Density: 5,572.6 people per square mile

Racial and ethnic characteristics

White: 58,816
Black or African American: 5,885
American Indian and Alaskan Native: 370
Asian: 190,481
Native Hawaiian and Other Pacific Islander: 29,365
Hispanic or Latino (may be of any race): 23,652
Other: 60,687

Percent of residents born in state: 48.5%

Age characteristics

Population under 5 years old: 17,482
Population 5 to 9 years old: 16,073
Population 10 to 14 years old: 17,028
Population 15 to 19 years old: 18,995
Population 20 to 24 years old: 28,016
Population 25 to 34 years old: 50,165
Population 35 to 44 years old: 44,021
Population 45 to 54 years old: 47,115
Population 55 to 59 years old: 23,539
Population 60 to 64 years old: 21,834
Population 65 to 74 years old: 28,820
Population 75 to 84 years old: 20,832
Population 85 years and over: 11,684
Median age: 40.4

Births (2010–11 Metropolitan Area)

Total number: 13,246

Deaths (2010–11 Metropolitan Area)

Total number: 6,870

Money income (2012)

Per capita income: $29,314
Median household income: $57,452
Total households: 127,145

Number of households with income of ...

less than $10,000: 9,141
$10,000 to $14,999: 5,913
$15,000 to $24,999: 10,773
$25,000 to $34,999: 11,863
$35,000 to $49,999: 17,626
$50,000 to $74,999: 23,637
$75,000 to $99,999: 16,857
$100,000 to $149,999: 18,162
$150,000 to $199,999: 7,106
$200,000 or more: 6,067

Percent of families below poverty level: 12.1%

■ Municipal Government

The city of Honolulu and the county of Honolulu are administered jointly by a mayor-council form of government. The mayor is elected to four-year terms. The nine council members are each elected from one of Oahu's nine separate geographic districts. Council members serve for a term of two or four years.

Head Official: Mayor Kirk Caldwell (D) (since 2013; current term expires 2017)

Total Number of City Employees: 8,361 (2013)

City Information: Mayor's Office, 530 South King Street, Honolulu, HI 96813; telephone (808) 768-4141.

■ Economy

Major Industries and Commercial Activity

Today, Honolulu is a tourist destination, known for its embodiment of the scenery of Hawaii while maintaining a cosmopolitan city, as well as a major hub for U.S. defense activity. However, Honolulu began its economic life in the mid-nineteenth century as a port for whalers; it was also a trade center for nations bordering the Pacific, dealing in such goods as sandalwood, whale oil, and fur. While markets for sandalwood and whale oil decreased, sugar and pineapple markets increased dramatically. Plantation agriculture has experienced a major decline since then. In fact, the powerful sugar industry, owned mainly by Americans, engineered the downfall of Hawaii's last monarch and the islands' annexation by the United States. One-fifth of the land in Honolulu County is zoned for agriculture, but fields are now giving way to new homes and commercial development. With the closure of sugar plantations, challenges arise to find the most productive use for these lands. Diversified agriculture has been on a steady upward trend. Aquaculture, which includes cultivated species of shellfish, finfish and algae, has grown in recent years. Honolulu County has over 45 aquaculture operations, which produced over $5 million in annual sales.

In addition to serving as the business and trading hub of the Hawaiian Islands, Honolulu is the transportation crossroads of the Pacific, connecting East with West. Several countries have diplomatic facilities in Honolulu, including consulates of Japan, South Korea, Philippines, Federated States of Micronesia, Australia, and the Marshall Islands.

The city's recently expanded harbor facilities handle cargo for several international steamship companies, and a Foreign Trade Zone is based there. Other important elements of Honolulu's economic base include tourism, military defense, research and development, and manufacturing. Inter-island airlines, such as Go! Mokulele, Hawaiian Airlines, Island Air, and Aloha Air Cargo are headquartered in the city.

Hawaii is recognized as a strategic military location with armed services expenditures amounting to 9.6 percent of the state's gross domestic product, making it the second largest source of economic wealth in the region. The military reportedly spends over $5 billion annually to maintain the nation's strategic presence in the Pacific Region. The state's share is the highest in the nation, overwhelmingly concentrated on Oahu.

The film and digital media industry is growing and is supported by the City and County Honolulu Film Office. In the 2000s, Honolulu and the island of Oahu became the backdrop to the major television series *Lost* produced by ABC. In the past, Hawaii has been known as Hollywood's "Tropical Backlot" due to a variety of high-profile films and shows in the area, such as *South Pacific, Jurassic Park, Pearl Harbor,* and *Lilo & Stitch.*

With millions of visitors coming each year to enjoy Honolulu's climate and beaches, tourism contributes significantly to the local economy. Pearl Harbor Naval Shipyard, Marine Corps Base Hawaii in Kaneohe, and Schofield Barracks Army base provide revenues that are unaffected by the normal business cycle. As the home of the University of Hawaii at Manoa, Honolulu is a center for research and development, especially in the areas of oceanography, astrophysics, geophysics, and biomedicine. The city and county of Honolulu also contains many commercial, industrial and retail properties. With available research centers at the University of Hawaii as well as the area's defense contracting industry, Honolulu is looking to diversify its economy in the following areas: alternate energies, astronomy and space sciences, defense-dual use technologies, diversified agriculture, information and communication technologies, life science-biotech, and marine sciences.

Items and goods produced: jewelry, clothing, food and beverages, rubber products, construction materials, and electronics and computer equipment

Incentive Programs—New and Existing Companies

Local programs: Honolulu's Office of Economic Development provides assistance to entrepreneurs; supports programs that stimulate business development; advocates for the removal of impediments to business; sponsors conferences and events to attract investments; underwrites marketing outreach; provides extensive international networking; provides advice and guidance to businesses; and reinforces Honolulu's position as an important player in the global economy. Enterprise Honolulu, a non-profit economic development organization, works to retain existing businesses and assist in their expansion; encourage growth and diversification amongst existing businesses; attract and recruit new businesses; and help entrepreneurs in their business development initiatives.

State programs: Most business incentives are offered at the state level. These include direct financial incentives such as Industrial Development Bonds, a Capital Loan Program, customized industrial training, and investment of public funds in return for equity or ownership positions in private businesses. Tax incentives are also offered along with the Hawaii Urban Enterprise Zones Program. Other tax incentives for businesses on the Big Island include no personal property taxes; no taxes on inventory, equipment, furniture and machinery; no tax on goods manufactured for export; no unincorporated business tax; and only one business tax for banks and financial institutions. High technology businesses can also take advantage of unparalleled tax breaks through legislative initiatives and the State Foreign Trade Zone program and

Enterprise Zone Partnership. Hawaii's economy relies heavily on small business entrepreneurs, as they account for over 96 percent of all businesses in the state. Hawaii's Small Business Development Center Network is a partnership of the University of Hawaii at Hilo and the U.S. Small Business Administration. With the aim of helping small business become established or expand, the Network offers one-on-one counseling, seminars, workshops and conferences. Three separate tax credits can be applied to film and television productions: the motion picture, digital media, and film production income tax credits, which range from 15 to 20 percent.

Job training programs: The Workforce Development Division of Hawaii's Department of Labor and Industrial Relations oversees One-Stop Workforce Assistance Centers, a job placement and training system to help people find work and employers find suitable workers, and the Employment & Training Fund (ETF), a job skills upgrade program for current workers. Employers can receive customized training grants for their workplace or they can nominate a current worker for an established training course. HireNet Hawaii was created as a "virtual one-stop employment center." The site allows individuals to post resumes online, search for available jobs in the state, and view current labor market data, among other features. Training providers can also use HireNet Hawaii as a tool to post program information.

Development Projects

The city's capital improvement budget of $620.1 million for fiscal year 2013 represented an increase of 13.3 percent compared to the preceding fiscal year. Funding for capital improvements in fiscal year 2013 was primarily for sanitation (53.5 percent), and highways and streets (20.1 percent).

In 2013 construction began on the Symphony Honolulu condominium project, a 388-unit mixed-use project that will combine residential units with commercial space. The project is scheduled for completion in 2015. Other construction projects include a new air cargo facility being built by Aloha Air Cargo. The 115,000-square-foot facility will consolidate existing cargo operations, aircraft maintenance, loading docks, support offices, and customer service operations. The new facility is part of the Hawaii Airports $1.7 billion Modernization Program. Renovations include a new terminal and new cargo and maintenance facilities. New Hawaii CC Kona Campus broke ground on a $25.5 million campus in West Hawaii, the only remaining major population center in the state without a permanent higher education facility. The new facility will include 24,000 square feet of learning space.

Honolulu is a resort town, and, as a result, many hotels and restaurants are developed and renovated regularly to cater to the crowd. The $535 million Waikiki Beach Walk redevelopment project rejuvenated walkways, hotels, retail complexes and entertainment areas along one of the most visited beaches in Honolulu. With its opening in 2007, the complex included 5 hotels and 47 restaurant and retail tenants.

The private and local government-supported "Second City" of Kapolei is constructed in an area 20 miles from downtown Honolulu. The Kapolei community, started in the 1980s, is one of the fastest growing areas in the state with projections of reaching 46,000 jobs by 2015. An office for the mayor and other government agencies is located there. New amenities to the area included shopping centers, golf courses, parks, and the Hawaiian Waters Adventures Park.

Construction on Honolulu's $5.2 billion dollar rail project, the largest public works project in Hawaii's history, resumed in 2013 after a one-year delay. The Hawaii Supreme Court halted construction because the project was not properly surveying for ancient Hawaiian burial grounds. The project is controversial, gaining the support of a bare minimum of voters. Some estimate cost overruns to top $1 billion, which has led to comparisons with Boston's disastrous Big Dig. It has been plagued by court challenges since its inception. As of early 2014, the project was scheduled for completion in 2019. The project, a 20-mile elevated rail line, will connect West Oahu with downtown Honolulu and Ala Moana Center. The system features electric trains capable of carrying more than 300 passengers each. Trains can carry more than 8,000 passengers per hour in each direction. New bus routes run by Honolulu's public transportation authority (TheBus) will provide direct connections to the stations, such as TheBus' $8 million Middle Street Intermodal Center which broke ground in 2010 (among other similar centers). The intention is that bus transit centers like these will ultimately be adjacent to a rail transit station adjacent, the first step toward a successful multi-modal transit system.

Economic Development Information: The Office of Economic Development, 530 South King Street, Suite 305, Honolulu, HI 96813; telephone (808) 527-5761; fax (808) 523-4242.

Commercial Shipping

Honolulu's location in the mid-Pacific makes it a major stopover for trans-Pacific sea and air shipments. Honolulu Harbor has a highly successful Foreign Trade Zone and several major shipping companies serving the port. The harbor also has terminals for commercial fishing, cruise ships, and ferries. In the "Oahu Commercial Harbors 2020 Master Plan," the development of a commercial fishing "village" was introduced. The finished "village" was expected to consolidate services scattered across the waterfront, producing more efficiency in the fishing market.

Labor Force and Employment Outlook

Honolulu County's four major industry sectors are government; trade, transportation, and utilities; leisure and hospitality; and professional and business services. These four industries account for the majority of the total employment in Honolulu County. Services and trade are considered the two largest growth industries for the County. The workforce is heavily bilingual; one out of every five adults in Hawaii is fluent in another language.

In 2013 Honolulu had the lowest unemployment rate among Hawaii's counties with a non-seasonally adjusted unemployment rate of 4.3 percent, compared to 4.7 percent statewide, and 7.0 percent nationally. That same year, personal income increased 2.8 percent. Construction jobs rose 7.9 percent in 2013. Non-agricultural jobs totaled 456,000, a slight 0.9 percent increase from the preceding year.

The following is a summary of data regarding the 2012 Honolulu labor force:

Size of civilian labor force: 180,603

Number of workers employed in . . .

agriculture and mining: 595
construction: 8,401
manufacturing: 4,719
wholesale trade: 3,742
retail trade: 22,041
transportation: 8,491
information systems: 2,798
finance: 12,451
professional administration: 18,036
education and social services: 36,793
arts and leisure: 30,638
other: 8,136
public administration: 13,427

Average hourly earnings of production workers: $17.76

Unemployment rate: 3.2% (2012)

Employers

Largest state employers (2012)	*Number of employees*
State of Hawaii	72,400
Federal Government	34,900
Local Governments	18,500
Hawaii Pacific Health	5,809
Starwood Hotels and Resorts	5,500
Hilton Hotels	5,400
Queen's Health System	5,281
Hawaiian Airlines	4,906

Kaiser Foundation
Health Plan and
Hospital 4,570
Hawaiian Electric
Industries, Inc. 3,870

Cost of Living

Because land is scarce and tourist development has driven up the cost of living, Hawaii is one of the top ranking states in housing costs. About 65 percent of housing in Honolulu is condominiums. Housing rentals, fuel, and food costs are among the highest in the country. These conditions force many Hawaiians to work two or three jobs to survive.

The following is a summary of data regarding several key cost of living factors in the area.

2013 ACCRA Average House Price: $766,114

2013 ACCRA Cost of Living Index: 175

State income tax rate: 1.4% to 11.00%

State sales tax rate: 4.0%

Local income tax rate: None

Local sales tax rate: 0.5%

Property tax rate: $3.50 per $1,000 assessed value (2013)

Economic Information: Chamber of Commerce of Hawaii, 1132 Bishop St. Suite 402, Honolulu, HI 96813; telephone (808) 545-4300; fax (808) 545-4369.

■ Education and Research

Elementary and Secondary Schools

Hawaii is the only state with a single, unified statewide school system, comprised of seven districts, four on the island of Oahu and three on the neighbor islands. The four districts on Oahu are in the city and county of Honolulu; metropolitan Honolulu falls in the Honolulu District. An elected board of education formulates educational policy and supervises the public school system. Seven members are elected according to geographic region and six are elected at-large. One non-voting student member is appointed.

A variety of private and special education schools are licensed by the state and serve the school-age population. There are six private schools in the Downtown Honolulu area. They are Hawaii Pacific University (post-secondary), Hongwanji Mission School, Kawaiahao School, Pacific Buddhist Academy, St. Andrew's Priory School, and Word of Life Academy.

The following is a summary of data regarding the Hawaii Department of Education.

Total enrollment: 179,601

Number of facilities
total: 204
elementary schools: 101
junior high schools: 55
high schools: 41
other: 7

Student/teacher ratio: 15.8:1

Teacher salaries
average (statewide): $55,063

Funding per pupil: $12,004

Public Schools Information: Hawaii State Department of Education, 390 Miller St. Honolulu, HI 96813; telephone (808) 586-3230.

Colleges and Universities

The University of Hawaii at Manoa, with an annual enrollment of more than 20,000, offers both undergraduate and graduate programs. It is especially known for its programs in the marine sciences, tropical agriculture, geophysics, astronomy, and Asian and Pacific cultures. The program reports to teach more Asian languages than any other U.S. university. Its School of Travel Industry Management is respected worldwide for its work in research and training new leaders in the field. On the campus of the University of Hawaii at Manoa is the East-West Center, which is an institution of technical and cultural exchange with Asian and Pacific countries.

Chaminade University of Honolulu is a small, private institution affiliated with the Society of Mary of the Roman Catholic Church. Also located in Honolulu is Hawaii Pacific University (HPU), Hawaii's largest private university. HPU was named "Best in the West" according to *The Princeton Review's* "Best Colleges: Region by Region" list and is ranked annually in the *U.S. News & World Report* as one of "America's Best Colleges." There are four community colleges.

Libraries and Research Centers

The Hawaii State Public Library System is based in Honolulu and operates 50 libraries throughout the state. Holdings consist of more than two million volumes (more than 1.5 million housed on Oahu) as well as newspapers, magazines, tapes, films, and special collections, including Hawaiian history and state and federal documents. The system also maintains the Library for the Blind and Physically Handicapped, located in Honolulu.

Specialized libraries are affiliated with local colleges and universities, government agencies, hospitals, and corporations. Research activities in such fields as agriculture, livestock, the environment, freshwater and marine ecology, marine biology, marine mammalogy, water resources, cancer, biomedicine, astronomy, geophysics, labor, and industrial relations are conducted primarily by the University of Hawaii and federal government agencies.

In 2013 Windward Community College broke ground on a new $41.6 million Library Learning Commons that will host media labs, learning and tutoring center, academic computing, and a Hawaiian collection.

Public Library Information: Hawaii State Public Library System, 478 South King Street, Honolulu, HI 96813; telephone (808) 586-3500.

■ Health Care

The city and county of Honolulu is served by 13 hospitals. The Queen's Medical Center in downtown Honolulu is the largest private hospital in the state, with 505 acute care beds and 28 sub-acute care beds. Cardiac rehabilitation centers are maintained at Kuakini Medical Center and Tripler Army Medical Center. Gamma Knife technology became available at the St. Francis Medical Center at the Gamma Knife Center of the Pacific. In 2006 more than 44,000 people were employed by the health-care and social assistance services in the Honolulu area.

■ Recreation

Sightseeing

The beauty of Honolulu's natural surroundings, its fascinating mix of cultures, and its unique layering of history offer much for the visitor to see and do. Honolulu abounds in the exotic flora and fauna of a semitropical island. The Honolulu Zoo houses an excellent collection of tropical birds as well as animals from around the world. A highlight of the zoo is the Kubuni Reserve. In this 12-acre African savanna, animals roam free within 30 different habitats. The Waikiki Aquarium has exhibits that educate visitors and promote conservation of marine life, including coral reef environments and endangered species such as the monk seal. In 2000, the Waikiki Aquarium was designated as a Coastal Ecosystem Learning Center. At Sea Life Park, visitors can watch dolphins, penguins, and sea lions perform as well as swim with stingrays and dolphins.

The University of Hawaii at Manoa maintains the 200-acre Lyon Arboretum, which offers paths and trails throughout its beautifully landscaped gardens. The Foster Botanical Garden was established in 1855 by Queen Kalama, wife of King Kamehameha III, and features a prehistoric glen planted with grasses, ferns, and palms. Other botanical gardens include Ho'omaluhia, Koko Crater, Liliuokalani, and Wahiawa. Exotic flowers can also be seen at the Queen Kapiolani Hibiscus Garden.

A number of historic buildings are located in Honolulu. The stately Iolani Palace is the only royal palace in the United States, although it was inhabited by Hawaiian royalty for only 11 years. Completed by King David Kalahaua in 1862, it served as a prison for Queen Liliuokalani. Honolulu's first church, the Kawaiahao Church, was built in 1841 from blocks of coral and was the place of worship for Hawaiian rulers. The State Capitol, resembling a volcano, is designed to reflect various facets of the state of Hawaii.

The exhibits at the Hawaii Maritime Center focus on Hawaii's whaling days, the history of the Honolulu Harbor and the *Falls of Clyde,* a four-masted sailing ship built in 1878, which carried passengers and cargo between Honolulu and San Francisco. An underwater park is located at Hanauma Bay Beach Park, where novices at snorkeling and SCUBA diving can view a coral reef. Other historical sites include Diamond Head State Monument, the U.S.S. Arizona Memorial, the Battleship Missouri Memorial, and the National Cemetery of the Pacific.

Visitors can climb to the top of Punchbowl Crater, the major geographic landmark seen behind Honolulu from the water and where the National Memorial Cemetery of the Pacific calls itself home. In addition to the general activities surrounding the beach and waterfront, in the 2000s, it became popular for tourists to seek out filming locations of the popular television drama *Lost.*

Arts and Culture

With a symphony, opera, theater groups, and numerous museums, Honolulu is the cultural center of the state of Hawaii. The Honolulu Symphony, the oldest U.S. symphony orchestra west of the Rocky Mountains, presents a classical concert series as well as a pop series at the Blaisdell Center Concert Hall. Also housed at Blaisdell Center is the Hawaii Opera Theater, which provides a season of grand opera and operettas. The Waikiki Shell is also a part of the Blaisdell Center and is an open-air amphitheater that hosts a variety of concerts and events. Broadway performances and dramatic classics are presented at Diamond Head Theatre and Manoa Valley Theatre, while the Kennedy Theatre at the University of Hawaii at Manoa is the site of student productions. Adjacent to the Waikiki Shell is a Hula Show Area where performances take place several times a week.

Honolulu's museums offer a range of experiences. The Bishop Museum is known for its collection of Polynesian artifacts, considered to be among the best in the world. The museum also presents hands-on exhibits and a planetarium where the constellations may be viewed as they appear from the island of Hawaii. The Bishop Museum is also home to the Science Adventure Center, which consists of 16,500 square feet of interactive displays and exhibits that feature volcanology, oceanography, and biodiversity. The Honolulu Academy of Arts houses permanent exhibits of oriental and occidental art, including the Kress collection of Italian Renaissance paintings and the Asian collection, featuring art and artifacts from throughout the Orient. It boasts the largest collection of Islamic art, housed at the Shangri La estate. The museum also has a $28 million Luce Pavilion Complex, providing two additional 4,000-square-foot galleries. The Mission Houses Museum is comprised of the three oldest American buildings in Hawaii; the Frame house, the oldest, was built in 1821 and is furnished with period pieces that help show how the missionaries lived.

Festivals and Holidays

A number of holidays and festivals celebrating Honolulu's unique mix of cultures are held throughout the year. The Narcissus Festival, in January or early February, marks the Chinese New Year with lion dances and pageants. The Cherry Blossom Festival runs from January to March and is the largest running ethnic celebration in the state. A highlight of the event is the selection of a Cherry Blossom Queen and Court. Prince Kuhio Day on March 26, a state holiday, is held in honor of the prince who served in the U.S. Congress for 20 years. The Honolulu Festival takes place in March and celebrates ethnic harmony. The Hawaii Invitational International Music Festival occurs in April with high school, junior high, and college band participants. Lei Day on May 1st is one of Honolulu's most popular unofficial holidays; festivities include hula dances, contests for the best lei, and the crowning of the Lei Queen. The Hawaii State Fair occurs on weekends from mid-May through mid-June at the Aloha Stadium. The Pan Pacific-Matsuri Festival held in June promotes cultural exchange between Hawaiian and Japanese cultures. In addition to dance, art, and music, the Festival includes a golf open and a half marathon run.

The King Kamehameha Celebration, a state holiday observed on June 11, honors the king who united the Hawaiian Islands. The Hawaii International Jazz Festival held in late July celebrates jazz with international artists. The Ukulele Festival held annually in July presents a variety of ukulele players during free concerts. The Prince Lot Hula Festival in July showcases ancient and modern versions of the dance at Queen Kapiolani Bandstand. The Aloha Festival celebrates *Makahiki,* the traditional harvest time when taxes were paid, with pageants and street parties known as *Ho'olaule'a*. The Annual Orchid Show in late October shows thousands of varieties of plants and flowers, especially the exotic orchids that grow in the area. The Hawaii International Film Festival in late November and early December brings together award-winning film directors from the nations that border the Pacific Ocean.

Sports for the Spectator

While there are no major professional sports in the city, Honolulu sports fans enjoy a variety of college sports, which include baseball, softball, basketball, soccer, golf, tennis, and track and field. The NFL Pro Bowl is held in February each year at the Aloha Stadium (with an interruption in 2010, when it was played in Miami). The NCAA Hawaii Bowl is played in Honolulu. The American Basketball Association welcomed the new Hawaii Hurricanes; the team began play in 2007n. Honolulu is also home to the Hawaii Winter Baseball League's Honolulu Sharks and Waikiki Beach Boys. Spectators can enjoy car racing at Hawaii Raceway Park.

Sports for the Participant

Honolulu's Waikiki beach draws more visitors than any other beach on the island, offering a host of water sports such as swimming, sailing, snorkeling, surfing, scuba diving, kayaking, or outrigger canoeing. Scuba equipment, surfboard and windsurf boards can be rented; lessons are also available. Charter boats for deep-sea fishing can be rented; during spring and summer there are particularly rich runs of game fish such as marlin and tuna. *Men's Fitness* magazine has named Honolulu the fittest city in the country. Several major road races are held in the city: the Great Aloha Run on Presidents' Day, the Honolulu Marathon in December, and the Honolulu Triathlon. The first ever Ironman World Championship was held in Honolulu, and has been held annually in Hawaii since 1978.

Honolulu is also popular for hang gliding and parasailing. Visitors can take helicopter tours or go whale watching. Other activities include hiking, jogging, biking, horseback riding, tennis, and golf.

Shopping and Dining

Shopping is a pleasurable pastime in Honolulu. Located in the city is Ala Moana, one of the largest open-air shopping centers in the world. After completion of a multi-million dollar expansion in 2008, Ala Moana will offer 290 stores, including 70 restaurants. Hotels along the beach in Waikiki are full of shops, and downtown Fort Street has been converted into a pedestrian mall. Also located within the city are the Royal Hawaiian and the Kahala Mall Shopping Centers. The Cultural Plaza in Chinatown Historic District features a variety of ethnic shops and stores. Temari, a center for Asian and Pacific arts that is not actually a store, offers two- to three-hour workshops to visitors. The former Dole Pineapple Cannery now houses retail shops oriented toward tourists. The newly developed Aloha Tower Marketplace next to the Hawaii Maritime Center offers many shops and restaurants catering to tourists.

Honolulu cuisine is truly international. Hawaiian specialties include *mahimahi* (dolphin fish), *poi* (rounded taro root), and *puaa kalua* (a whole pig slow-roasted in a pit). One restaurant in particular that boasts authentic Hawaiian cuisine is Alan Wong's Restaurant in Honolulu.

The restaurant has been ranked eighth on *Gourmet* magazine's "America's Top 50 Restaurants" and has won "Best Restaurant of the Year" in *Honolulu Magazine's* Hale Aina Awards more than eight times. Local restaurants offer a range of Oriental foods-Chinese, Japanese, Thai, and Korean-as well as European fare such as French, German, and Italian. Restaurants also serve popular Cajun and Creole dishes.

Visitor Information: Hawaii Visitors & Convention Bureau, 2270 Kalakaua Avenue, Suite 801, Honolulu, HI 96815; telephone (808) 923-1811; toll-free (800) 464-2924; fax (808) 923-0290.

■ Convention Facilities

Honolulu's principal meeting facility is the beautiful four-story Hawaii Convention Center, which offers a 200,000-square-foot ground floor exhibition hall; a second floor exclusively for parking; a third floor with meeting room space totaling 149,768 square feet; and a 35,000-square-foot grand ballroom and rooftop garden on the fourth floor. Inside, a $2 million Hawaiian art collection with paintings of volcanoes, mountains, ocean, waterfalls, taro, and fishponds are displayed alongside images of Hawaiian royalty, gods, and myths; above, soaring rooftop canopies recall images of Polynesian sailing canoes. The building is open to the outdoors and sits on landscaped grounds featuring terraces, lanais, and courtyards that occupy more than six acres of the 10-acre site. Honolulu is also home to plethora of hotels and facilities ripe for the choosing for meeting planners interested in this popular tourist and international business destination.

Convention Information: Hawaii Visitors & Convention Bureau, 2270 Kalakaua Avenue, Suite 801, Honolulu, HI 96815; telephone (808) 923-1811; fax (808) 923-0290.

■ Transportation

Approaching the City

Isolated from the mainland, Honolulu is reached primarily by plane. Honolulu International Airport, a major center for Pacific air travel, is served by over 20 domestic and foreign airlines as well as inter-island carriers. As of 2014, the airport was undergoing a $750 million modernization program. Improvements include a new concourse for wide body aircraft, a commuter terminal, cargo and maintenance facilities for Aloha Air Cargo and Hawaiian Airlines, taxiway widening, and a consolidated rental car facility.

Kalaeloa Airport is another available airport, used primarily by commuters for air taxis, general aviation, and military aircraft. Honolulu may also be reached by ship; cruise lines sail regularly between Honolulu and cities in California.

Traveling in the City

Because of the irregular shape of the city, Honolulu residents define directions according to landmarks such as the mountains and the sea rather than standard compass orientations. Honolulu's highways are among the most congested during peak commute hours. Interstate H-1 enters the city form the west, passing the Hickam Air Force Base and airport. H-201, also known as the Moanalua Freeway, is also a popular highway.

TheBus, owned by the City and County of Honolulu but operated separately, provides public transportation to the entire island on a fleet of over 530 buses providing daily service on over 100 routes. TheBus has been recognized twice by the American Public Transportation Association as America's best transit system, often noted for its dependability and frequency. Oahu Transit Service also provides a service called HandiVan that transports people with disabilities. The Waikiki Trolley Service, with a fleet of over 50 trolleys, provides transportation to shopping centers, museums, and other points of interest.

■ Communications

Newspapers and Magazines

Honolulu's only daily newspaper is *The Honolulu Star-Advertiser,* opened in 2010 following the merger of the city's former two daily newspapers, the *Honolulu Advertiser* and the *Honolulu Star-Bulletin.* There are also several non-English papers serving Honolulu. *Honolulu Magazine* features topics and events of local interest. Among the periodicals published in Honolulu are *Bamboo Ridge, The Hawaii Writers' Quarterly,* a literary magazine; *Biography,* a journal acting as a forum for learned articles dealing with life-writing; *Building Management Hawaii*; and *China Review International.* Business publications include *Hawaii Business* and *Pacific Business News.*

Television and Radio

Fifteen full power television stations broadcast from Honolulu; cable service is also available. An additional four low power television channels are available. Major networks such as Fox, ABC, CBS, NBC, and PBS are accompanied by several international and religious stations, among others. In 2009, Hawaii was the first state in the country to have its television stations switch from analog to digital. Over 42 FM and AM radio stations broadcast in Honolulu; several offer multilingual programming, from traditional Hawaiian to Chinese, Japanese, and Korean.

Media Information: *The Honolulu Advertiser;* telephone (808) 525-8090; fax (808) 525-8037. *Honolulu Star-Bulletin,* telephone (808) 529-4747; fax (808) 529-4750.

Honolulu Online

Chamber of Commerce of Hawaii. Available www.cochawaii.com

City and County of Honolulu. Available www.co.honolulu.hi.us

Hawaii Department of Education. Available www.doe.k12.hi.us

Hawaii Department of Labor and Industrial Relations. Available www.hawaii.gov/labor

Hawaii Visitors and Convention Bureau. Available www.gohawaii.com

*Honolulu Advertiser.*Available www.honoluluadvertiser.com

Honolulu Star-Bulletin. Available www.starbulletin.com

Oahu Visitors Bureau. Available www.visit-oahu.com

Social and economic trends. Available www.Hawaii.gov/dbedt

State of Hawaii. Available www.ehawaii.gov/dakine

BIBLIOGRAPHY

Cowing, Sue, ed., *Fire in the Sea: An Anthology of Poetry and Art* (Honolulu, HI: University of Hawaii Press in association with the Honolulu Academy of Arts, 1996)

Doughty, Andrew, *Oahu Revealed: The Ultimate Guide to Honolulu, Waikiki, and Beyond* 3rd ed. (Lihue, HI: Wizard Publications, 2010)

Shallenberger, Robert J., *Hawaiian Birds of the Sea* (Honolulu, HI: University of Hawaii Press, 2010)

Twain, Mark, *Letters from Honolulu* (Honolulu, HI: T. Nickerson, 1939)

Tyau, Kathleen, *A Little Too Much Is Enough* (New York: Norton, 1995)

Idaho

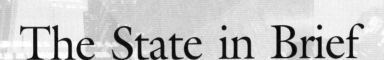

The State in Brief

Nickname: Gem State

Motto: Esto perpetua (Let it be perpetual)

Flower: Syringa

Bird: Mountain bluebird

Area: 83,569 square miles (2010; U.S. rank 14th)

Elevation: Ranges from 710 feet to 12,662 feet above sea level

Climate: Tempered by Pacific westerly winds, varying by altitude; hot summers in the arid south, cold snowy winters in the central and northern mountains

Admitted to Union: July 3, 1890

Capital: Boise

Head Official: C.L. "Butch" Otter (R) (until 2015)

Population
  1990: 1,006,749
  2000: 1,293,953
  2010: 1,567,582
  2012 estimate: 1,567,803
  Percent change, 2000–2010: 21.1%
  U.S. rank in 2012: 39th
  Percent of residents born in state: 46.6% (2012)
  Density: 19.0 people per square mile (2010)
  2012 FBI Crime Index Total: 34,969

Racial and Ethnic Characteristics (2012)
  White: 1,445,289
  Black or African American: 8,821
  American Indian and Alaska Native: 19,376
  Asian: 19,097
  Native Hawaiian and Pacific Islander: 2,213
  Hispanic or Latino (may be of any race): 175,512
  Other: 73,007

Age Characteristics (2012)
  Population under 5 years old: 119,601
  Population 5 to 19 years old: 351,889
  Percent of population 65 years and over: 12.5%
  Median age: 34.7

Vital Statistics
  Total number of births (2012–13): 22,187
  Total number of deaths (2012–13): 11,250
  AIDS cases reported through 2011: 776

Economy
  Major industries: Mining, lumbering, agriculture, high technology, tourism
  Unemployment rate (2012): 5.5%
  Per capita income (2012): $22,581
  Median household income (2012): $47,015
  Percentage of persons below poverty level (2012): 15.1%
  Income tax rate: 1.6% to 7.4%
  Sales tax rate: 6.0%

Boise

■ The City in Brief

Founded: 1834 (incorporated, 1864)

Head Official: Mayor David H. Bieter (D) (since 2004; current term expires 2016)

City Population
- 1990: 125,685
- 2000: 185,787
- 2010: 205,671
- 2012 estimate: 212,299
- Percent change, 2000–2010: 10.7%
- U.S. rank in 1990: 145th
- U.S. rank in 2000: 105th
- U.S. rank in 2010: 103rd (State rank: 1st)

Metropolitan Statistical Area Population
- 2000: 464,840
- 2010: 616,561
- 2012 estimate: 635,964
- Percent change, 2000–2010: 32.6%
- U.S. rank in 2000: 97th
- U.S. rank in 2010: 86th

Area: 63.8 square miles

Elevation: 2,842 feet above sea level

Average Annual Temperatures: January, 30.2° F; July, 74.7° F; annual average, 51.9° F

Average Annual Precipitation: 12.19 inches of rain; 20.7 inches of snow

Major Economic Sectors: services, agriculture, government, manufacturing, high-technology

Unemployment Rate: 6.1% (2012)

Per Capita Income: $27,681

2012 FBI Crime Index Property: 5,342

Major Colleges and Universities: Boise State University, University of Idaho–Boise Center

Daily Newspaper: *The Idaho Statesman*

■ Introduction

Boise, the capital of Idaho and the largest city in the state, is the commercial, financial, and cultural center of the northern Rockies region. Known as the "City of Trees," Boise is among the fastest-growing metropolitan areas in the nation, with growth peaking in the mid-2000s. At the same time, the city has maintained a high quality of life through cooperation between business, government, and citizens. An easy blending of historic structures and modern buildings in the downtown district attests to the fact that Boise remains close to its Western heritage while moving with the times. Boise is set in a fertile agricultural area called "Treasure Valley." Noted for its mild climate, clean environment, and friendly people, Boise is a place to treasure. The City of Boise was named the second most livable small city in the United States by *Forbes* magazine in 2012.

■ Geography and Climate

Boise is situated in a wide river valley at the foot of the Rocky Mountains. The Boise River runs out of a canyon to the south and through the center of the city, joining the Snake River about 40 miles to the north. The climate is tempered year-round by air from the Pacific Ocean. Summers are dry with hot periods that rarely last more than a few days; autumn weather is usually ideal. Winter storms produce much of the yearly precipitation; cold spells are common, but warm Chinook winds (moist air from the Pacific) bring periods of mild weather. Low humidity is raised slightly by agricultural irrigation.

Area: 63.8 square miles

The Idaho State Capitol building in Boise. *Randy Allphin/Shutterstock.com*

Elevation: 2,842 feet above sea level

Average Temperatures: January, 30.2° F; July, 74.7° F; annual average, 51.9° F

Average Annual Precipitation: 12.19 inches of rain; 20.7 inches of snow

■ History

Gold Brings Prospectors, Settlers

In 1834, the Hudson's Bay Company founded a trading post for wagon trains along the Oregon Trail on the Snake River northwest of Boise's present site. The region that is now Boise was originally a small-forested area along the Boise River, an oasis in the arid northwestern mountains. The spot was called "Les Bois," which means "wooded" in French, and thousands of emigrants passed through on their way to settle in Oregon. Gold was discovered in the area in 1862, bringing a number of prospectors, and the site became a convenient supply point for the mining camps in the mountains.

The U.S. Army constructed Fort Boise in 1863, and the town became the territorial capital in 1864, when it was also incorporated as a city. Several more gold strikes occurred in the next few years, and by1868 the town had more than four hundred permanent structures, more than half of which were residential. The Idaho Penitentiary was built in the town in 1870 and at one time or another housed many legendary western desperadoes.

Gold Dries Up; Irrigation Systems Bring Farms

After the gold boom ended, the population declined, and Boise faced an uphill battle for survival. The town was in an isolated location, far off the major lines of transportation, and the climate was too dry to support farming. A determined core of citizens set out to make the area livable by developing irrigation systems, planting crops, and mapping out a town with shady streets running along the river.

Boise approached the twentieth century as a remote place, reachable only by the difficult wagon trails. The city became the state capital when Idaho entered the Union, and the Capitol building was erected in 1920. A long struggle to obtain railway service finally succeeded when the elegant Union Pacific Depot (now the Boise Depot) was built in 1925. A number of dams and reservoirs were constructed in the years before World War II to improve the agricultural outlook and provide a water supply and hydroelectric power for the growing city.

During World War II the military became a strong presence in the Boise area when a flying and training base was established at Gowen Field. In the 1960s, a new city charter was drawn up, allowing the city to annex many of the suburban areas and doubling the population. The twenty-first century brought continued population growth due to Boise's urban renewal, job opportunities, quality of life, and favorable climate.

Historical Information: Idaho State Historical Society, Public Archives and Research Library, 2205 Old Penitentiary Road, Boise, ID 83712; telephone (208) 334-3356; fax (208) 334-3198.

■ Population Profile

Metropolitan Statistical Area Population

2000: 464,840
2010: 616,561
2012 estimate: 635,964
Percent change, 2000–2010: 32.6%
U.S. rank in 2000: 97th
U.S. rank in 2010: 86th

City Residents

1990: 125,685
2000: 185,787
2010: 205,671
2012 estimate: 212,299
Percent change, 2000–2010: 10.7%
U.S. rank in 1990: 145th
U.S. rank in 2000: 105th
U.S. rank in 2010: 103rd (State rank: 1st)

Density: 2,591.5 people per square mile

Racial and ethnic characteristics

White: 191,564
Black or African American: 2,530
American Indian and Alaskan Native: 2,056
Asian: 7,369
Native Hawaiian and Other Pacific Islander: 179
Hispanic or Latino (may be of any race): 15,433
Other: 8,601

Percent of residents born in state: 44.4%

Age characteristics

Population under 5 years old: 11,902
Population 5 to 9 years old: 10,758
Population 10 to 14 years old: 15,309
Population 15 to 19 years old: 14,207
Population 20 to 24 years old: 17,521
Population 25 to 34 years old: 31,661
Population 35 to 44 years old: 27,475
Population 45 to 54 years old: 30,631
Population 55 to 59 years old: 13,813
Population 60 to 64 years old: 13,778
Population 65 to 74 years old: 14,506
Population 75 to 84 years old: 6,473
Population 85 years and over: 4,265
Median age: 36.4

Births (2010–11 Metropolitan Area)

Total number: 8,500

Deaths (2010–11 Metropolitan Area)

Total number: 3,852

Money income (2012)

Per capita income: $27,681
Median household income: $45,985
Total households: 86,763

Number of households with income of . . .

less than $10,000: 6,064
$10,000 to $14,999: 5,554
$15,000 to $24,999: 10,032
$25,000 to $34,999: 11,155
$35,000 to $49,999: 13,817
$50,000 to $74,999: 15,130
$75,000 to $99,999: 8,952
$100,000 to $149,999: 9,774
$150,000 to $199,999: 3,657
$200,000 or more: 2,628

Percent of families below poverty level: 16.1%

FBI Crime Index Property: 5,342

FBI Crime Index Violent: 567

■ Municipal Government

Boise has been led by a mayor-council form of government since the adoption of a new city charter in 1961. The council is comprised of six part-time members, elected to four-year terms. A full-time mayor is elected every four years.

Head Official: Mayor David H. Bieter (D) (since 2004; current term expires 2016)

Total Number of City Employees: 1,605 (2013)

City Information: City of Boise Mayor's Office, P.O. Box 500, Boise, ID 83701; telephone (208) 384-4422; fax (208) 384-4420.

■ Economy

Major Industries and Commercial Activity

Boise began as a supply and service center for the mining camps in the nearby mountains. It continues today as an important commercial hub for smaller towns and agricultural establishments in the northern Rockies. In addition to mining, farming and timber have played important roles in the development of the Boise economy. Professional and business services, leisure and hospitality, and education and health services continue to drive growth.

Boise is the capital of Idaho and the city's most populated state. As one would expect, state government is one of the city's main employers. Law enforcement, education, and medical career opportunities also exist in Boise. Boise State University and Idaho State University are both located in Boise. The Army National Guard's Gowen Field also has an economic impact.

Private employers of note include Boise Inc., a nationwide provider of building materials and wood products. (The company sold its newspaper, paper, packaging, and transportation businesses in 2008.) Idaho Pacific Lumber Company also provides building materials, ranging from framing lumber to engineered wood products. Boise is home to Idaho Timber's national headquarters for sales, manufacture and distribution.

J.R. Simplot Company is one of the world's biggest privately held food and agribusiness companies specializing in frozen foods, phosphates, animal feeds, food processing, plant nutrition, and cattle. WinCo Foods is an employee-owned company with grocery store locations in various states.

The tech sector is represented by Micron Technology, which manufactures semiconductors. Other tech firms include Bodybuilding.com, the world's most visited website for sports nutrition and bodybuilding products, and Clearwater Analytics, headquartered in Boise, a provider of investment portfolio reporting solutions. In addition, Microsoft has a Boise location, as does Mark Monitor, Crucial.com, Balihoo.com, Mobile Data Force, Wire-stone.com and Sybase. Boise is also home to more than 20 call centers, including those for DIRECTV, EDS, T-Mobile, WDSGLobal, and Teleperformance.

Over 18,000 other businesses have major facilities in the area. Tourism is another large source of revenue for the Boise area.

Items and goods produced: building materials, wood, food, agricultural products, semiconductors

Incentive Programs—New and Existing Companies

Local programs: Boise advertises itself as business-friendly. The city's system for project management helps expedite permits, and a new online paperless review process reduces turnaround time for building and renovation projects. In addition, Boise State University provides various services for the business community through its Idaho Business and Economic Development Center's TECenter, Boise Future Foundation, Center for Professional Development, Simplot/Micron Instructional Technology Center, Small Business Development Center, and the College of Technology.

The Boise Capital City Development Corporation (CCDC) focuses on the revitalization of Boise's downtown and its neighborhoods through urban design and development initiatives in the city's urban renewal districts. CCDC's roles include planning, advocating, facilitating, partnering, managing facilities, developing and investing.

The Boise Valley Economic Partnership (BVEP) is the regional economic development organization with the mission of creating jobs, attracting new businesses to the region, and encouraging investment in the community. BVEP is a separately funded division of the Boise Metro Chamber of Commerce. The organization offers free, customized, confidential services and site location assistance to businesses and entrepreneurs interested in relocating, starting up, or expanding in the Boise Valley.

State programs: Idaho is an aggressive pro-business state. The Idaho Department of Commerce and Labor provides services to business owners to assist them in starting, relocating, running, and closing a business. The Idaho Corporate Advantage provides a comprehensive incentive package for large companies relocating headquarters or making major administrative expansions in the state.

Idaho has a variety of incentive programs designed to assist business start-up, business expansion, and business productivity, including financial incentives, business tax credits, and worker training programs. The Idaho Business Advantage program targets businesses that invest a minimum of $500,000 in new facilities and create at least 10 new jobs averaging $40,000 annually. Companies meeting these requirements may qualify for a variety of incentives, including an enhanced Investment Tax Credit of 3.75 percent up to $750,000 or 62.5 percent of tax liability in any one year; a new jobs tax credit starting at $1,500 and climbing to $3,000 per job; and a 2.5 percent real property improvement tax credit up to $125,000 in any one year along with a 25 percent rebate on sales tax paid on construction materials for the new facilities. In addition, businesses that make qualifying new investments may earn an income tax credit. This credit can be offset up to 50 percent of a company's state income tax liability and may be carried forward up to 14 years.

Other tax credits include the new jobs income tax credit, research and development income tax credit, and tax cap on certain excessive property values.

Job training programs: The state's workforce development training fund program provides up to $2,000 of new employee training reimbursement money. IdahoWorks is a combination of state and local workforce development groups. IdahoWorks provides career centers with over 17 programs geared toward those seeking employment or education. Programs include workshops on application and interview skills, resume and cover letter writing, and job fairs. The Boise State University Selland College of Applied Technology provides apprenticeship and job training programs to students who are enrolled in the college's Apprenticeship Programs offered by the Center for Workforce Training. Students receive on-the-job training while working as full-time, paid employees. Students also receive classroom training related to their chosen profession. The Center for Workforce Training offers career training programs for adults as well as programs to help businesses increase their productivity. In addition to training in the classroom, the Center offers online training programs and courses.

Development Projects

Boise is working on three major ongoing urban renewal projects. The oldest project, called the Central renewal project, focuses on downtown Boise's core and has resulted in the vibrant downtown Boise visitors and residents see today. Ongoing funding of the Central project was planned for use in additional infrastructure, beautification and public arts projects. The River Myrtle-Old Boise renewal project, also underway, is located south of downtown Boise. With a focus on attracting high-tech tenants, this urban renewal project is developing a technical infrastructure. The Westside renewal project encompasses 47 acres of downtown Boise. Renewal plans encompass a 25-year span with completion of all projects in 2025. The Westside project is expected to bring multi-use development to downtown, including office, residential, retail, restaurants, entertainment venues, and hotels.

Among the latest downtown plan announced in 2010 was the JUMP "parkscape," a redevelopment of four vacant city blocks. Jack's Urban Meeting Place (JUMP) is a $70 million project of the Simplot Family Foundation. Construction began in early 2012 and encompasses a 7.5-acre site near the heart of downtown. The project will house five working studios as well as civic event and meeting spaces, antique tractor sculptures, a dynamic urban park, and an outdoor amphitheater.

In 2011 Concordia Law School combined an existing LEED-certified 19,069-square-foot building with another 35,192 square feet in a three-story expansion. The approximately $10 million project opened in September 2011 and classes began in the fall of 2012.

As of 2014, new development projects in Boise amounted to $150 million in combined construction budgets. A new Whole Foods Market and Walgreens project on the east end of downtown was reported to be a $6 million investment. It covers 3.4 acres near Broadway and Front streets. A new 18-story Zion's Tower, also downtown, was estimated to be a $76 million investment. The building will be the tallest in the State of Idaho.

Economic Development Information: Boise Valley Economic Partnership, 250 S. 5th St., Suite 300, Boise, ID 83702; telephone (208) 472-5230.

Commercial Shipping

A Grant Thornton *General Manufacturing Climates* study ranked Idaho the best state in the nation for transportation because of its infrastructure and strategic location in the Pacific Northwest. Rail freight carriers serve the Boise metropolitan area via the Union Pacific Railroad. A variety of motor freight lines, air freight, package express companies, and air courier services are also part of Boise's commercial transportation industry.

Labor Force and Employment Outlook

Boise's skilled work force is educated above the national average and it remains diverse because of a high percentage of immigration. Thirty-four percent of residents have a bachelor's degree or higher; the Boise metro area has been ranked the fourth best place to do business in the nation by *Forbes* magazine. In the mid-2000s, although employment rates were on the rise, the city was experiencing difficulty finding qualified trade and skilled workers. In the late 2000s, the need for those employees dwindled slightly as unemployment got closer to the national averages during the recession. Nonetheless, Boise remains a top place for business and new growth in careers, with a low cost of doing business.

The following is a summary of data regarding the 2012 Boise labor force:

Size of civilian labor force: 115,846

Number of workers employed in . . .

    agriculture and mining: 929
    construction: 5,082
    manufacturing: 10,599
    wholesale trade: 2,400
    retail trade: 12,108
    transportation: 4,462
    information systems: 2,638
    finance: 6,108
    professional administration: 14,102
    education and social services: 24,271
    arts and leisure: 11,325
    other: 4,517
    public administration: 6,929

Average hourly earnings of production workers: $14.85

Unemployment rate: 6.1% (2012)

Employers

Largest employers (2012)	*Number of employees*
State of Idaho	12,968
St Luke's Health System Ltd.	4,250
Wal-Mart	7,100
Micron Technology Inc.	10,500
JR Simplot	3,800
Hewlett Packard	4,000
Saint Alphonsus Regional	3,373
Boise State University	1,784
DIRECTV Inc.	1,700
American Drug Stores Inc.	1,500

Cost of Living

Boise boasts rates for residential, commercial, and industrial electricity and natural gas that are below the national average. Home prices in the surrounding area are significantly less than national averages.

The following is a summary of data regarding several key cost of living factors in the area.

2013 ACCRA Average House Price: $262,914

2013 ACCRA Cost of Living Index: 93

State income tax rate: 1.6% to 7.4%

State sales tax rate: 6.0%

Local income tax rate: None

Local sales tax rate: None

Property tax rate: $8.036783 per $1,000 of assessed value (2013)

Economic Information: Idaho Department of Commerce, 700 West State Street, PO Box 83720, Boise, ID 83720-0093; telephone (208) 334-2470; toll-free (800) 842-5858; fax (208) 334-2631. Boise Metro Chamber of Commerce, 250 South 5th Street, PO Box 2368, Boise, ID 83702; telephone (208) 472-5200; fax (208) 472-5201; email info@boisechamber.org.

■ Education and Research

Elementary and Secondary Schools

The Boise School District serves 26,000 students and employs 3,900 people, of whom 1,700 are certified staff. Founded in 1865 under the auspices of the Idaho Territory, it is administered by a seven-member, nonpartisan board of trustees that appoints a superintendent.

The district maintains 33 elementary schools, 8 junior high schools, and 5 senior high schools. Specialized programs include Montessori, Dual Language, Classical, International, Harbor, Full-day and Highly Gifted programs at elementary grades, to the Treasure Valley Math and Science Center, Dennis Professional-Technical Center, and the state's pre-eminent Advanced Placement (AP) program at the secondary level.

The *Washington Post* has ranked all four of Boise's comprehensive high schools—Boise, Borah, Capital, and Timberline—among the top 9 percent in the country. Each high school offers at least 23 AP courses. Boise students took 37 percent of the statewide AP exams in 2012 and scored well above national and state averages, earning thousands of credit waivers and college credits at universities across the country.

Boise School District students perform well on standardized achievement tests. The percentage of students reading at grade level on the Idaho Reading Indicator and scoring proficient on the Idaho Standards Achievement Test continue to surpass Idaho results at all grade levels. In 2013, on the second statewide administration of the Scholastic Aptitude Test (SAT), Boise District juniors outperformed students in every other large district in the state of Idaho.

In addition to the public schools, there are 22 private and parochial schools, with a total enrollment of nearly about 3,100 students in the Boise area. The Diocese of Boise has 13 Catholic Grade Schools and one Catholic High School. The schools are dedicated to providing a Catholic environment for learning.

The following is a summary of data regarding the Boise Independent School District.

Total enrollment: 25,039

Number of facilities

    total: 46
    elementary schools: 33
    junior high schools: 8
    high schools: 5
    other: 0

Student/teacher ratio: 16:1

Teacher salaries

    average (statewide): $47,416

Funding per pupil: $8,218

Public Schools Information: Boise School District Public Information Specialist, 8169 W. Victory Rd., Boise, ID 83709; telephone (208) 338-3400; fax (208) 338-3487.

Colleges and Universities

Founded in 1932, Boise State is located in the state's population center and capital city. The 175-acre main campus is situated less than a mile from Boise's downtown. It is the largest university in Idaho with 22,678 students from 50 states and 65 countries. The university has undergraduate, graduate, and technical programs in seven colleges offering 82 master's degrees, 94 baccalaureates, 4 associates, 21 graduate certificates, and 9 doctoral programs. In 2012, 45 percent of new freshmen had a high school grade point average exceeding 3.5. The faculty-to-student ratio is 20 to 1.

Main academic facilities include Albertsons Library, Engineering Complex, Norco Building, Communication Building, Kinesiology Building and Annex, Liberal Arts Building, Math/Geosciences Building, Business Building, Education Building, Science/Nursing Building, Interactive Learning Center, Public Affairs and Arts West Building, and the Multipurpose Classroom Building. A five-story, 90,000-square-foot Environmental Research Building opened in 2011, and the Micron Business and Economics Building opened in fall 2012.

Entertainment and athletic facilities include Bronco Stadium (33,500 capacity), Taco Bell Arena (12,400), Morrison Center Main Hall (2,000) and Centennial Amphitheatre (800). Student Union venues are the Grace Jordan Ballroom (1,000), J.R. and Esther Simplot Grand Ballroom, (700) and Special Events Center (435), in addition to the Boise State Bookstore and Bronco Shop.

The College of Western Idaho (CWI) is a comprehensive community college providing higher education programs to residents of Western Idaho. The college offers courses leading to an associate of arts or science degree, transfer degrees, professional/technical degrees, continuing education, and certificates. CWI also offers basic academic skills to help prepare for a GED, dual credit for high school students, and fast-track career training for working professionals. Brown Mackie College is an independent college offering courses in health care and wellness, business and technology, legal studies, and veterinary technology.

The University of Idaho maintains a graduate, research, and professional development center in Boise hosting 120 faculty and staff members. The center focuses on water, natural resources, and the environment; community sustainability and design; organizational development and leadership; and the professions: law, medicine, architecture, engineering and education.

Three private colleges also serve the metropolitan area: Albertson College of Idaho in Caldwell, Northwest Nazarene University in Nampa, and Boise Bible College.

Libraries and Research Centers

Boise Public Library was founded in 1895 when the women of the Columbian Club opened a subscription library and free reading room in City Hall. A grant from Andrew Carnegie helped fund Boise's Carnegie Public Library, which opened its doors in 1905. In 1965 the bookmobile service was initiated to expand library service in the city and reduce crowding in the Carnegie building. Today, the bookmobile makes weekly stops at six locations throughout Boise. In addition to the main library, the system includes three neighborhood branch libraries. A fourth branch is planned for Southeast Boise.

In 2013 the library logged 1,432,014 in-person visits and 2,257,715 borrowed items. Public computer Internet sessions numbered 346,669, and 285,580 reference questions were answered by reference librarians.

As of 2014, the Boise Public Library is a part of the City of Boise government and is funded primarily through local property taxes. The Board of Trustees sets policy for operations, and the Friends of the Boise Public Library and the Boise Public Library Foundation provide additional financial support. The 2014 budget was $8.973 million.

The Idaho State Library contains more than 36,000 volumes; it also operates an extensive blind and physically handicapped service, providing more than 58,000 talking books as well as more than 5,000 large-print books.

Boise State University's library holds more than 530,000 books and more than 6,000 newspaper and serial subscriptions. A number of smaller private, corporate, and special interest libraries are also located in the Boise metropolitan area. Research activities in such fields as technology, audio and video production, computers, and data processing are conducted at centers in the Boise area.

Public Library Information: Boise Public Library, 715 South Capitol Boulevard, Boise, ID 83702-7115; telephone (208) 384-4076.

■ Health Care

The Boise medical community has two major regional medical facilities: Saint Alphonsus Regional Medical Center, an acute-care facility featuring a regional trauma center; and St. Luke's Regional Medical Center. St Luke's was the 2006 Microsoft "Hospital of the Year," awarded for use of technology in health care; the hospital provides general treatment, specialty care, and surgical services, as well as neonatal and pediatric intensive care. Both hospitals are among the city's largest employers with some 2,500 employees at St. Luke's and 1,800 at Saint Alphonsus. The Idaho Elks Rehabilitation Hospital specializes in rehabilitation services in the areas of audiology, brain injury, cardio-pulmonary, orthopedics, pediatrics and stroke/neurology. To better accommodate the growing community the hospital opened a new state of the art facility in 2001. The Veterans Administration Medical Center, a teaching hospital affiliated with the

University of Washington School of Medicine, offers general care and outpatient, mental health, and substance abuse clinics. Also located in Boise are Treasure Valley Hospital for patients needing surgery, Mountain States Tumor Institute, and several nursing homes.

■ Recreation

Sightseeing

The best way to see Boise is on the popular Tour Train, a replica of an 1890s steam-powered locomotive that originates in Julia Davis Park and takes an hour-long trip through the city's historic neighborhoods and the central business district. Other attractions in the park include Zoo Boise, the Julia Davis Park Rose Garden, and an outdoor band shell where summer concerts are performed.

The downtown area contains several historic points of interest. The Idaho State Capitol, erected in 1920, is a smaller version of the Capitol building in Washington D. C., and is the only statehouse in America heated by natural geothermal energy. The Capitol building underwent extensive exterior renovation, completed in 2006, and funding was put in place that same year for future interior renovations. At the other end of Capitol Boulevard is the Boise Depot, constructed in 1925 and modeled after a Spanish mission. The station is surrounded by the beautiful Platt Gardens. Other historic sites in Boise include the Old Boise district and the Eighth Street Marketplace, two restored neighborhoods. The O'Farrell Cabin, the first structure built in Boise, is located in Military Reserve Park. The area surrounding Boise offers many attractions, including restored wild west towns like Idaho City and the Snake River Birds of Prey area. Other pleasurable activities are scenic mountain and canyon drives and tours of the local vineyards in Idaho's wine country.

Arts and Culture

The Morrison Center for the Performing Arts, a 2,030-seat facility located on the Boise State University campus, is the site of much of the city's cultural activity. The center hosts performances by the Boise Philharmonic Orchestra, Ballet Idaho, and Opera Idaho as well as special events that range from rock concerts to touring Broadway productions. The city holds an annual Shakespearean festival, and several area theatrical groups perform throughout the year. Among them are the Boise Little Theater, the Idaho Theater for Youth, and the Stage Coach Theater.

The city is home to a number of museums and art galleries. The Idaho Historical Museum, located in Julia Davis Park, is a unique open-air museum that features an Old West saloon, a blacksmith's shop, and western and Native American artifacts. The restored Idaho State Penitentiary (called the "Old Pen") now houses several museums, including the Idaho Transportation Museum and the Electricity Museum. The Idaho Black History Museum relocated from the former penitentiary to St. Paul Baptist Church in Julia Davis Park; exhibits relate the importance of the African American culture to the heritage of Idaho and the nation. The Boise Art Museum, also in Julia Davis Park, contains a permanent collection of regional and national art; it also hosts a number of traveling exhibits each year. The Idaho Botanical Garden, featuring a variety of themed gardens, is adjacent to the Old Pen. Other art galleries in the city include the Art Attack Gallery, Brown's Galleries, Gallery 601, and the Art Source Gallery.

Festivals and Holidays

A number of special events are scheduled in the Boise area throughout the year. Spring is celebrated with the Apple Blossom Festival; seven days of festivities include a rodeo, parade, carnival, festival, and crowning of the Apple Blossom Queen. The National Old Time Fiddlers' Contest takes place for seven days each June in nearby Weiser, Idaho, one hour northwest of Boise. Summer also brings the Spirit of Boise Balloon Classic in late June; the Idaho Shakespeare Festival, featuring Shakespeare under the Stars; and the Western Idaho Fair, an old fashioned country fair that lasts for 10 days in August. Boise's Basque population, the largest concentration in North America, presents three days of cultural activities every July, including performances by the famous Oinkari Basque Dancers. Oktoberfest at the Idaho Botanical Garden includes music, dance, food and beverage.

Sports for the Spectator

The Boise Hawks, members of the Northwest League and affiliated with the Chicago Cubs, play baseball from mid-June through early September at Memorial Stadium. The Qwest Arena (formerly the Bank of America Center) hosts hockey action from the Idaho Steelheads of the East Coast Hockey League and satisfies basketball fans by also hosting the Idaho Stampede of the Continental Basketball Association.

A complete program of collegiate sports is offered at Boise State University, featuring a championship football team and a nationally recognized basketball team. The Boise State Bronco football team is often ranked among the top 25 in NCAA Division I college football polls and typically sells out Bronco Stadium, which has a unique blue playing field.

Thoroughbred and harness racing, along with pari-mutuel wagering, are featured at Les Bois Race Track. Championship drag racing is held at Firebird Raceway. Fans of rodeo enjoy the famous Snake River Stampede in Nampa and the Caldwell Night Rodeo in Caldwell.

Meridian Speedway offers drag racing and stock car racing. In women's sports action, there is the annual

St. Luke's Women's Fitness Celebration, a run/walk event that ranks among the largest of its kind in the nation. The Albertsons Boise Open golf tournament is part of the PGA Tour.

Sports for the Participant

Boise offers an abundance of outdoor activities. The area's 107 park sites feature facilities for boating, tennis, golf, swimming, jogging, cycling, and other recreational activities. The Boise River, which runs through downtown Boise, is a popular spot for tubing, canoeing, and fishing; 16 acres on both sides of the river form the Boise River Greenbelt offering 25 miles of paved and graveled paths. Many area reservoirs offer a full range of water activities. Both day and night skiing can be enjoyed at Bogus Basin, a 45-minute drive from downtown Boise; five other ski areas are within a three-hour drive. The nearby mountains are favorite hiking, fishing, and camping locations, while the nearby Payette and Salmon rivers are known worldwide by kayakers and rafters for their exciting white water.

Shopping and Dining

Old Boise and the Eighth Street Marketplace, two distinctive historical districts in Boise, have been converted into unique shopping areas. The Hyde Park district features a number of antique shops, and State Street marketplace is a group of specialty shops in a modern complex. Several shopping malls are open in the area, including Boise Towne Square, which offers more than 175 stores, and the Boise Factory Outlet Mall.

Dining opportunities in Boise are diverse and usually inexpensive. Cuisines range from simple yet filling Western fare to exotic international specialties such as Basque, Mexican, Chinese, Indian, Egyptian, and Vietnamese. Several elegant dining places feature French, Continental, and New American dishes.

Visitor Information: Boise Convention and Visitors Bureau, PO Box 2106, Boise, ID 83701; telephone (208) 344-7777; toll-free (800) 635-5240; fax (208) 344-6236; email info@boisechamber.org.

■ Convention Facilities

The Boise Center on the Grove offers over 80,000 square feet of meeting space and features a glass-fronted lobby, a 7,600-square-foot auditorium that will seat 350 people, and an almost 25,000-square-foot central meeting space. Other facilities include Boise State University's Taco Bell Arena, which seats up to 13,000 spectators and has 17,472 square feet of open floor space. The Morrison Center for the Performing Arts, also on the Boise State campus, has a 2,000 seat main hall and two teaching/studying halls. The Nampa Civic Center in nearby Nampa offers banquet seating for up to 1,000 people,

and a 648-seat auditorium. There are more than 4,600 hotel rooms in Boise; most of the major hotels provide meeting, banquet, and ballroom facilities.

Convention Information: Boise Convention and Visitors Bureau, PO Box 2106, Boise, ID 83701; telephone (208) 344-7777; toll-free (800) 635-5240; fax (208) 344-6236; email info@boisechamber.org.

■ Transportation

Approaching the City

Two major highways lead into Boise. I-84 runs east and west, connecting the metropolitan area with the West Coast and the Midwestern states. U.S. 20 and U.S. 26 runs diagonally west to southeast through the center of the city. Public bus transportation throughout Boise Valley is provided by ValleyRide. Van and carpooling services are offered by Commuteride.

The city-owned Boise Airport, located a few miles south of downtown, is served by eight airlines and offers non-stop daily service to 16 cities. The airport terminal is open 24 hours a day, 7 days a week. It has a covered parking garage and remote surface parking with shuttle service, food and beverage concessions, news and gifts concessions, and a conference center. Free Wi-Fi is available throughout Boise Airport. Each year more than three million passengers travel through Boise Airport, making it the gateway to southwestern Idaho and eastern Oregon.

The Boise Valley Railroad handles freight service in Boise Idaho. BVRR provides freight service through an agreement with Union Pacific Railroad and the City of Boise, both owners of railroad right-of-ways in the valley. The BVRR consists of 36 miles of track that travel two separate branches, the Wilder Branch and the Boise Cutoff. The major commodities shipped on the line include building materials, agricultural products and produce, lumber, fertilizer, and fuels.

Traveling in the City

Streets south of the Boise River tend to form a grid pattern; north of the river, streets follow the contours of the foothills of the Rocky Mountains and the streams that flow through town.

ValleyRide provides bus service on fixed routes as well as access services for people with disabilities.

■ Communications

Newspapers and Magazines

Boise is served by one daily newspaper, *The Idaho Statesman,* and two weekly papers. Locally-published magazines focus on religion, families, wildlife, farming, and sheep and cattle growing.

Television and Radio

Four television stations broadcast from Boise. Approximately 15 AM and FM radio stations serve the Boise area with a diverse blend of music, news, and information.

Media Information: *The Idaho Statesman,* P.O. Box 40, Boise, ID 83707; telephone (208) 377-6200; toll-free (800) 635-8934.

Boise Online

Boise Convention & Visitors Bureau home page. Available www.boise.org

Boise Metro Chamber of Commerce home page. Available www.boisechamber.org

Boise Public Library home page. Available www. boisepubliclibrary.org

Boise School District home page. Available www. boiseschools.org

City of Boise home page. Available www.cityofboise. org

Idaho Commerce & Labor home page. Available www.cl.idaho.gov

Idaho Commission for Libraries home page. Available www.libraries.idaho.gov

The Idaho Statesman. Available www. idahostatesman.com

BIBLIOGRAPHY

Egan, Timothy, *The Big Burn: Teddy Roosevelt and the Fire that Saved America* (Boston: Mariner Books, 2010)

Harris, Richard, *Hidden Idaho: Including Boise, Sun Valley and Yellowstone National Park* (Berkeley, CA: Ulysses, 2004)

MacGregor, Carol Lynn, *Boise, Idaho, 1882–1910 Prosperity in Isolation* (Missoula, MT: Mountain Press Pub., 2006)

Shallat, Todd, ed.*Quintessential Boise: An Architectural Journey* (Boise, ID: Boise State University College of Social Sciences and Public Affairs, 2010)

Idaho Falls

■ The City in Brief

Founded: 1891 (incorporated as Idaho Falls)

Head Official: Mayor Rebecca Casper (R) (since 2014; current term expires 2018)

City Population
- 1990: 43,929
- 2000: 50,730
- 2010: 56,813
- 2012 estimate: 57,478
- Percent change, 2000–2010: 12.0%
- U.S. rank in 2010: 607th (State rank: 4th)

Metropolitan Statistical Area Population
- 2000: 101,677
- 2010: 130,374
- 2012 estimate: 133,368
- Percent change, 2000–2010: 28.2%
- U.S. rank in 2000: 335th
- U.S. rank in 2010: 317th

Area: 17.4 square miles

Elevation: 4,739 feet above sea level

Average Annual Temperatures: January, 22.2° F; July, 70.2° F

Average Annual Precipitation: 14.3 inches of rain; 34.5 inches of snow

Major Economic Sectors: health care, agriculture, tourism, nuclear research

Unemployment Rate: 4.5% (2012)

Per Capita Income: $22,537

2012 FBI Crime Index Property: 1,705

Major Colleges and Universities: Eastern Idaho Technical College, University of Idaho, Idaho State University

Daily Newspaper: *Post Register*

■ Introduction

Idaho Falls, Idaho's fifth largest city, sits on the Snake River in the Snake River Plain, a wide valley surrounded by mountain ranges. The region has some of the richest agricultural land in the state. The Burbank Russet (Idaho Potato) is a major crop, while grain and alfalfa are also grown in abundance. The city is close to Yellowstone National Park, Grand Teton National Park, Sun Valley, Craters of the Moon National Monument, the Idaho Primitive Area, and many other skiing, hiking, fishing, picnicking and hunting areas. The city is the county seat of Bonneville County and serves as a regional center for health care, cultural events, and financial services. The community's economic base was expanded in 1949 when the Atomic Energy Commission opened the National Reactor Testing Station in the nearby desert. The facility brought high-income jobs to the area. As of 2014, the government facility, renamed the Idaho National Laboratory (INL) in 2005, continued to enrich the local economy. INL is 35 miles west of the Idaho Falls, and many residents commute to work in the nuclear research facilities.

■ Geography and Climate

Idaho Falls is located on the eastern edge of the Snake River Plain. The land is of volcanic origin, which provides for both a rich soil ideal for potatoes and the nearby hot springs and geysers of Yellowstone National Park. The area is surrounded by high desert sagebrush-grassland steppe. Idaho Falls enjoys all four seasons, with both seasonal and daily temperatures spanning a wide range, and annual precipitation falling primarily as snow during the winter months and rain in the fall and early spring.

Area: 17.4 square miles

Elevation: 4,739 feet above sea level

Average Temperatures: January, 22.2° F; July, 70.2° F

Average Annual Precipitation: 14.3 inches of rain; 34.5 inches of snow

■ History

Idaho Falls was originally the place where gold miners traveling the Montana Trial crossed the Snake River on their way to the boomtowns of Bannack and Virginia City. A ferry was established at the location in 1863, followed in 1865 by Taylor's Crossing, a timber frame toll bridge built by Matt Taylor. As travel increased, the site of the crossing evolved into a trading post. Businesses sprang up, including a post office, stage station, bank, and hotel. The site was close to a rocky island in the river that was home to an eagle with a nest high in a Juniper tree. The area became known as Eagle Rock.

In 1878 the robber baron and railroad tycoon Jay Gould was expanding rail service to the new copper mines in Butte. The railroad chose Taylor's Crossing for the location of an iron railroad bridge to span the Snake River. Construction crews set up camp nearby followed by saloons and dancehalls. With the arrival of the railroad, Eagle Rock became a distribution post for the surrounding area, then consisting mostly of ranchland.

To the miners and railroad workers passing through, the region seemed bleak and baron. However, in 1869, a geologist named Hayden noted that the valley was "composed of a rich, sandy loam, that needs but the addition of water to render it excellent farming land." It turned out that the surrounding countryside was ideally suited to growing a crop that would make Idaho famous, potatoes. Particularly well suited to the area was the "Idaho Russet," developed by Luther Burbank in 1872 in his New England garden.

Fueled by the Homestead Act (1862), the region began attracting farmers. The act gave 160 acres of free land to anyone over the age of 21 who was willing to live on it and cultivate it for five years. After the land was cleared, canals were dug to provide irrigation for wheat, barley, oats and corn, the staples of every farm. Acquiring water rights and digging canals was hard work. Sensing an opportunity, canal companies did a brisk business in bringing water from the Snake River and its feeder streams to the surrounding desert. Unfortunately, the canals built by these companies were at the mercy of the river. In the early spring, high water would wash out the diversion dams and changes in the course of the river would leave some canals without water altogether.

To solve the problem, in 1895 the Great Feeder Canal was built 20 miles northeast of Idaho Falls to divert water into the Dry Bed. It was the most ambitious irrigation project in the nation. At the time of its creation, its headgates were touted as the largest in the world. It is now part of one of America's largest irrigation systems. It helped turn tens of thousands of acres of desert into lush farmland.

As the farms became established, they began growing larger crops for the market, including the Idaho Russet. The town soon became the center of a great agricultural region. In 1891 the citizens changed the name of the city from Eagle Rock to Idaho Falls. In the early 1900s, Idaho Falls built a dam to tame the rough rapids of the Snake River that flowed through the center of town. The dam created the falls, now a scenic focal point of the city's historic downtown, and provided the city with its first power from hydroelectric turbines.

Idaho Falls remained an agricultural city until 1949, when the Atomic Energy Commission opened the National Reactor Testing Station in the desert west of the city. In 1951 a nuclear reactor at the site produced useful electricity for the first time in history. The site was renamed the Idaho National Laboratory (INL), and remains an important part of the Idaho Falls economy.

Historical Information: Idaho Historical Society, 2205 Old Penitentiary Road, Boise, ID 83712; telephone (208) 334-2682.

■ Population Profile

Metropolitan Statistical Area Population
> 2000: 101,677
> 2010: 130,374
> 2012 estimate: 133,368
> Percent change, 2000–2010: 28.2%
> U.S. rank in 2000: 335th
> U.S. rank in 2010: 317th

City Residents
> 1990: 43,929
> 2000: 50,730
> 2010: 56,813
> 2012 estimate: 57,478
> Percent change, 2000–2010: 12.0%
> U.S. rank in 2010: 607th (State rank: 4th)

Density: 1,690.7 people per square mile

Racial and ethnic characteristics
> White: 52,204
> Black or African American: 483
> American Indian and Alaskan Native: 488
> Asian: 322
> Native Hawaiian and Other Pacific Islander: 49

Hispanic or Latino (may be of any race): 6,814
Other: 3,932

Percent of residents born in state: 53.7%

Age characteristics

Population under 5 years old: 5,051
Population 5 to 9 years old: 4,862
Population 10 to 14 years old: 3,798
Population 15 to 19 years old: 4,200
Population 20 to 24 years old: 3,500
Population 25 to 34 years old: 8,456
Population 35 to 44 years old: 6,708
Population 45 to 54 years old: 7,252
Population 55 to 59 years old: 3,182
Population 60 to 64 years old: 3,421
Population 65 to 74 years old: 3,385
Population 75 to 84 years old: 2,369
Population 85 years and over: 1,294
Median age: 33.4

Births (2010–11 Metropolitan Area)

Total number: 2,428

Deaths (2010–11 Metropolitan Area)

Total number: 854

Money income (2012)

Per capita income: $22,537
Median household income: $45,582
Total households: 20,948

Number of households with income of ...

less than $10,000: 1,416
$10,000 to $14,999: 1,678
$15,000 to $24,999: 2,545
$25,000 to $34,999: 2,536
$35,000 to $49,999: 3,168
$50,000 to $74,999: 4,138
$75,000 to $99,999: 2,017
$100,000 to $149,999: 2,362
$150,000 to $199,999: 562
$200,000 or more: 526

Percent of families below poverty level: 16.4%

FBI Crime Index Property: 1,705

FBI Crime Index Violent: 139

■ Municipal Government

Idaho Falls has a mayor-council form of government, with the mayor serving as the chief executive officer. The city council consists of six members. Both the council members and the mayor are elected to four-year terms.

Head Official: Mayor Rebecca Casper (R) (since 2014; current term expires 2018)

Total Number of City Employees: 613 (2012)

City Information: City of Idaho Falls, 308 Constitution Way, Idaho Falls, Idaho 83402; telephone: (208) 612-8100.

■ Economy

Major Industries and Commercial Activity

Idaho Falls' location close to national parks, wilderness areas, and ski slopes has helped it develop a profitable industry based on tourism, including hospitality-based businesses, recreational equipment manufacturers, and all the attendant services required to meet the needs of the millions who pass through the region each year.

The traditional and still critically important agricultural sector provides an opportunity for an array of facilities for creating value-added products, including biofuels, distilled spirits, malt, and potato flakes. This has attracted some of the nation's leading food technology developers looking to add value to agricultural commodities, or to develop new products and processes for the food industry.

The city's position as a regional hub for medical services supports diagnostic facilities, medical laboratories, outpatient facilities, and medical support businesses.

Government facilities like the Idaho National Laboratory (INL) make the region a leader in the development and testing of nuclear energy technology.

Items and goods produced: agricultural products, especially potatoes; biofuels; food and beverage products

Incentive Programs—New and Existing Companies

Local programs: Grow Idaho Falls Inc. is the economic development agency for the City of Idaho Falls, the City of Ammon, the City of Ucon, and Bonneville County. The mission of the agency is to help expand the business base and facilitate the creation of high-quality jobs in the Idaho Falls area. The agency is focused on expanding its business presence in energy and high technology, including sustainable, carbon-free energy based on biofuels, wind, geothermal, and fossil resources. Other areas for development include medical technologies and services, agribusiness and food industries, and tourism and gateway community services.

The Downtown Development Corporation strives to create a unique and inviting atmosphere for Downtown Idaho Falls. Projects include a plan to reconfigure Memorial Drive to take advantage of the Snake River and the enhancement of Yellowstone Highway, which borders the east side of Historic Downtown Idaho Falls.

Opportunities and incentives also exist for energy-related companies, including commercialization programs between national labs and private industry that facilitate technology transfer, and a growing number of research parks and incubators.

State programs: Idaho is an aggressive pro-business state. The Idaho Department of Commerce and Labor provides services to business owners to assist them in starting, relocating, running, and closing a business. The Idaho Corporate Advantage provides a comprehensive incentive package for large companies relocating headquarters or making major administrative expansions in the state.

Idaho has a variety of incentive programs designed to assist business start-up, business expansion, and business productivity, including financial incentives, business tax credits, and worker training programs. The Idaho Business Advantage program targets businesses that invest a minimum of $500,000 in new facilities and create at least 10 new jobs averaging $40,000 annually. Companies meeting these requirements may qualify for a variety of incentives including an enhanced Investment Tax Credit of 3.75 percent up to $750,000 or 62.5 percent tax liability in any one year; a new jobs tax credit starting at $1,500 and climbing to $3,000 per job; and a 2.5 percent real property improvement tax credit up to $125,000 in any one year along with a 25 percent rebate on sales tax paid on construction materials for the new facilities. In addition, businesses that make qualifying new investments may earn an income tax credit. This credit can be offset up to 50 percent of a company's state income tax liability and may be carried forward up to 14 years.

Other tax credits include the new jobs income tax credit, research and development income tax credit, and tax cap on certain excessive property values.

Job training programs: WOTC is a federal income tax credit designed to help job seekers most in need of employment gain job experience and move towards economic self-sufficiency. Credits of up to $9,600 per employee are available for targeted groups. The maximum credit for most groups is $2,400. However, $4,800 is available for each new disabled veteran employee hired within one year of leaving service, $5,600 for each new veteran hired that is unemployed for at least six months, $9,000 for each new long-term family assistance recipient employee hired over a two-year period, and $9,600 for each new disabled veteran hired who is unemployed for six months.

Development Projects

Snake River Landing is a 400-acre master-planned waterfront community along the Snake River in close proximity to downtown Idaho Falls. Snake River Landing is also the chosen location for the planned Idaho Falls Event Center.

Scientech, a part of the Curtiss-Wright Flow Control Corporation, announced plans to locate their Idaho Falls office to new buildings under construction in 2014. The company is a global provider of commercial nuclear power safety and risk analyses, instrumentation, safety-related electrical components, specialty hardware, reactor and steam generator equipment and services, process control systems, and proprietary database solutions aimed at improving safety, plant performance, and reliability.

Like most downtown areas in the nation, downtown Idaho Falls struggled when businesses moved as the city expanded out of the central business district. To reverse this trend, the Idaho Falls Development Corporation and Grow Idaho Falls are working with business owners to revitalize the downtown area. Completed in 2012, the Memorial Drive Project takes advantage of the Snake River, while providing an attractive streetscape and needed parking. The Yellowstone Gateway, completed in 2007, adds visual appeal to the gateway to downtown by adding trees and replacing the islands with attractive landscape bricks. Future plans include the development of an amphitheater, a water feature, and a walking bridge. Funding for the project is in the beginning stages, with the water feature scheduled to be completed by 2015.

Economic Development Information: Idaho Falls Downtown Development Corporation, 440 N Capital Ave, Idaho Falls, ID 83402; telephone: (208) 535-0399. Grow Idaho Falls, 151 N Ridge Ave # A, Idaho Falls, ID 83402; telephone: (208) 522-2014.

Commercial Shipping

Idaho Falls is accessible by air, rail, or road. The comparatively low cost of real estate, as well as low energy costs, make the area attractive to prospective transportation and distribution companies. Idaho Falls Regional Airport is the largest area airport serving nearby resort communities such as Jackson Hole and Sun Valley. Union Pacific and Eastern Idaho Railroads both provide freight service. Transloading facilities are available.

Labor Force and Employment Outlook

Trade, utilities and transportation account for more than a quarter of Bonneville County's jobs, with trade by far the largest. Education and health care are next, followed by government. The county is economically stable and cooperates with one of the state's largest employment sites, the Idaho National Laboratory. Leisure and hospitality is growing, as the county becomes better known as a tourist destination.

Average employment in the Idaho Falls area increased nearly 2,900 between 2000 and 2010, while average annual wages increased by over $5,300. Although unemployment rates began to climb as the national recession took hold, county unemployment remained below national and state levels, helped by a skilled workforce that attracted new businesses and helped others expand. Nevertheless, in 2013, Bonneville County grew its local workforce by only 0.4%, considerably lower than the national average of 1.2%.

The following is a summary of data regarding the 2012 Idaho Falls labor force:

Size of civilian labor force: 28,018

Number of workers employed in ...

agriculture and mining: 699
construction: 1,282
manufacturing: 2,127
wholesale trade: 596
retail trade: 4,036
transportation: 774
information systems: 692
finance: 970
professional administration: 3,927
education and social services: 5,488
arts and leisure: 2,841
other: 932
public administration: 1,454

Average hourly earnings of production workers: $15.03

Unemployment rate: 4.5% (2012)

Employers

Largest employers (2012)	*Number of employees*
Bechtel BWXT Idaho	3,800
CH2M Hill WG, LLC	1,700
Idaho Falls School District 91	1,600
Eastern Idaho Regional Medical Center	1,300
Melaleuca, Inc.	1,300
City of Idaho Falls	860
Bonneville Joint School District 93	800
Center Partners	600
Wal-Mart	450
Bonneville County	550

Cost of Living

The following is a summary of data regarding several key cost of living factors in the area.

2013 ACCRA Average House Price: $194,300

2013 ACCRA Cost of Living Index: 86

State income tax rate: 1.6% to 7.4%

State sales tax rate: 6.0%

Local income tax rate: None

Local sales tax rate: None

Property tax rate: 0.938% of assessed value (city average, 2010)

Economic Information: Grow Idaho Falls Inc. 151 N Ridge Ave # A. Idaho Falls, ID; telephone: (208) 522-2014. Regional Development Alliance. 2300 N Yellowstone Hwy. Idaho Falls, ID; telephone: (208) 528-9400

■ Education and Research

Elementary and Secondary Schools

Idaho Falls has two public school districts: District 91 and 93. Idaho Falls School District 91 serves about 10,400 students. The district has 12 elementary schools, including a math and science magnet school, 2 junior high schools, and four high schools, including two comprehensive high schools, an alternative high school and Compass Academy, and a magnet high school through the New Tech Network. The high schools offer Advanced Placement classes in more than a dozen subjects from U.S. History to statistics.

Bonneville Joint School District No. 93 comprises a portion of the City of Idaho Falls along with the incorporated cities of Ammon, Iona, and Ucon, and the unincorporated county areas to the north, south, and east of Idaho Falls. The district has a student population of approximately 11,200. About 65 percent of students are transported to and from school. There are 21 buildings, including 14 elementary schools, 2 comprehensive middle schools, an alternative middle school, two comprehensive high schools, an alternative high school, and Teton Peaks Academy for special needs students. The district employs nearly 600 certified teachers and administrators.

Roman Catholic Diocese of Boise maintains Holy Rosary Catholic School serving students from preschool to sixth grade.

The following is a summary of data regarding the Idaho Falls School District 91.

Total enrollment: 10,174

Number of facilities

total: 19
elementary schools: 12
junior high schools: 2
high schools: 4
other: 1

Student/teacher ratio: 18.16:1

Teacher salaries

average (statewide): $Not available

Funding per pupil: $5,971

Public Schools Information: Idaho Falls School District #91, 690 John Adams Parkway, Idaho Falls, Idaho 83401; telephone (208) 525-7500; fax (208) 525-7596. Bonneville Joint School District #93, 3497 N. Ammon Road Idaho Falls, ID 83401; telephone (208) 525-4400, fax (208) 529-0104.

Colleges and Universities

Idaho Falls is home to Eastern Idaho Technical College, a two-year state college that offers hands-on technical programs, training, workforce, community and online education. University Place is a joint campus for the University of Idaho, Idaho State University, Eastern Idaho Technical College, Eastern Idaho Regional Medical Center, Mountain View Hospital, Melaleuca, Idahoan, Battelle Energy Alliance, and Wada Farms. University place is also home to the Idaho National Laboratory, Center for Advanced Energy Studies. University Place enables Idaho State University and University of Idaho students to pursue their degrees without leaving the city.

Libraries and Research Centers

The Idaho Falls Public Library has been in its current location since 1977. The building includes 42,000 square feet of finished space and 21,000 square feet of storage and expansion space. The Iona Community Library recently became a branch. In addition to a comprehensive reference collection, the library subscribes to more than 180 magazines and 26 newspapers. The library also keeps issues of the *Post Register* dating back to 1880.

Idaho National Laboratory (INL) is the largest research facility and a primary city employer. Its Center for Advanced Energy Studies is housed at University Place.

Public Library Information: Idaho Falls Public Library, 457 West Broadway, Idaho Falls, Idaho 83404; telephone (208) 612-8460.

■ Health Care

Eastern Idaho Regional Medical Center (EIRMC) is a 330-bed full-service hospital located in Idaho Falls. It has Idaho's only Level I intensive care unit. The largest medical facility in the region, it serves as the region's health-care hub, offering specialty services including cardiovascular surgery, leading-edge cancer treatment, trauma, neurosurgery, intensive care for adults and infants, and a helicopter and ground medical rescue service. It is also the only regional provider offering perinatalogy services (maternal-fetal medicine) for high-risk pregnancies; neonatology services for extremely premature and critically ill infants; gynecologic-oncology services provided by specialists who focus only on cervical, ovarian, uterine, and other reproductive cancers in women; and inpatient psychiatric services.

The Behavioral Health Center (BHC) is a 72-bed inpatient psychiatric facility for children, adolescents, and adults. Specialized staff provides 24-hour crisis intervention for people experiencing a variety of mental health problems.

Mountain View Hospital is a 40-bed facility owned and operated by local physicians. It offers inpatient, outpatient, diagnostic, and rehabilitative services for patients of all ages. The facility has 600 employees and underwent a $9 million expansion in 2010.

■ Recreation

Sightseeing

The surrounding mountains and national parks offer unlimited sightseeing opportunities. The Pier at Snake River Landing is a 4,000-square-foot pier with beautifully lit arches and a breathtaking view of the Snake River. The Central Valley offers views of waterfalls, streams and ponds along a winding pathway. In addition, the Idaho Falls Downtown Development Corporation sponsors a walking tour of over a dozen preserved buildings listed in the National Register of Historic Places. Minnetonka Cave in St. Charles Canyon offers a half-mile of stalactites, stalagmites, and banded travertine in nine rooms. From mid-June until Labor Day, over 20,000 people visit the cave and take guided tours. The cave stays at 40 degrees all year long. Minnetonka is one of two caverns administered by the Forest Service.

Arts and Culture

The city owned and operated Civic Auditorium is home to year-round, diverse music concerts, plays, and events.

The Idaho Falls Arts Council is a private non-profit organization that owns and operates the Colonial Theater, Willard Arts Center, and ARTitorum on Broadway. The Colonial Theater opened in 1919 to host traveling vaudeville acts, minstrel shows, and musical acts like John Phillips Sousa. In 1929 it was renamed the Paramount Theater and began showing motion pictures. It fell into disrepair in the late 1980s and was closed. In 1994 the nonprofit Idaho Falls Arts Council received the theater as a gift and spearheaded a $4.2 million renovation. Today the 988-seat theater is one of three large theaters of historical significance remaining in Idaho. The buildings adjacent to the theater were repurposed as the Willard Arts Center and now host a visual arts facility with galleries, classrooms, and meeting space for events. Scheduled for completion in 2014 is the ARTitorum on Broadway, an interactive display that will house an array of dynamic art stations.

The Museum of Idaho displays local artifacts and history and hosts traveling exhibits. Permanent exhibits include Eagle Rock, Race for Atomic Power, and Lewis and Clark in Idaho. Traveling exhibits hosted in 2012 included A Grateful Nation: A Look Back at WWII; Teeth, Tails, & Trouble: A T. Rex Named Sue; How to Raise a Dinosaur; and King Tut: Treasures of the Tomb.

The Tautphaus Park Zoo houses 325 animals, the largest collection in Idaho.

I.F. Symphony presents an annual concert to local venues including Freeman Park, the Colonial Theater, and the Civic Auditorium. Although the symphony has a full-time music director-conductor, it is a volunteer orchestra composed of people from all walks of life, with some traveling over 75 miles for rehearsals and concerts. It is one of few orchestras in Idaho not affiliated with a college or university.

Idaho Falls Opera was incorporated in 1978 and since then has produced over 50 fully staged productions and hundreds of other performances. Its first production was The Old Maid and the Thief, a one-act comedy by Menotti. In 2012 it performed a fully staged version of Hansel and Gretel at the Civic Auditorium.

The Actors' Repertory Theatre of Idaho (ARTI) is a nonprofit, all-volunteer organization. Since its beginnings, ARTI has been a dinner theatre venue, offering audiences both a theatre experience and an intimate dining experience including beer and wine service. Since 2001, ARTI has owned its theatre, located in downtown Idaho Falls, and recently named The Phoenix.

Festivals and Holidays

The greenbelt along the Snake River hosts many community events, such as the Melaleuca Freedom Celebration (on the Fourth of July), the Roaring Youth Jam, and the Farmers' Market, among others.

Sports for the Spectator

Idaho Falls loves baseball. The city has fielded a professional baseball team consecutively since 1940 (but for the suspension of league play during World War II). The minor league Idaho Falls Chukars currently play at Melaleuca Field, which opened in 2007. The ballpark seats 3,600. There are 1,300 box seats and 8 luxury suites. A select number of fans can watch the game from a hot tub down the right field line. The deepest part of the field is left center at 410 feet.

Sandy Downs Rodeo Grounds hosts various outdoor activities, including three major rodeos, circus performances, 4-H livestock programs, chariot racing in the winter, and other sporting events. A commissary is available for food and beverage service.

Sports for the Participant

Idaho Falls is 100 miles from Yellowstone and Grand Teton national parks and Craters of the Moon National Monument. Nearby sky resorts include Jackson Hole and Sun Valley. The area has 12 wilderness areas, 11 national forests, and an abundance of trout streams. There are also incredible opportunities for hunting, hiking, climbing, and kayaking.

The Snake River Greenbelt has more than two miles of paved trails bordering the river for walking and jogging.

The City of Idaho Falls maintains three 18-hole public golf courses, including Pinecrest, which was rated the best municipal golf course by *Golf Digest Idaho*. The par 27, 18-hole Freeman Park disc golf course averages 175–400 feet per hole. The city also maintains a public ice rink and skate park.

Shopping and Dining

Idaho Falls is home to the Grand Teton Mall, the largest shopping center in Southeastern Idaho. It and other national and local retail stores draw people from throughout southeastern Idaho, as well as parts of Montana and Wyoming.

Visitor Information: Eastern Idaho Visitor Information Center. 425 N Capital Ave, Idaho Falls, ID 83402. Phone: (208) 523-1010.

■ Convention Facilities

Idaho Falls meeting and convention facilities can support events with 800 people or fewer. Current convention facilities are limited to the motels and hotels in the area, the largest of which (Shilo Inn Suites Conference Hotel) has 18,000 square feet of meeting room facilities.

Under the leadership of the Greater Idaho Falls Chamber of Commerce, efforts are underway to build an Event Center to serve the surrounding area. The goal is to create a facility to attract larger events that currently cannot be accommodated with local facilities, including minor league sports, family shows like Disney on Ice, performing arts, rodeos, and tournaments (college, state, and local high school basketball, volleyball, wresting, etc.) Preliminary studies recommend a 140,000-square-foot facility in the city's Snake River Landing with 5,000 fixed seats and a project cost of $35 million to $40 million. It is envisioned that a sports team would be an anchor tenant. The preliminary design includes ice capability sufficient for professional hockey. Preliminary designs were unveiled in 2013.

■ Transportation

Approaching the City

Idaho Falls Regional Airport (IDA) is a regional air transportation center in Idaho Falls serving Eastern Idaho, Southern Montana, and Western Wyoming. The Airport is served by Skywest/Delta Airlines with frequent daily flights to Salt Lake City, Utah; United Express with daily non-stop flights to Denver, Colorado; and Allegiant

Air with weekly flights to Las Vegas, Nevada, and Phoenix/Mesa, Arizona.

Traveling in the City

Targhee Regional Public Transportation Authority (TRPTA) is a public transportation system that services Idaho Falls, Rexburg, Driggs, and Salmon areas with demand response (door-to-door) service. The region is also served by Holiday Motor Coach LLC, Greyhound Lines, and Rimrock Trailways.

■ Communications

Newspapers and Magazines

The *Post Register* has a daily print circulation of 22,000 (25,000 Sundays), a daily print readership of more than 70,000, and more than 7,000 online subscribers. The *Post Register* also owns three of eastern Idaho's weekly newspapers: *Jefferson Star, Shelley Pioneer,* and *Challis Messenger.*

Television and Radio

KIDK is a full-service television station in Idaho Falls and Pocatello, Idaho, broadcasting on local digital UHF channel 36 and on virtual channel 3. Founded in 1953 as KID, it is owned by Fisher Communications Inc. KIDK is affiliated with CBS. KIFI-TV is the ABC affiliate serving Idaho Falls.

Media Information: *Post Register,* 333 Northgate Mile, P.O. Box 1800, Idaho Falls, ID 83401; telephone: (208) 522-1800.

Idaho Falls Online

Grow Idaho Falls. Available www.growidahofalls.org

Idaho Falls Downtown Development Corporation. Available downtownidahofalls.com/

City of Idaho Falls. Available www.idahofallsidaho.gov/

Regional Development Alliance Inc. Available www.rdaidaho.org

Eastern Idaho Visitor Information Center. Available www.blm.gov/id/st/en/info/directory/eastern_idaho_visitor.html

Idaho Falls Public Library. Available www.ifpl.org.

BIBLIOGRAPHY

Egan, Timothy, *The Big Burn: Teddy Roosevelt and the Fire that Saved America* (Boston: Mariner Books, 2010)

Harris, Richard, *Hidden Idaho: Including Boise, Sun Valley and Yellowstone National Park* (Berkeley, CA: Ulysses, 2004)

Nampa

■ The City in Brief

Founded: 1891

Head Official: Mayor Tom Dale (since 2002; current term expires 2014)

City Population
- 1990: 28,365
- 2000: 51,876
- 2010: 81,557
- 2012 estimate: 83,932
- Percent change, 2000–2010: 57.2%
- U.S. rank in 2000: 688th (State rank: 2nd)
- U.S. rank in 2010: 376th (State rank: 2nd)

Metropolitan Statistical Area Population
- 2000: 432,345
- 2010: 616,561
- 2012 estimate: 635,964
- Percent change, 2000–2010: 42.6%
- U.S. rank in 2000: 97th
- U.S. rank in 2010: 86th

Area: 20 square miles

Elevation: Average 2,492 feet above sea level

Average Annual Temperatures: 64.4° F

Average Annual Precipitation: 11.7 inches of rain; 21.4 inches of snow

Major Economic Sectors: agriculture, manufacturing, education, health care

Unemployment Rate: 7.8% (2012)

Per Capita Income: $14,893

2012 FBI Crime Index Property: 2,180

Major Colleges and Universities: Northwest Nazarene University, Boise State University, Albertson College of Idaho

Daily Newspaper: *Idaho Press Tribune*

■ Introduction

About 20 miles west of Boise, Idaho, sits the second largest city in the state: Nampa. While it is now considered part of the Boise metropolitan area, Nampa has always been its own city, established in the late 1800s as a result of the completion of the Oregon Short Line railroad. Union Pacific main line operations continue to be significant to Nampa and the surrounding area. Although the origins of the name Nampa are unknown, it is believed to be a Shoshoni Indian word meaning "moccasin," or "footprint." Once highly dependent on agricultural production, the city's economy has become more diverse and now also relies on manufacturing. Nampa boasts a mild climate, excellent parks and recreation, and proximity to the state capital, Boise. Northwest Nazarene University is located in Nampa, and the Snake River Stampede, one of the nation's top 10 rodeos, is held every year in July. Located in the middle of Idaho's wine country, Nampa has grown from a population of 799 in 1900 to over 65,000 in 2014. As the population grows and diversifies, the city also benefits from a growing labor force and new economic developments. *Forbes* magazine has regularly listed the area in the Top 10 Places for Business and Careers.

■ Geography and Climate

Located in the heart of Idaho's Treasure Valley, or "Banana Belt," Nampa enjoys a mild climate year-round, with the average temperature at about 65 degrees. Its high desert location is bordered to the north by the Front

City of Nampa Economic Development

Range of the Rocky Mountains and to the south by the Owyhee Mountains. Nampa enjoys warm summers with an average temperature of 92° F, but the low humidity makes for a pleasant environment. Winter lows average 20.2° F. Nampa's winters are mild, with minimal snowfall. Blizzards are rare, and snow that does fall rarely stays on the ground for more than a few days. Nampa's climate is ideal for the production of agricultural goods, which make up a substantial part of the region's economy. Nampa is located about 20 miles from Boise, Idaho's state capital.

Area: 20 square miles

Elevation: Average 2,492 feet above sea level

Average Temperatures: 64.4° F

Average Annual Precipitation: 11.7 inches of rain; 21.4 inches of snow

■ History

Nampa's Early Years

Although Native American tribes had settled in Idaho for hundreds of years, little human settlement occurred in the area that is now Nampa until the late 1800s. Settlement in Nampa began in 1883, a direct result of the completion of the Oregon Short Line Railroad. At that time, Caldwell resident James A. McGee and businessman Alexander Duffes decided to invest in the development of this new town. Duffes filed a claim under the Idaho Homestead Act, and in 1886 McGee and Duffes formed the Nampa Land and Improvement Company and filed the town's articles of incorporation. Initially, the Short Line bypassed Boise, but due to increased traffic it soon became necessary to provide a connecting line between the Oregon Short Line and Boise in 1887. The Idaho Central Railway was built to make that connection, and Nampa was a stop along the way.

Nampa was incorporated in 1891. Population and business development continued to grow into the 1890s, mainly a result of irrigation made possible by the Phyllis Canal and the completion of the Ridenbaugh Canal extension. However, in 1894 Duffes mortgaged Nampa's unsold lots in an attempt to boost the slowing economy. The loan source defaulted and the town spiraled into debt. In 1896, Colonel W.H. Dewey paid the debt and received 2,000 deeds to town lots. He was crucial to the continued development of Nampa, as he began a survey of a route for the Boise, Nampa, Owyhee Railway that eventually linked Boise with the mining towns of the Owyhee Valley.

A Modern City Emerges

By 1900, 800 residents populated the town of Nampa. As the 20th century began, the Western Idaho Sugar Company and the Crescent Brewing Company were both established in Nampa. These companies utilized local farmers and created jobs at their processing plants. But a business decline was followed by a fire in 1909, which caused the destruction of more than 60 stores in downtown Nampa. By the 1920s, however, Nampa had once again established itself as a stable community. The Northwest Nazarene School, now Northwest Nazarene University, was established in 1913 by Eugene Emerson. During World War I, Nampa's farming community benefited from high crop prices. However, when the bottom of the market fell out after the war was over, many farmers were bankrupted. The economy was revived in 1942, when the Amalgamated Sugar Company opened a sugar beet plant in Nampa, which spurred farm productivity.

In 1946, Nampa was named "Main Street America," especially due to its main street retailers increasing their sales 121 percent in one year. In 1949, the Nampa Industrial Corporation (NIC) was formed to encourage other economic development beyond farming. By the 1970s, the NIC's investment in land and facility improvements had resulted in a more diverse economy, having encouraged new businesses and industries to locate in Nampa.

Nampa has grown to become Idaho's second-largest city, boasting a thriving economy and excellent quality of life. Building a strong and progressive community, Nampa was ranked as one of the "100 Best Communities for Young People" by America's Promise Alliance in 2007. The city also won a community achievement award from the City Achievement Program for its innovative training program designed to teach all citizens how to help keep drugs and other criminal activity off of their property. In the late 2000s, Nampa was hard hit by the economy, ending the decade with high unemployment. However, the cost of living in the city remains nearly 20 percent below the U.S. average. In addition, according to the local chamber of commerce, *Forbes* has listed Nampa in the Top 10 Places for Business and Careers eight times between 2001 and 2010.

Historical Information: Canyon County Historical Museum, 1200 Front Street, Nampa, ID 83651; telephone (208) 467-7611

■ Population Profile

Metropolitan Statistical Area Population

2000: 432,345
2010: 616,561
2012 estimate: 635,964

Percent change, 2000–2010: 42.6%
U.S. rank in 2000: 97th
U.S. rank in 2010: 86th

City Residents

1990: 28,365
2000: 51,876
2010: 81,557
2012 estimate: 83,932
Percent change, 2000–2010: 57.2%
U.S. rank in 2000: 688th (State rank: 2nd)
U.S. rank in 2010: 376th (State rank: 2nd)

Density: 2,614.7 people per square mile

Racial and ethnic characteristics

White: 74,821
Black or African American: 406
American Indian and Alaskan Native: 971
Asian: 800
Native Hawaiian and Other Pacific Islander: 105
Hispanic or Latino (may be of any race): 17,879
Other: 5,683

Percent of residents born in state: 44.3%

Age characteristics

Population under 5 years old: 7,674
Population 5 to 9 years old: 8,069
Population 10 to 14 years old: 7,632
Population 15 to 19 years old: 5,729
Population 20 to 24 years old: 5,801
Population 25 to 34 years old: 12,268
Population 35 to 44 years old: 10,733
Population 45 to 54 years old: 9,288
Population 55 to 59 years old: 3,215
Population 60 to 64 years old: 3,270
Population 65 to 74 years old: 5,188
Population 75 to 84 years old: 2,768
Population 85 years and over: 1,151
Median age: 30.3

Births (2010–11 Metropolitan Area)

Total number: 8,500

Deaths (2010–11 Metropolitan Area)

Total number: 3,852

Money income (2012)

Per capita income: $14,893
Median household income: $39,171
Total households: 27,068

Number of households with income of …

less than $10,000: 2,333
$10,000 to $14,999: 1,900
$15,000 to $24,999: 4,120
$25,000 to $34,999: 3,788

$35,000 to $49,999: 4,658
$50,000 to $74,999: 6,098
$75,000 to $99,999: 1,802
$100,000 to $149,999: 2,083
$150,000 to $199,999: 206
$200,000 or more: 80

Percent of families below poverty level: 24.1%

FBI Crime Index Property: 2,180

FBI Crime Index Violent: 203

■ Municipal Government

Nampa operates under a mayor-council form of government. In 2013 residents of the city voted to increase the size of the city council from four to six members. The mayor is elected at large every four years; the six council members serve staggered four-year terms.

Head Official: Mayor Tom Dale (since 2002; current term expires 2014)

Total Number of City Employees: 623 (2012)

City Information: City Hall, 411 3rd Street South, Nampa, ID 83651; telephone (208) 465-2200.

■ Economy

Major Industries and Commercial Activity

Historically, Nampa has been known as a strong agricultural base. Canyon County produces more than 90 percent of the world's sweet corn seed, and is also a leader in the production of livestock, dairy, and alfalfa. Nampa is home to the Amalgamated Sugar Company, one of the area's major employers. Located in the heart of Idaho's wine country, Nampa also produces its share of grapes. Vineyards in Nampa and surrounding areas grow Cabernet Sauvignon, Cabernet Franc, Roussanne, Pinot Gris, Merlot, and Syrah varietals. The climate, geography, and location along the Snake River make for ideal growing conditions. Nampa also has had a strong manufacturing base, with goods produced such as furniture, boxes, wood products, and computer chips. Nampa has benefited from the technology boom: computer equipment manufacturer Plexus' major manufacturing facility is located in Nampa. It is among the city's top employers. In 2010, total jobs in most industries declined, but education and health services increased by about seven percent. Education continues to be a major source of employment in Nampa, with Nampa School District 131 and higher education institutes Northwest Nazarene University and Boise State University's Canyon County Center providing jobs. Other major employers include Woodgrain Millwork Inc, J.R. Simplot, and Mercy Medical Center. The city is also dabbling in new technology.

Items and goods produced: bio-tech seeds, sugar, sweet corn, livestock, alfalfa, dairy products, grapes, frozen potatoes, CMOS image chips, computer equipment, cardboard boxes, and RV furniture

Incentive Programs—New and Existing Companies

Local programs: Several entities have been established to encourage business growth and development. The Nampa Industrial Corporation was formed in 1949 to create business opportunities in Nampa through the investment in and development of industrial property. The NIC also assists with community initiatives.

The Chamber of Commerce supports local businesses by providing services such as monthly luncheons, small business consultations, networking opportunities, marketing ideas, and sponsorship opportunities for its members.

The Boise Valley Economic Partnership (BVEP) serves the Boise-Nampa area with the goals of creating long-term jobs and encouraging economic development in the community. The BVEP provides free, customized services to businesses relocating, expanding, or establishing themselves in the Boise Valley Area.

The Nampa Development Corporation guides Nampa's revitalization and redevelopment efforts. NDC strategically invests public dollars in Nampa to spur private development. NDC projects include the Downtown and Boulevard Area and the North Commercial and Industrial Development Areas. In the North Commercial and Industrial Development Areas, NDC invests in retail or service sector projects in a new or existing structure of $3,000,000 or more and in small, new manufacturing, distribution or data center facilities with values between $1,000,000 and $3,000,000.

State programs: Idaho is an aggressive pro-business state. The Idaho Department of Commerce and Labor provides services to business owners to assist them in starting, relocating, running, and closing a business. The Idaho Corporate Advantage provides a comprehensive incentive package for large companies relocating headquarters or making major administrative expansions in the state.

Idaho has a variety of incentive programs designed to assist business start-up, business expansion, and business productivity, including financial incentives, business tax credits, and worker training programs. The Idaho Business Advantage program targets businesses that invest a minimum of $500,000 in new facilities and create at least 10 new jobs averaging $40,000 annually. Companies meeting these requirements may qualify for a variety of incentives, including an enhanced Investment Tax Credit of 3.75 percent up to $750,000 or 62.5 percent of tax liability in any one year; a new jobs tax credit starting at $1,500 and climbing to $3,000 per job; and a 2.5 percent real property improvement tax credit up to $125,000 in any one year along with a 25 percent rebate on sales tax paid on construction materials for the new facilities. In addition, businesses that make qualifying new investments may earn an income tax credit. This credit can be offset up to 50 percent of a company's state income tax liability and may be carried forward up to 14 years.

Other tax credits include the new jobs income tax credit, research and development income tax credit, and tax cap on certain excessive property values.

Job training programs: The state's workforce development training fund program provides up to $2,000 of new employee training reimbursement money. Jobs must pay at least $12 per hour with benefits, and the company must produce a product or service that is mainly marketed outside the region where the business is located. The Boise State University Selland College of Applied Technology provides apprenticeship and job training programs to students who are enrolled in the college's Apprenticeship Programs offered by the Center for Workforce Training. Students receive on-the-job training while working as full-time, paid employees. Students also receive classroom training related to their chosen profession. The Center for Workforce Training offers career training programs for adults as well as programs to help businesses increase their productivity. In addition to training in the classroom, the Center offers online training programs and courses. IdahoWorks is a combination of state and local workforce development groups. IdahoWorks provides career centers with over 17 programs geared towards those seeking employment or education. Programs include workshops on application and interview skills, resume and cover letter writing, and job fairs.

Development Projects

As Idaho's second-largest city and as part of the Boise metropolitan area, Nampa continues to attract new business development, although such activity has waned in the latter half of the 2000s.

In 2013 Saint Alphonsus Health System invested $33.5 million in its Nampa facility to expand and enhance medical services. Approximately 500 construction jobs and 85 new full-time staff positions were created with the Nampa expansion.

In 2014 the city was in the eighth year of a 24-year plan to revitalize the downtown area. The first major project was completed in 2012, with the opening of the Hugh Nichols Public Safety Building, which houses police and fire administration. The next phase, construction of the Library Square Project, was underway in 2014, and due for completion in early 2015. The site will

house a new 62,000-square-foot library, a new parking garage for the downtown neighborhood, retail and office space, and a public plaza.

Community Development Inc. of Caldwell purchased the Old Mercy Hospital with plans to transform the building into low-income senior housing. These programs require a match from the city. The plan to generate the local match is to create a single block Urban Renewal District. There will be only one property owner, one taxpayer in the district. A portion of the new taxes generated by their $7 million investment will be reimbursed to help cover the cost of sewer, water, and sidewalk upgrades needed on the block.

In 2014 Materne North America, the makers of GoGo squeeZ Applesauce On the Go, announced an $85 million investment in a new food processing facility that will create a minimum of 230 new jobs in the Treasure Valley. The new state-of-the-art facility, the company's second U.S. location, will be housed at a site formerly owned by Micron Technology Inc.

Economic Development Information: Idaho Department of Commerce, 700 West State Street, Boise, ID 83720; telephone (208) 334-2470. Idaho Department of Labor, 317 West Main Street, Boise, ID 83735; telephone (208) 332-3570; fax (208) 334-6300. Center for Workforce Training, Selland College of Applied Technology, Boise State University, 1464 University Drive, Technical Services Building, Boise, ID 83725; toll-free (800) 632-6586; fax (208) 426-4487.

Commercial Shipping

Nampa is served by the Union Pacific Railroad and several commercial truck lines that transport goods produced in Nampa throughout the country. Airfreight is handled at Nampa Municipal Airport.

Labor Force and Employment Outlook

Nampa's 300,000 strong area workforce contributes to a diversified economic base of agriculture, food processing, manufacturing, distribution and technology. In recent decades, Nampa's economy has become less dependent on agriculture as it has become a center for business and manufacturing. In 2012 residential construction experienced a strong recovery, increasing more than 140 percent. Construction permits totaled $93 million, which was an increase of nearly 40 percent over 2011. Numerous construction projects brought new jobs to Nampa, which boosted job growth to levels not experienced since the onset of the recession in 2008. In 2013 the unemployment rate for Nampa was 7.6 percent, the lowest since 2007.

The following is a summary of data regarding the 2012 Nampa labor force:

Size of civilian labor force: 37,149

Number of workers employed in . . .

agriculture and mining: 1,018

construction: 2,373

manufacturing: 4,493

wholesale trade: 1,148

retail trade: 3,946

transportation: 1,484

information systems: 584

finance: 1,685

professional administration: 2,865

education and social services: 7,428

arts and leisure: 2,213

other: 1,605

public administration: 1,785

Average hourly earnings of production workers: $14.85

Unemployment rate: 7.8% (2012)

Employers

Largest private employers (2012)	*Number of employees*
Nampa School District #131	1700
College of Western Idaho	800
Wal-Mart	700
Northwest Nazarene University	700
City of Nampa	600
St. Al's Nampa (Mercy Medical Center)	600
Sorrento Lactalis Inc.	500
Amalgamated Sugar Co. LLC	500
Plexus Corp.	400
Great American Appetizers	400
MicronPC	600
Conagra Fresh Meat	500

Cost of Living

Nampa's cost of living, as well as its housing prices, are below the national average.

The following is a summary of data regarding several key cost of living factors in the area.

State income tax rate: 1.6% to 7.4%

State sales tax rate: 6.0%

Local income tax rate: None

Local sales tax rate: None

Property tax rate: $14.062635 per $1,000 of assessed value (2013)

Economic Information: Nampa Chamber of Commerce, 312 13th Avenue, Nampa, ID 83651; telephone (208) 466-4641. Boise Valley Economic Partnership, 250 South 5th Street, Boise, ID 83702; telephone (208) 472-5230.

■ Education and Research

Elementary and Secondary Schools

Nampa School District (NSD) is the third largest school district in the state of Idaho. More than 15,200 students attend 27 schools. The district maintains 14 elementary schools, 4 middle schools, 3 high schools, 2 alternative high schools, 3 special education schools (preschool, elementary, secondary), and 1 district-authorized charter school (The Idaho Arts Charter School). The student body is 64 percent white, 32 percent Hispanic, 2 percent Native American, 1 percent black, and 1 percent Asian. About 65 percent of the students qualify for free or reduced price lunch and 9 percent for special education. The district is the county's largest employer with more than 1,500 full and part-time employees, including 850 certified teachers, administrators, and other professionals.

Nampa Christian Schools maintain an early childhood center, an elementary school, a middle school, and a high school. The Roman Catholic Diocese of Boise maintains St. Paul's School, which serves preschool through 8th grade with an average class size ranging from 14 to 20 students. A "before and after" school program is available to all students. Facilities include a state of the art science lab, computer lab, and mobile lab. Many St. Paul students continue their education at Bishop Kelly High School, located on the west side of Boise.

The following is a summary of data regarding the Nampa School District.

Total enrollment: 15,181

Number of facilities

total: 27

elementary schools: 14

junior high schools: 4

high schools: 3

other: 6

Student/teacher ratio: 19.2:1

Teacher salaries

average (statewide): $47,416

Funding per pupil: $6,081

Public Schools Information: Nampa School District 131, 619 S. Canyon, Nampa, ID 83686; telephone (208) 468-4600; fax (208) 468-4638.

Colleges and Universities

Five institutions of higher learning serve the Nampa area, including Northwest Nazarene College and Boise State University Selland College of Applied Technology, both located in Nampa. Boise State University is located in Boise, and Albertson College is in nearby Caldwell. Albertson College, in Caldwell, is the state's oldest four-year institution of higher education. The school is a private liberal arts college offering over 30majors. Northwest Nazarene University is a four-year, private Christian liberal arts university offering undergraduate and graduate degrees in such fields as arts, humanities, science, theology, and education. Boise State University is a public university that offers undergraduate, graduate, and technical programs. Courses are offered in eight colleges: applied technology, arts and sciences, business and economics, education, engineering, graduate studies, health sciences, and social sciences and public affairs. The Boise State University Selland College of Applied Technology, one of Boise State University's eight colleges, operates a campus at the Canyon County Center in Nampa. The college offers degree and certificate programs; it is the only public technical college in southwest Idaho. In 2009 the College of Western Idaho, located in the city, opened up to students. The college is the state's newest public, comprehensive community college

Libraries and Research Centers

The Nampa Public Library serves the Nampa community; non-residents may obtain a library card and utilize the library's resources for an annual fee. Nampa Public Library cardholders are allowed to borrow materials from six other area consortium libraries, including the Boise Public Library. The consortium has a collection of more than 500,000 books, videos, sound recordings, and other materials. In 2012 the library circulated 751,486 items, logged 27,892 patron visits, and answered 17,122 reference questions.

As of 2014, a new $30.8 million, 80,000-square-foot main library was under construction and due for completion in early 2015. The new library will be nearly three times the size of the current library with increased parking, allowing the library to serve more than twice as many daily patrons. Enhancements include a multi-purpose room with seating for 150; six smaller study or meeting rooms; a local history room with microfilm capabilities; an expanded Spanish-language area and collection; and access to a plaza, retail space, and restaurants.

The Northwest Nazarene University Riley Library is open to students and faculty, as well as members of the Nampa community. Materials at Albertsons Library at Boise State University are available to students, faculty, and staff, as well as "special borrowers" who meet certain criteria.

A variety of research centers, including one at the Technology and Entrepreneurial Center at Boise State University West, exist in Nampa and conduct research in the fields of biology and agriculture, among others.

Public Library Information: Nampa Public Library, 101 Eleventh Avenue South, Nampa, ID 83651; telephone (208) 468-5800.

■ Health Care

Saint Alphonsus Medical Center–Nampa is a not-for-profit, acute-care hospital licensed for up to 152 beds. As of 2014, it had 90 operational beds, with daily census of 40–50 patients. The hospital is part of the Saint Alphonsus Health System, a four-hospital regional, faith-based Catholic ministry with over 4,300 associates and a medical staff of nearly 1,000 that serves 700,000 people in Idaho and Oregon.

In 2013 the system committed $33.5 million to expand its Nampa facility. Improvements include construction of a new emergency room, a comprehensive heart-care center, and the Birkeland Maternity Center, all located at the Nampa Health Plaza (formerly Mercy North).

■ Recreation

Sightseeing

Visitors to Nampa enjoy a wealth of activities and recreational opportunities. Museums that celebrate Nampa's heritage, year-round outdoor activities, and a variety of shopping and dining experiences help make Nampa a great place to work and live.

Nampa museums celebrate the history of Nampa, Canyon County, and the United States. The Warhawk Air Museum is a 20,000-square-foot facility dedicated to preserving the country's World War II history from the home front to the war front, as well as to trace the history of flight from the advent of aviation through the space age. Its collection includes two of the few remaining Curtiss P-40 World War II fighter airplanes and a rare World War II P-510 razorback Mustang fighter plane. The museum also hosts traveling NASA space exhibits, and often hosts special events and ceremonies to honor veterans and commemorate World War II events.

The Canyon County Historical Museum, located in Canyon County's original train depot, displays both Canyon County and Union Pacific Railroad memorabilia. An authentic 1940s era caboose and model railroad are among the exhibits in the building that has been called "Idaho's finest example of Baroque architecture." A farmer's market is held outside the museum on Saturdays during the months of May through October.

Sawtooth winery, formerly known as Pintler Cellars, was founded in 1987 in the heart of the Canyon County region of the Idaho's Snake River Valley. The vineyards were once rich pastures. Since 1982, 15 acres of European vinifera vines have been planted, including Chenin Blanc, Riesling, Cabernet Sauvignon, Chardonnay and Semillon grapes. The winery's tasting room is open Wednesday to Sunday, 12 p.m.to 5 p.m.

The Van Slyke Agricultural Museum, located in Caldwell Memorial Park, is an open-air museum that features log cabin replicas and antique farm equipment. Visitors to the Deer Flat National Wildlife Refuge at Lake Lowell enjoy swimming, fishing, hunting, boating, and bird watching on more than 11,000 acres of land. In sum, Nampa has about 24 parks, the largest of which is Lakeview Park.

Arts and Culture

With several state of the art exhibit and performance facilities, Nampa is becoming known for its arts scene. The Brandt Center at Northwest Nazarene University is a performing arts center that attracts musical and dramatic performances attended by both students and the community at large. Its Samuel Swayne theatre can accommodate up to 1,500 people, and two guest suites accommodate up to 15 guests each for private viewings and receptions. The Brandt Center's Friesen Art Galleries provide gallery space for Northwest Nazarene University's art students to exhibit their work.

The Caldwell and Nampa Alliance of Community Theatre (CAN-ACT) was started in 1991 and is housed at the Caldwell Center for the Arts. The not-for-profit troupe performs comedies, dramas, and musicals in the CAN-ACT Theater located in the Karcher Mall. Auditions for CAN-ACT's four yearly plays are open to community members. Nampa is also home to the Majestic Entertainment Foundation, which restored the historic Pix Theater.

Festivals and Holidays

Parade America, Idaho's largest patriotic parade, is held in May. Each July, the Snake River Dayz Festival is held in conjunction with the Snake River Stampede rodeo. The week-long festival features concerts, a parade, a pageant and golf tournament, a fun zone for children, and a "movie under the stars" to cap off the pre-rodeo festivities. Nampa Community Fun Night is held in late August or early September and includes games for children, music, and food. The Nampa Festival of the Arts is held annually in August. The festival features live music performances ranging from jazz to Celtic, over 200 artists, and a variety of food vendors.

Sports for the Spectator

Although Nampa has no professional sports teams, Boise State University's indoor track team competes at Nampa's Idaho Center. The state-of-the-art track facility has also been used for other prestigious events such as the USA Masters Indoor Track and Field Championships and the Western Athletic Conference Indoor Championships. Sports fans can also take in collegiate-level sports played by Northwest Nazarene University's teams, including baseball and softball, basketball, cross country, track and field, men's golf, and women's volleyball.

The Snake River Stampede, held annually in July, is ranked among the country's top 10 professional rodeos. The arena at the Idaho Center seats up to 10,000 people who take in bull riding, barrel racing, mutton busting (for children), bareback riding, steer wrestling, and roping events.

Sports for the Participant

Nampa residents enjoy a wealth of outdoor activities year-round, and the city boasts that fitness is an integral part of the Nampa lifestyle. Nineteen city parks cover more than 120 acres of public parks. Available facilities include play areas, covered picnic shelters, baseball and softball fields, tennis courts, archery ranges, Little League fields, swimming pools, basketball courts, and a BMX track. A 140,000-square-foot recreation center provides residents with a climbing wall, basketball courts, an indoor track, six swimming pools, activity rooms, and a senior center.

Nampa has two public golf courses and one private golf course. Ridgecrest Golf Course has received a four-star rating from *Golf Digest* magazine. Runners can participate in a 5K fun run during July's Snake River Dayz festivities.

Shopping and Dining

Nampa, located along I-84, is well-situated as a shopping destination. Retailers range from national chains to locally owned specialty stores, ensuring something for everyone. In early 2004 Costco announced plans to build a retail center adjacent to the new Karcher Interchange off of Interstate 84. Karcher Mall, the tenants include Macy's, Radio Shack, Sam Goody, and Big 5 Sporting Goods. A Costco opened in 2006 as one of two anchors of the new, 700,000-square-foot Treasure Valley Marketplace, which was the only retail center on the I-84 interchange to date. Other major stores at the Marketplace include Target, Kohls, and Office Max. Mass retailers such as Ross, Old Navy, and Bed, Bath, & Beyond can be found in the Meridian Crossroads development. Downtown Nampa is home to many unique retailers, including antique, book, jewelry, and flower stores. The Boise Factory Outlet is just a short drive away, and includes outlet stores for companies such as Reebok and Eddie Bauer.

Nampa diners enjoy a variety of restaurants, from national chains to local establishments. The family-owned Generations restaurant offers steak and seafood, with their French dip sandwich among the more popular menu items. Copper Canyon is an upscale eatery known for its elegant presentation and extensive wine list. Asian restaurant House of Kim, located in downtown Nampa, serves Chinese, Thai, and Malaysian cuisine. The Dutch Inn, known for its salad bar, also serves breakfast, lunch, and dinner entrees. The Mona Lisa is a fondue restaurant that has found its niche as a special occasion restaurant. Cheese fondue appetizers and chocolate dessert fondues are part of a meal package that allows diners to cook their own main courses at pots on their table. Other area eateries include chains such as Applebee's, Denny's, Sizzler, and various fast food establishments.

Visitor Information: Nampa Chamber of Commerce, 312 13th Ave. So., Nampa, ID 83651; telephone (208) 466-4641; fax (208) 466-4677.

■ Convention Facilities

The Nampa Civic Center is Idaho's second largest full-service convention and performing arts center. With 42,500 square feet of space, the Civic Center hosts more than 750 events each year. Meetings, conventions, banquets, receptions, trade shows, and performing arts programs are among the events hosted there. Up to 14 separate meeting spaces can accommodate groups of up to 1,000. In addition to the 30,000 square feet of meeting space, the Civic Center boasts a 12,200 square foot exhibit area and a 640 seat theatre.

The Idaho Center Complex is comprised of four venues: an amphitheatre, an arena, the Idaho Horse Park, and the Idaho Sports Center. The arena can accommodate over 12,000 people, and the amphitheatre seats 10,500 people. Events such as concerts, basketball games, and ice shows, as well as trade shows and conventions, are held at the Idaho Center. The Idaho Horse Park, opened in 2002, consists of indoor and outdoor arenas, an English riding facility, warm-up pens, stalls, and stock pens. The Idaho Sports Center Complex is the newest addition to the Idaho Center. The 100,000 square foot multi-purpose building is the indoor track facility for Boise State University and is home to the only Mondo 200-meter banked track west of Nebraska.

Convention Information: Nampa Civic Center, 311 Third Street South, Nampa, ID 83651; telephone (208) 468-5500. Idaho Center, 16114 Idaho Center Blvd., Nampa, ID 83687; telephone (208) 468-1000.

■ Transportation

Approaching the City

The nearby Boise Airport is served by eleven major national and regional airlines and seven charter airlines carrying over three million passengers annually. The Nampa Municipal Airport, available for general aviation, handles only charter flights. About 280 aircraft are based at the facility, including 260 single-engine aircraft, 10 multi-engine aircraft, and 7 helicopters. In 2013 the State

of Idaho completed a $1.2 million project to rehabilitate the existing runway.

By car, Nampa is accessible via Interstate 84. Greyhound provides bus service to Nampa.

Traveling in the City

Nampa is accessible from Interstate 84 via three interchanges and is relatively easy to navigate. One major road in Nampa is the Nampa-Caldwell Boulevard, also known as Idaho State Route 55. Highway 45 extends through downtown Nampa toward the Snake River and Owyhee County. Roads in downtown Nampa are numbered, with avenues running north-south and streets running east-west. ValleyRide provides public transportation services for the Treasure Valley. Although ValleyRide provides transit service throughout Boise, it also provides fixed-line and door-to-door bus service in Nampa and Caldwell. The Ada County Highway District offers a commuter bus from Caldwell to Boise that stops in Nampa. The Treasure Valley Metro provides commuter service between Nampa, Meridian, and Boise during peak commute times.

■ Communications

Newspapers and Magazines

The *Idaho Press-Tribune* is published in Nampa and serves the Canyon County market. Published daily in the morning, the paper also maintains an Internet presence on its website. Since early 2009, the *Tribune*'s facility has also been the contract printer for *The Idaho Statesman*, Boise's daily newspaper.

Television and Radio

Nampa has one television station and four radio stations broadcasting within city limits; the city also receives programming from nearby Boise.

Media Information: Idaho Press-Tribune, PO Box 9399, Nampa, ID 83652; telephone (208) 467-9251.

Nampa Online

Boise State University Canyon County Center. Available www.boisestate.edu/bsuwest/ canyoncounty/studentservices.shtml

Boise Valley Economic Partnership. Available www. bvep.org

City of Nampa Home Page. Available www.ci. nampa.id.us

Idaho Center. Available www.idahocenter.com

Idaho Department of Commerce. Available www. commerce.idaho.gov

Idaho Department of Labor. Available www.labor. idaho.gov

Idaho Press-Tribune. Available www.idahopress.com

Nampa Chamber of Commerce. Available www.
nampa.com

Nampa Public Library. Available www.nampalibrary.
org

Nampa Public Schools. Available www.sd131.k12.id.us

Northwest Nazarene University. Available www.
nnu.edu

BIBLIOGRAPHY

Egan, Timothy, *The Big Burn: Teddy Roosevelt and the Fire that Saved America* (Boston: Mariner Books, 2010)

Harris, Richard, *Hidden Idaho: Including Boise, Sun Valley and Yellowstone National Park* (Berkeley, CA: Ulysses, 2004)

Montana

The State in Brief

Nickname: Treasure State

Motto: Oro y plata (Gold and silver)

Flower: Bitterroot

Bird: Western meadowlark

Area: 147,040 square miles (2010; U.S. rank 4th)

Elevation: Ranges from 1,800 feet to 12,799 feet above sea level

Climate: Continental; heavy snows in the west, hot dry summers in the east

Admitted to Union: November 8, 1889

Capital: Helena

Head Official: Steve Bullock (D) (until 2017)

Population
1990: 799,065
2000: 902,195
2010: 989,415
2012 estimate: 990,785
Percent change, 2000–2010: 9.7%
U.S. rank in 2012: 44th
Percent of residents born in state: 54.4% (2012)
Density: 6.8 people per square mile (2010)
2012 FBI Crime Index Total: 28,706

Racial and Ethnic Characteristics (2012)
White: 887,924
Black or African American: 4,145
American Indian and Alaska Native: 62,398
Asian: 6,034
Native Hawaiian and Pacific Islander: 674
Hispanic or Latino (may be of any race): 28,984
Other: 29,610

Age Characteristics (2012)
Population under 5 years old: 60,865
Population 5 to 19 years old: 190,100
Percent of population 65 years and over: 14.9%
Median age: 39.9

Vital Statistics
Total number of births (2012–13): 12,103
Total number of deaths (2012–13): 8,815
AIDS cases reported through 2011: 510

Economy
Major industries: Services, trade, energy, agriculture
Unemployment rate (2012): 4.5%
Per capita income (2012): $25,002
Median household income (2012): $45,456
Percentage of persons below poverty level (2012): 14.8%
Income tax rate: 1.0% to 6.9%
Sales tax rate: None

Billings

■ The City in Brief

Founded: 1882 (incorporated, 1885)

Head Official: Mayor Thomas W. Hanel (since 2009; current term expires 2017)

City Population

    1990: 81,125
    2000: 89,847
    2010: 104,170
    2012 estimate: 106,964
    Percent change, 2000–2010: 15.9%
    U.S. rank in 1990: 263rd (State rank: 1st)
    U.S. rank in 2000: 307th (State rank: 1st)
    U.S. rank in 2010: 260th (State rank: 1st)

Metropolitan Statistical Area Population

    2000: 139,946
    2010: 158,050
    2012 estimate: 161,487
    Percent change, 2000–2010: 12.9%
    U.S. rank in 2000: 264th
    U.S. rank in 2010: 259th

Area: 33.82 square miles

Elevation: 3,126 feet above sea level

Average Annual Temperatures: January, 24.0° F; July, 72.0° F; annual average, 47.4° F

Average Annual Precipitation: 14.77 inches of rain; 56.7 inches of snow

Major Economic Sectors: agriculture, services, government, finance, oil and gas

Unemployment Rate: 3.4% (2012)

Per Capita Income: $26,337

2012 FBI Crime Index Property: 4,812

Major Colleges and Universities: Montana State University-Billings, Rocky Mountain College

Daily Newspaper: *The Billings Gazette*

■ Introduction

Billings is the largest city in Montana and the commercial, cultural, and industrial center of a large region of the northern Rocky Mountains. Known as the "Magic City," Billings has grown phenomenally since its founding in 1882, until 1970 doubling in size every 30 years. As of 2012, the metropolitan area was home to over 163,000 people. About 100,000 people live in the city proper. The city is also the processing and distribution hub for a rich agricultural area that encompasses more than 125,000 miles. There are excellent road, rail, and air transportation networks. Many scenic attractions such as Yellowstone National Park are nearby, and the wide variety of recreation activities available make the Billings area a popular vacation spot. Booming with new development projects and ranked as having the number one housing market in the United States, it is abundantly clear why in 2013 *Kiplinger's Personal Finance* ranked Billings in its top 10 places to live nationwide.

■ Geography and Climate

Billings is located in southern Montana in the fertile Yellowstone River valley, with mountains on three sides. The Yellowstone River flows along the eastern boundary of the city. The mountains shelter the city from the most severe winter weather, but blizzard conditions are not uncommon in the spring and fall. Annual snowfall is about 56 inches but with only moderate accumulation since frequent thawing periods help to keep it at bay. Moist air from the Pacific Ocean, called "Chinook winds," often brings surprisingly warm weather in the winter and cooler temperatures in the summer. Spring

© Jon Arnold Images/Alamy

features the most unpredictable weather, and summers are typically dry with cool nights.

Area: 33.82 square miles

Elevation: 3,126 feet above sea level

Average Temperatures: January, 24.0° F; July, 72.0° F; annual average, 47.4° F

Average Annual Precipitation: 14.77 inches of rain; 56.7 inches of snow

■ History

Native Americans Resist Settlement

For thousands of years before the coming of European settlers, the site of present-day Billings was inhabited by migratory peoples. Traces of their camps and elaborate cave drawings have been discovered and preserved at many sites in the region. By the time of America's westward expansion, the predominant tribes in the area included the Crow, Sioux, and Cheyenne.

The Lewis and Clark Expedition of 1806 passed through the present site of Billings, and just 30 miles away William Clark climbed Pompey's Pillar, a 200-foot-high natural rock formation, which he named after the son of his female Indian guide. Although many Europeans explored the area, fierce resistance from the natives prevented any settlement. This led to the so-called "Sioux War," one of the more intense struggles between the U.S. Army and the native people. The infamous Battle of the Little Bighorn, where a large group of Sioux and Cheyenne warriors killed General George Custer and his entire 7th cavalry, took place 65 miles to the southeast of the future site of Billings.

Railroad Brings Ranchers, Farmers

Billings was founded in 1882 by the Northern Pacific Railroad as a rail head for the company's western line and named for the president of the railroad, Frederick Billings. Over the next six months more than 2,000 people settled in the town, which was incorporated as a city in 1885. The city was nicknamed the "Magic City" because of the immediate growth in population.

The wide-open prairie lands were ideal for cattle grazing, and a number of large ranches grew up around the town. During the early twentieth century, families of settlers known as "homesteaders" arrived in the area, taking advantage of the offer of free land. Typically, a family and all its possessions would arrive in one freight car and receive a 40-acre plot of land. Conditions were difficult, but many families struggled through their first years and eventually developed successful farms.

Irrigation had been introduced in the Yellowstone Valley in 1879. Sugar beet growing was thus made possible, and a sugar refinery was built in 1906. Immigrant laborers came to work the fields-first Japanese, then Russo-Germans, and finally Mexicans. The Russo-German workers were unusually industrious; soon they bought their own land at the Huntley Irrigation project outside Billings, where they constituted a third of the population by 1940.

Abundant Natural Resources Contribute to Growth

Billings grew steadily during the 1900s, spurred on by the development of vast natural resources such as minerals, coal, natural gas, and oil. At one time Billings was the largest inland wool shipping point in the United States. In 1933 pulp-drying equipment was installed at the sugar refinery; a thriving livestock industry developed around animals fed on beet pulp. By 1938 more than 600,000 acres of land around Billings was irrigated.

A true hub city and gateway to the West, Billings has become the commercial, health care, and cultural capital of the "Midland Empire," a vast area of agricultural, mountainous, wilderness, and sometimes forbidding terrain that includes eastern Montana, the western Dakotas, and northern Wyoming. It is also an important refining and shipping center for agricultural and energy products. As of 2014, it is home to the largest coal reserves in the nation and the nation's only palladium mine, continuing the city's reputation as the "Star of the Big Sky Country."

Historical Information: Montana State University-Billings Library, 1500 University Dr., Billings, MT 59101; telephone (406) 657-2011; toll-free (800) 565-6782.

■ Population Profile

Metropolitan Statistical Area Population

2000: 139,946
2010: 158,050
2012 estimate: 161,487
Percent change, 2000–2010: 12.9%
U.S. rank in 2000: 264th
U.S. rank in 2010: 259th

City Residents

1990: 81,125
2000: 89,847
2010: 104,170

2012 estimate: 106,964
Percent change, 2000–2010: 15.9%
U.S. rank in 1990: 263rd (State rank: 1st)
U.S. rank in 2000: 307th (State rank: 1st)
U.S. rank in 2010: 260th (State rank: 1st)

Density: 2,399.5 people per square mile

Racial and ethnic characteristics

White: 95,649
Black or African American: 517
American Indian and Alaskan Native: 5,038
Asian: 1,210
Native Hawaiian and Other Pacific Islander: 0
Hispanic or Latino (may be of any race): 5,097
Other: 4,550

Percent of residents born in state: 57.3%

Age characteristics

Population under 5 years old: 6,870
Population 5 to 9 years old: 7,156
Population 10 to 14 years old: 6,370
Population 15 to 19 years old: 6,119
Population 20 to 24 years old: 7,376
Population 25 to 34 years old: 15,413
Population 35 to 44 years old: 12,759
Population 45 to 54 years old: 15,110
Population 55 to 59 years old: 6,195
Population 60 to 64 years old: 7,663
Population 65 to 74 years old: 8,478
Population 75 to 84 years old: 4,790
Population 85 years and over: 2,665
Median age: 38.3

Births (2010–11 Metropolitan Area)

Total number: 2,001

Deaths (2010–11 Metropolitan Area)

Total number: 1,364

Money income (2012)

Per capita income: $26,337
Median household income: $46,655
Total households: 43,926

Number of households with income of . . .

less than $10,000: 2,924
$10,000 to $14,999: 3,069
$15,000 to $24,999: 5,414
$25,000 to $34,999: 5,077
$35,000 to $49,999: 6,660
$50,000 to $74,999: 8,288
$75,000 to $99,999: 5,346
$100,000 to $149,999: 4,519
$150,000 to $199,999: 1,494
$200,000 or more: 1,135

Percent of families below poverty level: 14.5%

FBI Crime Index Property: 4,812

FBI Crime Index Violent: 370

■ Municipal Government

Billings has a mayor-council form of government with ten council members elected to four-year terms. Until the 1995 election the mayor was elected to a two-year term; the mayor now serves a four-year term. The mayor and city council are the city's only policy-making bodies. A city administrator is hired by the mayor and city council and may be removed by a simple majority vote of the mayor and council. Billings is the seat of Yellowstone County.

Head Official: Mayor Thomas W. Hanel (since 2009; current term expires 2017)

Total Number of City Employees: 809 (2014)

City Information: City of Billings, 210 North 27th Street, Billings, MT 59101; telephone (406) 657-8433.

■ Economy

Major Industries and Commercial Activity

Montana's number one industry is agriculture, and Billings is a major contributor to that fact. Agriculture has been one of the leading economic forces in Billings since its founding, and it continues to play a major role today. Because of extensive irrigation, the Yellowstone Valley and the northern Great Plains are some of the nation's most fertile agricultural regions. The city is the transportation, processing, and packaging center for this large, productive area. The main agricultural products include sugar beets, grain, and livestock such as cattle and sheep. The Western Sugar Cooperative Plant, located in Billings, processes multi-million dollars of sugar beets annually.

The energy industry (oil, natural gas, and coal) is also an important part of the economic picture in Billings. The mountains around the city and throughout eastern Montana are a rich source of coal, oil, and natural gas. Billings boasts the largest coal reserves in the nation and the nation's only palladium mine, where the mineral used in catalytic converters can be found. Billings's three oil refineries-including ExxonMobil and ConocoPhillips-contribute to the city's standing as the oil-refining capital of the northern Rockies.

Billings is the retail and wholesale trade center for a vast area of land in the northern Rocky Mountain states and a primary and secondary market population of almost half a million people, reaching from Denver, Colorado to Calgary, Alberta, and from Minneapolis, Minnesota to Seattle, Washington.

Billings is also the medical and educational capital of the region. The city's medical community, including two major hospitals and more than 40 clinics, provides the most advanced health care in the four-state area. Two major colleges and a highly-rated public school system provide jobs and a well-trained workforce. The Billings Public School System is the state's largest. It is also difficult to underestimate the impact of tourism and recreational diversity on the area's economy. The proximity of nearby Yellowstone National Park, as well as a wide array of other wilderness territories, mountain trails, rivers, and streams in the area bring much-needed tourist dollars and act as a magnet to companies and workers looking to relocate.

Items and goods produced: raw and refined energy products, sugar, flour, farm machinery, electric signs, furniture, paint, metal ornaments, cereal, creamery and meat products, canned vegetables, concrete, sugar beets, wheat, beans, livestock

Incentive Programs—New and Existing Companies

Local programs: Big Sky Economic Development (BSED) is a public-private partnership. The Big Sky Economic Development Authority (EDA), the public agency, evolved from the Montana TradePort Authority, launched in 1989 by the Yellowstone County Board of Commissioners. Big Sky Economic Development Corporation (EDC), the private business side, was started in 2002. Services provided include both long-term fixed rate SBA 504 loan packages, business recruitment, expansion and retention, and management of the state sponsored Small Business Development Center. The Big Sky EDC has over 110 member investors committed to economic growth and development.

Additionally, the Business Development Council of the Chamber of Commerce maintains a comprehensive inventory of local and state programs. It also helps identify location alternatives, provides technical assistance, and maintains current information on Billings and its trade area.

State programs: The Montana Business Assistance Connection (MBAC) encourages and supports the creation of new jobs and relocation of existing jobs to various counties in Montana by helping with public and private revolving loan funds and providing training and access to capital for qualified start-up businesses or expanding businesses.

The Billings Small Business Development Center (SBDC) is part of a statewide network of resource and technical service providers that assist start-up and existing businesses. The SBDC staff provides confidential business counseling, training and information to small business leaders and entrepreneurs. Services are provided at no charge and are funded by the Small Business Administration, Montana Department of Commerce, Yellowstone County, and local organizations. Areas of assistance include technical assistance in writing business plans for new and existing businesses, financial analysis, planning and state and private capital sources; assistance with marketing research, analysis and strategy as well as advertising, packaging and promotion; business plan review and critique; pre-business workshops; and one-on-one counseling for existing and start-up business management.

The Montana Community Development Corporation (MCDC) provides support to businesses through business loans, trainings and one-on-one business consulting. In 2010, the MCDC was the recipient of a $750,000 grant from the U.S. Treasury Department to be used for businesses loans, and in 2009, MCDC was awarded $40 million dollars in federal New Markets Tax Credits to be used in eligible areas and projects. The New Markets Tax Credits Program provides a 39 percent federal income tax credit to businesses that choose to invest capital into qualified projects in eligible low-income areas. Loans provided by MCDC range from $1,000 to $1,000,000 to qualified businesses and projects.

Other State of Montana tax incentives include property tax reduction; no inventory, use, or sales tax; new industry income tax credits; small business investment tax credits; and tax reduction on pollution control equipment. The Big Sky Development Trust Fund can provide up to $5,000 in grant funding for each new eligible job created. The Primary Sector Workforce Training Grant offers direct reimbursement to eligible businesses for training costs up to $5,000 per eligible newly created job.

Job training programs: The Primary Sector Workforce Training Grant (WTG) program is a state-funded program; $3.9 million is available annually for this program. The WTG program is targeted to businesses that are creating at least one net, new job that pays at least the lower of the current county average wage or the state current average wage. Montana's JobLINC is the statewide coordination and collaboration of employment and training organizations, workforce development organizations, and other community service providers. Some of the organizations involved with JobLINC are workforce services divisions, local job service workforce centers, Chambers of Commerce, educational entities, economic development corporations, offices of public assistance, rural employment opportunities, human resource development councils, vocational rehabilitation, and other community-based organizations. One of JobLINC's many branches is located in Billings.

Development Projects

In 2010, the city broke ground on construction of an $80 million courthouse. The 146,000 square foot courthouse is a block long and five-stories high. It opened in 2012. It is home to the U.S. Marshal, the U.S. Attorney's office, and federal courtrooms.

Billings's TransTech Center is another recent development. It is a high-tech business park specifically designed to support the communication, power, and workforce needs of technology-based businesses and e-commerce. In 2009 GE opened its new operations center in the business park. The $7 million, 48,000-square-foot center employed some 100 workers in 2009, and the property has enough space on it to allow for expansions that could accommodate some 400 total employees. It is predicted to pump approximately $10 million into the local Billings economy. The business park's TransTech Data Center was recently completed as well; 9,100 square feet of the 11,000 square foot facility has been divided into individual suites for "Montana's Premiere Information Facility."

In 2014 work began on a Billings Heights facility for active seniors named Mission Ridge. The Heights complex will have 72 apartments, including 48 for independent living and 24 for seniors requiring some assistance. The 85,000-square-foot senior facility will have dining areas, a fitness center, and a pool. The facility will cost $13 million. Persons moving into the complex will pay an entrance fee ranging from $75,000 to $145,000, depending on the size of the apartment. The fee is 90 percent refundable. The monthly rent will range from $1,900 a month for smaller apartments to $2,800 for the largest.

Billings Clinic construction projects are expected to exceed $35 million in 2014. In addition to an $11.5 million new intensive care unit, and $13.5 million worth of expanded and renovated facilities for surgical services, construction is also underway on a 20,000-square-foot cardiac center in the heart of the downtown campus. The Clinic also is expanding its ambulatory telemetry unit from 10,000 to 27,000 square feet. The Cardiac Center and ATU combined will cost $10.9 million. The Clinic has also expanded and remodeled its neonatal intensive care unit and is expanding its Family Birth Center at a cost of at least $750,000.

As of 2014, CHS Inc. was upgrading its truck-loading facility at its Refinery in Laurel. Improvements in shipping conditions for Canadian tar sands oil, as well as crude from the Bakken, made the expansion economically feasible. Carl Casale, president of CHS Inc., reported, "There's so much crude oil trapped in the mid-continent right now and trapped up in Canada—and we have one refinery in Laurel that is served by a pipeline out of Canada. Pretty good place to have one," Casale said. "And we have one that sits in McPherson, Kansas, just north of Cushing, Oklahoma, where all the crude oil gets trapped. It's literally at the end of the pipe and you have to move it by rail or by train after that."

In response to the growth in Montana's oil, coal and agricultural economies, in 2013, Burlington Northern

Santa Fe Railroad opened an economic development office in Billings to accommodate rapidly increasing demand for oil transportation.

Economic Development Information: Billings Area Chamber of Commerce, 815 South 27th Street, Billings, MT 59107; telephone (406) 245-4111; fax (406) 245-7333; email info@billingschamber.com. Big Sky Economic Development Corporation, 222 North 32nd St., Suite 200, Billings, MT 59101; telephone (406) 256-6871; fax (406) 256-6877.

Commercial Shipping

About a dozen mail and cargo carriers provide service to the city via Billings Logan International Airport, including FedEx, UPS, and Airborne. Burlington Northern Railroad, Santa Fe Railway Company, and Montana Rail Link operate rail lines from the Billings area. Burlington Northern also operates an intermodal (surface, sea, and air transportation) hub in Billings.

Labor Force and Employment Outlook

The Billings-area work force is educated above the national average, and a recent study found that one in four workers was overqualified for the jobs they were performing, creating an excellent climate for technical and higher-wage businesses looking to relocate to the area. The unemployment rate in Billings is lower than the national average. The Billings area economy is service-based, which includes specialized manufacturing, processing, and professional services to support the region's rural agricultural and energy economies. Billings serves as the regional hub for medical services, higher education, professional business services, retail and distribution, and travel and lodging.

The following is a summary of data regarding the 2012 Billings labor force:

Size of civilian labor force: 56,637

Number of workers employed in . . .

agriculture and mining: 1,532
construction: 3,343
manufacturing: 2,291
wholesale trade: 2,198
retail trade: 6,970
transportation: 2,679
information systems: 1,191
finance: 3,674
professional administration: 5,089
education and social services: 12,005
arts and leisure: 7,427
other: 3,084
public administration: 2,160

Average hourly earnings of production workers: $17.73

Unemployment rate: 3.4% (2012)

Employers

Largest employers (2014)	Number of employees
Billings Clinic	2,500
St. Vincent Healthcare Foundation	1,850
School District #2	2,010
Sillwater Mining Company	1,570
Wal-Mart Stores Inc.	900
City of Billings	809
Avitus Group	580
County of Yellowstone	Not available
St John's Lutheran Ministries	412
Montana State University	540

Cost of Living

The following is a summary of data regarding several key cost of living factors in the area.

State income tax rate: 1.0% to 6.9%

State sales tax rate: None

Local income tax rate: None

Local sales tax rate: None

Property tax rate: $1,296 (statewide per capita average, 2010)

Economic Information: Billings Area Chamber of Commerce, 815 South 27th Street, Billings, MT 59107; telephone (406) 245-4111; fax (406) 245-7333; email info@billingschamber.com. Office of Research & Analysis, Montana Department of Labor & Industry, P.O. Box 1728, Helena, MT 59624; telephone (406) 444-2430; toll-free (800) 541-3904; fax (406) 444-2638.

■ Education and Research

Elementary and Secondary Schools

The Billings Public Schools District is governed by a nine-member School Board, which appoints a superintendent. With 16,328 students, it is the largest district in Montana. The District's instructional program encompasses pre-kindergarten through 12th grade. An Adult Education program offers GED accreditation, basic math, English, science, and other pre-collegiate coursework. There are 22 elementary schools, 4 middle schools, and 3 high schools. Billings Public Schools employs about 1,920 full-time equivalent positions. The 2013–14 budget is approximately $110.2 million dollars.

A number of private and parochial schools also serve the metropolitan area. Bishop W.J. Condon and the Catholic individuals of Billings undertook the task of building the first Catholic high school in Montana in December of 1944. In 1947 the first graduating class of Saint Patrick's High School consisted of 13 graduates: seven young women and six young men. Today, Billings Catholic Schools serve about 1,000 students in preschool through 12th grade. About 5 percent of Billings Catholic Schools' population is Black, Native American, or Asian. Another 4 percent is Hispanic.

The following is a summary of data regarding the Billings Public Schools District.

Total enrollment: 10,562

Number of facilities

> total: 29
> elementary schools: 22
> junior high schools: 4
> high schools: 3
> other: 0

Student/teacher ratio: 16.19:1

Teacher salaries

> average (statewide): $47,132

Funding per pupil: $8,598

Public Schools Information: Billings Public Schools, 415 North 30th St., Billings, MT 59101-1298; telephone (406) 281-5000.

Colleges and Universities

There are two four-year institutions of higher education in Billings, Montana State University-Billings and Rocky Mountain College.

Montana State University-Billings is a public, state-supported school with an enrollment of about 5,000 students. Of these, 3,389 (68 percent) attended full time and 1,580 (32 percent) attended part time. Women make up over 62 percent of the student body. Almost 83 percent of the students are white, about 1 percent are black, 1 percent are Asian, 6 percent American Indian, and almost 4 percent Hispanic. A satellite campus of Montana State University-Bozeman, the college offers two-year associate's and four-year bachelor's degrees in more than 100 programs of study on a 112 acre-campus in Montana's largest city. The University is strongest in areas of Arts and Sciences, Allied Health, Education, Business, and Technology (including nursing); students can earn master's degrees in education and business administration. The MSU Billings College of Technology offers training for many high-tech positions and hundreds of subjects from the medical field to computer support to the auto industry.

Rocky Mountain College, founded in 1878, is Montana's oldest higher-education institution. It is affiliated with the United Church of Christ, the United Methodist Church, and the United Presbyterian Church. It offers undergraduate degrees in more than 217 liberal arts and professionally-oriented majors and has an enrollment of about 1,000 students on a 60-acre Billings campus. It regularly ranks among the top ten most comprehensive colleges in the western portion of the nation.

Also located in Billings are the University of Mary Billings Center (which offers a non-traditional programming that requires only one night a week of classes and can be completed in as little as 15 months), the Yellowstone Baptist College (the only Southern Baptist College in the northwest), and Walla Walla University which offers social work education to interested students.

Libraries and Research Centers

The Parmly Billings Library contains more than 300,000 items, including 250,000 books (of these, more than 9,000 are large-print editions). There are also 190 magazine subscriptions, 7,000 music CDs, approximately 8,000 books on tape or CD, 11,000 videos, and 1,400 interactive CDs (games and other software). There are also five word processing centers and 18 Internet stations. Key collections include a full-text database research center, an Auto Repair Reference Center, Heritage Quest Online Genealogy Resources, and the NoveList Fiction Guide. There is an Outreach program and Infomobile for senior citizens. A new 66,000-square-foot building, designed by Will Bruder and Partners, opened on January 6, 2014. Funding for the new library was provided by a city voter-approved $16.3 million bond issue, with $3 million of bonds to be retired by a successful capital campaign conducted by the Billings Public Library Foundation, which also secured a $2 million initial gift from an anonymous donor for the architectural and engineering services through construction.

In 2010, the Montana State University Billings College of Technology opened its doors to the local community as a joint city-university branch library in conjunction with the Parmly Billings Library. The COT library has about 7,000 items in its collection. Other major libraries in the community also include the library at Rocky Mountain College.

Public Library Information: Parmly Billings Library, 510 North Broadway, Billings, MT 59101; telephone (406) 657-8258.

■ Health Care

Billings provides the main medical services for a four-state area, including Wyoming and the Dakotas, with state-of-the-art equipment and highly skilled personnel. Two fully equipped and modern hospitals—St. Vincent Health Care and the Billings Clinic—and 40 medical clinics, including some that focus on homeopathic care, serve the region. Most of the health care facilities are concentrated in a 114-acre medical corridor that encompasses both of the city's major hospitals and 20 other health-related facilities.

Billings Clinic, composed of more than 255 physicians and 85 non-physician providers, is a 285-bed Level II trauma center with general care and specialized services that include a cardiac care center, cancer services, an intensive care unit, the Kidney Center, a psychiatric center, pulmonary services, Women's Resource Center, occupational health and wellness, orthopedics and sports medicine, and a Research Institute. It also maintains and a 90-bed skilled nursing and assisted living facility. Off of the main campus are branch clinics, which include Billings Clinic Heights and Billings Clinic West. In addition, the Aspen Meadows Retirement Community is part of Billings Clinic. Billings Clinic was the first Montana Magnet-designated health-care organization and is a member of the Mayo Clinic Care Network.

A 286-bed Level II trauma center, St. Vincent Healthcare is operated by the Sisters of Charity of Leavenworth and provides comprehensive inpatient and outpatient services, special services for women and seniors, and expertise in cardiology, orthopedics, general internal medicine, pediatrics, emergency and trauma, neurosciences, rehabilitation, neonatology, and oncology. One of the region's largest healthcare providers, St. Vincent Healthcare serves the medical needs of more than 400,000 people in a four-state area. The hospital employees approximately 2,100 people. The medical staff of 511 individuals includes 105 physicians, 406 independent or privileged physicians, and 117 allied health professionals. It logs more than 400,000 patient visits per year.

Other medical facilities in Billings are the Northern Rockies Radiation Oncology Center; Rimrock Foundation, which provides treatment for addictive disorders such as chemical dependency, co-dependency, compulsive gambling, and eating disorders; RiverStone Health; Advanced Care Hospital of Montana; and several mental health facilities.

■ Recreation

Sightseeing

Downtown Billings contains the Billings Historical District, a renovated area that consists of most of the original business district. The Castle Corner is a replica of the Potter Palmer Mansion in Chicago, an interesting structure modeled after English castles. The railroad brought prosperity to Billings, and prosperity brought Preston B. Moss. In 1901, architect H.J. Hardenbergh (designer of the Waldorf-Astoria and Plaza Hotels in New York City) created the elegant Moss estate. The three-story Moss Mansion remains authentically furnished and is open year-round at 914 Division Street. The Black Otter Trail, beginning at the edge of the city, is a winding highway that follows the "rimrocks," natural sandstone cliffs that border the city on the north and east. Boothill Cemetery, burial ground for residents of the frontier town of Colson, and the Range Rider of Yellowstone, a life-sized bronze statue by artist Charles Christadora, are both located along the Black Otter Trail, as are Sacrifice Cliff and Yellowstone Kelly's gravesite. Pictograph Cave State Park, southeast of Billings, has cave paintings made by Indians who lived and hunted for wooly mammoth in the region some 4,500 years ago.

A number of national monuments, parks, and recreation areas are located near Billings, most within a two-hour drive. Little Bighorn Battlefield National Monument, site of Custer's Last Stand, is 65 miles southeast of the city, and Pompey's Pillar, a spectacular natural rock formation, is 28 miles east of Billings.

The Little Bighorn Battlefield National Monument lets visitors relive the clash between General George Custer's 7th Cavalry and more than 3,000 warriors led by Crazy Horse. Yellowstone National Park is the world's first such; President Theodore Roosevelt proclaimed it so during his presidential tenure, and visitors today can see its famous geysers, painted canyons, and wildlife much as the way Roosevelt saw it. On the way from Billings to Yellowstone, Montana's highest peak is on view from Highway 212 over the Beartooth Mountain Pass.

Arts and Culture

The main performing arts center in the region, the Alberta Bair Theater for the Performing Arts is the site of most of the cultural activity in Billings and the largest fully equipped performing arts center in the region. The Fox Committee for the Performing Arts and the Billings Community Concert Association are both responsible for bringing a wide range of cultural events to the city each year, including jazz, opera, ballet, and popular music concerts. The Billings Symphony Orchestra and Chorale performs approximately eleven concerts each season, including an annual free concert in the park.

The Billings Studio Theatre (BST), established in 1953, mounts a five-show Mainstage Season along with a major fall production at the Alberta Bair Theater, special events, and experimental plays in its Dark Night Series. BST also showcases two Rocky Mountain College productions annually and hosts many community events. In addition, BST operates a children's theatre, the Growing Stage. Montana Shakespeare in the Parks is the only professional theatre program in the state producing Shakespearean plays; it offers its performances free to the public. Since its inception in 1973, Montana Shakespeare in the Parks has traveled over 400,000 miles and presented over 1,500 performances to a cumulative audience of more than a half million people. It began as an amateur 12-city tour but has become a nationally known, professional company which presents an eight-week tour of 70 performances in 50 communities every summer throughout Montana, northern Wyoming, and eastern Idaho.

The Western Heritage Center features changing exhibits pertaining to the region's history, and the Yellowstone County Museum contains historical relics and dioramas depicting scenes from Billings's past. The Yellowstone Art Museum holds one of the region's best collections of contemporary and historic art, including an impressive collection of Western art particularly strong in the works of Montana artists Russell Chatham and Deborah Butterfield; it also sponsors lectures and concerts. In 2010 the Art Museum opened its new Visible Vault, the region's first publicly accessible art storage spaces. The Vault is unique in that it is one of only a meager handful of similar facilities in the United States.

MetraPark fairground holds concerts, rodeos, and the annual Montana Fair. Canyon Creek and a nature trail wind through ZooMontana's 70 acres of exotic animal exhibits.

Festivals and Holidays

Annual events in and around Billings include ArtWalk and the MSU-Billings Wine and Food Festival in May, the Moss Mansion County Fair and Strawberry Festival in June, and July's Crazy Days downtown and the Skyfest Parade and Balloon Rally. In August the Magic City Blues Festival graces downtown, and the MontanaFair is held at the MetraPark fairgrounds for nine days. On the fourth weekend in September the traditional German harvest festival, Herbstfest, is held in nearby Laurel. German foods, dancing, and music are featured. Downtown Billings is the site of Harvest Fest each October. Late November has the Holiday Parade, and Christmas Stroll occurs each December downtown.

Sports for the Spectator

Billings supports two professional sports teams. The Billings Mustangs, a baseball farm team of the Cincinnati Reds, play at Cobb Field; and the Billings Bulls play junior hockey at the Centennial Ice Arena. The city was also home to the Billings Outlaws, a United Indoor Football team, until they were forced to cease operations in 2010 due to lack of funding. The city features several rodeo events each year, including the Northern Rodeo Association finals, which have been held in Billings for 30 years. Auto racing takes place at Billings Motorsports Park. Billings also hosts the Big Sky State Games each year. In 2007, approximately 10,000 athletes participated in some 36 sports during the Big Sky State Games, and 2010 marked its 25th anniversary. Since its inception in 1986, more than 204,500 athletes from 250 Montana communities have participated in the multi-sport event.

Both Rocky Mountain College and Montana State University-Billings also offer up a plethora of spectator-sports for the community, including volleyball, basketball, and soccer, just to name a few.

Sports for the Participant

The mountains near Billings offer a complete range of year-round outdoor activity in some of America's most spectacular terrain: skiing (at nearby Red Lodge Mountain, and farther away Big Sky and the new Moonlight Basin resort); hiking; hunting; fishing (some of the world's legendary trout streams are nearby, such as Rock Creek and the Stillwater, Boulder, Musselshell, Big Horn, and Yellowstone rivers); camping; and a wide variety of water recreation. At a number of lakes and reservoirs, swimming, boating, sailing, and water skiing can be enjoyed. The city of Billings maintains and operates more than 2,300 acres in its 40 parks that feature swimming pools, tennis courts, athletic fields, jogging and biking paths, and other recreational facilities. The city's most popular park is Pioneer Park which offers the community 34 acres of wooded, hilly space, golf, tennis, and a wading pool. There are several public and private golf courses in the city.

Shopping and Dining

Rimrock Mall downtown is the largest shopping area, with more than 85 shops, including Dillard's, JCPenney, Eddie Bauer, Gap, and Bath and Body Works. West Park Plaza is another large enclosed shopping center, with more than 30 stores. There are at least a dozen smaller shopping areas in Billings. Western boutiques to specialty shops serve up quality merchandise and great bargains, all with no sales tax, in the historic downtown shopping district or the Billings Heights area on Main Street.

Restaurants in Billings feature traditional Western fare as well as exotic ethnic cuisine in settings ranging from casual and inexpensive to elegant and intimate. Most restaurants are clustered around the main shopping and commercial areas of downtown on Montana Avenue and North Broadway.

Visitor Information: Billings Area Chamber of Commerce, 815 South 27th St., Billings, MT 59107; telephone (406) 245-4111; fax (406) 245-7333; info@ billingschamber.com.

■ Convention Facilities

The primary meeting facility in Billings is MetraPark, a multipurpose major event center located on the Rimrocks overlooking downtown. The largest of its kind in a five-state region, MetraPark features a 10,000-seat arena, a 77,400 square-foot Expo Center, and a 28,800 square-foot Montana Pavilion. The complex contains an assortment of barns and small buildings as well as a covered grandstand for outdoor events and a half-mile track used for both horse racing and auto racing. The facility is diverse enough to hold large trade shows, professional sporting events for three local franchises, national touring shows and musical acts, and Gold Wing Road Riders Wing Ding gatherings.

The Billings Hotel and Convention Center specializes in groups of 10 to 1,400 people with over 30,000 square feet of meeting and banquet facilities. In addition to an indoor pool and hot tub, there are two amusement-style waterslides. A new ballroom and business center was also recently added to the facility. The R-Club offers live entertainment on the weekends.

The Holiday Inn Grand Montana Hotel & Convention Center is the largest facility in the four-state region to be built in conjunction with a hotel; recently renovated, it contains 50,000 square feet of meeting space in 17 rooms that accommodate groups from 10 to 4,670. Located downtown is the Alberta Bair Theater, which serves as the site of business meetings and conventions as well as performances, with a theater capacity of close to 1,400 people.

Conference and convention facilities for large and small groups are available in several hotels, motels, and bed-and-breakfast establishments throughout the Billings metropolitan area, including the Historic Northern Hotel and the Sheraton Billings Hotel. Billings offers more than 3,400 hotel rooms and nearly 350 million square feet of meeting space. Alternatives to city hotel accommodations can be found outside Billings at the Double Spear Ranch in Pryor, Montana.

Convention Information: Billings Area Chamber of Commerce, 815 South 27th Street, Billings, MT 59107; telephone (406) 245-4111; fax (406) 245-7333; email info@billingschamber.com.

■ Transportation

Approaching the City

Billings Logan International Airport is only two miles from the downtown district and serves most of eastern Montana and northern Wyoming with more than 50 flights daily from major airlines and regional carriers. It has been dubbed one of the nation's best-served small-market airports and provides non-stop flights to nine U.S. cities. Allegiant Air, Atlantic Southeast Airlines, Big Sky, Delta, Frontier, Horizon, Northwest, Skywest, and United all service Billings with planes as large as 757s.

Billings is at the junction of two interstate highways: I-90, connecting the city with the Pacific Northwest and the southern Rocky Mountain states; and I-94, providing a link with the Midwestern states. U.S. 87, 310, and 212 also meet in Billings.

Billings is served by Greyhound and Rimrock Trailways bus services. Billings lost Amtrak service in 1979 when the North Coast Hiawatha was discontinued. The nearest Amtrak stop is on the Hi-Line, 200 miles north of Billings. Plans to bring regular passenger rail service through Billings as part of a route through southern Montana have not materialized.

Traveling in the City

Billings Metropolitan Transit operates 18 routes within the city and serves approximately 5,000 customers. Auto traffic on major thoroughfares is light compared to most metropolitan areas. The downtown area is laid out in a grid pattern with numbered streets.

■ Communications

Newspapers and Magazines

Billings has one major daily newspaper, *The Billings Gazette* (morning). *Montana Land Magazine* is published quarterly.

Television and Radio

All four major television networks (ABC, CBS, NBC, and Fox) broadcast to the Billings area. Eleven FM and five AM radio stations broadcast from Billings.

Media Information: The Billings Gazette, 401 N. Broadway, Billings, MT 59101; telephone (406) 657-1200.

Billings Online

Big Sky Economic Development Authority. Available www.bigskyeda-edc.org/
Billings Area Chamber of Commerce. Available www.billingschamber.com
Billings Convention and Visitors Bureau. Available www.visitbillings.com
Billings Cultural Partners. Available www.billingsevents.com
The Billings Gazette. Available www.billingsgazette.com
Billings Public Schools. Available www.billingsschools.org
City of Billings home page. Available www.ci.billings.mt.us
Parmly Billings Library. Available www.billings.lib.mt.us

BIBLIOGRAPHY

Egan, Timothy, *The Big Burn: Teddy Roosevelt and the Fire that Saved America* (Boston: Mariner Books, 2010)

Raban, Jonathan, *Bad Land: An American Romance* (New York: Pantheon, 1996)

Van West, Carroll, *Capitalism on the Frontier: Billings and the Yellowstone Valley in the Nineteenth Century* (Lincoln, NE: University of Nebraska Press, 1993)

Butte

■ The City in Brief

Founded: 1864 (incorporated, 1879)

Head Official: Chief Executive Matt Vincent (since 2012; current term expires 2016)

City Population
> 1990: 33,336
> 2000: 33,892
> 2010: 33,525
> 2012 estimate: 33,344
> Percent change, 2000–2010: −1.1%

Micropolitan Statistical Area Population
> 2000: 34,606
> 2010: 34,200
> 2012 estimate: 34,334
> Percent change, 2000–2010: −1.2%
> U.S. rank in 2000: 1,262th
> U.S. rank in 2010: 787th

Area: 716.2 square miles

Elevation: ranges from 5,484 to 6,463 feet above sea level

Average Annual Temperatures: 53.2° F (maximum), 27.1° F (minimum)

Average Annual Precipitation: 12.75 inches

Major Economic Sectors: transportation, energy research, medicine, tourism

Unemployment Rate: 3.8% (2012)

Per Capita Income: $22,877

Major Colleges and Universities: Montana Tech of the University of Montana

Daily Newspaper: *The Montana Standard*

■ Introduction

For more than a century, copper was king in Butte, Montana. Once dependent almost solely on the mining industry-in the early 1900s it was called "the richest hill on earth" because of the valuable ores that lay beneath it-Butte, like many older American cities, is in the midst of a transition toward a more diversified economy. With easy access to western and Midwestern markets, Butte is one of the west's major transportation hubs; the city is also moving into enterprises related to energy research and high-altitude sports training. Butte is a community that juggles the old and new, maintaining a balance of history and modernity. The city has brought state-of-the-art technological resources to the area through newly established technology parks and rocket-testing facilities, and yet it also boasts the largest National Historical Landmark District in the nation, with over 5,000 buildings listed as national historic sites. Rimmed by the peaks of mountain ranges, Butte provides nearby access to trout fishing, world-class golf courses, hiking, hunting, skiing, soaking (in commercial hot springs), snowmobiling, and many other outdoor recreational opportunities. Despite all the changes underway in Butte, the city continues to retain its multiethnic heritage and its connection to the breathtaking natural beauty of the surrounding Rocky Mountains.

■ Geography and Climate

Butte is located in Summit Valley in the heart of the Rocky Mountains on the west slope of the Continental Divide in southwestern Montana. Silver Bow Creek, part of the Columbia River system-and called Clark Fork outside the city-runs through Butte. The climate is semi-arid, with a growing season of about 80 days.

Area: 716.2 square miles

Elevation: ranges from 5,484 to 6,463 feet above sea level

© Patti McCanville/Alamy

Average Temperatures: 53.2° F (maximum), 27.1° F (minimum)

Average Annual Precipitation: 12.75 inches

■ History

Discovery of Gold and Silver Brings Settlers to Region

The area surrounding Butte's present location remained uninhabited before gold was discovered in 1864 in Silver Bow Creek. Native Americans and explorers passed through the region, but found no attractions for permanent settlement until two prospectors detected placer deposits in the creek; they named the site the Missoula lode. Other prospectors came, and by 1867, the population of the mining settlement reached 500 people. Water was scarce, however, and the town began to decline; the 1870 census recorded only about 200 people.

One of the region's first prospectors, William Farlin, returned in 1874 to claim several outcrops of quartz that he had discovered previously. Before long a silver boom began, bringing a chaotic mix of claim staking and claim jumping as prospectors overran the site. Investors William Clark and Andrew Davis constructed mills for extracting

gold and silver, and by 1876, when a townsite patent was issued, the prosperous camp numbered 1,000 residents. Marcus Daly, representing Salt Lake City mining entrepreneurs, arrived that same year and bought the Alice Mine, naming it Walkerville for his employers. In 1879 Butte, which had been named for Big Butte, a volcanic cone to the northwest, was incorporated as a city.

Copper Discovered; Butte Thrives; Unions Formed

In 1880 Daly sold his interest in the Walker mining operations and bought the Anaconda Mine. As he was digging for silver, Daly struck copper, thus initiating the industry that eventually made him one of the country's wealthiest and most powerful men. Daly attracted investors from as far away as Boston and New York, and within a year the town had several mines and mining companies. In a lifelong rivalry with William Clark for control of Butte, Daly finally won out as the "boss" of a one-industry town. The arrival of the Union Pacific Railroad in 1881 ensured Butte's success as the leading producer of copper in the United States.

With a population of 14,000 people in 1885, Butte supported banks, schools, a hospital, a fire department, churches, and a water company. Copper production and the development of mining companies continued until the turn of the century, when Daly joined with the Rockefeller family to form the Amalgamated Copper Mining Company, one of the early twentieth-century trusts. By the first decade of the twentieth century Butte was a major rail hub, with four railroads connecting in the city. Amalgamated, having bought out other mining companies in Butte, changed its name back to the Anaconda Copper Mining Company in 1915.

The labor movement was important to Butte's history. The Butte Miner's Union was formed in 1878 to protect miners from the dangers of working underground. The Butte delegation was the largest at the 1906 founding convention of the International Workers of the World (IWW) in Chicago. During the early twentieth century the union's power began to decline when mining companies were consolidated and management became indifferent to worker demands. The dynamiting of the union hall in 1914 and the lynching of an IWW organizer in 1917 led to seven years of martial law in Butte. The worst hardrock mining disaster in American history, the Spectacular Mine Fire, also took place in 1917, killing 168 miners.

Present-day Butte neighborhoods such as Dublin Gulch, Finntown, Chinatown, and Corktown attest to the city's diverse ethnic roots. Since the community's earliest days immigrants from all over the world settled in Butte to work the mines. When the placer camp was started in 1864, Chinese miners were the first to arrive. Later came Cornish, Irish, and Welsh laborers, and for a time Irish workers formed the dominant group. Then Serbs, Croats, French Canadians, Finns, Scandinavians, Jews, Lebanese, Mexicans, Austrians, Germans, and African Americans added to the ranks of miners.

Mining Declines; Economy Diversifies

Throughout the first half of the twentieth century, the mining industry continued to dominate the Butte economy. Changes began to take place, however; underground mining gave way to pit mining in the 1950s when high-grade copper-ore deposits were exhausted and above-ground exploration for low-grade ore began. In 1976 Anaconda was bought by Atlantic Richfield Company; in 1983 the mines were completely closed. Unemployment rose to more than 17 percent and Butte's survival seemed threatened. That same year a task force composed of government and business leaders was formed to ensure a future for Butte through a concerted effort to diversify the city's economy. Since then, mines have reopened, a transportation hub was built at the Port of Montana, Cyber Village and Silicon Mountain Technology Park have opened, and several high-technology firms have established facilities in the area. Butte's economy is now powered by a variety of industries, including health care, retail trade, utilities, and a very successful "heritage tourism" industry supported by one of the largest historical districts in the nation.

The Montana Ambassadors, the Pacific Institute, the U.S. Corporation have recognized these efforts at economic stability, diversification, and growth for Economic Development, and *Newsweek* magazine, which commented in an article about the area's steady decline and stagnant economy, that "in Montana, Butte has engineered the most dramatic turnaround."

Historical Information: Butte Silver-Bow Public Archives, 17 W. Quartz St., Butte, MT 59703; telephone (406) 782-3280; email info@buttearchives.org.

■ Population Profile

Micropolitan Statistical Area Population

2000: 34,606
2010: 34,200
2012 estimate: 34,334
Percent change, 2000–2010: −1.2%
U.S. rank in 2000: 1,262th
U.S. rank in 2010: 787th

City Residents

1990: 33,336
2000: 33,892
2010: 33,525
2012 estimate: 33,344
Percent change, 2000–2010: −1.1%

Density: 46.8 people per square mile

Racial and ethnic characteristics

White: 31,896
Black or African American: 211
American Indian and Alaskan Native: 533
Asian: 158
Native Hawaiian and Other Pacific Islander: 0
Hispanic or Latino (may be of any race): 1,209
Other: 546

Percent of residents born in state: 68.6%

Age characteristics

Population under 5 years old: 1,699
Population 5 to 9 years old: 2,229
Population 10 to 14 years old: 1,731
Population 15 to 19 years old: 2,190
Population 20 to 24 years old: 2,562
Population 25 to 34 years old: 3,689
Population 35 to 44 years old: 3,796
Population 45 to 54 years old: 5,145
Population 55 to 59 years old: 2,710
Population 60 to 64 years old: 2,069
Population 65 to 74 years old: 2,973
Population 75 to 84 years old: 1,680
Population 85 years and over: 871
Median age: 42.1

Births (2010–11 Micropolitan Area)

Total number: 881

Deaths (2010–11 Micropolitan Area)

Total number: 665

Money income (2012)

Per capita income: $22,877
Median household income: $38,507
Total households: 14,500

Number of households with income of ...

less than $10,000: 1,399
$10,000 to $14,999: 1,336
$15,000 to $24,999: 2,020
$25,000 to $34,999: 1,888
$35,000 to $49,999: 2,299
$50,000 to $74,999: 2,364
$75,000 to $99,999: 1,493
$100,000 to $149,999: 1,229
$150,000 to $199,999: 257
$200,000 or more: 215

Percent of families below poverty level: 19.0%

■ Municipal Government

The governments of the city of Butte and Silver Bow County are combined and are administered by a Chief Executive and council. The twelve council members and the Chief Executive all serve four-year terms.

Head Official: Chief Executive Matt Vincent (since 2012; current term expires 2016)

Total Number of City Employees: 472 (2013)

City Information: Butte/Silver Bow Government Courthouse, 155 West Granite St., Butte, MT 59701; telephone (406) 497-6200; fax (406) 497-6328.

■ Economy

Major Industries and Commercial Activity

Since Butte's founding during a gold boom, its principal industry has been mining. From the mid-1880s to the 1980s, Butte produced an estimated $22 billion in minerals mined. More than 8 percent of the nation's copper continues to be produced in Butte, joining other important minerals such as lead, zinc, and magnesium. In the 1970s, when underground mines were closed, the copper industry began to decline; it reached its lowest point in 1983 when mining operations in the Butte area completely ceased for a time.

This recession began to ease in 1986 when copper mines were reopened, creating more than 300 jobs. This upsurge brought development in other areas such as transportation, tourism and recreation, small businesses, technology, energy research, medicine, and communications. Accolades have poured in during recent years, lauding Butte's economic resurgence, even earning the town a four-minute spot on the Paul Harvey radio program. Lou Tice of the Pacific Institute in Seattle hailed Butte as a "city on the move." Citing the economic rebirth of Butte, Tice attributed the successes to "its people-their tenacity, their hard work and the remarkable goals they set."

The reopening of Mountain Resources, which operates an open pit copper and molybdenum mine is evidence of the upswing that Butte's mining industry has seen in recent years. Although the major driving force behind Butte's economy was once mining, and despite the reopening of Mountain Resources, what once was a leading industry in Butte has since been replaced by a variety of other diverse industries, including healthcare and tourism. These new industries fostered a 2.6 percent growth in wages 2012. Growth in inflation-adjusted nonfarm earnings of between 2 and 2.5 percent was expected for the period 2013–16 as the economy continued to evolve.

In 2013, St. James Community Hospital was one of Silver-Bow County's largest employers, and the Healthcare and Social Assistance sector as a whole was Butte's largest industry sector, providing jobs for some 2,896 individuals. The Government sector and Retail Trade industry followed closely behind with some 2,461 and 2,149 individuals employed in these sectors respectively. Butte's focus on historic renovations-the city is home to more than 5,000 national historic sites and buildings–has played a key role in the development of Butte's "heritage tourism" industry over the years; in 2005, visitors to Butte–Silver Bow spent an estimated $67 million.

Home to technology parks such as Cyber Village and Silicon Mountain Technology Park, Butte has also seen a swell in its technology industry in recent years as well. Butte is currently home to quite a few technology-based businesses, including Advanced Silicon Materials LLC, Synesis7, Portlock Software, e-DOCS USA, and ITG World. In 2009, Butte Aerotec also began testing jet, rocket, and hybrid engines within the city limits. With the opening of the Rocky Mountain Supercomputing Center, it is predicted that the city will see a continued upsurge in the city's ability to attract even more technology companies to the area. The center offers supercomputing platforms as a service (SPaaS) and provides industry with standardized software packages, HPC services, application hosting, and support services. RMSC maximizes use of its resources and alliance partners in providing a Moab-enabled hybrid-OS (dual boot—RHE 5.2 and Windows HPC Server 2008) cloud-computing-on-demand model for academia, government, and industry as it emerges from the "Great American Supercomputing Desert."

Despite the impressive growth in information technologies, manufacturing, transportation, and health care, Butte's economic prospects continue to hinge crucially on the mining sector, especially copper. In 2013 the Montana Bureau of Economic Research reported that bonuses paid to miners exert a significant influence on overall growth. In the slowing global economy, which raises some concern as commodity prices continue to move sideways, their forecast reflects the expectation that prices remain high enough not to threaten the profitability at Butte's mining operations.

Items and goods produced: motors, dairy and food products, compressed and liquefied gases, beverages, optical goods, chemicals, steel fabrications, phosphate products

Incentive Programs—New and Existing Companies

Local programs: The Butte/Silver Bow Tax Increment Financing Industrial District (Butte has two, comprising 1,300 acres) directs new tax dollars accrued from new development within the district to assist further development within the boundaries of the district. There are four other tax incentive programs available to local businesses that qualify including a low-interest loan program designed to assist with facilities construction. The maximum loan amount is $400,000, and depending on the risk of the project and use of funds, carries an interest rate from 3 to 5 percent and term from 10 to 25 years.

The Butte Local Development Corporation (BLDC), a principal catalyst in the region's economic turnaround, is considered one of the best economic development organizations for its size in the country. Its mission is to create jobs through industrial development. The BLDC is the leading point of contact for individuals and companies wishing to save, expand, start, or locate a business in the Butte–Silver Bow area. BLDC accomplishes these goals through capital acquisition, land and infrastructure development, development and maintenance of informational tools, economic analysis and planning, and numerous other activities. The BLDC also works with Headwater RC&D to administer the BEAR Program (Business Expansion and Retention) to seven counties in Southwest Montana. The BEAR Program offers support to local businesses. The BLDC also administers five loan programs. In addition, property used by certain new or expanding industries is eligible for a reduced taxable valuation (up to 50 percent of its taxable valuation for the first five years) during the first nine years after construction or expansion. Thanks in great part to the efforts of the BLDC, Butte has been recognized as an "All America City" for its economic development efforts and its successful economic development team.

In 2009, Butte–Silver Bow County was designated a Foreign Trade Zone, allowing companies who import or export from the area a deferment or complete elimination of customs duties.

State programs: The Montana Economic Revitalization and Development Institute (MERDI) conducts energy research, commercialization for technology transfer, and economic development. MERDI manages the Thornton Technology and Enterprise Center, which is a renovated historic building, located in uptown Butte. The facility features cutting-edge information technology infrastructure and a data center offering a full suite of services, including access to high-speed and high-capacity broadband. The facility offers an IBM 1350 high-performance computing cluster. MERDI is currently leading an effort to build a hybrid-community fiber-optic network. Its goal is to provide Montana businesses, non-profits, educational and governmental organizations the increasingly necessary tools to thrive in the twenty-first century economy.

The Montana Business Assistance Connection (MBAC) encourages and supports the creation of new jobs and relocation of existing jobs to various counties in Montana by helping with public and private revolving loan funds and providing training and access to capital for qualified start-up businesses or expanding businesses. The New Markets Tax Credits Program provides a 39 percent federal income tax credit to businesses that choose to invest capital into qualified projects in eligible low-income areas. Loans provided by MCDC range from $1,000 to $1,000,000 to qualified businesses and projects.

Montana's Office of Economic Development was selected by the U.S. Department of Treasury to participate in their State Small Business Credit Initiative (SSBCI), making Montana eligible to receive $13,168,350 via transfer under the SSBCI. The funding was made possible through the Small Business Jobs Act of 2010. The legislation created the State Small Business Credit Initiative to strengthen state programs that support lending to small businesses and small manufacturers.

Other State of Montana tax incentives include property tax reduction; no inventory, use, or sales tax; new industry income tax credits; small business investment tax credits; and tax reduction on pollution control equipment. The Big Sky Development Trust Fund can provide up to $5,000 in grant funding for each new eligible job created. The Primary Sector Workforce Training Grant offers direct reimbursement to eligible businesses for training costs up to $5,000 per eligible new job.

In 2014 state regulators approved Butte's request for a new tax-increment financing district for Uptown and adjacent neighborhoods, a move that should eventually steer tens of millions of tax dollars into area development.

Job training programs: The Primary Sector Workforce Training Grant (WTG) program is a state-funded program; $3.9 million is available annually for this program. The WTG program is targeted to businesses that are creating at least one net, new job that pays at least the lower of the current county average wage or the state current average wage.

Development Projects

In 2009 alone, the BLDC devoted time to 38 different economic development projects. Renovations began on the historic Sears Building this same year in the heart of Uptown Butte. As of 2010, the renovation project was still underway to convert the space into a mix of urban housing and retail space. The $8.3 million renovations include approximately 34 modern apartments, a scenic rooftop deck, and a ground floor leased as commercial space. As of 2010, a grocery store was in the process of being built in a portion of this commercial space. The basement will be the future home of the Science Mine, a hands-on non-profit science museum. The project is predicted to have an economic impact of over $11 million and to yield some 45 new jobs in the next 10 years. The development project was a recipient of a 2010 "Development of Distinction" Award for its innovative financing through federal tax credits and its excellence in historic restoration. The nearby Leonard Hotel was also undergoing renovations in 2010. The $2.1 million project will yield some 40 apartments for the historic hotel once complete.

Butte has also been home to many recent technological developments. In 2010, Butte AeroTec Rocket & Jet Engine Test Facility was working on a new upgraded $386,000 rocket test facility that would allow for testing of 24-inch diameter rockets. The facility was scheduled for completion in the late summer of 2010. That same year, Chafin/Fuhrlander was solidifying plans to build their first U.S. wind turbine assembly plant in Butte. The $29 million plant could create jobs for 125 to 150 employees once construction is complete.

The Port of Montana, located in Butte, also underwent recent expansions as well. Its recently completed Port of Montana HUB, intended to facilitate the loading and transporting of minerals and forest products by rail and motor freight carriers, is expected to contribute significantly to the area's economic development. A separate project to expand the port's warehouse was completed in the summer of 2010. The $2.8 million expansion added some 40,000 square feet to its 80,000 square foot warehouse facility.

The facility is located in the only place in Montana where two Class I railroads and two interstate highways come together. The Business Development Park is zoned heavy industrial and has necessary infrastructure including, gas, electricity, and industrial water; potable water is available through wells. Construction on a waste water line was scheduled to begin in 2014. Businesses located in the Business Development Park include REC (Renewable Energy Corporation), SeaCast, Old Dominion Freight Line, Port of Montana, Rhodia, Montana Aerospace Development Association, and the Silver Bow Drive-In.

The South Butte Industrial Park saw new development in 2010 with the construction of the $10 million Army Reserve Center.

Other steps toward economic stabilization in Butte within the last decade include the opening of a small business incubator, the establishment of Butte's Cyber Village, and the development of the U.S. High Altitude Sports Center.

In 2013 Butte opened Montana's first community-hybrid fiber-optic network, the only one of its kind in the state. At an estimated cost of $1.6 million, the network rivals Google Fiber's much publicized one gigabit offering in certain U.S cities by delivering two gigabits of data transmission to each of the 14 Butte School District locations.

Economic Development Information: Butte Local Development Corporation, 480 East Park St., Butte, MT 59701; telephone (406) 723-4349; fax (406) 723-1539. Montana Department of Labor and Industry, 840 Helena Avenue, Helena, MT 59601; telephone (406) 444-2430; toll-free (800) 541-3904; fax (406) 444-2638.

Commercial Shipping

Butte is a major inland port from which imported cargo is shipped via rail and motor carrier to points throughout the Midwest. Butte is located at the only rail interline in the state of the Union Pacific and Burlington Northern railroads. Silver Bow County is served by Montana Western/Montana Rail Link/Burlington Northern; Rarus; and Union Pacific railroads. Piggyback service is provided, and trains run up to twelve times weekly from Butte. Several motor freight carriers regularly transport goods through facilities in Butte, with overnight and second-day delivery to major cities in the West and Midwest; in addition, well over 1,000 motor freight carriers serving the state have access to Butte. Some of the trucking firms serving the county are Western Transport Line, Yellow Freight, Molerway Freight Lines, Consolidated Freightways, Transystems, Roadway Express, ANA Transport, Biggers Transport, Irving Trucking, Americana Expressways, Highland, S&J Trucking, Prince, Kenyon-Noble, Rob Clark, RB&C Trucking, Solberg, and Ward Trucking.

Labor Force and Employment Outlook

When the Butte Job Service surveyed 10 major employers in the Butte area, they reported rates of absenteeism from 1 to 2 percent, and turnover rates that average 3 percent. The unemployment rate in Butte as of August 2010 was at 6.3 percent, still below the national average. Butte's labor force in August of 2010 was composed of some 17,167 employees included many well-trained workers with skills and experience beyond their present employment. Silver Bow County has experienced ups and downs in employment levels as it has made the difficult transition to a more diversified economy. Growth in the 1990s was driven in a large part by construction of the American Silicon Minerals corporate headquarters in Butte. Following the loss of construction jobs in 1999, employment losses were once again experienced with the shutdown of Montana Resources in mid-2000. However, in August 2003 Montana Resources' copper and molybdenum mine reopened; Montana Resources currently employs approximately 350 people residing in Butte and Anaconda and neighboring communities. By 2007 Butte and Montana's economy were growing steadily-predictions were for 4 percent growth a year until 2009. A particular bright spot has been the city's success in luring international firms to the Silicon Mountain Technology Park and Cyber Village.

The following is a summary of data regarding the 2012 Butte labor force:

Size of civilian labor force: 16,794

Number of workers employed in . . .

agriculture and mining: 884
construction: 984
manufacturing: 444
wholesale trade: 372
retail trade: 2,011
transportation: 1,093
information systems: 181
finance: 626
professional administration: 1,281
education and social services: 4,094
arts and leisure: 1,958
other: 745
public administration: 921

Average hourly earnings of production workers: $16.10

Unemployment rate: 3.8% (2012)

Employers

Largest employers (2013)	*Number of employees*
Northwestern Energy	500–999
St James Community Hospital	500–999
Acadia Montana	250–499
Advanced Silicon Materials	250–499
Montana Resources	250–499
Town Pump	250–499
Wal-Mart	250–499
Aware Inc.	100–249
BSW	100–249
Butte Convalescent Center	100–249
Community Counseling & Correctional Service	100–249
Community Health Center	100–249
Easter Seals–Goodwill	100–249
Lady of the Rockies Rehab and Living Center	100–249
Safeway	100–249
Silver House	100–249

Cost of Living

The following is a summary of data regarding several key cost of living factors in the area.

State income tax rate: 1.0% to 6.9%

State sales tax rate: None

Local income tax rate: None

Local sales tax rate: None

Property tax rate: $1,296 (statewide per capita average, 2010)

Economic Information: Butte/Silver Bow Chamber of Commerce, 1000 George St., Butte, MT 59701; telephone (406) 723-3177; toll-free (800) 735-6814; fax (406) 723-1215; email chamber@buttechamber.org. Montana Department of Labor & Industry, P.O. Box 1728, Helena, MT 59624; telephone (406) 444-2840; fax (406) 444-1394.

■ Education and Research

Elementary and Secondary Schools

The public elementary and secondary school system in Butte is Butte School District #1. The district is overseen by an eight-member elected school board and is administered by a superintendent appointed by the board. The district is home to seven elementary schools, one middle school, and one high school. The district considers itself one of the most technologically advanced in Montana, with 100 percent Internet access for all students. The district offers a full range of after-school latchkey and enrichment programs, adult education, homebound services, special education, and a unique Retired Seniors Volunteer Program (R.S.V.P.) that brings local retirees together with students to form tutoring and mentoring relationships. The 21st Century Community Learning Centers (R.O.C.K.I.E.S.) program offers elementary students and their parents such services as after-school childcare; enrichment activities; reading and math instruction; and recreational activities. In 2013 the district introduced a high-capacity fiber-optic broadband network to ensure that its students acquire the necessary skills to be successful in the twenty-first century.

Several religious and secular parochial elementary and high schools provide alternatives to public education in the Butte metropolitan area. Butte Central Catholic Schools have been active in providing secular and Catholic education for Butte's children for over 100 years. The system consists of Butte Central Grade School, Butte Central Middle School, and Butte Central High School. Butte Central Maroons Activities Center (MAC) is a newly built athletic facility.

The following is a summary of data regarding the Butte Elementary School District.

Total enrollment: 2,943

Number of facilities

    total: 20
    elementary schools: 11
    junior high schools: 5
    high schools: 4
    other: 8

Student/teacher ratio: 16.72:1

Teacher salaries

    average (statewide): $47,132

Funding per pupil: $8,619

Public Schools Information: Butte School District #1, 111 North Montana, Butte, MT 59701; telephone (406) 533-2500; fax (406) 533-2525.

Colleges and Universities

Montana Tech of the University of Montana, originally chartered as the Montana State School of Mines, boasts a reputation as one of the finest science, engineering, and technical colleges in the world. The school is comprised of the College of Humanities, Social Sciences, and Information Technology; the College of Mathematics and Sciences; the School of Mines and Engineering; the College of Technology; and the Graduate School. Montana Tech offers more than 60 academic degree programs at the master's, bachelor's, associate's, and certificate levels. It is 1 of only 2 U.S. schools that offer a bachelor's degree in geophysical engineering, 1 of 10 that offer a bachelor's degree in metallurgical engineering, 1 of 19 that offer a B.S. degree in mining engineering, and 1 of 20 that offer a bachelor's in petroleum engineering.

The student body presents a national and global snapshot with over 43 states and 13 foreign countries represented. The university has a total enrollment of over 2,800 students. Engineering attracts the most students (1062), followed by Arts & Sciences (1011). There are

about 150 graduate students and just over 300 students attend part-time. A $20 million dollar construction and renovation project was recently completed, which modernized laboratory, classroom, and office facilities for the biology and chemistry programs.

Both Montana State University-Bozeman and the University of Montana in Missoula are within a two-hour drive of Butte.

Libraries and Research Centers

In 2014, The Butte–Silver Bow Library is located in Butte with an annual budget of $869,423. Holdings consist of 77,374 items, including 51,907 print items and 9,908 E-books. Special collections relate to Montana architecture, historic preservation, and fishing. The library is the headquarters for the Montana Public Library Film Service. The Butte–Silver Bow Public Archives holds information on local families and history, plus more than 30 labor history and 70 personal collections. The Historic Hearst Free Library in Anaconda offers more than 43,000 volumes, 66 periodicals, 16 newspapers, and a repository of historic memorabilia.

The Montana Tech Library houses nearly 50,000 volumes, 80,000 maps, and 425,000 documents including paper, microform, and electronic media. The library is a depository for federal and state government documents. In addition, Montana Tech conducts research activities in such fields as water resources, earthquakes, mines, and geology. Butte is home to the National Center for Appropriate Technology Research Library. Most of the other libraries and research centers in the city also specialize in energy and technology.

Public Library Information: Butte–Silver Bow Library, 226 West Broadway Street, Butte, MT 59701; telephone (406) 723-3361.

■ Health Care

The chief medical provider for the Butte–Silver Bow area is the St. James Healthcare system, part of the Montana region of the Sisters of Charity of Leavenworth Health System, which also has operations in Billings and Miles City. St. James is the largest comprehensive hospital in Montana and provides health care for residents within the surrounding seven-county region. This state-of-the-art health-care facility is licensed for 98 beds and has a staff of approximately 480, including a medical staff of more than 60 physicians, 30 consulting and courtesy physicians, and 25 allied health professionals. In addition to serving as an ACS Level III Trauma facility, St. James Healthcare provides services in more than 30 specialties.

The Community Health Center (CHC) (Butte Silver-Bow Primary Health Care Clinic) has been providing care to the people of SW Montana since 1986. Over 13,000 patients are served each year. CHC has pediatricians, pediatric nurse practitioners, internal medicine physicians, family practice physicians, physician assistants, and nurse practitioners. General dentistry is provided at the main CHC dental clinic located in Butte. The CHC pharmacy provides clinical pharmacy services to all the medical and behavioral health providers at the CHC.

A number of other institutions provide mental health services, dental care, hospice care, chiropractic care, chemical dependency rehabilitation, and more.

■ Recreation

Sightseeing

A popular Trolley Tour takes visitors to all the key sights-Old No. 1, a replica of the city's original electric trolley car system, operates four times daily from the first of June through Labor Day. Both St. Lawrence Church and the Serbian Orthodox Church have stunning frescoes that are open to public viewing. Butte's historic district also showcases several homes built during the days of the mining barons. The Copper King Mansion, built in 1888, was the Elizabethan-Victorian-style home of William S. Clark, whose battle with Marcus Daly for control in Butte has become a local legend; the mansion is now a bed and breakfast inn. Another impressive structure is the Charles Clark Mansion, also called the W.A. Clark Chateau, home of William A. Clark's son and a replica of a French chateau; completely restored and housing an arts center and gallery, it has been designated as a National Historic Structure. On the west side of the city are other fashionable, late-nineteenth-century homes.

Overlooking Butte from Montana Tech Hill is a statue of Marcus Daly by Augustus Saint-Gaudens. North of the downtown district stands the "gallows frame" of the Original Mine, which was used to raise and lower miners and ores from the underground mine. To the east of the city is the Berkeley Pit, started in 1955, and once the largest truck-operated open pit copper mine in the United States; it is an example of the process that replaced underground vein mining. The Granite Mountain Memorial commemorates the 168 miners who died during a 1917 fire at the Granite Mountain and Speculator mines. Also east of Butte, atop the Continental Divide, is Our Lady of the Rockies, a statue of the Christian religion's Virgin Mary. Standing 90 feet high and floodlighted at night, the statue is a nondenominational monument to motherhood that was built with donated materials and labor and completed in 1985.

Among the points of interest within driving distance of Butte are ghost towns such as Alder Gulch, Cable, Granite, and Philipsburg, where legends were formed and fortunes made during the gold and silver booms.

Arts and Culture

A culturally active city, Butte supports a symphony, a community arts center, and a theater company. The

Mother Lode, completed in 1923 as a Masonic Temple but never occupied by Masons, has been rehabilitated and serves as southwest Montana's premier performing arts center. The Butte Symphony Orchestra programs a four-concert season featuring a choral group and soloists. Theater is presented by Orphan Girl Theater and the Mother Lode Theater. Opera productions and appearances by national touring groups and speakers are also scheduled in the city.

Butte's principal museums are related to the mining industry. The World Museum of Mining and Hell Roarin' Gulch, a popular attraction in the area, features indoor and outdoor exhibits that replicate an early mining environment. Among the indoor displays are models of mines, minerals, firefighting equipment, a Stanley steam engine, and an electric hoist. Outdoor exhibits include a reconstructed 1900 mining camp, with a print shop, Chinese laundry, bank, drug store, millinery shop, and other authentic structures. Also featured at the museum is a tour on the Neversweat and Washoe Railroad aboard a train drawn by an M-10 locomotive; the tour starts at the museum, traveling past mines and head frames, to nearby Kelly mine. Commentary on mine history is presented. The Dumas Brothel was the longest-running establishment of its kind in America; Butte once had as many as 2,400 ladies of the evening working in town. The Mineral Museum at Montana Tech exhibits 1,300 items from its collection of more than 15,000 mineral specimens gathered from throughout the world; a highlight is a display of fluorescent minerals. The Mai Wah preserves the history of Butte's Chinese miners.

The Piccadilly Museum of Transportation houses a fascinating array of exhibits about transportation in America, from antique cars to gas pumps to road signs. The Mother Bottego House honors Celestine Mary Bottego, who spent 15 years in Butte and has been nominated for beatification. The Butte–Silver Bow W.A. Clark Chateau, a professional art gallery, mounts changing exhibits of works by local and national artists. Several private art galleries are also located in the city.

Festivals and Holidays

The W.A. Clark Chateau holds a Wine Tasting Festival in February. The Winternational Sports Festival, a multi-sport event, begins in February and continues into March, when St. Patrick's Day festivities such as a parade and the Friendly Sons of St. Patrick Banquet also take place. On March 16 the Finnish-American community gives thanks to St. Urho for chasing the grasshoppers out of Finland. Ghost Walks takes place in April at the Mining Museum.

July is an event-filled month; included among the activities are Evel Knievel Days ("The world's greatest celebration for the world's greatest daredevil") and the Freedom Festival parade and community picnic. The annual National Folk Festival has been replaced by a new event named the Montana Folk Festival, featuring multiple stages with continuous live performances by some of the best local, regional, and national traditional musical performers, great ethnic and festival foods, a lively family area, and folk life demonstrations and workshops that focus on a theme that highlights Montana's heritage.

AnRi Ra—the Montana Irish Festival celebrating Irish culture and heritage in Butte—takes place each August. Mining Heritage Day happens in September. The year ends with the annual Christmas Stroll, Ice-Sculpting Contest, and Festival of Trees.

Sports for the Spectator

Butte's U.S. High Altitude Sports Center has three times been chosen as the site of the World Cup Speed skating competition. Other sporting events include state wrestling tournaments and rodeos.

Sports for the Participant

Butte has some 30 parks ranging from mini parks on lots to major parks such as Stodden and the recently built Copper Mountain Sports and Recreation Complex north of Timber Butte. Municipal parks located in Butte provide such facilities as a swimming pool, basketball courts, baseball and football fields, 24 public and private tennis courts, golf courses, an Olympic-sized skating rink, and running/walking tracks.

The United States High Altitude Sports Center, an outdoor Olympic-sized speed skating oval, is open to the public when not in use by the U.S. National Speed Skating Team.

Recreational areas outside the city include the Blacktail Creek and Alice Pit Walking Trails, the Red Mountain Highlands (a 10,000 foot peak), Humburg Spires rock climbing site, kayaking on Big Hole and Madison rivers, and downhill skiing at Maverick Mountain and Discovery Basin.

Butte–Silver Bow has four golf courses: one private 18-hole course, one public 18 hole course, one municipal 9-hole course, and one municipal par 3, 9-hole course. Several have layouts that offer spectacular scenery in the Butte foothills. There is also a Jack Nicklaus Signature golf course, Old Works, in Anaconda, located 12 miles from Butte. The course is built atop the ruins of a smelting plant.

Lakes, streams, and reservoirs surround Butte where trout fishing, boating, and waterskiing are popular pastimes. The nearest public access river is 25 miles away with swimming and fishing allowed.

Shopping and Dining

Historic Uptown has several unique stores that deal in antiques, toys, and tools, and art galleries that specialize in Western art. In addition to the Butte Plaza Mall, Butte's only enclosed shopping center, Butte's Harrison Avenue has small shops and stores with specialties ranging from locally made crafts and gifts to sporting equipment.

More than 80 restaurants in Butte provide a variety of choices that include fast food and family dining, as well as the more formal atmosphere of supper clubs. Many of these foods are influenced by Butte's historic past and diverse cultures. Among the cuisines offered are Chinese, Greek, Italian, and traditional American. Local favorites include The Acoma on Broadway, Gamer's Café on Park, the Gold Rush Casino and Restaurant on Galena, and Pork Chop John's (three locations). A local specialty is pasties, which are meat pies that were originally brought to Butte by Cornish miners in the 1870s.

Visitor Information: Butte Convention and Visitors Bureau, 1000 George St., Butte, MT 59701; telephone (406) 723-3177; toll-free (800) 735-6814; email chamber@buttecvb.com.

■ Convention Facilities

The Butte Civic Center, accessible to about 1,300 hotel and motel rooms and bed and breakfast inns in the metropolitan area, is a prime meeting facility both in the city and in the Northwest. Located in close proximity to major population centers, the complex offers a range of facilities for large and small group functions and sporting and recreational events. Total seating capacity in the civic center's arena is approximately 7,500 people, with parking for up to 1,500 vehicles on site. The theater seats up to another 5,000 visitors. Total exhibit space is 26,923 square feet.

Meeting and convention accommodations are also available at the city's two major hotels. The Copper King Park Hotel features ten multipurpose meeting rooms, including a recreation area with approximately 8,000 square feet of space; a convention center providing more than 5,000 square feet; smaller rooms with seating for small groups; and a ballroom accommodating up to 1,200 participants. The Best Western features large and small meeting rooms with a capacity of 80, indoor pool, spa, and fitness center, and the Hops Bar and Casino. The Fairmont Chalets and Fairmont Hot Springs Resort offer a more relaxed, country setting outside of Butte.

Convention Information: Butte Convention and Visitors Bureau, 1000 George St., Butte, MT 59701; telephone (406) 723-3177; toll-free (800) 735-6814; email chamber@buttecvb.com.

■ Transportation

Approaching the City

The Bert Mooney Airport is served by Alaska Airlines, Horizon Air, Sky West, and Delta Airlines. Most flights connect in Salt Lake City or through Bozeman/Seattle. Greyhound and Intermountain lines provide bus transportation.

The principal highways into Butte are Interstate-15, running north and south, and Interstate-90, approaching from the northwest, which intersect in the city. Two state highways also serve Butte.

Traveling in the City

Butte is laid out on a grid pattern, although some streets run diagonally to follow railroad or freeway routes. Harrison Avenue is the main north-south thoroughfare. Butte Transit System provides bus service.

■ Communications

Newspapers and Magazines

Butte's daily morning newspaper is *The Montana Standard*. Students at Montana Tech publish the *Technocrat. Butte Weekly* is a free weekly paper.

Television and Radio

In 2003, Bresnan Communications bought the rights to Butte cable television and invested several million dollars to upgrade the number of channels available and to bring high-speed Internet to Butte citizens. Viewers have access to ABC, CBS, and NBC television broadcasts. 91.3 FM is the city's Public Radio outlet. Seven other AM and FM radio stations originate their signals from Butte. A number of other radio stations can be picked up from neighboring communities.

Media Information: *The Montana Standard*, 25 W. Granite St., Butte, MT 59701; telephone (406) 496-5500; toll-free (800) 877-1074.

Butte Online

Butte Local Development Corporation. Available www.buttemontana.org

Butte Public School District #1. Available www.butte.k12.mt.us

Butte–Silver Bow Chamber of Commerce. Available www.buttechamber.org/

Butte–Silver Bow Local Government. Available www.co.silverbow.mt.us

The Montana Standard. Available www.mtstandard.com

Only in Butte. History stories about Butte's past. Available www.butteamerica.com/hist.

BIBLIOGRAPHY

Egan, Timothy, *The Big Burn: Teddy Roosevelt and the Fire that Saved America* (Boston: Mariner Books, 2010)

Hammett, Dashiell, *Red Harvest* (South Yarmouth, MA: J. Curley, 1983)

McGlashan, Zena Beth, *Buried in Butte* (Butte, MT: Wordz & Ink Publishing, 2010)

Morris, Patrick F., *Anaconda Montana: Copper Smelting Boomtown on the Western Frontier* (Bethesda, MD: Swann Pub., 1997)

Helena

■ The City in Brief

Founded: 1864 (chartered, 1881)

Head Official: Mayor James E. Smith (since November 2001; current term expires 2017)

City Population
1990: 24,699
2000: 25,780
2010: 28,190
2012 estimate: 28,722
Percent change, 2000–2010: 9.3%

Micropolitan Area Statistical Population
2000: 65,765
2010: 74,801
2012 estimate: 77,952
Percent change, 2000–2010: 13.7%
U.S. rank in 2010: 470th

Area: 14 square miles

Elevation: 4,090 feet above sea level

Average Annual Temperatures: January, 20.2° F; July, 67.8° F; annual average, 44.0° F

Average Annual Precipitation: 11.32 inches of rain; 46.9 inches of snow

Major Economic Sectors: government, services, finance

Unemployment Rate: 3.5% (2012)

Per Capita Income: $28,989

2012 FBI Crime Index Property: 1,015

Major Colleges and Universities: Carroll College

Daily Newspaper: *Helena Independent Record*

■ Introduction

Helena, known as the "City of Gold," lies at the heart of the Rocky Mountains in a fertile region with rolling hills. It was founded by four gold-seekers who decided to take one "last chance" at striking it rich. The miners found their gold and the name "Last Chance" became the name of the main street. The street's crooked path follows the gold-bearing creek (now underground), where other miners staked their claim and built their cabins. Today, this sophisticated and beautiful Victorian city is both the capital of Montana and the county seat for Lewis and Clark County. Helena is surrounded by pristine forests, alive with history and culture. On the outskirts of the city lies the giant Helena National Forest, this provides spectacular scenery and many opportunities for outdoor activities. Once a mining boomtown, Helena is now a major social and governmental center of the American west, offering amenities not usually found in a city of its size. It has also developed a reputation for its art scene in recent years, having been declared one of the 100 best small art towns in the United States.

■ Geography and Climate

Helena is located in west-central Montana in the foothills of the Big Belt Mountains on the eastern slope of the Continental Divide, 48 miles north-northeast of Butte, Montana. Helena is located midway between Glacier and Yellowstone national parks and fertile valleys lie to the north and east. The Missouri River flows northward nearly 10 miles east of the city.

Helena has a modified continental climate with warm, dry summers and moderately cold winters. Mountains located to the north and east of the city sometimes deflect shallow masses of arctic air to the east, but at times cold air can be trapped in the valley for days. During the coldest period, from November through February, temperatures sometimes drop to 0° F or below.

The Montana State Capitol building in Helena. *Alan Scheer/Shutterstock.com*

Summer temperatures are usually under 90° F and the mountains account for marked changes in temperature from day to night. April through July is the rainy season, while late summer, fall, and winter are quite dry.

Area: 14 square miles

Elevation: 4,090 feet above sea level

Average Temperatures: January, 20.2° F; July, 67.8° F; annual average, 44.0° F

Average Annual Precipitation: 11.32 inches of rain; 46.9 inches of snow

■ History

Land of the Prickly Pear

Archaeological evidence shows that Native Americans inhabited the valley in which greater Helena is situated more than 12,000 years ago. Although never serving as the permanent home of any particular tribe, the valley was a crossover area for Salish, Crow, Bannock, and Blackfeet tribal members.

In 1805, members of the Lewis and Clark expedition were the first white men to visit the valley. While investigating the area on foot, William Clark stepped on and had to remove 17 cactus spines from his feet. This caused him to name the nearby creek and valley Prickly Pear. In the early nineteenth century, trappers came to the area, later to be pushed aside by groups of white settlers.

In 1862, a group of immigrants in a wagon train decided to build houses for the winter in Prickly Pear Valley, but this settlement proved temporary. In 1864, four ex-Confederate soldiers from Georgia discovered placer gold in Last Chance Gulch, the heart of Helena's present-day downtown. The gold strike attracted hundreds of miners eager to find riches. Over the next 20 years, 3.5 billion dollars worth of gold was discovered in the gulch. By 1888, Helena was home to more millionaires per capita than anywhere else in the world.

Early settlers considered naming their new boomtown "Pumpkinville" or "Squashtown," but instead settled on the suggestion of John Somerville, who named the place after his hometown of Helena in Minnesota. The inhabitants chose to pronounce it HELL-uh-nuh, with the accent on the first syllable. Its original residents were mainly of English, Scottish, Irish, and German descent.

Becomes Territorial, Then State Capital

By 1870, Helena, with a population of 3,106 people, had become the most important town in the Montana

Territory. Other nearby settlements turned into ghost towns after gold supplies were exhausted. However, Helena's geographical location helped it become a business hub for other mining communities, such as Marysville to the west and Rimini to the southwest. It became a vital bank, trade and farming town.

In the late 1870s, the discovery of rich silver and lead deposits in nearby Wickes, Corbin, and Elkhorn further stimulated development in the area and helped Helena grow and prosper. The fact that Helena was on an important stagecoach route also spurred its growth as a hub city.

In 1875, Helena was made the capital of the Montana Territory. When Montana became a state in 1889, citizens disputed whether the capital should be Helena or Anaconda, another popular mining town. Copper rivals Marcus Daly, who supported Anaconda, and William A. Clark, who supported Helena, spent more than $3 million as each fought to have his city chosen for the honor. Helena finally won the vote in 1894. The city soon saw a tremendous amount of new construction. In time, Helena became the center of Montana political, social, and economic life. Between 1880 and 1890, the population grew from 3,624 to 13,834 people.

City Experiences Booms and Busts

By the late 1880s, wealthy Helena citizens had erected pretentious mansions and constructed a streetcar to transport them to the outskirts of town where they lived. They also drove about town, first in coaches driven by top-hatted drivers, and later in electric cars that stalled on the hills. Their Italianate, Romanesque, baroque, and Gothic-style houses featured cupolas, turrets, and hand-carved trim. A small army of maids and butlers served the inhabitants of the mansions.

The good times for many of the city's more than 13,000 residents continued until 1893, when the price of silver fell and many of the nouveau riche moved away. The spacious mansions were then taken over by members of the middle class who sometimes had problems paying to heat them. Many of the Mansion District homes can still be viewed today.

Like other Montana towns, Helena experienced boom-or-bust cycles. Prosperity returned once again between 1900 and 1910 when gold mining activity geared up at nearby Marysville and with the construction of the Canyon Ferry, Hauser, and Holter dams on the Missouri River, which employed a number of Helena residents. Then came a slump that lasted until the war years of 1914-1918, when once again the mines worked to meet the demand for metals during World War I. But another slump followed.

Helena in the Twentieth Century and Beyond

In the first part of the twentieth century, Helena's population showed modest growth, rising from 12,515 people in 1910 to 15,056 by 1940. This growth occurred despite several major fires and a 1935 earthquake that caused four deaths and $4 million in damages. Shocks of lesser intensity occurred in 1936 and 1937 but did no further harm.

During the mid-1930s, at the time of the Great Depression, the federal government employed hundreds of Helena citizens to repair the State Capitol and the county courthouse and to landscape a city park. New federal monetary policies increased the price of gold and silver and stimulated mining, which once again regained its importance in the life of the city.

The city's population stood at 17,581 people in 1950. During the 1960s, urban renewal changed the face of downtown Helena, and a pedestrian mall was built to attract tourists. Preservation fervor and urban renewal programs in the 1970s resulted in further downtown development. In recent decades, Montana residents have begun to truly appreciate and make efforts to preserve the beautiful terrain of their state. In 1992, the Montana House of Representatives voted to protect 1.5 million acres of Montana from development, including some local Helena area sites. In 2005, the National Trust for Historic Preservation named Helena one of America's Dozen Distinctive Destinations, recognizing the city as "unique and lovingly preserved."

Today, Helena is an attractive place that retains vintage residential and commercial structures while providing modern shops, distinctive restaurants, and entertainment centers for residents and visitors alike.

Historical Information: Montana Historical Society, PO Box 201201, 225 N. Roberts, Helena, MT, 59620-1201; telephone (406) 444-2694; email mhslibrary@mt.gov.

■ Population Profile

Micropolitan Area Statistical Population

2000: 65,765
2010: 74,801
2012 estimate: 77,952
Percent change, 2000–2010: 13.7%
U.S. rank in 2010: 470th

City Residents

1990: 24,699
2000: 25,780
2010: 28,190
2012 estimate: 28,722
Percent change, 2000–2010: 9.3%

Density: 1,724.3 people per square mile

Racial and ethnic characteristics

White: 27,042
Black or African American: 165

American Indian and Alaskan Native: 710
Asian: 96
Native Hawaiian and Other Pacific Islander: 0
Hispanic or Latino (may be of any race): 826
Other: 709

Percent of residents born in state: 57.4%

Age characteristics

Population under 5 years old: 2,048
Population 5 to 9 years old: 1,670
Population 10 to 14 years old: 944
Population 15 to 19 years old: 1,770
Population 20 to 24 years old: 2,346
Population 25 to 34 years old: 3,503
Population 35 to 44 years old: 3,309
Population 45 to 54 years old: 4,140
Population 55 to 59 years old: 2,312
Population 60 to 64 years old: 2,156
Population 65 to 74 years old: 2,217
Population 75 to 84 years old: 1,623
Population 85 years and over: 684
Median age: 40.4

Births (2010–11 Micropolitan Area)

Total number: 881

Deaths (2010–11 Micropolitan Area)

Total number: 665

Money income (2012)

Per capita income: $28,989
Median household income: $49,635
Total households: 12,799

Number of households with income of …

less than $10,000: 862
$10,000 to $14,999: 916
$15,000 to $24,999: 1,270
$25,000 to $34,999: 1,406
$35,000 to $49,999: 1,995
$50,000 to $74,999: 2,354
$75,000 to $99,999: 1,764
$100,000 to $149,999: 1,685
$150,000 to $199,999: 218
$200,000 or more: 329

Percent of families below poverty level: 12.7%

FBI Crime Index Property: 1,015

FBI Crime Index Violent: 127

■ Municipal Government

Helena, the capital of Montana and the seat of Lewis and Clark County, has a city charter form of government. The mayor and four commissioners are elected to the city commission, each serving four-year terms with two positions filled at each general election. A city manager, who is appointed by the commission, administers the daily affairs of the city.

Head Official: Mayor James E. Smith (since November 2001; current term expires 2017)

Total Number of City Employees: 304 (2014)

City Information: Mayor's Office, City of Helena, 316 N. Park Avenue, Helena, MT 59623; telephone (406) 447-8410.

■ Economy

Major Industries and Commercial Activity

For many years, Helena has enjoyed a record of economic stability. The city's largest employers are government-related, making the city a major governmental hub for the county, state, and federal government. Government positions account for 31 percent of Helena's workforce, while private sector jobs comprise 62 percent. However, reliance on a shrinking public sector is projected to lead to slower economic growth when compared with the rest of the state. The University of Montana's Bureau of Business and Economic Research projected nonfarm jobs earnings to grow by 1.7 percent in 2014, and by 2 percent in 2015 and 2016. Only moderate growth in residential and commercial construction was projected for Lewis and Clark County. Many of the private businesses rely on the government and its employees as their customers.

Helena is also a trading and transportation center for nearby livestock, mining, and farming enterprises. In an area rich in silver and lead deposits, Helena maintains an interest in mineral production and processing, and the nearby city of East Helena is the site of smelters, quartz crushers, and zinc reduction works. The Helena area is also a telephone communications center, and industries such as sand, gravel, and ranching remain important. Statewide, Montana's fastest-growing industries include education and instruction, waste management, and construction. Specific occupations showing significant growth include textile machinery operation, septic and sewer maintenance, and computer software engineering. Small businesses also provide a generous push to the local economy. The Helena Valley is home to over 3,700 businesses, and 78 percent of all the businesses in Helena have 10 or less employees.

Items and goods produced: refined and smelted metals, paints, ceramics, concrete, machine parts, baking products, sheet metal, prefabricated houses, bottled beverages

Incentive Programs—New and Existing Companies

Local programs: The Montana Business Information Center (BIC) in Helena is a one-stop center that provides a multitude of planning tools as well as free onsite counseling provided by the Service Corps of Retired Executives (SCORE), Small Business Development Center (SBDC), and other Small Business Administration resources.

The Montana BIC's resources include a reference library, a video center, and a computer lab designed specifically for small business research. The Small Business Administration offers a variety of financing options for small businesses, including long-term loans for machinery and equipment, general working capital loans, revolving lines of credit, and microloans. Similarly, the Montana Business Assistance Connection (MBAC), formerly known as the Gateway Economic Development Corporation, offers loans and tax rebates to new or expanding businesses in Lewis and Clark County and the surrounding area.

The Downtown Helena Business Improvement District offers grants up to $2,000 for retailers opening or expanding in the downtown area. The BID strives to build a stronger and more efficient collaboration among the existing property and business owners through multimedia and electronic-based communication and coordination; clean and safe projects; landscaping improvements; and stronger promotions.

State programs: The Montana Business Assistance Connection (MBAC) encourages and supports the creation of new jobs and relocation of existing jobs to various counties in Montana by helping with public and private revolving loan funds and providing training and access to capital for qualified start-up businesses or expanding businesses.

The Montana Community Development Corporation (MCDC) provides support to businesses through business loans, trainings and one-on-one business consulting. In 2010, the MCDC was the recipient of a $750,000 grant from the U.S. Treasury Department to be used for businesses loans, and in 2009, MCDC was awarded $40 million dollars in federal New Markets Tax Credits to be used in eligible areas and projects. The New Markets Tax Credits Program provides a 39 percent federal income tax credit to businesses that choose to invest capital into qualified projects in eligible low-income areas. Loans provided by MCDC range from $1,000 to $1,000,000 to qualified businesses and projects.

Other State of Montana tax incentives include property tax reduction; no inventory, use, or sales tax; new industry income tax credits; small business investment tax credits; and tax reduction on pollution control equipment. The Big Sky Development Trust Fund can provide up to $5,000 in grant funding for each new eligible job created. The Primary Sector Workforce Training Grant offers direct reimbursement to eligible businesses for training costs up to $5,000 per eligible newly created job.

In 2003 the Montana legislature created the Certified Regional Development Corporations (CRDC) program in the Montana Department of Commerce. The CRDC program is designed to encourage a regional approach to economic development. State law also provides for the creation of a tax increment financing (TIF) industrial district for industrial development projects. A local government can issue bonds for a wide variety of development purposes, such as financing land acquisition, industrial infrastructure, rail spurs, buildings, and personal property related to the public improvements.

Job training programs: The Small Business Development Center provides training, counseling, research, and other specialized assistance through its Helena office. NxLevel Entrepreneurial Training Programs, available through the Montana Department of Commerce, are in-depth training courses for entrepreneurs and business owners. NxLevel for Entrepreneurs is a 12-session course designed to help existing business owners improve growth and profits. NxLevel for Agricultural Entrepreneurs and NxLevel for Microentrepreneurs are similar programs aimed at new ventures and the self-employed.

Development Projects

Projects currently planned for Helena focus on business development, transportation, and branding. An ongoing downtown revitalization planning process has resulted in suggestions for an outdoor market, building restoration, and increased residential space. The City Commission voted to construct a new traffic lane on the Downtown Walking Mall, and to rename the road leading from the I-90 to downtown Last Chance Gulch (currently the name of the main downtown street only) to improve accessibility for tourists. Other plans call for new or upgraded freeway interchanges and improvements in water quality and availability.

Recently completed projects include the full restoration of the State Capitol building and construction of the Great Northern Town Center, a main street business and shopping district. During a five-year project, the Capitol building was restored to its original conditions from 1902. Not even the smallest detail was overlooked in the restoration; from doorknobs to the restroom flooring, everything is historically accurate to the original 1902 design. The two most awe-inspiring restorations include the original chandelier from the Senate chamber and the barrel vault ceiling made of 90 stained glass windows.

In 2013 Shodair Children's Hospital broke ground on a new $1.2 million Family House. The Family House provides room for families to stay near their children so the whole family can be part of the therapeutic process. The Crow Agency-Apsaalooke Nation announced financing for the construction of a 15-unit apartment complex that will serve homeless veterans of the Apsaalooke Nation. Construction was also completed on the new Intermountain Community Services Center. Services in the new 22,000-square-foot facility include children's psychological assessment and outpatient therapy, psychiatric clinic, in-home support for birth/kinship, adoptive and foster families, and school-based counseling and therapy.

Also in 2013, Boeing announced a $35 million expansion of its Helena manufacturing site and the hiring of 20 to 25 more employees there. The expansion adds 55,000 square feet of manufacturing space, increasing the size of the Boeing Helena facility near the Helena Regional Airport by about one-third, to 167,099 square feet. Construction was expected to be completed by the fourth quarter of 2014.

In January 2014, the Lewis & Clark County Cooperative Health Center broke ground on a new $5 million addition and renovation. Grant money came from the Affordable Care Act, funding a complete remodeling of the clinic and almost doubling its capacity to see patients. The entire project, which includes renovation of the dental clinic, will be completed by March 2015.

Three new bank and credit union offices opened in 2013. First Interstate Bank's $9 million branch; Helena Community Credit Union's $2 million branch; and Stockman Bank's new office.

Economic Development Information: Small Business Administration-Montana District Office, 10 West 15th Street, Suite 1100, Helena, Montana, 59626; telephone (406) 441-1081; fax (406) 441-1090. Montana Finance Information Center, 301 S. Park, Helena, MT 59601; telephone (406) 841-2732; fax (406) 841-2731. Downtown Helena, Inc., 225 Cruse Ave., Suite B, Helena, MT 59601; telephone (406) 447-1535. Montana Department of Commerce, 301 S Park Ave, Helena, MT 59601; telephone (406) 841-2700; fax (406) 841-2701.

Commercial Shipping

FedEx, Airborne Express, and UPS provide airfreight service. Freight service is also provided by Montana Rail Link, which provides national coverage in connection with Burlington Northern & Santa Fe Railway.

Labor Force and Employment Outlook

The Helena area labor force includes a high percentage of young, educated workers. The percentage of adults in the community who have received high school and college diplomas is considerably higher than state and national averages; 31 percent of the regional workforce has either a bachelor's degree or some other form of higher educational achievement. Helena's workforce is composed primarily of white-collar workers, professionals, and employees of small businesses. Helena's stable economy is based primarily on a range of government agencies and small businesses.

The city's unemployment rate is traditionally lower than Montana's due to the high number of jobs in the government sector. Government employment peaked in 2010 with the help of federal stimulus funds. Since then, however, government jobs have been on the decline. From the second quarter of 2011 to second quarter 2012, Lewis and Clark County lost about 1.6 percent of the state government workforce. As government employment decreased, jobs in the construction sector have shown strength. In 2013 Helena saw at least $27 million in commercial developments, according to the chamber of commerce. Despite this surge of activity, the housing industry in Helena is still struggling. It remains well below pre-recession levels and is not expected to recover fully until 2021.

Growth in the health-care industry has led to demand for a wide range of medical personnel. That trend is expected to continue for the foreseeable future. Demand for financial professionals, information technology specialists, and for persons with specific trade skills like electricians, plumbers, mechanics and carpenters, is also expected to remain strong. Economic analysts predict that because local applicants cannot fill many of those jobs, Helena will likely see steady population growth as people from around the country move to the area to fill those positions.

The following is a summary of data regarding the 2012 Helena labor force:

Size of civilian labor force: 15,866

Number of workers employed in . . .

  agriculture and mining: 220
  construction: 611
  manufacturing: 248
  wholesale trade: 170
  retail trade: 1,438
  transportation: 322
  information systems: 298
  finance: 814
  professional administration: 1,497
  education and social services: 3,874
  arts and leisure: 1,490
  other: 638
  public administration: 3,409

Average hourly earnings of production workers: $16.10

Unemployment rate: 3.5% (2012)

Employers

Largest employers (2012)	*Number of employees*
State of Montana	7,000
St. Peter's Hospital	1,175
Montana Rail Link Inc.	800
Blue Cross and Blue Shield Of MT	500
Wal-Mart Stores Inc.	400
Carroll College	250
Shodair Children's Hospital	220

Cost of Living

The following is a summary of data regarding several key cost of living factors in the area.

State income tax rate: 1.0% to 6.9%

State sales tax rate: None

Local income tax rate: None

Local sales tax rate: None

Property tax rate: $1,296 (statewide per capita average, 2010)

Economic Information: Montana Department of Commerce, Census and Economic Information Center, 301 S. Park Ave., PO Box 200505, Helena, MT 59620-0505; telephone (406) 841-2740; fax (406) 841-2731.

■ Education and Research

Elementary and Secondary Schools

Helena Public Schools states that its mission is to challenge and empower each student to become a competent, productive, responsible, caring citizen. Some 45 percent of the district's teachers have anywhere from one to three years of education beyond a bachelor's degree. Students consistently score above average in national standardized testing in all academic areas.

The Helena school district is composed of one special education preschool, 11 elementary schools, two middle schools, and three high schools (which include traditional and nontraditional high schools). The district also maintains one transitional school (NET), one Adult Learning Center, and one Community Education Program. The Helena school district enjoys one of the lowest teacher-to-pupil ratios in the state, with 15 students to each certified staff member. The curriculum includes many accelerated and advanced placement courses. In 2013 Capital High School had the highest graduation rate of all AA schools across the state at 93.5 percent. Nearly 57 percent of the district's graduating seniors attend four-year colleges or universities, earning over

$3 million annually in scholarships. Another 22 percent of high school graduates move on to trade school, two-year colleges or the military. Helena's public schools also receive a huge outpouring of support from the local community. In recent years, two mill levies were passed in support of operational expenses for the school district. Annually some 40,000 hours of volunteer time are donated to the school system as well.

There are also a number of private schools serving Helena's population. The Diocese of Helena maintains four elementary schools and two high schools. Enrollment in the elementary schools ranges from 72 students (grades 4–8) at De La Salle Blackfeet School to 264 (K–8) at Butte Central Elementary/Junior High School. Butte Central High School (9–12) has 131 students and Loyola Sacred Heart High School 172.

The following is a summary of data regarding the Helena School District.

Total enrollment: 5,107

Number of facilities
total: 19
elementary schools: 12
junior high schools: 2
high schools: 3
other: 2

Student/teacher ratio: 16.93:1

Teacher salaries
average (statewide): $47,132

Funding per pupil: $9,722

Public Schools Information: Helena Public Schools, 55 South Rodney, Helena, MT 59601; telephone (406) 324-2000; fax (406) 324-2022

Colleges and Universities

Helena's Carroll College, established in 1909, is a Catholic liberal arts college with an enrollment of about 1,500. Students enjoy small classes and easy access to faculty members, and half of the students go on to graduate school. *US News & World Report* placed Carroll first in their 2013 ranking of the best regional colleges in the West, and third in their best value rankings. Carroll College offers Bachelor of Arts degrees in about 40 different academic majors, as well as eight pre-professional programs and a variety of research and internship opportunities in the capital city.

Helena College of Technology is a two-year college that is part of the University of Montana. The school's full-time enrollment is at nearly one thousand students, and nearly 400 students receive technical education in accounting, computer science, aviation, construction, nursing, machine tooling, and other fields. The college also offers associate of science and arts degrees in general studies. Montana University also provides graduate programs and continuing education classes in Helena.

Libraries and Research Centers

The Lewis & Clark County Library's main facility is in downtown Helena and the system has three branches in nearby towns. The library contains 115,000 items, including books, periodicals, vertical files, and audio-visual tapes. Built in 1976, the library serves 50,000 patrons annually.

The Research Center of the Montana Historical Society, also in Helena, contains more than 40,000 books and pamphlets relating to Montana, 2,000 bound volumes of Montana newspapers, and more than 8,000 maps, as well as initial township plots, topographical maps, music scores, and other items. Its special collections focus on the Lewis & Clark expedition, fur trading, and General Custer and the Battle of the Little Big Horn. It also has an extensive photograph collection featuring approximately 400,000 images.

The Montana State Library is the primary facility for state government as well as for the blind, physically handicapped, and learning disabled. Its focus is on Montana's natural resources. Every Montanan is entitled to borrow from the State Library, although local libraries often borrow titles on behalf of their patrons.

Other local libraries include the college libraries of Carroll College and the Helena College of Technology, and those of St. Peter's Community and Shodair hospitals, the Montana state legislature, the Montana Department of Commerce, the Montana Natural Heritage Program, the Montana Department of Special Resources, the State Law Library, and the U.S. Geological Survey Water Resources Division Library.

Research institutions include the Montana Science Institute, which explores natural history and ecology of the Missouri River and conservation of native species, and the Nature Conservancy-Montana Chapter, which identifies rare plants and animals and works to protect rare species.

Public Library Information: Lewis & Clark County Library, 120 S. Last Chance Gulch, Helena, MT 59601; telephone (406) 447-1690; fax (406) 447-1687.

■ Health Care

Helena citizens have the service of two local hospitals, St. Peter's Community Hospital and Shodair Children's Hospital.

St. Peter's Community Hospital, a sole provider, non-profit, 123-bed facility, offers comprehensive inpatient, outpatient, and home-care service. St. Peter's employs approximately 1,180 staff members, including a medical staff of 110 physicians representing approximately 30 different specialties. The facility, founded in

1883, provides obstetrics, surgery, emergency care, a cancer treatment center, and a full range of diagnostic services. The hospital provides services to some 80,000 residents from Lewis and Clark and surrounding counties each year.

Shodair Children's Hospital began as a home for orphaned and abandoned children in 1896. It became the first facility in the state to treat children with polio, the first facility with a department of medical genetics, and the first with a chemical dependency unit dedicated to adolescents. Today, Shodair provides inpatient and outpatient psychiatric services, and treatment of genetic disorders. It is the only hospital in the state that offers both residential and acute treatment in one convenient location.

Located just outside Helena is Fort Harrison Veterans Hospital.

Health Care Information:

St. Peter's Community Hospital, 2475 Broadway, Helena, MT 59601; telephone (406) 442-2480. Shodair Hospital, 2755 Colonial Drive, PO Box 5539, Helena, MT 59604; telephone (406) 444-7500; toll-free (800) 447-6614.

■ Recreation

Sightseeing

The focal point of sightseeing in Helena is the 17-block Historic Downtown District. This part of town offers a mix of retail stores, galleries, lodging, restaurants, historic buildings, and entertainment centers. The imposing State Capitol Building is constructed of Montana granite and boasts a classic dome made of radiant copper. Courtesy of recent renovations, it has been restored to its original state back in 1902, down to even its historically accurate doorknobs. It now serves as the symbol of Montana. The interior is decorated with murals by artists E. S. Paxon, Charles M. Russell, and others. Russell depicts the meeting of Lewis and Clark with a group of Native Americans in a large mural.

Tours are offered of several impressive local structures. The original governor's mansion, which was built in 1888 in the Queen Anne style, contains furnishings popular during the early twentieth century. Helena Civic Center, built in 1921, is a Moorish-style edifice with a 175-foot minaret, an onion dome, and intricate exterior brickwork. Just outside Helena to the north is another impressive facility, Fort Harrison, which was once an army garrison and is now a veterans' hospital.

The Montana Historical Society Museum features the C.M. Russell painting collections, as well as temporary exhibits of western art. The Montana Homeland Exhibit portrays Montana history throughout the eras.

The imposing St. Helena Cathedral, with its white marble altar, stained-glass windows, and 230-foot spires, is modeled after famous churches in Austria and

Germany. Gold nuggets, gold wire, gold coins, and gold dust are on display at the Gold collection at downtown's Norwest Bank and the Federal Reserve Bank on Neill Avenue. The Guardian of the Gulch is a landmark fire tower built in 1876 and one of just five similar towers remaining in the United States.

Dotting the hillsides on Helena's west side are dozens of stately private homes, built by rich merchants and miners a century ago. The Last Chance Tour Train provides hour-long tours of the city. A guided Missouri riverboat tour follows the path taken by Lewis and Clark nearly two centuries ago. Northeast of Helena, Canyon Ferry Dam offers information and interactive displays of the region's wildlife as well as the Lewis and Clark expedition.

Arts and Culture

In 2008, Helena was ranked one of the 100 best small art towns in the U.S. The city is home to the Helena Institute, a unique non-profit that offers hands-on learning opportunities in art, science, history, and outdoor recreation. The institute's 2010 season featured 30 workshops in August and September, covering subjects such as the art of ceramics, fly-fishing, or ghostly history, to name just a few. Another major cultural facility in Helena is the Myrna Loy Center, named after the beloved Montana-born actress. It is housed in the city's 1880s-era former jailhouse and features performing arts activities, literary events, films, and art shows. The Carroll College Theatre presents live performances throughout the year. The Toadstone Theatre Company offers professional and community children's theater and Grandstreet Theatre offers live performances of Broadway shows using community-based volunteers. The Montana Shakespeare Company presents Shakespeare's classics in Performance Park Square, an outdoor venue.

Helena's Holter Museum of Art, which recently expanded its exhibit space, displays various works of art from historical to contemporary times. It also offers workshops, readings, and discussions and serves 30,000 visitors and 7,500 students annually. The Archie Bray Foundation for Ceramic Arts, which offers beautiful display pieces for sale, has attained a national reputation for training potters. The Ghost Art Gallery in Helena's old mining district features architecture and themes from nearby ghost towns, as well as western and wildlife art by fine local artists.

Music lovers attend performances of the Helena Symphony; in addition to a regular season of performances by its own chorale of 150 members, it offers community concerts. Four-part harmony is the focus of the Sweet Adelines Performing Chorus.

Festivals and Holidays

Downtown Helena is the site of many special events, including festivals, street dances, theater productions, sled dog races, car rallies, art exhibits, and street fairs. The annual Western Rendezvous of Art takes place in August, featuring art shows, seminars, an auction and a fixed price sale, and a gala awards banquet. Music fills the air in September during the Last Chance Bluegrass Festival, while October is enlivened by Bullfest and Oktoberfest celebrations. November brings the Bald Eagle Migration and Downtown Helena Fall Art Walk, while December hails the holidays with the Festival of Trees and Winter Fair.

The excitement of the Race to the Sky Sled Dog Race warms hearts in February, and children of all ages enjoy April's Railroad Fair and Kite Festival. The Governor's Cup Marathon and the Sleeping Giant Swing 'n Jazz Jubilee draw crowds in June, while July brings the excitement of the Last Chance Stampede & Rodeo and the Mt. Helena Music Festival.

Sports for the Spectator

Helena is the home of the Helena Brewers minor league baseball team of the Pioneer League; the Helena Bighorns hockey club, which plays NAHL hockey at the Helena Ice Arena; the Carroll College Fighting Saints; and high school teams that compete in tennis, baseball, football, soccer, hockey, golf, rugby, and basketball.

Sports for the Participant

Within easy access to Helena residents and visitors are millions of acres of public lands, top rated fisheries, and many lakes, rivers, and reservoirs that are used for boating, sailing, wind surfing, and other water sports. Also available are hunting, backpacking, biking, skiing, and snowmobiling. There are more than 25 area parks. Mount Helena City Park and Helena National Forest each have miles of hiking and biking trails. Mount Helena's City Park has various trails, many of which overlook gorgeous scenery, strewn across its 630 acres. Many of them climb to as high as 1,000 feet above downtown. The Helena National Forest also houses 10 campgrounds on its 976,000 acres. The local recreation department offers facilities for running, racquetball, weight training, and horseback riding. Centennial Water-slide Park is a family-focused indoor facility with slides and swimming pools. Helena Skate Park offers ledges, quarter pipes, and banks with free access for skateboarders and in-line skaters. There are two public golf courses and one private golf course, numerous tennis courts, and several health clubs. Hikers on the Blackfoot Meadows or the Continental Divide trails may spot such wildlife as elk, moose, mountain goats, bighorn sheep, black bears, otters, beavers, and mink. A few miles from the city, the Bob Marshall Wilderness Complex offers over 1,800 miles of hiking trails that take adventurous hikers as far as Glacier National Park.

Shopping and Dining

On the north side of town resides the Great Northern Town Center that offers tasteful shopping, a state of the art cinema center, and a carousel and ice cream shop for the downtown area. Helena's largest shopping center is Capital Hill Mall, which is located near the Capital complex and contains 40 specialty shops and two major department stores. What was once the Last Chance Gulch mine is now Helena's main street and a pedestrian mall. Downtown Helena is dotted with specialty shops and galleries, especially throughout the Walking Mall and Reeders' Alley, a complex of red brick buildings from the 1870s that once served as miners' shanties. Principal shopping centers include Northgate Plaza and Lundy Center. Discount shopping can be found at WalMart, Shopko, Target, Big-K and Gibson's.

For a small city, Helena has a varied selection of ethnic dining spots that feature Mexican, Thai, Chinese, Mediterranean, French, German, Italian, and classic American cuisines. Beer lovers can sample local micro brews from the Sleeping Giant Brewery, Kessler Brewery, or Blackfoot River Brewing Company.

Visitor Information: Helena Convention & Visitor Bureau, 225 Cruse Ave., Helena, MT 59601; telephone (406) 447-1530 or (800) 743-5362; fax (406) 447-1532.

■ Convention Facilities

Most conferences in Helena are held at one of three facilities. The Best Western Helena Great Northern Hotel offers sleeping accommodations in 101 rooms, and its 8,000 square feet of meeting and banquet space can hold groups of up to 500 people. Nestled amidst Last Chance Gulch, Helena's famous walking mall, the Holiday Inn Conference Center Downtown has 71 sleeping rooms and offers more than 6,000 square feet in its newly remodeled meeting and banquet facilities. Jorgenson's Inn and Suites has 116 sleeping rooms and can accommodate up to 250 people for banquets or conventions.

Convention Information: Helena Convention & Visitors Bureau, 225 Cruse Ave., Suite A, Helena, MT 59601; telephone (406) 447-1530 or (800) 743-5362; fax (406) 447-1532.

■ Transportation

Approaching the City

Interstate 15 runs along the east side of Helena, northward toward Great Falls and southward toward Butte. It intersects with U.S. Highways 12/287 that run east and west and extend toward East Helena. Helena Airport is located 2.5 miles from the center of the city. SkyWest, Comair, Horizon, and Big Sky Airlines provide 14 daily flights to the city. Bus service is provided by Rimrock Trailways, which connects with Greyhound.

Traveling in the City

The major north-south routes are U.S. 12, which is known as Montana Avenue, and North Last Chance Gulch, also known as Main Street. Neill Avenue, 6th, 9th and Lyndale are major east–west streets. Transportation is provided by door-to-door bus service through Helena Dial-a-Ride, along with many regular stops that connect the downtown with the east side of town. In-town transportation is also provided by the Helena Area Transit Service (HATS) trolley and a city taxi service

■ Communications

Newspapers and Magazines

Helena's local newspapers include the *Helena Independent Record,* a daily, and the *Adit,* a shopping weekly. Magazines published locally include *Montana Magazine,* a regional interest magazine, *The Montana Catholic, Montana, The Magazine of Western History,* and *Montana Outdoors,* as well as the *Montana Stockgrower,* the *Montana Food Distributor, Trial Trends,* and *Toy Collector Magazine.*

Television and Radio

Affiliates of NBC, CW, and CBS television broadcast in Helena. The city has four local FM radio stations and four AM stations. They feature adult contemporary, easy listening, country, classic rock, and news and talk formats.

Media Information: Independent-Record, P.O. Box 4249, Helena, MT 59604; telephone (406) 447-4000.

Helena Online

City of Helena. Available www.ci.helena.mt.us
Helena Chamber of Commerce. Available www.helenachamber.com/
Helena Convention & Visitors Bureau. Available www.gohelena.com
Helena Public Schools. Available www.helena.k12.mt.us
Independent-Record. Available helenair.com
Lewis & Clark County Library. Available www.lewisandclarklibrary.org

BIBLIOGRAPHY

Egan, Timothy, *The Big Burn: Teddy Roosevelt and the Fire that Saved America* (Boston: Mariner Books, 2010)

Evans, Nicholas, *The Horse Whisperer* (New York: Delacourte Press, 1995

Petrick, Paula Evans, *No Step Backward: Women and Family on the Rocky Mountain Mining Frontier, Helena, MT 1865–1900* (Helena, MT: Helena Montana Historical Society Press, 1987)

Spalding, Charleen, *Benton Avenue Cemetery: A Pioneer Resting Place, Helena, Montana* (Helena, MT: Pioneer Tales Publishing, 2010)

Missoula

■ The City in Brief

Founded: 1860 (incorporated, 1883)

Head Official: Mayor John Engen (since 2010; current term expires 2014)

City Population
1990: 42,918
2000: 57,053
2010: 66,788
2012 estimate: 68,386
Percent change, 2000–2010: 17.1%
U.S. rank in 2010: 490th (State rank: 2nd)

Metropolitan Statistical Area Population
2000: 95,802
2010: 109,299
2012 estimate: 110,977
Percent change, 2000–2010: 14.1%
U.S. rank in 2000: 342nd
U.S. rank in 2010: 364th

Area: 24 square miles

Elevation: 3,210 feet above sea level

Average Annual Temperatures: January, 23.5° F; July, 66.9° F; annual average, 44.8° F

Average Annual Precipitation: 13.82 inches of rain; 46.3 inches of snow

Major Economic Sectors: lumber, plywood, wood panels, food

Unemployment Rate: 6% (2012)

Per Capita Income: $24,964

2012 FBI Crime Index Property: 3,041

Major Colleges and Universities: University of Montana

Daily Newspaper: *Missoulian*

■ Introduction

The birthplace of Jeannette Rankin, the first woman elected to the U.S. House of Representatives (1916), Missoula has many claims to fame. Known as the "Garden City" for its dense trees and lush green landscape, and as the state's cultural capital, Missoula is a vibrant and friendly town. Surrounded by national forests and wilderness areas, Missoula is three hours south of Glacier National Park and three-and-a-half hours west of Yellowstone National Park. The Clark Fork River flows through the center of town, east to west. Perfect for outdoorsmen, Missoula offers much to those who cherish nature and wildlife. Indeed, the International Wildlife Film Festival, the largest animal-themed film festival in the world, is held annually at Missoula's historic Wilma Theatre. The main campus for the University of Montana, Missoula is a center of higher education, which tilts the town to the liberal end of the political spectrum. In 2013 the city was ranked a Top 10 Best College Towns by *Livability* magazine. That same year, it was named a Great Adventure Town by *National Geographic*, a Best River Towns In America by *Outside* magazine, and earned Bicycle Friendly Community Gold Status from the League of American Bicyclists.

■ Geography and Climate

Missoula is situated in a deep valley surrounded by the Bitterroot and Sapphire Mountains in western Montana. It is traversed by three rivers: the Clark Fork River, the Bitterroot River, and the Blackfoot River. The city is the namesake and center of the Glacial Lake Missoula, which caused tremendous flooding across the northwest between 15,000 and 13,000 years ago.

Dariusz Janczewski/BigStockPhoto.com

Missoula celebrates all four seasons. From December to February, temperatures average in the 20 degree range, with highs in the 30s and lows in the 10s. From June to September average monthly temperatures fall to the 50s and 60s, with highs in the 70s and 80s. Missoula gets between 12 to 15 inches of precipitation on average each year.

Because Missoula is located in a valley, there is a significant amount of smoke, soot, and fog during the winter months. Emissions restrictions have been placed on certain industries, and on the burning of wood in wood stoves. In recent years, the pollution problem has improved.

Area: 24 square miles

Elevation: 3,210 feet above sea level

Average Temperatures: January, 23.5° F; July, 66.9° F; annual average, 44.8° F

Average Annual Precipitation: 13.82 inches of rain; 46.3 inches of snow

■ History

"Nemissoolatakoo"

Native Americans from the Salish tribe originally inhabited the Missoula area. They called the area "Nemissoolatakoo," meaning "near the cold, chilling waters." In 1805 the Lewis and Clark expedition passed through the Missoula Valley, and 400 members of the Salish tribe met the whites south of what is now Darby, Montana. The Indians treated Lewis and Clark and their companions well, as they did later white settlers.

An Important Trading Center

In 1860, the Washington Territorial Legislature created Missoula County. C.P. Higgins and Francis Worden opened a trading post called the Hellgate Village on the Blackfoot River near the eastern edge of the Missoula Valley; this was the first white settlement in the area. Later a sawmill and a flourmill were built, which the settlers called the "Missoula Mills." The city began to grow and develop quickly when the Mullan Road connecting Fort Benton, Montana, with Walla Walla, Washington, was completed; the road passed through the Missoula Valley. The U.S. Army established Fort Missoula in 1877. In 1883 the Northern Pacific Railroad came through Missoula. These developments led to Missoula becoming an important trading center; produce and grain grown in the Bitterroot Valley could be easily transported. Businessmen A.B. Hammond, E.L. Bonner, and R.A. Eddy established the Missoula Mercantile

Company in the early 1880s. On March 8, 1883, Missoula became an officially incorporated town under the territory of Montana. Missoula reincorporated when Montana became a state in 1889.

Twentieth Century Developments

In September 1893 the University of Montana opened to serve as the center of public higher education for western Montana. In 1908 Missoula became a regional headquarters for the Forest Service. That year, Missoula experienced its worst natural disaster, a flood that washed away the Higgins Avenue Bridge, which had first been built in 1873.

Missoula is the birthplace of Jeannette Rankin, the first woman elected (in 1916) to the U.S. House of Representatives. Rankin was the only member of Congress to vote against U.S. entry into World War II and only one of 50 to vote against U.S. entry into World War I. A lifelong pacifist, she later led resistance to the Vietnam War.

In 1954, President Dwight D. Eisenhower dedicated the Aerial Fire Depot. Big industry came to Missoula in 1956, with the groundbreaking for the first pulp mill. Logging became a major industry, with log yards throughout the city. Many ran teepee burners to dispose of waste material, creating the smoky haze that sometimes covered the city. However, by the early 1990s changes in the economic fortunes in the city had shut down all the Missoula log yards.

In 1996, Missoula adopted a charter form of government; the charter went into effect in 1997. Missoula has a thriving tourism industry based on outdoor activities, such as hunting, fishing, and skiing. Missoula is located within the so-called fly-fishing "Golden Triangle" and is a popular area for hunting mule deer, elk, bear, moose, and other game animals.

Historical Information: Historical Museum of Fort Missoula, Building 322, Fort Missoula, Missoula, MT 59804; telephone (406) 728-3476; fax (406) 543-6277; e-mail ftmslamuseum@montana.com

■ Population Profile

Metropolitan Statistical Area Population

  2000: 95,802
  2010: 109,299
  2012 estimate: 110,977
  Percent change, 2000–2010: 14.1%
  U.S. rank in 2000: 342nd
  U.S. rank in 2010: 364th

City Residents

  1990: 42,918
  2000: 57,053
  2010: 66,788

  2012 estimate: 68,386
  Percent change, 2000–2010: 17.1%
  U.S. rank in 2010: 490th (State rank: 2nd)

Density: 2,427.6 people per square mile

Racial and ethnic characteristics

  White: 62,390
  Black or African American: 40
  American Indian and Alaskan Native: 720
  Asian: 1,131
  Native Hawaiian and Other Pacific Islander: 214
  Hispanic or Latino (may be of any race): 2,869
  Other: 3,891

Percent of residents born in state: 45.8%

Age characteristics

  Population under 5 years old: 4,349
  Population 5 to 9 years old: 3,346
  Population 10 to 14 years old: 3,028
  Population 15 to 19 years old: 4,505
  Population 20 to 24 years old: 10,214
  Population 25 to 34 years old: 12,447
  Population 35 to 44 years old: 7,987
  Population 45 to 54 years old: 7,799
  Population 55 to 59 years old: 3,880
  Population 60 to 64 years old: 2,933
  Population 65 to 74 years old: 4,124
  Population 75 to 84 years old: 2,414
  Population 85 years and over: 1,360
  Median age: 31.7

Births (2010–11 Metropolitan Area)

  Total number: 1,177

Deaths (2010–11 Metropolitan Area)

  Total number: 744

Money income (2012)

  Per capita income: $24,964
  Median household income: $40,369
  Total households: 28,776

Number of households with income of . . .

  less than $10,000: 2,603
  $10,000 to $14,999: 2,154
  $15,000 to $24,999: 4,441
  $25,000 to $34,999: 3,875
  $35,000 to $49,999: 4,032
  $50,000 to $74,999: 5,184
  $75,000 to $99,999: 2,707
  $100,000 to $149,999: 2,373
  $150,000 to $199,999: 824
  $200,000 or more: 583

Percent of families below poverty level: 19.5%

FBI Crime Index Property: 3,041

FBI Crime Index Violent: 221

■ Municipal Government

Missoula was originally incorporated in 1883 and re-incorporated in 1889. It operates under the mayor-council form of government and provides a wide range of municipal services including police, fire, recreation, public works, improvements, and general administration services. Private firms provide garbage, water, electric and gas services.

Missoula's chief elected official is the mayor who serves a four-year term. Both mayor and city council are elected on a non-partisan basis. There are 12 city council members. Each council member is elected in odd-numbered years for staggered four-year terms.

Head Official: Mayor John Engen (since 2010; current term expires 2014)

Total Number of City Employees: Approximately 520 (2013)

City Information: City Hall, 435 Ryman St., Missoula, MT 59802; telephone (406) 552-6000.

■ Economy

Major Industries and Commercial Activity

Missoula has long relied upon its lumber industry for its economic well-being. However, lumber mills in Missoula have had to implement curtailments and closures in the 21st century. Plywood plants in particular have had to close operations in response to burgeoning competition from a product called oriented strand board, or OSB. As a result of the decline in the nation's housing market in the mid-2000s, housing starts fell 12 percent through 2006 and were expected to fall an additional 15 percent by the end of 2007, to about 1.5 million units. That caused a substantial decline in lumber and plywood prices-15 to 25 percent depending on the grade or species of lumber. Likewise, government staffing decreased over the same time period and was replaced by an upsurge in medical-related facilities/services and the art industry, giving Missoula's economy a whole new look

As of 2009, Missoula's top four major employers were in the areas of healthcare and education. University of Montana employed some 3,651 individuals and Missoula County Public Schools approximately 1,424 in 2009. Patrick Hospital and Community Medical Center employed some 1,600 and 1,200 workers respectively this same year. Missoula benefits from the growth of the University of Montana, both economically and culturally. Throughout Montana, the average compensation per job is approximately $1,346 higher because of the University of Montana. The University of Montana alone accounts for 11 percent of Missoula County's economy. Visitors to the campus generate approximately $5.2 million in annual spending in the state of Montana.

Tourism and the arts are important industries for Missoula. Seasonal tourism in the summer months increases revenue. A 2007 study reported that Missoula's nonprofit arts and culture industry generated $34 million in economic activity annually, including 1,174 full-time equivalent jobs. More than 3.8 million nonresident travelers in Montana visit Missoula annually; that is nearly two out of every five. These tourists spend more than $300 million in Missoula County each year.

Missoula encourages sustainable development. Individuals, businesses, and organizations in the Missoula area aware of their relationship to the environment are utilizing sustainable business practices.

Items and goods produced: lumber, plywood, wood panels, food

Incentive Programs—New and Existing Companies

Local programs: The Missoula Area Economic Development Corporation (MAEDC) provides three loan fund programs for job creation and business retention. Loans can range from $20,000 to $400,000. MAEDC works on business recruitment and relocation, and can provide demographic and statistical area information. Other financing options are a Community Reinvestment Fund and a Community Development Block Grant. Also of help to local businesses is Missoula's Small Business Development Center (SBDC), provided by the Montana Community Development Corporation. The center offers entrepreneurial training programs and consultations with staff on how to get one's business started. The SBDC works statewide with more than 1,500 entrepreneurs annually.

MonTEC (Montana Technology Enterprise Center) is a joint program of the Missoula Economic Partnership, the University of Montana Innovation and Entrepreneurship Program, and Hellgate Venture Network. Housed in a 32,000-square-foot building situated across the river from the UM campus, the goal of the multitenant business incubator is to help startup companies thrive.

The University of Montana's Blackstone LaunchPad was opened in early 2014. Designed to spur entrepreneurship, the program is modeled after a University of Miami program that has generated 1,413 business proposals, created 210 new jobs, and drawn nearly 2,600 participants. Each new regional program will be linked together, drawing ideas and best practices from the existing programs, while giving student entrepreneurs at UM and MSU access to a national community of more than 200,000 peers across affiliated campuses, as well as expert advisers.

State programs: Montana Business Assistance Connection, Inc. (MBAC) encourages and supports the creation of new jobs and relocation of existing jobs to various counties in Montana by helping with public and private revolving loan funds and providing training and access to capital for qualified start-up businesses or expanding businesses.

The Montana Community Development Corporation (MCDC) provides support to businesses through business loans, trainings and one-on-one business consulting. In 2010, the MCDC was the recipient of a $750,000 grant from the U.S. Treasury Department to be used for businesses loans, and in 2009, MCDC was awarded $40 million dollars in federal New Markets Tax Credits to be used in eligible areas and projects. The New Markets Tax Credits Program provides a 39 percent federal income tax credit to businesses that choose to invest capital into qualified projects in eligible low-income areas. Loans provided by MCDC range from $1,000 to $1,000,000 to qualified businesses and projects.

Other State of Montana tax incentives include property tax reduction; no inventory, use, or sales tax; new industry income tax credits; small business investment tax credits; and tax reduction on pollution control equipment. The Big Sky Development Trust Fund can provide up to $5,000 in grant funding for each new eligible job created. The Primary Sector Workforce Training Grant offers direct reimbursement to eligible businesses for training costs up to $5,000 per eligible newly created job.

In 2003, the Montana legislature created the Certified Regional Development Corporations (CRDC) program in the Montana Department of Commerce. The CRDC program is designed to encourage a regional approach to economic development. State law also provides for the creation of a tax increment financing (TIF) industrial district for industrial development projects. A local government can issue bonds for a wide variety of development purposes, such as financing land acquisition, industrial infrastructure, rail spurs, buildings, and personal property related to the public improvements.

Job training programs: The Missoula Workforce Center assists job seekers, from resume reviews to mock interviews and other resources. The Workforce Center also has recruitment and selection services, comprehensive applicant testing capabilities, and interviewing facilities to offer employers the tools they need to attract and retain a superior workforce. Business consultants offer services that enable employers to stay abreast of changing regulatory issues, in order to avoid potential employer-related liability, and assist with management and employee training needs. Missoula's Lifelong Learning Center offers over 700 classes each year to an annual enrollment of approximately 11,500 registrants in preparation for Missoula's workforce. They offer a standard range of classes but will arrange customized training to meet an employer's needs when necessary. Montana's JobLINC is the statewide coordination and collaboration of employment and training organizations, workforce development organizations, and other community service providers. Some of the organizations involved with JobLINC are workforce services divisions, local job service workforce centers, Chambers of Commerce, educational entities, economic development corporations, offices of public assistance, rural employment opportunities, human resource development councils, vocational rehabilitation, and other community-based organizations.

Development Projects

Missoula improvements over the past decade include those made to the Technology District of the Missoula Development Park in 2007. The Missoula Development Park is located on 446 acres between Interstate 90 and the airport. It has a Special Zoning District, which accommodates hotel/conference centers, restaurants, convenience and specialty stores, gas stations, banks, cultural centers, research and development technical training facilities and business and technology parks, warehouses, manufacturing, parks, and trails. The Missoula Development Park is located within two Tax Increment Financing districts, one industrial and one for technology.

In 2013 the University of Montana (UM) announced that a new Missoula College building would be constructed on East Broadway near the entrance to Missoula and along the Clark Fork River. This places UM and Missoula College strongly in the public eye. The Montana Legislature approved $29 million for construction of the building, with the stipulation that UM match the funding with an additional $3 million.

The Old Sawmill District is a 46-acre urban renewal project along the Clark Fork River, in the heart of Missoula. Once a booming sawmill complex, this property long known as the "mill site" has sat vacant since the early 1990s. Ultimately, the site will be developed into a lively urban neighborhood where people live, work, shop, and play. Plans call for a dynamic combination of single- and multi-family residences, a mixed-use commercial office space, and Silver Park, a 14.5-acre city park that extends the Clark Fork trail system. Also in the works at the district is a senior living and learning community that would have a relationship with the University of Montana for lifelong learning.

Startup companies include Rocky Mountain Biologicals Inc., specializing in the development and production of high performance sera, protein fractions, and cell culture media supplements needed for both lab and diagnostic purposes, and FilmSpur, an entertainment, film distribution, marketing, and outreach company.

Economic Development Information: Missoula Area Chamber of Commerce, 825 E. Front St., Missoula, MT 59802; telephone (406) 543-6623; fax (406) 543-6625.

Commercial Shipping

Common carriers use Interstate 90, U.S. Highway 10/93, and Montana State Highway 200 to access Missoula. Missoula International Airport (Johnson-Bell Field) provides service for cargo operations.

Labor Force and Employment Outlook

Missoula is a university town and it provides employers with a high-quality workforce. Over 32 percent of Missoula residents over the age of 25 are college graduates. The highest percentage of Missoula's workforce is composed of individuals under the age 30. The Missoula unemployment rate has consistently held lower than the national rate over the past decade; with 5.2 percent of Missoula residents unemployed in October 2013, (the national rate that month was 7 percent).

The economy relies heavily on retail trade with people traveling hundreds of miles to Missoula for shopping and medical and other professional services. In 2014 economists reported Missoula's industries were growing, but at a slow pace. Job growth was hampered by cuts at the University of Montana and the city's two hospitals, which may have been affected by the Affordable Care Act. The government workforce was expected to remain stable with little or no growth.

Non-farm labor earning in Missoula County was expected to rise by 2.7 percent in 2014, somewhat lower than the projected state average of 3.1 percent. Similar annual growth was projected through 2017.

The fastest growing subsectors of the economy in recent years have included mining, utilities, finance and insurance, and real estate rental and leasing. An estimated $51 million in new construction projects at the University and the completion of the South Crossing shopping center will add a significant number of new jobs to the economy.

The following is a summary of data regarding the 2012 Missoula labor force:

Size of civilian labor force: 40,043

Number of workers employed in . . .

agriculture and mining: 657
construction: 2,261
manufacturing: 1,262
wholesale trade: 752
retail trade: 5,068
transportation: 851
information systems: 1,335
finance: 1,702
professional administration: 3,916
education and social services: 10,124
arts and leisure: 5,821
other: 1,548
public administration: 957

Average hourly earnings of production workers: $15.04

Unemployment rate: 6% (2012)

Employers

Largest employers (2013)	*Number of employees*
University of Montana	3,122
St. Patrick Hospital	1,698
Community Medical Center	1,174
Missoula County Public Schools	1,165
DirecTV	850
Missoula County	810
Us Forrest Service	745
Wal-Mart	585
Opportunity Resources Service	533
City of Missoula	521

Cost of Living

The following is a summary of data regarding several key cost of living factors in the area.

State income tax rate: 1.0% to 6.9%

State sales tax rate: None

Local income tax rate: None

Local sales tax rate: None

Property tax rate: $1,296 (statewide per capita average, 2010)

Economic Information: The Research & Analysis Bureau, Montana Department of Labor & Industry, P. O. Box 1728, Helena, MT 59624; telephone (406) 444-2430; toll-free (800) 541-3904; fax (406) 444-2638.

■ Education and Research

Elementary and Secondary Schools

In 2012 Missoula County Public Schools (MCPS) served 8,450 students in nine elementary schools, three middle schools, four high schools, an alternative high school program at Willard School, and a preschool program at Jefferson School. In addition, the district served hundreds of adult students in the community through its adult basic education, trade and technical, and special interest classes at The Lifelong Learning Center at the Emma Dickinson Building. The Montana Digital Academy offers high school students on-line courses.

MCPS offers an innovative, multi-disciplinary curriculum that is research-based and reflects the needs of all students. Their curriculum includes such programs as International Baccalaureate, dual-credit, and Advanced Placement classes. In 2011, MCPS was one of 400 districts in the nation honored by the College Board for simultaneously increasing access to Advanced Placement (AP) courses while maintaining the percentage of students earning scores of three or higher on AP exams.

MCPS also provides challenging programs to assist students with special needs and talents. These include agriculture education, bilingual education programs, a deaf education program, fine arts programs, gifted education programs, Indian education programs, special education programs, and Title I programs.

In addition to the public schools, Missoula has a variety of private schools, including Montessori and Catholic schools. Missoula Catholic Schools maintains St. Joseph Elementary and Middle School (300 students in grades K–8) and Loyola Sacred Heart High School (200 students in grades 9–12). About 70 percent of the students at the high school are Catholic.

The following is a summary of data regarding the Missoula Elementary School District.

Total enrollment: 4,880

Number of facilities

total: 17
elementary schools: 9
junior high schools: 3
high schools: 4
other: 1

Student/teacher ratio: 16.08:1

Teacher salaries

average (statewide): $47,132

Funding per pupil: $9,659

Public Schools Information: Missoula County Public Schools, Administrative Offices, 215 South Sixth West, Missoula, MT 59801; telephone (406) 728-2400, ext. 1030.

Colleges and Universities

Missoula is home to the University of Montana, which was founded in 1893. Since then some 14,921 students have been provided with a high-quality, well-rounded education and training for professional careers in the University's three colleges-arts and sciences, forestry and conservation, and technology-and six schools-journalism, law, business, education, pharmacy, and the fine arts. The university also has a strong commitment to adult-education, with nearly 10 percent of its students at age 35 or older. The 200-acre campus is one of the most beautiful in the nation.

Missoula is also home to the University of Montana College of Technology, a two-year college that offers

programs in 35 different disciplines, from healthcare to culinary arts to energy technology. An added bonus is that, as University of Montana students, those attending the College of Technology all have access to Mountain campus facilities, including the library, recreation facilities, student transportation, and health services. Also nestled in Missoula is Walla Walla University, a fully accredited private university affiliated with the Seventh-day Adventist church.

Libraries and Research Centers

Since 1894, the Missoula Public Library has been working to provide programs, materials, and services to meet the informational, cultural, recreational, and educational needs of its patrons. The library's collection numbers 230,000 items, and the library offers a variety of technological resources as well, including wireless internet access and more than 20 public internet stations to patrons. The main library and its two branches cooperate with other libraries, educational institutions, and agencies to gain information resources for residents within its service area.

The Maureen and Mike Mansfield Library at the University of Montana provides services to the university's student body. In 2000, the library added its millionth volume to its collection and currently offers a periodical and newspaper collection numbering in the thousands.

Public Library Information: Missoula Public Library, 301 E. Main St, Missoula, MT 59802; telephone (406) 721-2665; fax (406) 728-5900; email mslaplib@missoula.lib.mt.us.

■ Health Care

Missoula offers a wide range of medical services as the major medical hub between Minneapolis and Seattle. The city has over 9,700 people working in the health services industry. There are two major medical centers in Missoula: the 146-bed Community Medical Center and the 253-bed St. Patrick Hospital & Health Sciences Center.

Community Medical Center is the only facility in Missoula County that offers obstetrical and newborn care and one of only three facilities in the state offering neonatal intensive care and high-risk obstetrical care. The medical center provides services to nearly 6,000 inpatients and 151,000 outpatients each year. More than 97,000 visits are made to hospital physicians each year. The Center employs over 1,100 people and has an annual payroll of over $38 million. The staff includes 300 physicians and 57 allied health professionals.

St. Patrick Hospital & Health Sciences Center is home to some of the northern Rocky Mountain region's most advanced health care. The hospital opened in 1873 under the sponsorship of the Sisters of Providence. The present hospital facility opened in 1984. The hospital has 253 licensed beds. Each year it admits more than 7,900 patients and provides more than 37,902 days of patient care. The hospital boasts the only da Vinci robot in Montana; the robot is used to perform surgeries with less pain and recovery time. It is also the only Level II Trauma hospital in the region and a regular recipient of the Premier Award for Quality, which recognizes national leaders in healthcare.

■ Recreation

Sightseeing

The Missoula County Courthouse, designed by A.J. Gibson, Missoula's premier architect, was constructed between 1908 and 1910 and occupies an entire city block. The neoclassical sandstone block building has an integral ironclad dome that is crowned externally by a clock tower, with clocks on all four sides. Within the tower is a two-ton bell that rings on the half hour and the hour. The courthouse is listed on the National Register of Historic Places. The Historical Museum at Fort Missoula was established by community effort in 1975 to save what remained of the original Fort Missoula and to interpret the area's history. The museum's collection includes 24,000 objects. Also for the history enthusiast, located downtown is the Higgins Block, one of Missoula's uniquely designed and preserved buildings.

One of Missoula's most cherished attractions is A Carousel for Missoula; it is one of the first fully hand-carved carousels to be built in the United States since the Great Depression. The carousel has 38 horses and two chariots. The carousel's band organ is the largest band organ in continuous use in the nation. Its 400 square wooden pipes make the music of 23 instruments and 45 musicians. In 2001 over 4,000 volunteers gathered to build a play area next to the carousel, called Dragon Hollow. The playground is complete with a three-headed dragon, numerous slides (one over 25 feet tall), musical instruments, an obstacle course, and a variety of child-created artwork. Also for young ones, the Children's Museum offers fun, interactive learning opportunities that allow children to explore their interests and abilities through play. The museum provides hands-on exhibits and weekly programs for infants through 10-year-old children.

The Forest Service Smokejumper Visitor Center gives tours that look at the methods used to train smokejumpers, highly skilled firefighters who parachute into forested areas to stop the spread of wildfires. The Montana Natural History Center has great displays on the local and regional geology, flora and fauna and provides guided tours of the Philip L. Wright Zoological Museum on the University of Montana campus. The Museum of Mountain Flying seeks to interpret and preserve the history of mountain flying in Montana and the northern Rockies. There are aircraft displays as well as interactive history displays. The Rocky Mountain Elk Foundation Elk Country Visitor Center is one of the best conservation education facilities in the Northwest. The Elk Country Visitor Center features hands-on conservation and hunting heritage exhibits for all ages. The center also includes a Lewis and Clark display, a collection of world record elk mounts, a western wildlife diorama, and a conservation theater.

Arts and Culture

The MCT Center for the Performing Arts opened in 1998. It is home to the internationally renowned Missoula Children's Theatre, which takes original musical theater productions on the road to nearly 1,200 communities around the world each year. The Wilma Theatre is a historical landmark theater built in 1921 by William Simons, who produced an early Wild West show. He named it after his wife, Edna Wilma Simons, a renowned light-opera star who performed on the Pantages vaudeville circuit. The building has as a centerpiece a 1,067-seat theater, which shows first-run films and presents live events. It also has two smaller theaters of 125 seats each, which show second-run movies.

The Missoula Art Museum (MAM) is a free-admission museum dedicated to contemporary art. The MAM has grown from a summer arts festival to a thriving institution serving the Northwest. MAM develops and hosts approximately 25 exhibitions annually in six galleries located in its Carnegie building. MAM's exhibition programs encompass diverse media from local and international contemporary artists. It also provides two classrooms and a state-of-the-art collection vault to visitors.

The Montana Museum of Art & Culture serves the University of Montana community and the Missoula public at large. The permanent collection, begun in 1894, now includes more than 10,000 original works. It is among the largest and oldest collections in Montana and the Rocky Mountain Northwest.

Art galleries in Missoula include the Dana Gallery, the Clay Studio of Missoula, Monte Dolack Gallery, and dozens more worth exploring.

In the summer playgoers can enjoy Montana Shakespeare in the Parks, which is the only professional theater program in the state producing Shakespearean plays and the only company that offers its performances free to the public. Since its inception in 1973, Montana Shakespeare in the Parks has traveled over 400,000 miles and presented over 1,500 performances to a cumulative audience of more than half a million people. What began as an amateur 12-city tour has become a nationally known, professional company that presents an eight-week tour of 70 performances in 50 communities to approximately 30,000 people every summer throughout Montana, northern Wyoming, and eastern Idaho.

The Missoula Symphony Orchestra and Chorale was organized in 1954. Today, the orchestra puts on a five-concert season. In addition to the regular concert season, the orchestra performs a free outdoor summer concert in August in downtown Missoula, performs two youth concerts each year for 2,000 fourth grade students, performs an annual family concert, and provides educational performances in Missoula schools and in outlying communities.

Festivals and Holidays

In April the University of Montana holds its annual Buddy DeFranco Jazz Festival, which is a celebration of jazz performance and education. In May, the International Wildlife Film Festival is held; it is the largest animal-themed film festival in the world.

Summertime brims with activities in Missoula. At the Missoula Saturday Market each summer, the city of Missoula closes a downtown street for a Saturday craft and food market run by local artisans. From June through August at lunchtime, Out to Lunch is a weekly performing arts festival at Caras Park on the Clark Fork River, featuring musicians and over 20 varied food vendors. Downtown Tonight takes place Thursday evenings June through August, featuring live music, food vendors, and a beverage garden. The International Choral Festival is held in July.

In September Germanfest is held. It is an annual ethnic heritage celebration that highlights Missoula's Sister City relationship with Neckargemund, one of the oldest communities in Germany. In November the annual Renaissance Arts and Crafts Fair is held. This juried arts and crafts show features some of the Northwest's best artists and craftspeople. Jewelry, photography, sculpture, weaving, wooden toys, hand-made furniture, stained glass, glass beads, and pottery are displayed.

First Night Missoula is an all-day, alcohol-free celebration of the arts taking place on New Year's Eve. More than 100 music, theater, dance, children's programs, and visual arts performances and activities in more than 30 venues throughout downtown Missoula, the University of Montana campus, and Southgate Mall are held from noon until midnight.

Sports for the Spectator

The Missoula Osprey is a minor league baseball team affiliated with the Arizona Diamondbacks. They play at Ogren Park at Allegiance Field. The Missoula Maulers Junior "A" Hockey team play 48 games each year at Glacier Ice Rink on the Montana Fairgrounds. The University of Montana Grizzlies are the sports teams of the University of Montana. Men's teams include basketball, football, cross country, track and field, and tennis. Women's teams include basketball, tennis, soccer, volleyball, golf, cross country, and track and field.

Sports for the Participant

Recreational opportunities abound in the Missoula area; there are 50 parks (with more than 400 acres of parkland and 3,300 acres of conservation lands), 21 health clubs, 11 golf courses, three rivers, four ski areas, and miles of hiking and biking. In addition to hiking, biking, and skiing, outdoor activities include snowmobiling and ice skating, fishing, hunting, mountain climbing, river rafting, and wildlife viewing. The millions of acres of wilderness surrounding Missoula are home to a rich variety of trees, plants, flowers, and wildlife for the nature enthusiast.

Mount Sentinel, embellished by a huge concrete letter "M," offers a great view of the area, especially the rugged Hellgate River Canyon. Trails explore the Rattlesnake Wilderness, which, nonetheless, is free of snakes. The most developed of the city's ski areas is Montana Snowbowl, 12 miles northwest, which has a good range of slopes for all abilities and boasts a summer chairlift. Marshall Mountain, seven miles east of Missoula, is geared toward the novice.

Shopping and Dining

Missoula is home to western Montana's largest indoor shopping mall, national discount and department stores, and dozens of interesting and unique downtown stores and boutiques. North Reserve is Missoula's newest and fastest growing shopping district, and is also an excellent place to dine in a number of ethnic and traditional restaurants. Southgate Mall offers over 100 top specialty stores and many unique "Made in Montana" items.

Visitor Information: Missoula Convention & Visitors Bureau, 1121 E. Broadway, Number 103, Missoula, MT 59802; telephone (406) 532-3250; fax (406) 532-3252; toll-free (800) 526-3465.

■ Convention Facilities

The University of Montana's Adams Center offers 42,846 square feet of conference space and can seat 7,290 in theater- and classroom-capacity. The University Center has 37,000 square feet and 17 conference rooms; the University Center can seat 1,000 in theater-capacity and 400 in classroom-capacity.

The Best Inn & Conference Center, Doubletree Hotel Missoula Edgewater, the Hilton Garden Inn Missoula, the Holiday Inn Downtown at the Park, Ruby's Inn and Convention Center, and the Wingate Inn are some of the larger hotels and inns with both conference facilities and lodging.

Convention Information: Missoula Convention & Visitors Bureau, 1121 E. Broadway, Suite 103, Missoula, MT 59802; telephone (406) 532-3250; toll-free (800) 526-3465.

■ Transportation

Approaching the City

Interstate 90, U.S. Highway 10/93, and Montana State Highway 200 intersect in Missoula. Interstate 90 runs east–west right through the Missoula Valley. State Highway 93 runs north–south through the valley. Missoula is 345 miles from Billings, 476 miles from Seattle, 895 miles from Denver, and 2,247 miles from San Francisco.

Missoula International Airport (Johnson-Bell Field, MSO) is a primary commercial service airport with scheduled airline and air taxi service, military operations, U.S. Forest Service operations, cargo operations, and recreational flying services. Four airlines currently provide service to MSO, including Alaska Airlines–Horizon Air, Allegiant Airlines, United Express, and Delta.

Buses serving Missoula are Greyhound, Rimrock Trailways, and Beach Transportation.

Traveling in the City

Missoula Urban Transportation District does business as Mountain Line. Mountain Line operates regular route bus transit services within the Missoula urban area, and residents ride the bus about 20,000 miles per month within the city. In addition to a number of established bus stops around Missoula, a wave of the hand at any safe intersection along the bus routes will allow you to board.

■ Communications

Newspapers and Magazines

Missoulian is the city's daily newspaper. The *Missoula Independent* is western Montana's weekly alternative newspaper featuring political and arts coverage. The *Montana Kaimin* is the student daily of the University of Montana at Missoula. *Western Montana InBusiness Monthly* focuses on business news around the region.

Television and Radio

Affiliates of ABC, CBS, NBC, and PBS television broadcast in Missoula. Missoula also has a community access television station. Five AM and 13 FM radio stations broadcast everything from National Public Radio, talk radio, and sports, to country, classic rock, Christian, oldies, adult contemporary, and alternative music.

Media Information: Missoulian, 500 S. Higgins, Missoula, MT 59807; telephone (406) 523-5200; toll-free (800) 366-7102; fax (406) 523-5221.

Missoula Online

City of Missoula home page. Available www.ci. missoula.mt.us

Missoula Area Chamber of Commerce. Available www.missoulachamber.com

Missoula Convention and Visitors Bureau. Available www.missoulacvb.org

Missoula County Public Schools. Available www. mcps.k12.mt.us/portal

Missoula Public Library. Available www. missoulapubliclibrary.org

Missoula.com Magazine. Available www.missoula. com

Missoulian. Available www.missoulian.com

Montana Community Development Corporation. Available www.mtcdc.org

BIBLIOGRAPHY

Egan, Timothy, *The Big Burn: Teddy Roosevelt and the Fire that Saved America* (Boston: Mariner Books, 2010)

Koelbel, Lenora, *Missoula: the Way It Was A Portrait of an Early Town* (Helena, MT: Gateway Print and Litho, 1972)

Maechling, Philip, and Stan Cohen, *Missoula* (Charleston, SC: Arcadia Publishing, 2010)

Nevada

The State in Brief

Nickname: Silver State

Motto: All for our country

Flower: Sagebrush

Bird: Mountain bluebird

Area: 110,572 square miles (2010; U.S. rank 7th)

Elevation: 479 feet to 13,140 feet above sea level

Climate: Semi arid, with temperatures that vary with altitude as well as season; extremely cold winters in the north and west, ovenlike summer heat in parts of the south

Admitted to Union: October 31, 1864

Capital: Carson City

Head Official: Brian Sandoval (R) (until 2015)

Population

  1990: 1,201,833
  2000: 1,998,257
  2010: 2,700,551
  2012 estimate: 2,704,204
  Percent change, 2000–2010: 35.1%
  U.S. rank in 2012: 35th
  Percent of residents born in state: 24.3% (2012)
  Density: 24.6 people per square mile (2010)
  2012 FBI Crime Index Total: 94,273

Racial and Ethnic Characteristics (2012)

  White: 1,970,074
  Black or African American: 218,305
  American Indian and Alaska Native: 30,061
  Asian: 196,245
  Native Hawaiian and Pacific Islander: 16,472
  Hispanic or Latino (may be of any race): 717,835
  Other: 273,047

Age Characteristics (2012)

  Population under 5 years old: 187,513
  Population 5 to 19 years old: 544,629
  Percent of population 65 years and over: 12.2%
  Median age: 36.3

Vital Statistics

  Total number of births (2012–13): 35,504
  Total number of deaths (2012–13): 21,023
  AIDS cases reported through 2011: 7,199

Economy

  Major industries: Services; finance, insurance, and real estate; trade; manufacturing
  Unemployment rate (2012): 7.9%
  Per capita income (2012): $27,003
  Median household income (2012): $54,083
  Percentage of persons below poverty level (2012): 14.2%
  Income tax rate: None
  Sales tax rate: 6.85%

Carson City

■ The City in Brief

Founded: 1858 (incorporated, 1875)

Head Official: Mayor Robert Crowell (since 2008; current term expires 2016)

City Population

    1990: 40,443
    2000: 52,457
    2010: 55,274
    2012 estimate: 54,989
    Percent change, 2000–2010: 5.4%
    U.S. rank in 2000: 680th (State rank: 9th)
    U.S. rank in 2010: 635th (State rank: 10th)

Metropolitan Statistical Area Population

    2000: 52,457
    2010: 55,274
    2012 estimate: 54,838
    Percent change, 2000–2010: 5.4%
    U.S. rank in 2000: 365th
    U.S. rank in 2010: 567th

Area: 155.66 square miles

Elevation: 4,600 feet above sea level

Average Annual Temperatures: January, 33.6° F; July, 69.9° F

Average Annual Precipitation: 11.8 inches of rain, 22 inches of snow

Major Economic Sectors: services, government, trade, manufacturing

Unemployment Rate: 10.6% (2012)

Per Capita Income: $25,954

Major Colleges and Universities: Western Nevada Community College

Daily Newspaper: *Nevada Appeal*

■ Introduction

Carson City, often called the "hub of the Sierras," is Nevada's state capital. The city's distinct character was molded by the industries that dominated the mountainous region in the late 1800s—logging, mining, and the railroad. Though traces of its origins remain through tourist attractions such as an original working railroad, the city is mainly a center of government. Resident and visitors alike can experience Carson City's vast entertainment, shopping, and outdoor recreational activities. The city boasts a beautiful historic district, while lively casinos continue to flourish and complement the small-town feel of the community.

■ Geography and Climate

Carson City is located in northwestern Nevada in the foothills of the Sierra Nevada range. It lies 30 miles south of Reno, Nevada in the Carson River Valley near Lake Tahoe, which is 14 miles to the west. Carson City includes a 153-square-mile area that stretches across the Carson Range of the Sierra Mountains to Eagle Valley and the Pine Nut Mountains. It is bordered on the north by Washoe and Storey counties, and on the west by the state of California.

The mountains around Carson City intercept the moisture the Pacific Ocean air currents bring, leaving the area with a semi-desert climate. The area boasts an average of more than 260 sunny days annually. Summers are warm and dry with peak temperatures reaching into the 90° F range, while temperatures can drop into the 50° F range during the evenings. Winters are cold and dry with snow, but not in the amounts of nearby areas that are at a much higher elevation. The temperatures range from the high teens to the 40° F range. Annual snowfall in the city averages about 22 inches.

AP Images

Area: 155.66 square miles

Elevation: 4,600 feet above sea level

Average Temperatures: January, 33.6° F; July, 69.9° F

Average Annual Precipitation: 11.8 inches of rain, 22 inches of snow

■ History

Gold Leads the Way

For nearly 4,000 years before the coming of white settlers, the Washoe Indians occupied the land along the Sierra Nevada Mountain Range that borders Nevada and California. In 1851 a group of prospectors decided to look for gold in the area that is now Carson City. Unsuccessful in that attempt, they opened up a trading post called Eagle Station on the Overland Stagecoach route. It was used by wagon trains of people moving westward. The surrounding area came to be called Eagle Ranch, and the surrounding meadows as Eagle Valley. In time, a number of scattered settlements grew up in the area and the Eagle Ranch became its social center.

As a growing number of white settlers came to the area and began to develop the valleys and mountains, the Washoe people who for so long had occupied the area were overwhelmed. Although lands were allotted to individual Indians by the federal government starting in the 1880s, they did not offer sufficient water. As a result, the Washoe tended to set up camp at the edges of white settlements and ranches in order to work for food. It would not be until the twentieth century that parcels of reservation land were established for them.

Many of the earliest settlers in the Carson City area were Mormons led to Eagle Valley by Colonel John Reese. When the Mormons were summoned to Salt Lake City, Utah, by their leader, Brigham Young, many sold their land for a small amount to area resident John Mankin, who later laid claim to the entire Eagle Valley. In time he subdivided the land and sold tracts of it.

Birth of Carson City

In 1858, an ambitious New Yorker named Abraham Curry, along with three partners, bought most of Eagle Valley, including the ranch and trading post. Curry was correct in his prophecy that the western part of Utah Territory was soon to become a state, and he had the present-day site of Carson City surveyed. He promoted Eagle Valley, a fertile though rather deserted place, as the site of the future state capital.

Soon Major William M. Ormsby also became an enthusiastic promoter of a town that did not yet exist. He named it in honor of legendary mountain man Kit Carson, whose name was also borne by a nearby river. The town was laid out with wide streets and had a four-square city area that he named Capitol Square, but that later came to be called the Plaza.

In 1859 the rich Comstock Lode (chiefly silver) was discovered mere miles from the site of Carson City, setting off a rush to the area. Curry sold his claim to the Comstock for a few thousand dollars, but those who bought it became millionaires. Still, Curry is remembered in the name of the mine, the Gould and Curry.

By 1860 the town's population stood at 500 people. Soon Abe Curry took steps to have Carson City named territorial capital. He argued that it was close to the main lines of travel in the region. On November 25, 1861, Carson City was named the permanent capital of Nevada Territory and the Ormsby County seat. A plaza was established at the site for future public buildings.

Carson Named Capital of New State

Just one year later, the population of the town had nearly doubled. The year 1862 saw Carson become a station on the Pony Express and the eastern end of a telegraph line from San Francisco. Soon the town became a freighting and supply point for many mining and ranching communities in the central and southern part of Nevada.

About this time, both Carson and the entire surrounding area were having problems with cattle rustlers, claim jumpers, and other outlaws. As a result, the legislature passed laws designed to establish order. When the new legislature could not find a site large enough to accommodate its numbers, Abe Curry offered it the use of his Warm Springs Hotel, a rather primitive building located near the Carson River. In the early days a canvas curtain was used to divide the Nevada senate from the state assembly.

In October 1864, Nevada became a state, and Carson City was chosen to serve as the state capital. By then, Curry owned a sandstone quarry, a brickyard, a saloon, and the Great Basin Hotel. When a courthouse was needed, Curry again came to the rescue. He sold his Great Basin Hotel to the State of Nevada and it was used as a courthouse and legislature building into the 1870s. Because it was two miles out of town, Curry transported the legislators in Carson's first horse-drawn streetcar.

The Early Years of a Capital City

A few years later the Warm Springs building was converted into a territorial prison and Curry became its first warden. Prison labor used local sandstone to construct many of Carson City's early buildings. In 1870, a branch of the U.S. Mint was built in Carson and

Curry was appointed its first superintendent. The mint processed the rich ore found in nearby mines. In rapid succession, Curry resigned that position, lost a bid to become Nevada's lieutenant governor, and built the huge stone roundhouse and shops for the Virginia & Truckee Railroad. This became America's richest short-line railroad, connecting the Comstock mines with mills on the Carson River. In 1873 Curry died of a stroke.

During those early years, Nevada's legislative business was punctuated by fistfights, vote-buying, and other acts of political corruption. In 1872, a State Capitol building, a large square stone structure with rafters made of hewn logs, was completed. That same year saw the completion of a 52-mile railroad linking Carson City to Virginia City, and other lines were to follow. In 1880, the population stood at about 8,000 people.

As a New Century Dawned

During the last decades of the nineteenth century, Carson City experienced boom and bust cycles common to the area. With the decline of the nearby mines, the population too began to decline. Railroad traffic through Carson City came to a halt when the Southern Pacific Railroad built a branch rail line that bypassed the city. That, and the departure of the rootless, restless miners, resulted in Carson City's settling down into a quiet community. In the late 1800s Carson City became home to the Stewart Indian School, which educated thousands of native American children between 1890 and 1980, teaching them English and the ways of the white people.

In 1897, Carson City became the focus of worldwide attention when it became the site of a world heavyweight championship fight in which Britain Bob Fitzsimmons won over "Gentleman Jim" Corbett. A motion picture of the fight, the first of its kind, thrilled audiences, despite its bluish tint and flickering images. But soon after, between 1890 and 1900, the population of Carson City dropped from nearly 4,000 to a little more than 2,000 people.

Carson City in the Twentieth Century

Carson City's fortunes gradually declined through World War I and with the coming of the worldwide economic downturn known as the Great Depression. By 1930, the population had declined to only about 1,500 citizens, a quarter of what it had been 50 years earlier. Then in 1931 state legislation was enacted that permitted gambling in the area and provided for speedy divorce and simple marriage procedures. These moves brought more tourists into the area.

Soon the population began to grow again, reaching 2,478 in 1940, doubling to 5,163 by 1960, then tripling that figure by 1970, when the population stood at 15,468 people. In 1969, Ormsby County was merged with Carson City, and government services were consolidated. The population doubled again in 1980 to 32,022, then jumped by 20,000 more by 2010.

Today, as the site of a state prison, the Nevada Gaming Commission, and a variety of state department headquarters and federal agencies, the small city serves as the power center of Nevada. A national recession in the late 2000s that dwindled tax revenue and resulted in cutbacks in government employment hurt the city's economy. The recession failed to affect the pleasant weather conditions throughout the year that draw visitors to outdoor activities, in addition to the wide array of entertainment options in the city. As Carson City searched for ways to enhance its economy, it retained the strong sense of community that has made it one of the most pleasant small metropolitan areas in which to live.

Historical Information: Nevada Division of Museums and History, 708 N. Curry St., Carson City, NV 89703; telephone (775) 687-4340; fax (775) 687-4333.

■ Population Profile

Metropolitan Statistical Area Population

2000: 52,457
2010: 55,274
2012 estimate: 54,838
Percent change, 2000–2010: 5.4%
U.S. rank in 2000: 365th
U.S. rank in 2010: 567th

City Residents

1990: 40,443
2000: 52,457
2010: 55,274
2012 estimate: 54,989
Percent change, 2000–2010: 5.4%
U.S. rank in 2000: 680th (State rank: 9th)
U.S. rank in 2010: 635th (State rank: 10th)

Density: 3,285.4 people per square mile

Racial and ethnic characteristics

White: 46,512
Black or African American: 402
American Indian and Alaskan Native: 1,224
Asian: 1,651
Native Hawaiian and Other Pacific Islander: 259
Hispanic or Latino (may be of any race): 12,074
Other: 4,941

Percent of residents born in state: 28.4%

Age characteristics

Population under 5 years old: 3,212
Population 5 to 9 years old: 3,051
Population 10 to 14 years old: 3,318
Population 15 to 19 years old: 3,149
Population 20 to 24 years old: 3,611
Population 25 to 34 years old: 6,625
Population 35 to 44 years old: 7,161
Population 45 to 54 years old: 7,750
Population 55 to 59 years old: 3,529
Population 60 to 64 years old: 4,175
Population 65 to 74 years old: 5,085
Population 75 to 84 years old: 2,987
Population 85 years and over: 1,336
Median age: 41.7

Births (2010–11 Metropolitan Area)

Total number: 662

Deaths (2010–11 Metropolitan Area)

Total number: 614

Money income (2012)

Per capita income: $25,954
Median household income: $52,436
Total households: 21,212

Number of households with income of . . .

less than $10,000: 1,544
$10,000 to $14,999: 1,329
$15,000 to $24,999: 2,053
$25,000 to $34,999: 2,074
$35,000 to $49,999: 3,185
$50,000 to $74,999: 4,360
$75,000 to $99,999: 3,274
$100,000 to $149,999: 2,184
$150,000 to $199,999: 728
$200,000 or more: 481

Percent of families below poverty level: 16.3%

■ Municipal Government

The city and county of Carson, Nevada, have been coextensive since 1969, when the city merged with what was formerly Ormsby County to form a consolidated municipality. The city is governed by a council-manager form of government. Carson City has a mayor and a four-member board of supervisors, all elected to serve overlapping four-year terms. An appointed city manager performs administrative functions for the city's board of supervisors and oversees city staff and departments.

Head Official: Mayor Robert Crowell (since 2008; current term expires 2016)

Total Number of City Employees: 559 (2012)

City Information: City Hall, Carson City, 201 N. Carson St., Carson City, NV 89701; telephone (775) 887-2100; fax (775) 887-2286.

■ Economy

Major Industries and Commercial Activity

Carson City has a diverse economy. It is the regional retail and commercial center for northwestern Nevada, which is devoted to irrigated farming, livestock raising, and mining of silver and other minerals. It draws from a trade area of about one-quarter million people, with nearly 28,000 people working in the service sector, the city's largest.

As the seat of state government, which meets in the city for two months every two years, and a center for federal government, the government sector accounts for 11,500 area jobs and is the second-largest economic sector in the community. Cutbacks in state and local government employment during the late 2000s and early 2010s, largely in response to a national recession, had mixed effects. While residents enjoyed lower government operating costs, the city faced disproportionally large layoffs of state employees.

The retail industry is the city's third largest employer, followed by manufacturing. Trade is supported by the Airport Industrial Park and access to major highways and railways, and accommodating weather. The city's 176 manufacturers account for nearly one quarter of economic output and produce electronics, machinery, plastics and rubber, and chemicals.

Since gambling was legalized in 1931, tourism has also been important to the Carson City economy, and the resort city draws many visitors its casinos and hot springs. (The service industry includes hotel, gaming, and tourism workers.) In an effort to bolster the arts sector alongside tourism, the Carson City Arts and Culture Coalition provides advocacy for arts with the explicit goal of becoming the region's cultural hub.

Items and goods produced: electronics, machinery, plastics, rubber, chemicals

Incentive Programs—New and Existing Companies

Local programs: Carson City is able to save employers time and money through the major project review process, and a local one-stop shop that issues building permits. Both Nevada and Carson City rely heavily on having few taxes to make its cities very competitive in business. Accessible government and sensible regulations also draw business.

State programs: The state of Nevada has no personal state income tax, no unitary tax, no corporate income tax, no inventory tax, no estate and/or gift tax, no franchise tax, no inheritance tax, and no special intangible tax. Nevada is a Right to Work state, in which employees can choose to affiliate with or join labor unions; railway and airline employees, however, are not included in the law.

The state also guarantees Small Business Administration loans.

Tax abatements include a Sales and Use Tax Abatement, available on qualifying capital projects with reductions to as little as 2 percent; Modified Business Abatement of 50 percent of the 1.17 percent rate levied on quarterly wages above $85,000; Personal Property Abatement of up to 50 percent for 10 years; and Real Property Tax Abatement for Recycling, also up to 50 percent for 10 years.

The Nevada State Development Corporation (NSDC) provides loan financing for growth opportunities such as buying, building, or improving commercial real estate for new and existing businesses. The Nevada Microenterprise Initiative helps provide economic self-sufficiency for entrepreneurs through training, technical assistance, and access to credit. Loans can be used for start-up costs, equipment, inventory, supplies, working capital, fixtures and other furniture.

Job training programs: Nevada's "Train Employees Now" (TEN) program has customized short-term, industrial training programs to assist new and expanding businesses in training new or potential employees. Eligible businesses must contribute at least 25 percent of the total training costs, and must have at least 10 employees to train. The Silver State Works Employee Hiring Incentive offers employers up to $2,000 for each state-qualified employee hired.

Working to ensure that companies have an adequate workforce is Job Opportunities in Nevada (JOIN), which offers training and educational opportunities for job seekers; Nevadaworks assists employers in developing employee skills. Nevada Industry Excellence is an industrial outreach program affiliated with local community colleges and is dedicated to training employees to meet the hiring goals of specific companies.

Western Nevada College works closely with area businesses in providing specialized training courses for employees.

Development Projects

In 2003 the city held a groundbreaking for the new Carson City Freeway that was intended to provide another north–south option for local travelers. It was estimated that the challenging and long-discussed project would cost more than $70 million by final completion, which was originally planned for late 2010. The project was broken up into phases: Phase one, which included widening U.S. Highway 395, connecting U.S. Highway 50, and constructing interchanges, was completed in 2006. Phase two was under construction in 2013, with all construction scheduled to finish by 2016 as long as funding remained available.

In 2005 the Carson City Board of Supervisors approved a "Master Plan" for the city, which called for a new focus on better utilization of land through vertical development of properties and mixed-use developments, and also included plans to create a historic retail zoning district. In 2009 a plan was proposed for a nearly $100 million downtown redevelopment project that would create new jobs and help dwindling revenues. However, economic stagnation and a 2012 voter rejection of a quarter-cent increase in sales tax kept proposed projects in the planning stages, or terminated them completely.

As of 2014, the city was considering public investment in an athletic center and seeking a public-private partnership to establish a convention center. Independent of specific projects, a long-term development goal remained the creation of a more pedestrian-friendly downtown.

Economic Development Information: Carson City Office of Business Development, 108 E. Proctor Street, Carson City, NV 89701; phone (775) 887-2101; fax (775) 887-2286.

Commercial Shipping

Carson City enjoys a strategic location along three major highway corridors, including Interstate 80; more than 60 local, regional, and national carriers provide trucking services in nearby Reno. Shipments from Carson City are able to reach nine western states on a next-day basis. The Union Pacific Railroad provides regional freight service through Reno. Reno-Tahoe International Airport, just 30 miles to the north of Carson City, provides cargo air service through three carriers: FedEx, UPS, and DHL.

Labor Force and Employment Outlook

Carson City's average annual wage is above that of both Reno and Douglas County. Occupations in greatest demand are general and operations managers, construction managers, midscale and health service managers, business operations specialists, computer support specialists, lawyers, nurses, and carpenters.

Like much of the country, Carson City's job growth dwindled from 2006 to 2010, leaving the area with an unemployment rate hovering in the teens—a drastic increase compared to 5.1 percent in 2007. The rate slowly but steadily declined during the 2010s, but lingering unemployment continued to be a priority for the city government.

The following is a summary of data regarding the 2012 Carson City labor force:

Size of civilian labor force: 27,791

Number of workers employed in . . .

agriculture and mining: 242
construction: 943
manufacturing: 2,438
wholesale trade: 515
retail trade: 3,265
transportation: 881

information systems: 141
finance: 958
professional administration: 2,208
education and social services: 4,004
arts and leisure: 3,168
other: 1,241
public administration: 3,187

Average hourly earnings of production workers: $17.79

Unemployment rate: 10.6% (2012)

Employers

Largest employers (2012)	*Number of employees*
Carson City School District	1,000–1,499
Carson Tahoe Hospital	1,000–1,499
City of Carson City	600–699
State Department of Transportation	600–699
Western Nevada Community College	500–599
State Department of Corrections	300–399
State Department of Motor Vehicles	300–399
Casino Fandango	300–399
Wal-Mart Supercenter	300–399
Chromalloy Nevada	300–399

Cost of Living

The following is a summary of data regarding several key cost of living factors in the area.

State income tax rate: None

State sales tax rate: 6.85%

Local income tax rate: None

Local sales tax rate: 0.625%

Property tax rate: $3.53 per $100 assessed value (2013)

Economic Information: Carson City Chamber of Commerce, 1900 S. Carson St., Carson City, NV 89701; telephone (775) 882-1565; email ccchamber@ carsoncitychamber.com.

■ Education and Research

Elementary and Secondary Schools

The Carson City School District has seven elementary schools, two middle schools, and two high schools. One of the elementary schools, Carson Montessori, is a charter school, and Pioneer High School is the city's only alternative high school. Carson Online allows students to take courses from home.

Carson High School is one of the top-rated schools in Nevada. Since 1999 it has shared a $5 million joint-use project—the Jim Randolph High Tech Center—with Western Nevada Community College. It assists students in preparing for careers in electronics, automated technology, drafting, business, and allied health. The high school also offers small learning communities, specialized learning programs in which students can participate based on their own interests. The district provides adult education programs and learning opportunities for students with behavioral problems.

Carson City also has a number of private and parochial schools.

The following is a summary of data regarding the Carson City School District.

Total enrollment: 7,787

Number of facilities

    total: 11
    elementary schools: 7
    junior high schools: 2
    high schools: 2
    other: 0

Student/teacher ratio: 17.2:1

Teacher salaries

    average (statewide): $53,023

Funding per pupil: $9,907

Public Schools Information: Carson City School District, 1402 W. King St., Carson City, NV 89703; telephone (775) 283-2000; fax (775) 283-2090.

Colleges and Universities

Western Nevada College is a two-year public community college that offers about 40 academic degree programs, as well as basic education and job development skills programs. It enrolls more than 5,000 students each semester at its campuses in Carson City and in Fallon and Douglas counties, totaling an 18,000-square-foot service area. The college offers diverse degree and certificate programs, schedules evening and weekend as well as daytime classes, and provides small class sizes and one-on-one counseling opportunities for students.

The University of Nevada, Reno, is located 30 miles north of Carson City. It enrolls more than 18,000 students per semester and offers 145 programs of study. Specialties include earthquake expertise, which includes experts from fields of seismology, geology, geodesy, and civil engineering. The Master of Business Administration

degree program has been ranked among the top 25 national programs of its kind by *BusinessWeek*.

Other area schools include Truckee Meadows Community College and Sierra Nevada College.

Libraries and Research Centers

Carson City Library, built in 1966, offers more than 116,000 volumes, 200 periodical subscriptions, and 3,200 audio tapes. The library has a collection on Nevada history and a large print section.

Western Nevada College opened the 34,000-square-foot Dini Library and Student Center on its Carson City campus in 2004. The university's total holdings number more than 46,000 books, 185 magazines, 12 newspaper subscriptions, more than 1,000 maps, and other materials. The University of Nevada, Reno, is a major research center, with strong programs in Great Basin Studies, Basque Studies, and Genomics and Proteomics. Its library holdings include the Basque Library, Keck Earth Sciences and Mining Research Information Center, and the Nevada Inventors Database.

Other libraries in the city include the Nevada State Library & Archives, the library of the Nevada State Museum, and the Nevada Supreme Court Library.

Public Library Information: Carson City Library, 900 N. Roop St., Carson City, NV 89701; telephone (775) 887-2244.

■ Health Care

Carson Tahoe Health is the city's not-for-profit community health-care system. In 2005 the hospital opened the new Carson-Tahoe Regional Medical Center with 352,000 square feet, more than double the capacity of the previous building. The building contains 138 private rooms, a cardiovascular care unit, intensive care unit, women and children's center, and other medical capabilities. The hospital admits about 10,000 patients annually and treats some 25,000 in its emergency department. Besides Carson City, the system has other centers in Dayton, Minden, Gardnerville, Tahoe, and throughout Northern Nevada and California.

Other nearby hospitals include Saint Mary's Regional Medical Center in Reno; Renown Health, which operates a series of hospitals throughout Northern Nevada; and Nevada Health Centers Inc., which operates a community clinic in Carson City.

■ Recreation

Sightseeing

Carson City provides a number of historical sites and museums. The Governor's Mansion, a 1909 example of classic southern Colonial design, is on the 2.5-mile Kit

Carson Trail, a blue line painted on the sidewalk that takes visitors past a variety of historic sites. The route passes 60 historical homes, churches, and buildings featuring Victorian architecture. Also along the route are several museums. Visitors to the State Library and Archives Building can peruse its rich collection on Nevada history and view the original Nevada Constitution.

Historical homes that highlight the tour include the 1879 Bliss Mansion, a 15-room mansion with 7 marble fireplaces; the 1859 Foreman-Roberts House Museum, a Gothic revival structure that was moved to the city from its first site in Washoe City; and the 1876 Chartz House.

The silver-domed State Capitol, rebuilt during the 1970s, features portraits of Nevada governors, Nevada artifacts, and old Nevada Supreme Court and legislative chambers that are open to the public when not in use. The Federal Building, once the federal courthouse, a post office, and a state library, and now the Paul Laxalt State Office Building in honor of a popular Nevada politician, houses the state Tourism Commission.

The Nevada State Museum, inside the old Carson City Mint, has displays on the history of the area, an exhibit that illustrates the process of making coins, a realistic mock underground mine, and an exhibit showing bears, bobcats, and other animals native to the area. The Warren Engine Fire Museum displays a century's worth of fire-related memorabilia, including goggles, helmets, hose carts, and Currier & Ives prints of New York fires. The Children's Museum of Northern Nevada offers displays and activities for the younger set, such as hands-on exhibits and a walk-in kaleidoscope.

The Stewart Indian School Museum houses the Cassinelli arrowhead collection, traditional basketry, grinding rocks, Great Basin artifacts, and the Indian School collection, as well as a gift shop. The Dat So La Lee House features memorabilia of the famed Nevada basket weaver of the same name. Her original baskets, worth up to $250,000 each, remain on display at the Nevada State Museum and in other museums throughout the country.

Focusing on Nevada's rich railroad heritage, the Nevada State Railroad Museum's collection contains more than 60 pieces of rolling stock, including 6 steam locomotives and more than 50 passenger and freight cars, many of which once operated on the famous Virginia and Truckee line. The museum also contains an assortment of exhibits relating to railroading in Nevada.

A short drive from Carson City is Virginia City, site of the legendary Virginia City mining operation, which produced both gold and silver. Virginia City provides a glimpse into the days of the Old West. The booming mines there spurred the construction of quartz reduction mills along the Carson River and helped Carson City become a thriving commercial center beginning in the 1860s. Today's shops, saloons, museums, and rides on the Virginia & Truckee Railroad—which now reaches Carson City—are fun for visitors young and old. Major sites in Virginia City include the Comstock Fire Museum, with memorabilia from the Comstock Era; the mining and silver artifacts displayed at the MacKay Mansion; and the Territorial Enterprise, a newspaper office that gave famous writer Mark Twain his start in journalism.

Carson City draws visitors with its major gambling casinos, including Carson City Nugget, Slotworld, Silver Dollar Casino, Carson Horseshoe Club, Casino Fandango, Carson Station Casino, Carson Station Hotel-Casino, Cactus Jack's Casino, Comstock Casino, and Gold Dust West Casino Hotel.

Arts and Culture

The Brewery Arts Center Gallery, a showcase of the Nevada Artists Association, displays the works of many local artists. Western Nevada College's art galleries feature works by local and regional artists.

The Proscenium Players, Nevada's second-oldest year-round theater company, present dramas and comedies at the Children's Museum of Northern Nevada. Affiliated with Western Nevada College, the Western Nevada Musical Theatre Company stages plays and musicals on campus.

The Carson City Symphony presents five annual classical concerts. Residents also enjoy the music of the Carson Chamber Singers, who perform occasional concerts.

Festivals and Holidays

September calls for a trip to nearby Virginia City for the annual International Camel Races. Begun as a hoax, the event is now one of the most popular in the state. September has also been the time for the three-day Salsa y Salsas family celebration with food, entertainment, and dancing; in 2009, it was replaced by the Latino Cultural Fest. October's special events in Carson City include the Nevada Day Parade and four-day celebration, the La Ka Le'l Be Pow Wow, filled with arts, crafts, dancing, and the Ghost Walk tour of homes decorated for Halloween. The December holidays are ushered in by the Silver & Snowflake Festival of Lights, which includes caroling, and the Victorian Christmas Tour of houses on the Kit Carson Trail.

March features a traditional St. Patrick's Day parade. The Comstock Regional Chili Cook-Off takes place in Virginia City in May. June's big events are the Carson City Rendezvous, and the Stewart Indian Museum Powwow, as well as Taste of Downtown, which features a food tasting from the city's restaurants along with live music and dancing. The Kit Carson Rendezvous and Wagon Train event, also in June, features a mountain man encampment, trader's row, Indian pow wow, and mock gunfights, all in celebration of Nevada's history. Independence Day in July is hailed by a four-day celebration with the traditional fireworks and the Silver Dollar Car Classic, a street dance, and music concerts.

Sports for the Spectator

While no professional sports teams play in Carson City, nearby Reno offers viewing opportunities of several athletic programs. Reno is making a name for itself as the mountain golf capital of the world. Since 1999 the PGA Tour's Reno-Tahoe Open has taken place at Montreux Golf and Country Club in July, where some of the world's best professional golfers compete. A celebrity-packed golfing event, the American Century Celebrity Championship, is also held annually at Edgewood-Tahoe golf course in July. The country's largest bowling organizations, the American Bowling Congress (ABC), Women's International Bowling Congress (WIBC), Young American Bowling Alliance, and USA Bowling merged in 2005 to create the United States Bowling Congress (USBC), which holds tournaments at the National Bowling Stadium in Reno. Dubbed the "Taj Mahal of Tenpins" by the *Los Angeles Times*, the stadium draws thousands of bowlers to its high-technology facility on a regular basis.

The University of Nevada, Reno offers spectators the chance to cheer on Wolf Pack teams playing football, basketball, softball, volleyball, and other popular sports.

Sports for the Participant

Included within about 600 acres of city parks is Mills Park, which offers tennis courts, indoor and outdoor pools, a mini-golf course, and a children's one-mile train ride. The park is also the home of the Carson City Skateboard Park, which provides a skateboard area with platforms, ramps, and spectator seating. Centennial Park has several soccer and softball fields, tennis courts, a public golf course, and shady picnic sites. Residents and visitors can make use of the "Divine Nine" golf courses within the city limits. Horseback riding is also popular in the area, especially on the Mount Rose Wilderness trails. At the edge of town is an old hot springs where bathers can soak in a 100° F spring water pool, and make use of hot tubs, massage facilities, and an adjoining restaurant and motel.

Sports enthusiasts enjoy hunting for birds and big game such as elk, deer, antelope, and bighorn sheep. In addition, the city is only 45 minutes from several prime skiing areas at nearby Lake Tahoe.

Shopping and Dining

The once shabby block that houses the landmark St. Charles Hotel has been transformed into a delightful collection of shops and restaurants. Other major shopping areas include various downtown blocks, as well as Carson Mall, which includes small restaurants and non-commercial stores.

Diners in Carson City can choose from among more than 40 restaurants with American and ethnic cuisines,

including Basque, Asian, Southwestern, and Italian. Refurbished Victorian houses harbor quaint restaurants such as the French-inspired Adele's Restaurant near the town center.

Visitor Information: Carson City Convention & Visitors Bureau, 1900 S. Carson St., Carson City, NV 89701; telephone (775) 687-7410; toll-free (800) NEVADA-1; email cccvb@visitcarsoncity.com.

■ Convention Facilities

Carson City has a variety of meeting and convention facilities. The 31,020-square-foot Pony Express Pavilion can accommodate up to 3,000 people and offers table, theater, or bleacher-style seating. The Carson City Community Center's Bob Boldrick Theater can seat 803 people theater-style, and the Carson City Nugget has facilities of more than 7,600 square feet for banquets and meetings. The meeting room at the Carson City Plaza Hotel and Conference Center offers 4,000 square feet of event space, as well as an outstanding panoramic view of the city. Historic Brewery Arts Center offers its art gallery for smaller groups while its performance hall has space for up to 306 guests. Also at the center, the Maizie Harris Jesse Theater can seat up to 120 people, and the 1864 Grand Ballroom can hold up to 150 theater-style for banquets, meetings, and weddings.

Convention Information: Carson City Convention & Visitors Bureau, 1900 S. Carson St., Carson City, NV 89701; telephone (775) 687-7410; toll-free (800) NEVADA-1; email cccvb@visitcarsoncity.com.

■ Transportation

Approaching the City

The Carson City Airport does not provide commercial services, but Reno-Tahoe International Airport, just 30 miles to the north of Carson City, is served by seven major airlines and offers more than 100 flights daily to 15 non-stop destinations. Carson City is located at the intersection of U.S. Highway 395, which links cities from Canada to Mexico, and U.S. Highway 50, a direct route from west to east. Amtrak provides rail service to the Reno/Sparks area, 30 miles north of Carson City. The RTC Intercity provides express weekday intercity bus service among Carson City, Reno, North Douglas County, and the Reno/Tahoe International Airport. Greyhound bus lines offer daily service to Los Angeles, Sacramento, Las Vegas, Reno, and other destinations.

Traveling in the City

U.S. highways 395 and 50 serve as the main north–south and east–west highways, as well as the main streets in the city. The 9.7-mile Carson City Freeway project was adding access to Interstate 580 for residents and began in 2003, completing its first phase in 2006. The project completion date, originally expected to be in 2010, was pushed back to 2016. The city began operating its bus service, Jump Around Carson (JAC) in 2005, and a curb-to-curb service is available to residents.

■ Communications

Newspapers and Magazines

The *Nevada Appeal* is the daily newspaper and is the oldest paper in Nevada, first published in 1865. *Nevada Magazine*, a bimonthly that carries feature stories on events and people in the state, is also published in Carson City. Other locally published magazines include *Range Magazine*, a consumer magazine covering cowboys and people who work the land in the western United States.

Television and Radio

Carson City receives its television coverage from nearby Reno's network and public stations. The city has several AM and FM radio stations broadcasting religious, county, and oldies formats.

Media Information: *Nevada Appeal*, 580 Mallory Way, Carson City, NV 89702; telephone (775) 882-2515.

Carson City Online

Carson City Area Chamber of Commerce. Available www.carsoncitychamber.com

Carson City Convention & Visitors Bureau. Available www.visitcarsoncity.com

Carson City Office of Business Development. Available www.carson.org/index.aspx?page=2533

Carson City Library. Available www.carsoncitylibrary.org

Carson City home page. Available www.carson.org

Carson City School District. Available www.carsoncityschools.com

Nevada State Library and Archives. Available nsla.nevadaculture.org

BIBLIOGRAPHY

McLaughlin, Mark, *Sierra Stories: True Tales of Tahoe* (Carnelian Bay, CA: Mic Mac Publishers, 1997)

Rothman, Hal, *The Making of Modern Nevada* (Reno: University of Nevada Press, 2010)

Southerland, Cindy, *Cemeteries of Carson City and Carson Valley* (Charleston, SC: Arcadia Publishing, 2010)

Twain, Mark, *Roughing It* (Berkeley, CA: University of California Press, 1996)

Henderson

■ The City in Brief

Founded: 1941 (incorporated April 16, 1953)

Head Official: Mayor Andy A. Hafen (D) (since 2009; current term expires 2017)

City Population
> 1990: 62,942
> 2000: 175,381
> 2010: 257,729
> 2012 estimate: 265,688
> Percent change, 2000–2010: 47%
> U.S. rank in 2000: 118th (State rank: 2nd)
> U.S. rank in 2010: 73rd (State rank: 2nd)

Metropolitan Statistical Area Population
> 2000: 1,563,282
> 2010: 1,951,269
> 2012 estimate: 2,000,759
> Percent change, 2000–2010: 24.8%
> U.S. rank in 2000: 36th
> U.S. rank in 2010: 30th

Area: 80 square miles

Elevation: 1,940 feet above sea level

Average Annual Temperatures: 68.0° F

Average Annual Precipitation: 4.5 inches of rain

Major Economic Sectors: services, hospitality, retail, government, manufacturing, distribution

Unemployment Rate: 6.8% (2012)

Per Capita Income: $32,735

2012 FBI Crime Index Property: 5,295

Major Colleges and Universities: College of Southern Nevada; Nevada State College;, University of Nevada, Las Vegas

Daily Newspaper: *Las Vegas Review-Journal*

■ Introduction

Henderson was incorporated as a city during World War II. It had become known only 10 years prior when it began as the home of the Basic Magnesium Plant, which supplied U.S. forces with magnesium for munitions and airplane parts. The plant closed after the war ended, leaving many residents unemployed; quick thinking and creativity on the part of city leaders and developers brought success back to Henderson. An influx of money and new residents saved it from becoming a modern "ghost town." Henderson has crafted a quaint identity for itself, though it sits not far from the bustle of glamorous Las Vegas. Henderson's proximity to "Sin City" has helped establish the city as a major transportation hub, which in turn has attracted manufacturers. It has also helped Henderson support its own tourist industry, which includes several resorts and casinos.

■ Geography and Climate

Henderson sits at the southern rim of the Las Vegas Valley. At an elevation of 1,940 feet above sea level, the city is only seven miles southeast of Las Vegas and about midway between Las Vegas and Boulder City (home of the Hoover Dam). Residents and visitors enjoy warm weather, with an average temperature of just under 70 degrees most months of the year, low humidity, and very little rain. Winter snows are visible in the mountains, but snow is rare in the city.

Area: 80 square miles

ASSOCIATED PRESS

Elevation: 1,940 feet above sea level

Average Temperatures: 68.0° F

Average Annual Precipitation: 4.5 inches of rain

■ History

Spanish Move Through Area

Spanish explorers moved through Southern Nevada in the early 1800s, discovering and naming Las Vegas as a stop on their way to California. Mormon missionaries established a settlement and built a fort in 1855 in Las Vegas but didn't stay long. In the latter half of the century, Las Vegas, and with it the area that is now Henderson, was detached from Arizona territory to become part of Nevada. Small farming communities developed, but things were quiet in the area until construction on the Boulder Dam was begun in 1931, bringing thousands to the area for work.

A City Born Overnight

Southern Nevada had but a handful of residents in the early decades of the twentieth century. Henderson, quite

literally, was created almost overnight in 1941, as building began on a plant that was, at the time, a massive undertaking in the middle of desert land. Magnesium and its importance in munitions and to the brewing war were the key to the city's beginning.

In 1941 a Cleveland, Ohio manufacturer named Howard Eells and his newly formed Basic Magnesium Inc. (BMI) company signed a contract with the U.S. Defense Plant Corp. to build the Basic Magnesium Plant. Only days after signing, the government asked Eells to expand the planned site to 10 times its original size, making it 1.75 miles long and .75 miles wide, the largest such magnesium plant in the world. More than 13,000 workers—10 percent of the entire state's population at the time—lived in ramshackle housing or "tent cities" until construction began on a company town in 1942. Under scrutiny for attempting to profit from the war, Eells sold BMI to Anaconda Copper Mining Co. that year. Anaconda was charged with finishing the plant, and the burgeoning city was named not after Eells, but for former senator Charles P. Henderson for his role in helping to get the plant financed and built.

For the next few years, BMI exceeded its planned production rates and employees numbered 14,000 at peak production. However, by 1947 magnesium was no longer needed for defense; the plant closed, and more than half of the employees left. Almost as quickly as the city was built, it all but disappeared. Henderson stood in danger of becoming a ghost town, and in 1947 the U.S. War Asset Administration offered the entire city for sale as war surplus property. In a brochure created to help sell the city, a description was provided that outlined the housing, streets, alleys, sanitary systems, schools, general buildings, shops, churches, and other city amenities.

Last Ditch Effort Saves City

In an effort to save Henderson, the Chamber of Commerce convinced the Las Vegas Chamber of Commerce to issue an invitation to the entire Nevada Legislature to come visit Boulder Dam (now Hoover Dam). They were asked to evaluate the Basic Magnesium site and explore the possibility of construction of a power generator at the dam, which would bring new workers and provide work for those Henderson residents that remained. The plan worked—a bill was unanimously approved, giving the Colorado River Commission of Nevada authority to purchase the plant. By 1953 signs of improvement were well underway and the city was officially incorporated, with a population of 7,410 residents.

Modern Henderson Emerges

Throughout the 1960s and 1970s, Henderson remained a relatively small factory town. In the early 1980s, the first master planned community, Green Valley, was plotted. Henderson's population in 1980 was 24,363; by 1990 it had more than doubled, and by 1999 Henderson overtook Reno as Nevada's second largest city. The U.S. Census Bureau identified Henderson as the fastest-growing city in the nation from 1990 to 1998. In the early 2000s, Henderson celebrated its 50th birthday at a time when the city's growth showed little signs of slowing. Indeed, the city grew by another 47 percent between 2000 and 2010, reaching more than 250,000 residents.

A national recession in the late 2000s dampened the economy Between September 2007 and 2009, Clark County lost nearly 70,000 jobs. Population growth also slowed and the city's industrial and retail vacancy rate rose. Stability returned in the early 2010s, with the city's casinos, manufacturing, and distribution anchoring the local economy. In addition to attracting new businesses, city planners concentrated on the continued development of the Water Street District in downtown Henderson, hoping to establish it more firmly as the city's thriving urban core.

Historical Information: Nevada State Museum, 309 S. Valley View Blvd., Las Vegas, NV 89107; telephone (702) 486-5205.

■ Population Profile

Metropolitan Statistical Area Population

2000: 1,563,282
2010: 1,951,269
2012 estimate: 2,000,759
Percent change, 2000–2010: 24.8%
U.S. rank in 2000: 36th
U.S. rank in 2010: 30th

City Residents

1990: 62,942
2000: 175,381
2010: 257,729
2012 estimate: 265,688
Percent change, 2000–2010: 47%
U.S. rank in 2000: 118th (State rank: 2nd)
U.S. rank in 2010: 73rd (State rank: 2nd)

Density: 2,392.3 people per square mile

Racial and ethnic characteristics

White: 212,809
Black or African American: 14,575
American Indian and Alaskan Native: 1,057
Asian: 19,577
Native Hawaiian and Other Pacific Islander: 301
Hispanic or Latino (may be of any race): 39,033
Other: 17,369

Percent of residents born in state: 21.3%

Age characteristics

Population under 5 years old: 14,339
Population 5 to 9 years old: 15,839
Population 10 to 14 years old: 16,049
Population 15 to 19 years old: 15,332
Population 20 to 24 years old: 17,539
Population 25 to 34 years old: 32,594
Population 35 to 44 years old: 35,695
Population 45 to 54 years old: 39,557
Population 55 to 59 years old: 16,690
Population 60 to 64 years old: 17,642
Population 65 to 74 years old: 27,071
Population 75 to 84 years old: 13,523
Population 85 years and over: 3,818
Median age: 41.4

Births (2010–11 Metropolitan Area)

Total number: 27,563

Deaths (2010–11 Metropolitan Area)

Total number: 13,168

Money income (2012)

Per capita income: $32,735
Median household income: $62,720
Total households: 98,623

Number of households with income of ...

less than $10,000: 4,648
$10,000 to $14,999: 3,301
$15,000 to $24,999: 7,668
$25,000 to $34,999: 9,270
$35,000 to $49,999: 13,784
$50,000 to $74,999: 20,319
$75,000 to $99,999: 12,540
$100,000 to $149,999: 15,938
$150,000 to $199,999: 5,678
$200,000 or more: 5,477

Percent of families below poverty level: 10.3%

FBI Crime Index Property: 5,295

FBI Crime Index Violent: 445

■ Municipal Government

The city of Henderson received its charter only relatively recently, in 1953. The city operates under a council-manager form of government, with the mayor and city council having legislative power; the city manager is charged with executive duties and general administration of the city. The mayor and four city councilmen are elected at large on a nonpartisan basis, and councilmen each must be from one of the city's four wards. Elections are held on each odd-numbered year; the mayor is elected every four years. Majority vote by the mayor and city council decides all issues, including land use, business licensing, city ordinances, and city fund expenditures.

Head Official: Mayor Andy A. Hafen (D) (since 2009; current term expires 2017)

Total Number of City Employees: 3007 (2013)

City Information: City Hall, 240 Water St., Henderson, NV 89015; telephone (702) 267-2323.

■ Economy

Major Industries and Commercial Activity

For most of Henderson's short history, the city has been a manufacturing center. Though its beginnings were fast and furious as a magnesium producer for World War II efforts, Henderson's economy today has diversified. Still, the city is a manufacturing center and a producer of metals and industrial chemicals, aided by its proximity to major markets throughout the West that expedites distribution. Nevada's comparatively low tax burden also encourages distribution companies serving the West Coast to locate in Nevada. Major manufacturers and distributors in Henderson include Levi Strauss & Co., Webgistix, Vadatech, Ethel M. Chocolates, Good

Humor-Breyers, TH Foods Inc., Ocean Spray Cranberries, EMT West, Southwest Steel, Graham Packaging, and Specialty Vehicles.

Due in part to Henderson's proximity to Las Vegas, it goes without saying that a large portion of economic gain stems from the tourism and services industry. A growing population of retirees has helped to spur growth in health care. The military maintains a presence near Henderson; Nellis Air Force Base, located about 20 miles northeast of the city of Henderson, employs 5,000 civilian and military personnel.

The city has endured the departure of some companies and jobs from the immediate area in recent years, including online retailer Zappos, which had been headquartered in Henderson, but moved into new headquarters in downtown Las Vegas in 2013. Companies with back-office operations in Henderson include Toyota Financial Savings Bank, FirstComp Insurance, USCB, Burke Williams Spa, Credit Acceptance Corp., Amica Insurance, Promo Direct, and Vegas.com.

Items and goods produced: baked goods, clothing, food products, metal and chemical products

Incentive Programs—New and Existing Companies

Local programs: The City of Henderson can offer partial exemption from public utilities license or franchise fees for gas or electricity; businesses must meet stringent requirements to take advantage of this program. The city's department of economic development staff, along with community resource partners, work together to provide relocating or expanding businesses with needed resources. The city's Redevelopment Agency, as part of the Downtown Investment Strategy plan, offers development incentives via grants, low-interest loans, and other financing to businesses for building improvements, equipment, start-up capital, and other expenses; one of the most successful programs is the Facade Improvement Program. The agency is responsible for five development areas in the city, including downtown.

State programs: The state of Nevada has no personal state income tax, no unitary tax, no corporate income tax, no inventory tax, no estate and/or gift tax, no franchise tax, no inheritance tax, and no special intangible tax. Nevada is a Right to Work state, in which employees can choose to affiliate with or join labor unions; railway and airline employees, however, are not included in the law. The state also guarantees Small Business Administration loans.

Tax abatements include a Sales and Use Tax Abatement, available on qualifying capital projects with reductions to as little as 2 percent; Modified Business Abatement of 50 percent of the 1.17 percent rate levied on quarterly wages above $85,000; Personal Property

Abatement of up to 50 percent for 10 years; and Real Property Tax Abatement for Recycling, also up to 50 percent for 10 years.

The Nevada State Development Corporation (NSDC) provides loan financing for growth opportunities such as buying, building, or improving commercial real estate for new and existing businesses. The Nevada Microenterprise Initiative helps provide economic self-sufficiency for entrepreneurs through training, technical assistance, and access to credit. Loans can be used for start-up costs, equipment, inventory, supplies, working capital, fixtures and other furniture.

Job training programs: Nevada's "Train Employees Now" (TEN) program has customized short-term, industrial training programs to assist new and expanding businesses in training new or potential employees. Eligible businesses must contribute at least 25 percent of the total training costs, and must have at least 10 employees to train. The Silver State Works Employee Hiring Incentive offers employers up to $2,000 for each state-qualified employee hired.

Working to ensure that companies have an adequate workforce is Job Opportunities in Nevada (JOIN), which offers training and educational opportunities for job seekers; Nevadaworks assists employers in developing employee skills. Nevada Industry Excellence is an industrial outreach program affiliated with local community colleges and is dedicated to training employees to meet the hiring goals of specific companies.

The Airman and Family Readiness Center at Nellis Air Force Base offers job information and employer connections to spouses and family members of base personnel. A variety of programs exist through the area's educational institutions, including the College of Southern Nevada, which makes job training an explicitly stated part of its educational goals.

Development Projects

The Henderson Redevelopment Agency was created in 1985 and utilizes tax increment financing funds for projects in five designated areas of Henderson: Cornerstone, Downtown, Eastside, Lakemoor Canyon, and Tuscany. Finalization of a master plan for downtown was underway in 2014, with the central goal of making the Water Street district the city's main street. A key objective was connectivity between residential neighborhoods and the Water Street core, with new developments anticipated to create high quality public areas, accessible open space, and a variety of mixed-use projects.

In 2013 FedEx Ground construction a new 296,000-square-foot distribution facility in Henderson, which opened in 2014. The $50 million center was expected to provide as many as 300 additional jobs; some 200 employees were already working at a prior facility, also located in Henderson. In other private developments, Vadatech completed a new 70,000-square-foot

research and manufacturing facility in 2013 at a cost of $11.6 million. Cadence, a master-planned community that began construction in 2013, was expected to add as many as 1,100 homes. Brock Racing, Bluepoint Solutions, and Creative Tent all relocated to Henderson in 2012.

The Henderson Space and Science Center, an estimated $55 million project, was in the process of trying to raise $30 between 2011 an 2016. Funding from the city government remained uncertain, with setbacks to initial proposals endured in 2012. A proposal to build a multi-billion-dollar Las Vegas National Sports Complex—located in Henderson—collapsed in 2013 following city allegations of fraud against the developer.

A $1.6 billion Union Village health-care complex was expected to begin construction in 2015, with completion anticipated by 2022.

Economic Development Information: City of Henderson Economic Development, 280 S. Water St., City Hall Annex, Henderson, NV 89015; telephone (702) 267-1650.

Commercial Shipping

Southern Clark County is the hub of an extensive transportation network serviced by three highway corridors: Interstate 15, U.S. Highway 95, and U.S. Highway 93. More than 50 motor freight carriers serve the area. In addition, a variety of warehousing and support services are available in Clark County, including foreign trade zone accommodations, packaging support, and U.S. customs service. McCarran International Airport in Las Vegas handled in excess of 185 million pounds of arriving and departing cargo in 2013. Additionally, the McCarran International Air Cargo Center offers cargo storage and handling and operates in a designated Foreign Trade Zone (FTZ). Union Pacific Railroad runs northeast–southwest through Clark County, linking the area to markets in most states.

Labor Force and Employment Outlook

The array of vocational and technical trade schools, higher education institutions, and opportunities for customized training programs in the Henderson area enhance both business and employment prospects. Most of the labor force works in the arts, entertainment, recreation, and accommodation and foods services. Continued population growth—projected to reach nearly 400,000 by 2025—offered employers a steady stream of new workers. An estimated 31 percent of Henderson residents held at least a bachelor's degree, and more than 92 percent graduated from high school, rates that outpaced those of surrounding cities, such as Las Vegas.

The following is a summary of data regarding the 2012 Henderson labor force:

Size of civilian labor force: 136,444

Number of workers employed in ...

agriculture and mining: 264
construction: 6,693
manufacturing: 4,736
wholesale trade: 2,178
retail trade: 16,191
transportation: 5,840
information systems: 2,176
finance: 9,203
professional administration: 13,966
education and social services: 20,614
arts and leisure: 27,752
other: 5,520
public administration: 5,908

Average hourly earnings of production workers: $15.72

Unemployment rate: 6.8% (2012)

Employers

Largest employers (2013)	*Number of employees*
City of Henderson	3,007
St. Rose Dominican Hospital-Siena	1,500–1,999
Green Valley Ranch Station Casino	1,500–1,999
M Resort Spa and Casino	1,000–1,499
Sunset Station Hotel and Casino	1,000–1,499
St. Rose Dominican Hospital	700–799
Fiesta Henderson Casino Hotel	600–699
Zappos CLT Inc	600–699
Medico Health LLC	500–599
Titanium Metals Corp. of America	500–599

Cost of Living

Henderson's cost of living is equal to the national average. Within Nevada, Henderson residents pay one of the lowest base property tax rates.

The following is a summary of data regarding several key cost of living factors in the area.

2013 ACCRA Average House Price: $302,448

2013 ACCRA Cost of Living Index: 100

State income tax rate: None

State sales tax rate: 6.85%

Local income tax rate: None

Local sales tax rate: 1.25%

Property tax rate: $2.8968 per $100 assessed value (2013)

Economic Information: City of Henderson Economic Development, 280 S. Water St., City Hall Annex, Henderson, NV 89015; telephone (702) 267-1650.

■ Education and Research

Elementary and Secondary Schools

The Clark County School District serves more than 314,000 students in all of Clark County—a 7,910 square mile section of Nevada—which includes the city of Henderson and encompasses nearly three-quarters of all students in the state. The large system is divided into 15 performance zones. Hispanics comprise the single largest group of students, accounting for 44 percent of all students. A variety of magnet schools exist throughout the district, in addition to English as a Second Language programs, Gifted and Talented Education (GATE), adult education, and special education services. The school district is among the region's largest employers, with more than 39,000 people on its payroll.

The following is a summary of data regarding the Clark County School District.

Total enrollment: 314,059

Number of facilities

total: 357
elementary schools: 217
junior high schools: 59
high schools: 49
other: 32

Student/teacher ratio: 20.6:1

Teacher salaries

average (statewide): $53,023

Funding per pupil: $8,270

Public Schools Information: Clark County School District, 5100 W. Sahara Ave., Las Vegas, NV 89146; telephone (702) 799-5000.

Colleges and Universities

Henderson offers residents several major institutions of higher learning. The College of Southern Nevada (CSN) system, with a campus in Henderson, educates more than 43,000 students. It operates in three main campuses and also supports seven other learning centers. CSN's most popular degree programs include associate degrees in arts, business, nursing, general studies, science, education, psychology, criminal justice, hospitality management, and computer information technology. Twenty-eight degree programs are entirely accessible online. The Nevada State College at Henderson was founded in 2002, and places a particular focus on training in the nursing and healthcare industries.

The University of Nevada, Las Vegas (UNLV) in nearby Las Vegas enrolls nearly 28,000 students and supports a total staff of nearly 3,000. Colleges include those for business, education, engineering, fine arts, health sciences, hotel administration, liberal arts, sciences, and urban affairs, in addition to a graduate college and professional schools in dental medicine and law. The University of Nevada School of Medicine is located in Las Vegas. Also in Las Vegas, the International Academy of Design & Technology offers two- and four-year programs in Fashion Design, Interior Design, and Visual Communications.

Libraries and Research Centers

Henderson Libraries operate four main facilities in the city. The system had a circulation of more than 1.7 million items in 2012, with usage of electronic resources above 250,000. The Paseo Verde Library houses a Genealogy Collection, a Government Documents Collection, library administrative offices, and a Friends of Henderson Libraries Bookstore and Coffee Shop. Friends of the Henderson Libraries actively advocates for increased private donations, since population growth has far outpaced growth of the library system. The library within the Heritage Park Senior Facility opened in 2009 and is the system's newest development.

The Las Vegas-Clark County Library District serves all of Clark County with 25 branches and a comprehensive resource of informational materials. The district's Green Valley branch resides in Henderson. Its holdings include special collections on African-American history, Asian history, health and medicine, international language, gaming/local history, grants, government Documents, and patents. Total circulation in the Las Vegas-Clark County Library District was 14.4 million in 2012–13. The College of Southern Nevada library system, as well as the University of Nevada, Las Vegas libraries, are also available for public use.

The Desert Research Institute's (DRI) main research campus in Las Vegas carries out more than 300 scientific research projects at any given time. It is a stand-alone institution that falls under the umbrella of the Nevada System of Higher Education (NSHE), thanks to generous outside research funding. The institute generates $50 million in annual revenue. Environmental research programs focus on three core divisions of atmospheric sciences, earth and ecosystems sciences, and hydrologic sciences. DRI maintains a library that is available to researchers and scholars. A variety of other specialized libraries and research centers are located in the area.

Public Library Information: Henderson District Public Libraries, Paseo Verde Library, 280 S. Green Valley Parkway, Henderson, NV 89012; telephone (702) 492-7252.

■ Health Care

St. Rose Dominican Hospitals operates three medical campuses, with the Rose de Lima Campus and the Siena Campus both in Henderson. The third facility, the San Martín Campus in Las Vegas, opened in 2006. Rose de Lima, with 119 acute-care and 28 rehabilitation beds, offers emergency and surgical services, rehabilitation, obstetrical services, community outreach, and kidney stone treatment services, among others. Siena opened in 2000 and is a 230-bed acute-care facility with pediatrics services, neurosurgery, an open-heart surgery center, emergency department, obstetrics and surgical services, diagnostic imaging, and others. The hospital system also operates two WomensCare centers, one in Las Vegas and one in Henderson, which offer treatment and guidance on health and wellness to area women. A variety of hospitals and clinics exist in nearby Las Vegas. A $1.6 billion Union Village health-care complex was expected to begin construction in 2015, to be completed by 2022.

■ Recreation

Sightseeing

Less than 20 miles southeast of Henderson is the Hoover Dam. A National Historic Landmark, and recognized as one of America's Seven Modern Civil Engineering Wonders by the American Society of Civil Engineers, the dam entertains more than a million visitors and tourgoers annually. Lake Mead National Recreation Area in nearby Boulder City offers opportunities for a leisurely afternoon outdoors or multi-day, multi-activity trips, and dinner or dinner-and-dance cruises are available on a Mississippi-style paddlewheeler.

Ghost towns of the Old West are popular tourist destinations; several exist within an hour's drive of the city. Ethel M. Chocolates, a mainstay in Henderson though originating in Tacoma, Washington, offers tours of the chocolate factory (samples included) and the botanical cactus gardens on its grounds.

Henderson's Veterans Memorial Wall on Water Street honors not only those who have fought for their country, but those who played a part in Henderson's heritage. The wall was dedicated in 2004 and is inscribed with more than 1,500 names.

Arts and Culture

The Clark County Historical Museum tells the story of southern Nevada in a variety of exhibits, including prehistoric dioramas, Native American collections, a walk-in mine, and a pueblo. Heritage Street, an outdoor exhibit of the museum, offers a look at the structures and homes of the early 1900s, including a replicated newspaper print shop, historic homes, and the 1932 Boulder City Depot. The Howard W. Cannon Aviation Museum at the airport tells of the history of aviation in the region.

The Arts Council of Henderson, a nonprofit group, works to bring arts programming to Henderson residents. One of the Council's ventures is Henderson's annual Shakespeare in the Park, presented in cooperation with the city government, American Nevada Corporation, and the Clark County School District. Shakespeare in the Park, which celebrated its twenty-fifth anniversary in 2011, presents one play per season over one October weekend, with a performance each day. An Elizabethan Festival precedes each daily performance. Theatre in the Valley presents community theater in a season of four to five shows per year. The Henderson Symphony Orchestra performs at the Henderson Pavilion, Henderson Events Plaza, and Henderson Convention Center.

Festivals and Holidays

The St. Patrick's Day Parade and Block Party, which celebrated 45 years in 2011, takes place each March in downtown Henderson. For nearly a week in late March or early April the FLW Outdoors EverStart Series offers fishing competition action at Lake Mead. ArtFest happens over Mother's Day weekend in May in downtown Henderson's Water Street district, featuring more than 100 artists, music, food, and fun kids' events. Fourth of July events and fireworks happen citywide. September features the Super Run Car Show, with car cruises and drag racing, concerts, and food at Water Street and various locations throughout the city. In early October at the Lake Las Vegas Resort, crews compete in the Rose Regatta Dragon Boat Race and Festival. The Nevada Silverman, an iron-distance triathlon event in November, offers spectators and participants views of the Lake Mead National Recreation Area.

Sports for the Spectator

While no sports teams reside in the city of Henderson, nearby Las Vegas offers enthusiasts many opportunities to cheer for their favorite sports. The Las Vegas 51s, a Triple-A affiliate of the New York Mets, play minor league baseball at Cashman Field in Las Vegas. The Las Vegas Wranglers, members of the ECHL, play hockey at the Orleans Arena. The University of Las Vegas Rebels' most popular sports include basketball, football, baseball, and soccer. The Las Vegas Motor Speedway offers NASCAR and other motor sports events. High-profile boxing matches are often scheduled in Las Vegas. The Las Vegas Stallions FC, established in 2010, play in the National Premier Soccer League.

Sports for the Participant

Henderson and nearby areas are an outdoor lover's paradise. The city of Henderson offers visitors more than 1,200 acres of outdoor opportunities in 56 developed parks. Among Henderson's outdoor amenities in the park system and beyond are 11 pools, 93 athletic fields, 53 tennis courts, 6 recreation centers, more than 80 miles of trails, and many golf courses. The city of Henderson's bird viewing preserve is a 147-acre migratory bird and wetland area featuring basins, ponds, and lagoons; signs, kiosks and nature trails guide visitors.

The Lake Mead National Recreation Area consists of a man-made lake in a massive crater created during the building of the Hoover Dam, offering opportunities for boating, swimming, kayaking, hiking, horseback riding, and fishing. Bootleg Canyon, in nearby Boulder City, is heralded as one of the best mountain biking spots in the United States and offers more than 20 miles of challenging terrain. Red Rock Canyon, a 197,000-acre National Conservation Area, presents a variety of outdoor opportunities, including hiking and biking trails, rock climbing, a visitor's center with interpretive programs, and Spring Mountain State Park.

Shopping and Dining

The Galleria at Sunset mall, which was the first enclosed mall in the city, is anchored by Dillard's, JCPenney, and Macy's, and has two levels with fountains, skylights, and desert flowers in its indoor landscaping. The District at Green Valley Ranch, part residential development and part stylish shopping mecca, offers a "main street" shopping experience for its loft residents and visitors alike, with more than 40 upscale shops and restaurants on the development's street level. Shoppers looking for bargains can head to the Las Vegas Outlet Center, featuring more than 130 outlet shops. Shoppers in Henderson's Water Street District area will find a variety of unique shops, boutiques, galleries, and restaurants. The Country Fresh Farmers Market operates throughout the year on Thursdays in the Water Street District.

Henderson's variety of restaurants satisfy urges for area favorites like steak and Mexican food; other tastes tempted include French, Chinese, Italian, Japanese, Greek, and Thai.

Visitor Information: City of Henderson Department of Cultural Arts and Tourism, 200 Water St., Henderson, NV 89015; telephone (702) 267-2171; fax (702) 267-2177.

■ Convention Facilities

The Henderson Convention Center offers more than 10,000 feet of meeting space, and can accommodate wedding receptions, corporate and civic functions, class and family reunions, dances, and charity events. The

Hilton Lake Las Vegas Resort and Spa is located in the new resort development area of Lake Las Vegas in Henderson, offering a grand ballroom with 11,800 square feet and more than a dozen other flexible meeting spaces, ranging from 500 to nearly 8,000 square feet. Other hotels with convention facilities in Henderson include the Fiesta-Henderson Hotel Casino, Green Valley Ranch Resort, Westin Lake Las Vegas Resort, Wingate by Wyndham Henderson, and Sunset Station Hotel and Casino.

Convention Information: City of Henderson Department of Cultural Arts and Tourism, 200 Water St., Henderson, NV 89015; telephone (702) 267-2171; fax (702) 267-2177.

■ Transportation

Approaching the City

McCarran International Airport serves Henderson, Las Vegas, and all of Clark County and southern Nevada. In 2005 the airport completed a $125 million expansion, consisting of a new gate wing that allows the airport to handle an additional 3.1 million passengers annually. The 10th busiest airport in the United States and 16th busiest in the world in 2014, McCarran is served by more than 30 airlines and transported some 38.6 million passengers in 2013. The Henderson Executive Airport accommodates private and general aviation aircraft.

Four major highways bring travelers into and out of Henderson: Interstate 15, U.S. Highway 93/95, U.S. Highway 146, and the Southern Nevada Beltway (Interstate 215). North–south Interstate 15 links travelers west to California and east to the East Coast via Interstates 80, 70, and 40.

Amtrak Thruway provides bus service between Los Angeles, California, and Las Vegas. Greyhound provides bus service to and from nearby Las Vegas with connections throughout the west; in 2005 an additional stop was added in Henderson.

Traveling in the City

Major roads within the city include East Lake Mead Parkway (State Highway 564), which runs east–west, and North Boulder Highway (State Highway 582), which runs north–south. The city continues to work to make Water Street the city's "main street." The Regional Transportation Commission of Southern Nevada (RTC) serves the greater Las Vegas Valley region, transporting 60 million passengers on 42 routes annually. RTC also provides paratransit services to riders with disabilities.

■ Communications

Newspapers and Magazines

Henderson residents are served by the daily *Las Vegas Review-Journal*, the alternative *Las Vegas Weekly, Las Vegas Magazine*, which covers local entertainment, and a variety of other publications coming from Las Vegas.

Television and Radio

Henderson's one commercial television station is a Fox network; the area is served by Las Vegas's more than two-dozen television stations. One AM and seven FM radio stations broadcast from Henderson proper, although residents enjoy many more programming options from Las Vegas–based broadcasts.

Media Information: Las Vegas Review-Journal, 1111 W. Bonanza Road, P.O. Box 70, Las Vegas, NV 89125; telephone (702) 383-0211.

Henderson Online

Center for Business and Economic Research at the University of Nevada, Las Vegas. Available cber.unlv.edu

City of Henderson. Available www.cityofhenderson.com

Clark County School District. Available ccsd.net

Henderson Means Business. Available hendersonmeansbusiness.com

Henderson Nevada Chamber of Commerce. Available www.hendersonchamber.com

Las Vegas-Clark County Library District. Available www.lvccld.org

Las Vegas Review-Journal. Available www.reviewjournal.com

Nevada Division of Museums and History. Available museums.nevadaculture.org

Nevada Department of Tourism and Cultural Affairs. Available nevadaculture.org

BIBLIOGRAPHY

Bowers, Michael W., *The Sagebrush State: Nevada's History, Government, and Politics* (Reno, NV: University of Nevada Press, 2002)

City of Henderson, ed., *An American Journey: Henderson, 50 Years* (Henderson, NV: City of Henderson, 2004)

Hulse, James W., *The Silver State: Nevada's Heritage Reinterpreted* (Reno, NV: University of Nevada Press, 2004)

Rothman, Hal, *The Making of Modern Nevada* (Reno: University of Nevada Press, 2010)

Las Vegas

■ The City in Brief

Founded: 1905 (incorporated, 1911)

Head Official: Mayor Carolyn G. Goodman (since 2011; current term expires 2015)

City Population
> 1990: 258,877
> 2000: 478,434
> 2010: 583,756
> 2012 estimate: 596,440
> Percent change, 2000–2010: 22%
> U.S. rank in 1990: 63rd
> U.S. rank in 2000: 39th (State rank: 1st)
> U.S. rank in 2010: 30th (State rank: 1st)

Metropolitan Statistical Area Population
> 2000: 1,563,282
> 2010: 1,951,269
> 2012 estimate: 2,000,759
> Percent change, 2000–2010: 24.8%
> U.S. rank in 2000: 36th
> U.S. rank in 2010: 30th

Area: 113 square miles

Elevation: 2,180 feet above sea level

Average Annual Temperatures: January, 47.0° F; July, 91.2° F; annual average, 68.1° F

Average Annual Precipitation: 4.49 inches of rain; 1.2 inches of snow

Major Economic Sectors: gaming, tourism, mining, retailing, warehousing

Unemployment Rate: 8.4% (2012)

Per Capita Income: $24,899

2012 FBI Crime Index Property: 46,427

Major Colleges and Universities: University of Nevada, Las Vegas, College of Southern Nevada, Nevada State College

Daily Newspaper: *Las Vegas Review Journal*

■ Introduction

Las Vegas, also known as the "Entertainment Capital of the World," is unique among the nation's cities. Famous for lavish casinos and first-class entertainment, the city has over the years become synonymous with glitz and glamour. The non-stop recreation found on the "Strip" attracts tens of millions of visitors per year. Following a national recession in the late 2000s that decimated the local economy, Las Vegas focused on growth of other industries, especially high-technology ventures. Development projects continued to dot the landscape in the 2010s, and while the largest construction sites were tied to the ever-important gaming industry, developments by bioscience companies and online retailers showcased the successful efforts of the city to attract businesses from emerging industries.

■ Geography and Climate

Las Vegas is located in the center of Vegas Valley, a desert region of about 600 square miles, which is surrounded by the Sierra Nevada Mountains and the Spring Mountains. The seasons are hot, windy, and dry, with desert conditions and maximum temperatures of 100° F during the summer; because of the mountains, however, summer nights are cool. Winters are mild. The mountains around Las Vegas reach elevations of more than 10,000 feet, acting as barriers to moisture from the Pacific Ocean. Rainfall is minimal and there are approximately 215 clear days during the year. Snowfall is rare.

Area: 113 square miles

Sportstock/Getty Images

Elevation: 2,180 feet above sea level

Average Temperatures: January, 47.0° F; July, 91.2° F; annual average, 68.1° F

Average Annual Precipitation: 4.49 inches of rain; 1.2 inches of snow

■ History

Forts Built; Farmers Settle; Hoover Dam Built

Las Vegas was discovered by Spanish explorers, who gave the site its name-meaning "meadows"-because of the verdant grassland fed by natural aquifers. Las Vegas served as a watering place on the Spanish trail to California. In 1855 Mormon missionaries established a settlement, cultivating the land and building a fort to provide protection to travelers on the Salt Lake-Los Angeles Trail. They abandoned the place two years later when the enterprise became unprofitable, but their fort is still standing and is the oldest historical site in Las Vegas. In 1864 Fort Baker, a U.S. Army post, was built nearby; in 1867 Las Vegas was detached from the Arizona territory and became part of the Nevada territory.

Around that time Las Vegas began to expand as a series of farmers cultivated the land. The area encompassed 1,800 acres when it was sold to William Clark, a Montana senator. In 1905 Clark auctioned off parcels of land for the building of the Union Pacific Railroad link between Salt Lake City and Los Angeles. The town was incorporated in 1911. Construction on the Hoover Dam-originally the Boulder Dam-on the Colorado River was begun in 1931, bringing to the area thousands of men seeking employment. The 70-story dam, which is regarded as one of the wonders of the modern world, still supplies affordable power to parts of California, Arizona, and Nevada.

Gaming, Lenient Laws, Climate Attract Visitors, Settlers

Another significant event occurred in 1931: the legalization of casino gambling in Nevada. The gaming and entertainment industries boomed in Las Vegas after World War II. A street lined with large, glittering casino hotels came to be known as the "Strip"; downtown, in Casino Center, lavish palaces featured the country's top entertainers. By the 1950s Las Vegas, dubbed the "Entertainment Capital of the World," had become synonymous with the unique form of recreation it had created. Because of lenient state laws, Las Vegas also became popular as a wedding site; eventually wedding chapels were operating around the clock, and each year thousands of couples were coming to the city to be married.

Since the 1930s Las Vegas's population has steadily increased, jumping from slightly fewer than 8,500 people in 1940 to nearly 25,000 people in 1950. By 1960 almost 65,000 people lived in Las Vegas, and in 1980 the census figure was 164,674 people. Between 1980 and 1990 there was a more than 60 percent increase, or a total of 278,000 people. Newcomers, primarily from California, were attracted by the favorable climate, the high standard of living, low tax rate, and jobs produced by a boom in business and the entertainment and gaming industries. In the 1990s an average of 6,000 to 7,000 people moved into Clark County each month; in the mid 2000s, a quick rate of growth appeared to be a permanent fixture, but a national recession in the late 2000s slowed both economic and population growth.

In the immediate wake of the aforementioned recession, some development projects were abandoned due to bankruptcies, funding deficits, or loss of profit potential. The city government cut its budget in order to remain solvent, and job losses mounted. However, moderate economic and population growth returned in the 2010s. Importantly, new economic growth was not tied solely to the gaming, entertainment, and tourism ventures, but also included bioscience and other high-technology industries. Emerging industries were not about to displace the central role of business on the Strip, but they offered a path for the city to insulate itself against future economic uncertainty.

Historical Information: Nevada State Museum, 309 S. Valley View Blvd., Las Vegas, NV 89107; telephone (702) 486-5205.

■ Population Profile

Metropolitan Statistical Area Population

2000: 1,563,282
2010: 1,951,269
2012 estimate: 2,000,759
Percent change, 2000–2010: 24.8%
U.S. rank in 2000: 36th
U.S. rank in 2010: 30th

City Residents

1990: 258,877
2000: 478,434
2010: 583,756
2012 estimate: 596,440
Percent change, 2000–2010: 22%
U.S. rank in 1990: 63rd
U.S. rank in 2000: 39th (State rank: 1st)
U.S. rank in 2010: 30th (State rank: 1st)

Density: 4,298.2 people per square mile

Racial and ethnic characteristics

White: 400,931
Black or African American: 61,749
American Indian and Alaskan Native: 3,346
Asian: 36,402
Native Hawaiian and Other Pacific Islander: 2,099
Hispanic or Latino (may be of any race): 195,793
Other: 91,913

Percent of residents born in state: 24.1%

Age characteristics

Population under 5 years old: 38,588
Population 5 to 9 years old: 40,838
Population 10 to 14 years old: 40,236
Population 15 to 19 years old: 38,442
Population 20 to 24 years old: 41,081
Population 25 to 34 years old: 82,563
Population 35 to 44 years old: 84,543
Population 45 to 54 years old: 78,745
Population 55 to 59 years old: 38,431
Population 60 to 64 years old: 31,792
Population 65 to 74 years old: 47,774
Population 75 to 84 years old: 25,700
Population 85 years and over: 7,707
Median age: 37.1

Births (2010–11 Metropolitan Area)

Total number: 27,563

Deaths (2010–11 Metropolitan Area)

Total number: 13,168

Money income (2012)

Per capita income: $24,899
Median household income: $49,726
Total households: 210,927

Number of households with income of . . .

less than $10,000: 15,951
$10,000 to $14,999: 10,690
$15,000 to $24,999: 23,766
$25,000 to $34,999: 23,705
$35,000 to $49,999: 31,845
$50,000 to $74,999: 40,332
$75,000 to $99,999: 26,755
$100,000 to $149,999: 22,401
$150,000 to $199,999: 8,017
$200,000 or more: 7,465

Percent of families below poverty level: 17.7%

FBI Crime Index Property: 46,427

FBI Crime Index Violent: 11,598

■ Municipal Government

Las Vegas began as a "commission" form of government until 1944, when it became a council-manager form of government. Six council members and the mayor are elected to four-year terms. The city is divided into six ward areas, with one council member representing each ward.

Head Official: Mayor Carolyn G. Goodman (since 2011; current term expires 2015)

Total Number of City Employees: 3,000 (2012)

City Information: City of Las Vegas, City Hall, 495 S. Main Street, Las Vegas, NV 89101; telephone (702) 229-6011.

■ Economy

Major Industries and Commercial Activity

Tourism drives the economy in Las Vegas, with more than 42 million people visiting the city each year. The gaming Mecca includes four *Fortune* 500 companies: Las Vegas Sands, Caesars Entertainment, MGM Resorts International, and Wynn Resorts. The four gaming companies are also the only *Fortune* 500 companies in the state. Las Vegas also serves as a major convention center.

While the entertainment and service industries are the largest employers in Las Vegas, the major single employer is the Clark County School District. Other major employers, such as additional county personnel, the city's police department, and the University of Nevada, Las Vegas, are government-funded positions.

While the city's gleaming casinos are the most obvious signs of economic activity, Las Vegas has also developed other industries. Both Switch, a data and technology company, and Zappos, an online shoe retailer, have established headquarters in Las Vegas, and the InNEVation Center is a public-private partnership to further spur growth in the city's technology industry. Downtown Project also focuses on entrepreneurial creative and high-technology development in the heart of the city.

McCarron International Airport, a major aviation facility, supports manufacturing and distribution centers both in and around Las Vegas, which enjoys both proximity to and comparatively low operating costs from surrounding West Coast states. The rapid growth of the southern Nevada region has also supported growth in the health-care industry.

Nonetheless, Las Vegas's economy is still recovering from a national recession during the late 2000s. Nevada had the highest unemployment rate in the nation in late 2010, and a study by the Brookings Institution that year indicated that Las Vegas had the fifth worst economy in the world. Casino revenues dropped for 22 consecutive months. Las Vegas was also among cities leading the nation in foreclosures, with one out of every 60 households filing for foreclosure. The economy and housing market have since stabilized, and Nevada's push to attract and grow emerging industries speaks to its effort to diversify the local economy.

Items and goods produced: artisanal food products, crafts

Incentive Programs—New and Existing Companies

Local programs: To encourage industrial development, the Las Vegas business community works in cooperation with the state of Nevada to provide various incentives through minimal taxation, vocational training programs, no-cost site location services, special loan plans, and limited liability protection. The city is a foreign trade zone, making it an attractive foreign business destination. Las Vegas's Quick Start Program offers reimbursements of up to $50,000 for the rehabilitation of older buildings in Las Vegas Redevelopment Areas. The Visual Improvement Program, also specific to redevelopment areas, provides rebates for façade improvements or enhancements to bring existing facilities up to code. Tax Increment Financing is available for retail, hotel, mixed-use, and high-rise development projects in Las Vegas Redevelopment Areas.

State programs: The state of Nevada has no personal state income tax, no unitary tax, no corporate income tax, no inventory tax, no estate and/or gift tax, no franchise tax, no inheritance tax, and no special intangible tax. Nevada is a Right to Work state, in which employees can choose to affiliate with or join labor unions; railway and airline employees, however, are not included in the law. The state also guarantees Small Business Administration loans.

Tax abatements include a Sales and Use Tax Abatement, available on qualifying capital projects with reductions to as little as 2 percent; Modified Business Abatement of 50 percent of the 1.17 percent rate levied on quarterly wages above $85,000; Personal Property Abatement of up to 50 percent for 10 years; and Real Property Tax Abatement for Recycling, also up to 50 percent for 10 years.

The Nevada State Development Corporation (NSDC) provides loan financing for growth opportunities such as buying, building, or improving commercial real estate for new and existing businesses. The Nevada Microenterprise Initiative helps provide economic self-sufficiency for entrepreneurs through training, technical assistance, and access to credit. Loans can be used for start-up costs, equipment, inventory, supplies, working capital, fixtures and other furniture.

Job training programs: Nevada's "Train Employees Now" (TEN) program has customized short-term, industrial training programs to assist new and expanding businesses in training new or potential employees. Eligible businesses must contribute at least 25 percent of the total training costs, and must have at least 10 employees to train. The Silver State Works Employee Hiring Incentive offers employers up to $2,000 for each state-qualified employee hired.

Working to ensure that companies have an adequate workforce is Job Opportunities in Nevada (JOIN), which offers training and educational opportunities for job seekers; Nevadaworks assists employers in developing employee skills. Nevada Industry Excellence is an industrial outreach program affiliated with local community colleges and is dedicated to training employees to meet the hiring goals of specific companies.

The Airman and Family Readiness Center at Nellis Air Force Base offers job information and employer connections to spouses and family members of base personnel. A variety of programs exist through the area's educational institutions, including the College of Southern Nevada, which makes job training an explicitly stated part of its educational goals.

Development Projects

The 1990s saw major casino and resort developments in the area, with 18 new venues built in the last two years of the century alone, many themed after famous cities throughout the world. The race to build the most outrageous casino/resort in Las Vegas may be never-ending, but the area's more established resorts are quick to follow suit with expansions to match. A national recession in the late 2000s put many development projects on hold, or cancelled them entirely.

At any given time in Las Vegas, planned community developments are in various construction phases. The Octavius Tower, an $860 million, 668-room addition to Caesar's Palace, was delayed in 2009 but eventually completed in 2012. The proposed $4.8 billion Echelon, with 4,713 rooms divided among five towers; came to a halt in 2008, and its 87 acres were sold in 2013. Indicative of the value of land on the Las Vegas strip, the sale price of $350 million suggested a per-acre price of $4.02 million. A $2 billion development of the space by Malaysia-based Genting Group was set to complete in 2016 under the name Resorts World Las Vegas.

In 2007 work began on MGM Mirage's CityCenter Las Vegas, an $8.5 billion, 68-acre project on the Las Vegas Strip between Bellagio and Monte Carlo. It represents the largest privately financed building project in U.S. history. A national recession in the late 2000s threatened the project financially, but a deal with Dubai World secured financing to complete the project, although the Harmon Hotel—which suffered from construction defects—was eventually scrapped, although

plans to demolish the existing 26 floors were still on hold through 2013. CityCenter opened in 2009.

Major casino renovations included a $15 refurbishment of the former Fitzgerald's Casino into the new D Las Vegas Casino Hotel, and $100 million to transform the defunct Lady Luck casino into the Downtown Grand Hotel & Casino.

Not all development projects were casino-related. In 2010 MountainView Hospital, a part of Sunrise Health System, announced an expansion and renovation project to allow for better senior patient care. The expansion included construction of a 42,000-square-foot addition to the existing Emergency Room, and a 12-bed intensive care unit. Patient rooms were also to be updated. The project, which was estimated to cost $70 million, completed in 2013. In other medical developments, the Cleveland Clinic Foundation planned a $395 facility at Symphony Park to conduct research and provide medical treatment. Construction was expected to start in 2016 or 2017.

The $453 million Smith Center for the Performing Arts, $56 million Discovery Children's Museum, $1.9 million Neon Museum, and Mob Museum all opened in Las Vegas in 2012–13. The City of Las Vegas completed a new 309,000-square-foot City Hall in 2012. The Old City Hall enjoyed $58 million in renovations before becoming the new Zappos headquarters. An 11-story Federal Justice Tower on Las Vegas Boulevard was completed in 2013 at a cost of $35 million. It was set to house executive offices of the U.S. Department of Homeland Security, U.S. Immigration, and the U.S. Attorney's Office for the District of Nevada.

Economic Development Information: Economic and Urban Development, City of Las Vegas, 495 S. Main St., Las Vegas, NV 89101; telephone (702) 229-6551; fax (702) 385-3128. Las Vegas Metro Chamber of Commerce, 8363 W. Sunset Rd., Las Vegas, NV 89113; telephone (702) 641-5822; fax (702) 735-0406.

Commercial Shipping

Southern Clark County is the hub of an extensive transportation network serviced by three highway corridors: Interstate 15, U.S. Highway 95, and U.S. Highway 93. A proposed Interstate 11, running from Arizona northward through Nevada, offered the possibility of additional land routes. More than 50 motor freight carriers serve the area. In addition, a variety of warehousing and support services are available in Clark County, including foreign trade zone accommodations, packaging support, and U.S. customs service.

McCarran International Airport in Las Vegas handled in excess of 185 million pounds of arriving and departing cargo in 2013. Additionally, the McCarran International Air Cargo Center offers cargo storage and handling and operates in a designated Foreign Trade Zone (FTZ). Union Pacific Railroad runs northeast–

southwest through Clark County, linking the area to markets in most states.

Labor Force and Employment Outlook

Las Vegas used to expand as people moved into the region at a rate as high as 6,000 each month. Up until a national recession in the late 2000s, Las Vegas even boasted one of the highest rates of new job growth in the country; since then job growth and migration into the area has slowed. In the wake of the recession, the city experienced many layoffs and endured an unemployment rate of 14.7 percent in 2010. Housing prices fell significantly, and the city became among top national cities with the highest foreclosure rates.

Gaming and tourism-related jobs are still important to Las Vegas's economy. However jobs in highest demand in 2012 were registered nurses, with their need expected to grow by 26 percent by 2020, dental hygienists, computer engineers, accountants, and sales representatives.

The following is a summary of data regarding the 2012 Las Vegas labor force:

Size of civilian labor force: 295,024

Number of workers employed in . . .

agriculture and mining: 638
construction: 16,695
manufacturing: 7,278
wholesale trade: 4,890
retail trade: 28,539
transportation: 10,052
information systems: 4,698
finance: 17,079
professional administration: 32,102
education and social services: 39,285
arts and leisure: 69,324
other: 12,054
public administration: 11,092

Average hourly earnings of production workers: $15.72

Unemployment rate: 8.4% (2012)

Employers

Largest employers (2012)	*Number of employees*
Clark County School District	35,000
Clark County	8,000
Las Vegas Metropolitan Police	5,500
University of Nevada, Las Vegas	5,000
State of Nevada	4,500
UMC	3,500
City of Las Vegas	3,000
Sunrise Hospital	2,500
Golden Nugget Hotel & Casino	2,000
College of Southern Nevada	2,000
Stratosphere Tower/ American Casino	2,000

Cost of Living

The cost of living in Las Vegas is about equal to the national average, with the average cost of a house in 2013 estimated at $302,448.

The following is a summary of data regarding several key cost of living factors in the area.

2013 ACCRA Average House Price: $302,448

2013 ACCRA Cost of Living Index: 100

State income tax rate: None

State sales tax rate: 6.85%

Local income tax rate: None

Local sales tax rate: 1.25%

Property tax rate: $3.782 per $100 assessed value (2013)

Economic Information: Las Vegas Metro Chamber of Commerce, 8363 W. Sunset Rd., Las Vegas, NV 89113; telephone (702) 641-5822; fax (702) 735-0406. Las Vegas Global Economic Alliance, 6795 Edmond Street, Suite 260, Las Vegas, NV 89118; telephone (702) 791-0000.

■ Education and Research

Elementary and Secondary Schools

The Clark County School District serves more than 314,000 students in all of Clark County—a 7,910 square mile section of Nevada—which includes the city of Las Vegas and encompasses nearly three-quarters of all students in the state. The large system is divided into 15 performance zones. Hispanics comprise the single largest group of students, accounting for 44 percent of all students. A variety of magnet schools exist throughout the district, in addition to English as a Second Language programs, Gifted and Talented Education (GATE), adult education, and special education services. The school district is among the region's largest employers, with more than 39,000 people on its payroll.

More than 30 private and parochial elementary and secondary schools serve the Las Vegas metropolitan area.

There are also more than 90 preschools and day care centers.

The following is a summary of data regarding the Clark County School District.

Total enrollment: 314,059

Number of facilities

total: 357
elementary schools: 217
junior high schools: 59
high schools: 49
other: 32

Student/teacher ratio: 20.6:1

Teacher salaries

average (statewide): $53,023

Funding per pupil: $8,270

Public Schools Information: Clark County School District, 5100 W. Sahara Ave., Las Vegas, NV 89146; telephone (702) 799-5000.

Colleges and Universities

Officially opened in 1957 and occupying 350 acres in the metropolitan area, the University of Nevada at Las Vegas (UNLV) enrolls about 28,000 students and supports a total staff of nearly 3,000. Colleges include those for business, education, engineering, fine arts, health sciences, hotel administration, liberal arts, sciences, and urban affairs, in addition to a graduate college and professional schools in dental medicine and law. The University of Nevada School of Medicine is located in Las Vegas. Also in Las Vegas, the International Academy of Design & Technology offers two- and four-year programs in Fashion Design, Interior Design, and Visual Communications.

The College of Southern Nevada (CSN) system, with a campus in Las Vegas and North Las Vegas, educates more than 43,000 students. It operates another campus in Henderson and also supports seven learning centers. CSN's most popular degree programs include associate degrees in arts, business, nursing, general studies, science, education, psychology, criminal justice, hospitality management, and computer information technology. Twenty-eight degree programs are entirely accessible online. The Nevada State College at Henderson was founded in 2002, and places a particular focus on training in the nursing and healthcare industries.

Libraries and Research Centers

The Las Vegas-Clark County Library District serves all of Clark County with 25 branches and a comprehensive resource of informational materials. The district's Green Valley branch resides in Henderson. Its holdings include special collections on African-American history, Asian history, health and medicine, international language, gaming/local history, grants, government Documents, and patents. Total circulation in the Las Vegas-Clark County Library District was 14.4 million in 2012–13. The College of Southern Nevada library system, as well as the University of Nevada, Las Vegas libraries, are also available for public use.

The Desert Research Institute's (DRI) main research campus in Las Vegas carries out more than 300 scientific research projects at any given time. It is a stand-alone institution that falls under the umbrella of the Nevada System of Higher Education (NSHE), thanks to generous outside research funding. The institute generates $50 million in annual revenue. Environmental research programs focus on three core divisions of atmospheric sciences, earth and ecosystems sciences, and hydrologic sciences. DRI maintains a library that is available to researchers and scholars. The Church of Jesus Christ of Latter-Day Saints maintains a branch of its genealogical library in Las Vegas. A variety of other specialized libraries and research centers are located in the area.

Public Library Information: Las Vegas-Clark County Library District, 7060 W. Windmill Lane, Las Vegas, NV 89113; telephone (702) 382-7323.

■ Health Care

Among the major hospitals serving the area is the Sunrise Hospital and Medical Center. With more than 700 beds and 1,500 physicians, it also maintains centers for renal transplants, breast cancer, sleep disorders, and epilepsy. The hospital employs leading technologies such as the da Vinci Surgical Robot and GammaKnife Center, the only one in the state. The Sunrise Children's Hospital, also on the main campus, has a 24-hour emergency department and the largest neonatal and pediatric intensive care units in Nevada. MountainView Hospital, which is owned by Sunrise Health System, largely focuses on senior care and added a new 42,000-square-foot facility to its campus in 2013.

Affiliated with the University of Nevada School of Medicine, the University Medical Center (UMC) received high-performing marks from *U.S. News & World Report* in 2014. The facility is home to the Children's Hospital of Nevada and Lions Burn Care Center, the only such facility in Nevada, which has gained national recognition. UMC also maintains a free-standing trauma center and the state's first pediatric emergency department. The University of Nevada School of Medicine's genetics program offers counseling to prospective parents about inherited diseases and provides clinical care to children with birth defects.

Valley Health System has several facilities in Las Vegas. Desert Springs Hospital Medical Center has 346 beds and was the first diabetes treatment program in the nation to earn distinction for advanced inpatient diabetes care from The Joint Commission. The 171-bed Centennial Hills Hospital Medical Center offers many specialties but is highlighted by a comprehensive Women's Center that provides exceptional health and wellness services. Valley Hospital Medical Center has approximately 404 beds. Other hospitals include the Spring Valley Hospital Medical Center and Summerlin Hospital Medical Center.

The Cleveland Clinic's Lou Ruvo Center for Brain Health, a neurological disease research and treatment clinic, opened in Las Vegas in 2009. The Cleveland Clinic Foundation planned a $395 facility at Symphony Park to conduct research and provide medical treatment, with construction expected to start in 2016 or 2017.

■ Recreation

Sightseeing

Most people visit Las Vegas to see shows featuring world-famous entertainers and to try their luck at the gaming tables. But the city offers much more to see and do. The streets of Las Vegas, with neon and glittering lights, are themselves a popular attraction. Also within the city limits is the Old Mormon Fort; built in 1855, it is the oldest structure in the area and tours are offered daily.

East of the city, Lake Mead National Recreation area boasts 500 miles of scenic shoreline created when the Hoover Dam was constructed. Located 30 miles southeast of the city is Hoover Dam, the tallest concrete dam in the Western Hemisphere. The popular site draws about one million visitors annually to its tourist center while millions more drive over it. Only 15 miles west of Las Vegas is Red Rock Canyon, where a 13-mile scenic route winds through a natural landscape inhabited by wild burros and bighorn sheep; hikers and bicyclists can also enjoy 30 miles of trails in the nearly 196,000-acre National Conservation Area. Some 50 miles north, the Valley of Fire State Park contains beautiful desert land, rock formations, and rock drawings surviving from ancient civilizations. Tour buses travel from Las Vegas to Grand Canyon National Park in northern Arizona, where visitors can choose from hiking, camping, biking, fishing, and boating. Several ghost towns are within an hour's drive of Las Vegas; Bonnie Springs Old Nevada, southwest of the city, is a recreated town that evokes the lawless days of the Old West.

Arts and Culture

World famous for entertainment, Las Vegas is a city where nightlife lasts 24 hours a day and spectacular casino resorts and venues feature international stars. There is also an active and acclaimed arts community in Las Vegas; theater, dance, and concert performances as well as lectures are staged at the Reed Whipple Cultural Center,

and the new $453 million Smith Center for the Performing Arts, which opened in 2012, hosts the Las Vegas Philharmonic and Nevada Ballet Theatre. The Charleston Heights Arts Center presents theater and musical performances as well as exhibits by local and regional artists. The College of Southern Nevada offers dance, theater, and musical performances, and the University of Nevada, Las Vegas maintains three performing arts venues.

Several museums are located in the city. The Nevada State Museum specializes in the natural history of Southern Nevada, while the Las Vegas Natural History Museum focuses on the region's wildlife and natural environment, both past and present. The Discovery Children's Museum offers hands-on exhibits that let children explore science, arts, and humanities in a fun and educational way and moved to a new $56 million facility in 2013. Also that year, the Neon Museum opened; the Mob Museum opened in 2012.

The Gallery of Fine Art at Bellagio features two to three exhibitions annually, with works from top art museums and private collections. The University of Nevada at Las Vegas maintains an art gallery in the Ham Fine Arts Building on campus, featuring the work of faculty members, touring artists, and students. Las Vegas area commercial galleries show the work of local and nationally known artists.

Like many other areas of interest, the dire economic situation in Las Vegas took a toll on arts institutions in the late 2000s. The Las Vegas Art Museum, which was known for its contemporary art works, fell victim to the economy in 2009 when budget cuts and layoffs forced the museum to cease operations. The Liberace Museum, which exhibited a collection of rare pianos, including those owned by Frederic Chopin and George Gershwin, closed in 2010 after 31 years.

Festivals and Holidays

The World Archery Festival takes place each February in Las Vegas. Helldorado Days in May celebrate the Old West era with rodeos and parades. The Greek Festival in September features authentic food and dancing. The Wrangler National Finals Rodeo is held in December at the Thomas & Mack Center. The Lakes Festival of Lights, also held in December, is an annual community holiday gathering that kicks off holiday celebrations. Film festivals include the Nevada International Film Festival in December and Jewish Film Festival in January.

Sports for the Spectator

Las Vegas offers enthusiasts many opportunities to cheer for their favorite sports. The Las Vegas 51s, a Triple-A affiliate of the New York Mets, play minor league baseball at Cashman Field in Las Vegas. The Las Vegas Wranglers, members of the ECHL, play hockey at the Orleans Arena. The University of Las Vegas Rebels' most popular sports include basketball, football, baseball, and soccer. The Las Vegas Motor Speedway offers NASCAR and other motor sports events. High-profile boxing matches are often scheduled in Las Vegas. The Las Vegas Stallions FC, established in 2010, play in the National Premier Soccer League.

Sports for the Participant

Although Las Vegas is in the desert, there are facilities for a number of water sports, including fishing, boating, waterskiing, and canoeing at nearby Lake Mead and on the Colorado River. Nearby Henderson is nationally renowned for its recreational facilities. Las Vegas City parks and Clark County parks continue to be developed to meet the needs of an expanding population; both provide a variety of athletic programming, tennis courts and ballfields, swimming pools, golf courses, community centers, activities, classes, and workshops. The Clark County Wetlands Park Nature Preserve, which includes two miles of walking trails, is a habitat for numerous species of wildlife and seeks to create a cleaner natural water system in Southern Nevada. More than 30 golf courses exist in the area as well.

Shopping and Dining

Shopping center construction is constantly taking place in the city. A major attraction is the Forum Shops at Caesars, which opened in 1992 and occupies 675,000 square feet. Described as combining the opulence of Rodeo Drive with the glitter of the Las Vegas Strip, the Roman-inspired complex houses about 160 upscale shops, art galleries, and a $5 million animated fountain. The Galleria at Sunset Mall in nearby Henderson features one million square feet of enclosed mall space. The Boulevard Mall has about 140 shops and eateries. Fashion Show Mall has six anchor department stores: Saks Fifth Avenue, Dillard's, Neiman Marcus, Macy's, Nordstrom, and Forever 21. It also features "The Cloud," a canopy suspended 20 stories over the mall that serves the dual purpose as shade during the day and movie projection screen at night. An unusual shopping experience can be found at the Rue de la Paix center, featuring all that is French.

More than 750 restaurants with choices ranging from haute cuisine to inexpensive fare are located in Las Vegas. In the twenty-first century, Las Vegas has earned renown as a place to eat, with more master sommeliers than Los Angeles and New York City combined and a number of Michelin star restaurants. One of the most well-known restaurants is Spago, run by internationally-known chef Wolfgang Puck, who uses French cooking techniques to create an eclectic menu. Major resort hotels all feature gourmet menus; most hotels on "the Strip" and downtown offer buffet dining. Some examples of the culinary variety available include: Hard Rock Cafe, residing just outside of the hotel; Planet Hollywood, at

Caesars Palace; and the Eiffel Tower Restaurant, inside the Paris Las Vegas Hotel shaped to resemble the famous French structure.

Visitor Information: Las Vegas Visitor Information Center, 3150 Paradise Rd., Las Vegas, NV 89109; telephone (702) 892-0711; toll-free (877) 847-4858.

■ Convention Facilities

Las Vegas is among the nation's foremost meeting destinations, with convention trade being one of the city's major industries, generating $6.7 billion in non-gaming revenue 2012. Las Vegas hosted nearly 22,000 conventions and meetings that year, hosting in excess of 4.9 million delegates. Along with entertainment and recreation, well-appointed meeting facilities and luxury hotels and resorts are the attractions that consistently draw large and small groups to the city. There are more than 150,000 hotel rooms and 10.6 million square feet of meeting space in Las Vegas.

The Las Vegas Convention Center, after expansions in the late 1990s and then further expansion in the early 2000s, encompasses 3.2 million square feet. Nearly 2 million square feet is available for exhibit space in 16 exhibit halls, while 144 meeting rooms (more than 241,000 square feet) handle seating capacities ranging from 20 to 5,500 people. A grand lobby and concourse area of 225,000 square feet, catering services, state-of-the-art technological service, and ample parking round out the offerings.

Mandalay Bay Convention Center was the fifth-largest convention center in the United States when it opened in 2003, with 1.7 million square feet of meeting space. Sands Expo and Convention Center and Venetian Congress Facility provides another 1.8 million square feet of available space.

Convention Information: Las Vegas Visitor Information Center, 3150 Paradise Rd., Las Vegas, NV 89109; telephone (702) 892-0711; toll-free (877) 847-4858.

■ Transportation

Approaching the City

Seemingly isolated in the middle of the desert, Las Vegas is, in fact, easily accessible. McCarran International Airport, located five miles south of the business district, serves Las Vegas, Henderson, and all of Clark County and southern Nevada. In 2005 the airport completed a $125 million expansion, consisting of a new gate wing that allows the airport to handle an additional 3.1 million passengers annually. The 10th busiest airport in the United States and 16th busiest in the world in 2014, McCarran is served by more than 30 airlines and transported some 38.6 million passengers in 2013.

The city is served by three major highways. Interstate 15 connects Las Vegas with Los Angeles and Salt Lake City. U.S. Highway 95 leads into the city from the northwest, and U.S. Highway 93/95 enters from the southeast. Long-term plans for the potential creation of a new Interstate 11, to run from Arizona to Nevada, were under consideration in 2014.

Amtrak Thruway provides bus service between Los Angeles, California, and Las Vegas. Greyhound provides bus service to and from nearby Las Vegas with connections throughout the west.

Traveling in the City

The streets of Las Vegas are laid out in a grid system. The primary north–south routes are Main Street and Las Vegas Boulevard—locally known as the "Strip"—which runs parallel to Interstate 15. Main east–west thoroughfares are Flamingo Road, Tropicana Avenue, and Sahara Avenue. Within the city, U.S. Highway 95 is known as the Las Vegas Expressway.

The Regional Transportation Commission (RTC) of Southern Nevada serves 60 million annual passengers in the greater Las Vegas Valley region with 42 routes to points throughout the city and metropolitan area. Buses and trolleys serve the Strip every 15 minutes. RTC also provides paratransit services for riders with disabilities and environmentally-friendly transit alternatives to rail service. The Las Vegas Monorail runs along a four-mile route along the Strip, linking major resorts, hotels, attractions, and the convention center along its seven stops.

■ Communications

Newspapers and Magazines

The major daily newspaper is the *Las Vegas Review-Journal,* a morning paper. *Las Vegas Sentinel-Voice* is a weekly African American community newspaper, and the *Las Vegas Sun* is a general weekly community newspaper. Several small, special interest journals and magazines are also published in the city; among them are *Nevada Business Journal,* which focuses on the Nevada business climate, and *Las Vegas Magazine,* which provides coverage of local entertainment. Other publications include scholarly journals, Jewish publications, and those focused on art, foodservice, and business.

Television and Radio

More than two dozen television stations broadcast from the greater Las Vegas region. Cable television service is available by subscription. Several AM and FM radio stations broadcast from Las Vegas, featuring diverse programming, including news, information, and music ranging from jazz to classical. Additional stations are received from surrounding communities.

Media Information: Las Vegas Review-Journal, 1111 W. Bonanza Road, P.O. Box 70, Las Vegas, NV 89125; telephone (702) 383-0211.

Las Vegas Online

Center for Business and Economic Research at the University of Nevada, Las Vegas. Available cber. unlv.edu

City of Las Vegas home page. Available www. lasvegasnevada.gov

Clark County home page. Available www. clarkcountynv.gov

Clark County School District. Available ccsd.net

Las Vegas Metro Chamber of Commerce. Available www.lvchamber.com

Las Vegas-Clark County Library District. Available www.lvccld.org

Las Vegas Convention and Visitors Authority. Available www.lasvegas.com

Las Vegas Review-Journal. Available www. reviewjournal.com

Las Vegas Sun. Available www.lasvegassun.com

Nevada Division of Museums and History. Available museums.nevadaculture.org

BIBLIOGRAPHY

Hopkins, A.D., and K.J. Evans, eds., *The First 100: Portraits of the Men and Women Who Shaped Las Vegas* (Las Vegas, NV: Huntington Press, 2000)

Kraft, James P., *Vegas at Odds: Labor Conflict in a Leisure Economy* (Baltimore: Johns Hopkins University Press, 2010)

Kranes, David, *Low Tide in the Desert: Nevada Stories* (Las Vegas, NV: University of Nevada, 1996)

Pierce, Todd James, and Jarret Keene, eds., *Dead Neon: Tales of Near-future Las Vegas* (Reno: University of Nevada Press, 2010)

Rothman, Hal, *The Making of Modern Nevada* (Reno: University of Nevada Press, 2010)

Reno

■ The City in Brief

Founded: 1868 (incorporated, 1903)

Head Official: Mayor Robert Cashell (R) (since 2002; current term expires 2014)

City Population
 1990: 133,850
 2000: 180,480
 2010: 225,221
 2012 estimate: 231,004
 Percent change, 2000–2010: 24.8%
 U.S. rank in 1990: 132nd
 U.S. rank in 2000: 130th
 U.S. rank in 2010: 89th (State rank: 3rd)

Metropolitan Statistical Area Population
 2000: 339,486
 2010: 425,417
 2012 estimate: 433,612
 Percent change, 2000–2010: 25.3%
 U.S. rank in 2000: 132nd
 U.S. rank in 2010: 116th

Area: 69.34 square miles

Elevation: 4,400 feet above sea level

Average Annual Temperatures: January, 33.6° F; July, 71.3° F; annual average, 51.3° F

Average Annual Precipitation: 7.48 inches of rain; 24.3 inches of snow

Major Economic Sectors: tourism, gaming, manufacturing, distribution

Unemployment Rate: 7.2% (2012)

Per Capita Income: $24,043

2012 FBI Crime Index Property: 7,423

Major Colleges and Universities: University of Nevada, Reno; Truckee Meadows Community College; Morrison University; Sierra Nevada College

Daily Newspaper: *Reno Gazette-Journal*

■ Introduction

Often called "The Biggest Little City in the World," Reno has become popular for outstanding western hospitality, fine dining, entertaining stage shows, top-name performers, history, culture, and 24-hour gaming excitement. Adventurers can enjoy a wide variety of outdoor recreation including golf and skiing. Golfers can choose from courses in lake, high desert, and mountain settings. Lake Tahoe, located less than an hour's drive from downtown Reno, boasts the largest concentration of ski resorts in North America. Nevada's liberal tax structures, along with Reno's free port status and central location in the West, also make the area an important regional manufacturing, warehouse, and distribution center. Into the 2010s, the dry, sunny climate began attracting data centers seeking a safe environment for their facilities and clean technology businesses looking to exploit the state's abundant geothermal resources.

■ Geography and Climate

Reno is located at the western border of Nevada—in a valley known as the Truckee Meadows—about 20 miles east of the Sierra Nevada mountains and Lake Tahoe, the second largest alpine lake in the world. The Truckee River passes between Reno and its sister city, Sparks. Temperatures in the region are mild, but can fluctuate as much as 45 degrees between day and night. The temperature at night during the summer rarely rises above 60 degrees. More than half the annual precipitation

Craig Cozart/iStockPhoto.com

falls from December to March, in the form of mixed snow and rain, with snow accumulation seldom lasting longer than three or four days. Low humidity and sunny skies are prevalent throughout the year.

Area: 69.34 square miles

Elevation: 4,400 feet above sea level

Average Temperatures: January, 33.6° F; July, 71.3° F; annual average, 51.3° F

Average Annual Precipitation: 7.48 inches of rain; 24.3 inches of snow

■ History

Reno's Beginnings

Reno's history began when Charles William Fuller arrived in the Truckee Meadows in 1859 and occupied a piece of land on the south bank of the Truckee River. By early 1860, he had constructed a bridge and small hotel, and the place was known as Fuller's Crossing. In the following year, Fuller sold his bridge and hotel to Myron C. Lake, who renamed the spot Lake's Crossing and soon was charging a toll on the bridge. The Crossing became

an important station on one of the main routes between northern California and the silver mines of Virginia City and the Comstock Lode.

Lake was the crossing's only property owner until the Central Pacific Railroad (later renamed Union Railroad) crossed the Sierra Nevada in 1868 and pushed its tracks into the Truckee Meadows. Under terms of an agreement between Myron Lake and Central Pacific, a new town was laid out at the crossing; ownership was divided between Lake and the railroad. Almost overnight, buildings began to appear on the town site and the new settlement was named Reno in honor of General Jesse Lee Reno (1823–62), a Union army officer who was killed during the Civil War.

In 1871 the Nevada State Legislature moved the Washoe County seat to Reno, where one year later the Virginia & Truckee Railroad extended its line. The town soon became an important commercial center on the transcontinental railroad and a transfer point for the immense wealth coming out of the Comstock Lode. The University of Nevada was moved from Elko to Reno in 1885.

Gaming Gains Prominence; Modern Times

At the beginning of the twentieth century, Reno gained national notoriety after a number of famous people obtained divorces in the city under Nevada's lenient laws. Newspapers sensationalized the incidents, dubbing Reno the "divorce capital." Reno's sister city, Sparks, was established in 1904 as a division point on the Southern Pacific Railroad. After the legalization of casino gambling by the state legislature in 1931, Reno filled with gambling establishments—marking the start of a tourist industry that flourishes today.

In the shadow of the casinos, Reno has quietly grown into an important transportation hub for the western United States and has developed a diverse economic base. Emerging industries in the city included data warehousing, bolstered by the city's insulation from natural distasters, and clean technology companies anxious to capitalize on the state's geothermal resources. Modern Reno also boasts a thriving cultural scene, a refurbished downtown area, and an expanding tourist industry fueled not only by the casinos, but by the many year-round resorts in the nearby mountains.

Historical Information: Nevada Historical Society-Research Library, 1650 N. Virginia St., Reno, NV 89503; telephone (775) 688-1190; fax (775) 688-2917.

■ Population Profile

Metropolitan Statistical Area Population

2000: 339,486
2010: 425,417
2012 estimate: 433,612
Percent change, 2000–2010: 25.3%
U.S. rank in 2000: 132nd
U.S. rank in 2010: 116th

City Residents

1990: 133,850
2000: 180,480
2010: 225,221
2012 estimate: 231,004
Percent change, 2000–2010: 24.8%
U.S. rank in 1990: 132nd
U.S. rank in 2000: 130th
U.S. rank in 2010: 89th (State rank: 3rd)

Density: 2,186.4 people per square mile

Racial and ethnic characteristics

White: 182,512
Black or African American: 6,180
American Indian and Alaskan Native: 2,827
Asian: 15,340
Native Hawaiian and Other Pacific Islander: 1,768
Hispanic or Latino (may be of any race): 59,509
Other: 22,377

Percent of residents born in state: 28%

Age characteristics

Population under 5 years old: 16,433
Population 5 to 9 years old: 14,328
Population 10 to 14 years old: 13,236
Population 15 to 19 years old: 15,664
Population 20 to 24 years old: 22,575
Population 25 to 34 years old: 36,569
Population 35 to 44 years old: 26,578
Population 45 to 54 years old: 29,541
Population 55 to 59 years old: 13,599
Population 60 to 64 years old: 12,116
Population 65 to 74 years old: 17,497
Population 75 to 84 years old: 9,376
Population 85 years and over: 3,492
Median age: 34.2

Births (2010–11 Metropolitan Area)

Total number: 5,473

Deaths (2010–11 Metropolitan Area)

Total number: 3,122

Money income (2012)

Per capita income: $24,043
Median household income: $44,318
Total households: 89,155

Number of households with income of . . .

less than $10,000: 8,080
$10,000 to $14,999: 5,837
$15,000 to $24,999: 11,432
$25,000 to $34,999: 10,394
$35,000 to $49,999: 13,250
$50,000 to $74,999: 15,996
$75,000 to $99,999: 9,039
$100,000 to $149,999: 9,285
$150,000 to $199,999: 3,076
$200,000 or more: 2,766

Percent of families below poverty level: 19.5%

FBI Crime Index Property: 7,423

FBI Crime Index Violent: 1,192

■ Municipal Government

Reno operates under a council- manager form of government. The seven council members and the mayor, who appoint a city manager, all serve four-year terms.

Head Official: Mayor Robert Cashell (R) (since 2002; current term expires 2014)

Total Number of City Employees: 1,108 (2012)

City Information: Reno City Hall, 1 E. First Street, Reno, NV 89505; telephone (775) 334-2002; fax (775) 334-2097.

■ Economy

Major Industries and Commercial Activity

Tourism, especially casino-related, is a major industry in the Reno area. The nearby mountains draw many tourists to the highest concentration of ski resorts in America and contribute to the unlimited year-round recreational opportunities.The industry supports a wide range of restaurants and retail options, as well

The business climate also has a strong presence in manufacturing industries such as computers, electronics, financial services, and communications. Major manufacturers include IGT, Sierra Nevada Corporation, Kimmie Candy Company, Haws Corporation, Tyco, Trex, JamesHardie, Pacific Cheese, French Gourmet, Hidden Valley Ranch, Now, and Model Dairy.

Manufacturers benefit from Reno's central location among western states; the city is within 500 miles of 18 percent of the U.S. popoulation and can reach 56 million people in one day. Distribution or fulfillment centers for Walmart, Petsmart, Urban Outfitters, Barnes and Noble, JC Penney, Toys "R" Us, and K-Mart are all located in the area.

Growth in high-technology industries has coalesced around development of data centers. Reno is well isolated from regions prone to earthquakes, floods, and tornados, and the back-office support and data industry has grown 50 percent between 2011 and 2014. Both Apple and NJVC operate data centers in the area. Clean energy, another emerging industry in the area, utilizes the city's climate—with 250 days of sun each year—geothermal resources. Nevada has one of the most active geothermal landscapes in the world.

Items and goods produced: cement, labeling devices, valves, dairy and food products, pet food, electronic equipment, livestock, agricultural produce

Incentive Programs—New and Existing Companies

Local programs: To encourage industrial development, Reno offers tax deferral, exemption, and abatement programs, further reducing the already low tax rates in the state. Reno is part of northern Nevada's foreign trade zone, which, at nearly 7,500 acres, is one of the largest in the nation. The Made in Nevada non-profit program helps market and promote locally produced goods worldwide.

State programs: The state of Nevada has no personal state income tax, no unitary tax, no corporate income tax, no inventory tax, no estate and/or gift tax, no franchise tax, no inheritance tax, and no special intangible tax. Nevada is a Right to Work state, in which employees can choose to affiliate with or join labor unions; railway and airline employees, however, are not included in the law.

The state also guarantees Small Business Administration loans.

Tax abatements include a Sales and Use Tax Abatement, available on qualifying capital projects with reductions to as little as 2 percent; Modified Business Abatement of 50 percent of the 1.17 percent rate levied on quarterly wages above $85,000; Personal Property Abatement of up to 50 percent for 10 years; and Real Property Tax Abatement for Recycling, also up to 50 percent for 10 years.

The Nevada State Development Corporation (NSDC) provides loan financing for growth opportunities such as buying, building, or improving commercial real estate for new and existing businesses. The Nevada Microenterprise Initiative helps provide economic self-sufficiency for entrepreneurs through training, technical assistance, and access to credit. Loans can be used for start-up costs, equipment, inventory, supplies, working capital, fixtures and other furniture.

Job training programs: Nevada's "Train Employees Now" (TEN) program has customized short-term, industrial training programs to assist new and expanding businesses in training new or potential employees. Eligible businesses must contribute at least 25 percent of the total training costs, and must have at least 10 employees to train. The Silver State Works Employee Hiring Incentive offers employers up to $2,000 for each state-qualified employee hired.

Working to ensure that companies have an adequate workforce is Job Opportunities in Nevada (JOIN), which offers training and educational opportunities for job seekers; Nevadaworks assists employers in developing employee skills. Nevada Industry Excellence is an industrial outreach program affiliated with local community colleges and is dedicated to training employees to meet the hiring goals of specific companies.

The public school district's Glenn Hare Occupational Center provides training in areas identified by local employers. Training, recruiting, and continuing education resources in Reno also include Truckee Meadows Community College and the University of Nevada, Reno.

Development Projects

In 2012 and 2013, several companies relocated to or expanded in Reno. In March 2012 CustomInk, an online t-shirt design company, opened a new 25,000-square-foot facility in Reno set to employ up to 100 people. Urban Outfitters finished a 460,000-square-foot distribution center in Reno in 2012, built at a cost of $55 million.

Data center provider NJVC opened a 20,000-square-foot facility for operations that same year. In 2013 Myers Industries opened a new facility to employ some 150 new workers; Ardagh Metal Packaging opened a plant employing 140 people; Randa Accessories brought another 120 on board following a $25 million expansion; OLE Mexican Foods built a new manufacturing facility in Reno to employ 350; GreatCall Inc. opened a 400-person call center; One Contact announced 200 jobs at a new service support center; Video Gaming Technologies Inc. announced 70 new high-paying jobs at a new Reno location; and Schwabe North America and Valley Tech Systems both relocated to Reno.

These developments, while important, paled in comparison to a $1 billion, 10-year investment by Apple announced in 2012. Apple planned to build a 1.5-million-square-foot data center to support its iCloud services. The estimated economic impact of the total development was $343 million. Once fully completed, the facility was expected to employ 35 full-time workers with salaries of at least $25 per hour.

City investments included $100 million between 2008 and 2013 to improve the Reno-Tahoe International Airport. The final, $29 million phase completed in 2013 and renovated security checkpoints, baggage claim areas, and terminal amenities. The city has also worked on an array of signage and pavement enhancements to Interstate 80.

The shuttered Fitzgerald's Hotel and Casino, which went bankrupt in 2008, was set to reopen as the Whitney Peak Hotel in 2014. The multi-million-dollar redesign included 200 guest rooms in the non-gaming, non-smoking facility that sought to appeal to outdoor enthusiasts visiting Reno. Grand Sierra Resort and Casino, Peppermill Hotel Casino, and Silver Legacy Resort Casino all underwent renovations during the early 2010s.

Economic Development Information: Economic Development Authority of Western Nevada (EDAWN), 5190 Neil Rd., Ste. 110, Reno, NV 89502; telephone (775) 829-3700; toll-free (800) 256-9761; email Sidener@edawn.org.

Commercial Shipping

Reno/Sparks is situated at the hub of an extensive transportation network. Nevada borders five western states and provides overnight ground service to 10 of the 11 major West Coast markets.

The area is also located on two major highway corridors: Interstate 80 and U.S. Highway 395. Over 60 local, regional and national carriers provide trucking service in the Reno/Sparks area including the United Parcel Service (UPS) regional package-sorting hub in Sparks. Rail freight service is provided by Burlington Northern Santa Fe (BSNF) and Union Pacific Railroads.

The Reno/Tahoe International Airport provides cargo air service through three carriers: FedEx, UPS, and DHL. Daily cargo transport averages 310,000 pounds. The Reno/Sparks foreign trade zones are popular to business, as they provide economically favorable conditions and operational flexibility. Reno/Sparks has eight sites with more than 7,500 acres of building space.

Labor Force and Employment Outlook

State-supported training programs and pro-business policies helped make Nevada one the fastest growing states during the 2000s, and joblessness was as low as 4.5 percent in 2007. A national recession in the late 2000s both slowed population growth and ballooned the city's unemployment rate. However, stability and job growth returned during the early 2010s, though jobless rates remained well above those of pre-recessionary times. As a right-to-work state, Nevada's law states that no person shall be denied the opportunity to obtain or retain employment because of non-membership in a labor organization. As of 2012 trade, transportation, and utilities employed the most area workers, followed by leisure and hospitality, accommodation and food service, and government.

The following is a summary of data regarding the 2012 Reno-Sparks NV Metro Area labor force:

Size of civilian labor force: 119,892

Number of workers employed in . . .

agriculture and mining: 818
construction: 5,907
manufacturing: 6,901
wholesale trade: 3,395
retail trade: 12,512
transportation: 4,215
information systems: 1,688
finance: 6,654
professional administration: 12,705
education and social services: 20,663
arts and leisure: 19,812
other: 5,275
public administration: 5,090

Average hourly earnings of production workers: $16.32

Unemployment rate: 7.2% (2012)

Employers

Largest employers (2012)	*Number of employees*
Washoe County School District	8,250
University of Nevada–Reno	4,250
Washoe County	2,750
Renown Regional Medical Center	2,750
Peppermill Hotel Casino–Reno	2,250
Integrity Staffing Solutions	2,250
International Game Technology	2,250

Silver Legacy Hotel Casino	2,250
St. Mary's	1,750

Cost of Living

The cost of living in Reno is well below the national average, with the average cost of a home in 2013 estimated at $247,983. Reno compares favorably with other regional capitals such as Salt Lake City and Phoenix.

The following is a summary of data regarding several key cost of living factors in the area.

2013 ACCRA Average House Price: $247,983

2013 ACCRA Cost of Living Index: 90

State income tax rate: None

State sales tax rate: 6.85%

Local income tax rate: None

Local sales tax rate: 0.875%

Property tax rate: $3.66 per $100 assessed value (2013)

Economic Information: Economic Development Authority of Western Nevada (EDAWN), 5190 Neil Rd., Ste. 110, Reno, NV 89502; telephone (775) 829-3700; toll-free (800) 256-9761; email Sidener@edawn.org.

■ Education and Research

Elementary and Secondary Schools

Reno is part of the Washoe County School District, the second-largest district in the state. The district is governed by a board of trustees that consists of seven nonpartisan members. The superintendent is appointed by the board. Total district enrollment is more than 64,000 annually. White students make up nearly 54 percent of the student population, and hispanic students comprise 33 percent.

Reno public school students consistently score above state averages on standardized tests, including the Iowa Test of Basic Skills/Iowa Test of Educational Development (ITBS/ITED) and, for high school students, the ACT and SAT college entrance exams Most high schools offer honors and Advanced Placemetn Programs, and Wooster High School provides International Baccalaureate courses. Trukee Meadows Community College High School, available to juniors and seniors, allows students to take courses for college credit. English as a Second Language courses and Native American Education Programs are available to students, as are special services for students with disabilities.

The following is a summary of data regarding the Washoe County School District.

Total enrollment: 64,380

Number of facilities
total: 95
elementary schools: 64
junior high schools: 16
high schools: 12
other: 3

Student/teacher ratio: 19.1:1

Teacher salaries
average (statewide): $53,023

Funding per pupil: $8,487

Public Schools Information: Washoe County School District, 425 E. Ninth St., Reno, NV 89512; telephone (775) 348-0200.

Colleges and Universities

The University of Nevada, Reno, founded in 1874, enrolls more than 18,000 students per semester and offers 145 programs of study. Specialties include earthquake expertise, which includes experts from fields of seismology, geology, geodesy, and civil engineering. The Master of Business Administration degree program has been ranked among the top 25 national programs of its kind by *BusinessWeek*.

Truckee Meadows Community College offers two-year associate's degrees as well as adult education programs in more than 50 different fields of study. A number of business, vocational, and professional schools are also located in the Reno area. Morrison University focuses on business degrees while the Sierra Nevada College in Lake Tahoe takes advantage of its location by presenting many science and environmental programs, in addition to hosting nationally recognized speakers on various topics—from poetry to politics—from time to time.

Libraries and Research Centers

The Washoe County Library System consists of 13 library branches strategically placed around the county, as well as an Internet Branch. About half of the branches are "Partnership Libraries," housed in public school libraries but serving the entire public in their neighborhoods. Library holdings include thousands of books, videos, audios, and materials in microformat, CD-ROMs, database access, and several hundred periodical subscriptions. Special collections focus on gambling, Nevada history, and U.S. and Nevada documents.

The University of Nevada, Reno libraries offer resources in paper and electronic formats, including more than one million texts and journals available in-house, as well as electronic access to the full-text articles of more than 8,000 journals. Films, audio and video tapes, maps, and government documents are also available. Special collections include Basque materials, the photo-rich Nevada and the Great Basin collection, rare books and prints, and a collection of contemporary arts books.

The Desert Research Institute (DRI) maintains facilities in Reno (the 470-acre Dandini Research Park) and oversees about 300 separate projects throughout the state, conducting studies in areas such as air quality and climactic changes in the western United States over the last two million years. The University of Nevada, Reno, is a major research center, with strong programs in Great Basin Studies, Basque Studies, and Genomics and Proteomics. Its library holdings include the Basque Library, Keck Earth Sciences and Mining Research Information Center, and the Nevada Inventors Database.

Public Library Information: Washoe County Library, Downtown Reno, 301 S. Center St., Reno, NV 89501; telephone (775) 327-8312; fax (775) 327-8301.

■ Health Care

Renown Health, known as Washoe Med until 2006, is the primary health system in Reno. The system, which serves a 17-county area, features institutes for cancer, cardiac health, and neurosciences. Its hospitals provide 24-hour emergency room facilities and various specialized treatment programs. The Renown Regional Medical Center is the main campus, with the region's only Level II trauma center, only children's hospital, and most comprehensive cardiac care. The facility has 654 beds and admits about 27,000 patients annually.

Other health-related facilities include West Hills Hospital, which serves as a behavioral health center, and St. Mary's At Galena, an urgent care center. The University of Nevada School of Medicine, with a campus in Reno, is the state's only public medical school.

■ Recreation

Sightseeing

Downtown Reno glitters with brightly-lit casinos and 24-hour entertainment. In the middle of it all stands the city's best-known symbol, the Reno Arch. The arch welcomes visitors with its slogan, "The Biggest Little City In The World." There have been four arches since the original was erected in 1929; the current disco ball version has been there since 1987. The arch that welcomed visitors from 1934 to 1963 can now be seen on Lake Street, in front of the National Automobile Museum.

One of the country's finest and most extensive collections of antique cars is on display at the National Automobile Museum (The Harrah Collection). Opened in 1989, more than 220 vehicles are featured, including horseless carriages, cars owned by celebrities, and experimental cars of the future.

Described by the *Los Angeles Times* as the "Taj Mahal of Tenpins," the National Bowling Stadium is the only facility of its kind in the world. The stadium features 78-championship lanes, Paul Revere's Kick's Diner & Dance Club, and an IWERKS theater where giant screen movies are shown daily. The stadium announced $15 million in planned upgrades in 2012 following a deal to host at least 10 championship tournaments between 2019 and 2030.

The Wilbur D. May Center features a museum, an indoor arboretum, and a botanical garden surrounded by a beautiful park. During summer months, the center's Great Basin Adventure provides children with a full day of activities including pony rides, a "hands-on" discovery room, a log flume ride, a petting zoo, and a playground complete with dinosaurs. The Terry Lee Wells Nevada Discovery Museum opened in 2011, providing some 67,000 square feet of exhibits and activities for children.

Daytrip excursions also provide visitors with a number of sightseeing options. Reno serves as a base camp to some of the most unique attractions on the West Coast. Pyramid Lake, just east of Reno, is shrouded in the mysteries of Indian legend and prehistoric past; Virginia City, still the liveliest ghost town in the West, is only a 35-mile drive from Reno; Carson City, Nevada's State Capital, is only 30 miles from Reno; and nearby Lake Tahoe was described by Mark Twain as "surely the fairest picture the whole earth affords."

Arts and Culture

Reno offers a flourishing and diverse community of artistic talent. The 1,500-seat Pioneer Center for the Performing Arts is the home of the Reno Philharmonic Orchestra, AVA Ballet Theatre, and the Nevada Opera. Music concerts are also performed by the Sierra Nevada Master-Works Chorale. The University of Nevada, Reno presents a variety of art galleries, music, and performing arts.

The Nevada Museum of Art, originally called the Nevada Art Gallery in 1931, debuted its new four-level, 55,000 square foot location in 2003 and features a permanent collection along with video and experimental exhibitions. A library, cafe, sculpture garden, and store are among the other modern amenities offered.

Festivals and Holidays

Special events are plentiful and varied in Reno. The Reno Rodeo, the "wildest, richest rodeo in the west," takes place over nine days in June and infuses more than $40 million into the local economy. Reno's summer arts festival, Artown, has been named one of the top 100 Events in North America by the American Bus Association. The festival takes place every July, when more than 150 events at three dozen locations. In August, the Reno area celebrates America's love affair with cars and rock 'n' roll during the five-day Hot August Nights. The celebration features more than 5,000 classic cars, vintage music, parades, and drag racing. September is full of celebrations including the Great Reno Balloon Race, which features more than 100 hot air balloons; National Championship Air Races and Air Show; and Street Vibrations, which attracts thousands of motorcycle enthusiasts annually. October brings the Eldorado's Great Italian Festival and the Celtic Celebration.

Sports for the Spectator

Reno is making a name for itself as the mountain golf capital of the world. Since 1999 the PGA Tour's Reno-Tahoe Open has taken place at Montreux Golf and Country Club in July, where some of the world's best professional golfers compete. A celebrity-packed golfing event, the American Century Celebrity Championship, is also held annually at Edgewood-Tahoe golf course in July.

The country's largest bowling organizations the American Bowling Congress (ABC), the Women's International Bowling Congress (WIBC), Youth American Bowling Alliance, and USA Bowling merged in 2005 to create the United State Bowling Congress (USBC). The organization holds tournaments at the National Bowling Stadium. Dubbed the "Taj Mahal of Tenpins" by *The Los Angeles Times*, it draws thousands of bowlers to its high-technology facility on a regular basis.

The University of Nevada, Reno offers spectators the chance to cheer on Wolf Pack teams playing football, basketball, softball, volleyball, and other popular sports.

Sports for the Participant

Reno offers a seemingly limitless variety of indoor and outdoor activities. Snow-packed mountains, less than an hour from Reno, feature the largest concentration of world-class ski/snowboard resorts in North America. In the summer months, the same mountains, as well as the valley below, offer hiking and mountain biking. Since 1994 the three-day annual Mighty Tour De Nez Classic has featured different levels of regional bicyclers. Lake Tahoe, "the Jewel of the Sierra," is the perfect place for a day of canoeing, water skiing, swimming, and more.

High desert, rolling hills and mountainous alpine terrain make for some of the greatest golf courses found anywhere. The Reno-Tahoe area boasts more than 40 courses at 4,000 feet above sea level—golfers can watch their balls fly farther through the thin air. The Reno area also offers great fishing in a variety of streams, rivers, and lakes. Non-resident fishing licenses are available at most sporting goods stores.

Shopping and Dining

More than 90 area shopping centers sell items ranging from the usual designer apparel to Native American handicrafts and Western art and clothing. Popular centers

in Reno include Franktown Corners, Southwest Pavilion, and Meadowood Mall. Sparks is home to Victorian Square Plaza.

Restaurants in Reno range from simple to extravagant. A local specialty are family-style Basque dinners.

Visitor Information: Reno-Sparks Convention & Visitors Authority, 4590 S. Virginia Street, Reno, NV 89502; telephone (800) 367-7366.

■ Convention Facilities

In the heart of downtown is the two-floor Reno Events Center, which has a capacity of 7,000 and hosts everything from business conventions to rock concerts. In 2002 the Reno-Sparks Convention Center completed an extensive $100 million expansion to provide convention and meeting planners with a modern, high-tech facility. The convention center's total space increased to nearly 500,000 square feet, including 53 meeting rooms and exhibit space totaling 381,000 square feet.

Meeting attendees can visit the National Bowling Stadium in Reno, where customized tournaments on its 78 championship lanes can be arranged for groups from 100 to 2,000 people in the four-story facility that boasts a 172-seat theater. The Reno-Sparks Livestock Events Center provides space for livestock and equestrian events, as well as meetings. It features a 20,000-square-foot exhibition hall, and a climate-controlled main arena that seats 6,200. Theater-style seating for more than 1,500 people is available at the Pioneer Center for the Performing Arts in downtown Reno. The Lawlor Events Center, a large multipurpose arena on the campus of the University of Nevada, Reno, is also available for conventions and can seat around 12,000.

Reno has more than 20,000 first-class guestrooms all within minutes of the Reno-Sparks Convention Center and Reno-Tahoe International Airport. Many other local properties also offer facilities for meetings and conventions.

Convention Information: Reno-Sparks Convention & Visitors Authority, 4590 S. Virginia Street, Reno, NV 89502; telephone (800) 367-7366.

■ Transportation

Approaching the City

The Reno-Tahoe International Airport (RNO) is located three miles south of downtown Reno. The airport is served by seven major airlines and offers more than 100 flights daily to 15 non-stop destinations. It is also an international Port of Entry. The airport serves about four million passengers annually. Reno Stead Airport is a small general aviation airport located 15 miles north of Reno, with lengthened runways and an Air Tanker Facility.

Passenger rail service is available from Amtrak via the "California Zephyr," described as the most scenic train ride in the United States, with daily service from San Francisco and Chicago. The city is also served by commercial bus lines.

Interstate 80 runs through Reno's downtown region, west to San Francisco, and east to Salt Lake City. U.S. Highway 395 passes just east of the city, connecting Reno with Portland and Seattle to the north, and Los Angeles to the south.

Traveling in the City

Washoe County's Regional Transportation Commission (RTC) provides bus travel throughout the metropolitan area; most of its buses have wheelchair accessibility. RTC's ACCESS offers door-to-door service to those with special transportation needs. The Sierra Spirit bus line gives free rides to passengers in the downtown area. RTC began using low-floor, diesel-electric hybrid buses in 2010. Major thoroughfares in the city include Virginia Street, Plumb Lane, Kietzke Lane, and Mill Street.

■ Communications

Newspapers and Magazines

The *Reno Gazette-Journal* is the city's daily and Sunday newspaper, published in the morning. The *Daily Sparks Tribune* is a daily newspaper published in neighboring Sparks since 1910. Also published in Reno are the *Nevada Sagebrush* (a collegiate newspaper), and the alternative *Reno News and Review*.

Television and Radio

Commercial television station affiliates ABC, NBC, FOX, CBS, and PBS are based in the greater Reno area; a variety of channels are available from the local cable system. More than 20 radio stations broadcast from the Reno/Tahoe area.

Media Information: *Reno Gazette-Journal,* 995 Kuenzli St., Reno, NV 89502; telephone (775) 788-6200.

Reno Online

City of Reno. Available www. reno.gov
Economic Development Authority of Western Nevada. Available www.edawn.org
Nevada Department of Employment, Training & Rehabilitation. Available detr.state.nv.us
Reno Gazette-Journal. Available www.rgj.com
Northern Nevada Chamber of Commerce. Available www.renosparkschamber.org
Reno-Tahoe Convention & Visitors Authority. Available www.visitrenotahoe.com
Truckee Meadows Community College. Available www.tmcc.edu
Washoe County Library. Available www. washoecounty.us/library
Washoe County School District. Available www. washoe.k12.nv.us

BIBLIOGRAPHY

Betts, Doris, *The Sharp Teeth of Love: A Novel* (New York: Scribner, 1998)

Land, Barbara and Myrick Land, *A Short History of Reno* (Reno: University of Nevada Press, 1995)

Rothman, Hal, *The Making of Modern Nevada* (Reno: University of Nevada Press, 2010)

Twain, Mark, *Mark Twain of the Enterprise; Newspaper Articles and Other Documents, 1862–1864* (Berkeley, CA: U. of California Press, 1957)

Wilds, Leah J., *Water Politics in Northern Nevada: A Century of Struggle* (Reno: University of Nevada Press, 2010)

New Mexico

The State in Brief

Nickname: Land of Enchantment

Motto: Crescit eundo (It grows as it goes)

Flower: Yucca

Bird: Roadrunner

Area: 121,590 square miles (2010; U.S. rank 5th)

Elevation: Ranges from 2,842 feet to 13,161 feet above sea level

Climate: Semi arid and sunny, with temperatures varying according to elevation

Admitted to Union: January 6, 1912

Capital: Santa Fe

Head Official: Susana Martinez (R) (until 2015)

Population

1990: 1,515,069
2000: 1,819,046
2010: 2,059,179
2012 estimate: 2,055,287
Percent change, 2000–2010: 13.2%
U.S. rank in 2012: 36th
Percent of residents born in state: 52.1% (2012)
Density: 17.0 people per square mile (2010)
2012 FBI Crime Index Total: 86,754

Racial and Ethnic Characteristics (2012)

White: 1,492,641
Black or African American: 41,634
American Indian and Alaska Native: 189,785
Asian: 26,855
Native Hawaiian and Pacific Islander: 1,344
Hispanic or Latino (may be of any race): 952,569
Other: 303,028

Age Characteristics (2012)

Population under 5 years old: 143,937
Population 5 to 19 years old: 432,699
Percent of population 65 years and over: 13.4%
Median age: 36.6

Vital Statistics

Total number of births (2012–13): 27,146
Total number of deaths (2012–13): 16,472
AIDS cases reported through 2011: 3,268

Economy

Major industries: Government, manufacturing, services, aerospace, defense
Unemployment rate (2012): 5.5%
Per capita income (2012): $23,749
Median household income (2012): $44,886
Percentage of persons below poverty level (2012): 19.5%
Income tax rate: 1.7% to 4.9%
Sales tax rate: 5.125%

Albuquerque

■ The City in Brief

Founded: 1706 (incorporated, 1891)

Head Official: Mayor Richard J. Berry (since 2009; current term expires 2017)

City Population

    1990: 384,915
    2000: 448,607
    2010: 545,852
    2012 estimate: 555,419
    Percent change, 2000–2010: 21.7%
    U.S. rank in 1990: 38th (State rank: 1st)
    U.S. rank in 2000: 42nd (State rank: 1st)
    U.S. rank in 2010: 32nd (State rank: 1st)

Metropolitan Statistical Area Population

    2000: 729,649
    2010: 887,077
    2012 estimate: 902,794
    Percent change, 2000–2010: 21.6%
    U.S. rank in 2000: 65th
    U.S. rank in 2010: 57th

Area: 180.64 square miles

Elevation: 5,311 feet above sea level

Average Annual Temperatures: January, 35.7° F; July, 78.5° F; annual average, 56.8° F

Average Annual Precipitation: 9.47 inches of rain; 11.0 inches of snow

Major Economic Sectors: government, research, defense, health care, trade, manufacturing

Unemployment Rate: 5.3% (2012)

Per Capita Income: $25,786

2012 FBI Crime Index Property: 29,718

Major Colleges and Universities: University of New Mexico, University of Phoenix, Albuquerque Technical-Vocational Institute, College of Santa Fe at Albuquerque

Daily Newspaper: *Albuquerque Journal*

■ Introduction

Surrounded by natural beauty, Albuquerque is at the center of Native American pueblo country in New Mexico, the "Land of Enchantment." The state's largest city, Albuquerque retains deep roots in the past and simultaneously stands on the cutting edge of the future. The original Spanish town was built on the site of the oldest farming civilization in North America; modern Albuquerque is the focal point of the "Rio Grande Research Corridor," one of the nation's primary space-research complexes. The city's residents have maintained ethnic traditions and preserved a high quality of life, while at the same time fostering modern growth and economic development. Albuquerque's thriving arts scene comple-ments its rich heritage and is yet another reason why the city is consistently noted as one of the best places to live in America.

■ Geography and Climate

Albuquerque is situated in the middle of the Rio Grande valley. To the east of the city are the Sandia and Manzano mountains; to the west are five volcanic cones that mark the beginning of high plateau country. The climate in Albuquerque, termed "arid-continental," is sunny and dry with very low humidity. Half of the annual precipitation falls between July and September in heavy afternoon thundershowers. During the winter one can ski on Sandia Peak and play a round of golf on the same day.

Area: 180.64 square miles

David Liu/Getty Images

Elevation: 5,311 feet above sea level

Average Temperatures: January, 35.7° F; July, 78.5° F; annual average, 56.8° F

Average Annual Precipitation: 9.47 inches of rain; 11.0 inches of snow

■ History

Early Native American and Spanish Influences

The region surrounding present-day Albuquerque was home to several groups of Native American peoples, including "Sandia Man," who lived there and hunted mastodon during the ice age 25,000 years ago. Albuquerque was later inhabited by the ancient Anasazi Indians. Their huge apartment-like buildings, constructed 3,000 years ago of stone and adobe, are still standing. The city continues to be a center of Native American culture; most of New Mexico's 19 pueblos—including the thousand-year-old, still-inhabited Acoma Pueblo—are within an hour's drive. To the north is Sandia Pueblo Indian Reservation. Albuquerque's modern architecture, particularly buildings on the University of New Mexico campus, combines modern design elements with Native American and Hispanic motifs.

Albuquerque was founded as a villa in 1706 by Spanish colonists, who were attracted to the banks of the Rio Grande by the green pastures they needed to graze their sheep. The city is named for a Spanish Duke, the tenth Duke of Albuquerque (over time the first "r" in his name was dropped). The first structure built in Albuquerque was a church named for the city's patron saint, San Felipe de Neri. The original adobe walls remain standing in the part of the city known as Old Town.

City Becomes Distribution Center

Although the topography of the land—the mountains to the east and the Rio Grande to the west—afforded the settlement natural protection, Albuquerque was regularly threatened during the nineteenth century by hostile attacks, particularly from the Navajo and Apache. In the meantime, the town assumed a role as purveyor of goods to the West and served as a link in trade with Mexico. Situated on the Old Chihuahua trail, an extension of the Santa Fe Trail, Albuquerque's stores and warehouses were perfectly positioned to supply forts that were established in the Southwest to protect westward-moving settlers. Albuquerque became a U.S. Army post in 1846 and was occupied by the Confederacy for two months during the Civil War.

In 1880 rail travel arrived in Albuquerque. The town's strength as a transportation and trade center grew as manufactured goods were shipped in from the East and raw materials and livestock were transported from the West. A bustling new town quickly sprang up around the railroad and then grew to take in historic Old Town. In 1883 Albuquerque became the seat of Bernalillo County, and in 1891 it was incorporated as a city. Already an established oasis of civilization, Albuquerque, unlike other southwestern towns, never suffered from the boisterousness of the Old West.

Development of Atomic Bomb Brings High Technology

Until World War II, Albuquerque remained a small, quiet city. Then the development of the atomic bomb at nearby Los Alamos brought the town into the nuclear age. Now an important part of the Rio Grande Research Corridor, Albuquerque has undergone record population growth. It is a center of large high-technology industries that have evolved around the research and development of atomic energy and space exploration, drawing as well hundreds of smaller research firms.

The city celebrated its tricentennial in 2006 with events and exhibits honoring Albuquerque's art, history, and culture. Into the 2010s, the city continued to gain notoriety for growth in its high-technology industries, both through expansion of existing companies and relocation of others. The city became a pop-culture icon following the success of the television series *Breaking Bad*, which was filmed and set in Albuquerque.

■ Population Profile

Metropolitan Statistical Area Population

2000: 729,649
2010: 887,077
2012 estimate: 902,794
Percent change, 2000–2010: 21.6%
U.S. rank in 2000: 65th
U.S. rank in 2010: 57th

City Residents

1990: 384,915
2000: 448,607
2010: 545,852
2012 estimate: 555,419
Percent change, 2000–2010: 21.7%
U.S. rank in 1990: 38th (State rank: 1st)
U.S. rank in 2000: 42nd (State rank: 1st)
U.S. rank in 2010: 32nd (State rank: 1st)

Density: 2,907.6 people per square mile

Racial and ethnic characteristics

White: 384,566
Black or African American: 18,373
American Indian and Alaskan Native: 23,905
Asian: 14,026
Native Hawaiian and Other Pacific Islander: 665
Hispanic or Latino (may be of any race): 259,184
Other: 113,884

Percent of residents born in state: 51.6%

Age characteristics

Population under 5 years old: 36,986
Population 5 to 9 years old: 38,384
Population 10 to 14 years old: 35,547
Population 15 to 19 years old: 35,660
Population 20 to 24 years old: 43,052
Population 25 to 34 years old: 86,465
Population 35 to 44 years old: 70,145
Population 45 to 54 years old: 72,321
Population 55 to 59 years old: 33,251
Population 60 to 64 years old: 32,625
Population 65 to 74 years old: 39,778
Population 75 to 84 years old: 21,766
Population 85 years and over: 9,439
Median age: 35.3

Births (2010–11 Metropolitan Area)

Total number: 11,693

Deaths (2010–11 Metropolitan Area)

Total number: 6,590

Money income (2012)

Per capita income: $25,786
Median household income: $46,060
Total households: 224,766

Number of households with income of ...

less than $10,000: 20,756
$10,000 to $14,999: 13,611
$15,000 to $24,999: 27,280
$25,000 to $34,999: 26,435
$35,000 to $49,999: 31,451
$50,000 to $74,999: 40,107
$75,000 to $99,999: 24,897
$100,000 to $149,999: 25,027
$150,000 to $199,999: 8,544
$200,000 or more: 6,658

Percent of families below poverty level: 18.3%

FBI Crime Index Property: 29,718

FBI Crime Index Violent: 4,151

■ Municipal Government

Albuquerque operates under a mayor-council form of government, with a full-time mayor, nine council members—all of whom serve staggered four-year terms— and a chief administrative officer, who is appointed by the mayor. The city is the seat of Bernalillo County.

Head Official: Mayor Richard J. Berry (since 2009; current term expires 2017)

Total Number of City Employees: More than 5,854 (2012)

City Information: City of Albuquerque, PO Box 1293, Albuquerque, NM 87103; telephone (505) 768-3000.

■ Economy

Major Industries and Commercial Activity

The largest city in New Mexico, Albuquerque is also its economic center; it accounts for nearly half of the state's economic activity. The city is most noted as a manufacturing and high-tech research center, namely due to its mix of public research institutions and major manufacturers. Its economic success is also attributed to a diverse economic base consisting of government, services, trade, agriculture, and tourism. In 2013–14 the city was ranked 9th among mid-sized American Cities of the Future by *fDi Magazine*.

Albuquerque is home to hundreds of manufacturing firms—many of them located in well-planned industrial parks—that produce such goods as trailers, food products, electronic components, neon and electric signs, hardware, and machine tools. Among the major manufacturing firms that call Albuquerque home are General Mills and Tempur-Pedic. Intel maintains one of its largest semiconductor manufacturing plants in Albuquerque.

The Rio Grande Research Corridor is a constellation of high-technology industries. The corridor sprang up in the wake of the development of nuclear research during and after World War II, with its focal point in Albuquerque. Each year, more than $4 billion is spent on research and development in the region. Several of the area's major employers are part of this complex, namely Sandia National Laboratories and the Kirtland U.S. Air Force Base. Sandia National Laboratories, a government research and development lab, is involved in laser- and nanotechnology and solar energy, and employs nearly 9,000 residents. New Mexico's many sunny days have drawn private solar energy firms as well, such as UniRac, Emcore, Array Technologies, Sacred Power, and Fraunhofer CFV Solar Test Laboratory.

In part due to the influence of Sandia National Laboratories, New Mexico has consistently ranked as a national leader in Microsystems and nanotechnology. Development of the industry can also be traced to efforts by Central New Mexico Community College to become the first community college nationwide to offer a full curriculum of Micro Electromechanical Systems courses. NanoPore, NanoCool, Qynergy, and HT Micro, Inc., represent private industry.

Kirtland U.S. Air Force Base is a weapons research center and includes the Air Force Research Laboratory's Space Vehicles Directorate. The presence of the defense installation has attracted several major private companies, including Honeywell Aerospace, Devore Aviation, Eclipse Aerospace, Bendix/King, Aspen Avionics, Sun Country Industries, and Lockheed Martin.

For nearly a century people have valued Albuquerque for its dry air, which is especially beneficial to those with respiratory problems. Today the city's medical services and facilities are a vital part of the local economy. The biotechnology and biomedicine industry has more than 100 companies located in the area. Major medical based companies in Albuquerque include Johnson & Johnson's, Ethicon Endo-Surgery (medical instruments), and Cardinal Health (pharmaceuticals).

The year-round sunny weather attracts pleasure seekers as well; some $5 billion in direct expenditures are tied to the tourist industry each year, and it provides residents with 55,000 jobs.

Items and goods produced: machine tools, fabricated structural steel, furniture, hardware, textiles, paints, varnishes, fertilizers, scientific instruments, electronic equipment, neon and electric signs, Native American jewelry and curios

Incentive Programs—New and Existing Companies

Local programs: Among the factors that draw businesses to Albuquerque are the city's affordable cost of living (based on cost of labor, energy, taxes, and office space) and its highly-educated workforce. Albuquerque Economic Development, Inc. (AED) is a private, nonprofit organization that recruits companies to the Albuquerque area. AED works with the city of Albuquerque Economic Development Department to provide site-selection assistance, labor market analysis, business incentive analysis, workforce recruitment and job-training assistance, and coordination of state and local assistance, among other services. Technology Ventures Corporation, a non-profit organization, serves as a bridge between the public and private sectors for the commercialization of technologies developed at the national labs and research universities, and assists in the expansion of existing businesses.

The city of Albuquerque also issues industrial revenue bonds (IRBs) to companies looking to fund construction and renovation of manufacturing plants, research and development facilities, and corporate headquarters. Projects using IRBs may be exempt for up to 20 years from property taxes on land, buildings, and equipment.

State programs: New Mexico offers a variety of incentives to all new and expanding businesses. The High-Wage Jobs Tax Credit allows qualified businesses to take a generous tax credit for each new job created with a salary of at least $28,000 a year (in areas where the population does not exceed 40,000) or $40,000 a year (in areas where the population exceeds 40,000).

Other tax credit incentives include a Manufacturer's Investment Tax Credit, a New Markets Tax Credit, a Technology Jobs Tax Credit, Aircraft Manufacturing Tax Deduction, Aircraft Maintenance or Remodeling Tax Deduction, Space Gross Receipts Tax Credit, Alternative Energy Product Manufacturer's Tax Credit, New Mexico Refundable Film Production Tax Credit, and State Film Investment Loan Program. New Mexico's property taxes are among the lowest in the nation.

Job training programs: New Mexico is home to one of the most aggressive training incentive packages in the nation. Through the Job Training Incentive Program (JTIP) expanding or relocated businesses can receive up to six months of funds for classroom and on-the-job-training for newly created jobs. The JTIP reimburses required travel expenses and up to 65 percent of employee wages.

In 2007 the Governor's Office of Workforce Training & Development merged with the New Mexico Department of Labor to create a new branch called the New Mexico Department of Workforce Solutions. The combined department focuses on preparing job seekers to meet current standards in the labor market as well as effectively matching citizens with businesses in need of help. Services available include job fairs, local workforce development centers, online job searches, and online registration for employment services.

Albuquerque's Central New Mexico Community College (CNM) also meets companies' needs in the area with their customized training programs. The community college supplies local manufacturing companies with a continual stream of trained personnel composed of graduates of their two-year Advanced Manufacturing program. It also helps bolster Albuquerque's high-tech workforce with its programs dedicated to training students for the microelectronics industry and as micro-systems technicians.

Development Projects

Several businesses were relocating or expanding in the Albuquerque area during 2012–13. These included Admiral Beverage Corporation, which in 2012 built a $15 million, 219,000-square-foot distribution facility in the South Valley area just outside Albuquerque. In 2013 Canon U.S.A. announced plans for a 33,682-square-foot customer support center, expected to open in 2014 and create 150 new jobs. Lowe's completed a $25 million customer support center in Albuquerque, set to employ some 900, in 2013.

City-sponsored projects included improvements to the Paseo del Norte and Interstate 25 interchange, expected to complete in 2015, and a two-phase renovation of the Albuquerque Convention Center, the first of which completed in 2013, with the second stage scheduled to finish in 2014.The Bare Canyon Senior Center enjoyed $1.8 million in renovations in 2013.

The University of New Mexico planned to establish its Innovate ABQ initiative at an existing downtown property, which it purchased in 2013. Total investment was expected to reach more than $7 million. A 10-month renovation of the retail outlet Coronado Center was expected to complete in late 2014.

Economic Development Information: Albuquerque Economic Development, 851 University Boulevard SE, Suite 203, Albuquerque, NM 87106; telephone (505) 246-6200; toll-free (800) 451-2933.

Commercial Shipping

Since the days of the Santa Fe Trail, Albuquerque has been an important center for the transportation of goods. The city's economy benefits from the Burlington Northern Santa Fe Railroad, which operates a north–south line that connects in Albuquerque, as well as an east–west line connecting about 40 miles south of the city in Belen.

New Mexico is a Freeport State, meaning that business inventories for resale, raw materials, and inter-state commerce products stored there temporarily are not subject to state or local property taxes. Albuquerque, a registered U.S. Port of Entry, has its own customs facility. This allows freight cargo to be shipped directly with duties paid locally.

Albuquerque offers an international airport, Albuquerque International Sunport, with a port of entry from Mexico; the airport is served by three all-cargo service providers: DHL, FedEx, and UPS. Foreign trade zones operate in Albuquerque, which allow goods to be manufactured or stored in these zones without the imposition of a U.S. customs duty.

Labor Force and Employment Outlook

The city's labor force is relatively young, skilled, and educated; Albuquerque is notable for its high percentage of advanced degree holders thanks to the large student population affiliated with the University of New Mexico, Central New Mexico Community College, and the Albuquerque Public School District. Albuquerque's work force is also routinely cited for its productivity, and the metropolitan area accounts for 45 percent of the state's total employment. While government employs the greatest number of residents, five sectors employ at least 10 percent of the population, highlighting the city's diversified economy. During 2012–13, the strongest growth industry was information, followed by the combined demographic of mining, lodging, and construction.

The following is a summary of data regarding the 2012 Albuquerque labor force:

Size of civilian labor force: 284,240

Number of workers employed in ...

agriculture and mining: 2,497
construction: 15,461
manufacturing: 13,513
wholesale trade: 6,030
retail trade: 29,623
transportation: 8,463
information systems: 5,325
finance: 13,599
professional administration: 36,602
education and social services: 67,382
arts and leisure: 29,360
other: 11,482
public administration: 19,052

Average hourly earnings of production workers: $16.84

Unemployment rate: 5.3% (2012)

Employers

Largest employers (2012)	*Number of employees*
Albuquerque Public Schools	14,810
University of New Mexico	14,644
Sandia National Labs	8,930
Presbyterian Hospital	8,217
Kirtland Air Force Base (civilian)	6,095
UNM Hospital	5,959
City of Albuquerque	5,854
State of New Mexico	5,590
Kirtland Air Force Base (military)	4,520
Lovelace Health System	4,000

Cost of Living

Albuquerque's cost of living is slightly below the national average. The city has been noted as one of the least expensive in which to live a high-end lifestyle.

The following is a summary of data regarding several key cost of living factors in the area.

2013 ACCRA Average House Price: $253,038

2013 ACCRA Cost of Living Index: 93

State income tax rate: 1.7% to 4.9%

State sales tax rate: 5.125%

Local income tax rate: None

Local sales tax rate: 1.875%

Property tax rate: 46.801 mills (2013)

Economic Information: Greater Albuquerque Chamber of Commerce, 115 Gold Avenue SW, Suite 201, Albuquerque, NM 87102; telephone (505) 764-3700; fax (505) 764-3714.

■ Education and Research

Elementary and Secondary Schools

The Albuquerque Public Schools (APS) system, one of the largest in the nation and the largest in New Mexico, is administered by a nonpartisan, seven-member school board and a superintendency team. The Albuquerque Public School system serves Albuquerque, Rio Rancho, Corrales, Los Ranchos de Albuquerque, Tijeras, San Antonito, and Edgewood as well as Laguna and Isleta pueblos, Chilili, Tohajiilee, and the Atrisco Land Grant. The APS is composed of some 140 schools and an astounding more than 90,000 students. Some 6,080 students in the district attend one of the city's additional 33 charter schools. The Albuquerque Institute for Math & Science at UNM Charter School was named a National Blue Ribbon School in 2013 by the U.S. Department of Education.

The Albuquerque area has more than 70 private or parochial schools. Among these schools, Albuquerque Academy—a prep school for talented students in grades six through 12—is regarded as one of the top private schools in the nation.

The following is a summary of data regarding the Albuquerque Public Schools.

Total enrollment: 95,415

Number of facilities

total: 140
elementary schools: 89
junior high schools: 27
high schools: 13
other: 11

Student/teacher ratio: 15:1

Teacher salaries

average (statewide): $46,950

Funding per pupil: $8,662

Public Schools Information: Albuquerque Public Schools, 6400 Uptown Blvd., NE,, Albuquerque, NM 87110; telephone (505) 880-3700.

Colleges and Universities

The University of New Mexico (UNM), the state's largest institution of higher learning and part of the Rio

Grande Research Corridor complex, is based in Albuquerque, with branch campuses in Gallup, Los Alamos, Taos, Valencia, and west Albuquerque. The main campus had an enrollment of nearly 30,000 students in 2013. The university offers more than 210 degree and certificate programs and is particularly strong in Latin American studies, flamenco dance, anthropology, and medicine—its rural medicine and family medicine programs consistently are ranked among the best nationally.

The city is also home to Central New Mexico Community College (CNM), formerly Albuquerque Technical-Vocational Institute, the largest community college in New Mexico with more than 28,000 students. The community college offers associate's degrees in about 50 occupational and liberal arts fields. Central New Mexico Community College and the University of New Mexico passed a joint agreement in 2007 to give students access to several services at both schools. Plans for this new collaboration included dual enrollment, easier transition for CNM students to finish a four-year degree at UNM, and allowing CNM students to access UNM dorms and recreational services.

Other institutions in Albuquerque include the New Mexico campus of the University of Phoenix, offering bachelor's and advanced degrees across eight main fields; a campus of ITT Technical Institute, which offers degrees in information technology, electronics technology, drafting and design, business, and criminal justice; and National American University, which offers associate and bachelor's degrees in dozens of programs.

Libraries and Research Centers

The Albuquerque Bernalillo County Library system is a consortium of the City of Albuquerque, Bernalillo County, and the City of Rio Rancho. Public library service is available through a large main library and 16 branches throughout the Albuquerque area, including a Special Collections Library specializing in genealogy and regional history and the Erne Pyle Branch, former home of the famed World War II correspondent, displaying a collection of his memorabilia. The library system has a collection of more than 1.4 million items, including periodicals and audio-visual materials.

The University of New Mexico libraries include six branches that collectively maintain more than 2.2 million volumes. The branches include the Health Sciences Library and Informatics, Law Library, Centennial Science and Engineering Library, Fine Arts and Design Library, Parish Memorial Library for Business and Economics, and the Zimmerman Library. Collection strengths include Latin American history, regional photography, music and architecture, American Indian affairs, and maps. The Health Sciences Library serves the medical school and the health professions statewide. The Law Library is the primary legal library in the state and has

special collections in American Indian and Latin American Law.

Research activities in such fields as water resources, Southwestern biology, power systems, alternative energy, artificial intelligence, robotics, anthropology, satellite data analysis, business and economics, Native American law, aging and health policy issues, Latin America, and Hispanic and Chicano studies are conducted at centers in the Albuquerque area. The University of New Mexico (UNM) is the state's primary research university. Among its research units are the Center for Advanced Studies (quantum optics, laser physics, etc.), Center of Biomedical Engineering, New Mexico Engineering Research Institute, Center for High Technology Materials, Center for Advanced Research Computing, Center for Micro-Engineered Materials, and the Latin American and Iberian Institute. Many of UNM's research centers work in alliance with industry partners such as Toyota Motor Company, Delphi, and Sandia National Laboratories. The school's Health Sciences Center for treatment, research, and education receives more than $145 in annual grant money.

Other research centers based in Albuquerque include the Behavioral Health Research Center of the Southwest, which conducts research on substance abuse and other behavioral health issues, and the Air Force Research Lab at Kirtland Air Force Base, where space- and missile-related research is performed. Sandia National Laboratories, based in nearby Sandia, performs national security research.

Public Library Information: Main Library, 501 Copper NW, Albuquerque, NM 87102; telephone (505) 768-5170.

■ Health Care

In the 1920s Albuquerque, like many other cities in the Southwest, became a mecca for people suffering from respiratory diseases and allergies who seek relief in the warm, dry climate. Today, advanced medical care is available at the University of New Mexico Health Sciences Center, which encompasses UNM Hospital, UNM Carrie Tingley Hospital, UNM Children's Hospital, UNM Children's Psychiatric Center, UNM Psychiatric Center, and UNM Cancer Center. UNM opened a new $233.8 million, 476,555-square-foot expansion of its children's hospital in 2007.

Albuquerque's other major hospitals are the 552-bed Presbyterian Hospital, New Mexico's largest acute-care hospital, and the 263-bed Lovelace Medical Center, which specializes in orthopedics, ophthalmology, neurology and neurosurgery, oncology, and cardiology. In 1959 the first Americans in space underwent a newly developed test series at the Lovelace Clinic in preparation for their mission.

■ Recreation

Sightseeing

Albuquerque's unique mixture of Native American, Hispanic, and Anglo heritages provides visitors with a variety of activities. Albuquerque's spiritual heart is Old Town, dating to the city's founding in 1706, where an arts community flourishes. Old Town is an atmospheric area of quaint adobe-style buildings with flat roofs and rounded edges, with windows frequently decorated with strings of dried chili peppers for good luck, and winding cobblestone or brick walkways leading to tucked-away patios and gardens. Old Town's Plaza features an outdoor Native American market offering traditional arts and crafts such as textiles, jewelry, and pottery. Also located in Old Town is San Felipe de Neri church, the city's oldest building, enclosing the adobe walls of the original presidio (fort). The area is also home to some 150 shops and galleries.

The landscape surrounding the city is particularly scenic and provides some of the area's principal attractions. To the west are a high mesa and five extinct volcanoes; to the east are the magnificent Sandia and Manzano mountains. Sandia Crest in the Cibola National Forest, 30 miles from Albuquerque, offers a breathtaking view that encompasses 11,000 square miles. A skylift operates there throughout the year, carrying skiers and hikers up the mountain. The Aerial Tramway, 2.7 miles in length and one of the longest in the world, runs to the top of 10,378-foot Sandia Peak.

Evidence of Albuquerque's Native American roots can be found in the numerous pueblos around the city, many of them at least 1,000 years old and some still inhabited. Active pueblos within an hour's drive of Albuquerque include Acoma, Cochiti, Isleta, Jemez, Laguna, Sandia, San Felipe, Santa Ana, Santo Domingo, and Zia. Acoma is perhaps the most spectacular; a walled adobe village atop a sheer rock mesa, the community dates to the eleventh century or earlier and is thought to be the longest continuously occupied community in the country. Reminders of the ancient native civilization also exist in dozens of ruins and archaeological sites, among them Petroglyph State Monument, where some 17,000 petroglyphs (images carved in rock) dating back as far as 1300, can be found.

The Rio Grande Nature Center State Park, located a few miles north of Old Town, offers several miles of nature trails through the Southwest *bosque* (the grove of cottonwood growing along the Rio Grande). The Albuquerque Biological Park consists of four separate facilities: Rio Grande Zoo, Albuquerque Aquarium, Rio Grande Botanic Garden, and Tingley Beach. The zoo sits on 64 acres and is an oasis for both exotic and native species, such as seals and sea lions, gorillas, orangutans, elephants, polar bears, giraffes, camels, tamarinds, koalas, Mexican wolves, mountain lions, monkeys, jaguars, zebras, and rhinoceros; one of the missions of the zoo is the breeding of endangered species. At the Albuquerque Aquarium visitors can follow the story of a drop of water as it enters the upper Rio Grande high in the San Juan Mountains of Colorado and flows past canyons, deserts, and valleys in New Mexico, Texas, and Mexico, before reaching the Gulf of Mexico. The aquarium features exhibits of Gulf of Mexico saltwater species. The Botanic Garden is 36 acres of developed land that includes a 10,000-square-foot conservatory divided into a Desert Pavilion and a Mediterranean Pavilion. Tingley Beach offers three fishing lakes, a train station, a model boating pond, and pedal boat and bicycle rentals.

Glancing skyward in Albuquerque, spectators frequently see the colorful spectacle of hang-gliders and hot-air balloons drifting slowly past. A combination of sunshine and topography produces steady geothermal winds, making the area ideal for wind sports and earning the city the nickname "Hot Air Balloon Capital of the World."

Albuquerque's Central Avenue, which runs east–west through the city, is considered one of the best-preserved sections of historic Route 66 in the state. Along the avenue are more than 100 classic structures, including diners, motor courts, and theaters, in architectural styles ranging from Streamline Moderne to Pueblo Deco.

Arts and Culture

Albuquerque actively promotes its rich cultural community. In 1979 the city council created an ordinance that assigns 1 percent of monies generated by revenue bonds and general obligation bonds to public construction and public art. Consequently, Albuquerque abounds with sculptures and murals attesting to the city's artistic energies. Along Central Avenue, from historic Old Town on the east through downtown and the university area to Nob Hill on the west, is Albuquerque's "cultural corridor." In the numerous theaters, museums, galleries, and cafes, and at other sites along this route, the stimulating and diverse cultural life of Albuquerque is on view.

Albuquerque has more than 30 performing arts centers and groups. The KiMo Theatre, an ornate 1927 Pueblo Deco-style landmark downtown, is on the National Register of Historic Places; it serves as a performing arts theater, hosting a number of groups, with seating for 700. The Albuquerque Little Theatre presents comedies, mysteries, and light classics in its own playhouse near Old Town. Vortex Theatre offers off-Broadway original and classic plays. A new African American Performing Arts Center opened in 2007. The 23,000-square-foot facility hosts permanent and traveling art exhibits, music, theater, and dance performances, as well as educational programs about the history, culture, and arts of people of African descent.

Albuquerque is home to the New Mexico Ballet Company, founded in 1972, which performs classic dances in the KiMo Theatre and in Popejoy Hall on the University of New Mexico campus. Dance performances by visiting artists and groups can also be seen at KiMo Theatre. Popejoy Hall, the primary facility in the city for the performance of orchestral music and opera, is home to the Ovation Series—which offers a variety of events including drama and comedy, and ballet and modern dance—and the New Mexico Philharmonic. Based in the city and one of the Southwest's most prestigious orchestras, the symphony presents classical, baroque, and pops, as well as Symphony Under the Stars and other special concerts. Musical Theatre Southwest performs classical and new musicals and is one of the largest producers of community theater in the country. Chamber Music Albuquerque, established in 1942, brings chamber ensembles from around the world to Albuquerque.

Many of Albuquerque's museums concentrate on area history and culture. The New Mexico Museum of Natural History and Science features exhibits exploring the geological and anthropological history of New Mexico, through Paleozoic-era fossils, full-scale dinosaur models, a walk-through volcano, and a replica of an ice-age cave. The Indian Pueblo Cultural Center specializes in the authentic history and culture of the Pueblo peoples. The center includes exhibits tracing the history, artifacts, and contemporary art of New Mexico's 19 pueblos; the Pueblo House Children's Museum; a restaurant serving Native American foods; and an outdoor arena where Native American dancers perform on weekends. The National Hispanic Cultural Center, opened in 2000, explores Hispanic history and literature as well as visual, performing, media, and culinary arts. Located on the University of New Mexico campus, the Maxwell Museum of Anthropology holds over 10 million ethnic, anthropological, and archaeological artifacts. Some date back 10,000 years, with especially strong collections from Southwestern cultures. The National Museum of Nuclear Science & History reopened in the Old Town region of Albuquerque in 2009 and exhibits the history of atomic energy, including the Manhattan Project that produced the first atomic bomb, as well as non-military applications of nuclear energy. The museum is also home to the five-acre Heritage Park, one of its most popular attractions and New Mexico's largest aircraft collection available for public viewing. The collection includes rockets, planes, missiles, the biggest cannon built by the United States, and part of a submarine.

The Albuquerque Museum of Art and History displays southwest art and explores 400 years of Albuquerque history. The museum features works by New Mexican artists from the early twentieth century to the present, and numerous artifacts from the area's Spanish-American period, such as swords, helmets, and horse armor. A 40,000-square-foot expansion, completed in 2005, allowed the museum to display more of its permanent collection. With an emphasis on the early

modernist period, the University of New Mexico Art Museum houses a collection of nineteenth- and twentieth-century American and European art, including one of the largest university-owned photography collections in the nation. It completed a 9,000 square-foot expansion in 2010. The National Hispanic Cultural Center's 11,000-square-foot gallery space displays contemporary and traditional Hispanic art. The KiMo Gallery at KiMo Theatre presents the work of local artists. The South Broadway Cultural Center Gallery mounts exhibitions by local and regional artists; workshops are available for emerging artists of all ages.

Festivals and Holidays
Many of Albuquerque's yearly events celebrate the city's ethnic heritage. At the National Fiery Foods and Barbeque Show, held in early March, attendees can sample spicy sauces, salsas, candies, and more. The Rio Grande Arts and Crafts Festival, held in mid-March, features some 200 artists and crafters from across the country. Native American dancing and feast-day observances take place at numerous pueblos located within an hour's drive of the city. In April, the Gathering of Nations Pow Wow, held on the University of New Mexico campus, features more than 3,000 Native American dancers and singers representing some 500 tribes; more than 800 artists, crafters, and traders at its Indian Traders Market; and a Miss Indian World pageant. The New Mexico Arts and Crafts Fair, in June, showcases the works of some 200 New Mexican artisans. Each Saturday during the summer, Summerfest at Civic Plaza celebrates the food and culture of the city's various ethnic groups, and presents live music and entertainment.

In September, the New Mexico Wine Festival in nearby Bernillo offers wine tastings, an art show, and entertainment. Also in September, the 17-day New Mexico State Fair, regarded as one of the top fairs in the United States, presents a professional rodeo, concerts, livestock shows, and other events. The annual Albuquerque International Balloon Fiesta is one of the most-photographed events in the world. A nine-day festival in October, it features the mass ascension of some 700 hot air balloons; at night, balloons filled with luminous gas light the sky. The Weems International Artfest, in November, is billed as New Mexico's number-one arts and crafts festival; a three-day event, the Artfest shows the works of approximately 260 artisans from around the world. Albuquerque is known as the "City of Little Lights" during the annual Luminaria festival in December. Luminaria bus tours are available as well as maps of noted luminarias neighborhoods for self walking tours.

Sports for the Spectator
The Albuquerque Isotopes, part of the Pacific Coast League, are a Triple-A affiliate of the Los Angeles

Dodgers that play at Isotopes Park, which seats 11,124. The city is famous for the University of New Mexico Lobos, especially the football and basketball teams; the football team plays a September to November season at the 37,370 seat University Stadium, and the basketball team plays from November to March at "The Pit," the university's Arena. The New Mexico Renegades, part of the Western States Hockey League, began operations in 2012. Rodeos and horse racing are other popular spectator sports in Albuquerque.

Sports for the Participant

With more than 286 park sites, 113 miles of developed urban and soft trails, and more than 28,000 acres of dedicated open-space, Albuquerque has much to offer the outdoor enthusiast. Los Altos Park, the city's largest park, offers baseball and softball diamonds, an enclosed heated pool, tennis courts, a lighted golf course, and a children's recreational area. The Los Altos Skate Park is designed for BMX bikers, skateboarders, and in-line skaters. The city opened a covered BMX track in 2007 as part of the new Albuquerque VeloPort. Once the indoor velodrome, a track cycling arena, the VeloPort is an indoor center for cycling training and competition available for novice and professional cyclers alike. Biking trails can be found at Sandia Peak and the Rio Grande Nature Center. Fishing is available in irrigation and drainage ditches, stocked with trout by the state, and in nearby mountain streams.

Among other favorite outdoor adventures are hiking the trails in Cibola National Forest, camping, horseback riding, and downhill and cross-country skiing at Sandia Peak Ski area. Albuquerque's calm, steady winds also provide perfect conditions for hang gliding and hot-air ballooning.

Shopping and Dining

Albuquerque is a shopper's paradise. Numerous shops and galleries in Old Town specialize in art items and crafts produced by local artisans, such as textiles and the turquoise and silver jewelry for which the region is famous. Authentic pre-historic, historic, and contemporary Native American pottery, paintings, photography, and furniture are also for sale in Albuquerque. Sandia Pueblo, just north of Albuquerque, runs its own crafts market, Bien Mur Indian Market Center.

The new Uptown area of Albuquerque is considered the heart of the city's business and shopping districts. It is home to ABQ Uptown, an outdoor mall that offers over 220,000 square feet of shops and restaurants, and Coronado Center, New Mexico's biggest mall. Expo New Mexico, home of the state fairgrounds, also resides here and hosts a popular flea market every weekend. Other shopping needs can be met at Cottonwood Mall, one of New Mexico's largest shopping centers; the

historic Nob Hill district, offering some 130 shops, galleries, and restaurants.

For dining pleasure Albuquerque offers a diverse range of restaurants, from family to fancy. Many feature regional specialties, including authentic Native American food, Hispanic and Mexican cuisine, and western barbecue. The core ingredients of what is known as Northern New Mexican Cuisine-a blending of Hispanic and Pueblo cuisines-are beans, corn, and chili. Several restaurants in Old Town are housed in picturesque adobe buildings.

Visitor Information: Albuquerque Convention and Visitors Bureau, 20 First Plaza NW, Suite 601, Albuquerque, NM 87102; telephone (505) 842-9918; toll-free (800) 284-2282.

■ Convention Facilities

As the economic and industrial heart of New Mexico, and as a city known for its commitment to the past and to the future, Albuquerque is an ideal meeting place for conferences and conventions. Albuquerque's unique ethnic heritage and spectacular setting, plus its generous meeting facilities and hotel guest rooms, promote the mixing of business with pleasure.

The city's primary meeting place is the Albuquerque Convention Center. Located in the heart of downtown, it was undergoing $20 million in design improvements during 2013–14. The 600,000-square-foot complex offers over 270,000 square feet of exhibition space, a 31,000-square-foot ballroom, and a 2,300-seat auditorium. It can accommodate more than 9,000 attendees and has banquet space for up to 6,000 people. The convention center is within walking distance of more than 900 guest rooms, as well as restaurants and clubs offering a variety of entertainment. Facilities for large groups are also available at Expo New Mexico on the State Fairgrounds, which offers flexible indoor and outdoor space, with an indoor capacity of 12,000 and outdoor capacity of 20,000 people.

Convention Information: Albuquerque Convention and Visitors Bureau, 20 First Plaza NW, Suite 601, Albuquerque, NM 87102; telephone (505) 842-9918; toll-free (800) 284-2282.

■ Transportation

Approaching the City

Albuquerque is a designated Port of Entry into the United States. When arriving in Albuquerque by plane, visitors are greeted by the Albuquerque International Sunport terminal, which introduces them to local art and pueblo architecture. Located within the city limits, the airport is served by six major commercial airlines, although Southwest Airlines handles more than 50 percent of all passenger service. The airport provides 6.1 million annual passengers with non-stop service to 21 cities across the country.

Albuquerque is at the crossroads of two major highway routes: Interstate 25, running from Canada to Mexico, and Interstate 40 (formerly Route 66), intersecting the city from east to west.

Passenger bus transportation into Albuquerque is available through commercial bus companies. Train service is provided by Amtrak; Albuquerque is a stop along its Southwest Chief route, a daily line between Los Angeles and Chicago.

Traveling in the City

The landscape surrounding Albuquerque—the Sandia Mountains to the east and mesas to the west—provides convenient landmarks for finding direction in the city. Dividing Albuquerque into quadrants are Interstate 40, which runs east to west, and Interstate 25, known as the Pan American Freeway, which runs north to south. The streets form a grid accommodating this intersection.

Albuquerque's mass transit service is provided by ABQ Ride. During the major festivals, ABQ Ride supplies special service to and from event venues. A trolley serves shoppers and tourists, running between Old Town, the zoo, and downtown. The New Mexico Rail Runner Express, a commuter rail system, started operations in 2006 and his 14 stations stretching from Belen in the south to Santa Fe in the north.

The city also maintains more than 400 miles of bike paths and trails.

■ Communications

Newspapers and Magazines

Albuquerque is served by its daily newspaper, the *Albuquerque Journal,* and by the weekly newspaper *Albuquerque Business First,* which covers business media. *El Hispano News,* a Spanish-language newspaper, printed its last issue in 2011 after 25 years of publication. Magazines include *abqARTS & Entertainment.*

Television and Radio

Numerous television stations, including affiliates for the major commercial networks and public television, serve metropolitan Albuquerque. Cable television is available by subscription. Nineteen FM and 11 AM radio stations broadcast from Albuquerque, offering a wide variety of programming, including Spanish- and Navajo-language features. Albuquerque Public Schools operates an instructional radio station that features educational programming as well as jazz and Latin music.

Media Information: *Albuquerque Journal,* 7777 Jefferson Street NE, Albuquerque, NM, 87109; telephone (505) 823-3800.

Albuquerque Online

Albuquerque Convention & Visitors Bureau. Available www.itsatrip.org

Albuquerque Journal. Available www.abqjournal.com

Albuquerque Public Schools. Available www.aps.edu

Bernalillo County home page. Available www.bernco.gov

City of Albuquerque home page. Available www.cabq.gov

Greater Albuquerque Chamber of Commerce. Available www.abqchamber.com

New Mexico Department of Workforce Solutions. Available www.dws.state.nm.us

Albuquerque/Bernalillo County Library System. Available abclibrary.org/home

BIBLIOGRAPHY

Anaya, Rudolfo A., *Alburquerque* (Albuquerque: University of New Mexico Press, 1992)

Parent, Laurence, *Scenic Driving New Mexico,* 3rd ed. (Guilford, CT: Globe Pequot Press, 2011)

Randall, Margaret, *My Town: A Memoir of Albuquerque, New Mexico, in Poems, Prose, and Photographs* (San Antonio, TX: Wings Press, 2010)

Simmons, Mark, *Albuquerque: A Narrative History* (Albuquerque: University of New Mexico Press, 1982)

Las Cruces

■ The City in Brief

Founded: 1848; incorporated 1907

Head Official: Mayor Ken Miyagishima (D) (since 2007; current term expires 2015)

City Population
> 1990: 62,648
> 2000: 74,267
> 2010: 97,618
> 2012 estimate: 101,053
> Percent change, 2000–2010: 31.4%
> U.S. rank in 1990: 396th (State rank: 2nd)
> U.S. rank in 2000: 408th (State rank: 2nd)
> U.S. rank in 2010: 288th (State rank: 2nd)

Metropolitan Statistical Area Population
> 2000: 174,682
> 2010: 209,233
> 2012 estimate: 214,445
> Percent change, 2000–2010: 19.8%
> U.S. rank in 2000: 213th
> U.S. rank in 2010: 203rd

Area: 52.22 square miles

Elevation: 3,909 feet above sea level

Average Annual Temperatures: 64.0° F

Average Annual Precipitation: 8.5 inches rain, 3.2 inches snow

Major Economic Sectors: government, education, aerospace, services, trade, agriculture

Unemployment Rate: 7% (2012)

Per Capita Income: $19,923

2012 FBI Crime Index Property: 4,419

Major Colleges and Universities: New Mexico State University, Doña Ana Community College

Daily Newspaper: *Las Cruces Sun-News*

■ Introduction

Las Cruces, the "city of crosses," is located in the Mesilla Valley, a wonderfully varied area of forests, river valley, and vast desert. The seat of Doña Ana County, the city is near White Sands Missile Range, where the first atomic bomb was tested. The city's spectacular setting boasts the Organ Mountains to the east and the surrounding Chihuahua Desert, with the Rio Grande running through the middle. Since the end of the nineteenth century, the city has been the political, social, and business hub for southern New Mexico. With the development of Spaceport America in the 2010s, the first commercial spaceport in the world, the city eyed a high-technology future that would make it a focal point of transportation far beyond the U.S.-Mexico border.

■ Geography and Climate

Las Cruces is located 45 miles from the Mexican border and 40 miles northwest of El Paso, Texas. Bordered by the Organ Mountains in the east and the legendary Rio Grande on the west, Las Cruces is located in the heart of the fertile Mesilla Valley.

Las Cruces enjoys 350 days of sunshine annually, with less than 9 inches of average annual rainfall, which happens mostly at night, and only 3.2 inches of snowfall. Because it is situated over a natural underground aquifer, it does not suffer the water problems of a number of southwestern cities. Also, unlike many desert cities, Las Cruces experiences four mildly distinct seasons, with the harder part of the winter occurring during December and January, when the average daytime temperature is

Historic mail stage stop, plaza of Las Cruces. *Chris Faivre/Courtesy of the Las Cruces Convention and Visitors Bureau*

57 degrees. Light snow does fall in the winter but seldom lasts longer than one day. June is generally the hottest month, with an average temperature of 94 degrees. The monsoon season, when heavy thunderstorms can occur daily, takes place in July and August.

Area: 52.22 square miles

Elevation: 3,909 feet above sea level

Average Temperatures: 64.0° F

Average Annual Precipitation: 8.5 inches rain, 3.2 inches snow

■ History

Long Before Humans

Before the first human inhabitants, the area around Las Cruces was populated by a teeming variety of reptiles and amphibians, which left many fossils when the great inland sea that once covered southern New Mexico retreated 600 million years ago. The Smithsonian has stated that the area holds "the world's best-fossilized footprints from the Permian Period."

Early Paleolithic Indians traversed the area about 20,000 years ago, and Anasazi tribes built cliff dwellings over most of New Mexico 10,000 years ago. The Mogollon tribe thrived in the Las Cruces region until they mysteriously disappeared around 1450 A.D. They left many petroglyphs, or rock drawings, scattered around the vicinity for scientists to gain a glimpse into their way of life.

Blazing a Trail

The first European visitors came to the Las Cruces area in 1535 when Spanish explorers, led by Cabeza de Vaca, passed through. In 1589, the first colonists arrived, led by Don Juan Onate, motivated by legends of seven ancient cities of gold. The group's livestock were driven in front of them, blazing a trail called El Camino Real, which led from Chihuahua, Mexico to Santa Fe. Another trail blazed by this same group was dubbed Jornado del Muerto, or Journey of Death. As they attempted to forge a path more direct than the one that followed the meandering Rio Grande, the brutal desert conditions claimed the lives of many men and the Apaches claimed more.

Control of the region changed hands often from the 1600s to about 1850. The Pueblo Indians rebelled against their Spanish conquerors in the late seventeenth century and enjoyed self-rule for a time. In 1821 the Mexican Revolution overthrew the Spanish and created the Republic of Mexico. Soon after that, U.S. westward expansion caused friction and an eventual war with Mexico. This was resolved with the 1848 Treaty of Guadalupe Hidalgo, followed by the 1854 Gadsden Purchase, which claimed much of northern Mexico's land as U.S. territory. The region was even briefly under Confederate rule when Texas troops marched on it in 1862. They were later defeated by Union soldiers near Santa Fe.

After the Civil War ended, the Army installed Fort Selden to help guard travelers against attacks by the Apache. The Buffalo Soldiers of the 125th Infantry, African Americans, were among the first to man the fort. With the coming of the railroad and more and more new immigrants, the Apache threat abated and the fort officially closed in 1891.

The small town of Mesilla is intertwined with the history of Las Cruces. Mesilla was founded by residents who were not happy with the Treaty of Guadalupe Hidalgo and wished to remain Mexican citizens, hence moving across the Rio Grande. Ironically, the Gadsden Purchase a few years later placed them back under U.S. rule.

A Glimpse of Modern Las Cruces

In 1849 the first blocks of the city were laid out with rawhide ropes and stakes. Plots were quickly claimed by settlers and gold miners hoping to find their fortune in the Organ Mountains. The coming of the railroad increased growth of the town quickly. The Santa Fe Railroad had planned to lay track through Mesilla, which had been a depot of the Butterfield Stage Coach, but someone in Las Cruces offered them free land. From then on, Las Cruces grew rapidly while Mesilla remained a sleepy little border town.

Las Cruces continued to grow quickly yet rather quietly into the 1900s as New Mexico became the 47th state in 1912. The quiet was suddenly disturbed when the first atomic bomb was tested north of Las Cruces on July 16, 1945. The area used for the test site, fittingly, was the Jornado del Muerto area. The following year World War II ended and Las Cruces was officially incorporated as a city.

Las Cruces celebrated its 150th birthday in 1998 with festivities that carried on into the millennium. Today, Las Cruces remains the second largest city in New Mexico. In addition to thriving business in trade, government, and agriculture, the unique and stunning scenery of the region has made it an attractive place to film movies and music videos. Spaceport America hosted some 20 rocket launches between 2006 and 2013, by which time most major work had completed. The world's first commercial spaceport, it put Las Cruces on the cutting edge of an industry that promised to offer spaceflight to the ordinary person.

Historical Information: Archives and Special Collections, New Mexico State University Library, PO Box 30006, Dept. 3475, Las Cruces, NM 88003-3006; telephone (575) 646-3839; fax (575) 646-7477.

■ Population Profile

Metropolitan Statistical Area Population
2000: 174,682
2010: 209,233
2012 estimate: 214,445
Percent change, 2000–2010: 19.8%
U.S. rank in 2000: 213th
U.S. rank in 2010: 203rd

City Residents
1990: 62,648
2000: 74,267
2010: 97,618
2012 estimate: 101,053
Percent change, 2000–2010: 31.4%
U.S. rank in 1990: 396th (State rank: 2nd)
U.S. rank in 2000: 408th (State rank: 2nd)
U.S. rank in 2010: 288th (State rank: 2nd)

Density: 1,276.2 people per square mile

Racial and ethnic characteristics
White: 87,275
Black or African American: 1,767
American Indian and Alaskan Native: 1,982
Asian: 2,201
Native Hawaiian and Other Pacific Islander: 0
Hispanic or Latino (may be of any race): 58,575
Other: 7,828

Percent of residents born in state: 48.8%

Age characteristics
Population under 5 years old: 9,539
Population 5 to 9 years old: 7,603
Population 10 to 14 years old: 5,695
Population 15 to 19 years old: 7,491
Population 20 to 24 years old: 8,533
Population 25 to 34 years old: 16,562
Population 35 to 44 years old: 11,870
Population 45 to 54 years old: 11,148
Population 55 to 59 years old: 5,348
Population 60 to 64 years old: 3,755
Population 65 to 74 years old: 6,673
Population 75 to 84 years old: 4,783
Population 85 years and over: 2,053
Median age: 31.1

Births (2010–11 Metropolitan Area)
Total number: 3,281

Deaths (2010–11 Metropolitan Area)

Total number: 1,387

Money income (2012)

Per capita income: $19,923
Median household income: $39,319
Total households: 37,828

Number of households with income of ...

less than $10,000: 4,828
$10,000 to $14,999: 2,379
$15,000 to $24,999: 6,173
$25,000 to $34,999: 4,003
$35,000 to $49,999: 5,371
$50,000 to $74,999: 6,295
$75,000 to $99,999: 4,176
$100,000 to $149,999: 2,996
$150,000 to $199,999: 1,086
$200,000 or more: 521

Percent of families below poverty level: 24.4%

FBI Crime Index Property: 4,419

FBI Crime Index Violent: 394

■ Municipal Government

Las Cruces has a council-manager form of government with six council members, elected by district, serving staggered terms. Both the mayor, elected at-large, and the council members serve four-year terms.

Head Official: Mayor Ken Miyagishima (D) (since 2007; current term expires 2015)

Total Number of City Employees: 1,279 (2012)

City Information: City of Las Cruces; PO Box 20000, Las Cruces, NM 88004; telephone (575) 541-2000.

■ Economy

Major Industries and Commercial Activity

Since World War II, federal, state, and local government jobs—including those in public education—have been a main source of jobs in the area. The city's two largest employers, Las Cruces Public Schools and New Mexico State University, are within that sector. Las Cruces Public Schools is the second largest school district in New Mexico and employs more than 3,600, including about 2,200 classroom teachers and educational assistants. New Mexico State University is the city's largest employer with 1,168 faculty and another 2,845 staff members on its Las Cruces campus as of 2012. The university also provides training and education for research facilities at White Sands.

White Sands Missile Range is the Army's largest installation and the largest military installation in the Western Hemisphere, covering more than 4,000 miles, and is used by the Navy, Air Force, and NASA. Other government agencies, universities, private industries, and even foreign militaries conduct research there as well. Headquartered about 20 miles east of Las Cruces, the base has 600 active duty members, 1,637 family members, and another 3,640 civilians.

White Sands Missile Range anchors a larger aerospace and defense industry. Spaceport America, the world's first purpose-built commercial spaceport, is located just outside Las Cruces. Spaceport completed most aspects of its $209 million facility in 2013 and attracted a number of private companies to the area that supported efforts to establish regular commercial flights to space. Two different studies, conducted by New Mexico State University and Futron Corporation, have predicted that within five years of start-up operations, expected during 2014, Spaceport America will employ approximately 2,300 people, and by 2020 it will employ more than 3,500, with some $750 million in total revenue. The growing unmanned aerial vehicle industry also supported growth in the aerospace industry.

Although Las Cruces was never primarily an industrial town, manufacturing and commerce has been growing in importance. The North American Free Trade Agreement, or NAFTA, passed in 1994, has influenced this trend, as has the opening in 1991 of the border crossing at Santa Teresa, just 40 miles south of Las Cruces. Many companies relocate in the Mesilla Valley area to do business with maquiladoras (factories) in Mexico. NAFTA and the Mexican government's maquiladora program, enacted in the 1960s, encourage this type of trade by lowering or completely eliminating tariffs. Completion of a major Union Pacific intermodal facility in 2014 was expected to increase the region's stature as a trade gateway to the Southwest. On the U.S. side of the border, industrial and research parks abound in Doña Ana County, including Arrowhead Research Park on the New Mexico State University campus, the 1,820-acre West Mesa Industrial Park, Santa Teresa Logistics Park, the 230-acre Bi-National Park, and the 58.2-acre Hatch Industrial Park.

Agricultural and value-added food manufacturing are other important sectors. Las Cruces is a land of peppers. Chile, cayenne, jalapeno, and bell peppers in every color imaginable are all raised locally. Stahmann Farms, which originally focused on cotton and tomatoes, is now one of the world's largest producers of pecans. Other agricultural products include cotton, onions and various vegetables, and dairy products. There are some 1,700 farms across nearly 600,000 acres in Doña Ana County. Research into preserving species of chiles and developing new strains takes place at New Mexico State University at the Chile Pepper Institute.

Emerging industries included renewable energy, especially solar given the area's 340 annual days of sunshine, and digital media such as film and gaming, which is supported by programs at local colleges.

Items and goods produced: peppers, pecans, cotton and other agricultural products; electronics; airplane and automobile parts

Incentive Programs—New and Existing Companies

Local programs: The city of Las Cruces Local Economic Development Act allows the city to offer incentive packages, particular for new or expanding businesses in the city's target sectors: aerospace, manufacturing, high technology, advanced business and financial services, and value-added food processing. New jobs created in these sectors must offer above-average wage and salary to qualify for local incentives, and must also equal a three-to-one ratio of private to public investment, create at least one new job for every $10,000 to $30,000 of public assistance, and be completed within two years. Central to the city's incentive package was an offer of land at the West Mesa Industrial Park for qualifying companies.

State programs: New Mexico offers a variety of incentives to all new and expanding businesses. The High-Wage Jobs Tax Credit allows qualified businesses to take a generous tax credit for each new job created with a salary of at least $28,000 a year (in areas where the population does not exceed 40,000) or $40,000 a year (in areas where the population exceeds 40,000).

Other tax credit incentives include a Manufacturer's Investment Tax Credit, a New Markets Tax Credit, a Technology Jobs Tax Credit, Aircraft Manufacturing Tax Deduction, Aircraft Maintenance or Remodeling Tax Deduction, Space Gross Receipts Tax Credit, Alternative Energy Product Manufacturer's Tax Credit, New Mexico Refundable Film Production Tax Credit, and State Film Investment Loan Program. New Mexico's property taxes are among the lowest in the nation.

Job training programs: New Mexico is home to one of the most aggressive training incentive packages in the nation. Through the Job Training Incentive Program (JTIP) expanding or relocated businesses can receive up to six months of funds for classroom and on-the-job-training for newly created jobs. The JTIP reimburses required travel expenses and up to 65 percent of employee wages.

In 2007 the Governor's Office of Workforce Training & Development merged with the New Mexico Department of Labor to create a new branch called the New Mexico Department of Workforce Solutions. The combined department focuses on preparing job seekers to meet current standards in the labor market as well as effectively matching citizens with businesses in need of help. Services available include job fairs, local workforce development centers, online job searches, and online registration for employment services.

Las Cruces is also home to The Bridge of Southern New Mexico, a nonprofit working towards developing a stronger and well-qualified workforce in Doña Ana County through a focus on business, economic development, government, and education. The organization's goal is to bridge the gap between young people looking for a career path and businesses looking to develop a skilled workforce.

Development Projects

Las Cruces most notable and unique development project is $209 million Spaceport America, the world's first purpose-built commercial spaceport, which completed major construction in 2013. Private companies planned to offer commercial space flights as soon as 2014 and included Virgin Galactic, UP Aerospace, and SpaceX. By 2020, studies predicted that the spaceport would employ more than 3,500 people and generate some $750 million in annual revenue. Spaceport America was funded and owned by the state, with management through the New Mexico Spaceport Authority.

In 2010 Las Cruces unveiled a new city hall and federal courthouse downtown. The new city hall facility cost approximately $34 million and covers 117,000 square feet. The 230,000-square-foot federal courthouse was built at a cost of $81 million. Also in 2010, Las Cruces finished construction on a $26 million convention center.

In nearby Santa Teresa, Southwest Steel Coil expanded its operations in both 2012 and 2013, adding 20,000 and 35,000 square feet during each expansion, respectively. The second expansion represented an investment of $5 million. Also in 2013, aerospace and defense company General Dynamics announced it was adding some 200 jobs in back-office support in Las Cruces. A major Union Pacific railroad facility, built at a cost of $400 million, was expected to open in Santa Teresa in 2014. The project included a crew change point, fueling station, and intermodal facility.

Economic Development Information: Mesilla Valley Economic Development Alliance, 277 E. Amador, Suite 304, P.O. Box 1299, Las Cruces, NM 88004; telephone (575) 525-2852; toll-free (800) 523-6833; fax (575) 523-5707.

Commercial Shipping

Cargo services are provided by Las Cruces International Airport and the Doña Ana County Airport at Santa Teresa. Air freight service is provided by all major companies. Overnight shipping is available to most major western cities, including Dallas, Houston, San Antonio, Phoenix, San Diego, Los Angeles, and Denver. Two railroads provide direct rail services: Burlington Northern-Santa Fe and Union Pacific; Union Pacific was expected to complete a massive new intermodal facility in 2014. The Santa Teresa Intermodal Terminal was to be New Mexico's first inland port. Several major commercial trucking firms offer freight service for the area.

Labor Force and Employment Outlook

Las Cruces is within close proximity to 11 post-secondary institutions that create a young, abundant workforce. Area institutions enroll more than 90,000 students annually, and several early college high schools offer course credit for associate or bachelor's degrees. An estimated 84 percent of the Las Cruces labor force had graduated from high school, with 30 percent having earned at least a bachelor's degree. The labor force within a one-hour commute of Las Cruces numbers more than 450,000.

The following is a summary of data regarding the 2012 Las Cruces labor force:

Size of civilian labor force: 47,447

Number of workers employed in . . .

agriculture and mining: 467
construction: 2,204
manufacturing: 917
wholesale trade: 660
retail trade: 4,611
transportation: 1,430
information systems: 1,155
finance: 1,635
professional administration: 3,747
education and social services: 13,797
arts and leisure: 4,133
other: 1,815
public administration: 4,422

Average hourly earnings of production workers: $14.47

Unemployment rate: 7% (2012)

Employers

Largest employers (2012)	*Number of employees*
New Mexico State University	Not available
Las Cruces Public Schools	Not available
City of Las Cruces	Not available
Memorial Medical Center	Not available
Doña Ana Branch Community College	Not available
Doña Ana County	Not available
Mountain View Regional Medical Center	Not available
Wal-Mart	Not available
Coordinated Care Corporation	Not available
National Aeronautics & Space	Not available

Cost of Living

The following is a summary of data regarding several key cost of living factors in the area.

State income tax rate: 1.7% to 4.9%

State sales tax rate: 5.125%

Local income tax rate: None

Local sales tax rate: 2.4375%

Property tax rate: $29.170 per $1,000 of 33% of assessed value (2013)

Economic Information: Greater Las Cruces Chamber of Commerce, 505 S. Main St. #134, Las Cruces, NM 88001; telephone (575) 524-1968; (575) 527-5546. Mesilla Valley Economic Development Alliance, 277 E. Amador, Suite 304, P.O. Box 1299, Las Cruces, NM 88004; telephone (575) 525-2852; toll-free (800) 523-6833; fax (575) 523-5707.

■ Education and Research

Elementary and Secondary Schools

Las Cruces Public Schools is the state's second largest school district and one of the largest employers in Doña Ana County. The district is governed by five members of the board of education, elected to four year terms, who select a superintendent. The district covers the City of Las Cruces, the villages of Doña Ana and La Mesilla, and the middle third of Doña Ana County. Nearly 75 percent of the student population is Hispanic.

The Early College High School, which opened in the district in 2010, was the state's first high school offering courses for college credit to secondary students; additional early college high schools were under construction during 2013. A curriculum focused on science, technology, engineering, and math—often referred to as STEM—supports students seeking to earn technical degrees. Other specialized programs within the district include a bilingual education program, preschool program, in-school program for pregnant teens, and a drug abuse prevention program. There are also special vocational/technical programs featuring nontraditional, nonacademic training for fields such as construction.

Programs for special education students and for the gifted or talented are strong.

The following is a summary of data regarding the Las Cruces Public Schools.

Total enrollment: 25,488

Number of facilities

    total: 38
    elementary schools: 25
    junior high schools: 8
    high schools: 4
    other: 1

Student/teacher ratio: 15.4:1

Teacher salaries

    average (statewide): $46,950

Funding per pupil: $8,703

Public Schools Information: Las Cruces Public Schools, 505 S. Main, Suite 249, Las Cruces, NM 88001; telephone (575) 527-5800.

Colleges and Universities

New Mexico State University (NMSU), with an enrollment of more than 18,000 at its Las Cruces campus, is home to eight colleges: Agricultural, Consumer and Environmental Sciences; Arts and Sciences; Business; Education; Engineering; Extended Learning; Health and Social Services; Honors and the Graduate School. In addition to nearly 100 undergraduate degree programs and nearly 20 master's degree programs, NMSU offers doctorate degrees in economic development, nursing, education, and doctorate degrees of philosophy in 20 fields. NMSU is also a NASA Space Grant College and hosts 12 research and science centers.

Doña Ana Branch Community College (DABCC), actually a branch of New Mexico State University and located on NMSU's campus, was instituted in 1973 to meet the needs of students who wish to achieve one-year certificates and two-year associate's degrees in medical, technical, and business fields. DABCC also has programs for high school students in Doña Ana County in which students can earn credits toward an associate's or bachelor's degree. Enrollment averages nearly 10,000 students enrolled in credit programs, with about 6,000 of those attending as full-time students. Noncredit enrollment in the college's adult and community education classes numbers more than 7,000.

Libraries and Research Centers

The Las Cruces public library, called Thomas Branigan Memorial Library, has more than 200,000 items, which include audio, video, and microform media as well as print materials. It is the fourth largest library in the state of New Mexico. The library provides free Internet access seven days a week, a Bookmobile, a Spanish Language Collection, and a genealogy collection. While the Branigan Library is the only full-service library in Las Cruces, the system maintains the Munson Senior Center Library and the San Andres High School Library.

The New Mexico State University Library holds over a million volumes housed in two buildings on the Las Cruces main campus. The Branson Library houses items pertaining to engineering, agriculture, business, government publications, and special collections, while the Zuhl Library houses the arts, humanities, and sciences collections.

Major research areas at New Mexico State University include Animal and Range Science; Biochemistry, Molecular Biology, and Genetics; Computer Science, and Computer and Electrical Engineering; Energy and Biofuels; Environment and Ecology; Medical and Health Sciences; Plant and Soil Sciences; Space; and Water. Two important institutes include the New Mexico Water Resource Research Institute and the Freeport-McMoRan Copper & Gold Water Quality Laboratory. New Mexico State University received $133 million in research funding in 2013.

A number of federal and private research entities operate research facilities in Doña Ana County, including White Sands Missile Range, NASA LBJ Space Center, Honeywell Technology, Jacobs Technology, Boeing, General Dynamics, Raytheon, Calculex, Trax International, and Physical Science Laboratory.

Public Library Information: Thomas Branigan Memorial Library, 200 E. Picacho, Las Cruces, NM 88001; telephone (575) 528-4000; fax (575) 528-4030.

■ Health Care

Las Cruces has three main medical facilities serving its health-care needs. Memorial Medical Center (MMC) is the city's primary facility and has 224 beds. The hospital admits nearly 11,000 patients annually, while also treating some 40,000 in its emergency department. MMC offers comprehensive cancer care at Ikard Cancer Treatment Center, imaging services, maternal/infant care, lab services, Memorial Heart Center for Heart and Vascular Care, outpatient surgery, Women's Health and Wellness, pediatrics, a neonatal care center, behavioral services, and various rehabilitation services. Additional services are offered at its freestanding annex, Memorial HealthPlex, an outpatient surgery center with diagnostic imaging, lab services, and endoscopy.

The Mesilla Valley Hospital, with 126 beds, offers adult and child psychiatric care, and chemical dependency treatment. The 142-bed MountainView Regional Medical Center opened in 2002. It includes a full-service emergency room and all-private inpatient rooms. Among other key services at MountainView are the Comprehensive Women's Center, cardiology services, surgery services, diagnostic imaging, inpatient rehabilitation, a pain management center, and an ADA certified diabetes program. The MountainView Surgical Center allows patients to have gastrointestinal, orthopedic, and pediatric surgeries in a relaxed outpatient setting. The Southern New Mexico Cancer Center, which also opened in 2002, providing patients with services including radiation therapy, medical oncology, and diagnostic radiology.

■ Recreation

Sightseeing

A popular attraction is the monument and white crosses that mark the graves of the travelers from Taos who were ambushed and killed by Apaches in 1830, and for which the city is purported to be named. White Sands Missile Range displays missiles and weapons at its visitor's center. Its museum traces the origins of space and nuclear research. Separate and distinct from the missile range is White Sands National Monument, an area of over 275 square miles of pure gypsum. Nature tours, including tours of Lake Lucero, are given. Visitors can explore the world's largest pecan farms at Stahmann Farms, about seven miles south of the city. History buffs of the Old West will enjoy the Basilica of San Albino, one of the oldest missions in the region; the Fort Selden State Monument on the site of the former cavalry fort; and the Historical Museum of Lawmen, located at the Doña Ana County Sheriff's Department, which displays law enforcement memorabilia. The only federally funded monument to the Bataan Death March heroes can be found in Veterans Park in Las Cruces along Roadrunner Parkway. It was sculpted by local artist Kelly Hester and dedicated in 2001.

Arts and Culture

Founded by Tony-award-winning playwright Mark Medoff, The American Southwest Theatre Company performs five or six regular season productions a year, plus a children's show at New Mexico State University. Professional actors are hired each season through the Guest Artist Program and work alongside the resident company and New Mexico State University actors. The Las Cruces Community Theatre group produces five shows annually and holds a one-act festival of experimental plays in the winter. After more than 70 years as a cinema house, the Rio Grande Theatre was reopened as a state-of-the-art performing arts center in downtown Las Cruces in 2005.

Las Cruces boasts a number of interesting museums. Four are run by the city itself: the Branigan Cultural Center, Museum of Natural History, Museum of Art, and the Railroad Museum. The Branigan Cultural Center displays both historical and fine arts items in a building that was constructed as the city's main library during the Great Depression. The museum of Natural History displays plants and animals from the Chihuahuan Desert region and has programs running the gamut from dinosaurs to astronomy. The Museum of Art was completed in spring of 1999. The Las Cruces Railroad Museum holds artifacts from New Mexico's railroading past.

The New Mexico Farm and Ranch Heritage Museum is the largest of its kind in the world and educates the public on everything in the 3,000-year history of agriculture in New Mexico. New Mexico State University has its own University Museum in Kent Hall on the main campus, which holds mostly anthropological artifacts including historic and prehistoric art objects. Space Murals Inc. is a combination giant water tower mural and museum honoring space exploration and astronauts. Visitors to the Gadsden Museum get a taste of the life and times of the Albert Jennings Fountain family, who played a crucial role in Las Cruces history. The museum exhibits Indian artifacts and objects from the Civil War, paintings and china, and outlines the history of the Gadsden Purchase.

Festivals and Holidays

Las Cruces hosts holidays and fiestas year round, many of them celebrating the city's Hispanic culture. Starting in mid-January is the Mesilla Valley Balloon Rally, when 70 or more colorful hot air balloons fill the sky. April offers four happenings: the La Vina Blues and Jazz Thing features cool music sponsored by New Mexico's oldest winery; the Trinity Site Tour in White Sands Missile Range, where the first atomic explosion was set off; the Border Book Festival, featuring renowned visiting authors, food, fun, and live acts; and the annual Frontier Days at Fort Selden. Cinco de Mayo festivities take place in May, with Mexican food, dancing, and music in old Mesilla. The Southern New Mexico Wine Festival is held at the end of May.

Fourth of July is celebrated with the Electric Light Parade and fireworks. In September and October, kids and grown-ups alike enjoy the Mesilla Valley Maze, which includes hay rides to a pumpkin patch and finding one's way through twists and turns cut into a corn field. In early September is the Hatch Chile Festival, honoring the Mesilla Valley as the chile capital of the world with food, crafts, an auction, and more. An hour north of Las Cruces, Hillsboro holds its apple festival the first week of September. Diez y Seis de Septiembre commemorates Mexican Independence day with folk dances, mariachi music, and traditional Mexican foods. The world's largest enchilada is constructed each year at the Whole Enchilada Fiesta, with an accompanying parade and other festivities. The end of September and the beginning of October bring the Southern New Mexico State Fair, with food, music, an auction, livestock shows, and a rodeo. La Vina, New Mexico's oldest winery, holds its namesake festival in October. The annual Mesilla Jazz Happening holds court in two places—the old Historic Plaza and the Mercado Plaza—with horse-drawn shuttles giving free rides between the two plazas.

While the Anglo world celebrates Halloween, in Las Cruces there is Dia de los Muertos, or Day of the Dead, with candlelit processions, homemade altars in the streets, and a giant piñata. November brings the Annual Renaissance Artsfaire, where artisans present their works in a juried art show and exhibition. In mid-November the International Mariachi Conference and Concert arrives at New Mexico State University and Young Park. Finally, in December, Luminarias and Christmas Carols set historic old Mesilla aglow.

Sports for the Spectator

The Las Cruces Vaqueros is the city's first professional sports team. The professional baseball team had its first season in 2010 and plays at Apodoca Park. New Mexico State University offers National Collegiate Athletic Association Division I sports, with six men's and 11 women's teams. Many games are held at Aggie Memorial Stadium, with a capacity of more than 30,000 people. The city is home to over 25 sport facilities that host a variety of games. Las Cruces also hosts sporting events such as the American Bicycle Association National BMX Tournament and the American Junior Golf Association Nike All Stars Tournament.

Sports for the Participant

Las Cruces is home to 34 parks, many of which have playgrounds, picnic tables, and special events throughout the year. The city's seven recreation centers have weight rooms, racquetball and basketball courts, and indoor and outdoor pools. Therapeutic recreation is offered at Mesilla Park Recreation Center. Summer programs include swimming, tennis, track and field, and computer camp. Other city recreation department offerings are soccer, football, softball, basketball, BMX, track and field, swimming lessons, volleyball, and boxing.

Shopping and Dining

Shopping in Las Cruces can be a delightfully varied experience. Mesilla Valley Mall houses 115 stores, including national chain stores and small boutiques, representing the largest selection of stores in southern New Mexico. Rated as one of the top open-air markets in the country, the Las Cruces Farmers & Crafts Market presents more than 250 local artisans and farmers twice a week, year round. Visitors to Las Cruces are drawn to Old Mesilla, a picturesque village of more than 40 galleries, unique stores, and restaurants built around the town plaza, with buildings dating to the 1850s. Mesilla is only five minutes from downtown Las Cruces.

Besides the wonderful Southwestern cuisine featuring dishes of local peppers and other produce, Las Cruces has more than 70 restaurants running the gamut from fast food and deli fare to Chinese, Japanese, continental, Italian, and, of course, Mexican fare.

Visitor Information: Las Cruces Convention and Visitors Bureau, 211 N. Water St., Las Cruces, NM 88001; telephone (575) 541-2444; fax (575) 541-2164; email cvb@lascrucescvb.org.

■ Convention Facilities

The city of Las Cruces has more than 3,000 hotel rooms, 128,000 square feet of meeting space, and can accommodate groups from 10 to 1,400. Las Cruces state-of-the-art convention center, which opened in 2010, covers approximately 55,000 square feet, with over 30,000 square feet dedicated to meeting space. The Las Cruces Convention Center has an exhibition hall, ballroom, and six break-out rooms, and also offers an additional 5,000 square feet of outdoor space.

Convention Information: Las Cruces Convention and Visitors Bureau, 211 N. Water St., Las Cruces, NM 88001; telephone (575) 541-2444; fax (575) 541-2164; email cvb@lascrucescvb.org.

■ Transportation

Approaching the City

Interstate 10, which is a direct route to Phoenix, Los Angeles, Houston, and Dallas; and Interstate 25, which is the direct route to Albuquerque and Denver, traverse the city's south end. U.S. Highway 70 presents a direct route to Interstate 40 at Amarillo. The Las Cruces International Airport, eight miles west of the city, no longer offers commercial services; the last commercial flight was in July 2005. Air travel takes place at the El Paso International Airport in Texas, about 52 miles to the south of Las Cruces. El Paso International Airport offers non-stop flights to more than a dozen cities and is served by five major airlines: American, Delta, Southwest, United, and US Airways. It provides an average of 136 daily arrivals and departures, serving about 3 million passengers annually.

Bus and shuttle service is offered by Greyhound-Trailways and the Las Cruces Shuttle Taxi.

Traveling in the City

Local bus service is offered by Roadrunner Transit, which provides morning through evening service Monday through Saturday on eight routes. Taxis are available from the Checker/Yellow Cab Company.

■ Communications

Newspapers and Magazines

The city is served by the *Las Cruces Sun-News,* which is published every morning, and *The Las Cruces Bulletin,* a community newspaper that comes out each Thursday. The scholarly journal *Tamara* covers organization science and is published out of New Mexico State University's Department of Management.

Television and Radio

Las Cruces broadcasts 2 AM and 12 FM radio stations. The stations have a variety of formats including country, Hispanic news/talk, adult contemporary, and public radio programming. Six area television stations serve the city. Television and satellite service is available.

Media Information: *Las Cruces Sun-News,* 256 West Las Cruces Avenue, P.O. Box 1749, Las Cruces, NM 88004; telephone (575) 541-5400; fax (575) 541-5498.

Las Cruces Online

City of Las Cruces home page. Available www. las-cruces.org

Greater Las Cruces Chamber of Commerce. Available www.lascruces.org

Las Cruces Convention and Visitors Bureau. Available www.lascrucescvb.org

Las Cruces Sun-News. Available www.lcsun-news. com

Mesilla Valley Economic Development Alliance. Available www.mveda.com

New Mexico Department of Workforce Solutions. Available www.dws.state.nm.us

New Mexico Magazine. Available www.nmmagazine. com

New Mexico State University Library. Available lib. nmsu.edu

BIBLIOGRAPHY

Holmes, Allan J., *Fort Selden, 1865–1891: The Birth, Life, and Death of a Frontier Fort in New Mexico* (Santa Fe, NM: Sunstone Press, 2010)

Harris, Linda G., *Las Cruces: An Illustrated History* (Las Cruces, NM: Arroyo Press, 1993

Parent, Laurence, *Scenic Driving New Mexico,* 3rd ed. (Guilford, CT: Globe Pequot Press, 2011)

Santa Fe

■ The City in Brief

Founded: 1607 (incorporated, 1846)

Head Official: Mayor David Coss (since 2006; current term expires 2014)

City Population
1990: 56,537
2000: 62,203
2010: 67,947
2012 estimate: 69,211
Percent change, 2000–2010: 9.2%
U.S. rank in 1990: 428th
U.S. rank in 2000: 508th (State rank: 3rd)
U.S. rank in 2010: 476th (State rank: 4th)

Metropolitan Statistical Area Population
2000: 129,292
2010: 144,170
2012 estimate: 146,375
Percent change, 2000–2010: 11.5%
U.S. rank in 2000: 275th
U.S. rank in 2010: 285th

Area: 37.33 square miles

Elevation: 7,000 feet above sea level

Average Annual Temperatures: 49.3° F

Average Annual Precipitation: 14 inches, 32 inches of snow

Major Economic Sectors: government, tourism, health care

Unemployment Rate: 5.9% (2012)

Per Capita Income: $33,034

2012 FBI Crime Index Property: 3,897

Major Colleges and Universities: Santa Fe University of Art and Design, St. John's College, Santa Fe Community College

Daily Newspaper: *The Santa Fe New Mexican*

■ Introduction

Founded before Massachusetts's Plymouth Colony and the second oldest city in the United States, Santa Fe—which means "holy faith" in Spanish—is a cultural center for the Southwest with its blend of Native American, Spanish, and Anglo heritage. The architectural integrity of the city's high-walled adobe structures and narrow, winding streets have been preserved through careful planning, attracting travelers worldwide and gaining the city recognition as one of the top destinations in the United States. The Santa Fe Opera is known throughout the world, and the city is a gathering place for writers and artists. As the capital of New Mexico, Santa Fe is also a state center for government and regional health-care hub.

■ Geography and Climate

Santa Fe is located in the northern Rio Grande Valley at the southern end of the Rocky Mountains. Situated in the foothills of the Sangre de Cristo mountain range, the city has a nearby pine forest. Because of the mountain setting, Santa Fe enjoys a semi-arid continental climate, with moderate summers and winters. Humidity is low and the sun shines approximately 300 days per year. Snowfall averages 32 inches annually in the city; deep snow does remain at higher altitudes during the winter.

Area: 37.33 square miles

Elevation: 7,000 feet above sea level

Average Temperatures: 49.3° F

© Jorg Hackemann/Shutterstock.com

Average Annual Precipitation: 14 inches, 32 inches of snow

■ History

Native American and Spanish Influences

During prehistoric times a village built by the Tano tribe stood on the site now occupied by Santa Fe. Evidence from the Tano culture, uncovered in the few ruins left by Spanish settlers, indicates that civilization existed on the site as far back as 1050 to 1150 A.D. The settlement was abandoned around 200 years before the arrival of the Spanish. The spot was called Kuapoga—"place of the shell beads near the water"—by the Pueblos. Santa Fe was founded in either 1607 or 1609 (there is some confusion about the year) by Don Pedre de Peralta, the third governor of the Province of New Mexico, who built the Palace of Governors and the Plaza and planned a walled city. The palace was occupied by a succession of sixty Spanish governors for more than 200 years, and Santa Fe has been a seat of government since its founding.

Throughout Spanish rule of the territory Santa Fe was a center for exploration and mission work. Franciscan friars built eleven churches and by 1617 had converted more than 14,000 Native Americans to their form of Christianity. Conflict arose, however, when the Native Americans continued to practice their own religion. In 1680 a number of the Spanish settlers were killed in a conflict with natives; the survivors fled to El Paso del Norte, abandoning the town. The Native Americans established their own community in Santa Fe; occupying the palace and appointing a governor, they held the town for twelve years until the arrival of De Vargas, Spanish governor of the province. He made peace and returned the following year with a statue of the Christian New Testament's Virgin Mary. Making his entry on the site of present day Rosario Chapel, he vowed to pay yearly homage to "Our Lady of Victory." Since that time, in fulfillment of this vow the De Vargas Procession has been held in Santa Fe.

Mexico and United States Claim Santa Fe

When Mexico won independence from Spain in 1821, Santa Fe came under the control of Mexico. Trade was then opened between Santa Fe and the United States over a route that came to be known as the Santa Fe Trail. In 1846 the United States claimed Santa Fe; the city has been under U.S. jurisdiction ever since, except for two weeks during the Civil War when the Confederates seized control after the Battle of Valverde. The Santa Fe Trail eventually fell into disuse when rail travel advanced to the region. Santa Fe flourished, however, benefiting from the new trade connections that were made possible by the railroad.

City Becomes Art Colony, Capital of State

Around the turn of the century, artists, attracted by the climate and the beauty of the area, moved to Santa Fe, and the city soon became popular as an art colony. When New Mexico attained statehood in 1912, Santa Fe, as the capital, entered a period of prosperity; government workers arrived to live in the city and federal and state buildings were constructed around the Plaza. By 1920 the population had grown from 5,000 to more than 7,000 people, and by the 1940s it was over 20,000 people.

In 1957 the city established zoning codes designed to maintain a uniform architectural style. Two types of architecture are permitted: Pueblo, characterized by rounded parapets and rough-hewn woodwork, and Territorial, featuring brick coping and milled, often decorative woodworking.

Santa Fe's populace reflects the city's Native American, Spanish, and Anglo heritage, and the cultural traditions of these groups have been retained. However, after an influx of new residents in the 1980s, the 1990 census reported that for the first time since the city's founding, Hispanic residents were a minority. During the 1990s the city experienced tension between locals—many of them poor—and newcomers, who drove up the cost of housing and otherwise altered the landscape.

Economic frustrations continued into the 2000s, as wages lingered almost 20 percent below the national average, while the cost of living remained well above the national average. In an effort to remedy the issue, the city passed a "living wage" ordinance in 2003 to periodically raise minimum wages for employers with 25 or more employees. In 2012 the living wage was $10.29 per hour. Nonetheless, the city's cultural importance remains undiminished, and the introduction of light rail connecting Santa Fe with Albuquerque in 2008 offered the possibility of greater economic ties in the future.

Historical Information: Fray Angelico Chavez History Library and Photographic Archive, 120 Washington Ave., Santa Fe, NM 87501; telephone (505) 476-5090; fax (505) 476-5104.

■ Population Profile

Metropolitan Statistical Area Population

2000: 129,292
2010: 144,170
2012 estimate: 146,375

Percent change, 2000–2010: 11.5%
U.S. rank in 2000: 275th
U.S. rank in 2010: 285th

City Residents

1990: 56,537
2000: 62,203
2010: 67,947
2012 estimate: 69,211
Percent change, 2000–2010: 9.2%
U.S. rank in 1990: 428th
U.S. rank in 2000: 508th (State rank: 3rd)
U.S. rank in 2010: 476th (State rank: 4th)

Density: 1,477.8 people per square mile

Racial and ethnic characteristics

White: 59,339
Black or African American: 829
American Indian and Alaskan Native: 1,120
Asian: 1,019
Native Hawaiian and Other Pacific Islander: 0
Hispanic or Latino (may be of any race): 34,601
Other: 6,904

Percent of residents born in state: 43.8%

Age characteristics

Population under 5 years old: 4,207
Population 5 to 9 years old: 4,035
Population 10 to 14 years old: 3,350
Population 15 to 19 years old: 3,971
Population 20 to 24 years old: 3,151
Population 25 to 34 years old: 8,899
Population 35 to 44 years old: 7,492
Population 45 to 54 years old: 9,563
Population 55 to 59 years old: 4,673
Population 60 to 64 years old: 6,357
Population 65 to 74 years old: 7,730
Population 75 to 84 years old: 3,859
Population 85 years and over: 1,924
Median age: 44.3

Births (2010–11 Metropolitan Area)

Total number: 1,411

Deaths (2010–11 Metropolitan Area)

Total number: 924

Money income (2012)

Per capita income: $33,034
Median household income: $47,105
Total households: 31,570

Number of households with income of . . .

less than $10,000: 2,819
$10,000 to $14,999: 1,970
$15,000 to $24,999: 3,709

$25,000 to $34,999: 3,474
$35,000 to $49,999: 4,260
$50,000 to $74,999: 5,836
$75,000 to $99,999: 3,838
$100,000 to $149,999: 2,953
$150,000 to $199,999: 1,098
$200,000 or more: 1,613

Percent of families below poverty level: 19.0%

FBI Crime Index Property: 3,897

FBI Crime Index Violent: 331

■ Municipal Government

Santa Fe operates under a council-mayor form of government, administered by an eight-member council and a mayor elected to four-year terms. The mayor appoints a city manager, who is approved by the council. Santa Fe is the seat of Santa Fe County and, as the state capital, the site of meetings of the state legislature.

Head Official: Mayor David Coss (since 2006; current term expires 2014)

Total Number of City Employees: 1,719 (2013)

City Information: City of Santa Fe, 200 Lincoln Avenue, Santa Fe, NM 87504; telephone (505) 955-6549.

■ Economy

Major Industries and Commercial Activity

Santa Fe's economy has been based largely on government and tourism. As capital of New Mexico, the government is the largest employer in the area, with city, county, and state officials accounting for more than 14,000 jobs in 2014. Federal employment added nearly 2,000 more.

Santa Fe's hospitality industry is the city's second largest employer. Santa Fe attracted an average of two million overnight visitors annually from 2007 to 2012. Many visitors are attracted by the city's arts market, which annually ranks among the top arts markets of any U.S. city. The United Nations Educational Scientific and Cultural Organization (UNESCO) designated Santa Fe a "Creative City" in 2005 as part of the "Creative Cities Network." It was the first U.S. city to receive the honor. Other accolades, all in 2012, include a *Travel + Leisure* honor as the number-one cultural getaway, designation by *U.S. News* as the number-five U.S. Historic Destination, and an award by the American Lung Association for the cleanest air of any U.S. city.

Health care is another of Santa Fe's significant economic sectors. In recent years, Santa Fe has emerged as a regional medical center; CHRISTUS St. Vincent Regional Medical Center is the city's largest private employer and serves a 19,000-square-mile area in seven counties. The Cancer Institute of New Mexico is also located in Santa Fe.

Items and goods produced: art, pumice products, weavings, Native American arts and crafts, textiles, electronic instruments, aluminum ware

Incentive Programs—New and Existing Companies

Local programs: The Santa Fe Business Incubator, considered one of the best of its kind in the nation, assists new businesses with all aspects of start-up. Since they began in 1997, the SFBI has helped launch and nurture over 100 local businesses. The Santa Fe Small Business Development Center provides one-on-one business advising, encourages and instructs entrepreneurs, and is a strong advocate for local business growth and development. For over 20 years, Small Business Development Centers throughout the state have provided some 94,000 New Mexico businesses with affordable workshops, free small business consulting, and business training. SCORE (Service Corps of Retired Executives) provides business counseling and support as well. Microloans are available from the Santa Fe Small Business Development Loan Fund, Tri-County Revolving Loan Fund, and WESST Corp, ranging from $300 to $200,000 in value.

State programs: New Mexico offers a variety of incentives to all new and expanding businesses. The High-Wage Jobs Tax Credit allows qualified businesses to take a generous tax credit for each new job created with a salary of at least $28,000 a year (in areas where the population does not exceed 40,000) or $40,000 a year (in areas where the population exceeds 40,000).

Other tax credit incentives include a Manufacturer's Investment Tax Credit, a New Markets Tax Credit, a Technology Jobs Tax Credit, Aircraft Manufacturing Tax Deduction, Aircraft Maintenance or Remodeling Tax Deduction, Space Gross Receipts Tax Credit, Alternative Energy Product Manufacturer's Tax Credit, New Mexico Refundable Film Production Tax Credit, and State Film Investment Loan Program. New Mexico's property taxes are among the lowest in the nation.

Job training programs: New Mexico is home to one of the most aggressive training incentive packages in the nation. Through the Job Training Incentive Program (JTIP) expanding or relocated businesses can receive up to six months of funds for classroom and on-the-job-training for newly created jobs. The JTIP reimburses required travel expenses and up to 65 percent of employee wages.

In 2007 the Governor's Office of Workforce Training & Development merged with the New Mexico Department of Labor to create a new branch called the New Mexico Department of Workforce Solutions. The combined department focuses on preparing job seekers to meet current standards in the labor market as well as effectively matching citizens with businesses in need of help. Services available include job fairs, local workforce development centers, online job searches, and online registration for employment services.

Santa Fe Community College also works with local businesses to develop any specialized workforce training and education programs they require. The community college is also home base for the Santa Fe Small Business Development Center.

Development Projects

The grand opening of one of Santa Fe's newest retail spaces, the Santa Fe Railyard, a 50-acre mixed-use neighborhood and retail destination, occurred in 2008. The Railyard is a shopping area, park, and transportation hub all rolled into one. It features retail stores, art galleries, outdoor performance space, a park and public plaza, and a new Santa Fe Farmers Market building. Back in 2002, the Railyard Master Plan was approved by the governing body Santa Fe, and 2008 through 2010 saw the completion of the Park's infrastructure as well as the continued development of building sites. Plans for a 25,800-square-foot cinema and connected 4,447-square-foot restaurant were approved in 2013, with completion expected by 2014 or 2015.

Road congestion in Santa Fe has long been a longstanding problem, so a large portion of construction projects in 2009 dealt with road improvements. The Siler Road Bridge crossing and connection to West Alameda was built in 2009; the bridge is noteworthy as the first city-built bridge constructed over the Santa Fe River in 50 years. The Sandoval Street Bridge located in downtown Santa Fe was also renovated. Other road improvements included the construction of medians, pedestrian improvements, and new sidewalks. Santa Fe's General Plan also includes proposals for new roads to help combat local congestion.

Construction on a 280-room Drury Plaza Hotel began in 2012, with a projected completion in 2014. The hotel was to be the largest (by number of rooms) in the downtown area, which has strict building codes limiting construction to five stories. Partly because of these construction restrictions, the hotel was set to be the first new hotel in the downtown since the early 2000s. Estimated costs were estimated around $50 million. Several other downtown hotels, including the Eldorado, Hilton, and La Fonda, underwent renovations during 2012 and 2013.

In 2013 Santa Fe Gold announced plans to open a gold mine in the Ortiz Mountains, some 30 miles south of Santa Fe. The mine, which was controversial due its potential impact on the pristine environment, was a two billion dollar project.

Economic Development Information: Santa Fe Economic Development, 120 South Federal Place, Room 314, Santa Fe, NM 87501; telephone 505-955-6912.

Commercial Shipping

Santa Fe is linked with major western and Midwestern markets via rail freight service provided by the Santa Fe Southern Railroad, which maintains a main line through nearby Lamy. Several rail sidings are conveniently located in the city's industrial areas. Several interstate motor freight carriers connect Santa Fe with markets on both the East and West Coasts; major parcel express lines also serve the city. Air cargo service is available at Santa Fe Municipal Airport.

Labor Force and Employment Outlook

Santa Fe's economy is lead by government and tourism. Corporations of substantial size are absent from the economy, with more than half of all local businesses having fewer than five employees. Approximately 41 percent of adult residents in Santa Fe have a college degree or higher, providing the city with a well-educated work force. A "living wage" ordinance, passed in 2003, attempts to raise minimum wages to remedy the imbalance of low wages with a high cost of living index. In 2012 the living wage was $10.29 per hour, an increase from $9.50 in 2007 and $9.85 in 2010. Santa Fe draws an important part of its workforce from the surrounding counties of Rio Arriba, Los Alamos, Sandoval, and San Miguel.

The following is a summary of data regarding the 2012 Santa Fe labor force:

Size of civilian labor force: 36,966

Number of workers employed in . . .

    agriculture and mining: 340
    construction: 1,609
    manufacturing: 686
    wholesale trade: 392
    retail trade: 4,263
    transportation: 1,034
    information systems: 460
    finance: 2,040
    professional administration: 5,433
    education and social services: 7,193
    arts and leisure: 5,060
    other: 1,725
    public administration: 2,916

Average hourly earnings of production workers: $15.08

Unemployment rate: 5.9% (2012)

Employers

Largest employers (2013)	*Number of employees*
State of New Mexico	9,443
Santa Fe School District	1,850
U.S. Federal Government	1,750
City of Santa Fe	1,719
CHRISTUS St. Vincent Hospital	1,450
Santa Fe County	815
Santa Fe Community College	717
Santa Fe Opera	650
Santa Fe University of Art and Design	564
Santa Fe Ski Company	437

Cost of Living

The following is a summary of data regarding several key cost of living factors in the area.

State income tax rate: 1.7% to 4.9%

State sales tax rate: 5.125%

Local income tax rate: None

Local sales tax rate: 3.0625%

Property tax rate: $669.70 per $100,000 of assessed value (2012)

Economic Information: Santa Fe County Chamber of Commerce, 1644 St. Michael's Drive, Santa Fe, NM 87501; telephone (505) 988-3279; fax (505) 984-2205; email info@santafechamber.com. University of New Mexico, Bureau of Business and Economic Research, 303 Girard Blvd. NE #116, Albuquerque, NM 87131; telephone (505) 277-2216.

■ Education and Research

Elementary and Secondary Schools

The Santa Fe Public Schools system is one of the largest districts in the state of New Mexico. It is administered by an elected, five-member board of education that establishes educational policies and appoints a superintendent. The district oversees the operations of four charter schools.

Additionally, Santa Fe has a large network of private schools, consisting of over 30 schools ranging from pre-Kindergarten through 12th grade, one of which—the Santa Fe Indian School—is a federally funded boarding school for Native Americans, run by the All Indian Pueblo Council.

The following is a summary of data regarding the Santa Fe Public Schools.

Total enrollment: 14,188

Number of facilities

total: 30
elementary schools: 17
junior high schools: 5
high schools: 3
other: 5

Student/teacher ratio: 15.5:1

Teacher salaries

average (statewide): $46,950

Funding per pupil: $8,476

Public Schools Information: Santa Fe Public Schools, 610 Alta Vista Street, Santa Fe, NM 87505; telephone (505) 467-2000.

Colleges and Universities

Santa Fe has several institutes of higher learning, including the Santa Fe University of Art and Design, St. John's College, and Santa Fe Community College. The Santa Fe University of Art and Design, known as the College of Santa Fe until 2010, is a 151-year-old private college offering associate and bachelor's degrees. Programs meld practical experience with core theory in areas such as contemporary music, creative writing, theater, art, graphic design, film and video, photography, business, and education. Students have the ability to design their own majors by working with faculty and advisors if they choose.

St. John's College, which has a campus in Annapolis, Maryland, as well as in Santa Fe, offers undergraduate and graduate degrees. St. John's is distinctive for its "great books" curriculum; learning is based upon the study of important books of the Western tradition, and no textbooks are used. There are no majors or departments; all students follow the same path of study including four years of language, four years of math, four years of interdisciplinary study, three years of laboratory science, and one year of music. The school tries to keep its enrollment at a maximum of 475 students in an effort to foster learning through smaller classes and a better student-teacher ratio.

Santa Fe Community College serves area residents with two-year college preparatory and technical and vocational curricula for its 6,700 students enrolled each semester. The Institute of American Indian Arts, a fine arts college offering associate and baccalaureate degrees in creative writing, studio arts, new media arts, and museum studies, serves Native American students from across the country. Southwestern College, devoted to the study of mental health, offers master's degrees in counseling; counseling with a concentration in grief, loss, and trauma; and art therapy. Southwest Acupuncture College offers a Master of Science in Oriental Medicine.

Libraries and Research Centers

The Santa Fe Public Library operates two branches in addition to its main facility downtown. Holdings include over 345,000 separate items, from books to videos to DVDs and CDs. Circulation in 2013 totaled nearly 760,000 items.

Research libraries located in Santa Fe house special collections pertaining to such diverse topics as Southwestern culture, comparative religion, and Sherlock Holmes; other libraries are affiliated with local colleges and government agencies. The New Mexico State Library, with over two million items, is a federal and state documents depository.

The Santa Fe Institute conducts research activities in the physical, biological, computational, and social sciences, in areas such as cognitive neuroscience, computation in physical and biological systems, economic and social interactions, evolutionary dynamics, network dynamics, and robustness. The National Center for Genome Resources examines the influence of genetic variability on infectious disease progression. The Georgia O'Keefe Museum Research Center, in downtown Santa Fe, provides a research library and archived materials supporting research in American Modernism. The Indian Arts Research Center (IARC) holds one of the most prominent collections of authentic Southwest Indian arts and artifacts in the world; most research focuses on the existing collection.

Public Library Information: Santa Fe Public Library, 145 Washington Street, Santa Fe, NM 87501; telephone (505) 955-6781.

■ Health Care

In 2012 the American Lung Association honored Santa Fe as having the cleanest air of any U.S. city. The range of outdoor activities in the area also contributes to active, healthy lifestyles by the city's residents. Santa Fe's CHRISTUS St. Vincent Regional Medical Center is the largest medical center in Northern New Mexico, and has the region's only Level III Trauma Center. In April 2008, St. Vincent and CHRISTUS Health formed a partnership allowing St. Vincent to benefit from the international hospital system's resources. CHRISTUS St. Vincent is the major regional medical center for a 19,000-square-mile area covering seven counties and serving some 300,000

New Mexico residents. St. Vincent has 268 licensed beds, and employs some 380 physicians representing 34 medical specialties. Non-profit and non-affiliated, it was established in 1865 and is the oldest hospital in the state. The medical center is known for its heart and vascular center, which has the first rural EKG network in the nation; it allows rural EMS personnel to transmit an electrocardiogram directly to the medical center.

The Cancer Institute of New Mexico, the combination of the New Mexico Cancer Care Associates and Radiation Oncology Associates, opened in 2003 in Santa Fe. It is New Mexico's newest and most advanced cancer-care facility. Cancer patients are able to access doctors specializing in medical oncology, radiation oncology, diagnostic imaging, clinical research, and administrative support all in one facility.

■ Recreation

Sightseeing

Santa Fe's historic downtown plaza, once the terminus of the Santa Fe Trail, has been a center of activity in Santa Fe since the city's founding. The plaza area is full of restaurants, shops, art galleries, and museums. Also here is St. Francis Cathedral, a grand structure built in the French Romanesque style, unusual in this city of Spanish-Pueblo architecture. Santa Fe's first Roman Catholic archbishop, Jean Baptiste Lamy, started the cathedral; both the bishop and the building were the inspiration for Willa Cather's novel, *Death Comes to the Archbishop*. A wooden icon in the cathedral's north chapel is the oldest representation of the Madonna in the United States.

Other historical buildings include Santuario de Nuestra Señora de Guadalupe, the nation's oldest shrine dedicated to Our Lady of Guadalupe; built in the late 1700s, its adobe walls are three feet thick. Our Lady of Light Chapel, also known as Loretto Chapel, was built between 1873 and 1878 and is the oldest stone masonry building in the city; it is known for its spiral wooden Miraculous Staircase, made without nails (only wooden pegs) or a visible support structure. San Miguel Mission, one of the oldest mission churches in the nation, was built in 1610 by the Tlaxcala natives, who were servants of Spanish soldiers and missionaries; on display is a bell that was cast in Spain in 1356 and brought to Santa Fe in the early nineteenth century. The New Mexico State Capitol building, the only round capitol building in the United States, was built in the shape of a Southwestern Indian *zia*, which represents the circle of life. The Palace of the Governors has been home to 60 Spanish, Mexican, and American governors, among them Lew Wallace, who wrote the novel *Ben Hur* there during his 1877–81 tenure. Built in 1610, it became a history museum in 1909.

Canyon Road, just north of the capitol building, was once a Native American trail and defines one of the oldest districts in the city. Just west of Canyon Road is Barrio de Analco, now called East de Vargas Street, among the oldest continuously inhabited streets in the nation; many historic homes are located here. The Cross of the Martyrs, overlooking the city, is a large white cross built in 1920 to commemorate the Franciscans killed by native Pueblos in 1680. The Commemorative Walkway leading to the monument has been the route for various religious processions, particularly in September during Fiesta, the celebration of the return of the Spanish to Santa Fe in 1692.

Santa Fe is surrounded by 12 Pueblo villages, each of which retains its own distinct culture and holds special events relating to its unique traditions; all are located within an hour's drive of the city.

Arts and Culture

Home of more than 20 music groups, theater companies, and dance groups, Santa Fe supports one of the best and most active arts communities in the country. The famous Santa Fe Opera, which attracts audiences from throughout the world, presents its performances in a partially open-air amphitheater located on a wooded hill north of the city. The open-air structure allows viewers to watch both the show as well as sunsets, rainstorms, or the night sky. It is known for its performances of the classics, obscure works by classical composers, and American premiers of modern works. Its eight-week season runs from June to August.

The Santa Fe Symphony Orchestra and Chorus performs classical and popular works at the Lensic Performing Arts Center; the center's lavish Lensic Theater, built in 1931 as a film and vaudeville house, received an $8.2 million restoration in 2001. The Desert Chorale choral group performs at venues throughout the city and is known for blending Renaissance melodies and avant-garde compositions. The Desert Chorale also has a children's chorus. Children ages 8 to 14 can participate and take part in several public performances each season.

Students at the Santa Fe University of Art and Design stage their productions in the Greer Garson Theatre. Their season, which runs from October to May, consists of several presentations of four plays. Santa Fe Playhouse, established in the 1920s, performs dramas, avant-garde works, and musical comedy in a historic adobe theater.

The María Benitez Teatro Flamenco performs flamenco music and dance in a summer season at the María Benitez Theatre at the Lodge at Santa Fe. The company is comprised of Benitez, who has been named the best flamenco dancer of her generation by *Dance* magazine, and flamenco dancers and musicians from throughout the United States and Spain.

Santa Fe is home to several museums specializing in a variety of fields. The Museum of New Mexico, which reopened in its newest location on the historic Santa Fe Plaza in 2009, is described as the most important modern cultural institution in the state. It serves as an anchor to a campus that houses the Palace of Governors, the Palace Press, and the Fray Angelico Chavez History Library and Photo Archives. The Palace of the Governors, the nation's oldest continually used building, houses exhibits relating to Native American, Spanish, Mexican, and American frontier history. Its governor offices have been restored and preserved. The Palace Press is an exhibit focused on the history of the state's printing traditions. It houses a collection of artifacts and a research library of more than 400 volumes related to the arts of the book. It also is home to a fully functional historic press that prints award-winning, limited editions. The Fray Angélico Chávez History Library and Photo Archives is a close-stacked, non-circulating research library.

One block to the west of the New Mexico History Museum is the New Mexico Museum of Art. Built in 1917, it is the oldest art museum in the state; it was built in the style of the mission church at nearby Acoma Pueblo. The museum maintains a collection of more than 23,000 works, with a specialty in regional art from throughout the 20th century to the present. The Museum of Indian Arts and Culture/Laboratory of Anthropology and the Museum of International Folk Art are located on Museum Hill. The Museum of Indian Arts and Culture showcases exhibits pertaining to the history and contemporary culture of the Pueblo, Navajo, and Apache peoples, including pottery, basketry, woven fabrics, jewelry, and contemporary crafts. Opened in 1987, its massive collection has been built over the course of nearly 80 years of research and acquisition by the Laboratory of Anthropology. The Museum of International Folk Art, the largest of its kind in the world, has more than 135,000 items of folk art from around the world, including dolls and puppets, masks, textiles, ceramics, furniture, clothing, and Spanish colonial artworks.

The Wheelwright Museum of the American Indian, housed in a building shaped like a Navajo hogan, features rotating single-subject displays of jewelry, tapestry, pottery, baskets, and paintings crafted by Native Americans throughout the Southwest. The Institute of American Indian Arts Museum focuses on works by students and faculty members; with more than 7,000 works, it is one of the largest collections of contemporary American Indian art in the world.

The Georgia O'Keeffe Museum houses the largest collection of the artist's work in the world. The museum features revolving exhibits of O'Keeffe's paintings, watercolors, pastels, charcoals, and sculptures, and also hosts exhibitions of works by some of O'Keeffe's contemporaries. In July 2001 the Georgia O'Keeffe Research Center opened as the only museum-related, American Modernism–dedicated research facility in the world. Santa Fe's Museum of Spanish Colonial Art presents a variety of Hispanic media—including santos (painted and sculpted images of saints), textiles, tinwork, silverwork, goldwork, ironwork, straw appliqué, ceramics, furniture, and books—dating from the Middle Ages through the present. In total, it is home to some 3,000 items.

The Santa Fe Children's Museum was developed to offer hands-on exhibits for the whole family.

Festivals and Holidays

Many of Santa Fe's events reflect the cultural diversity of the city. During the Chimayo Pilgrimage, on Good Friday, thousands walk on foot to the Santuario de Chimayo, a small church believed to aid in miracles. The Rodeo de Santa Fe, a popular regional competition, is held in June; the four-night rodeo features entrants from several states competing in such events as bareback bronco riding, calf roping, steer wrestling, and barrel racing.

The annual Traditional Spanish Market is held in July; it is the oldest and largest market in the country for Spanish Colonial artists. More than 300 Hispanic artisans offer traditional art forms, including santos, textiles, tinwork, furniture, straw appliqué, and metalwork. The market also presents live music, art demonstrations, and regional foods. The Santa Fe Indian Market, held in August, is the country's largest and most prestigious Native American art show. More than 1,000 artisans offer basketry, blankets, jewelry, pottery, woodcarvings, rugs, sand paintings, and sculptures. Tribal dancing and craft demonstrations are also presented.

Santa Fe Fiesta in September, which dates to 1712, is the oldest community celebration in the country. Highlights include Spanish dancing, mariachi music, food and craft booths, and parades and ceremonies including a pet parade, a historical/hysterical parade, and a fiesta mass of thanksgiving held at St. Francis Cathedral, followed by a candle-lit procession from the cathedral to the Cross of the Martyrs. The Santa Fe Wine and Chile Fiesta, a five-day event, is also held in September. The Winter Spanish Market, in December, is a smaller version of July's market; more than 100 artisans offer their wares.

Drawing on the traditions of three cultures—Native American, Spanish, and Anglo—Christmas celebrations in Santa Fe take on a special flair. As part of the festivities, *farolitos*—luminaries made of paper bags, sand, and candles—set the town aglow on Christmas Eve. The city also celebrates Las Posadas, the traditional Spanish play depicting the Christmas Eve plight of Mary and Joseph. Indian pueblos schedule winter dances, bonfires, and processions in late December and January.

Sports for the Spectator

The Santa Fe Fuego began playing baseball at Fort Mercy Park in 2012 as part of the Pecos League.

Sports for the Participant

Outdoor activities can be pursued throughout most of the year in Santa Fe. Outdoor enthusiasts can mountain-bike through the area's high-desert terrain, hike in the area's 1,002 miles of national forest trails, golf at one of Santa Fe's six golf courses, or play tennis at one of several tennis courts. The city maintains 68 developed parks, 26 undeveloped parks, and 170 miles of trails. Parks cover a total of 2,500 acres.

Within the Santa Fe National Forest are wilderness areas—Pecos, Dome, and San Pedro parks, and the Chama River Canyon—that are ideal for hiking, camping, fishing, and hunting. Resorts at Ojo Caliente and Jemez Springs furnish bath houses for the enjoyment of the natural hot springs for which northern New Mexico is famous. Skiing is a flourishing sport in Santa Fe. Seven ski areas within a two-hour drive provide facilities for every level of skiing expertise. Ski Santa Fe, a 30-minute drive through the Sangre De Cristo Mountains from Santa Fe, is an especially popular spot. Cross-country skiing areas are also nearby.

Shopping and Dining

Santa Fe has been described as a shopper's "Shangri-La." With hundreds of stores in the downtown area alone, the city offers boutiques and specialty shops, art galleries, and several large shopping centers. Locally designed and crafted items such as clothing, jewelry, pottery, and furniture are featured. *Travel + Leisure* magazine ranked Santa Fe first among all U.S. cities for independent boutiques in 2012.

Prime shopping areas include the city's newest shopping area, the Railyard District, home to a new shopping complex and numerous local art galleries. Just southeast of downtown is the historic Canyon Road area, home to a large, eclectic mix of small shops and galleries; the plaza area, which features the greatest concentration of Native American crafts; and the Santa Fe Arcade, a three-story shopping center. The Guadalupe district, a redeveloped area close to the railyard, features numerous specialty stores and cafes. Located in this area is the Sanbusco Market Center, a remodeled warehouse occupied by unique shops and restaurants. Other Santa Fe shopping highlights include the local treats at the Santa Fe Farmer's Market and the variety of wares at the Tesuque Flea Market.

A specialty of Santa Fe is northern New Mexico cuisine, which is a mixture of Pueblo Indian, Spanish Colonial, and Anglo frontier cooking. It differs from "Tex-Mex" food in that northern New Mexican cooks use heavy meats for such dishes as *carne adovada*, or marinated pork. Green chiles, pinto beans, and blue corn tortillas are also used in local dishes. *Sopaipillas*, deep-fried puff pastries drizzled with honey, are especially popular. Among other dining options are Western-style steak and barbeque, vegetarian cuisine, and Italian, Chinese, Sushi, Thai, Indian, Korean, Mediterranean, French, and Native American restaurants.

Visitor Information: Santa Fe Convention and Visitors Bureau, 201 West Marcy, Santa Fe, NM 87501; telephone (800) 777-2489.

■ Convention Facilities

The principal meeting facility in its newly built Santa Fe Community Convention Center, which replaced the Sweeney Convention Center when it opened in 2008. The new 72,500-square-foot venue offers more than 40,000 square feet of exhibit space and is located in the heart of downtown Santa Fe. Within walking distance of the facility are some 1,500 hotel rooms, fine Santa Fe restaurants, museums, and shopping. The Convention Center also has an underground garage that can hold approximately 512 vehicles.

Convention Information: Santa Fe Convention and Visitors Bureau, 201 West Marcy, Santa Fe, NM 87501; telephone (800) 777-2489.

■ Transportation

Approaching the City

The major airport closest to Santa Fe is Albuquerque International Sunport, 65 minutes away. Shuttle companies offer transportation between the airport and Santa Fe. The airport is served by six major commercial airlines, although Southwest Airlines handles more than 50 percent of all passenger service. The airport provides 6.1 million annual passengers with non-stop service to 21 cities across the country. Santa Fe Municipal Airport, located nine miles southwest of the city's central business district, accommodates commuter flights and private aircraft. The Roadrunner Shuttle meets every flight to transport travelers to any Santa Fe location.

The principal highway routes into Santa Fe are Interstate 25, running east and west along the southern perimeter of the city, and Interstate 84/285, which bisects the city from north to south.

Amtrak's Southwest Chief, a line running between Chicago and Los Angeles, schedules twice-daily arrivals and departures at Lamy, about 20 miles south of Santa Fe; regular shuttle service is provided from the village to Santa Fe. The New Mexico Rail Runner Express, a commuter rail system, began service from Santa Fe in 2008 with more than one dozen stations heading southward through Albuquerque to Belen.

Intercity commercial bus transportation is available through two bus lines.

Traveling in the City

Santa Fe Trails bus system provides affordable public transportation on 10 routes throughout the city.

■ Communications

Newspapers and Magazines

Santa Fe's major daily newspaper is *The Santa Fe New Mexican,* the oldest newspaper in the West. The alternative weekly *Santa Fe Reporter* is published on Wednesdays. Magazines published in Santa Fe include the *Santa Fean,* featuring articles on New Mexico history and travel, restaurants, events, and attractions; and *New Mexico Magazine,* founded in 1923, which covers such topics as the state's multicultural heritage, arts, climate, environment and diverse people.

Television and Radio

Several television stations broadcast from Santa Fe; others, including network affiliates, are broadcast from nearby Albuquerque. Cable service is available by subscription. Eleven FM and four AM radio stations broadcast in Santa Fe, at least one of which plays Spanish music. Santa Fe also receives programming from Albuquerque and other nearby cities.

Media Information: *The Santa Fe New Mexican,* 202 E. Marcy Street, Santa Fe, NM 87501; telephone (505) 983-3303.

Santa Fe Online

> Bureau of Business and Economic Research, University of New Mexico. Available bber.unm.edu
>
> City of Santa Fe home page. Available www.santafenm.gov
>
> New Mexico Department of Workforce Solutions. Available www.dws.state.nm.us
>
> Santa Fe Economic Development. Available santafebiz.org
>
> *The Santa Fe New Mexican.* Available www.santafenewmexican.com
>
> Santa Fe Public Library. Available www.santafelibrary.org
>
> Santa Fe Public Schools. Available www.sfps.info

BIBLIOGRAPHY

All Trails Lead to Santa Fe: An Anthology Commemorating the 400th Anniversary of the Founding of Santa Fe, New Mexico, in 1610 (Santa Fe, NM: Sunstone Press, 2010)

Parent, Laurence, *Scenic Driving New Mexico,* 3rd ed. (Guilford, CT: Globe Pequot Press, 2011)

Taos

■ The City in Brief

Founded: 1934 (incorporated)

Head Official: Darren Cordova (since 2010; current term expires 2014)

City Population
> 1990: 4,401
> 2000: 4,700
> 2010: 5,716
> 2012 estimate: 5,661
> Percent change, 2000–2010: 21.6%

Micropolitan Statistical Area Population
> 2000: 29,979
> 2010: 32,937
> 2012 estimate: 32,872
> Percent change, 2000–2010: 9.9%
> U.S. rank in 2010: 799th

Area: 5.4 square miles

Elevation: 8,998 feet above sea level

Average Annual Temperatures: January, 25.2° F; July, 68.3° F

Average Annual Precipitation: 12.3 inches of rain; 89.2 inches of snow

Major Economic Sectors: government, tourism, retail, health care

Unemployment Rate: 12.8% (2012)

Per Capita Income: $20,813

2012 FBI Crime Index Property: 460

Major Colleges and Universities: University of New Mexico Taos

Daily Newspaper: *The Taos News*

■ Introduction

Since Spanish explorers first saw the multi-tiered adobe structures of the Taos Pueblo, the area has been a focal point of cultural and artistic history in New Mexico. As time passed, both rail lines and major U.S. interstate highways bypassed the area, preserving the town's identity but also isolating it from high-tech development in cities such as Santa Fe and Albuquerque, both located to the south. As a result, Taos's reputation as an artistic hub, as well as year-round opportunities to enjoy its unblemished natural environment, have defined the town's economy, supporting local artists in good times, while also challenging the city to expand its economic base during lean years.

■ Geography and Climate

Taos enjoys dry and sunny summers and far cooler winters, frequently accompanied by snow. Greater snowfall in the Taos Ski Valley supports winter activities several months each year. Precipitation during warmer months comes in the form of occasional afternoon thunderstorms.

Area: 5.4 square miles

Elevation: 8,998 feet above sea level

Average Temperatures: January, 25.2° F; July, 68.3° F

Average Annual Precipitation: 12.3 inches of rain; 89.2 inches of snow

■ History

Evidence of human civilization in Taos dates to 12,000 B.C., with small-scale farming beginning in the area around 3000 B.C. Pottery and structures appeared by 200 A.D.,

© Ian Dagnall/Alamy

and the first multi-storied pueblos were believed to have been constructed around 1050. Taos Pueblo structures were built between 1300 and 1450.

A Spanish Colonial Possession

Contact between Native Americans and Spanish explorers occurred in 1540 during an expedition of Spanish Captain Hernando Alvarado. Alvarado was sent by superiors to explore a region that included the Taos Valley. At the time, the valley was inhabited by the Tiwa Indians, who had created large pueblo structures at the historic Taos Pueblo. Alvarado encountered several establishments of friendly Indians, the most remote of which was the Taos Pueblo. The eventual name of the city first appeared in a 1598 report by a Spanish secretary, who included a reference by locals to their "Tao" relatives who lived nearby.

Taos officially became a Spanish village in 1615 and was governed by a Spanish *alcalde*, or mayor. Indian groups signed allegiances to Spanish authority in exchange for military protection and access to Spanish missionaries. Passive acceptance of Spanish rule ended in 1680, when a major revolt led by Popé, a San Juan

Pueblo Indian, expelled the Spanish from New Mexico. Relations had soured over treatment of Indians and religious intolerance. The Spanish re-conquered most of the area in 1692, primarily to secure famed silver mines in the area. The Taos Pueblo Indians surrendered in 1696.

In 1760 the Taos Pueblo was named Don Fernando de Taos by Spanish settlers, a reference to Captain Don Fernando de Chavez, a prominent settler expelled from the area during the initial rebellion. By the formation of the United States in the late eighteenth century, the area had about 67 families, including 306 Spanish settlers. By the early 1800s, most settlers had moved to the present-day location of the city, a couple miles southwest of the Taos Pueblo. While Mexican independence from Spain in 1821 had little effect on the area, the opening of the Santa Fe Trail allowed for considerable in-migration.

Incorporation into the United States

The U.S. presence in Taos dates to 1846, when Colonel Stephen W. Kearney and the Army of the West occupied New Mexico during the Mexican War (1846–48) and appointed American Charles Bent as governor. Locals revolted against U.S. control, and Bent was murdered. Nonetheless, the U.S. victory against Mexico ceded the territory, and much of the Southwest, to the United States in the 1848 Treaty of Guadalupe Hidalgo.

Into the late 1800s, attempts to connect Taos via railways proved unsuccessful, maintaining a degree of isolation still present in contemporary Taos. New Mexico was admitted as the 47th state in 1912, and the Town of Taos was incorporated as a general law municipality on May 7, 1934.

The city's arts culture had been established years prior, when American artist Ernest Blumenschien stayed in Taos after his family's wagon broke down in 1898. The Taos Society of Artists (1915–27) further solidified the city's arts base, which later connected with the counter-culture of the 1960s; the New Buffalo commune was founded there by Arroyo Hondo in 1967, and it became a mecca for the hippie movement of that generation.

By the late twentieth century, Taos had become a prime destination for tourists looking to enjoy the city's historical, cultural, and artistic legacy. A major fire on July 4, 2003, sparked by a lightning strike, threatened many of the Taos Pueblo historic buildings, but 13 days and thousands of firefighters were able to preserve all buildings and avoid any loss of life. Taos was not as lucky regarding the effects of a national recession during the late 2000s, which crippled the economy and exposed the area's dependency on tourist dollars.

Economic stability returned by 2013. That year, some 242,500 acres of public land near Taos was designated as Río Grande del Norte National Monument, which secured the area's protection and was also likely to drive tourist interest.

■ Population Profile

Micropolitan Statistical Area Population

   2000: 29,979
   2010: 32,937
   2012 estimate: 32,872
   Percent change, 2000–2010: 9.9%
   U.S. rank in 2010: 799th

City Residents

   1990: 4,401
   2000: 4,700
   2010: 5,716
   2012 estimate: 5,661
   Percent change, 2000–2010: 21.6%

Density: 1,048.3 people per square mile

Racial and ethnic characteristics

   White: 3,678
   Black or African American: 12
   American Indian and Alaskan Native: 418

   Asian: 57
   Native Hawaiian and Other Pacific Islander: 4
   Hispanic or Latino (may be of any race): 2,721
   Other: 1,492

Percent of residents born in state: 47.9%

Age characteristics

   Population under 5 years old: 391
   Population 5 to 9 years old: 395
   Population 10 to 14 years old: 207
   Population 15 to 19 years old: 349
   Population 20 to 24 years old: 288
   Population 25 to 34 years old: 739
   Population 35 to 44 years old: 749
   Population 45 to 54 years old: 983
   Population 55 to 59 years old: 427
   Population 60 to 64 years old: 327
   Population 65 to 74 years old: 473
   Population 75 to 84 years old: 187
   Population 85 years and over: 146
   Median age: 41.3

Births (2010–11 Micropolitan Area)

   Total number: 320

Deaths (2010–11 Micropolitan Area)

   Total number: 259

Money income (2012)

   Per capita income: $20,813
   Median household income: $41,165
   Total households: 2,368

Number of households with income of …

   less than $10,000: 422
   $10,000 to $14,999: 241
   $15,000 to $24,999: 330
   $25,000 to $34,999: 282
   $35,000 to $49,999: 340
   $50,000 to $74,999: 457
   $75,000 to $99,999: 167
   $100,000 to $149,999: 66
   $150,000 to $199,999: 19
   $200,000 or more: 44

Percent of families below poverty level: 24.4%

FBI Crime Index Property: 460

FBI Crime Index Violent: 56

■ Municipal Government

Taos has a mayor-council form of government, with an appointed town manager. Four council members and the mayor serve four-year terms and are elected at-large.

Head Official: Darren Cordova (since 2010; current term expires 2014)

Total Number of City Employees: 1,587 (2011)

City Information: Town of Taos, 400 Camino de la Placita, Taos, NM 87571; telephone (575) 751-2000; fax (575) 751-2026.

■ Economy

Major Industries and Commercial Activity

Taos's main industry is tourism and the associated activities of retail trade, restaurants, and hotels. Tourism contributes about $75 million annually to the economy, with visitor arrivals averaging around 120,000. Taos markets itself on the natural scenic beauty of the surrounding area and the region's rich history, particularly as it relates to indigenous culture. When tourism revenues declined beginning in 2006, the economy plunged into a deep recession; the economy began to recover by 2012.

Economic development priorities as of 2013, apart from seeking to stabilize and expand the tourist market, focused on the retention, expansion, and incubation of new and existing businesses, and support of technology-based companies. Other industries contributing to the local economy included manufacturing, with an impact of about $20 million annually, and agriculture, forestry, and fishing, worth about $4 million to the local economy.

Items and goods produced: agricultural products, soap, crafts

Incentive Programs—New and Existing Companies

Local programs: Business support and information is provided through the Taos County Chamber of Commerce.

State programs: New Mexico offers a variety of incentives to all new and expanding businesses. The High-Wage Jobs Tax Credit allows qualified businesses to take a generous tax credit for each new job created with a salary of at least $28,000 a year (in areas where the population does not exceed 40,000) or $40,000 a year (in areas where the population exceeds 40,000).

Other tax credit incentives include a Manufacturer's Investment Tax Credit, a New Markets Tax Credit, a Technology Jobs Tax Credit, Aircraft Manufacturing Tax Deduction, Aircraft Maintenance or Remodeling Tax Deduction, Space Gross Receipts Tax Credit, Alternative Energy Product Manufacturer's Tax Credit, New Mexico Refundable Film Production Tax Credit, and State Film Investment Loan Program. New Mexico's property taxes are among the lowest in the nation.

Job training programs: New Mexico is home to one of the most aggressive training incentive packages in the nation. Through the Job Training Incentive Program (JTIP) expanding or relocated businesses can receive up to six months of funds for classroom and on-the-job-training for newly created jobs. The JTIP reimburses required travel expenses and up to 65 percent of employee wages.

In 2007 the Governor's Office of Workforce Training & Development merged with the New Mexico Department of Labor to create a new branch called the New Mexico Department of Workforce Solutions. The combined department focuses on preparing job seekers to meet current standards in the labor market as well as effectively matching citizens with businesses in need of help. Services available include job fairs, local workforce development centers, online job searches, and online registration for employment services.

The Taos Business and Education Collaborative provides youth in Taos with training in life skills and personal development, as well as opportunities for work exposure, internships, and entrepreneurial development.

Development Projects

In 2013 the local Kit Carson Electric Cooperative began testing a new fiber-optic network set to provide inexpensive broadband access to Taos residents. The $63 million broadband project received a $44 million federal grant to support the effort. After completion, expected in 2014, the bandwidth was to be sold to all Internet Service Providers, include Kit Carson Cooperative.

A dispute between the Town of Taos and the county government over control of the Taos Regional Airport was decided in favor of the county by a judge in late 2013. The Town of Taos had annexed county land on which the airport—which the town owns—sat, in expectation of a federally funded $22 million expansion project that required $1.4 million in matching funds from the town. In order to obtain sufficient tax revenue, the town annexed the land so that it could collect gross receipts tax revenue from the expansion activities; the judge rejected the legality of the annexation. The county had offered to provide the town with the related tax revenue without annexation, but distrust led town officials to reject the offer. Final resolution of the issue, expected to go to the New Mexico Municipal Boundary Commission, was needed before expansion could take place.

Economic Development Information: Taos County Chamber of Commerce, 1139 Paseo del Pueblo Sur, Taos, NM 87571; telephone (575) 751-8800; email info@taoschamber.com.

Commercial Shipping

Taos remains a relatively isolated city, with no rail links or direct interstate access. Major commercial shipping needs are met by nearby Santa Fe and Albuquerque, both located to southwest of Taos.

Labor Force and Employment Outlook

Most of the Taos labor force works in support of the tourist industry, which includes those in the restaurant, hospitality, or creative industries. Government and health care are also important employers. Steady economic decline between 2006 and 2012 resulted in significant job losses, with some leaving the city to find work elsewhere. The lack of skilled labor in Taos has threatened the development of some Taos-based industries, which struggle to find a sufficiently skilled workforce for operations.

The following is a summary of data regarding the 2012 Taos labor force:

Size of civilian labor force: 2,978

Number of workers employed in . . .

agriculture and mining: 29
construction: 221
manufacturing: 62
wholesale trade: 63
retail trade: 233
transportation: 41
information systems: 39
finance: 34
professional administration: 224
education and social services: 625
arts and leisure: 477
other: 177
public administration: 165

Average hourly earnings of production workers: $14.20

Unemployment rate: 12.8% (2012)

Cost of Living

The following is a summary of data regarding several key cost of living factors in the area.

State income tax rate: 1.7% to 4.9%

State sales tax rate: 5.125%

Local income tax rate: None

Local sales tax rate: 3.0625%

Property tax rate: 16.798 mills (2013)

Economic Information: Taos County Chamber of Commerce, 1139 Paseo del Pueblo Sur, Taos, NM 87571; telephone (575) 751-8800; email info@taoschamber.com.

■ Education and Research

Elementary and Secondary Schools

Taos Municipal Schools are governed by a three-member school board and a superintendent. The district operates five regular schools, oversees one charter school, and offers the Taos Cyber Magnet School. Vista Grande High School, the town's charter school, utilizes a project-based environment and expeditionary learning model to provide customized learning experiences for its students. The Taos Cyber Magnet School offers online courses through the National Network of Digital Schools, and also partners with the University of New Mexico Taos Branch to allow high school students to earn credit toward college degrees.

Two other charter schools, Taos Academy and Taos Integrated School of the Arts , are also available to area residents.

The following is a summary of data regarding Taos Municipal Schools.

Total enrollment: 3,014

Number of facilities

total: 6
elementary schools: 3
junior high schools: 1
high schools: 2
other: 0

Student/teacher ratio: 14.12:1

Funding per pupil: $9,768

Public Schools Information: Taos Municipal Schools, 310 Camino de la Placita, Taos, NM 87571; telephone (575) 758-5200.

Colleges and Universities

The University of New Mexico Taos, established in 2003, is the primary center of higher education in Taos. The campus offers associate degrees in education, fine art, liberal arts, pre-business administration, pre-science, general studies, and nursing. Also available are certificates in more than a dozen fields, including culinary arts, dental assistant, and woodworking, among others.

Southern Methodist University maintains a 423-acre Taos campus offering credit courses in arts, sciences, business, and other disciplines. The focus area of the campus is Southwest Studies; it also serves as a retreat location for university receptions and alumni events.

Libraries and Research Centers

The Taos Public Library opened its present facility in 1996, although long-term plans seek construction of an even larger space. The library maintains 17 Internet terminals, and wireless Internet is available throughout the building. The children's library has programs for children of all ages and a collection that includes audiobooks, CDs, DVDs, and videos. Some 1,500 books in the library's collection are specific to the interests in teenage patrons.

The University of New Mexico Taos library supports an interlibrary loan program that provides users with access to materials at 10,000 additional libraries. Online databases provide students with thousands of additional resources, primarily scholarly journals and periodicals. The Fort Burgwin Library of Southern Methodist University in Taos contains some 9,000 books, as well as a small collection of journals and maps. The library collection focuses on the history, literature, culture, and environment of New Mexico.

Public Library Information: Taos Public Library, 402 Camino de la Placita, Taos, NM 87571; telephone (575) 758-3063; email librarian@taosgov.com.

■ Health Care

The main health-care facility in Taos is Holy Cross Hospital, which is part of the broader Taos Health Systems. Medical services offered include diagnostic imaging, emergency services, inpatient services, integrative medicine and wellness, observation unit, surgical services, and women's health services. Outpatient services include anticoagulation and dermatology clinics, as well as diabetes management services, nutritional counseling, and wound care. The hospital employs 80 physicians in specialties that include internal medicine, cardiology, obstetrics and gynecology, orthopedics, general surgery, urology, and emergency services. Other facilities in the Taos Health Systems network include Taos Surgical Specialties, Women's Health Institute, and Peñasco Health Clinic.

■ Recreation

Sightseeing

The primary landmark in Taos is the Taos Pueblo, the site of pre-colonial indigenous habitation and the only living Native American community designated both as a UNESCO World Heritage Site and a National Historic Landmark. The adobe structures that comprise the pueblo have been continuously inhabited for more than 1,000 years, with most of the present buildings likely constructed between 1000 and 1450 A.D. Picuris Pueblo, located about 24 miles southeast of Taos, was the largest pueblo at the time of Spanish colonization, although it is now one of the smallest remaining Tiwa pueblos.

Built in the late 1700s, San Francisco de Asis Church, also known as Ranchos Church, remains an active church and was made famous by artist Georgia O'Keeffe and photographer Ansel Adams. Community members still add a layer of adobe to the building annually to preserve its appearance. The church is surrounded by shops, art galleries, and restaurants.

Around the same time the church was constructed, Spanish colonists formed the Don Fernando de Taos Plaza; all doors and windows face inward, a protective measure

that limited access to the settlement. Hotel La Fonda, located within the plaza, has two D.H. Lawrence paintings.

The Blumenschein Home and Museum was built in 1797 but earned its name from Ernest Blumenschein, the artist who established the Taos Society of Artists after moving to the area in 1919. The house is filled with artwork by the former owner, as well as additional works by other local and international artists. European antiques from the colonial era are also on display. The Couse-Sharp Historic Site showcases the home and studio of E.I. Couse, who was also a founding member of the Taos Society of Artists and its first president. The Kit Carson Home and Museum near Taos Plaza maintains the four-room house built in 1825 where prominent Taos residents Kit and Josefa Carson lived.

The Rio Grande Gorge Bridge, completed in 1965, is the second highest bridge in the U.S. highway system and fifth highest bridge in the United States. It is 650 feet above the Rio Grande and spans some 1,280 feet; the center span is 600 feet long. The bridge has been popular with film crews, appearing in the movies *Natural Born Killers, Twins, She's Having a Baby, Wild Hogs,* and *Terminator Salvation.*

Twenty miles north of Taos is the D.H. Lawrence Ranch, which is open to visitors by appointment. The ranch was left to the University of New Mexico by the author's widow in her will, for the purpose of establishing a public memorial to Lawrence.

Arts and Culture

The arts culture of Taos, along with the historic pueblo, remains the most distinctive feature of the city. A popular truism among residents is that Taos has more artists per capita than any other city in the world. There are more than 80 art galleries in Taos, and murals and sculptures throughout the downtown area add original artwork to nearly every wall in the city.

The Harwood Museum of Art is the principal art museum of Taos. The museum, founded by Burt and Elizabeth Harwood in the early twentieth century, features works from major Taos artists—both past and present—as well as a collection of Hispanic art dating from the eighteenth century onward. Native American arts are on display at the Millicent Rogers Museum, which includes both historic and contemporary pottery, paintings, photography, crafts, and jewelry from Native American communities throughout northern New Mexico. The Taos Art Museum at the Fechin House, located in the former home of Russian-born artist Nicolai Fechin, features many works by local artists.

The Taos Chamber Music Group performs seven times from September through March. Performances mix classical masterpieces with seldom-heard works and multidisciplinary collaborations. Concerts take place at Arthur Bell Auditorium in the Harwood Museum of Art. The Taos School of Music hosts a summer concert series featuring top guest performers from around the world.

The Town of Taos maintains Kit Carson Park, Taos Plaza, and Fred Baca Park.

Shopping and Dining

Taos shopping focuses on the unique, locally made crafts of the town's residents. Don Fernando de Taos Plaza features an array of shops and galleries with locally made goods. Guadalupe Plaza, adjacent to the main Taos plaza, and Ledoux Street offer additional art galleries. Other galleries are concentrated on East Kit Carson Road, North Pueblo Road, Bent Street, and the John Dunn Shops. Taos Canyon allows shoppers to watch artists at work, and Ranchos de Taos, a few miles south of the main plaza, showcases still more local Taos artists. Native American crafts and jewelry can be found throughout Taos Pueblo, as well as in the northern communities of Questa and Costilla.

Ski resorts located within 10 miles of Taos sell locally produced goods and the necessary apparel and equipment for winter sports.

Visitor Information: Taos Visitor Center, 1139 Paseo del Pueblo Sur, Taos, NM 87571; telephone (575) 758-3873; toll-free (800) 348-0696; email information@taos-visitor.com.

■ Convention Facilities

The Taos Convention Center has two main facilities: Coronado Hall has four breakout rooms, each of which accommodates between 45 and 75 people; Don Fernando Hall is an unbroken space capable of hosting as many as 600 people theater-style. Two outdoor patios offer an additional 5,400 square feet of space.

Other meeting facilities in Taos are Kachina Lodge and Meetings Center, with 7,000 square feet of space, and Sagebrush Inn and Conference Center, with 12,200 square feet. Ski resorts in surrounding areas provide additional capacity for meetings and conventions.

Convention Information: Taos Convention Center, 120 Civic Plaza Drive, Taos, NM 87571; telephone (575) 737-2617; fax (575) 751-1432.

■ Transportation

Approaching the City

The Taos Municipal Airport has a 5,800-foot runway about six miles from the city limit, although no commercial flights operate to or from the airport. Albuquerque International Sunport is 135 miles south of Taos. Taos Ski Valley Inc. operates a year-round daily shuttle from Albuquerque International Sunport. Other regional airports include Colorado Springs Airport, 230 miles to the north, and Denver International Airport, 300 miles north of Taos.

Interstate 25 runs north–south about 50 miles east of Taos, and Interstate 40 runs east–west through Albuquerque, more than 100 miles to the south. Most methods of approach take Interstate 25 to U.S. Highway 285, to State Highway 68, which follows the Rio Grande into Taos. U.S. Highway 64 runs east–west to the north of the city.

Traveling in the City

Upon entering the Town of Taos, State Highway 68 becomes the Paseo del Pueblo, running north–south through the city center. (It is Paseo del Pueblo Sur south of U.S. Highway 68 and Paseo del Pueblo Norte thereafter.) Downtown roads are not laid out in any particular pattern, given the lack of population density. Main thoroughfares include Camino de la Placita and Ranchitos Road.

The Taos Chile Line is the town's public transit service, which has a main route running from the southern edge of the city northward to the Taos Pueblo along the Paseo del Pueblo.

■ Communications

Newspapers and Magazines

The Taos News is a weekly newspaper serving Taos County and the Moreno valley.

Televisio
Seven loca
does one *A*

Media I
Street, Ta
email web

Taos Onl
Río G
Ava
Taos (
tao
Taos (
tao
Taos
Taos
The T

BIBLIOGRA

Martinez
Mount.
2010)

Summer,
(Chape
2010)

CITIES (

Oregon

The State in Brief

Nickname: Beaver State

Motto: Alis Volat Propriis (She flies with her own wings)

Flower: Oregon grape

Bird: Western meadowlark

Area: 98,379 square miles (2010; U.S. rank 9th)

Elevation: Ranges from sea level to 11,239 feet above sea level

Climate: Mild and humid with frequent rainfall in western third; dry with extremes of temperature in the interior two-thirds

Admitted to Union: February 14, 1859

Capital: Salem

Head Official: John Kitzhaber (D) (until 2015)

Population
1990: 2,842,321
2000: 3,421,399
2010: 3,831,074
2012 estimate: 3,836,628
Percent change, 2000–2010: 12.0%
U.S. rank in 2012: 27th
Percent of residents born in state: 45.7% (2012)
Density: 39.9 people per square mile (2010)
2012 FBI Crime Index Total: 135,376

Racial and Ethnic Characteristics (2012)
White: 3,272,707
Black or African American: 69,377
American Indian and Alaska Native: 52,637
Asian: 143,652
Native Hawaiian and Pacific Islander: 14,132
Hispanic or Latino (may be of any race): 449,888
Other: 284,123

Age Characteristics (2012)
Population under 5 years old: 234,979
Population 5 to 19 years old: 732,657
Percent of population 65 years and over: 14.1%
Median age: 38.4

Vital Statistics
Total number of births (2012–13): 45,135
Total number of deaths (2012–13): 32,529
AIDS cases reported through 2011: 7,141

Economy
Major industries: Manufacturing; finance, insurance, and real estate; trade; agriculture
Unemployment rate (2012): 6.8%
Per capita income (2012): $26,702
Median household income (2012): $50,036
Percentage of persons below poverty level (2012): 15.5%
Income tax rate: 5.0% to 9.9%
Sales tax rate: None

Eugene

■ The City in Brief

Founded: 1846 (incorporated, 1862)

Head Official: Mayor Kitty Piercy (D) (since 2005; current term expires January 2017)

City Population
 1990: 112,733
 2000: 137,893
 2010: 156,185
 2012 estimate: 157,984
 Percent change, 2000–2010: 13.3%
 U.S. rank in 1990: 159th (State rank: 2nd)
 U.S. rank in 2000: 160th (State rank: 2nd)
 U.S. rank in 2010: 148th (State rank: 2nd)

Metropolitan Statistical Area Population
 2000: 322,959
 2010: 351,715
 2012 estimate: 354,542
 Percent change, 2000–2010: 8.9%
 U.S. rank in 2000: 139th
 U.S. rank in 2010: 143rd

Area: 41.0 square miles

Elevation: 369 feet above sea level

Average Annual Temperatures: January, 39.8° F; July, 66.2° F; annual average, 52.1° F

Average Annual Precipitation: 50.9 inches of rain; 6.4 inches of snow

Major Economic Sectors: services, trade, government, agriculture

Unemployment Rate: 6.3% (2012)

Per Capita Income: $26,186

2012 FBI Crime Index Property: 8,004

Major Colleges and Universities: University of Oregon, Lane Community College, Northwest Christian College, Gutenberg College, Eugene Bible College

Daily Newspaper: *The Register-Guard*

■ Introduction

The seat of Lane County, Eugene is Oregon's second largest city. Together with Springfield, it is also the second largest metropolitan area in the state. The city has been a commercial and cultural hub for a large agricultural and timber region, as well as an important retail trade and transportation hub in the state of Oregon. However, as the lumber industry weakened during the 2000s, the city sought to better incubate its existing businesses and target high-technology companies. Situated halfway between the ocean and the mountains, Eugene offers many recreational opportunities year round. The University of Oregon continues to serve as an intellectual and cultural anchor for the community.

■ Geography and Climate

Eugene is located in the center of western Oregon, about 100 miles south of Portland and halfway between the Pacific Ocean and the Cascade Mountains in the broad Willamette River valley. Temperatures are usually moderate throughout the year, with most rainfall occurring from October to May. Winters are warmed by prevailing winds from the southwest, and summers are kept mild and dry by cooling northwestern winds.

Area: 41.0 square miles

Elevation: 369 feet above sea level

© Len Stolfo/upshotz.com

Average Temperatures: January, 39.8° F; July, 66.2° F; annual average, 52.1° F

Average Annual Precipitation: 50.9 inches of rain; 6.4 inches of snow

■ History

A site near present-day Eugene was settled in 1846 by Eugene F. Skinner at the base of a mountain peak called Ya-po-ah by the Calapooya tribe. The settlement was named Skinner's after its founder, and in 1852 a townsite was laid out by Skinner and Judge D. M. Risdon, who erected the first house within the corporate limits. Attempts to establish the town were foiled by heavy rains, however, and resulted in the nickname "Skinner's Mudhole." The settlers moved to higher ground where construction succeeded, and in 1853 the town, taking its founder's first name, was chosen as the seat of newly created Lane County. The first post office in the region was built there the same year; Eugene was incorporated in 1862.

Agriculture, milling, and transportation were the principal industries during Eugene's early years. A steady steamship trade was conducted between the town and Portland from the late 1850s until 1871, when construction of the Oregon & California Railroad brought an end to water transportation. By the end of the Civil War, Eugene's population had reached 1,200 residents and the city was becoming highly industrialized. With lumbering as a principal industry, the city was the site of sawmills, shingle mills, planing mills, and box factories. Cotton-wood and balm trees indigenous to the area were used to produce excelsior. Mining was also an important part of the economy. Agriculture continued to expand; wheat had been the major crop, and many farmers soon turned to fruit growing and dairy farming as well. Creameries, canneries, and flour mills were built for the processing of agricultural goods. A major influence on the city as a cultural and education center began in 1876, when the University of Oregon was founded.

Along with industrial development, however, Eugene maintained a livable environment for its residents. By the 1940s the city was noted for its park-like appearance: comfortable, well-kept homes were set in landscaped lawns and trees lined the streets. Business districts occupied impressive brick and concrete buildings. Eugene's population expanded steadily throughout the first half of the twentieth century, reaching nearly

51,000 people in 1967. By 1980, the population had nearly doubled. A slowdown in the timber industry during the early 1980s halted expansion.

Into the 2000s, the city continued to serve as a lumber and wood-products center, where a high percentage of the nation's plywood was produced. A national recession in the late 2000s significantly curtailed construction projects—and demand for Eugene's most lucrative product. In response, the city has sought to become a hub for Oregon's high-technology businesses and industries. The state government's strong push for renewable energy production and adoption has supported these efforts. The lumber market showed signs of recovery by the mid-2010s, which offered a more promising future for many Eugene residents.

Historical Information: Lane County Historical Society and Museum, 740 W. 13th Avenue, Eugene, OR 97402; telephone (541) 682-4242.

■ Population Profile

Metropolitan Statistical Area Population

2000: 322,959
2010: 351,715
2012 estimate: 354,542
Percent change, 2000–2010: 8.9%
U.S. rank in 2000: 139th
U.S. rank in 2010: 143rd

City Residents

1990: 112,733
2000: 137,893
2010: 156,185
2012 estimate: 157,984
Percent change, 2000–2010: 13.3%
U.S. rank in 1990: 159th (State rank: 2nd)
U.S. rank in 2000: 160th (State rank: 2nd)
U.S. rank in 2010: 148th (State rank: 2nd)

Density: 3,572.2 people per square mile

Racial and ethnic characteristics

White: 135,505
Black or African American: 2,519
American Indian and Alaskan Native: 968
Asian: 6,713
Native Hawaiian and Other Pacific Islander: 492
Hispanic or Latino (may be of any race): 11,834
Other: 11,787

Percent of residents born in state: 41.5%

Age characteristics

Population under 5 years old: 6,276
Population 5 to 9 years old: 6,117
Population 10 to 14 years old: 7,361
Population 15 to 19 years old: 12,797
Population 20 to 24 years old: 25,603
Population 25 to 34 years old: 22,248
Population 35 to 44 years old: 18,708
Population 45 to 54 years old: 18,876
Population 55 to 59 years old: 9,266
Population 60 to 64 years old: 9,686
Population 65 to 74 years old: 10,804
Population 75 to 84 years old: 6,130
Population 85 years and over: 4,112
Median age: 34.2

Births (2010–11 Metropolitan Area)

Total number: 3,481

Deaths (2010–11 Metropolitan Area)

Total number: 3,060

Money income (2012)

Per capita income: $26,186
Median household income: $40,435
Total households: 65,952

Number of households with income of ...

less than $10,000: 9,187
$10,000 to $14,999: 4,577
$15,000 to $24,999: 7,608
$25,000 to $34,999: 8,015
$35,000 to $49,999: 8,901
$50,000 to $74,999: 10,781
$75,000 to $99,999: 6,373
$100,000 to $149,999: 6,777
$150,000 to $199,999: 2,007
$200,000 or more: 1,726

Percent of families below poverty level: 25.1%

FBI Crime Index Property: 8,004

FBI Crime Index Violent: 430

■ Municipal Government

Eugene operates under a council-manager form of government with a mayor and eight council members elected to four-year terms in non-partisan elections. Half the council is elected every two years. The council hires the city manager.

Head Official: Mayor Kitty Piercy (D) (since 2005; current term expires January 2017)

Total Number of City Employees: 1,378 (2012)

City Information: City of Eugene, 125 East 8th Avenue, 2nd Floor, Eugene, OR 97401; telephone (541) 682-5010.

■ Economy

Major Industries and Commercial Activity

Historically lumber has been the largest industry in the Eugene area, where a number of manufacturing companies produce lumber and wood products. The region is the nation's largest producer of softwood lumber and plywood products; weak prices in the 2000s, coupled with higher fuel costs, hurt the industry. A decline in housing construction associated with a national recession in the late 2000s also weakened demand, although the market had stabilized and showed some signs of growth by the mid-2010s.

Partly in response to the decline in lumber's economic impact, the high-technology industry has become increasingly important to the economic well-being of the area. As part of its economic plan for 2020, the city targeted high technology industries like renewable energy, advanced manufacturing, software, and biomedical. A sizable food processing industry has grown up around the agricultural activity, and the area is also known for its RV coach production.

Small businesses form the core of the Lane County economy; businesses with fewer than five employees account for 60 percent of all companies. Still, Eugene is home to several large businesses, among them Bi-Mart, Farwest Steel, Tyree Oil, Willamette Valley Company, States Industries, and McDonald Wholesale Co.

Eugene serves central and southern Oregon as a retail and wholesale trade center. Services, government, and tourism are also contributors to the overall economy.

Items and goods produced: lumber, recreational vehicles, canned fruits and vegetables, dairy and meat products, chickens and chicken fryers, sheep, grass seed, metals, machinery, compact discs, computer software, plastics, electronic instruments, computer memory disks

Incentive Programs—New and Existing Companies

Local programs: In recent years the emphasis in the Willamette Valley has switched from business recruitment to business retention and expansion programs designed to help resident companies "stay put and stay healthy." Among the many incentives available to businesses in Eugene are financial programs offered at the local level, such as the Eugene Business Development Funds. Cascades West Microloan Program provides new or existing businesses in Lane County with up to $25,000 for any purpose with a 20 percent match from owner equity, while the Cascades West Revolving Loans finance land and buildings, equipment and machinery, and working capital. Other incentives include enterprise zones, new construction exemptions, and tax credits. Workforce incentive programs include employee recruiting, screening, and evaluating; customized training at

Lane Community College; on-the-job training reimbursement; and certification services.

State programs: The state of Oregon offers a number of incentive programs to attract new and expanding businesses to the state. Tax incentives include Enterprise Zones, Strategic Investment Program, Construction-in-Process, Oregon Investment Advantage, Employer-provided Dependent Care Tax Credit, Work Opportunity Tax Credit, Research Tax Credits, and Film & Video Incentives.

State-supported finance programs include the Oregon Business Oregon Business Development Fund, Oregon Capital Access Program, Oregon Credit Enhancement Fund, Oregon Industrial Development Bonds, Entrepreneurial Development Loan Fund, Business Retention Program, and Brownfields Redevelopment Fund.

Oregon supports an array of incentives that support renewable energy projects, including tax credits for equipment purchases, property tax exemptions for wind farms, a state energy loan program, and other grants and credits. The state's Renewable Portfolio Standard helps support demand for renewable energy by requiring energy providers to meet at least 25 percent of their Oregon load with renewable energy by 2025.

Job training programs: The state of Oregon's education program includes a statewide apprenticeship program that offers many opportunities for individuals to learn trades. The Employer Workforce Training Fund is an Oregon grant program for employers wanting to upgrade the skills of their employees in the trade or health-care sectors. The Lane Workforce Partnership oversees programs based on those grants, while the state runs the JOBS For Oregon's Future program. WorkSource Oregon centers not only help match employees and their skills with employers, but also help bring workers to training programs, such as those at Lane Community College.

Development Projects

The Eugene area has seen growth in the medical industry, with PeaceHealth Medical Group opening two new branches in the greater Eugene area; the first, Sacred Heart Medical Center and Level II trauma center at RiverBend near Springfield, opened in 2008, while Eugene's Sacred Heart Medical Center in the University District underwent a $97 million update involving 450,000 square feet of its campus expected to continue through 2015. As part of that project, construction for a $13.6 million new behavioral health center began in 2013.

In recent years Eugene has also seen an increase in sports-related developments. PK Park, the new home of the Eugene Emeralds baseball team, was completed in 2010. The park, which includes luxury seats, a bleacher section, concessions and other ballpark amenities, seats 4,000 and cost $19.2 million to build. The University of

Oregon's Matthew Knight Arena, a 352,000-square-foot multi-purpose venue with 12,500 seats, finished in 2011.

Lane Community College planned a major renovation to the 184,000-square-foot Center Building in 2013. The building was to be completed by 2016, with funding for the project totaling $35 million. The college opened a $53.4 million, 90,000-square-foot campus in downtown Eugene 2012. Richardson Sports, a Eugene-based maker of athletic hats, announced a doubling in size of its facilities in 2012, which included the addition of an existing 136,000-square-foot building.

City-sponsored projects primarily targeted street improvements, as well as bicycle and pedestrian paths and stormwater systems. Renovations to Amazon Park, Charnel Mulligan Park, and Spencer Butte Summit Trail were planned for 2014, as was completion of a skatepark.

Economic Development Information: Eugene Area Chamber of Commerce, 1401 Willamette St., Eugene, OR 97401; telephone (541) 484-1314; fax (541) 484-4942. Lane Metro Partnership, 1401 Willamette St., Eugene, OR 97401; telephone (541) 686-2741; fax (541) 686-2325; email business@lanemetro.com.

Commercial Shipping

A number of air-freight services operate out of Eugene Airport, notably Alaska Air Cargo. A new LEED certified air cargo facility at the airport was completed in 2008. More than 50 interstate truck carriers serve metropolitan Eugene and the West Coast via Interstate 5. Eugene is close to three deep-water ports, including the Port of Portland and the International Port of Coos Bay, for shipping to Asia. The Union Pacific and Burlington Northern Santa Fe railroads run through the area for shipping goods throughout North America.

Labor Force and Employment Outlook

Eugene boasts a skilled labor force with a good work ethic and low turnover rates. Just over one-quarter of Eugene residents have completed four or more years of college. A national recession in the late 2000s caused many job losses and an unemployment rate above state average lingered into 2014. Economic plans projecting to the year 2020 sought to lower the unemployment rate to at or below both state and national averages.

The following is a summary of data regarding the 2012 Eugene labor force:

Size of civilian labor force: 79,969

Number of workers employed in . . .

  agriculture and mining: 969
  construction: 2,463
  manufacturing: 5,069
  wholesale trade: 1,851
  retail trade: 8,659
  transportation: 1,901

  information systems: 1,694
  finance: 3,789
  professional administration: 7,354
  education and social services: 22,925
  arts and leisure: 8,119
  other: 3,784
  public administration: 2,346

Average hourly earnings of production workers: $16.32

Unemployment rate: 6.3% (2012)

Employers

Largest employers (2012)	*Number of employees*
PeaceHealth Medical Group	4,212
University of Oregon	4,038
Eugene School District 4J	2,794
Lane County	2,000
State of Oregon	1,781
U.S. Government	1,667
City of Eugene	1,378
Springfield School District	1,300
Lane Community College	1,118
Walmart	1,050

Cost of Living

The Chamber of Commerce describes Eugene housing as "plentiful, varied and built to last." Eugene is the center of many environmentally friendly housing construction projects and developments.

The following is a summary of data regarding several key cost of living factors in the area.

State income tax rate: 5.0% to 9.9%

State sales tax rate: None

Local income tax rate: 0.7% (paid by employer)

Local sales tax rate: None

Property tax rate: $18.9952 per $1,000 assessed value (2013)

Economic Information: Eugene Area Chamber of Commerce, 1401 Willamette St., Eugene, OR 97401; telephone (541) 484-1314; fax (541) 484-4942. Lane Metro Partnership, 1401 Willamette St., Eugene, OR 97401; telephone (541) 686-2741; fax (541) 686-2325; email business@lanemetro.com.

■ Education and Research

Elementary and Secondary Schools

Eugene is home to three school districts, with the largest being Eugene School District 4J, which serves about 85 percent of Eugene residents. A seven-member board, elected at large, governs the district. The board employs the superintendent. Parents residing within the Eugene District may choose any 4J school for their child, provided that space is available.

Unique programs include the elementary and middle Yujin Gakuen Japanese immersion schools, Spanish Immersion Middle School, and Eugene International High School. Eugene's public school students consistently score higher on standardized tests than the state and national averages. Oregon state standards are among the highest in the world. Among the district's schools are four public charter schools.

Eugene is also served by private high schools and many other private schools from pre-kindergarten to eighth grade, including religious and special education centers, as well as schools for the gifted and the physically and mentally challenged.

The following is a summary of data regarding the Eugene School District.

Total enrollment: 17,379

Number of facilities

    total: 33
    elementary schools: 18
    junior high schools: 9
    high schools: 4
    other: 2

Student/teacher ratio: 21.3:1

Teacher salaries

    average (statewide): $56,387

Funding per pupil: $9,626

Public Schools Information: School District 4J, Eugene Public Schools, 200 North Monroe St., Eugene, OR 97402; telephone (541) 790-7700; fax (541) 790-7711.

Colleges and Universities

The University of Oregon, a major research and educational institution with an enrollment of about 24,500 students, is located in Eugene. The university has 268 academic programs of study that span the arts and sciences, architecture, arts, business, education, journalism, law, music, and dance.

Lane Community College offers two-year associate and vocational degrees, serving more than 37,000 students in both credit and non-credit course study. It added a new

downtown Eugene campus in 2012. Gutenberg College, which enrolled 22 students in 2012-13, offers liberal arts education from a Protestant Christian base and follows a "great books" program. Other educational institutions in Eugene are Northwest Christian University, and New Hope Christian College (formerly Eugene Bible College.

Libraries and Research Centers

The Eugene Public Library consists of three locations: the Downtown Library, the Bethel Branch, and the Sheldon Branch. The system contains more than 400,000 items including books, CDs, DVDs, audio and video tapes, and art reproductions, in addition to magazine and newspaper subscriptions. The library's special collections include fine children's literature and a state documents department. The library was given the Star Library award by *Library Journal* in 2013 for ranking among the top 3 percent of libraries in the United States for cost-effective services.

The University of Oregon's Knight Library holds more than 3 million volumes, nearly 17,000 periodical subscriptions, and special collections on the American West, American missions and missionaries, Esperanto, Oriental literature and art, politics, and zeppelins. It is the largest library facility in Oregon. Other libraries at the university specialize in law, architecture, science, and mathematics. New Hope Christian College's library holds about 74,000 volumes, and Lane Community College holds 62,000 books.

Research activities in such fields as the environment, botany of the Pacific Northwest, molecular biology, marine biology, cellular biology, neuroscience, materials science, solar energy, chemical physics, applied materials, forest industries, labor, industrial relations, work organizations, ocean and coastal law, women and gender roles, human development, communication, recreation, mental retardation, and mass communications are conducted at centers in the Eugene area primarily through the University of Oregon. Technicians at Eugene's Riverfront Research Park engage in industrial research and development, data processing, and computer software development.

Public Library Information: Eugene Public Library, 100 West 10th Avenue, Eugene, OR 97401; telephone (541) 682-5450.

■ Health Care

Two major hospitals serve Eugene. The largest is Sacred Heart Medical Center, a general-care facility with 93 beds that features an emergency department, Gamma Knife center, and orthopedics and rehabilitation services. Sacred Heart opened another branch, a comprehensive regional medical center and Level II trauma center, at RiverBend in 2008. The RiverBend facility received high-performing marks in three specialties—diabetes and endocrinology, gynecology, and pulmonology—from *U.S. News & World Report* in 2013. The Cottage Grove Community Hospital offers imaging, laboratory, physical therapy, and 24-hour emergency care services with 14 patient beds. All three branches fall under the umbrella of the PeaceHealth Medical Group, which operates facilities in Oregon, Washington, and Alaska.

The McKenzie-Willamette Medical Center is a full-care hospital and Level III Trauma Center containing 113 beds and 15 mother/newborn units; it offers short-stay surgery and home care services with a staff of 218 healthcare professionals. Traditional and alternative physical and mental health care services are offered at area clinics.

■ Recreation

Sightseeing

Eugene's Willamette River banks are lined with miles of paths and a number of picnic areas and scenic parks, including the five-acre Owen Memorial Rose Garden. The Hendricks Park Rhododendron Garden features thousands of rhododendrons and azaleas. Culminating at Spencer Butte, the city's highest point, the South Hills Ridgeline Trail showcases a variety of plants and wildlife. The Mount Pisgah Arboretum has trails throughout its 209 acres and multiple habitats. Tours of many historic homes and buildings, such as the Shelton McMurphey-Johnson House from 1888, are also available in Eugene.

The surrounding area offers a number of attractions, such as scenic drives, a national park, wildlife and natural areas, mine and winery tours, and historic sites.

Arts and Culture

Eugene has a large and varied arts community. Companies that perform music include the Eugene Symphony, Eugene Opera, Oregon Mozart Players Chamber Orchestra, and the Eugene-Springfield Youth Orchestras; most of these groups call the Hult Center for the Performing Arts home. The Shedd Institute for the Arts is home to the Oregon Festival of American Music, which runs year round and features an eclectic variety of performers. Summer music concerts are held at the Cuthbert Amphitheater in Alton Baker Park. The McDonald Theatre, a historic restored movie house, presents touring and local musicians and performers.

The Eugene Ballet Company performs several times during the year at the Hult Center. The Actors Cabaret of Eugene has been presenting plays and musicals since 1979. The Very Little Theatre is a volunteer community theater group that dates back to 1929. The Lord Leebrick Theatre Company presents five plays a year. The Hult Center is also home to the Eugene Concert Choir.

The University of Oregon Museum of Natural and Cultural History contains exhibits in archeology, paleontology, and zoology. The Science Factory Children's

Museum and Exploration Dome, formerly the Willamette Science and Technology Center, re-opened in 2002 with interactive exhibits and planetarium shows. Relics and memorabilia pertaining to the history of the Eugene area can be viewed at the Lane County Historical Society and Museum. The Maude Kerns Art Center displays a number of works by local artists as well as traveling exhibits. The University of Oregon's Jordan Schnitzer Museum of Art reopened in 2005 with a new addition that doubled the size of the museum. It houses a famous collection of Asian art and hosts numerous special exhibits each year.

Festivals and Holidays

The Oregon Bach Festival is an annual highlight of Eugene's special events calendar. Held for two weeks in late June and early July, the festival is hosted on the University of Oregon campus and at the Hult Center. It features performances by internationally acclaimed soloists and orchestral, choral, and chamber music groups interpreting the compositions of eighteenth-century German composer Johann Sebastian Bach. Eugene also celebrates with the Asian Kite Festival in May, the Oregon Country Fair in July, and Eugene Celebration, taking place for three days beginning in late August. The city also hosts "Summer in the City," a series of free community concerts during summer evenings.

Sports for the Spectator

Professional baseball is represented in Eugene by the minor league Eugene Emeralds, a Class-A farm club for the San Diego Padres that plays at PK Park, which can accommodate up to 4,000 fans. The University of Oregon fields teams in every major sport, competing at the National Collegiate Athletic Association (NCAA) Division I level; football games are played at the 54,000-seat Autzen Stadium, while track and field events take place at Hayward Field. The 12,500-seat Matthew Knight Arena, which was completed in early 2011, became the new home of the University of Oregon basketball teams. Eugene is also a major center of track and field events, hosting the NCAA Track and Field Outdoor Championships on a regular basis at Hayward Field. The championships are scheduled to be held there through at least 2021.

Sports for the Participant

A wide range of outdoor recreation activities are available in and around Eugene, located only 60 miles away from either the mountains or the ocean. The Cascade Mountains offer opportunities for winter skiing and summer hiking, camping, and rafting. The glacier-fed McKenzie and Willamette rivers offer water sports such as fishing, boating, and kayaking. The city maintains more than 3,000 acres of park land, with jogging trails, bike paths, pools, athletic fields, tennis courts, bowling alleys, a roller rink, an outdoor skateboard facility, and a major lighted softball complex. KIDSPORTS provides about 24,000 young people with organized sports programs such as soccer, baseball, softball, football, basketball, and volleyball. Eugene was ranked the ninth best city for bicycling by *Bicycling* magazine in 2012.

Shopping and Dining

Valley River Center is an enclosed mall with more than 120 retail, food, and specialty businesses. The Fifth Street Public Market is a collection of specialty and craft shops and restaurants, and hosts musicians, artists, and special events. Boutiques can be found in downtown Eugene. Saturday Market, an open-air market featuring fresh produce, handcrafted goods, and ethnic foods, is open from April to mid-November; the Holiday Market is open through Christmas. Gateway Mall, in nearby Springfield, has about 80 stores and a 29-screen movie complex. Hundreds of area restaurants present fresh Oregon salmon, lamb, wines, apples, pears, and berries among their offerings. Coffee shops and cafes abound.

Visitor Information: Travel Lane County, 754 Olive St., Eugene OR 97401; telephone (541) 484-5307; toll-free (800) 547-5445.

■ Convention Facilities

The Lane Events Center at the Fairgrounds in Eugene offers a convention center, an equestrian and livestock pavilion, a state-of-the-art ice arena, 2,500 parking spaces, and full catering service. The convention center itself has 75,000 square feet of available space, and an exhibit hall that can seat 4,000 guests.

Other Eugene venues include the Hult Center for the Performing Arts, Florence Events Center in Florence, Oregon, and the Valley River Inn. In addition, there are numerous hotels, motels, resorts, lodges, and conference facilities throughout Lane County, including the Hilton Eugene & Conference Center, one of the largest convention centers between San Francisco and Portland. It offers more than 30,000 square feet of meeting and exhibit space ranging from intimate boardrooms to convention halls and ballrooms.

Convention Information: Travel Lane County, 754 Olive St., Eugene OR 97401; telephone (541) 484-5307; toll-free (800) 547-5445.

■ Transportation

Approaching the City

Eugene Airport is located seven miles northwest of Eugene by Interstate 5, and is served by six major air carriers. It offers non-stop service to Seattle, Portland, San Francisco, Oakland, Los Angeles, Las Vegas, Salt Lake City, Phoenix, Denver, and Honolulu. Amtrak provides passenger rail service north to Vancouver on the Amtrak Cascades Line, and south to Los Angeles on the Coast Starlight.

The major north–south route from Canada to Mexico along the West Coast, Interstate 5, runs through Eugene. U.S. Highway 126 connects the city with the Pacific coast and eastern Oregon.

Traveling in the City

Public transportation is provided by Lane Transit District buses to all parts of the city and to some rural areas. The system provides convenient stops at schools and downtown, and is completely wheelchair accessible. The city maintains 42 miles of shared-use bicycle paths, 81 miles of on-street bicycle lanes, and 35 miles of signed bikeways.

■ Communications

Newspapers and Magazines

Eugene is served by one daily morning newspaper, *The Register-Guard,* which also serves Springfield and Lane County. *Eugene Weekly,* a Thursday paper, presents arts and entertainment information along with news. There are also several smaller neighborhood and special-interest weekly newspapers. The University of Oregon publishes the *Oregon Daily Emerald.* Magazines published in Eugene include *Skipping Stones,* an international, multicultural magazine for children; *Alternatives,* an environmental and political quarterly; *Oregon Voice,* a general interest magazine by students from the University of Oregon; and several scholarly journals.

Television and Radio

Television stations broadcasting from Eugene include ABC, NBC, CBS, FOX, and PBS, as well as commercial/religious programming. AM and FM radio stations broadcast music, information, Christian and sports programs from Eugene, and many other stations are received from other communities in the metropolitan area.

Media Information: The *Register-Guard,* 3500 Chad Drive, Eugene, OR 97408; telephone (541) 485-1234.

Eugene Online

City of Eugene home page. Available www.eugene-or.gov

Travel Lane County. Available www. eugenecascadescoast.org

Eugene Area Chamber of Commerce. Available www.eugenechamber.com

Eugene School District 4J. Available www.4j.lane.edu

Lane Metro Partnership. Available lanemetro.com

Oregon Business Development Department. Available www.oregon.gov/OBDD

The Register-Guard. Available www.registerguard.com

BIBLIOGRAPHY

Card, Douglas, *From Camas to Courthouse: Early Lane County History* (Eugene, OR: Lane County Historical Society, 2008)

Eugene 1945–2000: Decisions that Made a Community (Eugene, OR: The City Club of Eugene, 2000)

Moore, Lucia W., *The Story of Eugene* (Eugene, OR: Lane County Historical Society, 1995)

Portland

■ The City in Brief

Founded: 1845 (incorporated 1851)

Head Official: Mayor Charlie Hales (since 2012; current term expires 2016)

City Population
1990: 485,975
2000: 529,121
2010: 583,776
2012 estimate: 603,650
Percent change, 2000–2010: 10.3%
U.S. rank in 1990: 30th (State rank: 1st)
U.S. rank in 2000: 35th (State rank: 1st)
U.S. rank in 2010: 29th (State rank: 1st)

Metropolitan Statistical Area Population
2000: 1,927,881
2010: 2,226,009
2012 estimate: 2,289,651
Percent change, 2000–2010: 15.5%
U.S. rank in 2000: 25th
U.S. rank in 2010: 23rd

Area: 130 square miles

Elevation: Averages 173 feet above sea level

Average Annual Temperatures: January, 39.9° F; July, 68.1° F; annual average, 53.5° F

Average Annual Precipitation: 37.07 inches of rain; 6.5 inches of snow

Major Economic Sectors: services, trade, manufacturing, government

Unemployment Rate: 7.1% (2012)

Per Capita Income: $31,203

2012 FBI Crime Index Property: 30,454

Major Colleges and Universities: Portland State University, Oregon Health Sciences University, Reed College, Lewis & Clark College, University of Portland, Marylhurst University

Daily Newspaper: *The Oregonian*

■ Introduction

Portland, known as the "City of Roses," lacks many of the problems that plague other cities. Traffic congestion, pollution, and litter problems have been avoided both by chance and planning. Portland's natural forest setting, along with parks, gardens, and fountains dispersed throughout the area make it a beautiful, clean place to visit and live. The Port of Portland, which consists of marine and airport facilities, makes for a thriving commercial center; the diverse economy includes high-technology software and computer businesses, too, as well as a robust manufacturing sector. The city has retained its individuality by controlling growth and development while encouraging a healthy and friendly region.

■ Geography and Climate

Located 110 miles from the Pacific Ocean, Portland lies between two mountain ranges, the Cascade Range to the east and the lower Coast Range to the west, in the Willamette River valley, one of the world's most fertile river valleys. The city is divided by the Willamette River, which flows into the Columbia River just to the north. Winters are rainy in Portland, with 55 percent of the annual rainfall occurring between the months of November and February, but the marine air keeps temperatures moderate, and the summers are mild, with temperatures rarely more than 90 degrees.

© Rigucci/Shutterstock.com

Area: 130 square miles

Elevation: Averages 173 feet above sea level

Average Temperatures: January, 39.9° F; July, 68.1° F; annual average, 53.5° F

Average Annual Precipitation: 37.07 inches of rain; 6.5 inches of snow

■ History

The area surrounding present-day Portland was originally inhabited by the Multnomah and Clackamas tribes, who had established several villages by the 1830s. Most of these people died from smallpox epidemics and other diseases. Meriwether Lewis and William Clark were the first settlers of European descent to travel through the Portland area during their 1806 expedition. Clark named the Willamette River after the Multnomah village he found on Sauvie Island.

The future site of Portland was originally a clearing in the woods, appropriately known as "The Clearing," where Native Americans and traders stopped to rest on trips between Oregon City and Fort Vancouver. The land underwent a series of ownerships until Amos Lovejoy and Francis Pettygrove bought it and mapped out a town called "Stumptown" in 1845. Four years later the two men, Lovejoy from Boston and Pettygrove from Portland, Maine, decided to flip a coin to determine the town's new name. Pettygrove won and the town became Portland.

Portland grew steadily through the California gold rush, reporting a population of 821 residents, a post office, and a newspaper—the *Weekly Oregonian*—in the 1850 census. Portland was incorporated in 1851 and became the seat of newly created Washington County (later renamed Multnomah County) in 1854. That same year the town advanced toward becoming a major trade center when its harbor was selected as the West Coast terminal for *The Petonia,* the U.S. mail steamer. Prior to the Civil War the salmon industry began to grow, enhancing Portland's economic status. The city experienced catastrophe when, in 1872 and 1873, the downtown area was heavily damaged by fire; civic leaders subsequently decided to rebuild only with cast iron, brick, and stone. The construction of the first transcontinental railroad in 1883, linking Portland with the East Coast, brought renewed prosperity. By the turn of the century the population had grown to 90,000 people.

Portland continued to expand steadily through the early decades of the twentieth century; the Alaska gold rush, the 1905 Lewis and Clark Centennial Exposition, and the construction of the Bonneville Dam in the 1930s were important factors in its growth. During World War II the city was a ship-building and manufacturing center.

In the 1960s and 1970s Portland's city leaders were able to avoid problems experienced by other large metropolitan areas through economic diversification, controlled growth, and environmental planning. A precedent had already been set by early planners who had integrated parks and green spaces into the city's layout; later, city planners instituted an ordinance to protect scenic views.

Local government continues to work on the Region 2040 growth plan to manage all aspects of growth in the metropolitan area, with a focus on urban renewal and expansion of mass transit. The city has been nationally recognized for its unique character and attention to the quality of life of its residents.

Historical Information: Oregon Historical Society Research Library, 1200 SW Park Avenue, Portland, OR 97205; telephone (503) 222-1741; fax (503) 221-2035.

■ Population Profile

Metropolitan Statistical Area Population

2000: 1,927,881
2010: 2,226,009
2012 estimate: 2,289,651
Percent change, 2000–2010: 15.5%
U.S. rank in 2000: 25th
U.S. rank in 2010: 23rd

City Residents

1990: 485,975
2000: 529,121
2010: 583,776
2012 estimate: 603,650
Percent change, 2000–2010: 10.3%
U.S. rank in 1990: 30th (State rank: 1st)
U.S. rank in 2000: 35th (State rank: 1st)
U.S. rank in 2010: 29th (State rank: 1st)

Density: 4,375.3 people per square mile

Racial and ethnic characteristics

White: 475,727
Black or African American: 36,746
American Indian and Alaskan Native: 3,581
Asian: 42,465
Native Hawaiian and Other Pacific Islander: 4,730
Hispanic or Latino (may be of any race): 57,049
Other: 40,401

Percent of residents born in state: 40.8%

Age characteristics

Population under 5 years old: 34,646
Population 5 to 9 years old: 35,340
Population 10 to 14 years old: 29,800
Population 15 to 19 years old: 28,777
Population 20 to 24 years old: 38,150
Population 25 to 34 years old: 118,124
Population 35 to 44 years old: 101,815
Population 45 to 54 years old: 77,151
Population 55 to 59 years old: 39,275
Population 60 to 64 years old: 35,128
Population 65 to 74 years old: 36,777
Population 75 to 84 years old: 17,884
Population 85 years and over: 10,783
Median age: 36.6

Births (2010–11 Metropolitan Area)

Total number: 28,672

Deaths (2010–11 Metropolitan Area)

Total number: 15,161

Money income (2012)

Per capita income: $31,203
Median household income: $49,958
Total households: 248,701

Number of households with income of ...

less than $10,000: 23,133
$10,000 to $14,999: 15,249
$15,000 to $24,999: 26,437
$25,000 to $34,999: 26,548
$35,000 to $49,999: 33,065
$50,000 to $74,999: 42,674
$75,000 to $99,999: 28,601
$100,000 to $149,999: 30,941
$150,000 to $199,999: 10,824
$200,000 or more: 11,229

Percent of families below poverty level: 18.6%

FBI Crime Index Property: 30,454

FBI Crime Index Violent: 3,093

■ Municipal Government

Portland is the last large city in the United States to operate under a commission form of government, with four commissioners, an auditor, and the mayor elected to staggered four-year terms. Each member casts an equal vote in council, and each undertakes administrative responsibilities for a group of city bureaus. The mayor receives the authority to make budget assignments and traditionally proposes the annual budget for council approval; otherwise, governing power is invested in the council as a whole.

Portland is also home to the nation's only directly elected regional government. The body, known as Metro, controls growth by wielding authority over land use, transportation, and the environment throughout the metropolitan area.

Head Official: Mayor Charlie Hales (since 2012; current term expires 2016)

Total Number of City Employees: 8,951 (2013)

City Information: Portland City Hall, 1221 SW 4th Avenue, Portland, OR 97204; telephone (503) 823-6868; email cityinfo@portlandoregon.gov.

■ Economy

Major Industries and Commercial Activity

Early in its history, Portland's economy was based on the Columbia and Willamette rivers and their access to the Pacific Ocean. The town was a supply hub for area farming communities and a regional shipping center. The deep, fresh-water port helped the city grow into an important part of the lumber industry, and a number of manufacturing concerns settled there because of the ease of transportation.

Today, Portland is the fourth largest export tonnage port on the West Coast and the largest wheat export port in the nation. Easy access to the north–south and east–west interstate freeway system, international air service, and both West Coast intercontinental railroads make Portland an important distribution center. Both Port of Portland marine and aviation facilities have an economic impact of $3.7 billion for the region.

Portland enjoys a long history of association with high-technology industries, beginning with Tektronix in 1946. There are now more than 1,400 technology companies currently operating in Portland. Technology companies with area operations include Fios, Google, IBM, Intel, McAfee, Survey Monkey, Symantec, WebMD, and many others. Software start-ups are common, with three-quarters of all software companies in Portland employing fewer than five people. The clean technology also maintains a presence in Portland, primarily in the solar and wind power industries. Notable firms include SolarWorld, Vestas, Ch2M Hill, PECI, and Solaicx, among several others.

Portland's manufacturing base centers on metals and transport equipment. Advanced manufacturing firms employ about 34,000 area residents; specialty products include flatbed railcars, streetcars, industrial trucks and tractors, mining equipment, aircraft parts, and shipbuilding and repair. Employment in advanced manufacturing grew 16 percent between 2010 and 2012.

Outdoor equipment and apparel is unique niche of Portland. Some 700 athletic and outdoor industry firms operate in Portland, lured by the city's strong workforce and distribution network. Additionally, the city has a strong cultural identity with outdoor activities and weather that permits year-round testing. Nike, Columbia Sportswear, and Adidas all have major operations in Portland, as do smaller firms such as Keen Footwear, Icebreaker, and Nutcase Helmets.

Items and goods produced: electronics, machinery, food products, beverages, transportation equipment

Incentive Programs—New and Existing Companies

Local programs: Portland Business Alliance allows area businesses to access valuable information to help them succeed, including site location assistance, storefront improvement grants, contract opportunities, and economic and demographic data. The Portland Development Commission administers a variety of programs to assist new, existing, and expanding businesses, such as tenant improvements, equipment purchases, façade improvements, real estate acquisition, and working capital. The Portland Enterprise Zone is a tax abatement program for firms making major investments in the region.

State programs: The state of Oregon offers a number of incentive programs to attract new and expanding businesses to the state. Tax incentives include Enterprise Zones, Strategic Investment Program, Construction-in-Process, Oregon Investment Advantage, Employer-provided Dependent Care Tax Credit, Work Opportunity Tax Credit, Research Tax Credits, and Film & Video Incentives.

State-supported finance programs include the Oregon Business Oregon Business Development Fund, Oregon Capital Access Program, Oregon Credit Enhancement Fund, Oregon Industrial Development Bonds, Entrepreneurial Development Loan Fund, Business Retention Program, and Brownfields Redevelopment Fund.

Oregon supports an array of incentives that support renewable energy projects, including tax credits for equipment purchases, property tax exemptions for wind farms, a state energy loan program, and other grants and credits. The state's Renewable Portfolio Standard helps support demand for renewable energy by requiring energy providers to meet at least 25 percent of their Oregon load with renewable energy by 2025.

Job training programs: The state of Oregon's education program includes a statewide apprenticeship program that offers many opportunities for individuals to learn trades. The Employer Workforce Training Fund is an Oregon grant program for employers wanting to upgrade the skills of their employees in the trade or health-care sectors. The state also runs the JOBS for Oregon's Future program.

The Portland Development Commission's Economic Opportunity Initiative focuses on training and placing young adults in jobs so they will succeed. Worksystems Inc. funds providers of career placement and training services. The WorkSource Portland Metro network offers job-seekers assistance with their career planning and job search activities. Due to an increase in the non-native English speaking population, services are also provided in Spanish, Russian, Vietnamese, and Chinese. Portland Community College assists in training and certifying area students.

Development Projects

In 1999 the North Macadam Urban Renewal Plan was adopted by the city government. The plan seeks to develop vacant and underdeveloped land in the North Macadam area. Technical, environmental, and transportation difficulties had prevented previous efforts to develop the land. Redevelopment efforts, expected to continue through 2019, have focused on providing transportation connections, space for housing and businesses, and greenway and open space connections. The city has since designated a number of other neighborhoods as Urban Renewal Areas, which are targeted for improvement projects by the Portland Development Commission.

A MAX light-rail line from Portland to Milwaukie was approved in 2010, to begin service upon completion in 2015. The projected was to add 7.3 miles of rail between Portland State University, inner southeast Portland, Milwaukie, and Oak Grove in north Clackamas County. The project fell under the umbrella of the North Macadam Urban Renewal Plan and required an investment of $1.4 billion. Projections to 2030 suggested that the line would carry 27,400 daily trips by 2030 and reduce vehicle traffic by more than 60,000 daily miles.

Oregon Health and Science University broke ground in 2011 on its Collaborative Life Sciences Building, located on the university's Schnitzer Campus. Expected to complete in 2014, the $295 million, 500,000-square-foot Skourtes Tower was to serve as a teaching, clinic, and research space, and would include housing of the university's School of Dentistry. The building was expected to receive LEED Platinum certification for its environmentally conscious design.

A major private development, Park Avenue West, began construction in 2013 after several stalled years caused by a national recession. The 30-story tower, to be built at a cost of $175 million, was to include office and retail space on its lower floors, as well as 211 apartment units on the remaining, upper floors.

Economic Development Information: Portland Business Alliance, 200 SW Market Street, Ste 150, Portland, OR 97201; telephone (503) 224-8684; fax (503) 323-9186; email info@portlandalliance.com.

Commercial Shipping

Portland's comprehensive transportation system comprises ocean shipping, transcontinental railways and highways, river barging, and a major international airport. The shipping industry is keyed to a lifeline of ship, rail, air, and truck services. Both West Coast transcontinental railroads and more than 100 trucking lines provide shippers with options for moving cargo. At the Port of Portland's four marine terminals, container ships, grain ships, bulk and breakbulk carriers, and auto carriers work around the clock. The Port of Portland leads the nation in wheat exports and is a leader in auto imports. In addition, barges ply the Columbia/Snake river system, the second largest waterway in the nation, feeding the Port's Terminal 6 from as far upriver as Lewiston, Idaho, more than 300 river miles away. Foreign Trade Zone #45, administered by the Port of Portland, provides an additional incentive for international trade activity. Six all-cargo airlines serve the Portland International Airport, which handles nearly 200,000 tons of cargo annually.

Labor Force and Employment Outlook

The work force in Portland is young and well-educated. The job turnover rate is low and productivity is high, compared with other metropolitan areas. The unemployment rate has generally remained below the national average; during recessionary times of the late 2000s, the unemployment rate in Portland was above the national average but below that of other large cities in Oregon. Into the 2010s, the labor force showed signs of shrinking

The following is a summary of data regarding the 2012 Portland labor force:

Size of civilian labor force: 341,018

Number of workers employed in . . .

    agriculture and mining: 1,544
    construction: 12,003
    manufacturing: 28,591
    wholesale trade: 9,956
    retail trade: 33,186
    transportation: 12,238
    information systems: 7,785
    finance: 18,523
    professional administration: 40,429
    education and social services: 77,603
    arts and leisure: 36,128
    other: 16,590
    public administration: 10,516

Average hourly earnings of production workers: $17.62

Unemployment rate: 7.1% (2012)

Employers

Largest employers (2013)	*Number of employees*
Intel Corporation	16,250
Providence Health System	14,389
U.S. Government	13,900
Oregon Health and Science University	13,733
Fred Meyer Stores	10,389
Legacy Health System	9,662
Kaiser Permanente NW	9,195
City of Portland	8,951
State of Oregon	7,559
NIKE, Inc.	7,000
Portland School District	6,544
Evergreen School District	6,282

Cost of Living

The cost of living in Portland is above the national average, with the average cost of a house in 2013 estimated at $344,079. Still, the city can claim a lower cost of living compared to most major cities in California.

The following is a summary of data regarding several key cost of living factors in the area.

2013 ACCRA Average House Price: $344,079

2013 ACCRA Cost of Living Index: 116

State income tax rate: 5.0% to 9.9%

State sales tax rate: None

Local income tax rate: 0.7218% (paid by employer)

Local sales tax rate: None

Property tax rate: $15.00 to $20.30 per $1,000 assessed value (metropolitan area, 2013)

Economic Information: Portland Business Alliance, 200 SW Market Street, Ste 150, Portland, OR 97201; telephone (503) 224-8684; fax (503) 323-9186; email info@portlandalliance.com. Oregon Employment Department, 875 Union St. NE, Salem, OR 97311; telephone (800) 237-3710.

■ Education and Research

Elementary and Secondary Schools

Portland Public Schools, the largest district in the state of Oregon, is governed by a nonpartisan, seven-member board that appoints a superintendent. Special programs offered by the district include a gifted and talented program, summer school remedial and enrichment classes, special education, and career education. Magnet schools in the district offer dual language immersion programs in Spanish, Japanese, and Chinese; a living history curriculum; schools for the performing arts; and early intervention programs. Students can also apply to attend any school in the district outside of their geographically-assigned one, including the alternative schools listed previously. The district supports seven charter schools.

A variety of private education options exist in the Portland metro area, including the well-known Oregon Episcopal School and the Catlin Gabel School. Seven Catholic schools, several Montessori and Waldorf schools, and arts-centered schools serve the area's students.

The following is a summary of data regarding the Portland School District.

Total enrollment: 45,818

Number of facilities

total: 78
elementary schools: 42
junior high schools: 25
high schools: 10
other: 1

Student/teacher ratio: 18.36:1

Teacher salaries

average (statewide): $56,387

Funding per pupil: $11,137

Public Schools Information: Portland Public Schools, 501 North Dixon St., Portland, OR 97227; telephone (503) 916-2000; email pubinfo@pps.net.

Colleges and Universities

Portland is home to several accredited institutions of higher education. The University of Portland, a Catholic university, offers many majors and graduate degrees in its College of Arts and Sciences and four professional schools—Business, Education, Engineering, and Nursing. Portland State University offers strong liberal arts and sciences programs to augment its concentration on engineering, computer science, international trade, and business. The school also boasts Oregon's most diverse college campus.

Lewis & Clark College, founded by Presbyterian pioneers and set on 137 wooded acres, offers 29 majors. It was ranked among the top 75 national liberal arts colleges in America in 2013–14 by *U.S. News & World Report*. Reed College is an independent liberal arts and sciences college, and was also ranked among the top 75 national liberal arts colleges in America in 2013–14 by *U.S. News & World Report.*

Concordia University is a private four-year college affiliated with the Lutheran Church, Missouri Synod, that offers bachelor's degrees in accounting, biology, business, chemistry, education, English, exercise and sport science, history, marketing, music, nursing, psychology, social work, and theology. It has a total enrollment of 5,000 students. Marylhurst University is a private Catholic institution offering coursework leading to master's and bachelor's degrees to students of all ages.

Oregon Health & Science University houses schools of medicine, nursing, and dentistry, and is Oregon's only academic health center. In 2013–14 it was honored by *U.S. News & World Report* as among the top three medical schools for primary care training, and also ranked 31st for research.

Libraries and Research Centers

The Multnomah County Library, the oldest public library west of the Mississippi, maintains a Central Library and 18 other branches throughout the metropolitan area. Total holdings include more than two million items including books, periodicals, videos, audio cassettes, compact discs, films, records, and maps. The County Library and its branches together host nearly 900 computer work stations. The Multnomah County Library is Oregon's largest public library system and serves nearly a fifth of the total state population. Area universities also offer extensive library services, and there are a number of special interest and research libraries in the area, serving science, industry, and business interests.

Oregon Health & Science University is where both the artificial heart valve and cardiac angioplasty were developed; research there continues to be the catalyst for clinical and educational advancements in heart treatment. Cancer research in the areas of cancer biology, hematologic malignancies, solid tumors, and cancer prevention and control is also performed at Oregon Health & Science University. The Vollum Institute studies brain function at the molecular level, in addition to sponsoring a new center for the study of weight loss. At Oregon Medical Laser Center, researchers study the use of lasers in medicine. Other areas of medical research include cancer research at the Robert W. Franz Cancer Research Center in the Earl A. Chiles Research Institute at Providence Cancer Center.

Research activities in such fields as public health, computing and information systems, nuclear science, urban studies, population and census, sociology, psychology, aging, human services, and the Middle East are conducted at other centers in the Portland area.

Public Library Information: Multnomah County Library, 801 SW Tenth Avenue, Portland, OR 97205; telephone (503) 988-5123.

■ Health Care

Portland is the center for health care in the state of Oregon, with major hospitals collaborating to offer quality care at a moderate cost. Playing a prominent role is the Oregon Health & Science University (OHSU), which includes the OHSU Hospital and Doernbecher Children's Hospital, as well as the Casey Eye Institute, the Child Development and Rehabilitation Center, primary care clinics, and numerous specialty and dental clinics. OHSU also operates interdisciplinary centers that focus on aging, women's health, cancer, and interventional therapy. OHSU shares technology, personnel, and training with the Portland Veterans Affairs Medical Center to help keep health-care costs down. OHSU was the top-ranked health-care center in the state in 2013 according to *U.S. News & World Report*, and was also ranked nationally in five adult specialties. Doernbecher Children's Hospital was ranked nationally in eight pediatric specialties.

Providence Health and Services, a non-profit Catholic health-care ministry, merged with Swedish Health Services in 2012 for a combined operation of 32 hospitals throughout a region that includes Alaska, California, Montana, Oregon, and Washington. Providence hospitals specialize in cancer care, rehabilitation, cardiac care, children's emergency care, surgical services, sports medicine, and maternity care.

Residents who seek nontraditional medical treatment have access to licensed acupuncturists and to practitioners trained at a local naturopathic college, the National College of Natural Medicine. Senior services are coordinated by the Multnomah County Aging and Disability Services Division to help senior citizens remain active in the community.

■ Recreation

Sightseeing

Portland offers sightseeing attractions both in the city itself and in the surrounding area. A walking tour of downtown encompasses two separate national historical districts, including the largest preserved example of nineteenth-century cast iron architecture in the West, and a number of other nineteenth-century landmarks intermixed with distinctive modern buildings. The controversial Portland Building was the first major postmodern architectural structure in the country. The award-winning Pioneer Courthouse Square, which hosts more than 300 events a year, bustles with activity from outdoor art exhibits, concerts, and sidewalk vendors.

Portland is proud of its outdoor public art and fountains, including Portlandia, a 36-foot tall hammered copper sculpture of a kneeling woman, and Ira's Fountain, a cascading water sculpture dotted with islands and terraces across from Keller Auditorium. Other attractions include The Grotto, a 62-acre shrine; the Japanese Garden, the most authentic example of Japanese gardens outside of Japan; the International Rose Test Garden; and the Lan Su Chinese Garden in the Old Town/Chinatown district.

Many other attractions can be found just outside of the city. Vineyards in the Willamette Valley are open to the public for tours and wine tastings. Some of the nation's most beautiful natural scenery can be found around nearby Mount Hood and the Columbia Gorge. Portland is 110 miles from the Pacific Ocean.

Arts and Culture

Portland's Centers for the Arts are at the center of art activity in the city, presenting more than 900 annual events and featuring the Arlene Schnitzer Concert Hall, Newmark Theatre, Dolores Winningstad Theatre, Brunish Theatre, and Keller Auditorium. Portland's performing arts groups include the Oregon Symphony, Portland Opera, Oregon Ballet Theatre, Portland Center Stage, Portland Youth Philharmonic, Portland Gay Men's Chorus, and Chamber Music Northwest.

The Oregon History Museum, run by the Oregon Historical Society, houses exhibits tracing the history of the Pacific Northwest from prehistoric times to the present. The Oregon Maritime Museum features ship models, navigational instruments, hardware, and historical exhibits. The Oregon Museum of Science and Industry (OMSI), one of the nation's largest, offers hands-on displays pertaining to science, including a walk-in replica of a space station, a planetarium, and a computer center. The World Forestry Center has recreational and educational exhibits relating to the forestry industry; a special attraction is a 70-foot talking tree.

Washington Park is home to many children's attractions, including the Portland Children's Museum. It features hands-on exhibits for children through 10 years of age. The Oregon Zoo, which opened in 1887, houses animals from around the world. Also of interest to children and book-lovers alike is the Beverly Cleary Sculpture Garden in Grant Park, which showcases bronze statues of Ramona Quimby and Henry Huggins and his dog Ribsy—characters made famous in the Portland author's classic children's books.

The Portland Art Museum houses collections of 35 centuries of world art, including European works from the Renaissance to the present, nineteenth- and twentieth-century American art, and Native American, Asian, and West African art. In 2000 the museum unveiled three new centers in its Millennium Project expansion: the Center for Native American Art, Center for Northwest Art, and the outdoor public sculpture gardens. A 2005 renovation of the Mark Building added a new Center for Modern and Contemporary Art, two ballrooms, a 33,000-volume Art Study Center and Library, and

headquarters for the Northwest Film Center, which features traditional, historical, and experimental exhibits in the media of film and video. The museum's current collection comprises more than 42,000 works.

The Museum of Contemporary Craft displays artworks in clay, fiber, glass, wood, and metal.

Festivals and Holidays

The centerpiece of Portland's special events schedule is the annual Portland Rose Festival, which is held each May into June and celebrated its 100th anniversary in 2007. The festival features many different events, including the Grand Floral Parade (second largest all-floral parade in the nation), a waterfront carnival, and a juried fine arts festival, among many other events. The festival attracts more than two million visitors annually.

There are several area jazz festivals, including the Portland Jazz Festival in February and the Mt. Hood Jazz Festival in August, which brings renowned jazz musicians from all over the country to the Portland area.

The Oregon Brewers Festival celebrates the works of more than 80 craft brewers from around the United States in late July. In August the Bite of Oregon presents a three-day extravaganza of music while Portland's finest restaurants and cafes, wineries, and microbreweries demonstrate their specialties. The Christmas holidays are highlighted by the spectacular Christmas Ships Parade.

Sports for the Spectator

Professional sports in Portland are led by the National Basketball Association's Portland Trail Blazers, who play at the Moda Center, formerly known as the Rose Garden. The Portland Timbers are Portland's professional soccer franchise that joined Major League Soccer in 2011 after playing in the United Soccer Leagues first division for a number of years. The Timbers play their home games to boisterous, sold-crowds at Jeld-Wen Field. Hockey action is brought to fans by the Portland Winterhawks of the Western Hockey League, which is a major source of talent for the National Hockey League. A wide range of other sports activities can be viewed at several of the area's universities. Professional minor league baseball was represented by the Triple-A Portland Beavers until 2010.

Portland Meadows features quarter horse and thoroughbred racing from October through April. Auto racing takes place at the Portland International Raceway.

Sports for the Participant

Portland offers a variety of ways to satisfy the sporting urge. The mountains provide opportunities for outdoor sports such as rock climbing and hiking. Timberline Lodge, a National Historic Landmark, serves one of Mt. Hood's five ski areas and offers the only lift-serviced summer skiing in the country. Local rivers feature all water sports; the Portland area is a fishing paradise, offering everything from fly fishing for trout in mountain streams and salmon-fishing in the rivers to all-day deep-sea excursions on charter boats. Hood River, Oregon, is a windsurfing mecca on the Columbia Gorge. The Portland Marathon, held in early October, ranks as one of the premier marathon events in the country; its 26.2-mile course is open to walkers as well as runners.

The Portland Parks & Recreation department maintains 10,000 acres at more than 250 locations throughout the city. Parks range in size from the 5,000-acre Forest Park to Mill Ends Park, the world's smallest park at 36 inches in diameter. Facilities include two amphitheaters; a skateboard park; tennis courts; sports fields; playgrounds; arts, music, and dance centers; and sports, fitness, and arts programming. There are some 152 miles of regional trails.

Shopping and Dining

Lloyd Center, Portland's first and largest shopping center, is located in the downtown core in the city's northeast section. Here, more than 200 stores surround an indoor ice rink. Washington Square, Jantzen Beach Super Center, and Clackamas Town Center are all located within a 20-minute drive of downtown. The Galleria includes several floors of unique urban shopping and dining. Pioneer Place Mall in the heart of downtown features four city blocks of dining, shopping, and entertainment. Powell's City of Books, the world's largest new and used independent bookstore, is located in downtown Portland and stocks more than a million books.

The Skidmore/Old Town National Historic District at the north end of downtown offers many shopping possibilities. Saturday Market is open Saturday and Sunday, March through December, and features more than 300 vendors. The Water Tower at John's Landing is the home of a unique blend of shops and restaurants. The Sellwood and Hawthorne Boulevard Districts in southeast Portland and the Multnomah District in southwest Portland are favorites of antique hunters.

Portland features a number of restaurants specializing in fresh, grown-in-Oregon foods, as well as spots to sample famous Pacific seafood. The Chinatown district offers regional Chinese cuisine; a large number of other restaurants specialize in many ethnic foods. More than a dozen nationally ranked restaurants emphasize elegance and formal dining, and there are many informal bistros and other places to mix dining with nightlife. Portland's up-and-coming fine dining has earned six local chefs nominations for prestigious James Beard awards between 2008 and 2012.

Visitor Information: Portland Oregon Visitors Association, 1000 SW Broadway, Suite 2300, Portland, OR 97205; telephone (503) 275-9750; toll-free (800) 962-3700; fax (503) 275-9284; email info@travelport land.com.

■ Convention Facilities

The Oregon Convention Center, which completed a major expansion in 2003, is located in the center of downtown along the Willamette River. It contains nearly one million square feet of enclosed space, with 255,000 square feet of exhibit space, 50 meeting rooms, two grand ballrooms, and an 800-space parking garage. The facility can accommodate groups of up to 10,000. Offering greater flexibility and more options than ever before, the Oregon Convention Center is the largest meeting facility in the Pacific Northwest.

The Veterans Memorial Coliseum, in the Rose Quarter, features 108,000 square feet of exhibit space. In 2007 the City of Portland outlined a number of improvements to the coliseum, including new large-screen televisions and beer gardens, but implementation was still on hold through 2013. The arena can seat up to 12,000 guests.

Portland offers several convention complexes that are all within a few minutes of more than 11,000 hotel rooms. Montgomery Park is a unique trade center located five minutes northwest of downtown Portland. It contains 4,900 square feet of exhibition and meeting space complemented by a 135-foot-high glass atrium that consists of 6,000 square feet.

Brunish Theatre at Portland'5 Centers for the Arts can accommodate 200 people for meetings, conferences, or other events. Other meeting and exhibition facilities include the Portland Expo Center and the Washington County Fair Complex (also referred to as Fairplex). Most major hotels in the city offer extensive meeting, banquet, and ballroom facilities.

Convention Information: Portland Oregon Visitors Association, 1000 SW Broadway, Suite 2300, Portland, OR 97205; telephone (503) 275-9750; toll-free (800) 962-3700; fax (503) 275-9284; email info@ travelportland.com.

■ Transportation

Approaching the City

Portland's airport, Portland International Airport (PDX), is one of the fastest-growing major airports on the West Coast, with 13 commercial carriers offering daily nonstop flights from Portland to various destinations. Serving more than 13 million passengers annually, PDX offers nearly 550 passenger flights daily. The airport is nine miles east of the central city, a 15-minute car ride. Portland International Airport is owned and operated by the Port of Portland.

Two major interstate highways intersect in Portland: Interstate 5, running north–south from southern California into Canada, and Interstate 84, running east–west. U.S. highways 26 and 30 are other east–west routes.

Portland is bypassed by Interstate 405, on the western edge of the downtown area, and Interstate 205, running through the eastern suburbs.

Amtrak serves the Portland area with daily train service; commercial bus service is also available.

Traveling in the City

Portland is divided into five areas—southwest, southeast, north, northeast and northwest—with the Willamette River bisecting the city. Street addresses match the location of these areas. Eleven bridges cross the river. Major streets are Grand Avenue, Martin Luther King Jr. Boulevard, Sandy Boulevard, and 82nd Avenue. Downtown, streets are mostly one way, with adjacent streets flowing in opposite directions.

TriMet, Portland's mass transit system, is ultramodern and efficient, highlighted by MAX, a 52-mile light-rail system that connects the downtown area with three counties. Westside MAX serves commuters in suburbs west of town as far west as Hillsboro. This line boasts the deepest subterranean transit station in North America. A Portland-Milwaukie expansion was approved in late 2010; the line was to span 7.3 miles and was expected to become functional in 2015. TriMet has a total 625 buses that serve Multnomah, Clackamas, and Washington counties, in addition to commuter rail line WES (Westside Express Service), and the Portland Street Car, which connects the Cultural District, the Pearl District, the Nob Hill/Northwest Neighborhood, and other areas.

■ Communications

Newspapers and Magazines

Portland's major daily newspaper, *The Oregonian,* has been in publication since the 1850s. The paper's affiliated website provides news and local coverage online as well as archives to past stories. *Willamette Week* and many smaller neighborhood weeklies, as well as *The Portland Observer* and *The Skanner* (online), both serving the African American community, are among the other Portland area newspapers. The *Portland Business Journal* provides news pertaining to the Portland business community. Local magazines include *Oregon Business Magazine* and a quarterly publication of the Oregon Historical Society.

Television and Radio

Portland is represented by commercial networks and public television; affiliates include ABC, CW, CBS, NBC, PBS, and FOX. Other channels are available on cable and from neighboring communities. Ten AM and 21 FM radio stations serve the Portland area with a variety of music and other programming.

Media Information: *The Oregonian,* 1320 SW Broadway, Portland, OR 97201; telephone (503) 221-8327.

Portland Online

City of Portland home page. Available www.portland online.com

Multnomah County Library. Available multcolib.org

The Oregonian. Available www.oregonlive.com

Portland Art Museum. Available www.portlandart museum.org

Portland Business Alliance. Available www.portland alliance.com

Portland Public Schools. Available www.pps.k12. or.us

Travel Portland. Available www.travelportland.com

BIBLIOGRAPHY

Hawkins, William John, and William F. Willingham, *Classic Houses of Portland, Oregon: 1850–1950* (Portland, OR: Timber Press, 1999)

Heying, Charles, *Brew to Bikes: Portland's Artisan Economy* (Portland, OR: Ooligan Press, 2010)

Will, Robin, *Beauty of Portland* (Portland, OR: LTA Publishing, 1989)

Salem

■ The City in Brief

Founded: 1848 (incorporated, 1860)

Head Official: Mayor Anna M. Peterson (since 2010; current term expires 2014)

City Population
1990: 107,793
2000: 136,924
2010: 154,637
2012 estimate: 157,425
Percent change, 2000–2010: 12.9%
U.S. rank in 1990: 178th (State rank: 3rd)
U.S. rank in 2000: 162nd (State rank: 3rd)
U.S. rank in 2010: 150th (State rank: 3rd)

Metropolitan Statistical Area Population
2000: 347,214
2010: 390,738
2012 estimate: 396,338
Percent change, 2000–2010: 12.5%
U.S. rank in 2000: 129th
U.S. rank in 2010: 131st

Area: 46.37 square miles

Elevation: 171 feet above sea level at State Capitol

Average Annual Temperatures: January, 40.3° F; July, 66.8° F; annual average, 52.6° F

Average Annual Precipitation: 40 inches of rain, 6.6 inches of snow

Major Economic Sectors: government, agriculture, food processing, manufacturing

Unemployment Rate: 7.8% (2012)

Per Capita Income: $21,459

2012 FBI Crime Index Property: 6,731

Major Colleges and Universities: Willamette University, Chemeketa Community College

Daily Newspaper: *Statesman Journal*

■ Introduction

Salem is the capital of Oregon and the third largest city in the state. Situated in the middle of a large, fertile agricultural region and known as the "Cherry City," Salem is the processing and governmental center for the surrounding area and the state. A clean environment, the natural scenic beauty of its location, and the recreational activities afforded by the nearby mountains contribute to the high quality of life for which Salem is noted. In addition, careful planning and intelligent zoning have made the city attractive to new business and industry, particularly those involved in solar power production and advanced manufacturing.

■ Geography and Climate

Salem is located about 60 miles inland from the Pacific Ocean in the Willamette Valley and about halfway between Portland and Eugene. The Willamette River flows on the western edge of the central city. The city is bounded by the Coast Range of mountains on the west and the Cascade Range on the east. Moist Pacific air is the dominant weather feature, moderating temperatures year round. The city and especially the nearby mountains receive a large amount of rainfall; more than 70 percent occurs between November and March and only about 6 percent during the summer. Severe storms and extreme temperatures are uncommon.

Area: 46.37 square miles

The State Capitol building in Salem. *Jim Corwin/Stone/Getty Images*

Elevation: 171 feet above sea level at State Capitol

Average Temperatures: January, 40.3° F; July, 66.8° F; annual average, 52.6° F

Average Annual Precipitation: 40 inches of rain, 6.6 inches of snow

■ History

The site of present-day Salem was called "Chemeketa" by the Calapooya tribe. The word means "meeting" or "resting place," and the tribe used the region for many years in that capacity. In 1840, Jason Lee, a Methodist-Episcopal missionary, moved his mission to the area and called it "Chemeketa," but most settlers referred to it as "The Mill," because of its proximity to Mill Creek. Two years later, the mission established the Oregon Institute, a training school for the local Native Americans that eventually became Willamette University.

The mission was closed in 1844, but in 1848, a town was laid out on the site and called Salem. Some controversy remains over who actually named the town Salem, but historians agree that it was either David Leslie or W. H. Wilson. A fierce battle over where to locate the

capital of the Oregon Territory began when the capital was moved from Oregon City to Salem in 1851. In 1853 the Oregon State Legislature began debate on whether to change the town's name to Thurston, Valena, or Corvallis, but a vote in 1855 retained the town's original name. The capital was moved again in 1855, but it returned to Salem later that same year. A suspicious fire that destroyed the Capitol building in late 1855 added to the controversy. When Oregon became a state in 1859, Salem was named the tentative capital, but it was not until 1864 that the city was officially chosen as the capital by election. Salem was incorporated as a city in 1860, and the present Capitol building was built in 1938, after the previous building was destroyed by fire in 1935.

Beginning as a wool processing center, Salem has grown to be an important center for the processing of agricultural products and lumber, as well as a remaining the governmental center of the state. Industrial parks inaugurated during the 2000s have sought to attract companies involved in distribution, advanced manufacturing, and solar energy. The city's historic buildings, surrounding natural beauty, and modern amenities make it a draw for new residents and businesses alike.

Historical Information: Marion County Historical Society Museum, 260 Twelfth St., SE, Salem, Oregon

97301; telephone (503) 364-2128; email director@marionhistory.org.

■ Population Profile

Metropolitan Statistical Area Population

2000: 347,214
2010: 390,738
2012 estimate: 396,338
Percent change, 2000–2010: 12.5%
U.S. rank in 2000: 129th
U.S. rank in 2010: 131st

City Residents

1990: 107,793
2000: 136,924
2010: 154,637
2012 estimate: 157,425
Percent change, 2000–2010: 12.9%
U.S. rank in 1990: 178th (State rank: 3rd)
U.S. rank in 2000: 162nd (State rank: 3rd)
U.S. rank in 2010: 150th (State rank: 3rd)

Density: 3,228.6 people per square mile

Racial and ethnic characteristics

White: 128,450
Black or African American: 1,885
American Indian and Alaskan Native: 1,381
Asian: 5,154
Native Hawaiian and Other Pacific Islander: 2,028
Hispanic or Latino (may be of any race): 33,609
Other: 18,527

Percent of residents born in state: 47.8%

Age characteristics

Population under 5 years old: 11,375
Population 5 to 9 years old: 11,379
Population 10 to 14 years old: 11,613
Population 15 to 19 years old: 10,240
Population 20 to 24 years old: 13,301
Population 25 to 34 years old: 23,409
Population 35 to 44 years old: 18,001
Population 45 to 54 years old: 20,278
Population 55 to 59 years old: 9,263
Population 60 to 64 years old: 9,408
Population 65 to 74 years old: 10,625
Population 75 to 84 years old: 5,447
Population 85 years and over: 3,086
Median age: 34.0

Births (2010–11 Metropolitan Area)

Total number: 5,470

Deaths (2010–11 Metropolitan Area)

Total number: 3,183

Money income (2012)

Per capita income: $21,459
Median household income: $45,215
Total households: 57,838

Number of households with income of ...

less than $10,000: 4,829
$10,000 to $14,999: 3,666
$15,000 to $24,999: 6,749
$25,000 to $34,999: 7,110
$35,000 to $49,999: 9,437
$50,000 to $74,999: 11,087
$75,000 to $99,999: 6,420
$100,000 to $149,999: 5,764
$150,000 to $199,999: 1,539
$200,000 or more: 1,237

Percent of families below poverty level: 20.4%

FBI Crime Index Property: 6,731

FBI Crime Index Violent: 564

■ Municipal Government

Salem operates under a council-manager form of government with eight council members elected by wards to four-year terms; half of the council is elected every two years. The mayor serves for two years. The entire council hires the city manager. Salem is the seat of Marion County.

Head Official: Mayor Anna M. Peterson (since 2010; current term expires 2014)

Total Number of City Employees: 1,312 (2013)

City Information: City of Salem, 555 Liberty Street SE, Salem, OR 97301; telephone (503) 588-6255; email manager@cityofsalem.net.

■ Economy

Major Industries and Commercial Activity

The major industry in Salem, as the state's capital and county seat of Marion County, is government, where state, local, and federal governments employ nearly one third of Salem's workers. There were more than 31,000 government jobs throughout Salem in 2013. The service and trade industries comprise significant other portions of the economy.

Agriculture and livestock, which is a highly diversified industry in the Salem area, has a total estimated economic impact of $1.4 billion dollars annually. More than 150 different cash crops are produced in the area. Vegetables and fruits, nursery and greenhouse crops, grass seed, and dairy products account for more than 50 percent of the total agricultural value.

Manufacturing in the Salem area has become increasingly diverse. The food product industry is the largest single manufacturing sector, employing up to 10,000 during the peak of the processing season. Major manufacturing employers also include those that produce fabricated metal products and high-technology equipment, from cell phones to snowboards. Most employment pertaining to lumber and wood products is actually in the manufactured building industry making prefabricated structures. The addition of SANYO Solar, which makes silicon parts for solar products, to the area in 2009 diversified the manufacturing industry.

Items and goods produced: high-tech components, vegetable and fruit products, wood and paper products, grass seed, ornamental plants, dairy products, manufactured homes, metal products, and solar products

Incentive Programs—New and Existing Companies

Local programs: In recent years the emphasis in the Willamette Valley has switched from business recruitment to business retention and expansion programs designed to help resident companies "stay put and stay healthy." Most incentive programs are run through the Mid-Willamette Valley Council of Governments or the Strategic Economic Development Corp. (SEDCOR). The Salem area has three enterprise zones for qualified manufacturing and wholesale distribution firms that allow a three- to five-year property tax exemption on improvements. Additional financial incentives center on related urban renewal projects.

State programs: The state of Oregon offers a number of incentive programs to attract new and expanding businesses to the state. Tax incentives include Enterprise Zones, Strategic Investment Program, Construction-in-Process, Oregon Investment Advantage, Employer-provided Dependent Care Tax Credit, Work Opportunity Tax Credit, Research Tax Credits, and Film & Video Incentives.

State-supported finance programs include the Oregon Business Oregon Business Development Fund, Oregon Capital Access Program, Oregon Credit Enhancement Fund, Oregon Industrial Development Bonds, Entrepreneurial Development Loan Fund, Business Retention Program, and Brownfields Redevelopment Fund.

Oregon supports an array of incentives that support renewable energy projects, including tax credits for equipment purchases, property tax exemptions for wind farms, a state energy loan program, and other grants and credits. The state's Renewable Portfolio Standard helps support demand for renewable energy by requiring energy providers to meet at least 25 percent of their Oregon load with renewable energy by 2025.

Job training programs: The state of Oregon's education program includes a statewide apprenticeship program that offers many opportunities for individuals to learn trades. The Employer Workforce Training Fund is an Oregon grant program for employers wanting to upgrade the skills of their employees in the trade or health-care sectors. The state also runs the JOBS for Oregon's Future program.

Chemeketa Community College's Center for Business and Industry has a variety of programs, such as the MicroEnterprise Resources, Initiatives and Training program, to help small businesses develop and to assist existing businesses to expand.

Development Projects

Private developments centered on two industrial parks, Salem Renewable Energy and Technology Center, which opened in 2009, and Mill Creek Corporate Center. The 80-acre Salem Renewable Energy and Technology Center's main tenant, SANYO Solar, established an $80 million manufacturing facility on the premises. The 130,000-square-foot building makes silicon products for solar components. The Mill Creek Corporate Center is a 514-acre area consisting of business and industry parks. In 2011 Home Depot opened a 465,000-square-foot Rapid Deployment Center on the premises. Assessed valuation of Mill Creek Corporate Center in 2012 was nearly $48 million; valuation was just over $1 million when it opened in 2005.

City projects in 2012–13 included $18.5 million of investments in highway widening, water and sewer improvements, new parks, and flood repairs. Funds from the Federal Emergency Management Agency (FEMA) supported work, as many of the repairs were necessary following flooding in January 2012. Plans to build a pedestrian bridge connecting Minto Brown Park and Riverfront Park were approved in 2013, with the $9 million project expected to begin construction as early as 2014, pending funding.

Economic Development Information: SEDCOR, Chemeketa Center for Business and Industry, 626 High St. NE, Ste 200, Salem, OR 97301; telephone (503) 588-6225; fax (503) 588-6240. Salem Area Chamber of Commerce, 1110 Commercial Street NE, Salem, OR 97301; telephone (503) 581-1466; fax (503) 581-0972; email info@salemchamber.org. City of Salem, 555 Liberty Street SE, Salem, OR 97301; telephone (503) 588-6255; email manager@cityofsalem.net.

Commercial Shipping

Salem is located on the main lines of the Union Pacific and Burlington Northern Santa Fe railroads. Located in Salem are about 25 long haul truck lines with seven terminals. Interstate 5, the primary north–south highway of the West Coast, passes through the east side of Salem, and Interstate 84 connects to states in the east. Nearby

Portland has marine terminals and deep water ports, and is one of the busiest ports on the West Coast in terms of cargo shipped. The Salem Municipal Airport at McNary Field is a 750-acre facility with a 5,800-foot ILS, precision runway that has full facilities for corporate and general aviation aircraft.

Labor Force and Employment Outlook

The Salem area labor force is diversified, with skilled and semi-skilled components including metal workers, assemblers, electrical/electronic technicians, machine operators, computer operators, and programmers. As in cities throughout the country, a national recession in the late 2000s increased unemployment. Nonfram employment declined 7.2 percent between 2008 and 2012 in the Salem metropolitan area, amounting to a loss of some 11,000 jobs. Construction jobs were hardest hit, followed by manufacturing. Within the government sector, local government suffered the highest attrition rate, with about 10 percent of all local government jobs cut during that same time period. Employment in educational and health services grew despite the economic downtown, and occupational projections through 2016 showed the fastest growing competitive industry in the region to be ambulatory health-care services, with an expected growth of 35.7 percent.

The following is a summary of data regarding the 2012 Salem labor force:

Size of civilian labor force: 74,635

Number of workers employed in . . .

> agriculture and mining: 2,564
> construction: 2,920
> manufacturing: 5,020
> wholesale trade: 1,322
> retail trade: 7,523
> transportation: 1,626
> information systems: 748
> finance: 3,624
> professional administration: 6,133
> education and social services: 16,204
> arts and leisure: 5,583
> other: 3,019
> public administration: 7,050

Average hourly earnings of production workers: $14.55

Unemployment rate: 7.8% (2012)

Employers

Largest employers (2013)	*Number of employees*
State of Oregon	21,000
Salem-Keizer School District	4,638
Salem Hospital	3,900
Chemeketa Community College	1,651
Marion County	1,487
Federal Government	1,400
City of Salem	1,312
Norpac Foods Incorporated	1,097
Kaiser Permanente	1,048
State Accident Insurance Fund	837

Cost of Living

The following is a summary of data regarding several key cost of living factors in the area.

State income tax rate: 5.0% to 9.9%

State sales tax rate: None

Local income tax rate: None

Local sales tax rate: None

Property tax rate: $19.00 per $1,000 assessed value (2013)

Economic Information: SEDCOR, Chemeketa Center for Business and Industry, 626 High St. NE, Ste 200, Salem, OR 97301; telephone (503) 588-6225; fax (503) 588-6240. Oregon Employment Department, 875 Union St. NE, Salem, OR 97311; telephone (800) 237-3710.

■ Education and Research

Elementary and Secondary Schools

Salem-Keizer Public Schools comprises the second largest school district in the state. It is governed by a seven-member, nonpartisan school board that appoints the superintendent. The district includes four charter schools and two alternative high schools. Special programs include a Teen Parent Program and Salem Family Literacy. The district's Early College High School provides students with a pathway to college-credit courses at Chemeketa Community College.

Salem is also served by more than 20 parochial and private schools spanning pre-kindergarten to 12th grade.

The following is a summary of data regarding the Salem-Keizer School DIstrict.

Total enrollment: 40,403

Number of facilities

> total: 65
> elementary schools: 42

junior high schools: 11
high schools: 8
other: 4

Student/teacher ratio: 19.37:1

Teacher salaries

average (statewide): $56,387

Funding per pupil: $9,331

Public Schools Information: Salem-Keizer Public Schools, 2450 Lancaster Dr. NE, Salem, OR 97305; telephone (503) 399-3000.

Colleges and Universities

Salem boasts more than 13 universities and colleges within a 70-mile radius. Salem is home to Willamette University, a private school affiliated with the Methodist Church that traces its roots back to 1842 and calls itself the first university in the West. With an enrollment of more than 2,700, the university offers a wide range of undergraduate degrees in many fields and a number of postgraduate programs, including law (the first program in the Pacific Northwest), teaching, and management. A 2013 review by *U.S. News & World Report* ranked the school 61st among national liberal arts colleges.

Chemeketa Community College enrolled nearly 39,000 students in 2012-13; it offers one- and two-year associate degrees. The school also boasts more than 450 full-time staff members. A branch of Tokyo International University of America opened in Salem in 1989 to meet Japanese corporations' increased demand for a culturally adapted workforce. The branch is located directly across from Willamette University.

Other area colleges and universities are Corban College (formerly Western Baptist College), George Fox University–Salem, and Western Oregon University in Monmouth. In 2013 Corban College was ranked sixth among regional colleges in the West by *U.S. News & World Report.*

Libraries and Research Centers

The Salem Public Library maintains a main library and one branch, with a total of more than 350,000 items, including more than 800 periodical titles. The library features a special photographic history collection. Around 1.3 million items circulate annually from the library. At Willamette University the Mark O. Hatfield Library houses more than 425,000 volumes and more than 25,000 print and electronic subscriptions; the J.W. Long Law Library houses collections of Oregonian, national, and international law titles.

The Oregon State Library provides quality information service to Oregon state government, provides reading materials to blind and print-disabled Oregonians, and provides leadership, grants, and other assistance to improve local library service for all Oregonians. Among its more than one million items are in-depth collections in business, history, political and social sciences, federal and state government publications, genealogy, and a comprehensive collection of materials about Oregon. In addition, it's Talking Book and Braille Services collection consists of more than 60,000 cassette, large print, Braille, and talking book titles.

Public Library Information: Salem Public Library, 585 Liberty Street SE, Salem, OR 97301; telephone (503) 588-6071.

■ Health Care

Salem Hospital, with 469 physicians and 454 acute-care beds, is the major health-care facility in the city, providing a wide range of services in several locations. The hospital is part of a larger network called Salem Health. Salem Hospital's service area includes Marion, Polk, and portions of Yamhill counties. Salem Hospital is one of the largest of Oregon's 59 acute-care hospitals and is home to the state's busiest Emergency Room. The hospital's Center for Outpatient Medicine, just east of the hospital, houses outpatient programs, outpatient surgery, imaging, a Sleep Disorders Center, a SHAPES clinic, and other programs. In 2012 the facility admitted nearly 21,000 patients and treated more than 114,000 in its emergency department.

The Salem Hospital Regional Rehabilitation Center provides comprehensive inpatient and outpatient rehabilitation services as well as home care. Other Salem Hospital facilities include a Psychiatric Medicine Center, Infusion and Wound Care center, and a Convenient Care Center.

Additional community health care providers are the Willamette Valley Hospice, Northbank Surgical Center, skilled nursing and adult foster care providers, and a number of physician clinics also furnishing care to Salem residents. Kaiser Permanente runs two medical office buildings in the city.

■ Recreation

Sightseeing

The State Capitol building in downtown Salem is constructed of white marble and features a 22-foot bronze and gold leaf statue, "The Oregon Pioneer." Willson Park, next to the Capitol, contains the Waite Fountain, a replica of the Liberty Bell, and a gazebo for open-air concerts. Bush's Pasture Park is a large park near the Willamette River and downtown Salem that features the Bush House, a Victorian mansion; Historic Deepwood Estate, a four-acre estate built in the Queen Anne style; Bush Barn Art Center; and Bush Conservatory, renovated in 2010. The Salem Municipal Rose Garden is also located in the park.

Riverfront Park on the Willamette River has an amphitheatre, a playground and picnic areas, and is home to Salem's Riverfront Carousel, featuring hand-carved horses. A.C. Gilbert's Discovery Village, a children's museum, is also in Riverfront Park. Half of the museum is housed in a Victorian home once occupied by Gilbert's uncle, and the other half is in a Victorian building separated from the first by a charming outdoor activity center. Salem Saturday Market brings local farmers and artisans to the corner of Marion and Summers streets April through October. The Reed Opera House, built in 1869, has been renovated and now contains a number of shops and restaurants.

Mission Mill Museum is a five-acre site that is home to the Thomas Kay Woolen Mill, the historic buildings of the Jason Lee House, the Parsonage, the John D. Boon House, and Pleasant Grove Church. The modern PGE Waterpower Interpretive Center showcases the importance of waterpower to Salem's textile industry.

Attractions at Enchanted Forest, a family-run amusement park, include Storybook Lane in a woodland setting, a Western mining town, summer comedy theater, a haunted house, the Ice Mountain Bobsleds roller coaster, and bumper car and log flume rides. The Salem area features more than 20 wineries within an hour's drive.

Arts and Culture

Theatrical performances are held year-round by the Pentacle Theatre, a community theater group. The Elsinore Theatre presents international and national tours of musicians and theatrical performances, hosts a children's play series, and presents films on Wednesdays. The Willamette University Playhouse is where theatre majors from Willamette University perform, along with the university's Distinguished Artists Series that brings speakers, concerts, and plays to the venue.

Musical performances by local groups include classical and pops concerts backed by the Oregon Symphony Association in Salem. The Willamette Falls Symphony presents four concerts a year. Salem is also home to concert and jazz bands, a chamber music group, and men's and women's barbershop choirs.

The Hallie Ford Museum of Art, the state's largest art museum, opened in 1998. It houses Willamette University's collection of Indian baskets, Northwest paintings, prints, photographs, sculptures, and European, Asian, and American art.

Festivals and Holidays

The Oregon Wine, Food, and Brew Festival, billed as "The first taste of the wine season," is held at the Oregon State Fairgrounds in January. In April, the Oregon Ag Fest at the State Fairgrounds brings more than 17,000

visitors a year to enjoy the Trade, Garden and Craft Show, live entertainment, food, and petting zoo. In June, Riverfront Park hosts the Salem World Beat Festival, with music, dance, crafts, and food from around the world. The Salem Art Fair and Festival occurs annually in the third weekend in July and exhibits the works of artists from throughout the Northwest. Also in July is Oregon National Guard Hoopla, an all-ages three-on-three basketball tournament held right on Court Street, and the Marion County Fair takes place at the State Fairgrounds. The Oregon State Fair is a 12-day celebration each August that features floral and art exhibits, agricultural displays, a midway, and live entertainment. The nearby Bavarian-style community of Mt. Angel holds a popular Oktoberfest each fall. The Festival of Lights Parade in December features floats and marching bands on a route through downtown at night.

Sports for the Spectator

The Salem-Keizer Volcanoes are a Class-A affiliate of the San Francisco Giants and play home games at Volcanoes Stadium in Keizer.

Sports for the Participant

More than 1,600 acres across 46 developed parks in Salem offer a variety of outdoor recreational activities. Water sports include fishing, swimming, and boating. Nearly 30 parks maintain ball fields, and there are also more than 20 public tennis courts and three public golf courses; some provide accommodations for the handicapped. Minto-Brown Island Park, the largest park at 900 acres, is located along the river about a mile from Salem's center city and contains picnic grounds, jogging and bike paths, and a wildlife refuge. Construction to connect Salem's major parks with a pedestrian bridge over the Willamette River was expected to begin as early as 2014. Within 50 miles of Salem are coastal beaches and state and federal recreational areas and parks.

Shopping and Dining

The downtown Salem Center Mall, Lancaster Mall, and Woodburn Company Stores outlet mall are the three main shopping areas in Salem. A system of skywalks connects the four major department stores downtown. A number of other specialty stores and smaller shops, such as Mission Mill Village, featuring antiques and crafts in a historic village setting, are scattered throughout the area.

Salem restaurants specialize in fresh, grown-in-Oregon foods and famous Pacific seafood along with cuisine from around the world. The Willamette Valley's vineyards produce a variety of fine wines that area restaurants proudly feature.

Visitor Information: Salem Convention and Visitors Association, 181 N. High St. NE, Salem, OR 97301;

telephone (503) 581-4325; toll-free (800) 874-7012; fax (503) 581-4540; information@travelsalem.com.

■ Convention Facilities

There are numerous options when deciding where to meet and stay in Oregon's capital city. The Salem Convention Center, which opened in 2005, has more than 30,000 square feet of meeting and exhibition space in 14 rooms, and is attached to the all-suite, 193-room Phoenix Grand Hotel. The Pavilion at the Oregon State Fair & Expo Center offers more than 30,500 square feet of meeting and exhibit space. There are five other buildings available at the Fairgrounds, including a horse barn, a livestock building, and an amphitheater, all available for events or meetings. The historic Reed Opera House in downtown Salem has two ballrooms with catering facilities for elegant receptions for up to 300 people, and the Elsinore Theatre can be rented for events.

Convention Information: Salem Convention and Visitors Association, 181 N. High St. NE, Salem, OR 97301; telephone (503) 581-4325; toll-free (800) 874-7012; fax (503) 581-4540; information@travelsalem.com.

■ Transportation

Approaching the City

Airport shuttles make round trips from Portland International Airport, 61 miles from Salem. Salem Municipal Airport, also known as McNalty Field, is located two miles outside the city. It is a general aviation facility, largely serving private flights and the Oregon Army National Guard. Interstate 5, the major West Coast interstate highway, and Interstate 84, for destinations to the east, run through Salem. Passenger rail service is available from Amtrak with two trains daily. The city is also served by Greyhound bus line.

Traveling in the City

The downtown area and much of the rest of Salem is laid out in a grid pattern. Major thoroughfares include State Street, Center Street, Commercial Street, and River Road. Salem-Keizer Transit, also known as Cherriots, provides more than four million rides annually on 64 buses throughout the metropolitan area, and also supports a Rideshare program.

■ Communications

Newspapers and Magazines

Salem readers support one major daily morning newspaper, the *Statesman Journal,* and a number of weekly papers that provide business, agricultural, government, and general news, including Willamette University's *Collegian.* Among the magazines published in Salem are *Dialogue,* a magazine for the visually impaired, and the *Capital Press,* a farming newspaper for the Pacific Northwest.

Television and Radio

Salem is served by six local television stations, in addition to those broadcasting from Portland, as well as cable television. Three FM and three AM radio stations are located in Salem, which, along with broadcasters from the surrounding communities, serve the area with an assortment of music, news, and informational programming.

Media Information: Statesman Journal, 280 Church St. NE, Salem, OR 97309; telephone (503) 399-6611.

Salem Online

City of Salem home page. Available www.cityofsalem.net

Salem Area Chamber of Commerce. Available www.salemchamber.org

Salem Convention & Visitors Association. Available www.travelsalem.com

Strategic Economic Development Corporation. Available www.sedcor.org

Salem-Keizer Public Schools. Available www.salkeiz.k12.or.us

Salem Public Library. Available www.salemlibrary.org

Statesman Journal. Available www.statesmanjournal.com

BIBLIOGRAPHY

Lim, Tyrone, and Dolly Pangan-Specht, *Filipinos in the Willamette Valley* (Charleston, SC: Arcadia Publishing Company, 2010)

Northwest 2010: Alaska, Idaho, Montana, Oregon, Washington, and Wyoming (Chicago, IL: Five Star Travel Corp., 2010)

Price, Lorna, ed., *Oregon Biennial* (Portland, OR: Portland Art Museum, 2006)

Utah

The State in Brief

Nickname: Beehive State

Motto: Industry

Flower: Sego lily

Bird: California gull

Area: 84,897 square miles (2010; U.S. rank 13th)

Elevation: Ranges from 2,000 feet to 13,528 feet above sea level

Climate: Generally arid with abundant sunshine, higher temperatures in the southwestern desert, cooler weather and lower temperatures in high plateaus and mountains

Admitted to Union: January 4, 1896

Capital: Salt Lake City

Head Official: Gary R. Herbert (R) (until 2017)

Population
> 1990: 1,722,850
> 2000: 2,233,169
> 2010: 2,763,885
> 2012 estimate: 2,766,233
> Percent change, 2000–2010: 23.8%
> U.S. rank in 2012: 34th
> Percent of residents born in state: 61.9% (2012)
> Density: 33.6 people per square mile (2010)
> 2012 FBI Crime Index Total: 91,300

Racial and Ethnic Characteristics (2012)
> White: 2,465,277
> Black or African American: 29,912
> American Indian and Alaska Native: 30,823
> Asian: 56,081
> Native Hawaiian and Pacific Islander: 25,766
> Hispanic or Latino (may be of any race): 357,893
> Other: 158,374

Age Characteristics (2012)
> Population under 5 years old: 260,218
> Population 5 to 19 years old: 696,387
> Percent of population 65 years and over: 9.1%
> Median age: 29.3

Vital Statistics
> Total number of births (2012–13): 50,840
> Total number of deaths (2012–13): 14,875
> AIDS cases reported through 2011: 2,690

Economy
> Major industries: Manufacturing; trade; finance, insurance, and real estate; services; mining; agriculture; tourism
> Unemployment rate (2012): 4.9%
> Per capita income (2012): $23,794
> Median household income (2012): $58,164
> Percentage of persons below poverty level (2012): 12.1%
> Income tax rate: 5.0%
> Sales tax rate: 4.7%

Provo

■ The City in Brief

Founded: 1849 (incorporated, 1851)

Head Official: Mayor John Curtis (since 2010; current term expires 2014)

City Population
>1990: 86,835
>2000: 105,166
>2010: 112,488
>2012 estimate: 115,925
>Percent change, 2000–2010: 7%
>U.S. rank in 1990: 239th
>U.S. rank in 2000: 244th (State rank: 3rd)
>U.S. rank in 2010: 231st (State rank: 3rd)

Metropolitan Statistical Area Population
>2000: 368,536
>2010: 526,810
>2012 estimate: 550,461
>Percent change, 2000–2010: 42.9%
>U.S. rank in 2000: 120th
>U.S. rank in 2010: 98th

Area: 41.79 square miles

Elevation: 4,540 feet above sea level

Average Annual Temperatures: 53.3° F

Average Annual Precipitation: 20.13 inches of rain; 60.40 inches of snow

Major Economic Sectors: services, technology, bioscience, education

Unemployment Rate: 5.3% (2012)

Per Capita Income: $15,346

2012 FBI Crime Index Property: 2,465

Major Colleges and Universities: Brigham Young University, Utah Valley University

Daily Newspaper: *Daily Herald*

■ Introduction

Provo is the commercial center and county seat of Utah County and second largest metropolitan area in the state. A high-technology mecca, the Provo area is home to one of the largest concentrations of computer software in the nation after California's Silicon Valley. The city is also an agricultural center producing berries and orchard fruit. Many ski areas, campgrounds, state parks, lakes, and rivers are located within Utah County. Fishing, camping, hiking, and hunting facilities are nearby. Brigham Young University is the center for many local activities in the city, which is the headquarters of the Uinta National Forest with its many scenic drives through the Wasatch Mountains and Provo Canyon. The city has a highly educated population—both an explanation for and result of its many high-technology companies. Housing is affordable and the crime rate is two to three times lower than in most comparable cities.

■ Geography and Climate

Provo is located in Utah Valley, 38 miles south of Salt Lake City, 263 miles northeast of St. George, and 80 miles south of Ogden. It is situated on the Provo River between Utah Lake to the west and the scenic Wasatch Mountain Range to the east. It sits on a shelf along the famous shoreline of prehistoric Lake Bonneville and is nurtured by the Provo River.

The area experiences four seasons with low humidity that makes the air cool rapidly after sunset, resulting in comfortably cool evenings. The temperature dips below zero on only three days per year on average. Generally

Photograph by Ron H. MacDonald. Provo City Corporation, Economic Development Office. Reproduced by permission.

57 days of the year are above 90 degrees and 15 days are below freezing. The wettest month of the year is usually May while June is the driest month.

Area: 41.79 square miles

Elevation: 4,540 feet above sea level

Average Temperatures: 53.3° F

Average Annual Precipitation: 20.13 inches of rain; 60.40 inches of snow

■ History

Two Franciscan friars, Francisco Dominguez and Silvestre de Escalante, were the first Spaniards to visit the area that makes up present-day Utah County. They arrived in the area from Santa Fe, New Mexico, in search of a direct route to Monterey, California. Arriving in 1776, Father Escalante described the Provo/Orem Valley as having comfortable weather both day and night. "This place is the most pleasant, beautiful, and fertile land in all New Spain," he wrote. The two priests instructed the Native Americans in Christian teachings, and though they promised to return, no further record of them remains.

Etienne Provost, a French Canadian trapper, was the next recorded European visitor. He arrived in the area in 1825 with a band of men in search of fur-bearing animals. The trappers were visited by 20 or 30 natives, whose leader told them that they could not smoke peace pipes together because there was iron in the vicinity. Provost and his men moved their knives and guns further away, and subsequently the natives attacked them with hidden knives and tomahawks, killing 17 of the 22 men. Provost and four other men escaped and made their way to the mountains.

The Mormon pioneers, fleeing religious persecution in Illinois, were the next European visitors to the area.

Brigham Young led his followers to Salt Lake Valley in 1847, where they immediately began planting crops and constructing houses. In 1849 a permanent settlement in Provo was established by Mormon pioneers.

Provo was founded in 1849 as Fort Utah, named after the Ute tribe that inhabited the region. Later, the name was changed to Fort Provo in honor of Provost, the French trapper.

A war between the settlers and the native tribes took place in 1850, and the Walker War followed in 1853. The Mormons built a fort that they called Fort Utah as a protection against their native enemies. Shortly after, settlers began building houses around the fort. By 1852 hotels and businesses had been established.

By 1861 all of the Utah Valley was being settled. Even though lack of water remained a problem, many of the earlier settlers from nearby valleys began living on the lands that now comprise the city of Orem. When railroad connections were built from Salt Lake City (1873) and Scofield (1878), Provo became a shipping point for the region's mines. Provo is the seat of Brigham Young University (founded in 1875) and Utah Valley University (formerly Utah Valley State College). Nearby are the Uinta National Forest, with headquarters in Provo; a state fish hatchery; a wild bird refuge; and Provo Peak.

Today, Provo has a rapidly growing metropolitan population, with gains of more than 40 percent during the 2000s. The area boasts a high quality of life due in part to its proximity to an abundance of recreational and leisure options in the nearby Wasatch Mountains and Utah Lake. Provo is a family-friendly city, too, frequently listed in national rankings of best places to raise a family.

Historical Information: Department of History, Brigham Young University, 2130 JFSB, Provo, UT 84602; telephone (801) 422-4335.

■ Population Profile

Metropolitan Statistical Area Population
> 2000: 368,536
> 2010: 526,810
> 2012 estimate: 550,461
> Percent change, 2000–2010: 42.9%
> U.S. rank in 2000: 120th
> U.S. rank in 2010: 98th

City Residents
> 1990: 86,835
> 2000: 105,166
> 2010: 112,488
> 2012 estimate: 115,925
> Percent change, 2000–2010: 7%
> U.S. rank in 1990: 239th
> U.S. rank in 2000: 244th (State rank: 3rd)
> U.S. rank in 2010: 231st (State rank: 3rd)

Density: 2,699.3 people per square mile

Racial and ethnic characteristics
> White: 102,933
> Black or African American: 325
> American Indian and Alaskan Native: 198
> Asian: 3,367
> Native Hawaiian and Other Pacific Islander: 1,614
> Hispanic or Latino (may be of any race): 21,229
> Other: 7,488

Percent of residents born in state: 44.5%

Age characteristics
> Population under 5 years old: 9,006
> Population 5 to 9 years old: 7,817
> Population 10 to 14 years old: 6,176
> Population 15 to 19 years old: 12,057
> Population 20 to 24 years old: 30,654
> Population 25 to 34 years old: 18,329
> Population 35 to 44 years old: 9,587
> Population 45 to 54 years old: 7,113
> Population 55 to 59 years old: 4,390
> Population 60 to 64 years old: 2,599
> Population 65 to 74 years old: 3,508
> Population 75 to 84 years old: 3,071
> Population 85 years and over: 1,618
> Median age: 23.7

Births (2010–11 Metropolitan Area)
> Total number: 12,100

Deaths (2010–11 Metropolitan Area)
> Total number: 1,963

Money income (2012)
> Per capita income: $15,346
> Median household income: $38,338
> Total households: 31,937

Number of households with income of ...
> less than $10,000: 2,986
> $10,000 to $14,999: 3,029
> $15,000 to $24,999: 4,578
> $25,000 to $34,999: 4,089
> $35,000 to $49,999: 4,709
> $50,000 to $74,999: 6,010
> $75,000 to $99,999: 2,859
> $100,000 to $149,999: 2,222
> $150,000 to $199,999: 811
> $200,000 or more: 644

Percent of families below poverty level: 32.7%

FBI Crime Index Property: 2,465

FBI Crime Index Violent: 149

■ Municipal Government

Provo has a council-mayor form of government. Seven members make up the Provo Municipal Council—five representing municipal districts and two at-large representatives. These elected officials serve a term of four years, with elections alternating every two years.

Head Official: Mayor John Curtis (since 2010; current term expires 2014)

Total Number of City Employees: 773 (2013)

City Information: City Center Building, 351 West Center St., Provo, UT 84603; telephone (801) 852-6100.

■ Economy

Major Industries and Commercial Activity

With low unemployment and high job growth, the Provo-Orem area has a diverse economy with every employment sector well represented. The area is home to one of the largest concentrations of high-tech and software technologies companies in the United States. There is also a large concentration of biotech companies located in the area.

Some of the world's major software companies are located in the area, including Novell Inc. and Symantec, creating opportunities for more than 400 small to mid-range high-technology companies. Provo is also home to such giants as Nestle Frozen Foods and Nu Skin. High-technology companies in the Provo/Orem area include Micron Technology, Ameritech Library Systems, Folio Corporation, Viewsoft, and Nimbus Manufacturing, among others.

The notable work ethic of local employees and the appeal of a serene mountain community have made Provo ideal for a wide variety of manufacturers, communications firms, and marketing and retail organizations, including Nature's Sunshine, PowerQuest Corp., and Powder River Manufacturing. Many industrial parks offer a variety of settings for light to heavy industry with abundant, low-cost utilities.

Tourism is also an important industry. Provo is a magnet for many surrounding counties, and the major shopping areas are easily accessible from Interstate 15 and other main routes. In addition, Provo's standing as a college town, with one of the largest privately funded university's in the world, has helped provide a steady, highly educated workforce.

Items and goods produced: software, medical products, electronics

Incentive Programs—New and Existing Companies

Local programs: Most incentive programs are at the state level. Provo City's Redevelopment Agency provides support for starting a new business by offering assistance in preparing a business plan and demographic information necessary for decision making. The agency has the authority to implement Tax Increment Financing to support development projects and funds the Business Development Corporation of Provo, which offers loans and mentoring to start-up companies, primarily in new technology and exports. Provo also offers a city-wide broadband high-speed Internet capacity fiber network in an effort to entice new businesses.

State programs: Business financing options offered by the state of Utah include Private Activity Bonds, available to small manufacturers looking to expand their business, with Utah averaging about $275 million in funding annually; Opportunity Finance Network, which provides capital and financial services to bridge market gaps with loans of up to $5 million; Utah Microenterprise Loan Fund, with loans of between $1,000 and $25,000 repaid over five years at 5 percent above prime interest rates; and Utah Technology Finance Corporation, which invests in small, mostly information technology–related companies. Grants and venture capital are supplied by the Utah Angel Network, with investments of up to $2 million, Grow Utah Ventures, and the Wayne Brown Institute. Technical and planning assistance is offered by Utah Procurement Technical Assistance, Utah Department of Commerce, Utah Small Business Development Center, Utah Supplier Development Council, Utah U.S. Export Assistance Center, and local community colleges.

Sales tax exemptions are offered for manufacturing equipment, in designated enterprise zones, and in designated economic development zones. Research tax credits may cover up to 100 percent of sales, corporate, and withholding taxes for the life of a project, typically 5 to 10 years.

Job training programs: Custom Fit is an employee training program offered through the Utah College of Applied Technology, state colleges, and the local business community. It provides training in specific technologies, computer skills, safety certification, leadership, management and team-building. The Utah State Legislature allocates annual funding to Custom Fit, covering a substantial portion of the cost to employers. State funding is also provided for Short Term Intensive Training programs across Utah. Training is offered at the state college level at a discount to potential employers or employees. The program is customized to match full-time job seekers with the needs of specific companies.

The Small Business Development Center in Orem/Provo provides free personal consulting services and low-cost skill-based training to owners and managers of small businesses and to prospective entrepreneurs.

Development Projects

Downtown revitalization efforts in Provo were anchored by the 2012 opening of the Utah Valley Convention

Center. The $42 million facility was funded by the county and anticipated to generate some $18 million in annual revenue, as well as to act as a stimulus for further downtown development. The convention center featured more than 85,000 square feet of meeting and garden space, including 19,620 square feet of exhibit space and a nearly 17,000-square-foot grand ballroom. The west side of the building was constructed with temporary materials to allow for expansion in future years.

The Provo Tabernacle of the Church of Jesus Christ of Latter-day Saints endured a catastrophic fire in 2010, necessitating a complete rebuilding. The church decided to convert the historic tabernacle—in use since 1886—into a temple, and construction began in 2012, with an anticipated completion date of 2015.

In 2013 Nu Skin opened an $85 million Innovation Center in downtown Provo. The facility expanded existing corporate headquarters and housed 900 employees. A total of 164,000 square feet were added to the corporate campus, more than doubling its previous size. Research and development facilities focusing on anti-aging were a central feature of the expansion.

Economic Development Information: Provo City Economic Redevelopment Agency, 351 West Center St., Provo, UT 84603; telephone (801) 852-6161.

Commercial Shipping

Provo is served by the Union Pacific railroad, which offers second-morning service to the majority of the Western markets. The Provo area is served by approximately 40 major trucking lines. The expanding Provo Municipal Airport can serve and handle most aircraft and is equipped with an instrument-landing system and a weather-reporting capability. Nearby Salt Lake International Airport is served by 30 air cargo companies.

Labor Force and Employment Outlook

The Provo/Orem area boasts low unemployment; favorable taxes; a young, educated, "internationally skilled" work force; and a growing metropolitan population. Valley remains one of the hottest high-tech areas in the nation, which continues to bring in entrepreneurs, big business, and new and higher-paying jobs. Utah is a right-to-work state.

The following is a summary of data regarding the 2012 Provo labor force:

Size of civilian labor force: 63,119

Number of workers employed in . . .

agriculture and mining: 198
construction: 2,687
manufacturing: 3,862
wholesale trade: 873
retail trade: 6,308
transportation: 902

information systems: 1,684
finance: 1,935
professional administration: 8,154
education and social services: 21,354
arts and leisure: 5,422
other: 3,435
public administration: 1,129

Average hourly earnings of production workers: $15.93

Unemployment rate: 5.3% (2012)

Employers

Largest employers (2013)	*Number of employees*
Brigham Young University	5,000–6,999
Utah Valley Regional Medical Center	3,000–3,999
Vivint Inc.	2,000–2,999
Central Utah Medical Clinic	500–999
FindItInUtah	500–999
MyFamily.com	500–999
Provo City Inc.	500–999
RBD Acquisition Sub, Inc.	500–999
Utah State Hospital	500–999
Provo City Administrative	250–499
Bluehost.com	250–499
Deseret Industries	250–499
Heritage Schools Inc.	250–499

Cost of Living

Overall cost of living in the Salt Lake City area, which includes Provo, ranks close to—but slightly below—the national average. Utility costs are some 15 percent below the national average.

The following is a summary of data regarding several key cost of living factors in the area.

2013 ACCRA Average House Price: $238,871

2013 ACCRA Cost of Living Index: 96

State income tax rate: 5.0%

State sales tax rate: 4.7%

Local income tax rate: None

Local sales tax rate: 2.05%

Property tax rate: 0.0117550% of 55% of assessed value (2013)

Economic Information: Utah Valley Chamber of Commerce, 111 South University Avenue, Provo, UT 84601; telephone (801) 851-2555.

■ Education and Research

Elementary and Secondary Schools

In addition to educating students from kindergarten to grade 12, the Provo City School District assists students in preschool and latch-key programs, as well as through programs for the physically challenged. Provo also has one school for children with physical and emotional challenges too severe for mainstreaming. The graduation rate in 2012–13 was just under 70 percent. The system is home to several charter schools; one, the Walden School of Liberal Arts, is consistently ranked among the best high schools in the state.

Because public education in the Utah Valley is highly regarded, there are few private schools. Among the private schools are Challenger School, a K–12 school based on a structured learning environment; Provo Canyon School, an alternative school; and several Montessori Schools.

The following is a summary of data regarding the Provo City School District.

Total enrollment: 13,753

Number of facilities

    total: 22
    elementary schools: 13
    junior high schools: 2
    high schools: 3
    other: 4

Student/teacher ratio: 20.95:1

Teacher salaries

    average (statewide): $46,571

Funding per pupil: $6,619

Public Schools Information: Provo City School District, 280 West 940 North, Provo, UT 84604-3394; telephone (801) 374-4800.

Colleges and Universities

Brigham Young University (BYU) is located in the city at the base of the Wasatch Mountains. Founded in 1875 by Brigham Young, BYU is one of the largest private universities in the United States. Owned by the Mormon Church (Church of Jesus Christ of Latter-day Saints), the university enrolls about 27,000 undergraduates annually. The vast majority of its students are members of the Church of Jesus Christ of Latter-day Saints. Particularly notable are its business administration programs,

broadcast journalism program, and law and engineering schools. *U.S News & World Report* consistently recognizes BYU as one of the nation's best universities; it ranked 62nd among national universities in 2013. The university has a major impact on the community.

Utah Valley University enrolls more than 31,000 students annually and awards bachelor's degrees in dozens of fields, from biology to cinema production to world politics. Other Provo institutions of higher learning include Provo College (with Schools of Healthcare, Business, Health & Wellness, Justice, and Design & Technology) and Stevens-Henager College, which trains students in health care, business, graphic arts, and information technology.

Libraries and Research Centers

The Provo City Library at Academy Square holds more than 270,000 volumes, records and audio tapes, video tapes, and compact discs. Its special collections center on Utah and Utah County history. Other libraries in the city include the Utah State Hospital's Patient Library and Brigham Young University's Harold B. Lee Library, which houses more than 4.2 million volumes and features special collections on linguistics, poetry, children's literature, Victorian literature, and oral history. The library serves nearly three million patrons per year.

Provo has many research centers affiliated with Brigham Young University. They encompass such areas as engineering, computers, cancer, sociology, literature, thermodynamics, Western studies, communications, international studies, earth science, agriculture, psychology, religion, life science, anthropology, business, religion, and women's studies. BYU maintains an Office of Research and Creative Activities that apportions grants annually. The U.S. Forest Service has a Shrub Sciences Laboratory maintained in cooperation with Brigham Young University.

Public Library Information: Provo City Library at Academy Square, 550 North University Ave., Provo, UT 84601; telephone (801) 852-6650.

■ Health Care

The Provo/Orem area is served by three major hospitals—Utah Valley Regional Medical Center (UVRMC) in Provo, Orem Community Hospital in Orem (OHC), and Timpanogos Regional Hospital in Orem. The majority of health-care facilities in the area are run by Intermountain Health Care (IHC), the regional health-care provider that operates UVRMC and Orem Community Hospital, in addition to other facilities.

UVRMC is a 330-bed tertiary and acute-care facility. UVRMC is a Level II trauma center and includes specialty programs for heart and vascular care, newborn intensive care unit, cancer and stroke services, weight loss surgery, behavioral health, and rehabilitation. OCH specializes in same-day surgery and obstetrics. IHC facilities in Provo are the Utah Valley Heart Center and the Utah Valley Rehabilitation Center.

MountainStar Health Care operates Timpanogos Regional Hospital in Orem, built in 1999; services include open heart surgery, obstetrics, and a variety of health and wellness centers. Surgical facilities in Provo include the Central Utah Surgical Center. Mental health services are available at Utah State Hospital and Wasatch Mental Health Center.

■ Recreation

Sightseeing

The Provo/Orem area is one of the most scenic in the country. Visitors can view the breathtaking Bridal Veil Falls from the Provo Canyon floor. The falls can be seen from Highway 189, which curves alongside the Provo River up the beautiful Provo Canyon Scenic Byway. A turn onto the Alpine Loop Scenic Backway (Highway 92) goes past the Sundance Resort and the Timpanogos Cave National Monument. Located in American Fork Canyon, the cave is actually three highly decorated limestone caverns that can be observed on a 1.5-mile hike.

Built in 1972, Provo Latter Day Saints Temple is located on a hillside above the Brigham Young University campus. It is an architecturally striking building faced with white cast stone and topped with a segmented spire. The Provo Latter Day Saints Tabernacle, a historic structure dating to the late 1800s, suffered severe fire damage in 2010; while the building's brick frame was being preserved, a new temple was slated to replace the tabernacle in 2015.

The award-winning McCurdy Historical Doll Museum has more than 4,000 dolls, 47 miniature rooms, toys, and a toy shop. The Monte L. Bean Life Science Museum on the Brigham Young University campus contains a large collection of trophy animals and displays of animal habitats. The Brigham Young University Museum of Paleontology features animals large and small from dinosaurs to ancient forms of sea life.

The Sundance Resort, 15 miles northeast of Provo, provides fine dining, a spa, plays, art workshops, and nature experiences throughout the summer in addition to excellent skiing in winter.

The Trafalga Family Fun Center in Orem contains a 400-foot waterslide, indoor and outdoor miniature golf courses, and a game room. Thanksgiving Point in nearby Lehi is a 700-acre oasis featuring restaurants, a visitor center and gift shop, a professional golf course, academy driving range, clubhouse, tennis ranch, animal farm, equestrian center, shopping village, North American Museum of Ancient Life, and acres and acres of awe-inspiring gardens.

Arts and Culture

Hundreds of cultural events are sponsored annually in Provo, including concerts, symposiums, plays, lectures, classes, art exhibits, and museum displays. The Museum of Art at Brigham Young University (BYU) is one of the largest of its kind in the intermountain West and houses an impressive permanent collection of fine art. The B. F. Larson Gallery at BYU exhibits works by contemporary artists. Fine art is on display at the Brownstone Gallery. The Springville Museum of Art in nearby Springville houses an extensive collection of the works of Utah artists, highlighted by the month-long National Art Exhibit in April.

The Sundance Institute, an arts community near Provo, fosters creativity in film and visual and performing arts, and presents arts events throughout the year, including children's theater.

The historic Latter Day Saints Tabernacle hosted a roster of internationally known performers as well as the Utah Valley Symphony, an 80-member community orchestra, until it burned in 2010. The symphony now plays at the Covey Center for the Arts. Brigham Young University is a major source of music, dance, and drama events at its Harris Fine Arts Center. Utah Regional Ballet is the resident ballet company at Utah Valley University in Orem. The Center Street Musical Theater presents dinner theater in downtown Provo. The Provo Theatre Company stages five to six musical, comedy, and dramatic productions from September through July.

Festivals and Holidays

Provo kicks off the New Year with its First Night community celebration of the arts in an alcohol-free setting. Utah Pioneer Days in May features the Miss Orem Pageant. America's Freedom Festival in Provo on July 4 is the largest Independence Day celebration in the country. This grand three-week event begins with balloon festivals; gala balls; clogging competitions; 10K, 5K, and one-mile runs; and explodes with an enormous parade and a "Stadium of Fire" concert and fireworks display.

More than 700 folk dancers from many countries gather at the Springville World Folkfest in July for the largest event of its kind in the country. From May through September, many cities in Utah County hold individual city festivals. Winter Fest in downtown Provo during the month of December celebrates the holiday season with concerts, a parade, living nativity, decorated storefronts and a "Lights On" celebration.

Sports for the Spectator

Brigham Young University's (BYU) basketball team plays its games throughout the winter at the 23,000-seat Marriott Center arena. The BYU Cougars hold home football games at their 65,000-seat stadium on campus. The Utah Valley Wolverines play basketball at the UCCU

Center in Orem. Some of the other sports presented at BYU and Utah Valley are basketball, baseball, track, volleyball, gymnastics, rugby, wrestling, and swimming.

Sports for the Participant

The city of Provo has five parks with public tennis courts, seven baseball/softball complexes, and ice rinks among its more than 30 facilities. The city maintains a rifle and pistol shooting range year-round for public use. Within an hour's drive from Provo are seven downhill ski resorts, including Park City and Snowbird. Sundance Resort, which offers mountain biking trails as well as skiing, is 20 minutes from the city of Provo Canyon. Nearby Utah Lake State Park and Deer Creek Reservoir in Heber Valley provide water skiing, fishing, boating, camping, canoeing, and other water sports, in addition to being popular spots for hiking. Fly-fishing in the Provo River is popular, and hunting of elk, deer, moose, and bighorn sheep is also possible. Maps and trail guides to the area can be obtained at the U.S. Forest Service's main office in Provo. Climbers have access to both indoor and outdoor ropes courses at the CLAS (Challenging Leadership Adventure Systems, Inc.) Ropes Course facility. The High Uintas Mountain Range is a challenge for climbers and home to the highest Boy Scout Camp in the country.

Seven Peaks Resort, located at the foot of Maple Mountain in Provo, is a waterpark with a variety of water amusements including some of the world's tallest water slides, a wave pool, and children's activity areas. The park's acres of lush lawns and pavilions make it a favorite site for picnics and parties. Thanksgiving Point in nearby Lehi is a 700-acre oasis featuring a variety of outdoor activities.

Shopping and Dining

Provo boasts two newer malls: the modern Provo Towne Center and The Shops at Riverwoods. Provo Town Center is anchored by major department stores. The Shops at Riverwoods features modern, upscale shops in a nostalgic Main Street U.S.A. setting. Provo Town Square is a specialty theme mall in the heart of the city. All the buildings are restored historic structures housing restaurants, shops, and entertainment facilities. Provo University Parkway has recently developed into a major shopping area with large department stores and small specialty shops. University Mall in the University Parkway corridor in Orem contains 185 stores and restaurants.

The city of Provo has more than 200 eating places. The Provo/Orem area hosts a variety of ethnic restaurants including American, Chinese, Japanese, Indian, Italian, and Mexican establishments. Vegetarian fare, bars/nightclubs, and fast foods of all kinds are also popular. Los Hermanos and Magelby's Fresh are local favorites for dining. At Sundance Resort, The Tree Room offers elegant dining by candlelight; the Foundry Grill Room features lighter, bistro-style dining; and the Owl Bar offers spirits, local brews, and a bistro-style menu for the benefit of private club members (temporary memberships are available); all rooms are known for their exceptional fare.

Visitor Information: Utah County Convention & Visitors Bureau, 220 West Center Street, Suite 100, Provo, UT 84601; telephone (801) 851-2100.

■ Convention Facilities

The Utah County Convention Center's groundbreaking occurred in 2010, and the facility opened in 2012. The convention center featured more than 85,000 square feet of meeting and garden space, including 19,620 square feet of exhibit space and a nearly 17,000-square-foot grand ballroom. The west side of the building was constructed with temporary materials to allow for expansion in future years.

The Provo Marriott Hotel and Conference Center has 21 meeting rooms for a total of more than 28,000 square feet, and 330 sleeping rooms, including more than 100 suites. The Brigham Young University Conference Center is a full-service facility featuring 34 conference rooms. It can be scheduled for programs that are consistent with BYU's educational mission and is a smoke- and alcohol-free facility.

In addition to the conference centers, the Provo area offers many options for hosting large groups, including the Provo City Library at Academy Square, Historic County Courthouse, Springville Museum of Art, Thanksgiving Point, Alpine Art Center, and SCERA Center for the Arts in Orem, among others.

The UCCC Center at Utah Valley University features an 8,500-seat arena, four multipurpose athletic courts of 5,000 square feet each, two 2,500-square-foot meeting spaces, four concession stands, six locker rooms, in-house catering, full equipment rental, and ticketing services. Sundance Resort's facilities include more than 11,000 square feet of meeting space and 102 sleeping units in a rustic, alpine atmosphere. The fairground facilities at Spanish Fork include a 7,000-seat main arena, plus two additional arenas totaling more than 60,000 square feet.

Convention Information: Utah County Convention & Visitors Bureau, 220 West Center Street, Suite 100, Provo, UT 84601; telephone (801) 851-2100.

■ Transportation

Approaching the City

Provo/Orem is intersected by U.S. highways 50, 89, 91, and 189, as well as by Interstate 15. Provo is located within an hour's drive of Salt Lake International Airport, which offers over 645 daily flights on nine airlines. In

2012 the airport served 20 million customers as the 26th busiest airport in the United States. Bus service to the city is also available.

Traveling in the City

The Utah Transit Authority provides daily mass transit service to both the Provo/Orem and Salt Lake City metropolitan areas. It offers complete routes serving all of the major business areas in Provo. The metropolitan area is served by 10 taxi and for-hire car service companies.

■ Communications

Newspapers and Magazines

The *Daily Herald* is Provo's daily newspaper. The *Daily Universe* newspaper is published by the students at Brigham Young University. Magazines published in Provo include *BYU Studies, BYU Magazine, Al-Arabiyya* (a scholarly journal for Arabic language teachers), *The Western North American Naturalist,* and *Scandinavian Studies.*

Television and Radio

Provo has three AM and 17 FM radio stations that encompass religion, music, talk, and public broadcasting, and three television stations, including one that broadcasts from the campus of Brigham Young University.

Media Information: *Daily Herald,* 1555 North Freedom Blvd., PO Box 717, Provo, UT 84603; telephone (801) 375-5050; toll-free (800) 880-8075.

Provo Online

City of Provo home page. Available www.provo.org
Daily Herald. Available www.harktheherald.com
Provo City Economic Development. Available www.provo.org/departments/economic-development
Provo City Library. Available www.provolibrary.com
Provo City School District. Available provo.edu
Utah Chamber of Commerce. Available www.thechamber.org
Utah County Convention & Visitors Bureau. Available www.utahvalley.org
Utah State Office of Education. Available www.schools.utah.gov

BIBLIOGRAPHY

Balaz, Christine, *Salt Lake City, Park City, Provo, and Utah's High Country Resorts,* 2nd ed. (Countryman Press, 2010)

Handley, George B., *Home Waters: A Year of Recompenses on the Provo River* (Salt Lake City: University of Utah Press, 2010)

Smoot, L. Douglas, *The Miracle at Academy Square* (Provo, UT: Brigham Young University Press, 2003)

Salt Lake City

■ The City in Brief

Founded: 1847 (incorporated, 1851)

Head Official: Mayor Ralph Becker (D) (since 2007; current term expires 2015)

City Population
1990: 159,928
2000: 181,743
2010: 186,440
2012 estimate: 189,311
Percent change, 2000–2010: 2.6%
U.S. rank in 1990: 108th (State rank: 1st)
U.S. rank in 2000: 129th (State rank: 1st)
U.S. rank in 2010: 124th (State rank: 1st)

Metropolitan Statistical Area Population
2000: 939,122
2010: 1,124,197
2012 estimate: 1,161,715
Percent change, 2000–2010: 19.7%
U.S. rank in 2000: 50th
U.S. rank in 2010: 50th

Area: 109 square miles

Elevation: 4,330 feet above sea level

Average Annual Temperatures: January, 29.2° F; July, 77.0° F; annual average, 52.0° F

Average Annual Precipitation: 16.50 inches of rain; 58.5 inches of snow

Major Economic Sectors: government, education, health care, finance, transportation

Unemployment Rate: 5.7% (2012)

Per Capita Income: $27,430

2012 FBI Crime Index Property: 14,357

Major Colleges and Universities: University of Utah, Westminster College

Daily Newspaper: *The Salt Lake Tribune; Deseret News*

■ Introduction

Salt Lake City is the state capital and largest city in Utah. Founded in 1847 by religious leader Brigham Young, the city is the world headquarters of the Church of Jesus Christ of Latter-day Saints (Mormons). From its early days as a mining and railroad town, Salt Lake City has emerged as the commercial and cultural hub for a large area of the western mountain region. The city played host to the 2002 Winter Olympics, which proved to be an economic boon to the area and raised the international profile of the city. The nearby mountains, historical and religious landmarks, and the uniqueness of the Great Salt Lake also make the city a prominent tourist attraction.

■ Geography and Climate

Salt Lake City is bounded on three sides by mountain ranges and on the northwest by the Great Salt Lake. The Jordan River flows just to the west of the downtown district. Mountains shield the city from much of the severe winter weather common to the area, and the lake also serves to moderate the temperatures. Summer days are typically hot and dry, with cool nights and little precipitation. The winters are cold but not severe, with snow remaining on the ground through most of the season. Spring, especially in March, is the season of heavy rain and high winds from Pacific storms.

Area: 109 square miles

Elevation: 4,330 feet above sea level

Salt Lake City skyline in early spring. © *strickke/Getty Images*

Average Temperatures: January, 29.2° F; July, 77.0° F; annual average, 52.0° F

Average Annual Precipitation: 16.50 inches of rain; 58.5 inches of snow

■ History

European Explorers Replace Native Americans

For thousands of years, the inhabitants of the northern Utah region were hunter-gatherers. Artifacts dating as far back as 12,000 years have been found in caves near the Great Salt Lake. About 500 B.C. the Fremont tribe, a less nomadic, agricultural society, settled in the area, building impressive cliff dwellings and drawing elaborate rock paintings, many of which can still be viewed today. Changing environmental conditions eventually made primitive farming impossible, and by the twelfth century, the area was populated mainly by the Ute, Paiute, and Shoshone tribes of nomadic hunters.

The first Europeans to travel through the area were the Spanish, coming from New Mexico in search of a direct route to Monterey, California, in 1776. In the early 1800s, fur trappers and "mountain men" explored the region, discovering the Great Salt Lake and mapping the mountain passes. A number of government expeditions explored the area, and a steady stream of settlers bound for California began to pass through.

Mormons Settle, Lay Out Town; Religious Beliefs Questioned

A group of Mormon pioneers led by Brigham Young settled in the Salt Lake Valley in 1847, laying out a town they called Great Salt Lake City. From the beginning the city was well planned, with a grid of 10-acre plots separated by streets 132 feet wide. The industrious settlers began planting crops and developing intricate irrigation systems, eventually forming more than 500 settlements in the Utah area. Disaster was averted in 1848 when, as drought and plagues of insects threatened the crops, flocks of seagulls arrived to consume the insects, thereby saving the harvest.

In 1848 the settlers organized the State of Deseret and applied for statehood with a government headed by the Mormon Church. Congress denied the petition and instead created Utah Territory in 1850. Salt Lake City was incorporated in 1851, and in 1856 it replaced Fillmore as the territorial capital. Misunderstandings about Mormon religious beliefs and political outrage at the Mormon practice of polygamy led to the so-called "Utah War" in 1857 between the Mormon settlers and the U.S. government. Although the dispute was settled peacefully in 1858, relations between the church and the territorial government were strained for many years.

City Becomes State Capital; Regional Mines, Industry Thrive

The two ends of the transcontinental railroad met just 40 miles north of Salt Lake City in 1869, tying Utah with the outside world. Over the next 20 years, hundreds of copper, silver, and lead mines were developed in the region, bringing a large number of non-Mormon settlers. Under continued pressure, the practice of polygamy was officially stopped by the church in 1890. This paved the way for women's suffrage in Utah, which had been a political lever in the national polygamy debate. The majestic Mormon Temple, begun in 1853, was completed in 1892, and Utah entered the Union in 1896 as the third suffrage state, with Salt Lake City as the capital.

During the early twentieth century Salt Lake City assumed the look of a modern city. The State Capitol building and a number of other impressive structures were built, electric trolley cars began service on the city's streets, and large residential sections developed around the city. Like most cities, Salt Lake City suffered during the Great Depression, but prosperity returned during World War II amidst a construction boom and increased demand for metals. Industrial expansion continued postwar with downtown development and beautification projects becoming a focus in the 1970s and 1980s.

In 2002 Salt Lake City hosted the "best attended" Olympic Winter Games in history, with 1.6 billion tickets sold and another four billion television viewers. The city continues to reap the benefits of improved infrastructure and a significant increase in tourism. A building boom that followed included the 2012 opening of City Creek Center, a $1.5 billion mixed-use facility. Still pending was a new $116 million performing arts center, expected to begin operations in 2016.

Historical Information: Utah State Historical Society Library, 300 South Rio Grande Street, Salt Lake City, UT 84101; telephone (801) 245-7225; fax (801) 533-3567.

■ Population Profile

Metropolitan Statistical Area Population

2000: 939,122
2010: 1,124,197
2012 estimate: 1,161,715
Percent change, 2000–2010: 19.7%
U.S. rank in 2000: 50th
U.S. rank in 2010: 50th

City Residents

1990: 159,928
2000: 181,743
2010: 186,440
2012 estimate: 189,311
Percent change, 2000–2010: 2.6%
U.S. rank in 1990: 108th (State rank: 1st)
U.S. rank in 2000: 129th (State rank: 1st)
U.S. rank in 2010: 124th (State rank: 1st)

Density: 1,678.0 people per square mile

Racial and ethnic characteristics

White: 136,245
Black or African American: 6,215
American Indian and Alaskan Native: 1,706
Asian: 11,696
Native Hawaiian and Other Pacific Islander: 5,131
Hispanic or Latino (may be of any race): 39,808
Other: 28,318

Percent of residents born in state: 46.8%

Age characteristics

Population under 5 years old: 14,223
Population 5 to 9 years old: 11,550
Population 10 to 14 years old: 9,216
Population 15 to 19 years old: 10,734
Population 20 to 24 years old: 19,626
Population 25 to 34 years old: 42,492
Population 35 to 44 years old: 25,571
Population 45 to 54 years old: 19,398
Population 55 to 59 years old: 9,713
Population 60 to 64 years old: 7,707
Population 65 to 74 years old: 10,262
Population 75 to 84 years old: 5,415
Population 85 years and over: 3,404
Median age: 31.4

Births (2010–11 Metropolitan Area)

Total number: 19,631

Deaths (2010–11 Metropolitan Area)

Total number: 5,957

Money income (2012)

Per capita income: $27,430
Median household income: $42,267
Total households: 74,037

Number of households with income of ...

less than $10,000: 8,240
$10,000 to $14,999: 4,606
$15,000 to $24,999: 9,741
$25,000 to $34,999: 8,367
$35,000 to $49,999: 10,612
$50,000 to $74,999: 12,544

$75,000 to $99,999: 7,441
$100,000 to $149,999: 6,803
$150,000 to $199,999: 2,823
$200,000 or more: 2,860

Percent of families below poverty level: 21.9%

FBI Crime Index Property: 14,357

FBI Crime Index Violent: 1,300

■ Municipal Government

Salt Lake City has a council-mayor form of government with the mayor elected at large. The mayor and seven council members serve four-year terms. The city is also the seat of Salt Lake County and the capital of Utah.

Head Official: Mayor Ralph Becker (D) (since 2007; current term expires 2015)

Total Number of City Employees: 2,770 (2013)

City Information: Salt Lake City Corporation, 451 South State Street, Salt Lake City, UT 84111; telephone (801) 535-6333.

■ Economy

Major Industries and Commercial Activity

Salt Lake City was originally a farming community; it also depended on mining until the early 1980s when foreign competition began to erode profits from that industry. Today, it has grown into a diverse economic region. As the state capital, county seat of Salt Lake County, and the largest city in the four-county Wasatch Front metropolitan area, the city is a governmental, commercial, and industrial center for Utah and much of the Intermountain West.

The service sector produces the most jobs in the city, especially education and health-care services. Government employment is considerable, with the State of Utah, University of Utah, and Salt Lake County among the city's top employers. The University of Utah alone accounts for more than 10 percent of all city employment.

A number of national financial institutions have established branch offices in Salt Lake City, making it the center of banking and finance for the region. The high number of residents who speak a language other than English makes Salt Lake City ideal for international financial institutions. Companies with a significant presence in Salt Lake City include American Express, Providian Financial Corporation, Morgan Stanley/Discover Card, Fidelity Investments, and JP Morgan Chase.

Known as the "Crossroads of the West," Salt Lake City's transportation and distribution network is extensive and includes easy access to major air cargo and rail

services. Virtually every major Western city—from Denver to Los Angeles to Seattle—can be reached by plane in two hours or by truck within 14. Major distribution operations in Salt Lake County include RC Willey Furnishings, Nicholas & Company Inc., Costco Western Distribution Center, and Schiff Nutrition International Inc.

Salt Lake City is the largest retail and wholesale market in Utah. The city supports a thriving tourism industry, especially in the wake of the 2002 Olympics, which brought in over $2 billion dollars of directly related spending; the industry continues to benefit from the city's increased international profile, with tourism generating some $1.2 billion in annual economic impact.

Salt Lake City is the international headquarters of the Church of Jesus Christ of Latter-day Saints. The city boasts a lower-than-the-national average cost of doing business.

Items and goods produced: petroleum products, electronics, pharmaceuticals, communications satellites, medical products

Incentive Programs—New and Existing Companies

Local programs: The Salt Lake County Office of Business Economic Development offers incentives to new and existing companies in the form of loans, grants, and on-the-job training. Most incentives are targeted toward the unincorporated areas of the county. The Salt Lake City Department of Economic Development offers incentives that include a revolving loan fund, redevelopment tax credits and tax increment financing, and industrial revenue bonds.

State programs: Business financing options offered by the state of Utah include Private Activity Bonds, available to small manufacturers looking to expand their business, with Utah averaging about $275 million in funding annually; Opportunity Finance Network, which provides capital and financial services to bridge market gaps with loans of up to $5 million; Utah Microenterprise Loan Fund, with loans of between $1,000 and $25,000 repaid over five years at 5 percent above prime interest rates; and Utah Technology Finance Corporation, which invests in small, mostly information technology–related companies. Grants and venture capital are supplied by the Utah Angel Network, with investments of up to $2 million, Grow Utah Ventures, and the Wayne Brown Institute. Technical and planning assistance is offered by Utah Procurement Technical Assistance, Utah Department of Commerce, Utah Small Business Development Center, Utah Supplier Development Council, Utah U.S. Export Assistance Center, and local community colleges.

Sales tax exemptions are offered for manufacturing equipment, in designated enterprise zones, and in designated economic development zones. Research tax credits may cover up to 100 percent of sales, corporate, and withholding taxes for the life of a project, typically 5 to 10 years.

Job training programs: Custom Fit is an employee training program offered through the Utah College of Applied Technology, state colleges, and the local business community. It provides training in specific technologies, computer skills, safety certification, leadership, management and team-building. The Utah State Legislature allocates annual funding to Custom Fit, covering a substantial portion of the cost to employers. State funding is also provided for Short Term Intensive Training programs across Utah. Training is offered at the state college level at a discount to potential employers or employees. The program is customized to match full-time job seekers with the needs of specific companies.

Development Projects

City Creek Center, a $1.5 billion mixed-use development in downtown Salt Lake City, opened in 2012. The 23-acre site included 1.2 million square feet of office space, 800 residential units, and 700,000 square feet of retail space. An artificial recreation of historic City Creek runs through the center of the development. The space also was the first U.S. shopping center built with a retractable roof.

A new Frank E. Moss Courthouse, covering 410,000 square feet, completed in late 2013. Ground was broken in 2011 after a 20-year funding and planning effort. The total cost was estimated at $226 million. The 10-story building houses 10 courtrooms, 14 judges' chambers, and provides office space for a U.S. Marshals Office, U.S. Probation Office, and records library. The new building replaced an older courthouse of the same name, constructed in 1905.

Plans for a new performing arts center were unveiled in 2013. The projected $116 million facility was to include a 2,500-seat theater capable of hosting Broadway shows and other major musical, comedy, and family entertainment. The facility was projected to open in 2016.

The University of Utah broke ground on a $36.5 million, 80,000-square-foot building to house its School of Dentistry in 2013, with an anticipated completion date of 2014. To be known as the Ray and Tye Noorda Oral Health Education Building, it was to feature a state-of-the-art laboratory and classroom facility that included a dental clinic.

Economic Development Information: Economic Development Corporation of Utah, 201 South Main Street, Suite 2010, Salt Lake City, UT 84111; telephone (801) 328-8824; fax (801) 531-1460. Downtown Alliance, 175 East 400 South, Suite 600, Salt Lake City, UT 84111; telephone (801) 359-5118.

Commercial Shipping

Utah's free port law makes it an ideal location for the import and export of goods. Salt Lake City is a full-service customs port city with a foreign trade zone. The Salt Lake International Airport is served by 30 air cargo companies.

Southern Pacific and Union Pacific railways offer freight service throughout Utah. The state's railroad lines all converge in the Salt Lake–Ogden area, making it a convenient interline switching route for destinations across the country. About 2,300 interstate and intrastate motor freight carriers operate in Utah.

Labor Force and Employment Outlook

The services sector is Salt Lake City's largest employment division. Health-care and computer technology are two dominant subsections of growth. The Salt Lake City labor force is young, well-educated, and possesses a strong work ethic. A low cost of living allows for lower-than-average wages, an attractive element for prospective businesses. Strong population growth, fueled both by above-average family size and in-migration, have spurred job growth as well. Throughout the twenty-first century, Salt Lake City has generally enjoyed above average job growth and low unemployment rates.

The following is a summary of data regarding the 2012 Salt Lake City labor force:

Size of civilian labor force: 105,777

Number of workers employed in . . .

agriculture and mining: 715
construction: 4,299
manufacturing: 8,771
wholesale trade: 2,200
retail trade: 9,661
transportation: 3,336
information systems: 2,226
finance: 6,468
professional administration: 12,491
education and social services: 25,212
arts and leisure: 12,503
other: 4,725
public administration: 3,007

Average hourly earnings of production workers: $16.45

Unemployment rate: 5.7% (2012)

Employers

Largest employers (2013)	*Number of employees*
University of Utah	20,000–24,000
State of Utah	7,000–9,000
Salt Lake County	5,000–7,000
Salt Lake City School District	5,000–6,200

Intermountain	
Health Care	4,000–5,000
L3 Communications	
Systems West	3,000–4,000
Wells Fargo	3,000–4,000
Salt Lake City	
Corporation	2,500–3,000
ARUP	2,000–2,500
Delta	2,000–2,500

Cost of Living

Overall cost of living in the Salt Lake City area ranks slightly below the national average. Power and natural gas rates throughout the state are among the lowest nationwide.

The following is a summary of data regarding several key cost of living factors in the area.

2013 ACCRA Average House Price: $257,400

2013 ACCRA Cost of Living Index: 97

State income tax rate: 5.0%

State sales tax rate: 4.7%

Local income tax rate: None

Local sales tax rate: 2.15%

Property tax rate: 0.0045750% of assessed value (2011)

Economic Information: Economic Development Corporation of Utah, 201 South Main Street, Suite 2010, Salt Lake City, UT 84111; telephone (801) 328-8824; fax (801) 531-1460.

■ Education and Research

Elementary and Secondary Schools

The Salt Lake City School District serves more than 24,000 students from diverse socioeconomic backgrounds. Caucasian and Hispanic students constitute the two largest ethnic groups, collectively representing more than 80 percent of the student body. More than 80 languages are spoken by students in the district, and about 63 percent qualify for free or reduced lunch. The district oversees four charter schools, including the Academy for Math, Engineering, and Science, and Salt Lake Center for Science Education.

The following is a summary of data regarding the Salt Lake City School District.

Total enrollment: 24,647

Number of facilities

    total: 36

    elementary schools: 27

    junior high schools: 5

    high schools: 3

    other: 1

Student/teacher ratio: 21.28:1

Teacher salaries

    average (statewide): $46,571

Funding per pupil: $7,534

Public Schools Information: Salt Lake City School District, 440 East 100 South, Salt Lake City, Utah 84111-1891; telephone (801) 578-8599; fax (801) 578-8248.

Colleges and Universities

Salt Lake City is home to the University of Utah, the oldest university in the West. Founded in 1850, the university covers more than 1,000 acres and includes the Red Butte Garden and Arboretum. One of the country's top 30 public research universities, the University of Utah is known for its technology transfer program to move research into practical applications in the business world; it also has a medical school. Annual enrollment exceeds 31,000. As part of an environmental stewardship program, the university planned to be carbon neutral by 2050.

Salt Lake City is also home to prestigious Westminster College, a private non-denominational institution founded in 1875, offering 38 undergraduate majors and a range of post-graduate degree and certificate programs. It enrolls approximately 2,300 undergraduate students each year in its four colleges: School of Arts and Sciences, Bill and Vieve Gore School of Business, School of Education, and the School of Nursing and Health Sciences.

Other local colleges include the Salt Lake Community College and LDS Business College. Adult education is available through the Salt Lake City campus of the University of Phoenix.

Libraries and Research Centers

The Salt Lake City Public Library System consists of a main library and five branch locations, with an annual circulation of nearly four million items and 140,000 registered library card holders. The total library system collection numbers in excess of one million items, with about 120,000 new items added annually. The library also contains special collections of old and rare material from the region's past. A new Main Library was unveiled in 2003, featuring a six-story curving, climbable wall, spiraling fireplaces, a multi-level reading area and a rooftop garden. The 240,000-square-foot space is double the size of the previous library.

The Salt Lake County Library System consists of a main library and 18 branches offering a variety of exhibits, events and collections. Salt Lake City is also home to the Utah State Library Program for the Blind and Disabled, which serves visually impaired, physically disabled, and reading disabled patrons across the western states with Braille books, books on cassette, and large-print books. The University of Utah maintains a large library system. A number of private, research, and special interest libraries also serve the city.

The Church of Jesus Christ of Latter-day Saints Library houses a genealogical library, considered to be the largest of its kind in the world. Open to the public free of charge, the collection contains family history, local history, and vital records. The library is visited by approximately 1,900 patrons each day.

Centers in the Salt Lake City area conduct research activities in such fields as the environment, entomology, engineering design, biomedical engineering, toxicology, lasers, radiobiology, occupational and environmental health, astrophysics, astronomy, communications, nuclear engineering, physical electronics, remote sensing and cartography, mineral technology, isotope geology, seismology, mining, business and economics, finance, public affairs, politics, energy law, gerontology, the American West, the Middle East, and archaeology.

Public Library Information: Salt Lake City Public Library, 210 East 400 South, Salt Lake City, UT 84111; telephone (801) 524-8200. Salt Lake County Library System, 2197 Fort Union Blvd, Salt Lake City, UT 84121-3139; telephone (801) 943-4636; fax (801) 942-6323.

■ Health Care

Utah boasts some of the healthiest people in the country. In 2013 the state was ranked sixth-healthiest in the United States by the United Health Foundation. Utah has the lowest smoking rate in the nation and also records some of the lowest cancer, heart disease, and infant mortality rates.

The University of Utah Health Care system operates several facilities, including its University Hospital, and is the teaching and research hospital for the University of Utah Medical School. The system includes more than 1,100 board certified physicians involved in both patient care and research. In addition to the University Hospital, other main facilities include Huntsman Cancer Hospital, University Orthopaedic Center, and the University Neuropsychiatric Institute.

Intermountain Health Care is a non-profit organization based in Salt Lake City. It includes 22 hospitals and has a mandate to provide quality care regardless of a patients' abilities to pay. In 2013 the Intermountain Medical Center in Murray was ranked the top hospital in Utah by *U.S. News & World Report*. The Intermountain Shriners Hospital for Children provides no-cost care and services for children with disorders of the bones, muscles and joints.

■ Recreation

Sightseeing

Downtown Salt Lake City boasts a number of popular attractions. The State Capitol with its spectacular copper-clad dome is located on Capitol Hill, which offers a view of the city and surrounding area. At Temple Square, the headquarters of the Mormon Church, the Salt Lake Temple displays six spires, 15-foot-thick granite walls, and a golden statue of the Angel Moroni. Also on the square are the famous Mormon Tabernacle, built in 1867 with no interior supports, and the Seagull Monument, honoring the birds that saved the settlers' first crops.

Other sights in the city include Beehive House, the restored residence of Brigham Young, who gave it the name because he wanted his followers to be as industrious as bees. Fort Douglas, a 9,000-acre historical fort, is filled with interesting military architecture dating from 1862. Utah's Hogle Zoo contains a collection of exotic birds and animals in a natural setting, including an elephant habitat and an Asian Highlands exhibit. This Is The Place Heritage Park contains an operational pioneer community as it was in 1847, as well as the "This Is The Place" Monument, marking the spot where Brigham Young chose the area as a home for the Mormons.

The Great Salt Lake, over 90 miles long and 48 miles wide, is the second saltiest body of water in the world. The high salinity makes it a unique swimming experience: it is almost impossible for a person to sink in the water. A different type of aquatic entertainment is found at Raging Waters, a family-oriented theme park with more than 30 water rides and a picnic area. Clark Planetarium presents daily star shows and images from the Hubble Telescope. Olympic Cauldron Park is a stunning addition to the city, featuring the 72-foot Olympic Cauldron, which housed the Olympic Flame; the Hoberman Arch, where athletes stood to receive their medals; a visitor center; and a theatre dedicated to the memory of the 2002 Olympic Winter Games.

Arts and Culture

Salt Lake City is home to a number of acclaimed cultural organizations. The world-famous Mormon Tabernacle Choir, an American institution for many years, is based in Salt Lake City. The Utah Symphony performs over 260 concerts nationally and internationally each year; the orchestra performs locally in Maurice Abravanel Hall, a world-class acoustic space. The historic Capitol Theatre is home to the Utah Opera and Ballet West, one of the nation's leading companies. The Rose Wagner Performing Arts Center includes an art gallery and several performance spaces for new and established artists.

Theatrical performances are scheduled at Desert Star Playhouse, featuring live musical comedy melodrama, honky-tonk piano, and audience participation; Hale Centre Theatre, offering comedies and musicals for the whole family to enjoy; Off Broadway Theatre, staging comedy and improvisation; Promised Valley Playhouse, presenting theater in a restored turn-of-the-century showplace; and Salt Lake Community College Grand Theatre, featuring Broadway musicals.

Several interesting museums are located in Salt Lake City. The Daughters of Utah Pioneers Museum houses a collection of dolls, textiles, and frontier furniture in a replica of the famous Salt Palace. Located in a restored nineteenth century railroad station, the Utah Historical Society features exhibits on the history of Utah's various ethnic groups. The Fort Douglas Military Museum inside the restored fort displays items relating to the military history of the state. Hill Air Force Base Aerospace Museum maintains a collection of military aircraft, missiles, vehicles and uniforms. The Natural History Museum of Utah contains a large collection of dinosaur skeletons excavated from many local sites, as well as exhibits on animals and minerals of the region.

The Utah Museum of Contemporary Art (formerly the Salt Lake Art Center) houses traveling art exhibits from around the world as well as a permanent collection and a sculpture garden. On the campus of the University of Utah, the Utah Museum of Fine Arts contains paintings by artists such as Rubens, antique tapestries, and Louis XIV furniture. The Church History Museum chronicles the early development of the Church of Jesus Christ of Latter-day Saints. The Chase Home Museum of Utah Folk Arts is dedicated to the work of Utah's ethnic, native, and rural artists.

Festivals and Holidays

The Utah Arts Festival, the nation's first statewide arts festival, takes place in June and provides exciting performances and visual art, crafts, and ethnic foods. June is also the time for the prestigious Gina Bachauer International Piano Foundation Festival and Competition. Days of '47 features parades, pageants, and a rodeo to celebrate the city's founding pioneers. September is a busy month in Salt Lake City, with the Salt Lake City International Jazz Festival and the Utah State Fair, which features midway rides, livestock and art exhibits, and special entertainment nightly. The Christmas season begins the day after Thanksgiving, when more than 300,000 lights are turned on in Temple Square. The Sundance Film Festival takes place in the Salt Lake area every January. The Madeleine Festival takes place at the Cathedral of the Madeleine each spring, offering free cultural performances to the community. The annual Great Salt Lake Bird Festival takes place in May, as well as Living Traditions, a three-day festival honoring folk artists of the Salt Lake Valley.

Sports for the Spectator

Salt Lake City is home to the Utah Jazz of the National Basketball Association, who play at the state-of-the-art EnergySolutions Arena. Salt Lake City is also host to Major League Soccer's Real Salt Lake. The Salt Lake Bees, a Triple-A affiliate of the Anaheim Angels, play baseball at Spring Mobile Ballpark from April through mid-September. Hockey is represented by the Utah Grizzlies, members of the ECHL. The University of Utah fields competitive teams in most major collegiate sports, and a number of events on the national rodeo circuit occur in Salt Lake City. The nearby Bonneville Salt Flats is the site of numerous auto races and frequent attempts to set the land speed record.

Sports for the Participant

The Salt Lake City area offers an abundance of outdoor activities. The nearby mountains provide year-round recreation: hiking, fishing, camping, and winter skiing. Some of the nation's most popular ski resorts such as Snowbird, Park City, Deer Valley, Sundance, Alta, and Solitude are within a 40-minute drive of the city. Non-traditional sports such as ski-jumping and luge are offered at facilities constructed for the 2002 Olympic Winter Games. The area's rivers offer white-water rafting, canoeing, and inner-tubing. Many area lakes are ideal spots for all forms of water activity-boating, sailing, water skiing, and swimming.

Gallivan Center, a four-acre public plaza in downtown Salt Lake, has a skating rink. Salt Lake City operates a number of parks that feature swimming pools, jogging trails, playing fields, tennis courts, and other recreational facilities. Several championship golf courses are located in the city as well.

Shopping and Dining

America's first department store, the Zions Cooperative Mercantile Institution, opened in Salt Lake City in 1868. A number of major shopping centers are located in the city, including Trolley Square, a theme mall located in a group of restored trolley barns. The Gateway, Salt Lake's first open-air entertainment, dining, and shopping venue, was completed in 2001. Set on 30 acres, it features 90 shops and restaurants, a restored 1908 Union Pacific Depot, and the Olympic Legacy Plaza. City Creek Center, a $1.5 billion mixed-use development with 700,000 square feet of retail space, opened in 2012. Many small shops and boutiques are scattered throughout the metropolitan area.

Because of its diverse ethnic population, Salt Lake City features a variety of international restaurants; many are prominent nationally. Everything from inexpensive fast food to elegant, intimate dining can be found in the more than 300 restaurants located in the valley.

Visitor Information: Salt Lake City Convention & Visitors Bureau, 90 South West Temple, Salt Lake City, Utah 84101; telephone (801) 534-4900; toll-free (800) 541-4955.

■ Convention Facilities

The Salt Palace Convention Center, located in the center of the downtown district, is the city's major convention facility. After an extensive renovation completed in 2006, the Palace features 515,000 square feet of continuous exhibition space, catering services, and a business center. The largest ballroom has 45,000 square feet of space; an additional 119,000 square feet of meeting space is available. The South Towne Exposition Center as 243,000 square feet of exhibit space and another 15,000 square feet of meeting space.

There are nearly 7,000 hotel rooms throughout the city, with some 17,300 available county wide. Several major hotels also contain extensive meeting, banquet, and ballroom accommodations. The EnergySolutions Arena offers meeting rooms ranging in size from 400 to 10,000 square feet.

Convention Information: Salt Lake City Convention & Visitors Bureau, 90 South West Temple, Salt Lake City, Utah 84101; telephone (801) 534-4900; toll-free (800) 541-4955.

■ Transportation

Approaching the City

The Salt Lake International Airport offers over 645 daily flights on nine airlines and is located just minutes from downtown Salt Lake City. In 2012 the airport served 20 million customers as the 26th busiest airport in the United States. The Utah Transit Authority provides transportation to and from the airport; taxis are available, and many area hotels provide complimentary shuttle service.

Salt Lake City is at the junction of two major interstate highways, Interstate 15 running north–south and Interstate 80 running east–west. Interstate 215 forms a commuter loop and bypass around the inner city.

Amtrak provides national passenger rail service from Salt Lake City's Gateway area. The TRAX light rail system serves Salt Lake County.

Traveling in the City

Walking is perhaps the best way to see the city's sights. Salt Lake City was laid out in a grid pattern with exceptionally wide streets by the early Mormon pioneers, which makes automobile travel easy and pleasurable compared to most larger metropolitan areas. Streets are named according to their distance and relationship to Temple Square. Salt Lake City recently implemented an intelligent CommuterLink system to decrease traffic congestion.

The Utah Transit Authority (UTA) operates 146 light rail vehicles, 63 commuter rail cars and more than 600 buses. UTA has a 1,600-mile service area across six counties serving 1.8 million passengers annually. UTA also provides service to ski resorts in winter and door-to-door transportation for the disabled.

■ Communications

Newspapers and Magazines

Salt Lake City is served by two major daily newspapers, *The Salt Lake Tribune* and *Deseret News.* The Latter-Day Saints publish three titles: *Church News,* a weekly newspaper; *The Friend,* a magazine for children aged 3 to 11; and *New Era,* a magazine for teens. Other magazines published in the city include *Salt Lake Magazine* and several scholarly, medical, and industry magazines.

Television and Radio

Salt Lake City's 14 television stations represent the commercial networks and independent and instructional channels. The city is also served by a variety of cable channels. Six AM and 22 FM radio stations broadcast from Salt Lake City, providing a wide range of music, news, and informational programming.

Media Information: The Salt Lake Tribune, 143 S. Main Street, Salt Lake City, UT 84111; telephone (801) 257-8742. *Deseret News,* 55 North 300 West, Salt Lake City, UT 84101; telephone (801) 204-6100.

Salt Lake City Online

City of Salt Lake City home page. Available www.ci. slc.ut.us

Deseret News. Available www.deseretnews.com

Salt Lake City Public Library. Available www.slcpl. org

Salt Lake City Public Schools. Available www. slcschools.org

Salt Lake Convention and Visitors Bureau. Available www.visitsaltlake.com

The Salt Lake Tribune. Available www.sltrib.com

BIBLIOGRAPHY

Balaz, Christine, *Salt Lake City, Park City, Provo, and Utah's High Country Resorts,* 2nd ed. (Countryman Press, 2010)

Bradley, Martha Sonntag, *Salt Lake City Yesterday & Today* (Lincolnwood, IL: Publications International, Ltd., 2010)

Miller, Marjorie, *Salt Lake City: Jewel of the Wasatch* (Yellow Cat Flats, UT Yellow Cat Publishing, 2000)

Naifeh, Steven W., *The Mormon Murders: A True Story of Greed, Deceit, and Death* (New York: Weidenfeld and Nicolson, 1988)

Washington

The State in Brief

Nickname: Evergreen State

Motto: Al-Ki (By and by)

Flower: Coast rhododendron

Bird: Willow goldfinch

Area: 71,298 square miles (2010; U.S. rank 18th)

Elevation: Ranges from sea level to 14,410 feet above sea level

Climate: Generally mild and humid in the western region dominated by the Pacific Ocean; semi arid in the eastern region; heavy snows in higher elevation

Admitted to Union: November 11, 1889

Capital: Olympia

Head Official: Jay Inslee (D) (until 2017)

Population

1990: 4,866,692
2000: 5,894,121
2010: 6,724,540
2012 estimate: 6,738,714
Percent change, 2000–2010: 14.1%
U.S. rank in 2012: 13th
Percent of residents born in state: 47.1% (2012)
Density: 101.2 people per square mile (2010)
2012 FBI Crime Index Total: 272,719

Racial and Ethnic Characteristics (2012)

White: 5,304,864
Black or African American: 238,255
American Indian and Alaska Native: 93,416
Asian: 484,047
Native Hawaiian and Pacific Islander: 39,246
Hispanic or Latino (may be of any race): 754,366
Other: 578,886

Age Characteristics (2012)

Population under 5 years old: 437,979
Population 5 to 19 years old: 1,323,095
Percent of population 65 years and over: 12.4%
Median age: 37.2

Vital Statistics

Total number of births (2012–13): 87,554
Total number of deaths (2012–13): 51,052
AIDS cases reported through 2011: 13,796

Economy

Major industries: Trade; manufacturing; finance, insurance, and real estate; government; services; agriculture; technology
Unemployment rate (2012): 5.8%
Per capita income (2012): $30,661
Median household income (2012): $59,374
Percentage of persons below poverty level (2012): 12.9%
Income tax rate: None
Sales tax rate: 6.5%

Bellingham

■ The City in Brief

Founded: as Whatcom (1852); renamed Bellingham (1903)

Head Official: Mayor Kelli Linville (since 2012; current term expires 2016)

City Population
> 1990: 52,179
> 2000: 67,171
> 2010: 80,885
> 2012 estimate: 82,234
> Percent change, 2000–2010: 20.4%
> U.S. rank in 1990: 477th (State rank: 9th)
> U.S. rank in 2000: 461st (State rank: 10th)
> U.S. rank in 2010: 382nd (State rank: 12th)

Metropolitan Statistical Area Population
> 2000: 166,814
> 2010: 201,140
> 2012 estimate: 205,262
> Percent change, 2000–2010: 20.6%
> U.S. rank in 2000: 222nd
> U.S. rank in 2010: 210th

Area: 31.74 square miles

Elevation: 68 feet above sea level

Average Annual Temperatures: 51.5° F

Average Annual Precipitation: 58 inches

Major Economic Sectors: trade, services, government

Unemployment Rate: 6.7% (2012)

Per Capita Income: $24,114

2012 FBI Crime Index Property: 3,975

Major Colleges and Universities: Western Washington University, Whatcom Community College, Northwest Indian College

Daily Newspaper: *The Bellingham Herald*

■ Introduction

Bellingham, a coastal city built around the deep-water harbor of Bellingham Bay, is set against the backdrop of the Cascade Mountains. Bellingham is the last major city before the coast of Washington state meets the border of Canada. It was named in honor of Sir William Bellingham, who was director of stores for the British Admiralty. The renovated old, historic buildings, views of the water and the mountains, and gorgeous sunsets make for a picture-postcard setting. The city's economy depends in large part on its manufacturing and distribution network, as well as the tourists—from both sides of the border—that come to enjoy the city's charm and outdoor activities.

■ Geography and Climate

Bellingham is the seat of Whatcom County, the most northwestern county in the United States. The city is located 90 miles north of Seattle, 50 miles south of Vancouver, British Columbia, and 20 miles from the Canadian border at Baline. Bellingham, situated at the foot of 10,788-foot Mount Baker, is set on several hills overlooking the 172 San Juan Islands.

Bellingham has a mild, maritime climate with temperatures ranging from 45 to 60 degrees in spring and fall, 30 to 50 degrees in winter, and 60 to 80 degrees in summer. Most days have at least partial sunshine and snow; sleet and hail occur only about 15 days per year.

Area: 31.74 square miles

© US Coast Guard Photo/Alamy

Elevation: 68 feet above sea level

Average Temperatures: 51.5° F

Average Annual Precipitation: 58 inches

■ History

European Contact with Natives Minimal at First

Long before the coming of Europeans, ancestors of local Bellingham tribes-the Lummi, the Nooksack, and the Semiahmoo-established camps along the bay as part of the great migration over the land bridge that once extended from Asia to North America. Salmon from the surrounding waters was their dietary mainstay, supplemented by roots, berries, and shellfish. The tribes engaged in both warfare and trade at various times. Some historians contend that Spanish explorers were the first white men to visit the area; if so, little evidence of them remains. The Lummi and Semiahmoo still live in the area and salmon remains their chief source of sustenance.

British Captain George Vancouver weighed anchor in nearby Birch Bay during his explorations of the Puget Sound in 1792, and Lt. Joseph Widbey charted Vancouver Bay. Widbey and his men may have seen a community of more than 3,000 natives living near the bay. Vancouver is said to have named the site of present-day Bellingham after the British admiralty controller who outfitted his ships.

As a result of reports carried back to Europe about the bounty of the region, traders began to arrive and a fur industry burgeoned in the early 1800s. From 1825 to 1846 the Hudson's Bay Company held domain over the region, but in the latter year the United States and Great Britain established a boundary at the 49th Parallel, and the Hudson's Bay Company relocated to Vancouver.

Industries Emerge; A Rush for Gold

In 1852, assisted by Lummi tribesmen, Henry Roeder built a sawmill on what is now Whatcom Creek. This initiated a period of coal mining and milling that continued for many decades. Whatcom County was established in 1854. Although the area of Bellingham remained untouched during the Indian War of 1855-1856, an infantry group was sent to Bellingham Bay in 1856 to establish Fort Bellingham.

More than 10,000 people were drawn to Bellingham during the Fraser River Gold Rush of 1858. A tent city mushroomed until would-be prospectors were advised by Canadian officials that before starting their digging, they had to report to Victoria, British Columbia. Eventually, fire and fatalities brought difficult times to the mining industry, and Roeder's mill site was sold to a company from Kansas City. Soon after, a boom was initiated by the building of a railroad that connected Bellingham to the trans-Canada railroad line. Other major segments of the economy at that time were farming, fishing, and canning. In the late 1880s the town of Fairhaven, now part of Bellingham, was promoted as the "next Chicago" by entrepreneur Nelson Bennett, and hundreds of workers were hired to build hotels, homes, and office buildings. People began arriving at the rate of 300 per month, among them gamblers and prostitutes. A vigilante group tried to keep the peace until a police force was finally formed in 1890. In 1902 a brewery was founded in Bellingham that at its height produced more than 100,000 barrels of beer annually. However, the Bellingham Bay Brewery disappeared forever with the beginning of prohibition in 1917.

Bellingham was formed in 1903 with the consolidation of four towns-Whatcom, New Whatcom, Fairhaven, and Bellingham-into one town with the name Bellingham. During the late 1800s tall ships could be seen loading coal, salmon, and timber for transport to cities around the globe. Prosperous businessmen began building impressive homes in the Sehome Hill section of the city, many of which are now used for student housing. The Whatcom Normal School opened in 1899, later to become Western Washington College of Education in 1937, Western Washington Sate College in 1961, and finally Western Washington University within the following decade.

Bellingham in the New Millennium

In June 1999 a fuel pipeline exploded along Whatcom Creek, killing three people along with thousands of fish and other wildlife. The tragedy resulted in major changes to federal pipeline laws and the creation of a Washington State Office of Pipeline Safety.

During the 2000s, the city made protection of Lake Whatcom a high priority. The Lake Whatcom Reservoir is the source of drinking water for about 95,000 people in Whatcom County, including the 82,000 served in Bellingham. The health of the reservoir has declined, as algae growth is requiring more expensive treatment to keep the water safe. Steps to be taken to protect the lake include protecting more undeveloped land in the watershed, improving stormwater treatment, and helping watershed residents become better stewards of the lake.

Plans to clean up and develop Bellingham's waterfront continued into 2014. The waterfront is home to the 137-acre site of Georgia Pacific's former pulp and chemical plant and tissue mill. Efforts to redevelop the site remain preliminary, although lots were first sold to private developers in 2013.

Historical Information: Center for Pacific Northwest Studies, Goltz-Murray Archives Building, Western Washington University, 808 25th St., Bellingham, WA 98225-9123; telephone (360) 650-7747; fax (360) 650-3323; email cpnws@wwu.edu.

■ Population Profile

Metropolitan Statistical Area Population
2000: 166,814
2010: 201,140
2012 estimate: 205,262
Percent change, 2000–2010: 20.6%
U.S. rank in 2000: 222nd
U.S. rank in 2010: 210th

City Residents
1990: 52,179
2000: 67,171
2010: 80,885
2012 estimate: 82,234
Percent change, 2000–2010: 20.4%
U.S. rank in 1990: 477th (State rank: 9th)
U.S. rank in 2000: 461st (State rank: 10th)
U.S. rank in 2010: 382nd (State rank: 12th)

Density: 2,987.0 people per square mile

Racial and ethnic characteristics
White: 71,526
Black or African American: 669
American Indian and Alaskan Native: 1,879
Asian: 3,422
Native Hawaiian and Other Pacific Islander: 109
Hispanic or Latino (may be of any race): 5,954
Other: 4,629

Percent of residents born in state: 47.6%

Age characteristics
Population under 5 years old: 3,400
Population 5 to 9 years old: 3,672
Population 10 to 14 years old: 3,723
Population 15 to 19 years old: 6,682
Population 20 to 24 years old: 11,939
Population 25 to 34 years old: 12,201
Population 35 to 44 years old: 8,648
Population 45 to 54 years old: 7,786
Population 55 to 59 years old: 5,178
Population 60 to 64 years old: 6,045
Population 65 to 74 years old: 6,832
Population 75 to 84 years old: 4,072
Population 85 years and over: 2,056
Median age: 34.6

Births (2010–11 Metropolitan Area)
Total number: 2,270

Deaths (2010–11 Metropolitan Area)

Total number: 1,366

Money income (2012)

Per capita income: $24,114
Median household income: $41,594
Total households: 33,873

Number of households with income of ...

less than $10,000: 3,890
$10,000 to $14,999: 2,548
$15,000 to $24,999: 3,818
$25,000 to $34,999: 4,321
$35,000 to $49,999: 4,415
$50,000 to $74,999: 6,126
$75,000 to $99,999: 4,141
$100,000 to $149,999: 3,085
$150,000 to $199,999: 850
$200,000 or more: 679

Percent of families below poverty level: 22.7%

FBI Crime Index Property: 3,975

FBI Crime Index Violent: 220

■ Municipal Government

Bellingham has a mayor-council form of government. Six council members serve four-year terms and a seventh council member serves a two-year term as a council person-at-large. The mayor serves a four-year term.

Head Official: Mayor Kelli Linville (since 2012; current term expires 2016)

Total Number of City Employees: 807 (2012)

City Information: City Hall, 210 Lottie Street, Bellingham, WA 98225; telephone (360) 778-8000; fax (360) 778-8001; email info@cob.org.

■ Economy

Major Industries and Commercial Activity

The economies of both Bellingham and Whatcom County have moved away from their traditional roots in agriculture, fishing, and timber to rely more heavily on government, retail trade, health care, and manufacturing.

In 2001 the area economy was negatively impacted by Georgia-Pacific Corporation's closure of a pulp and paper mill, resulting in the loss of 420 high-paying jobs, and Alcoa's Intalco Works shuttering of an aluminum plant. Heightened border security following terrorist attacks in the United States that same year also curtailed the number of Canadian visitors that spent their retail and entertainment dollars in Whatcom County.

Nonetheless, manufacturing remains an important industry in Whatcom County, as does tourism. Boatbuilding is a crucial segment of the transportation equipment sector, as its focus has shifted from fishing vessels to the production of luxury yachts and military boats. Tourism's economic impact amounts to more than $430 million annually, which in turn generates $7 million in city and county tax revenue.

Whatcom County's government sector, which includes public school educators such as Western Washington University as well as tribal governments, is the largest in both percentage of employment and wages in the county. Another major employer, St. Joseph Hospital, supports 2,753 area jobs.

Items and goods produced: boats, lumber and wood products, tissue paper, refined oil and petroleum products, blueberries, strawberries, raspberries, seed potatoes, apples, processed frozen foods, baked goods

Incentive Programs—New and Existing Companies

Local programs: The non-profit Northwest Economic Council, which operates throughout Whatcom County, promotes local businesses, products, and services, and helps firms in interfacing with regional, national, and international markets. It assists businesses by providing information on expansion and investment decisions, and by providing liaison with government officials and community leaders. The local Small Business Development Center (SBDC), a combined effort of Western Washington University, the City of Bellingham, and the Bellingham/Whatcom Chamber of Commerce and Industry, offers businesses free consulting services adapted to the needs of each particular business. The city of Bellingham incentivizes development with expedited building permit review, technical assistance, urban village traffic impact fee reductions, water conservation and low-impact development support, and assistance for development efforts to refurbish historic buildings.

State programs: The state of Washington offers a number of incentive programs to attract new and expanding businesses to the state, with most targeted to specific industries or geographic areas. Industry-specific incentives include sales and use tax exemptions for general manufacturing and agriculture; sales and use tax deferrals and waivers, and business and occupation tax credits for high-technology industries, including biotechnology and medical device manufacturing; business and occupation tax rate reductions and credits for the aerospace, timber, food manufacturing, biofuel, semiconductor, and aluminum industries; and a range of credits and exemptions for renewable energy firms.

Geography-based incentives are available in designated Community Empowerment Zones, high unemployment counties, and Main Street areas. Other incentives support economic activity that reduces commuter travel; produces television or film; or relates to newspaper publishing.

Job training programs: Job training programs offered by the state of Washington include the Washington Customized Employment Training Program, which offers a business and occupation tax credit to qualifying companies for job-training expenses. The WorkSource partnership is a collaboration among local, state, and federal agencies to recruit, screen, test, and refer potential employees.

Training programs for a variety of industries, including health care and manufacturing, are offered by such institutions of higher learning as Bellingham Technical College, Northwest Indian College, Western Washington University, and Whatcom Community College.

Development Projects

A major expansion at the Bellingham International Airport began in 2010, with an expected completion of 2014. The $26 million project was to nearly triple the size of the 30,000-square-foot airport terminal. Phase I of the project, completed in 2011, doubled the seating capacity within the airport's pre-boarding lobby area and strengthened the airport runway. Phase II began in 2012 and was set to expand the main passenger terminal, specifically ticketing area, baggage claim, baggage make up, and the Transportation Security Administration screening checkpoint.

Plans to develop Bellingham's waterfront also were still in early planning stages as of 2013, although the sale of lots to private developers began that year. The waterfront is home to the site of Georgia Pacific's former pulp and chemical plant and tissue mill. The Port of Bellingham is working to clean up and develop 237 acres of property along the waterfront that has been contaminated by mercury. The tentative master plan, a combined effort of the Port and the city of Bellingham, is predicted to be a decades-long project and include new public parks and trails as well as mixed use residential, corporate, and educational facilities, with a goal of transforming the land into a thriving part of the Bellingham community. Western Washington University planned to expand the school to the waterfront as well.

Elsewhere in Bellingham, Bellwether on the Bay is a mixed-use complex occupying 15 acres of waterfront property. Phase I completed in 2007 and included two office buildings, the four-star Hotel Bellwether, a fitness center and spa, and a variety of restaurants and shops. Construction of a third office building occurred in 2012, with a fourth and final building in 2013.

A $3.2 million improvement project to the Bakerview interchange at Interstate 5 in Bellingham was largely completed in 2013. The project represented a public-private partnership among several local and state organizations, as improvements were expected to support local commerce in the heavily trafficked area.

Economic Development Information: Bellingham/Whatcom Chamber of Commerce & Industry, 119 N. Commercial Street | Suite 110, Bellingham, WA 98225; telephone (360) 734-1330. Whatcom Council of Governments, 314 E. Champion Street, Bellingham, WA 98225; telephone (360) 676-6974; email wcog@wcog.org.

Commercial Shipping

Whatcom County has four major locations for U.S.-Canada border crossings: two in Blaine, one in Lynden, and one in Sumas. Freight rail service is offered in Bellingham by the Burlington Northern Santa Fe, Canadian Rail, and Canadian Pacific railroads. Among its motor freight companies are Puget Sound Truck Lines, Roadway Express, Yellow Transportation, LTI Inc., AES Transportation, JIT Transport, Oak Harbor Freight Lines, and Peninsula Truck Lines. The area is also home to freight brokers.

Bellingham International Airport (BIA) serves as a base for charter airlines and is a port of entry for general aviation aircraft. The airport is home to Foreign Trade Zone #129, an area where foreign goods bound for international destinations can be temporarily stored without incurring an import duty. BIA also offers customs brokerage and air cargo services, and houses a U.S. Customs office.

The Port of Bellingham, a municipal corporation dedicated to fulfilling the essential transportation needs of the region, operates a cargo terminal with three ship berths, backed up by two warehouses. The port administers five federally designated foreign trade zones to promote manufacturing, warehousing, and trade in the region.

Labor Force and Employment Outlook

Bellingham's workforce is highly educated. Some 31.9 percent of residents held at least a bachelor's degree, above both state and national averages. Washington is a "right to work" state. Unions are primarily active in the public sector, health care, and construction trades. Whatcom County employers are mostly small business operations and experience little union activity. Most Whatcom County businesses are non-union shops.

Unemployment in Whatcom County, a product of a national recession during the late 2000s, peaked in February 2010 at 10.5 percent before gradually declining in 2012 and 2013. Manufacturing employment returned to 2008 levels during 2012.

The following is a summary of data regarding the 2012 Bellingham labor force:

Size of civilian labor force: 45,406

Number of workers employed in . . .

agriculture and mining: 628
construction: 1,509
manufacturing: 3,283
wholesale trade: 1,096
retail trade: 6,189
transportation: 1,397
information systems: 790
finance: 2,246
professional administration: 3,747
education and social services: 11,485
arts and leisure: 4,449
other: 1,547
public administration: 1,930

Average hourly earnings of production workers:
$18.45

Unemployment rate: 6.7% (2012)

Employers

Largest employers (2012)	Number of employees
St. Joseph Hospital / Madrona Medical Group	2,753
Western Washington University	1,575
Bellingham School District	1,200
Health Techna Inc.	850
City of Bellingham	807
Whatcom County	805
Haggen Inc.	787
Fred Meyer	660
Aramark Food Services (formerly Sodexho)	620
The Market's LLC (formerly Brown & Cole)	522

Cost of Living

Bellingham's average home sales price in 2013 was $387,844. The cost of doing business in Bellingham is far lower than Seattle and many of its adjacent counties.

The following is a summary of data regarding several key cost of living factors in the area.

2013 ACCRA Average House Price: $387,844

2013 ACCRA Cost of Living Index: 109

State income tax rate: None

State sales tax rate: 6.5%

Local income tax rate: None

Local sales tax rate: 2.2%

Property tax rate: $10.91 per $1,000 of assessed value (2013)

Economic Information: Bellingham/Whatcom Chamber of Commerce & Industry, 119 N. Commercial Street | Suite 110, Bellingham, WA 98225; telephone (360) 734-1330.

■ Education and Research

Elementary and Secondary Schools

Bellingham Public Schools has 23 total facilities and employs 1,300 staff members. The district offers special programs for disabled students, those with learning disabilities, and exceptionally capable students. The schools have computers and related technology in every classroom. An early childhood preschool program and Head Start classes are offered, as is the GRADS teen parent program.

In 2010 the Bellingham School board adopted a unique approach to handling the policies in the district by establishing a policy governance model, which focuses on results and holds the superintendent accountable for monitoring the results through the use of data, reports, and focused discussions.

Bellingham has 15 private schools, including both religious and independent schools ranging from pre-kindergarten through 12th grade.

The following is a summary of data regarding the Bellingham School District.

Total enrollment: 10,936

Number of facilities

total: 23
elementary schools: 15
junior high schools: 4
high schools: 3
other: 1

Student/teacher ratio: 20.2:1

Teacher salaries

average (statewide): $53,796

Funding per pupil: $9,477

Public Schools Information: Bellingham Public Schools, 1306 Dupont St., Bellingham, WA 98225-3118; telephone (360) 676-6400; fax (360) 676-2793.

Colleges and Universities

Western Washington University, with nearly 15,000 students, overlooks the city on Sehome Hill. Founded in 1893, the school became a regional university in 1977.

College programs number more than 160, including business and economics, fine and performing arts, humanities and social sciences, science and technology, the Huxley College of the Environment, the Woodring College of Education, and Fairhaven College, an interdisciplinary liberal arts college. Western Washington University's graduate school offers master's degrees in art, business administration, accounting, education, music, science, and teaching. In 2013–14 the school was ranked 22nd among regional universities in the West by *U.S. News & World Report.*

Nearly 7,000 students are enrolled quarterly in Whatcom Community College, which offers a variety of two-year programs in areas such as business, finance, accounting, social sciences, humanities, sciences and environmental sciences, nursing, and engineering and engineering technology. The college employs 72 full-time faculty and 212 part-time faculty.

Accredited as a four-year institution in 2010, Northwest Indian College offers its more than 1,400 students associate degrees in unique fields such as Native Environmental Science and Native Oksale Education, and bachelor's degrees in Native Studies Leadership and Tribal Governance. Degree and certificate programs in more than 50 fields, from culinary arts to radiologic technology, are offered at Bellingham Technical College. Washington State University, based in Pullman, has a Whatcom County Extension that offers non-credit education and degree programs in the fields of gardening and agriculture, family living, and environment and natural resources.

Libraries and Research Centers

The Bellingham Public Library's main building was built in 1949 and was remodeled and expanded in 1985. Its Fairhaven branch occupies an original 1912 Carnegie building on the south side of the city. In addition to the Fairhaven Branch and Central Library, the public library system has another full-service Branch, the Barkley Branch, as well as three connection libraries and community drop boxes. The library system circulates 1.6 million items annually, from original manuscripts to CDs, videos, books on tape, and nearly 10,000 e-books. Its collection totals nearly 237,000 items. The library offers free Internet access to patrons, quality programs for children, reference services for adults, and an online local newspaper index and catalogue, as well as a complete database of community resources. The library has a special collection on local history and is a U.S. and state documents depository.

Bellingham's colleges and universities maintain a number of libraries, many of which are open to the public. Western Washington University has a number of research institutes and libraries, including those focusing on such areas as Canadian-American studies, Pacific Northwest studies, demographics, watershed studies,

economic education and research, environmental toxicology, and vehicle research. Its special collections include the Ford Fly Fishing Collection, Northwest Collection, Rare Books Collection, and the Western Collection. The Whatcom County Law Library houses more than 15,000 books and CDs covering Washington laws and practice guides, federal laws, U.S. Supreme Court reports, and regional case law, as well as legal reference materials. Bellingham Technical College maintains an Information Technology Resource Center.

Public Library Information: Bellingham Public Library, 210 Central Ave., CS-9710, Bellingham, WA 98227; telephone (360) 778-7323.

■ Health Care

Bellingham residents are served by PeaceHealth St. Joseph Medical Center, which has 253 beds across two campuses. The hospital has 253 beds, a medical surgical intensive care unit, a trauma center, and emergency, obstetrics, and oncology departments. Services offered include open-heart surgery, outpatient surgery, psychiatric and addiction care for children and adults, and geriatric services. St. Joseph's Cardiovascular Center was ranked the top center for cardiac surgery in the state in 2013 by Healthgrades.

The Interfaith Community Health Center provides primary care and preventative medical, dental, behavioral health, and pharmacy services to adults and children in the area.

■ Recreation

Sightseeing

Bellingham's museums are devoted to an array of topics. The Whatcom Museum of History & Art, located in downtown Bellingham, is comprised of three buildings, each with its own theme: the 1892 Old City Hall, Syre Education Center, and the Lightcatcher. The SPARK Museum of Electrical Invention is the only one of its kind in North America. This museum, which completed an expansion in 2001, houses artifacts and interactive exhibits in 11 galleries, spanning a period of nearly 400 years, from the onset of the scientific exploration of electricity in the seventeenth century to the evolution of broadcast radio and its impact on American culture. The Bellingham Railway Museum chronicles the heritage and operation of railroads in Whatcom and Skagit counties. Mindport Exhibits is a collection of interactive and fine arts exhibits designed to encourage exploration, discovery, and thought. Nearby, the Lynden Pioneer Museum focuses on the heritage of Whatcom County prior to World War II, with exhibits covering Front Street, agriculture, rural Victorian lifestyles, transportation, natural resources, veterans, and the military.

The International Peace Arch, located about 20 miles north of Bellingham, is one of the world's few landmarks to be listed on the national historic registries of two countries. The 67-foot-tall arch has one foot in Canada and the other in the United States, and represents the longest undefended boundary—3,000 miles—in the world. It commemorates the signing of the Treaty of the Ghent, which ended the war between Britain and the United States. A number of celebrations take place there each year. From May to September, a sculpture exhibition of both Canadian and American artists includes festivities each weekend. The Peace Arch Celebration, also known as Hands Across the Border, is held in June. September brings the annual Peace Arch Dedication Days, or "Sam Hill Days," that reenact the anniversary of the arch.

Arts and Culture

The Mt. Baker Theatre has been offering theatrical entertainment since 1927. The Moorish-Spanish style former vaudeville movie palace, which is on the National Historic Register, seats 1,500 people. The theater boasts a 100-foot Moorish tower, open-beamed lobby, 80-foot interior dome, an original 215-pipe organ, state-of-the-art staging capabilities, and, some speculate, a resident ghost. The theater hosts more than 100 live events annually, including touring Broadway shows. The Studio Theatre, a 2004 addition to the Mt. Baker Theatre, stages performances in an intimate setting. Mt. Baker Theatre is also the site for performances by the Whatcom Symphony Orchestra, Mt. Baker Youth Symphony, and Mt. Baker Organ Society.

The oldest community theater company in the Northwest, the Bellingham Theatre Guild, presents a year-round venue of comedies, dramas, and musicals. Western Washington University offers a wide range of performances, including its summer stock season, a theatre arts series of dramas and comedies, and a performing arts series featuring world-renowned musicians and dance companies. Other theaters include the iDiOM Theater and the Upfront Theatre.

Bellingham is also home to a number of art galleries, including Artwood (a gallery of fine woodworking), Barbo Furniture, and the Chuckanut Bay Gallery and Sculpture Garden, just to name a few. The first two weekends in October are dedicated to the Whatcom Artist Free Studio Tour where some 50 Whatcom artists open their studio doors for two weekend's worth of tours. The Free Studio Tour was in its 20th year as of 2014.

Festivals and Holidays

The highlight of Memorial Day weekend is Bellingham's annual Sea to Ski Race, an athletic contest dating from the 1800s that is accompanied by parades, carnivals, art and garden shows, house tours, and street fairs. The race saw its 100th anniversary in 2011. The Bellingham Scottish Highland Games take place in early June. July brings the Northwest Raspberry Festival at the Bellingham Farmers Market. The Mount Baker Blues Festival, also in July, has been voted the best blues event in the state. The Bellingham Festival of Music that same month features classical, chamber, jazz, and world music. Families flock to downtown's Chalk ArtFest in August.

For hundreds if not thousands of years, Native Americans in the Pacific Northwest have held ceremonies in honor of the salmon each fall. Also in autumn is the Eldridge Area Historical Home Tour. In December the Holiday Port Festival and Holiday Festival of the Arts are held.

Sports for the Spectator

The Bellingham Bells, with a season that runs from June through August, are a part of the West Coast Collegiate Baseball League. The Bellingham Slam, the city's professional basketball team, plays at the Whatcom Pavilion. The Western Washington University Vikings compete in cross country, football, softball, track and field, volleyball, rowing, golf, soccer and basketball. Students of Whatcom Community College participate in men's and women's basketball and soccer, and women's volleyball. Bellingham has a roller derby team, the Bellingham Roller Betties, which play at the Bellingham Sportsplex.

Sports for the Participant

The city has an extensive network of hiking and biking trails, swimming pools and beaches, picnic grounds, fishing sites, softball and soccer fields, and beautiful gardens. At 10,788 feet, Mt. Baker is the highest peak in the North Cascade mountain range. It not only offers some spectacular views, it has the longest ski season in the state, with runs that curve below Mt. Shuksan. The Mt. Baker Ski Area also boasts the most snowfall ever in a single season with a world record of 1,140 inches. Whatcom County boasts the largest concentration of public golf courses in the Pacific Northwest. Water sports abound, with sailing, kayaking, rafting, and whale watching among the favorites. Charter trips are available to the San Juan Islands or Victoria, British Columbia.

More than 110,000 athletes from around the world participate in the annual Sea to Ski Race, an 82.5-mile relay for teams of eight. The race begins with cross-country skiing at Mount Baker, followed by downhill skiing, running, road cycling, canoeing, mountain biking, and kayaking to the finish at Bellingham Bay. The Human Race, held each June, is a 5K/10K walk-run event in which participants raise money for their favorite charities. The course of the Baker's Healthy Start Foundation Triathlon, held each August, begins from the banks of Lake Whatcom and ends at Bloedel Donovan Park. September brings the Bellingham Traverse, a team event involving running, mountain and road biking, and canoeing/kayaking around downtown Bellingham.

Shopping and Dining

Shopping opportunities in Bellingham encompass both large regional malls and charming boutiques. Downtown Bellingham boasts two million square feet of businesses and shops. It is also the seasonal home of the Bellingham Farmers' Market. The Victorian buildings in the city's Fairhaven District hold a variety of specialty shops and eateries. Bellis Fair, the regional shopping mall, has Macy's, Kohl's, Target, JCPenney, Sports Authority, and 150 small shops, plus a six-screen cinema. Outlet centers just a few miles from the town center draw bargain hunters. The Sunset Square Shopping Center houses more than 40 stores and restaurants, as well as a movie theater. Barkley Village is a newer shopping village with old-world charm and features specialty shops as well as restaurants and a wine shop. Unique shops can be found at the new Bellwether on the Bay development on Squalicum Harbor, and West Holly Street provides a plethora of antique and secondhand stores.

Beer-lovers enjoy the fare at the Boundary Bay Brewery Company, where hand-crafted ales and lagers are served in a historic warehouse. Local eateries range from casual cafes and burger joints to restaurants offering Italian, Mexican, and Chinese cuisine, to an upscale steak house with scenic views. The Silver Reef Casino, located in Ferndale, offers food and drink, live entertainment, and gaming, as does the Skagit Valley Casino Resort.

Visitor Information: Bellingham/Whatcom County Tourism, 904 Potter St., Bellingham, WA 98229; telephone (360) 671-3990; toll-free (800) 487-2032; fax (360) 647-7873; email tourism@bellingham.org.

■ Convention Facilities

The Bellingham and Mt. Baker region offers more than 2,200 guest rooms and 175,000 square feet of meeting space. Northwest Washington Fairgrounds, located in nearby Lynden, offers more than 46,000 square feet of meeting space in eight rooms, the largest of which can seat 5,000 people. Within the city of Bellingham, the Mt. Baker Theatre offers three meetings rooms that can accommodate up to 1,500 people. Whatcom Community College has 18,400 square feet of space with a capacity of 1,200 people, and Western Washington University offers facilities able to hold up to 1,000 attendees.

A number of area facilities provide both meeting space and lodging. Semiahmoo Resort offers 6,500 square feet in the largest of its 12 meeting rooms. The Best Western Lakeway Inn & Conference Center has 12

meeting rooms that can seat up to 500. The Homestead Farms Golf Resort & Convention Center, located 20 miles north of Bellingham in Lynden, has 7 meeting rooms, the largest of which is 2,400 square feet in size.

Convention Information: Bellingham/Whatcom County Tourism, 904 Potter St., Bellingham, WA 98229; telephone (360) 671-3990; toll-free (800) 487-2032; fax (360) 647-7873; email tourism@bellingham.org.

■ Transportation

Approaching the City

Bellingham is located along western America's Interstate 5 corridor, nearly equidistant from Seattle and Vancouver, British Columbia. State routes 11, 539, 542, and 544 form a highway grid that covers most of the interior of western Whatcom County, linking with Interstate 5 near Bellingham.

Bellingham International Airport provides service from Alaska Air, Allegiant Air, and Frontier Airlines. Charter or air-taxi services are available from Island Air Inc., Northwest Sky Ferry, and Xtra Airways. The Airporter Shuttle delivers passengers to local points. At the Port of Bellingham, the Bellingham Cruise Terminal and Fairhaven Station launch cruises by ferry to Alaska, the San Juan Islands, and Victoria, British Columbia. Amtrak provides passenger rail service to Seattle and Vancouver, British Columbia, and Canadian Pacific and Rail Canada travel east through Canada. Regional bus service is offered by Greyhound Bus Lines.

Traveling in the City

Interstate 5 runs north and south through the center of Bellingham. State Highway 11 runs north and south down the coast of Bellingham Bay at the south end of town. The Whatcom Transportation Authority (WTA) provides local bus service around Bellingham and to Blaine, Ferndale, and Lynden, offering more than 30 routes.

■ Communications

Newspapers and Magazines

Bellingham's daily paper is *The Bellingham Herald,* which appears every morning. *The Western Front* is published twice weekly from fall to spring by students of Western Washington University. The *Bellingham Business Journal, Northwest Business Monthly,* and *Business Pulse* focus on local business news and features each month. Other papers published in Bellingham include *Cascadia Weekly,* and *Whatcom Watch.*

Television and Radio

Three television stations broadcast out of Bellingham. Bellingham has three AM and 11 FM radio stations, covering classical music, jazz, rock, news, talk, and public radio.

Media Information: *The Bellingham Herald,* 1155 N. State St., Bellingham, WA 98225; telephone (360) 676-2660.

Bellingham Online

The Bellingham Herald. Available www. bellinghamherald.com

Bellingham Public Library. Available www. bellinghampubliclibrary.org

Bellingham Public Schools. Available bellinghamschools.org

Bellingham/Whatcom Chamber of Commerce and Industry. Available www.bellingham.com

Bellingham/Whatcom County Tourism. Available www.bellingham.org

City of Bellingham home page. Available www.cob. org

Northwest Economic Council. Available www. nwecon.org

Western Washington University College of Business and Economics, Center for Economics and Business Research. Available www.cbe.wwu.edu/ cebr

BIBLIOGRAPHY

Dillard, Annie, *The Living* (New York: HarperCollins Publishers, 1992)

Gilliland, Miki, *Entering Bellingham* (Bellingham, WA: Bayside Press, 1989)

Holsather, Kent *Bays to Bells: The Story of Baseball in Whatcom County from the Earliest Known References through 2011* (Bellingham, WA: Lonejack Mountain Press, 2011)

Manning, Harvey, *Walking the Beach to Bellingham* (Corvallis, OR: Oregon State University Press, Reprint Edition, 2002)

Roth, Lottie Roeder, *The History of Whatcom County* (Seattle, WA: Pioneer Historical Publishing Co., 1926)

Olympia

■ The City in Brief

Founded: 1846 (incorporated, 1859)

Head Official: Mayor Stephen H. Buxbaum (since 2012; current term expires 2016)

City Population
- 1990: 33,729
- 2000: 42,514
- 2010: 46,478
- 2012 estimate: 47,250
- Percent change, 2000–2010: 9.3%

Metropolitan Statistical Area Population
- 2000: 207,355
- 2010: 252,264
- 2012 estimate: 258,332
- Percent change, 2000–2010: 21.7%
- U.S. rank in 2000: 189th
- U.S. rank in 2010: 181st

Area: 18.52 square miles

Elevation: 221 feet above sea level

Average Annual Temperatures: January, 38.1° F; July, 62.8° F; annual average, 49.6° F

Average Annual Precipitation: 50.79 inches of rain; 16.7 inches of snow

Major Economic Sectors: government, services, trade

Unemployment Rate: 5.9% (2012)

Per Capita Income: $29,097

2012 FBI Crime Index Property: 2,085

Major Colleges and Universities: The Evergreen State College, South Puget Sound Community College, Saint Martin's University

Daily Newspaper: *The Olympian*

■ Introduction

Olympia, Washington's capital, is a city rich in history and natural beauty. Known for its spectacular view of the Olympic Mountains, the city serves as the gateway to Olympic National Park and headquarters for the Olympic National Forest. Local residents enjoy quiet neighborhoods with lovely tree-lined streets, an abundance of parks, good schools, and a high overall quality of life. In the twenty-first century, the city continued its transition from processing and manufacturing tied to natural resources, such as lumber, to nascent information technology, bioscience, and renewable energy industries.

■ Geography and Climate

Olympia sits on a low flat at the southern end of Puget Sound on the shores of Budd Inlet's two bays, between Seattle and the Olympic Mountains to the north, Mt. Rainier to the northeast, and Mt. Saint Helens to the south. The city is further divided by Capitol Lake.

The city and the surrounding area experience fair-weather summers and the gray, overcast winters of the Pacific Northwest. Tempered by the Japanese trade current, the mild northwest climate favors lushly forested landscapes replete with ferns and mosses. Olympia sees some 50 inches of average rainfall each year, but the rainfall tends to be spread out over a large number of days. With about 52 clear days out of every 365, Thurston County residents live under some form of cloud cover 86 percent of the year, with more than a trace of rain falling on almost half of the days of the year.

Area: 18.52 square miles

Elevation: 221 feet above sea level

The State Capitol building in Olympia. © *James Blank*

Average Temperatures: January, 38.1° F; July, 62.8° F; annual average, 49.6° F

Average Annual Precipitation: 50.79 inches of rain; 16.7 inches of snow

■ History

Territorial Days

Before British Captain George Vancouver sailed into Puget Sound Bay in 1791 and made the first known European contact with the native tribes, the Nisqually, Duwamish, Suquamish, and Puyallup Indians hunted, gathered, and fished in the region where Olympia now stands. The United States and Great Britain jointly controlled the region until the boundary between U.S. territory and Canada was established in 1846. The Pacific Northwest Region was then called Oregon Territory.

White settlement of what later became Olympia began in 1846 with a joint claim filed under a homestead law by partners Edmund Sylvester, a Maine fisherman, and Levi Lathrop Smith, an easterner who wanted to be a minister but was prevented by epilepsy from pursuing that career. Smith called his portion of the claim Smithfield. For two years, Smith and Sylvester were the only white residents in Smithfield (then Oregon Territory); the area was covered with virgin forest. When Smith drowned in Puget Sound in 1848, Sylvester took over his partner's claim. By the end of 1848, a trail had been cleared between Smithfield and New Market to the south (now Tumwater), and four families, about fifteen single men, and Father Pascal Ricard and his small band of Oblate missionaries had settled in Smithfield. In 1850 a city was laid out and Smithfield was renamed Olympia after the Olympic Mountains that can be seen in the distance. In 1853 Washington Territory became separate from Oregon Territory. Olympia (population 150), the largest settlement in Washington Territory, was named its capital and Isaac Stevens arrived to serve as Washington's first territorial governor.

Governor Stevens predicted a golden future for Washington Territory. He moved quickly to open up the area to white settlement, promising to survey a route for a transcontinental railway and to convince the natives to cede their land and move to reservations. By 1854 most of the tribes had done so, but intermittent outbreaks of hostility throughout the 1850s deterred extensive settlement. Delays in constructing a transcontinental railroad and the 1849 discovery of gold in California drew prospective settlers from the Northwest. The outbreak of the Civil War in 1861 nearly halted the westward migration of settlers.

City's Desire for Prominence Thwarted

Blessed with abundant natural resources, Olympia remained small but prospered. The year 1852 marked many firsts for the town. Coal was discovered, saw mills

were built, a fledgling trade industry was started with California, road and school districts were established, and Washington's first newspaper, the weekly *Columbian*, published its first issue. In 1853 a Methodist minister took up residence and began to build a church, classes began at the Olympia Public School, and the city's first theatrical performance was held. Olympia's population grew from fewer than 1,000 people in 1860 to 1,203 residents in 1870. By 1872 Olympia seemed on its way to becoming Washington's great city; that year, however, a severe earthquake shook Olympia, as did the decision by the Northern Pacific railroad not to end the line at Olympia. Instead, the railway went to Tacoma, taking with it much of Olympia's trade and industry.

Meanwhile, people began moving to Seattle instead of Olympia. Still, with its strategic location near virgin forestland and the waterfalls at Tumwater, Olympia flourished as a sawmill town. Furniture, shingles, timber, pilings, and coal were loaded aboard ships bound from Olympia Harbor to California. Olympia served as a social center for isolated settlers throughout Washington, who traveled by steamboat to attend picnics and fairs there. By 1890 Olympia's population stood at 4,698 inhabitants. A year earlier, in 1889, Washington had become a state; Olympia fought bids by several other cities for the right to remain state capital and won in a statewide vote. At the time, state government was housed in a single frame building.

The decade of the 1890s was marked by progress and disappointments. The Olympia Brewing Company, which would become one of Olympia's greatest claims to fame, was founded in 1896 in Tumwater. Telephone lines and electric light poles were erected, dredging began for a modern port, a street railway system was built, and the elegant Olympia Hotel was completed (but destroyed by fire in 1904); however, an economic depression left citizens complaining that their diet consisted of nothing but clams, and Olympia's population fell to 3,863 residents by 1900. By this time, Seattle and Tacoma had surpassed Olympia as the big cities of the Puget Sound area.

Twentieth-Century Advances

In 1901 the state bought Olympia's Thurston County Court House to serve as the Capitol building, but Olympians could not rest easy with their title of state capital until the present Capitol complex was finally completed in 1935, after delays due to the 1890 and 1930 depressions.

Olympia had escaped the worst of the Indian wars of the 1850s, and in the twentieth century managed to escape the labor troubles and various upheavals that beset other Washington cities. The city benefited when World War I brought a huge demand for Olympic peninsula spruce to make airplanes. Waterborne trade lost by 1920 to other Puget Sound ports picked up after a 1925 revitalization of the Port of Olympia, and ships once again began loading lumber bound for the Orient.

Olympia suffered a severe earthquake in 1949. A year later the city celebrated its centennial, 100 years from the date Olympia was laid out. By then Olympia ranked twelfth among Washington's cities in population and boasted one high school, one radio station, a "video" station, and two newspapers. With a population in 1953 of 16,800 people, Olympia was a typical small town where the sidewalks were "rolled up" each evening. One by one, state government offices were moving from Olympia to Seattle, and the city feared it would lose its capital status. Finally, four local businessmen filed a lawsuit against the state to stop the exodus; the eighteen state agencies were ordered back to Olympia in a decision that opined: "it was not the intention of the framers of the constitution that the state capital should be composed of empty buildings to collect cobwebs and stand in disuse."

Then began a flurry of construction of government buildings on what had once been residential streets. Despite decades of effort, Olympia was less successful in luring industry, thus managing to escape the attendant smog and pollution. In the 1960s and 1970s Olympia lost many of its downtown retail businesses to shopping malls in the then-rural towns of Lacey and Tumwater.

Challenges in the New Century

The turn of the century brought several challenges to Olympia. Some, like a national recession and terrorist attacks in 2001, affected the entire United States and beyond. Others were more specific to the region. On February 28, 2001, the 6.8-magnitude Nisqually Earthquake occurred, with an epicenter only 10 miles from Olympia. A gradual yet significant loss of manufacturing jobs forced diversification, particularly in technology—a segment in which Olympia lagged behind the state's other regions.

Into the twenty-first century, efforts to preserve the downtown have emphasized people-friendly projects while discouraging skyscrapers. A new city hall, completed in 2011, anchored the East Bay district, which was home to several public and private development projects during the 2010s. It was also an appropriate metaphor for the city, demonstrating officials' recognition of the importance of government jobs to the economy, while also attempting to leverage that sector to spur private investments.

Historical Information: Washington State Capital Museum, SW 211 21st Ave., Olympia, WA 98501; telephone (360) 753-2580.

■ Population Profile

Metropolitan Statistical Area Population

2000: 207,355
2010: 252,264

2012 estimate: 258,332
Percent change, 2000–2010: 21.7%
U.S. rank in 2000: 189th
U.S. rank in 2010: 181st

City Residents

1990: 33,729
2000: 42,514
2010: 46,478
2012 estimate: 47,250
Percent change, 2000–2010: 9.3%

Density: 1,702.9 people per square mile

Racial and ethnic characteristics

White: 40,308
Black or African American: 610
American Indian and Alaskan Native: 356
Asian: 3,283
Native Hawaiian and Other Pacific Islander: 149
Hispanic or Latino (may be of any race): 3,950
Other: 2,544

Percent of residents born in state: 46.0%

Age characteristics

Population under 5 years old: 2,751
Population 5 to 9 years old: 2,601
Population 10 to 14 years old: 2,291
Population 15 to 19 years old: 2,223
Population 20 to 24 years old: 4,700
Population 25 to 34 years old: 7,247
Population 35 to 44 years old: 6,724
Population 45 to 54 years old: 6,053
Population 55 to 59 years old: 3,158
Population 60 to 64 years old: 3,044
Population 65 to 74 years old: 3,497
Population 75 to 84 years old: 1,777
Population 85 years and over: 1,184
Median age: 37.1

Births (2010–11 Metropolitan Area)

Total number: 3,015

Deaths (2010–11 Metropolitan Area)

Total number: 1,815

Money income (2012)

Per capita income: $29,097
Median household income: $50,934
Total households: 20,549

Number of households with income of …

less than $10,000: 1,921
$10,000 to $14,999: 1,067
$15,000 to $24,999: 2,127
$25,000 to $34,999: 2,257
$35,000 to $49,999: 2,771

$50,000 to $74,999: 3,496
$75,000 to $99,999: 2,777
$100,000 to $149,999: 2,845
$150,000 to $199,999: 718
$200,000 or more: 570

Percent of families below poverty level: 14.0%

FBI Crime Index Property: 2,085

FBI Crime Index Violent: 150

■ Municipal Government

Olympia has a council-manager form of government. Power lies with the council, which sets policy and makes budgetary decisions. Seven elected, nonpartisan council members representing the community at-large, not individual districts, serve staggered four-year terms, with Position 1 designated as the mayor's position. A city manager is hired by the council to advise and administer all city affairs.

Head Official: Mayor Stephen H. Buxbaum (since 2012; current term expires 2016)

Total Number of City Employees: 583 (2012)

City Information: City of Olympia, PO Box 1967, Olympia, WA 98507-1967; telephone (360) 753-8447; fax (360) 709-2791; email cityhall@ci.olympia.wa.us.

■ Economy

Major Industries and Commercial Activity

The city's early development was based on its port facilities and lumber-based industries, and later oyster farming and dairying. Following World War II, Olympia served as a major service center for lumber communities west of Thurston County, while the Port of Olympia remained a major transportation center for shipping logs and finished lumber. But during the mid-twentieth century, the decline of the local timber industry resulted in the loss of many of the local associated milling and secondary operations.

During the 1970s, Olympia expanded as a center of offices and homes for state employees, military personnel, and their respective families. This further diminished Thurston County's already modest farm sector as housing development pushed into the remaining fertile prairies. Dairy and truck (mostly berry) farming continued in the south county, interspersed with small hobby farms.

In the late 1960s and early 1970s, the state legislature approved and financed construction of the Evergreen State College. The four-year public institution became and remains an economic and cultural fixture in Thurston County with faculty, staff, and students contributing to the local housing and retail sectors. On a smaller scale, South Puget Sound Community College and Saint Martin's University in nearby Lacey also drove the housing demand. In the late 1980s the Olympia waterfront and downtown were revitalized, and an effort began to draw new businesses to the area.

Manufacturing, mostly tied to the wood product, paper, and agribusiness industries, continued to be a major industry into the 2010s. Major purchasers of wood products were hospitals and soft drink packagers. As with agriculture, the timber industry is dominated by smaller, family-owned operations. Chemical product and plastics manufacturing is also important to the local economy.

As the capital of the state of Washington, Olympia relies on the state government to stabilize the local economy; combined with local and federal government positions, government jobs number roughly 40,000. Tours of state government buildings and monuments play their part in supporting Olympia's tourist industry as well.

In recent years, Thurston County has seen a change in workforce, with professional services—which includes everything from technical Internet and Web design firms to legal and consultant companies—moving up the rungs of the city's most important industries. Programming, data processing, and Internet hosting make up the core of the information technology sector, which is supported mainly by start-up companies and the self-employed.

Health-care services, from traditional hospitals to stand-alone specialty facilities, are also important to Olympia's economy.

Items and goods produced: wood products, processed foods, metal and paper containers

Incentive Programs—New and Existing Companies

Local programs: Olympia has no corporate or personal income tax, and no inventory tax. Thurston County offers exemptions on sales and use tax for manufacturing equipment, repair and replacement parts, and labor; for manufacturing machinery and equipment used for research and development; and for warehouse/distribution facilities and equipment. A tax credit of up to $2 million is available for research and development in the high technology industry. Tax exempt revenue bonds for manufacturing, ranging from $1 million to $10 million, are also available.

State programs: The state of Washington offers a number of incentive programs to attract new and expanding businesses to the state, with most targeted to specific industries or geographic areas. Industry-specific incentives include sales and use tax exemptions for general manufacturing and agriculture; sales and use tax deferrals and waivers, and business and occupation tax credits for high-technology industries, including biotechnology and medical device manufacturing; business and occupation tax rate reductions and credits for the aerospace, timber, food manufacturing, biofuel, semiconductor, and aluminum industries; and a range of credits and exemptions for renewable energy firms.

Geography-based incentives are available in designated Community Empowerment Zones, high unemployment counties, and Main Street areas. Other incentives support economic activity that reduces commuter travel; produces television or film; or relates to newspaper publishing.

Job training programs: Job training programs offered by the state of Washington include the Washington Customized Employment Training Program, which offers a business and occupation tax credit to qualifying companies for job-training expenses. The WorkSource partnership is a collaboration among local, state, and federal agencies to recruit, screen, test, and refer potential employees.

South Puget Sound Community College provides specialized job training for public and private employees, contracts with businesses to provide specialized job training, and operates a comprehensive Cooperative Work Experience program.

Development Projects

Olympia's City Hall was relocated in 2010–11 to the 600 block of Fourth Avenue East in downtown Olympia. The City Hall project cost $35.6 million and opened in January 2011. The old City Hall was then converted into the city's new Criminal Justice Center. The new City Hall satisfies one of the council's four primary goals: to invest in downtown.

Construction of the new city hall intended to spur additional public and private development. As of 2014, projects included a new $18.5 million Hands On Children's Museum, completed in 2012; WET Science Center for the LOTT Alliance, which opened in 2010; a destination hotel, still working to raise capital in 2014; and shops and restaurants. Collectively, the redevelopment was referred to as the city's East Bay property.

In 2013 Red Wind Casino announced plans to nearly double in size with a $45 million expansion to add 42,700 square feet and a 600-space parking structure. The expansion was to house additional gaming and restaurant spaces.

Several home and apartment projects were planned or underway during 2014, including 170 age-restricted units at Affinity of Olympia Apartments; 120 lots of single-family development at Chestnut Village; 260 multifamily units at Copper Trail; 150 single-family lots at Evergreen Hills Plat; 100 single-family lots at Cyrene; and several others.

Economic Development Information: Thurston County Economic Development Council, 665 Woodland Square Loop SE, Ste. 201, Lacey, WA 98503; telephone (360) 754-6320; fax (360) 407-3980. Thurston Regional Planning Council, 2424 Heritage Ct. SW, Ste. A, Olympia, WA 98502; telephone (360) 956-7575; fax (360) 956-7815; email info@trpc.org.

Commercial Shipping

After years of struggling with an identity as a failing bastion of log exporting, the Port of Olympia produced operating income in 2013 for the first time since 2001. The turnaround was primarily due to diversification into such bulk commodities as metals and limestone; the port was named Port of the Year by the Washington Public Ports Association in 2013. The 66-acre, deepwater port offers three berths, a U.S. Customs bonded warehouse, and a complete container yard for breakbulk, bulk, rolling stock, and containerized cargoes. The Port of Olympia is also the site of Foreign Trade Zone #216, an area where foreign goods bound for international destinations can be temporarily stored without incurring an import duty.

The Port of Olympia owns and operates Olympia Regional Airport, a general aviation-transport facility for corporate, commercial, and recreational users. The airport is 20 minutes by air to the Seattle-Tacoma International Airport and 50 minutes away from Vancouver, British Columbia. Nearly 90 miles of active rail lines lie in Thurston County. Burlington Northern Santa Fe, Union Pacific, and the Puget Sound & Pacific Railroad serve the area, with the Tri-City & Olympia Railroad also serving the Port of Olympia.

Labor Force and Employment Outlook

Olympia's workforce surpasses much of the nation in educational attainment. Nearly 94 percent of residents had graduated from high school, and almost 43 percent held a bachelor's degree or higher—nearly 11 percentage points above the state average. The cost of living and working in Olympia is about 10–15 percent lower than Seattle, drawing both an increased labor force and employers to Olympia. Geographically, Olympia is also located midway between Seattle and Portland.

The following is a summary of data regarding the 2012 Olympia labor force:

Size of civilian labor force: 25,638

Number of workers employed in . . .

    agriculture and mining: 281
    construction: 1,114
    manufacturing: 1,133
    wholesale trade: 306
    retail trade: 2,439
    transportation: 782
    information systems: 348
    finance: 1,235

professional administration: 2,199
education and social services: 5,791
arts and leisure: 2,346
other: 1,507
public administration: 3,773

Average hourly earnings of production workers: $16.94

Unemployment rate: 5.9% (2012)

Employers

Largest employers (2012)	Number of employees
State of Washington, including education	20,000–25,000
Local Government, including education	10,000–15,000
Providence St. Peter Hospital	1,000–5,000
Tribal Government	1,000–5,000
Federal Government	500–1,000
Group Health Cooperative	500–1,000
Walmart	500–1,000
Great Wolf Lodge	500–1,000
Columbia Capital Medical Center	100–500
Saint Martin's College	100–500

Cost of Living

Real estate prices in the area have been driven by people migrating from more crowded and costly counties to the north, resulting in a cost of living slightly above the national average.

The following is a summary of data regarding several key cost of living factors in the area.

2013 ACCRA Average House Price: $303,238

2013 ACCRA Cost of Living Index: 102

State income tax rate: None

State sales tax rate: 6.5%

Local income tax rate: None

Local sales tax rate: 2.3%

Property tax rate: $15.00 per $1,000 of assessed value (2013)

Economic Information: Thurston County Chamber, 809 Legion Way SE, Olympia, WA 98507; telephone (360) 357-3362; fax (360) 357-3362.

■ Education and Research

Elementary and Secondary Schools

One of the oldest districts in the state of Washington, the Olympia School District was founded in 1852, nearly 40 years before Washington statehood. The district offers special education, alternative education, gifted education, and career and technical education. The district has strong programs in Advanced Placement, the International Baccalaureate, fine arts, technology, and athletics. The district's 2013–18 strategic plan had four goals: high standards for student success, best practices, supportive work environment to meet student needs, and family and community support.

Beginning with the graduating class of 2008, all students enrolled in the Olympia School District were required to meet new graduation requirements that include the earning of 22 credits, completion of the "High School and Beyond" plan, the attainment of a Certificate of Academic Achievement, and the completion of a culminating project.

Olympia is home to a number of private and religious schools.

The following is a summary of data regarding the Olympia School District.

Total enrollment: 9,369

Number of facilities
total: 19
elementary schools: 11
junior high schools: 4
high schools: 3
other: 1

Student/teacher ratio: 20:1

Teacher salaries
average (statewide): $53,796

Funding per pupil: $9,197

Public Schools Information: Olympia School District, 1113 Legion Way SE, Olympia, WA 98501; telephone (360) 596-6100.

Colleges and Universities

The Evergreen State College, a public liberal arts and sciences institution founded in 1969, enrolled about 4,200 undergraduate students in 2013, with an additional 300 graduate students. The Olympia campus accounts for the vast majority of enrollment, with Grays Harbor, Tacoma, and Tribal Reservations sharing the remainder. Emphasizing interdisciplinary studies rather than traditional majors, Evergreen offers a Bachelor's of Arts and a Bachelor's of Science in Liberal Arts and Sciences, with the opportunity to concentrate in biology and life sciences, environmental studies, psychology, visual and media arts, and writing. In 2013 *U.S. News & World Report* ranked the college 27th among regional universities in the West.

South Puget Sound Community College is a two-year, public institution that serves all adults regardless of their previous education. More than 6,000 students each semester pursue associate's degrees in arts, general studies, applied science, business, elementary education, biology, and nursing. Some 47 percent of the school's full-time students are there in preparation for transferring to a four-year college; however, nearly that same number, 42 percent, receive technical training that allows them to immediately enter the work force. The college also offers non-credit community education classes, adult literacy, and high school completion programs. In addition to its main campus in Olympia, it has a satellite facility in Lacey.

U.S. News & World Report ranked Saint Martin's University 49th among regional universities in the West in 2013. Located in nearby Lacey, Saint Martin's is a four-year, co-educational college with a strong liberal arts foundation that also encompasses business, education, and engineering. Known as Saint Martin's College until changing its name in August 2005, the school offers about 20 undergraduate programs, seven graduate programs, and numerous pre-professional and certification programs. One of 18 U.S. Benedictine Catholic colleges, Saint Martin's enrolls more than 1,800 full- and part-time students. It has extension campuses at the Fort Lewis Army Post, McChord Air Force Base, and Centralia Community College, as well as partnerships with Tacoma Community College and Olympic College at Bremerton.

Libraries and Research Centers

The Timberland Regional Library system has 27 community libraries, including the Olympia branch, two cooperative library centers, and four library kiosks in Grays Harbor, Lewis, Mason, Pacific, and Thurston counties. The system provides some 475,000 patrons with 1.2 million items, including books, electronic books, magazines, online reference databases, and numerous videos, CDs, audio books, pamphlets, CD-ROMs, and DVDs. The Olympia Timberland Library was founded in 1909 with a collection of 900 books. The library underwent extensive renovations in 2008, including refurbished computer stations and a new circulation area. In 2003 the Timberland Regional Library system became the state's first public library system to join with the Library of Congress as a partner in the national Veterans History Project.

Other local libraries include college libraries at The Evergreen State College, whose special collections include a Rare Books room and the Chicano/Latino Archive, South Puget Sound Community College, Providence St. Peter Hospital, and the Washington State Capital Museum. The Washington State Library has more than half a million volumes and periodicals, with special collections on Washington newspapers, Washington authors, and Washington state documents. It is a U.S. government and Washington State depository library.

Local research institutes or organizations conducting research include the Cascadia Research Collective, the Evergreen Freedom Foundation, Washington State Labor Education and Research Center, Washington State Institute for Public Policy, and the Washington Department of Fish and Wildlife Fish.

Public Library Information: Olympia Timberland Library, 313 8th Ave. SE, Olympia, WA 98501; telephone (360) 352-0595. Washington State Library, Point Plaza East, 6880 Capitol Blvd. Tumwater, PO Box 42460, Olympia, WA 98504-2460; telephone (360) 704-5200.

■ Health Care

Olympia has two hospitals and functions as the regional medical center for five surrounding counties. The Providence Health System operates the 390-bed Providence St. Peter Hospital and the 127-bed Providence Centralia Hospital, each of which have served the community's health care needs for a century. Providence St. Peter is the largest hospital in the region, offering a full spectrum of acute care, specialty and outpatient services, including cardiac surgery, obstetrics, medical rehabilitation, emergency care, and outpatient surgery. Providence St. Peter admits more than 21,000 patients each year as of 2013, while also treating some 65,500 in its emergency department.

Capital Medical Center, established in 1985, has 110 beds. The full-service hospital includes emergency care, private birthing suites, a same-day private-room surgery center, pain management services, a lymphedema program, senior programs, and a sleep disorder center. Capital Medical Center is part of the Capella Healthcare network based in Franklin, Tennessee.

■ Recreation

Sightseeing

Located on the Olympic Peninsula, nearby Olympic National Park encompasses the Olympic Mountains and Pacific Ocean beaches. Beautiful Olympic National Forest, which surrounds the park, is the site of three rain forests.

Capitol Lake Park provides a spectacular view of the state capitol buildings, the lake, and surrounding wooded bluffs. The Capitol grounds feature the Executive Mansion, the campus gardens, war memorials, and a conservatory. The Capitol group of buildings, completed in 1935, consists of six white sandstone structures located on a hill in the city's southern section. The marble interior Legislative Building at the center of the cluster has a 287-foot high dome, similar to that of the U.S. Capitol, and one of the highest of its kind in the world.

Heritage Fountain invites children and adults to don a swimsuit and splash among its 47 waterspouts. The fountain is part of the Heritage Park, a scenic pedestrian district stretching from the Capitol Grounds to Percival Landing. Percival Landing, on the city's waterfront, has a nearly one-mile boardwalk featuring works of art and interpretive displays outlining the history of the harbor. A walk along the Port Plaza provides mountain views from the working waterfront and a visit to the nationally recognized Batdorf and Bronson Coffee roasters shop.

Yashiro Japanese Garden, a traditional Asian garden designed in the ancient hill and pond style, honors Olympia's sister city of Yashiro, Japan. The walled garden features classic gates built without nails. The City of Yashiro presented two cutstone lanterns and a 13-tier pagoda as gifts to the garden.

Chief William Shelton's Story Pole, located on the Washington State Capitol Campus, was dedicated in 1940 to commemorate the relationship between Northwest Native tribal governments and the State of Washington. The American Revolution is remembered in downtown Sylvester Park with a monument to the End of the Oregon Trail, a leg of a pioneer trail that ran to the shores of Puget Sound.

The Nisqually National Wildlife Refuge has 3,000 acres of land and waters to provide refuge and nesting places for migratory waterfowl, songbirds, raptors, and wading birds. The Woodard Bay Natural Resource Conservation Area is a wildlife sanctuary for bald eagles, seals, otters, and bats, and is one of the most important heron rookeries in Washington.

Four tribal casinos operate in Thurston County. Located in Olympia, the Red Wind Casino features slot machines, table games, dining, and live entertainment. The area's other casinos are Hawks Prairie, Little Creek, and Lucky Eagle.

Arts and Culture

Olympia residents enjoy a variety of arts and cultural facilities and events. Each year, the Capitol Campus draws more than half a million visitors who tour the Legislature as well as the stately buildings, grounds, gardens, and artwork. The State Capital Museum, adjacent to the Capitol Campus, houses exhibits that document the story and political and cultural life of the city and state. Built in the 1850s, the Bigelow House Museum, one of the oldest homes in the Pacific Northwest, offers tours of the house's original furnishings. Exhibits at the Hands On Children's Museum, which opened a new facility in the East Bay area in 2012, allow children to enjoy a first-hand experience of science and art. At the east side of the

Olympia Airport, the Olympic Flight Museum features historic aircraft from around the world.

The Washington Center for the Performing Arts presents a full season of performances by resident and touring groups, offering music, dance, theater, and family entertainment. Groups in residence at the center include Ballet Northwest, Youth Orchestra, Olympia Chamber Orchestra, Olympia Symphony Orchestra, and Opera Pacifica. The Masterworks Choral Ensemble is a southwest Washington chorus based in Olympia. The Capital Playhouse, a semi-professional theater company, presents five musical performances in its season. The State Theater is the venue for Harlequin Productions, whose eclectic performances include both new works and innovative treatments of classics. The Olympia Film Society shows independent, international, and classic film year-round at the Capital Theater, offers special live performances, and annually produces a nationally recognized film festival.

The city's popular Music in the Park program takes place at noon each Friday from mid-July through August. The largest Art Walk in the state occurs in Olympia in April and October, with businesses featuring visual arts, performances, and poetry of local artists.

Olympia's downtown art galleries include the Childhood's End Gallery, Side Door Studio, Van Tuinen Art, Matter! Gallery, and State of the Arts Gallery. The Evergreen Galleries on that college's campus feature changing exhibits.

Olympia is known as a center for independent rock and punk music produced and performed locally. Cover charges are generally low or non-existent, venues are often no-frills, and shows are frequently all-ages events. Folk, jazz, and bluegrass are traditionally strong draws as well. The Capitol Theater Backstage offers all-ages shows.

Festivals and Holidays

Olympia's first celebration of the year is April's Procession of the Species, a celebration of arts and the natural world that culminates in a procession of residents in masks and costumes. Percival Landing is the site of May's annual Wooden Boat Fair, which features wooden boats, international foods, and craft booths. Also in May is the annual Swantown Boatswap & Chowder Challenge, a day dedicated to boats, marine equipment, and clam chowder. It restarted in 2013 following a five-year hiatus. Nearby that same month are the annual Grays Harbor Shorebird Festival at the Grays Harbor National Wildlife Refuge, and the Lacey Alternative Energy Fair.

Evergreen State College sponsors Super Saturday, a free festival for all ages, in June. Also in June is the annual Olympic Air Show, held at the Olympic Flight Museum. July brings the Dixieland Jazz Festival, a four-day event, and Capital Lakefair, one of the largest community festivals in the state. The Thurston County Fair is held over the first weekend of August. For more than 60 years, the Pet Parade has invited the children of the city to parade the downtown streets with their favorite pets or toys, costumes, or creations of their own. Sand in the City, Washington's largest sand sculpting competition, takes place at the Hands On Children's Museum.

Olympia Harbor Days is held over Labor Day weekend, and features the Tugboat Races & Festival. The fall Arts Walk takes place in October. In December the spotlight is on the Parade of Lighted Ships at the city's waterfront.

Sports for the Spectator

Olympia is home to the Oly Rollers, the local women's flat track roller derby league and 2009 and 2010 national champions of the Women's Flat Track Derby Association. The Geoducks, the sports teams of The Evergreen State College, compete in cross country, track and field, volleyball, men's and women's basketball and soccer, and volleyball. Saint Martin's University teams, nicknamed the Saints, participate in baseball and softball, cross country, track and field, volleyball, and men's and women's basketball, soccer, and golf. Nearby Tacoma is home to the Tacoma Rainiers baseball team, a Triple-A affiliate of the Seattle Mariners.

Sports for the Participant

Olympia's location on the Puget Sound and nearby mountains make outdoor recreation very popular, especially hiking, kayaking, skiing, and sailboating. Olympia is home to nearly 40 city parks totaling more than 900 acres. Thurston County boasts a number of golf courses, including Vicwood, a championship-rated course. An abundance of parks and forests nearby and in the city include the very popular Tolmie State Park and Millersylvania State Park. Burfoot Park, which covers 50 acres of property with 1,100 feet of saltwater beach frontage on Budd Inlet, offers nature trails and beach access that feature beautiful views of the State Capitol and the Olympic Mountains.

The Capital City Marathon winds through various parts of town each May. The Washington State Senior Games take place throughout Thurston County, with a series of athletic competitions in 20 sports for men and women aged 50 and older.

Shopping and Dining

Capital Mall encompasses more than 100 stores and restaurants, and is anchored by JCPenney and Macy's. More than 100 specialty stores are located throughout the downtown area. Olympia's Farmers Market, the second largest in the state, offers the finest in handicrafts, baked goods, and fresh produce. It is located on Budd Inlet, the southernmost reach of the Puget Sound.

Naturally, the stars of Olympia's cuisine are the wonderful fish and seafood that have made the area famous. In addition to Northwest fare, diners may choose from ethnic cuisine, oven fired pizza, or family dining spots.

Visitor Information: Olympia-Thurston County Visitor & Convention Bureau, PO Box 7338, Olympia, WA 98507; telephone (360) 704-7544; toll-free (877) 704-7500; fax (360) 7 04-7533; email georgesharp@ visitolympia.com.

■ Convention Facilities

Thurston County offers more than 2,500 hotel rooms and over 100,000 square feet of meeting space. The Thurston County Fairgrounds, located in Olympia, feature three buildings including the Thurston Expo Center which can hold up to 288 people. The Olympia Center and the Washington Center for the Performing Arts each offer facilities for a variety of meeting and exhibition events. The Washington State Capital Museum houses several venues for conferences, among them the Coach House and the Conference Room. The Norman Worthington Conference Center on the St. Martin's University campus in nearby Lacey has 4,752 square feet of open area that can be partitioned into four smaller rooms of approximately 1,100 square feet each.

Other meeting venues include the Heritage Room on Capitol Lake, Jacob Smith House, Lucky Eagle Casino, Lacey Community Center, facilities at The Evergreen State College, Indian Summer Golf and Country Club, Masonic Center and New Masonic Center, Olympic Flight Museum, Squaxin Island Museum, Library, and Research Center, Stampfer Center, State Theater, Tugboat Annie's, Olympia Tumwater Foundation Schmidt House, Pavilion at American Heritage Campground, and Tumwater Valley Lodge.

Convention Information: Olympia-Thurston County Visitor & Convention Bureau, PO Box 7338, Olympia, WA 98507; telephone (360) 704-7544; toll-free (877) 704-7500; fax (360) 704-7533; email georgesharp@visitolympia.com.

■ Transportation

Approaching the City

Olympia can be approached from the east by Interstate 5. In the center of the city, Interstate 5 turns southward. State Highway 12 runs westward beginning at the center of the city. State Highway 101 runs northward from the west side of Olympia.

Olympia is served by Seattle-Tacoma International Airport. Located 45 miles northwest of downtown Olympia, Sea-Tac is a modern facility that served over 33.2 million passengers in 2012 on more than 309,000 passenger flights. Sea-Tac is the 15th busiest airport in the United States. The Olympia Regional Airport, situated in Tumwater, is home to aircraft service operations, hangars, corporate offices, and a modern public terminal. The airport provides tower-controlled and full-instrument approach access for a variety of recreational, commercial, and corporate users.

Traveling in the City

Olympia's downtown streets are arranged in a grid to the east of Budd Inlet. Local bus transportation is available on Dash, the free Capitol Shuttle. The Intercity Transit has routes to nearby cities. Amtrak provides rail transportation, and bus service is provided by Greyhound.

■ Communications

Newspapers and Magazines

The Olympian is the city's daily newspaper. Three monthly newspapers published locally are *The Thurston-Mason Senior News; Washington State Grange News,* an agricultural paper; and *Works in Progress,* a community newspaper.

Television and Radio

Olympia has one locally broadcasttelevision station, as well as seven FM and two AM radio stations with nostalgia, country music, classical, soft rock, and eclectic programming.

Media Information: The Olympian, 111 Bethel St. NE, Olympia, WA; 98507; telephone (360) 754-5400; fax (360) 754-5408.

Olympia Online

City of Olympia. Available www.olympiawa.gov
Olympia-Thurston County Visitor & Convention Bureau. Available www.visitolympia.com
The Olympian. Available www.theolympian.com
Thurston County Chamber. Available thurstonchamber.com
Thurston County Economic Development Council. Available www.thurstonedc.com
Thurston Regional Planning Council. Available www.trpc.org
Timberland Regional Library. Available www.trl.org

BIBLIOGRAPHY

Christie, Rebecca A., *Workingman's Hill: A History of an Olympia Neighborhood* (Olympia, WA: Bigelow House Preservation Association, 2001)

Hannum, James S., *Gone but not Forgotten: Abandoned Railroads of Thurston County, Washington* (Olympia, WA: Hannum House Publications, 2012)

Newell, Gordon, *So Fair a Dwelling Place A History of Olympia and Thurston County, Washington* (Olympia, WA: Gordon Newell and F. George Warren, 1984)

Seattle

■ The City in Brief

Founded: 1851 (incorporated, 1869)

Head Official: Mayor Ed Murray (since 2014; current term expires 2018)

City Population

    1990: 516,259
    2000: 563,374
    2010: 608,660
    2012 estimate: 634,541
    Percent change, 2000–2010: 8%
    U.S. rank in 1990: 21st (State rank: 1st)
    U.S. rank in 2000: 30th (State rank: 1st)
    U.S. rank in 2010: 23rd (State rank: 1st)

Metropolitan Statistical Area Population

    2000: 3,043,878
    2010: 3,439,809
    2012 estimate: 3,552,157
    Percent change, 2000–2010: 13.0%
    U.S. rank in 2000: 15th
    U.S. rank in 2010: 15th

Area: 83.9 square miles

Elevation: Ranges from sea level to 450 feet above sea level

Average Annual Temperatures: January, 41.5° F; July, 65.5° F; annual average, 52.9° F

Average Annual Precipitation: 38.25 inches of rain; 7.3 inches of snow

Major Economic Sectors: services, trade, manufacturing, government

Unemployment Rate: 4.9% (2012)

Per Capita Income: $42,280

2012 FBI Crime Index Property: 31,931

Major Colleges and Universities: University of Washington, Seattle Pacific University, Seattle University

Daily Newspaper: *The Seattle Times; Seattle Post-Intelligencer*

■ Introduction

Little more than a century ago, Seattle—nicknamed "The Emerald City"—was a pioneer outpost and a quiet lumbering town. Transformed by the Yukon gold rush into a thriving metropolis, Seattle has become the transportation, manufacturing, commercial, and services hub for the Pacific Northwest as well as the largest urban area north of San Francisco, California. The city's arts community has gained an international reputation, boasting hundreds of galleries, highly-regarded art museums, and drawing audiences from around the world for its musical and theatrical performances. Nestled between two magnificent mountain ranges with a breathtaking view of a lake and bay, Seattle enjoys a climate one observer has likened to "an airborne ocean bath." The geography supports a robust transportation and distribution network, complemented by the city's importance in the aerospace and technology sectors.

■ Geography and Climate

Seattle is situated on a series of hills in a lowland area on Puget Sound's eastern shore between the Olympic Mountains to the west and the Cascade Mountains to the east. Westerly air currents from the ocean and the shielding effects of the Cascade range produce a mild and moderately moist climate, with warm winters and cool summers. Extremes in temperature are rare and of short duration, and the daily fluctuation is slight. While Seattle is known for its pronounced rainy season and frequent

Alex Stepanov/Shutterstock.com

cloudy weather, the average annual rainfall is actually less than that of many other cities in the United States, including New York and Atlanta.

Area: 83.9 square miles

Elevation: Ranges from sea level to 450 feet above sea level

Average Temperatures: January, 41.5° F; July, 65.5° F; annual average, 52.9° F

Average Annual Precipitation: 38.25 inches of rain; 7.3 inches of snow

■ History

Illinois Farmers Build Sawmills in Seattle

The original inhabitants of the region surrounding the site of present-day Seattle were the Suquamish tribe. Their chief, Sealth, befriended a group of Illinois farmers who settled in the area in 1851. These settlers, the first people of European descent to arrive north of the Columbia River, had established a town at Alki Point on Elliott Bay then moved to the location of present-day

Pioneer Square. They named their new town Seattle in gratitude to Chief Sealth.

Finding an abundant lumber resource in the rich forests, the settlers set up sawmills for the preparation of logs for export to San Francisco, where the 1849 gold rush had generated a building boom. By 1853 the lumber industry was thriving in the area, and for several years it provided the sole economic base of Seattle, which was incorporated in 1869.

City Rebuilds After Fire; Becomes Commercial Center

In 1889 a great fire, ignited by a flaming glue pot in a print shop, destroyed the entire business district, consuming sixty blocks. Damaged wood-frame buildings were replaced by masonry structures on a higher elevation than the original storefronts, resulting in the creation of an underground city that is a popular tourist attraction in modern Seattle. The city recovered fairly quickly from the setback caused by the fire.

During the last decade of the nineteenth century Seattle became a rail and maritime commercial center when the Great Northern Railroad reached town and the city was selected by a major shipping line as the port of entry for trade with the Orient. The Alaska gold rush brought further growth and development, and Seattle, dubbed the "gateway to the Klondike," increased in population from 56,842 people in 1897 to 80,600 people in 1900. Prosperity continued and within the next decade the population grew to 240,000 residents.

Rise of Aerospace Industry; World's Fair Brings Tourists

Seattle's aerospace industry began when a small local firm that became the Boeing Company—now the world's foremost manufacturer of jet aircraft and spacecraft—started making two-seater biplanes in 1916. The shipping and aircraft industries continued to play an important role in the city's economy during both world wars and into the 1960s. Boeing moved its corporate headquarters from Seattle to Chicago in 2001.

The Seattle World's Fair in 1962 brought new economic dimensions to the region, establishing Seattle as a tourist and entertainment center. As a result of the reduction of federal support for aerospace projects in the 1970s, the city's reliance on the aircraft industry shifted to development of its position as a transportation hub in the international market. Since 1975 Seattle has undergone renewed economic expansion to become the financial, industrial, and trade center for the Pacific Northwest.

Seattle made international headlines in 1999 when the city played host to the World Trade Organization meeting. Forty thousand demonstrators gathered to protest globalization; city leaders had hoped that the summit would showcase Seattle as a world-class friend to free trade. The event highlighted the tension between those who liked the new high-tech, high-wealth Seattle, and those who believed Seattle was losing its small-town charm.

Today, Seattle is a hotbed of activity in the Pacific Northwest. Located just two hours south of Vancouver, Canada, the city of Seattle is an international port that boasts hundreds of restaurants, two professional sports teams, a myriad of cultural venues, and a lifestyle that unique to the region.

Historical Information: Historic Seattle, Dearborn House, 1117 Minor Avenue, Seattle, WA 98101; telephone (206) 622-6952; fax (206) 622-1197.

■ Population Profile

Metropolitan Statistical Area Population

2000: 3,043,878
2010: 3,439,809
2012 estimate: 3,552,157
Percent change, 2000–2010: 13.0%
U.S. rank in 2000: 15th
U.S. rank in 2010: 15th

City Residents

1990: 516,259
2000: 563,374
2010: 608,660
2012 estimate: 634,541
Percent change, 2000–2010: 8%
U.S. rank in 1990: 21st (State rank: 1st)
U.S. rank in 2000: 30th (State rank: 1st)
U.S. rank in 2010: 23rd (State rank: 1st)

Density: 7,250.9 people per square mile

Racial and ethnic characteristics

White: 441,308
Black or African American: 45,715
American Indian and Alaskan Native: 5,103
Asian: 92,535
Native Hawaiian and Other Pacific Islander: 1,327
Hispanic or Latino (may be of any race): 46,413
Other: 48,553

Percent of residents born in state: 38.7%

Age characteristics

Population under 5 years old: 34,281
Population 5 to 9 years old: 25,742
Population 10 to 14 years old: 25,080
Population 15 to 19 years old: 27,986
Population 20 to 24 years old: 54,025
Population 25 to 34 years old: 140,431
Population 35 to 44 years old: 99,318
Population 45 to 54 years old: 80,724
Population 55 to 59 years old: 39,049
Population 60 to 64 years old: 35,454
Population 65 to 74 years old: 41,586
Population 75 to 84 years old: 19,987
Population 85 years and over: 10,878
Median age: 35.9

Births (2010–11 Metropolitan Area)

Total number: 44,416

Deaths (2010–11 Metropolitan Area)

Total number: 22,136

Money income (2012)

Per capita income: $42,280
Median household income: $62,617
Total households: 284,559

Number of households with income of ...

less than $10,000: 23,478
$10,000 to $14,999: 12,039
$15,000 to $24,999: 22,104
$25,000 to $34,999: 24,456
$35,000 to $49,999: 33,780
$50,000 to $74,999: 48,349

$75,000 to $99,999: 33,811
$100,000 to $149,999: 43,416
$150,000 to $199,999: 19,355
$200,000 or more: 23,771

Percent of families below poverty level: 14.4%

FBI Crime Index Property: 31,931

FBI Crime Index Violent: 3,746

■ Municipal Government

Seattle operates under a mayor-council form of government. The mayor is elected to a four-year term; the nine council members, elected at large, serve staggered four-year terms. Seattle is the seat of King County.

Head Official: Mayor Ed Murray (since 2014; current term expires 2018)

Total Number of City Employees: 10,870 (2012)

City Information: City Hall, 600 Fourth Avenue, PO Box 94749, Seattle, WA 98124; telephone (206) 684-4000.

■ Economy

Major Industries and Commercial Activity

While Seattle had in the past been largely dependent on the aerospace industry, the city's diverse economy is also based on the manufacture of transportation equipment and forest products, as well as food processing and advanced technology in computer software, biotechnology, electronics, medical equipment, and environmental engineering.

Still aerospace remains vitally important, with some 650 related companies operating in the Seattle metropolitan area, directly supporting 650 jobs. Even when Boeing moved its headquarters from Seattle to Chicago in 2001, tens of thousands of Boeing jobs remained in the Seattle area, and it remains the city's largest private employer. Washington state is then nation's largest exporter of aerospace products, worth more than $23 billion annually, with half of all aerospace jobs located in King County.

The maritime industry in Seattle is another huge contributor to Seattle's economy. Part of the manufacturing and industrial sector, maritime industries account for more than 21,000 jobs in the city. The Port of Seattle, the eighth largest handler of container cargo in the country, provides a direct connection to the Orient—Seattle is located midway between London and Tokyo—and serves as a major link in trade with markets in Alaska, on the Gulf of Mexico, and on the Atlantic Coast. In 2012, 16.1 million tons of goods worth $38 billion

passed through the port. Sea-Tac, Seattle's international airport, ranks among the top 25 cargo airports in North America. Add to that Seattle's multifaceted transportation network of freeways, railroads, and a ferry system, and it explains why Seattle is the principal trade, distribution, financial, and services center for the Northwest.

The city's information and communications technology industry, which is composed of programmers, administrators, analysts, graphic designers, and software developers and engineers, directly employs more than 100,000 area residents. Washington state has more people working in software publishing than any other state, and King County is home to Microsoft, Amazon, and Expedia, in addition to major operations of Google, Facebook, Intel, Hewlett Packard, Oracle, Yahoo!, and Adobe. Also included in the sector is the interactive media industry—producers of video games—which are represented by some 150 companies that have produced classics such as *Myst, Half Life, and Halo.*

Seattle is also emerging as a hub for global biotechnology, ranking as one of the nation's top-five clusters for life science. About 160 companies employ more than 22,000 people in Seattle's biotechnology sector. Some of the largest researchers and developers are tied to the University of Washington, Fred Hutchinson Cancer Research Center, and Bill and Melinda Gates Foundation. The South Lake Union neighborhood serves as the center for the city's biotechnology industry. Clean-energy companies, another high-technology emerging industry, employ more than 30,000.

Tourism continues to be another vital part of the city's economy. Every year, nearly 9 million visitors spend some $7 billion in Seattle and King County.

Fortune 500 businesses headquartered in Seattle include Internet retailer Amazon.com, department store Nordstrom, coffee chain Starbucks, and logistics company Expeditors International of Washington.

Items and goods produced: food products, textiles, aluminum, iron and steel products, lumber, flour, clothing, airplanes, canned fish and fruit

Incentive Programs—New and Existing Companies

Local programs: Incentives available to businesses in Seattle and King County include tax exemptions and credits, customized employee training, and low interest loans. The Grow Seattle Fund, available to small and medium businesses, provides below-market financing to support business growth in amounts from $100,000 to $5 million, with a total annual fund of $8 million. Financing for businesses that create jobs in low-income areas can be obtained through the Craft3 project; the Alliance of Angels seeks to match investors with young companies in search of capital. Rebates are also available to businesses that install energy efficiency improvements.

State programs: The state of Washington offers a number of incentive programs to attract new and expanding businesses to the state, with most targeted to specific industries or geographic areas. Industry-specific incentives include sales and use tax exemptions for general manufacturing and agriculture; sales and use tax deferrals and waivers, and business and occupation tax credits for high-technology industries, including biotechnology and medical device manufacturing; business and occupation tax rate reductions and credits for the aerospace, timber, food manufacturing, biofuel, semiconductor, and aluminum industries; and a range of credits and exemptions for renewable energy firms.

Geography-based incentives are available in designated Community Empowerment Zones, high unemployment counties, and Main Street areas. Other incentives support economic activity that reduces commuter travel; produces television or film; or relates to newspaper publishing.

Job training programs: The state of Washington offers a number of incentive programs to attract new and expanding businesses to the state, with most targeted to specific industries or geographic areas. Industry-specific incentives include sales and use tax exemptions for general manufacturing and agriculture; sales and use tax deferrals and waivers, and business and occupation tax credits for high-technology industries, including biotechnology and medical device manufacturing; business and occupation tax rate reductions and credits for the aerospace, timber, food manufacturing, biofuel, semiconductor, and aluminum industries; and a range of credits and exemptions for renewable energy firms.

The two major contributors to Seattle workforce development are the Workforce Development Council of Seattle (WDC) and the Seattle Jobs Initiative (SJI). The WDC helps with job placement and provides training programs that help residents find living wage jobs. The SJI partners community colleges, community-based organizations, and employers in an effort to recruit, train, place and retain residents with low-income in living wage jobs.

Development Projects

Perhaps one of the area's most ambitious projects is the replacement of the Alaskan Way Viaduct with a tunnel. Because the adjacent seawall has deteriorating and the viaduct itself was severely damaged in the 2001 Nisqually earthquake, both structures need to be rebuilt in order to remove a threat to public safety and the economy. The viaduct is one of the state's most important transportation corridors. Initial construction began 2007, and construction on the viaduct's central waterfront portion began in 2013. All of the project was expected to be completed by 2016, when the viaduct along the central waterfront will be removed. The Alaskan Way Viaduct replacement projects are estimated to cost $3.1 billion.

Quite a few development projects have taken place for the betterment of Seattle's transportations in recent years as well. In 2009 the Sound Transit's Link light rail line stretching from downtown Seattle to the Seattle-Tacoma International Airport was finally completed; the year prior, the Seattle-Tacoma International Airport opened a third runway. In 2010 the airport began construction on a new $419 million rental car facility that completed in 2012 and could accommodate 5,400 vehicles.

The Seattle Center has seen recent additions to its campus. In honor of the 50th anniversary of the 1962 World's Fair, the Seattle Center constructed a 175-foot-tall observation wheel that offers panoramic views of the Seattle Center and opened in 2012. The Seattle Center also became home to a new Chihuly Garden and Glass Museum, which also opened in 2012. The museum houses a collection of artist Dale Chihuly 's work. Total redevelopment at the Seattle Center, expected to continue through 2023, amounted to $570 million.

Residential projects boomed in 2013, with nine major construction efforts adding 1,300 units to the downtown area in the first half of the year. An additional 30 projects were permitted or under construction in 2013, expected to add an additional 5,400 units. Total investment in residential construction was estimated at $2.8 billion. The two largest projects were the 717-unit, $255 million Stadium Place West, and the 670-unit, $450 million Insignia Towers.

The largest office project was a 43-story building known as Fifth + Columbia, which was to also include a 180-room hotel. With 525,000 square feet of office space, the $300 million private investment was expected to complete in 2016.

Economic Development Information: City of Seattle Office of Economic Development, 700 Fifth Avenue, Suite 5752, Seattle, WA 98124-4708; telephone (206) 684-8090; fax (206) 684-0379. Trade Development Alliance of Greater Seattle, 1301 Fifth Avenue, Suite 1500, Seattle, WA 98101; telephone (206) 389-7301; fax (206) 624-5689; email tdags@seattlechamber.com

Commercial Shipping

Seattle's economy benefits from Seattle-Tacoma International Airport (Sea-Tac); total air cargo for 2012 was 283,500 metric tons. Sea-Tac perennially ranks among the top-25 airports for cargo volume in North America. The city's most important commercial asset is Elliott Bay, one of the finest deep-water ports in the world. The Port of Seattle handled 16.1 million tons of goods in 2012, making it the 8th largest U.S. container port and 73rd largest in the world. Two transcontinental railroads and more than 170 motor freight carriers transport goods to and from Seattle.

Labor Force and Employment Outlook

Seattle offers a very highly-educated, skilled, productive, and stable work force, and workers are attracted to the area by the quality of life. The city and its residents are consistently ranked at the top in national polls for college degrees per capita, with more than 54 percent of residents holding a bachelor's degree or higher—twice the national average. A Central Connecticut State University survey ranked Seattle second among the Most Literate Cities in North America, which polled residents in the 79 largest U.S. cities. *Forbes* magazine has ranked Seattle first in the nation for technology jobs.

The following is a summary of data regarding the 2012 Seattle labor force:

Size of civilian labor force: 386,171

Number of workers employed in...

agriculture and mining: 1,740
construction: 10,818
manufacturing: 24,730
wholesale trade: 6,793
retail trade: 38,863
transportation: 10,658
information systems: 12,427
finance: 21,804
professional administration: 71,028
education and social services: 87,272
arts and leisure: 40,922
other: 18,125
public administration: 12,442

Average hourly earnings of production workers: $20.92

Unemployment rate: 4.9% (2012)

Employers

Largest county employers (2011)	*Number of employees*
The Boeing Co.	76,452
Microsoft	40,311
University of Washington	27,920
Providence Health and Services	19,091
King County Government	13,382
United States Postal Service	12,367
City of Seattle	10,627
Costco Wholesale Corp.	8,224
Group Health Cooperative	8,125
Nordstrom Inc.	7,343
Swedish	7,069

Cost of Living

The cost of living in Seattle is not inexpensive, given the relatively high price of housing. Still, it is far less expensive than major Californian cities, and high median income levels compensate in part for Seattle's greater cost of living.

The following is a summary of data regarding several key cost of living factors in the area.

2013 ACCRA Average House Price: $381,471

2013 ACCRA Cost of Living Index: 118

State income tax rate: None

State sales tax rate: 6.5%

Local income tax rate: None

Local sales tax rate: 3.0%

Property tax rate: $10.29168 to $13.39768 per $1,000 assessed value (2013)

Economic Information: Economic Development Council of Seattle and King County, 1301 5th Avenue, Suite 1500, Seattle, WA 98101; telephone (206) 389-8650; email info@edc-seaking.org.

■ Education and Research

Elementary and Secondary Schools

Seattle Public Schools is the largest district in the state. The system is administered by a nonpartisan, seven-member school board that appoints a superintendent. The district serves students that speak some 120 languages, and 12 percent of students are English-language learners. Top foreign languages spoken by students were Spanish, Somali, Chinese, Vietnamese, and Tagalog, in that order. Roughly 40 percent of students are eligible for free or reduced lunch. The district employs 2,730 teachers, including 227 National Board–Certified teachers. The 2011–12 four-year high school graduation rate was 74 percent.

More than 300 private and parochial schools, preschools, and special schools also operate in the Seattle metropolitan area.

The following is a summary of data regarding the Seattle Public Schools.

Total enrollment: 47,735

Number of facilities

total: 95
elementary schools: 63
junior high schools: 15
high schools: 12
other: 5

Student/teacher ratio: 18.5:1

Teacher salaries
  average (statewide): $53,796

Funding per pupil: $11,154

Public Schools Information: Seattle Public Schools, 2445 3rd Avenue, S. Seattle, WA 98134; telephone (206) 252-0000.

Colleges and Universities

The University of Washington, Seattle Pacific University, and Seattle University are the major four-year accredited institutions of higher learning in Seattle. They offer baccalaureate degrees in a wide range of disciplines and graduate degrees in such fields as education, law, software engineering, and medicine.

The University of Washington offers over 250 degree options, and its Seattle campus had over 42,000 students enrolled in fall of 2013. For nearly 40 consecutive years, the school has received more federal research funding than any other public university in the nation. It received $1.47 billion in total sponsored grants and contracts in 2012, with just over $1 billion coming from federal funds.

Seattle Pacific University, a Christian university founded in 1891 by Free Methodist pioneers, has an enrollment of approximately 4,300 students. The university offers 62 undergraduate majors and 20 master's degree programs. Seattle University, one of the largest independent educational institutions in the Pacific Northwest, is a Jesuit university that serves approximately 7,500 students. It is regularly ranked as one of *U.S. News & World Report*'s top ten universities in the West; it ranked sixth in 2013.

A number of community colleges, vocational schools, and adult-education centers serve Seattle residents as well.

Libraries and Research Centers

In addition to its main branch downtown, the Seattle Public Library system operates 26 branches throughout the city and also provides bookmobile services. Its collection consists of more than two million items. Special collections focus on aeronautics, African Americans, and Northwest history. In 1998 Seattle voters approved a $290.7 million bond measure to upgrade the Seattle Public Library system with new facilities, technology, and books. The 362,987-square-foot main facility, which opened in 2004, includes a 275-seat auditorium and parking for 143 vehicles. All construction completed by 2008.

The University of Washington's library, said to be the largest and most comprehensive in the Northwest, holds more than 7 million volumes. Special libraries there are affiliated with universities, government agencies, hospitals, and local corporations, concentrating on such fields as medicine, business, banking, law, and science.

The University of Washington is the heart of research study in Seattle, boasting more than 270 specialized research centers, with focuses in the areas of microcomputer architecture, digital systems theory, speech and image processing, artificial intelligence, and metallurgical and ceramic engineering. Other major research facilities are the Fred Hutchinson Cancer Research Center and the Battelle Memorial Institute.

Public Library Information: Seattle Public Library, 1000 Fourth Avenue, Seattle, WA 98104-1109; telephone (206) 386-4636.

■ Health Care

With a national reputation for diagnostic and treatment facilities, Seattle-King County is the health-care center for the Pacific Northwest. The metropolitan area offers 45 general acute-care hospitals providing some 9,400 beds, staffed by more than 15,000 medical professionals.

The University of Washington's main facilities, Harborview Medical Center and UW Medical Center, treat more than one million patients annually in their emergency rooms and outpatient clinics, and while admitting a combined 41,000 patients. The University of Washington also operates the Northwest Hospital and Medical Center and Valley Medical Center. UW Medical Center, a teaching hospital, was ranked nationally by *U.S. News & World Report* in 2013 in ten adult specialties, including top-10 rankings in cancer, diabetes and endocrinology, and rehabilitation.

Among Seattle's other leading health-care institutions are the Seattle Children's Hospital, a 250-bed facility ranked nationally in 10 pediatric specialties by *U.S. News & World Report* in 2013. Also in Seattle are the Fred Hutchinson Cancer Research Center, Virginia Mason Hospital and Medical Center, and Swedish Medical Center. Bailey-Boushay House is a nationally recognized residence where people with HIV can be treated less expensively than at traditional centers. The Seattle Cancer Treatment and Wellness Center is the only cancer center in the Pacific Northwest where medical oncologists work side by side with practitioners of alternative medicine.

■ Recreation

Sightseeing

Seattle is consistently ranked among the top U.S. tourist destinations. Many attractions are located in the pedestrian-scale downtown area or within easy access by bus and monorail. Tourists can choose from several diversions, including historical sites, internationally acclaimed cultural events, and outdoor activities in the spectacular mountains, forests, and waters surrounding the city.

A popular Seattle landmark is the Space Needle, focal point of the Seattle Center, the 74-acre park and building complex constructed for the 1962 World's Fair. The 605-foot Space Needle features an observation deck for viewing the city, Puget Sound, and adjacent Cascade and Olympic mountains. At its base is the $100 million Experience Music Project, a nonprofit interactive museum tracing the history of American music, which was funded entirely by Microsoft co-founder Paul Allen. The Seattle Center, linked to the central business district by free bus service and the high-speed monorail, contains an amusement park and sponsors outdoor concerts as well as other events. In celebration of the 50th anniversary of the 1962 World's Fair, the Seattle Center opened a 200-foot-tall observation wheel and the Chihuly Garden and Glass Museum in 2012.

Pioneer Square, near the waterfront downtown, is the city's historic district. This area offers a trip back to late-1800s Seattle via cobblestone streets, the original Skid Road (an expression that later evolved into Skid Row), and restored brick and sandstone buildings, many of them housing shops and restaurants. A unique point of interest beneath Pioneer Square is the "underground city," five blocks of sidewalks and storefronts that were left standing after the 1889 fire, when the street levels were raised.

Seattle offers an abundance of attractions related to the maritime industry. Harbor traffic on Elliott Bay can be observed from Waterfront Park, located in the pier area just off Alaskan Way. South of the park at Pier 53, the Seattle Fire Department boats *Chief Seattle, Leschi,* and *Marine One* are berthed; a favorite local event is practice day, when the fireboats shoot high water arcs into the bay. At Fishermen's Terminal, a working commercial fishing port, residents and visitors enjoy watching fishermen mend nets and tend their boats. Hiram M. Chittenden Locks (Ballard Locks), among the busiest locks in the world, furnish diversion for navigation enthusiasts as scores of large and small vessels are transferred daily between salt and fresh water. The Seattle Aquarium on the downtown waterfront links the waterfront to First Avenue, which lies just above. For those wanting to go out onto the water, ferries provide rides along the coast and across the sound; tour boats offer longer cruises and excursions to points of interest in the area.

Seattle is known for the Woodland Park Zoo, which contains about 1,100 animals in their natural habitats with minimal fencing and barriers; special features are 50 endangered species and the world's largest group of lion-tailed macaques. In 2009, it opened its Humboldt penguin exhibit, home to 20 endangered Humboldt penguins. Washington Park on the University of Washington campus is the setting for the Arboretum, 200 acres of public gardens, including a Japanese tea garden, with especially striking displays of blossoms and foliage during spring and fall.

Arts and Culture

Seattle is the cultural and entertainment hub of the Pacific Northwest as well as one of the nation's leading cities for theater and opera. Rivaled only by New York in the number of equity theaters based in the area and considered one of the leading U.S. cities for opera performances, Seattle is an international leader for annual productions from Wagner's *Ring* cycle. Attaining wide recognition has in fact become a Seattle tradition, yet cultural events also emphasize regional artists and performers.

The Seattle Opera, recognized internationally for its compelling and accomplished performances, moved into its new state-of-the-art home, Marion Oliver McCaw Hall, in 2003. The Seattle Repertory Theatre Company, the city's principal and nationally acclaimed professional theater company, stages its annual productions at the Bagley Wright Theater at Seattle Center. Downtown's Paramount Theatre houses both the 5th Avenue Theatre and visiting Broadway shows, and the Moore Theatre, the oldest remaining theater in Seattle, hosts community events, local dance troupes, local bands, and nontraditional music and theater. Live theater is presented by area companies, including A Contemporary Theater (ACT), now housed at the renovated Eagle's Auditorium and Intiman. Several small theaters are also active in the Seattle metropolitan area. Dramatic and musical performances are regularly scheduled at the University of Washington. Seattle hosts large-scale musical concerts and has gained international attention as the place of origin of many trend-setting rock and pop groups. Pacific Northwest Ballet is the area's main ballet company.

Seattle supports nearly 400 galleries and four art museums. The Seattle Art Museum displays a large collection of Oriental, Asian, African, and modern art; of special interest is a collection of paintings by the Northwest Mystics school. The Seattle Art Museum is responsible for the award-winning nine-acre Olympic Sculpture Park, which opened in 2007. The park is located on the Seattle waterfront and is the home of outdoor art framed against a backdrop of the Olympic Mountains and Puget Sound. The Frye Art Museum downtown features exhibits of eighteenth- and nineteenth-century and contemporary paintings. The Bellevue Arts Museum in Bellevue Square specializes in works by regional artists. The city is also home to the Seattle Asian Art Museum. The Henry Art Gallery at the University of Washington is one of the oldest art museums in the state. Commercial galleries, most of them clustered around Pioneer Square, regularly schedule shows.

The Museum of Flight, home to more than 85 aircraft, traces the history of flight from Leonardo da Vinci to the present with such exhibits as "Apollo," which chronicles manned space exploration and displays more than 40 aircraft. The Suquamish Museum is devoted to the preservation of Puget Sound native culture; artifacts, photographs, and oral histories are featured. Daybreak

Star Indian Cultural Center in Discovery Park pays homage to Northwest Coast tribes through indoor and outdoor displays of paintings and carvings. The Burke Museum of Natural History and Culture displays artifacts and geological materials relating to Northwest Coast native and Pacific Rim cultures; dinosaur exhibits are a highlight. The Museum of History and Industry (MOHAI) concentrates on the heritage of Seattle, King County, and the Pacific Northwest. The Pacific Science Center, located at Seattle Center, presents exhibits pertaining to science; laser shows and films are shown at the Eames/IMAX Theater. The Seattle Children's Museum, also at Seattle Center, offers such hands-on activities as a child-size neighborhood for both adults and children.

Festivals and Holidays

Seattle and its environs, a major attraction for the television and film industry, support an annual, world-famous international film festival. Other festival celebrations include the Bite of Seattle food festival and the Northwest Folklife Festival, held at Seattle Center on Memorial Day weekend in May. Held annually for 23 days from mid-July to early August, the Seafair includes boat races and exhibitions, parades, a queen coronation and pageant, fishing derbies, food, and entertainment. Also in July and August is the famous Wagner Festival, presenting performances from the composer's *Ring* cycle, staged at Marion Oliver McCaw Hall. Seattle Center is the site on Labor Day weekend of the Seattle Arts Festival, popularly known as "Bumbershoot"; rated as one of the top festivals in the nation, it is a celebration of the city's arts community, with more than 400 performances ranging from grunge bands to Russian tightrope walkers. The year closes with the Argosy Christmas Ships Festival in December.

Sports for the Spectator

Seattle was once the only city in the Northwest to support professional teams in three major sports. However, in 2008 the SuperSonics, Seattle's National Basketball Association team, moved to Oklahoma City. Seattle is still home to both National Football League and Major League Baseball franchises. The Seattle Seahawks play football at CenturyLink Field, a 72,000-seat, open-air stadium. The Seattle Mariners play American League baseball at Safeco Field, which has a retractable roof. Soccer fans enjoy Major League Soccer matches featuring the Seattle Sounders at CenturyLink Field. The Seattle Thunderbirds of the Western Hockey League play at the Seattle Center, and the Seattle Storm are part of the Women's National Basketball Association. Area colleges and universities field teams in all primary sports. There is also horse racing at Emerald Downs, minor league baseball with the Everett AquaSox (Single A) and Tacoma Rainiers (Triple A), and Professional Rodeo Cowboys Association (PRCA) events.

Sports for the Participant

Seattle describes itself as a "metronatural" city, meaning that it has characteristics of a major metropolis tucked away within wild, natural, and breathtaking surroundings. Considered one of the best recreational cities in the United States, Seattle offers a variety of outdoor activities. Especially popular are water sports such as fresh- and salt-water fishing, boating, swimming, scuba diving, and whitewater rafting on lakes and waterways within an hour of downtown. Hiking and horseback riding can be enjoyed on miles of forest trails maintained in area parks and mountains; skiing and mountain climbing, including guided climbs to the top of Mount Rainier, can be pursued at several locations in the mountains surrounding Seattle. Seattle is also a bicyclist's dream, with a plethora of recreational trails, such as Cheshiahud Lake Union Loop, a six-mile path that circles Lake Union. Four municipal golf courses, more than 150 tennis courts, 12 beaches, 10 swimming pools, and more than 180 athletic fields can be found in the area's more than 400 parks and open spaces, which total in excess of 6,200 acres.

Shopping and Dining

Shopping can be a unique experience in Seattle, where high-fashion merchandise and recreational gear coexist on shop counters. Major department stores and designer boutiques are located downtown within walking distance of hotels and in suburban shopping centers throughout the area. Seattle is the nation's primary manufacturing and retail center for recreational and outdoor equipment. Northwest Native American handicrafts and art items are available at local artisan centers, specialty shops, and galleries and museums; goods imported from the Orient are featured at shops in Seattle's International District, where Chinatown is located. Historic Pike Place Market near Pioneer Square is one of the few remaining authentic farmer's markets in the nation. A terraced walkway leads from the market to Alaskan Way, a colorful waterfront streetcar route lined with piers, marine equipment shops, and seafood restaurants.

Seafood is a Seattle specialty, and seafood stands and restaurants featuring dishes prepared from daily catches abound. The city has also gained a national reputation as the center for "Northwest cuisine": Olympia oysters, geoduck clams, wild mushrooms, fresh produce, whole-grain breads, and local cheeses and wines. Many restaurants feature scenic locations that enhance dining pleasure, and opportunities for alfresco dining are plentiful. Asian food is found on many local menus, and citizens have gone wild for coffee-coffee shops and espresso carts can be found in the usual locations and even in gas stations and hardware stores.

Visitor Information: Seattle/King County Convention & Visitors Bureau, 701 Pike Street, Suite 800, Seattle, WA 98101; telephone (206) 461-5800; fax (206) 461-5855.

■ Convention Facilities

The Washington State Convention Center is the city's major meeting and conference facility. The facility offers up to 61 meeting rooms and ballrooms totaling approximately 105,000 square feet of space, and exhibit space totaling 205,700 square feet. Coupled with the Convention Center's 71,000-square-foot Conference Center that opened in 2010, the center offers a total of 414,000 square feet of function space. The center sits on top of Interstate 5, within walking distance of more than 9,000 hotel rooms. The 74-acre Seattle Center also hosts conventions and meetings.

Lynnwood Convention Center, Meydenbauer Center, and Bell Harbor International Conference Center are among other locations used for trade shows and meetings. Hotels and motels throughout the metropolitan area provide a total of some 25,000 rooms as well as additional convention and meeting accommodations.

Convention Information: Seattle/King County Convention & Visitors Bureau, 701 Pike Street, Suite 800, Seattle, WA 98101; telephone (206) 461-5800; fax (206) 461-5855.

■ Transportation

Approaching the City

Air travelers to Seattle are served by the Seattle-Tacoma International Airport (Sea-Tac), the 15th busiest commercial airport in the United States. Sea-Tac is a modern facility that served over 33.2 million passengers in 2012 on more than 20 airlines. It offers non-stop flights to roughly 100 domestic and international destinations. In 2008 the airport completed a third runway that enables aircraft to land in any weather conditions.

Two interstate highways serve Seattle: Interstate 5 (north–south) and Interstate 90 (east–west). Seattle is the southern terminus of the Alaska Marine Highway System; ferries transporting passengers and motor vehicles operate year round from points in southeast Alaska. Passenger rail service to major U.S. destinations is provided by Amtrak, and buses connect Seattle with U.S. and Canadian cities and with Tijuana, Mexico.

Traveling in the City

Avenues in Seattle run north and south and streets run east and west. The city center is perhaps best explored on foot. Seattle's bus- and trolley-based mass transit system, Metro Transit, operates routes throughout the Seattle-King County area. Metro Transit has 220 routes serving 115 million passengers annually within a 2,134-square-mile area. Metro Transit operates the largest publicly owned vanpool program in the country, with more than 1,300 vans making more than 3.5 million trips per year.

■ Communications

Newspapers and Magazines

Seattle's major daily newspapers are the evening *The Seattle Times* and the morning *Seattle Post-Intelligencer*. Seattle is also the headquarters for several weekly, biweekly, or monthly publications appealing to ethnic groups, such as *Northwest Asian Weekly* and *Korea Daily*. *Slate,* an online publication developed by Microsoft, started in Seattle.

Television and Radio

All major television networks have affiliates in Seattle, and cable service is available. Some 13 AM and 15 FM radio stations are based in Seattle, providing music, news, and features; other stations broadcast from neighboring communities.

Media Information: *The Seattle Times,* 1120 John St., Seattle, WA 98109; telephone (206) 464-2111. *Seattle Post-Intelligencer,* 101 Elliott Ave. W, Suite 540, Seattle, WA 98119; telephone (206) 448-8000.

Seattle Online

City of Seattle home page. Available www.seattle.gov
Economic Development Council of Seattle and King County. Available www.edc-seaking.org
Greater Seattle Chamber of Commerce. Available www.seattlechamber.com
Seattle Daily Journal of Commerce. Available www.djc.com
Seattle-King County Convention & Visitors Bureau. Available www.visitseattle.org
Seattle Post-Intelligencer. Available www.seattlepi.com
Seattle Public Library. Available www.spl.org
Seattle Public Schools. Available www.seattleschools.org
The Seattle Times. Available seattletimes.com
Washington State Tourism home page. Available www.experiencewa.com

BIBLIOGRAPHY

Dillard, Annie, *The Living* (New York: HarperCollins, 1992)

Mullins, William H., *Becoming Big League: Seattle, the Pilots, and Stadium Politics* (Seattle, WA: University of Washington Press, 2013)

Pomper, Steve *It Happened in Seattle: Remarkable Events that Shaped History* (Guilford, CT: Globe Pequot Press, 2010)

Sanders, Jeffrey C., *Seattle and the Roots of Urban Sustainability: Inventing Ecotopia* (Pittsburgh: University of Pittsburgh Press, 2010)

Spokane

■ The City in Brief

Founded: 1878 (incorporated, 1881)

Head Official: Mayor David A. Condon (since 2012; current term expires 2016)

City Population
> 1990: 177,196
> 2000: 195,629
> 2010: 208,916
> 2012 estimate: 209,504
> Percent change, 2000–2010: 6.8%
> U.S. rank in 1990: 94th (State rank: 2nd)
> U.S. rank in 2000: 110th (State rank: 2nd)
> U.S. rank in 2010: 100th (State rank: 2nd)

Metropolitan Statistical Area Population
> 2000: 417,939
> 2010: 471,221
> 2012 estimate: 475,735
> Percent change, 2000–2010: 12.7%
> U.S. rank in 2000: 107th
> U.S. rank in 2010: 107th

Area: 58 square miles

Elevation: Ranges from 1,898 to 2,356 feet above sea level

Average Annual Temperatures: January, 27.3° F; July, 68.6° F; annual average, 47.3° F

Average Annual Precipitation: 16.67 inches of rain; 48.8 inches of snow

Major Economic Sectors: services, manufacturing, health care, retail trade

Unemployment Rate: 6.6% (2012)

Per Capita Income: $23,533

2012 FBI Crime Index Property: 18,522

Major Colleges and Universities: Eastern Washington University, Gonzaga University, Whitworth University, Washington State University–Spokane, Spokane Community Colleges

Daily Newspaper: *The Spokesman-Review*

■ Introduction

Spokane is the commercial and cultural hub of a large area known as the "Inland Empire" or the "Inland Northwest," a rich agricultural region. The second largest city in the state of Washington, Spokane is home to more than 200,000 residents with a metropolitan population reaching nearly 500,000. The picturesque beauty of its surroundings makes the city an attractive vacation spot, and population and economic growth have brought many metropolitan amenities to the once quiet, out-of-the-way town. Although the city suffered from decay during the late 1980s and early 1990s, Spokane has undergone an impressive $1 billion urban renaissance and, through its many development projects, including its University District, has ensured its status as an economic, recreational, and cultural hub in the Pacific Northwest.

■ Geography and Climate

Spokane is located near the eastern border of Washington, about 20 miles from Idaho and 110 miles south of the Canadian border. The city lies on the eastern edge of the Columbia Basin, a wide sloping plain that rises sharply to the east toward the Rocky Mountains. The Spokane River and its waterfalls bisect the city. Summers are typically dry and mild, and winters can bring periods of cold, wet weather. Snowfall rarely accumulates to depths greater than one foot.

SolidagoliStockPhoto.com

Area: 58 square miles

Elevation: Ranges from 1,898 to 2,356 feet above sea level

Average Temperatures: January, 27.3° F; July, 68.6° F; annual average, 47.3° F

Average Annual Precipitation: 16.67 inches of rain; 48.8 inches of snow

■ History

Spokane Area Popular with Traders

For years before the coming of European explorers, the land around the present-day city was settled by the Spokane tribe. Explorers and trappers passed through the area, but no settlements were built until 1810, when Finan McDonald and Joco Finlay built a trading post called Spokane House at the junction of the Spokane and Little Spokane rivers. In 1812 John Clarke of the Pacific Fur Company built Fort Spokane not far from the trading post. The house and fort soon became a popular meeting place for traders, trappers, and Native Americans, and the buildings were sold to the North West Company in 1813.

The Hudson's Bay Company bought the North West Company in 1821 and dismantled Spokane House. The area was once again left to local tribes. Chief Garry, the leader of the Middle and Upper Spokane tribes, had been educated at the Red River Mission school and converted to Presbyterianism. He built a school for his people and taught them English and religion, as well as modern agricultural methods. At about the same time, the first missionaries arrived in the area, establishing a mission on Walker's Prairie, 25 miles north of Spokane Falls.

The great westward expansion of the 1840s attracted a number of settlers to the area, but a clash with local tribes, culminating in the Whitman Massacre, led to the closing of eastern Oregon (the Spokane area was then part of the Oregon Territory) to settlement in the 1850s. In 1871 J. J. Downing and his family located a claim on the banks of the Spokane River. Within a year, the small settlement included a sawmill, a post office, and a general store. In 1873 James N. Glover, who is called the "father of Spokane," rode through the area on horseback. He was, he wrote, "enchanted . . . overwhelmed . . . with the beauty and grandeur of everything." Glover bought the rights to Downing's land and sawmill and opened a store and stable. His early trade was with the Spokane and

Coeur d'Alene Indians who lived in the region. The town was registered as Spokane Falls in 1878. By 1880, the town had a population of 75 people, a weekly newspaper, and several baseball teams. In 1881 it was incorporated.

Rapid Population Growth Builds Sophisticated City

Spokane Falls grew steadily throughout the ensuing decades, changing from a rough frontier community into a solid city, complete with all the trappings of Eastern culture: a college, a library, and a number of theaters. The transcontinental railroad reached Spokane Falls in 1883, ensuring the town's success. Fire destroyed much of the town in 1889, but residents quickly rebuilt. By 1890, the city had a population of 30,000 people and changed its name to Spokane when Oregon entered the Union. By 1910 the population had jumped to over 100,000 people.

In 1974 the city was host to the World's Fair, Expo '74, which focused the world's attention on Spokane. Development of Expo '74 buildings and other improvements at the fair site in downtown Spokane created a modern city center with an extensive system of enclosed skywalks. Expansion and development continued through the 1990s and into the new century. Faced with the possibility of losing important downtown retailers, Spokane embarked upon an ambitious and large-scale effort at renewing the city center.

These efforts have been enormously successful, as Spokane has continued to attract new retailers and businesses as well as residents who are fleeing high prices in California and in Seattle. The city's next economic growth engine was tied to the opening of a medical school affiliated with the University of Washington, which accepted its first class of medical students in the fall of 2013.

Historical Information: Eastern Washington State Historical Society/Northwest Museum of Arts and Culture, Joel E. Ferris Research Library and Archives, 2316 W. First Avenue, Spokane, WA 99201; telephone (509) 363-5342; fax (509) 363-5303; themac@ northwestmuseum.org

■ Population Profile

Metropolitan Statistical Area Population

2000: 417,939
2010: 471,221
2012 estimate: 475,735
Percent change, 2000–2010: 12.7%
U.S. rank in 2000: 107th
U.S. rank in 2010: 107th

City Residents

1990: 177,196
2000: 195,629
2010: 208,916
2012 estimate: 209,504
Percent change, 2000–2010: 6.8%
U.S. rank in 1990: 94th (State rank: 2nd)
U.S. rank in 2000: 110th (State rank: 2nd)
U.S. rank in 2010: 100th (State rank: 2nd)

Density: 3,526.2 people per square mile

Racial and ethnic characteristics

White: 183,521
Black or African American: 4,098
American Indian and Alaskan Native: 3,997
Asian: 6,649
Native Hawaiian and Other Pacific Islander: 470
Hispanic or Latino (may be of any race): 10,421
Other: 10,769

Percent of residents born in state: 54.4%

Age characteristics

Population under 5 years old: 15,285
Population 5 to 9 years old: 12,534
Population 10 to 14 years old: 12,337
Population 15 to 19 years old: 12,277
Population 20 to 24 years old: 17,510
Population 25 to 34 years old: 32,578
Population 35 to 44 years old: 24,488
Population 45 to 54 years old: 26,222
Population 55 to 59 years old: 13,428
Population 60 to 64 years old: 12,399
Population 65 to 74 years old: 16,180
Population 75 to 84 years old: 9,910
Population 85 years and over: 4,356
Median age: 35.8

Births (2010–11 Metropolitan Area)

Total number: 5,873

Deaths (2010–11 Metropolitan Area)

Total number: 3,964

Money income (2012)

Per capita income: $23,533
Median household income: $41,593
Total households: 88,184

Number of households with income of ...

less than $10,000: 8,610
$10,000 to $14,999: 5,987
$15,000 to $24,999: 11,977
$25,000 to $34,999: 11,271
$35,000 to $49,999: 12,923
$50,000 to $74,999: 16,769
$75,000 to $99,999: 9,705
$100,000 to $149,999: 7,093
$150,000 to $199,999: 2,001
$200,000 or more: 1,848

Percent of families below poverty level: 18.7%

FBI Crime Index Property: 18,522

FBI Crime Index Violent: 1,369

■ Municipal Government

Spokane's mayor-council form of government formerly elected a mayor and six other council members to four-year terms; the council employed a city manager for the day-to-day operation of the city. In 1999 Spokane voters adopted a strong-mayor form of government, eliminating the city manager position. The city council still has seven members; a council president now presides over meetings instead of the mayor, so there are eight elected city officials instead of seven.

Head Official: Mayor David A. Condon (since 2012; current term expires 2016)

Total Number of City Employees: 1,864 (2012)

City Information: City of Spokane, 808 W. Spokane Falls Blvd., Spokane, WA 99201; telephone (509) 755-2489.

■ Economy

Major Industries and Commercial Activity

Natural resources have traditionally provided much of the economic activity for the Spokane area, a major center for the timber, agriculture, and mining industries in the region. A number of manufacturing companies have located in Spokane, drawn by the easy access to raw materials. Aluminum casting, computers and electronic equipment, medical supplies, and paper and plastic products are among the leaders in manufacturing. Even though manufacturing only accounts for about 10 percent of the nonfarm workforce, over 500 manufacturing businesses provide jobs to 15,000 workers. The aerospace industry is a particularly noteworthy facet of the manufacturing sector, providing jobs to over 1,500 workers with an annual payroll of some $77.4 million.

The outlying areas of Spokane are part of an abundant agricultural system, providing a large amount of the nation's apples, peas, hops, pears, asparagus, lentils, soft wheat, and sweet cherries. A number of wineries and breweries also operate in the area. These industries continue to be important elements in the local economy, generating $117 million in annual economic impact and employing more than 1,500 people.

Health-related industries employ more people than any other industry in Spokane, making it no surprise that Spokane is considered the health-care hub of the Inland Northwest. Health care accounts for 18.5 percent of the local employment base. The city provides specialized care to many patients from the surrounding areas, as far north as the Canadian border. A workforce of 34,000 individuals, including 900 physicians, runs over 1,100 businesses and five major hospitals within the city.

Spokane has also seen the recent development of economic activity in the lucrative high-tech and biotech sectors. The city is the site of a 100-block wireless network (the Spokane Hot Zone), among the largest of its kind in the country, which is seen as symbolic of its dedication to the development of technological opportunities and resources. Innovate Washington (formerly Sirti Technology Center) has been a hub for attracting high-tech companies; in 2012 there were 38 companies and organizations operating at the center, with 10 companies having invested at least $1 million. Major technology businesses based in the area include Purcell Systems, Itron Inc., Telect, AdvantageIQ, Critical Logic, NextIT, Agilent, and Inland Northwest Health Services. There are also some 50 clean technology or energy efficiency companies in the Spokane region.

Spokane County's other largest industry sectors are government, distribution, and retail trade. Fairchild Air Force Base is one of the city's largest employers.

Items and goods produced: silver, lead, zinc, timber, poultry, dairy, vegetable, fruit, meat products, aluminum, magnesium, clay and cement products, machinery and metal products, flour, feed, cereal, petroleum products, paper, electrical fixtures

Incentive Programs—New and Existing Companies

Local programs: Greater Spokane Incorporated works with businesses to locate and utilize local and state business incentives. The Spokane Neighborhood Economic Development Alliance offers two revolving loans to businesses and nonprofits expanding or creating new jobs in Spokane.

State programs: The state of Washington offers a number of incentive programs to attract new and expanding businesses to the state, with most targeted to specific industries or geographic areas. Industry-specific incentives include sales and use tax exemptions for general manufacturing and agriculture; sales and use tax deferrals and waivers, and business and occupation tax credits for high-technology industries, including biotechnology and medical device manufacturing; business and occupation tax rate reductions and credits for the aerospace, timber, food manufacturing, biofuel, semiconductor, and aluminum industries; and a range of credits and exemptions for renewable energy firms.

Geography-based incentives are available in designated Community Empowerment Zones, high unemployment counties, and Main Street areas. Other incentives support economic activity that reduces commuter travel;

produces television or film; or relates to newspaper publishing.

Job training programs: The state of Washington offers a number of incentive programs to attract new and expanding businesses to the state, with most targeted to specific industries or geographic areas. Industry-specific incentives include sales and use tax exemptions for general manufacturing and agriculture; sales and use tax deferrals and waivers, and business and occupation tax credits for high-technology industries, including biotechnology and medical device manufacturing; business and occupation tax rate reductions and credits for the aerospace, timber, food manufacturing, biofuel, semiconductor, and aluminum industries; and a range of credits and exemptions for renewable energy firms.

Spokane businesses are assisted largely by working with the higher education community. The Community Colleges of Spokane's Training and Education Coordinating Center (TECC), a one-stop training coordinator, helps match up client training needs with resources provided by Spokane Falls Community College, Spokane Community College, and the Institute of Extended Learning. The Business Training and Applied Technology Center (BTATC), also run by Community Colleges of Spokane, helps businesses learn how to inexpensively and quickly incorporate technological advances into their operations. Other similar organizations include the Applied Technology Center, also part of the Community Colleges of Spokane. The Spokane Area Workforce Development Council administers employment and training programs for local economically disadvantaged youths and adults through the Spokane City-County Employment and Training Consortium. The council also supports local economic growth by working to improve the workforce development system.

Development Projects

The Spokane's University District is an ongoing revitalization project for the city of Spokane, with a goal of promoting economic development in the area located east of downtown. Five institutions occupy space in the U-district, including Washington State University, Gonzaga, Eastern Washington University, Whitworth University, and the Community Colleges of Spokane. While hundreds of millions of dollars were invested in the area during the late 2000s and early 2010s, perhaps the most notable project was expansion of the University of Washington's School of Medicine to Spokane. Construction of a $60 million facility completed in 2013, with the anticipation of annually graduating as many as 120 physicians. The school was to focus on delivery primary care in small communities, the largest need for the surrounding region that includes Wyoming, Alaska, Montana, and Idaho, in addition to Washington.

Despite a major expansion in 2007, the Spokane Convention Center's master plan included additional expansions of the convention district into the 2020s. Previous expansions included $80 million in renovations and construction of new amenities in the existing areas, and a new 100,000-square-foot exhibition hall. Construction during 2013–14 included replacement and addition of arena seats, as well as improvements to the riverbank and adjacent Centennial Trail.

In 2012 the Honor Point Museum Military and Aerospace Museum obtained a lease for a 14,400-square-foot piece of land near Felts Field in Spokane to construct a museum honoring the achievements and importance of both the armed forces and aviation in the city's history. With the signing of the lease, the museum began a $6 million fundraising campaign to construct the museum, which was estimated to have a $5 million annual economic impact. The Spokane Public Market, an arena for food vendors and local artisans, opened in 2011.

The city of Spokane set aside $117 million for street improvements over a 10-year period between 2005 and 2015. The project is expected to repair about 110 miles of residential streets and arterials throughout Spokane.

The Spokane tribe announced plans in 2011 for a new $400 million casino and retail space in nearby Airway Heights, which still awaited state and federal approval in 2014. Development of the project, advocated by the tribe as a means to create more than 2,000 jobs and achieve economic self-sufficiency, remained controversial for opponents of gambling and those concerned about the development's environmental and quality-of-life impacts.

Economic Development Information: Greater Spokane Incorporated, 801 West Riverside, Suite 100, Spokane, WA 99201; telephone (509) 624-1393; toll-free (800) SPOKANE; email info@greaterspokane.org.

Commercial Shipping

Two air cargo carriers fly out of Spokane International Airport: Federal Express and United Parcel Service. The airport processed more than 61,000 tons of air cargo tons in 2012. The Burlington Northern Santa Fe and Union Pacific/Southern Pacific railroads also serve the city. Many motor freight concerns operate regularly scheduled trucks in and out of Spokane. Once completed, the North Spokane Corridor is predicted to increase freight transportation between Spokane and Canada as well; the corridor was half-completed by the end of 2013.

Labor Force and Employment Outlook

A large, experienced work force is available in Spokane; about 80 percent of workers are native Washingtonians. Greater than 90 percent of the Spokane County population over 25 years of age had high school degrees or higher as of 2013. Nearly 20 percent had obtained at least a bachelor's degree, while more than 11 percent held graduate diplomas.

The following is a summary of data regarding the 2012 Spokane labor force:

Size of civilian labor force: 105,400

Number of workers employed in . . .

agriculture and mining: 704
construction: 4,414
manufacturing: 6,548
wholesale trade: 3,659
retail trade: 11,481
transportation: 4,811
information systems: 1,898
finance: 5,792
professional administration: 9,636
education and social services: 25,638
arts and leisure: 10,236
other: 4,570
public administration: 4,135

Average hourly earnings of production workers: $16.55

Unemployment rate: 6.6% (2012)

Employers

Largest county employers (2012)	*Number of employees*
State of Washington	4,202
Spokane Public Schools	3,025
Providence Sacred Heart Medical Center	3,010
92nd Air Refueling Wing, Fairchild Air Force Base	2,892
Spokane County	1,908
City of Spokane	1,864
Walmart	1,484
Northern Quest Casino & Resort	1,359
URM Stores	1,322
Central Valley School District	1,270

Cost of Living

The cost of living in Spokane is slightly below the national average, and housing prices are significantly less expensive than those in major cities in the western part of the state.

The following is a summary of data regarding several key cost of living factors in the area.

2013 ACCRA Average House Price: $261,111

2013 ACCRA Cost of Living Index: 97

State income tax rate: None

State sales tax rate: 6.5%

Local income tax rate: None

Local sales tax rate: 2.2%

Property tax rate: $13.00 per $1,000 of assessed value (county average, 2013)

Economic Information: Greater Spokane Incorporated, 801 West Riverside, Suite 100, Spokane, WA 99201; telephone (509) 624-1393; toll-free (800) SPOKANE; email info@greaterspokane.org. Greater Spokane Valley Chamber of Commerce, 1421 North Meadowwood Lane, Suite #10, Liberty Lake, WA 99019; telephone (509) 924-4994; toll-free (866) 475-1436; fax (509) 924-4992.

■ Education and Research

Elementary and Secondary Schools

Spokane School District Number 81, representing all city schools, is the second largest in the state and the largest in eastern Washington. The district is composed of 34 elementary, six middle, and six high schools. It is also home to the NEWTECH Skills Center, which partners with local high schools to offer advanced technical and professional training. The district boasts a number of alternative schools, including a homeless education program, school-parent partnerships, and a Montessori school. Some 74 percent of teachers hold at least a master's degree.

In 2009 voters approved a $288 million bond for the district to allow for improvement of facilities and technology at local schools. Construction projects through 2015 included renovations of a high school, four elementary schools, and a middle school gym, as well as safety, maintenance, and technology upgrades for the district.

A variety of state-approved private elementary and secondary schools augment the public school system, including parochial schools, special schools such as the Lilac Services for the Blind, Montessori programs, and the Spokane Guild's School and Neuromuscular Center. The Spokane Art School offers classes, workshops, and master classes.

The following is a summary of data regarding the Spokane School District.

Total enrollment: 29,446

Number of facilities

total: 51
elementary schools: 34
junior high schools: 6

high schools: 6

other: 5

Student/teacher ratio: 17.5:1

Teacher salaries

average (statewide): $53,796

Funding per pupil: $9,998

Public Schools Information: Spokane Public Schools, 200 North Bernard, Spokane, WA 99201; telephone (509) 354-5900.

Colleges and Universities

The Spokane region boasts an enrollment of approximately 62,000 students in its area colleges and universities. Eastern Washington University (EWU), a state-operated school located 16 miles from Spokane in Cheney, Washington, offers 135 areas of study, two engineering degrees, nine master's degrees, 12 graduate certificates, 39 graduate programs, an educational specialist degree, and one applied doctorate. The school offers the only physical therapy doctorate program in Washington. The university operates a branch in downtown Spokane and enrolls close to 13,000 students.

Gonzaga University, founded by the Jesuits in 1887, offers 75 fields of study, 25 master's degrees, two doctoral degrees, and a juris doctorate. It was ranked fourth among regional universities in the West by *U.S. News & World Report* in 2013. The university's law school and engineering program have a particularly good reputation; the law school was ranked among the top 115 law schools in the nation by *U.S. News & World Report* in 2013. The school enrolls more than 7,600 students.

Washington State University–Spokane, a multi-campus research university, enrolls more than 27,500 students throughout the university system, 1,367 of whom study at the Spokane campus. There are 90 majors, 67 master's degree programs, and 46 doctoral programs.

Whitworth University, a Presbyterian institution founded in 1890, enrolls about 2,300 students annually. The Community Colleges of Spokane, with nearly 13,000 students, serve students in a six-county region, awarding degrees in 126 programs of study including 99 associate degrees and 100 professional certificates. Spokane Falls Community College focuses on a liberal arts education and provides students with a means of transferring to a four-year college or university.

The University of Washington began operating a medical school in Spokane in 2013.

Libraries and Research Centers

Founded in 1904, the Spokane Public Library system comprises a Downtown Library overlooking Spokane Falls and five branch libraries. Total holdings include approximately 600,000 volumes; more than 35,000 video, music, and audiotapes and CDs; and a periodicals collection numbering more than 700 titles. Special collections include Northwest history; history of the book; genealogy; oral history; an African American collection; and U.S., Washington state, and Spokane County government documents. The downtown library features a gallery, three works of permanent public art, a skywalk connection to downtown shopping and restaurants, and wireless Internet service. The library system also sponsors community programs for residents of all ages as well as computer classes.

Special libraries in Spokane include the Crosby Collection at Gonzaga University, which contains a collection of Bing Crosby records and other memorabilia. The Area Health Education Center at Washington State University–Spokane develops clinical and applied research in biomedical and social health areas. The Washington Institute for Mental Illness Research and Training, based in Tacoma, recruits and retrains qualified professionals at state hospitals in the use of modern treatments.

Public Library Information: Spokane Public Library, 906 West Main Avenue, Spokane, WA 99201; telephone (509) 444-5300.

■ Health Care

Spokane is the center of specialized care for the entire Inland Northwest area, offering an expert team of cardiac surgeons and more than 900 physicians. Sacred Heart, a 644-bed facility, is a leader in heart, lung, and kidney transplant services. Sacred Heart, which is a non-profit Catholic institution, has over 4,000 employees, 800 of whom are medical specialists and primary care doctors. Another 400 individuals volunteer at the hospital throughout the year. In 2003 the hospital opened the region's first full-service children's hospital; a Women's Health Center was added in 2004.

Other health-care facilities include Providence Holy Family Hospital, St. Luke's Rehabilitation Institute, Deaconess Medical Center–Spokane, and Spokane Veterans Affairs Medical Center. The Shriners Hospital for Children, a pediatric hospital focusing on orthopedic surgery, is also based in Spokane. Frontier Behavioral Health offers mental health services to area residents.

■ Recreation

Sightseeing

Riverfront Park, the site of Expo '74, is a 100-acre urban park that has been developed into a collection of cultural and recreational attractions including an IMAX theater, art gallery, a skating rink, an antique carousel composed of 54 hand-carved horses, a train, and an exciting gondola ride over Spokane Falls, one of the largest urban waterfalls in the nation. Historic Fort George Wright, a 1,500-acre complex, was established in 1894 on a plateau overlooking the river. Other points of interest in the city include Manito Park, with its beautiful Rose Hill and Japanese garden, and Cliff Park, site of Review Rock, a large formation with steps cut into the sides that offers a beautiful view of the city.

The area around Spokane offers a number of attractions, including several ghost towns, the Spokane Plains Battlefield, and the Turnbull National Wildlife Refuge. A variety of historic homes, churches, and architecture are available for touring in the Spokane area. Spokane's local wineries have won prestigious awards and offer tours, tastings, and sales.

Arts and Culture

Spokane's 12,500-seat Veteran's Memorial Arena is a focal point for special events. In addition, the 2,700-seat INB Performing Arts Center and the more intimate Bing Crosby Theater host national and international touring companies and entertainers. Music is provided by the Spokane Symphony, which presents a full season of classical music, including special children's performances and Super Pops! by the Spokane Jazz Orchestra, at the newly renovated Martin Woldson Theatre at the Fox; and by Allegro Baroque & Beyond, Connoisseur Concerts, Spokane Chamber Music Association, and Uptown Opera.

Theater is represented by the region's only resident professional company, Interplayers Ensemble, whose seven-play season runs from September to June; by Spokane Civic Theatre; and by several amateur community theaters and smaller groups. The Big Easy Concert House, home to a concert hall and dance club, occupies a renovated office block adjacent to the arts district. Area colleges and universities also contribute to the cultural scene.

The Northwest Museum of Arts and Culture (formerly the Cheney Cowles Museum) reopened in 2009 after a $28 million expansion. The museum houses permanent collections of regional history and American Indian artifacts, as well as five art galleries and educational facilities. The historic Campbell House, a museum since 1925, is now a part of the Northwest Museum complex, with tours of the home available by reservation. Additionally, the Jundt Art Museum on the campus of Gonzaga University includes two large gallery spaces and an exhibition lounge.

Festivals and Holidays

Bloomsday, one of the country's largest timed road races, is held on the first Sunday in May and attract some 60,000 runners. Later that month, the Spokane Lilac Festival runs for 10 days and features such activities as a flower show, parades, concerts, games, and other entertainment. Begun in 1938, the festival also showcases local foods and crowns a lilac queen. In June, Spokane plays host to Hoopfest, one of the world's largest three-on-three basketball tournaments. Celebrating the end of summer, Pig Out in the Park festival is a five-day event that occurs over Labor Day weekend featuring live entertainment and food vendors. The Spokane County Fair, a tradition since the late 1800s, also happens in September. The Northwest Bach Festival celebrates the music of J.S. Bach in venues throughout the city for one week at the end of January or early February.

Sports for the Spectator

The remodeled Spokane Veteran's Memorial Arena hosts the Spokane Chiefs of the Western Hockey Association. The Spokane Indians, a Single-A affiliate of Major League Baseball's Texas Rangers, play at Avista Stadium. In 2009, the Spokane Shock became part of the Arena Football League. The Gonzaga Bulldogs athletic teams, Division I members of the National Collegiate Athletic Association (NCAA), engage in intercollegiate competition at Gonzaga University. Spokane County Raceway Park offers stock car and drag racing.

Sports for the Participant

Seventy-six lakes and four major rivers within a 50-mile radius of Spokane offer a wide variety of water activity. For hikers and nature lovers, a 70-mile pathway called Centennial Trail begins near the old Spokane House fur trading post and winds through Riverside State Park, Riverfront Park in downtown Spokane, and eastward past Coeur d'Alene, Idaho. The Trail includes 37 paved miles on the Spokane River. The city and county maintain more than 75 parks, many of which feature athletic fields, tennis courts, swimming pools, skating rinks, recreational programming, and other facilities. In total, the city boasts 4,100 acres of protected green space. The region is home to 13 ski areas, with more than 1,000 skiable acres, and more than 30 public and private golf courses. The nearby mountains offer year-round recreation: skiing in the winter and fishing, hunting, camping, canoeing, hiking, and other outdoor activities in the warmer months. In the summer months, floating excursions are available on the Spokane River, while several nearby rivers provide whitewater rafting opportunities. Rock climbing is available just outside of Spokane, and ski areas are within a two-hour drive.

Shopping and Dining

Spokane shoppers are served by several major shopping centers in the city and a number of smaller plazas and specialty shopping districts. Retail establishments in downtown Spokane are connected by a 16-block system of enclosed skywalks. The shopping opportunities at River Park Square and in the retail district are unmatched in the Inland Northwest. Spokane's restaurants offer fine international and traditional American dishes. Specialties include fresh salmon and locally-produced wines. More than 500 dining establishments can be found in the Spokane area.

Visitor Information: Spokane Area Visitor Information Center, 201 W. Main, Spokane, WA 99201; telephone (509) 747-3230; toll-free (888) SPOKANE.

■ Convention Facilities

The Spokane Convention Center is located on the banks of the Spokane River in the downtown district. The campus is composed of the INB Performing Arts Center and the Spokane Convention Center, which is home to the Council Group Health Exhibit Hall. The exhibit hall, which opened in 2006, offers 100,160 square feet of meeting space. The Convention Center, whose major renovations were completed in 2007, provides over 320,000 square feet of meeting space and was the third convention center in the nation to become Silver LEED Certified. Its meeting space includes 24 state of the art meeting rooms, a 13,730 square foot junior ballroom, and a 25,310 square foot fully finished ballroom. A roof deck can hold another 500 people and provides a panoramic view of the city.

The Spokane Veterans Memorial Arena provides 30,000 square feet of meeting space and festival seating for 12,500 people. The Spokane County Fair and Expo Center, located just five miles outside of downtown Spokane, offers some 127,428 square feet of exhibit space and four arenas including a covered grandstand. Center-Place, located in the Spokane Valley, boasts a 54,000 square foot conference center that includes meeting rooms, a banquet hall, an auditorium, a computer lab, classrooms, and a greenhouse.

More than 2,000 hotel rooms are available within walking distance of the major convention sites in Spokane; nearly 7,000 hotel rooms total exist in the surrounding area. Most of the larger hotels maintain ample facilities for conventions, such as banquet space, conference rooms, and ballrooms.

Convention Information: Spokane Area Visitor Information Center, 201 W. Main, Spokane, WA 99201; telephone (509) 747-3230; toll-free (888) SPOKANE.

■ Transportation

Approaching the City

The Spokane International Airport is a multimillion-dollar complex located a few minutes from the downtown area and served by seven major airlines. It serves in excess of three million passenger annually. The city is also served by commercial bus lines and Amtrak.

Interstate 90 passes through Spokane, connecting the city with Seattle to the west and with points east. U.S. Highway 2 also runs east and west through the city. U.S. Highway 395 continues north out of Spokane into Canada, and U.S. Highway 195 leads south from the city. Spokane is also home to the North Spokane Corridor, which had a preliminary opening in 2009 and was to connect to both U.S. Highway 2 and U.S. Highway 395. Upon completion—the total project was roughly half finished by the end of 2013—the North Spokane Corridor was expected to be a major corridor for freight transportation between Spokane and Canada.

Traveling in the City

Generally in Spokane, the east–west roads are designated as avenues, and the north–south roads are referred to as streets. Major east–west thoroughfares in the city include Francis, Wellesley, Mission, Sprague, and 29th avenues. North–south arteries include Maple, Monroe, Division, Hamilton, Greene-Market, Argonne, and Sullivan streets. The city offers pedestrians one of the largest skywalk systems in the nation; those who want to rest their feet are provided for by the Spokane Transit Authority, which offers trolley shuttles along with 36 bus routes. Spokane was also awarded bronze recognition as a bicycle-friendly community by the League of American Bicyclists each year between 2010 and 2014 for promoting biking as a means of transportation and recreation and also providing safe accommodations for cyclists.

■ Communications

Newspapers and Magazines

Spokane readers are served by one daily newspaper, *The Spokesman-Review*, which presents a special entertainment section on Friday. *Journal of Business* is among the biweekly business journals published in the city. *The Pacific Northwest Inlander*, a weekly newspaper, has an extensive arts and entertainment section. Other newspapers focus on senior living, the outdoors, and collegiate interests.

Television and Radio

Spokane has 14 television stations representing the major commercial networks and public television. The area is also served by a cable system that provides a wide variety of viewing options. Eight AM and 18 FM radio stations broadcast in Spokane, which also receives programming from neighboring communities.

Media Information: *The Spokesman-Review*, 999 W. Riverside Avenue, PO Box 2160, Spokane, WA 99210; telephone (509) 459-5000; toll-free (800) 338-8801.

Spokane Online

City of Spokane home page. Available www. spokanecity.org

Greater Spokane Incorporated. Available www. greaterspokfane.org

Spokane Area Convention & Visitors Bureau. Available www.visitspokane.com

Spokane Public Library. Available www. spokanelibrary.org/

Spokane Public Schools. Available www. spokaneschools.org

Spokane Veterans Memorial Arena. Available www. spokanearena.com

The Spokesman-Review. Available www.spokesman. com

BIBLIOGRAPHY

Barmonte, Tony, *Spokane, Our Early History: Under All Is Land* (Spokane, WA: Tornado Creek Publications, 2011)

Ross, John Alan *The Spokan Indians* (Spokane, WA: Michael J. Ross, 2011)

Tacoma

■ The City in Brief

Founded: 1852 (incorporated, 1884)

Head Official: Mayor Mary Strickland (since 2010; current term expires 2018)

City Population
>1990: 176,664
>2000: 193,556
>2010: 198,397
>2012 estimate: 201,999
>Percent change, 2000–2010: 2.5%
>U.S. rank in 1990: 95th (State rank: 3rd)
>U.S. rank in 2000: 114th (State rank: 3rd)
>U.S. rank in 2010: 110th (State rank: 3rd)

Metropolitan Statistical Area Population
>2000: 3,043,878
>2010: 3,439,809
>2012 estimate: 3,552,157
>Percent change, 2000–2010: 13.0%
>U.S. rank in 2000: 15th
>U.S. rank in 2010: 15th

Area: 50 square miles

Elevation: 380 feet above sea level

Average Annual Temperatures: 53.1° F

Average Annual Precipitation: 39.2 inches

Major Economic Sectors: health care, trade and distribution, military, high technology

Unemployment Rate: 7.2% (2012)

Per Capita Income: $24,182

2012 FBI Crime Index Property: 12,866

Major Colleges and Universities: University of Washington Tacoma, Pacific Lutheran University, University of Puget Sound

Daily Newspaper: *The News Tribune*

■ Introduction

Tacoma's name is derived from the Native American word "Tahoma," meaning "Mother of the Waters," referring to Mt. Tacoma, which is now known as Mt. Rainier. Tacoma's beautiful natural setting affords views of the nearby Cascade Range and the more distant Olympic Mountains. Tacoma is home to a deep-water harbor that is among the busiest in the nation and has played an important role in the city's economic development. Into the twenty-first century, health care became the city's fastest growing industry. Nationally recognized for careful municipal planning, Tacoma has been nicknamed the "City of Destiny."

■ Geography and Climate

Situated on Commencement Bay, an inlet of Puget Sound, Tacoma lies at the foot of Mt. Rainier in the Puyallup River valley, bordered by mountains. The Tacoma Narrows Bridge links the city to the Olympic Peninsula. Tacoma is about 36 miles south of Seattle. The climate is quite mild throughout the year. Although the area has the reputation of being rainy, Tacoma actually receives less rain than New York City. Most of the precipitation falls in the winter, when snow blankets the mountains. Tacoma is the seat of Pierce County. The city lies near active fault lines making the area susceptible to earthquakes; however, very few damaging quakes have occurred in the recent past.

Area: 50 square miles

Ron Lassen/Shutterstock.com

Elevation: 380 feet above sea level

Average Temperatures: 53.1° F

Average Annual Precipitation: 39.2 inches

■ History

Slow Rise of Lumber Industry; Arrival of Settlers

The first people to live in the Puyallup Valley on the shore of Commencement Bay were the Nisqually and Puyallup Native American tribes. Captain George Vancouver was the first person of European descent to explore the area when, in 1792, he sailed his ship up Puget Sound and named Mt. Rainier for Peter Rainier, an officer in the British Navy. Commencement Bay was charted and named in 1841 by a member of the Charles Wilkes Expedition. Permanent European settlement was achieved in the region in 1852 when a Swedish immigrant, Nicholas De Lin, built a sawmill at the

junction of two creeks and soon conducted a thriving lumber business.

Settlers fled the area in 1855 after hearing rumors of native hostilities; they returned when the Commencement Bay tribe was relocated to a nearby reservation, leaving the area free for other settlers. General Morton Matthew McCarver, who named the settlement Tacoma, was responsible for promoting extensive development by buying tracts of land and bringing in other settlers.

When the Hanson & Ackerman Mill was built in 1869 by a group of San Francisco investors, Tacoma became established in the lumber industry. The mill started a boom, as laborers, artisans, and shopkeepers arrived with their families to settle in Tacoma; with a population of 200 people, the town soon boasted mail service, electric lights, and a telegraph. In 1873 Tacoma was selected as the terminus for the Northern Pacific Railroad; construction was stopped 20 miles short of Tacoma, however, when an economic crash forced the railroad's investors to pull out of the project. The government recalled the workers, who insisted upon being paid thousands of dollars in back wages before they completed the line.

Railroad Assists Industrial Development

The railroad increased Tacoma's industrial development. Coal mines were opened and Tacoma became the major coaling station on the Pacific Coast. The lumber industry expanded while new industries included a flour mill, a salmon cannery, and machine shops. The town continued to grow, and with a population of 4,400 residents, Tacoma was incorporated in 1884. During the following year a group of residents, who blamed Chinese workers for an employment recession that came with the completion of the railroad, formed the Law and Order League and forcibly deported the Chinese. The insurgents were tried in court but were later acquitted.

Transcontinental rail service to Tacoma was completed in 1887, bringing further development; the completion of the Stamford Pass Tunnel and the establishment of the Northern Pacific Railroad general offices in Tacoma gave an even greater boost to the lumber and coal industries. Record numbers of settlers arrived and the town flourished. Since Tacoma's economy was closely tied to the railroad industry, however, more than half of the city's banks closed when the Reading Railroad went bankrupt. The economy recovered to some degree with the creation of the Weyerhaeuser Timber Company in 1900. During World War I the shipping industry boomed, and the city profited from its proximity to Camp Lewis (later renamed Fort Lewis). Commencement Bay was declared an official U.S. Port of Entry in 1918.

Although the Great Depression of the 1930s brought hard times to Tacoma, World War II stimulated industrial growth and prosperity because of the city's location near Fort Lewis and McChord U.S. Air Force Base. During the 1950s Tacoma underwent extensive city planning. Voters adopted a progressive council-manager form of government, and massive renovation of the city's infrastructure was implemented.

While the presence of the military has long had a stabilizing effect on the city economy, economic diversification into the early 2000s has offered the promise of continued growth. In particular, health-care and financial services industries have gained importance to the local economy. Educational institutions have expanded in the area, most notably through the University of Washington Tacoma, which opened its campus in 1990 as a degree completion site and expanded to a four-year institution by 2006. The City of Tacoma, along with investors from the private sector, have spent over $300 million on the city's telecommunications infrastructure through Click! Network. Becoming a "wired" city has helped attract new industries while balancing environmental and quality-of-life concerns.

From 2000 to 2007, over 74 new projects were completed or under construction in downtown Tacoma. These included expansion and development of the Foss Waterway, with many residential, retail, and business locations; construction of a new convention and trade center; and hundreds of new residential units. While development slowed beginning in 2008—a result of a national recession—final planning for additional public and private projects had returned by 2013.

Historical Information: Washington State History Museum, 1911 Pacific Avenue, Tacoma, WA 98402; telephone (253) 272-3500; fax (253) 272-9518.

■ Population Profile

Metropolitan Statistical Area Population

2000: 3,043,878
2010: 3,439,809
2012 estimate: 3,552,157
Percent change, 2000–2010: 13.0%
U.S. rank in 2000: 15th
U.S. rank in 2010: 15th

City Residents

1990: 176,664
2000: 193,556
2010: 198,397
2012 estimate: 201,999
Percent change, 2000–2010: 2.5%
U.S. rank in 1990: 95th (State rank: 3rd)
U.S. rank in 2000: 114th (State rank: 3rd)
U.S. rank in 2010: 110th (State rank: 3rd)

Density: 3,990.2 people per square mile

Racial and ethnic characteristics

White: 127,766
Black or African American: 21,381
American Indian and Alaskan Native: 3,565
Asian: 16,263
Native Hawaiian and Other Pacific Islander: 2,634
Hispanic or Latino (may be of any race): 23,166
Other: 30,390

Percent of residents born in state: 50.6%

Age characteristics

Population under 5 years old: 14,907
Population 5 to 9 years old: 12,525
Population 10 to 14 years old: 13,512
Population 15 to 19 years old: 12,969
Population 20 to 24 years old: 15,193
Population 25 to 34 years old: 30,683
Population 35 to 44 years old: 28,571
Population 45 to 54 years old: 28,347
Population 55 to 59 years old: 11,916
Population 60 to 64 years old: 10,514
Population 65 to 74 years old: 12,626
Population 75 to 84 years old: 6,419

Population 85 years and over: 3,817
Median age: 35.3

Births (2010–11 Metropolitan Area)

Total number: 44,416

Deaths (2010–11 Metropolitan Area)

Total number: 22,136

Money income (2012)

Per capita income: $24,182
Median household income: $49,556
Total households: 77,704

Number of households with income of ...

less than $10,000: 6,275
$10,000 to $14,999: 3,980
$15,000 to $24,999: 8,867
$25,000 to $34,999: 8,109
$35,000 to $49,999: 11,939
$50,000 to $74,999: 15,482
$75,000 to $99,999: 8,756
$100,000 to $149,999: 9,496
$150,000 to $199,999: 2,961
$200,000 or more: 1,839

Percent of families below poverty level: 17.8%

FBI Crime Index Property: 12,866

FBI Crime Index Violent: 1,615

■ Municipal Government

Tacoma's council-manager form of government provides for the election of a mayor and eight city council members—five members serving districts and three at-large members. All serve four-year terms. The council hires a city manager.

Head Official: Mayor Mary Strickland (since 2010; current term expires 2018)

Total Number of City Employees: 3,620 (2012)

City Information: City of Tacoma, 747 Market Street, Tacoma, WA 98402; telephone (253) 591-5000.

■ Economy

Major Industries and Commercial Activity

During the early twenty-first century, the health-care industry has quickly gained ground in Tacoma. Franciscan Health System (with headquarters in Tacoma) and Multi-Care Health System both operate hospitals and health clinics in the city and have become top employers for both the city and the county. InVivo Health Partners, offering

support services to hospitals and physician groups, has also made Tacoma the site of regional headquarters. DaVita, a *Fortune* 500 company that provides dialysis services, is headquartered in Denver, Colorado, but also maintains corporate offices in Tacoma.

The Port of Tacoma continues to have a major impact on the local economy. One of the top-10 container handling ports in the United States, it moved 1.89 million units in 2013. Top imports include industrial machinery, vehicles and parts, electronics, toys and sports equipment, and furniture. Top exports include oil seeds and grains, industrial machinery, cereals, meat, and vehicles and parts. A major gateway port for international trade in Asia, the Port of Tacoma covers more than 2,400 acres of land. Port activities generate more than 43,000 jobs in Pierce County, and more than 113,000 jobs in Washington are related to Port activities. Port activities generate over $637 million in annual wages.

The military and defense industry also has a strong foothold in the local economy through the presence of Joint Base Lewis-McChord, a 2010 merger of Fort Lewis and McChord Air Force Base. The joint base accounted for 56,624 jobs in 2012, which had a payroll of more than $350 million and generated nearly $500 million in local economic impact.

Industries involved in satellite imaging, cyber security, and Internet and computer services have been lured to Tacoma because of multiple broadband telecommunications systems, including the city's fiber-optic Click! Network. Launched in 1998, Click! is the nation's largest municipally owned telecommunications network. The City of Tacoma, along with investors from the private sector, have spent over $300 million on the city's telecommunications infrastructure, offering affordable high-speed Internet access for personal and professional use.

Tacoma's economy is still heavily involved with timber. Regional enterprises produce more flower bulbs than the Netherlands, as well as crops, such as berries and rhubarb, which require heavy seasonal employment. Tourism is also important to Tacoma's economy. Visitors are attracted to the waters of Commencement Bay and the state and national parks surrounding Tacoma.

Items and goods produced: lumber products, pulp, paper, clothing, chemicals, furniture, flour, furnaces, railroad car wheels, candy, food products, meat and fish

Incentive Programs—New and Existing Companies

Local programs: The City of Tacoma offers a variety of business loan programs, tax credits for new job creation, industrial revenue bonds, sales and use tax exemption on machinery and equipment, a variety of housing-related programs, financial incentives for historic properties, and others.

State programs: The state of Washington offers a number of incentive programs to attract new and expanding businesses to the state, with most targeted to specific industries or geographic areas. Industry-specific incentives include sales and use tax exemptions for general manufacturing and agriculture; sales and use tax deferrals and waivers, and business and occupation tax credits for high-technology industries, including biotechnology and medical device manufacturing; business and occupation tax rate reductions and credits for the aerospace, timber, food manufacturing, biofuel, semiconductor, and aluminum industries; and a range of credits and exemptions for renewable energy firms.

Geography-based incentives are available in designated Community Empowerment Zones, high unemployment counties, and Main Street areas. Other incentives support economic activity that reduces commuter travel; produces television or film; or relates to newspaper publishing.

Job training programs: The state of Washington offers a number of incentive programs to attract new and expanding businesses to the state, with most targeted to specific industries or geographic areas. Industry-specific incentives include sales and use tax exemptions for general manufacturing and agriculture; sales and use tax deferrals and waivers, and business and occupation tax credits for high-technology industries, including biotechnology and medical device manufacturing; business and occupation tax rate reductions and credits for the aerospace, timber, food manufacturing, biofuel, semiconductor, and aluminum industries; and a range of credits and exemptions for renewable energy firms.

The Local Employment and Apprenticeship Training Program (LEAP) provides Tacoma residents with opportunities to access training, enter apprenticeship programs, acquire skills, and perform work on city public works projects that provide living wages. Clover Park Technical College also offers on-site training programs for local businesses.

Development Projects

The Seattle-Tacoma International Airport opened a third runway in November 2008. In 2010 the airport began construction on a new $419 million rental car facility that completed in 2012 and could accommodate 5,400 vehicles. A voter-approved Sound Transit (ST2) plan was approved in November 2008, which devoted 15 years to the expansion of bus and rail commuter services in the three counties of the Sound Transit District. The project was set to increase rail service between Tacoma and Seattle by some 65 percent. The $17.9 billion project was expected to be complete by 2023.

Development of the downtown waterfront has been ongoing since 2000 through the efforts of the Foss Waterway Development Authority. Projects slowed beginning in 2008 as the result of a national recession, but development initiatives returned by 2013, with plans for a 161-unit apartment building known as The Henry, a waterfront hotel, and renovations to existing facilities all announced that year. Also in 2013, the development authority purchased waterfront land south of Murray Morgan Bridge to develop additional public spaces in the area.

Two recent projects expected to help generate tourist dollars for the local economy include a new museum and a renovated ball field. The LeMay Car Museum, a $60 million project, broke ground in 2010 and opened in 2012. The interactive automotive museum and educational center houses approximately 500 different vehicles and was estimated to generate $34 million for the local economy annually. Cheney Stadium completed $30 million in renovations in 2011. The stadium added a 4,000-square-foot club and restaurant, 16 new luxury suites, new restrooms and concessions, and new team clubhouse facilities.

The University of Washington Tacoma has grown considerably since it opened as a degree completion center in 1990. The school began Phase 3 of expansion plans in 2010, which were highlighted by construction of the four-story Tioga Library Building, completed in 2012.

Private investments were highlighted by construction of a plant for California-based Niagara Bottling. The 311,000-square-foot facility, built at a cost of $50 million, was expected to complete in 2014. The Tacoma Art Museum broke ground on a $15.5 million expansion in late 2013.

Economic Development Information: Tacoma-Pierce County Chamber, 950 Pacific Ave., Ste. 300, Tacoma, WA 98402; telephone (253) 627-2175. Community and Economic Development, City of Tacoma, 747 Market Street, 9th Floor, Tacoma, WA 98402; telephone (253) 591-5624 fax (253) 591-5232.

Commercial Shipping

The 2,400-acre Port of Tacoma is one of the top-10 container ports in North America. It serves as one of the country's primary gateways for trade with China, Japan, South Korea, Taiwan, Canada, and Vietnam. Tacoma is also strongly tied to Alaska's economy, with annual trade estimated at $3 billion. Top export commodities included oil seeds and grains, industrial machinery, cereals, meat, and vehicles and parts. Top imports were industrial machinery, vehicles and parts, electronics, toys and sports equipment, and furniture. The port transported nearly 1.9 million units in 2013, with the value of all international trade approaching $50 billion.

The city is also an important rail shipping hub and is served by two major transcontinental railroads: Burlington Northern-Santa Fe and Union Pacific. These two railroads link Tacoma to major markets in the Midwest and East Coast. Rail is also used to move a variety of export commodities through Tacoma—everything from Midwest corn to John Deere tractors. Tacoma Rail, which is governed by Tacoma's Public Utility, connects these two transcontinental railroads and directly serves the Port of Tacoma, the Port of Olympia, and the Frederickson Industrial Area. More than 200 trucking companies work to move goods through the city and major air freight carriers serve Seattle-Tacoma International Airport (Sea-Tac), which is located about 30 minutes from Tacoma. Sea-Tac perennially ranks among the top-25 airports for cargo volume in North America.

Labor Force and Employment Outlook

Tacoma draws from a stable work force of skilled and unskilled workers that has steadily attracted new business and industry. Local firms can rely on more than one million workers who live within an hour's commute of the city. The large military presence regularly adds laborers to the work force, both through the exit of military servicemen and the presence of non-military spouses. About 22 percent of Tacoma residents hold at least a bachelor's degree, a figure below the state average.

The following is a summary of data regarding the 2012 Tacoma labor force:

Size of civilian labor force: 101,681

Number of workers employed in . . .

agriculture and mining: 465
construction: 5,368
manufacturing: 7,047
wholesale trade: 2,636
retail trade: 10,522
transportation: 4,705
information systems: 1,607
finance: 5,438
professional administration: 8,311
education and social services: 23,172
arts and leisure: 9,067
other: 4,648
public administration: 5,441

Average hourly earnings of production workers: $18.9

Unemployment rate: 7.2% (2012)

Employers

Largest county employers (2012)	*Number of employees*
Joint Base Lewis McChord	56,624
Local Public School Districts (K–12)	13,352
MultiCare Health System	6,547
Washington State Employees	6,488
Franciscan Health System	5,709
City of Tacoma	3,620
Pierce County Government	2,872
Washington State Higher Education	2,632
Emerald Queen Casino	2,200
Walmart	1,785

Cost of Living

The following is a summary of data regarding several key cost of living factors in the area.

State income tax rate: None

State sales tax rate: 6.5%

Local income tax rate: None

Local sales tax rate: 3.0%

Property tax rate: $11.6205 per $1,000 assessed value (2009)

Economic Information: Tacoma-Pierce County Chamber, 950 Pacific Ave., Ste. 300, P.O. Box 1933, Tacoma, WA 98401-1933; telephone (253) 627-2175. Washington State Workforce Explorer, P.O. Box 9046, Olympia, WA; telephone (800) 215-1617; fax (360) 438-4109.

■ Education and Research

Elementary and Secondary Schools

Tacoma Public Schools offer a wide range of academic services for its more than 27,000 students. The district is composed of 37 elementary schools, 9 middle schools, and 5 comprehensive high schools. It also includes 14 alternative learning sites. High school students may participate in dual credit programs through which they may gain up to two years of college credits while completing their graduation requirements. Foss High School offers an International Baccalaureate program. Magnet schools are also available. Oakland Alternative High School assists children with learning differences. The Tacoma School of the Arts offers a focus on arts education for eligible high school students. In 2009, the district opened its Science and Math Institute, a collaboration between the school district and Metro Parks Tacoma. Some 61 percent of students are eligible for free or reduced lunches; 7.6 percent are bilingual.

Many private and parochial schools in Tacoma offer alternative and religious curricula.

The following is a summary of data regarding the Tacoma School District.

Total enrollment: 27,407

Number of facilities

total: 65
elementary schools: 37
junior high schools: 9
high schools: 5
other: 14

Student/teacher ratio: 16.7:1

Teacher salaries

average (statewide): $53,796

Funding per pupil: $11,806

Public Schools Information: Tacoma Public Schools, Central Administration Building, PO Box 1357, Tacoma, WA 98401-1357; telephone (253) 571-1000; email info@tacoma.k12.wa.us.

Colleges and Universities

The University of Washington Tacoma opened in 1990 to offer bachelor's and master's degree completion programs for students with two or four years of college. The school welcomed its first freshman class in 2006 with a total enrollment of about 2,292 students. As of 2013, the school had a total enrollment of some 4,309 students. Bachelor's and master's degrees are available through 11 schools and programs: Education; Global Honors; Healthcare Leadership; Institute of Technology; Interdisciplinary Arts & Sciences; International Programs; Milgard School of Business; Nursing; Social Work; Undergraduate Education; and Urban Studies.

Pacific Lutheran University is affiliated with the Evangelical Lutheran Church in America. The school has an enrollment of about 3,500 students and offers bachelor's degrees in a wide variety of majors through eight academic divisions. It is perennially ranked among the top 15 regional universities in the West by *U.S. News & World Report*. The University of Puget Sound is a private liberal arts college with an enrollment of about 2,600. The school offers more than 50 traditional and interdisciplinary programs.

Tacoma Community College, Bates Technical College, Clover Park Technical College, and Pierce College provide occupational training and college preparatory curricula, as well as two-year degree programs and certificates. The Tacoma Campus of Evergreen State College offers bachelor's degree completion programs with flexible class schedules. Evergreen has a bridge program with Tacoma Community College.

Libraries and Research Centers

Tacoma is served by two public library systems. The Tacoma Public Library, with a downtown Main Library housed in a renovated 1903 Carnegie Library building, has two regional libraries and five neighborhood libraries that maintain holdings of nearly one million items including books, periodical subscriptions, records, slides, tapes, films, maps, and art reproductions. Special collections include city archives and World War I books and posters; the library is a depository for federal and state government documents. The Pierce County Library System operates 18 branches and bookmobiles; holdings consist of one million items. Several specialized libraries in the city are affiliated with government agencies, universities, corporations, churches, and a local newspaper.

The UW Tacoma Library is part of the University of Washington Library System. Students and researchers with borrowing privileges through the library have access to over 6 million items available through 33 regional consortium libraries. The Collins Memorial Library at the University of Puget Sound has a stock of 530,281 books, 47,432 periodical subscriptions, and over 16,000 tapes, CDs, and DVDs.

Research activities in such fields as invertebrate zoology, herpetology, and ornithology are conducted at the University of Puget Sound's James R. Slater Museum of Natural History in Tacoma. The Franciscan Health System Research Center at St. Joseph Medical Center conducts clinical trials. The Center for Urban Waters conducts research to protect and restore local waterways, namely Puget Sound.

Public Library Information: Tacoma Public Library, 1102 Tacoma Avenue South, Tacoma, WA 98402; telephone (253) 292-2001. Pierce County Library System, 3005 112th Street East, Tacoma, WA 98446; telephone (253) 548-3300; fax (253) 537-4600.

■ Health Care

Tacoma-based Franciscan Health System (FHS) operates eight full-service hospitals, including the 361-bed St. Joseph Medical Center in Tacoma. St. Joseph Medical Center offers a comprehensive range of medical and surgical services including a burn clinic, endoscopy center, the Franciscan Spine Center, the St. Joseph Heart and Vascular Center, a Wound Care Center, Hyperbaric Oxygen Center, and a cancer treatment center that is affiliated with the Fred Hutchinson Cancer Research Center in Seattle. An outpatient clinic and mental health services are available, as is a hospice program. In 2009 FHS opened St. Anthony Hospital, located in Gig Harbor. The hospital offers 24-hour emergency services and a variety of inpatient and outpatient care. Other FHS facilities provide hospice and palliative care, dialysis, occupational health and physical therapy services, women's care, and heart and vascular treatment.

MultiCare Health System (MHS) is the largest provider of medical services in Pierce County. MultiCare sponsors the Mary Bridge Children's Hospital and Health Center, which is the only dedicated pediatric hospital in southwest Washington. The MHS Tacoma General Hospital is a 420-bed facility that features a Level II adult trauma center and a Level III neonatal intensive care unit. Tacoma General has a special Family Birth Center. The Mary Bridge Children's Hospital and Tacoma General each opened a new emergency department and Express Care Center in 2010, both of which are five times the size of the previous facilities. Allenmore Hospital, a 130-bed facility, features the Kelley Eye Center, a regional cancer center, orthopedic services, and a pulmonary conditioning department.

Governmental agencies provide a number of programs that assist in substance abuse care, mental health, preventive medicine, and family planning.

■ Recreation

Sightseeing

Tacoma offers the sightseer a variety of diversions. The city is bordered by miles of waterfront parks and beaches. One of several parks located in the city is the 702-acre Point Defiance Park, which includes miles of walking trails through the wilderness and along the waterfront. Its Point Defiance Zoo and Aquarium includes animals native to the Puget Sound area as well as such exotic animals as Sumatran tigers and polar bears. Other attractions within Point Defiance Park include the Fort Nisqually Living History Museum, a restored trading post, and Camp 6, a re-creation of a logging camp. The city's first off-leash dog park is located at Rogers Park. The Narrows Bridge, spanning the Sound between Tacoma and the Gig Harbor Peninsula, is the fifth longest suspension bridge in the United States.

Wright Park downtown offers lawn bowling and horseshoe pitching; it is also the site of the Seymour Botanical Conservatory, a 1908 Victorian-style conservatory that contains about 500 species of exotic tropical flowers and foliage. Other points of interest are Union Station and the Old City Hall, built in the style of the Italian Renaissance; both are National Historic Landmarks.

A little more than an hour from Tacoma is Mt. Rainier National Park, which provides a closer view of the mountain that dominates the city's landscape. More than 300 miles of trails in the park provide plenty of opportunity for hiking and exploring. Climbing courses and skiing instruction are available. Kopachuck State Park and Penrose Point State Park are also in the vicinity.

Arts and Culture

Tacoma has a vibrant arts community with excellent museums and professional theater and opera companies. Downtown Tacoma, which in recent years has been attempting to re-establish the theater district as the "heart of the city," has revitalized its Broadway Center for the Performing Arts. The Broadway Center, which includes the historic Pantages Theater, Rialto Theater, and Theatre on the Square, is home to many performances year-round and is the largest performing arts center between Portland and Seattle. Often programs at the Broadway Center feature companion education activities for school children. In addition, the University of Puget Sound and Pacific Lutheran University offer ongoing performances from September through June.

The Museum of Glass, opened in 2002, features works of glass artists from throughout the world. Recognized glass artist Dale Chihuly is a Tacoma native. His work can be viewed in the historic Union Station on Pacific Avenue. The Tacoma Art Museum has a rich collection of American, European, and Asian art and offers stimulating rotating exhibits on an ongoing schedule. It opened a new facility in May 2003, twice the size of its previous location, and broke ground on a more than $15 million expansion in 2013. The Antoine Predock-designed building features a unique flexible exhibition area that wraps around an indoor, open-air stone garden.

The Washington State History Museum has the largest collection of Northwest artifacts in the state. Its interactive exhibits chronicle the natural, social, and industrial history of the Pacific Northwest. The Washington State Capitol Museum features exhibits that reflect regional Native American history. The Karpeles Manuscript Library Museum has a collection of original manuscripts from American authors of the nineteenth century.

Tacoma's anchor arts groups include the Northwest Sinfonietta, Tacoma Philharmonic (which merged operations with the Broadway Center for the Performing Arts in 2012), Tacoma Symphony Orchestra, Tacoma Little Theatre, Children's Museum of Tacoma, and Tacoma Youth Symphony. Visitors to Tacoma can also enjoy a variety of public art. Highlights not to be missed include displayed public art projects on the Ruston Way waterfront and the literary, visual, and sound art forms at the walkway at Point Defiance. The University of Washington Tacoma campus is located in the middle of downtown Tacoma. A stroll through the campus takes the visitor past a variety of contemporary art created by some of Washington state's finest artists, including Buster Simpson, Dan Senn, and the aforementioned Dale Chihuly. The city is also home to the Tollbooth Gallery, the world's smallest gallery dedicated solely to experimental video and fine arts.

Festivals and Holidays

Tacoma's special events calendar is filled throughout the year. The Tacoma Home and Garden Show is held in January. The Wintergrass Bluegrass Festival takes place in

February, followed by the Northwest Antique Show in March. The annual Daffodil Festival and the Spring Barrel Wine Tasting Tour are fun April events. The Sound to Narrows Race draws crowds annually in June, as does Taste of Tacoma at the end of the month. July in Tacoma is especially festive, with the Fourth of July Celebration in Old Town and the Tacoma Freedom Fair and Fireworks Display. Summer festivals continue with the Pierce County Fair, Downtown Farmers Market, and Tall Ships Festival, which includes world-class sailing ships at the waterfront. Fall brings the Western Washington Fair, Oktoberfest, the Puyallup Canine Fest, and the Holiday Food and Gift Festival. The year closes with the Victorian Country Christmas in December, followed by the Downtown Tacoma Tree Lighting Ceremony, and First Night Celebrations on New Year's Eve.

Sports for the Spectator

The Tacoma Rainiers, the Triple-A affiliate of Major League Baseball's Seattle Mariners, play at Cheney Stadium. The Tacoma Stars are the state's only professional indoor soccer team. Both Pacific Lutheran University and the University of Puget Sound field teams in major sports.

Sports for the Participant

In addition to the recreational opportunities provided by the Cascade Mountains and the 361 freshwater lakes in Pierce County, Tacoma operates several public golf courses, and tennis courts are located in the public parks. There are more than 20 golf courses in Pierce County to choose from as well, including Chambers Bay, the first public course to host the 2010 U.S. Amateur Championship. MetroParks Tacoma maintains 68 parks, including the Point Defiance Park Zoo and Aquarium, with a total of nearly 3,000 acres of astounding acres of parks and gardens throughout the city. The city has five municipal pools. There are nine parks with spraygrounds. The city also maintains a number of public beaches and piers for swimming and fishing. Six skateparks are available.

Shopping and Dining

Boutiques and antique shops can be found at Tacoma's Old Town Historic District, the city's original business district. The downtown business district has shops, boutiques, and galleries. Freighthouse Square is a public market with restaurants, specialty shops, an antique mall, and special events. The Tacoma Mall, one of the largest in the Northwest, contains about 150 specialty stores, 5 department stores and a food court. In 2008, the mall opened a new 56,000 square foot lifestyle building that added a number of new businesses and restaurants. The Pacific Northwest Shop in the historic Proctor District features "Gifts Made in Our Corner of America," including wine and specialty foods.

Tacoma is salmon country, and the city is home to numerous seafood restaurants. Ruston Way, along the western side of the peninsula, is dotted with restaurants and is referred to as "Restaurant Row." There are some 2,500 restaurants within a 15-mile radius of Tacoma.

Visitor Information: Tacoma Regional Convention and Visitor Bureau, 1516 Pacific Ave., Tacoma, WA 98402; telephone (253) 284-3254; toll-free (800) 272-2662.

■ Convention Facilities

The Greater Tacoma Convention and Trade Center in the heart of downtown features a 50,000-square-foot Exhibition Hall, a 13,650-square-foot ballroom (which can be divided into 4 smaller rooms), and 15 meeting rooms, with the capacity to handle conferences of up to 4,000 people. An 18,000-square-foot outdoor event space is also available. A light rail train connects the center to the Tacoma Dome.

Meeting facilities are available at the 6.1-acre Tacoma Dome Entertainment Complex, which can accommodate as many as 23,000 people. The Dome, located near Commencement Bay in downtown Tacoma, contains a 30,000-square-foot Convention Hall with a seating capacity for 2,000 participants. The hall can be divided into six soundproof rooms, providing seminar space. The dome's arena can provide additional seating space for 3,000 persons. The Shanaman Sports Museum, which aims to preserve the area's sports heritage, is also located inside the Dome.

Tacoma's Landmark Catering and Convention Center is located in the historic Stadium District, and its Temple Theater Ballroom provides facilities with cabaret-style seating for 600 or theater-style seating for 1,400. Several other hotels and motels providing additional meeting space are located in the Tacoma area.

Convention Information: Tacoma Regional Convention and Visitor Bureau, 1516 Pacific Ave., Tacoma, WA 98402; telephone (253) 284-3254; toll-free (800) 272-2662.

■ Transportation

Approaching the City

Air travelers to Seattle are served by the Seattle-Tacoma International Airport (Sea-Tac), the 15th busiest commercial airport in the United States. Sea-Tac is a modern facility that served over 33.2 million passengers in 2012 on more than 20 airlines. It offers non-stop flights to roughly 100 domestic and international destinations. In 2008 the airport completed a third runway that enables aircraft to land in any weather conditions. Tacoma Narrows Airport is a municipally-owned field approximately six miles from Tacoma that handles corporate commuter flights.

The primary north–south motor route to Tacoma is Interstate 5, which runs between Canada and Mexico. East–west access is provided by State Route 16. Amtrak furnishes rail service into Tacoma with two daily routes. Greyhound also stops in the city.

Traveling in the City

Tacoma occupies an irregular peninsula with its street pattern conforming roughly to a grid within those constraints. The principle north–south arteries are Pacific Avenue, North Pearl, and Ruston Way. The major east–west thoroughfares are Sixth Avenue and S.R. 16, which enters Tacoma across the Narrows Bridge. Interstate 5 bisects the city on a southwest to northeast axis.

Sound Transit (ST) offers several ways of getting around. ST Express buses run from Tacoma, Gig Harbor, and Lakewood to downtown Seattle and back. ST Express buses also run from Lakewood and Tacoma to Seattle-Tacoma International Airport. Sounder commuter trains run some 80 miles on weekdays, connecting from Everett and Tacoma into Seattle and back. The Tacoma Link light rail trains began operating in August 2003 and have encouraged the renaissance of downtown Tacoma. The light rail system connects the Tacoma Dome station to five other stations in downtown Tacoma with trains that run every 10 to 20 minutes.

Pierce Transit (PT) is another regional public transportation service serving Tacoma and Pierce County. The county's transit system provides 36 routes. PT offers daily commuter buses to Seattle and Olympia as well as dozens of fixed routes in and around the city. Washington State Ferries offer service between Pt. Defiance Park and Vashon Island.

■ Communications

Newspapers and Magazines

The major daily newspaper in Tacoma is *The News Tribune.* The *Fort Lewis Ranger* is a weekly paper for military personnel. The *Pierce County Business Examiner* is available in a print edition once a week; an email daily subscription is also available. The *Northwest Dispatch* is a weekly serving the African American community.

Television and Radio

Five television stations are based in Tacoma; because of the city's proximity to Seattle, broadcasts from Seattle television stations are also received in the metropolitan area. Two AM and nine FM radio stations broadcast from Tacoma with music, news, and special interest programming.

Media Information: *The News Tribune,* 1950 South State Street, Tacoma, WA 98405; telephone (253) 597-8742.

Tacoma Online

City of Tacoma home page. Available www. cityoftacoma.org

Economic Development Board for Tacoma-Pierce County. Available www.edbtacomapierce.org

The News Tribune. Available www.thenewstribune. com

Pierce County Library System. Available www. piercecountylibrary.org

Tacoma-Pierce County Chamber of Commerce. Available www.tacomachamber.org

Tacoma Public Library. Available www.tpl.lib.wa.us

Tacoma Public Schools. Available www.tacoma.k12. wa.us

Tacoma Regional Convention and Visitor Bureau. Available www.traveltacoma.com

BIBLIOGRAPHY

McGinnis, Melissa, Doreen Beard-Simpkins, and the Metropolitan Park District of Tacoma *Tacoma's Point Defiance Park* (Charleston, SC: Arcadia Publishing, 2012)

Stover, Karla Wakefield *Hidden History of Tacoma: Little-known Tales from the City of Destiny* (Charleston, SC: The History Press, 2012)

Vancouver

■ The City in Brief

Founded: 1825 (incorporated, 1857)

Head Official: Mayor Timothy D. Leavitt (since 2009; current term expires 2017)

City Population

1990: 46,380
2000: 143,560
2010: 161,791
2012 estimate: 165,502
Percent change, 2000–2010: 12.7%
U.S. rank in 2000: 145th
U.S. rank in 2010: 144th

Metropolitan Statistical Area Population

2000: 1,927,881
2010: 2,226,009
2012 estimate: 2,289,651
Percent change, 2000–2010: 15.5%
U.S. rank in 2000: 25th
U.S. rank in 2010: 23rd

Area: Not available

Elevation: Not available

Average Annual Temperatures: 51.8° F

Average Annual Precipitation: 41.92 Inches

Major Economic Sectors: manufacturing, agriculture, health care, transportation

Unemployment Rate: 7.9% (2012)

Per Capita Income: $24,621

2012 FBI Crime Index Property: 6,478

Major Colleges and Universities: Clark College, Washington State University–Vancouver

Daily Newspaper: *The Columbian*

■ Introduction

Washington's fourth largest city and the county seat of Clark County, Vancouver celebrated its 150th anniversary as an incorporated city in 2007. Vancouver is a historic and cultural gem of southwest Washington, replete with natural beauty. It offers the services of a large metropolitan city with the charm and hospitality of a small urban town. Residents and visitors can engage in a wide variety of outdoor recreational activities and be entertained by a symphony orchestra, different theater troupes, or popular musical and comedy acts. Vancouver's proximity to Portland, Oregon, also offers residents and visitors additional opportunities for business and pleasure. The economy is diversifying, with growth in health-care and high-technology industries. Coupled with Vancouver's efforts to develop its downtown—highlighted by city investment in the waterfront to make way for more than $1 billion in private development—the future looks promising for the Columbia River city.

■ Geography and Climate

Vancouver sits on the north bank of the Columbia River directly across from Portland, Oregon. The Pacific Coast is less than 90 miles to the west. The Cascade Mountain Range rises on the east. The city has a total area of 46.1 square miles. Vancouver has a climate similar to Portland—temperate and seasonal. The rainy season lasts from November through April, with 80 percent of the total annual rainfall occurring in those months. Winter low temperatures hover around 35 degrees and summer highs average around 80 degrees. Summers are usually very pleasant with abundant sunshine. However, Vancouver's climate is different from Portland's in a few key ways. Being unsheltered by the Willamette Valley, high pressures

© *Josef Hanus/Shutterstock.com*

east of the Cascade Range lead to cold east winds down the Columbia River Gorge. Vancouver can experience freezing rain. Until the building of dams, close proximity to the river was a concern for flooding, destroying features such as Celilo Falls. Two of the most destructive floods took place in June 1894 and May 1948. Offsetting the cold gorge winds is a subtropical jet stream that brings warm moist air from the southern Pacific Ocean.

Area: Not available

Elevation: Not available

Average Temperatures: 51.8° F

Average Annual Precipitation: 41.92 Inches

■ History

A Habitable Place

For thousands of years, the Vancouver area was home to native people, including the Chinook and Klickitat nations. In May 1792 American trader and sailor Robert Gray became the first non-native to enter the Columbia River. Later that year, British Lieutenant William Broughton, serving under Captain George Vancouver, explored 100 miles upriver. Broughton named a point of land along the shore in honor of Vancouver. In 1806 Meriwether Lewis and William Clark camped near the Vancouver waterfront on the return trip of their western expedition. Lewis called the area "the only desired situation for settlement west of the Rocky Mountains."

In 1825 Dr. John McLoughlin, the chief agent of the Hudson Bay Company's Columbia District, made a decision to move the company's northwest headquarters from Astoria (now Oregon) upriver. He named the site after Point Vancouver on Broughton's original map. This was the founding of Fort Vancouver.

From a Fur Trading Center to Military Headquarters

For many years, Fort Vancouver was the main location for fur trading in the Pacific Northwest. It was settled by both Americans and British under a "joint occupation" agreement. Fort Vancouver was a center of British control over the Oregon Territory. However, in 1846 American control was extended north to the 49th parallel with the Oregon Treaty. The northwest became part of the United States.

In 1849 American troops arrived to establish Columbia (later Vancouver) Barracks. It served as military headquarters for much of the Pacific Northwest. U.S. Army Captain Ulysses S. Grant was quartermaster at the Columbia Barracks for 15 months beginning in September 1852. The neighboring settlement was named the "City of Columbia." The city of Vancouver was incorporated on January 23, 1857. Through the rest of nineteenth century, Vancouver developed and grew. In 1908 the first rail line east through the Washington side of the Columbia River Gorge reached Vancouver. In 1910 a railroad bridge was opened south across the Columbia River. In 1917 the Interstate Bridge was completed, which replaced ferries.

Wartime Activities

During World War I, the site later named Pearson Field was the location of the world's largest spruce cut-up mill. The mill cut raw timber into the lumber used to build planes that fought in World War I. After the bombing of Pearl Harbor, Henry Kaiser opened a shipyard next to the U.S. Army reserve, which by 1944 employed as many as 36,000 people. Vancouver's Kaiser Shipyard built a variety of craft that were used in World War II. The large number of shipyard workers who came to work in Vancouver increased the population from 18,000 to over 80,000 in just a few months. This led to the creation of the Vancouver Housing Authority and six new residential developments that became neighborhoods.

Sesquicentennial Celebration

Vancouver celebrated its 150th anniversary as an incorporated city in 2007. Vancouver has gone through many transformations in its history, including growing from a population of about 250 people in 1857 to more than 165,000 during the twenty-first century. Population growth has been sustained by an economic resiliency that has switched from an agricultural and manufacturing base to one focused on attracting and retaining health-care, financial services, and high-technology companies. As its motto says, Vancouver, with a colorful past, has a bright future.

Historical Information: Clark County Historical Museum, 1511 Main Street, Vancouver, WA 98660; telephone (360) 993-5679; fax (360) 993-5683; email info@cchmuseum.org.

■ Population Profile

Metropolitan Statistical Area Population
2000: 1,927,881
2010: 2,226,009

2012 estimate: 2,289,651
Percent change, 2000–2010: 15.5%
U.S. rank in 2000: 25th
U.S. rank in 2010: 23rd

City Residents
1990: 46,380
2000: 143,560
2010: 161,791
2012 estimate: 165,502
Percent change, 2000–2010: 12.7%
U.S. rank in 2000: 145th
U.S. rank in 2010: 144th

Density: 3,482.6 people per square mile

Racial and ethnic characteristics
White: 126,688
Black or African American: 5,302
American Indian and Alaskan Native: 1,361
Asian: 12,286
Native Hawaiian and Other Pacific Islander: 3,115
Hispanic or Latino (may be of any race): 19,654
Other: 16,750

Percent of residents born in state: 29.9%

Age characteristics
Population under 5 years old: 11,881
Population 5 to 9 years old: 9,664
Population 10 to 14 years old: 11,148
Population 15 to 19 years old: 9,311
Population 20 to 24 years old: 12,988
Population 25 to 34 years old: 26,034
Population 35 to 44 years old: 21,963
Population 45 to 54 years old: 20,660
Population 55 to 59 years old: 10,287
Population 60 to 64 years old: 8,735
Population 65 to 74 years old: 12,502
Population 75 to 84 years old: 7,809
Population 85 years and over: 2,520
Median age: 36.0

Births (2010–11 Metropolitan Area)
Total number: 28,672

Deaths (2010–11 Metropolitan Area)
Total number: 15,161

Money income (2012)
Per capita income: $24,621
Median household income: $48,273
Total households: 65,449

Number of households with income of …
less than $10,000: 4,378
$10,000 to $14,999: 3,687
$15,000 to $24,999: 7,277

$25,000 to $34,999: 7,643
$35,000 to $49,999: 11,013
$50,000 to $74,999: 13,595
$75,000 to $99,999: 7,876
$100,000 to $149,999: 6,568
$150,000 to $199,999: 1,975
$200,000 or more: 1,437

Percent of families below poverty level: 16.7%

FBI Crime Index Property: 6,478

FBI Crime Index Violent: 592

■ Municipal Government

The city has a council/manager form of government. Seven council members—including a mayor—are elected to staggered four-year terms.

Head Official: Mayor Timothy D. Leavitt (since 2009; current term expires 2017)

Total Number of City Employees: 962 (2012)

City Information: City of Vancouver, 415 West 6th Street, Vancouver, WA 98660; telephone (360) 487-8629; email vancmo@cityofvancouver.us.

■ Economy

Major Industries and Commercial Activity

Vancouver's economy has diversified over the past two decades, resulting in a healthy climate for business investment, as well as creating markets for a wide array of products and services. The expansion of the manufacturing base and growth in high-technology and service sectors has improved the economic outlook. Despite diversification, manufacturing suffered during a national recession in the late 2000s, exemplified by Carlisle Interconnect Technologies, which closed its doors in 2010. Manufacturing targets into the 2010s focused on medical devices and scientific instruments, as well as aerospace components and semiconductors.

Although traditional industries like agriculture, wood products, and natural resources and mining no longer contribute materially to job growth, industries such as construction, professional and scientific services, software publishing, biotechnology, education, health care, and retail trade have recently seen measurable gains, due in part to regional employees' high level of educational attainment. Southwest Washington Health System joined the broader PeaceHealth network in 2011; PeaceHealth moved its corporate offices to Vancouver during 2012–14.

Clark County is also home to more than 300 high-technology companies that employ some 8,000 workers. Quite a few of these are based in Vancouver, including SEH America and offices of Hewlett-Packard. Vancouver is also home to nLight, a leader in the production of high-power semiconductor lasers, which was named one of the nation's 5,000 fastest growing companies in 2012 by *Inc.*

The Port of Vancouver contributes to the health of the local economy as well, generating $1.6 billion in economic benefit to the community annually. Related businesses employ some 2,300 individuals.

Over 50,000 Clark County residents commute to Portland, Oregon, on a daily basis.

Items and goods produced: electronic goods, software, agricultural products, foodstuffs, wood products, fitness equipment

Incentive Programs—New and Existing Companies

Local programs: The Columbia River Economic Development Council (CREDC) helps companies find profitable locations in the Vancouver and Portland Metropolitan area. The council offers such services as site location and acquisition, business demographics, and permit and process facilitation. It helps businesses relocate, expand, and increase their competitiveness in a cost-effective manner. CREDC markets tax-exempt industrial revenue bonds on behalf of the Industrial Revenue Bonds Public Corporation of Clark County. IRBs can be used to finance real estate, machinery, and equipment for eligible manufacturing companies. The CREDC also has connections that can introduce businesses to private equity and government-backed financing for projects. CREDC promotes funding programs that leverage research and development support for targeted industries.

The City of Vancouver's Economic Development Services also works with the CREDC to help diversify the city's business climate. The city offers streamlined permitting which allows for a more efficient development review process for local businesses.

State programs: The state of Washington offers a number of incentive programs to attract new and expanding businesses to the state, with most targeted to specific industries or geographic areas. Industry-specific incentives include sales and use tax exemptions for general manufacturing and agriculture; sales and use tax deferrals and waivers, and business and occupation tax credits for high-technology industries, including biotechnology and medical device manufacturing; business and occupation tax rate reductions and credits for the aerospace, timber, food manufacturing, biofuel, semiconductor, and aluminum industries; and a range of credits and exemptions for renewable energy firms.

Geography-based incentives are available in designated Community Empowerment Zones, high unemployment counties, and Main Street areas. Other incentives support economic activity that reduces commuter travel; produces television or film; or relates to newspaper publishing.

Job training programs: The state of Washington offers a number of incentive programs to attract new and expanding businesses to the state, with most targeted to specific industries or geographic areas. Industry-specific incentives include sales and use tax exemptions for general manufacturing and agriculture; sales and use tax deferrals and waivers, and business and occupation tax credits for high-technology industries, including biotechnology and medical device manufacturing; business and occupation tax rate reductions and credits for the aerospace, timber, food manufacturing, biofuel, semiconductor, and aluminum industries; and a range of credits and exemptions for renewable energy firms.

The Southwest Washington Workforce Development Council (SWWDC) provides leadership and resources to increase economic development with a trained and productive workforce in Clark, Cowlitz, and Wahkiakum Counties. WorkSource and other partners offer resources and a variety of services to help youth, adults, and dislocated workers secure gainful employment. There is a WorkSource center in Vancouver, which offers job search assistance, access to current job openings, career development and assistance, and training and skill development.

Development Projects

In June 2007 the City Council adopted the Vancouver City Center Vision and Subarea Plan for future development. The boundary of the City Center Plan was expanded to approximately 130 city blocks including the city center waterfront. The plan will encourage residential development; the creation and support of what the city calls "messy vitality," a mix of residential, civic, retail, and entertainment places that will attract growth, jobs, and activity; focused waterfront redevelopment; protection of key historic buildings and established residential neighborhoods; and revitalization of the Main Street Corridor to establish downtown as a regional center for commerce, culture, and urban living.

The largest development project in Vancouver's history began in 2010, a $44.6 million waterfront-access project to connect downtown Vancouver to the Columbia River waterfront, formerly occupied by the industrial site of Boise Cascade. The 35-acre Boise Cascade site was expected to see $1.3 billion invested in converting its acreage into 22 city blocks dedicated to commerce, including residential and office spaces intermingled with restaurants, shops, public parks, and hotels. The project's infrastructure was expected to be completed in 2014.

Nautilus opened a 52,000-square-foot headquarters in 2012 near the Columbia Tech Center. Financial difficulties several years earlier had led the company to vacate its space in the center, which subsequently was taken by Hewlett Packard and PeaceHealth. Other commercial projects in 2012 included a $4.1 million investment by Great Western Malting, a $10.5 million project by Cinetopia, and a $6.5 million development by Quarry Senior Living.

The Columbia River Crossing Project is a joint, phased effort between governments in Oregon and Vancouver to reduce congestion and also improve safety for a portion of Interstate 5, which included construction of a new bridge and extension of light rail lines. The project began in 2008 and continued through 2014. Total cost of the project was estimated at more than $3 billion.

Economic Development Information: City of Vancouver, Community and Economic Development, City Hall, 415 West 6th Street, Vancouver, WA 98660; telephone (360) 487-7800. Columbia River Economic Development Council, 805 Broadway, Suite 412, Vancouver, WA 98660-3237; telephone (360) 694-5006.

Commercial Shipping

The Port of Vancouver is a multi-purpose port authority located along the banks of the Columbia River. Annually the port handles more five million metric tons of total cargo from between 400 and 500 ocean vessels and river barges. The Port has over 1,000 acres available for expansion and development of heavy and light industry, manufacturing, distribution warehousing, research and business-park uses. The Port also has versatile cargo handling facilities, a skilled labor force, personal customer service, and extensive transportation networks. The Port is a hub of marine, rail, highway, and air cargo transportation connections. The Port of Vancouver has handled a variety of bulk and break bulk cargo since 1912.

Labor Force and Employment Outlook

Many Vancouverites work in Portland. Job opportunities are increasing in the high technology, education, health care, and other service sectors, while employment in traditional industries such as agriculture, wood products, and natural resources and mining has declined.

The following is a summary of data regarding the 2012 Vancouver labor force:

Size of civilian labor force: 83,863

Number of workers employed in . . .

    agriculture and mining: 276
    construction: 4,454
    manufacturing: 9,101
    wholesale trade: 2,144

retail trade: 9,281
transportation: 4,987
information systems: 1,650
finance: 4,716
professional administration: 8,853
education and social services: 14,984
arts and leisure: 6,109
other: 3,678
public administration: 2,744

Average hourly earnings of production workers: $17.62

Unemployment rate: 7.9% (2012)

Employers

Largest employers (2012)	*Number of employees*
PeaceHealth SW Medical Center	2,841
Evergreen School District	2,455
Vancouver School District	2,203
Clark County	1,561
Fred Meyer Stores	1,500
Clark College	985
City of Vancouver	962
Vancouver Clinic Inc. PS	912
BNSF Railway Railroad	800
Kaiser Permanente NW	724

Cost of Living

Vancouver's median home price in 2013 was $306,600. That year, Vancouver's cost of living was slightly above the national average, although it was still less than Portland, Oregon, its immediate neighbor to the south.

The following is a summary of data regarding several key cost of living factors in the area.

2013 ACCRA Average House Price: $306,600

2013 ACCRA Cost of Living Index: 102

State income tax rate: None

State sales tax rate: 6.5%

Local income tax rate: None

Local sales tax rate: 1.9%

Property tax rate: $13.17 per $1,000 of assessed value (county average, 2013)

Economic Information: City of Vancouver, Community and Economic Development, City Hall, 415 West 6th Street, Vancouver, WA 98660; telephone (360) 487-7800. Columbia River Economic Development Council, 805 Broadway, Suite 412, Vancouver, WA 98660-3237; telephone (360) 694-5006.

■ Education and Research

Elementary and Secondary Schools

Vancouver Public Schools are composed of 21 elementary schools, 6 middle schools, and 5 high schools, and serve nearly 23,000 students. The district employs 3,200 people full time, with some 1,144 of those employees classroom teachers. More than one-fifth of all students speak a language other than English at home, and transitional bilingual enrollment constitutes 11 percent of the student population. Some 53 percent of students are eligible for free or reduced lunches. Specialty schools and programs within the district include the Vancouver School of Arts and Academics, Vancouver iTech Preparatory, Fir Grove/Vista Program, and Vancouver Home Connection.

Private schools include the Cascadia Montessori School, Clark County Christian School, Columbia Adventist Academy, Columbia Ridge Baptist Academy, Cornerstone Christian School, Firm Foundation Christian School, Gardner School of Arts and Sciences, King's Way Christian School, Our Lady of Lourdes Catholic School, Vancouver Christian High School, Christ Community Vancouver, and St. Joseph Catholic Grade School. The Washington School for the Deaf and the Washington State School for the Blind are also located in Vancouver.

The following is a summary of data regarding the Vancouver School District.

Total enrollment: 22,669

Number of facilities

total: 36
elementary schools: 21
junior high schools: 6
high schools: 5
other: 4

Student/teacher ratio: 20.9:1

Teacher salaries

average (statewide): $53,796

Funding per pupil: $9,122

Public Schools Information: Vancouver School District, 2901 Falk Road, Vancouver, WA 98661; telephone (360) 313-1000.

Colleges and Universities

Originally founded as a private two-year junior college in 1932, Clark College provides a variety of associate degrees, general adult education, and preparation for four-year university degrees. Clark College has well-regarded programs in nursing, dental hygiene, and industrial arts such as welding and auto maintenance. One of the largest community/technical colleges in the state of Washington, it enrolls nearly 16,000 students annually.

Washington State University (WSU), a major public research university with a main campus in Pullman, Washington, has a regional 351-acre campus in Vancouver. WSU–Vancouver is a non-residential research university with access to the resources of the WSU system. WSU–Vancouver offers 20 bachelor's degrees, 9 master's degrees, 2 doctorate degrees, and more than 37 fields of study. Enrollment in 2013 was 3,062 students. WSU–Vancouver has more than 150 full-time, Ph.D. faculty.

Libraries and Research Centers

Fort Vancouver Regional Library District serves southwest Washington state. With a library collection that includes more than 730,000 books, magazines, videotapes, DVDs, CDs, and tapes, the library district serves all of Clark, Skamania, and Klickitat counties, and the city of Woodland and the independent Yale Valley Library District in Cowlitz County. The district has 16 libraries, with branch libraries in Vancouver located in Cascade Park, Three Creeks, the former Vancouver Mall, and downtown.

Washington State University–Vancouver's library has more than 30,000 books and media, including 300 print and more than 20,000 electronic journals. It also provides access to 125 online research databases. The library participates in several local and regional library consortia, including the Portland Area Library System and Orbis Cascade Alliance (the Oregon and Washington Cooperative Library Project). It also houses the Environmental Information Cooperative Library.

Public Library Information: Vancouver Community Library, 901 C Street, Vancouver, WA 98660; telephone (360) 906-5106.

■ Health Care

PeaceHealth Southwest Medical Center in Vancouver offers comprehensive hospital services, with special heart and vascular, cancer, brain and spine, bone and joint, and trauma centers. It has 450 beds and admits nearly 13,000 patients annually. Originally established in 1858 as the first permanent hospital in the Northwest Territories, PeaceHealth Southwest Medical Center is the largest private employer in Clark County and one of the major employers in the Portland metropolitan region. Prior to a merger with PeaceHealth that took effect in 2011, the hospital was known as Southwest Washington Medical Center.

Legacy Salmon Creek Hospital is part of the Legacy Health System. The 194-bed, full-service community hospital celebrated its fifth anniversary in 2011. Medical centers in Portland within a 10-mile radius of Vancouver include the Providence Portland Medical Center and Legacy Emanuel Medical Center.

■ Recreation

Sightseeing

A must-see for any visitor to the city is the Fort Vancouver National Historic Site. Headquarters for the British Hudson's Bay Company, the fort was once the center of political, cultural, and commercial activities in the Pacific Northwest. Interpreters in period clothing re-enact daily fort life in this reconstructed mid-nineteenth-century fur trading outpost. Officers Row is the location for 22 preserved Victorian homes on the National Historic Register. Built in the mid- to late-1800s, these beautifully restored homes were built to house U.S. Army officers and their families stationed at Vancouver Barracks. They include the Marshall House, the O.O. Howard House, and the Grant House (featuring the Restaurant at the Historic Reserve and Commander's Whiskey and Wine Bar). On Main Street, the Clark County Historical Museum showcases the history of Clark County housed in a former Carnegie Library that was built in 1909. Exhibits feature a Native American gallery, railroad exhibit, American military memorabilia, and other artifacts dating back to the thirteenth century.

Located at the oldest continually operating airfield in the nation, the Pearson Air Museum houses a collection of vintage airplanes, interpretive displays, an interactive children's center, theater presentations, a restoration shop, and gift shop. The Water Resources Education Center teaches people of all ages about water resources and includes hands-on activities in the Exhibit Hall, artwork in the Center's White Sturgeon Art Gallery, live sturgeon in a 350-gallon aquarium, and a panoramic view of the Columbia River. The Salmon Run Bell Tower and Glockenspiel is located in Esther Short Park. The bells were cast in the Netherlands, and there are four five-foot bronze jumping salmon on the tower and several jets that spray water down the column. A Chinook Indian story is inscribed in the basalt column around the base of the tower and a glockenspiel with a fully animated three-scene diorama depicts Chinook Indian legend. The Ilchee Monument features a seven-foot tall statue, overlooking the Columbia River, honoring the daughter of Comcomly, a nineteenth-century Chinook chief. According to Native American lore, Ilchee had the power of a shaman, and she paddled her own canoe, the sign of a chief. The Waterfront Renaissance Trail connects downtown Vancouver with retail shops and restaurants along the Columbia River waterfront.

The Ridgefield National Wildlife Refuge offers over 5,200 acres of vital migration and wintering habitat for spring and fall migrating birds. The mild winter climate and wetlands along the Columbia River create ideal resting and feeding areas for 180 species of birds such as Canada Geese, Sandhill Cranes, Great Blue Herons, swans, shore and song birds, and a variety of waterfowl.

The Cedar Creek Grist Mill in Woodland is the only grain-grinding mill in Washington that has maintained its original structural integrity, grinds with stones, and is water-powered. Built in 1876, the mill has been fully restored as a working museum and is registered as a National Historic Site. The covered bridge spanning Cedar Creek adjacent to the mill was rebuilt in 1994. Cathlapotle Plankhouse is a full-scale replica of a Chinookan-style cedar plankhouse located at the Ridgefield National Wildlife Refuge at the location of Cathlapotle, one of the largest Chinookan villages in the area. At Hulda Klager Lilac Gardens in Woodland, visitors can step back in time to discover an 1880s Victorian farmhouse and country garden with more than 150 varieties of lilacs and some rare and unusual plants and trees. The 1889 farmhouse contains many of the original furnishings as well as featured displays of handmade quilts, artwork, antiques, and collectibles.

In Yacolt visitors can experience 1920s farm life at the Pomeroy Living History Farm. Period-dressed interpreters help visitors participate in farm activities such as grinding grain, washing clothes, feeding livestock, and making rope. Also in Yacolt, the Chelatchie Prairie Railroad is pulled by an 1841 diesel locomotive, transporting passengers through scenic northern Clark County from Yacolt to Mouton Falls and Chelatchie Prairie and back. Special events include casino nights, murder mysteries, staged hold-ups, and barbeque trips.

Arts and Culture

The Vancouver Symphony Orchestra, with critically acclaimed music director and conductor Salvador Brotons, puts on musical performances from October through May, plus a summer outdoor evening concert in Esther Short Park. The Bravo! Vancouver Concert Series is one of the premiere choral groups in the Pacific Northwest. Singers perform a diverse repertoire, and are equally at home performing jazz and popular music. In Ridgefield the Sleep Country Amphitheater, previously known as the Amphitheater at Clark County, is a 60,000-square-foot live music venue located next to the Clark County Event Center and Fairgrounds. The facility seats almost 8,000 in the covered pavilion and an additional 10,000 on the lawn. The Camas

Performing Arts Series presents five musical concerts between September and May. The 90-minute concerts feature national and international artists in a variety of musical genres.

The Clark College Theatre blends theatre, music, dance, and art into entertaining and award-winning productions. For more than two decades, the theatre has been recognized as a leader in Southwest Washington. The Kiggins Theatre offers an intimate venue in downtown Vancouver for live performances.

Festivals and Holidays

True to its reputation as a great city for walking, Vancouver hosts the International Discovery Walk Festival each April. The Discovery Walk Festival is sponsored by International Walk Fest and the city of Vancouver to foster international friendship. Walkers and military units come from a dozen different nations to participate.

The Sturgeon Festival is held at the Water Resources Education Center in June. The festival is a celebration of the sturgeon and its Columbia River ecosystem. Each Fourth of July, fireworks are set off on the grounds of Fort Vancouver National Historic Site. The display is one of the largest west of the Mississippi River. In late August the Vancouver Wine and Jazz Festival is held in Esther Short Park, where attendees can sample excellent wine and food while listening to great music. Also in August, Founder's Day is held to commemorate the anniversary of the founding of the National Park System. Admission to Fort Vancouver National Historic Site is free, and there are craft demonstrations by carpenters, blacksmiths, bakers, and cooks.

St. Joseph Catholic School hosts the Vancouver Sausage Fest in September; more than 100,000 people attend the festival over three days. October brings the Old Apple Tree Celebration, an annual celebration in honor of the Northwest's oldest living apple tree, originally planted at Fort Vancouver in 1826. The celebration features a Heritage Tree bike ride, children's activities, tree expert presentations, a fruit tree pruning workshop, and a chance to sample apples from the Old Apple Tree itself.

In December visitors can experience the festive traditional sights, smells, and sounds of the holiday season at Fort Vancouver, just as the employees of Hudson's Bay Company may have been doing in preparation for the holidays.

Sports for the Spectator

When not rooting for other Washington teams, Vancouverites and visitors can take advantage of the city's close proximity to Portland, Oregon, to watch spectator sports. Portland hosts National Basketball Association, Major League Soccer, and minor league hockey. The Moda Center is home to the NBA's Portland Trail Blazers. The

Portland Timbers are Portland's professional soccer franchise that joined Major League Soccer in 2011 after playing in the United Soccer Leagues first division for a number of years. The Timbers play their home games to boisterous, sold-crowds at Jeld-Wen Field. Hockey action is brought to fans by the Portland Winterhawks of the Western Hockey League, which is a major source of talent for the National Hockey League. Portland Meadows features quarter horse and thoroughbred racing from October through April. Auto racing takes place at the Portland International Raceway.

Washington State University-Vancouver belongs to the Pacific-10 Conference for football, basketball, baseball, and track and field.

Sports for the Participant

Vancouver offers recreation and sports programs for residents of all ages. There are nearly 7,000 acres of parkland, over 44 miles of trails, and facilities including pools, a tennis/racquetball center, and community centers. Opportunities for hiking, biking, camping, fishing, boating, swimming, kayaking, golf, windsurfing, skiing, and snowboarding abound. The rivers and lakes in southwest Washington offer tremendous fishing opportunities. There are many fine steelhead streams and one of the only wild Fall Chinook salmon runs in the state. The Columbia River also offers some of the best sturgeon fishing.

The Columbia River Gorge has become known as one of the best locations worldwide for windsurfing—some even call it the windsurfing capital of the world. There are approximately 50 approved windsurfing sites along the east and west sides of the Gorge. Hikers can climb in Gifford Pinchot National Forest to the east. Trails range from easy nature trails to rugged terrain at varying difficulties. Mt. Hood in Oregon, about an hour's drive away from Vancouver, offers everything from the best powder skiing and snowboarding, to tubing, sleigh rides, and dog sled rides. Mt. Hood Skibowl also offers the nation's largest night ski area. For golf, the county has eight 18-hole courses and numerous driving ranges. For those who like to camp, the area also has two state parks with tent and RV sites, as well as a number of well-kept RV campgrounds.

Shopping and Dining

Vancouver offers a variety of shopping opportunities. The Vancouver Farmers Market operates year-round indoors in the Esther Short Commons next to Esther Short Park. It features an eclectic mixture of food, high-end crafts, farm-direct produce, and nursery stock. From April through October, the market expands outdoors into the streets with more than 150 vendors offering local produce, plants, and arts and crafts. There are also food booths with local and international specialties, and entertainers provide live music.

If one is shopping for antiques, gifts, or in boutique shops, Uptown Village in the upper Main Street area is the place to go. In downtown Vancouver, there are many art galleries, clothing and shoe stores, and gift and specialty shops. Westfield Vancouver is Southwest Washington's largest mall. It features more than 140 specialty shops, 5 major anchor retailers, and a food court with 11 restaurants. Downtown Camas, just east of Vancouver, boasts a variety of shops where one can find antiques, ladies fashions, accessories, jewelry, and home décor.

There are many wonderful restaurants in the heart of Vancouver and surrounding areas. From seafood restaurants, steak houses, vegetarian restaurants, pubs, wine bars, delis, and coffee shops to such ethnic specialties as Italian, Greek, Mexican, Thai, Chinese, and Japanese, diners have a wide variety of choices from which to sate their palates.

Visitor Information: Southwest Washington Convention & Visitors Bureau, 101 East 8th Street, Suite 240, Vancouver, WA 98660-3294; toll-free (877) 600-0800; telephone (360) 750-1553; fax (360) 750-1933; email admin@VisitVancouverUSA.com.

■ Convention Facilities

Conveniently located only 15 minutes from Portland International Airport, Vancouver is an ideal setting for conventions. In the heart of downtown, the Hilton Vancouver Washington and Vancouver Convention Center provide 226 guest rooms and 30,000 square feet of flexible meeting space for conferences and events, with a meeting capacity of 1,500. The Exhibition Hall at the Clark County Event Center has 97,200 square feet of space with a maximum occupancy of 13,844 people and up to 551 booths. Outdoor venues include Esther Short Park and Alderbrook Park, which can each accommodate 10,000 people. Facilities at Pearson Air Museum can accommodate 450; Clark Community College can accommodate 350; and the Marshall House can accommodate 225, in addition to other off-site venues.

Convention Information: Southwest Washington Convention & Visitors Bureau, 101 East 8th Street, Suite 240, Vancouver, WA 98660-3294; toll-free (877) 600-0800; telephone (360) 750-1553; fax (360) 750-1933; email admin@VisitVancouverUSA.com.

■ Transportation

Approaching the City

Portland's airport, Portland International Airport (PDX), is one of the fastest-growing major airports on the West Coast, with 13 commercial carriers offering daily nonstop flights from Portland to various destinations. Serving more than 13 million passengers annually, PDX offers nearly 550 passenger flights daily. Clark County has two airfields that accommodate private aircraft: Pearson Airfield, near downtown Vancouver, and Grove Field, near the Port of Camas/Washougal.

Interstate 5, the major north-south artery, goes directly through the Vancouver area. Interstate 84, running along the Oregon side of the Columbia River, provides easy access from the West. A number of other state highways provide southwest Washington with access from the northwest and southwest.

Amtrak provides passenger rail service and Greyhound provides bus service to Vancouver.

Traveling in the City

C-Tran is Clark County's public bus service. C-Tran has 28 routes covering Clark County and connecting into Portland. C-Tran also offers curb-to-curb service for people who are unable to use regular service, as well as carpool and vanpool services. Two transit centers and five park-and-ride facilities serve the area.

■ Communications

Newspapers and Magazines

The Columbian is Vancouver's daily newspaper. The *Vancouver Business Journal* and *Vancouver Family Magazine* are also published in the city.

Television and Radio

Two television stations, three FM radio stations, and three AM radio stations broadcast from Vancouver, but the city also receives broadcasts from surrounding areas, especially Portland, Oregon.

Media Information: *The Columbian*, 701 West 8th St., Vancouver, WA 98660; telephone (360) 694-3391; toll-free (800) 743-3391.

Vancouver Online

City of Vancouver home page. Available www. cityofvancouver.us

The Columbian. Available www.columbian.com

Fort Vancouver Regional Library District. Available www.fvrl.org

Greater Vancouver U.S.A. Chamber of Commerce. Available www.vancouverusa.com

Southwest Washington Convention and Visitors Bureau. Available www.visitvancouverusa.com

Vancouver School District. Available www.vansd.org

BIBLIOGRAPHY

Blumenthal, Richard W., ed., *With Vancouver in Inland Washington Waters: Journals of 12 Crewmen, April–June 1792* (Jefferson, NC: McFarland and Co., 2007)

Northwest 2010: Alaska, Idaho, Montana, Oregon, Washington, and Wyoming (Chicago, IL: Five Star Travel Corp., 2010)

Wyoming

The State in Brief

Nickname: Equality State, Cowboy State

Motto: Equal rights

Flower: Indian paintbrush

Bird: Meadowlark

Area: 97,813 square miles (2010; U.S. rank 10th)

Elevation: Ranges from 3,100 feet to 13,084 feet above sea level

Climate: Continental; semi arid and cool, with mild summers and severe winters; temperature varies with elevation

Admitted to Union: July 10, 1890

Capital: Cheyenne

Head Official: Mathew Mead (R) (until 2015)

Population
    1990: 453,588
    2000: 493,782
    2010: 563,626
    2012 estimate: 562,803
    Percent change, 2000–2010: 14.1%
    U.S. rank in 2012: 50th
    Percent of residents born in state: 41.3% (2012)
    Density: 5.8 people per square mile (2010)
    2012 FBI Crime Index Total: 14,383

Racial and Ethnic Characteristics (2012)
    White: 513,021
    Black or African American: 4,689
    American Indian and Alaska Native: 12,951
    Asian: 4,392
    Native Hawaiian and Pacific Islander: 206
    Hispanic or Latino (may be of any race): 50,313
    Other: 27,544

Age Characteristics (2012)
    Population under 5 years old: 39,192
    Population 5 to 19 years old: 112,025
    Percent of population 65 years and over: 12.5%
    Median age: 36.9

Vital Statistics
    Total number of births (2012–13): 7,549
    Total number of deaths (2012–13): 4,409
    AIDS cases reported through 2011: 307

Economy
    Major industries: Mining; finance, insurance, and real estate; trade; research and technology
    Unemployment rate (2012): 3.5%
    Per capita income (2012): $28,858
    Median household income (2012): $56,573
    Percentage of persons below poverty level (2012): 11.0%
    Income tax rate: None
    Sales tax rate: 4.0%

Casper

■ The City in Brief

Founded: 1888 (incorporated in 1889)

Head Official: City Manager John C. Patterson (since 2011)

City Population

    1990: 46,742
    2000: 49,644
    2010: 55,316
    2012 estimate: 56,391
    Percent change, 2000–2010: 11.4%
    U.S. rank in 1990: 559th (State rank: 2nd)
    U.S. rank in 2000: Not available (State rank: 2nd)
    U.S. rank in 2010: 632nd (State rank: 2nd)

Metropolitan Statistical Area Population

    2000: 66,533
    2010: 75,450
    2012 estimate: 78,621
    Percent change, 2000–2010: 13.4%
    U.S. rank in 2000: 363rd
    U.S. rank in 2010: 469th

Area: 23.9 square miles

Elevation: 5,140 feet above sea level

Average Annual Temperatures: January, 22.3° F; July, 70.0° F; annual average, 44.9° F

Average Annual Precipitation: 13.03 inches rainfall; 77.9 inches snowfall

Major Economic Sectors: mining, education, health care, social services, retail trade, tourism

Unemployment Rate: 3.6% (2012)

Per Capita Income: $28,782

2012 FBI Crime Index Property: 1,968

Major Colleges and Universities: Casper College, University of Wyoming–Casper College Center

Daily Newspaper: *Casper Star-Tribune*

■ Introduction

In the days of the Wild West and Manifest Destiny, all roads led to Casper. The city was sited at the nexus of a number of important trails of the time, including the Oregon Trail, the Pony Express route, the Mormon Trail, the Bozeman Trail, the California Trail, and the Bridger Trail. The city remains a crossroads today, but of several major state and federal highways not trails. While the economy of the surrounding area still centers on oil and petroleum exploration, new developments have strengthened the city in fields such as health care, a product of the city's aging population, and tourism, which draws upon the city's rich history.

■ Geography and Climate

At almost a mile above sea level, Casper rests at the foot of Casper Mountain and follows the contours of the North Platte River. With the Laramie Mountain Range of the Rocky Mountains to the west and the Wyoming plains to the east, Casper has been uniquely situated between natural resources for energy and outdoor adventure exploration on the one hand and agricultural endeavors on the other.

Casper sits within the area characterized by the National Weather Service as the "comfort zone," with year-round low humidity moderating the cold of winter and the heat of summer. Casper averages 275 days of sunshine every year and experiences an average wind speed of 12.9 miles per hour. The city's location and climate make it a jumping-off point for outdoor adventures, such as golf, hiking, biking, and skiing. The

Casper Area Casper Convention and Visitors Bureau. Reproduced by permission.

city is the seat of Natrona County and is near the center of the state.

Area: 23.9 square miles

Elevation: 5,140 feet above sea level

Average Temperatures: January, 22.3° F; July, 70.0° F; annual average, 44.9° F

Average Annual Precipitation: 13.03 inches rainfall; 77.9 inches snowfall

■ History

Back to the Source

Before there were people, there was the river. The North Platte River begins its meandering journey in the mountains near Casper, running east across the Great Plains to merge with its sister river, the South Platte, to become simply the Platte River. Water, mountains, and

plains were a lure from the beginning. Evidence of human occupation dates back more than 12,000 years with the Clovis peoples, followed by the Folsom and the Eden Valley peoples. A mix of hunting and gathering tribes occupied the area until approximately 500 A.D., eventually morphing into Native American tribes more familiar in today's world.

The original residents of Wyoming were nomadic Plains Indians, including tribes as disparate as the Arapaho, Sioux, Cheyenne, Crow, Lakota, Blackfeet, Kiowa, Nez Perce, and Shoshone. The tribes relied on the land and the roaming buffalo herds for sustenance. When European explorers and hunters began a wholesale slaughter of the buffalo that coincided with an interest in herding native peoples to a containment area in Oklahoma, armed conflicts escalated in the clash of cultures and interests. In 1812 fur trappers had followed beaver and buffalo populations to the northern Rockies. The Oregon Trail had been scouted out in 1823 and its ever-deepening ruts reflected the entrenched U.S. belief in its manifest destiny to expand westward.

The Western Civil War

By 1847 a network of travel routes converged at a spot just west of present-day Casper. Here the Emigrant Trail crossed from the south side to the north side of the North Platte River. When the first Mormon wagon train passed through this area on its way to what would become Utah, Brigham Young arranged for a ferry to be set up for the use of future travelers. The Mormon Ferry soon faced competition as more emigrants passed that way and decided to cash in on a good idea. One entrepreneurial French Canadian trader named John Baptiste Richard decided to build a bridge across the North Platte and charge a toll for crossing it. The area was now not just a way-station but an encampment.

Local residents established a trading post along the Emigrant Trail in 1859, taking advantage of the growing stream of wagon trains. As the local population grew along with the number of emigrants, friction developed with local tribes of Lakota, Arapaho, and Cheyenne. As a result, the trading post was transformed into a fort by the military, and two pitched battles between the army and the native tribes took place in 1865. In the first conflict, Lieutenant Caspar Collins was killed while attempting to rescue another soldier. Lt. Collins' father already had a fort named after him in Colorado, so the military named the Wyoming fort "Casper" in his honor, inadvertently using a misspelling that had been transmitted by telegraph. The seeds of present-day Casper had been planted.

Black Gold, Texas Tea

Casper in 1888 was a true Wild West town. A railroad had been built through the town in an effort to ease travel to riches of gold in California and fertile land in Oregon. Isolation and lawlessness attracted a rough crowd of renegades and outlaws and the original township developed a main street lined with saloons on one side. By necessity, the first public building in Casper was a jail. Lynchings were not an uncommon occurrence.

Oil was struck in nearby Salt Creek Field in 1889, an event that has come to define Casper as the "oil capital of the Rockies." The city was flooded with an influx of claim jumpers looking to capitalize on the promised wealth. In 1895 the first oil refinery was constructed. Oil workers known as "roughnecks" followed, along with gamblers, prostitutes and corrupt businessmen. Cattlemen went to war against the sheepmen. The local law struggled to keep up with the shenanigans of the populace, passing laws to prevent women from walking on the saloon side of Main Street and to make illegal the discharge of firearms within city limits.

Local municipal leaders were set on Casper becoming the state capitol and a centerpiece of the West. As the economy continued to thrive, construction began on some of the tallest buildings in Wyoming during the early 20th century. But, a city that lives on oil can die on oil.

Nearly a Ghost Town

Few communities escaped the repercussions of the Great Depression and Casper was not an exception. In 1929 the city's population diminished by 50 percent. The struggle continued until World War II spurred renewed demand for oil and gas supplies. The city experienced a 10-year cycle of boom and bust beginning in the 1960s, riding the wave of oil and gas prices. Then in 1991 the Casper Refinery, operated by Amoco, closed down. The city began to consider redevelopment efforts that would diversify the economy in fields such as health care, social services, and tourism, in part through revitalization of its downtown areas.

Beginning in 1998, city residents and officials teamed up with British Petroleum (the new owners of Amoco) and the state Wyoming Department of Environmental Quality to clean up and redevelop the old refinery site. In 2000 the city council established the West Central Corridor (from David Street to Poplar Street and from West 1st to Collins Drive) as an urban renewal zone, offering special funding incentives for development. The result by 2005 was a new development that included the Robert Trent Jones-designed Three Crowns Golf Course, the Casper White-water Park, and three commercial parks.

In 2006 the city created the Urban Renewal Division within the city government structure to implement redevelopment plans for these and future renewal districts. The city began focusing specifically on the possibilities of mixed-use developments, renovation of historic buildings through tax incentive programs, and the recruitment of commercial and residential businesses to the downtown area. The program was successful at beautifying the Old Yellowstone District, improving roads, and attracting new local businesses. Construction of the taxpayer-funded Casper Area Innovation Center, a business incubator completed in 2012, offered additional prospects for economic development.

Historical Information: Fort Caspar Museum, 4001 Fort Caspar Road, Casper, WY 83604; telephone (307) 235-8462.

■ Population Profile

Metropolitan Statistical Area Population
2000: 66,533
2010: 75,450
2012 estimate: 78,621
Percent change, 2000–2010: 13.4%
U.S. rank in 2000: 363rd
U.S. rank in 2010: 469th

City Residents
1990: 46,742
2000: 49,644
2010: 55,316

2012 estimate: 56,391
Percent change, 2000–2010: 11.4%
U.S. rank in 1990: 559th (State rank: 2nd)
U.S. rank in 2000: Not available (State rank: 2nd)
U.S. rank in 2010: 632nd (State rank: 2nd)

Density: 2,003.6 people per square mile

Racial and ethnic characteristics

White: 51,618
Black or African American: 459
American Indian and Alaskan Native: 857
Asian: 634
Native Hawaiian and Other Pacific Islander: 0
Hispanic or Latino (may be of any race): 4,358
Other: 2,823

Percent of residents born in state: 45.3%

Age characteristics

Population under 5 years old: 3,925
Population 5 to 9 years old: 3,819
Population 10 to 14 years old: 3,389
Population 15 to 19 years old: 3,743
Population 20 to 24 years old: 4,218
Population 25 to 34 years old: 8,857
Population 35 to 44 years old: 6,564
Population 45 to 54 years old: 7,485
Population 55 to 59 years old: 3,755
Population 60 to 64 years old: 3,449
Population 65 to 74 years old: 3,594
Population 75 to 84 years old: 2,578
Population 85 years and over: 1,015
Median age: 35.3

Births (2010–11 Metropolitan Area)

Total number: 1,033

Deaths (2010–11 Metropolitan Area)

Total number: 667

Money income (2012)

Per capita income: $28,782
Median household income: $54,618
Total households: 23,191

Number of households with income of ...

less than $10,000: 1,029
$10,000 to $14,999: 882
$15,000 to $24,999: 2,412
$25,000 to $34,999: 2,672
$35,000 to $49,999: 3,348
$50,000 to $74,999: 5,167
$75,000 to $99,999: 3,014
$100,000 to $149,999: 3,300
$150,000 to $199,999: 609
$200,000 or more: 758

Percent of families below poverty level: 9.2%

FBI Crime Index Property: 1,968

FBI Crime Index Violent: 86

■ Municipal Government

The City of Casper has a council-manager form of government with a nine-member city council. The city is divided into three wards. Three council members are elected for each ward with staggered four-year terms. The council appoints a mayor and vice president from among the members. The mayor and vice president each serve for one year. The council hires a city manager.

Head Official: City Manager John C. Patterson (since 2011)

Total Number of City Employees: 700 (2012)

City Information: City of Casper, 200 N. David, Casper, WY 82601; telephone (307) 235-8400.

■ Economy

Major Industries and Commercial Activity

Casper has often been recognized for its comparatively low costs of doing business. The city's central location and proximity to a wealth of natural resources have attracted mining and petroleum exploration industries to the area, which remain the economic backbone of the community. Casper grew up as a cattle and sheep ranching town, and the industry remains today, although its cultural and touristic value now outweigh that of its direct economic impact. The tourism trade is further grounded by local Wild West history, rodeos, and proximity to natural wonders such as Grand Teton National Park and Yellowstone National Park.

Propped up by an aging population, the health-care industry is robust, as Casper serves as the site for a Department of Veterans Affairs Clinic in addition to the Wyoming Medical Center, the largest hospital in the region.

Items and goods produced: oil, natural gas, coal, gravel, agricultural products

Incentive Programs—New and Existing Companies

Local programs: The lack of a local income tax and a low municipal sales tax rate are the main business incentives employed by the City of Casper. General assistance to local business owners can be found through the Casper Area Chamber of Commerce, the Casper Area

Economic Development Alliance, and the Downtown Development Authority.

State programs: Wyoming's primary business incentive is a non-existent corporate income tax rate, coupled with relatively minimal sales tax rates. The state also does not tax intangibles or inventory and has kept property taxes low. The Wyoming Business Council provides several financing programs for businesses, including the Business Ready Community Grant and Loan Program and the Wyoming Partnership Challenge Loan Program. The Challenge Loan and Industrial Development Revenue Bonds programs are also administered by the Wyoming Business Council; the former allows the state to match loans with local economic development agencies, and the latter are tax-exempt bonds available to municipalities for the creation of in-state jobs. The Foreign Trade Zone at Natrona County International Airport provides further encouragement for importers to frequent Casper, as international goods can be warehoused at the airport without undergoing full U.S. Customs scrutiny. In 2013 the Wyoming Business Council and Powder River Energy Corporation began offering discounted renewable energy credits to companies seeking to power operations from renewable sources.

Job training programs: The Wyoming Department of Workforce Services manages a statewide network of workforce development resources, including services for businesses, job seekers and employment data researchers. Expanding and new businesses can tap into the Business Training Grant program through which employers may receive up to $2,000 per trainee per year for existing employees and $4,000 per employee per year for new hires. Large and small business owners can take advantage of Wyoming at Work, an online network for job-seekers and employers. State workforce centers additionally operate a Foreign Labor Certification program, which allows employers to utilize immigrant labor for positions that are difficult to fill with U.S. citizens. The state sponsors a Pre-Hire Economic Development Grant program to offer training for new hires in particular businesses and industries.

Casper College offers training programs to assist the local workforce. The McMurray Training Center is a program of the Wyoming Contractor's Association designed to offer job training for those interested in certain heavy-industry trades. Contractors and other businesses may seek help through the center for specialized employee training programs.

Development Projects

The Casper Area Economic Development Alliance completed a $10.5 million taxpayer-funded business incubator in 2012, the Casper Area Innovation Center. Operations of the incubator were transferred to the University of Wyoming in 2013, at which time five businesses operated in the nearly 40,000-square-foot center.

The Urban Renewal Division of the city government, established in 2006, was well into their 10-year plan to renew, beautify and clean-up the historic Old Yellowstone District in Casper. Other city projects underway in 2013 included efforts to make the city more pedestrian and cyclist friendly. Casper was in the process of developing a park and open space master plan as well.

The Wyoming High School Activities Association opened a new 7,000-square-foot building in Casper in 2013.

Economic Development Information: Casper Area Economic Development Alliance, 300 South Wolcott Suite 300, Casper, WY 82601; telephone (307) 577-7011; toll-free (800) 634-5012.

Commercial Shipping

The largest airport in Wyoming, the Natrona County International Airport, is located in Casper and encompasses Foreign Trade Zone No. 157, which allows imported goods to remain onsite without undergoing full U.S. Customs processing. The zone comprises 1,476 acres. A full-time U.S. Customs Agent is onsite.

Burlington Northern Santa Fe (BNSF) Railway passes through Casper, with routes to the West Coast, the Southwest, the Midwest, and other points west of the Mississippi River. Freight services are available for agricultural, mineral, industrial, and consumer goods. Freight forwarding and direct connections with dock spurs are available. The Casper Logistics Hub, a 700-acre rail park is home to several businesses and offers tailored lots and services 24 hours a day, seven days a week with access to the Foreign Trade Zone.

Casper's central location makes it a highway hub, with Interstate 25, U.S. highways 20/26 and 87, and state routes 220, 254 and 20 all meeting within its city limits. Casper has access to package delivery services such as UPS, FedEx and DHL.

Labor Force and Employment Outlook

While it is expected that Wyoming will remain identified with production of natural gas and coal, a slight decline in total mining jobs is anticipated. Wyoming is a right-to-work state, with union membership primarily in the industrial and manufacturing sectors. During 2013, the strongest job gains were in trade, transportation, and utilities, leisure and hospitality, education and health services, and government.

The following is a summary of data regarding the 2012 Casper labor force:

Size of civilian labor force: 31,143

Number of workers employed in . . .
  agriculture and mining: 2,355
  construction: 2,368

manufacturing: 1,549
wholesale trade: 1,007
retail trade: 3,789
transportation: 1,973
information systems: 526
finance: 1,202
professional administration: 2,492
education and social services: 6,743
arts and leisure: 2,763
other: 1,697
public administration: 1,012

Average hourly earnings of production workers: $19.87

Unemployment rate: 3.6% (2012)

Employers

Largest private employers (2012)	*Number of employees*
Wyoming Medical Center	1,018
Key Energy Services	540
Unit Drilling Company	500
Walmart	400
Wyoming Machinery Company	350
DHS Drilling	300
Keyhole Technologies	270
Johnson Restaurant Group	250
Luthercare Inc.	230
JW Williams Inc.	203

Cost of Living

The overall cost of living in the state of Wyoming is slightly below the national average. The cost of living in Casper is roughly equal to that of living elsewhere in the state, including Cheyenne and Laramie.

The following is a summary of data regarding several key cost of living factors in the area.

State income tax rate: None

State sales tax rate: 4.0%

Local income tax rate: None

Local sales tax rate: 1.0%

Property tax rate: 72.890 mills on 9.5% of assessed value (2013)

Economic Information: Casper Area Economic Development Alliance, 300 South Wolcott Suite 300, Casper, WY 82601; telephone (307) 577-7011; toll-free (800) 634-5012.

■ Education and Research

Elementary and Secondary Schools

The Natrona County School District serves more than 12,000 students not just in Casper but also the communities of Midwest, Edgerton, Mills, Evansville, Bar Nunn, Alcova, Mountain View, and Powder River. The school district emphasizes site-based decision-making in schools of choice, a system that allows parents to enroll students in any school without regard to location. Ideally, this encourages a cooperative approach between school administration, parents, and students in targeting an educational environment that best fits the needs of the individual.

The district operates a K–12 substance abuse program that has been recognized at the national level, along with specialized services for English language learners. Since 2001, the school district has offered an after-school program and community learning center at two elementary schools, with stated goals of retention, improved academic performance, life-long learning, and a safe drug-free environment. Outreach is also conducted for students who are homebound and those who are homeless. The district has adopted the Common Core State Standards.

The Natrona County School District created a planetarium in 1966, which over the years has brought the stars and planets to more than 500,000 students.

There are a few private schools in the city, primarily church-based.

The following is a summary of data regarding the Natrona County School District.

Total enrollment: 12,153

Number of facilities

total: 43
elementary schools: 23
junior high schools: 4
high schools: 4
other: 12

Student/teacher ratio: 9.99:1

Teacher salaries

average (statewide): $56,978

Funding per pupil: $15,206

Public Schools Information: Natrona County School District, 970 N. Glenn Rd., Casper, WY 82601; telephone (307) 253-5200.

Colleges and Universities

Perched in the foothills of Casper Mountain, Casper College—one of the largest community colleges in the region—offers students a choice of 140 academic transfer and technical and career programs. The college enrolls about 5,000 students in small, personal classes in five schools: business and industry, fine arts and humanities, health science, science, and social and behavioral sciences. The college also provides Adult Basic Education and General Educational Development (GED) assistance in the Werner Technical Center.

The University of Wyoming (UW) in nearby Laramie maintains an outreach school as the UW Casper College Center. Students typically complete their first two years of study as Casper College students and then enroll as students of the University of Wyoming. Coursework is completed onsite, via teleconferencing, or through web-based instruction, with internships and educational travel experiences offered in various degree programs. About 17 baccalaureate degrees, 12 master's programs, and a variety of certification programs are available through the UW Casper College Center.

The McMurray Training Center, a program of the Wyoming Contractor's Association, offers training programs for heavy industry trades. At the Natrona County International Airport, the Aircraft Rescue Firefighting training program offers classroom and hands-on experience with firefighting techniques unique to aeronautical equipment. Small classes ensure individual attention as students learn to deal with hazardous materials, ventilation issues, fire behavior, and search and rescue procedures.

Libraries and Research Centers

The Natrona County Public Library's Main Library is located in the heart of Casper with branch libraries maintained in the communities of Edgerton and Mills and a bookmobile. The library has an average annual circulation of some 700,000 items and serves more than 1,000 patrons daily. Children's programs include a Reader's Advisory program that recommends books tailored to particular ages and interests; outreach programs to schools and community groups; educational games and reference programs; story time; a summer reading program; and Dial-a-Story, with a new story available by phone every week. The library also maintains a special multicultural literature collection for children. As part of a strategic initiative to improve services for the senior population, the library offers a Books by Mail program.

The Goodstein Foundation Library at Casper College contains a collection of 88,000 volumes. The library subscribes to more than 140 print journals, with access to more than 46,000 full-text periodicals available online in addition to 440 library databases. A statewide interlibrary loan service is available, and library cards are available to both students and members of the community around the college. The library is also home to a Western history collection, with materials focused on Casper and Natrona County.

Public Library Information: Natrona County Public Library (Main Library), 307 East Second Street, Casper, WY 82601; telephone (307) 577-7323.

■ Health Care

The Wyoming Medical Center in Casper serves the Natrona County area and also draws patients from rural communities of greater distances. The state's largest medical facility is a full-service hospital licensed for 191 beds. Staffed by 1,200 medical professionals, including 160 licensed physicians, the medical center offers a range of specialty services, from heart and vascular care to oncology, weigh management, and maternity care. The center was the first in the state to feature a 64-slice CT scanner and Stealth Station System, supporting treatment for major head and spine injuries. The emergency room treats some 38,000 patients annually.

The main campus of the Wyoming Behavioral Institute is located in Casper, with substance abuse and mental health services for seniors, adults, adolescents, and children. The 90-bed facility offers initial assessment, intensive inpatient treatment, detoxification programs, and outpatient therapy. The Wyoming Orthopedic Institute in Casper sponsors the Wyoming Orthopedic and Sports Therapy Center and the Wyoming Surgical Center. These facilities offer a wide range of programs in orthopedic injury diagnosis and care, rehabilitation, and sports medicine. There are five skilled nursing care facilities in the city.

The Department of Veterans Affairs Casper Outpatient Clinic serves as an outreach center connecting military veterans to health-care and counseling services, including making arrangements for bus travel to Veterans Affairs hospitals in Cheyenne or Sheridan.

■ Recreation

Sightseeing

A sightseeing tour of Casper would start where the town started—at the convergence of the multiple travel routes to the West. The National Historic Trails Interpretive Center accurately portrays the experiences of emigrants who traversed the Oregon, California, Mormon, Bridger, Bozeman, and Pony Express Trails. The museum has incorporated the history of Wyoming's native peoples in displays that include a simulated crossing of the North Platte River in a replica Conestoga wagon. An award-winning audiovisual feature recreates the days of early Casper in a way that brings pioneer existence alive for modern visitors.

The natural segue is to next visit the Fort Caspar Museum and Historical Site, located along the historical trail system. The buildings of the original fort have been reconstructed, with structures including the 1859

Guinard Bridge and the 1847 Mormon ferry utilized in crossings of the North Platte. Exhibits range from prehistoric natural history items to recent regional development in central Wyoming.

While in the vicinity, visitors can enjoy a leisurely ramble along the Platte River Parkway, an 11-mile paved path that connects residential neighborhoods to natural areas. The Platte River Commons in downtown Casper continues along the riverbank; within the downtown area, the Art for the Streets program has sprinkled the historic area with 31 sculptures. "Painted Past" Living History Tours through the downtown area highlight myths, legends, and true stories of Casper's checkered past.

The Mormon Handcart Visitors' Center commemorates the hardships and survival of members of the Church of Jesus Christ of Latter-day Saints traveling as part of the Martin and Willie Handcart Companies in 1856. As the group traveled westward, it encountered a raging blizzard that forced the company to hole up in a local cove for four days. During the ensuing wait for rescuers, many members of the group died from exposure. Visitors to the site today can pull a handcart to the cove or can participate in guided camping treks.

Arts and Culture

The Nicolaysen Art Museum and Discovery Center contains one large and six small galleries exhibiting art from or about the Rocky Mountain Region. Exhibitors at "the Nic" often include contemporary living artists from the area. The Discovery Center allows visitors to create their own art in a self-guided studio containing interactive exhibits, and the Wyoming Science Zone generates interest in sciences through fun, interactive displays. Workshops and educational programs are offered throughout the year as well, with a special emphasis on quilting.

The West Wind Gallery is operated by the Casper Artists' Guild, the members of which show and sell their works under the gallery's roof. The gallery occasionally hosts artists from out of state and also offers classes.

The Tate Geological Museum is located on the grounds of Casper College and is home to a collection of more than 3,000 fossil and mineral specimens. The museum offers a Saturday Club experience for local youth in which they study local geology and animal fossils. Adults can take part in paleontology and geology fieldwork expeditions coordinated through the museum, with visits to Wind River Reservation, and the Morrison and Lance Formation sites. Casper College also houses the Werner Wildlife Museum, featuring more than 285 birds and 100 other various species.

The formative history of Casper is further represented at the Salt Creek Museum in the city of Midwest, where books, memorabilia and reminiscences reflect on more than 100 years of oil field action in the area. The

Wyoming Veteran's Memorial Museum at the airport is located in the building where bombing crews trained during World War II.

The Wyoming Symphony Orchestra performs six annual concerts at the John F. Welsh Auditorium. Young musicians from 4th graders to 21-year-olds participate in The Troopers Drum and Bugle Corps, regardless of musical experience. The Troopers travel around the United States throughout the summer, performing and competing in drum and bugle corps contests. Further musical offerings are provided through the Casper Chamber Music Society, Casper Children's Chorale, Casper Civic Chorale, Casper Fiddle Club, Casper Municipal Band, Choral Arts Ensemble, Oil City Slickers, and ARTCORE.

Productions ranging from the classical to the contemporary are performed by the players of Stage III, an all-volunteer community theater located in historic downtown Casper. The theater department at Casper College presents similarly varied fare to audiences in the Gertrude Krampert Theatre. A musical and three plays are presented each academic year, while the summer season offerings are often musicals or comedies.

Festivals and Holidays

The Kinzer Jazz Festival occurs each February at Casper College. Casper sees a local version of March Madness with the 1A–2A state basketball tournament held at the Casper Events Center early in the month. Casper College hosts the College National Finals Rodeo at the Casper Events Center in June. The festivities continue that month with the Casper Antique Show early in the June and the Governor's Cup Sailboat Regatta at Alcova Lake a few weeks later. Casper residents fire up for the Wyoming State Games in June, an Olympic-style event composed of a mix of indoor and outdoor competitive sports.

The Fourth of July blasts off with the Central Wyoming Fair and a Professional Rodeo Cowboys Association event, both of which continue for a full week. The Wyoming State Mineral and Gem Society sponsors a gem and mineral show in July as well. The Community Recreation Foundation holds its annual Craft Fair in November. Also that month, the National Women's Junior College Volleyball Championship takes place in Casper. Rodeo returns in late December for a New Year's Eve Rodeo Match.

Sports for the Spectator

Casper grew up around the livestock industry, so it's no surprise that rodeo is the major spectator sport. Casper hosts two large rodeo events: the College National Finals Rodeo and the Central Wyoming Fair and Rodeo. The College National Finals Rodeo takes place in mid-June each year and features the top rodeo event qualifiers from colleges and universities from across the United States.

Events include barrel racing, calf roping, and bull riding. The Central Wyoming Fair and Rodeo is held in July, with Pro Rodeo Cowboys Association competitions in roping, bareback riding, saddle bronco and bull riding events among others.

Until 2011, baseball fans could see tomorrow's stars playing for the Casper Ghosts, a minor league affiliate of the Colorado Rockies; the team moved to Grand Junction, Colorado, that year. The Wyoming Cavalry of the National Indoor Football League play from February to June at the Casper Events Center. The Casper College Thunderbirds play volleyball and basketball at the Erickson Thunderbird Gymnasium.

Sports for the Participant

Aficionados of the Wild West will relish the opportunity to participate in historic wagon train trips arranged through local companies. A similar desire to experience pioneer Casper could spur a visit to a working cattle and guest ranch located about 65 miles southwest of the city. For folks who prefer to provide their own locomotion, the Casper Marathon takes place in early June, with marathon, half-marathon, and marathon relay options.

A slightly less strenuous workout can be found at the Casper Municipal Golf Course, an 18-hole course with a practice range, putting and chipping greens, and a 19th Hole Restaurant and Lounge. The course is open from April 1st to November 1st each year. The City of Casper also operates close to 50 parks totaling over 1,500 acres of developed and undeveloped land, including athletic fields and playgrounds. The city also maintains the Casper Recreation Center and the Casper Ice Arena with racquetball and volleyball courts, indoor playground, public skating, and health and fitness classes.

The North Platte River offers ample outdoor recreation opportunities, such as kayaking through the Platte River Parkway Whitewater Park. This man-made whitewater facility runs for half a mile over structures that create turbulent water for kayak maneuvers. Canoes and rafts can also navigate through the Whitewater Park or pursue a more relaxed pace on other stretches of the North Platte. Fly fishing along the river can yield large brown and rainbow trout. Birding excursions at the Audubon Center, Edness Kimball Wilkins State Park, and Jackson Canyon may produce sightings of bald and golden eagles, hummingbirds, bluebirds, hawks, sandpipers, wild turkeys, and grosbeaks.

Casper Mountain is the scene of outdoor adventure year-round, with alpine skiing, Nordic skiing and snowshoeing in the winter and hiking during the spring, summer and fall seasons. Casper is within an easy day's drive of Yellowstone National Park, Grand Teton National Park, and Devil's Tower Monument, all of which offer a range of trails in addition to campsites. Serious rock climbers can head east a few hours to Vedauwoo in southeast Wyoming; this startling and

impressive collection of rock formations has something for everyone, from the scrambler to the multi-pitch climber.

Shopping and Dining

Casper's historic downtown area contains a mix of antique shops and other retailers, including the largest western merchandise store in Wyoming. The Eastridge Mall is the site of over 60 stores including a number of national franchise stores combined with shops owned locally. Fast-food outlets, grocery stores, and home supply stores are located nearby. Based near the foothills of Casper Mountain, the Sunrise Shopping Center is anchored by a restaurant and a bowling alley at one end and a gym at the other. The Hilltop Shopping Center focuses on local businesses, while the Beverly Plaza Shopping Center is home to national franchises.

Traditional American cuisine rules in Casper, with at least 36 restaurants offering down-home and family-style cooking. Ethnic culinary options are dominated by Mexican and Asian fare. As might be expected in cattle country, steakhouses are popular as well. A handful of fine dining, Italian, seafood, and barbecue restaurants round out the dining options in Casper. Basic and gourmet coffees are available at several city coffeehouses.

Visitor Information: Casper Area Convention & Visitors Bureau, 139 West 2nd St., Suite 1B, Casper, WY 82601; telephone (307) 234-5362; toll-free (800) 852-1889.

■ Convention Facilities

The Casper Events Center was constructed high on a hill overlooking the city, and its massive maroon roof is visible from practically all points in Casper. The arena is shaped like a horseshoe, with a 28,200-square-foot main floor that can hold up to 154 exhibition booths. Concourse exhibit space encompasses 7,900 square feet, while meeting rooms add another 6,204 square feet of usable space. Sound and lighting systems can be configured for many diverse events from rodeos and ice shows to trade shows and banquets. The Parkway Plaza Hotel and Convention Centre has three large exhibit rooms and a grand ballroom that can be divided into three smaller sections totaling about 25,000 square feet of space.

The Central Wyoming Fairgrounds can accommodate trade shows, conferences, receptions, rodeos, and RV parking. A multi-purpose sports facility covers 76,875 square feet, while the Grandstand and Outdoor Arena have seating capacity for 5,200.

Several local hotels offer meeting, convention, and conference space, including the Holiday Inn on the River and the Best Western Ramkota Hotel Casper. The

Natrona County International Airport also offers meeting and reception rooms as well, offering views of the airfield.

Convention Information: Casper Area Convention & Visitors Bureau, 139 West 2nd St., Suite 1B, Casper, WY 82601; telephone (307) 234-5362; toll-free (800) 852-1889.

■ Transportation

Approaching the City

Natrona County International Airport (NCIA), about seven miles to the northwest of Casper, is Wyoming's largest airport and is located at the geographic center of the state. Three regional carriers provide service through NCIA, Delta, United, and Allegiant Airlines, and operate direct flights to Denver, Salt Lake City, and Las Vegas. There are about seven daily departures, with a majority of the flights going to Denver.

Casper's central location makes it a highway hub, with Interstate 25, U.S. highways 20/26 and 87, and state routes 220, 254, and 20 all meeting within its city limits. Casper is served by Greyhound, which maintains a station at the Casper Bus Depot.

Traveling in the City

While Casper is fitted to the meandering contours of the North Platte River, the streets are laid out on a straightforward north–south, east–west grid pattern. Numbered streets run east and west, while name streets run north and south for the most part, making navigation simpler.

The Casper Area Transportation Coalition, a nonprofit corporation, operates The Bus with seven buses on six routes that make over 186 stops, serving Casper, Mills and Evansville. The Bus offers reduced fares and dial-a-ride services to elderly and disabled patrons. Children five years or younger ride free. Service is available Monday through Saturday.

The 11-mile Platte River Parkway provides a safe and fast route for bike commuters to ride into downtown Casper.

■ Communications

Newspapers and Magazines

Casper's daily paper is the *Casper Star-Tribune,* delivered mornings and providing comprehensive coverage of international, national, regional, and local news stories. A special insert on Saturdays conveys community events and special features. Billed as "Casper's community newspaper," the *Casper Journal* is a weekly focused on local news, sports, and community events. The *Wyoming Business Report* is a monthly paper that provides coverage of banking, technology, energy, investing, and agribusiness issues.

Television and Radio

Eleven television stations broadcast from Casper; the community has relays for transmissions of public television and other network stations. Casper's 3 AM and 17 FM radio stations offer a variety of programming, including classic rock, country, top 40, talk radio, news, public radio, and Christian music.

Media Information: *Casper Star-Tribune,* 170 Star Lane, Casper, WY 82601; telephone (866) 981-6397.

Casper Online

Casper Area Chamber of Commerce. Available www.casperwyoming.org

Casper Star-Tribune. Available trib.com

Casper Wyoming Convention & Visitors Bureau. Available visitcasper.com

City of Casper. Available www.casperwy.gov

Natrona County School District. Available www. natronaschools.org

BIBLIOGRAPHY

Casper Chronicles (Casper, WY: Casper Zonta Club, 1964)

Lewis, Norma, and Jay de Vries, *Wyoming* (Charleston, SC: Arcadia Publishing, 2010)

Cheyenne

■ The City in Brief

Founded: 1867 (incorporated, 1867)

Head Official: Mayor Richard L. Kaysen (since 2009; term expires 2017)

City Population
   1990: 50,008
   2000: 53,011
   2010: 59,466
   2012 estimate: 60,497
   Percent change, 2000–2010: 12.2%
   U.S. rank in 1990: 504th (State rank: 1st)
   U.S. rank in 2000: 520th (State rank: 1st)
   U.S. rank in 2010: 573rd (State rank: 1st)

Metropolitan Statistical Area Population
   2000: 81,607
   2010: 91,738
   2012 estimate: 94,483
   Percent change, 2000–2010: 12.4%
   U.S. rank in 2000: 356th
   U.S. rank in 2010: 413th

Area: 21.19 square miles

Elevation: 6,062 feet above sea level

Average Annual Temperatures: January, 25.9° F; July, 67.7° F; annual average, 44.9° F

Average Annual Precipitation: 15.45 inches of rain; 55.6 inches of snow

Major Economic Sectors: public administration, wholesale and retail trade, services, technology

Unemployment Rate: 3.6% (2012)

Per Capita Income: $27,431

2012 FBI Crime Index Property: 2,081

Major Colleges and Universities: Laramie County Community College, University of Wyoming–Laramie

Daily Newspaper: *Wyoming Tribune-Eagle*

■ Introduction

Cheyenne, the capital of Wyoming, began as a railroad town and, during the height of the colorful cattle days, became the wealthiest city in the world. Cheyenne has retained its Western frontier traditions while keeping pace with the twenty-first century. The seat of Laramie County, Cheyenne continues to be a railroad and transportation center. While F.E. Warren Air Force Base and various government agencies remain the city's primary employers in the past decade, the growth of data centers has birthed a nascent high-technology industry. Cheyenne continues to be known for its quality of life, politeness of residents, and for high clean air ratings.

■ Geography and Climate

Surrounded by rolling prairie, Cheyenne is located between the North and South Platte rivers. The Laramie Mountains 30 miles west of the city form a ridge that is part of the Rocky Mountain range and that significantly influences local temperature and weather. Winds passing over the ridge from the northwest through the west to southwest produce a Chinook effect, particularly during the winter. (Chinooks are warm, moist winds from the sea.) Because of the terrain and wind patterns, Cheyenne experiences wide daily temperature fluctuations of 30 degrees in the summer and about 23 degrees in the winter. Snow falls during late winter and early spring, with yearly snowfall averaging 55.6 inches. Cheyenne is the seat of Laramie County.

The Wyoming State Capitol building in Cheyenne. *Jonathan Lenz/Shutterstock.com*

Area: 21.19 square miles

Elevation: 6,062 feet above sea level

Average Temperatures: January, 25.9° F; July, 67.7° F; annual average, 44.9° F

Average Annual Precipitation: 15.45 inches of rain; 55.6 inches of snow

■ History

Rough-and-Tumble Beginnings of Railroad Terminus

The region where present-day Cheyenne stands was originally occupied by a Native American Plains tribe in the Algonquian linguistic family. The townsite was initially a campsite for the U.S. Army's Major General

Grenville M. Dodge and his troops, who were charged in 1865 with finding a railroad route over the Laramie Mountains. In 1867, when Dodge became chief engineer for the Union Pacific Railroad, he established a terminal town there; he named it Cheyenne for the local tribe. Dodge received some criticism in the local press for his mispronunciation of the word, which was actually "shai-en-na;" but his two-syllable version was accepted through usage.

Fort D. A. Russell was built in 1867 to protect railroad construction crews. Soon real estate speculators, merchants, gamblers, and tradesmen converged on Cheyenne in hopes of profiting from the construction project. Violent disputes arose over ownership of the land, since the railroad had already claimed it and citizens questioned the company's right to do so. Eventually troops from Fort Russell were called in; land jumpers were run out of town and could not return until they promised to acknowledge the railroad's claim.

A town charter was accepted by the Dakota Territorial Legislature in 1867 and Cheyenne was thereupon incorporated. By the end of that year the population had risen to 4,000 people, and lots were selling for $2,500. Makeshift buildings gave the town a raffish appearance, but even before railroad construction began, Cheyenne enjoyed the elements of a stable community; churches had been built and the first school, with 114 pupils, was opened in 1867. Within a year Cheyenne was thriving. More than 300 businesses were in operation, and the diverse citizenry included engineers, lawyers, artists, Native Americans, trappers, hunters, laborers, gamblers, and gunslingers. The town, however, was soon overrun by lawlessness.

The early Cheyenne closely resembled the Wild West towns depicted in novels and films. Dodge named it the gambling center of the world and some dubbed it "Hell on Wheels." Mayhem and violence were a way of life with the saloon and the cemetery being the most important places in town. In an attempt to impose order, the churches backed an ordinance that closed saloons for four hours on Sundays; another ruling required visitors to check their guns. But laws were virtually unenforceable, so the vigilante "committee" became a substitute for the courts. Although the city government had been given powers by the Dakota Legislature upon incorporation, civic leaders found the vigilante approach to be more effective. When the jail became full, for instance, prisoners were driven from town with a whip or a six-shooter; frequently the committee executed perpetrators of severe crimes.

Riches Flow from Cattle, Sheep, Gold

A degree of peacefulness returned when railroad construction moved on toward Sherman Pass and transients followed. But then the first Sioux War broke out north of the Platte River, and Fort Russell became the supply depot for the Rocky Mountain region. In 1868 Cheyenne was made the seat of Laramie County; the following year it was named the capital of the new Wyoming territory. By the 1870s Cheyenne was the center of a prosperous ranching area where cattle were bred for a European beef market. Visiting Englishmen, who spent summers in Cheyenne and winters in Europe, joined wealthy cattle owners to found the Cheyenne Club, where they dined in luxury and struck deals that affected the cattle industry throughout the West. Furnished in the English style and serving the finest liquors in the world, the club employed a foreign chef whose cuisine was known nationwide.

With the opening of the Black Hills gold fields in 1875, the town profited from a new industry as Cheyenne merchants supplied miners and prospectors with provisions and equipment. The Cheyenne and Black Hills Stage Company was formed to transport passengers and cargo between the railroad and the mines. When electric lights were installed in 1882, Cheyenne was the wealthiest city per capita in the world. Cheyenne was named the capital of the new state of Wyoming in 1890 and the Capitol building was erected in the city. By 1890 the population had reached 10,000 people.

Before the turn of the century many ranchers had begun raising sheep, which adapted well to the climate and the native grasses; sheep raising continues to be an important industry in the area. During the twentieth century Cheyenne became an industrial and manufacturing center. The Francis E. Warren U.S. Air Force Base was established at Fort Russell in 1947. While undergoing several realignment plans through the early 2000s, the base continued to remain active and was still one of the largest employers in the city. State government also maintained a large number of employees.

In the late 1990s and early 2000s city officials began making plans to expand and encourage new business, primarily through the revitalization of the downtown areas with mixed-use developments. Through the efforts of Cheyenne LEADS, a local development organization, they city welcomed two new business parks and helped recruit new technology-based companies to the area, in efforts to further diversify the economy. In 1994 EchoStar Communications selected the Cheyenne Business Parkway as the site for its multimillion dollar satellite uplink center. In 2006 Nanomaterials Discovery Corporation agreed to build a specialized laboratory at Cheyenne Business Parkway. In 2012 the National Center for Atmospheric Research completed a new supercomputer in Cheyenne to study climate and weather, and in 2013 Microsoft was constructing a $112 million data center.

Historical Information: Wyoming State Archives, 2301 Central Avenue, Cheyenne, WY 82002; telephone (307) 777-7826; fax (307) 777-7044.

■ Population Profile

Metropolitan Statistical Area Population
2000: 81,607
2010: 91,738
2012 estimate: 94,483
Percent change, 2000–2010: 12.4%
U.S. rank in 2000: 356th
U.S. rank in 2010: 413th

City Residents
1990: 50,008
2000: 53,011
2010: 59,466
2012 estimate: 60,497
Percent change, 2000–2010: 12.2%
U.S. rank in 1990: 504th (State rank: 1st)
U.S. rank in 2000: 520th (State rank: 1st)
U.S. rank in 2010: 573rd (State rank: 1st)

Density: 1,817.7 people per square mile

Racial and ethnic characteristics

> White: 51,720
> Black or African American: 1,784
> American Indian and Alaskan Native: 703
> Asian: 810
> Native Hawaiian and Other Pacific Islander: 9
> Hispanic or Latino (may be of any race): 8,454
> Other: 5,471

Percent of residents born in state: 40.5%

Age characteristics

> Population under 5 years old: 4,249
> Population 5 to 9 years old: 4,140
> Population 10 to 14 years old: 4,035
> Population 15 to 19 years old: 3,693
> Population 20 to 24 years old: 4,476
> Population 25 to 34 years old: 9,411
> Population 35 to 44 years old: 7,118
> Population 45 to 54 years old: 7,457
> Population 55 to 59 years old: 4,070
> Population 60 to 64 years old: 3,452
> Population 65 to 74 years old: 4,313
> Population 75 to 84 years old: 2,969
> Population 85 years and over: 1,114
> Median age: 35.7

Births (2010–11 Metropolitan Area)

> Total number: 1,264

Deaths (2010–11 Metropolitan Area)

> Total number: 720

Money income (2012)

> Per capita income: $27,431
> Median household income: $50,420
> Total households: 24,849

Number of households with income of . . .

> less than $10,000: 1,216
> $10,000 to $14,999: 1,900
> $15,000 to $24,999: 2,405
> $25,000 to $34,999: 2,838
> $35,000 to $49,999: 3,988
> $50,000 to $74,999: 4,446
> $75,000 to $99,999: 3,496
> $100,000 to $149,999: 3,015
> $150,000 to $199,999: 1,060
> $200,000 or more: 485

Percent of families below poverty level: 12.1%

FBI Crime Index Property: 2,081

FBI Crime Index Violent: 140

■ Municipal Government

Cheyenne operates under a mayor-council form of government; the nine council members and the mayor serve four-year terms. Three council members are elected to represent each of the three city wards and serve staggered terms. A council president and vice-president elected from among the council members each serve one-year terms. The mayor and council members serve as Cheyenne's governing body, which is responsible for regulating city growth and development, enacting ordinances, appropriating city funds, and establishing city rules and regulations.

Head Official: Mayor Richard L. Kaysen (since 2009; term expires 2017)

Total Number of City Employees: 129 (2013)

City Information: City of Cheyenne, 2101 O'Neil Avenue, Cheyenne, WY 82001; telephone (307) 637-6200.

■ Economy

Major Industries and Commercial Activity

F. E. Warren Air Force Base, site of a major installation of the Strategic Air Command, is the city's largest employer; federal, state, and county government offices are also located in Cheyenne.

Major private sector employers included Cheyenne Regional Medical Center, Lowe's Companies Inc., Union Pacific Railroad, Sierra Trading Post, Walmart, Frontier Refining Inc., EchoStar Broadcasting Corporation, HollyFrontier Oil, Great Lakes Aviation, Magic City Enterprises, Allstate Insurance, Blue Cross/Blue Shield, and Dyno Nobel/Coastel Chemical.

Several developments during the early 2010s grew the area's high-technology industry. The National Center for Atmospheric Research opened a $70 million supercomputing facility, and several companies, including giant Microsoft, opened or expanded data centers in the area.

Items and goods produced: oil refining, fertilizer, food service equipment, rail switching equipment

Incentive Programs—New and Existing Companies

Local programs: At the local level, Cheyenne LEADS, a private, not-for-profit economic development organization, assists non-retail businesses through such services as site location, employee training, and demographic and financial assistance. Since the formation of LEADS in 1985, the organization has helped over 70 companies relocate to or expand in Cheyenne, creating over 4,000 jobs in that time period. The Cheyenne Workforce Center, a regional office of the Wyoming Business

Council, offers expansion assistance for current businesses, and relocation assistance for businesses looking to expand into the area. Most local business incentive packages are customized for the particular needs of the business.

State programs: Wyoming's primary business incentive is a non-existent corporate income tax rate, coupled with relatively minimal sales tax rates. The state also does not tax intangibles or inventory and has kept property taxes low. The Wyoming Business Council provides several financing programs for businesses, including the Business Ready Community Grant and Loan Program and the Wyoming Partnership Challenge Loan Program. The Challenge Loan and Industrial Development Revenue Bonds programs are also administered by the Wyoming Business Council; the former allows the state to match loans with local economic development agencies, and the latter are tax-exempt bonds available to municipalities for the creation of in-state jobs. The Foreign Trade Zone at Natrona County International Airport provides further encouragement for importers to frequent Casper, as international goods can be warehoused at the airport without undergoing full U.S. Customs scrutiny. In 2013 the Wyoming Business Council and Powder River Energy Corporation began offering discounted renewable energy credits to companies seeking to power operations from renewable sources.

Job training programs: The Wyoming Department of Workforce Services manages a statewide network of workforce development resources, including services for businesses, job seekers and employment data researchers. Expanding and new businesses can tap into the Business Training Grant program through which employers may receive up to $2,000 per trainee per year for existing employees and $4,000 per employee per year for new hires. Large and small business owners can take advantage of Wyoming at Work, an online network for job-seekers and employers. State workforce centers additionally operate a Foreign Labor Certification program, which allows employers to utilize immigrant labor for positions that are difficult to fill with U.S. citizens. The state sponsors a Pre-Hire Economic Development Grant program to offer training for new hires in particular businesses and industries.

Laramie County School District provides education programs at the secondary level in areas such as agricultural science, industrial technology, business and marketing education, health occupations, and core employability skills. Laramie County Community College offers career skills training in the Internet and computing through the Adult Career and Education System, as well as workforce and professional development in many fields.

Our Families Our Future in Cheyenne provides assistance to populations living below poverty through training programs and job search help. Our Families Our Future works with Wyoming agencies, community colleges, and employers; the organization began the CLIMB program in 2004 to train eligible single mothers in the field of medical transcription.

Development Projects

In 2001, city leaders, the chamber of commerce, and other individuals and organizations got together to begin a development planning process known as Vision 2020 plan. That process led to the adoption of a community-driven Cheyenne Area Master Plan commonly referred to as PlanCheyenne, adopted in 2006. PlanCheyenne serves as a guiding principle for development in three key areas: community, transportation, and parks and recreation.

In 2007 the National Center for Atmospheric Research announced plans to build a new supercomputing facility at North Range. Construction started in 2010 and completed in 2012. The $70 million building and its $30 million computer was to focus on research topics covering the underground effects of earthquakes, the flow of rain from the sky toward the ground, and movement of winds around natural and man-made structures.

In 2013 Microsoft was building a $112 million data center in Cheyenne, capable of being powered by a fuel cell running on biogas generated from landfills and water treatment plants. Green House Data announced a $35 million expansion of its data center in Cheyenne in 2013.

Cheyenne Regional Medical Center opened a $30 million cancer center in 2013. It opened a new 39,000-square-foot emergency department that same year.

Economic Development Information: Cheyenne LEADS, 1 Depot Square, 121 W. 15th Street, Suite 304, Cheyenne, WY 82001; telephone (307) 638-6000; toll-free (800) 255-0742.

Commercial Shipping

With access to two railroads, two interstate freeways, and to commercial air service, the city is a vital transportation center for the state of Wyoming. Great Lakes Airlines routes light cargo through Cheyenne Regional Airport. Union Pacific and Burlington Northern Santa Fe provide daily freight transportation and a variety of motor freight carriers move goods through facilities in Cheyenne and onto interstates 80 and 25.

Labor Force and Employment Outlook

Cheyenne's labor force is described as available, educated, and productive. Cheyenne's budding technology sector has increased demand for high-technology workers, creating new job opportunities. Wyoming is a right-to-work state with low unionization rates. The presence of F.E. Warren Air Force Base creates a ready labor supply as local residents exit the military, or when new military residents bring their nonmilitary spouses into the workforce.

The following is a summary of data regarding the 2012 Cheyenne labor force:

Size of civilian labor force: 31,304

Number of workers employed in...

  agriculture and mining: 641
  construction: 2,049
  manufacturing: 1,244
  wholesale trade: 520
  retail trade: 3,598
  transportation: 1,930
  information systems: 903
  finance: 1,434
  professional administration: 2,098
  education and social services: 5,906
  arts and leisure: 3,241
  other: 1,337
  public administration: 4,463

Average hourly earnings of production workers: $16.81

Unemployment rate: 3.6% (2012)

Employers

Largest employers (2013)	Number of employees
F.E. Warren AFB	3,660
State of Wyoming	3,409
Laramie County School District No. 1	2,178
Federal Government	1,814
Cheyenne Regional Medical Center	1,763
Wyoming National Guard	1,230
Laramie County Community College	800
Sierra Trading Post	684
Veterans Affairs Medical Center	650
Union Pacific Railroad	600

Cost of Living

The following is a summary of data regarding several key cost of living factors in the area.

State income tax rate: None

State sales tax rate: 4.0%

Local income tax rate: None

Local sales tax rate: 2.0%

Property tax rate: 71.00 mills on 9.5% of assessed value (2013)

Economic Information: Greater Cheyenne Chamber of Commerce, 121 West 15th Street, Suite 204, Cheyenne, WY 82001; telephone (307) 638-3388; fax (307) 778-1407.

■ Education and Research

Elementary and Secondary Schools

Public elementary and secondary schools in Cheyenne are part of Laramie County School District No. 1 (LCSD1). The district, the largest in the state with over 13,000 students, is administered by a seven-member Board of Trustees and a superintendent. The Cheyenne Schools Foundation works "to engage community interest and support for enhanced academic, personal, and vocational opportunities for LCSD1 students beyond the capacity of the local school district budget." The Foundation also provides grants to benefit district and school-wide projects as well as teachers for classroom projects that address student needs.

Among the special programs offered by the school district is a magnet school for high-potential elementary students. Four-year graduation rates in the district average more than 72 percent, with about three-quarters of graduates going on to attend either two- or four-year colleges.

There are a few private schools located in Cheyenne, primarily affiliated with Christian churches.

The following is a summary of data regarding the Laramie County School District.

Total enrollment: 13,171

Number of facilities

  total: 33
  elementary schools: 26
  junior high schools: 3
  high schools: 4
  other: 0

Student/teacher ratio: 10.44:1

Teacher salaries

  average (statewide): $56,978

Funding per pupil: $14,767

Public Schools Information: Laramie County School District No. 1, 2810 House Avenue, Cheyenne, WY 82001; telephone (307) 771-2100.

Colleges and Universities

Laramie County Community College (LCCC), which provides a two-year curriculum, is based in Cheyenne with an additional campus in Laramie and outreach centers at Pine Bluffs and F.E. Warren Air Force Base. The college offers associate's degrees in 76 academic programs and 25 certificate programs. Enrollment is about 4,200 full-time students per year. The Adult Career Education Center at LCCC offers basic adult education and English as a second language programs.

The University of Wyoming is the state's only public provider of baccalaureate and graduate education, research, and outreach services. The main campus at Laramie is less than 45 miles west of Cheyenne. Popular majors there are elementary and secondary education and social work. The University of Wyoming Family Medicine Residency Program is based in Cheyenne at the Cheyenne Regional Medical Center.

The Cheyenne Campus of Embry-Riddle Aeronautical University is located at the F.E. Warren Air Force Base. Students there may achieve a bachelor's degree in professional aeronautics or technical management or a master's degree in aeronautical science and management. F.E. Warren Air Force Base is also the site for the Cheyenne Campus of Park University.

Libraries and Research Centers

The Laramie County Library System, established in 1886, is the oldest continually operating county library system in the country. In addition to its main library in Cheyenne, the Laramie County Library System operates two branches and a bookmobile serving the rural eastern portion of the county. Its holdings include more than 305,000 books, periodicals, microfiche, maps, CDs, videos, DVDs, and music CDs. The library also offers Internet connectivity, books-on-tape, video games, and art reproductions. Special collections are the Carpenter Collection of Western Americana and material on the elk of North America. The library's genealogy collection includes extensive materials that are part of a joint collection with the Family History Library of the Church of Jesus Christ of Latter Day Saints. In 2008, the Laramie County Public Library was named Library of the Year by the *Library Journal*.

The Wyoming State Library is also located in Cheyenne. It contains more than 130,000 volumes and is a federal, state, and regional document depository. It is also the site of the Wyoming Patent and Trademark Depository Library. The Wyoming Center for the Book, established in 1995, operates as a program within the Wyoming State Library. A state affiliate of the Library of Congress Center for the Book, it "promotes the values of a literate and learned society through a variety of programs including a database of Wyoming writers and literary guide."

The Ludden Library at Laramie County Community College has over 60,000 items and a continually growing collection of e-books and research databases.

The University of Wyoming-Laramie conducts research activities in dozens of disciplines, such as education; biological, physical, and social sciences;

business and economics; mathematics; and politics and government in Wyoming. At the university's Archaeological Dig Site in Pine Bluffs, researchers extract relics and prehistoric artifacts dating back 8,000 years. External funding for research at the university neared $86 million in 2012.

The National Center for Atmospheric Research began work at its Wyoming Supercomputing Center in 2012, focusing on advanced computing services studying a broad range of disciplines, including weather, climate, oceanography, air pollution, space weather, computational science, energy production, and carbon sequestration. It also houses a data storage and archival facility that stores historical climate records, among other things.

Public Library Information: Laramie County Library System, 2200 Pioneer Avenue, Cheyenne, WY 82001; telephone (307) 634-3561.

■ Health Care

The Cheyenne Regional Medical Center (CRMC) is a nonprofit county hospital system. The two main facilities, CRMC West and CRMC East, have a combined total of 222-beds. CRMC West contains Wyoming's first Level II Trauma Center, the Wyoming Heart & Vascular Institute, inpatient and outpatient surgery units, a birthing center with a Level II neonatal intensive care unit, the Women's Imaging Center, physical therapy services, and a radiology department. CRMC East contains the Behavioral Health Services, a transitional care unit, home care and hospice services, the Rehabilitation Center, the Sleep Disorders Lab, and Home Away From Home, a nine-room facility to house out-of-town family guests. CRMC Health and Fitness Center offers physical and occupational therapy, sports medicine services, cardiac and pulmonary rehabilitation programs, as well as a full-service fitness center. Construction to add a new cancer center and emergency department completed in 2013.

The Cheyenne Veteran's Administration Medical Center provides care to military personnel and their families. Facilities at the F.E. Warren U.S. Air Force Base also offer medical and dental care.

■ Recreation

Sightseeing

Cheyenne features several sites that recall the city's past. The Tivoli Building was completed in 1892. It is among the best examples of Victorian architecture in the Rocky Mountain region. The former Union Pacific Depot is an equally fine example of Romanesque architecture. Located on Capitol Avenue, the Wyoming State Capitol building contains historic photographs and a display of native wildlife; near the Capitol is a statue of Esther

Hobart Morris, a pioneer in the women's suffrage movement. A guided walking tour of historic Cheyenne is available.

The French Merci Train was sent to the American people by French citizens in 1946 as a "thank-you" for the Friendship Train that carried food from America to France during World War II. The Big Boy steam engine, "Old Number 4004," is the world's largest steam locomotive and was retired from the Union Pacific Railroad in 1956. F. E. Warren Air Force Base houses intercontinental ballistic missiles; free tours are conducted.

Recalling the days of cattle barons, the Wyoming Hereford Ranch east of Cheyenne was established in 1883; still in operation and producing Hereford cattle, it is the oldest continuous registered livestock operation in the county. The ranch hosts visitors and community events. Terry Bison Ranch is a working guest ranch that offers chuckwagon dinners, trout fishing, and horse-drawn wagon tours into a bison herd.

The Cheyenne Botanic Gardens in Lions Park, open 365 days a year, is a public botanical garden as well as a municipal nursery and community garden. The conservatory is entirely solar heated; 50 percent of the garden's electricity is also solar-generated. Displays include rose, cacti, and herbs, and plants native to the area. In 2009 the gardens opened the Paul Smith Children's Village, a state-of-the-art, interactive site that offers outdoor fun for the whole family.

Other points of interest are historic Lakeview Cemetery and the Wyoming Game & Fish Visitors Center, featuring wildlife exhibits ranging from grizzly bears to big horn sheep.

Arts and Culture

Cheyenne supports an active cultural community. The Civic Center is the site of performances by Broadway touring companies, major symphony orchestras, and popular entertainers. Residents also enjoy concerts by the Cheyenne Symphony Orchestra at the Civic Center from September through May and occasionally in the summer. The Cheyenne Little Theatre stages plays with local directors and actors at its own playhouse; in the summer it stages melodramas at the historic Atlas Theater. The Cheyenne All-City Children's Chorus highlights the talents of children in grades four through eight, offering performances at the Laramie County School District Auditorium.

Several museums are located in Cheyenne. The Wyoming State Capitol and State Museum displays western memorabilia and chronicles the history of Wyoming. The Wyoming Arts Council Gallery displays the works of Wyoming artists. The Nelson Museum of the West houses cowboy and Indian collectibles and wildlife trophies from around the world. The Governors' Mansion, a state historic site and an example of colonial-revival architecture, was home to the state's governors from 1905 to 1976; guided tours are available. At the Cheyenne Frontier Days Old West Museum, highlights include Oglala Sioux artifacts, a Union Pacific railroad exhibit, and a collection of horse-drawn vehicles.

The Cheyenne Depot Museum is a restored Union Pacific Depot with a visitor center, restaurant, and exhibits of railroad history. For a unique tour of public art, maps are available at the Depot Visitor's Center to show the locations of the Cheyenne Big Boots. These eight-feet-tall cowboy boots have been decorated by local artists to reflect local and state history.

Local art galleries include the Painted Pony Gallery at Wyoming Home, the Wild Goose Gallery, and Manitou Galleries. Audio tours of many of the city's museums and sites are available via cell phone.

Festivals and Holidays

The foremost event in the Cheyenne area is Cheyenne Frontier Days. Taking place during the last full week in July, it is billed as the world's largest outdoor rodeo. Frontier Days features daily rodeos, concerts, parades, pancake breakfasts, Native American dances, shootouts, and a carnival. The festivities attract hundreds of thousands of people. Running concurrently is the annual Western Art Show at the Old West Museum in Frontier Park. In June and July Cheyenne Gunslingers gunfights are enacted. In August Cheyenne hosts the Laramie County Fair. Oktoberfest and the Goblin Walk are held in the fall. Highlights of the Christmas season are the Christmas Parade, Craft Show, and Concert, held at the end of November. An annual Festival of Trees event is sponsored as a fundraiser for the MentorAbility Program, a local group benefiting citizens with disabilities.

Sports for the Spectator

There are no major professional sports teams in Wyoming. Cheyenne is home of the oldest rodeo event in the world, celebrated as part of the Cheyenne Frontier Days in July. Other rodeos are presented in the city throughout the year. The Wyoming State Open Golf Tournament is held at the Airport Golf Club, and Holiday Park in Cheyenne is host to the Wyoming Governor's Cup Tennis Tournament. The Cheyenne Stampede are part of the Western States Hockey League.

Sports for the Participant

Cheyenne maintains 24 city parks which cover more than 600 acres, plus 37 miles of the Cheyenne Greenway Trail. Lion's Park features a special physical fitness course with activities at all levels of physical ability. The city maintains 23 baseball and softball fields, 13 soccer fields, 12 tennis courts, 2 golf courses, and 2 public swimming pools. A Spray Park is located at Lion's Park. Sloans Lake offers swimming, paddleboats, kayaks, and canoes. Curt Gowdy State Park is located 25 miles outside of the city, while the Vedauwoo and Happy Jack recreational areas are approximately 30 miles away. Taco John's Events Center offers recreation such as ice and roller skating, miniature golf, laser tag, and an arcade. Facilities for such sports as hunting, fishing, boating, camping, trap-shooting, snow-mobiling, polo, tennis, and waterskiing are available.

Shopping and Dining

Shopping in downtown Cheyenne is enhanced by a sense of tradition; among the wide selection of stores, shops, and boutiques are several that have been in the city for many years. Nine shopping areas are located throughout the city. Frontier Mall features national retailers such as JCPenney, Dillard's, and Sears, but also has local and regional stores such as Daky Native Treasures and All Wild and Western. Visitors wanting to find a wide selection of Western clothing can visit Wrangler on Capitol Avenue. Cheyenne Farmer's Market, open half-days from August to October, sells fresh fruits, vegetables, and more.

Cheyenne offers a range of dining experience from traditional Southwestern specialties to Continental and ethnic cuisine such as Italian, Greek, Chinese, and Japanese. There are a large number of local Mexican restaurants. The Outlaw Saloon has live country music seven nights a week.

Visitor Information: Cheyenne Area Convention and Visitors Bureau, One Depot Square, 121 W. 15th Street, Suite 202, Cheyenne WY 82001; telephone (800) 426-5009; fax (307) 778-3190.

■ Convention Facilities

Little America Hotel and Resort offers a 10,360-square-foot meeting room at a facility that also includes 188 guest rooms and a nine-hole golf course. The Hitching Post Inn has 14,000 square feet of meeting space that can be divided into 10 smaller rooms. The Holiday Inn has 18,000 square feet of banquet and exhibition space. About 9,000 square feet of conference space is available at the Historic Plains Hotel. Other event and meeting venues include the Cheyenne Frontier Days Arena and Exhibit Hall, the City of Cheyenne-Kiwanis Community House, Cheyenne Civic Center, Terry Bison Ranch, and Taco John's Event Center.

Convention Information: Cheyenne Area Convention and Visitors Bureau, One Depot Square, 121 W. 15th Street, Suite 202, Cheyenne WY 82001; telephone (800) 426-5009; fax (307) 778-3190.

■ Transportation

Approaching the City

The major routes into Cheyenne are Interstate 25, which runs north and south; the east–west Interstate 80; and U.S. Highway 30, which bisects the city southwest to east. U.S. Highway 85 provides access from the northeast and southeast.

Out of Cheyenne Regional Airport, Great Lakes Airlines operates daily shuttle flights to Denver International Airport. From there travelers may connect to flights around the world. SuperShuttle offers shuttle service from the Denver Airport to Cheyenne. Greyhound bus service is available into the city. Thruway bus service is provided by Amtrak as well. Powder River Coach offers bus service from Cheyenne to Denver with stops at Fort Collins, Greeley, Longmont, and Boulder. Service from Cheyenne to Gillette includes stops at Douglas and Wheatland.

Traveling in the City

The Cheyenne Transit Program is Cheyenne's city-operated bus system. It serves Cheyenne and surrounding areas with six routes operating Monday through Saturday. For disabled passengers, the Transit Program offers Curb-to-Curb travel by reservation. Children under five years old ride for free, and students, seniors and disabled veterans travel at a discounted fare. The Cheyenne Street Railway Trolley takes visitors through the downtown and historic districts and to the air force base from mid-May through mid-September. Occasionally the governor will greet riders as they pass his residence.

■ Communications

Newspapers and Magazines

Cheyenne's daily newspaper is the *Wyoming Tribune-Eagle*, which has a circulation of about 16,500 daily and 18,500 on Sunday. With headquarters in Cheyenne, the paper is distributed throughout southeast Wyoming and into western Nebraska. *Warren Sentinel* is a weekly paper published by News Media Corporation for F.E. Warren Air Force Base. Also published in Cheyenne is the award winning *Wyoming Wildlife,* a Wyoming Fish and Game Department magazine on hunting, fishing, and environmental issues.

Television and Radio

Eleven licensed television stations broadcast from Cheyenne. The city also receives stations from Denver and surrounding areas; cable service is available. The area is served by 3 AM and 12 FM radio stations that feature news and information, music, and special programming.

Media Information: *Wyoming Tribune-Eagle,* 702 West Lincolnway, Cheyenne, WY 82001; telephone (307) 634-3361.

Cheyenne Online

Cheyenne Area Convention and Visitors Bureau. Available www.cheyenne.org

City of Cheyenne. Available www.cheyennecity.org

Greater Cheyenne Chamber of Commerce. Available www.cheyennechamber.org

Laramie County School District. Available www.laramie1.org

Wyoming Tribune-Eagle. Available www.wyomingnews.com

BIBLIOGRAPHY

Dubois, William Robert, *We've Worked Hard to Get Here: The First 100 Years of the Greater Cheyenne Chamber of Commerce* (Cheyenne, WY: Greater Cheyenne Chamber of Commerce, 2007)

Lewis, Norma, and Jay de Vries, *Wyoming* (Charleston, SC: Arcadia Publishing, 2010)

O'Neal, Bill, *Cheyenne: A Biography of the Magic City of the Old West* (Austin, TX: Eakin Press, 2006)

Laramie

■ The City in Brief

Founded: 1868

Head Official: Mayor Dave Paulekas (since 2013; current term expires 2015)

City Population
> 1990: 26,687
> 2000: 27,298
> 2010: 30,816
> 2012 estimate: 32,074
> Percent change, 2000–2010: 12.9%

Micropolitan Statistical Area Population
> 2000: 32,014
> 2010: 36,299
> 2012 estimate: 36,849
> Percent change, 2000–2010: 13.4%
> U.S. rank in 2010: 765th

Area: Not available

Elevation: 7,200 feet above sea level

Average Annual Temperatures: January, 10° F; July, 80° F

Average Annual Precipitation: 10 inches of precipitation

Major Economic Sectors: education, government, research, health care, technology

Unemployment Rate: 3.3% (2012)

Per Capita Income: $21,621

2012 FBI Crime Index Property: 710

Major Colleges and Universities: University of Wyoming, Laramie County Community College

Daily Newspaper: *The Laramie Boomerang*

■ Introduction

The seat of Albany County, Laramie is home to an important governmental center. The state's only public four-year educational institution, the University of Wyoming, is also located in the city. Although Laramie has excelled in educational and technological endeavors that have furthered progress in recent years, it continues to maintain an Old West feel by hosting an array of historic sites and local traditions. A historic downtown area, ranches, and occasional rodeos are reminiscent of the city's origins as a town of outlaws. The surrounding terrain provides both residents and visitors access to several recreational opportunities, such as biking, running, skiing, and fishing.

■ Geography and Climate

Laramie is located in southeast Wyoming. It is 49 miles from Cheyenne, which is the capital of Wyoming, and 130 miles from Denver. Situated on the edge of the Laramie Plains plateau, the city is 7,200 feet above sea level. The city's stance between two mountain ranges, the Snowy Range and Laramie Range, shields it from extreme temperatures. Summers are mild, and winters are cold and long. However, precipitation is scarce with only about an average 10 inches annually. There are more than 250 days of sunshine annually.

Area: Not available

Elevation: 7,200 feet above sea level

Average Temperatures: January, 10° F; July, 80° F

Average Annual Precipitation: 10 inches of precipitation

© Andre Jenny/Alamy

■ History

Railroad Delivers First Settlers to Area

Laramie was named after French-Canadian trapper Jacques LaRamie, who was one of the first visitors to the area, but mysteriously disappeared into the mountains in the 1800s. Long after his disappearance in the 1860s, a tent city was established along the Overland Trail, just south of what is now Laramie, for the purpose of creating the first transcontinental railroad. The makeshift fort that housed and protected railroad builders was named Fort Buford. Building the railroad track happened simultaneously with tents and cabins being erected to accommodate a growing population. The first train arrived at the Laramie station in 1868. The rail line brought travelers into town, and like other towns in the area, people began to settle there as Laramie was not a travel-through stop at the time.

Outlaws Threaten Young City, Order Prevails and City Flourishes

Melville C. Brown, a lawyer, became the first mayor of Laramie after its establishment in 1868. However, his term was short lived: he resigned in three weeks after failed attempts to govern the town's outlaws. Afterwards, a committee, led by Tom Sears, John Wright, and Nathaniel K. Boswell set to work driving the bad seeds out of town. Lynchings ensued, and soon the town was saved from its chronic lawlessness. Boswell went on to become the first sheriff of Albany County. In the fall, a school, churches and retail stores sprang up in town. Business got their start, run by the town's many permanent residents. An electric plant was built in 1886, making Laramie one of the first cities west of the Mississippi to provide power to subscribers. The University of Wyoming was also established in 1886

Women Earn Right to Vote

Wyoming officially became a territory in 1869. The first legislative session established protection of property rights for married women, equal consideration alongside men for teaching jobs, followed by women's suffrage that December. Wyoming became the first of the United States that gave women a vote in each election. Louisa Swain, an older woman of 70, was thought to be the first woman voter. The years that followed also allowed women to sit on the jury during trial. Railroads that served the region were also erected in Laramie, including the Laramie, North Park and Western Railroad in 1901.

Local Hate Crime Leads to National Legislation

Nearly a century later in 1998, Laramie experience tragedy when University of Wyoming student Matthew Shepard was murdered. Shepard, who identified himself as homosexual, was beaten, tortured, and left for dead by two men who had robbed him. The murder incited a national campaign against hate crimes, leading to legislation passed against them in 2009. The Laramie Project, a controversial play based on the 1998 events, was first performed in 2000 to commemorate Matthew Shepard and addresses issues surrounding homophobia and violent crimes.

Historical Information: Laramie Plains Museum, 603 Ivinson St, Laramie, WY 82070; telephone (307) 742-4448.

■ Population Profile

Micropolitan Statistical Area Population

2000: 32,014
2010: 36,299
2012 estimate: 36,849
Percent change, 2000–2010: 13.4%
U.S. rank in 2010: 765th

City Residents

1990: 26,687
2000: 27,298
2010: 30,816
2012 estimate: 32,074
Percent change, 2000–2010: 12.9%

Density: 1,737.5 people per square mile

Racial and ethnic characteristics

White: 28,402
Black or African American: 537
American Indian and Alaskan Native: 90
Asian: 1,166
Native Hawaiian and Other Pacific Islander: 9
Hispanic or Latino (may be of any race): 2,762
Other: 1,870

Percent of residents born in state: 39.0%

Age characteristics

Population under 5 years old: 1,757
Population 5 to 9 years old: 1,604
Population 10 to 14 years old: 1,232
Population 15 to 19 years old: 3,543
Population 20 to 24 years old: 7,472

Population 25 to 34 years old: 5,720
Population 35 to 44 years old: 3,404
Population 45 to 54 years old: 2,618
Population 55 to 59 years old: 1,333
Population 60 to 64 years old: 1,205
Population 65 to 74 years old: 1,092
Population 75 to 84 years old: 664
Population 85 years and over: 430
Median age: 25.5

Births (2010–11 Micropolitan Area)

Total number: 424

Deaths (2010–11 Micropolitan Area)

Total number: 176

Money income (2012)

Per capita income: $21,621
Median household income: $36,540
Total households: 13,081

Number of households with income of ...

less than $10,000: 1,497
$10,000 to $14,999: 1,202
$15,000 to $24,999: 1,896
$25,000 to $34,999: 1,786
$35,000 to $49,999: 1,551
$50,000 to $74,999: 2,114
$75,000 to $99,999: 1,237
$100,000 to $149,999: 1,136
$150,000 to $199,999: 435
$200,000 or more: 227

Percent of families below poverty level: 30.9%

FBI Crime Index Property: 710

FBI Crime Index Violent: 34

■ Municipal Government

Laramie is the seat of Albany County, and operates under a council-manager form of government. The council consists of nine members who are elected from three wards. Before the ward system was established in 2002, the entire council was elected at large. The nine council members serve overlapping four-year terms. The mayor and vice-mayor are elected by the council from among its members every two years in January.

Head Official: Mayor Dave Paulekas (since 2013; current term expires 2015)

Total Number of City Employees: 408 (2013)

City Information: City of Laramie, City Hall, 406 Ivinson Street, Laramie, Wyoming 82070; telephone (307) 721-5200.

■ Economy

Major Industries and Commercial Activity

Laramie's economy derives from its education, health, and government institutions. With nearly 7,000 employees, the University of Wyoming remains Laramie's largest employer; it is also the only four-year university in the state. Other major public employers are the city of Laramie, Albany County School District No. 1, and Albany County. All have a significant impact on the local economy. A 2009 economic impact report showed that Laramie Regional Airport generated about $18.6 million annually for the state economy.

Technology has become an important industrial sector for Laramie. The city welcomes and fosters technology-based companies, which boast high wages and benefits for the workforce and overall economy. The Laramie Technology Workforce Project has the goal of developing and maintaining southeast Wyoming's technology sector. Important technology employers in the area are Coffey Engineering and Surveying, Falcon Technologies, Firehole Technologies, Handel Information Technologies, Happy Jack Software, Intevac Photonics DeltaNu, Medicine Bow Technologies, and Proghorn Technologies. Environmental consulting firm Trihydro Corporation has headquarters in the Laramie River Business Park.

Items and goods produced: Geographic Information Systems (GIS), cable assemblies, software, water treatment products, environmental planning design

Incentive Programs—New and Existing Companies

Local programs: The Laramie Economic Development Corporation both attracts and retains businesses in the area by offering training and incentives, including a Revolving Loan Fund.

State programs: Wyoming's primary business incentive is a non-existent corporate income tax rate, coupled with relatively minimal sales tax rates. The state also does not tax intangibles or inventory and has kept property taxes low. The Wyoming Business Council provides several financing programs for businesses, including the Business Ready Community Grant and Loan Program and the Wyoming Partnership Challenge Loan Program. The Challenge Loan and Industrial Development Revenue Bonds programs are also administered by the Wyoming Business Council; the former allows the state to match loans with local economic development agencies, and the latter are tax-exempt bonds available to municipalities for the creation of in-state jobs. The Foreign Trade Zone at Natrona County International Airport provides further encouragement for importers to frequent Casper, as international goods can be warehoused at the airport

without undergoing full U.S. Customs scrutiny. In 2013 the Wyoming Business Council and Powder River Energy Corporation began offering discounted renewable energy credits to companies seeking to power operations from renewable sources.

Job training programs: The Wyoming Department of Workforce Services manages a statewide network of workforce development resources, including services for businesses, job seekers and employment data researchers. Expanding and new businesses can tap into the Business Training Grant program through which employers may receive up to $2,000 per trainee per year for existing employees and $4,000 per employee per year for new hires. Large and small business owners can take advantage of Wyoming at Work, an online network for job-seekers and employers. State workforce centers additionally operate a Foreign Labor Certification program, which allows employers to utilize immigrant labor for positions that are difficult to fill with U.S. citizens. The state sponsors a Pre-Hire Economic Development Grant program to offer training for new hires in particular businesses and industries.

Development Projects

The Lincoln Community Center, originally opened in 1924 as a public school, began renovations in 2010. The center, which was funded by a $1.5 million Community Facilities grant received in 2009, reopened to the public in late 2011. In addition, more than $200,000 in community investment made the renovation possible.

In 2013 Maverick Ammunition announced plans to open an ammunition manufacturing facility in Laramie capable of producing 1.8 million rounds per week. The plant was expected to begin operations by 2014. HiViz Shooting Systems, a rifle sight manufacturing, announced plans to relocate to Laramie earlier that year with a new 20,000-square-foot facility.

The University of Wyoming opened a new 80,000-square-foot, $25 million visual arts center in 2012. The building received LEED certification for its environmentally conscious design.

Economic Development Information: Laramie Economic Development Corporation, 800 South 3rd Street, Laramie, WY 82070; telephone (307) 742-2212; fax (307) 742-8200; email ledc@laramiewy.org.

Commercial Shipping

Although Laramie has no airports nearby that provide commercial shipping services, the city is served by many truck lines that transport freight to major destinations such as Denver. The closest international airport is Denver International Airport. Denver International Airport handled 410 million pounds of cargo in 2012. Major cargo carriers are the U.S. Postal Service, DHL, UPS, FedEx, and United Airlines. Cargo and mail facilities cover some 375,000 square feet. The airport is the site of Foreign Trade Zone #123, as well as areas for U.S. Customs and Department of Agriculture clearance. WorldPort at DIA, adjacent to the freight operations site, provides an additional 100,000 feet of office space.

Although Laramie historically has not been served by rail, the Laramie Economic Development Corporation (LEDC) has spearheaded a South Laramie Rail Spur project to create a trans-modal site off of rail spur 107, which was formerly used by the Union Pacific railway. The project was estimated to be complete by 2014.

Labor Force and Employment Outlook

The top 10 employers in the city of Laramie account for nearly half of all jobs in the city. The vast majority of that employment is tied to the University of Wyoming. Almost half of all residents over the age of 25 hold at least a four-year college degree, an impressive statistic indicative of the major influence of the university. The highest wages in the city were in fields tied to professional, scientific, and technical services, educational services, public administration, finance and insurance, and information.

The following is a summary of data regarding the 2008 Laramie WY Micro Area labor force:

Size of civilian labor force: 18,255

Number of workers employed in . . .

    agriculture and mining: 330
    construction: 682
    manufacturing: 600
    wholesale trade: 44
    retail trade: 1,867
    transportation: 501
    information systems: 193
    finance: 558
    professional administration: 1,235
    education and social services: 7,807
    arts and leisure: 1,609
    other: 719
    public administration: 965

Average hourly earnings of production workers: $16.81

Unemployment rate: 3.3% (2012)

Employers

Largest county employers (2013) — *Number of employees*

	Number of employees
University of Wyoming	6,737
Albany County School District No. 1	800
Ivinson Memorial Hospital	448
City of Laramie	408
Wal-Mart Stores, Inc.	340
ARK Regional Services	255
Wyoming Technical Institute	203
Cathedral Home for Children	195
Albany County	146
Trihydro	145

Cost of Living

The cost of living in Laramie and throughout Albany County falls just below national and state averages.

The following is a summary of data regarding several key cost of living factors in the area.

2013 ACCRA Average House Price: $326,000

2013 ACCRA Cost of Living Index: 99

State income tax rate: None

State sales tax rate: 4.0%

Local income tax rate: None

Local sales tax rate: 2.0%

Property tax rate: 69.00 mills on 9.5% of assessed value (county average, 2013)

Economic Information: Laramie Economic Development Corporation, 800 South 3rd Street, Laramie, WY 82070; telephone (307) 742-2212; fax (307) 742-8200; email ledc@laramiewy.org.

■ Education and Research

Elementary and Secondary Schools

Albany County School District No. 1 serves Laramie and all of Albany County. The district enrolls about 3,600 students annually. The district is served by a nine-member school board and a superintendent. The district offers several programs including "Child Find," which helps to identify students five and older who might have disabilities, as well as programs for students with hearing loss, and a variety of other educational services.

The following is a summary of data regarding the Albany County School District.

Total enrollment: 3,654

Number of facilities

    total: 14
    elementary schools: 8
    junior high schools: 1

high schools: 2
other: 3

Teacher salaries
average (statewide): $56,978

Funding per pupil: $15,163

Public Schools Information: Albany County School District One, 1948 Grand Ave., Laramie, WY 82070; telephone (307) 721-4400; fax (307) 721-4408.

Colleges and Universities

Founded in 1886, the University of Wyoming has the state's only four-year baccalaureate program. It enrolls about 13,000 undergraduate and graduate students from 75 countries. Students can choose from more than 200 areas of study throughout its many colleges, including the School of Energy Resources that teaches energy-related science and research. The school has the largest single scholarship endowment for study abroad programs in the nation. The university has been recognized among top national colleges by *U.S. News & World Report. Forbes* magazine recognized the university as the nation's 11th best college value in 2013. Besides the main campus in Laramie, the university also has remote branches in the state: the Casper College Center and a branch on the Wind River Indian Reservation.

Laramie County Community College (LCCC) has campuses in Cheyenne and Laramie. Less than 10 minutes from downtown Laramie, the Albany County Campus enrolls about 600 students per semester. As a whole system, LCCC offers 76 academic programs culminating in associate degrees, and 25 certificate programs. Workforce training programs are also offered.

WyoTech (formerly Wyoming Technical Institute) is a trade school that provides short-term skills education primarily in cars, motorcycles, marine engines, collision and refinishing, as well as other areas. Students can earn diplomas or associate degrees in less than 16 months. The institute has five campuses: Blairsville, PA; Daytona, FL; Fremont, CA; Long Beach, CA; and Laramie. The Laramie campus consists of 370,000 square feet of shop, classroom, and administrative facilities. Not every campus offers all programs; the Laramie campus offers training in diesel applications, collision and refinishing, and automotive technology.

Libraries and Research Centers

The Albany County Public Library has one main library, a branch in Rock River, and another in Centennial. The main library includes of the Wyoming Room, which contains historical information accessible through books, microfilm, and directories. The Wyoming Room is a non-circulating section, but permits copying of materials. The collection also includes the Wyoming Pamphlet File, with biographies, news, and photographs from the past. The library system offers programming that includes children's story time, a "Teen Pad," to engage young adults, enrichment activities for adults, and select programs for senior citizens.

The University of Wyoming's William Robertson Coe Library, named after the British financier who originally funded the library, opened in 1957 and is the university's main library. Also on campus, the Brinkerhoff Geology Library focuses on geological studies and is located next to the Geological Museum. The Rocky Mountain Herbarium is a non-circulating university library branch that contains the Meckler Collection, which includes more than 4,500 book titles. The Learning Resource Center consists of close to 30,000 items. It is the library and media center for Albany County School District One's Laboratory School, and serves the university's College of Education as well as the overall community. Began in 1945, the American Heritage Center at the University of Wyoming is a repository for more than 55,000 rare books, manuscripts, and the university archives. In 2010 the American Heritage Center was honored with the Distinguished Service Award by the Society of American Archivists (SAA). The George W. Hooper Law Library and the Library Annex are also included in the University Library system.

Also on the University of Wyoming campus, the Western Research Institute performs energy systems research. The institute also runs an Advanced Technology Center to the north on 22 acres of laboratories and additional space.

Public Library Information: Albany County Public Library, Laramie Main Library, 310 S. 8th St., Laramie, WY 82070; telephone (307) 721-2580.

■ Health Care

Ivinson Memorial Hospital is Laramie's major health-care provider. Ivinson Memorial Hospital offers 24-hour emergency services, rehabilitation services, imaging services, intensive care, oncology services at the Meredith and Jeannie Ray Cancer Center, and Family Care Unit that includes a Level I nursery, as well as obstetrics, gynecology, and pediatric services. In 2010 the dialysis unit was awarded disease-specific care certification for end-stage renal disease by the Joint Commission. The Meredith and Jeannie Ray Cancer Center opened in March 2002. Ivinson also has an extended care facility for those needing constant care. Affiliated with Ivinson, Laramie Physicians for Women and Children operates a women's and children's clinic on Harney Street. Children's services include care for injuries, acute illnesses, psychiatric evaluations, allergy treatment, vaccinations, physicals, and adolescent care. Women's services include obstetrics and gynecological care, including minor surgery options.

■ Recreation

Sightseeing

Laramie offers several historic sites that attract visitors to the area. The Wyoming Territorial Prison, built in 1872, is also known as the Wyoming State Penitentiary. The prison once held western legendary outlaws such as Butch Cassidy, Clark "The Kid" Pelton, and Dan Parker. After it ceased to be a prison in 1903, it was used as a stock farm for University of Wyoming until 1989. The restored prison displays prison cells, the warden's house, horse barn exhibit hall, broom factory, and box car house, among other exhibits.

The Ames Monument is a granite pyramid that stands 60 feet high. The structure, which was built by the Union Pacific Railroad Company, was made in honor of Oakes and Oliver Ames who played integral roles in building the first railroad that stretched from coast to coast.

The Geological Museum at the University of Wyoming houses a collection of more than 40,000 catalogued fossil specimens that date back to the university's founding. It also holds a dinosaur exhibit that features six different species including a Tyrannosaurus rex, and the Allosaurus "Big Al."

The Laramie Historic Railroad Depot dates back to 1924 when the Union Pacific Railroad transported passengers into town. Before that, the original railroad station began service in 1868. The current structure at 1st and Kearney serves as a museum dedicated to the railroad after it stopped passenger service to Laramie in 1997. The Ivinson Mansion, which houses the Laramie Plains Museum, pays tribute to the city of Laramie, a girls boarding school, and the Ivinson family, who had a tremendous role in the town's establishments.

The Wyoming House for Historic Women, located downtown, was established by the Louisa Swain Foundation. A statue of Louisa Swain, the first woman to vote for women's equality, stands in front of the building. The museum itself pays homage to Swain and 12 others who have made significant strides for women around the world.

Arts and Culture

University of Wyoming Symphony Orchestra consists of 90 members and performs at the Fine Arts Concert Hall. The Art Museum at the University of Wyoming features 7,000 pieces that encompass a variety of cultures. Modern and contemporary art, American, European, Asian, and African works are displayed, as well as photographs. The University's Centennial Complex houses both the Art Museum and the American Heritage Center.

Festivals and Holidays

Events in Laramie during the year center on its Old West origins. Laramie Jubilee Days takes place throughout the month of July, and includes bull riding, a rodeo, a chili cook off, and various events in the downtown area. The three-day Snowy Range Music Festival occurs over Labor Day weekend. The Jubilee Days Fall Brawl happens later that month. The University of Wyoming hosts various events throughout the year as well.

Sports for the Spectator

Although there are no professional sports teams serving the area, the University of Wyoming Cowboys offer entertainment in basketball, track, wrestling, tennis, football, swimming, and several other sports. Jonah Field at War Memorial Stadium, home of the Cowboys football team, can accommodate 30,514 fans and is the highest National Collegiate Athletic Association Division I football stadium in the nation at 7,220 feet. Club seats and luxury suites were added for the 2010 season. The Glenn "Red" Jacoby Golf Course accommodates both the university's men's and women's golf teams. The $15 million Arena-Auditorium, called the "Dome of Doom" by team opponents because of the university basketball team's notorious home court advantage, can seat more than 15,000 individuals. Local high schools also offer many athletic events throughout the academic year.

Sports for the Participant

There are 15 parks in Laramie with an assortment of playgrounds, picnic facilities, biking paths, a skateboard park, and fishing pond. The Laramie Community Ice and Event Center is available for hockey leagues, figure skating, speed skating, free skating, broomball, and curling. The Laramie Community Recreation Center features aquatic facilities such as an indoor pool, lap pool, whirlpool, outdoor pool with water slides, and a lazy river. The center also has a fitness center with cardio machines, circuit weights, a gymnasium, and other amenities. Adults and youths can participate in several seasonal community leagues offered through the recreation center. Golfers can play at the University of Wyoming's 18-hole Glenn "Red" Jacoby Golf Course. The Laramie Country Club hosts a private, nine-hole course.

Located between two mountain ranges, the area boasts many opportunities for outdoor enthusiasts. Located 32 miles west of Laramie, the Snowy Range Ski and Recreation Area rises 10,000 feet at summit elevation and boasts 250 acres of skiing. It offers four chairlifts and a surface lift that lead to 7 easy, 12 intermediate, and 8 expert trails. The longest hill stretches 1.8 miles. Snowboarding opportunities are also offered. Other ski areas are located north or northwest of

Laramie. Many other ski resorts lie at least two hours away from the area. Colorado ski resorts Vail and Breckenridge are each about four hours south of Laramie.

Laramie's mountainous area provides a challenging terrain for endurance running and biking. Adventurers can hike and rock climb at Vedauwoo Recreation Area. The Wyoming Marathon Races are held in May in the Medicine Bow National Forest, and include the Vedauwoo 5K, Medicine Bow Half Marathon, Wyoming Marathon, and Rocky Mountain 50K. The Laramie Enduro 111K, a 500-person mountain bike race of more than 70 miles on both flat and uneven terrain, takes place in late July throughout the Laramie Range.

Lake Hattie, the largest of the Laramie Plains Lakes, is located 20 miles west from Laramie. The lake accommodates campers and is an ample body of water for fishing, as it contains rainbows, browns, perch, and Kokanee salmon.

Shopping and Dining

There are no major malls in Laramie, but visitors and residents alike can peruse the area's unique shops. Murdoch's, Hastings book store, Wal-Mart, and Kmart are among the area's largest retailers. In the downtown district, smaller antique shops and specialty clothing stores are also favorites among shoppers. About an hour away, Cheyenne offers more shopping options, including Frontier Mall that is the major shopping area for six counties. The mall is anchored by Dillard's, JCPenney, and Sears, and has more than 75 retail stores.

Dining offerings in Laramie include American, Mexican, Chinese, Japanese, Italian, and Thai influences, along with chain restaurants. Breweries and pubs are also among the area's popular offerings.

Visitor Information: Albany County Tourism Board Convention and Visitor Bureau, 210 Custer St., Laramie, WY 82070; telephone (800) 445-5303.

■ Convention Facilities

Event planners and guests to Laramie can access a variety of facilities for meetings and special occasions. The Laramie Hilton Garden Inn & University of Wyoming Conference Center has more than 13,000 square feet of meeting space consisting of 12 meeting rooms. Space is flexible, and can make two ballrooms totaling 9,000 square feet of space: the Grand Ballroom has more than 7,000 square feet of space, and the Garden Ballroom is more than 2,000 square feet. Facilities have audio/visual capabilities.

The historic Ivinson Mansion can be rented out for different occasions such as meetings, parties, and weddings, as well as the train depot. Other area hotels include AmericInn Lodge and Suites, Holiday Inn, Days Inn, and Hampton Inn, which contribute to the total 1,800 hotel rooms throughout the Laramie area. A number of guest and dude ranches in the area, including the historical Vee Bar Guest Ranch, accommodate guests for day meetings and overnight retreats. Bed and breakfasts and cabins serve as rustic retreats.

Convention Information: Albany County Tourism Board Convention and Visitor Bureau, 210 Custer St., Laramie, WY 82070; telephone (800) 445-5303.

■ Transportation

Approaching the City

Travelers to Laramie are served through Laramie Regional Airport, which accommodates 40 private and corporate aircrafts, including Cowboy Aviation. United transports passengers on 40-minute flights to Denver International Airport. The airport is funded and operated by both the city of Laramie and Albany County, and has its own five-member airport board of directors. The airport sits about three miles from the central business district. Greyhound Bus also has a stop in Laramie. There is no passenger rail service to the area since the Union Pacific stopped serving Laramie in 1997.

Traveling in the City

Transportation throughout the city is offered by the University of Wyoming, which has buses that transport people to and from the university and other parts of the city. The Eppson Center for Seniors offers Public Assisted Transportation Service (PATS), which includes two buses that transport riders to points of interest throughout the city. The first bus goes to West Laramie, toward Iverson Memorial Hospital; the bus originates at the Eppson Center every hour. The second bus, also originating at the Eppson Center, goes along Grand Avenue toward the Civic Center and Laramie County Community College. The Grand Avenue bus line departs every thirty minutes. The buses operate Monday through Friday. Paratransit services are available for disabled residents or those who cannot physically get to the Eppson Center.

■ Communications

Newspapers and Magazines

The *Laramie Boomerang* is a daily newspaper that circulates throughout southeast Wyoming and parts of northern Colorado; the most readership remains in Albany County. Students at the University of Wyoming in Laramie have produced the *Branding Iron* newspaper daily since 1898. The *Laramie Free Press* is an online news publication that covers regional news and sports.

Television and Radio

Six licensed television stations operate from Laramie, with other stations available from nearby communities. Cable television is available. Four AM and 22 FM radio stations serve the Laramie area, including the University of Wyoming radio stations. Programming includes public radio, Spanish, country, contemporary, oldies, and classic rock.

Media Information: *Laramie Boomerang,* 320 E. Grand Ave., Laramie, WY 82070; telephone (307) 742-2176; toll-free (877) 452-3789; fax (307) 742-2046; email online@laramieboomerang.com.

Laramie Online

Albany County Public Library. Available www. albanycountylibrary.org

Albany County School District One. Available www. acsd1.org

Albany County Tourism Board Convention and Visitor Bureau. Available www.visitlaramie. org

City of Laramie. Available www.ci.laramie.wy.us

Laramie Area Chamber of Commerce. Available www.laramie.org

Laramie Economic Development Corporation. Available laramiewy.org

The Laramie Boomerang. Available www. laramieboomerang.com

BIBLIOGRAPHY

Lewis, Norma, and Jay de Vries, *Wyoming* (Charleston, SC: Arcadia Publishing, 2010)

Cumulative Index

The 219 cities featured in *Cities of the United States*, Volume 1: *The South*, Volume 2: *The West*, Volume 3: *The Midwest*, and Volume 4: *The Northeast*, along with names of individuals, organizations, historical events, etc., are designated in this Cumulative Index by name of the appropriate regional volume, or volumes, followed by the page number(s) on which the term appears in that volume.